THE ENEMY COMBATANT PAPERS: AMERICAN JUSTICE, THE COURTS, AND THE WAR ON TERROR

This volume presents the five major enemy combatant cases of the post–9/11 era. Assembled in narrative form, the documents tell the story of the legal arguments upon which the U.S. government and the defense attorneys have based their respective sides in what has become a complex and philosophically important debate among American lawyers, political scientists, and citizens. These cases involve two U.S. citizens, one Qatari citizen enrolled at an Illinois university, and two of the most prominent cases regarding Guantanamo detainees. Viewed together, the documents assembled herein in digested form illustrate the judicial struggle between the needs of national security and the constitutional and international legal protections regarding the rights of individuals. Legal issues, including habeas corpus, presidential powers, and the applicability of the Geneva Conventions; administrative issues such as the plenary executive and the roles of the Departments of Defense, State, and Justice; and moral questions, including conditions of detention and how to define the "enemy," all coalesce in providing one of the most comprehensive and compelling portraits of the U.S. engagement in the war on terror.

Karen J. Greenberg is the Executive Director of the Center on Law and Security at the New York University School of Law. She is the editor of the *NYU Review of Law and Security*; co-editor of *The Torture Papers: The Road to Abu Ghraib*, with Joshua L. Dratel; editor of the books *Al Qaeda Now* and *The Torture Debate in America*; and author of the forthcoming *The Least Worst Place: Guantanamo's First Hundred Days*. Her work on terrorism, international law, the war on terror, and detainee issues has been featured in *Financial Times*, the *Guardian*, the *Los Angeles Times*, the *San Francisco Chronicle*, *The Washington Post*, the *Nation*, the *American Prospect*, and on major media outlets.

Joshua L. Dratel is an attorney in New York City. Dratel, a past President of the New York State Association of Criminal Defense Lawyers and member of the Board of Directors of the National Association of Criminal Defense Lawyers, has been defense counsel in several terrorism and national security prosecutions, including that of Sami Omar Al-Hussayen, who was acquitted in federal court in Idaho in 2004, and Wadih El-Hage, a defendant in *United States v. Usama bin Laden*, which involved the August 1998 bombings of the United States embassies in Kenya and Tanzania. He was also lead and civilian counsel for David Hicks, an Australian detained at Guantanamo Bay, Cuba, in Hicks's prosecution by U.S. military commission. Dratel currently represents Mohamed El-Mezain, a defendant in the federal prosecution of the Holy Land Foundation for Relief and Development, and, on appeal, Lynne Stewart, a New York lawyer convicted of material support for terrorism. He is co-editor with Karen J. Greenberg of *The Torture Papers: The Road to Abu Ghraib*, a compendium of government memoranda.

THE ENEMY COMBATANT PAPERS

American Justice, the Courts, and the War on Terror

Edited by

Karen J. Greenberg

and

Joshua L. Dratel

with

Jeffrey S. Grossman

CAMBRIDGE
UNIVERSITY PRESS

CAMBRIDGE UNIVERSITY PRESS
Cambridge, New York, Melbourne, Madrid, Cape Town, Singapore, São Paulo, Delhi

Cambridge University Press
32 Avenue of the Americas, New York, NY 10013-2473, USA

www.cambridge.org
Information on this title: www.cambridge.org/9780521886475

First published 2008

Printed in the United States of America

A catalog record for this publication is available from the British Library.

Library of Congress Cataloging in Publication Data

The enemy combatant papers : American justice, the courts, and the War on Terror /
edited by Karen J. Greenberg, Joshua Dratel.
    p.   cm.
Includes bibliographical references and index.
ISBN 978-0-521-88647-5 (hardback)
1. War on Terrorism, 2001 – Law and legislation – United States.
2. Detention of persons – United States.   3. Combatants and noncombatants –
Legal status, laws, etc. – United States.   4. Combatants and noncombatants
(International law)   I. Greenberg, Karen J.   II. Dratel, Joshua L., 1957–   III. Title.
KF9430.E53   2008
345.73′02–dc22   2008013105

ISBN 978-0-521-88647-5 hardback

Contents

PART TWO. MILITARY COMMISSIONS

PART THREE. U.S. CAPTURES

Acknowledgments

This volume could not have been produced without the assistance of many of our colleagues, including Neal Katyal, Paul Clement, Donna Newman, Stephen Holmes, John Berger, and Joan Dim. New York University law student Erik Paulsen ('07) deserves especial credit for coordinating the early stages of this project and scrupulously gathering and analyzing the many thousands of pages of primary source material. We are also indebted to the researchers and staff of the Center on Law and Security and New York University law students and undergraduates for their dedication in assembling, editing, and proofing the documents herein. They include Meredith Angelson, Katie Brodsky, Keith Chapman, Nicholas Colten, Elizabeth Dettori, Daniel Freifeld, Divya Khosla, Francesca Laguardia, Susan MacDougall, Adam Maltz, Christopher McGuire, Jason Porta, Jackie Randell, Elizabeth Rothstein, Gunjan Sharma, Zachary Stern, and Katie Sticklor. We would also like to thank Jim Diggins for his thorough work in compiling the index.

Caught in the War on Terror: Redefining Prisoners in the Post–9/11 Era

Karen J. Greenberg

A dramatic story unfolds through the pages of this volume. From the narrative digest of the five major enemy combatant cases that have come to define the role of the federal courts in the war on terror, one predominant fact leaps out. These documents tell a story less about the dynamics of judicial process than about human beings. It is a tale of individuals, both Americans citizens and non-citizens, who have found themselves ensnared in a radically novel legal system, and who, as suspected terrorists, have been locked up, often held incommunicado and denied the elemental protections usually provided by American law.

For over six years, as these cases have made their way from court to court and have been batted from the Supreme Court to Congress and back again, debate has raged over a central burning issue. These cases are not essentially about releasing or continuing to detain individuals who may possibly be terrorists, though that is indeed an underlying thread in the larger strand of arguments. Instead, the existential tension at the heart of these cases concerns the basic constitutional guarantee that no person (including non-citizens) shall be deprived of liberty without due process of law.

Throughout American history, wartime presidents have stepped beyond their customary constitutional powers while Congress and the courts have stepped back, yielding to the prevailing winds of wartime discretion. For Presidents Lincoln, Wilson, and Franklin Roosevelt, the nation in arms opened the door to restricting fundamental liberties – habeas corpus, freedom of speech, and freedom from unreasonable search and seizure. Under these earlier presidents, however, the historic balance of power was always restored at war's end. Owing to the predictable cessation of hostilities, the nation has managed to survive crises of national security while continuing, in the main, to honor the Bill of the Rights and to treat as inviolable the basic principles of the Constitution. Americans, as a result, have accepted the pendulum swing that war can bring, tolerating the wartime Constitution, secure in the knowledge that the peacetime Constitution will be waiting on the shelf, ready to be retrieved and revived.

Like previous conflicts, the war on terror has encouraged and permitted the executive to demand deference from the other branches of government. In the name of national security, as he defines it, President George W. Bush has claimed the power to make decisions without consulting or even informing either Congress or the courts. Sidelining traditional restraints on executive power, his presidency has altered the relationship not only between the branches of government but also between the government and the public. Secrecy, national security concerns, and the administration's publicly announced willingness to use law enforcement in disregard of an American tradition of civil liberties appear to have cowed the citizenry into political paralysis. And six years after its onset, the war on terror rages on, mostly out of sight and seemingly without end. As President Bush predicted in a speech delivered on the South Lawn of the White House on September 16th, 2001, the response to 9/11 promises to be "a long campaign." Accordingly, the pendulum-swing back to constitutional normality hovers in defiance of physics, waiting for a sign that such a return is viable.

At the center of this reorganization of power, symbolically and legally, has been the creation of a new category of person, applicable to U.S. citizens as well as to non-citizens. The nomenclature used to designate this new category is "enemy combatant," a term that mixes confusingly several legal and military concepts. What those who adopted it were searching for was a term that could indicate prisoners in the war on terror who were not conventional prisoners of war. Although it conflates a number of previously well-defined categories (especially "enemy prisoner of war," "combatant" and "civilian combatant"), "enemy combatant" apparently seemed to anonymous administration linguists to be the best option at the time.

In creating this nebulous class, the Bush administration exploited a lack of clarity in international law. Although the term "unlawful combatant," is not part of any written international law or code, the idea has long been recognized in practice. Legal interpretation, military protocol, and case law have all led to the widely shared acceptance of the distinction between lawful combatants and unlawful combatants, a distinction that has specific implications for the legal treatment of prisoners in either group. Lawful combatants include those members of militias and volunteer forces who, in the words of the Geneva Convention Relative to the Treatment of Prisoners of War, are "commanded by a person responsible for his subordinates," "have a fixed distinctive sign," and carry "arms openly." Essentially, they are battlefield captives who qualify as lawful combatants and are entitled to prisoner of war status, defined according to widely accepted international norms. As "enemy prisoners of war," or "EPW" (as they are called by Army regulations), they are able to be legally detained for the duration of the war and, as such, are subject to a lengthy set of international and U.S. military codes that ensure humane treatment on the part of the detaining authorities, in this case the United States.

Unlawful combatants, such as the Nazi saboteurs whose fate was decided by the Supreme Court in the *Quirin* case, are prisoners "likewise subject to capture and detention, but in addition they are subject to trial and punishment by military tribunals for acts which render their belligerency unlawful," as Chief Justice Harlan Fiske Stone wrote for the Court. The *Quirin* defendants were caught behind enemy lines, having landed in Florida and Long Island by submarine, burying their uniforms so as to defy identification as combatants and intending to sabotage American industrial targets.

Citing *Quirin* as precedent, the government's lawyers laid out their radical strategy, asserting that the demands of national security, given the unprecedented threat of Islamic fundamentalist terrorism, required a re-reading of the law. In a series of memos drafted by the Office of Legal Counsel beginning in the fall of 2001 and continuing throughout the Bush presidency, the administration asserted that not only were the Geneva Conventions on the categorization and treatment of prisoners "quaint" and "obsolete," but so too were the traditional guarantees of right to counsel, right to habeas corpus, and the right to humane and decent treatment. As a basis for later determinations in court, the administration's lawyers concluded early in 2002 that the laws of armed conflict "do not protect" members of al Qaeda and the Taliban militia. Furthermore, government lawyers concluded that al Qaeda and the Taliban militia were not covered by the Geneva Conventions. The Taliban, the administration asserted by way of explanation, represented a failed state. "Afghanistan's status as a failed state is ground alone to find that members of the Taliban militia are not entitled to enemy POW status," as Deputy Assistant Attorney General John Yoo and Special Counsel Robert J. Delahunty wrote in a draft memo on January 9, 2002. As a non-state actor, al Qaeda was similarly held to be not covered by international law in general and the Geneva Conventions in particular. "Al Qaeda is merely a violent political movement organization and not a nation-state," echoed Assistant Attorney General Jay S. Bybee in a January 22, 2002, memo. With one fell swoop, the administration thus extricated the United States from the international obligations that have governed the treatment of prisoners in armed conflict since the middle of the nineteenth century.

Publicly defying tradition to an extent rarely, and perhaps never, seen in American history, the administration embraced the shattering of established rules and norms. In speeches and memos, the president and his lawyers would later use these baseline deviations from previously settled law to defend coercive interrogation techniques, to redefine torture so narrowly as to allow for techniques accepted from medieval times forward as torture – e.g., waterboarding – and to denounce proper judicial processes, both in the military and the civilian context, as posing unaffordable risks to national security. Lawyers, courts, and the law, when exercised on behalf of individuals classified as enemy combatants, were considered impediments to the nation's safety and well-being. The 2005 National Defense Strategy echoed this attitude toward the courts, including "judicial processes" among the country's "vulnerabilities," and labeling them part of a "strategy of the weak."

The cases digested in this volume present the riveting story of five conversations on the politics of the war on terror. Clearly presented are the justifications for reneging upon basic rights and liberties that are traditionally guaranteed to Americans. For government lawyers, it has largely been a story of deference to the executive branch in time of war. Equally thought-provoking is the argument of the defense attorneys who have relentlessly insisted that to create unheard-of categories of prisoners and to constantly change the rules for their treatment threatens overarching principles of legality, both domestic and international.

As the petitioners in *Hamdi* argued in their Supreme Court brief, "Hamdi's detention is offensive to the most basic and unimpeachable rule of due process: that no citizen may be incarcerated at the will of the Executive without recourse to a timely proceeding before an independent tribunal to determine whether the Executive's asserted justifications for the detention have a basis in fact and a warrant in law."

The government has claimed that, in time of war, the courts need to step aside and grant the institutions responsible for national security – the executive and the military – the ability to do what they think they need to do to protect the country adequately. Is judicial abdication in time of war either justifiable or necessary? Might it not weaken the country's defenses in the face of a serious foreign threat? These are the fundamental *political* questions posed by the enemy combatant cases. As the Fourth Circuit explained in July of 2002, in deciding *Hamdi*, "The federal courts have many strengths, but the conduct of combat operations has been left to others." In other words, if the armed struggle with al Qaeda involves war rather than crime, then it is for the military and political branches of government alone, not for the courts.

Attorneys representing the detainees have repeatedly countered these arguments by claiming that judicial deference to the executive will dangerously undermines fundamental rights. In response to the administration's dire warnings, the attorneys have invoked fear of another sort, namely the fear that American citizens will no longer be shielded from their government's overreaching. Lawyers for Mr. al-Marri similarly invoked the egregious violations of fundamental rights. "The government's claim that the President can, without authorization from Congress, direct the military to seize a person off the streets of the United States and confine him indefinitely, without charges, in a military prison contravenes the Suspension Clause's protection against the arbitrary exercise of executive power. The President cannot circumvent this constitutional guarantee simply by labeling Mr. al-Marri an 'enemy combatant.'"

Neither fears about national security nor consideration of rights seem to have been decisive in shaping the thinking of the Supreme Court, however. Instead, the Justices have focused on presidential power. As Sandra Day O'Connor wrote in her opinion in *Hamdi*, "a state of war" cannot be "a blank check for the President." The Court has invoked the responsibilities of Congress several times over the course of the litigation. Congress's response has been a codification of the power that the president has sought – first with the Detainee Treatment Act and then with the Military Commissions Act, a direct response to the decision in *Hamdan*, which declared that the types of military tribunals then in use at Guantanamo did not meet the accepted standards for military commissions.

Arguably, this legal and legislative back-and-forth has brought to the fore a nation at its best, reasoning and debating, trying to make sense of a world increasingly difficult to fathom, searching its fundamental philosophical treatises and its knowledge of its own past for usable precedents and explanatory principles, in an effort to find a guide to going forward. You will find in this volume attempts by both the government and the defense attorneys to navigate treacherous political waters while keeping within the confines of the law. Yet you will also see revealed here a nation struggling to find a shared language and, beyond that, a shared vision of how to proceed in bringing the war on terror to a resolution that provides both a sense of security and a trust in the inviolability of the law.

The cases of Mr. Rasul, Mr. Hamdi, Mr. Hamdan, Mr. Padilla, and Mr. al-Marri have inspired a new and rich conversation for understanding the politics of America at war. Perhaps the story of the detained men presented here will help the American citizenry understand better what is at stake, how best we as a nation can resolve these cases, and how we should rethink what it means to create a new category of individual situated outside the protections of American law.

Repeating History: Rights and Security in the War on Terror

Joshua L. Dratel

Since September 11, 2001, much has been made of the supposedly unprecedented nature of the threat presented by international terrorism. Indeed, it has been a refrain commonly used to justify an unprecedented response in the form of invented legal systems and doctrine, "aggressive" interrogation methods, novel detention schemes, and an invigorated quest for unfettered executive authority.

All of those elements have converged in these five cases as they have percolated their way through the U.S. civilian court system. They constitute the "enemy combatant" cases – involving persons the U.S. executive department has unilaterally designated "enemy combatants," and therefore reputedly outside the rules of the law of war, international law, and U.S. law, including the Constitution. Each case presents a different wrinkle. *Rasul v. Bush* involves detainees at Guantanamo Bay, all aliens, who still seek, even after a Supreme Court victory, the right to institute habeas corpus actions to test the validity of their detention. *Hamdi v. Rumsfeld* involved a U.S. citizen apprehended in Afghanistan but held in military custody in the U.S. *Padilla v. Hanft* also involved a U.S. citizen in military custody, but one who had been arrested disembarking a flight in Chicago and initially held as a material witness pursuant to the ordinary rules of federal criminal procedure. *Hamdan v. Rumsfeld* involves a Guantanamo detainee who had been charged in the military commission process devised just for the Guantanamo population. *Al-Marri v. Hanft* involves an alien who was initially indicted in the federal criminal system but plucked from there on the eve of trial and transferred to military custody.

What the cases have shared is the government's approach: that the courts do not possess any role in the process; that only the executive can exercise any discretion in deciding who to detain, on what evidence, pursuant to what process, and for how long. Yet in that sense the cases are not unprecedented. Rather, they have repeated the same cycle that has existed during and after every war the U.S. has fought. At first, there is deference to executive authority in the name of security and solidarity in the prosecution of the war. That deference invariably extends beyond that which peacetime principles find tolerable and results in postwar retrenchment.

Whether the chosen analog is *Ex parte Milligan* and *Ex parte Merryman* (the Civil War), the Espionage Act of 1917 prosecution of Eugene Debs (World War I), *Korematsu* and *Quirin* (World War II), the Smith Act cases (the Cold War), or the Chicago Eight and Dr. Spock cases (the Vietnam War), the current controversy replicates the tensions between executive power and civil liberties about which the courts have had to decide during a series of crises. Perhaps it is a sign of progress that while the administration insists that the conflict is ongoing – indeed, without any end in sight – the pendulum swing toward greater protection for civil liberties and human rights appears already to be occurring.

In three of the cases profiled in this volume – *Rasul*, *Hamdi*, and *Hamdan* – the Supreme Court reversed lower court decisions dismissing the particular detainees' law suits and vindicated at least some of the rights and principles the detainees had invoked. In *Padilla*, the detainee's loss was purely procedural. At the time of this writing, Mr. al-Marri's case has not yet reached the Court (although he has won a victory before a panel of the Court of Appeals for the Fourth Circuit – the first in that court for an "enemy combatant" among the four cases it has decided).

Thus, unlike cases related to previous wars, court victories have not had to await the end of hostilities and the elimination of the perceived danger to U.S. national security. Indeed, it is ironic that the cycle from judicial deference to defiance has been shorter in the context of a conflict that does not appear to have any discernible end and that is not susceptible to a clear point at which victory can be confidently and conclusively declared.

Also ironic is the manner in which the administration has refused to apply *any* law to its treatment of "enemy combatants" and has as a result ushered in a resurgence of attention and fidelity to international law principles and normative concepts of universal human rights – two legal systems that had been roundly dismissed as irrelevant to U.S. jurisprudence during the past two decades. The abandonment of ordinary protections, such as the U.S. Constitution and conventional statutory protections (i.e., habeas corpus, the Third Geneva Convention, and the Convention Against Torture), has had the unintended consequence of forcing the courts to address broader, traditional protections that have global application.

Much about this conflict has generated unanticipated developments. Before September 11th, who would have thought it would be the United States that would, in effect, repudiate the fundamental values incorporated in the Geneva Convention and, as a result, precipitate a crisis that would threaten to turn the clock back more than a century with respect to treatment of prisoners taken in armed conflict?

Nevertheless, those values, so long in developing into formal rules and protections – after all, the international conventions are less than a century old, while warfare is as old as humanity – have proven more durable than the U.S. government hoped. Placed in jeopardy by U.S. actions since September 11th, those values have experienced a resurgence, reminding everyone of the compelling reasons they were enacted in the first place. Along with resuscitating those internationally acknowledged limits on the treatment of prisoners, these five cases have also served as an important reminder of the founding principles of the U.S. itself: separation of powers, including an independent judiciary and constitutional rights that cannot be abrogated at the discretion of the executive or even with the imprimatur of Congress.

The governmental structure the Framers created, on full display not only in these five cases themselves but also in the rich historical and legal analyses explicated in the briefs and court opinions presented in this volume, continues more than 200 years later to strike an extraordinarily sensitive yet enduring balance between security in a physical sense – in immediate terms, within the natural purview of the executive – and security in terms of the values that make that physical security worth preserving – the checks applied by the legislative and judicial branches.

Thus, perhaps the triumph of these five cases in the historical context is not just their timing, coming *during* the conflict as opposed to after the danger has passed, but also in how collectively they turn not so much on hypertechnical textual constructions – whether a person is a citizen or alien, whether territory is or is not sovereign U.S. soil conferring jurisdiction – as they do on the threshold requirements for the humane treatment of individuals apprehended in a conflict that has transcended ordinary geographical boundaries as well as on the definition of the "enemy."

In many ways, these five cases share an attempt by the detainees, their lawyers, and the courts to render stationary many of the concepts and definitions the administration wishes to leave in a fluid state and has therefore resisted articulating with any specificity: *Where* is the battlefield? *Who* is the enemy? *What* is an "enemy combatant"? To *what process* are detainees entitled? *Which* laws and principles apply?

The administration has made the answers to these questions moving targets rather than fixed principles, in effect arguing that it should be free to decide these issues on an *ad hoc* basis, free from any meaningful or independent review. The result is not only the attempted thwarting of judicial intervention but also the attempted evasion of accountability in both the legal and electoral sense. Already we have on the record *mea culpas* from some of the participants as the rhetoric of executive hegemony fades in the waning days of the Bush administration. Ultimate accountability, however, awaits further investigation and review. These cases provide a legal and historical primer on the important civic discussion that will likely ensue in the coming years.

Each of the five cases featured in this volume is important in its own right, both legally and historically. The process of reviewing them, and choosing what portions of the record, briefs, and opinions to include, has provided us the opportunity to reflect on them as a group and has enabled us to recognize with a good measure of clarity the intellectual, legal, and political drama that has unfolded over the fate of the enemy combatant cases. For the reader as well, we hope that reading through these narratives will bring greater understanding of the post–9/11 era and the challenges – legal, political, and philosophical – that await this nation in the days ahead.

Enemy-Criminals: The Law and the War on Terror

Noah Feldman

I.

Almost as soon as the towers fell on September 11, lawyers began to ask and advise on the question of whether the U.S. government should engage with those responsible – and their associates – as criminals or as enemies in war. Both options seemed logically possible. On the one hand, the attacks perpetrated by al Qaeda certainly violated U.S. laws, and previous terrorists, including those who planned and executed the attack on the World Trade Center in 1991, had been tried as criminals. On the other hand, these attacks were on an unprecedented scale, came from outside the country, and were understood as acts of war by those who planned them out. The attacks of 9–11 were not the acts of a state, but, at least according to al Qaeda, they were directed *at* a state.

As it turned out, the U.S. government's approach to the crime/war dilemma was to treat alleged members of al Qaeda as both criminals and as wartime enemies, sometimes alternately, and sometimes simultaneously. The Congress leapt into action within a week, passing on September 18, 2001, a resolution authorizing the use of military force against those responsible for 9–11, their associates, and those who harbored them. This document, known to initiates through its acronym "AUMF," was based in part upon other resolutions that have come to do the legal and political work that a declaration of war did for an earlier generation. Where it differed from its predecessors was in its extraordinarily open-ended description of the adversary. To fight an asymmetric, non-state enemy, Congress seemed to say, the executive branch must be able to range far and wide in targeting, unconstrained by the niceties of a more ordinary war which the enemy forces can be identified by their uniforms and their nation of origin.

The executive branch, we now know, adopted for itself an interpretation of the congressional resolution that was at once embracing and dismissive. It was embracing insofar as the Bush administration read the AUMF as allowing it to detain any suspected al Qaeda members or associates wherever they might be, to hold them indefinitely and without counsel wherever it chose, and, in some cases, to interrogate them using methods and techniques that would otherwise have been prohibited by U.S. and international law. It was dismissive in that the same government that relied on the AUMF for these extraordinary powers also maintained that it would have had all the same powers even if Congress had never passed the resolution. The reason given was that, as the sole holder of the executive power and as commander in chief, the president had the inherent constitutional right to do what was necessary to defend a nation under attack – a power that Congress might confirm or even enhance but lacked the power to restrict.

With the two justifications of congressional and constitutional authority in hand, the executive branch undertook its own offensive in the global war on terror. Afghanistan was invaded and the Taliban, who had harbored senior al Qaeda figures, including Osama bin Laden and Ayman al-Zawahiri, fell quickly. In the aftermath, several hundred non-Afghan Muslims who were found in or near Afghanistan were detained, many of them handed to U.S. authorities in exchange for bounty. The status of these men posed obvious legal problems. They wore no uniforms, and though most carried weapons, so did every herdsman in Afghanistan who could afford one. Their presence as non-Afghans in Taliban Afghanistan strongly suggested some degree of al Qaeda affiliation, but it was not as if al Qaeda fighters wore dog tags or carried identification. They did not fit the paradigm of ordinary prisoners of war, but neither could it be said immediately that they had committed any crimes.

These men, and some other suspected al Qaeda members apprehended elsewhere in the world, were transferred in short order to detention facilities hastily constructed on the U.S. naval base in Guantanamo Bay, Cuba – a twilight zone for men whose legal status was itself of a twilight hue. The U.S. had leased Guantanamo in perpetuity when Cuba was little more than an American-controlled banana republic. Since Castro's revolution, the U.S. had continued to claim and exercise control there over Cuban protest – but, crucially for the Bush administration's legal strategy, not sovereignty. Guantanamo was therefore of the United States but not in it. The idea was that the government could do what it wanted there without falling inside the reach of U.S. law, whether statutory or constitutional.

By happenstance, one of these new detainees was American born. This accident meant that Yaser Esam Hamdi came in for special treatment. He was transferred to a military brig in the U.S. There he was joined, metaphorically though not literally (since both men were kept in solitary confinement in different locations), by another American, a Muslim convert named Jose Padilla. Padilla had not been to Afghanistan, but he had apparently consorted with terrorist types in Yemen and Pakistan, and may have been planning attacks on U.S. soil. He was arrested at O'Hare airport in Chicago on his return to the U.S., on information apparently obtained through the secret interrogation of Khalid Shaikh Mohammed, the purported mastermind of 9–11. What Padilla had most in common with Hamdi was that both were held on U.S. soil without criminal charges or access to attorneys or indeed to anyone else. If the Guantanamo detainees were in a place that was off the grid, Hamdi and Padilla were off the legal grid even inside the United States.

II.

To this point in our story, more than a year after 9–11, Congress and the president had acted in the war on terror, but the third branch of government, the judiciary, had done exactly nothing. It is a peculiar and quirky – though by no means necessary – feature of the American system of government that the courts only act when they are asked to consider the case of a particular individual who either has been harmed or has been placed in jeopardy of life, limb, or liberty by the state. To be sure, the *law* was constantly on the minds of various government actors. Yet despite popular perceptions to the contrary, the courts do not always have the chance to say what the law is. First a case must come before them.

Over the next several years, however, cases did begin to come to the U.S. courts, and, to one degree or another, these cases have been heard and decided. Through them, we are beginning to develop a picture of the how the law and the war on terror truly interact. The cases of the two Americans, Hamdi and Padilla, were among the first to be dealt with in definitive terms, and they generated some important, disturbing, and fascinating results. First, the executive branch needed to explain how it could hold them incommunicado without any time horizon. To do so the Bush administration gave them a legal name, one that has stuck: illegal enemy combatants. The term makes them more than ordinary criminals and less than soldiers in an enemy army. An illegal enemy combatant is one who has taken up arms against the U.S. but failed to follow the laws of war. According to the Supreme Court, the AUMF authorized the president to detain such combatants until the end of hostilities – which could be indefinitely.

Nevertheless, the Supreme Court held in Hamdi's case, an enemy combatant has at least some rights. A plurality of the Court – four justices – said that Hamdi was entitled to due process of law under the Constitution, which usually means the chance to be given notice of the charges against him and the chance to refute them before a nominally neutral decisionmaker. This was an important precedent because, at least in principle, it denied the president the authority to hold detainees with no formal review whatever. Two justices – the unlikely combination of the arch-conservative Justice Scalia and the ultra-liberal Justice Stevens – thought that when a U.S. citizen was on U.S. soil where the courts were open for business, he had to be tried as a criminal in a regular trial, not held as an enemy combatant. But inspiring as it sounded, this view did not carry the day.

Another principle emerged from Padilla's case as it played itself out in the Supreme Court and the lower courts: that the government may treat a suspected terrorist as an enemy or a criminal or both. Padilla had been captured in the U.S., and since the Supreme Court ducked his case by saying it had been brought in the wrong court, it was unclear whether he needed the full-dress trial that had been denied to his countryman Hamdi. The government ultimately announced it was transferring Padilla's case to the ordinary courts and charging him with conspiracy. Although an appellate court expressed its outrage – the government had, after all, been claiming all along that Padilla could not be charged in federal court because of the circumstances of his case – the Supreme Court allowed the transfer from military to civilian control.

The phenomenon of the enemy-criminal, though, is not limited to Padilla. In Guantanamo, where those detained are held as enemy combatants, the process of putting them on trial for war crimes has begun. This process had its birth when the Supreme Court held that, despite the Bush administration's best efforts to put the detainees out of the range of U.S. law, the federal statute conferring the right of habeas corpus on detained persons applied to them even in Guantanamo. This meant that, unless Congress changed the law, the detainees would have their day in court to hear why they were being held and to give reasons for their release.

Congress did subsequently change the law to exclude the Guantanamo detainees from seeking habeas corpus. Nevertheless, the symbolic significance of the Court's holding was profound. In effect, the Supreme Court said it would not recognize the claim that the U.S. could hold human beings in a place where no law at all would protect them. And in some form, the message got through to the White House. The president put in place tribunals in Guantanamo to try the detainees for war crimes. In another landmark case involving Salim Ahmed Hamdan, Osama bin Laden's driver, the Supreme Court found those tribunals not to have been authorized by the AUMF in the special form they took. In the aftermath of the *Hamdan* decision, Congress drafted a new statute delineating the terms of the tribunals, and the president signed it into law.

Practically speaking, then, the Guantanamo detainees have been afforded limited rights to limited tribunals, in which secret evidence may be used and the verdict is rendered by servants of the same military that brings the charges. They are not entitled to lawyers, although some have them anyway. This is hardly due process of the kind recognized in ordinary U.S. criminal trials. It is also true, however, that smart and aggressive lawyers have in some cases managed to publicize their clients' circumstances effectively enough to get them released to their home countries, which in some cases at least would doubtless mean an improvement in their circumstances.

It is probably too soon to render a final verdict on the way the law and the war on terror have interacted in the U.S. in the immediate post–9–11 years. More litigation remains. But it is not too soon to draw some conclusions. Congress has, for the most part, given the president almost everything he could ask for in terms of authority. That has not stopped the executive from in almost every instance trying to grab more even than Congress offered, stretching the law to its limits and then beyond, often without thinking through the likely consequences of its actions. Meanwhile, the courts have adopted a split strategy. In well-publicized decisions, they have confronted the president and reined in some of his excesses, thus standing up for the rule of law. In practical terms, though, they have largely accommodated the executive and Congress by charting legal ways for them to do what they had previously sought to do unlawfully. The law stands for our aspirations to fairness and justice – but remains, in the end, in the service of the state.

Readers' Guide

We have necessarily been selective in assembling the documents for this volume. Our guiding principal in deciding what to include has been to accurately reflect the legal theories as they have won, lost, evolved, and manifested themselves in various forms among the cases. We have also tried to provide a complete narrative so that the reader can follow the sequence of events as they occurred.

Background materials, including executive orders; amicus briefs; precedent cases such as *ex parte Milligan*, *ex parte Quirin*, and *Johnson v. Eisentrager*; and statutes such as the Authorization for Use of Military Force, the Detainee Treatment Act, and the Military Commissions Act are available online at www.lawandsecurity.org.

The conventions that we used in editing the documents are as follows:

- The documents are presented in two formats, either as text or as an image of the original. Text documents have been converted to a standard typeface throughout, but we have retained the original heading structure, citation style, and typographic errors.

- Three centered dots indicate that an entire paragraph or a block of successive paragraphs has been deleted. Ellipses indicate that text within a paragraph, or at the beginning or end of a paragraph, has been deleted.

- Timestamps and signature images have been removed from documents from which we have made substantive deletions. Typed signatures preceded by an "s/" are as they are in the original.

- No alterations have been made to direct quotes. All ellipses and brackets within quotation marks are as they are in the original.

- Footnote numbering corresponds to the original. As a result, some footnotes appear to be non-consecutive. Footnote one may be followed by footnote three, for example, where we have deleted footnote two and its accompanying text.

We hope that our edits are transparent and enhance the readers' ability to assess the arguments made on both sides of the cases presented herein.

Timeline

	Date	Events/Executive Branch Action	Rasul v. Bush	Hamdi v. Rumsfeld	Hamdan v. Rumsfeld	Padilla v. Bush	al-Marri v. Hanft
2001	9/10/2001						al-Marri arrives in the U.S.
	9/11/2001	9/11 attacks					
	9/18/2001	AUMF signed					
	10/7/2001	U.S. attacks Afghanistan					
	10/26/2001	PATRIOT Act signed					
	11/13/2001	Taliban retreats from Kabul/Military order authorizing detentions & mil. comms.					
	12/12/2001						al-Marri arrested in IL on a NY material witness warrant; then transferred to NY
	12/28/2001	DoJ memo: GTMO detainees lack habeas rights					
2002	1/11/2002	GTMO receives 1st detainees					
	2/6/2002						Indictment in NY for credit card fraud
	2/7/2002	Pres. memo: Third Geneva Conv. Art. 3 & 4 don't apply to al Q'da or Taliban					
	2/19/2002		Pet. for habeas filed in DC				
	3/21/2002	Mil. Comm. Ord. No. 1 establishes mil. comm. procedures					
	4/5/2002			Hamdi transferred from GTMO to brig in VA			

Date					
5/8/2002					Padilla arrested at O'Hare on a NY material witness warrant; then transferred to NY
5/10/2002			Pet. for habeas filed		
6/2002				Hamdan transferred to GTMO	
6/9/2002					Padilla classified as an enemy combatant; then transferred to Charleston, SC brig
6/12/2002					Pet. for habeas filed in NY
7/30/2002		*Dist. ct. dismisses habeas pet.: lack of jurisdiction*			
8/1/2002	DoJ memo: "torture" reqs. pain equivalent to "organ failure, impairment of bodily function, or even death."				
8/16/2002			*Dist. ct.: additional factfinding needed*		
12/2/2002	Rumsfeld approves "mild, non-injurious physical contact"				
12/4/2002					*South. Dist. of NY: court has jurisdiction; Padilla's detention is not per se unlawful but Padilla must have access to counsel*
2003 1/8/2003			*4th Cir. dismisses habeas pet.: Hamdi not entitled to challenge Mobbs dec.*		

Date	Events/Executive Branch Action	Rasul v. Bush	Hamdi v. Rumsfeld	Hamdan v. Rumsfeld	Padilla v. Bush	al-Marri v. Hanft
1/15/2003	Rumsfeld rescinds 12/2/02 approval; will consider such methods for individual cases where justified					
1/22/2003						Indictment in NY for false statements & false ID
3/11/2003		*DC Cir. affirms dismissal*				
3/19/2003	U.S. attacks Iraq					
4/4/2003	DoD working group report: interrogation methods beyond what Geneva Conv. would allow for POWs may be required					
5/12/2003						NY indictment dismissed; then re-indicted in IL
5/20/2003						al-Marri transferred to Peoria
6/23/2003						al-Marri classified as an enemy combatant & transferred to Charleston, SC brig; criminal indictment dismissed
7/3/2003		Hicks and 5 others designated for trial		Pres.: Hamdan & 5 others subject to order authorizing mil. comms.		
7/8/2003						Pet. for habeas filed in IL
7/9/2003			*4th Cir. denies rehearing*			

Date					
7/19/2003	Proceedings against Hicks and 2 others suspended pending diplomacy				
7/30/2003		Hamdi transferred to Charleston, SC brig			
8/1/2003					*Dist. ct. in IL dismisses habeas pet.: improper venue*
11/10/2003	*S. Ct. agrees to hear case*				
11/30/2003	*Time*: military official says that at least 140 detainees are scheduled for release				
12/2/2003		DoD agrees to allow access to counsel			
12/3/2003	Military counsel assigned to Hicks				
12/2003			Hamdan moved to pre-commission segregation		
12/13/2003			Military counsel assigned		
12/18/2003				*2nd Cir. remands to grant writ of habeas: Padilla's detention is not authorized by statute or the Const.*	
2004 1/9/2004		*S. Ct. agrees to hear case*			
1/30/2004			Hamdan meets with counsel		
2/3/2004		Hamdi meets with counsel			
2/11/2004				DoD agrees to allow access to counsel	

Date	Events/Executive Branch Action	Rasul v. Bush	Hamdi v. Rumsfeld	Hamdan v. Rumsfeld	Padilla v. Bush	al-Marri v. Hanft
2/13/2004	Rumsfeld describes screening process; DoD briefing on Admin. Review Panel					
2/20/2004					*S. Ct. agrees to hear case*	
2/24/2004	Two detainees charged with conspiracy to commit war crimes					
3/3/2004	DoD releases draft of admin. review process					
3/8/2004						*7th Cir. affirms dismissal: Dist. ct. lacked jurisdiction*
3/9/2004		Rasul, Iqbal, and 3 others returned to the UK & released				
4/6/2004				Pet. filed in West. Dist. of WA		
4/28/2004	Abu Ghraib photos shown on *60 Minutes II*					
5/12/2004	Adm. Church reports infractions at GTMO					
6/1/2004					Dep. AG holds press conf.	
6/07/04 & 6/08/04	Press reports on DoJ torture memos					
6/28/2004		*S. Ct. remands: courts have jurisdiction to hear the habeas claims*	*S. Ct. remands: citizens must have meaningful chance to dispute facts*		*S. Ct. orders habeas pet. dismissed: Dist. ct. in NY lacked jurisdiction*	
7/2/2004					Pet. for habeas filed in SC	

Date				
7/7/2004	Order establishing CSRTs for foreign nationals			
7/8/2004				*Petition for habeas filed in SC*
7/13/2004			Hamdan charged with conspiracy	
7/29/2004	Memo by the Sec. of the Navy describes the CSRT process			
8/9/2004			*Dist. judge in Seattle transfers case to DC*	
8/24/2004	Schlesinger report: stress positions, isolation, & stripping used in GTMO interrogations			
10/3/2004			*CSRT conducts hearing leading to determination that Hamdan is an enemy combatant*	
10/4/2004		Hamdi released w/agreement to return to Saudi Arabia & renounce U.S. nationality		
10/11/2004				*S. Ct. declines case regarding IL petition*

Date	Events/Executive Branch Action	Rasul v. Bush	Hamdi v. Rumsfeld	Hamdan v. Rumsfeld	Padilla v. Bush	al-Marri v. Hanft
10/14/2004						al-Marri meets with counsel
11/2/2004	Pres. Bush re-elected					
11/8/2004				*Dist. ct. in DC grants habeas in part: no mil. comm. unless a tribunal finds that Hamdan is not entitled to POW status; mil. comm. must comply with UCMJ Art. 39*		
11/10/2004	Ashcroft resignation announced					
1/31/2005		*Dist. judge in DC: CSRTs don't meet 5th Amend. reqs &, for Taliban detainees, Geneva Conv. reqs*				
2/3/2005	Gonzales confirmed					
2/28/2005					*Dist. ct. in SC grants habeas pet.: Pres. lacked authority to detain Padilla as an enemy combatant*	
7/15/2005				*DC Cir. reverses: mil. comm. is a "competent tribunal"*		
8/31/2005	New Mil. Comm. Ord. No. 1					
9/3/2005	Justice Rehnquist dies					
9/8/2005		Cases argued in D.C. Cir.				

2005

Date			
9/9/2005			*4th Cir. reverses: AUMF authorizes detention*
9/29/2005	**Justice Roberts sworn in (previously on D.C. Cir.)**		
11/7/2005		S. Ct. agrees to hear case	
11/17/2005			Indictment in FL
11/20/2005			Pres. orders transfer to civilian custody for trial
12/21/2005			*4th Cir. denies transfer*
12/30/2005	**DTA signed**		
2006 1/4/2006			*S. Ct. grants transfer*
1/31/2005	**Justice Alito replaces Justice O'Connor**		
4/3/2006			S. Ct. declines case
5/8/2006			*Magistrate recommends that habeas pet. be dismissed: al-Marri didn't present rebuttal evidence*
6/29/2005		*S. Ct. remands: DTA did not strip jurisdiction over pending cases; mil. comm. violates the UCMJ & Geneva Conv. (Roberts recused)*	
8/8/2006			**Dist. ct. dismisses habeas pet.: government met its burden**
9/6/2006	**Pres. Bush announces transfer of high-value detainees to GTMO**		

Date		Events/Executive Branch Action	Rasul v. Bush	Hamdi v. Rumsfeld	Hamdan v. Rumsfeld	Padilla v. Bush	al-Marri v. Hanft
	10/17/2006	MCA signed					
	11/7/2006	U.S. elections					
	11/8/2006	Rumsfeld resignation announced					
	11/13/2006						Dep. Sec. of Def.: al-Marri to be provided a CSRT upon dismissal
	12/5/2006	Gates confirmed					
	12/13/2006				*Dist. ct. in DC dismisses habeas pet.: MCA stripped jurisdiction & Hamdan has no constitutional right to habeas*		
2007	2/20/2007		*D.C. Cir. dismisses habeas petitions: MCA stripped jurisdiction*				
	3/26/2007		Hicks pleads guilty to material support for terrorism; then sentenced to serve 9 months				
	4/2/2007		*S. Ct. declines cases*		*S. Ct. declines case*		
	4/30/2007						
	5/14/2007					Criminal trial begins	
	5/20/2007		Hicks returned to Australia				

Date			
6/4/2007	Mil. comm. dismisses charges against Omar Khadr: CSRT held prior to the MCA did not meet MCA reqs for classifying him as an unlawful enemy combatant	Mil. comm. dismisses charges: CSRT held prior to the MCA did not meet MCA reqs for classifying Hamdan as an unlawful enemy combatant	
6/11/2007			*4th Cir. remands to grant writ of habeas: MCA doesn't apply to al-Marri; military cannot hold civilians indefinitely*
6/22/2007	Abraham dec. filed		
6/29/2007	*S. Ct. agrees to hear cases*		
8/16/2007		*Padilla convicted of terrorism support*	
8/22/2007			*4th Cir. agrees to rehear case before full panel*
8/27/2007	**Gonzales resignation announced**		
9/8/2007	**Mukasey confirmed**		
9/24/2007	Court of Mil. Comm. Review reverses *Khadr* decision, cases proceed		

THE ENEMY COMBATANT PAPERS: AMERICAN JUSTICE, THE COURTS, AND THE WAR ON TERROR

PART ONE. "BATTLEFIELD" CAPTURES

Rasul v. Bush

On January 11, 2002, an army transport plane descended from a cloudless Caribbean sky and touched down at the U.S. naval base at Guantanamo Bay, Cuba. Heavily armed Marines surrounded the plane as it taxied to a stop. A Navy helicopter hovered overhead with a gunner hanging off the side. Twenty prisoners stepped unsteadily from the plane. Shackles at their wrists were linked to chains encircling their waists, which connected to chains that ran down their legs and around their ankles – what the military calls a "three-piece suit." They were dressed in orange jumpsuits and wore oversize, blacked-out goggles so they could not see, soundproof earmuffs so they could not hear and heavy mitts strapped to their hands so they could not feel. One official described them as "wobbly and disoriented." In the days and weeks to come, more planes would drop from the sky, delivering their human cargo in much the same fashion.

In time, each of the prisoners was allowed to send a single-page letter to his family, censored by the United States and delivered by the International Red Cross. Australian David Hicks wrote to his father, Terry, who in turn contacted Stephen Kenny, a lawyer in Adelaide. Mr. Kenny contacted a group of attorneys nationwide that had come together in recent weeks – Michael Ratner and Steven Watt from the Center for Constitutional Rights, based in New York; Clive Stafford Smith, from New Orleans; and me, a civil rights lawyer in Minneapolis. We met in New York in late January to organize a law suit in response to the plan for military tribunals as described by the president and senior administration officials.

Mr. Kenny, who joined us by phone from Australia, pressed us to challenge Hicks's detention as quickly as possible. When he first learned that Mr. Hicks had been brought to Guantanamo, Mr. Kenny asked the U.S. government for word about his welfare, and for an immediate statement of the allegations against him that justified his detention. Mr. Kenny's inquiries were met with silence. The United States did not even officially acknowledge that Mr. Hicks was their prisoner, let alone permit him any contact with the outside world. This legal limbo could not be allowed to persist, Mr. Kenny said, and had to be challenged in court.

But Mr. Hicks had not yet been brought before a military tribunal. I wondered whether we could challenge a process that had not yet begun. Mr. Kenny was indignant. "They'll never start the tribunals if they don't have to," he said. The rules governing the tribunals were still years from completion. Should we do nothing until the trials began? And what incentive did the United States have to start costly and potentially embarrassing military trials if they could hold the prisoners for as long as they saw fit, with no means by which a prisoner could challenge the lawfulness of his detention? In short, what did they lose by simply maintaining the status quo? The immediate legal challenge, Mr. Kenny said, was not to some tribunal that loomed in the uncertain future, but to Mr. Hicks's present, indefinite detention without legal process. He was quite right. The litigation in *Rasul, et al. v. Bush* – named for Shafiq Rasul, a British prisoner who arrived three days after Hicks, and which was brought on behalf of two British citizens and two Australians – began with that call.

The team of attorneys filed *Rasul* on February 19, 2002, in the United States District Court for the District of Columbia. We sought a writ of habeas corpus, the time-honored means by which a prisoner may challenge the factual and legal basis for his incarceration. We argued, and have always argued, that while the president may have the authority to hold people seized in connection with the conflict in Afghanistan, he cannot hold them without a lawful process before a neutral tribunal that rationally separates wheat from chaff. A few weeks later, I received a call from Neil Koslowe, an attorney at the Washington, D.C., office of Shearman and Sterling. His firm had been retained to represent a group of Kuwaiti prisoners at Guantanamo and he wanted to know whether our team would be willing to collaborate with theirs. I readily agreed, and the two groups have worked shoulder to shoulder ever since. They filed their case that April.

The litigation eventually made its way to the Supreme Court. Theodore Olson, the solicitor general of the United States whose wife was killed in the 9/11 attacks, represented the government. The federal courts, he insisted, were powerless in this matter. The prisoners could be held under any conditions that the military may devise, for as long as the president saw fit, because the petitioners – like all the men and boys at Guantanamo – were foreigners beyond the technical sovereignty of the United States.

For more than 100 years, the United States has leased Guantanamo from Cuba. The lease says that Cuba retains "ultimate sovereignty" over the base while the United States exercises "complete jurisdiction and control" for as long as it wants. No one quite knows what these terms mean but, in practice, they mean nothing – former Cuban President Fidel Castro ordered the United States to close the base and leave Cuba, to no avail. In the meantime, Guantanamo has developed into a fully American enclave, with all the trappings of a small American city. For years, the Untied States has described it as "practically . . . a part of the Government of the United States." It is entirely self-sufficient, with its own water plant, power supply, schools, and transportation system. It has a number of commercial centers with a McDonalds, a movie theater and a Starbucks. With a total area of over 45 square miles, the base is larger than the island of Manhattan and nearly half the size of the District of Columbia, with a full time population of nearly 10,000. At one court appearance, a lawyer for the government protested that even Paris has a Starbucks, which does not suggest that Paris is part of the United States. I whispered to my colleague that Guantanamo is much more like Paris, Texas than Paris, France. During the course of the litigation, I came to refer to the suggestion that the base was – despite all appearances to the contrary – really just like Paris as "the Guantanamo fiction."

On June 28, 2004, the Supreme Court issued its decision. By a six-to-three margin, the Court held that the prisoners could challenge the lawfulness of their detention in federal court, a stunning reversal for the president. The Court quickly dispatched the Guantanamo fiction, concluding that Cuba's "ultimate sovereignty" did not deprive the federal courts of the power to act. "What matters," Justice Anthony Kennedy explained in a thoughtful concurrence, "is the unchallenged and indefinite control that the United States has long exercised over Guantanamo Bay. From a practical perspective, the indefinite lease of Guantanamo Bay has produced a place that belongs to the United States. . . ."

The decision in *Rasul* did not end our struggle to bring the rule of law to Guantanamo. Instead, the administration created "Combatant Status Review Tribunals" that purported to review the cases there. At the same time, Congress has become involved. In December 2005, the Republican Congress passed the Detainee Treatment Act (or "DTA"), with provisions to strip the courts of jurisdiction over habeas actions brought by prisoners at Guantanamo. In June 2006, the Supreme Court held in *Hamdan v. Rumsfeld* that the DTA did not apply to cases that were already pending when the act was passed. Congress responded the following October, just before the November elections, by passing the Military Commissions Act (or "MCA"). On February 20, 2007, five years and a day after we filed the litigation in *Rasul*, the D.C. Circuit Court of Appeals held that the MCA stripped the federal courts of jurisdiction over all habeas actions filed by prisoners at Guantanamo. As of this writing, the Supreme Court has again heard oral arguments. When it issues its decision, we will once again learn – one hopes for all time – whether Guantanamo is a prison beyond the law.

Joseph Margulies
MacArthur Justice Center
Northwestern University School of Law
Chicago, Illinois

2/19/2002: PETITION FOR WRIT OF HABEAS CORPUS*

IN THE UNITED STATES DISTRICT COURT
FOR THE DISTRICT OF COLUMBIA

SHAFIQ RASUL,
    Detainee, Camp X-Ray
    Guantanamo Bay Naval Base
    Guantanamo Bay, Cuba
	))))

SKINA BIBI,
    as Next Friend of Shafiq Rasul
    █████████████████
	))))))

ASIF IQBAL,
    Detainee, Camp X-Ray
    Guantanamo Bay Naval Base
    Guantanamo Bay, Cuba
	))))

MOHAMMED IQBAL,
    as Next Friend of Asif Iqbal
    █████████████████
	))))))

DAVID HICKS,
    Detainee, Camp X-Ray
    Guantanamo Bay Naval Base
    Guantanamo Bay, Cuba
	))))

TERRY HICKS,
    as Next Friend of David Hicks
    █████████████████
	))))))

Petitioners,	)

**PETITION FOR WRIT
OF HABEAS CORPUS**

No. _____

v.

GEORGE WALKER BUSH,
    President of the United States
    The White House
    ███████████████████
	)))))

DONALD RUMSFELD,
    Secretary, United States
    Department of Defense
    ███████████████████
	)))))

BRIGADIER GEN. MICHAEL LEHNERT,
    Commander, Joint Task Force-160
    Guantanamo Bay Naval Base
    Guantanamo Bay, Cuba
	))))

COLONEL TERRY CARRICO,
    Commander, Camp X-Ray,
    Guantanamo Bay Naval Base
    Guantanamo Bay, Cuba
	))))

Respondents
        All sued in their official
        and individual capacities.
	))))

---

* Redactions on this page have been added for privacy purposes. – *Eds.*

PETITION FOR WRIT OF HABEAS CORPUS

1. Petitioners David Hicks, Asif Iqbal, and Shafiq Rasul seek the Great Writ. They act on their own behalf and through their Next Friends: Skina Bibi acts for her son Shafiq Rasul, Mohammed Iqbal acts for his son Asif, and Terry Hicks acts for his son David. David Hicks is a citizen of Australia. Mr. Iqbal and Mr. Rasul are citizens of the United Kingdom. They are being held virtually *incommunicado* in respondents' unlawful custody.

I.
JURISDICTION

2. Petitioners bring this action under 28 U.S.C. §§2241 and 2242, and invoke this Court's jurisdiction under 28 U.S.C. §§1331, 1350, 1651, 2201, and 2202; 5 U.S.C. §702; as well as the Fifth and Fourteenth Amendments to the United States Constitution, the International Covenant on Civil and Political Rights ("ICCPR"), the American Declaration on the Rights and Duties of Man ("ADRDM"), and Customary International Law. Because they seek declaratory relief, Petitioners also rely on F. R. Civ. P. 57.

3. This Court is empowered under 28 U.S.C. §2241 to grant the Writ of Habeas Corpus, and to entertain the Petition filed by Terry Hicks, Mohammed Iqbal, and Skina Bibi as Next Friend under 28 U.S.C. §2242. This Court is further empowered to declare the rights and other legal relations of the parties herein by 28 U.S.C. §2201, and to effectuate and enforce declaratory relief by all necessary and proper means by 28 U.S.C. §2202, as this case involves an actual controversy within the Court's jurisdiction.

II.
VENUE

4. Venue is proper in the United States District Court for the District of Columbia, since at least one respondent resides in the district, a substantial part of the events or omissions giving rise to the claim occurred in the district, at least one respondent may be found in the district, and all respondents are either officers or employees of the United States or any agency thereof acting in their official capacities. 28 U.S.C. §§1391(b); 1391(e).

III.
PARTIES

5. Petitioner David Hicks is an Australian citizen presently incarcerated and held in respondents' unlawful custody at Camp X-Ray, United States Naval Base, Guantanamo Bay, Cuba. *See* . . . Birth Certificate of David Hicks.

6. Petitioner Terry Hicks is David Hicks' father. He too is an Australian citizen. Terry Hicks has received a letter from his son, delivered through the Australian Red Cross, asking for legal assistance. Because his son cannot secure access either to legal counsel or the courts of the United States, the elder Mr. Hicks acts as Next Friend. *See* . . . Affidavit of Terry Hicks, incorporated by reference herein.

7. Through counsel, Terry Hicks has tried repeatedly to contact his son, and to learn more about his condition and status. The United States has either rebuffed or ignored counsel's requests. In a letter dated January 17, 2002, for instance, Steven Kenny, Australian counsel for Terry and David Hicks, asked the Australian Government to confirm, *inter alia*, whether David Hicks was being held at Guantanamo, whether the United

States intended to charge him with any offense, and whether the Australian Government could work with counsel to secure representation for Mr. Hicks. In the same letter, Mr. Kenny asked the Australian Government to "arrange contact between David and his family." *See* Exhibit C, Affidavit of Stephen Kenny, Australian Counsel for Petitioners; Letter from Stephen Kenny to Hon. Daryl Williams, Attorney-General (Jan. 17, 2002), all correspondence incorporated herein by reference. The following day, the Australian Government advised counsel that Mr. Hicks was being held in Guantanamo, that he "does not currently have legal representation due to the nature and circumstances of his detention," and that "the matter of access to Mr. Hicks by his family" was "ultimately a matter for the United States." *Id.* at Letter from Robert Cornall, Attorney-General's Department (Jan. 18, 2002).

8. Mr. Kenny responded the same day, repeating his request for information about Mr. Hicks, and seeking the assistance of the Australian Government "with a view to arranging" legal advice for Mr. Hicks. On February 1, 2002, Mr. Kenny renewed his request for "access by [Terry Hicks] to his son. He wishes to see his son face to face but would appreciate being able to make even a telephone call to him. Will you please make a direct request to the United States authorities for such a meeting." *Id.* at Letter from Stephen Kenny (Feb. 1, 2002). On February 8, 2002, the Australian Government left no doubt that David Hicks, and all detainees, were cut off:

> Your request for Mr. Hicks' family to have access to him was referred to the United States authorities. *The United States has advised that, at this stage, no family access will be allowed any of the detainees held at Guantanamo Bay.*

Id. at Letter from Robert Cornall (Feb. 8, 2002)(emphasis added).

9. In addition to his correspondence with the Australian Government, on January 25, Mr. Kenny wrote to President Bush, asking, *inter alia*, if he would "permit David to be seen by legal counsel," and if he would allow Terry Hicks "to have contact with his son." To date, the United States Government has not responded to this request.

10. Petitioner Asif Iqbal is a citizen of the United Kingdom presently incarcerated and held in respondents' unlawful custody at Camp X-Ray, Guantanamo Bay Naval Station, Guantanamo Bay, Cuba. *See* . . . Birth Certificate of Asif Iqbal.

11. Petitioner Mohammed Iqbal is Asif Iqbal's father. He too is a British citizen. Mohammed Iqbal received a telephone call from the Foreign and Commonwealth Office on January 21, 2002, during which he was informed that his son was being detained in Guantanamo Bay. Because his son cannot secure access either to legal counsel or the courts of the United States, Mohammed Iqbal acts as his Next Friend. *See* . . . Affidavit of Mohammed Iqbal, incorporated by reference herein.

12. Through counsel, Mohammed Iqbal has attempted to gain access to his son. The United States has declined to accede to counsel's requests. *See* . . . First Affidavit of Gareth Peirce, United Kingdom Counsel for Petitioners Asif and Mohammed Iqbal and Shafiq Rasul and Skina Bibi.

13. The British Foreign and Commonwealth Office advised Ms. Peirce that any request for access to Mr. Iqbal must be made to the United States Ambassador in London. Immediately upon receiving instructions from Mr Iqbal's family, on January 25, 2002, Ms. Peirce telephoned and also sent a faxed request to the Ambassador, seeking immediate access to Mr. Iqbal in Guantanamo Bay in order to provide legal advice. In addition, she asked the Foreign and Commonwealth Office in London to pursue this request directly with the United States government. Ms. Peirce has been advised by the Foreign and Commonwealth Office that this request has been passed to the United States government on behalf of Mr Iqbal, together with requests by Mr Iqbal's Member of Parliament that he and Mr Iqbal's family be permitted access to him. Counsel is

advised by the Foreign and Commonwealth Office that as of February 13, 2002, these requests have not received a response, and nor has a request for further consular access to Mr Iqbal, i.e. a second consular visit, been granted.

14. Petitioner Shafiq Rasul is a citizen of the United Kingdom presently incarcerated and held in respondents' unlawful custody at Camp X-Ray, Guantanamo Bay Naval Station, Guantanamo Bay, Cuba. *See* . . . Birth Certificate of Shafiq Rasul.

15. Petitioner Skina Bibi is Shafiq Rasul's mother. She too is a British citizen. Ms. Bibi received a telephone call from the Foreign and Commonwealth Office on January 21, 2002, during which she was informed that her son was being detained in Guantanamo Bay. Skina Bibi has also received news of a message from her son, delivered through the Red Cross, asking for legal representation. Because her son cannot secure access either to legal counsel or the courts of the United States, she acts as his Next Friend. *See* . . . Affidavit of Skina Bibi, incorporated by reference herein.

16. Through counsel, Skina Bibi has attempted to gain access to her son. The United States has declined to accede to counsel's requests. *See* . . . Second Affidavit of Gareth Peirce, United Kingdom Counsel for the Petitioners Asif and Mohammed Iqbal and Shafiq Rasul and Skina Bibi.

17. The British Foreign and Commonwealth Office advised Ms. Peirce that any request for access to Mr. Rasul must be made to the United States Ambassador in London. Immediately upon receiving instructions from Mr. Rasul's family, on January 25, 2002, Ms. Peirce telephoned and also sent a faxed request to the Ambassador, seeking immediate access to Mr. Rasul in Guantanamo Bay in order to provide legal advice. In addition, she asked the Foreign and Commonwealth Office in London to pursue this request directly with the United States government. Ms. Peirce has been advised by the Foreign and Commonwealth Office that this request has been passed to the United States government on behalf of Mr. Rasul, together with requests by Mr. Rasul's Member of Parliament that he and Mr. Rasul's family be permitted access to him. Counsel is advised by the Foreign and Commonwealth Office that as of February 13, 2002, these requests have not received a response, and nor has a request for further consular access to Mr Rasul, i.e. a second consular visit, been granted.

18. Respondent Bush is the President of the United States and Commander in Chief of the United States Military. He is the author of the Order directing that David Hicks, Asif Iqbal, and Shafiq Rasul be detained, and is ultimately responsible for their unlawful detention. He is sued in his official and personal capacities.

19. Respondent Rumsfeld is the Secretary of the United States Department of Defense. Pursuant to the Order described in Para. 18, respondent Rumsfeld has been charged with maintaining the custody and control of the detained petitioners. Respondent Rumsfeld is sued in his official and personal capacities.

20. Respondent Lehnert is the Commander of Joint Task Force-160, the task force running the detention operation at the Guantanamo Naval Station, Guantanamo Bay, Cuba. He has supervisory responsibility for the detained petitioners and is sued in his official and personal capacities.

21. Respondent Carrico is the Commandant of Camp X-Ray, where the detained petitioners are presently held. He is the immediate custodian responsible for their detention, and is sued in his official and personal capacities.

IV.

STATEMENT OF FACTS

22. The detained petitioners are not enemy aliens. David Hicks is an Australian citizen in respondents' unlawful custody. At the time of his seizure by the United States

Government, Mr. Hicks was living in Afghanistan. On information and belief, he had no involvement , direct or indirect, in either the terrorist at tacks on the United States September 11, 2001, or any act of international terrorism attributed by the United States to al Qaida or any terrorist group. He is not properly subject to the detention Order issued by respondent Bush, and discussed *infra* in Paras. 28–33.

23. Petitioners Asif Iqbal and Shafiq Rasul are UK citizens in respondents' unlawful custody. No proper or adequate information has been provided by the United States government as to the circumstances of their seizure by U.S . forces. They were in the United Kingdom at all material times before and on September 11, 2001. On information and belief, they had no involvement, direct or indirect, in either the terrorist attacks on the United States on September 11, 2001, or any act of international terrorism attributed by the United States to al Qaida or any terrorist group. They are not properly subject to the detention Order issued by respondent Bush, and discussed *infra* in Paras. 28–33.

Petitioners' Seizure By The United States

24. In the wake of September 11, 2001, the United States, at the direction of respondent Bush, began a massive military campaign against the Taliban, then in power in Afghanistan. On September 18, 2001, a Joint Resolution of Congress authorized the President to use force against the "nations, organizations, or persons" that "planned, authorized, committed, or aided the terrorist attacks on September 11, 2001, or [that] harbored such organizations or persons." Joint Resolution 23, Authorization for Use of Military Force, Public Law 107–40, 115 Stat. 224 (Jan. 18, 2001). The Resolution did not authorize the indefinite detention of persons seized on the field of battle.

25. In the course of the military campaign, and as part of their effort to overthrow the Taliban, the United States provided military assistance to the Northern Alliance, a loosely knit coalition of Afghani and other military groups opposed to the Taliban Government. On information and belief, no American casualties were caused by the Taliban prior to when Mr. Hicks, Mr. Iqbal, and Mr. Rasul were apprehended, and the detained petitioners neither caused nor attempted to cause any harm to American personnel prior to their capture.

26. On or about December 9, 2001, the precise date unknown to counsel but known to respondents, the Northern Alliance captured David Hicks in Afghanistan. On December 17, 2001, the Northern Alliance transferred him to the custody of the United States military. *See* . . . Joint News Release of the Australian Attorney General and the Minister for Defense (December 17, 2001). David Hicks has been held in United States custody since that time.

27. No proper or adequate information has been provided by the United States government as to the date or circumstances of Mr. Iqbal's and Mr. Rasul's seizure by U.S. forces. The precise date of their capture by U.S. forces is unknown to counsel but known to respondents. They have been held in United States custody since that time.

The Detention Order

28. On November 13, 2001, respondent Bush issued a Military Order authorizing indefinite detention without due process of law. The Order authorizes respondent Rumsfeld to detain anyone respondent Bush has "reason to believe":

i. is or was a member of the organization known as al Qaida;

ii. has engaged in, aided or abetted, or conspired to commit, acts of international terrorism, or acts in preparation therefor, that have caused, threaten to cause, or have as their aim to cause, injury to or adverse effects on the United States, its citizens, national security, foreign policy, or economy; or

iii. has knowingly harbored one or more individuals described in subparagraphs (i) and (ii)

See...Military Order of November 13, 2001. President Bush must make this determination in writing. The Order was neither authorized nor directed by Congress, and is beyond the scope of the Joint Resolution of September 18, 2001.

29. The Military Order vests the President with complete discretion to identify the individuals that fall within its scope. It establishes no standards governing the use of his discretion. Once a person has been detained, the Order contains no provision for him to be notified of the charges he may face. On the contrary, the Order authorizes detainees to be held without charges. It contains no provision for detainees to be notified of their rights under domestic and international law, and provides neither the right to counsel, nor the right to consular access. It provides no right to appear before a neutral tribunal to review the legality of a detainee's continued detention, and no provision for appeal to an Article III court. In fact, the Order expressly bars review by any court. Though the Order directs respondent Rumsfeld to create military tribunals, it sets no deadline for his task. And for those detainees who will not be tried before a tribunal, the Order authorizes indefinite and unreviewable detention, based on nothing more than the President's written determination that an individual is subject to its terms.

30. The United States Government has advised the Australian Government that Mr. Hicks is being held at Camp X-Ray, Guantanamo Bay Naval Station, Guantanamo Bay, Cuba, pursuant to this Order. *See*...Letter from Robert Cornall, Australian Attorney General's Department, to Stephen Kenny, Australian counsel for Petitioners (Jan. 18, 2002).

31. British Foreign Office Minister Ben Bradshaw advised Parliament on January 21, 2002, that British officials had visited three British citizens being detained at Camp X-Ray, Guantanamo Bay Naval Station, Guantanamo Bay, Cuba, who were held pursuant to this Order. Only one of the detainees was named; the name given was neither Mr. Iqbal nor Mr. Rasul. However, Petitioners Mohammed Iqbal and Skina Bibi received telephone calls from the Foreign and Commonwealth Office January 21, 2002, during which they were informed that their sons were being detained at Camp X-Ray, in Guantanamo Bay.

32. On information and belief, respondent Bush has never certified or determined in any manner, in writing or otherwise, that the detained petitioners are subject to this detention order.

33. The detained petitioners are not properly subject to this detention order.

Guantanamo Bay Naval Station

34. On or about January 11, 2002, the United States military began transporting prisoners captured in Afghanistan to Camp X-Ray, at the United States Naval Base, in Guantanamo Bay, Cuba. Guantanamo Bay is a self-sufficient and essentially permanent city with approximately 7,000 military and civilian residents under the complete jurisdiction and control of the United States. Guantanamo Bay occupies nearly thirty-one square miles of land, an area larger than Manhattan, and nearly half the size of the District of Columbia. It has its own schools, generates its own power, provides its own internal transportation, and supplies its own water. Offenses committed by both civilians and foreign nationals living on Guantanamo are brought before federal courts on the mainland, where respondents enjoy the full panoply of Constitutional rights. The

United States has occupied Guantanamo Bay since 1903, and has repeatedly declared its intention to remain there indefinitely. For several decades, the United States has resisted claims of national sovereignty made by Cuba over Guantanamo Bay.

35. On or about January 11, 2002, the precise date unknown to counsel but known to respondents, the United States military transferred the detained petitioners to Camp X-Ray, Guantanamo Bay, where they have been held ever since, in the custody of respondents Bush, Rumsfeld, Lehnert, and Carrico.

36. Since gaining control of the detained petitioners, the United States military has held them virtually *incommunicado*. They have been or will be interrogated repeatedly by agents of the United States Departments of Defense and Justice, though they have not been charged with an offense, nor have they been notified of any pending or contemplated charges. They have made no appearance before either a military or civilian tribunal of any sort, nor have they been provided counsel or the means to contact counsel. They have not been informed of their rights under the United States Constitution, the regulations of the United States Military, the Geneva Convention, the International Covenant on Civil and Political Rights, or the American Declaration on the Rights and Duties of Man. Indeed, the respondents have taken the position that the detainees should not be told of these rights. As a result, the detained petitioners are completely unable either to protect, or to vindicate their rights under domestic and international law.

37. David Hicks has been allowed to write a single, brief letter to his father, which was delivered by the Australian Red Cross. In that letter, he asked his father for legal assistance. *See* . . . Affidavit of Terry Hicks.

38. Shafiq Rasul has attempted to pass messages to his family, through the Red Cross. The U.S. authorities did not permit the details of these messages to be delivered. A summary was provided, however, indicating that Mr. Rasul was well and that he had asked for legal representation. *See* . . . Affidavit of Skina Bibi. Asif Iqbal communicated with his family, through the Red Cross, when he was detained in Afghanistan. It is unknown whether he has attempted to communicate with his family since his detention in Guantanamo.

39. In published statements, respondents Bush, Rumsfeld, Lehnert and Carrico have indicated the United States may hold the detained petitioners under these conditions indefinitely. *See, e.g.,* Roland Watson, *The Times (London)*, Jan. 18, 2002 ("Donald Rumsfeld, the U.S. Defence Secretary, suggested last night that al-Qaeda prisoners could be held indefinitely at the base. He said that the detention of some would be open-ended as the United States tried to build a case against them."); Lynne Sladky, Associated Press, Jan. 22, 2002 ("Marine Brig. Gen. Mike Lehnert, who is in charge of the detention mission, defended the temporary cells where detainees are being held . . . 'We have to look at Camp X-ray as a work in progress . . .,' Lehnert told CNN. . . . Lehnert said plans are to build a more permanent prison 'exactly in accordance with federal prison standards'"); John Mintz, THE WASHINGTON POST, "Extended Detention In Cuba Mulled," Feb. 13, 2002 ("As the Bush administration nears completion of new rules for conducting military trials of foreign detainees, U.S. officials say they envision the naval base at Gantanamo Bay, Cuba, as a site for the tribunals and as a terrorist penal colony for many years to come.")[1]

---

[1] *See also* Time Magazine, "Welcome to Camp X-Ray" (February 3, 2002):

"More curious still is the matter of the prisoners' ultimate fate. Rumsfeld has laid out four options: a military trial, a trial in U.S. criminal courts, return to their home countries for prosecution, or continued detention 'while additional intelligence is gathered.' The last seems a distinct possibility; the Pentagon plans to build 2,000 cells at Camp X-Ray."

V.

CAUSES OF ACTION

FIRST CLAIM FOR RELIEF
(DUE PROCESS —FIFTH AND FOURTEENTH AMENDMENTS
TO THE UNITED STATES CONSTITUTION)

. . .

41. By the actions described above, respondents, acting under color of law, have violated and continue to violate the Fifth and Fourteenth Amendments to the United States Constitution. Respondent Bush has ordered the prolonged, indefinite, and arbitrary detention of individuals, without Due Process of Law. Respondents Rumsfeld, Lehnert, and Carrico are likewise acting in violation of the Fifth Amendment, since they act at the President's direction. On its face, the Executive Order violates the Fifth and Fourteenth Amendments.

SECOND CLAIM FOR RELIEF
(DUE PROCESS —FIFTH AND FOURTEENTH AMENDMENTS
TO THE UNITED STATES CONSTITUTION)

. . .

43. By the actions described above, respondents, acting under color of law, have violated and continue to violate the right of the detained petitioners to be free from arbitrary, prolonged, and indefinite detention, in violation of the Due Process Clause of the Fifth and Fourteenth Amendments to the United States Constitution. The Executive Order, as applied to Mr. Hicks, Mr. Iqbal, and Mr. Rasul, violates the Fifth and Fourteenth Amendments.

THIRD CLAIM FOR RELIEF
(DUE PROCESS —INTERNATIONAL LAW)

. . .

45. By the actions described above, respondents, acting under color of law, have violated and continue to violate Customary International Law, Arts. 9 & 14 of the International Covenant on Civil and Political Rights, and Arts. 18, 25, & 26 of the American Declaration on the Rights and Duties of Man. Respondent Bush has ordered the prolonged, indefinite, and arbitrary detention of individuals, without legal process, in violation of binding obligations of the United States under International Law. Respondents Rumsfeld, Lehnert, and Carrico are likewise acting in violation of International Law, since they act at the President's direction. On its face, the Executive Order violates International Law.

FOURTH CLAIM FOR RELIEF
(DUE PROCESS —INTERNATIONAL LAW)

. . .

47. By the actions described above, respondents, acting under color of law, have violated and continue to violate the right of the detained petitioners to be free from arbitrary,

prolonged, and indefinite detention, in violation of Customary International Law, Arts. 9 & 14 of the International Covenant on Civil and Political Rights, and Arts. 18, 25, & 26 of the American Declaration on the Rights and Duties of Man. The Executive Order, as applied to the detained petitioners, violates these and other binding obligations of the United States under International Law.

FIFTH CLAIM FOR RELIEF
(DUE PROCESS —FAILURE TO COMPLY
WITH U.S. MILITARY REGULATIONS AND
INTERNATIONAL HUMANITARIAN LAW)

. . .

49. By the actions described above, respondents, acting under color of law, have violated and continue to violate the rights accorded to persons seized by the United States Military in times of armed conflict, as established by, *inter alia*, the regulations of the United States Military, Articles 4 and 5 of Geneva Convention III, Geneva Convention IV, and Customary International Law.

SIXTH CLAIM FOR RELIEF
(WAR POWERS CLAUSE)

. . .

51. By the actions described above, respondents, acting under color of law, have exceeded the constitutional authority of the Executive and have violated and continue to violate the War Powers Clause by ordering the prolonged and indefinite detention of the detained petitioners without Congressional authorization.

SEVENTH CLAIM FOR RELIEF
(SUSPENSION OF THE WRIT)

. . .

53. To the extent the order of November 13, 2001, disallows any challenge to the legality of the detained petitioners' detention by way of habeas corpus, the Order and its enforcement constitute an unlawful Suspension of the Writ, in violation of Article I of the United States Constitution.

VI.
PRAYER FOR RELIEF

WHEREFORE, Petitioners pray for relief as follows:

1. Grant Petitioner Terry Hicks Next Friend status, as Next Friend of David Hicks;
2. Grant Petitioner Mohammed Iqbal Next Friend status, as Next Friend of Asif Iqbal;
3. Grant Petitioner Skina Bibi Next Friend status, as Next Friend of Shafiq Rasul;
4. Order the detained petitioners released from respondents' unlawful custody;
5. Order respondents to allow counsel to meet and confer with the detained petitioners, in private and unmonitored attorney-client conversations;
6. Order respondents to cease all interrogations of the detained petitioners, direct or indirect, while this litigation is pending;

7. Order and declare the Executive Order of November 13, 2001, unlawful as a violation of the Fifth and Fourteenth Amendments to the United States Constitution;

8. Order and declare that the detained petitioners are being held in violation of the Fifth and Fourteenth Amendments to the United States Constitution;

9. Order and declare the Executive Order of November 13, 2001, unlawful as a violation of Customary International Law, the International Covenant on Civil and Political Rights, and the American Declaration on the Rights and Duties of Man;

10. Order and declare that the detained petitioners are being held in violation of Customary International Law, the International Covenant on Civil and Political Rights, and the American Declaration on the Rights and Duties of Man;

11. Order and declare that the detained petitioners are being held in violation of the regulations of the United States Military, the Geneva Convention, and International Humanitarian Law;

12. Order and declare that the Executive Order of November 13, 2001, violates the War Powers Clause;

13. Order and declare that the provision of the Executive Order that bars the detained petitioners from seeking relief in this Court is an unlawful Suspension of the Writ, in violation of Article I of the United States Constitution;

14. To the extent respondents contest any material factual allegations in this Petition, schedule an evidentiary hearing, at which Petitioners may adduce proof in support of their allegations;

15. Such other relief as the Court may deem necessary and appropriate to protect Petitioners' rights under the United States Constitution and International Law.

Dated: 2/19/02   Respectfully submitted,

Counsel for Petitioners:

_____

Joseph Margulies*

. . .

MARGULIES & RICHMAN, plc

. . .

Clive A. Stafford Smith**

. . .

_____

Gareth Peirce**
Birnberg, Peirce and Partners, Solicitors

. . .

_____

Michael Ratner*
William Goodman
Anthony DiCaprio
Center for Constitutional Rights

. . .

_____

Jon W. Norris

. . .

The Law Office of Jon W. Norris

. . .

_____

Stephen Kenny*
CAMATTA LEMPENS, PTY LTD.
BARRISTERS AND SOLICITORS

. . .

_____

L. Barrett Boss

. . .

ASBILL MOFFITT & BOSS, Chtd.

. . .

*Mr. Margulies, Mr. Kenny, and the Center for Constitutional Rights appear for Petitioners Terry and David Hicks.

**Mr. Stafford Smith and Ms. Peirce appear for Petitioners Asif and Mohammed Iqbal, as well as Petitioners Rasul and Bibi.

Mr. Norris and Mr. Boss appear as local counsel for all attorneys.

. . .

IN THE UNITED STATES DISTRICT COURT
FOR THE DISTRICT OF COLUMBIA

SHAFIQ RASUL,
    Detainee, Camp X-Ray
    Guantanamo Bay Naval Base
    Guantanamo Bay, Cuba
	)
	)
	)
	)
	)	

SKINA BIBI, as Next Friend of Shafiq Rasul ███████████	))))))	
	)	**FIRST AMENDED** **PETITION FOR WRIT** **OF HABEAS CORPUS**

ASIF IQBAL,
    Detainee, Camp X-Ray
    Guantanamo Bay Naval Base
    Guantanamo Bay, Cuba
	)
	)
	)
	)
		No. CV: 02-0299 (CKK)

MOHAMMED IQBAL, as Next Friend of Asif Iqbal ███████████	))) ,))	

DAVID HICKS,
    Detainee, Camp X-Ray
    Guantanamo Bay Naval Base
    Guantanamo Bay, Cuba
	)
	)
	)
	)	

TERRY HICKS, as Next Friend of David Hicks ███████████	)))))	
Petitioners,	)	
v.		

GEORGE WALKER BUSH,
    President of the United States
    The White House
 ███████████
	)
	)
	)
	)
	)
	)

DONALD RUMSFELD,
    Secretary, United States
    Department of Defense
 ███████████
	)
	)
	)
	)
	)
	)

BRIGADIER GEN. MICHAEL LEHNERT,
    Commander, Joint Task Force-160
    Guantanamo Bay Naval Base
    Guantanamo Bay, Cuba
	)
	)
	)
	)

COLONEL TERRY CARRICO,
    Commander, Camp X-Ray,
    Guantanamo Bay Naval Base
    Guantanamo Bay, Cuba
	)
	)
	)
	)
	)

Respondents
         All sued in their official
         and individual capacities.
	)
	)
	)
	)

---

* Redactions on this page of this document have been added for privacy purposes. – *Eds.*

<u>FIRST AMENDED PETITION FOR WRIT OF HABEAS CORPUS</u>

· · ·

IV.
STATEMENT OF FACTS

22. The detained petitioners are not, nor have they ever been, enemy aliens or unlawful combatants. David Hicks is an Australian citizen in respondents' unlawful custody. At the time of his seizure by the United States Government, Mr. Hicks was living in Afghanistan.

23. Petitioner Asif Iqbal is a UK citizen in respondent's unlawful custody. In July, 2001, Iqbal's family arranged for him to marry a woman living in the same village in Pakistan as Iqbal's father. He left Britain after September 11, 2001, and traveled to Pakistan solely for the purpose of this arranged marriage. In early October, 2001, shortly before the arranged marriage, Petitioner Iqbal's father allowed him to leave the village briefly. On information and belief, after he left the village, Petitoner Iqbal was captured and kidnapped by groups working in opposition to the United States in Afghanistan and Pakistan.

24. Petitioner Shafiq Rasul is a UK citizen in respondents' unlawful custody. In the summer of 2001, Petitioner Rasul decided to take time off from his computer engineering degree to travel. His brother persuaded him to visit Pakistan. Petitioner Rasul traveled to Pakistan to visit relatives and explore his culture. He also hoped to continue his education, and wanted to find computer courses equivalent to, but more reasonably priced, than those he could take in Britain. He left Britain after September 11, 2001, and traveled to Pakistan solely for these purposes. Following his arrival in Pakistan, he stayed with an aunt in Lahore before beginning further travel in the country. On information and belief, after he left Lahore, Petitioner Rasul was captured and kidnapped by groups working in opposition to the United States in Afghanistan and Pakistan.

Petitioners' Seizure By The United States

· · ·

29. The detained petitioners are not, and have never been, members of Al Qaida or any other terrorist group. Prior to their detention, they did not commit any violent act against any American person, nor espouse any violent act against any American person or property. On information and belief, they had no involvement, direct or indirect, in either the terrorist attacks on the United States September 11, 2001, or any act of international terrorism attributed by the United States to al Qaida or any terrorist group. They are not properly subject to the detention Order issued by respondent Bush, and discussed *infra* in Paras. 34–38.

30. On information and belief, the detained petitioners at no time voluntarily joined any terrorist force. On information and belief, if any of the detained petitioners ever took up arms in the Afghani struggle, it was only on the approach of the enemy, when they spontaneously took up arms to resist the invading forces, without having had time to form themselves into regular armed units, and carrying their arms openly and respecting all laws and customs of war.

31. On information and belief, the detained petitioners were not initially taken into custody by American forces. They were taken into custody against their will, and handed over to the Americans. There is no evidence they engaged in combat against American forces. On information and belief, if the detained petitioners were ever in Afghanistan prior to being taken involuntarily into custody, it was in order to facilitate humanitarian assistance to the Afghani people. The detained petitioners have taken no step that was not fully protected as their free exercise of their religious and personal beliefs.

32. On information and belief, the detained petitioners promptly identified themselves by correct name and nationality to the United States. They requested that the United States provide them with access to their families and to legal counsel. On information and belief, the detained petitioners were kept blindfolded, and sedated against their will for lengthy periods while they were taken involuntarily to Guantanamo Bay. On information and belief, in the course of being taken to Guantanamo Bay, the detained petitioners were transported via other American territory. On information and belief, the detained petitioners have been forced to provide involuntary statements to Respondents' agents in Guantanamo Bay.

33. On information and belief, the detained petitioners have been held under conditions that violate their international and constitutional rights to dignity and freedom from cruel, unusual and degrading punishment. They have not been provided with housing that even has proper walls. They have been forced to use a bucket for a toilet, and have not been provided with basic hygienic facilities. They have not been provided with meaningful access to their families. They have not been provided with the opportunity fully to exercise their religious beliefs. They have been exposed to the indignity and humiliation of the cameras of the national and international press, brought to Guantanamo Bay with the express consent and control of Respondents. Anyone who has seen them has been under instructions not to tell them even where they are being held.

The Detention Order

. . .

36. The Military Order was promulgated in the United States and in this judicial district, the decision to detain petitioners was made by respondents in the United States and in this judicial district, the decision to detain petitioners on Guantanamo Bay was made in the United States and in this judicial district, and the decision to continue detaining petitioners was, and is, being made by respondents in the United States and in this judicial district.

. . .

Guantanamo Bay Naval Station

41. On or about January 11, 2002, the United States military began transporting prisoners captured in Afghanistan to Camp X-Ray, at the United States Naval Base, in Guantanamo Bay, Cuba. Guantanamo Bay is a self-sufficient and essentially permanent city with approximately 7,000 military and civilian residents under the complete jurisdiction and control of the United States. Guantanamo Bay occupies nearly thirty-one square miles of land, an area larger than Manhattan, and nearly half the size of the District of Columbia. It has its own schools, generates its own power, provides its own internal transportation, and supplies its own water. Offenses committed by both civilians and foreign nationals living on Guantanamo are brought before federal courts on the mainland, where defendants enjoy the full panoply of Constitutional rights.

42. The United States has occupied Guantanamo Bay since 1903, and has repeatedly declared its intention to remain there indefinitely. For several decades, the United States has resisted claims of national sovereignty made by Cuba over Guantanamo Bay, insisting that its occupation of the land is legal and will remain so in perpetuity, so long as the United States chooses to exercise dominion and control over the land. The area is now, and has been for many years, under exclusive United States jurisdiction.

43. Guantanamo Bay has developed into a fully American enclave with all the residential, commercial, and recreational trappings of a small American city. The infrastructure is permanent and complex, providing for a wholly self-sufficient American community. The "Gitmo Guide", available online, lists fifteen restaurants, a bowling alley, and a Baskin Robbins. *See* The Gitmo Guide, at http://www.geocities.com/Pentagon/ 6625/dining.html. Guantanamo Bay contains an outdoor movie theater, a McDonald's and a mini-mall. http://www.cubanet.org/CNews/y02/jan02/15e5.htm. Residents, as well as their children, enjoy a number of recreational activities and clubs, including the Boys Scouts, Cub Scouts, USA Girl Scouts, the Guantanamo Bay Little Theater Company, an Archery Club, a golf club and even a Star Trek club. Residents may participate in a number of different sports including golf, hunting, tennis, horseback riding, football, softball and soccer.

44. A small children's zoo has been established on the naval base which contains "goats, donkeys, iguanas and banana rats. To facilitate water recreation for the residents, the bay side beaches have been dredged and pooled to protect bathers from the undertow and swift tidal current in the bay. "Gitmo boasts its own yatch club, which conducts races nearly every week . . . [requiring] all boats . . . to fly the United States flag"[1] The United States has established 'America's Slice of Cuba,'[2] where the residents "live in American-style homes, shop for American products and drive American cars. They have cable TV and radio stations, and their children attend schools that could be found in any suburban neighborhood."[3]

45. In light of the foregoing, the United States Navy has accurately described Guantanamo Bay as "a Naval reservation *which, for all practical purposes, is American territory.* Under the [lease] agreements, *the United States has for approximately [ninety] years exercised the essential elements of sovereignty over this territory*, without actually owning it. Unless we abandon the area or agree to a modification of the terms of our occupancy, we can continue in the present status as long as we like. [According to the United States p]ersons on the reservation are amenable only to United States legislative enactments." *See* The History of Guantanamo Bay: An Online Edition (1964), available at http://www.nsgtmo.navy.mil/history.htm.

. . .

---

[1] Theodore K Mason, "Across the Cactus Curtain" at 106 (1984) (Library of Congress Cataloging in Publication Data).

[2] *See* Tom Gibbs, "World Americas, America's Slice of Cuba" (BBC Online Network, Friday January 1, 1999).

[3] http://www.sun-sentinel.com/news/local/cuba/sns-gitmo-galleryindex.photogallery?coll=sfla-news-cuba- (Inside Guantanamo Bay Naval Station).

Dated: 3/12/02   Respectfully submitted,

Counsel for Petitioners:

_____

Joseph Margulies*

. . .

MARGULIES & RICHMAN, plc

. . .

_____

Clive A. Stafford Smith**

. . .

_____

Michael Ratner*
William Goodman
Anthony DiCaprio
Center for Constitutional Rights

. . .

_____

Gareth Peirce**
Birnberg, Peirce and Partners, Solicitors

. . .

_____

Stephen Kenny*
CAMATTA LEMPENS, PTY LTD.
BARRISTERS AND SOLICITORS

. . .

_____

Jon W. Norris

. . .

The Law Office of Jon W. Norris

. . .

_____

L. Barrett Boss

. . .

ASBILL MOFFITT & BOSS, Chtd.

. . .

*Mr. Margulies, Mr. Kenny, and the Center for Constitutional Rights appear for
Petitioners Terry and David Hicks.

**Mr. Stafford Smith and Ms. Peirce appear for Petitioners Asif and Mohammed Iqbal,
as well as Petitioners Rasul and Bibi.

Mr. Norris and Mr. Boss appear as local counsel for all attorneys.

. . .

UNITED STATES DISTRICT COURT
FOR THE DISTRICT OF COLUMBIA

SHAFIQ RASUL, SKINA BIBI, as Next Friend of Shafiq Rasul, et al., Petitioners v. GEORGE WALKER BUSH, President of the United States, et al., Respondents.	)))))))) Civil Action No. 02-0299(CKK))))))))

RESPONDENTS' MOTION TO DISMISS PETITIONERS' FIRST AMENDED PETITION FOR WRIT OF HABEAS CORPUS

Respondents hereby move to dismiss petitioners' first amended petition for a writ of habeas corpus, for the reasons set forth below, and submit the following points and authorities in support of this motion to dismiss.[1]

INTRODUCTION

While the hostilities in Afghanistan remain active and ongoing, petitioners, who are aliens captured abroad during those hostilities and their representatives, ask this Court to intervene to examine the legality of the President's military actions and ultimately seek to have this Court order their release. A number of legal doctrines, as well as common sense, make clear that this Court does not have jurisdiction to consider this petition for a writ of habeas corpus, or to order the relief petitioners seek. This Court should dismiss the petition for four reasons.

First, none of the detained petitioners is being held pursuant to the military order that is the focal point of their petition. The petition is largely directed at the President's Military Order of November 13, 2001 (Military Order) concerning the detention, treatment, and military trial of aliens captured overseas in connection with the current hostilities. But, as petitioners themselves acknowledge . . . , the President has not designated any of them for detention or military trial pursuant to that Order. Accordingly, to the extent that petitioners challenge the Military Order, their challenge is premature and jurisdictionally barred under both the standing and ripeness doctrines. Moreover, if any of the detained petitioners is designated for trial by military commission, the military commissions would provide the proper forum for their complaints.

---

[1] This motion to dismiss is addressed to the Court's lack of jurisdiction to entertain the petition. If the Court denies respondents' motion to dismiss and determines that it has jurisdiction to address the merits of some of the claims raised by petitioners, respondents would address the merits of any such claims at that time.

Second, the detained petitioners are aliens held abroad. Accordingly, none of their claims – including their premature challenges to the Military Order – are within the subject matter jurisdiction of this Court, or <u>any</u> United States court. The Supreme Court has squarely held that the United States courts lack jurisdiction over the habeas petitions of aliens detained outside the sovereign territory of the United States. See <u>Johnson</u> v. <u>Eisentrager</u>, 339 U.S. 763 (1950). As the District Court for the Central District of California recently concluded in considering a petition for habeas corpus filed on behalf of the detainees at Guantanamo (including the detained petitioners here), <u>Eisentrager</u> is "controlling" here, because "[i]n all key respects, the Guantanamo detainees are like the petitioners in <u>Johnson</u>." <u>Coalition of Clergy</u> v. <u>Bush</u>, No. CV 02-570, 2002 WL 272428 (C.D. Cal. Feb. 21, 2002), slip op. at 16, 19, appeal filed (No. 02-55367) (slip op. attached).

Third, the extraordinary circumstances in which this action arises and the particular relief that petitioners seek implicate core political questions about the conduct of the war on terrorism that the Constitution leaves to the President as Commander in Chief. Petitioners ask this Court to opine on the legality of the President's military operations and to release individuals who were captured during hostilities and the military has determined should be detained. Particularly where the hostilities that led to their capture remain ongoing, the courts have no jurisdiction, and no judicially-manageable standards, to evaluate or second-guess the conduct of the President and the military. These questions are constitutionally committed to the Executive Branch.

Fourth and finally, even if this Court found that it would otherwise have jurisdiction over this petition, it would need to transfer the case because no custodian responsible for the detained petitioners is present within the District of Columbia. Federal courts can only grant habeas relief within "their respective jurisdictions." 28 U.S.C. 2241(a). The only respondent named in the petition who is both present in the United States and amenable to suit is the Secretary of Defense, who is present for habeas purposes where the Pentagon is located, i.e., within the Eastern District of Virginia. However, because the transfer statute, 28 U.S.C. 1631, requires the transferee court to have subject matter jurisdiction, this Court need not reach the transfer issue if it agrees that – consistent with principles of ripeness, standing, the Supreme Court's decision in <u>Eisentrager</u>, and the political question doctrine – no United States court has jurisdiction over this petition.

BACKGROUND

1. On September 11, 2001, members of the al Qaida terrorist network savagely attacked the United States, killing thousands of United States citizens. In the wake of those attacks, the President, acting in his capacity as Commander in Chief and with the full backing of Congress (see Authorization for Use of Military Force, Pub.L.No. 107-40, 115 Stat. 224), dispatched the armed forces of the United States to Afghanistan to seek out and debilitate the al Qaida terrorist network and the Taliban regime in Afghanistan that had chosen to support and protect that network. In the course of those ongoing military operations, the United States military and its allies have captured or secured the surrender of thousands of persons fighting as part of the al Qaida terrorist network or to support, protect, or defend the al Qaida terrorists. United States armed forces have taken control of many such persons, who are being held under the President's authority as Commander in Chief and under the laws and usages of war, which permit holding combatants in connection with an armed conflict.

Some of the individuals of which the United States military has taken control in connection with the military campaign in Afghanistan have been transferred by the military to the United States Naval Base at Guantanamo Bay, Cuba (Guantanamo). The

Guantanamo Naval Base is in the sovereign territory of the Republic of Cuba. The United States uses and occupies the base under a 1903 lease agreement with Cuba continued in effect by a 1934 treaty.[2] The Lease Agreement provides that Cuba retains sovereignty over the leased lands:

> While on the one hand the United States recognizes the continuance of the ultimate sovereignty of the Republic of Cuba over the [leased area], on the other hand the Republic of Cuba consents that during the period of the occupation by the United States of said areas under the terms of this agreement the United States shall exercise complete jurisdiction and control over and within said areas ***.

Under a supplementary agreement, the United States agreed to additional lease terms, including a limit on establishing commercial or industrial enterprises on the lands. See Lease of Certain Areas for Naval or Coaling Stations, July 2, 1903, U.S.-Cuba, art. III, T.S. No. 426.

2. On November 13, 2001, the President, acting in his capacity as Commander in Chief, issued a Military Order concerning the "Detention, Treatment, and Trial of Certain Non-Citizens in the War Against Terrorism." 66 Fed. Reg. 57,831. In the Order, the President recounted the grave acts of terrorism inflicted on the Nation and found, inter alia, that "[t]he ability of the United States to protect the United States and its citizens *** from *** further terrorist attacks depends in significant part upon using the United States Armed Forces to identify terrorists and those who support them," and that "[t]o protect the United States and its citizens, and for the effective conduct of military operations and prevention of terrorist attacks, it is necessary for individuals subject to this order *** to be detained, and, when tried, to be tried for violations of the laws of war and other applicable laws by military tribunals." §1(d) and (e), 66 Fed. Reg. at 57,833. The Order further states that "an extraordinary emergency exists for national defense purposes." §1(g), 66 Fed. Reg. at 57,833–57,834. The Order delegates to the Secretary of Defense the authority to promulgate "orders and regulations as may be necessary to carry out any of the provisions of th[e] order." §6(a), 66 Fed. Reg. at 57,835; see also §4(b), (c), 66 Fed. Reg. at 57,834.

The Military Order applies only to individuals who are expressly designated by the President. The Order states that "[t]he term 'individual subject to this order' shall mean any individual who is not a United States citizen with respect to whom I determine from time to time in writing that:

> (1) there is reason to believe that such individual, at the relevant times,
>
> (i) is or was a member of the organization known as al Qaida;
>
> (ii) has engaged in, aided or abetted, or conspired to commit, acts of international terrorism, or acts in preparation therefor, that have caused, threaten to cause, or have as their aim to cause, injury to or adverse effects on the United States, its citizens, national security, foreign policy, or economy; or
>
> (iii) has knowingly harbored one or more individuals described in subparagraphs (i) or (ii) of subsection 2(a)(1) of this order; and
>
> (2) it is in the interest of the United States that such individual be subject to this order.

---

[2] See Lease of Lands for Coaling and Naval Stations, Feb. 16–23, 1903, U.S.-Cuba, T.S. No. 418, 6 Bevans 1113 (Lease Agreement); Treaty on Relations with Cuba, May 29, 1934, U.S.-Cuba, art. III, 48 Stat. 1682, 1683, T.S. No. 866 (extending lease "[u]ntil the two contracting parties agree to the modification or abrogation of the stipulations").

§2(a), 66 Fed. Reg. at 57,834. The President has not yet made such a determination with respect to anyone detained at Guantanamo. The United States military and other authorities are gathering and evaluating information concerning whether individuals should be made subject to the Order. That process is complicated not only by the scope and urgency of the military operations underway, but also by the refusal of many of the detainees to cooperate with military authorities.

   3. On February 19, 2002, petitioners filed a petition for a writ of habeas corpus in this Court. The petition was filed by individuals claiming to be the parents of three Guantanamo detainees, petitioners Shafiq Rasul, Asif Iqbal, and David Hicks. Amend. Pet. ¶¶1, 5–17.[3] Rasul, Iqbal, and Hicks (collectively, the "detained petitioners") are aliens who were apprehended during the course of the military campaign in Afghanistan. Amend. Pet. ¶¶26–27. The petition alleges that Iqbal and Rasul are citizens of the United Kingdom, and that Hicks is a citizen of Australia, and that they have conveyed requests to their parents to obtain legal assistance on their behalf. Amend. Pet. ¶¶22–24, 48–49. The petition seeks, inter alia, an order releasing them from custody, an order declaring the President's Military Order unlawful, an order preventing the United States military from interrogating petitioners, and certain other relief. Amend. Pet. 23–24. The named respondents are the President of the United States, Secretary of Defense, and two military commanders present at Guantanamo. Amend. Pet. ¶¶18–21.[4]

   4. Two days after the petition in this case was filed, the District Court for the Central District of California dismissed a habeas petition filed in January 2002, purportedly on behalf of all Guantanamo detainees captured in Afghanistan (including the detained petitioners here), by a coalition of clergy, lawyers, and law professors. Coalition of Clergy v. Bush, supra. The court concluded both that the coalition lacked standing to proceed on behalf of the detainees on a next-friend basis, and that even if the coalition possessed such standing, the court lacked habeas jurisdiction because none of the named respondents was within the court's territorial jurisdiction. Slip op. at 3–4. In considering whether it could transfer the case to another forum pursuant to 28 U.S.C. 1631, the Coalition of Clergy court further held that "[n]o federal court would have jurisdiction over petitioners' claims" (Slip op. at 4) under the rule of Johnson v. Eisentrager, 339 U.S. 763 (1950), which, as explained below, holds that the United States courts lack jurisdiction to consider the claims of aliens held outside the United States.

ARGUMENT

. . .

II. THE COURT LACKS JURISDICTION UNDER JOHNSON V. EISENTRAGER TO CONSIDER A HABEAS PETITION FILED ON BEHALF OF ALIENS WHO HAVE BEEN SEIZED AND HELD OUTSIDE THE UNITED STATES

Wholly apart from the standing and ripeness defects inherent in petitioners' central challenge to the Military Order, Johnson v. Eisentrager, 339 U.S. 763 (1950), precludes any attempt by petitioners to secure habeas relief in any United States court, for any

---

   [3] On March 12, 2002, petitioners filed a First Amended Petition for Writ of Habeas Corpus. . . . The citations in this memorandum are to the amended petition. Petitioners also have filed a Motion for Access to Counsel and Motion to Provide the Detained Clients with Notice of the Pending Litigation. A separate response opposing both of those motions is filed with this motion to dismiss.

   [4] The petition also seeks an order granting the parents of Rasul, Iqbal, and Hicks next-friend status to proceed on behalf of the detained petitioners. . . . Because the petition should be dismissed for the reasons explained below, the Court need not consider that request.

claim. In Eisentrager, the Supreme Court ruled emphatically that the courts of the United States lack jurisdiction to entertain habeas corpus petitions filed on behalf of aliens who are held outside the sovereign territory of the United States. These detainees are aliens, and Guantanamo lies outside the sovereign territory of the United States. Eisentrager thus forecloses jurisdiction with respect to claims made by the detainees in this or any other United States court.

Eisentrager declined to exercise jurisdiction over a habeas petition filed by German nationals who had been seized by United States armed forces in China after the German surrender in World War II and subsequently imprisoned in a United States military prison in Landsberg, Germany. See 339 U.S. at 765–767. The Court held that the prisoners could not file a petition for habeas corpus in any United States court because they were aliens without connection to the United States who had been seized and held outside the sovereign territory of the United States. The Court emphasized that aliens have been accorded rights under the Constitution and laws of the United States only as a consequence of their presence within the United States. As the Court put it, "in extending constitutional protections beyond the citizenry, the Court has been at pains to point out that it was the alien's presence within its territorial jurisdiction that gave the Judiciary power to act." Id. at 771. Eisentrager held that the writ of habeas corpus was unavailable because "these prisoners at no relevant time were within any territory over which the United States is sovereign, and the scenes of their offense, their capture, their trial and their punishment were all beyond the territorial jurisdiction of any court of the United States." Id. at 778. The Court also held that the prisoners could not invoke the writ to vindicate the Fifth Amendment, because, as aliens abroad, they had no Fifth Amendment rights. See id. at 781.[6]

Eisentrager also emphasized that entertaining a petition of enemy aliens seized by the military in an armed conflict would raise grave questions of interference with the President's powers as Commander in Chief. The writ of habeas corpus by its very nature contemplates that the custodian may be required to produce the prisoner before the court – which in cases like this and Eisentrager would require the military, at the direction of a civilian court, to find means of transporting combatants intent on destroying the United States into the territorial confines of the Nation. As the Court explained, "[i]t would be difficult to devise more effective fettering of a field commander than to allow the very enemies he is ordered to reduce to submission to call him to account in his own civil courts and divert his efforts and attention from the military offensive abroad to the legal defensive at home." 339 U.S. at 779.

Eisentrager controls this case and makes clear that there is "no basis for invoking federal judicial power in any district." 339 U.S. at 790. The holding in Eisentrager rested on the dual factors that the prisoners were aliens without connection to the United States and they were held outside United States territory. Both factors apply equally to the detainees here. Indeed, another court recently considered the application of Eisentrager to these very detainees, and found the case "controlling." Coalition of Clergy, slip op. at 16. As Judge Matz concluded: "In all key respects, the Guantanamo detainees are like the petitioners in Johnson: They are aliens; they were enemy combatants; they were captured in combat; they were abroad when captured; they are abroad now; since their

---

[6] Eisentrager remains one of the pivotal decisions delimiting the territorial reach of constitutional protections and the rights of aliens, and the Court continues to rely on it in addressing those issues. See, e.g., Zadvydas v. Davis, 121 S. Ct. 2491 (2001) (relying on Eisentrager); United States v. Verdugo-Urquidez, 494 U.S. 259, 269 (1990) (relying on Eisentrager to hold that the Fourth Amendment does not apply extraterritorially); see also Harbury v. Deutch, 233 F.3d 596, 602–604 (D.C. Cir. 2000), cert. granted on other grounds, 122 S. Ct. 663 (2001).

capture, they have been under the control of only the military; they have not stepped foot on American soil; and there are no legal or judicial precedents entitling them to pursue a writ of habeas corpus in an American civilian court." Id. at 19. Petitioners' efforts to distinguish Eisentrager are unavailing.

A.   The Detainees Were Seized And Held Outside The United States

Petitioners state that the detained petitioners are being held "at the United States Naval Base, in Guantanamo Bay, Cuba." Amend. Pet. ¶41; see Amend. Pet. ¶42. By filing their habeas petition in the District of Columbia, petitioners have implicitly acknowledged that there is no district court with territorial jurisdiction over Guantanamo or the detained petitioners. The territory of every federal district court is defined by statute, see 28 U.S.C. 81–131 (1994); 48 U.S.C. 1424, 1424b, 1821–1826 (1994 & Supp. V. 1999), and Guantanamo is not within the territory defined for any district. Petitioners, nonetheless, insist that "Guantanamo is within the territorial jurisdiction of the United States." Mem. 6. However, the relevant international agreements make clear that Guantanamo Bay lies outside the sovereign territory of the United States and outside the territorial jurisdiction of any United States court.

The United States uses and occupies the land and waters forming the Guantanamo Bay Naval Base under a lease from the Republic of Cuba entered into in 1903. See note 2, supra. That Lease Agreement makes plain that the United States has no claim of sovereignty over the leased areas. It expressly provides that, although Cuba "consents" that the "United States shall exercise complete jurisdiction and control over" the leased areas, at the same time the "the United States recognizes the continuance of the ultimate sovereignty of the Republic of Cuba over" the land. Lease Agreement art. III, T.S. No. 418 (6 Bevans 1113). The "jurisdiction and control" that the United States exercises is plainly distinct from the concept of sovereignty that the Lease Agreement expressly reserves to the Republic of Cuba.

The terms of the Lease Agreement are definitive on the question of sovereignty. As the Supreme Court has explained, the "determination of sovereignty over an area is for the legislative and 17 executive departments," and not a question on which a court may second-guess the political branches. Vermilya-Brown Co. v. Connell, 335 U.S. 377, 380 (1948); see United States v. Spelar, 338 U.S. 217, 221–222 (1949); Jones v. United States, 137 U.S. 202, 212 (1890). Accordingly, as in Eisentrager, the detainees are not "within any territory over which the United States is sovereign" (as the Lease Agreement makes explicit), and the "scenes" of their detention are "beyond the territorial jurisdiction of any court of the United States." 339 U.S. at 778.

The Supreme Court has already addressed the status of leased United States military installations abroad and held that they lie outside the sovereign territory of the United States. In Spelar, the Supreme Court held that the Federal Tort Claims Act (FTCA) does not apply to a United States base leased in Newfoundland because the lease "effected no transfer of sovereignty with respect to the military bases concerned." 338 U.S. at 221–222. The Court held that the base was a "foreign country" under the FTCA, and concluded that, "[w]e know of no more accurate phrase in common English usage than 'foreign country' to denote territory subject to the sovereignty of another nation," and not "to the sovereignty of the United States." Id. at 219.[7]

---

[7] There is no basis for distinguishing Guantanamo from the base at issue in Spelar. Indeed, Spelar noted that the lease between the United States and Great Britain governing the Newfoundland base involved "the same executive agreement and leases discussed at length in Vermilya-Brown," which addressed the United States

To the extent that there is direct precedential authority on the question, courts have reached the unremarkable conclusion that Guantanamo is <u>not</u> part of the sovereign territory of the United States.[8] The Eleventh Circuit, for example, relied on the terms of the Lease Agreement to hold that Guantanamo is not "United States territory," and flatly rejected any suggestion that "'control and jurisdiction' is equivalent to sovereignty." <u>Cuban Am. Bar Ass'n</u> v. <u>Christopher</u>, 43 F.3d 1412, 1425 (11th Cir.), cert. denied, 515 U.S. 1142 (1995); see <u>ibid</u>. (noting that Guantanamo was a leased base "under the sovereignty of [a] foreign nation[]"); <u>Bird</u> v. <u>United States</u>, 923 F. Supp. 338, 343 (D. Conn. 1996) ("sovereignty over the Guantanamo Bay does not rest with the United States"). Most recently, the district court in <u>Coalition of Clergy</u> held that "sovereignty over Guantanamo Bay remains with Cuba." <u>Coalition of Clergy</u>, slip op. at 23. As a result, the court concluded that, "petitioners' claim that the Guantanamo detainees are entitled to a writ of habeas corpus is foreclosed by the Supreme Court's holding in <u>Johnson</u> [v. <u>Eisentrager</u>]." <u>Ibid</u>.

B.   There Is No Basis For Distinguishing <u>Eisentrager</u>

Petitioners insist that the detained petitioners "are not, nor have they ever been, enemy aliens," Amend. Pet. ¶22, but the result in <u>Eisentrager</u> did not depend on the fact that the prisoners were "enemy aliens." Although the Court addressed the long tradition of limiting the legal rights of enemy aliens, see 339 U.S. at 769–777 & n.2, in stressing that the key to its analysis was that the prisoners before it were aliens held abroad, the Court emphasized that "the privilege of litigation has been extended to aliens, <u>whether friendly or enemy</u>, only because permitting their presence in the country implied protection," <u>id</u>. at 777–778 (emphasis added); see also <u>Bridges</u> v. <u>Wixon</u>, 326 U.S. 135, 161 (1945) (Murphy, J., concurring) (noting that "an alien obviously brings with him no constitutional rights"). The Court, moreover, has not subsequently treated the analysis in <u>Eisentrager</u> as somehow limited to the narrow class of "enemy aliens." Rather, the Court has cited <u>Eisentrager</u> as a seminal decision defining the application of the Constitution to all aliens outside the territory of the United States. See, <u>e.g.</u>, <u>Zadvydas</u> v. <u>Davis</u>, 121 S. Ct.2491, 2500 (2001); <u>United States</u> v. <u>Verdugo-Urquidez</u>, 494 U.S. 259, 269 (1990). For example, in <u>Verdugo-Urquidez</u>, the Court both reaffirmed <u>Eisentrager</u> and applied its reasoning to the Fourth Amendment claims of a Mexican citizen, who was quite obviously not an enemy alien. The D.C. Circuit, moreover, in affirming this Court in relevant part has expressly rejected the argument that <u>Eisentrager</u> applies only to the "rights of enemy aliens during wartime." <u>Harbury</u> v. <u>Deutch</u>, 233 F.3d 596, 604 (2000). "[T]he

---

base in Bermuda. 338 U.S. at 218. And in <u>Vermilya-Brown</u>, the Supreme Court noted that "[t]he United States was granted by the Cuban lease substantially the same rights as it has in the Bermuda lease." 335 U.S. at 383; see <u>id</u>. at 405 (Jackson, J., dissenting) (relying on the similarities of Guantanamo and the base in Bermuda). Moreover, although petitioners attempt to rely on cases applying United States law extraterritorially, see Mem. 6, <u>Spelar</u> makes clear that the questions whether laws apply outside the United States and whether territory is part of the sovereign territory of the United States are different questions. 338 U.S. at 221–222. The former issue was implicated in <u>Vermilya-Brown</u>, while the latter concept was at issue in <u>Spelar</u> and is what is relevant under <u>Eisentrager</u>.

[8] The three cases on which petitioners primarily rely for their claim that Guantanamo should be considered part of sovereign United States territory, see Mem. 4–8, have all been vacated or reversed and have no precedential value. See <u>Haitian Ctrs. Council, Inc.</u> v. <u>McNary</u>, 969 F.2d 1326 (2d Cir. 1992), vacated as moot, <u>Sale</u> v. <u>Haitian Ctrs. Council, Inc.</u>, 509 U.S. 918 (1993); <u>United States</u> v. <u>Wilmot</u>, 29 C.M.R. 777, 781 (U.S.A.F. Rev. Bd. 1960), reversed, <u>United States</u> v. <u>Wilmot</u>, 29 C.M.R. 514 (Ct. Mil. App. 1960); see also <u>Cuban Am. Bar Ass'n</u>, 43 F.3d at 1424 n.8 (noting that the decision in <u>Haitian Centers Council, Inc.</u> v. <u>Sale</u>, 823 F. Supp. 1028 (E.D.N.Y. 1993) – the district court decision in <u>McNary</u> – was also vacated by stipulated order).

Supreme Court's extended and approving citation of Eisentrager [in Verdugo-Urquidez] suggests that its conclusions regarding extraterritorial application of the Fifth Amendment are not so limited." Ibid.[9]

In any event, despite the petitioners' bare assertions to the contrary, the detained petitioners here plainly qualify as "enemy aliens" for purposes of Eisentrager. Petitioners acknowledge that "Mr. Hicks, Mr. Iqbal, and Mr. Rasul were apprehended," "[i]n the course of the military campaign" conducted by United States forces in Afghanistan, Amend. Pet. ¶26, and allege that "the Northern Alliance captured David Hicks in Afghanistan," Amend. Pet. ¶27. The detained petitioners were seized in the course of hostilities against United States and allied forces. That is sufficient to establish their status as enemies under Eisentrager. See Coalition of Clergy, slip op. at 19.[10] Nothing in Eisentrager suggests that an "enemy alien" is limited to a national of a country that has formally declared war on the United States. Although the Court noted that under international law all nationals of a belligerent nation become "enemies" of the other upon a declaration of war, see 339 U.S. at 769–773 & n.2, the Court stressed that it did not need to rely on that "fiction" because the prisoners were "actual enemies, active in the hostile service of an enemy power." Id. at 778. The same is true of the detained petitioners here. Moreover, any suggestion that Eisentrager should apply only to the forces of a nation in a declared war with the United States would be irrational. It would suggest that those involved in the attack on Pearl Harbor would be eligible for more favorable treatment than Japanese soldiers captured after war had been declared by Congress, or that while lawful combatants of a nation that had declared war could seek no recourse in our courts, the courts would somehow be more accessible to rogue forces or members of an international terrorist network. Nothing in Eisentrager suggests that bizarre result.

As in Eisentrager, exercise of habeas jurisdiction over these detainees would interfere with the foreign affairs and Commander-in-Chief powers of the Executive. Indeed, the interference here would be even greater because this habeas petition has been filed within months of the detainees' capture and detention, while the Eisentrager petition, in contrast, did not reach the Court until years after hostilities had ceased. Recognizing the jurisdiction denied in Eisentrager would allow "the very enemies [that the Secretary of Defense] is ordered to reduce to submission to call him to account in his own civil courts," and would divert the military's "efforts and attention from the military offensive abroad to the legal defensive at home." 339 U.S. at 779. This Court should not allow that unprecedented intrusion into the President's Commander-in-Chief authority.

III. THE COURT SHOULD DISMISS THE PETITION AS NONJUSTICIABLE UNDER THE POLITICAL QUESTION DOCTRINE

Even in the absence of Eisentrager, the political question doctrine would prohibit the Court from exercising jurisdiction and granting the extraordinary relief requested by petitioners in the circumstances of this case. The detained petitioners are aliens captured overseas who seek access to American courts while the same hostilities that led to their

---

[9] The relevant constitutional line is not between enemy aliens and non-enemy aliens, but between aliens abroad and citizens abroad. "Neither the Constitution nor the laws passed in pursuance of it have any force in foreign territory unless in respect of our own citizens." United States v. Curtiss-Wright Export Co., 299 U.S. 304, 318 (1936).

[10] Cf. United States v. Terry, 36 C.M.R. 756, 761 (N.B.R. 1965) ("The term 'enemy' applies to any forces engaged in combat against our own forces."), aff'd, 36 C.M.R. 348 (C.M.A. 1966). Moreover, the status of forces as enemies is a political question on which the courts are bound by the actions of the political branches, see, e.g., The Three Friends, 166 U.S. 1, 63 (1897); The Prize Cases, 67 U.S. (2 Black) 635, 670 (1862).

capture are still being waged. Justifiably, courts have allowed the President to make the difficult decisions concerning the capture, detention, and questioning of such captives in the course of conducting the war, including the decision whether to try such individuals before a military tribunal. Petitioners here seek to involve this Court in the conduct of the war immediately on the heels of their capture, while the fighting continues and before any military trials have been conducted. The threat of interference with the delicate and vital military and foreign affairs determinations that continue to be made fully justifies application of the political question doctrine in this case.

The political question doctrine is one of a number of principles "that cluster about Article III" to give effect to the case-or-controversy requirement and its underlying separation-of-powers "concern about the proper – and properly limited – role of the courts in a democratic society." Allen v. Wright, 468 U.S. 737, 751 (1984) (internal quotation marks omitted); see Schlesinger v. Reservists Comm. to Stop the War, 418 U.S. 208, 215 (1974). In Baker v. Carr, 369 U.S. 186 (1962), the Supreme Court identified several factors that may render a case nonjusticiable under the political question doctrine, including:

> [1] a textually demonstrable constitutional commitment of the issue to a coordinate political department; [2] a lack of judicially discoverable and manageable standards for resolving it; [3] the impossibility of deciding without an initial policy determination of a kind clearly for nonjudicial discretion; [4] the impossibility of a court's undertaking independent resolution without expressing lack of the respect due coordinate branches of government; [5] an unusual need for unquestioning adherence to a political decision already made; or [6] the potentiality of embarrassment from multifarious pronouncements by various departments on one question.

Id. at 217. The presence of any one of these factors may justify dismissal of a case as nonjusticiable. Ibid. In this case, petitioners' claims implicate all the Baker factors.

The Constitution makes the President Commander in Chief of the armed forces and commits to his discretion their use in defense of national security. U.S. Const. Art. II, §2, Cl. 1. See, e.g., Orloff v. Willoughby, 345 U.S. 83, 90–92 (1953) (holding commissioning and control of military officers "is a matter of discretion within the province of the President as Commander in Chief"); Industria Panificadora, S.A. v. United States, 763 F. Supp. 1154, 1161 (D.D.C. 1991) ("[J]udicial review of executive branch decisions pertaining to the nature, conduct, and implementation of a presidentially-directed military operation in a foreign country***goes to the heart of the political question doctrine."). The President is also "the sole organ of the federal government in the field of international relations." United States v. Curtiss-Wright Export Corp., 299 U.S. 304, 320 (1936). Accordingly, courts will avoid intrusions upon the authority of the Executive in military and national security affairs, particularly where, as here, that authority involves ongoing United States military operations abroad. Luther v. Borden, 48 U.S. (7 How.) 1, 43 (1849) ("After the President has acted and called out the militia," if "a Circuit Court of the United States [is] authorized to inquire whether his decision was right," then "the guarantee contained in the Constitution *** is a guarantee of anarchy, and not of order."); see also Sanchez-Espinoza v. Reagan, 770 F.2d 202, 209 (D.C. Cir. 1985) (challenge to President's decision to provide military support to Contras in Nicaragua presented nonjusticiable political question); Crockett v. Reagan, 720 F.2d 1355 (D.C. Cir. 1983) (per curiam) (action challenging military aid to El Salvador raised nonjusticiable political question), aff'd, 558 F. Supp. 893 (D.D.C. 1982).[11]

---

[11] Furthermore, as the D.C. Circuit has emphasized, the Supreme Court has long recognized that "'any policy toward aliens is vitally and intricately interwoven with contemporaneous policies in regard to the conduct of

Petitioners' challenge to their capture and detention clearly implicates the President's core Commander-in-Chief and foreign-affairs powers and questions determinations left to the President's sole discretion. The hostilities in Afghanistan against al Qaida and Taliban forces are ongoing, and the United States military continues to capture aliens in connection with those hostilities and hold them for questioning pending an eventual determination as to how individual captives will be processed. The President's actions are based on his determination as to what is necessary for the successful conduct of the war and the protection of innocent Americans both at home and abroad. A judicial inquiry into the exact circumstances of the detained petitioners' capture could intrude into his conduct of the war by, for example, requiring the testimony of military personnel currently engaged in the field of combat or in interfering with the questioning of detainees to discover information necessary to his successful conduct of the war and protection of America and its allies from further terrorist threats. Where armed conflict is ongoing and the detainees captured on the battlefield are being held abroad for questioning and have not yet been designated as subject to any particular procedure for trial or punishment, any exercise of jurisdiction would intolerably interfere with determinations that the Constitution commits to the political branches.[12]

Nor do courts have any discoverable or manageable standards for assessing the propriety of the discretionary military and national security determinations that the President and the Armed Forces have made concerning the control and handling of the detainees under the circumstances of this case. The very fact that decisions about the location of troops, the need to detain captured combatants, and the value of interrogating them are committed to Executive branch and military officials means that courts have no standards by which to assess such actions. See Crockett, 720 F.2d 1356–1357 (affirming trial court holding that it "did not have the resources or expertise" to resolve issues regarding the legality of military aid to El Salvador).

As the Supreme Court recognized long ago, the President as Commander in Chief "is necessarily constituted the judge of the existence of the exigency [requiring particular military actions] in the first instance, and is bound to act according to his belief of the facts." Martin v. Mott, 25 U.S. (12 Wheat) 19, 31 (1829). Indeed, courts have found the absence of judicially manageable standards in a variety of foreign affairs settings. See, e.g., Aktepe v. United States, 105 F.3d 1400, 1404 (11th Cir. 1997) (suit for injuries caused by NATO training exercise), cert. denied, 522 U.S. 1045 (1998); DaCosta v. Laird, 471 F.2d 1146, 1155 (2d Cir. 1973) (challenge to President's decision to mine harbors and bomb targets in North Vietnam); Holtzman v. Schlesinger, 484 F.2d 1307, 1310 (2d Cir. 1973) (challenge to American bombing and other military activity in Cambodia),

---

foreign relations, the war power, and the maintenance of a republican form of government. Such matters are so exclusively entrusted to the political branches of government as to be largely immune from judicial query or interference.'" Bruno v. Albright, 197 F.3d 1153, 1159 (D.C. Cir. 1999) (quoting Harisiades v. Shaughnessy, 342 U.S. 580, 588–589 (1952)); see Eisentrager, 339 U.S. at 774 ("Executive power over enemy aliens, undelayed and unhampered by litigation, has been deemed, throughout our history, essential to war-time security.").

[12] The President's authority to act in this sphere is only bolstered by the Joint Resolution of Congress recognizing the President's "authority under the Constitution to take action to deter and prevent acts of international terrorism against the United States," and stating that "the President is authorized to use all necessary and appropriate force against those nations, organizations, or persons he determines planned, authorized, committed, or aided the terrorist attacks that occurred on September 11, 2001, or harbored such organizations or persons." Authorization for Use of Military Force, Pub. L. No. 107-40, 115 Stat. 224; see Dames & Moore v. Regan, 453 U.S. 654, 668–669 (1981); Youngstown Sheet & Tube Co. v. Sawyer, 343 U.S. 579, 635–638 (1952) (Jackson, J., concurring). The detention and interrogation of aliens captured in the midst of the ongoing hostilities is a necessary component of that charge, not to mention an elementary responsibility in fulfilling the President's constitutional role as Commander in Chief.

cert. denied, 416 U.S. 936 (1974); In re Korean Air Lines Disaster of Sept. 1, 1983, 597 F. Supp. 613, 616 (D.D.C. 1984) (national security decisions with respect to the U.S.S.R.); Greenham Women Against Cruise Missiles v. Reagan, 591 F. Supp. 1332, 1337–1338 (S.D.N.Y. 1984) (action seeking injunction against deployment of cruise missiles overseas). Especially where hostilities and military actions are ongoing, the civilian courts of this Nation cannot be a forum for second-guessing the sensitive military and foreign-affairs decisions challenged by petitioners without undermining the President's ability to conduct the war on terrorism.

Moreover, any order granting petitioners the relief they seek would also necessarily implicate the other Baker factors. Such an order would run counter to, and substantially undermine, the President's foreign policy determinations and military orders at issue in this case, which necessarily involve the exercise of nonjudicial discretion; it would evince a lack of respect for those determinations and orders and would question adherence to vital political decisions already made by the President; it would embarrass the United States in the exercise of its foreign affairs. See Baker, 369 U.S. at 217. The President has determined that the capture and detention of the Guantanamo detainees is necessary to the successful prosecution of the ongoing war on terrorism and vital to the identification and deterrence of additional terrorist threats. Under the circumstances of this case, judicial review of petitioners' claims would detract from and show a lack of respect for the credibility of these Executive Branch determinations, which as discussed above are not appropriate subjects for judicial discretion. See, e.g., Industria Panificadora S.A. v. United States, 763 F. Supp. 1154, 1161 (D.D.C. 1991) (judicial resolution of challenge to reasonableness of military conduct in Panama would "require that this Court second-guess Executive Branch decisions, some of which were made while military personnel were engaged in combat" and "would show a lack of respect due to a coordinate branch").

Further, any such review would also violate the principle that the United States can have only one voice when it speaks in the national security sphere. See Lowry v. Reagan, 676 F. Supp. 333, 340 (D.D.C. 1987) (because a judicial pronouncement on existence of "hostilities" in Persian Gulf "could impact on statements by the Executive that the United States is neutral in the Iran-Iraq war" and "might create doubts in the international community regarding the resolve of the United States to adhere to this position," court must adhere to rule that Constitution requires a 'single-voiced statement of the Government's views'" in foreign affairs) (citation omitted). As then-Circuit Judge Scalia warned in Sanchez-Espinoza, courts must recognize and guard against "the danger of foreign citizens' using the courts *** to obstruct the foreign policy of our government." 770 F.2d at 209. He further cautioned that suits such as petitioners have a dramatic ability "to produce *** 'embarrassment of our government' through 'multifarious pronouncements by various departments on one question.'" Ibid. (internal citations omitted). It is precisely such embarrassment in the conduct of foreign affairs that the political question doctrine is designed to prevent.

IV. THE COURT LACKS HABEAS JURISDICTION BECAUSE NO CUSTODIAN IS WITHIN ITS TERRITORIAL JURISDICTION

This Court also lacks habeas jurisdiction over petitioners' claims because no custodian responsible for the detainees is present within this Court's territorial jurisdiction. The only respondent named in the petition who is both in the United States and amenable to suit in this action is Secretary of Defense Donald Rumsfeld. Secretary Rumsfeld is present for purposes of habeas jurisdiction where the Pentagon is located, in the Eastern

District of Virginia, not in the District of Columbia. Accordingly, if this Court concludes, contrary to the arguments discussed above, that this Court has subject matter jurisdiction over petitioners' claims, the Court should transfer the case to the Eastern District of Virginia pursuant to 28 U.S.C. 1631, and allow that court to determine whether it is appropriate to proceed with this action. Of course, Section 1631 permits transfer only where the transferee court would in fact have jurisdiction to hear the case, and thus this Court need not reach issues of territorial jurisdiction and transfer unless it disagrees with respondents' other jurisdictional arguments. See 28 U.S.C. 1631 (limiting transfer to "court in which the action***could have been brought at the time it was filed"); Hadera v. INS, 136 F.3d 1338, 1341 (D.C. Cir. 1998) (rejecting transfer where claims would have been untimely if filed in the transferee court).

The federal habeas statute provides that courts may grant the writ of habeas corpus only "within their respective jurisdictions." 28 U.S.C. 2241(a) (emphasis added). Because the writ acts "upon the person who holds [the detainee] in what is alleged to be unlawful custody," Braden v. 30th Judicial Circuit Court, 410 U.S. 484, 494–495 (1973), a district court lacks jurisdiction to issue the writ unless the detainee's custodian is present within the territorial jurisdiction of the court. See Schlanger v. Seamans, 401 U.S. 487, 491 (1971) ("the absence of [the] custodian is fatal to ***jurisdiction"). Generally, habeas jurisdiction exists only in the district in which the "immediate custodian" – e.g., the local prison warden – is present. See Monk v. Secretary of the Navy, 793 F.2d 364, 368 (D.C. Cir. 1986); Guerra v. Meese, 786 F.2d 414 (D.C. Cir. 1986); Blair-Bey v. Quick, 151 F.3d 1036, 1039 (D.C. Cir. 1998); Sanders v. Bennett, 148 F.2d 19, 20 (D.C. Cir. 1945). In very limited circumstances, where the immediate custodian is unknown or unavailable, courts have permitted other officials in the chain of custody to be treated as the "custodian" for jurisdictional purposes. See Demjanjuk v. Meese, 784 F.2d 1114, 1116 (D.C. Cir. 1986) (Bork, J., in chambers) (Attorney General may be treated as "custodian" in the "very limited and special circumstances" where the location of the petitioner was kept confidential); cf. Ex parte Hayes, 414 U.S. 1327, 1328 (1973) (Douglas, J., in chambers); Hirota v. MacArthur, 338 U.S. 197, 202 (1949) (Douglas, J., concurring). But even then, there must be a proper custodian present in the territorial jurisdiction of the district court for that court to exercise jurisdiction. Schlanger, 401 U.S. at 491.

Respondents acknowledge that the "immediate" custodians of the Guantanamo detainees are outside the territorial jurisdiction of the United States and are therefore unavailable. Petitioners, however, have named only two respondents who are present in the United States – President George W. Bush and Secretary of Defense Donald Rumsfeld – neither of whom is subject to this Court's habeas jurisdiction.

It is well settled that the President cannot be compelled by judicial process to perform any official act. See Franklin v. Massachusetts, 505 U.S. 788, 802–803 (1992); Id. at 825 (Scalia, J., concurring); Mississippi v. Johnson, 71 U.S. (4 Wall.) 475, 501 (1866); Swan v. Clinton, 100 F.3d 973, 976–977 (D.C. Cir. 1996). Although the Supreme Court has left open the question whether the President may be subject to an order requiring performance of a purely "ministerial" duty, Franklin, 505 U.S. at 802, the relief petitioners seek is far from "ministerial." See Johnson, 71 U.S.(4 Wall.) at 499 (holding that "duties [that] must necessarily be performed under the supervision of the President as commander-in-chief" are "in no just sense ministerial" but rather are "purely executive and political").

As for Secretary Rumsfeld, even if he can be sued as a "custodian" of the Guantanamo detainees, he is not present within this Court's territorial jurisdiction for habeas purposes. Rather, as the D.C. Circuit has indicated, Pentagon officials such as the Secretary of Defense are "located" in the Eastern District of Virginia for habeas purposes, not in the District of Columbia. Monk, 793 F.2d at 369 n.1 ("Of course, the Secretary of the Navy is located at the Pentagon, which is in Virginia, not the District of Columbia.") (emphasis added); see also Watkis v. West, 36 F.3d 127 (D.C. Cir. 1994) (ordering transfer of Title VII suit against Pentagon officials to the Eastern District of Virginia); Donnell v. National Guard Bureau, 568 F. Supp. 93, 94–95 (D.D.C. 1983) (same); Townsend v. Carmel, 494 F. Supp. 30, 32 (D.D.C. 1979) (Pentagon located in Arlington, Virginia and so Virginia state law applies under 18 U.S.C. 13); cf. Terry v. United States Parole Comm'n, 741 F. Supp. 282, 283–284 (D.D.C. 1990) (holding that territorial nature of habeas jurisdiction precluded jurisdiction in this Court "[b]ecause both the Parole Commission, whose principal offices are located in Chevy Chase, Maryland, and the Southeast Regional Parole Board, located in Atlanta, Georgia, are outside the territorial confines of the District of Columbia").[13]

None of the "custodians" over the Guantanamo detainees is present in this district. Their absence is "fatal" to this Court's jurisdiction. Schlanger, 401 U.S. at 491. Accordingly, if (and only if) the Court concludes that, contrary to Eisentrager and the jurisdictional limitations discussed above, United States courts may exercise jurisdiction over petitioners' habeas claims, the Court should transfer the case to the Eastern District of Virginia pursuant to 28 U.S.C. 1631.

---

[13] In Eisentrager, the court of appeals, after concluding that a United States court could exercise subject matter jurisdiction over the habeas petition in that case, remanded for a determination as to whether any of the named respondents (who included the Secretary of Defense) were within the District of Columbia's habeas jurisdiction. 339 U.S. at 767; see 174 F.2d 961, 967–968. The Supreme Court then reversed and observed that, because there was "no basis for invoking federal judicial power in any district," it would not "debate as to where, if the case were otherwise, the petition should be filed." 339 U.S. at 790–791 (emphasis added).

Some cases have permitted suits against Pentagon officials in non-habeas contexts to be brought in this Court under 28 U.S.C. 1391(e), which permits nationwide service of process on government officers in civil cases. See, e.g., Smith v. Dalton, 927 F. Supp. 1, 6 (D.D.C. 1996); Bartman v. Cheney, 827 F. Supp. 1, 2 (D.D.C. 1993); Mundy v. Weinberger, 554 F. Supp. 811, 817 & n.23 (D.D.C. 1982). However, Section 1391(e)'s liberal venue requirements do not apply to habeas claims. Schlanger, 401 U.S. at 490 n.4 (Section 1391(e) does not "exten[d] habeas corpus jurisdiction"); Chatman-Bey [v. Thornburgh], 864 F.2d [804,] 813 n.7 [(1988)] (same). Moreover, because the D.C. Circuit treats defenses based on territorial jurisdiction as waivable, see Chatman-Bey, 864 F.2d at 813, the mere fact that a court may have entertained a habeas petition in the District of Columbia does not establish this Court's jurisdiction in the present case, where respondents have timely challenged this Court's territorial jurisdiction. Cf. United States ex rel. Albertson v. Truman, 103 F. Supp. 617, 618 (D.D.C. 1951) (exercising jurisdiction in habeas case brought by overseas citizen because government had entered "general appearance," but noting "the proper respondents***are not located in the District of Columbia in their official capacity, but maintain their offices in the Pentagon Building in the State of Virginia").

CONCLUSION

For the foregoing reasons, petitioners' first amended petition for writ of habeas corpus should be dismissed.

Respectfully submitted,

_____

ROSCOE C. HOWARD, JR.
United States Attorney

_____

PAUL D. CLEMENT
Deputy Solicitor General

_____

ALICE S. FISHER
Deputy Assistant Attorney General

_____

ROBERT D. OKUN
. . .
Chief, Special Proceedings Section
. . .

Attorneys for Respondents
GEORGE WALKER BUSH, et al.

. . .

UNITED STATES DISTRICT COURT
FOR THE DISTRICT OF COLUMBIA

SHAFIQ RASUL, SKINA BIBI, as Next
Friend of Shafiq Rasul, *et al.*,

    Petitioners,

    v.

GEORGE WALKER BUSH, President of the
United States, *et al.*,

    Respondents.

Civil Action No. 02-299 (CKK)

FAWZI KHALID ABDULLAH FAHAD AL
ODAH, *et al.*,

    Plaintiffs,

    v.

UNITED STATES OF AMERICA, *et al.*,

    Defendants.

Civil Action No. 02-828 (CKK)

MEMORANDUM OPINION
(July 30, 2002)

I. INTRODUCTION

Presently before the Court are two cases involving the federal government's detention of certain individuals at the United States Naval Base at Guantanamo Bay, Cuba. The question presented to the Court by these two cases is whether aliens held outside the sovereign territory of the United States can use the courts of the United States to pursue claims brought under the United States Constitution. The Court answers that question in the negative and finds that it is without jurisdiction to consider the merits of these two cases. Additionally, as the Court finds that no court would have jurisdiction to hear these actions, the Court shall dismiss both suits with prejudice.

    Throughout their pleadings and at oral argument, Petitioners and Plaintiffs contend that unless the Court assumes jurisdiction over their suits, they will be left without any rights and thereby be held *incommunicado*. In response to this admittedly serious concern, the government at oral argument, conceded that "there's a body of international

law that governs the rights of people who are seized during the course of combative activities." Transcript of Motion Hearing, June 26, 2002 ("Tr.") at 92. It is the government's
position that "the scope of those rights are for the miliary and political branches to
determine – and certainly that reflects the idea that other countries would play a role in
that process." *Id.* at 91. Therefore, the government recognizes that these aliens fall within
the protections of certain provisions of international law and that diplomatic channels
remain an ongoing and viable means to address the claims raised by these aliens.[1] While
these two cases provide no opportunity for the Court to address these issues, the Court
would point out that the notion that these aliens could be held *incommunicado* from
the rest of the world would appear to be inaccurate.

After reviewing the extensive briefings in these cases, considering the oral arguments of the parties and their oral responses to the Court's questions, and reflecting
on the relevant case law, the Court shall grant the government's motion to dismiss
in both cases on the ground that the Court is without jurisdiction to entertain these
claims.[2]

II. PROCEDURAL HISTORY

. . .

Plaintiffs in *Odah v. United States,* Civil Action No. 02-828, filed their action on May
1, 2002. The *Odah* case involves the detention of twelve Kuwaiti nationals who are
currently being held in the custody of the United States at the United States Naval Base
at Guantanamo Bay, Cuba. Am. Compl. at 4. The action is concurrently brought by
twelve of their family members who join the suit and speak on behalf of the individuals
in United States custody. *Id.* Unlike Petitioners in *Rasul*, the *Odah* Plaintiffs disclaim that
their suit seeks release from confinement. Rather, Plaintiffs in *Odah* ask this Court to
enter a preliminary and permanent injunction prohibiting the government from refusing
to allow the Kuwaiti nationals to "meet with their families," "be informed of the charges,
if any, against them," "designate and consult with counsel of their choice," and "have
access to the courts or some other impartial tribunal." *Id.* ¶40.[3] Plaintiffs' Amended
Complaint contains three counts. First, Plaintiffs contend that Defendants' conduct
denies the twelve Kuwaiti nationals due process in violation of the Fifth Amendment to
the Constitution. *Id.* ¶37. Second, Plaintiffs argue that Defendants' actions violate the
Alien Tort Claims Act, 28 U.S.C. §1350. *Id.* ¶38. Lastly, Plaintiffs allege that Defendants'
conduct constitutes arbitrary, unlawful, and unconstitutional behavior in violation of
the Administrative Procedure Act, 5 U.S.C. §§555, 702, 706. *Id.* ¶39.

. . .

At the time the Court received the motion to dismiss in the *Odah* matter, it became obvious to the Court that the government was moving to dismiss both cases primarily on

---

[1] The Court notes that, at least for Petitioner David Hicks in the *Rasul* case, diplomatic efforts by the Australian
government have already commenced. First Am. Pet. for Writ of Habeas Corpus ("Am.Pet."), Ex. C., "Affidavit
of Stephen James Kenny," Attach. 2 (Letter from Robert Cornall, Australian Attorney-General's Office to
Stephen Kenny, counsel for Petitioner Terry Hicks) ("Australia has indicated to the United States that it is
appropriate that Mr Hicks remain in U.S. military custody with other detainees while Australia works through
complex legal issues and conducts further investigations. . . . Australian authorities have been granted access
to Mr Hicks and will be granted further access if required.").

[2] . . .

[3] . . .

jurisdictional grounds. Accordingly, the Court found it appropriate to make a threshold ruling on the jurisdictional question in both cases before conducting any further proceedings. Mindful of the importance of these suits, which raise concerns about the actions of the Executive Branch, the Court heard oral argument on the government's motion to dismiss in both cases on June 26, 2002.

III. FACTUAL BACKGROUND[5]

A.   *Rasul v. Bush*

. . .[6]

B.   *Odah v. United States*

The twelve Kuwaiti nationals in the *Odah* case, who are in United States custody at the military base at Guantanamo Bay, were in Afghanistan and Pakistan, some before and some after, September 11, 2001. Am. Compl. ¶14. These individuals were allegedly in those countries as volunteers for charitable purposes to provide humanitarian aid to the people of those countries. *Id.* The government of Kuwait allegedly supports such volunteer service by continuing to pay the salaries of its Kuwaiti employees while they engage in this type of volunteer service abroad. *Id.*

According to the Amended Complaint, none of those held in United States custody are, or have ever been, a combatant or belligerent against the United States, or a supporter of the Taliban or any terrorist organization. *Id.* ¶15. Villagers seeking bounties or other promised financial rewards allegedly seized the twelve Kuwaiti Plaintiffs against their will in Afghanistan or Pakistan. *Id.* ¶16. Subsequently these twelve Plaintiffs were transferred into the custody of the United States. *Id.* At various points in time, beginning in January of 2002, these twelve Plaintiffs were transferred to Guantanamo Bay. *Id.* ¶¶19–21.[7]

. . .

V. DISCUSSION

. . .

B.   The Ability of Courts to Entertain Petitions for Writs of Habeas Corpus Made By Aliens Held Outside the Sovereign Territory of the United States

The Court, therefore, considers both cases as petitions for writs of habeas corpus on behalf of aliens detained by the United States at the military base at Guantanamo Bay,

---

[5] . . .

[6] While denying a role in any terrorist activity, Petitioners in their Amended Petition for Writ of Habeas Corpus conspicuously neglect to deny that they took up arms for the Taliban. In fact, in an exhibit attached to the Amended Petition, Petitioner Terry Hicks, who has brought this suit on behalf of his son, indicates that his son had joined the Taliban forces. Am. Pet., Ex. C., "Affidavit of Stephen James Kenny," Attach. 8 (Letter from Stephen Kenny, counsel for Petitioner Terry Hicks to Respondent Bush) ("It is our client's understanding that his son subsequently joined the Taliban forces and on 8 December 2001 was captured by members of the Northern Alliance."). Interestingly, this fact has been omitted from the text of the Amended Petition, but can be found only by a careful reading of an exhibit attached to the Amended Petition. *Id.*

[7] It has not been confirmed that Plaintiff Mohammed Funaitel Al Dihani is currently in custody at Guantanamo Bay. Am. Compl. ¶21.

Cuba. In viewing both cases from this perspective, the Court concludes that the Supreme Court's ruling in *Johnson v. Eisentrager*, 339 U.S. 763 (1950), and its progeny, are controlling and bars the Court's consideration of the merits of these two cases. The Court shall briefly provide an overview of the *Eisentrager* decision, discuss the distinction in *Eisentrager* between the rights of citizens and aliens, analyze whether *Eisentrager* applies only to enemy aliens, and lastly, discuss the meaning of the concept of "sovereign territory" as presented in *Eisentrager*.

1. Johnson v. Eisentrager

The *Eisentrager* case involved a petition for writs of habeas corpus filed by twenty-one German nationals in the United States District Court for the District of Columbia. *Eisentrager*, 339 U.S. at 765. The prisoners in *Eisentrager* had been captured in China for engaging in espionage against the United States following the surrender of Germany, but before the surrender of Japan, at the end of World War II. *Id.* at 766. Since the United States was at peace with Germany, the actions of the *Eisentrager* petitioners violated the laws of war. *Id.* Following a trial and conviction by a United States military commission sitting in China, with the express permission of the Chinese government, the prisoners were repatriated to Germany to serve their sentences at Landsberg Prison. *Id.* Their immediate custodian at Landsberg Prison was a United States Army officer under the Commanding General, Third United States Army, and the Commanding General, European Command. *Id.*

The district court dismissed the petition for want of jurisdiction. *Id.* at 767. An appellate panel reversed the decision of the district court and remanded the case for further proceedings. *See Eisentrager v. Forrestal*, 174 F.2d 961 (D.C.Cir.1949). In an opinion by Judge E. Barrett Prettyman, the Court of Appeals for the District of Columbia Circuit held that "any person who is deprived of his liberty by officials of the United States, acting under purported authority of that Government, and who can show that his confinement is in violation of a prohibition of the Constitution, has a right to the writ." *Id.* at 963.

A divided panel of the Supreme Court reversed the decision of the District of Columbia Circuit and affirmed the judgment of the district court. *Eisentrager*, 339 U.S. at 791. In finding that *no* court had jurisdiction to entertain the claims of the German nationals, the Supreme Court, in an opinion by Justice Robert Jackson, found that a court was unable to extend the writ of habeas corpus to aliens held outside the sovereign territory of the United States. *Id.* at 778.

2. The Critical Distinction Between Citizens and Aliens

Justice Jackson began his opinion by noting the legal differences between citizens and aliens, and between friendly aliens and enemy aliens. *Id.* at 769. Noting that citizenship provides its own basis for jurisdiction, Justice Jackson observed that "[c]itizenship as a head of jurisdiction and a ground of protection was old when Paul invoked it in his appeal to Caesar." *Id.* Such protections, Justice Jackson noted, also apply to an individual seeking a fair hearing on his or her claim to citizenship. *Id.* 769–70 (citing *Chin Yow v. United States*, 208 U.S. 8 (1908)).

In the case of the alien, Justice Jackson wrote that "[t]he alien, to whom the United States has been traditionally hospitable, has been accorded a generous and ascending scale of rights as he increases his identity with our society." *Id.* at 770. For example, presence within the country provides an alien with certain rights that expand and become more secure as he or she declares an intent to become a citizen, culminating in the full panoply of rights afforded to the citizen upon the alien's naturalization. *Id.* In extending constitutional protections beyond the citizenry, Justice Jackson noted that the Supreme Court "has been at pains to point out that it was the alien's presence within its territorial jurisdiction that gave the Judiciary power to act." *Id.* at 771.

Justice Jackson's sentiment is borne out by the case law. Courts of the United States have exercised jurisdiction in cases involving individuals seeking to prove their citizenship, *Chin Yow*, 208 U.S. at 13 (1908) (habeas action permitted for one seeking admission to the country to assure a hearing on his claims to citizenship), or in situations where aliens held in a port of the United States sought entry into the country, *Nishimura Ekiu v. United States*, 142 U.S. 651, 660 (1892) ("An alien immigrant, prevented from landing by any such officer claiming authority to do so under an act of congress, and thereby restrained of his liberty, is doubtless entitled to a writ of *habeas corpus* to ascertain whether the restraint is lawful."). In the cases at bar it is undisputed that the individuals held at Guantanamo Bay do not seek to become citizens. Nor have Petitioners or Plaintiffs suggested that they have ever been to the United States or have any desire to enter the country. Petitioners and Plaintiffs do not fall into any of the categories of cases where the courts have entertained the claims of individuals seeking access to the country.

3. Does the *Eisentrager* Opinion Apply Only to "Enemy" Aliens?

Justice Jackson continued his analysis in *Eisentrager* by noting that enemy aliens captured incident to war do not have even a qualified access to the courts of the United States as compared to an alien who has lawful residence within the United States. *Eisentrager*, 339 U.S. at 776 ("[T]he nonresident enemy alien, especially one who has remained in the service of the enemy, does not have . . . this qualified access to our courts, for he neither has comparable claims upon our institutions nor could his use of them fail to be helpful to the enemy."); *id.* (quoting *Clarke v. Morey*, 10 Johns. 69, 72 (N.Y. Sup. Ct. 1813) ("A lawful residence implies protection, and a capacity to sue and be sued. A contrary doctrine would be repugnant to sound policy, no less than to justice and humanity.")). Petitioners in *Rasul* and Plaintiffs in *Odah* argue that the determination by the military commission in China that the petitioners in *Eisentrager* were enemy aliens is fatal to the government's reliance on *Eisentrager*. Pet'rs Mem. in Opp'n to Resp'ts Mot. to Dismiss ("Pet'rs Opp'n") at 12; Pls.' Opp'n at 6–7. Insisting that no determination has been made about the aliens presently held by the government at Guantanamo Bay, Plaintiffs and Petitioners argue that the holding in *Eisentrager* is inapplicable to the instant cases.

To the contrary, the Supreme Court's conclusion in *Eisentrager*, that the district court was without jurisdiction to consider the petition for writs of habeas corpus on behalf of the twenty-one German nationals, did not hinge on the fact that the petitioners were enemy aliens, but on the fact that they were aliens outside territory over which the United States was sovereign. The Supreme Court held:

> We have pointed out that the privilege of litigation has been extended to aliens, whether friendly or enemy, only because permitting their presence in the country implied protection. No such basis can be invoked here, for these prisoners at no relevant time were within any territory over which the United States is sovereign, and the sences of their offense, their capture, their trial and their punishment were all beyond the territorial jurisdiction of any court of the United States.

Id. at 777–78. In fact, the Supreme Court has consistently taken the position that *Eisentrager* does not apply only to those aliens deemed to be "enemies" by a competent tribunal. *See Zadvydas v. Davis*, 533 U.S. 678, 693 (2001) (Breyer, J.); *United States v. Verdugo-Urquidez*, 494 U.S. 259, 270 (1990) (Rehnquist, C.J.). These later Supreme Court cases reinforce the conclusion that there is no meaningful distinction between the cases at bar and the *Eisentrager* decision on the mere basis that the petitioners in *Eisentrager* had been found by a military commission to be "enemy" aliens.[12]

In *Zadvydas*, the Court cited *Eisentrager* for the proposition that "[i]t is well established that certain constitutional protections available to persons inside the United States are unavailable to aliens outside of our geographic borders." *Zadvydas*, 533 U.S. at 693 (discussing also that "once an alien enters the country, the legal circumstance changes, for the Due Process Clause applies to all 'persons' within the United States, including aliens, whether their presence here is lawful, unlawful, temporary, or permanent"). In *Verdugo-Urquidez*, the Court quoted a passage from *Eisentrager* for the proposition that the Supreme Court has emphatically rejected "extraterritorial application of the Fifth Amendment." *Verdugo-Urquidez*, 494 U.S. at 269. The Court of Appeals for the District of Columbia Circuit has taken a similarly broad view of *Eisentrager*. *Harbury v. Deutch*, 233 F.3d 596, 605 (D.C. Cir.2000), *rev'd on other grounds sub nom. Christopher v. Harbury*, 122 S.Ct. 2179 (2002) (observing that the Supreme Court's citation to *Eisentrager* in *Verdugo-Urquidez* was binding, and expressing its view that extraterritorial application of the Fifth Amendment was not available for aliens).

If there exists any doubt as to the sweeping nature of the holding in *Eisentrager*, the dissent in that opinion clearly crystalizes the extent of the decision. Justice Douglas, writing for himself and two other Justices, stated:

> If the [majority's] opinion thus means, and it apparently does, that these petitioners are deprived of the privilege of habeas corpus solely because they were convicted and imprisoned overseas, the Court is adopting a broad and dangerous principle.... [T]he Court's opinion inescapably denies courts power to afford the least bit of protection for any alien who is subject to our occupation government abroad, even if he is neither enemy nor belligerent and even after peace is officially declared.

Eisentrager, 339 U.S. at 795–96 (Douglas, J., dissenting). Thus, even Justice Douglas noted that according to the majority's opinion in *Eisentrager*, the Great Writ had no extraterritorial application to aliens.

Accordingly, the Court finds that *Eisentrager* is applicable to the aliens in these cases, who are held at Guantanamo Bay, even in the absence of a determination by a military commission that they are "enemies."[13] While it is true that the petitioners in *Eisentrager*

---

[12] The government has encouraged this Court to take "judicial notice" that these individuals are "enemy combatants." Tr. 9–10. In reviewing this case, the Court has taken the allegations in the Amended Petition and Amended Complaint as true as required by Rule 12(b)(1). Petitioners and Plaintiffs allege that the individuals held at Guantanamo Bay were initially taken into custody and detained in Afghanistan and Pakistan where military hostilities were in progress. Am. Pet. ¶¶22–24; Am. Compl. ¶16. David Hicks, who had joined the Taliban, *see supra* note 6, arguably may be appropriately considered an "enemy combatant." The paucity, ambiguity, and contradictory information provided by the Amended Petition and the Amended Complaint about Petitioners Rasul and Iqbal and the twelve Kuwaiti Plaintiffs held at the military base at Guantanamo Bay prevents the Court from likewise concluding that these individuals were engaged in hostilities against the United States, or were instead participating in the benign activities suggested in the pleadings. While another court with apparently the same factual record has labeled, without explanation, the individuals held at Guantanamo Bay "enemy combatants," *Coalition of Clergy v. Bush*, 189 F. Supp. 2d, 1036, 1048 (C.D. Cal. 2002), this Court on the record before it, declines to take that step because taking judicial notice of a fact requires that the fact be "not subject to reasonable dispute." Fed. R. Evid. 201.

[13] The United States confronts an untraditional war that presents unique challenges in identifying a nebulous enemy. In earlier times when the United States was at war, discerning "the enemy" was far easier than today. "[I]n war 'every individual of the one nation must acknowledge every individual of the other nation as his

had already been convicted by a military commission, *id.* at 766, the *Eisentrager* Court did not base its decision on that distinction. Rather, *Eisentrager* broadly applies to prevent aliens detained outside the sovereign territory of the United States from invoking a petition for a writ of habeas corpus.

In sum, the *Eisentrager* decision establishes a two-dimensional paradigm for determining the rights of an individual under the habeas laws. If an individual is a citizen or falls within a narrow class of individuals who are akin to citizens, i.e. those persons seeking to prove their citizenship and those aliens detained at the nation's ports, courts have focused on status and have not been as concerned with the situs of the individual. However, if the individual is an alien without any connection to the United States, courts have generally focused on the location of the alien seeking to invoke the jurisdiction of the courts of the United States. If an alien is outside the country's sovereign territory, then courts have generally concluded that the alien is not permitted access to the courts of the United States to enforce the Constitution. Given that *Eisentrager* applies to the aliens presently detained at the military base at Guantanamo Bay, the only question remaining for the Court's resolution is whether Guantanamo Bay, Cuba is part of the sovereign territory of the United States.

4.   Is Guantanamo Bay Part of the Sovereign Territory of the United States?

The Court in *Eisentrager* discusses the territory of the United States in terms of sovereignty. *Id.* at 778 ("for these prisoners at no relevant time were within any territory over which the United States is sovereign"). It is undisputed, even by the parties, that Guantanamo Bay is not part of the sovereign territory of the United States.[14] Thus, the only question remaining for resolution is whether this fact alone is an absolute bar to these suits, or whether aliens on a United States military base situated in a foreign country are considered to be within the territorial jurisdiction of the United States, under a *de facto* theory of sovereignty.

Petitioners and Plaintiffs assert that the United States has *de facto* sovereignty over the military base at Guantanamo Bay, and that this provides the Court with the basis needed to assert jurisdiction. Pet'rs Opp'n at 21; Pls.' Opp'n at 11. In other words, Petitioners and Plaintiffs argue that even if the United States does not have *de jure* sovereignty over the military facility at Guantanamo Bay, it maintains *de facto* sovereignty due to the unique nature of the control and jurisdiction the United States exercises over this military base. According to Petitioners and Plaintiffs, if the United States has *de facto* sovereignty over the military facility at Guantanamo Bay, then

---

own enemy.'" *Eisentrager* 339 U.S. at 772 (quoting *The Rapid*, 8 Cranch 155, 161 (1814)). The two cases at bar contain nationals from three friendly countries at peace with the United States, demonstrating the difficulty in determining who is the "enemy."

[14] The United States occupies Guantanamo Bay under a lease entered into with the Cuban government in 1903. Agreement Between the United States and Cuba for the Lease of Lands for Coaling and Naval Stations, Feb. 16–23, 1903, U.S.-Cuba, art. III, T.S. 418. The lease provides:

> While on the one hand the United States recognizes the continuance of the ultimate sovereignty of the Republic of Cuba over [the military base at Guantanamo Bay], on the other hand the Republic of Cuba consents that during the period of occupation by the United States of said areas under the terms of this agreement the United States shall exercise complete jurisdiction and control over and within said areas with the right to acquire . . . for the public purposes of the United States any land or other property therein by purchase or by exercise of eminent domain with full compensation to the owners thereof.

Id. As is clear from this agreement, the United States does not have sovereignty over the military base at Guantanamo Bay.

Eisentrager is inapplicable to their cases and the Court is able to assume jurisdiction over their claims. However, the cases relied on by Petitioners and Plaintiffs to support their thesis are belied not only by *Eisentrager*, which never qualified its definition of sovereignty in such a manner, but also by the very case law relied on by Petitioners and Plaintiffs.

At oral argument, when asked for a case that supported the view that *de facto* sovereignty would suffice to provide the Court with jurisdiction, both Petitioners and Plaintiffs directed the Court to *Ralpho v. Bell*, 569 F.2d 607 (D.C. Cir.1977). Tr. at 33, 62–63. The *Ralpho* case involves a claim brought under the Micronesian Claims Act of 1971, which was enacted by the United States Congress to establish a fund to compensate Micronesians for losses incurred during the hostilities of World War II. *Ralpho*, 569 F.2d at 611. The plaintiff in that case, a citizen of Micronesia, argued that the Micronesian Claims Commission, established by the Act to adjudicate settlement claims, violated his due process rights by relying on secret evidence in deciding his claim. *Id.* at 615. While the United States did not have sovereignty over Micronesia, the District of Columbia Circuit found that the plaintiff was entitled to the protections of the due process clause. *Id.* at 618–19.

. . .

As clearly set forth in the case, the *Ralpho* Court treated Micronesia as the equivalent of a United States territory, such as Puerto Rico or Guam. In fact, *Ralpho* relies solely on the cases establishing constitutional rights for persons living in the territories of the United States as support for the view that the plaintiff located in Micronesia was deserving of certain due process rights. *Ralpho*, 569 F.2d at 619 n.70 (citing, *inter alia*, *Balzac v. Porto Rico*, 258 U.S. 298, 313 (1922)). The *Balzac* case, which predates *Eisentrager*, stands for the proposition that the limits of due process apply to the sovereign territories of the United States. *Balzac*, 258 U.S. at 313; *id* at 312 ("The Constitution, however, contains grants of power, and limitations which in the nature of things are not always and everywhere applicable and the real issue in the Insular Cases was not whether the Constitution extended to the Philippines or [Puerto] Rico when we went there, but which ones of its provisions were applicable by way of limitation upon the exercise of executive and legislative power in dealing with new conditions and requirements.").[15]

Thus, the Court in *Ralpho* analogized the situation before it to those cases granting constitutional rights to the peoples of United States territories, even though the trust agreement with the United Nations did not provide for sovereignty over Micronesia. *Ralpho*, 569 F.2d at 619 n.71. The cases involving the territories of the United States, relied on by the *Ralpho* Court, are fundamentally different from the two cases presently before the Court. The military base at Guantanamo Bay, Cuba, is nothing remotely akin to a territory of the United States, where the United States provides certain rights to the inhabitants. Rather, the United States merely leases an area of land for use as a naval base. Accordingly, the Court is hard-pressed to adopt Petitioners' and Plaintiffs' view that the holding in *Ralpho* favors their claims.

In fact, another district court considering whether a *de facto* sovereignty test should be used to analyze claims occurring at the military base at Guantanamo Bay flatly rejected the idea. *Bird v. United States*, 923 F.Supp. 338 (D.Conn. 1996). In *Bird*, a plaintiff alleged a misdiagnosis of a brain tumor at the United States Medical Facility at Guantanamo Bay. *Id.* at 339. Seeking to sue under the Federal Tort Claims Act ("FTCA"), the plaintiff sought to distinguish prior case law which held that injuries occurring on leased military bases were exempt from the FTCA under the "foreign country" exemption. In

---

15 . . .

order to circumvent this case law, the plaintiff in *Bird* argued that the unique territorial status of the military base at Guantanamo Bay brought injuries occurring on its soil within the FTCA. *Id.* at 340. Rejecting the plaintiff's argument that the United States had *de facto* sovereignty over the military base at Guantanamo Bay, the court wrote, "[b]ecause the 1903 Lease of Lands Agreement clearly establishes Cuba as the *de jure* sovereign over Guantanamo Bay, this Court need not speculate whether the United States is the *de facto* sovereign over the area." *Id.* at 343. While *Bird* dealt with the foreign country exemption to the FTCA, it expressly disavowed a *de facto* sovereignty test, when it was clear that Cuba was the *de jure* sovereign over Guantanamo Bay.

The *Bird* case is not the only court to reject a *de facto* sovereignty test for claims involving aliens located at the military base at Guantanamo Bay. *Cuban American Bar Ass'n, Inc. v. Christopher*, 43 F.3d 1412 (11th Cir.1995), *cert. denied*, 515 U.S. 1142 (1995). The *Cuban American Bar Association* case involved Cuban and Haitian migrants held in "safe haven" at Guantanamo Bay after they left their respective countries and were intercepted in international waters by the United States Coast Guard. *Id.* at 1417, 1419. The Eleventh Circuit specifically addressed the question of whether migrants "outside the physical borders of the United States have any cognizable statutory or constitutional rights." *Id.* at 1421. In *Cuban American Bar Association*, the Eleventh Circuit held:

> The district court here erred in concluding that Guantanamo Bay was a "United States territory." We disagree that "control and jurisdiction" [as set forth in the lease between the United States and Cuba] is equivalent to sovereignty. . . . [W]e again reject the argument that our leased military bases abroad which continue under the sovereignty of foreign nations, hostile or friendly, are "functional[ly] equivalent" to being land borders or ports of entry of the United States or otherwise within the United States.

Id. at 1425 (internal citations omitted). Thus, *Cuban American Bar Association* stands for the proposition that the military base at Guantanamo Bay is not within the territorial jurisdiction of the United States simply because the United States exercises jurisdiction and control over that facility.

Plaintiffs seek to distinguish *Cuban American Bar Assoication* by citing a Second Circuit opinion that has been vacated as moot by the Supreme Court. Pls.' Opp'n at 12–13 (citing *Haitian Centers Council, Inc. v. McNary*, 969 F.2d 1326 (2d Cir.1992), *vacated as moot sub nom. Sale v. Haitian Centers Council, Inc.*, 509 U.S. 918 (1993) [hereinafter "*HCC*"]). Ordinarily the Court would give short shrift to a case that has been vacated by the Supreme Court and not issued by the District of Columbia Circuit. However, since Plaintiffs in their papers, emphasize the importance of the reasoning in this vacated decision, the Court considers it necessary to briefly address the case.

The Court determines that *HCC* is distinguishable on its facts. In *HCC*, migrants were housed at the military base on Guantanamo Bay and determinations were made by Immigration and Naturalization Service ("INS") officers regarding their status. *Id.* at 1332–33. Those migrants that an INS officer deemed to have a credible fear of political persecution were "screened in" and were to be brought to the United States to pursue asylum claims. Those who did not fit within this class were repatriated to Haiti. *Id.*

The crucial distinction in their rights as aliens is that the aliens in *HCC* had been given some form of process by the government of the United States. Once the United States made determinations that the migrants had a credible fear of political persecution and could claim asylum in the United States, these migrants became vested with a liberty interest that the government was unable to simply deny without due process of law. The situation in *HCC* is fundamentally different from the cases presently before the Court. The individuals held at Guantanamo Bay have no desire to enter the United States and no final decision as to their status has been made. At this stage of their detention, those held at Guantanamo Bay more closely approximate the migrants in *Cuban American Bar Association* than the migrants "screened in" for admission to the United States in *HCC*.[16]

VI. CONCLUSION

The Court concludes that the military base at Guantanamo Bay, Cuba is outside the sovereign territory of the United States. Given that under *Eisentrager*, writs of habeas corpus are not available to aliens held outside the sovereign territory of the United States, this Court does not have jurisdiction to entertain the claims made by Petitioners in *Rasul* or Plaintiffs in *Odah*. Of course, just as the *Eisentrager* Court did not hold "that these prisoners have no right which the military authorities are bound to respect," *Eisentrager*, 339 U.S. at 789 n.14, this opinion, too, should not be read as stating that these aliens do not have some form of rights under international law. Rather, the Court's decision solely involves whether it has jurisdiction to consider the constitutional claims that are presented to the Court for resolution.

Petitioners and Plaintiffs argue that as long as the United States has *de facto* sovereignty over Guantanamo Bay, Fifth Amendment protections should apply. For this proposition, Petitioners and Plaintiffs rely on *Ralpho*, a case that involves land so similar to United States territory that the District of Columbia Circuit extended constitutional protections to its inhabitants. Clearly, Guantanamo Bay does not fall into that category. The Court, therefore, rejects the holding in *Ralpho* as a basis for this Court to exercise jurisdiction over the claims made by Petitioners and Plaintiffs. Accordingly, both cases shall be dismissed for want of jurisdiction.

COLLEEN KOLLAR-KOTELLY
United States District Judge

. . .

---

[16] While there is dicta in the *HCC* opinion which indicates a broader holding with regard to the constitutional rights of individuals detained at the military base on Guantanamo Bay, such dicta in *HCC* is not persuasive and not binding. *HCC*, 969 F.2d at 1343. The Supreme Court in *Eisentrager*, *Verdugo-Urquidez*, and *Zadvydas*, and the District of Columbia Circuit in *Harbury*, have all held that there is no extraterritorial application of the Fifth Amendment to aliens.

· · ·

United States Court of Appeals

FOR THE DISTRICT OF COLUMBIA CIRCUIT

———

Argued December 2, 2002   Decided March 11, 2003

———

No. 02-5251

KHALED A. F. AL ODAH, ET AL.,
APPELLANTS

v.

UNITED STATES OF AMERICA, ET AL.,
APPELLEES

———

Consolidated with
Nos. 02-5284, 02-5288

———

Appeals from the United States District Court
for the District of Columbia
(02cv00299)
(02cv00828)
(02cv01130)

———

· · ·

Thomas B. Wilner and *Joseph Margulies* argued the cause for appellants. With them on the briefs were *Neil H. Koslowe, Michael Ratner, Beth Stephens,* and *L. Barrett Boss.*

· · ·

Paul D. Clement, Deputy Solicitor General, U.S. Department of Justice, argued the cause for appellees. With him on the brief were *Roscoe C. Howard, Jr.,* U.S. Attorney, *Gregory G. Katsas,* Deputy Assistant Attorney General, U.S. Department of Justice, *Gregory G. Garre* and *David B. Salmons,* Assistants to the Solicitor General, *Douglas N. Letter, Robert M. Loeb* and *Katherine S. Dawson,* Attorneys.

· · ·

Before: RANDOLPH and GARLAND, *Circuit Judges,* and WILLIAMS, *Senior Circuit Judge.*

Opinion for the Court filed by *Circuit Judge* RANDOLPH.

Concurring opinion filed by *Circuit Judge* RANDOLPH.

· · ·

RANDOLPH, *Circuit Judge*: Through their "next friends," aliens captured abroad during hostilities in Afghanistan and held abroad in United States military custody at the Guantanamo Bay Naval Base in Cuba brought three actions contesting the legality and conditions of their confinement. The ultimate question presented in each case is whether the district court had jurisdiction to adjudicate their actions.

I.

. . .

The district court held that it lacked jurisdiction. Believing no court would have jurisdiction, it dismissed the complaint and the two habeas corpus petitions with prejudice. *Rasul v. Bush,* 215 F. Supp. 2d 55, 56 (D.D.C. 2002). In the court's view all of the detainees' claims went to the lawfulness of their custody and thus were cognizable only in habeas corpus. *Id.* at 62–64. Relying upon *Johnson v. Eisentrager*, 339 U.S. 763 (1950), the court ruled that it did not have jurisdiction to issue writs of habeas corpus for aliens detained outside the sovereign territory of the United States. *Rasul*, 215 F. Supp. 2d at 72–73.

II.

. . .

In each of the three cases, the detainees deny that they are enemy combatants or *enemy* aliens. Typical of the denials is this paragraph from the petition in *Rasul*:

> The detained petitioners are not, and have never been, members of Al Qaida or any other terrorist group. Prior to their detention, they did not commit any violent act against any American person, nor espouse any violent act against any American person or property. On information and belief, they had no involvement, direct or indirect, in either the terrorist attacks on the United States September 11, 2001, or any act of international terrorism attributed by the United States to al Qaida or any terrorist group.

(As the district court pointed out, an affidavit from the father of the Australian detainee in *Rasul* admitted that his son had joined the Taliban forces. *Rasul*, 215 F. Supp. 2d at 60 n.6.) Although the government asked the district court to take judicial notice that the detainees are "enemy combatants," the court declined and assumed the truth of their denials. *Id.* at 67 n.12.

This brings us to the first issue: whether the Supreme Court's decision in *Johnson v. Eisentrager*, which the district court found dispositive, is distinguishable on the ground that the prisoners there were "enemy aliens." In the two and a half years leading up to the 1950 *Eisentrager* decision, "German enemy aliens confined by American military authorities abroad" filed more than 200 habeas corpus petitions invoking the Supreme Court's original jurisdiction. 339 U.S. at 768 n.1. The Court denied each petition, often with four Justices announcing that they would dismiss for lack of jurisdiction. *Id.*; *see* Charles Fairman, *Some New Problems of the Constitution Following the Flag*, 1 STAN. L. REV. 587, 593–600 (1949). Justice Jackson, the author of the *Eisentrager* opinion, recused himself from each of the cases, doubtless because of his service (after his appointment to the Court) as Representative and Chief Counsel at the Nazi war crime trials in Nuremberg from 1945 to 1946. *See* Telford Taylor, *The Nuremberg Trials*, 55 COLUM. L. REV. 488 (1955).

Eisentrager differed from the earlier World War II habeas petitions. The case started not in the Supreme Court, but in a district court; and the Germans seeking the writ had not been convicted at Nuremberg. After Germany's surrender on May 8, 1945, but before the surrender of Japan, twenty-one German nationals in China assisted Japanese forces fighting against the United States. The Germans were captured, tried by an American military commission headquartered in Nanking, convicted of violating the laws of war, and transferred to the Landsberg prison in Germany, which was under the control of the United States Army. 339 U.S. at 765–66. One of the prisoners, on behalf of himself and the twenty others, sought writs of habeas corpus in the United States District Court for the District of Columbia, claiming violations of the Constitution, other laws of the United States, and the 1929 Geneva Convention. *Id.* at 767. The district court dismissed for lack of jurisdiction, but the court of appeals reversed. *Eisentrager v. Forrestal*, 174 F.2d 961 (D.C. Cir.1949).

The Supreme Court, agreeing with the district court, held that "the privilege of litigation" had not been extended to the German prisoners. 339 U.S. at 777–78. (Although *Eisentrager* discussed only the jurisdiction of federal courts, state courts do not have jurisdiction to issue writs of habeas corpus for the discharge of a person held under the authority of the United States. *Tarble's Case*, 80 U.S. (13 Wall.) 397 (1872).) The prisoners therefore had no right to petition for a writ of habeas corpus: "these prisoners at no relevant time were within any territory over which the United States is sovereign, and the scenes of their offense, their capture, their trial and their punishment were all beyond the territorial jurisdiction of any court of the United States." 339 U.S. at 778. Moreover, "trials would hamper the war effort and bring aid and comfort to the enemy." *Id.* at 779. Witnesses, including military officials, might have to travel to the United States from overseas. Judicial proceedings would engender a "conflict between judicial and military opinion" and "would diminish the prestige of" any field commander as he was called "to account in his own civil courts" and would "divert his efforts and attention from the military offensive abroad to the legal defensive at home." *Id.*

The detainees here are quite right that throughout its opinion, the Supreme Court referred to the *Eisentrager* prisoners as "enemy aliens." The petitioners in *Habib* and *Rasul* distinguish themselves from the German prisoners on the ground that they have not been charged and that the charges in *Eisentrager* are what rendered the prisoners "enemies." For this they rely on Justice Brennan's dissenting opinion in *United States v. Verdugo-Urquidez*, 494 U.S. 259, 290–91 (1990). Brief for Appellants at 29 (No. 02-5284 et al.). *Eisentrager*, Justice Brennan wrote, "rejected the German nationals' efforts to obtain writs of habeas corpus not because they were foreign nationals, but because they were enemy soldiers." 494 U.S. at 291 (Brennan, J., dissenting). This seems to us doubly mistaken. In the first place, the German prisoners were not alleged to be "soldiers." They were civilian employees of the German government convicted of furnishing intelligence to the Japanese about the movement of American forces in China. *Eisentrager*, 339 U.S. at 765–66; *Eisentrager*, 174 F.2d at 962. In the second place, it was not their convictions – which they contested – that rendered them "enemy aliens." The Supreme Court made this explicit: "It is not for us to say whether these prisoners were or were not guilty of a war crime," 339 U.S. at 786; "the petition of these prisoners admits[ ] that they are really alien enemies," *id.* at 784. The Court's description of the prisoners as "enemy aliens" rested instead on their status as nationals of a country at war with the United States. *Id.* at 769 n.2 (quoting *Techt v. Hughes*, 229 N.Y. 222, 229 (1920) (Cardozo, J.)). (Although Germany surrendered in 1945, the state of war with Germany did not end until October 19, 1951. Pub.L. No. 82–181, 65 Stat. 451; *see United States ex rel. Jaegeler v. Carusi*, 342 U.S. 347, 348 (1952) (per curiam).) This is the time-honored meaning of the term. "Every individual of the one nation must acknowledge every individual of the other nation as his own enemy – because the enemy of his country." *The Rapid*, 12 U.S. (8 Cranch) 155, 161 (1814); *see Guessefeldt v. McGrath*, 342 U.S. 308 (1952); *Lamar v. Browne*, 92 U.S. 187, 194 (1875); J. Gregory Sidak, *War, Liberty, and Enemy Aliens*, 67 N.Y.U. L. REV. 1402, 1406 (1992); *see also* The Alien Enemy Act of 1798, 50 U.S.C. §§21–24. Despite the government's argument to the contrary, it follows that none of the Guantanamo detainees are within the category of "enemy aliens," at least as *Eisentrager* used the term. They are nationals of Kuwait, Australia, or the United Kingdom. Our war in response to the attacks of September 11, 2001, obviously is not against these countries. It is against a network of terrorists operating in secret throughout the world and often hiding among civilian populations. An "alien friend" may become an "alien enemy" by taking up arms against the United States, but the cases before us were decided on the pleadings, each of which denied that the detainees had engaged in hostilities against America.

Nonetheless the Guantanamo detainees have much in common with the German prisoners in *Eisentrager*. They too are aliens, they too were captured during military operations, they were in a foreign country when captured, they are now abroad, they are in the custody of the American military, and they have never had any presence in the United States. For the reasons that follow we believe that under *Eisentrager* these factors preclude the detainees from seeking habeas relief in the courts of the United States.

The court of appeals in *Eisentrager* had ruled that "any person who is deprived of his liberty by officials of the United States, acting under the purported authority of that Government," and who can establish a violation of the Constitution, "has a right to the writ." 174 F.2d at 963. This statement of law, unconstrained by the petitioner's citizenship or residence, by where he is confined, by whom or for what, "necessarily" followed – thought the court of appeals – from the Fifth Amendment's application to "any person" and from the court's view that no distinction could be made between "citizens and aliens." *Id*. at 963–65. As the Supreme Court described it, the court of appeals thus treated the right to a writ of habeas corpus as a "subsidiary procedural right that follows from the possession of substantive constitutional rights." 339 U.S. at 781.

In answer the Supreme Court rejected the proposition "that the Fifth Amendment confers rights upon all persons, whatever their nationality, wherever they are located and whatever their offenses," *id*. at 783. The Court continued: "If the Fifth Amendment confers its rights on all the world ... [it] would mean that during military occupation irreconcilable enemy elements, guerrilla fighters, and 'werewolves' could require the American Judiciary to assure them freedoms of speech, press, and assembly as in our First Amendment, right to bear arms as in the Second, security against 'unreasonable' searches and seizures as in the Fourth, as well as rights to jury trial as in the Fifth and Sixth Amendments." *Id*. at 784. (Shortly before Germany's surrender, the Nazis began training covert forces called "werewolves" to conduct terrorist activities during the Allied occupation. *See, e.g.*, http://www.archives.gov/iwg/declassified_records/oss_records_263_wilhelm_hoettl.html.) The passage of the opinion just quoted may be read to mean that the constitutional rights mentioned are not held by aliens outside the sovereign territory of the United States, regardless of whether they are enemy aliens. That is how later Supreme Court cases have viewed *Eisentrager*.

In 1990, for instance, the Court stated that *Eisentrager* "rejected the claim that aliens are entitled to Fifth Amendment rights outside the sovereign territory of the United States." *Verdugo-Urquidez*, 494 U.S. at 269. After describing the facts of *Eisentrager* and quoting from the opinion, the Court concluded that with respect to aliens "our rejection of the extraterritorial application of the Fifth Amendment was emphatic." *Id*. By analogy, the Court held that the Fourth Amendment did not protect nonresident aliens against unreasonable searches or seizures conducted outside the sovereign territory of the United States. Citing *Eisentrager* again, the Court explained that to extend the Fourth Amendment to aliens abroad "would have serious and deleterious consequences for the United States in conducting activities beyond its borders," particularly since the government "frequently employs Armed Forces outside this country," *id*. at 273. A decade after *Verdugo-Urquidez*, the Court – again citing *Eisentrager* – found it "well established that certain constitutional protections available to persons inside the United States are unavailable to aliens outside of our geographic borders." *Zadvydas v. Davis*, 533 U.S. 678, 693 (2001).

Although the Supreme Court's statement in *Verdugo-Urquidez* about the Fifth Amendment was dictum, our court has followed it. In *Harbury v. Deutch*, 233 F.3d 596, 604 (D.C. Cir. 2000), *rev'd on other grounds sub nom. Christopher v. Harbury*, 536 U.S. 403 (2002), we quoted extensively from *Verdugo-Urquidez* and held that the Court's description of *Eisentrager* was "firm and considered dicta that binds this court." Other decisions of this court are firmer still. Citing *Eisentrager*, we held in *Pauling v. McElroy*, 278 F.2d 252, 254 n.3 (D.C. Cir. 1960), that "non-resident aliens . . . plainly cannot appeal to the protection of the Constitution or laws of the United States." The law of the circuit now is that a "foreign entity without property or presence in this country has no constitutional rights, under the due process clause or otherwise." *People's Mojahedin Org. v. Dep't of State*, 182 F.3d 17, 22 (D.C. Cir. 1999); *see also 32 County Sovereignty Comm. v. Dep't of State*, 292 F.3d 797, 799 (D.C. Cir. 2002).

The consequence is that no court in this country has jurisdiction to grant habeas relief, under 28 U.S.C. §2241, to the Guantanamo detainees, even if they have not been adjudicated enemies of the United States. We cannot see why, or how, the writ may be made available to aliens abroad when basic constitutional protections are not. This much is at the heart of *Eisentrager*. If the Constitution does not entitle the detainees to due process, and it does not, they cannot invoke the jurisdiction of our courts to test the constitutionality or the legality of restraints on their liberty. *Eisentrager* itself directly tied jurisdiction to the extension of constitutional provisions: "in extending constitutional protections beyond the citizenry, the Court has been at pains to point out that it was the alien's presence within its territorial jurisdiction that gave the Judiciary power to act." 339 U.S. at 771. Thus, the "privilege of litigation has been extended to aliens, *whether friendly or enemy*, only because permitting their presence in the country implied protection." *Id*. at 777–78 (emphasis added). In arguing that *Eisentrager* turned on the status of the prisoners as enemies, the detainees do not deny that if they are in fact in that category, if they engaged in international terrorism or were affiliated with al Qaeda, the courts would not be open to them. Their position is that the district court should have made these factual determinations at the threshold, before dismissing for lack of jurisdiction. But the Court in *Eisentrager* did not decide to avoid all the problems exercising jurisdiction would have caused, only to confront the same problems in determining whether jurisdiction exists in the first place.

It is true that after deciding jurisdiction did not exist, the Supreme Court, in part IV of its *Eisentrager* opinion, went on to consider and reject the merits of the prisoners' claims. From this the detainees reason that the Court's holding must have been merely that the military courts, rather than the civilian courts, had jurisdiction to try charges of war crimes, not that the district court lacked jurisdiction to adjudicate the habeas petition. We find it impossible to read the Court's statements – many of which we have already quoted – about the courts not being open to the prisoners as so limited. The discussion in part IV of the Court's opinion was extraneous. The dissenting Justices viewed it as such, calling part IV "gratuitous," "wholly irrelevant," lending "no support whatever to the Court's holding that the District Court was without jurisdiction." 339 U.S. at 792, 794 (Black, J., joined by Douglas and Burton, JJ., dissenting). There is a ready explanation for the *Eisentrager* Court's method. Before *Steel Co. v. Citizens for a Better Environment*, 523 U.S. 83 (1998), the Supreme Court (and the lower federal courts) were not always punctilious in treating jurisdiction as an antecedent question to the merits. The Court in *Steel Co.* acknowledged as much. *See* 523 U.S. at 101. Part IV of *Eisentrager*, whether an advisory opinion (*see* 523 U.S. at 101) or an alternative holding, does not detract from the central meaning of the decision that the district court did not have jurisdiction to issue writs of habeas corpus.

We have thus far assumed that the detainees are not "within any territory over which the United States is sovereign," *Eisentrager*, 339 U.S. at 778. The detainees dispute the assumption. They say the military controls Guantanamo Bay, that it is in essence a territory of the United States, that the government exercises sovereignty over it, and that in any event *Eisentrager* does not turn on technical definitions of sovereignty or territory.

The United States has occupied the Guantanamo Bay Naval Base under a lease with Cuba since 1903, as modified in 1934. Lease of Lands for Coaling and Naval Stations, Feb. 23, 1903, U.S.-Cuba, T.S. No. 418 (6 Bevans 1113) ("1903 Lease"); Relations With Cuba, May 9, 1934, U.S.-Cuba, T.S. No. 866 (6 Bevans 1161) ("1934 Lease"). In the 1903 Lease, "the United States recognizes the continuance of the ultimate sovereignty of the Republic of Cuba" over the naval base. 1903 Lease, art. III. The term of the lease is indefinite. 1903 Lease, art. I; 1934 Lease, art. III ("So long as the United States of America shall not abandon the said naval station at Guantanamo or the two Governments shall not agree to a modification of its present limits, the station shall continue to have the territorial area that it now has. . . .").

The detainees think criminal cases involving aliens and United States citizens for activities at Guantanamo Bay support their position. But those cases arose under the special maritime and territorial jurisdiction, *see* 18 U.S.C. §7. In *United States v. Lee*, 906 F.2d 117 (4th Cir. 1990) (per curiam), a Jamaican national was charged with committing a crime at Guantanamo. The indictment invoked the special maritime and territorial jurisdiction of the United States pursuant to 18 U.S.C. §7 and 18 U.S.C. §3238. *Id.* at 117 n.1. Extension of federal criminal law pursuant to these provisions does not give the United States sovereignty over Guantanamo Bay any more than it gives the United States sovereignty over foreign vessels destined for this country because crimes committed onboard are also covered. *See* 18 U.S.C. §7(8).

The text of the leases, quoted above, shows that Cuba – not the United States – has sovereignty over Guantanamo Bay. This is the conclusion of *Cuban Am. Bar Ass'n v. Christopher*, 43 F.3d 1412 (11th Cir. 1995). The Eleventh Circuit there rejected the argument – which the detainees make in this case – that with respect to Guantanamo Bay "'control and jurisdiction' is equivalent to sovereignty." *Id.* at 1425. The Supreme Court reached the same conclusion in *Vermilya-Brown Co. v. Connell*, 335 U.S. 377, 381 (1948). In holding that a naval base in Bermuda, controlled by the United States under a lease with Great Britain, was outside United States sovereignty, the Court took notice of the lease with Cuba for the Guantanamo Bay Naval Base and the fact that it granted the United States "substantially the same rights as it has in the Bermuda lease." *Id.* at 383.

The "determination of sovereignty over an area," the Court held, "is for the legislative and executive departments." *Id.* at 380. The contrary decision of the Second Circuit, on which the detainees rely – *Haitian Centers Council, Inc. v. McNary*, 969 F.2d 1326 (2d Cir. 1992), *vacated as moot, Sale v. Haitian Centers Council, Inc.*, 509 U.S. 918 (1993) – has no precedential value because the Supreme Court vacated it. The decision was, in any event, at odds with the Supreme Court's reasoning not only in *Vermilya-Brown*, but also in *Spelar v. United States*, 338 U.S. 217 (1949). The Second Circuit's result rested in very large measure on its extraterritorial application of the Fifth Amendment to non-resident aliens, *see* 969 F.2d at 1342–43, a position we rejected in *People's Mojahedin Org. v. Dep't of State*, 182 F.3d at 22, and in *Harbury v. Deutch*, 233 F.3d at 604, and a position we reject again today. And the Second Circuit thought it important that the United States controlled Guantanamo Bay. 969 F.2d at 1342–44. But under *Eisentrager*, control is surely not the test. Our military forces may have control over the naval base at Guantanamo, but our military forces also had control over the Landsberg prison in Germany.

We also disagree with the detainees that the *Eisentrager* opinion interchanged "territorial jurisdiction" with "sovereignty," without attaching any particular significance to either term. When the Court referred to "territorial jurisdiction," it meant the territorial jurisdiction of the United States courts, as for example in these passages quoted earlier: "in extending constitutional protections beyond the citizenry, the Court has been at pains to point out that it was the alien's presence within its territorial jurisdiction that gave the Judiciary power to act" (339 U.S. at 771); and "the scenes of their offense, their capture, their trial and their punishment were all beyond the territorial jurisdiction of United States courts" (*id.* at 778). Sovereignty, on the other hand, meant then – and means now – supreme dominion exercised by a nation. The United States has sovereignty over the geographic area of the States and, as the *Eisentrager* Court recognized, over insular possessions, *id.* at 780. Guantanamo Bay fits within neither category.

As against this the detainees point to *Ralpho v. Bell*, 569 F.2d 607 (D.C. Cir. 1977). After World War II, the United Nations designated the United States as administrator of the Trust Territory of Micronesia. *Id.* at 612. No country had sovereignty over the region, but the court treated Micronesia as if it were a territory of the United States, over which Congress could and did exercise its power under Article IV of the Constitution. (The United States did not hold the Trust Territory "in fee simple . . . but rather as trustee," a difference the court considered irrelevant. *Id.* at 619.) The court therefore described the residents of Micronesia as being "as much American subjects as those in other American territories." *Id.* In the Micronesian Claims Act, Congress established a commission to distribute a fund for claims against the United States for damages suffered during World War II. Because Congress intended the Micronesia Trust Territory to be treated as if it were a territory of the United States, the court held that the right of due process applied to the commission's actions. *Id.* at 629–30. Given the premises on which the court acted, its holding is hardly surprising. "Fundamental personal rights" found in the Constitution apply in territories. *See, e.g., Balzac v. Porto Rico*, 258 U.S. 298, 312–13 (1922); *see also Dorr v. United States*, 195 U.S. 138, 148 (1904) (considering the law applicable in the Philippines); 48 U.S.C. §1421b (Guam). *Ralpho* thus establishes nothing about the sort of *de facto* sovereignty the detainees say exists at Guantanamo. And its reasoning does not justify this court, or any other, to assert habeas corpus jurisdiction at the behest of an alien held at a military base leased from another nation, a military base outside the sovereignty of the United States.

. . .

IV.

We have considered and rejected the other arguments the detainees have made to the court. The judgment of the district court dismissing the complaint in No. 02-5251 and the petitions for writs of habeas corpus in Nos. 02-5284 and 02-5288 for lack of jurisdiction is

Affirmed.[*]

. . .

---

[*] . . .

No. 03-334

In The

Supreme Court of the United States

SHAFIQ RASUL, *et al.*,

Petitioners,

v.

GEORGE W. BUSH, *et al.*,

Respondents.

**On Writ of Certiorari
to the United States Court of Appeals
for the District of Columbia Circuit**

PETITIONERS' BRIEF ON THE MERITS

JOSEPH MARGULIES
Counsel of Record
MARGULIES & RICHMAN, PLC

BARBARA J. OLSHANSKY
STEVEN MACPHERSON WATT
MICHAEL RATNER
CENTER FOR
    CONSTITUTIONAL RIGHTS

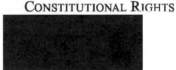

MACARTHUR JUSTICE CENTER
UNIVERSITY OF CHICAGO
    LAW SCHOOL

JOHN J. GIBBONS
GITANJALI S. GUTIERREZ
GIBBONS, DEL DEO,
    DOLAN, GRIFFINGER
    & VECCHIONE, P.C.

Attorneys for Petitioners

---

* Redactions on this page have been added for privacy purposes. – *Eds.*

QUESTION PRESENTED

Whether United States courts lack jurisdiction to consider challenges to the legality of the detention of foreign nationals captured abroad in connection with hostilities and incarcerated at the Guantánamo Bay Naval Base, Cuba.

. . .

STATEMENT OF THE CASE

Seized in ostensible connection with hostilities abroad, the petitioners are in United States custody at Guantánamo Bay Naval Station, Cuba. They have been confined for two years without charges, access to counsel or courts, or recourse to any legal process. The Executive has presented no evidence to justify the detentions, and claims it is under no obligation to do so. It claims it may hold the petitioners under these conditions indefinitely.

. . .

The four Petitioners have never been enemy aliens or unlawful combatants. Prior to their detention, the Taliban had caused no American casualties, and the Petitioners neither caused nor attempted to cause harm to American personnel. The four Petitioners had no involvement, direct or indirect, in any terrorist act, including the attacks of September 11, 2001. They maintain today, as they have throughout this litigation, that they are innocent of wrongdoing, and the United States has never presented evidence to the contrary. . . .

. . .[3]

ARGUMENT

I.   THE HABEAS STATUTE GIVES THE DISTRICT COURT JURISDICTION

The Great Writ stands as "the precious safeguard of personal liberty and there is no higher duty than to maintain it unimpaired." *Bowen v. Johnston*, 306 U.S. 19, 26 (1939). Since the founding, it has been the indispensable means for the judiciary to test the legality of executive detention. *Ex parte Bollman*, 8 U.S. (4 Cranch) 75, 99 (1807); *Ex parte Lange*, 85 U.S. (18 Wall.) 163 (1874); *Johnson v. Zerbst*, 304. U.S. 458, 465–67 (1938); *Zadvydas v. Davis*, 533 U.S. 678, 699 (2001); *INS v. St. Cyr*, 533 U.S. 289, 301–304 (2001).

   Yet the Executive argues that the federal courts are powerless to review these prisoners' indefinite detentions because they are foreign nationals brought by the military to a prison beyond the "ultimate sovereignty" of the United States. The

---

[3] In the lower courts, the Executive took the position the prisoners were held pursuant to the President's power as Commander in Chief "and under the laws and usages of war." *E.g. Rasul v. Bush*, Government's Motion to Dismiss at 4. On July 3, 2003, the President designated David Hicks and five other detainees as being held pursuant to the President's Military Order of November 13, 2001, concerning the "Detention, Treatment, and Trial of Certain Non-Citizens in the War Against Terrorism." 66 Fed. Reg. 57,831. Mike Allen & Glenn Frankel, *Bush Halts Military Proceedings Against 3*, WASH. POST, Jul. 19, 2003, at A15. According to the Government, this means Hicks *may*, but need not, be brought before a military commission. On December 3, 2003, the Executive assigned military counsel for Petitioner Hicks, and counsel has since visited with Hicks. John Mintz, *Guantanamo Bay Detainee Is First to Be Given a Lawyer*, WASH. POST, Dec. 4, 2003, at A8. At present, however, Hicks has not been charged, has no recourse to any procedure for demonstrating his innocence or seeking his release, and remains subject to indefinite detention without legal process.

Government is mistaken. First, nothing in the habeas statute supports such a limitation, nor has Congress manifested an intention to strip the federal courts of their jurisdiction under these circumstances. The Court has routinely taken jurisdiction of habeas petitions filed by persons in custody under the authority of the United States in places beyond its "ultimate sovereignty," even during times of armed conflict. And the Court has never suggested that the Executive can incarcerate people indefinitely, beyond the reach of judicial recourse, simply by confining them in a facility that the United States Government controls through some arrangement other than "ultimate sovereignty."[6]

Second, the Executive's argument – if accepted – would raise "serious constitutional problem[s]." *Zadvydas*, 533 U.S. at 692. It would permit "an indefinite, perhaps permanent, deprivation of human liberty without any [judicial] protection," *id.*, and would suspend the writ for an entire class of detainees on no firmer basis than Executive fiat. The Executive would have the Court "close our doors to a class of habeas petitioners seeking review without any clear indication that such was Congress' intent." *United States v. Castro*, 124 S.Ct. 786, 791 (2003). This country has rejected imprisonment without legal process, even during times of war, and the Court should not interpret the habeas statute in a manner that permits the creation of an offshore prison for foreign nationals that operates entirely outside the law.[7] *Id.*; *St. Cyr*, 533 U.S. at 314.

Third, construing the statute to exclude habeas jurisdiction would violate the well-established canon that "an act of Congress ought never to be construed to violate the law of nations if any other possible construction remains." *Murray v. Schooner Charming Betsy*, 6 U.S. (2 Cranch) 64, 118 (1804). In recent decades 151 nations, including this one, have ratified the International Covenant on Civil and Political Rights, which guarantees judicial review of executive detentions, even in wartime. And 191 nations, including the United States, have joined the 1949 Geneva Conventions, which require that prisoners captured in combat zones have the right to be brought before a "competent tribunal" whenever there is "any doubt" as to their status. The Executive's strained construction of the habeas statute, permitting indefinite incarceration with no legal process, would violate these fundamental precepts of international law. The statute should not be so construed.

A. Habeas Turns On Executive Detention, Not The Accident of Nationality or Situs

Title 28 U.S.C. §2241 (c)(1) and (c)(3) confer jurisdiction on the district court to hear applications for habeas corpus filed by any person imprisoned "under or by color of the authority of the United States," or "in violation of the Constitution or laws or treaties of the United States." Nothing in the text purports to exclude habeas jurisdiction on the basis of nationality or territory. On the contrary, "[t]his legislation is of the most comprehensive character. It brings within the *habeas corpus* jurisdiction of every court and of every judge every possible case of privation of liberty contrary to the National

---

[6] The Executive leans heavily on *Johnson v. Eisentrager*, 339 U.S. 763 (1950). But *Johnson* cannot bear the weight, as we demonstrate at pages 30–46 *infra*.

[7] Even the prospect of judicial review is salutary. Only after this Court granted *certiorari* did the Executive announce its apparent intention to release 140 detainees. *Cf. Walling v. Helmerich & Payne, Inc.*, 323 U.S. 37, 42–43 (1944) ("Respondent has consistently urged the validity of [its] plan and would presumably be free to resume the use of this illegal plan were not some effective restraint made.").

Constitution, treaties, or laws. It is impossible to widen this jurisdiction."[8] *Ex parte McCardle*, 73 U.S. (6 Wall.) 318, 325–26 (1868).

The history of the statute is well known. In 1789, Congress granted habeas jurisdiction over prisoners "in custody, under or by colour of the authority of the United States." Act of Sept. 24, 1789, ch. 20, §14, 1 Stat. 73, 81–82. In 1842, Congress made explicit that federal habeas included foreign nationals. Act of Aug. 29, 1842, ch. 257, 5 Stat. 539, 539. In 1867, Congress expanded habeas review to include "all cases where any person may be restrained of his or her liberty in violation of the constitution or of any treaty or law of the United States." Act of Feb. 5, 1867, ch. 28, 14 Stat. 385, 385. The 1867 Act is the "direct ancestor" of 28 U.S.C. §2241(c).[9] *Felker v. Turpin*, 518 U.S. 651, 659 (1996).

Though habeas today often involves collateral review of criminal convictions (as in *Johnson v. Eisentrager*), "[a]t its historical core, the writ of habeas corpus has served as a means of reviewing the legality of Executive detention, and it is in that context that its protections have been strongest." *St. Cyr*, 533 U.S. at 301; *Swain v. Pressley*, 430 U.S. 372, 380 n. 13 (1977); *Brown v. Allen*, 344 U.S. 443, 533 (1953) (Jackson, J., concurring in result) ("The historic purpose of the writ has been to relieve detention by executive authorities without judicial trial"). Indeed, at common law, "[w]hile habeas review of a court judgment was limited to the issue of the sentencing court's jurisdictional competency, an attack on an executive order could raise all issues relating to the legality of the detention." *St. Cyr*, 533 U.S. at 301 n.14 (internal citations omitted).[10]

The Court has always jealously guarded its power to review Executive detention. It has consistently required a clear and unequivocal statement of legislative intent before concluding that Congress stripped the federal courts of their habeas jurisdiction. *Ex parte Yerger*, 75 U.S. (8 Wall.) 85, 102 (1869); *DeMore v. Kim.*, 538 U.S. 510 (2003); *see also St. Cyr*, 533 U.S. at 308–09. In *Kim*, the Court held that Congress had not removed habeas jurisdiction despite statutory language which provided that "[n]o court may set aside any action or decision by the Attorney General" to detain criminal aliens while removal proceedings are ongoing. *Kim*, 123 S.Ct. at 1714. And in *St. Cyr*, the Court preserved habeas jurisdiction in the face of four statutory provisions that could have been read as excluding it, including one entitled "Elimination of Custody Review by Habeas Corpus." 533 U.S. at 308–311, 314.[11]

---

[8] Section 2241(a) empowers federal judges to grant the writ "within their respective jurisdictions." 28 U.S.C. §2241(a). At one time, the Court interpreted this language to require the petitioner's presence within the jurisdiction. *See Ahrens v. Clark*, 335 U.S. 188, 189–93 (1948). This is no longer the law, however, *see Braden v. 30ᵗʰ Judicial Cir. Ct.*, 410 U.S. 484, 494–95 (1973), and petitions challenging military detention overseas are properly filed in the District of Columbia because the courts have jurisdiction over the custodian. *E.g., McElroy v. United States ex rel. Guagliardo*, 361 U.S. 281, 282–83 (1960) (habeas filed in the District Court for the District of Columbia against Secretary of Defense by petitioner detained in Morocco at time of filing); *Toth v. Quarles*, 350 U.S. 11, 13 n.3 (1955) (habeas filed in the District Court of the District of Columbia against Secretary of the Air Force by sister of petitioner detained in Korea); *Ex parte Hayes*, 414 U.S. 1327, 1328–29 (1973) (Douglas, J., in chambers) (habeas filed in District Court of the District of Columbia against Secretary of the Army by petitioner detained in Germany).

[9] The historical foundations of the writ are canvassed in greater detail by several *amici*. *See* Brief of the Commonwealth Lawyers Association as *Amicus Curiae*; Brief of Legal Historians as *Amici Curiae*.

[10] In addition to the habeas statute, Petitioners relied on 28 U.S.C. §1331 and 5 U.S.C. §702 in the lower courts to establish jurisdiction. . . . Jurisdiction under these provisions is discussed by the Petitioners in *Al Odah v. United States*, No. 03-343, and we adopt their arguments.

[11] Other statutory language considered in *St. Cyr* provided that "judicial review" was available "only" by means other than habeas, and that "no court shall have jurisdiction to review" any final agency order. 533 U.S. at 308–311. Yet the Court found a "lack of clear, unambiguous, and express statement of congressional intent to preclude judicial consideration on habeas of such an important question of law." *Id.* at 314; *see also, e.g., Ex parte Yerger*, 75 U.S. at 102 ("We are not at liberty to except from [habeas corpus jurisdiction] any cases

Unlike *Kim* and *St. Cyr*, where the Court was faced with explicit – although insufficiently categorical – statutory provisions appearing to restrict the courts' habeas jurisdiction, the present case involves no remotely perceptible attempt by Congress to abridge jurisdiction.[12] And certainly, the Executive cannot amend the statute by fiat. *Cf. Youngstown Sheet & Tube Co. v. Sawyer*, 343 U.S. 579, 637 (1952) (Jackson, J., concurring) ("When the President takes measures incompatible with the expressed or implied will of Congress, his power is at its lowest ebb...."); *Brown v. Allen*, 344 U.S. at 533 (Jackson, J., concurring) ("[I]f Congress intended a reversal of this traditional concept of habeas corpus it would have said so.").

Over time, Executive detention has taken countless forms, limited only by the perceived demands of the day. But the genius of habeas is "its capacity to reach all manner of illegal detention – its ability to cut through barriers of form and procedural mazes." *Harris v. Nelson*, 394 U.S. 286, 291 (1969).[13] To that end, the Court has long recognized that federal courts have the power to review every species of Executive imprisonment, wherever it occurs and whatever form it takes. The Court has entertained habeas petitions by aliens detained on ships at sea, *e.g., Chew Heong v. United States.*, 112 U.S. 536 (1884);[14] by United States citizens detained at American military installations overseas, *e.g., McElroy v. United States ex rel. Guagliardo*, 361 U.S. 281 (1960);[15] and even by enemy aliens convicted of war crimes during a declared war, whether in the United States, *Ex parte Quirin*, 317 U.S. 1 (1942), or in territories overseas, *In re Yamashita*, 327 U.S. 1 (1948). Even the Executive has conceded that the federal courts would have habeas jurisdiction over an American citizen imprisoned at Guantánamo.[16]

Yet the Executive insists the prior decisions count for naught because no single case embraces all the circumstances presented here. This, of course, testifies to the unprecedented character of the Executive's position. Detention without legal process is the very antithesis of this country's wartime experience, as shown below.[17] It is not surprising, therefore, that the Court has had no occasion to consider whether the Executive may unilaterally strip the federal courts of their statutory power to review the indefinite

---

not plainly excepted by law...."); *Felker*, 518 U.S. at 660–61 (statutory provisions purporting to strip federal courts of jurisdiction did not foreclose habeas review).

[12] On the contrary, available evidence suggests that Congress *refused* to suspend the writ as part of the "war on terrorism." Published accounts indicate the earliest drafts of the USA PATRIOT Act, Uniting and Strengthening America by Providing Appropriate Tools Required to Intercept and Obstruct Terrorism Act of 2001, 107 Pub. L. No. 56, 115 Stat. 272 (2001), included a provision entitled 'Suspension of the Writ of Habeas Corpus.' Representative James Sensenbrenner, Chairman of the House Judiciary Committee, later told reporters "[t]hat stuck out like a sore thumb. It was the first thing I crossed out." Roland Watson, *Bush Law Chief Tried to Drop Habeas Corpus*, THE TIMES (London), Dec. 3, 2001, at 14; *see also* Steven Brill, *After: How America Confronted the Sept. 12 Era*, NEWSWEEK, Mar. 10, 2003, at 66 (same). The USA PATRIOT Act passed by Congress does not alter §2241. *See* USA PATRIOT Act §412(b)(1) (codified at 8 U.S.C. §1226a(b)(1)).

[13] As discussed in Part II, the Court on occasion limits the *extent* of habeas review, but distinguishes these limitations from a restriction on its *power* to review executive detention. *See, e.g., Burns v. Wilson*, 346 U.S. 137, 139 (1953) (plurality) (question is "not whether the District Court has any power at all to consider petitioners' applications; rather our concern is with the manner in which the Court should proceed to exercise its power").

[14] *See also, e.g., Nishimura Ekiu v. United States*, 142 U.S. 651, 660 (1892) ("An alien immigrant, prevented from landing by any such officer claiming authority to do so under an act of congress, and thereby restrained of his liberty, *is doubtless entitled to a writ of habeas corpus to ascertain whether the restraint is lawful.*" (emphasis added)).

[15] *See supra* note 8 (collecting additional cases).

[16] Tr. of Nov. 17, 2003 Oral Argument at 16:25-19:8, *Padilla v. Rumsfeld*, _F.3d_, 2003 U.S. App. LEXIS 25616 (Nos. 03-2235, 03-2438), *at* http://news.findlaw.com/hdocs/docs/padilla/padrums111703trans.pdf.

[17] *See also* Brief of Former American Prisoners of War as *Amicus Curiae*; Brief of the National Institute of Military Justice as *Amicus Curiae*.

detention of foreign nationals without legal process, simply by deciding to detain them in an offshore prison.

B. The Habeas Statute Should Not Be Read To Condone Creating A Prison Outside The Law

The lower court did not discuss the scope of the habeas statute. Instead, it resolved the jurisdictional question by concluding the prisoners have no rights that may be vindicated in federal court, "under the due process clause or otherwise." . . . In its view, foreign nationals may be subjected to an "indefinite, perhaps permanent, deprivation of human liberty without any [judicial] protection," *Zadvydas*, 533 U.S. at 692, so long as the Executive elects to detain them outside the "ultimate sovereignty" of the United States. This holding creates a "serious constitutional problem," *id.*, both by approving prolonged detention without legal process, and by suspending the writ in the absence of any indication of congressional intent. To avoid these results, the Court should interpret the habeas statute to allow the prisoners to bring this challenge in federal court. *See St. Cyr*, 533 U.S. at 314.

1. The Executive's Interpretation of The Habeas Statute Would Raise Serious Doubts Under The Due Process Clause

At its core, the Due Process Clause protects against unlawful bodily restraint. *See, e.g.*, *Zadvydas*, 533 U.S. at 690 ("Freedom from imprisonment – from government custody, detention, or other forms of physical restraint – lies at the heart of the liberty that Clause protects."). The Executive may not imprison people for more than brief periods unless it acts pursuant to narrowly circumscribed criteria and strict procedural restraints. *Id.* at 690–91 ("[W]e have upheld preventive detention based on dangerousness only when limited to specially dangerous individuals and subject to strong procedural protections."); *cf. Kim*, 123 S.Ct. at 1720 (contrasting the "indefinite" and "potentially permanent" detention condemned in *Zadvydas* with the "brief" detention upheld in *Kim*).[18]

Statutory schemes that subject a particular class of aliens to potential restraint have consistently been interpreted so as to respect these principles. Aliens detained pursuant to these schemes enjoy at least the right to a fair hearing to determine whether they fall within the defined class. *See, e.g.*, *Ludecke v. Watkins*, 335 U.S. 160, 171 n.17 (1948) (administrative hearing followed by judicial review to determine whether person detained was in fact an "enemy alien"); *Carlson v. Landon*, 342 U.S. 524, 540–41 (1952) (administrative hearing followed by judicial review to determine whether detained alien was an active member of the communist party); *Kim*, 123 S.Ct. at 1722 (Kennedy, J., concurring) (detainee entitled to hearing "to demonstrate that he was not improperly included in a mandatory detention category."); *Zadvydas*, 533 U.S. at 721 (Kennedy, J., dissenting on other grounds) ("[I]nadmissible aliens are entitled to be free from detention that is arbitrary or capricious.").

During the Second World War, the Court repeatedly agreed that even convicted saboteurs and war criminals, seized here and abroad, were entitled at least to a hearing to

---

[18] *See also United States v. Salerno*, 481 U.S. 739, 747, 750–52 (1987) (stressing stringent time limitations and presence of judicial safeguards); *Addington v. Texas*, 441 U.S. 418, 425–27 (1979); *Kansas v. Hendricks*, 521 U.S. 346, 356–58 (1977) (emphasizing strict procedural protections); *Gerstein v. Pugh*, 420 U.S. 103, 117–18 (1975); *Jackson v. Indiana*, 406 U.S. 715, 737–39 (1972).

determine their status. *See Quirin*, 317 U.S. at 24–25; *Yamashita*, 327 U.S. at 8; *Johnson*, 339 U.S. at 780–81 (prisoners received "the same preliminary hearing as to sufficiency of application that was extended in *Quirin*.... [and] *Yamashita*"). In this respect, the Executive "is certainly not immune from the historic requirements of fairness merely because he acts, however conscientiously, in the name of security." *Joint Anti-Fascist Refugee Committee v. McGrath*, 341 U.S. 123, 173 (1951) (Frankfurter, J., concurring).

Yet the Executive takes the position now that foreign nationals imprisoned by the military beyond the "ultimate sovereignty" of the United States have no rights that can be protected by a federal court and may be detained indefinitely without legal process. This has never been the law:

> The proposition is, of course, not that the Constitution "does not apply" overseas, but that there are provisions in the Constitution which do not *necessarily* apply in all circumstances in every foreign place.

* * *

> [T]he question of which specific safeguards of the Constitution are appropriately to be applied in a particular context overseas can be reduced to the issue of what process is "due" a defendant in the particular circumstances of a particular case.

Reid v. Covert, 354 U.S. 1, 74–75 (1957) (Harlan, J., concurring).[19] The Court later quoted this language with approval in a case involving a non-resident alien. *United States v. Verdugo-Urquidez*, 494 U.S. 259, 270 (1990); *see also id.* at 277–78 (Kennedy, J., concurring).[20]

The suggestion, therefore, that the Constitution tolerates the creation of a prison beyond the reach of the judiciary, reserved for foreign nationals who may be held on mere Executive fiat, is mistaken. Rather, the courts must undertake a more discriminating

---

[19] *See also Reid*, 354 U.S. at 56 (Frankfurter, J., concurring) ("Governmental action abroad is performed under both the authority and the restrictions of the Constitution – for example, proceedings before American military tribunals, whether in Great Britain or in the United States, are subject to the applicable restrictions of the Constitution.").

[20] In *Verdugo*, the Court held that the warrant clause of the Fourth Amendment does not apply to the search of a foreign national in Mexico by Mexican agents. *Dicta* cited *Johnson v. Eisentrager* for the "emphatic" rejection of the "extraterritorial application of the Fifth Amendment." *Verdugo*, 494 U.S. at 269. But this language cannot be read in isolation. *Verdugo* cited the *Insular Cases, id.* at 268–69, in which the Court repeatedly recognized that the Due Process Clause embodies a fundamental right that constrains the Executive, even when it acts with respect to an alien outside the United States. As the Court stated in *Balzac v. Porto Rico*, 258 U.S. 298, 312–13 (1922):

> [T]he real issue in the *Insular Cases* was not whether the Constitution extended to the Philippines or Porto Rico when we went there, but which of its provisions were applicable by way of limitation upon the exercise of executive and legislative power.... *The guaranties of certain fundamental personal rights declared in the Constitution, as for instance that no person could be deprived of life, liberty or property without due process of law*, had from the beginning full application in the Philippines and Porto Rico....

Id. at 312–13 (emphasis added).

   Verdugo then approvingly quoted Justice Harlan's *Reid* concurrence insisting that the extra-territorial reach of the Constitution depended on what process was due in a particular case. Although *Reid* had involved a U.S. citizen overseas, *Verdugo* did not hesitate to endorse Justice Harlan's guiding principle in a case involving a foreign national, just as it had in the *Insular Cases. E.g., Downes v. Bidwell*, 182 U.S. 244, 283 (1901) (rejecting theory that aliens in unincorporated territories "have no rights which [Congress] is bound to respect."). It is thus incorrect to read *Verdugo* as establishing a categorical rule that the Due Process Clause cannot apply to aliens overseas. Indeed, Justice Kennedy's concurring opinion in *Verdugo* made explicit that the Court had not yet resolved the Constitution's extra-territorial reach "when the Government acts, in reference to an alien, within its sphere of foreign operations." 494 U.S. at 277.

analysis of the interests at stake. Here, that analysis can wait for another day. For while "there is no table of weights and measures for ascertaining what constitutes due process," *Burns v. Wilson*, 346 U.S. 137, 149 (1953) (opinion of Frankfurter, J.), the Executive's claim that courts lack jurisdiction even to undertake the weighing misreads the habeas statute and would raise serious questions under the Due Process Clause.

2.   The Executive's Interpretation of The Habeas Statute Would Also Raise
     Serious Doubts Under The Suspension Clause

The Court should also avoid an interpretation of the habeas statute that suspends the writ for an entire class of claimants based solely on Executive proclamation. In *St. Cyr*, the Government argued that certain provisions of the Anti-Terrorism and Effective Death Penalty Act of 1996, 110 Stat. 1214, should be construed as denying the alien petitioners the right to habeas review of their deportation proceedings. *St. Cyr*, 533 U.S. at 308–11. The Court rejected this position, noting that such a construction would raise grave constitutional doubts under the Suspension Clause. *Id.* at 305.

It was common ground among the parties in *St. Cyr* that Executive detention struck at the "historical core" of the writ, "and it is in that context that its protections have been strongest." *Id.* at 301. Furthermore, as the Court observed, "[i]n England prior to 1789, in the Colonies, and in this Nation during the formative years of our Government, *the writ of habeas corpus was available to nonenemy aliens as well as to citizens.*" *Id.* at 301–02 (emphasis added) (footnote omitted). While the Government acknowledged this historical understanding, it argued there was no unlawful suspension as long as "'an official had statutory authorization to detain the individual.'" *Id.* at 303 (quoting Brief for Respondent at 33, *Calcano-Martinez v. INS*, 533 U.S. 348 (2001) (No. 00-1011)). It acknowledged "that the writ protected an individual who was held without legal authority, *id.*, but because the deportation statutes at issue in *St. Cyr* gave the Government authority to detain, the Government argued that the alien could complain of nothing more than a failure by the official detaining him to exercise his "discretionary power to determine whether the person should be released," – a failing which, in the Government's view, raised no concern protected by the Suspension Clause. *Id.*

The Court rejected this argument. While acknowledging that the Government's "historical arguments are not insubstantial," the Court found that "the ambiguities in the scope of the exercise of the writ at common law identified by St. Cyr, and the suggestions in this Court's prior decisions as to the extent to which habeas review could be limited consistent with the Constitution," convinced the Court "that the Suspension Clause questions that would be presented by the INS' reading of the immigration statutes before us are difficult and significant." *Id.* at 304.

The constitutional questions are even more "difficult and significant" here. Because the prisoners in this case "are nonenemy aliens" – they are citizens of allied nations – the writ would have been available to them even at the Founding.[21] *St. Cyr*, 533 U.S. at 301; *see also id.* ("[A]t the absolute minimum, the Suspension Clause protects the writ as it existed in 1789." (quotation marks omitted)). In addition, the detentions here are the very sort that the Government conceded in *St. Cyr* must, under the Suspension Clause, be subject to testing by habeas corpus because they are supported by no statutory authorization. There is no evidence that Congress meant to suspend the writ during the

---

[21] The historic right of aliens to test their status as alleged "enemies" in habeas proceedings, even when detained beyond the "ultimate sovereignty" of the United States, is canvassed by the Brief of Legal Historians *Amici Curiae*.

current hostilities, let alone the plain and unambiguous statement required by the Court. *See supra* 14 and note 11.[22]

These grave constitutional questions would confront the Court if the habeas statute were read as the Executive suggests – to close the courthouse doors to an entire class of habeas petitioners "without any clear indication that such was Congress' intent." *United States v. Castro*, 124 S.Ct. at 791. It should not be read that way.

C. Unreviewable Executive Detention Is Rejected Not Only By Anglo-American Tradition, But Also By "Every Modern Government"

Few canons of international law are now more universally accepted that the prohibition against prolonged, arbitrary detention. For centuries, the law in Anglo-American countries has not only prohibited indefinite detention without legal process, but allowed petitioners to challenge that detention by habeas.[23] The Executive's position that the prisoners at Guantánamo occupy a law-free zone recently prompted the English Court of Appeal to note its "deep concern that, in apparent contravention of fundamental principles of law, [the prisoners] may be subject to indefinite detention in territory over which the United States has exclusive control with no opportunity to challenge the legitimacy of [their] detention before any court or tribunal." *R. v. Sec'y of State for Foreign and Commonwealth Affairs*, 2002 EWCA Civ 1598, at ¶66. A senior judge in the United Kingdom recently described the detentions on Guantánamo as "a monstrous failure of justice."[24] This common tradition is further reflected in the holding of the Supreme Court of Canada. In *R. v. Cook*, 2 S.C.R. 587 (1998), ¶¶25, 44, 46, 48, that Court held that the Canadian constitution protects foreign nationals outside Canadian territory, so long as the conduct in question is that of Canadian Government officials, and application of the constitution will not interfere with the sovereign authority of a foreign state.[25]

Judicial review of executive detentions is not limited to common law jurisdictions. This principle is enshrined in the Constitutions of nearly every country in the civilized world,[26] as well as every major human rights instrument in force today, including the Universal Declaration of Human Rights,[27] the International Covenant on Civil and

---

[22] The Use of Force Resolution that authorized the present military action hardly qualifies as explicit "statutory authorization" for a suspension of the writ. Congress' Authorization for Use of Military Force Joint Resolution, Pub. L. No. 107–40, 115 Stat. 224 (2001). During the Second World War, the Court held that the Articles of War did not strip the federal courts of habeas jurisdiction even though they explicitly purported to do so. *Yamashita*, 327 U.S. at 9 ("[Congress] has not withdrawn, and the Executive branch of the Government could not, unless there was suspension of the writ, withdraw from the courts the duty and power to make such inquiry into the authority of the commission as may be made by habeas corpus."); *Quirin*, 317 U.S. at 24–25 (despite Articles of War, federal courts retained habeas jurisdiction). *Johnson* is not to the contrary, since the prisoners in *Johnson* had the opportunity to litigate their claims in the military commission. *See Swain v. Pressley*, 430 U.S. at 381–83 (no suspension of the writ if petitioner had an adequate chance to mount a collateral attack in coordinate court system); *St. Cyr*, 533 U.S. at 305 (suspension clause problem arises if writ is suspended with "no adequate substitute for its exercise."). *See* Part II *infra*.

[23] *See* Brief for the Commonwealth Lawyers Association as *Amicus Curiae* and Brief of Legal Historians as *Amici Curiae*.

[24] Lord Johan Steyn, Address to the British Institute of International and Comparative Law for the Twenty-Seventh F.A. Mann Lecture, *at* www.nimj.org (Nov. 25, 2003).

[25] *See* the discussion of *R. v. Cook* in the Brief of Omar Ahmed Khadr as *Amicus Curiae*.

[26] *See* M. Cherif Bassiouni, *Human Rights in The Context of Criminal Justice: Identifying International Procedural Protections And Equivalent Protections in National Constitutions*, 3 DUKE J. COMP. & INT'L L. 235, 261 n. 177 (1993) (listing 119 national constitutions that protect the right to be free from arbitrary arrest and detention.).

[27] Universal Declaration of Human Rights, art. 9, G.A. Res. 217A (III), U.N. Doc. A/810 at 71, 73 (Dec. 10, 1948). Though the Universal Declaration is not a treaty, the United States recognizes that Article 9 embodies a rule of

Political Rights (ICCPR),[28] and the American Declaration of the Rights and Duties of Man.[29] In 1950, when the Court decided *Johnson* – upon which the Executive places dispositive reliance – the Court took pains to note that "[t]he practice of every modern Government" is to refuse the protection of the "organic law" to enemy aliens convicted by a military trial. 339 U.S. at 784–85. In the present circumstances, the reverse is true: "the practice of every modern Government" condemns prolonged Executive detention without legal process.

War works no exception to this settled principle of international law. The International Court of Justice has observed that "the protection of the [ICCPR] does not cease in times of war."[30] *See Legality of the Threat or Use of Nuclear Weapons*, 1996 I.C.J. 226, 240 (Advisory Opinion of July 8, 1996) *reprinted in* 35 I.L.M. 809, 820. The United Nations Human Rights Committee, which monitors compliance with the ICCPR, has held that Articles 9(1) (prohibiting arbitrary detentions) and 9(4) (guaranteeing judicial review of detentions) apply to all deprivations of liberty, and that Article 9(4) is non-derogable, even in times of armed conflict.[31] In any event, the United States has not declared any derogation from the Covenant. *See also Ocalan v. Turkey*, Eur. Ct. H. R. No. 46221/99 (Mar. 2003), ¶¶45, 66–76 (prompt judicial review required of detention of alleged terrorist accused of responsibility for more than 4,000 deaths).[32]

International humanitarian law – part of the law of war – similarly provides that even during hostilities, prisoners may not be held without legal process. Over 190

---

customary international law. Richard B. Lillich & Hurst Hannum, INTERNATIONAL HUMAN RIGHTS: PROBLEMS OF LAW, POLICY AND PRACTICE 136 (3d ed. 1995).

[28] International Covenant on Civil and Political Rights, G.A. Res. 2200A (XXI), 21 U.N. GAOR Supp. No. 16, at 15, U.N. Dec. A/6316 (1966), 999 U.N.T.S. 171 [ICCPR]. The relevant provisions of the ICCPR, which the United States ratified in 1992, are unambiguous:

> Article 9(1): Everyone has the right to liberty and security of the person. No one shall be subjected to arbitrary arrest or detention. No one shall be deprived of his liberty except on such grounds and in according with such procedure as are established by law.

> ***

> Article 9(4): Anyone who is deprived of his liberty by arrest or detention shall be entitled to take proceedings before a court, in other that that court may decide without delay on the lawfulness of his detention and order his release if the detention is not lawful.

ICCPR, art. 9(1), 9(4); *Senate Resolution of Ratification of International Covenant on Civil and Political Rights*, 138 Cong. Rec. S4781, S4784, 102nd Cong. (1992) (ratified Apr. 2, 1992). Of the one hundred fifty-one states, including the United States, that have ratified the ICCPR, none has made a relevant reservation to these provisions. *See* United Nations Treaty Collection, *at* http:// www.unhchr.ch/html/menu3/b/treaty4_asp.htm.) (last visited January 5, 2004).

[29] American Declaration of the Rights and Duties of Man, art. XXV, O.A.S.T.S. XXX, adopted by the Ninth International Conference of American States (1948), *reprinted in* Basic Documents Pertaining to Human Rights in the Inter-American System, OEA/Ser.L/V/II82 Doc. 6 rev.1 at 17 (1992).

[30] Unlike this Court, the International Court of Justice is expressly charged to render advisory opinions at the request of an authorized body. *See* Statute of the International Court of Justice, arts. 65–68, *available at* http://www.icj-cij.org/icjwww/ibasicdocuments/ibasictext/ibasicstatute.htm (last visited January 5, 2004).

[31] *See* Human Rights Committee, Gen. Cmt. 8, art. 9 (Sixteenth session, 1982), Compilation of General Comments and General Recommendations Adopted by Human Rights Treaty Bodies, U.N. Doc. HRI\GEN\1\Rev.1 at 8 (1994) at para. 1; Human Rights Committee, Gen. Cmt. 29, States of Emergency (art. 4), U.N. Doc. CCPR/C/21/Rev.1/Add.11 (2001) at. para. 16.

[32] *See also Aksoy v. Turkey*, 23 Eur. H.R. 553 (1996) (though Turkey had lawfully declared a national emergency, it could not hold a suspected terrorist for fourteen days without judicial intervention); *Chahal v. United Kingdom*, 23 Eur. H.R. 413, ¶131 (1997) (concern for national security, though legitimate, "does not mean . . . that the national authorities can be free from effective control by the domestic courts whenever they choose to assert that national security and terrorism are involved").

countries, including the United States, are parties to the Geneva Conventions.[33] Under the Conventions, the rights due to an individual vary with the person's legal status. The Official Commentary to the Fourth Geneva Convention,[34] makes clear that "every person in enemy hands must have some status under international law . . . [N]obody in enemy hands can be outside the law." COMMENTARY ON GENEVA CONVENTION IV OF AUG. 12, 1949, at 51 (Jean S. Pictet ed., 1958). To implement this command, Article 5 of the Third Geneva Convention, governing prisoners of war, requires that any doubt regarding the status of a person captured by the detaining power must be resolved by a "competent tribunal," and that all detainees enjoy prisoner of war status unless and until an Article 5 tribunal determines otherwise.[35]

In light of these settled principles, it is not surprising that the detentions at Guantánamo have come under sharp criticism from the international community, including the International Committee of the Red Cross, the United Nations, and the European Parliament. In 2002, the Inter-American Commission on Human Rights of the Organization of American States, of which the United States is a member, decided that the Guantánamo prisoners may not be held "entirely at the unfettered discretion of the United States Government" and that the Government must convene competent tribunals to determine the legal status of the prisoners under its control. Decision on Request for Precautionary Measures (Detainees at Guantánamo Bay, Cuba), Inter-Am.C.H.R. (Mar. 12, 2002), *reprinted in* 41 I.L.M. 532, 533 (2002).[36]

The Executive's proposed reading of the habeas statute would thus put the United States in flagrant disregard of globally recognized norms. Just as the Court should avoid an interpretation of the statute that runs afoul of the Constitution, it should avoid an interpretation in conflict with international law. *Schooner Charming Betsy*, 6 U.S.

---

[33] *See* International Committee of the Red Cross (ICRC), *States Party to the Geneva Conventions and their Additional Protocols, at* http:// www.icrc.org/Web/Eng/siteeng0.nsf/htmlall/party_gc#a7 (May 20, 2003). The requirements of the Geneva Conventions are discussed in detail by several *amici*. *See* Brief of Former American Prisoners of War as *Amicus Curiae*; Brief of Retired Military Officials as *Amicus Curiae*.

[34] Geneva Convention IV Relative to the Protection of Civilians in Time of War, Aug. 12, 1949, 6 U.S.T. 3516, 75 U.N.T.S. 287.

[35] Geneva Convention III Relative to the Treatment of Prisoners of War, art. 5, Aug. 12, 1949, 6 U.S.T. 3316, U.N.T.S. 135 This provision was not part of the 1929 Convention, which the Court considered in *Johnson v. Eisentrager*, 339 U.S. 763 (1950).

[36] The United States has also rejected the view of the United Nations High Commissioner for Human Rights, the United Nations Working Group on Arbitrary Detention, the United Nations Special Rapporteur on the Independence of Judges and Lawyers, the European Parliament, the Parliamentary Assembly of the Council of Europe, the Parliamentary Assembly of the Organization for Security and Co-operation in Europe, and the International Committee of the Red Cross (ICRC), all of which disagree with the Government's position on Guantánamo. *See* Statement of High Commissioner for Human Rights on Detention of Taliban and Al Qaida Prisoners at U.S. Base in Guantánamo Bay, Cuba (Jan. 16, 2002). P.A. 75a–76a; Report on the Working Group on Arbitrary Detention, U.N. GAOR, Hum. Rts. Comm., 59th Sess., U.N. Doc. E/CN.4/2003/8 at 19–21 (Dec. 16, 2002). P.A.77a–82a, Statement of Special Rapporteur on the Independence of Judges and Lawyers, Dato' Param Cumaraswamy, *at* http://www.unhchr.ch/huricane/huricane.nsf/0/ 0C5F3E732DBFC069C1256CE8002D76C0? opendocument (Mar. 12, 2003); European Parliament Resolution on the European Union's Rights, Priorities and Recommendations for the 59th Session of the U.N. Commission on Human Rights in Geneva (Mar. 17–Apr. 25, 2003), *available at* http://europa.eu.int/abc/doc/ off/bull/en/200301/p102001.htm; Rights of Persons Held in the Custody of the United States in Afghanistan and Guantánamo Bay, Parliamentary Assembly Resolution No. 1340 (2003) (Adopted June 26, 2003), *available at* http:// assembly.coe.int/Documents/AdoptedTexts; Organization for Security and Co-operation in Europe Parliamentary Assembly Rotterdam Declaration and Resolutions Adopted during the 12th Annual Session (Rotterdam, July 5–9, 2003), *available at* http://www.osce.org/documents/pa/2003/07/495_cn.pdf; International Committee of the Red Cross, Overview of the ICRC's Work for Internees, *at* http://www. icrc.org/Web/Eng/siteeng0.nsf/iwpList454/951C74F20D2A2148C1256D8D002CA8DC (November 6, 2003).

(2 Cranch) at 18; *Restatement (Third) of Foreign Relations Law of the United States* §114 (2000) ("Where fairly possible, a United States statute is to be construed so as not to conflict with international law or with an international agreement of the United States.").[37]

II. THE GOVERNMENT OFFERS NO PERSUASIVE REASON TO IGNORE THE UNAMBIGUOUS COMMAND OF THE HABEAS STATUTE

The Executive argues that the current hostilities demand indefinite detention without legal process. Indeed, the argument is broader still; the contention is made that Executive action has become "proof of its own necessity," and that no court may inquire into the lawfulness of the detentions on Guantánamo. *Duncan v. Kahanamoku*, 327 U.S. 304, 336 (1946) (Stone, J., concurring); see also Sterling v. Constantin, 287 U.S. 378, 401 (1932) ("What are the allowable limits of military discretion, and whether or not they have been overstepped in a particular case, are judicial questions.").

The Executive makes this argument despite the text of the habeas statute, the absence of any Congressional indication that federal courts should be stripped of their habeas jurisdiction, the settled practice of this Court to take jurisdiction of habeas petitions filed by people imprisoned beyond the "ultimate sovereignty" of the United States, and the considerable weight of constitutional doubt. To support its argument, the Executive relies heavily on Johnson v. Eisentrager, 339 U.S. 763 (1950). But as demonstrated below, this reliance is misplaced.

A.   Introduction

In *Johnson*, the Court was asked to grant post-conviction habeas review to enemy aliens who were convicted of war crimes by a military commission. The commission had been created pursuant to explicit Congressional authorization during a declared war. The prisoners were convicted, sentenced, and imprisoned in occupied enemy territory temporarily controlled by the U.S. military as an incident of our wartime operations. At trial, the prisoners had the right to challenge the lawfulness of their detention. They also enjoyed due process protections that insured against the conviction of an innocent person. In fact, six of the original twenty-seven defendants were acquitted and released.

The Court held that these convicted war criminals did not enjoy the "privilege of litigation" in the federal courts. *Id.* at 777. It couched some portions of its opinion in jurisdictional terms.[38] *See, e.g., id.* at 791 (prisoners present "no basis for invoking federal judicial power in any district."). Seizing on this language, the Executive assigns the broadest possible reading to the case: federal courts are always powerless to review executive detention of aliens outside the "ultimate sovereignty" of the United States, regardless of the circumstances. See Government's Brief In Opposition to Certiorari at 16, 18–19. But *Johnson* is more ambiguous than that. It is useful to examine what the Court *did*, not merely what it occasionally said.

---

[37] As the Court has recently observed, these international norms may also provide persuasive authority for the interpretation of constitutional values. *E.g., Lawrence v. Texas*, 123 S.Ct. 2472, 2481, 2483 (2003); *Atkins v. Virginia*, 536 U.S. 304, 316 n.21 (2002); *see also* Brief *Amicus Curiae* of the Human Rights Institute of the International Bar Association (discussing obligations imposed by international law).

[38] *See also, e.g., Chin Yow v. United States*, 208 U.S. 8, 11–13 (1908) (if alien had a fair exclusion hearing, district court would not have jurisdiction to consider habeas application; but if petitioner did not have a fair hearing, district court had jurisdiction and could grant habeas relief); *see also infra* 40–41 and note 40.

Johnson is best understood not as a limitation on the *power* of the federal judiciary, but as a restraint on the *exercise* of habeas based on the factors present in that case. The Court limited the exercise of habeas to a determination that the prisoners were enemy aliens imprisoned in occupied territory who had received a lawful trial before a properly constituted military commission. Because these threshold questions were not in dispute, the Court refused to countenance any further interference with the operation of a lawful and independent system of military justice.

The present case stands on entirely different footing. Congress has not authorized trials by military commission, and, even if it had, the prisoners here have been detained for two years with no legal process. They are not enemy aliens, but citizens of our closest allies who allege they have committed no wrong against the United States, and whose allegations at this stage must be accepted as true. Because there have been no proceedings, they do not seek post-conviction relief from an overseas trial by a lawfully constituted tribunal. Instead, they challenge the fact that they have been cast into a legal limbo, held by the Executive without charges, without recourse to any legal process, and with no opportunity to establish their innocence.

B. The Court In *Johnson* Restrained The Exercise Of Habeas Where A Lawful And Independent System of Justice Had Allowed The Prisoners To Challenge Their Detention

By December 11, 1941, Congress had declared war on Germany and Japan. Within weeks, Congress passed the Articles of War. 10 U.S.C. §§1471–1593. These Articles authorized the President to convene military commissions to try suspected war criminals. *Quirin*, 317 U.S. at 28 ("Congress has explicitly provided, so far as it may constitutionally do so, that military tribunals shall have jurisdiction to try offenders or offenses against the law of war in appropriate cases.").

Throughout the Second World War, the Executive repeatedly invoked the power given it by Congress, creating military commissions to try suspected war criminals captured here and abroad. *See, e.g., id.* ("[T]he President, as Commander in Chief, by his Proclamation in time of war has invoked [the Articles of War]"); *Yamashita*, 327 U.S at 7–12 (Articles of War authorized creation of military commission in the Philippines); *Johnson*, 339 U.S. at 766, 786 (military commission had authority to preside over trials in Nanking, China). On January 21, 1946, the Executive invoked this power and convened a military commission to try alleged war criminals in the China Theater. *Johnson v. Eisentrager*, 339 U.S. 763 (1950) (Case No. 306), Index to Pleadings filed in Supreme Court, Ex. F "Regulations Governing the Trial of War Criminals in the China Theater," at 34 [hereinfter *Johnson*, Index to Pleadings].....

Each commission consisted of at least three service members who had to be free from "personal interest or prejudice" and who could not preside over "a case which he personally investigated, nor if he [was] required as a witness in that case." ... Whenever feasible, every commission was to include "one or more members" with legal training..... No sentence could be executed until approved by a commanding officer, who also had the power to reduce the sentence or order a new trial....

The prisoners in *Johnson* were tried by these commissions. After Japan surrendered, the military arrested twenty-seven German nationals in China. A Bill of Particulars accused them of violating the laws of war. *Johnson*, Index to Pleadings, Ex. C "Charge and Bill of Particulars Against Lothar Eisentrager, *et al.*, at 25–34..... Prior to trial, the commission conducted a two-day hearing, where the prisoners unsuccessfully urged the same Constitutional issues they would later raise before the Supreme Court. *Johnson*,

Index to Pleadings, Petition for Writ of Habeas Corpus, at 4–5. . . . . After four weeks
of trial, the commission granted motions for judgment of acquittal with respect to six
prisoners. . . . The defense case for the remaining prisoners lasted an additional eight
weeks. . . .

The commission found each prisoner guilty of war crimes "by engaging in, permitting or ordering continued military activity against the United States after surrender of
Germany and before surrender of Japan." *Johnson*, 339 U.S. at 766. After the commission
sentenced the prisoners to various terms, the reviewing authority reduced the sentences
for three prisoners and approved the remainder. . . . Throughout these proceedings, the
prisoners enjoyed the right to notice of the charges against them, to prompt appointment
of counsel of choice, to prepare a defense, to call and confront witnesses, to compul-
sory process, to discover and introduce evidence, and to make an opening statement
and closing argument. . . . After they were repatriated to Germany, the prisoners sought
post-conviction relief in the District of Columbia, claiming unspecified violations of the
Fifth Amendment and other provisions of the Constitution and the 1929 Geneva Convention. 339 U.S. at 767. In addition, the prisoners admitted they were enemy aliens.
Id. at 784.

Thus, the prisoners in *Johnson* were tried by a lawfully constituted and independent
military court that provided them an opportunity to challenge the lawfulness of their
detention. The Court has long held that lawfully created military courts, sanctioned by
Congress in the valid exercise of their Article I power, represent an independent judicial
system whose lawful judgments are not subject to plenary review by the civilian courts.
See, e.g., In re Grimley, 137 U.S. 147, 150 (1890) ("[The] civil courts exercise no supervisory or correcting power over the proceedings of a court-martial"); *Hiatt v. Brown*,
339 U.S. 103, 111 (1950) (same) (collecting cases). The Court reaffirmed this principle
throughout the Second World War, and repeatedly applied it to military commissions.
As the Court explained in *Yamashita*:

> [O]n application for habeas corpus we are not concerned with the guilt or innocence
> of the petitioners. We consider here only the lawful power of the commission to try
> the petitioner for the offense charged. . . . The military tribunals which Congress has
> sanctioned by the Articles of War are not courts whose rulings and judgments are made
> subject to review by this Court. . . . Congress conferred on the courts no power to review
> their determinations save only as it has granted judicial power "to grant writs of habeas
> corpus for the purpose of an inquiry into the cause of the restraint of liberty." 28 U.S.C.
> §§451, 452. The courts may inquire whether the detention complained of is within the
> authority of those detaining the petitioner. If the military tribunals have lawful authority
> to hear, decide and condemn, their action is not subject to judicial review merely because
> they have made a wrong decision on disputed facts.

Yamashita, 327 U.S. at 8; *see also Quirin*, 317 U.S. at 24.

The Court has often restrained the exercise of habeas to avoid interference with lawful and independent military judicial systems. For example, three years after *Johnson*,
the Court considered a habeas application from American servicemen court-martialed
in Guam. *Burns*, 346 U.S at 138. The Court readily concluded that the habeas statute
provided jurisdiction. *Id.* at 139. The question was "not whether the District Court has
any power at all to consider petitioners' applications; rather our concern is with the
manner in which the Court should proceed to exercise its power." *Id.*

In answering this question, the plurality noted that "[t]he military courts, like
the state courts, have the same responsibilities as do the federal courts to protect a
person from a violation of his constitutional rights." *Id.* at 142. Consistent with this

responsibility, the military had provided the petitioners in *Burns* with repeated opportunities to litigate their claims. *Id.* at 140–42. The Court concluded "it would be in disregard of the statutory scheme if the federal civil courts failed to take account of the prior proceedings – of the fair determinations of the military tribunals after all military remedies have been exhausted." *Id.* at 142. This military process

> does not displace the civil courts' jurisdiction over an application for habeas corpus from the military prisoner. But . . . *when a military decision has dealt fully and fairly with an allegation . . . it is not open to a federal civil court to grant the writ simply to reevaluate the evidence.*

Id. (emphasis added) (citation omitted); *see also Gusik v. Schilder*, 340 U.S. 128, 131–132 (1950) (habeas petitioner must first exhaust available remedies in military system: "The procedure established to police the errors of the tribunal whose judgment is challenged may be adequate for the occasion. If it is, any friction between the federal court and the military or state tribunal is saved.").

As *Burns* intimates, the Court has sometimes limited the substantive claims for relief that the federal courts should entertain in habeas, in order to recognize an appropriate division of responsibility between those courts and another competent adjudicatory system. But these limitations have been imposed *only* when the habeas petitioners were challenging their confinement under orders issued by a lawfully created and convened coordinate system of tribunals in which they enjoyed a full and fair opportunity to present their claims; and the Court has always made clear that the limitations are upon the *extent of habeas review*, not upon the *existence of habeas jurisdiction*. *See, e.g., Ex parte Royall*, 117 U.S. 241, 252 (1886) (to avoid interference with the "courts of co-ordinate jurisdiction, administered under a single system," and in the absence of any indication that the state court had abused its authority, Court declines to exercise its undisputed power under the habeas statute); *Stone v. Powell*, 428 U.S. 465, 481–82 (1976) (federal court has jurisdiction under habeas statute, but will restrain exercise of judicial power for Fourth Amendment claims fully and fairly adjudicated in state court); *Frank v. Mangum*, 237 U.S. 309, 329, 334–36 (1915).[39] Indeed, if the petitioner has been denied that opportunity, it is well settled that "a federal court should entertain his petition for habeas corpus, else he would be remediless." *Ex parte Hawk*, 321 U.S. 114, 118 (1944) (per curiam) (citations omitted).[40]

As on these other occasions, the Court in *Johnson* restrained the exercise of habeas to avoid interfering with the military commissions. Thus, the Court refused to provide the prisoners with the right to appear before the District Court, "[a] basic consideration

---

[39] *See also Withrow v. Williams*, 507 U.S. 680, 716 (1993) (Scalia, J., dissenting on other grounds) ("[T]he most powerful equitable consideration [in deciding whether to restrain the exercise of habeas is whether petitioner] has already had full and fair opportunity to litigate [his] claim.").

[40] The Court has long recognized that federal habeas is available to fill the void created by an inadequate remedy in the coordinate system of justice. *See, e.g., Chin Yow*, 208 U.S. at 11–13; *Kwack Jan Fat v. White*, 253 U.S. 454, 457–58 (1920) (immigration findings by Executive are conclusive unless petitioner establishes in habeas that "the proceedings were manifestly unfair, were such as to prevent a fair investigation, or show manifest abuse of the discretion committed to the executive officers by the statute, or that their authority was not fairly exercised, that is, consistently with the fundamental principles of justice embraced within the conception of due process of law.") (internal citations and quotations omitted); *Moore v. Dempsey*, 261 U.S. 86, 91 (1923)(if state fails to provide an adequate "corrective process" to a trial dominated by mob sentiment, petitioner may seek review and secure relief by federal habeas); *Johnson v. Zerbst*, 304 U.S. at 467 (habeas must be available to provide remedy for constitutional violations that, through no fault of the petitioner, cannot be remedied elsewhere); *Burns*, 346 U.S. at 142 (plurality) ("Had the military courts manifestly refused to consider [petitioners' claims], the District Court was empowered to review them *de novo*.").

in habeas corpus practice" as it existed at that time.[41] 339 U.S. at 778. The Court, however, did not consider itself powerless to inquire into the lawfulness of the prisoners' detention. On the contrary, the Court stated that "the doors of our courts have not been summarily closed upon these prisoners," *id.* at 780.

First, the Court reviewed at great length the legal disabilities imposed upon enemy aliens, and took pains to emphasize that these disabilities are "imposed temporarily as an incident of war and not as an incident of alienage." *Id.* at 772. Beginning with this historical understanding, the Court then undertook "the same preliminary hearing as to sufficiency of application" that was extended in *Quirin*, *Yamashita*, and *Hirota v. McArthur*, 338 U.S. 197 (1949). This review established, without the need for further inquiry, that the prisoners "are really enemy aliens," *id.* at 784, who hav been "active in the hostile service of an enemy power," *id.* at 778, and who were convicted by a lawful military commission, *id.* at 777. Having heard "all contentions [the prisoners] have seen fit to advance and considering every contention we can base on their application and the holding below," the Court arrived "at the same conclusion" as in *Quirin*, *Yamashita*, and *Hirota*: "that no right to the writ of habeas corpus appears." *Id.* at 781.

Second, the Court reviewed the prisoners' challenge to the "jurisdiction" of the military commissions, and ultimately concluded that it failed. *Id.* at 785–788; *see also id.* at 790 ("We are unable to find that the petition alleges any fact showing lack of jurisdiction in the military authorities...."). Two months before *Johnson*, the Court used this 'jurisdictional' formulation to describe its *merits* review of a habeas petition challenging military detention. *Hiatt v. Brown*, 339 U.S. at 110 ("[I]t is well settled that by habeas corpus the civil courts exercise no supervisory or correcting power over the proceedings of a court-martial .... The single inquiry, the test, is jurisdiction" (internal quotations omitted)). The Court also used this articulation to describe its *merits* review of the habeas petitions brought in *Quirin* and *Yamashita*. *Quirin*, 317 U.S. at 27–29; *Yamashita*, 327 U.S. at 8–9. Yet in all of these cases, federal habeas jurisdiction was not in dispute. *See also Burns*, 346 U.S. at 142 ("We have held before that this [military process] does not displace the civil courts' jurisdiction over an application for habeas corpus from the military prisoner.").

And third, the Court in *Johnson* adjudicated the merits of the prisoners' claims under both the Constitution and the 1929 Geneva Convention. The Court rejected the prisoners' contention that the Fifth Amendment conferred "a right of personal security or an immunity from military trial and punishment upon an enemy alien engaged in the hostile service of a government at war with the United States," *Johnson*, 339 U.S. at 785, as well as their other arguments under the Constitution and the Convention. *Id.* at 788–790.

This extensive and multi-faceted review of the prisoners' claims cannot be squared with the Government's contention that the Court did not have jurisdiction. "Without jurisdiction the court cannot proceed at all in any cause. Jurisdiction is power to declare the law, and when it ceases to exist, the only function remaining to the court is that of announcing the fact and dismissing the cause." *Ex parte McCardle*, 74 U.S. (7 Wall.) 506, 514 (1869).

To be sure, *Johnson* occasionally uses the term "jurisdiction" in its modern sense – *i.e.*, "the courts' statutory or constitutional *power* to adjudicate the case," *Steel Co. v. Citizens for a Better Env't*, 523 U.S. 83, 89 (1998) – and the decision is ambiguous

---

[41] The habeas statute has been amended since *Johnson* and this is no longer an essential feature of habeas practice. *30ᵗʰ Judicial Cir. Ct.*, 410 U.S. at 497–98.

for this reason.[42] But the better reading – the reading that is faithful to the language of the habeas statute, that considers what the Court *did*, and that avoids needless conflict with a lawfully created coordinate system of military justice – is to view *Johnson* as a restraint on the exercise of habeas, not as a limitation on the courts' power to act.

The formal denial of post-conviction review in *Johnson* is, in any event, no bar to habeas jurisdiction where, as here, the petitioners have been held completely without legal process for two years. They have had no opportunity to challenge the lawfulness of their detention and there has been no proceeding in a lawfully created coordinate system of justice to which this Court can defer. They are not enemy aliens, but citizens of our closest allies. Just as the habeas statute gave the Court the power to act in *Johnson*, the statute provides the power to act in this case; but the very factors that called for restraint in *Johnson* are notable here for their absence, and now call for the opposite result.[43]

C.　Guantánamo Is Not Like Wartime China or Germany

Here, unlike in *Johnson*, the petitioners are held at Guantánamo. The Executive concedes that if the petitioners were being held in the United States, the federal courts would be open to them. *Gherebi v. Bush*, _F.3d_, 2003 WL 22971053, at *4 (9th Cir. Dec. 18, 2003). It offers no persuasive reason why an area subject to the complete, exclusive, and indefinite jurisdiction and control of the United States, where this country alone has wielded power for more than a century, should be treated the same as occupied enemy territory, temporarily controlled as an incident of wartime operations.

The Executive also concedes that if the prisoners at Guantánamo were U.S. citizens, federal habeas would lie.[44] It offers no persuasive reason why the courthouse doors should be open to citizens detained at Guantánamo but not to citizens of our closest allies who allege they have committed no wrong against this country.

Once again, the Executive relies heavily on stray language in *Johnson*. And again the reliance is misplaced. The Court in *Johnson* repeatedly noted the prisoners' lack of connection to this country's "territory," or "territorial jurisdiction." *See, e.g., Johnson*,

---

[42] *Johnson* thus confirms that jurisdiction "is a word of many, too many, meanings." *Citizens for a Better Env't*, 523 U.S. at 90 (internal quotations omitted). Elsewhere, *Johnson* uses the term "jurisdiction" to refer to "the territorial jurisdiction" of the United States. *E.g., id.* at 768 ("We are cited to no instance where a court . . . has issued [the writ] on behalf of an alien enemy who, at no relevant time and at no stage of his captivity, has been within its territorial jurisdiction.").

[43] Even if *Johnson* were a jurisdictional holding – that federal courts do not have habeas jurisdiction over enemy aliens lawfully tried, convicted, and imprisoned in areas equivalent to post-war China and Germany – federal courts have at least the power to inquire whether these factors are present. Indeed, the Court in *Johnson* undertook precisely this inquiry. The Court has long recognized the power of a habeas court to inquire into the "jurisdictional facts" that mark the outer bounds of its power. *See, e.g., Ludecke*, 335 U.S. at 163 n.5 (whether petitioner is alien enemy is a jurisdictional fact that may be tested in habeas); *Johnson*, 333 U.S. at 775 (same); *Ng Fung Ho v. White*, 259 U.S. 276, 284 (1922) (claim of citizenship is a jurisdictional fact that may be tested in habeas prior to alleged alien's deportation: "The situation bears some resemblance to that which arises where one against whom proceedings are being taken under the military law denies that he is in the military service. It is well settled that in such a case a writ of habeas corpus will issue to determine the status."); *see also* Brief *Amici Curiae* of Legal Historians (at common law, habeas courts had jurisdiction to resolve whether the prisoner was in fact an enemy alien).

　　As demonstrated below, Guantánamo is in no relevant respect akin to post-war China and Germany. But even if it were, the prisoners in this case, unlike the prisoners in *Johnson*, are not enemy aliens, have not been provided the benefit of the Geneva Conventions, and have not been tried by a military commission. The factors that led to the result in *Johnson* have never been established in this case, and the Petitioners' allegations are all to the contrary.

[44] *See supra* 16 & note 16 (citing oral arguments in *Padilla*).

339 U.S. at 768 ("We are cited to no instance where a court...has issued [the writ] on behalf of an alien enemy who, at no relevant time and at no stage of his captivity, has been within its territorial jurisdiction."); *id.* at 771 ("[I]n extending constitutional protections beyond the citizenry, the Court has been at pains to point out that it was the alien's presence within its territorial jurisdiction that gave the Judiciary power to act."); *id.* at 781 (criticizing lower court for dispensing with "all requirement of territorial jurisdiction."); *id.* at 777 (writ should not extend to enemy alien detained "outside of our territory and there held in military custody as a prisoner of war.") The Court also observed that the prisoners had not come within United States sovereignty. *Id.* at 778. At no time did the Court indicate that this observation was essential to the result.[45] Still, the Executive seizes on this language and argues that this Nation's relationship to Guantánamo brings the case within *Johnson* because the lease governing the base grants Cuba "ultimate sovereignty" over the territory.

To suggest that because of these undefined terms, Guantánamo is no more amenable to federal habeas jurisdiction than occupied enemy territory defies reality.[46] The Government has long considered Guantánamo to be "practically...a part of the Government of the United States." 25 Op. Att'y Gen. 157 (1904). Solicitor General Olson once described the base as part of our "territorial jurisdiction" and "under exclusive United States jurisdiction." 6 Op. Off. Legal Counsel. 236, 242 (1982) (opinion of Asst. Attorney General Olson). The same treaty article that reserves an undefined quantum of "ultimate sovereignty" for Cuba grants the United States "complete jurisdiction and control" over the base. Agreement for the Lease to the United States of Lands in Cuba for Coaling and Naval Stations, Feb. 16–23, 1903, art. III, T.S. No. 418, 6 Bevans 1113. The Executive determines who may enter and leave the base, and enjoys the power "to acquire.... any land or other property therein by purchase or by exercise of eminent domain." *Id.*; *see United States v. Carmack*, 329 U.S. 230, 236 (1946) ("The power of eminent domain is essential to a sovereign government."). United States law governs the conduct of all who are present on the base, citizen and alien alike; and violations of criminal statutes are prosecuted in the Government's name. *See, e.g., United States v. Lee*, 906 F.2d 117 (4ᵗʰ Cir. 1990).

Consistent with the Treaty language, the United States has long exercised prescriptive and adjudicative jurisdiction over Guantánamo. In *Vermilya-Brown v. Connell*, 335 U.S. 377 (1948), the Court made clear that Guantánamo is presumptively covered by federal statutes regulating conduct in "territories and possessions" and that the rule against "extraterritorial application" of federal law has no provenance in a case arising from Guantánamo. *Id.* at 390 ("[W]here [the statute's] purpose is to regulate labor relations in an area vital to our national life, it seems reasonable to interpret its provisions to have force where the nation has sole power.").

Unlike the conditions that prevailed in *Johnson*, Congress governs Guantánamo pursuant to its Article I and IV powers. Courts routinely take jurisdiction of cases that arise from the base, and have long exercised their power to test Government action on the base against the requirements of the Constitution. *See, e.g., Kirchdorfer, Inc. v. United States*, 6 F.3d 1573, 1583 (Fed. Cir. 1993) (finding violation of Takings Clause by Navy);

---

[45] The *Johnson* dissenters certainly did not believe the holding depended on whether the petitioners had set foot within the "ultimate sovereignty" of the United States. The dissent never uses the word 'sovereignty' and criticizes the majority for making the result turn on whether the prisoners had come within the "territorial jurisdiction." 339 U.S. at 796 (Black, J., dissenting) ("a majority may hereafter find citizenship a sufficient substitute for territorial jurisdiction.").

[46] A number of *amici* discuss the nature and history of Guantánamo in detail. *See* Brief of Former Guantánamo Officials as *Amicus Curiae*; Brief of National Institute of Military Justice as *Amicus Curiae*.

Burtt v. Schick, 23 M.J. 140, 142–43 (U.S.C.M.A. 1986) (granting writ of habeas corpus and holding that impending court martial proceeding on Guantánamo would constitute double jeopardy, in violation of 10 U.S.C. §844(a)). *Cf. Johnson*, 339 U.S. at 780 ("[T]he scenes of [petitioners'] offense, their capture, their trial and their punishment were all beyond the territorial jurisdiction of any court of the United States."). And while Guantánamo is a military installation, it is eight thousand miles from the theater of operations, and manifestly not under martial law. *Compare Padilla v. Rumsfeld*, _F.3d_, 2003 U.S. App. LEXIS 25616 at *57–58 (2d Cir. Dec. 18 2003) (Chicago not in theater of operations), *with Johnson*, 339 U.S. at 780 (events in *Johnson* took place within "a zone of active military operations or under martial law").

Equally important, Cuba's laws are wholly ineffectual in Guantánamo. United States governance, now entering its second century, is potentially permanent and in no way dependent on the wishes or consent of the Cuban Government. Treaty Defining Relations with Cuba, May 29, 1934 U.S. – Cuba, art. III, 48 Stat. 1682, 1683, T.S. No. 866. Indeed, the Cuban Government has long characterized the United States presence as "illegal" and refuses to cash the annual rent payment of $4,085 the United States has tendered pursuant to the lease. *See Bird v. United States*, 923 F. Supp. 338, 341 n.6 (D. Conn. 1996). Recently, the Cuban Government added its voice to the chorus of governments criticizing the detentions on Guantánamo. Anita Snow, *Cuba Rants About Use of U.S. Navy Base*, FT. WORTH STAR-TELEGRAM, Dec. 27, 2003, at 14. However, "ultimate sovereignty" does not imply actual authority, as the United States has ignored Cuba's complaints and "continues to recognize the validity of these treaties." *Bird*, 923 F. Supp. at 341 (citing U.S. Dep't of State, *Treaties in Force* (1995); U.S. Dep't of State, "Fact Sheet: Cuba," Feb. 22, 1993, *available at* 1993 WL 2977391.

The extent of our jurisdiction and control in Guantánamo, and its amenability to judicial process, stands in stark contrast to the situation in *Johnson*. The Executive could not convene a military commission to try the *Johnson* petitioners unless it first secured permission from the Chinese Government. *Johnson*, Index to Pleadings, Ex. 4 – Message of 6 July 1946 to Wedemeyer from Joint Chiefs of Staff. J.A. 167. The same is true of Landsberg prison, where the *Johnson* petitioners were detained. The United States shared jurisdiction and control over detentions in occupied Germany with the United Kingdom and France. *See* Basic Principles for Merger of the Three Western German Zones of Occupation and Creation of an Allied High Commission, *reprinted in* DOCUMENTS ON GERMANY, 1944–70, Comm. on Foreign Relations, 92nd Cong., (Comm. Print 1971), at 150–51, and the occupation in Germany was avowedly temporary. *See* Protocol of the Proceedings of the Berlin (Potsdam) Conference, Aug. 1, 1945, *reprinted in* DOCUMENTS ON GERMANY, 1944–1961, Comm. on Foreign Relations, United States Senate, 87th Cog., 1st Sess. 8 (Comm. Print 1961); *see also Johnson*, 339 U.S. at 797 (Black, J., dissenting)(China and Germany were "temporarily occupied countries.").[47]

---

[47] The Government also relies on *United States v. Spelar*, 338 U.S. 217, 200 (1949), which held that plaintiffs injured on a United States base in Canada could not sue under the Federal Tort Claims Act ("FTCA") because the base was in a foreign country. That case involved the interpretation of a particular statute; Congress's authority to legislate was not in question, and the possibility that territory is "foreign" for some purposes and not for others is uncontroversial. *See Downes v. Bidwell*, 182 U.S. 244, 341 (1901) ("Porto Rico . . . was foreign to the United States in a domestic sense"); *see also Vermilya-Brown*, 335 U.S. at 386–390 (presumption against extraterritorial application does not govern in United States "possessions"). For that reason, courts have held that Government action in a territory is constrained by the Constitution, even though the territory may be in a foreign country, which precludes litigation under the FTCA. *Compare Ralpho v. Bell*, 569 F.2d 607, *reh'g denied*, 569 F.2d 636 (D.C. Cir. 1977) (fundamental constitutional rights apply in Pacific Trust Territories), *with Callas v. United States*, 253 F.2d 838, 839–40 (2d Cir.), *cert. denied*, 357 U.S. 936 (1958) (FTCA does not extend to Pacific Trust Territory).

D. The Current Hostilities Do Not Justify A Departure From Settled Practice

Lastly, the Executive makes vague reference to the ongoing hostilities in Afghanistan, as though this were sufficient reason to permit the creation of a prison beyond the law, eight thousand miles away. But until this litigation began, the United States had never proposed that military necessity demanded indefinite detention without legal process for prisoners captured during hostilities, nor does the military take that position during the present conflict in Iraq.

On the contrary, the military has adopted a comprehensive set of regulations to insure that no person be detained without legal process. *Enemy Prisoners of War, Detained Personnel, Civilian Internees, and Other Detainees*, U.S. Army Regulation 190–8 (applicable to the Departments of the Army, the Navy, the Air Force, and the Marine Corps (October 1, 1997)). . . . . These regulations trace their origin to the Vietnam conflict, when the United States often captured people whose status under the Convention was in doubt. "[R]arely did the Viet Cong wear a recognizable uniform, and only occasionally did the guerrillas carry their arms openly. Additionally, some combat captives were compelled to act for the Viet Cong out of fear of harm to themselves or their families." Frederic L. Borch, Judge Advocates in Combat 21 (Office of the Judge Advocate General 2001); Howard S. Levie, Prisoners of War 57 (Naval War College Press 1978). The nature of the conflict, in other words, created a distinct risk of capturing innocent civilians.

Rather than allow innocent detainees to languish in custody, the military created "Article 5 tribunals" to resolve all doubtful cases.[48] Levie, Prisoners of War at 57. These tribunals, which operated during hostilities within the theater of operations, consisted of at least three officers, including one who was "a judge advocate or other military lawyer familiar with the Geneva Convention." Directive Number 20-5, United States Military Assistance Command, Vietnam (March 15, 1968), *reprinted in* 62 Am. J. Int'l L. 765 (1968). Detainees enjoyed the "fundamental rights considered to be essential to a fair hearing," including the right to counsel and an interpreter. *Id.* at 771. Counsel had "free access" to his client, was given at least one week to prepare, and, at the hearing had the right to call and cross-examine witnesses, to present evidence, and to make an opening and closing statement. The tribunal determined whether a detainee was a prisoner of war, a "civil defendant" subject to Vietnamese law, or an innocent civilian who should be released. *Id.* at 767; Borch, Judge Advocates in Combat, at 21. No one was held without a legal status. Directive Number 20-5, *reprinted in* 62 Am. J. Intl. Law at 768.

Today, Article 5 tribunals consist of three commissioned officers. Prisoners may attend all open sessions and they enjoy the services of a qualified interpreter. They may testify on their own behalf, call witnesses, present documentary evidence, and question witnesses called by the tribunal. Prisoners may also remain silent and cannot be compelled to testify. At the close of the hearing, the tribunal determines, in a written report, whether the person is a prisoner of war, who enjoys the full protections of the Geneva Convention, a religious person who is likewise "entitled to" POW protections, an innocent civilian "who should immediately be returned to his home or released," or a civilian internee "who for reasons of operational security, or probable cause incident

---

[48] So named because they implement Article 5 of the Third Geneva Convention. As noted above, Article 5 requires that "any doubt" regarding the status of a person captured by the detaining power be resolved by a "competent tribunal," and that all detainees enjoy POW status unless and until an Article 5 tribunal determines otherwise. Geneva III, art. 5, 6 U.S.T. at 3324, 75 U.N.T.S. at 142.

to criminal investigation, should be detained." U.S. Army Regulation 190-8, at 1-6e. The tribunal may reach no other possible outcome, and no one is held without some defined status. *Id.* at 1-6e(10). Persons in the civilian-internee category may not be punished "without further proceedings to determine what acts they may have committed and what penalty should be imposed." *Id.* at 1-6g. Finally, any decision denying POW status "shall be reviewed for legal sufficiency" by the office of the Judge Advocate General. *Id.*

   Since Vietnam, Article 5 tribunals have been a settled part of military practice. During the first Persian Gulf War, the United States conducted nearly 1,200 Article 5 tribunals, finding that 310 detainees were entitled to POW status, with the remainder entitled to refugee status. *See* Dep't of Defense, Conduct of the Persian Gulf War: Final Report to Congress Pursuant to Title V of the Persian Gulf Conflict Supplemental Authorization and Personnel Benefits Act of 1991 (Public Law 102-25) App. L. at 577 (Apr. 1992). Even during the present conflict in Iraq, within the field of battle, the military continues to conduct these tribunals. War Briefing, Army Col. John Della Jacono, Enemy Prisoner of War Briefing from Umm Qar, Iraq (May 8, 2003), *available at* 2003 WL 1864306. Why the same process should be denied to citizens of our closest allies who have done no harm to the United States and who remain imprisoned half a world away, is a mystery.

* * *

In sum, whatever may have been the justification for restricting the exercise of habeas in *Johnson* – a matter on which the prisoners here take no position – the prisoners in *Johnson* were enemy aliens who were given the opportunity to litigate their claims in a coordinate system of justice created by the valid exercise of Congressional authority during a declared war. They were charged, tried, convicted, and held in occupied territory temporarily controlled by the military. The considerations that counseled in favor of restraint in that case now call for the opposite result – judicial exercise of jurisdiction to review indefinite detentions.

CONCLUSION

The Court should reverse the judgment below and remand to the D.C. Circuit to allow the prisoners to challenge the lawfulness of their detention in the district court.

. . .

Nos. 03-334 and 03-343

In the Supreme Court of the United States

SHAFIQ RASUL, ET AL., PETITIONERS

v.

GEORGE W. BUSH,
PRESIDENT OF THE UNITED STATES, ET AL.

FAWZI KHALID ABDULLAH FAHAD AL ODAH,
ET AL., PETITIONERS

v.

UNITED STATES OF AMERICA, ET AL.

ON WRIT OF CERTIORARI TO THE
UNITED STATES COURT OF APPEALS
FOR THE DISTRICT OF COLUMBIA CIRCUIT

BRIEF FOR THE RESPONDENTS

THEODORE B. OLSON
Solicitor General
Counsel of Record

PETER D. KEISLER
Assistant Attorney General

PAUL D. CLEMENT
Deputy Solicitor General

GREGORY G. KATSAS
Deputy Assistant Attorney
General

GREGORY G. GARRE
DAVID B. SALMONS
Assistants to the Solicitor
General

DOUGLAS N. LETTER
ROBERT M. LOEB
SHARON SWINGLE
Attorneys
Department of Justice

WILLIAM H. TAFT IV
Legal Adviser
Department of State

---

* Redactions on this page have been added for privacy purposes. – *Eds.*

QUESTION PRESENTED

Whether United States courts lack jurisdiction to consider challenges to the legality of detention of foreign nationals captured abroad in connection with hostilities and incarcerated at the Guantanamo Bay Naval Base, Cuba.

. . .

This case arises in the midst of the global armed conflict in which the United States is currently engaged against the al Qaeda terrorist network and its supporters. At issue is whether U.S. courts have jurisdiction to consider challenges to the detention of aliens who were captured abroad in connection with the ongoing combat operations in Afghanistan and determined to be enemy combatants, and who are being detained by the U.S. military to prevent them from rejoining the conflict and for other military purposes at the U.S. Naval Base at Guantanamo Bay, Cuba. Applying the principles recognized by this Court in *Johnson v. Eisentrager*, 339 U.S. 763 (1950), the court of appeals correctly held that U.S. courts lack jurisdiction over such claims.

STATEMENT

. . .

    1. a. . . .

. . .

The President dispatched the U.S. armed forces to Afghanistan to seek out and subdue the al Qaeda terrorist network and the Taliban regime that had supported it. During the course of those operations, U.S. and coalition forces have removed the Taliban from power, eliminated the "primary source of support to the terrorists who viciously attacked our Nation on September 11, 2001" and "seriously degraded" al Qaeda's training capability. . . . However, "[p]ockets of al Qaeda and Taliban forces remain a threat to United States and coalition forces and to the Afghan government," and "[w]hat is left of both the Taliban and the al Qaeda fighters is being pursued actively and engaged by United States and coalition forces." *Ibid.* An American-led force of approximately 11,500 soldiers and a NATO-led force of 5000 remain engaged in active combat operations in Afghanistan. Fighting has intensified in recent months, as al Qaeda and Taliban combatants have continued to launch attacks on U.S. troops, foreign aid workers, and Afghan government officials.[1] At the same time, Osama bin Laden, the leader of al Qaeda, has continued to call on al Qaeda and its supporters to continue their terrorist holy war, or jihad, against the United States, and the United States and other nations have been subject to attacks throughout the world. . . .

. . .

b. U.S. and coalition forces have captured or taken control of thousands of individuals in connection with the ongoing hostilities in Afghanistan. As in virtually every other armed conflict in the Nation's history, the military has determined that many of those individuals should be detained during the conflict as enemy combatants. Such detention serves the vital military objectives of preventing captured combatants from rejoining the conflict and gathering intelligence to further the overall war effort and prevent additional attacks. The military's authority to capture and detain such combatants is both well-established and time-honored. See, *e.g.*, *Duncan v. Kahanamoku*, 327 U.S. 304, 313–314 (1946); *Ex parte Quirin*, 317 U.S. 1, 30–31 & n.8 (1942); *Hamdi v. Rumsfeld*,

---

[1] . . .

316 F.3d 450, 465–466 (4th Cir. 2003), cert. granted, 124 S. Ct. 981 (2004); 2 L. Oppen-heim, *International Law* 368–369 (H. Lauterpacht ed., 7th ed. 1952); William Winthrop, *Military Law and Precedents* 788 (2d ed. 1920).

Individuals taken into U.S. control in connection with the ongoing hostilities un-dergo a multi-step screening process to determine if their detention is necessary. When an individual is captured, commanders in the field, using all available information, make a determination as to whether the individual is an enemy combatant, *i.e.*, whether the individual is "part of or supporting forces hostile to the United States or coalition part-ners, and engaged in an armed conflict against the United States." Dep't of Defense, *Fact Sheet: Guantanamo Detainees* (<www.defenselink.mil/news/detainees.html.>) (*Guan-tanamo Detainees*).[3] Individuals who are not enemy combatants are released by the military.

Individuals who are determined to be enemy combatants are sent to a centralized holding in the area of operations where a military screening team reviews all available information with respect to the detainees, including information derived from inter-views of the detainee. That screening team looks at the circumstances of capture, the threat the individual poses, his intelligence value, and with the assistance from other U.S. government officials on the ground, determines whether continued detention is warranted. Detainees whom the U.S. military determines, after conducting this screen-ing process, have a high potential intelligence value or pose a particular threat may be transferred to the U.S. Naval Base at Guantanamo Bay, Cuba. A general officer re-views the screening team's recommendations. Any recommendations for transfer for continued detention at Guantanamo are further reviewed by a Department of Defense review panel. Approximately 10,000 individuals have been screened in Afghanistan and released from U.S. custody. See *Guantanamo Detainees, supra.*

c. Only a small fraction of those captured in connection with the current conflict and subjected to this screening process have been designated for detention at Guan-tanamo. Upon their arrival at Guantanamo, detainees are subject to an additional assess-ment by military commanders regarding the need for their detention. That assessment is based on information obtained from the field, detainee interviews, and intelligence and law enforcement sources. In addition, there is a thorough process in place for de-termining whether a detainee may be released or transferred to another government, consistent with the interests of national security. That process includes an initial re-view by a team of interrogators, analysts, behavioral scientists, and regional experts, and a further round of review by the commander of the Southern Command, who for-wards a recommendation to an interagency group composed of representatives from, *inter alia*, the Department of Defense, Department of Justice, and Department of State. The recommendation is then reviewed by the Secretary of Defense or his designee. See *Guantanamo Detainees, supra.*[4]

---

[3] Additional information on the military's screening procedures and the Guantanamo detentions is available at Department of Defense, Detainees at Guantanamo Bay (<www.defenselink.mil/news/detainees.html>); Secretary Rumsfeld Remarks to Greater Miami Chamber of Commerce (Feb. 13, 2004) (<www.defenselink.mil/transcripts/2004/tr20040213-0445.html>); Briefing on Detainee Operations at Guantanamo (Feb. 13, 2004) (<www.defenselink.mil/transcripts/2004/tr20040213-0443.html>).

[4] In addition to these existing procedures, the Department of Defense has recently announced that it will, on a going-forward basis, establish administrative review boards to review at least annually the need to detain each enemy combatant. Detainees will be afforded an opportunity to appear before the panel and the detainee's foreign government will be able to submit information to the panel. The panel will make an independent recommendation on whether continued detention is appropriate. See Dep't of Defense, News Release (Mar. 3, 2004) (<www.defenselink.mil/releases/2004/nr20040303-0403.html>).

The military is currently detaining about 650 aliens at Guantanamo. They include direct associates of Osama Bin Laden; al Qaeda operatives with specialized training; bodyguards, recruiters, and intelligence operatives for al Qaeda; and Taliban leaders. The intelligence gathered at Guantanamo has been vital to the ongoing combat operations in Afghanistan and elsewhere around the world, and to efforts to disrupt the al Qaeda terrorist network and prevent additional attacks on the United States and its allies. Among other things, Guantanamo detainees have revealed al Qaeda leadership structures, funding mechanisms, training and selection programs, and potential modes of attack. In addition, detainees have provided a continuous source of information to confirm other intelligence reports concerning unfolding terrorist plots or other developments in the conflict. See *Guantanamo Detainees, supra.*

The President has determined that neither al Qaeda nor Taliban detainees are entitled to prisoner-of-war status under the Geneva Convention Relative to the Treatment of Prisoners of War, Aug. 12, 1949, 75 U.N.T.S. No. 972 (GPW). See *Guantanamo Detainees, supra*; Office of the White House Press Secretary, *Fact Sheet, Status of Detainees at Guantanamo* (Feb. 7, 2002) (<www.whitehouse.gov/news/releases/2002/02/20020207-13.html>); note 18, *infra*. However, the Department of Defense has made clear that it is treating detainees at Guantanamo humanely and providing them with many privileges similar to those accorded to prisoners of war, including three meals a day that meet Muslim dietary laws, specialized medical care, religious worship privileges, means to send and receive mail, and visits from representatives of the International Red Cross. See *Guantanamo Detainees, supra.* . . .

The Guantanamo detentions already have been the subject of extensive diplomatic discussions between the Executive and officials of the foreign governments of detainees' home countries. To date, more than 90 detainees have been released (or designated for release) from Guantanamo to foreign governments. See note 25, *infra*. In addition, the President has determined that six detainees are subject to the Military Order of November 13, 2001, making them eligible for prosecution by a military commission for violations of the laws of war. See *Detention, Treatment, and Trial of Certain Non-Citizens in the War Against Terrorism*, 66 Fed. Reg. 57,833 (2001). The United States has charged two of those detainees with conspiracy to commit war crimes. See *Guantanamo Detainees Charged With Conspiracy to Commit War Crimes* (Feb. 24, 2004) (<www.dod.mil/news/Feb2004/n02242004_200402246.html>).

. . .

SUMMARY OF ARGUMENT

The court of appeals correctly held that U.S. courts lack jurisdiction over challenges to the legality of the detention of aliens captured abroad and detained by the U.S. military at the U.S. Naval Base at Guantanamo Bay, Cuba.

I. The fundamental jurisdictional question presented in this case is governed by this Court's decision in *Johnson v. Eisentrager*, 339 U.S. 763 (1950). In *Eisentrager*, the Court held that U.S. courts lacked jurisdiction to consider a habeas petition filed on behalf of German nationals who had been seized overseas following the German surrender in World War II, tried by a military commission, and imprisoned at a U.S.-controlled facility in Germany. The Court concluded that neither the federal habeas statutes nor the Constitution conferred such jurisdiction. In addition, the Court emphatically rejected the argument that the Fifth Amendment confers rights on aliens held outside the sovereign territory of the United States. *Id.* at 784.

Subsequent developments have only reinforced *Eisentrager's* analytical foundation. First, Congress has not amended the habeas statutes to confer the jurisdiction that this Court held was absent in *Eisentrager* and, indeed, did not enact a proposed amendment in the wake of *Eisentrager* that would have explicitly conferred such jurisdiction. Second, this Court has repeatedly reaffirmed *Eisentrager's* constitutional holding that the Fifth Amendment does not apply to aliens abroad. See, *e.g.*, *United States* v. *Verdugo-Urquidez*, 494 U.S. 259 (1990). Third, the U.S. military has detained thousands of aliens abroad in connection with several conflicts since 1950, but the U.S. courts have not entertained any habeas petition filed on such an alien's behalf.

Eisentrager controls the outcome in this case. The Guantanamo detainees, like the detainees in *Eisentrager*, are aliens who were captured overseas in connection with an armed conflict and have no connection to the United States. In addition, the Guantanamo detainees, like the detainees in *Eisentrager*, are being held by the U.S. military outside the sovereign territory of the United States. It is "undisputed" that Guantanamo is not part of the sovereign United States . . . and that conclusion is compelled by the express terms of the Lease Agreements between the United States and Cuba and the Executive Branch's definitive construction of those agreements. Accordingly, U.S. courts lack jurisdiction to consider claims filed on behalf of aliens held at Guantanamo.

II. Petitioners' efforts to recast and evade this Court's decision in *Eisentrager* are unavailing. *Eisentrager* is not distinguishable on the ground that the Guantanamo Naval Base is under the control of the United States. *Eisentrager* itself makes clear that sovereignty, not mere control, is the touchstone of its jurisdictional rule. Thus, even though the U.S. military controlled the Landsberg prison in post-war Germany, the *Eisentrager* Court held that the alien prisoners in that facility lacked access to our courts because they were outside the sovereign territory of the United States. The same is equally true with respect to the Guantanamo detainees.

Nor did the Court's jurisdictional ruling in *Eisentrager* turn on the fact that the prisoners were "enemy" aliens. *Eisentrager* addressed the restrictions on "the privilege of litigation" that apply to "aliens, *whether friendly or enemy*." 339 U.S. at 777–778 (emphasis added). Moreover, this Court has recognized in subsequent cases that *Eisentrager* is a seminal decision defining the rights of *all* aliens abroad, and not just "enemy" aliens. See, *e.g.*, *Zadvydas v. Davis*, 533 U.S. 678 (2001). And, in any event, the detainees in this case – who were captured in connection with the fighting in Afghanistan and who have been determined by the U.S. military to be enemy combatants – plainly qualify as enemy aliens for any relevant purposes.

· · ·

III. Deviating from the principles recognized in *Eisentrager* in this case would raise grave constitutional concerns. The Constitution commits to the political branches and, in particular, the President, the responsibility for conducting the Nation's foreign affairs and military operations. Exercising jurisdiction over claims filed on behalf of aliens held at Guantanamo would place the federal courts in the unprecedented position of micromanaging the Executive's handling of captured enemy combatants from a distant combat zone where American troops are still fighting; require U.S. soldiers to divert their attention from the combat operations overseas; and strike a serious blow to the military's intelligence-gathering operations at Guantanamo. At the same time, recognizing jurisdiction over petitioners' claims would intrude on Congress's ability to delineate the subject-matter jurisdiction of the federal courts.

IV. The Guantanamo detentions are the subject of intense diplomatic, congressional, and public consideration. As this Court observed in *Eisentrager*, a recognition of the established jurisdictional limits of the U.S. courts does not mean that detainees are without rights. Rather, the "responsibility for observance and enforcement" of the rights of aliens held abroad under the law of armed conflict "is upon political and military authorities," 339 U.S. at 789 n.14, not the courts.

ARGUMENT

U.S. COURTS LACK JURISDICITON TO CONSIDER CLAIMS FILED ON BEHALF
OF ALIENS CAPTURED ABROAD AND HELD AT GUANTANAMO

. . .

I.   UNDER THE FUNDAMENTAL PRINCIPLES RECOGNIZED IN
     EISTENTRAGER, U.S. COURTS LACK JURISDICTION OVER CLAIMS
     FILED ON BEHALF OF GUANTANAMO DETAINEES

. . .

B.   The Analytical Foundation Of *Eisentrager* Has Only Been Reinforced
     During The Past Half Century

In at least three key respects, the force of the Court's decision in *Eisentrager* has only grown with time.

1. As explained above, the Court in *Eisentrager* held that "nothing *** in our statutes" conferred jurisdiction over the habeas petition at issue. 339 U.S. at 768. Congress is presumed to be aware of this Court's decisions. It has legislated in the area of federal habeas jurisdiction on several occasions since 1950. Yet Congress has never amended the habeas statutes to provide the jurisdiction that this Court held was absent in *Eisentrager*. See *Lorillard* v. *Pons*, 434 U.S. 575, 580 (1978) ("Congress is presumed to be aware of an administrative or judicial interpretation of a statute and to adopt that interpretation when it re-enacts a statute without change"); see also *Keene Corp.* v. *United States*, 508 U.S. 200, 212 (1993).

At the same time, the current habeas statute is "very much the same" as the statute in effect at the time of *Eisentrager*. Pet. App. 18a; see 49-306 U.S. Br. at 2–3 n.1. Section 2241 of title 28 has been amended only once since 1950. In 1966, Congress added subsection (d), which relates to federal jurisdiction over claims filed on behalf of prisoners detained pursuant to state-court convictions. See 28 U.S.C. 2241 amendments; Act of Sept. 19, 1966, Pub. L. No. 89-590, 80 Stat. 811. Although Congress has narrowed federal habeas jurisdiction since 1950 over certain types of claims, see, *e.g.*, Antiterrorism and Effective Death Penalty Act, Pub. L. No. 104-132, 110 Stat. 811, it has never *broadened* habeas jurisdiction to cover the sort of claims at issue in *Eisentrager*.

There was, however, one failed legislative attempt to create such jurisdiction in the immediate aftermath of *Eisentrager*. In February 1951, a bill was introduced in Congress "[p]roviding for the increased jurisdiction of Federal courts in regard to the power to issue writs of habeas corpus in cases where officers of the United States are detaining persons in foreign countries, regardless of their status as citizens." H.R. 2812, 82d Cong., 1st Sess. The bill provided "[t]hat the district court of the United States is given jurisdiction to issue writs of habeas corpus inquiring into the legality of any detention by any officer, agent, or employee of the United States, *irrespective of whether the detention is in the United States or in any other part of the world, and irrespective of whether the person seeking the writ is a citizen or an alien." Ibid.* (emphasis added). The bill was never voted out of committee, much less enacted into law.

Principles of separation of powers and stare decisis strongly counsel against revisiting *Eisentrager* and revising the habeas statutes in a manner that Congress itself considered and rejected. See *Patterson v. McLean Credit Union*, 491 U.S. 164, 175 n.1 (1989) ("As we reaffirm today, considerations of *stare decisis* have added force in statutory cases because Congress may alter what we have done by amending the statute."); *id.* at 172; accord *Hilton v. South Carolina Pub. Ry.*, 502 U.S. 197, 202 (1991) ("Congress has had almost 30 years in which it could have corrected our decision*** if it disagreed with it, and has chosen not to do so.").

Since *Eisentrager*, this Court also has repeatedly emphasized its reluctance to presume that Congress intends a federal statute to have extraterritorial application. As the Court observed in *Sale v. Haitian Centers Council, Inc.*, 509 U.S. 155 (1993), a case involving a challenge to the United States' treatment of Haitian refugees who were intercepted on the high seas and temporarily detained at Guantanamo, "Acts of Congress normally do not have extraterritorial application unless such an intent is clearly manifested," and "[t]hat presumption has special force when we are construing treaty and statutory provisions that may involve foreign and military affairs for which the President has unique responsibility." *Id.* at 188 (citing *United States v. Curtiss-Wright Export Corp.*, 299 U.S. 304, 319 (1936)). Those decisions bolster the *Eisentrager* Court's refusal to interpret the federal habeas statutes to confer jurisdiction over challenges by aliens held *outside* the United States.

. . .

II. PETIONERS ATTEMPTS TO RELITIGATE AND EVADE *EISENTRAGER* ARE UNAVAILING

. . .

B. There Is No Basis For Carving A "Guantanamo Exception" Out Of *Eisentrager*'s Sovereignty-Based Rule

Although they have conceded that Guantanamo is outside the sovereignty territory of the United States, . . . petitioners nonetheless argue that *Eisentrager* is inapplicable on the ground that Guantanamo is "under U.S. jurisdiction and control." . . . . The panel majority in *Gherebi* distinguished *Eisentrager* on similar grounds. See 352 F.3d at 1286–1290. For several reasons, the courts below . . . , as well as Judge Graber in *Gherebi* (see 352 F.3d at 1305–1306), correctly rejected that argument.

1. To begin with, petitioners' argument cannot be squared with *Eisentrager*'s own terms. As discussed above, *Eisentrager* makes clear that its jurisdictional holding is based on sovereignty, and not on malleable concepts like de facto control. See Pet. App. 16a; *id.* at 55a; *Gherebi* [v. *Bush*], 352 F.3d [1278,] 1305 [(9th Cir. 2003)] ("A straightforward reading of [*Eisentrager*] makes it clear that 'sovereignty' is the touchstone *** for the exercise of federal courts' jurisdiction.") (Graber, J., dissenting). In particular, in explaining why "the privilege of litigation" did not extend to the aliens in *Eisentrager*, the Court stated that the "prisoners at no relevant time were within any *territory over which the United States is sovereign.*" 339 U.S. at 777–778 (emphasis added).

The *Eisentrager* Court's treatment of *Ex parte Quirin*, 317 U.S. 1 (1942), and *In re Yamashita*, 327 U.S. 1 (1946), underscores that sovereignty, not merely jurisdiction or control, is the key, and that petitioners' efforts to rely on cases like *Quirin* and *Yamashita* are misguided. In *Quirin* and *Yamashita*, the Court exercised jurisdiction over habeas petitions of enemy aliens (and, in *Quirin*, an enemy combatant who was presumed to be a U.S. citizen). The *Eisentrager* Court, however, distinguished those cases on the ground that the aliens were captured and detained *within* U.S. territory. As the Court noted, *Quirin* was brought by aliens who were apprehended "in the United States." 339 U.S. at 780. Similarly, the habeas petition in *Yamashita* was brought by an alien who was captured and detained in the Philippine Islands – then an insular possession of the United States. As the Court explained, "[b]y reason of our *sovereignty* at that time over these insular possessions, *Yamashita* stood much as did *Quirin* before American courts" – *i.e.*, he was "within territory of the United States." *Ibid*. (emphasis added). The dissenters in *Eisentrager* likewise understood that sovereignty was the key to the Court's distinction of *Quirin* and *Yamashita*. See *id.* at 795 ("Since the Court expressly disavows conflict with the *Quirin* and *Yamashita* decisions, it must be relying not on the status of these petitioners as alien enemy belligerents but rather on the fact that they were captured, tried and imprisoned outside our territory."). *Eisentrager's* treatment of *Quirin* and *Yamashita* thus reaffirms that the key to the Court's decision was the prisoners' status as aliens outside U.S. sovereign territory, and demonstrates that petitioners' efforts to rely on *Quirin* and *Yamashita* (and habeas petitions filed by citizens) are misguided. See R. Br. 15–16.

2. Similarly, if U.S. jurisdiction or control over foreign territory, and not sovereignty, were the benchmark, then the prisoners in *Eisentrager* themselves would have been entitled to judicial review of their habeas claims. The Landsberg prison in Germany was unmistakably under the control of the United States when Eisentrager was held there. Indeed, it is hard to imagine that the United States would ever detain military prisoners in a facility over which it *lacked* control. The Court in *Eisentrager* noted that the prisoners at issue in *Eisentrager* were under the custody of the "American Army officer" who was the "Commandant of Landsberg Prison" and it referred to the hundreds of cases – like *Eisentrager* – involving "aliens confined by *American* military authorities abroad." 339 U.S. at 766, 768 n.1 (emphasis added). Justice Black was even more direct in his dissenting opinion, stating that "[w]e control that part of Germany we occupy." *Id.* at 797. The United States controls Guantanamo subject to the terms and conditions of its Lease Agreements with Cuba, but – as this Court made clear in *Eisentrager* – in the absence of *sovereignty*, the exercise of such control does not entitle the aliens held at Guantanamo to the privilege of litigating in U.S. courts.[12]

3. This Court has recognized that leased U.S. military installations abroad are outside the sovereign territory of the United States, even though such facilities are vital to the conduct of the United States' foreign affairs abroad precisely because they provide an area removed from the sovereign territory of the United States, yet indisputably within the control of U.S. armed forces. In *United States* v. *Spelar*, 338 U.S. 217, 219 (1949), the Court held that a U.S. military base leased in Newfoundland was "subject to the sovereignty of another nation," not "to the sovereignty of the United States," and

---

[12] The conclusion that the United States exercised control over the Landsberg military prison is further demonstrated by the instruments governing the allied occupation of Germany. Paragraph 2(i) of the Occupation Statute (C.A. App. 332) explicitly reserved "[c]ontrol" over the "German prisons" to the occupying powers. And the United States, through the U.S. High Commissioner for Germany, exercised exclusive control as an occupying force over the American zone in Germany, including the Landsberg prison. See Staff of the Senate Comm. on Foreign Relations, 92d Cong., 1st Sess., *Documents on Germany, 1944–1970*, at 165 (Comm. Print 1971) (Charter of the Allied (Western) High Commission for Germany, para. 3, signed by the Foreign Ministers of France, the United Kingdom, and the United States, June 20, 1949).

therefore fell within the "foreign country" exception to the Federal Tort Claims Act. The base in *Spelar* was governed by "the same executive agreement and leases" as the U.S. military base in Bermuda. *Id.* at 218. This Court in *Vermilya-Brown* recognized in turn that the United States' rights over the base in Guantanamo are "substantially the same" as its rights over the base in Bermuda. 335 U.S. at 383;....

4. Petitioners' reliance on the "Insular Cases" – in which the Court has recognized that certain constitutional rights or privileges may extend to inhabitants of American territories or insular possessions – is misplaced. Guantanamo is not a U.S. territory, or even an unincorporated territory like Guam or Puerto Rico. The Constitution gives to Congress the power to recognize and regulate American territories. See U.S. Const. Art. IV, §3, Cl. 2; *Torres v. Puerto Rico*, 442 U.S. 465, 469–470 (1979). Congress has exercised that authority and an entire title of the United States Code (Title 48) is devoted to "Territories and Insular Possessions."[13] Guantanamo is not addressed in Title 48 because it is not a U.S. territory or insular possession. It is a leased military base on foreign soil, just like numerous other military bases occupied by the United States around the world. See *Spelar*, 338 U.S. at 219; *Vermilya-Brown*, 335 U.S. at 385.

Guantanamo is not comparable to the former Trust Territory of Micronesia. See ... 48 U.S.C. 1901 *et seq*. Quite unlike the Trust Territory of Micronesia, the United States occupies Guantanamo pursuant to a lease that explicitly recognizes that Cuba retains sovereignty over Guantanamo. By contrast, no other sovereign authority existed at the time of the appointment of the United States as administrator of the Micronesia Trust Territory. See Trusteeship Agreement for the Former Japanese Mandated Islands, July 18, 1947, 61 Stat. 3301, T.I.A.S. No. 1665. Likewise, the United States' operation of Guantanamo does not share any of the civilian governmental attributes of its special role with respect to the Trust Territory in Micronesia, and responsibility to "nurture the Trust Territory toward self-government." *Gale v. Andrus*, 643 F.2d 826, 830 (D.C. Cir. 1980); see 48 U.S.C. 1681(a).[14]

Nor is Guantanamo comparable to the Panama Canal Zone, which, until the United States withdrew from the Zone, was viewed as an unincorporated territory of the United States and was the subject of extensive legislation. See 48 U.S.C. 1301 *et seq*. (1946). The Fifth Circuit held that Congress had extended some constitutional rights to the Panama Canal Zone, but the exercise of jurisdiction in those cases was based on the fact that Congress had established a U.S. federal district court of the Canal Zone with appellate

---

[13] When Congress recognizes U.S. territories, it carefully delineates the rights and privileges that extend to the residents of such territories. See, *e.g.*, 48 U.S.C. 734 ("statutory laws of the United States not locally inapplicable *** shall have the same force and effect in Puerto Rico as in the United States"); 48 U.S.C. 737 (stating that "rights, privileges, and immunities" of U.S. citizens shall be respected in Puerto Rico "to the same extent as though Puerto Rico were a State of the Union"); 48 U.S.C. 1421b(l) ("Bill of rights" governing Guam; includes "privilege of the writ of habeas corpus"); 48 U.S.C. 1561 ("Bill of rights" governing Virgin Islands; includes "privilege of the writ of habeas corpus"); 48 U.S.C. 1661, 1662, 1662a (recognizing U.S. sovereignty over Tutuila, Manua, eastern Samoa, and Swains Island; stating that amendments to the constitution of American Samoa, as approved by the Secretary of the Interior pursuant to executive order, and which includes privilege of the writ of habeas corpus, may be made only by Act of Congress); 48 U.S.C. 1801 (historical and statutory notes) (approving Covenant to Establish a Commonwealth of the Northern Mariana Islands in Political Union with the United States of America and incorporating Constitution of the Northern Mariana Islands which includes privilege of writ of habeas corpus). Congress has not enacted any such legislation with respect to Guantanamo.

[14] See, *e.g.*, Proclamation No. 5564, 51 Fed. Reg. 40,399 (1986) (establishing the Northern Mariana Islands as U.S. territory); J. Res. of Mar. 24, 1976, Pub. L. No. 94-241, 90 Stat. 263 (Covenant to Establish a Commonwealth of the Northern Mariana Islands in Political Union with the United States of America); Act of Nov. 8, 1977, Pub. L. No. 95–157, 91 Stat. 1265 (establishing a U.S. District Court in the Northern Mariana Islands).

review by the Fifth Circuit. See 22 U.S.C. 3841(a) (repealed).[15] Obviously there is no analogous district court with jurisdiction over Guantanamo, nor has Guantanamo ever been treated as an unincorporated territory of the United States. Moreover, as Judge Graber explained in *Gherebi*, the differences between the language of the Guantanamo Lease Agreements and the Panama Canal Treaty if anything only bolster the conclusion that *Cuba* retained sovereignty over Guantanamo. 352 F.3d at 1311 (dissenting).[16]

5. When the United States is occupying a foreign land for general military purposes, the Court has held that the occupied area remains foreign soil and "cannot be regarded, in any constitutional, legal, or international sense, a part of the territory of the United States." *Neely* v. *Henkel*, 180 U.S. 109, 119 (1901). In *Neely*, this Court considered the military's occupation and control of Cuba following the Spanish-American War – the war that led to the current Guantanamo lease arrangement. When *Neely* arose, "the Island of Cuba was 'occupied by' and was 'under the control of the United States.'" *Id.* at 115. Moreover, the treaty pursuant to which the United States occupied Cuba did not place a limit on the term of such occupancy. *Id.* at 116 (quoting treaty provisions). But this Court nonetheless held that Cuba was "a *foreign* country or territory," *id.* at 115 (emphasis in original), and not, "in any *** sense, a part of the territory of the United States," *id.* at 119.

If the island of Cuba was not U.S. territory when the United States occupied and controlled it after the Spanish-American War, then *a fortiori* Cuba (including Guantanamo) is not U.S. territory today. That conclusion is underscored by the terms pursuant to which the United States *leases* Guantanamo from Cuba, which place the United States in an inferior position at Guantanamo than the one that it occupied with respect to Cuba at the time of *Neely*. See also *Fleming* v. *Page*, 50 U.S. (9 How.) 603, 614–615 (1850).

· · ·

CONCLUSION

The judgment of the court of appeals should be affirmed.

· · ·

---

[15] See *United States* v. *Husband R. (Roach)*, 453 F.2d 1054, 1057 (5th Cir. 1971), cert. denied, 406 U.S. 935 (1972); *Government of the Canal Zone* v. *Scott*, 502 F.2d 566, 568, 570 (5th Cir. 1974); *Government of the Canal Zone* v. *Yanez P. (Pinto)*, 590 F.2d 1344, 1351 (5th Cir. 1979).

[16] Petitioners cite *United States* v. *Lee*, 906 F.2d 117 (4th Cir. 1990) (per curiam), for the proposition that crimes committed at Guantanamo may be prosecuted in the U.S. courts. But petitioners overlook that the court in *Lee* exercised jurisdiction over an indictment pursuant to 18 U.S.C. 7 (1988), which extended the criminal law extraterritorially to "crimes committed *outside* the jurisdiction of a state or district court." 906 F.2d at 117 n.1 (emphasis added). That certain laws may apply *extra*territorially to Guantanamo only reinforces the conclusion that the base lies outside the United States. . . . .

No. 03-334

In The
Supreme Court of the United States

SHAFIQ RASUL, *et al.*,

Petitioners,

v.

GEORGE W. BUSH, *et al.*,

Respondents.

**On Writ of Certiorari
to the United States Court of Appeals
for the District of Columbia Circuit**

PETITIONERS' REPLY BRIEF

JOSEPH MARGULIES	MICHAEL RATNER
Counsel of Record	BARBARA J. OLSHANSKY
MARGULIES & RICHMAN, PLC	CENTER FOR
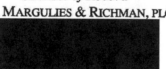	CONSTITUTIONAL RIGHTS

	JOHN J. GIBBONS
MACARTHUR JUSTICE CENTER	GITANJALI S. GUTIERREZ
UNIVERSITY OF CHICAGO	GIBBONS, DEL DEO,
LAW SCHOOL	DOLAN, GRIFFINGER
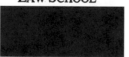	& VECCHIONE, P.C.

Attorneys for Petitioners

* Redactions on this page have been added for privacy purposes. – *Eds.*

· · ·

APPENDIX

Chronology

Date	Prison Population at Guantánamo	Litigation Developments
1/15/2002	50 detainees held.[1]	
1/28/2002	158 detainees held.[2]	
2/8/2002	186 detainees held.[3]	
2/19/2002		*Rasul* Petitioners file habeas petition in D.C. District Court.
2/28/2002	300 detainees held.[4]	
5/1/2002		*Al Odah* Plaintiffs file civil action in D.C. District Court.
5/20/2002		District court orders military to permit Federal Public Defender unmonitored access to Hamdi.
5/23/2002		Respondents move in district court to stay counsel access order in *Hamdi*.
5/29/2002		District court orders counsel access meeting with Hamdi to go forward within 72 hours of order.
5/30/2002		Respondents file notice of appeal in Fourth Circuit of Hamdi counsel access order.
6/9/2002		President issues order designating Padilla as an enemy combatant. Padilla transferred to naval brig.
6/10/2002		Habib files habeas petition in D.C. District Court.
6/10/2002	Appx. 400 detainees held.[5]	
6/12/2002		Padilla files habeas petition in Southern District of New York District Court.
6/21/2002	564 detainees held.[6] 180 detainees added this month.	
7/12/2002		Court of Appeals for the Fourth Circuit reverses counsel access order in *Hamdi* and remands.
7/22/02		Respondents refuse to make initial disclosures in *Hamdi*.

[1] Jim Garamone, *50 Detainees Now at Gitmo: All Treated Humanely*, Am. Forces Press Serv., Jan. 15, 2002, http://www.defenselink.mil/news/Jan2002/n01152002_200201151.html.

[2] Linda D. Kozaryn, *U.S. Gains Custody of More Detainees*, Am. Forces Info. Serv., Jan. 28, 2002, http://www.defenselink.mil/news/Jan2002/n01282002_200201284.html.

[3] Linda D. Kozaryn, *U.S. Following Up on Predator Strike; More Detainees Headed for GITMO*, Feb. 8, 2002, http://www.defenselink.mil/news/Feb2002/n02082002_200202083.html.

[4] Sgt. 1st Class Kathleen T. Rhem, *Some Al Qaeda, Taliban Detainees Refuse Food*, Am. Forces Press Serv., Feb. 28, 2002, http://www.defenselink.mil/news/Feb2002/n02282002_200202284.html.

[5] Sgt. 1st Class Kathleen T. Rhem, *Rumsfeld Invites Kuwaitis to Visit Their Citizens at Guantánamo*, Am. Forces Press Serv., June 10, 2002, http://www.dod.mil/news/Jun2002/n06102002_200206104.html.

[6] Rudi Williams, *GITMO General Rates Force Protection High With Detainee Care*, Am. Forces Press Serv., June 21, 2002, http://www.dod.mil/news/Jun2002/n06212002_200206212.html.

Date	Prison Population at Guantánamo	Litigation Developments
7/23/2002		Respondents move to terminate appointment of counsel in *Hamdi*.
10/26/2002	4 detainees released.[7]	
10/28/2002	34 detainees added.[8] Appx. 625 detainees held.[9]	
12/26/2002		Respondents refuse counsel access to Padilla.
1/10/2003	Appx. 625 detainees held.[10]	
3/11/2003		D.C. Court of Appeals affirms dismissal in *Rasul* & *Al Odah*.
5/14/2003	5 detainees released.[11]	
7/3/2003		President designates 6 detainees under his Military Order of November 13, 2001,[12] including *Rasul* Petitioner David Hicks.[13]
7/18/2003	27 detainees released.[14] 10 detainees added.[15] Appx. 660 detainees held.[16]	
9/2/2003		Rasul and Al Odah file petition for certiorari in United States Supreme Court.
10/1/2003		Hamdi files petition for certiorari in United States Supreme Court.
11/10/2003		**United States Supreme Court grants petition for certiorari in *Rasul* and *Al Odah*.**
11/21/2003	20 detainees released.[17]	
11/23/2003	20 detainees added.[18] Appx. 660 detainees held.[19]	

[7] Kathleen T. Rhem, *Four Detainees Released, New Group Brought to Cuba*, Oct. 28, 2002, http://www.dod.mil/news/Oct2002/n10282002_200210282.html.

[8] Kathleen T. Rhem, *Four Detainees Released, New Group Brought to Cuba*, Oct. 28, 2002, http://www.dod.mil/news/Oct2002/n10282002_200210282.html.

[9] Kathleen T. Rhem, *Four Detainees Released, New Group Brought to Cuba*, Oct. 28, 2002, http://www.dod.mil/news/Oct2002/n10282002_200210282.html.

[10] Kathleen T. Rhem, *Intel of 'Enormous Value' Gleaned From Guantánamo Detainees*, Jan. 10, 2003, http://www.dod.mil/news/Jan2003/n01102003_ 200301107.html.

[11] U.S. Dep't of Defense, *Release/Transfer of Detainees Completed*, News Release, May 16, 2003, http://www.dod.mil/news/May2003/b05162003_bt33803.html.

[12] U.S. Dep't of Defense, *President Determines Enemy Combatants Subject to His Military Order*, News Release, Jul. 3, 2003, http://www.defenselink.mil/releases/2003/nr20030703-0173.html.

[13] U.S. Dep't of Defense, *DoD Assigns Legal Counsel for Guantánamo Detainee*, News Release, Dec. 3, 2003, http://www.defenselink.mil/releases/2003/nr200312030721.html.

[14] U.S. Dep't of Defense, *Transfer of Detainees Completed*, New Release, July 18, 2003, http://www.defenselink.mil/releases/2003/nr20030718-0207.html.

[15] U.S. Dep't of Defense, *Transfer of Detainees Completed*, New Release, July 18, 2003, http://www.defenselink.mil/releases/2003/nr20030718-0207.html.

[16] U.S. Dep't of Defense, *Transfer of Detainees Completed*, New Release, July 18, 2003, http://www.defenselink.mil/releases/2003/nr20030718-0207.html.

[17] U.S. Dep't of Defense, *Transfer of Guantánamo Detainees Complete*, Nov. 24, 2003, http://www.defenselink.mil/releases/2003/nr20031124-0685.html.

[18] U.S. Dep't of Defense, *Transfer of Guantánamo Detainees Complete*, Nov. 24, 2003, http://www.defenselink.mil/releases/2003/nr20031124-0685.html.

[19] U.S. Dep't of Defense, *Transfer of Guantánamo Detainees Complete*, Nov. 24, 2003, http://www.defenselink.mil/releases/2003/nr20031124-0685.html.

Date	Prison Population at Guantánamo	Litigation Developments
11/25/2003		United States and Australia agree on military commission procedures for any charged Australian detainee.[20]
11/30/2003		Official speaking on condition of anonymity states that military expects to release additional 100 to 140 detainees by the end of January 2004.[21]
12/2/2003		Defense Department announces Hamdi will be allowed access to counsel.[22]
12/3/2003		Government files opposition to Hamdi's petition for certiorari.
12/3/2003		Department of Defense assigns counsel to *Rasul* Petitioner David Hicks.[23]
1/9/2004		**United States Supreme Court grants petition for certiorari in *Hamdi*.**
1/14/2004		Rasul and Al Odah file merit briefs in support of petition.
1/16/2004		Government files petition for certiorari in *Padilla*.
1/26/2004	3 detainees released.[24]	
2/4/2004		Padilla files opposition to petition for certiorari.
2/11/2004		Defense Department announces that Padilla will be allowed access to counsel.[25]
2/11/2004		Government files reply brief *Padilla* in support of petition for certiorari.
2/13/2004		Defense Secretary Donald Rumsfeld and Deputy Assistant Secretary of Defense Paul Butler announce plans for annual administrative review panel for Guantánamo detainees.[26]
2/13/2004		Paul Butler, Deputy Assistant Secretary of Defense, announces that screening process "takes place" in Afghanistan.[27]
2/16/2004	87 detainees released to date and "a few" transferred for detention in home country.[28]	

[20] U.S. Dep't of Defense, *U.S. and Australia Announce Agreements on Guantánamo Detainees*, News Release, Nov. 25, 2003, http://www.defenselink.mil/releases/2003/nr20031125-0702.html.

[21] Nancy Gibbs, *Inside "The Wire,"* TIME MAG., Dec. 8, 2003, at 40. Frank Griffiths, *Official: More than 100 terror suspects at Guantánamo to be released by January, including juvenile detainees*, AP Wire, Nov. 30, 2003.

[22] U.S. Dep't of Defense, *DoD Announces Detainee Allowed Access to Lawyer*, News Release, Dec. 2, 2003, http://www.defenselink.mil/releases/2003/nr20031202-0717.html.

[23] U.S. Dep't of Defense, *DoD Assigns Legal Counsel for Guantánamo Detainee*, News Release, Dec. 3, 2003, http://www.defenselink.mil/releases/2003/nr20031203-0721.html.

[24] U.S. Dep't of Defense, *Transfer of Juvenile Detainees Completed*, News Release, Jan. 29, 2004, http://www.defenselink.mil/releases/2004/nr20040129-0934.html.

[25] U.S. Dep't of Defense, *Padilla Allowed Access to Lawyer*, News Release, Feb. 11, 2004, http://www.defenselink.mil/releases/2004/nr20040211-0341.html.

[26] U.S. Dep't of Defense, News Transcript, Secretary Rumsfeld Remarks to Greater Miami Chamber of Commerce, Feb. 13, 2004; K.L. Vantran, *Panel to Review Guantánamo Detainees*, Am. Forces Press Serv., Feb. 13, 2004, http://www.dod.mil/news/Feb2004/n02132004_200402137.html.

[27] U.S. Dep't of Defense, *Briefing on Detainee Operations at Guantánamo Bay*, News Transcript, Feb. 13, 2004, http://www.defenselink.mil/transcripts/2004/tr20040213-0443.html.

[28] Linda D. Kozaryn, *Dangerous Detainees Important to Intelligence Effort, Rumsfeld Says*, Am. Forces Press Serv., Feb. 16, 2004, http://www.dod.mil/news/Feb2004/n02162004_200402161.html.

Date	Prison Population at Guantánamo	Litigation Developments
2/20/2004		**United States Supreme Court grants petition for certiorari in *Padilla***
2/24/2004		Department of Defense charges 2 detainees.[29]
2/25/2004	1 detainee released.[30]	
3/1/2004	7 detainees released.[31]	
3/3/2004		Department of Defense releases memo outlining draft administrative review process in Guantánamo.[32]
3/3/2004		Respondents file reply brief in *Rasul/Al Odah.*
3/9/2004	5 detainees transferred, including *Rasul* Petitioners Shafiq Rasul and Asif Iqbal.[33]	
3/15/2004	26 detainees released[34] Appx. 610 detainees held.[35]	
4/2/2004	15 detainees released. A total of 119 detainees release to date.[36] Appx. 595 detainees held.[37]	

[29] K.L. Vantran, *Guantánamo Detainees Charged With Conspiracy to Commit War Crimes*, Am. Forces Press Serv., Feb. 24, 2004, http://www.dod.mil/news/Feb2004/n02242004_200402246.html.

[30] U.S. Dep't of Defense, *Transfer of Detainee Complete*, News Release, Feb. 25, 2004, http://www.defenselink.mil/releases/2004/nr20040225-0365.html.

[31] U.S. Dep't of Defense, *Transfer of Detainees Complete*, News Release, Mar. 1, 2004, http://www.defenselink.mil/releases/2004/nr20040301-0389.html.

[32] U.S. Dep't of Defense, *DoD Announces Draft Detainee Review Policy*, News Releases, Mar. 3, 2004, http://www.defenselink.mil/releases/2004/nr20040303_0403.html. *See also* U.S. Dep't of Defense, Draft Memorandum, *Administrative Review Procedures for Enemy Combatants in the Custody of the Department of Defense at Guantánamo Bay Naval Base, Cuba*, http://www.defenselink.mil/news/Mar2004/d20040303ar.pdf.

[33] U.S. Dep't of Defense, *Transfer of British Detainees Complete*, News Release, Mar. 9, 2004, http://www.defenselink.mil/releases/2004/nr20040309-0443.html.

[34] U.S. Dep't of Defense, *Transfer of Afghani and Pakistani Detainees Complete*, News Release, Mar. 15, 2004, http://www.defenselink.mil/releases/2004/nr20040315-0462.html.

[35] U.S. Dep't of Defense, *Transfer of Afghani and Pakistani Detainees Complete*, News Release, Mar. 15, 2004, http://www.defenselink.mil/releases/2004/nr20040315-0462.html.

[36] U.S. Dep't of Defense, *Detainee Transfer Completed*, News Release, Apr. 2, 2004, http://www.defenselink.mil/releases/2004/nr20040402-0505.html.

[37] U.S. Dep't of Defense, *Detainee Transfer Completed*, News Release, Apr. 2, 2004, http://www.defenselink.mil/releases/2004/nr20040402-0505.html.

Opinion of the Court

SUPREME COURT OF THE UNITED STATES

Nos. 03–334 and 03–343

SHAFIQ RASUL, ET AL., PETITIONERS

03–334   *v.*

GEORGE W. BUSH, PRESIDENT OF THE UNITED
STATES, ET AL.

FAWZI KHALID ABDULLAH FAHAD AL ODAH, ET AL.,
PETITIONERS

03–343   *v.*

UNITED STATES ET AL.

ON WRITS OF CERTIORARI TO THE UNITED STATES COURT OF
APPEALS FOR THE DISTRICT OF COLUMBIA CIRCUIT

[June 28, 2004]

JUSTICE STEVENS delivered the opinion of the Court.

These two cases present the narrow but important question whether United States courts lack jurisdiction to consider challenges to the legality of the detention of foreign nationals captured abroad in connection with hostilities and incarcerated at the Guantanamo Bay Naval Base, Cuba.

I

On September 11, 2001, agents of the al Qaeda terrorist network hijacked four commercial airliners and used them as missiles to attack American targets. While one of the four attacks was foiled by the heroism of the plane's passengers, the other three killed approximately 3,000 innocent civilians, destroyed hundreds of millions of dollars of property, and severely damaged the U.S. economy. In response to the attacks, Congress passed a joint resolution authorizing the President to use "all necessary and appropriate force against those nations, organizations, or persons he determines planned, authorized, committed, or aided the terrorist attacks . . . or harbored such organizations or persons." Authorization for Use of Military Force, Pub.L. 107–40, §§1–2, 115 Stat. 224. Acting pursuant to that authorization, the President sent U.S. Armed Forces into Afghanistan to wage a military campaign against al Qaeda and the Taliban regime that had supported it.

Petitioners in these cases are 2 Australian citizens and 12 Kuwaiti citizens who were captured abroad during hostilities between the United States and the Taliban.[1] Since

---

[1] When we granted certiorari, the petitioners also included two British citizens, Shafiq Rasul and Asif Iqbal. These petitioners have since been released from custody.

91

early 2002, the U.S. military has held them – along with, according to the Government's estimate, approximately 640 other non-Americans captured abroad – at the Naval Base at Guantanamo Bay. Brief for United States 6. The United States occupies the Base, which comprises 45 square miles of land and water along the southeast coast of Cuba, pursuant to a 1903 Lease Agreement executed with the newly independent Republic of Cuba in the aftermath of the Spanish-American War. Under the Agreement, "the United States recognizes the continuance of the ultimate sovereignty of the Republic of Cuba over the [leased areas]," while "the Republic of Cuba consents that during the period of the occupation by the United States...the United States shall exercise complete jurisdiction and control over and within said areas."[2] In 1934, the parties entered into a treaty providing that, absent an agreement to modify or abrogate the lease, the lease would remain in effect "[s]o long as the United States of America shall not abandon the...naval station of Guantanamo."[3]

In 2002, petitioners, through relatives acting as their next friends, filed various actions in the U.S. District Court for the District of Columbia challenging the legality of their detention at the Base. All alleged that none of the petitioners has ever been a combatant against the United States or has ever engaged in any terrorist acts.[4] They also alleged that none has been charged with any wrongdoing, permitted to consult with counsel, or provided access to the courts or any other tribunal. App. 29, 77, 108.[5]

The two Australians, Mamdouh Habib and David Hicks, each filed a petition for writ of habeas corpus, seeking release from custody, access to counsel, freedom from interrogations, and other relief. *Id.*, at 98–99, 124–126. Fawzi Khalid Abdullah Fahad Al Odah and the 11 other Kuwaiti detainees filed a complaint seeking to be informed of the charges against them, to be allowed to meet with their families and with counsel, and to have access to the courts or some other impartial tribunal. *Id.*, at 34. They claimed that denial of these rights violates the Constitution, international law, and treaties of the United States. Invoking the court's jurisdiction under 28 U.S.C. §§1331 and 1350, among other statutory bases, they asserted causes of action under the Administrative Procedure Act, 5 U.S.C. §§555, 702, 706; the Alien Tort Statute, 28 U.S.C. §1350; and the general federal habeas corpus statute, §§2241–2243. App. 19.

Construing all three actions as petitions for writs of habeas corpus, the District Court dismissed them for want of jurisdiction. The court held, in reliance on our opinion in *Johnson v. Eisentrager*, 339 U.S. 763 (1950), that "aliens detained outside the sovereign territory of the United States [may not] invok[e] a petition for a writ of habeas corpus." 215 F. Supp. 2d 55, 68 (DC 2002). The Court of Appeals affirmed. Reading *Eisentrager* to hold that "'the privilege of litigation' does not extend to aliens in military custody

---

[2] Lease of Lands for Coaling and Naval Stations, Feb. 23, 1903, U.S.-Cuba, Art. III, T.S. No. 418 (hereinafter 1903 Lease Agreement). A supplemental lease agreement, executed in July 1903, obligates the United States to pay an annual rent in the amount of "two thousand dollars, in gold coin of the United States" and to maintain "permanent fences" around the base. Lease of Certain Areas for Naval or Coaling Stations, July 2, 1903, U.S.-Cuba, Arts. I–II, T.S. No. 426.

[3] Treaty Defining Relations with Cuba, May 29, 1934, U.S.-Cuba, Art. III, 48 Stat. 1683, T.S. No. 866 (hereinafter 1934 Treaty).

[4] Relatives of the Kuwaiti detainees allege that the detainees were taken captive "by local villagers seeking promised bounties or other financial rewards" while they were providing humanitarian aid in Afghanistan and Pakistan, and were subsequently turned over to U.S. custody. App. 24–25. The Australian David Hicks was allegedly captured in Afghanistan by the Northern Alliance, a coalition of Afghan groups opposed to the Taliban, before he was turned over to the United States. *Id.*, at 84. The Australian Mamdouh Habib was allegedly arrested in Pakistan by Pakistani authorities and turned over to Egyptian authorities, who in turn transferred him to U.S. custody. *Id.*, at 110–111.

[5] David Hicks has since been permitted to meet with counsel. Brief for United States 9.

who have no presence in 'any territory over which the United States is sovereign,'" 321 F. 3d 1134, 1144 (CADC 2003) (quoting *Eisentrager*, 339 U.S., at 777–778), it held that the District Court lacked jurisdiction over petitioners' habeas actions, as well as their remaining federal statutory claims that do not sound in habeas. We granted certiorari, 540 U.S. 1003 (2003), and now reverse.

II

Congress has granted federal district courts, "within their respective jurisdictions," the authority to hear applications for habeas corpus by any person who claims to be held "in custody in violation of the Constitution or laws or treaties of the United States." 28 U.S.C. §§2241(a), (c)(3). The statute traces its ancestry to the first grant of federal court jurisdiction: Section 14 of the Judiciary Act of 1789 authorized federal courts to issue the writ of habeas corpus to prisoners "in custody, under or by colour of the authority of the United States, or committed for trial before some court of the same." Act of Sept. 24, 1789, ch. 20, §14, 1 Stat. 82. In 1867, Congress extended the protections of the writ to "all cases where any person may be restrained of his or her liberty in violation of the constitution, or of any treaty or law of the United States." Act of Feb. 5, 1867, ch. 28, 14 Stat. 385. See *Felker* v. *Turpin*, 518 U.S. 651, 659–660 (1996).

Habeas corpus is, however, "a writ antecedent to statute, . . . throwing its root deep into the genius of our common law." *Williams* v. *Kaiser*, 323 U.S. 471, 484, n. 2 (1945) (internal quotation marks omitted). The writ appeared in English law several centuries ago, became "an integral part of our common-law heritage" by the time the Colonies achieved independence, *Preiser* v. *Rodriguez*, 411 U.S. 475, 485 (1973), and received explicit recognition in the Constitution, which forbids suspension of "[t]he Privilege of the Writ of Habeas Corpus . . . unless when in Cases of Rebellion or Invasion the public Safety may require it," Art. I, §9, cl. 2.

As it has evolved over the past two centuries, the habeas statute clearly has expanded habeas corpus "beyond the limits that obtained during the 17th and 18th centuries." *Swain* v. *Pressley*, 430 U.S. 372, 380, n. 13 (1977). But "[a]t its historical core, the writ of habeas corpus has served as a means of reviewing the legality of Executive detention, and it is in that context that its protections have been strongest." *INS* v. *St. Cyr*, 533 U.S. 289, 301 (2001). See also *Brown* v. *Allen*, 344 U.S. 443, 533 (1953) (Jackson, J., concurring in result) ("The historic purpose of the writ has been to relieve detention by executive authorities without judicial trial"). As Justice Jackson wrote in an opinion respecting the availability of habeas corpus to aliens held in U.S. custody:

> "Executive imprisonment has been considered oppressive and lawless since John, at Runnymede, pledged that no free man should be imprisoned, dispossessed, outlawed, or exiled save by the judgment of his peers or by the law of the land. The judges of England developed the writ of habeas corpus largely to preserve these immunities from executive restraint." *Shaughnessy* v. *United States ex rel. Mezei*, 345 U.S. 206, 218–219 (1953) (dissenting opinion).

Consistent with the historic purpose of the writ, this Court has recognized the federal courts' power to review applications for habeas relief in a wide variety of cases involving Executive detention, in wartime as well as in times of peace. The Court has, for example, entertained the habeas petitions of an American citizen who plotted an attack on military installations during the Civil War, *Ex parte Milligan*, 4 Wall. 2 (1866), and of admitted enemy aliens convicted of war crimes during a declared war and held in the United

States, *Ex parte Quirin*, 317 U.S. 1 (1942), and its insular possessions, *In re Yamashita*, 327 U.S. 1 (1946).

The question now before us is whether the habeas statute confers a right to judicial review of the legality of Executive detention of aliens in a territory over which the United States exercises plenary and exclusive jurisdiction, but not "ultimate sovereignty."[6]

III

Respondents' primary submission is that the answer to the jurisdictional question is controlled by our decision in *Eisentrager*. In that case, we held that a Federal District Court lacked authority to issue a writ of habeas corpus to 21 German citizens who had been captured by U.S. forces in China, tried and convicted of war crimes by an American military commission headquartered in Nanking, and incarcerated in the Landsberg Prison in occupied Germany. The Court of Appeals in *Eisentrager* had found jurisdiction, reasoning that "any person who is deprived of his liberty by officials of the United States, acting under purported authority of that Government, and who can show that his confinement is in violation of a prohibition of the Constitution, has a right to the writ." *Eisentrager* v. *Forrestal*, 174 F.2d 961, 963 (CADC 1949). In reversing that determination, this Court summarized the six critical facts in the case:

> "We are here confronted with a decision whose basic premise is that these prisoners are entitled, as a constitutional right, to sue in some court of the United States for a writ of *habeas corpus*. To support that assumption we must hold that a prisoner of our military authorities is constitutionally entitled to the writ, even though he (a) is an enemy alien; (b) has never been or resided in the United States; (c) was captured outside of our territory and there held in military custody as a prisoner of war; (d) was tried and convicted by a Military Commission sitting outside the United States; (e) for offenses against laws of war committed outside the United States; (f) and is at all times imprisoned outside the United States." 339 U.S., at 777.

On this set of facts, the Court concluded, "no right to the writ of *habeas corpus* appears." *Id.*, at 781.

Petitioners in these cases differ from the *Eisentrager* detainees in important respects: They are not nationals of countries at war with the United States, and they deny that they have engaged in or plotted acts of aggression against the United States; they have never been afforded access to any tribunal, much less charged with and convicted of wrongdoing; and for more than two years they have been imprisoned in territory over which the United States exercises exclusive jurisdiction and control.

Not only are petitioners differently situated from the *Eisentrager* detainees, but the Court in *Eisentrager* made quite clear that all six of the facts critical to its disposition were relevant only to the question of the prisoners' *constitutional* entitlement to habeas corpus. *Id.*, at 777. The Court had far less to say on the question of the petitioners' *statutory* entitlement to habeas review. Its only statement on the subject was a passing reference to the absence of statutory authorization: "Nothing in the text of the Constitution extends such a right, nor does anything in our statutes." *Id.*, at 768.

Reference to the historical context in which *Eisentrager* was decided explains why the opinion devoted so little attention to question of statutory jurisdiction. In 1948, just two months after the *Eisentrager* petitioners filed their petition for habeas corpus in the U.S. District Court for the District of Columbia, this Court issued its decision in

---

[6] 1903 Lease Agreement, Art. III.

Ahrens v. *Clark*, 335 U.S. 188, a case concerning the application of the habeas statute to the petitions of 120 Germans who were then being detained at Ellis Island, New York, for deportation to Germany. The *Ahrens* detainees had also filed their petitions in the U.S. District Court for the District of Columbia, naming the Attorney General as the respondent. Reading the phrase "within their respective jurisdictions" as used in the habeas statute to require the petitioners' presence within the district court's territorial jurisdiction, the Court held that the District of Columbia court lacked jurisdiction to entertain the detainees' claims. *Id.*, at 192. *Ahrens* expressly reserved the question "of what process, if any, a person confined in an area not subject to the jurisdiction of any district court may employ to assert federal rights." *Id.*, 192, n.4. But as the dissent noted, if the presence of the petitioner in the territorial jurisdiction of a federal district court were truly a jurisdictional requirement, there could be only one response to that question. *Id.*, at 209 (opinion of Rutledge, J.).[7]

When the District Court for the District of Columbia reviewed the German prisoners' habeas application in *Eisentrager*, it thus dismissed their action on the authority of *Ahrens*. See *Eisentrager*, 339 U.S., at 767, 790. Although the Court of Appeals reversed the District Court, it implicitly conceded that the District Court lacked jurisdiction under the habeas statute as it had been interpreted in *Ahrens*. The Court of Appeals instead held that petitioners had a constitutional right to habeas corpus secured by the Suspension Clause, U.S. Const., Art. I, §9, cl. 2, reasoning that "if a person has a right to a writ of habeas corpus, he cannot be deprived of the privilege by an omission in a federal jurisdictional statute." *Eisentrager* v. *Forrestal*, 174 F. 2d, at 965. In essence, the Court of Appeals concluded that the habeas statute, as construed in *Ahrens*, had created an unconstitutional gap that had to be filled by reference to "fundamentals." 174 F. 2d, at 963. In its review of that decision, this Court, like the Court of Appeals, proceeded from the premise that "nothing in our statutes" conferred federal-court jurisdiction, and accordingly evaluated the Court of Appeals' resort to "fundamentals" on its own terms. 339 U.S., at 768.[8]

Because subsequent decisions of this Court have filled the statutory gap that had occasioned *Eisentrager's* resort to "fundamentals," persons detained outside the territorial jurisdiction of any federal district court no longer need rely on the Constitution as the source of their right to federal habeas review. In *Braden* v. *30th Judicial Circuit Court of Ky.*, 410 U.S. 484, 495 (1973), this Court held, contrary to *Ahrens*, that the prisoner's presence within the territorial jurisdiction of the district court is not "an invariable prerequisite" to the exercise of district court jurisdiction under the federal habeas statute. Rather, because "the writ of habeas corpus does not act upon the prisoner who seeks relief, but upon the person who holds him in what is alleged to be unlawful custody,"

---

[7] Justice Rutledge wrote:

> "[I]f absence of the body detained from the territorial jurisdiction of the court having jurisdiction of the jailer creates a total and irremediable void in the court's capacity to act,... then it is hard to see how that gap can be filled by such extraneous considerations as whether there is no other court in the place of detention from which remedy might be had...." 335 U.S., at 209.

[8] Although JUSTICE SCALIA disputes the basis for the Court of Appeals' holding, *post*, at 4, what is most pertinent for present purposes is that this Court clearly understood the Court of Appeals' decision to rest on constitutional and not statutory grounds. *Eisentrager*, 339 U.S., at 767. ("[The Court of Appeals] concluded that any person, including an enemy alien, deprived of his liberty anywhere under any purported authority of the United States is entitled to the writ if he can show that extension to his case of any constitutional rights or limitations would show his imprisonment illegal; [and] that, *although no statutory jurisdiction of such cases is given*, courts must be held to possess it as part of the judicial power of the United States..." (emphasis added)).

a district court acts "within [its] respective jurisdiction" within the meaning of §2241 as long as "the custodian can be reached by service of process." 410 U.S., at 494–495. *Braden* reasoned that its departure from the rule of *Ahrens* was warranted in light of developments that "had a profound impact on the continuing vitality of that decision." 410 U.S., at 497. These developments included, notably, decisions of this Court in cases involving habeas petitioners "confined overseas (and thus outside the territory of any district court)," in which the Court "held, if only implicitly, that the petitioners' absence from the district does not present a jurisdictional obstacle to the consideration of the claim." *Id.*, at 498 (citing *Burns* v. *Wilson*, 346 U.S. 137 (1953), rehearing denied, 346 U.S. 844, 851–852 (opinion of Frankfurter, J.); *United States ex rel. Toth* v. *Quarles*, 350 U.S. 11 (1955); *Hirota* v. *MacArthur*, 338 U.S. 197, 199 (1948) (Douglas, J., concurring)). *Braden* thus established that *Ahrens* can no longer be viewed as establishing "an inflexible jurisdictional rule," and is strictly relevant only to the question of the appropriate forum, not to whether the claim can be heard at all. 410 U.S., at 499–500.

Because *Braden* overruled the statutory predicate to *Eisentrager's* holding, *Eisentrager* plainly does not preclude the exercise of §2241 jurisdiction over petitioners' claims.[9]

IV

Putting *Eisentrager* and *Ahrens* to one side, respondents contend that we can discern a limit on §2241 through application of the "longstanding principle of American law" that congressional legislation is presumed not to have extraterritorial application unless such intent is clearly manifested. *EEOC* v. *Arabian American Oil Co.*, 499 U.S. 244, 248 (1991). Whatever traction the presumption against extraterritoriality might have in other contexts, it certainly has no application to the operation of the habeas statute with respect to persons detained within "the territorial jurisdiction" of the United States. *Foley Bros., Inc.* v. *Filardo*, 336 U.S. 281, 285 (1949). By the express terms of its agreements with Cuba, the United States exercises "complete jurisdiction and control" over the

---

[9] The dissent argues that *Braden* did not overrule *Ahrens'* jurisdictional holding, but simply distinguished it. *Post*, at 7. Of course, *Braden* itself indicated otherwise, 410 U.S., at 495–500, and a long line of judicial and scholarly interpretations, beginning with then-JUSTICE REHNQUIST's dissenting opinion, have so understood the decision. See, *e.g., id.*, at 502 ("Today the Court overrules *Ahrens*"); *Moore* v. *Olson*, 368 F. 3d 757, 758 (CA7 2004) ("[A]fter *Braden* . . . , which overruled *Ahrens*, the location of a collateral attack is best understood as a matter of venue"); *Armentero* v. *INS*, 340 F. 3d 1058, 1063 (CA.9 2003) ("[T]he Court in [*Braden*] declared that *Ahrens* was overruled" (citations omitted)); *Henderson* v. *INS*, 157 F. 3d 106, 126, n. 20 (CA.2 1998) ("On the issue of territorial jurisdiction, *Ahrens* was subsequently overruled by *Braden*"); *Chatman-Bey* v. *Thornburgh*, 864 F. 2d 804, 811 (CADC 1988) (en banc) ("[I]n *Braden*, the Court cut back substantially on *Ahrens* (and indeed overruled its territorially-based jurisdictional holding)"). See also, *e.g., Patterson* v. *McLean Credit Union*, 485 U.S. 617, 618, (1988) (*per curiam*); Eskridge, Overruling Statutory Precedents, 76 Geo. L.J. 1361, App. A (1988).

The dissent also disingenuously contends that the continuing vitality of *Ahrens'* jurisdictional holding is irrelevant to the question presented in these cases, "inasmuch as *Ahrens* did not pass upon any of the statutory issues decided by *Eisentrager*." *Post*, at 7. But what JUSTICE SCALIA describes as *Eisentrager's* statutory holding – "that, unaided by the canon of constitutional avoidance, the statute did not confer jurisdiction over an alien detained outside the territorial jurisdiction of the courts of the United States," *post*, at 6 – is little more than the rule of *Ahrens* cloaked in the garb of *Eisentrager's* facts. To contend plausibly that this holding survived *Braden*, JUSTICE SCALIA at a minimum must find a textual basis for the rule other than the phrase "within their respective jurisdictions" – a phrase which, after *Braden*, can no longer be read to require the habeas petitioner's physical presence within the territorial jurisdiction of a federal district court. Two references to the district of confinement in provisions relating to recordkeeping and pleading requirements in proceedings before circuit judges hardly suffice in that regard. See *post*, at 2 (citing 28 U.S.C. §§2241(a), 2242).

Guantanamo Bay Naval Base, and may continue to exercise such control permanently if it so chooses. 1903 Lease Agreement, Art. III; 1934 Treaty, Art. III. Respondents themselves concede that the habeas statute would create federal-court jurisdiction over the claims of an American citizen held at the base. Tr. of Oral Arg. 27. Considering that the statute draws no distinction between Americans and aliens held in federal custody, there is little reason to think that Congress intended the geographical coverage of the statute to vary depending on the detainee's citizenship.[10] Aliens held at the base, no less than American citizens, are entitled to invoke the federal courts' authority under §2241.

Application of the habeas statute to persons detained at the base is consistent with the historical reach of the writ of habeas corpus. At common law, courts exercised habeas jurisdiction over the claims of aliens detained within sovereign territory of the realm,[11] as well as the claims of persons detained in the so-called "exempt jurisdictions," where ordinary writs did not run,[12] and all other dominions under the sovereign's control.[13] As Lord Mansfield wrote in 1759, even if a territory was "no part of the realm," there was "no doubt" as to the court's power to issue writs of habeas corpus if the territory was "under the subjection of the Crown." *King* v. *Cowle*, 2 Burr. 834, 854–855, 97 Eng. Rep. 587, 598–599 (K. B.). Later cases confirmed that the reach of the writ depended not on formal notions of territorial sovereignty, but rather on the practical question of "the exact extent and nature of the jurisdiction or dominion exercised in fact by the Crown." *Ex parte Mwenya*, [1960] 1 Q. B. 241, 303 (C.A.) (Lord Evershed, M. R.).[14]

---

[10] JUSTICE SCALIA appears to agree that neither the plain text of the statute nor his interpretation of that text provides a basis for treating American citizens differently from aliens. *Post*, at 10. But resisting the practical consequences of his position, he suggests that he might nevertheless recognize an "atextual exception" to his statutory rule for citizens held beyond the territorial jurisdiction of the federal district courts. *Ibid.*

[11] See, *e.g.*, *King* v. *Schiever*, 2 Burr. 765, 97 Eng. Rep. 551 (K. B. 1759) (reviewing the habeas petition of a neutral alien deemed a prisoner of war because he was captured aboard an enemy French privateer during a war between England and France); *Sommersett* v. *Stewart*, 20 How. St. Tr. 1, 79 82 (K. B. 1772) (releasing on habeas an African slave purchased in Virginia and detained on a ship docked in England and bound for Jamaica); *Case of the Hottentot Venus*, 13 East 195, 104 Eng. Rep. 344 (K. B. 1810) (reviewing the habeas petition of a "native of *South Africa*" allegedly held in private custody).

American courts followed a similar practice in the early years of the Republic. See, *e.g.*, *United States* v. *Villato*, 2 Dall. 370 (CC Pa. 1797) (granting habeas relief to Spanish-born prisoner charged with treason on the ground that he had never become a citizen of the United States); *Ex parte D'Olivera*, 7 F. Cas. 853 (No, 3,967) (CC Mass. 1813) (Story, J., on circuit) (ordering the release of Portuguese sailors arrested for deserting their ship); *Wilson* v. *Izard*, 30 F. Cas. 131 (No. 17,810) (CC NY 1815) (Livingston, J., on circuit) (reviewing the habeas petition of enlistees who claimed that they were entitled to discharge because of their status as enemy aliens).

[12] See, *e.g.*, *Bourn's Case*, Cro. Jac. 543, 79 Eng. Rep. 465 (K. B. 1619) (writ issued to the Cinque-Ports town of Dover); *Alder* v. *Puisy*, 1 Freeman 12, 89 Eng. Rep. 10 (K. B. 1671) (same); *Jobson's Case*, Latch 160, 82 Eng. Rep. 325 (K. B. 1626) (entertaining the habeas petition of a prisoner held in the County Palatine of Durham). See also 3 W. Blackstone, Commentaries on the Laws of England 79 (1769) (hereinafter Blackstone) ("[A]ll prerogative writs (as those of *habeas corpus,* prohibition, *certiorari,* and *mandamus*) may issue . . . to all these exempt jurisdictions; because the privilege, that the king's writ runs not, must be intended between party and party, for there can be no such privilege against the king" (footnotes omitted)); R. Sharpe, Law of Habeas Corpus 188–189 (2d ed. 1989) (describing the "extraordinary territorial ambit" of the writ at common law).

[13] See, *e.g.*, *King* v. *Overton*, 1 Sid. 387, 82 Eng. Rep. 1173 (K. B. 1668) (writ issued to Isle of Jersey); *King* v. *Salmon*, 2 Keble 450, 84 Eng. Rep. 282 (K. B. 1669) (same). See also 3 Blackstone 131 (habeas corpus "run[s] into all parts of the king's dominions: for the king is at all times [e]ntitled to have an account, why the liberty of any of his subjects is restrained, wherever that restraint may be inflicted" (footnotes omitted)); M. Hale, History of the Common Law 120–121 (C. Gray ed.1971) (writ of habeas corpus runs to the Channel Islands, even though "they are not Parcel of the Realm of England").

[14] *Ex parte Mwenya* held that the writ ran to a territory described as a "foreign country within which [the Crown] ha[d] power and jurisdiction by treaty, grant, usage, sufferance, and other lawful means." *Ex parte Mwenya*, 1 Q. B., at 265 (internal quotation marks omitted). See also *King* v. *The Earl of Crewe ex parte Sekgome*, [1910] 2 K. B. 576, 606 (C.A.) (Williams, L.J.) (concluding that the writ would run to such a territory); *id.*, at 618 (Farwell, L.J.) (same). As Lord Justice Sellers explained:

In the end, the answer to the question presented is clear. Petitioners contend that they are being held in federal custody in violation of the laws of the United States.[15] No party questions the District Court's jurisdiction over petitioners' custodians. Cf. *Braden*, 410 U.S., at 495. Section 2241, by its terms, requires nothing more. We therefore hold that §2241 confers on the District Court jurisdiction to hear petitioners' habeas corpus challenges to the legality of their detention at the Guantanamo Bay Naval Base.

V

In addition to invoking the District Court's jurisdiction under §2241, the *Al Odah* petitioners' complaint invoked the court's jurisdiction under 28 U.S.C. §1331, the federal question statute, as well as §1350, the Alien Tort Statute. The Court of Appeals, again relying on *Eisentrager*, held that the District Court correctly dismissed the claims founded on §1331 and §1350 for lack of jurisdiction, even to the extent that these claims "deal only with conditions of confinement and do not sound in habeas," because petitioners lack the "privilege of litigation" in U.S. courts. 321 F.3d, at 1144 (internal quotation marks omitted). Specifically, the court held that because petitioners' §1331 and §1350 claims "necessarily rest on alleged violations of the same category of laws listed in the habeas corpus statute," they, like claims founded on the habeas statute itself, must be "beyond the jurisdiction of the federal courts." *Id.*, at 1144–1145.

As explained above, *Eisentrager* itself erects no bar to the exercise of federal court jurisdiction over the petitioners' habeas corpus claims. It therefore certainly does not bar the exercise of federal-court jurisdiction over claims that merely implicate the "same category of laws listed in the habeas corpus statute." But in any event, nothing in *Eisentrager* or in any of our other cases categorically excludes aliens detained in military custody outside the United States from the "'privilege of litigation'" in U.S. courts. 321 F.3d, at 1139. The courts of the United States have traditionally been open to nonresident aliens. Cf. *Disconto Gesellschaft* v. *Umbreit*, 208 U.S. 570, 578 (1908) ("Alien citizens, by the policy and practice of the courts of this country, are ordinarily permitted to resort to the courts for the redress of wrongs and the protection of their rights"). And indeed, 28 U.S.C. §1350 explicitly confers the privilege of suing for an actionable

---

"Lord Mansfield gave the writ the greatest breadth of application which in the then circumstances could well be conceived. . . . 'Subjection' is fully appropriate to the powers exercised or exercisable by this country irrespective of territorial sovereignty or dominion, and it embraces in outlook the power of the Crown in the place concerned." 1 Q. B., at 310.

JUSTICE SCALIA cites *In re Ning Yi-Ching*, 56 T. L. R. 3 (Vacation Ct. 1939), for the broad proposition that habeas corpus has been categorically unavailable to aliens held outside sovereign territory. *Post*, at 18. *Ex parte Mwenya*, however, casts considerable doubt on this narrow view of the territorial reach of the writ. See *Ex parte Mwenya*, 1 Q. B., at 295 (Lord Evershed, M. R.) (noting that *In re Ning Yi-Ching* relied on Lord Justice Kennedy's opinion in *Ex parte Sekgome* concerning the territorial reach of the writ, despite the opinions of two members of the court who "took a different view upon this matter"). And *In re Ning Yi-Ching* itself made quite clear that "the remedy of *habeas corpus* was not confined to British subjects," but would extend to "any person . . . detained" within reach of the writ. 56 T. L. R., at 5 (citing *Ex parte Sekgome*, 2 K. B., at 620 (Kennedy, L.J.)). Moreover, the result in that case can be explained by the peculiar nature of British control over the area where the petitioners, four Chinese nationals accused of various criminal offenses, were being held pending transfer to the local district court. Although the treaties governing the British Concession at Tientsin did confer on Britain "certain rights of administration and control," "the right to administer justice" to Chinese nationals was not among them. 56 T. L. R., at 4–6.

[15] Petitioners' allegations – that, although they have engaged neither in combat nor in acts of terrorism against the United States, they have been held in Executive detention for more than two years in territory subject to the long-term, exclusive jurisdiction and control of the United States, without access to counsel and without being charged with any wrongdoing – unquestionably describe "custody in violation of the Constitution or laws or treaties of the United States." 28 U.S.C. §2241(c)(3). Cf. *United States* v. *Verdugo-Urquidez*, 494 U.S. 259, 277–278 (1990) (KENNEDY, J., concurring), and cases cited therein.

"tort . . . committed in violation of the law of nations or a treaty of the United States" on aliens alone. The fact that petitioners in these cases are being held in military custody is immaterial to the question of the District Court's jurisdiction over their nonhabeas statutory claims.

VI

Whether and what further proceedings may become necessary after respondents make their response to the merits of petitioners' claims are matters that we need not address now. What is presently at stake is only whether the federal courts have jurisdiction to determine the legality of the Executive's potentially indefinite detention of individuals who claim to be wholly innocent of wrongdoing. Answering that question in the affirmative, we reverse the judgment of the Court of Appeals and remand for the District Court to consider in the first instance the merits of petitioners' claims.

It is so ordered.

. . .

JUSTICE KENNEDY, concurring in the judgment.

The Court is correct, in my view, to conclude that federal courts have jurisdiction to consider challenges to the legality of the detention of foreign nationals held at the Guantanamo Bay Naval Base in Cuba. While I reach the same conclusion, my analysis follows a different course. JUSTICE SCALIA exposes the weakness in the Court's conclusion that *Braden* v. *30th Judicial Circuit Court of Ky.*, 410 U.S. 484 (1973), "overruled the statutory predicate to *Eisentrager*'s holding," *ante*, at 10–11. As he explains, the Court's approach is not a plausible reading of *Braden* or *Johnson* v. *Eisentrager*, 339 U.S. 763 (1950). In my view, the correct course is to follow the framework of *Eisentrager*.

Eisentrager considered the scope of the right to petition for a writ of habeas corpus against the backdrop of the constitutional command of the separation of powers. The issue before the Court was whether the Judiciary could exercise jurisdiction over the claims of German prisoners held in the Landsberg prison in Germany following the cessation of hostilities in Europe. The Court concluded the petition could not be entertained. The petition was not within the proper realm of the judicial power. It concerned matters within the exclusive province of the Executive, or the Executive and Congress, to determine.

The Court began by noting the "ascending scale of rights" that courts have recognized for individuals depending on their connection to the United States. *Id.*, at 770. Citizenship provides a longstanding basis for jurisdiction, the Court noted, and among aliens physical presence within the United States also "gave the Judiciary power to act." *Id.*, at 769, 771. This contrasted with the "essential pattern for seasonable Executive constraint of enemy aliens." *Id.*, at 773. The place of the detention was also important to the jurisdictional question, the Court noted. Physical presence in the United States "implied protection," *id.*, at 777–778, whereas in *Eisentrager* "th[e] prisoners at no relevant time were within any territory over which the United States is sovereign," *id.*, at 778. The Court next noted that the prisoners in *Eisentrager* "were actual enemies" of the United States, proven to be so at trial, and thus could not justify "a limited opening of our courts" to distinguish the "many [aliens] of friendly personal disposition to whom the status of enemy" was unproven. *Id.*, at 778. Finally, the Court considered the extent to which jurisdiction would "hamper the war effort and bring aid and comfort to the enemy." *Id.*, at 779. Because the prisoners in *Eisentrager* were proven enemy aliens found and detained outside the United States, and because the existence of jurisdiction would have had a clear harmful effect on the Nation's military affairs, the matter was appropriately left to the Executive Branch and there was no jurisdiction for the courts to hear the prisoner's claims.

The decision in *Eisentrager* indicates that there is a realm of political authority over military affairs where the judicial power may not enter. The existence of this realm acknowledges the power of the President as Commander in Chief, and the joint role of the President and the Congress, in the conduct of military affairs. A faithful application of *Eisentrager*, then, requires an initial inquiry into the general circumstances of the detention to determine whether the Court has the authority to entertain the petition and to grant relief after considering all of the facts presented. A necessary corollary of *Eisentrager* is that there are circumstances in which the courts maintain the power and the responsibility to protect persons from unlawful detention even where military affairs are implicated. See also *Ex parte Milligan*, 4 Wall. 2 (1866).

The facts here are distinguishable from those in *Eisentrager* in two critical ways, leading to the conclusion that a federal court may entertain the petitions. First, Guantanamo Bay is in every practical respect a United States territory, and it is one far removed from any hostilities. The opinion of the Court well explains the history of its possession by the United States. In a formal sense, the United States leases the Bay; the 1903 lease agreement states that Cuba retains "ultimate sovereignty" over it. Lease of Lands for Coaling and Naval Stations, Feb. 23, 1903, U.S.-Cuba, Art. III, T.S. No. 418. At the same time, this lease is no ordinary lease. Its term is indefinite and at the discretion of the United States. What matters is the unchallenged and indefinite control that the United States has long exercised over Guantanamo Bay. From a practical perspective, the indefinite lease of Guantanamo Bay has produced a place that belongs to the United States, extending the "implied protection" of the United States to it. *Eisentrager*, *supra*, at 777–778.

The second critical set of facts is that the detainees at Guantanamo Bay are being held indefinitely, and without benefit of any legal proceeding to determine their status. In *Eisentrager*, the prisoners were tried and convicted by a military commission of violating the laws of war and were sentenced to prison terms. Having already been subject to procedures establishing their status, they could not justify "a limited opening of our courts" to show that they were "of friendly personal disposition" and not enemy aliens. 339 U.S., at 778. Indefinite detention without trial or other proceeding presents altogether different considerations. It allows friends and foes alike to remain in detention. It suggests a weaker case of military necessity and much greater alignment with the traditional function of habeas corpus. Perhaps, where detainees are taken from a zone of hostilities, detention without proceedings or trial would be justified by military necessity for a matter of weeks; but as the period of detention stretches from months to years, the case for continued detention to meet military exigencies becomes weaker.

In light of the status of Guantanamo Bay and the indefinite pretrial detention of the detainees, I would hold that federal-court jurisdiction is permitted in these cases. This approach would avoid creating automatic statutory authority to adjudicate the claims of persons located outside the United States, and remains true to the reasoning of *Eisentrager*. For these reasons, I concur in the judgment of the Court.

. . .

JUSTICE SCALIA, with whom THE CHIEF JUSTICE and JUSTICE THOMAS join, dissenting.

The Court today holds that the habeas statute, 28 U.S.C. §2241, extends to aliens detained by the United States military overseas, outside the sovereign borders of the United States and beyond the territorial jurisdictions of all its courts. This is not only a novel holding; it contradicts a half-century-old precedent on which the military undoubtedly relied, *Johnson* v. *Eisentrager*, 339 U.S. 763 (1950). The Court's contention that *Eisentrager* was somehow negated by *Braden* v. *30th Judicial Circuit Court of Ky.*, 410 U.S. 484 (1973) – a decision that dealt with a different issue and did not so much as mention *Eisentrager* – is implausible in the extreme. This is an irresponsible overturning of settled law in a matter of extreme importance to our forces currently in the field. I would leave it to Congress to change §2241, and dissent from the Court's unprecedented holding.

I

As we have repeatedly said: "Federal courts are courts of limited jurisdiction. They possess only that power authorized by Constitution and statute, which is not to be expanded by judicial decree. It is to be presumed that a cause lies outside this limited jurisdiction...." *Kokkonen* v. *Guardian Life Ins. Co. of America*, 511 U.S. 375, 377 (1994) (citations omitted). The petitioners do not argue that the Constitution independently requires jurisdiction here.[1] Accordingly, this case turns on the words of §2241, a text the Court today largely ignores. Even a cursory reading of the habeas statute shows that it presupposes a federal district court with territorial jurisdiction over the detainee. Section 2241(a) states:

> "Writs of habeas corpus may be granted by the Supreme Court, any justice thereof, the district courts and any circuit judge *within their respective jurisdictions*." (Emphasis added).

It further requires that "[t]he order of a circuit judge shall be entered in the records of *the* district court of *the district wherein the restraint complained of is had*." 28 U.S.C. §2241(a) (emphases added). And §2242 provides that a petition "addressed to the Supreme Court, a justice thereof or a circuit judge . . . shall state the reasons for not making application to *the* district court of *the district in which the applicant is held*." (Emphases added). No matter to whom the writ is directed, custodian or detainee, the statute could not be clearer that a necessary requirement for issuing the writ is that *some* federal district court have territorial jurisdiction over the detainee. Here, as the Court allows, see *ante*, at 10, the Guantanamo Bay detainees are not located within the territorial jurisdiction of any federal district court. One would think that is the end of this case.

The Court asserts, however, that the decisions of this Court have placed a gloss on the phrase "within their respective jurisdictions" in §2241 which allows jurisdiction in this case. That is not so. In fact, the only case in point holds just the opposite (and just what the statute plainly says). That case is *Eisentrager*, but to fully understand its implications for the present dispute, I must also discuss our decisions in the earlier case of *Ahrens* v. *Clark*, 335 U.S. 188 (1948), and the later case of *Braden*.

In *Ahrens*, the Court considered "whether the presence within the territorial jurisdiction of the District Court of the person detained is prerequisite to filing a petition for a writ of habeas corpus." 335 U.S., at 189 (construing 28 U.S.C. §452, the statutory precursor to §2241). The *Ahrens* detainees were held at Ellis Island, New York, but brought their petitions in the District Court for the District of Columbia. Interpreting "within their respective jurisdictions," the Court held that a district court has jurisdiction to issue the writ only on behalf of petitioners detained within its territorial jurisdiction.

---

[1] See Tr. of Oral Arg. 5 ("Question: And you don't raise the issue of any potential jurisdiction on the basis of the Constitution alone. We are here debating the jurisdiction under the Habeas Statute, is that right? [Answer]: That's correct . . .").

It was "not sufficient . . . that the jailer or custodian alone be found in the jurisdiction." 335 U.S., at 190.

Ahrens explicitly reserved "the question of what process, if any, a person confined in an area not subject to the jurisdiction of any district court may employ to assert federal rights." *Id.*, at 192, n. 4. That question, the same question presented to this Court today, was shortly thereafter resolved in *Eisentrager* insofar as noncitizens are concerned. *Eisentrager* involved petitions for writs of habeas corpus filed in the District Court for the District of Columbia by German nationals imprisoned in Landsberg Prison, Germany. The District Court, relying on *Ahrens*, dismissed the petitions because the petitioners were not located within its territorial jurisdiction. The Court of Appeals reversed. According to the Court today, the Court of Appeals "implicitly conceded that the District Court lacked jurisdiction under the habeas statute as it had been interpreted in *Ahrens*," and "[i]n essence . . . concluded that the habeas statute, as construed in *Ahrens*, had created an unconstitutional gap that had to be filled by reference to 'fundamentals.'" *Ante*, at 9. That is not so. The Court of Appeals concluded that there *was* statutory jurisdiction. It arrived at that conclusion by applying the canon of constitutional avoidance: "[I]f the existing jurisdictional act be construed to deny the writ to a person entitled to it as a substantive right, the act would be unconstitutional. It should be construed, if possible, to avoid that result." *Eisentrager* v. *Forrestal*, 174 F. 2d 961, 966 (CADC 1949). In cases where there was no territorial jurisdiction over the detainee, the Court of Appeals held, the writ would lie at the place of a respondent with directive power over the detainee. "It is not too violent an interpretation of 'custody' to construe it as including those who have directive custody, as well as those who have immediate custody, where such interpretation is necessary to comply with constitutional requirements. . . . *The statute must be so construed*, lest it be invalid as constituting a suspension of the writ in violation of the constitutional provision." *Id.*, at 967 (emphasis added).[2]

This Court's judgment in *Eisentrager* reversed the Court of Appeals. The opinion was largely devoted to rejecting the lower court's constitutional analysis, since the doctrine of constitutional avoidance underlay its statutory conclusion. But the opinion *had* to pass judgment on whether the statute granted jurisdiction, since that was the basis for the judgments of both lower courts. A conclusion of no constitutionally conferred right would obviously not support reversal of a judgment that rested upon a statutorily conferred right.[3] And absence of a right to the writ under the clear wording of the habeas

---

[2] The parties' submissions to the Court in *Eisentrager* construed the Court of Appeals' decision as I do. See Pet. for Cert., O.T.1949, No. 306, pp. 8–9 ("[T]he court felt constrained to construe the habeas corpus jurisdictional statute – despite its reference to the 'respective jurisdictions' of the various courts and the gloss put on that terminology in the *Ahrens* and previous decisions – to permit a petition to be filed in the district court with territorial jurisdiction over the officials who have directive authority over the immediate jailer in Germany"); Brief for Respondent, O.T.1949, No. 306, p. 9 ("Respondent contends that the U.S. Court of Appeals . . . was correct in its holding that the statute, 28 U.S.C. 2241, provides that the U.S. District Court for the District of Columbia has jurisdiction to entertain the petition for a writ of habeas corpus in the case at bar"). Indeed, the briefing in *Eisentrager* was mainly devoted to the question of whether there was statutory jurisdiction. See, *e.g.*, Brief for Petitioner, O.T.1949, No. 306, pp. 15–59; Brief for Respondent, O.T.1949, No. 306, pp. 9–27, 38–49.

[3] The Court does not seriously dispute my analysis of the Court of Appeals' holding in *Eisentrager*. Instead, it argues that this Court in *Eisentrager* "understood the Court of Appeals' decision to rest on constitutional and not statutory grounds." *Ante*, at 10, n. 8. That is inherently implausible, given that the Court of Appeals' opinion clearly reached a statutory holding, and that both parties argued the case to this Court on that basis, see n. 2, *supra*. The only evidence of misunderstanding the Court adduces today is the *Eisentrager* Court's description of the Court of Appeals' reasoning as "that, although no statutory jurisdiction of such cases is given, courts must be held to possess it as part of the judicial power of the United States. . . ." 339 U.S., at 767. That is no misunderstanding, but an entirely accurate description of the Court of Appeals' reasoning – the

statute is what the *Eisentrager* opinion held: "Nothing in the text of the Constitution extends such a right, *nor does anything in our statutes.*" 339 U.S., at 768 (emphasis added). "[T]hese prisoners at no relevant time were within any territory over which the United States is sovereign, and the scenes of their offense, their capture, their trial and their punishment *were all beyond the territorial jurisdiction of any court of the United States.*" *Id.*, at 777–778. See also *id.*, at 781 (concluding that "no right to the writ of *habeas corpus* appears"); *id.*, at 790 (finding "no basis for invoking federal judicial power in any district"). The brevity of the Court's statutory analysis signifies nothing more than that the Court considered it obvious (as indeed it is) that, unaided by the canon of constitutional avoidance, the statute did not confer jurisdiction over an alien detained outside the territorial jurisdiction of the courts of the United States.

Eisentrager's directly-on-point statutory holding makes it exceedingly difficult for the Court to reach the result it desires today. To do so neatly and cleanly, it must either argue that our decision in *Braden* overruled *Eisentrager*, or admit that *it* is overruling *Eisentrager.* The former course would not pass the laugh test, inasmuch as *Braden* dealt with a detainee held within the territorial jurisdiction of a district court, and never *mentioned Eisentrager*. And the latter course would require the Court to explain why our almost categorical rule of *stare decisis* in statutory cases should be set aside in order to complicate the present war, *and*, having set it aside, to explain why the habeas statute does not mean what it plainly says. So instead the Court tries an oblique course: "*Braden*," it claims, "overruled *the statutory predicate* to *Eisentrager*'s holding," *ante*, at 11 (emphasis added), by which it means the statutory analysis of *Ahrens*. Even assuming, for the moment, that *Braden* overruled some aspect of *Ahrens*, inasmuch as *Ahrens* did not pass upon any of the statutory issues decided by *Eisentrager*, it is hard to see how any of that case's "statutory predicate" could have been impaired.

But in fact *Braden* did not overrule *Ahrens;* it distinguished *Ahrens. Braden* dealt with a habeas petitioner incarcerated in Alabama. The petitioner filed an application for a writ of habeas corpus in Kentucky, challenging an indictment that had been filed against him in that Commonwealth and naming as respondent the Kentucky court in which the proceedings were pending. This Court held that Braden was in custody because a detainer had been issued against him by Kentucky, and was being executed by Alabama, serving as an agent for Kentucky. We found that jurisdiction existed in Kentucky for Braden's petition challenging the Kentucky detainer, notwithstanding his physical confinement in Alabama. *Braden* was careful to *distinguish* that situation from the general rule established in *Ahrens.*

> "A further, *critical* development since our decision in *Ahrens* is the emergence of *new classes of prisoners* who are able to petition for habeas corpus because of the adoption of a more expansive definition of the 'custody' requirement of the habeas statute. The overruling of *McNally* v. *Hill*, 293 U.S. 131 (1934), made it possible for prisoners in custody under one sentence to attack a sentence which they had not yet begun to serve. And it also enabled a petitioner held in one State to attack a detainer lodged against him by another State. In such a case, the State holding the prisoner in immediate confinement

---

penultimate step of that reasoning rather than its conclusion. The Court of Appeals went on to hold that, in light of the constitutional imperative, the statute should be interpreted as supplying jurisdiction. See *Eisentrager* v. *Forrestal*, 174 F. 2d 961, 965–967 (CADC 1949). This Court in *Eisentrager* undoubtedly understood that, which is why it immediately followed the foregoing description with a description of the Court of Appeals' *conclusion* tied to the language of the habeas statute: "[w]here deprivation of liberty by an official act occurs outside the territorial jurisdiction of any District Court, the petition will lie in the District Court which has territorial jurisdiction over officials who have directive power over the immediate jailer." 339 U.S., at 767.

acts as agent for the demanding State, and the custodian State is presumably indifferent to the resolution of the prisoner's attack on the detainer. Here, for example, the petitioner is confined in Alabama, but his dispute is with the Commonwealth of Kentucky, not the State of Alabama. *Under these circumstances*, it would serve no useful purpose to apply the *Ahrens* rule and require that the action be brought in Alabama." 410 U.S., at 498–499 (citations and footnotes omitted; emphases added).

This cannot conceivably be construed as an overturning of the *Ahrens* rule *in other circumstances*. See also *Braden, supra*, at 499–500 (noting that *Ahrens* does not establish "an inflexible jurisdictional rule dictating the choice of an inconvenient forum *even in a class of cases which could not have been foreseen at the time of that decision*" (emphasis added)). Thus, *Braden* stands for the proposition, and only the proposition, that where a petitioner is in custody in multiple jurisdictions within the United States, he may seek a writ of habeas corpus in a jurisdiction in which he suffers legal confinement, though not physical confinement, if his challenge is to that legal confinement. Outside that class of cases, *Braden* did not question the general rule of *Ahrens* (much less that of *Eisentrager*). Where, as here, present physical custody is at issue, *Braden* is inapposite, and *Eisentrager* unquestionably controls.[4]

The considerations of forum convenience that drove the analysis in *Braden* do not call into question *Eisentrager*'s holding. The *Braden* opinion is littered with venue reasoning of the following sort: "The expense and risk of transporting the petitioner to the Western District of Kentucky, should his presence at a hearing prove necessary, would in all likelihood be outweighed by the difficulties of transporting records and witnesses from Kentucky to the district where petitioner is confined." 410 U.S., at 494. Of course nothing could be *more* inconvenient than what the Court (on the alleged authority of *Braden*) prescribes today: a domestic hearing for persons held abroad, dealing with events that transpired abroad.

Attempting to paint *Braden* as a refutation of *Ahrens* (and thereby, it is suggested, *Eisentrager*), today's Court imprecisely describes *Braden* as citing with approval post-*Ahrens* cases in which "habeas petitioners" located overseas were allowed to proceed (without consideration of the jurisdictional issue) in the District Court for the District of Columbia. *Ante*, at 10. In fact, what *Braden* said is that "[w]here *American citizens* confined overseas (and thus outside the territory of any district court) have sought relief

---

[4] The Court points to Court of Appeals cases that have described *Braden* as "overruling" *Ahrens*. See *ante*, at 11, n. 9. Even if that description (rather than what I think the correct one, "distinguishing") is accepted, it would not support the Court's view that *Ahrens* was overruled *with regard to the point on which Eisentrager relied*. The *ratio decidendi* of *Braden* does not call into question the principle of *Ahrens* applied in *Eisentrager*: that habeas challenge to present physical confinement must be made in the district where the physical confinement exists. The Court is unable to produce a single authority that agrees with its conclusion that *Braden* overruled *Eisentrager*.

Justice Kennedy recognizes that *Eisentrager* controls, *ante*, at 1 (opinion concurring in judgment), but misconstrues that opinion. He thinks it makes jurisdiction under the habeas statute turn on the circumstances of the detainees' confinement – including, apparently, the availability of legal proceedings and the length of detention, see *ante*, at 3–4. The *Eisentrager* Court mentioned those circumstances, however, only in the course of its *constitutional* analysis, and not in its application of the statute. It is quite impossible to read §2241 as conditioning its geographic scope upon them. Among the consequences of making jurisdiction turn upon circumstances of confinement are (1) that courts would *always* have authority to inquire into circumstances of confinement, and (2) that the Executive would be unable to know with certainty that any given prisoner-of-war camp is immune from writs of habeas corpus. And among the questions this approach raises: When does definite detention become indefinite? How much process will suffice to stave off jurisdiction? If there is a terrorist attack at Guantanamo Bay, will the area suddenly fall outside the habeas statute because it is no longer "far removed from any hostilities," *ante*, at 3? Justice Kennedy's approach provides enticing law-school-exam imponderables in an area where certainty is called for.

in habeas corpus, we have held, if only implicitly, that the petitioners' absence from the district does not present a jurisdictional obstacle to consideration of the claim." 410 U.S., at 498 (emphasis added). Of course "the existence of unaddressed jurisdictional defects has no precedential effect," *Lewis* v. *Casey*, 518 U.S. 343, 352, n. 2 (1996) (citing cases), but we need not "overrule" those implicit holdings to decide this case. Since *Eisentrager itself* made an exception for such cases, they in no way impugn its holding. "With the citizen," *Eisentrager* said, "we are now little concerned, except to set his case apart *as untouched by this decision* and to take measure of the difference between his status and that of all categories of aliens." 339 U.S., at 769. The constitutional doubt that the Court of Appeals in *Eisentrager* had erroneously attributed to the lack of habeas for an alien abroad might indeed exist with regard to a *citizen* abroad – justifying a strained construction of the habeas statute, or (more honestly) a determination of constitutional right to habeas. Neither party to the present case challenges the atextual extension of the habeas statute to United States citizens held beyond the territorial jurisdictions of the United States courts; but the possibility of one atextual exception thought to be required by the Constitution is no justification for abandoning the clear application of the text to a situation in which it raises no constitutional doubt.

The reality is this: Today's opinion, and today's opinion alone, overrules *Eisentrager;* today's opinion, and today's opinion alone, extends the habeas statute, for the first time, to aliens held beyond the sovereign territory of the United States and beyond the territorial jurisdiction of its courts. No reasons are given for this result; no acknowledgment of its consequences made. By spurious reliance on *Braden* the Court evades explaining why *stare decisis* can be disregarded, *and why Eisentrager was wrong.* Normally, we consider the interests of those who have relied on our decisions. Today, the Court springs a trap on the Executive, subjecting Guantanamo Bay to the oversight of the federal courts even though it has never before been thought to be within their jurisdiction – and thus making it a foolish place to have housed alien wartime detainees.

II

In abandoning the venerable statutory line drawn in *Eisentrager,* the Court boldly extends the scope of the habeas statute to the four corners of the earth. Part III of its opinion asserts that *Braden* stands for the proposition that "a district court acts 'within [its] respective jurisdiction' within the meaning of §2241 as long as 'the custodian can be reached by service of process.'" *Ante,* at 10. Endorsement of that proposition is repeated in Part IV. *Ante,* at 16 ("Section 2241, by its terms, requires nothing more [than the District Court's jurisdiction over petitioners' custodians]").

The consequence of this holding, as applied to aliens outside the country, is breathtaking. It permits an alien captured in a foreign theater of active combat to bring a §2241 petition against the Secretary of Defense. Over the course of the last century, the United States has held millions of alien prisoners abroad. See, *e.g.,* Department of Army, G. Lewis & J. Mewha, History of Prisoner of War Utilization by the United States Army 1776–1945, Pamphlet No. 20-213, p. 244 (1955) (noting that, "[b]y the end of hostilities [in World War II], U.S. forces had in custody approximately two million enemy soldiers"). A great many of these prisoners would no doubt have complained about the circumstances of their capture and the terms of their confinement. The military is currently detaining over 600 prisoners at Guantanamo Bay alone; each detainee undoubtedly has complaints – real or contrived – about those terms and circumstances. The Court's unheralded expansion of federal-court jurisdiction is not even mitigated by a comforting assurance that the legion of ensuing claims will be easily resolved on the merits. To the contrary, the Court says that the "[p]etitioners' allegations ... unquestionably describe 'custody in violation of the Constitution or laws or treaties of the United States.'" *Ante*, at 15, n. 15 (citing *United States* v. *Verdugo-Urquidez*, 494 U.S. 259, 277–278 (1990) (KENNEDY, J., concurring)). From this point forward, federal courts will entertain petitions from these prisoners, and others like them around the world, challenging actions and events far away, and forcing the courts to oversee one aspect of the Executive's conduct of a foreign war.

Today's carefree Court disregards, without a word of acknowledgment, the dire warning of a more circumspect Court in *Eisentrager:*

> "To grant the writ to these prisoners might mean that our army must transport them across the seas for hearing. This would require allocation for shipping space, guarding personnel, billeting and rations. It might also require transportation for whatever witnesses the prisoners desired to call as well as transportation for those necessary to defend legality of the sentence. The writ, since it is held to be a matter of right, would be equally available to enemies during active hostilities as in the present twilight between war and peace. Such trials would hamper the war effort and bring aid and comfort to the enemy. They would diminish the prestige of our commanders, not only with enemies but with wavering neutrals. It would be difficult to devise more effective fettering of a field commander than to allow the very enemies he is ordered to reduce to submission to call him to account in his own civil courts and divert his efforts and attention from the military offensive abroad to the legal defensive at home. Nor is it unlikely that the result of such enemy litigiousness would be conflict between judicial and military opinion highly comforting to enemies of the United States." 339 U.S., at 778–779.

These results should not be brought about lightly, and certainly not without a textual basis in the statute and on the strength of nothing more than a decision dealing with an Alabama prisoner's ability to seek habeas in Kentucky.

III

Part IV of the Court's opinion, dealing with the status of Guantanamo Bay, is a puzzlement. The Court might have made an effort (a vain one, as I shall discuss) to distinguish *Eisentrager* on the basis of a difference between the status of Landsberg Prison in Germany and Guantanamo Bay Naval Base. But Part III flatly rejected such an approach, holding that the place of detention of an alien has no bearing on the statutory availability of habeas relief, but "is strictly relevant only to the question of the appropriate forum." *Ante*, at 11. That rejection is repeated at the end of Part IV: "In the end, the answer to the question presented is clear. . . . No party questions the District Court's jurisdiction over petitioners' custodians. . . . Section 2241, by its terms, requires nothing more." *Ante*, at 15–16. Once that has been said, the status of Guantanamo Bay is entirely irrelevant to the issue here. The habeas statute is (according to the Court) being applied *domestically*, to "petitioners' custodians," and the doctrine that statutes are presumed to have no extraterritorial effect simply has no application.

Nevertheless, the Court spends most of Part IV rejecting respondents' invocation of that doctrine on the peculiar ground that it has no application to Guantanamo Bay. Of course if the Court is right about that, not only §2241 but presumably *all* United States law applies there – including, for example, the federal cause of action recognized in *Bivens* v. *Six Unknown Fed. Narcotics Agents*, 403 U.S. 388 (1971), which would allow prisoners to sue their captors for damages. Fortunately, however, the Court's irrelevant discussion also happens to be wrong.

The Court gives only two reasons why the presumption against extraterritorial effect does not apply to Guantanamo Bay. First, the Court says (without any further elaboration) that "the United States exercises 'complete jurisdiction and control' over the Guantanamo Bay Naval Base [under the terms of a 1903 lease agreement], and may continue to exercise such control permanently if it so chooses [under the terms of a 1934 Treaty]." *Ante*, at 12; see *ante*, at 2–3. But that lease agreement explicitly recognized "the continuance of the ultimate sovereignty of the Republic of Cuba over the [leased areas]," Lease of Lands for Coaling and Naval Stations, Feb. 23, 1903, U.S.-Cuba, Art. III, T.S. No. 418, and the Executive Branch – whose head is "exclusively responsible" for the "conduct of diplomatic and foreign affairs," *Eisentrager, supra*, at 789 – affirms that the lease and treaty do not render Guantanamo Bay the sovereign territory of the United States, see Brief for Respondents 21.

The Court does not explain how "complete jurisdiction and control" without sovereignty causes an enclave to be part of the United States for purposes of its domestic laws. Since "jurisdiction and control" obtained through a lease is no different in effect from "jurisdiction and control" acquired by lawful force of arms, parts of Afghanistan and Iraq should logically be regarded as subject to our domestic laws. Indeed, if "jurisdiction and control" rather than sovereignty were the test, so should the Landsberg Prison in Germany, where the United States held the *Eisentrager* detainees.

The second and last reason the Court gives for the proposition that domestic law applies to Guantanamo Bay is the Solicitor General's concession that there would be habeas jurisdiction over a United States citizen in Guantanamo Bay. "Considering that the statute draws no distinction between Americans and aliens held in federal custody, there is little reason to think that Congress intended the geographical coverage of the statute to vary depending on the detainee's citizenship." *Ante*, at 12–13. But the reason the Solicitor General conceded there would be jurisdiction over a detainee who was a United States citizen had *nothing to do* with the special status of Guantanamo Bay. "Our answer to that question, Justice Souter, is that citizens of the United States, because of their constitutional circumstances, may have greater rights with respect to the scope and reach of the Habeas Statute as the Court has or would interpret it." Tr. of Oral Arg. 40. See also *id.*, at 27–28. And *that* position – the position that United States citizens throughout the world may be entitled to habeas corpus rights – is precisely the position that this Court adopted in *Eisentrager*, see 339 U.S., at 769–770, even while holding that aliens abroad *did not have* habeas corpus rights. Quite obviously, the Court's second reason has no force whatever.

The last part of the Court's Part IV analysis digresses from the point that the presumption against extraterritorial application does not apply to Guantanamo Bay. Rather, it is directed to the contention that the Court's approach to habeas jurisdiction – applying it to aliens abroad – is "consistent with the historical reach of the writ." *Ante*, at 13. None of the authorities it cites comes close to supporting that claim. Its first set of authorities involves claims by aliens detained in what is indisputably domestic territory. *Ante*, at 13, n. 11. Those cases are irrelevant because they do not purport to address the territorial reach of the writ. The remaining cases involve issuance of the writ to "'exempt jurisdictions'" and "other dominions under the sovereign's control." *Ante*, at 13–14, and nn. 12–13. These cases are inapposite for two reasons: Guantanamo Bay is not a sovereign dominion, and even if it were, jurisdiction would be limited to subjects.

"Exempt jurisdictions" – the Cinque Ports and Counties Palatine (located in modern-day England) – were local franchises granted by the Crown. See 1 W. Holdsworth, History of English Law 108, 532 (7th ed. rev.1956); 3 W. Blackstone, Commentaries *78–*79 (hereinafter Blackstone). These jurisdictions were "exempt" in

the sense that the Crown had ceded management of municipal affairs to local authorities, whose courts had exclusive jurisdiction over private disputes among residents
(although review was still available in the royal courts by writ of error). See *id.*, at *79.
Habeas jurisdiction nevertheless extended to those regions on the theory that the delegation of the King's authority did not include his own prerogative writs. *Ibid.*; R. Sharpe,
Law of Habeas Corpus 188–189 (2d ed. 1989) (hereinafter Sharpe). Guantanamo Bay
involves no comparable local delegation of pre-existing sovereign authority.

The cases involving "other dominions under the sovereign's control" fare no better.
These cases stand only for the proposition that the writ extended to dominions of the
Crown outside England proper. The authorities relating to Jersey and the other Channel
Islands, for example, see *ante*, at 14, n. 13, involve territories that are "dominions of the
crown of Great Britain" even though not "part of the kingdom of England," 1 Blackstone
*102–*105, much as were the colonies in America, *id.*, at *104–*105, and Scotland,
Ireland, and Wales, *id.*, at *93. See also *King* v. *Cowle*, 2 Burr. 834, 853–854, 97 Eng.
Rep. 587, 598 (K.B.1759) (even if Berwick was "no part of the realm of England," it
was still a "dominion of the Crown"). All of the dominions in the cases the Court cites –
and all of the territories Blackstone lists as dominions, see 1 Blackstone *93–*106 – are
the sovereign territory of the Crown: colonies, acquisitions and conquests, and so on.
It is an enormous extension of the term to apply it to installations merely leased for a
particular use from another nation that still retains ultimate sovereignty.

The Court's historical analysis fails for yet another reason: To the extent the writ's
"extraordinary territorial ambit" did extend to exempt jurisdictions, outlying dominions, and the like, that extension applied only to British *subjects*. The very sources the
majority relies on say so: Sharpe explains the "broader ambit" of the writ on the ground
that it is "said to depend not on the ordinary jurisdiction of the court for its effectiveness, but upon the authority of the sovereign over all her *subjects*." Sharpe, *supra*,
at 188 (emphasis added). Likewise, Blackstone explained that the writ "run[s] into all
parts of the king's dominions" because "the king is at all times entitled to have an account why the liberty of any of his *subjects* is restrained." 3 Blackstone *131 (emphasis
added). *Ex parte Mwenya*, [1960] 1 Q. B. 241 (C. A.), which can hardly be viewed as
evidence of the *historic* scope of the writ, only confirms the ongoing relevance of the
sovereign-subject relationship to the scope of the writ. There, the question was whether
"the Court of Queen's Bench can be debarred from making an order in favour of a
British citizen unlawfully or arbitrarily detained" in Northern Rhodesia, which was at
the time a protectorate of the Crown. *Id.*, at 300 (Lord Evershed M. R.). Each judge
made clear that the detainee's status as a subject was material to the resolution of the
case. See *id.*, at 300, 302 (Lord Evershed, M. R.); *id.*, at 305 (Romer, L. J.) ("[I]t is difficult to see why the sovereign should be deprived of her right to be informed through
her High Court as to the validity of the detention of her subjects in that territory");
id., at 311 (Sellers, L.J.) ("I am not prepared to say, as we are solely asked to say on
this appeal, that the English courts have no jurisdiction in any circumstances to entertain an application for a writ of habeas corpus ad subjiciendum in respect of an
unlawful detention of a British subject in a British protectorate"). None of the exempt-
jurisdiction or dominion cases the Court cites involves someone not a subject of the
Crown.

The rule against issuing the writ to aliens in foreign lands was still the law when,
in *In re Ning Yi-Ching*, 56 T. L. R. 3 (Vacation Ct. 1939), an English court considered the
habeas claims of four Chinese subjects detained on criminal charges in Tientsin, China,
an area over which Britain had by treaty acquired a lease and "therewith exercised
certain rights of administration and control." *Id.*, at 4. The court held that Tientsin was

a foreign territory, and that the writ would not issue to a foreigner detained there. The Solicitor-General had argued that "[t]here was no case on record in which a writ of *habeas corpus* had been obtained on behalf of a foreign subject on foreign territory," *id.*, at 5, and the court "listened in vain for a case in which the writ of *habeas corpus* had issued in respect of a foreigner detained in a part of the world which was not a part of the King's dominions or realm," *id.*, at 6.[5]

In sum, the Court's treatment of Guantanamo Bay, like its treatment of §2241, is a wrenching departure from precedent.[6]

* * *

Departure from our rule of *stare decisis* in statutory cases is always extraordinary; it ought to be unthinkable when the departure has a potentially harmful effect upon the Nation's conduct of a war. The Commander in Chief and his subordinates had every reason to expect that the internment of combatants at Guantanamo Bay would not have the consequence of bringing the cumbersome machinery of our domestic courts into military affairs. Congress is in session. If it wished to change federal judges' habeas jurisdiction from what this Court had previously held that to be, it could have done so. And it could have done so by intelligent revision of the statute,[7] instead of by today's clumsy, countertextual reinterpretation that confers upon wartime prisoners greater habeas rights than domestic detainees. The latter must challenge their present physical confinement in the district of their confinement, see *Rumsfeld* v. *Padilla*, *ante*, whereas under today's strange holding Guantanamo Bay detainees can petition in any of the 94 federal judicial districts. The fact that extraterritorially located detainees lack the district of detention that the statute requires has been converted from a factor that precludes their ability to bring a petition at all into a factor that frees them to petition wherever they wish – and, as a result, to forum shop. For this Court to create such a monstrous scheme in time of war, and in frustration of our military commanders' reliance upon clearly stated prior law, is judicial adventurism of the worst sort. I dissent.

---

[5] The Court argues at some length that *Ex parte Mwenya*, [1960] 1 Q. B. 241 (C. A.), calls into question my reliance on *In re Ning Yi-Ching*. See *ante*, at 15, n. 14. But as I have explained, see *supra*, at 17–18, *Mwenya* dealt with a British subject and the court went out of its way to explain that its expansive description of the scope of the writ was premised on that fact. The Court cites not a single case holding that aliens held outside the territory of the sovereign were within reach of the writ.

[6] The Court grasps at two other bases for jurisdiction: the Alien Tort Statute (ATS), 28 U.S.C. §1350, and the federal-question statute, 28 U.S.C. §1331. The former is not presented to us. The ATS, while invoked below, was repudiated as a basis for jurisdiction by all petitioners, either in their petition for certiorari, in their briefing before this Court, or at oral argument. See Pet. for Cert. in No. 03-334, p. 2, n. 1 ("Petitioners withdraw any reliance on the Alien Tort Claims Act . . ."); Brief for Petitioners in No. 03-343, p. 13; Tr. of Oral Arg. 6.

   With respect to §1331, petitioners assert a variety of claims arising under the Constitution, treaties, and laws of the United States. In *Eisentrager*, though the Court's holding focused on §2241, its analysis spoke more broadly: "We have pointed out that the privilege of litigation has been extended to aliens, whether friendly or enemy, only because permitting their presence in the country implied protection. No such basis can be invoked here, for these prisoners at no relevant time were within any territory over which the United States is sovereign, and the scenes of their offense, their capture, their trial and their punishment were all beyond the territorial jurisdiction of any court of the United States." 339 U.S., at 777–778. That reasoning dooms petitioners' claims under §1331, at least where Congress has erected a jurisdictional bar to their raising such claims in habeas.

[7] It could, for example, provide for jurisdiction by placing Guantanamo Bay within the territory of an existing district court; or by creating a district court for Guantanamo Bay, as it did for the Panama Canal Zone, see 22 U.S.C. §3841(a) (repealed 1979).

1/31/2005: DISTRICT COURT MEMO *IN RE* GUANTANAMO DETAINEE CASES*

**UNITED STATES DISTRICT COURT
FOR THE DISTRICT OF COLUMBIA**

	)
	)
	)
	)
In re **Guantanamo Detainee Cases**	)
	)
	)
	)
	)
	)

Civil Action Nos.
02-CV-0299 (CKK), 02-CV-0828 (CKK),
02-CV-1130 (CKK), 04-CV-1135 (ESH),
04-CV-1136 (JDB), 04-CV-1137 (RMC),
04-CV-1144 (RWR), 04-CV-1164 (RBW),
04-CV-1194 (HHK), 04-CV-1227 (RBW),
04-CV-1254 (HHK)

**MEMORANDUM OPINION DENYING IN PART AND
GRANTING IN PART RESPONDENTS' MOTION TO DISMISS
OR FOR JUDGMENT AS A MATTER OF LAW**

These eleven coordinated habeas cases were filed by detainees held as "enemy combatants" at the United States Naval Base at Guantanamo Bay, Cuba. Presently pending is the government's motion to dismiss or for judgment as a matter of law regarding all claims filed by all petitioners, including claims based on the United States Constitution, treaties, statutes, regulations, the common law, and customary international law. Counsel filed numerous briefs addressing issues raised in the motion and argued their positions at a hearing in early December 2004. Upon consideration of all filings submitted in these cases and the arguments made at the hearing, and for the reasons stated below, the Court concludes that the petitioners have stated valid claims under the Fifth Amendment to the United States Constitution and that the procedures implemented by the government to confirm that the petitioners are "enemy combatants" subject to indefinite detention violate the petitioners' rights to due process of law. The Court also holds that at least some of the petitioners have stated valid claims under the Third Geneva Convention. Finally, the Court holds that the government is entitled to the dismissal of the petitioners' remaining claims.

Because this Memorandum Opinion references classified material, it is being issued in two versions. The official version is unredacted and is being filed with the Court Security Officer at the U.S. Department of Justice responsible for the management of classified information in these cases. The Court Security Officer will maintain possession of the original, distribute copies to counsel with the appropriate security clearances in accordance with the procedures earlier established in these cases, and ensure that the document is transmitted to the Court of Appeals should an appeal be taken. Classified information in the official version is highlighted in gray to alert the reader to the specific material that may not be released to the public. The other version of the Memorandum Opinion contains redactions of all classified information and, in an abundance of caution, portions of any discussions that might lead to the discovery of classified

---

* Redactions in the text of this document are in the original. The original is stamped "UNCLASSIFIED VERSION FOR PUBLIC RELEASE" on each page. – *Eds.*

information. The redacted version is being posted in the electronic dockets of the cases and is available for public review.

I. BACKGROUND

In response to the horrific and unprecedented terrorist attacks by al Qaeda against the United States of America on September 11, 2001, Congress passed a joint resolution authorizing the President "to use all necessary and appropriate force against those nations, organizations, or persons he determines planned, authorized, committed, or aided the terrorist attacks . . . , or harbored such organizations or persons, in order to prevent any future acts of international terrorism against the United States by such nations, organizations or persons." Authorization for Use of Military Force, Pub. L. No. 107–40, §2(a), 115 Stat. 224 (2001) (hereinafter "AUMF"). In accordance with the AUMF, President George W. Bush ordered the commencement of military operations in Afghanistan against al Qaeda and the Taliban regime, which harbored the terrorist organization. During the course of the military campaign, United States forces took custody of numerous individuals who were actively fighting against allied forces on Afghan soil. Many of these individuals were deemed by military authorities to be "enemy combatants" and, beginning in early 2002, were transferred to facilities at the United States Naval Base at Guantanamo Bay, Cuba, where they continue to be detained by U.S. authorities.

In addition to belligerents captured during the heat of war in Afghanistan, the U.S. authorities are also detaining at Guantanamo Bay pursuant to the AUMF numerous individuals who were captured hundreds or thousands of miles from a battle zone in the traditional sense of that term. For example, detainees at Guantanamo Bay who are presently seeking habeas relief in the United States District Court for the District of Columbia include men who were taken into custody as far away from Afghanistan as Gambia,[1] Zambia,[2] Bosnia,[3] and Thailand.[4] Some have already been detained as long as three years[5] while others have been captured as recently as September 2004.[6] Although many of these individuals may never have been close to an actual battlefield and may never have raised conventional arms against the United States or its allies, the military nonetheless has deemed them detainable as "enemy combatants" based on conclusions that they have ties to al Qaeda or other terrorist organizations.

All of the individuals who have been detained at Guantanamo Bay have been categorized to fall within a general class of people the administration calls "enemy combatants." It is the government's position that once someone has been properly designated as such, that person can be held indefinitely until the end of America's war on terrorism or until the military determines on a case by case basis that the particular detainee no longer poses a threat to the United States or its allies. Within the general set of "enemy combatants" is a subset of individuals whom the administration decided to prosecute for war crimes before a military commission established pursuant to a Military Order issued by President Bush on November 13, 2001. Detention, Treatment, and Trial of Certain Non-Citizens in the War Against Terrorism, 66 Fed. Reg. 57,833 (Nov. 13, 2001). Should individuals be prosecuted and convicted in accordance with the Military Order,

---

[1] Jamil El-Banna and Bisher Al-Rawi, petitioners in El-Banna v. Bush, 04-CV-1144 (RWR).

[2] Martin Mubanga, petitioner in El-Banna v. Bush, 04-CV-1 144 (RWR).

[3] Lakhdar Boumediene, Mohammed Nechle, Hadj Boudella, Belkacem Bensayah, Mustafa Ait Idr, and Saber Lahmar, petitioners in Boumediene v. Bush, 04-CV-1166 (RJL).

[4] Saifullah Paracha, petitioner in Paracha v. Bush, 04-CV-2022 (PLF).

[5] E.g., the petitioners in Al Odah v. Bush, 02-CV-0828 (CKK).

[6] E.g. Saifullah Paracha in Paracha v. Bush, 04-CV-2022 (PLF).

they would be subject to sentences with fixed terms of incarceration or other specific penalties.

Since the beginning of the military's detention operations at Guantanamo Bay in early 2002, detainees subject to criminal prosecution have been bestowed with more rights than detainees whom the military did not intend to prosecute formally for war crimes. For example, the military regulations governing the prosecutions of detainees required a formal notice of charges, a presumption of innocence of any crime until proven guilty, a right to counsel, pretrial disclosure to the defense team of exculpatory evidence and of evidence the prosecution intends to use at trial, the right to call reasonably available witnesses, the right to have defense counsel cross-examine prosecution witnesses, the right to have defense counsel attend every portion of the trial proceedings even where classified information is presented, and the right to an open trial with the press present, at least for those portions not involving classified information. See Procedures for Trials by Military Commissions of Certain Non-United States Citizens in the War Against Terrorism, 32 C.F.R. §§9.1 et seq. (2005). Although detainees at Guantanamo Bay not subject to prosecution could suffer the same fate as those convicted of war crimes – potentially life in prison, depending on how long America's war on terrorism lasts – they were not given any significant procedural rights to challenge their status as alleged "enemy combatants," at least until relatively recently. From the beginning of 2002 through at least June 2004, the substantial majority of detainees not charged with war crimes were not informed of the bases upon which they were detained, were not permitted access to counsel, were not given a formal opportunity to challenge their "enemy combatant" status, and were alleged to be held virtually incommunicado from the outside world. Whether those individuals deemed "enemy combatants" are entitled under the United States Constitution and other laws to any rights and, if so, the scope of those rights is the focus of the government's motion to dismiss and this Memorandum Opinion.[7]

In the wake of the Supreme Court's decision in Rasul, several new habeas cases were filed on behalf of Guantanamo detainees in addition to those cases that were remanded by the Court as part of Rasul. As of the end of July 2004, thirteen cases involving more than sixty detainees were pending before eight Judges in this District Court. On July 23, 2004, the respondents filed a motion to consolidate all of the cases pending at that time. The motion was denied without prejudice three days later. On August 4, 2004, the respondents filed a motion seeking coordination of legal issues common to all cases. By order dated August 17, 2004, Judge Gladys Kessler on behalf of the Calendar and Case Management Committee granted the motion in part, designating this Judge to coordinate and manage all proceedings in the pending matters and, to the extent necessary, rule on procedural and substantive issues common to the cases. An Executive Session Resolution dated September 15, 2004 further clarified that this Judge would

---

[7] In a decision issued on November 8, 2004, Judge James Robertson ruled that the procedures for trying Guantanamo detainees for alleged war crimes by military commission were unlawful for failing to comply with the requirements for courts martial set forth in the Uniform Code of Military Justice. Hamdan v. Rumsfeld, 344 F. Supp.2d 152 (D.D.C. 2004). Only one of the detainees in the above-captioned cases has been given notice that he will be tried for war crimes. That detainee, David Hicks, a petitioner in Hicks v. Bush, 02-CV-0299 (CKK), has filed a separate motion for partial summary judgment challenging the legality of the military commission procedures. Pursuant to an order issued in that case on December 15, 2004, resolution of that motion is being held in abeyance pending final resolution of all appeals in Hamdan. This Memorandum Opinion does not address the legality of the military commission proceedings but rather focuses on the issue of the rights of detainees with respect to their classification as "enemy combatants" regardless of whether they have been formally charged with a war crime.

identify and delineate both procedural and substantive issues common to all or some of these cases and, as consented to by the transferring judge in each case, rule on common procedural issues. The Resolution also provided that to the extent additional consent was given by the transferring Judges, this Judge would address specified common substantive issues. The Resolution concluded by stating that any Judge who did not agree with any substantive decision made by this Judge could resolve the issue in his or her own case as he or she deemed appropriate. Although issues and motions were transferred to this Judge, the cases themselves have remained before the assigned Judges.

After two informal status conferences discussing, among other issues, the factual bases for the government's detention of the petitioners, this Judge issued a scheduling order requiring the respondents to file responsive pleadings showing cause why writs of habeas corpus and the relief sought by petitioners should not be granted. The order also incorporated the respondents' proposed schedule for the filing of factual returns identifying the specific bases upon which they claim the government is entitled to detain each petitioner at Guantanamo Bay as an "enemy combatant." Although most of the detainees had already been held as "enemy combatants" for more than two years and had been subjected to unspecified "multiple levels of review," the respondents chose to submit as factual support for their detention of the petitioners the records from the CSRT proceedings, which had only commenced in late August or early September 2004. Those factual returns were filed with the Court on a rolling basis as the CSRT proceedings were completed, with the earliest submitted on September 17, 2004 and the latest on December 30, 2004. Because every complete CSRT record contained classified information, respondents filed redacted, unclassified versions on the public record, submitted the full, classified versions for the Court's in camera review, and served on counsel for the petitioners with appropriate security clearances versions containing most of the classified information disclosed in the Court's copies but redacting some classified information that respondents alleged would not exculpate the detainees from their "enemy combatant" status.

During the fall, the Court resolved numerous procedural issues common to all cases, Among other matters, the Court ruled that the cases should not be transferred to the Eastern District of Virginia, where the primary respondent, Secretary of Defense Donald Rumsfeld, maintains his office,[11] ruled on protective order issues,[12] and granted the petitioners certain rights relating to access to counsel to assist in the litigation of these cases.[13]

On October 4, 2004, the respondents filed their Response to Petitions for Writ of Habeas Corpus and Motion to Dismiss or for Judgment as a Matter of Law in all thirteen cases pending before the Court at that time. Counsel for petitioners filed a joint opposition on November 5, 2004, which was supplemented by additional filings specific to the petitions filed in Al Odah v. United States, 02-CV-0828 (CKK); El-Banna v. Bush, 04-CV-1144 (RWR); and Boumediene v. Bush, 04-CV-1166 (RJL). Respondents filed replies in support of their original motion. The motions to dismiss in eleven of the thirteen cases were transferred by separate orders issued by the assigned Judges in accordance with the procedures set forth for the resolution of substantive matters in

---

[11] Gherebi v. Bush, 338 F. Supp.2d 91 (D.D.C. 2004).

[12] November 8, 2004 Amended Protective Order and Procedures for Counsel Access to Detainees at the United States Naval Base in Guantanamo Bay, Cuba, 344 F. Supp.2d 174 (D.D.C. 2004).

[13] Id.

the September 15, 2004 Executive Resolution.[14] This Court held oral argument for the eleven cases with transferred motions on December 1, 2004. Subsequently, eight more habeas cases were filed on behalf of Guantanamo detainees.[15] Although this Memorandum Opinion addresses issues common to those new cases, counsel in those cases have not yet had the opportunity to fully brief or argue the issues on their own behalf. Accordingly, while the Judges assigned to those cases are free, of course, to adopt the reasoning contained in this Memorandum Opinion in resolving those motions, this Memorandum Opinion technically applies only to the eleven cases contained in the above caption.

II. ANALYSIS

The petitioners in these eleven cases allege that the detention at Guantanamo Bay and the conditions thereof violate a variety of laws. All petitions assert violations of the Fifth Amendment, and a majority claim violations of the Alien Tort Claims Act,[16] the Administrative Procedure Act,[17] and the Geneva Conventions.[18] In addition, certain petitions allege violations of the Sixth, Eighth, and Fourteenth Amendments; the War Powers Clause;[19] the Suspension Clause;[20] Army Regulation 190–8, entitled "Enemy Prisoners of War, Retained Personnel, Civilian Internees and Other Detainees;" the International Covenant on Civil and Political Rights ("ICCPR");[21] the American Declaration on the Rights and Duties of Man ("ADRDM");[22] the Optional Protocol to the Convention on the Rights of the Child on the Involvement of Children in Armed Conflict;[23] the International Labour Organization's Convention 182, Concerning the Prohibition and Immediate Action for the Elimination of the Worst Forms of Child Labour;[24] and customary international law. The respondents contend that none of these provisions constitutes a valid basis for any of the petitioners' claims and seek dismissal of all counts as a matter of law under Fed. R. Civ. P. 12(b)(6) for failing to state a claim upon which relief can be granted. In the alternative, the respondents seek a judgment based on the pleadings pursuant to Fed. R. Civ. P.12(c). The respondents have not requested entry of summary judgment pursuant to Fed. R. Civ. P. 56, and they have opposed requests for discovery made by counsel for the petitioners on the ground that those requests are premature at this stage of the proceedings. See, e.g., Respondents' Memorandum in Opposition to Petitioners' Motion for Leave to Take Discovery and For Preservation Order, filed January 12, 2005, at 6.

In addressing a motion to dismiss for failure to state a claim upon which relief can be granted pursuant to Fed. R. Civ. P. 12(b)(6), the Court must accept as true all factual allegations contained in a petition and must resolve every factual inference in

---

[14] As was his prerogative, Judge Richard Leon did not transfer the motions to dismiss in his two Guantanamo cases, Khalid v. Bush, 04-CV-1142 (RJL) and Boumediene v. Bush, 04CV-1166 (RJL), and this Memorandum Opinion therefore does not apply to those two cases.

[15] Belmar v. Bush, 04-CV-1897 (RMC); Al Qosi v. Bush, 04-CV-1937 (PLF); Paracha v. Bush, 04-CV-2022 (PLF); Al-Marri v. Bush, 04-CV-2035 (GK); Zemiri v. Bush, 04-CV-2046 (CKK); Deghayes v. Bush, 04-CV-2215 (RMC); Mustapha v. Bush, 05-CV-0022 (JR); and Abdullah v. Bush, 05-CV-0023 (RWR).

[16] 28 U.S.C. §1350 (1993).

[17] 5 U.S.C. §§555, 702, 706 (1996).

[18] (Third) Geneva Convention Relative to the Treatment of Prisoners of War of Aug. 12, 1949, 6 U.S.T. 3316; and Fourth Geneva Convention, 1956 WL 54810 (U.S. Treaty), T.I.A.S. No. 3365, 6 U.S.T. 3516.

[19] U.S. Const. art. I, §8, cl. 11.

[20] U.S. Const. art. I, §9, cl. 2.

[21] 999 U.N.T.S. 171, 6 I.L.M. 368 (1992), and 102d Cong., 138 Cong. Rec. S4781 (Apr. 2, 1992).

[22] O.A.S. Off. Rec. OEA/Ser. LV/I.4 Rev. (1965).

[23] S. Treaty Doc. No. 106–37, 2000 WL 33366017.

[24] S. Treaty Doc. No. 106-5, 1999 WL 33292717.

the petitioner's favor. Sparrow v. United Air Lines, Inc., 216 F.3d 1111, 1113 (D.C. Cir. 2000). The moving party is entitled to dismissal "only if it is clear that no relief could be granted under any set of facts that could be proved consistent with the allegations." Croixland Properties Ltd. Partnership v. Corcoran, 174 F.3d 213, 215 (D.C. Cir. 1999) (quoting Hishon v. King & Spalding, 467 U.S. 69 (1984)). Similarly, in resolving a motion for judgment on the pleadings pursuant to Fed. R. Civ. P. 12(c), the Court must "accept as true the allegations in the opponent's pleadings, and as false all controverted assertions of the movant" and must "accord the benefit of all reasonable inferences to the non-moving party." Haynesworth v. Miller, 820 F.2d 1245, 1249 n.11 (D.C. Cir. 1987).

. . .

B. SPECIFIC REQUIREMENTS OF THE FIFTH AMENDMENT'S DUE PROCESS CLAUSE

Having found that the Guantanamo detainees are entitled to due process under the Fifth Amendment to the United States Constitution, the Court must now address the exact contours of that right as it applies to the government's determinations that they are "enemy combatants." Due process is an inherently flexible concept, and the specific process due in a particular circumstance depends upon the context in which the right is asserted. Morrissey v. Brewer, 408 U.S. 471, 481 (1972). Resolution of a due process challenge requires the consideration and weighing of three factors: the private interest of the person asserting the lack of due process; the risk of erroneous deprivation of that interest through use of existing procedures and the probable value of additional or substitute procedural safeguards; and the competing interests of the government, including the financial, administrative, and other burdens that would be incurred were additional safeguards to be provided. Mathews v. Eldridge, 424 U.S 319, 335 (1976).

The Supreme Court applied a Mathews v. Eldridge analysis in Hamdi v. Rumsfeld, ____ U.S. ____, 124 S. Ct. 2633 (2004), a decision issued the same day as Rasul which consideredan American citizen's due process challenge to the U.S. military's designation of him as an "enemy combatant." Although none of the detainees in the cases before this Court is an American citizen, the facts under Hamdi are otherwise identical in all material respects to those in Rasul. Accordingly, Hamdi forms both the starting point and core of this Court's consideration of what process is due to the Guantanamo detainees in these cases.

In addressing the detainee's private interest in Hamdi for purposes of the Mathews v. Eldridge analysis, the plurality opinion called it "the most elemental of liberty interests – the interest in being free from physical detention by one's own government." 124 S. Ct. at 2646. Although the detainees in the cases before this Court are aliens and are therefore not being detained by their own governments, that fact does not lessen the significance of their interests in freedom from incarceration and from being held virtually incommunicado from the outside world. There is no practical difference between incarceration at the hands of one's own government and incarceration at the hands of a foreign government; significant liberty is deprived in both situations regardless of the jailer's nationality.

As was the case in Hamdi, the potential length of incarceration is highly relevant to the weighing of the individual interests at stake here. The government asserts the right to detain an "enemy combatant" until the wax on terrorism has concluded or until the Executive, in its sole discretion, has determined that the individual no longer poses a threat to national security. The government, however, has been unable to inform the

Court how long it believes the war on terrorism will last. See December 1, 2004 Transcript of Motion to Dismiss (hereinafter "Transcript") at 22–23. Indeed, the government cannot even articulate at this moment how it will determine when the war on terrorism has ended. Id. at 24. At a minimum, the government has conceded that the war could last several generations, thereby making it possible, if not likely, that "enemy combatants" will be subject to terms of life imprisonment at Guantanamo Bay. Id. at 21; Hamdi, 124. S. Ct. at 2641. Short of the death penalty, life imprisonment is the ultimate deprivation of liberty, and the uncertainty of whether the war on terror – and thus the period of incarceration – will last a lifetime may be even worse than if the detainees had been tried, convicted, and definitively sentenced to a fixed term.

It must be added that the liberty interests of the detainees cannot be minimized for purposes of applying the Mathews v. Eldridge balancing test by the government's allegations that they are in fact terrorists or are affiliated with terrorist organizations. The purpose of imposing a due process requirement is to prevent mistaken characterizations and erroneous detentions, and the government is not entitled to short circuit this inquiry by claiming ab initio that the individuals are alleged to have committed bad acts. See Hamdi, 124 S. Ct. at 2647 ("our starting point for the Mathews v. Eldridge analysis is unaltered by the allegations surrounding the particular detainee or the organizations with which he is alleged to have associated"). Moreover, all petitioners in these cases have asserted that they are not terrorists and have not been involved in terrorist activities, and under the standards provided by the applicable rules of procedure, those allegations must be accepted as true for purposes of resolving the government's motion to dismiss.

On the other side of the Mathews v. Eldridge analysis is the government's significant interest in safeguarding national security. Having served as the Chief Judge of the United States Foreign Intelligence Surveillance Court (also known as "the FISA Court"), the focus of which involves national security and international terrorism,[29] this Judge is keenly aware of the determined efforts of terrorist groups and others to attack this country and to harm American citizens both at home and abroad. Utmost vigilance is crucial for the protection of the United States of America. Of course, one of the government's most important obligations is to safeguard this country and its citizens by ensuring that those who have brought harm upon U.S. interests are not permitted to do so again. Congress itself expressly recognized this when it enacted the AUMF authorizing the President to use all necessary and appropriate force against those responsible for the September 11 attacks. The Supreme Court also gave significant weight to this governmental concern and responsibility in Hamdi when it addressed the "interests in ensuring that those who have in fact fought with the enemy during a war do not return to battle against the United States." 124 S. Ct. at 2647. The plurality warned against naivete regarding the dangers posed to the United States by terrorists and noted that the legislative and executive branches were in the best positions to deal with those dangers. As articulated by the plurality, "[T]he law of war and the realities of combat may render . . . detentions both necessary and appropriate, and our due process analysis need not blink at those realities. Without doubt, our Constitution recognizes that core strategic matters of warmaking belong in the hands of those who are best positioned and most politically accountable for making them." Id. Indeed, a majority of the Court affirmed the Executive's authority to seize and detain Taliban fighters as long as the conflict in

---

[29] See 50 U.S.C. §1803 (2003).

Afghanistan continues, regardless of how indefinite the length of that war may be. See the plurality opinion, id. at 2641–42, and the dissenting opinion of Justice Thomas, id. at 2674.

Given the existence of competing, highly significant interests on both sides of the equation – the liberty of individuals asserting complete innocence of any terrorist activity versus the obligation of the government to protect this country against terrorist attacks – the question becomes what procedures will help ensure that innocents are not indefinitely held as "enemy combatants" without imposing undue burdens on the military to ensure the security of this nation and its citizens. The four member Hamdi plurality answered this question in some detail, and although the two concurring members of the Court, Justice Souter and Justice Ginsburg, emphasized a different basis for ruling in favor of Mr. Hamdi, they indicated their agreement that, at a minimum, he was entitled to the procedural protections set forth by the plurality. Id. at 2660.

According to the plurality in Hamdi, an individual detained by the government on the ground that he is an "enemy combatant" "must receive notice of the factual basis for his classification, and a fair opportunity to rebut the Government's factual assertions before a neutral decisionmaker." Id. at 2648. Noting the potential burden these requirements might cause the government at a time of ongoing military conflict, the plurality stated that it would not violate due process for the decision maker to consider hearsay as the most reliable available evidence. Id. at 2649. In addition, the plurality declared it permissible to adopt a presumption in favor of "enemy combatant" status, "so long as that presumption remained a rebuttable one and fair opportunity for rebuttal were provided." Id. For that presumption to apply and for the onus to shift to the detainee, however, the plurality clarified that the government first would have to "put[] forth credible evidence that the [detainee] meets the enemy-combatant criteria." Id.[30]

After setting forth these standards, the plurality suggested the "possibility" that constitutional requirements of due process could be met by an "appropriately authorized and properly constituted military tribunal" and referenced the military tribunals used to determine whether an individual is entitled to prisoner of war status under the Geneva Convention. Id. at 2651 (citing Enemy Prisoners of War, Retained Personnel, Civilian Internees and Other Detainees, Army Regulation 190–8, §1–6 (1997)). In the absence of a tribunal following constitutionally mandated procedures, however, the plurality declared that it was the District Court's obligation to provide those procedural rights to the detainee in a habeas action. Again recognizing the enormous significance of the interests of both detainees and the government, the plurality affirmed the proper role of the judiciary in these matters, stating "We have no reason to doubt that courts faced with these sensitive matters will pay proper heed both to the matters of national security that might arise in an individual case and to the constitutional limitations safeguarding essential liberties that remain vibrant even in times of security concerns." Id. at 2652. The plurality concluded by affirming that the detainee "unquestionably [had] the right to access to counsel in connection with the proceedings on remand." Id.

Hamdi was decided before the creation of the Combatant Status Review Tribunal, and the respondents contend in their motion to dismiss that were this Court

---

[30] Justice Souter, whose opinion was joined by Justice Ginsburg, indicated he did not believe that such a presumption was constitutionally permissible when he wrote, "I do not mean to imply agreement that the Government could claim an evidentiary presumption casting the burden of rebuttal on [the detainee]." Id. at 2660.

to conclude that the detainees are entitled to due process under the Fifth Amendment, the CSRT proceedings would fully comply with all constitutional requirements. More specifically, the respondents claim that the CSRT regulations were modeled after Army Regulation 190–8 governing the determination of prisoner of war status, referenced in <u>Hamdi</u>, and actually exceed the requirements set forth by the <u>Hamdi</u> plurality. For example, respondents cite the facts that under CSRT rules, tribunal members must certify that they have not been involved in the "apprehension, detention, interrogation, or previous determination of status of the detainee[s]," that detainees are provided a "Personal Representative" to assist in the preparation of their cases, that the "Recorder" – that is, the person who presents evidence in support of "enemy combatant" status – must search for exculpatory evidence, that the detainee is entitled to an unclassified summary of the evidence against him, and that the tribunal's decisions are reviewed by a higher authority. Motion to Dismiss at 34–35. Notwithstanding the procedures cited by the respondents, the Court finds that the procedures provided in the CSRT regulations fail to satisfy constitutional due process requirements in several respects.

C. SPECIFIC CONSTITUTIONAL DEFECTS IN THE CSRT PROCESS AS WRITTEN IN THE REGULATIONS AND AS APPLIED TO THE DETAINEES

The constitutional defects in the CSRT procedures can be separated into two categories. The first category consists of defects which apply across the board to all detainees in the cases before this Judge. Specifically, those deficiencies are the CSRT's failure to provide the detainees with access to material evidence upon which the tribunal affirmed their "enemy combatant" status and the failure to permit the assistance of counsel to compensate for the government's refusal to disclose classified information directly to the detainees. The second category of defects involves those which are detainee specific and may or may not apply to every petitioner in this litigation. Those defects include the manner in which the CSRT handled accusations of torture and the vague and potentially overbroad definition of "enemy combatant" in the CSRT regulations. While additional specific defects may or may not exist, further inquiry is unnecessary at this stage of the litigation given the fundamental deficiencies detailed below.

1. General Defects Existing in All Cases Before the Court: Failure to Provide Detainees Access to Material Evidence Upon Which the CSRT Affirmed "Enemy Combatant" Status and Failure to Permit the Assistance of Counsel

The CSRT reviewed classified information when considering whether each detainee presently before this Court should be considered an "enemy combatant," and it appears that all of the CSRT's decisions substantially relied upon classified evidence. No detainee, however, was ever permitted access to any classified information nor was any detainee permitted to have an advocate review and challenge the classified evidence on his behalf. Accordingly, the CSRT failed to provide any detainee with sufficient notice of the factual basis for which he is being detained and with a fair opportunity to rebut the government's evidence supporting the determination that he is an "enemy combatant."

The inherent lack of fairness of the CSRT's consideration of classified information not disclosed to the detainees is perhaps most vividly illustrated in the following unclassified colloquy, which, though taken from a case not presently before this Judge, exemplifies the practical and severe disadvantages faced by all Guantanamo prisoners. In reading a list of allegations forming the basis for the detention of Mustafa Ait Idr,[31] a petitioner in Boumediene v. Bush, 04-CV-1166 (RJL), the Recorder of the CSRT asserted, "While living in Bosnia, the Detainee associated with a known Al Qaida operative." In response, the following exchange occurred:

> Detainee: Give me his name.
>
> Tribunal President: I do not know.
>
> Detainee: How can I respond to this?
>
> Tribunal President: Did you know of anybody that was a member of Al Qaida?
>
> Detainee: No, no.
>
> Tribunal President: I'm sorry, what was your response?
>
> Detainee: No.
>
> Tribunal President: No?
>
> Detainee: No. This is something the interrogators told me a long while ago. I asked the interrogators to tell me who this person was. Then I could tell you if I might have known this person, but not if this person is a terrorist. Maybe I knew this person as a friend. Maybe it was a person that worked with me. Maybe it was a person that was on my team. But I do not know if this person is Bosnian, Indian or whatever. If you tell me the name, then I can respond and defend myself against this accusation.
>
> Tribunal President: We are asking you the questions and we need you to respond to what is on the unclassified summary.

Respondents' Factual Return to Petition for Writ of Habeas Corpus by Petitioner Mustafa Air Idir, filed October 27, 2004, Enclosure (3) at 13. Subsequently, after the Recorder read the allegation that the detainee was arrested because of his alleged involvement in a plan to attack the U.S. Embassy in Sarajevo, the detainee expressly asked in the following colloquy to see the evidence upon which the government's assertion relied:

> Detainee: …The only thing I can tell you is I did not plan or even think of [attacking the Embassy]. Did you find any explosives with me? Any weapons? Did you find me in front of the embassy? Did you find me in contact with the Americans? Did I threaten anyone? I am prepared now to tell you, if you have anything or any evidence, even if it is just very little, that proves I went to the embassy and looked like that [Detainee made a gesture with his head and neck as if he were looking into a building or a window] at the embassy, then I am ready to be punished. I can just tell you that I did not plan anything. Point by point, when we get to the point that I am associated with Al Qaida, but we already did that one.
>
> Recorder: It was [the] statement that preceded the first point.
>
> Detainee: If it is the same point, but I do not want to repeat myself. These accusations, my answer to all of them is I did not do these things. But I do not have anything to

---

[31] Although the petition for writ of habeas corpus filed on behalf of this detainee and related documents refer to him as "Mustafa Ait Idir," the proper spelling of his name appears to be "Mustafa Ait Idr."

prove this. The only thing is the citizenship. I can tell you where I was and I had the papers to prove so. But to tell me I planned to bomb, I can only tell you that I did not plan.

Tribunal President: Mustafa, does that conclude your statement?

Detainee: That is it, but I was hoping you had evidence that you can give me. If I was in your place – and I apologize in advance for these words – but if a supervisor came to me and showed me accusations like these, I would take these accusations and I would hit him in the face with them. Sorry about that.

[Everyone in the Tribunal room laughs.]

Tribunal President: We had to laugh, but it is okay.

Detainee: Why? Because these are accusations that I can't even answer. I am not able to answer them. You tell me I am from Al Qaida, but I am not an Al Qaida. I don't have any proof to give you except to ask you to catch Bin Laden and ask him if I am a part of Al Qaida. To tell me that I thought, I'll just tell you that I did not. I don't have proof regarding this. What should be done is you should give me evidence regarding these accusations because I am not able to give you any evidence. I can just tell you no, and that is it.

Id. at 14–15. The laughter reflected in the transcript is understandable, and this exchange might have been truly humorous had the consequences of the detainee's "enemy combatant" status not been so terribly serious and had the detainee's criticism of the process not been so piercingly accurate.[32]

Another illustration of the fundamental unfairness of the CSRT's reliance on classified information not disclosed to the detainees arises in the government's classified factual return to the petition filed by Murat Kurnaz in Kurnaz v. Bush, 04-CV-1135 (ESH). Mr. Kurnaz is a Turkish citizen and permanent resident of Germany who was arrested by police in Pakistan and turned over to American authorities. The CSRT concluded that he was a member of al Qaeda and stated that this determination was based on unclassified evidence and on one classified document, attached to the factual return as Exhibit R19. Respondents' Factual Return to Petition for Writ of Habeas Corpus by Petitioner Murat Kurnaz (hereinafter "Kurnaz Factual Return"), filed October 18, 2004, Enclosure (2).[33]

The Court does not find that the unclassified evidence alone is sufficiently convincing in supporting the CSRT's conclusion that he is a member of al Qaeda.[34] That evidence establishes that Mr. Kurnaz attended a mosque in Bremen, Germany which the CSRT

---

[32] This is not to say whether or not the government was able to present any inculpatory evidence during the CSRT proceeding against the detainee. The primary purpose of the Memorandum Opinion's reference to the transcript at this stage of the litigation is to illustrate the detainees' lack of any reasonable opportunity to confront the government's evidence against them and not to resolve whether or not this particular detainee did in fact plan to attack the U.S. Embassy.

[33] Although the tribunal makes several references to its reliance on Exhibit R12, those references were typographical errors and the document actually relied upon was Exhibit R19, as recognized by the tribunal's Legal Advisor. See October 14, 2004 Memorandum from James R. Crisfield Jr. to the Director, Combatant Status Review Tribunal, attached to the Kumaz Factual Return.

[34] In fact, for reasons stated later in this opinion, even if all of the unclassified evidence were accepted as true, it alone would not form a constitutionally permissible basis for the indefinite detention of the petitioner. See infra section II.C.2.b.

found to be moderate in its views but also to have housed a branch of Jama'at-Al-Tabliq (hereinafter "JT"), a missionary organization alleged to have supported terrorist organizations. Kurnaz Factual Return, Enclosure (1) at 2. The unclassified evidence also establishes that Mr. Kurnaz had been friends with an individual named Selcuk Belgin, who is alleged to have been a suicide bomber, and that the detainee traveled to Pakistan to attend a JT school. Id at 2–3. Nowhere does the CSRT express any finding based on unclassified evidence that the detainee planned to be a suicide bomber himself, took up arms against the United States, or otherwise intended to attack American interests. Thus, the most reasonable interpretation of the record is that the classified document formed the most important basis for the CSRT's ultimate determination. That document, however, was never provided to the detainee, and had he received it, he would have had the opportunity to challenge its credibility and significance.

call into serious question the nature and thoroughness of the prior "multiple levels of review" of "enemy combatant" status referenced in Deputy

Secretary of Defense Paul Wolfowitz's July 7, 2004 Order establishing the CSRT system. At a minimum, the documents raise the question of

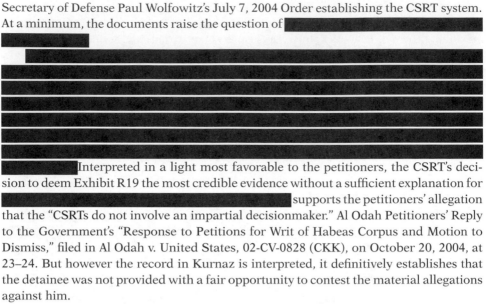

Interpreted in a light most favorable to the petitioners, the CSRT's decision to deem Exhibit R19 the most credible evidence without a sufficient explanation for ▮▮▮▮▮▮▮▮▮▮▮▮▮▮▮▮▮▮ supports the petitioners' allegation that the "CSRTs do not involve an impartial decisionmaker." Al Odah Petitioners' Reply to the Government's "Response to Petitions for Writ of Habeas Corpus and Motion to Dismiss," filed in Al Odah v. United States, 02-CV-0828 (CKK), on October 20, 2004, at 23–24. But however the record in Kurnaz is interpreted, it definitively establishes that the detainee was not provided with a fair opportunity to contest the material allegations against him.

The Court fully appreciates the strong governmental interest in not disclosing classified evidence to individuals believed to be terrorists intent on causing great harm to the United States. Indeed, this Court's protective order prohibits the disclosure of any classified information to any of the petitioners in these habeas cases. Amended Protective Order and Procedures for Counsel Access to Detainees at the United States Naval Base in Guantanamo Bay, Cuba, 344 F. Supp.2d 174 (D.D.C. 2004) at ¶30. To compensate for the resulting hardship to the petitioners and to ensure due process in the litigation of these cases, however, the protective order requires the disclosure of all relevant classified information to the petitioners' counsel who have the appropriate security clearances. Id. at ¶¶17–34. Although counsel are not permitted to share any classified information with their clients, they at least have the opportunity to examine all evidence relied upon by the government in making an "enemy combatant" status determination and to investigate and ensure the accuracy, reliability and relevance of that evidence. Thus, the governmental and private interests have been fairly balanced in a manner satisfying constitutional due process requirements. In a similar fashion, the rules regulating the military commission proceedings for aliens – rules which the government so vigorously defended in Hamdan v. Rumsfeld – expressly provide that although classified evidence may be withheld from the defendant, it may not be withheld from defense counsel. Procedures for Trials by Military Commissions of Certain Non-United States Citizens in the War Against Terrorism, 32 C.F.R. §9.6(b)(3) ("A decision to close a proceeding or portion thereof may include a decision to exclude the Accused, Civilian Defense Counsel, or any other person, but Detailed Defense Counsel may not be excluded from any trial proceeding or portion thereof."). In contrast, the CSRT regulations do not properly balance the detainees' need for access to material evidence considered by the tribunal against the government's interest in protecting classified information.

The CSRT regulations do acknowledge to some extent the detainees' need for assistance during the tribunal process, but they fall far short of the procedural protections that would have existed had counsel been permitted to participate. The implementing regulations create the position of "Personal Representative" for the purpose of "assist[ing] the detainee in reviewing all relevant unclassified information, in preparing and presenting information, and in questioning witnesses at the CSRT." July 29, 2004

Implementing Regulations at Enclosure (1), ¶C. (3). But notwithstanding the fact that the Personal Representative may review classified information considered by the tribunal, that person is neither a lawyer nor an advocate and thus cannot be considered an effective surrogate to compensate for a detainee's inability to personally review and contest classified evidence against him. Id. at Enclosure (3), ¶D. Additionally, there is no confidential relationship between the detainee and the Personal Representative, and the Personal Representative is obligated to disclose to the tribunal any relevant inculpatory information he obtains from the detainee. Id. Consequently, there is inherent risk and little corresponding benefit should the detainee decide to use the services of the Personal Representative.

The lack of any significant advantage to working with the Personal Representative is illustrated by the record of Kurnaz. Despite the existence of █████████████ the Personal Representative made no request for further inquiry regarding ████████ ███ ████████ ██

███████ Kurnaz Factual Return, Enclosure (5). Clearly, the presence of counsel for the detainee, even one who could not disclose classified evidence to his client, would have ensured a fairer process in the matter by highlighting weaknesses in evidence considered by the tribunal and helping to ensure that erroneous decisions were not made regarding the detainee's "enemy combatant" status. The CSRT rules, however, prohibited that opportunity.

In sum, the CSRT's extensive reliance on classified information in its resolution of "enemy combatant" status, the detainees' inability to review that information, and the prohibition of assistance by counsel jointly deprive the detainees of sufficient notice of the factual bases for their detention and deny them a fair opportunity to challenge their incarceration. These grounds alone are sufficient to find a violation of due process rights and to require the denial of the respondents' motion to dismiss these cases.

2. Specific Defects That May Exist in Individual Cases: Reliance on Statements Possibly Obtained Through Torture or Other Coercion and a Vague and Overly Broad Definition of "Enemy Combatant"

Additional defects in the CSRT procedures support the denial of the respondents' motion to dismiss at least some of the petitions, though these grounds may or may not exist in every case before the Court and though the respondents might ultimately prevail on these issues once the petitioners have been given an opportunity to litigate them fully in the habeas proceedings.

a. Reliance on Statements Possibly Obtained Through Torture or Other Coercion

The first of these specific grounds involves the CSRT's reliance on statements allegedly obtained through torture or otherwise alleged to have been provided by some detainees involuntarily. The Supreme Court has long held that due process prohibits the government's use of involuntary statements obtained through torture or other mistreatment. In the landmark case of Jackson v. Denno, 378 U.S. 368 (1964), the Court gave two rationales for this rule: first, "because of the probable unreliability of confessions that are obtained in a manner deemed coercive," and second "because of the 'strongly felt attitude of our society that important human values are sacrificed where an agency of the government, in the course of securing a conviction, wrings a confession out of an accused against his will.'" 378 U.S. at 386 (quoting Blackburn v. Alabama, 361 U.S. 199 (1960)). See also Lam v. Kelchner, 304 F.3d 256, 264 (3'd Cir. 2002) ("The voluntariness standard is intended to ensure the reliability of incriminating statements and to deter improper police conduct."). Arguably, the second rationale may not be as relevant to these habeas cases as it is to criminal prosecutions in U.S. courts, given that the judiciary clearly does not have the supervisory powers over the U.S. military as it does over prosecutors, who are officers of the court. Cf. United States v. Toscanino, 500 F.2d 267, 276 (2d Cir. 1974) (the supervisory power of the district courts "may legitimately be used to prevent [them] from themselves becoming 'accomplices in willful disobedience of law'") (quoting McNabb v. United States, 318 U.S. 332, 345 (1943)). At a minimum, however, due process requires a thorough inquiry into the accuracy and reliability of statements alleged to have been obtained through torture. See Clanton v. Cooper, 129 F.3d 1147, 1157–58 (10th Cir. 1997) ("[B]ecause the evidence is unreliable and its use offends the Constitution, a person may challenge the government's use against him or her of a coerced confession given by another person."); Buckley v. Fitzsimmons, 20 F.3d 789, 795 (7th Cir. 1994) ("Confessions wrung out of their makers may be less reliable than voluntary confessions, so that using one person's coerced confession at another's trial violates his rights under the due process clause.").

Interpreting the evidence in a light most favorable to the petitioners as the Court must when considering the respondents' motion to dismiss, it can be reasonably inferred that the CSRT did not sufficiently consider whether the evidence upon which the tribunal relied in making its "enemy combatant" determinations was coerced from the detainees. The allegations and factual return of Mamdouh Habib, a petitioner in Habib v. Bush, 02-CV-1130 (CKK) are illustrative in this regard. Mr. Habib has alleged that after his capture by allied forces in Pakistan, he was sent to Egypt for interrogation and was subjected to torture there, including routine beatings to the point of unconsciousness. Petitioner's Memorandum of Points and Authorities in Support of His Application for Injunctive Relief, filed with the Court Security Officer on November 23, 2004 and on the public record on January 5, 2005. Additionally, the petitioner contends that he was locked in a room that would gradually be filled with water to a level just below his chin as he stood for hours on the tips of his toes. Id. He further claims that he was suspended from a wall with his feet resting on the side of a large electrified cylindrical drum, which forced him either to suffer pain from hanging from his arms or pain from electric shocks to his feet. Id. The petitioner asserts that as a result of this treatment, he made numerous "confessions" that can be proven false. Id. at n.3. According to the classified factual return for Mr. Habib, ███ ██ ██ ██ ██ ██ ██ and the CSRT found the allegations of torture serious enough to refer the matter on September 22, 2004 to the Criminal Investigation Task Force. Id., Enclosure (1) at 3. ███████ ████████████████████████████████████ Examined in the light most favorable to the petitioner, this reliance cannot be viewed to have satisfied the requirements of due process. Examined in the light most favorable to the petitioner, this reliance cannot be viewed to have satisfied the requirements of due process.

Mr. Habib is not the only detainee before this Court to have alleged making confessions to interrogators as a result of torture. ███████████████████████████

███████████ Notwithstanding the inability of counsel for petitioners to take formal discovery beyond interviewing their clients at Guantanamo Bay, they have introduced evidence into the public record indicating that abuse of detainees occurred during interrogations not only in foreign countries but at Guantanamo Bay itself. One illustration of alleged mistreatment during interrogation by U.S. authorities is Exhibit D to the petitioners' Motion for Leave to Take Discovery and for Preservation Order, filed in several of these cases with the Court Security Officer on January 6, 2005 and filed on the public record on January 10, 2005. In that document, dated August 2, 2004, the author apparently affiliated with the Federal Bureau of Investigation but whose identity has been redacted, summarized his or her observations of interrogation activities at Guantanamo Bay as follows:

> On a couple of occassions [sic], I entered interview rooms to find a detainee chained hand and foot in a fetal position to the floor, with no chair, food, or water. Most times they had urinated or defacated [sic] on themselves, and had been left there for 18–24 hours or more. On one occasion [sic], the air conditioning had been turned down so far and the temperature was so cold in the room, that the barefooted detainee was shaking with cold. When I asked the MP's what was going on, I was told that interrogators from the day prior had ordered this treatment, and the detainee was not to be moved. On another occassion [sic], the A/C had been turned off, making the temperature in the unventilated room probably well over 100 degrees. The detainee was almost unconcious [sic] on the floor, with a pile of hair next to him. He had apparently been literally pulling his own hair out throughout the night. On another occassion [sic], not only was the temperature unbearably hot, but extremely loud rap music was being played in the room, and had been since the day before, with the detainee chained hand and foot in the fetal position on the tile floor.

The identities of the detainees referenced in this document are unknown to the Court and therefore, it is not certain whether they are even petitioners in any of these cases and, if so, whether the results of the above-described interrogations were used against them in CSRT proceedings. Of course, the veracity of Exhibit D itself must be investigated before it can be definitively relied upon. Indeed, at this stage of the litigation it is premature to make any final determination as to whether any information acquired during interrogations of any petitioner in these cases and relied upon by the CSRT was in fact the result of torture or other mistreatment. What this Court needs to resolve at this juncture, however, is whether the petitioners have made sufficient allegations to allow their claims to survive the respondents' motion to dismiss. On that count, the Court concludes that the petitioners have done so.

b.   Vague and Overly Broad Definition of "Enemy Combatant"

Although the government has been detaining individuals as "enemy combatants" since the issuance of the AUMF in 2001, it apparently did not formally define the term until the July 7, 2004 Order creating the CSRT. The lack of a formal definition seemed to have troubled at least the plurality of the Supreme Court in <u>Hamdi</u>, but for purposes of resolving the issues in that case, the plurality considered the government's definition to be an individual who was "'part of or supporting forces hostile to the United States or coalition partners' in Afghanistan <u>and</u> who 'engaged in an armed conflict against the United States' there." 124 S. Ct. 2633, 2639 (<u>quoting</u> Brief for the Respondents) (emphasis added). The Court agreed with the government that the AUMF authorizes the Executive to detain individuals falling within that limited definition, <u>id.</u>, with the plurality explaining that "[b]ecause detention to prevent a combatant's return to the battlefield is a fundamental incident of waging war, in permitting the use of 'necessary and appropriate force,' Congress has clearly and unmistakably authorized detention in the narrow circumstances considered here." <u>Id.</u> at 2641. The plurality cautioned, however, "that indefinite detention for the purpose of interrogation is not authorized" by the AUMF, and added that a congressional grant of authority to the President to use "necessary and appropriate force" might not be properly interpreted to include the authority to detain individuals for the duration of a particular conflict if that conflict does not take a form that is based on "longstanding law-of-war principles." <u>Id.</u>

The definition of "enemy combatant" contained in the Order creating the CSRT is significantly broader than the definition considered in <u>Hamdi</u>. According to the definition currently applied by the government, an "enemy combatant" "shall mean an individual who was part of or supporting Taliban or al Qaeda forces, or associated forces that are engaged in hostilities against the United States or its coalition partners. This <u>includes</u> any person who has committed a belligerent act or has directly supported hostilities in aid of enemy armed forces." July 7, 2004 Order at 1 (emphasis added). Use of the word "includes" indicates that the government interprets the AUMF to permit the indefinite detention of individuals who never committed a belligerent act or who never directly supported hostilities against the U.S. or its allies. This Court explored the government's position on the matter by posing a series of hypothetical questions to counsel at the December 1, 2004 hearing on the motion to dismiss. In response to the hypotheticals, counsel for the respondents argued that the Executive has the authority to detain the following individuals until the conclusion of the war on terrorism: "[a] little old lady in Switzerland who writes checks to what she thinks is a charity that helps orphans in Afghanistan but [what] really is a front to finance al-Qaeda activities," Transcript at 25, a person who teaches English to the son of an al Qaeda member, <u>id.</u> at 27, and a journalist who knows the location of Osama Bin Laden but refuses to disclose it to protect her source. <u>Id.</u> at 29.

The Court can unequivocally report that no factual return submitted by the government in this litigation reveals the detention of a Swiss philanthropist, an English teacher, or a journalist. The Court can also acknowledge the existence of specific factual returns containing evidence indicating that certain detainees fit the narrower definition of "enemy combatant" approved by the Supreme Court in <u>Hamdi</u>. The petitioners have argued in opposition to the respondents' motion to dismiss, however, that at least with respect to some detainees, the expansive definition of "enemy combatant" currently in use in the CSRT proceedings violates long standing principles of due process by permitting the detention of individuals based solely on their membership in anti-American organizations rather than on actual activities supporting the use of violence or harm against the United States. Al Odah Petitioners' Reply to the Government's "Response to Petitions for Writ of Habeas Corpus and Motion to Dismiss" at 25–26 (citing <u>Scales v. United States</u>, 367 U.S. 203, 224–225 (1961); <u>Carlson v. Landon</u>, 342 U.S. 524, 541 (1952)).

Whether the detention of each individual petitioner is authorized by the AUMF and satisfies the mandates of due process must ultimately be determined on a detainee by detainee basis. At this stage of the litigation, however, sufficient allegations have been made by at least some of the petitioners and certain evidence exists in some CSRT factual returns to warrant the denial of the respondents' motion to dismiss on the ground that the respondents have employed an overly broad definition of "enemy combatant." Examples of cases where this issue is readily apparent are <u>Kurnaz v. Bush</u>, 04-CV-1135 (ESH), and <u>El-Banna v. Bush</u>, 04-CV-1144 (RWR).

As already discussed above, the unclassified evidence upon which the CSRT relied in determining Murat Kurnaz's "enemy combatant" status consisted of findings that he was "associated" with an Islamic missionary group named Jama'at-Al-Tabliq, that he was an "associate" of and planned to travel to Pakistan with an individual who later engaged in a suicide bombing, and that he accepted free food, lodging, and schooling in Pakistan from an organization known to support terrorist acts. Kurnaz Factual Return, Enclosure (1) at 1. While these facts may be probative and could be used to bolster the credibility of other evidence, if any, establishing actual activities undertaken to harm American interests, by themselves they fall short of establishing that the detainee took any action or provided any direct support for terrorist actions against the U.S. or its allies. Nowhere does any unclassified evidence reveal that the detainee even had knowledge of his associate's planned suicide bombing, let alone establish that the detainee assisted in the bombing in any way. In fact, the detainee expressly denied knowledge of a bombing plan when he was informed of it by the American authorities. <u>Id.</u>, Enclosure (3) at 1. ██

██
██
██
██
██
██
██
██
██
██
██

███████ Absent other evidence,[36] it would appear that the government is indefinitely holding the detainee – possibly for life – solely because of his contacts with individuals or organizations tied to terrorism and not because of any terrorist activities that the detainee aided, abetted, or undertook himself. Such detention, even if found to be authorized by the AUMF, would be a violation of due process. Accordingly, the detainee is entitled to fully litigate the factual basis for his detention in these habeas proceedings and to have a fair opportunity to prove that he is being detained on improper grounds.

---

[35] ██
████████████████████████████████████

[36] It is true that Exhibit R19 to the Kurnaz Factual Return does assert that ████████████ ██████ and the respondents urge this Court to uphold the detention of any petitioner, including Mr. Kurnaz, as long as "some evidence" exists to support a conclusion that he actively participated in terrorist activities. Motion to Dismiss at 47–51. <u>Hamdi</u>, however, holds that the "some evidence" standard cannot be applied where the detainee was not given an opportunity to challenge the evidence in an administrative proceeding, 124 S. Ct. at 2651, and Mr. Kurnaz was never provided access to Exhibit R19. Additionally, in resolving a motion to dismiss, the Court must accept as true the petitioner's allegations and must interpret the evidence in the record in the light most favorable to the nonmoving party. Because Exhibit R19 ████████████ ███ ███████████████████████████████ the Court cannot at this stage of the litigation give the document the weight the CSRT afforded it.

Similar defects might also exist with respect to the detention of Jamil El-Banna, a petitioner in El-Banna v. Bush, 04-CV-1144 (RWR). At the CSRT proceedings, the tribunal concluded that the detainee was an "enemy combatant" on the ground that he was "part of or supporting Al Qaida forces." Respondents' In Camera Factual Return to Petition for Writ of Habeas Corpus by Petitioner Jamil El-Banna (hereinafter "El-Banna Factual Return"), filed December 17, 2004, Enclosure (1) at 5. The CSRT reached this conclusion notwithstanding the Personal Representative's position that it was unsupported by the record before the tribunal. See October 16, 2004 Memorandum of James R. Crisfield Jr., attached to the El-Banna Factual Return. During the CSRT proceedings, the tribunal rejected two grounds cited by the Recorder in support of the detainee's "enemy combatant" status. First, although the detainee was alleged to have been indicted by a Spanish National High Court Judge for membership in a terrorist organization, id., Enclosure (3) at 2, the tribunal did not find any evidence relating to that indictment "helpful in establishing the detainee's association with Al Qaida." Id., Enclosure (1) at 4. ███ ███ Second, although the detainee was alleged to have attempted "to board an airplane with equipment that resembled a homemade electronic device," id., Enclosure (3) at 3, ████████████

███ Even accepting these factual conclusions as true, a serious legal question exists as to whether such activities would be sufficient to detain the petitioner at Guantanamo Bay indefinitely without formally charging him with a crime. See Hamdi, 124 S. Ct. at 2640 ("The purpose of detention is to prevent captured individuals from returning to the field of battle and taking up arms once again.") and at 2642 ("If the practical circumstances of a given conflict are entirely unlike those of the conflicts that informed the development of the law of war, that understanding [that the AUMF allows indefinite detention] may unravel."). In any event, however, final resolution of that question must be left for another day because at this stage of the proceedings, the Court must interpret the facts in the light most favorable to the party opposing a motion to dismiss. Under that approach, evidence in the record can be fairly interpreted to conclude that the petitioner- is being detained indefinitely not because ████████████████

It may well turn out that after the detainee is given a fair opportunity to challenge his detention in a habeas proceeding, the legality of his detention as an "enemy combatant" will be upheld and he will continue to be held at Guantanamo Bay until the end of the war on terrorism or until the government determines he no longer poses a threat to U.S. security. It is also possible, however, that once given a fair opportunity to litigate his case, the detainee will establish that he is being indefinitely detained not because of anything he has done and not to prevent his return to any "battlefield," metaphorical or otherwise, but simply because ███████████████████████████ ███████████████████ such detention is not permissible ███████████████ ██████ and the respondents' motion to dismiss must therefore be denied.

This concludes the Court's analysis of the due process issues arising from the respondents' motion to dismiss. Nothing written above should be interpreted to require the immediate release of any detainee, nor should the conclusions reached be considered to have fully resolved whether or not sufficient evidence exists to support the continued detention of any petitioner. The respondents' motion to dismiss asserted that no evidence exists and that the petitioners could make no factual allegations which, if taken as true, would permit the litigation of these habeas cases to proceed further. For the reasons stated above, the Court has concluded otherwise. The Court, however, has not addressed all arguments made by the petitioners in opposition to the respondents' motion to dismiss, and it may be that the CSRT procedures violate due process requirements for additional reasons not addressed in this Memorandum Opinion. In any event, and as Hamdi acknowledged, in the absence of military tribunal proceedings that comport with constitutional due process requirements, it is the obligation of the court receiving a habeas petition to provide the petitioner with a fair opportunity to challenge the government's factual basis for his detention. Id. at 2651–52. Accordingly, the accompanying Order requests input from counsel regarding how these cases should proceed in light of this Memorandum Opinion.

D. CLAIMS BASED ON THE GENEVA CONVENTIONS

The petitioners in all of the above captioned cases except Al Odah v. United States, 02-CV-0828, have also asserted claims based on the Geneva Conventions, which regulate the treatment of certain prisoners of war and civilians. The respondents contend that all Geneva Convention claims filed by the petitioners must be dismissed because Congress has not enacted any separate legislation specifically granting individuals the right to file private lawsuits based on the Conventions and because the Conventions are not "self-executing," meaning they do not by themselves create such a private right of action. Motion to Dismiss at 68–71. In the alternative, the respondents argue that even if the Geneva Conventions are self-executing, they do not apply to members of al Qaeda because that international terrorist organization is not a state party to the Conventions. Id. at 70 n.80. Finally, although respondents concede that Afghanistan is a state party to the Conventions and admit that the Geneva Conventions apply to Taliban detainees, they emphasize that President Bush has determined that Taliban fighters are not entitled to prisoner of war status under the Third Geneva Convention and contend that this decision is the final word on the matter. Id.

The Constitution provides that "all Treaties made...under the Authority of the United States, shall be the supreme Law of the Land." U.S. Const. art. VI, cl. 2. Unless Congress enacts authorizing legislation, however, an individual may seek to enforce a treaty provision only if the treaty expressly or impliedly grants such a right. See Head Money Cases, 112 U.S. 580, 598–99 (1884). If a treaty does not create an express right of private enforcement, an implied right might be found by examining the treaty as a whole. See Diggs v. Richardson, 555 F.2d 848, 851 (D.C. Cir. 1976).

The Third and Fourth Geneva Conventions do not expressly grant private rights of action, and whether they impliedly create such rights has never been definitively resolved by the D.C. Circuit.[37] The Court of Appeals is currently reviewing the matter in the appeal of Hamdan v. Rumsfeld, 344 F. Supp.2d 152 (D.D.C. 2004), but until that court issues a definitive ruling,[38] this Court must make its own determination. After reviewing Hamdan and the briefs filed by petitioners and respondents in the instant cases, the Court concludes that the Conventions are self-executing and adopts the following reasoning provided by Judge Robertson:

> Because the Geneva Conventions were written to protect individuals, because the Executive Branch of our government has implemented the Geneva Conventions for fifty years without questioning the absence of implementing legislation, because Congress clearly understood that the Conventions did not require implementing legislation except in a few specific areas, and because nothing in the Third Geneva Convention itself manifests the contracting parties' intention that it not become effective as domestic law without the enactment of implementing legislation, I conclude that, insofar as it is pertinent here, the Third Geneva Convention is a self-executing treaty.

Id. at 165.

---

[37] The closest the Court of Appeals came to ruling on the issue was the case of Tel-Oren v. Libyan Arab Republic, 726 F.2d 774 (D.C. Cir. 1984), a suit brought by victims of a brutal attack in Israel by the Palestinian Liberation Organization. The main issue on appeal was whether the District Court correctly ruled that there was no subject-matter jurisdiction to hear the case, and although the three judge panel ultimately affirmed the lower court's decision, each judge relied on a separate rationale and no judge joined any other judge's opinion. In reaching his own conclusion, Judge Robert Bork determined that the Third Geneva Convention was not self-executing. Id. at 808–09. The other two judges on the panel did not address the issue, however, and the matter remains unsettled as of this date.

[38] Oral argument on the respondents' appeal in Hamdan is currently scheduled for March 8, 2005.

Although the Court rejects the primary basis argued by the respondents for dismissal of claims based on the Geneva Conventions, it does accept one of the alternative grounds put forth in their motion, namely that the Geneva Conventions do not apply to al Qaeda. Article 2 of the Third and Fourth Geneva Conventions provides, "In addition to the provisions which shall be implemented in peacetime, the present Convention shall apply to all cases of declared war or of any other armed conflict which may arise between two or more of the High Contracting Parties, even if the state of war is not recognized by one of them." Clearly, al Qaeda is not a "High Contracting Party" to the Conventions, and thus individuals detained on the ground that they are members of that terrorist organization are not entitled to the protections of the treaties.

This does not end the analysis for purposes of resolving the respondents' motion to dismiss, however, because some of the petitioners in the above-captioned cases are being detained either solely because they were Taliban fighters or because they were associated with both the Taliban and al Qaeda. Significantly, the respondents concede that the Geneva Conventions apply to the Taliban detainees in light of the fact that Afghanistan is a High Contracting Party to the Conventions. Motion to Dismiss at 70–71 n.80 (citing White House Fact Sheet (Feb. 7, 2002), available at http://www.whitehouse.gov/news/releases/2002/02120020207-13.html). They argue in their motion to dismiss, however, that notwithstanding the application of the Third Geneva Convention to Taliban detainees, the treaty does not protect Taliban detainees because the President has declared that no Taliban fighter is a "prisoner of war" as defined by the Convention. Id. The respondents' argument in this regard must be rejected, however, for the Third Geneva Convention does not permit the determination of prisoner of war status in such a conclusory fashion.

Article 4 of the Third Geneva Convention defines who is considered a "prisoner of war" under the treaty. Paragraph (1) provides that the term "prisoners of war" includes "[m]embers of the armed forces of a Party to the conflict, as well as members of militias or volunteer corps forming part of such armed forces." As provided in Paragraph (2), the definition of "prisoners of war" also includes "[m]embers of other militias and members of other volunteer corps, including those of organized resistance movements," but only if they fulfill the following conditions: "(a) that of being commanded by a person responsible for his subordinates; (b) that of having a fixed distinctive sign recognizable at a distance; (c) that of carrying arms openly; (d) that of conducting their operations in accordance with the laws and customs of war." If there is any doubt as to whether individuals satisfy the Article 4 prerequisites, Article 5 entitles them to be treated as prisoners of war "until such time as their status has been determined by a competent tribunal." Army Regulation 190–8 created the rules for the "competent tribunal" referenced in Article 5 of the Third. Geneva Convention, and the CSRT was established in accordance with that provision. See Army Regulation 490–8 §1-1.b, Motion to Dismiss at 32.

Nothing in the Convention itself or in Army Regulation 190–8 authorizes the President of the United States to rule by fiat that an entire group of fighters covered by the Third Geneva Convention falls outside of the Article 4 definitions of "prisoners of war." To the contrary, and as Judge Robertson ruled in Hamdan, the President's broad characterization of how the Taliban generally fought the war in Afghanistan cannot substitute for an Article 5 tribunal's determination on an individualized basis of whether a particular fighter complied with the laws of war or otherwise falls within an exception denying him prisoner of war status. 344 F. Supp.2d at 161–62. Clearly, had an appropriate determination been properly made by an Article 5 tribunal that a petitioner was not a prisoner of war, that petitioner's claims based on the Third Geneva Convention could not survive the respondents' motion to dismiss. But although numerous petitioners in the above-captioned cases were found by the CSRT to have been Taliban fighters, nowhere do the CSRT records for many of those petitioners reveal specific findings that they committed some particular act or failed to satisfy some defined prerequisite entitling the respondents to deprive them of prisoner of war status.[39] Accordingly, the Court denies that portion of the respondents' motion to dismiss addressing the Geneva Convention claims of those petitioners who were found to be Taliban fighters but who were not specifically determined to be excluded from prisoner of war status by a competent Article 5 tribunal.

. . .

III. CONCLUSION

For the reasons provided above, the Court holds that the petitioners have stated valid claims under the Fifth Amendment and that the CSRT procedures are unconstitutional for failing to comport with the requirements of due process. Additionally, the Court holds that Taliban fighters who have not been specifically determined to be excluded from prisoner of war status by a competent Article 5 tribunal have also stated valid claims under the Third Geneva Convention. Finally, the Court concludes that the remaining claims of the petitioners must be denied. Accordingly, this Memorandum Opinion is accompanied by a separate Order denying in part and granting in part the respondents' Motion to Dismiss or for Judgment as a Matter of Law.

This Judge began her participation as the coordinator of these cases on August 17, 2004, and her involvement will soon be ending. These cases have always remained before the original Judges assigned to them and only particular issues or motions were referred to this Judge for resolution. Therefore, there will be no need to transfer the cases back to those Judges. In the interest of the effective management of this litigation, however, the accompanying Order requests briefing from counsel on an expedited basis regarding their views as to how these cases should proceed in light of this Memorandum Opinion and this Judge's imminent departure.

January 31, 2005

_____

JOYCE HENS GREEN
United States District Judge

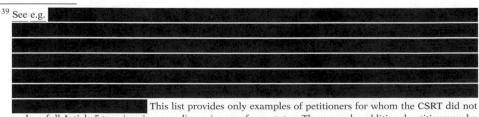

[39] See e.g. ▮▮▮▮▮▮ This list provides only examples of petitioners for whom the CSRT did not make a full Article 5 type inquiry regarding prisoner of war status. There may be additional petitioners who fought for the Taliban and who were not given individualized determinations as to their prisoner of war status. Absence from this list should not be interpreted to imply that a petitioner can no longer assert his Geneva Convention claims in this habeas litigation.

United States Court of Appeals

FOR THE DISTRICT OF COLUMBIA CIRCUIT

———

Argued September 8, 2005   Decided February 20, 2007

No. 05-5062

LAKHDAR BOUMEDIENE, DETAINEE, CAMP DELTA, ET AL.,
APPELLANTS

v.

GEORGE W. BUSH, PRESIDENT OF THE UNITED STATES, ET AL.,
APPELLEES

———

Consolidated with
05-5063

———

Appeals from the United States District Court
for the District of Columbia
(No. 04cv01142)
(No. 04cv01166)

No. 05-5064

KHALED A. F. AL ODAH, NEXT FRIEND OF FAWZI KHALID
ABDULLAH FAHAD AL ODAH ET AL.,
APPELLEES/CROSS-APPELLANTS

UNITED STATES OF AMERICA, ET AL.,
APPELLANTS/CROSS-APPELLEES

———

Consolidated with
05-5095, 05-5096, 05-5097, 05-5098, 05-5099, 05-5100,
05-5101, 05-5102, 05-5103, 05-5104, 05-5105, 05-5106,
05-5107, 05-5108, 05-5109, 05-5110, 05-5111, 05-5112,
05-5113, 05-5114, 05-5115, 05-5116

———

Appeals from the United States District Court
for the District of Columbia
(No. 02cv00828)
(No. 02cv00299)
(No. 02cv01130)
(No. 02cv01135)
(No. 02cv01136)
(No. 02cv01137)
(No. 02cv01144)
(No. 02cv01164)
(No. 02cv01194)
(No. 02cv01227)
(No. 02cv01254)

———

Stephen H. Oleskey argued the causes for appellants in
Nos. 05-5062, et al. With him on the briefs were *Louis R.
Cohen, Robert C. Kirsch, Douglas F. Curtis, Mark C. Fleming,
Wesley R. Powell, Julia Symon,* and *Christopher Land.*

133

Thomas B. Wilner argued the causes for the appellees/cross-appellants in Nos. 05-5064, et al. With him on the briefs were *Barbara J. Olshansky, Joe Margulies, Neil H. Koslowe, Jared A. Goldstein, L. Barrett Boss, Adrian Lee Steel, Jr., Baher Azmy, Shayana Devendra Kadidal, Barry J. Pollak, Eric M. Freedman, Richard J. Wilson, George Brent Mickum, IV, Douglas James Behr, Erwin Chemerinsky, Jonathan L. Hafetz, Muneer I. Ahmad, Pamela Rogers Chepiga, Ralph A. Taylor, Seth B. Waxman, Kevin B. Bedell, David H. Remes, Marc Falkoff, Marc A. Goldman, David J. Cynamon,* and *Osman Handoo.*

· · ·

Gregory G. Katsas, Deputy Assistant Attorney General, U.S. Department of Justice, argued the cause for the United States of America, et al. in Nos. 05-5062, et al. and 05-5064, et al. With him on the briefs were *Paul D. Clement,* Solicitor General, *Peter D. Keisler,* Assistant Attorney General, and *Douglas N. Letter, Robert M. Loeb, Eric D. Miller,* and *Catherine Y. Hancock,* Attorneys. *Kenneth L. Wainstein,* U.S. Attorney at the time the briefs were filed, entered an appearance.

· · ·

Before: SENTELLE, RANDOLPH and ROGERS, *Circuit Judges.*

Opinion for the court filed by *Circuit Judge* RANDOLPH.

Dissenting opinion filed by *Circuit Judge* ROGERS.

RANDOLPH, *Circuit Judge*: Do federal courts have jurisdiction over petitions for writs of habeas corpus filed by aliens captured abroad and detained as enemy combatants at the Guantanamo Bay Naval Base in Cuba? The question has been the recurring subject of legislation and litigation. In these consolidated appeals, foreign nationals held at Guantanamo filed petitions for writs of habeas corpus alleging violations of the Constitution, treaties, statutes, regulations, the common law, and the law of nations. Some detainees also raised non-habeas claims under the federal question statute, 28 U.S.C. §1331, and the Alien Tort Act, *id.* §1350. In the "Al Odah" cases (Nos. 05-5064, 05-5095 through 05-5116), which consist of eleven cases involving fifty-six detainees, Judge Green denied the government's motion to dismiss with respect to the claims arising from alleged violations of the Fifth Amendment's Due Process Clause and the Third Geneva Convention, but dismissed all other claims. *See In re Guantanamo Detainee Cases*, 355

F. Supp. 2d 443 (D.D.C. 2005). After Judge Green certified the order for interlocutory appeal under 28 U.S.C. §1292(b), the government appealed and the detainees cross-appealed. In the "Boumediene" cases (Nos. 05-5062 and 05-5063) – two cases involving seven detainees – Judge Leon granted the government's motion and dismissed the cases in their entirety. *See Khalid v. Bush*, 355 F. Supp. 2d 311 (D.D.C. 2005).

In the two years since the district court's decisions the law has undergone several changes. As a result, we have had two oral arguments and four rounds of briefing in these cases during that period. The developments that have brought us to this point are as follows.

In *Al Odah v. United States*, 321 F.3d 1134 (D.C. Cir. 2003), *rev'd sub nom. Rasul v. Bush*, 542 U.S. 466 (2004), we affirmed the district court's dismissal of various claims – habeas and non-habeas – raised by Guantanamo detainees. With respect to the habeas claims, we held that "no court in this country has jurisdiction to grant habeas relief, under 28 U.S.C. §2241, to the Guantanamo detainees." 321 F.3d at 1141. The habeas statute then stated that "Writs of habeas corpus may be granted by the Supreme Court, any justice thereof, the district courts and any circuit judge within their respective jurisdictions."

28 U.S.C. §2241(a) (2004). Because Guantanamo Bay was not part of the sovereign territory of the United States, but rather land the United States leases from Cuba, *see Al Odah*, 321 F.3d at 1142–43, we determined it was not within the "respective jurisdictions" of the district court or any other court in the United States. We therefore held that §2241 did not provide statutory jurisdiction to consider habeas relief for any alien – enemy or not – held at Guantanamo. *Id.* at 1141. Regarding the non-habeas claims, we noted that "'the privilege of litigation' does not extend to aliens in military custody who have no presence in 'any territory over which the United States is sovereign,'" *id.* at 1144 (quoting *Johnson v. Eisentrager*, 339 U.S. 763, 777–78 (1950)), and held that the district court properly dismissed those claims.

The Supreme Court reversed in *Rasul v. Bush*, 542 U. S. 466 (2004), holding that the habeas statute extended to aliens at Guantanamo. Although the detainees themselves were beyond the district court's jurisdiction, the Court determined that the district court's jurisdiction over the detainees' custodians was sufficient to provide subject-matter jurisdiction under §2241. *See Rasul*, 542 U.S. at 483–84. The Court further held that the district court had jurisdiction over the detainees' non-habeas claims because nothing in the federal question statute or the Alien Tort Act categorically excluded aliens outside the United States from bringing such claims. *See Rasul*, 542 U. S. at 484–85. The Court remanded the cases to us, and we remanded them to the district court.

In the meantime Congress responded with the Detainee Treatment Act of 2005, Pub. L. No. 109–148, 119 Stat. 2680 (2005) (DTA), which the President signed into law on December 30, 2005. The DTA added a subsection (e) to the habeas statute. This new provision stated that, "[e]xcept as provided in section 1005 of the [DTA], no court, justice, or judge" may exercise jurisdiction over

(1) an application for a writ of habeas corpus filed by or on behalf of an alien detained by the Department of Defense at Guantanamo Bay, Cuba; or

(2) any other action against the United States or its agents relating to anyaspect of the detention by the Department of Defense of an alien atGuantanamo Bay, Cuba, who

(A) is currently in military custody; or

(B) has been determined by the United States Court of Appeals for theDistrict of Columbia Circuit . . . to have been properly detained as an enemy combatant.

DTA §1005(e)(1) (internal quotation marks omitted). The "except as provided" referred to subsections (e)(2) and (e)(3) of section 1005 of the DTA, which provided for exclusive judicial review of Combatant Status Review Tribunal determinations and military commission decisions in the D.C. Circuit. *See* DTA §1005(e)(2), (e)(3).

The following June, the Supreme Court decided *Hamdan v. Rumsfeld*, 126 S. Ct. 2749 (2006). Among other things, the Court held that the DTA did not strip federal courts of jurisdiction over habeas cases pending at the time of the DTA's enactment. The Court pointed to a provision of the DTA stating that subsections (e)(2) and (e)(3) of section 1005 "shall apply with respect to any claim . . . that is pending on or after the date of the enactment of this Act. " DTA §1005(h). In contrast, no provision of the DTA stated whether subsection (e)(1) applied to pending cases. Finding that Congress "chose not to so provide . . . after having been presented with the option," the Court concluded "[t]he omission [wa]s an integral part of the statutory scheme." *Hamdan*, 126 S. Ct. at 2769.

In response to *Hamdan*, Congress passed the Military Commissions Act of 2006, Pub. L. No. 109–366, 120 Stat. 2600 (2006) (MCA), which the President signed into law on October 17, 2006. Section 7 of the MCA is entitled "Habeas Corpus Matters." In subsection (a), Congress again amended §2241(e). The new amendment reads:

> (1) No court, justice, or judge shall have jurisdiction to hear or consider an application for a writ of habeas corpus filed by or on behalf of an alien detained by the United States who has been determined by the United States to have been properly detained as an enemy combatant or is awaiting such determination.
>
> (2) Except as provided in [section 1005(e)(2) and (e)(3) of the DTA], no court, justice, or judge shall have jurisdiction to hear or consider any other action against the United States or its agents relating to any aspect of the detention, transfer, treatment, trial, or conditions of confinement of an alien who is or was detained by the United States and has been determined by the United States to have been properly detained as an enemy combatant or is awaiting such determination.

MCA §7(a) (internal quotation marks omitted). Subsection (b) states:

> The amendment made by subsection (a) shall take effect on the date of the enactment of this Act, and shall apply to *all cases, without exception, pending on or after the date of the enactment* of this Act which relate to any aspect of the detention, transfer, treatment, trial, or conditions of detention of an alien detained by the United States since September 11, 2001.

MCA §7(b) (emphasis added).

The first question is whether the MCA applies to the detainees' habeas petitions. If the MCA does apply, the second question is whether the statute is an unconstitutional suspension of the writ of habeas corpus.[1]

I.

As to the application of the MCA to these lawsuits, section 7(b) states that the amendment to the habeas corpus statute, 28 U.S.C. §2241(e), "shall apply to all cases, without exception, pending on or after the date of the enactment" that relate to certain subjects. The detainees' lawsuits fall within the subject matter covered by the amended §2241(e);

---

[1] Section 7(a) of the MCA eliminates jurisdiction over non-habeas claims by aliens detained as enemy combatants. That alone is sufficient to require dismissal even of pending non-habeas claims. *See Bruner v. United States*, 343 U.S. 112, 116–17 (1952). Section 7(b) reinforces this result.

each case relates to an "aspect" of detention and each deals with the detention of an "alien" after September 11, 2001. The MCA brings all such "cases, without exception" within the new law.

Everyone who has followed the interaction between Congress and the Supreme Court knows full well that one of the primary purposes of the MCA was to overrule *Hamdan*.[2]

Everyone, that is, except the detainees. Their cases, they argue, are not covered. The arguments are creative but not cogent. To accept them would be to defy the will of Congress. Section 7(b) could not be clearer. It states that "the amendment made by subsection (a) " – which repeals habeas jurisdiction – applies to "all cases, without exception" relating to any aspect of detention. It is almost as if the proponents of these words were slamming their fists on the table shouting "When we say 'all,' we mean all – **without exception!**"[3]

The detainees of course do not see it that way. They say Congress should have expressly stated in section 7(b) that habeas cases were included among "all cases, without exception, pending on or after" the MCA became law. Otherwise, the MCA does not represent an "unambiguous statutory directive[]" to repeal habeas corpus jurisdiction. *INS v. St. Cyr*, 533 U.S. 289, 299 (2001). This is nonsense. Section 7(b) specifies the effective date of section 7(a). The detainees' argument means that Congress, in amending the habeas statute (28 U.S.C. §2241), specified an effective date only for non-habeas cases. Of course Congress did nothing of the sort. Habeas cases are simply a subset of cases dealing with detention. *See, e.g., Preiser v. Rodriguez*, 411 U.S. 475, 484 (1973).[4] Congress did not have to say that "the amendment made by subsection (a) " – which already *expressly* includes habeas cases – shall take effect on the date of enactment and shall apply to "all cases, without exception, *including habeas cases.*" The *St. Cyr* rule of interpretation the detainees invoke demands clarity, not redundancy.

---

[2] Without exception, both the proponents and opponents of section 7 understood the provision to eliminate habeas jurisdiction over pending cases. *See, e.g.,* 152 Cong. Rec. S10357 (daily ed. Sept. 28, 2006) (statement of Sen. Leahy) ("The habeas stripping provisions in the bill go far beyond what Congress did in the Detainee Treatment Act. . . . This new bill strips habeas jurisdiction retroactively, even for pending cases."); *id.* at S10367 (statement of Sen. Graham) ("The only reason we are here is because of the *Hamdan* decision. The *Hamdan* decision did not apply . . . the [DTA] retroactively, so we have about 200 and some habeas cases left unattended and we are going to attend to them now."); *id.* at S10403 (statement of Sen. Cornyn) ("[O]nce . . . section 7 is effective, Congress will finally accomplish what it sought to do through the [DTA] last year. It will finally get the lawyers out of Guantanamo Bay. It will substitute the blizzard of litigation instigated by Rasul v. Bush with a narrow DC Circuit-only review of the [CSRT] hearings."); *id.* at S10404 (statement of Sen. Sessions) ("It certainly was not my intent, when I voted for the DTA, to exempt all of the pending Guantanamo lawsuits from the provisions of that act.*** Section 7 of the [MCA] fixes this feature of the DTA and ensures that there is no possibility of confusion in the future. . . . I don't see how there could be any confusion as to the effect of this act on the pending Guantanamo litigation. The MCA's jurisdictional bar applies to that litigation 'without exception.'"); 152 Cong. Rec. H7938 (daily ed. Sept. 29, 2006) (statement of Rep. Hunter) ("The practical effect of [section 7] will be to eliminate the hundreds of detainee lawsuits that are pending in courts throughout the country and to consolidate all detainee treatment cases in the D.C. Circuit."); *id.* at H7942 (Rep. Jackson-Lee) ("The habeas provisions in the legislation are contrary to congressional intent in the [DTA]. In that act, Congress did not intend to strip the courts of jurisdiction over the pending habeas [cases].").

[3] Congress has rarely found it necessary to emphasize the *absence* of exceptions to a clear rule. Indeed, the use of "without exception" to emphasize the word "all" occurs in only one other provision of the U.S. Code. *See* 48 U.S.C. §526(a).

[4] If section 7(b) did not include habeas cases among cases "which relate to any aspect of the detention, transfer, treatment, trial, or conditions of detention," it would be inconsistent with section 7(a). Section 7(a) of the MCA first repeals jurisdiction "to hear or consider an application for a writ of habeas corpus" by detainees. 28 U.S.C. §2241(e)(1). It then repeals jurisdiction over "any *other* action . . . relating to any aspect of the detention, transfer, treatment, trial, or conditions of confinement" of a detainee, *id.* §2241(e)(2) (emphasis added), thus signifying that Congress considered habeas cases as cases relating to detention, as indeed they are.

The detainees also ask us to compare the language of section 7(b) to that of section 3 of the MCA. Section 3, entitled "Military Commissions," creates jurisdiction in the D.C. Circuit for review of military commission decisions, *see* 10 U.S.C. §950g. It then adds 10 U.S.C. §950j, which deals with the finality of military commission decisions. Section 950j strips federal courts of jurisdiction over any pending or future cases that would involve review of such decisions:

> Except as otherwise provided in this chapter and notwithstanding any other provision of law *(including section 2241 of title 28 or any other habeas corpus provision)*, no court, justice, or judge shall have jurisdiction to hear or consider any claim or cause of action whatsoever, including any action pending on or filed after the date of the enactment of the Military Commissions Act of 2006, relating to the prosecution, trial, or judgment of a military commission under this chapter, including challenges to the lawfulness of procedures of military commissions under this chapter.

10 U.S.C. §950j(b) (emphasis added). The detainees maintain that §950j calls into question Congress's intention to apply section 7(b) to pending habeas cases.

The argument goes nowhere. Section 7(b), read in conjunction with section 7(a), is no less explicit than §950j. Section 7(a) strips jurisdiction over detainee cases, including habeas cases, and section 7(b) makes section 7(a) applicable to pending cases. Section 950j accomplishes the same thing, but in one sentence. A drafting decision to separate section 7 into two subsections – one addressing the scope of the jurisdictional bar, the other addressing how the bar applies to pending cases – makes no legal difference.[5]

II.

This brings us to the constitutional issue: whether the MCA, in depriving the courts of jurisdiction over the detainees' habeas petitions, violates the Suspension Clause of the Constitution, U.S. CONST. art. I, §9, cl. 2, which states that "The Privilege of the Writ of Habeas Corpus shall not be suspended, unless when in Cases of Rebellion or Invasion the public Safety may require it."

The Supreme Court has stated the Suspension Clause protects the writ "as it existed in 1789," when the first Judiciary Act created the federal courts and granted jurisdiction to issue writs of habeas corpus. *St. Cyr*, 533 U.S. at 301; *cf.* Henry J. Friendly, *Is Innocence Irrelevant? Collateral Attack on Criminal Judgments*, 38 U. CHI. L. REV. 142, 170 (1970). The detainees rely mainly on three cases to claim that in 1789 the privilege of the writ extended to aliens outside the sovereign's territory. In *Lockington's Case*, Bright. (N.P.) 269 (Pa. 1813), a British resident of Philadelphia had been imprisoned after failing to comply with a federal marshal's order to relocate. The War of 1812 made Lockington

---

[5] The detainees suggest that federal courts retain some form of residual common law jurisdiction over habeas petitions. *Ex parte Bollman*, 8 U.S. (4 Cranch) 75, 95 (1807), holds the opposite. *See Ex parte McCardle*, 74 U.S. 506 (1868). "Jurisdiction of the lower federal courts is . . . limited to those subjects encompassed within a statutory grant of jurisdiction." *Ins. Corp. of Ireland, Ltd. v. Compagnie des Bauxites de Guinee*, 456 U.S. 694, 701 (1982). The observations about common law habeas in *Rasul*, 542 U.S. at 481–82, referred to the practice in England. Even if there were such a thing as common law jurisdiction in the federal courts, §2241(e)(1) quite clearly eliminates all "jurisdiction to hear or consider an application for a writ of habeas corpus" by a detainee, whatever the source of that jurisdiction.

In order to avoid "serious 'due process,' Suspension Clause, and Article III problems," the detainees also urge us not to read section 7 of the MCA to eliminate habeas jurisdiction over Geneva Convention claims. But that reading is unavoidable. Section 7 is unambiguous, as is section 5(a), which states that "No person may invoke the Geneva Conventions or any protocols thereto in any habeas corpus or other civil action or proceeding . . . as a source of rights in any court of the United States."

an "enemy alien" under the Alien Enemies Act of 1798. Although he lost on the merits of his petition for habeas corpus before the Pennsylvania Supreme Court, two of three Pennsylvania justices held that he was entitled to review of his detention.[6] In *The Case of Three Spanish Sailors*, 96 Eng. Rep. 775 (C.P. 1779), three Spanish seamen had boarded a merchant vessel bound for England with a promise of wages on arrival. After arriving in England, the English captain refused to pay their wages and turned them over to a warship as prisoners of war. The King's Bench denied the sailors' petitions because they were "alien enemies and prisoners of war, and therefore not entitled to any of the privileges of Englishmen; much less to be set at liberty on a habeas corpus." *Id.* at 776. The detainees claim that, as in *Lockington's Case*, the King's Bench exercised jurisdiction and reached the merits. The third case – *Rex v. Schiever*, 97 Eng. Rep. 551 (K.B. 1759) – involved a citizen of Sweden intent on entering the English merchant trade. While at sea on an English merchant's ship, a French privateer took Schiever along with the rest of the crew as prisoners, transferred the crew to another French ship, and let the English prisoners go free. An English ship thereafter captured the French ship and its crew, and carried them to Liverpool where Schiever was imprisoned. From Liverpool Schiever petitioned for habeas corpus, claiming he was a citizen of Sweden and only by force entered the service of the French. The court denied him relief because it found ample evidence that he was a prisoner of war. *Id.* at 552.

None of these cases involved an alien outside the territory of the sovereign. Lockington was a resident of Philadelphia. And the three Spanish sailors and Schiever were all held within English sovereign territory.[7] The detainees cite no case and no historical treatise showing that the English common law writ of habeas corpus extended to aliens beyond the Crown's dominions. Our review shows the contrary. *See* WILLIAM F. DUKER, A CONSTITUTIONAL HISTORY OF HABEAS CORPUS 53 (1980); 9 WILLIAM HOLDSWORTH, A HISTORY OF ENGLISH LAW 116–17, 124 (1982 ed.); 3 BLACKSTONE COMMENTARIES 131 (1768); *see also* 1 Op. Att'y Gen. 47 (1794); *In re Ning Yi-Ching*, 56 T. L. R. 3, 5 (Vacation Ct. 1939) (noting prior judge "had listened in vain for a case in which the writ of *habeas corpus* had issued in respect of a foreigner detained in a part of the world which was not a part of the King's dominions or realm"). Robert Chambers, the successor to Blackstone at Oxford, wrote in his lectures that the writ of habeas corpus extended only to the King's dominions. 2 ROBERT CHAMBERS, A COURSE OF LECTURES ON THE ENGLISH LAW DELIVERED AT OXFORD 1767–1773 (composed in association with Samuel Johnson), at 7–8 (Thomas M. Curley ed., 1986). Chambers cited *Rex v. Cowle*, 97 Eng. Rep. (2 Burr.) 587 (K.B. 1759), in which Lord Mansfield stated that "[t]o foreign dominions . . . this Court has no power to send any writ of any kind. We cannot send a habeas corpus to Scotland, or to the electorate; but to Ireland, the Isle of Man, the plantations [American colonies] . . . we may. " Every territory that Mansfield, Blackstone, and Chambers cited as a jurisdiction to which the writ extended (e.g., Ireland, the Isle of Man, the colonies, the Cinque Ports, and Wales) was a sovereign territory of the Crown.

When agents of the Crown detained prisoners outside the Crown's dominions, it was understood that they were outside the jurisdiction of the writ. *See* HOLDSWORTH, *supra*, at 116–17. Even British citizens imprisoned in "remote islands, garrisons, and other places"

---

[6] During this period, state courts often employed the writ of habeas corpus to inquire into the legality of federal detention. The Supreme Court later held in *Ableman v. Booth*, 62 U.S. (21 How.) 506 (1859), and *Tarble's Case*, 80 U.S. (13 Wall.) 397 (1871), that state courts had no such power.

[7] The dissent claims that the difference between Schiever and the detainees is "exceedingly narrow," Dissent at 14, because Schiever was brought involuntarily to Liverpool. For this proposition, the dissent cites *United States v. Verdugo-Urquidez*, 494 U.S. 259, 271 (1990). *Verdugo-Urquidez* was a Fourth Amendment case. Obviously, it had nothing to say about habeas corpus in Eighteenth Century England.

were "prevent[ed] from the benefit of the law," 2 HENRY HALLAM, THE CONSTITUTIONAL HISTORY OF ENGLAND 127–28 (William S. Hein Co. 1989) (1827), which included access to habeas corpus, *see* DUKER *supra*, at 51–53; HOLDSWORTH, *supra*, at 116; *see also* Johan Steyn, *Guantanamo Bay: The Legal Black Hole*, 53 INT'L & COMP. L.Q. 1, 8 (2004) ("the writ of habeas corpus would not be available" in "remote islands, garrisons, and other places" (internal quotation marks omitted)). Compliance with a writ from overseas was also completely impractical given the habeas law at the time. In *Cowle*, Lord Mansfield explained that even in the far off territories "annexed to the Crown," the Court would not send the writ, "notwithstanding the power." 97 Eng. Rep. at 600. This is doubtless because of the Habeas Corpus Act of 1679. The great innovation of this statute was in setting time limits for producing the prisoner and imposing fines on the custodian if those limits were not met. *See* CHAMBERS, *supra*, at 11. For a prisoner detained over 100 miles from the court, the detaining officer had twenty days after receiving the writ to produce the body before the court. *See id.* If he did not produce the body, he incurred a fine. One can easily imagine the practical problems this would have entailed if the writ had run outside the sovereign territory of the Crown and reached British soldiers holding foreign prisoners in overseas conflicts, such as the War of 1812. The short of the matter is that given the history of the writ in England prior to the founding, habeas corpus would not have been available in 1789 to aliens without presence or property within the United States.

Johnson v. Eisentrager, 339 U.S. 763 (1950), ends any doubt about the scope of common law habeas. "We are cited to no instance where a court, in this or any other country where the writ is known, has issued it on behalf of an alien enemy who, at no relevant time and in no stage of his captivity, has been within its territorial jurisdiction. Nothing in the text of the Constitution extends such a right, nor does anything in our statutes." *Id.* at 768; *see also* Note, *Habeas Corpus Protection Against Illegal Extraterritorial Detention*, 51 COLUM. L. REV. 368, 368 (1951). The detainees claim they are in a different position than the prisoners in *Eisentrager*, and that this difference is material for purposes of common law habeas.[8] They point to dicta in *Rasul*, 542 U. S. 481–82, in which the Court discussed English habeas cases and the "historical reach of the writ." *Rasul* refers to several English and American cases involving varying combinations of territories of the Crown and relationships between the petitioner and the country in which the writ was sought. *See id.* But as Judge Robertson found in *Hamdan*, "[n]ot one of the cases mentioned in *Rasul* held that an alien captured abroad and detained outside the United States – or in 'territory over which the United States exercises exclusive jurisdiction and control,' *Rasul*, 542 U.S. at 475 – had a common law or constitutionally protected right to the writ of habeas corpus." *Hamdan v. Rumsfeld*, No. 04-1519, 2006 WL 3625015, at *7 (D.D.C. Dec. 13, 2006). Justice Scalia made the same point in his *Rasul* dissent, *see Rasul*, 542 U. S. at 502-05 & n.5 (Scalia, J., dissenting) (noting the absence of "a single case holding that aliens held outside the territory of the sovereign were within reach of the writ"), and the dissent acknowledges it here, *see* Dissent at 12. We are aware of no case prior to 1789 going the detainees' way,[9] and we are convinced that the writ in 1789

---

[8] The detainees are correct that they are not "enemy aliens." That term refers to citizens of a country with which the United States is at war. *See Al Odah*, 321 F.3d at 1139–40. But under the common law, the dispositive fact was not a petitioner's enemy alien status, but his lack of presence within any sovereign territory.

[9] The dissent claims the lack of any case on point is a result of the unique combination of circumstances in this case. But extraterritorial detention was not unknown in Eighteenth Century England. *See* HOLDSWORTH, *supra*, at 116–17; DUKER, *supra*, at 51–53. As noted, *supra*, these prisoners were beyond the protection of the law, which included access to habeas corpus. And *Eisentrager* (and the two hundred other alien petitioners the court noted, *see* 339 U.S. at 768 n.1) involved both extraterritorial detention and alien petitioners.

would not have been available to aliens held at an overseas military base leased from a foreign government.

The detainees encounter another difficulty with their Suspension Clause claim. Precedent in this court and the Supreme Court holds that the Constitution does not confer rights on aliens without property or presence within the United States. As we explained in *Al Odah*, 321 F.3d at 1140–41, the controlling case is *Johnson v. Eisentrager*. There twenty-one German nationals confined in custody of the U.S. Army in Germany filed habeas corpus petitions. Although the German prisoners alleged they were civilian agents of the German government, a military commission convicted them of war crimes arising from military activity against the United States in China after Germany's surrender. They claimed their convictions and imprisonment violated various constitutional provisions and the Geneva Conventions. The Supreme Court rejected the proposition "that the Fifth Amendment confers rights upon all persons, whatever their nationality, wherever they are located and whatever their offenses," 339 U.S. at 783. The Court continued: "If the Fifth Amendment confers its rights on all the world . . . [it] would mean that during military occupation irreconcilable enemy elements, guerrilla fighters, and 'werewolves' could require the American Judiciary to assure them freedoms of speech, press, and assembly as in the First Amendment, right to bear arms as in the Second, security against 'unreasonable' searches and seizures as in the Fourth, as well as rights to jury trial as in the Fifth and Sixth Amendments." *Id.* at 784. (Shortly before Germany's surrender, the Nazis began training covert forces called "werewolves" to conduct terrorist activities during the Allied occupation. *See* http://www.archives.gov/iwg/ declassified_records/oss_ records_263_wilhelm_hoettl.html.)

Later Supreme Court decisions have followed *Eisentrager*. In 1990, for instance, the Court stated that *Eisentrager* "rejected the claim that aliens are entitled to Fifth Amendment rights outside the sovereign territory of the United States." *United States v. Verdugo-Urquidez*, 494 U.S. 259, 269 (1990). After describing the facts of *Eisentrager* and quoting from the opinion, the Court concluded that with respect to aliens, "our rejection of extraterritorial application of the Fifth Amendment was emphatic." *Id.* By analogy, the Court held that the Fourth Amendment did not protect nonresident aliens against unreasonable searches or seizures conducted outside the sovereign territory of the United States. *Id.* at 274–75. Citing *Eisentrager* again, the Court explained that to extend the Fourth Amendment to aliens abroad "would have significant and deleterious consequences for the United States in conducting activities beyond its boundaries," particularly since the government "frequently employs Armed Forces outside this country," *id.* at 273. A decade after *Verdugo-Urquidez*, the Court – again citing *Eisentrager* – found it "well established that certain constitutional protections available to persons inside the United States are unavailable to aliens outside of our geographic borders." *Zadvydas v. Davis*, 533 U.S. 678, 693 (2001).[10]

Any distinction between the naval base at Guantanamo Bay and the prison in Landsberg, Germany, where the petitioners in *Eisentrager* were held, is immaterial to the application of the Suspension Clause. The United States occupies the Guantanamo Bay Naval Base under an indefinite lease it entered into in 1903. *See Al Odah*, 321 F.3d at 1142. The text of the lease and decisions of circuit courts and the Supreme Court all make clear that Cuba – not the United States – has sovereignty over Guantanamo Bay.

---

[10] The *Rasul* decision, resting as it did on statutory interpretation, *see* 542 U.S. at 475, 483–84, could not possibly have affected the constitutional holding of *Eisentrager*. Even if *Rasul* somehow calls *Eisentrager*'s constitutional holding into question, as the detainees suppose, we would be bound to follow *Eisentrager*. *See Rodriguez de Quijas v. Shearson/American Exp., Inc.*, 490 U.S. 477, 484–85 (1989).

See Vermilya-Brown Co. v. Connell, 335 U.S. 377, 381 (1948); *Cuban Am. Bar Ass'n v. Christopher*, 43 F.3d 1412 (11th Cir. 1995). The "determination of sovereignty over an area," the Supreme Court has held, "is for the legislative and executive departments." *Vermilya-Brown*, 335 U.S. at 380. Here the political departments have firmly and clearly spoken: "'United States,' when used in a geographic sense . . . does not include the United States Naval Station, Guantanamo Bay, Cuba." DTA §1005(g).

The detainees cite the *Insular Cases* in which "fundamental personal rights" extended to U.S. territories. *See Balzac v. Porto Rico*, 258 U.S. 298, 312–13 (1922); *Dorr v. United States*, 195 U.S. 138, 148 (1904); *see also Ralpho v. Bell*, 569 F.2d 607 (D.C. Cir. 1977). But in each of those cases, Congress had exercised its power under Article IV, Section 3 of the Constitution to regulate "Territory or other Property belonging to the United States," U. S. CONST., art. IV, §3, cl. 2. These cases do not establish anything regarding the sort of *de facto* sovereignty the detainees say exists at Guantanamo. Here Congress and the President have specifically disclaimed the sort of territorial jurisdiction they asserted in Puerto Rico, the Philippines, and Guam.

Precedent in this circuit also forecloses the detainees' claims to constitutional rights. In *Harbury v. Deutch*, 233 F.3d 596, 604 (D.C. Cir. 2000), *rev'd on other grounds sub nom. Christopher v. Harbury*, 536 U.S. 403 (2002), we quoted extensively from *Verdugo-Urquidez* and held that the Court's description of *Eisentrager* was "firm and considered dicta that binds this court." Other decisions of this court are firmer still. Citing *Eisentrager*, we held in *Pauling v. McElroy*, 278 F.2d 252, 254 n.3 (D.C. Cir. 1960) (per curiam), that "non-resident aliens . . . plainly cannot appeal to the protection of the Constitution or laws of the United States." The law of this circuit is that a "foreign entity without property or presence in this country has no constitutional rights, under the due process clause or otherwise." *People's Mojahedin Org. of Iran v. U.S. Dep't of State*, 182 F.3d 17, 22 (D.C. Cir. 1999); *see also 32 County Sovereignty Comm. v. U.S. Dep't of State*, 292 F.3d 797, 799 (D.C. Cir. 2002).[11]

As against this line of authority, the dissent offers the distinction that the Suspension Clause is a limitation on congressional power rather than a constitutional right. But this is no distinction at all. Constitutional rights are rights against the government and, as such, *are* restrictions on governmental power. *See H.P. Hood & Sons, Inc. v. Du Mond*, 336 U.S. 525, 534 (1949) ("Even the Bill of Rights amendments were framed only as a limitation upon the powers of Congress.").[12] Consider the First Amendment. (In contrasting the Suspension Clause with provisions in the Bill of Rights, *see* Dissent at 3, the dissent is careful to ignore the First Amendment.) Like the Suspension Clause, the First Amendment is framed as a limitation on Congress: "Congress shall make no law. . . ." Yet no one would deny that the First Amendment protects the rights to free speech and religion and assembly.

The dissent's other arguments are also filled with holes. It is enough to point out three of the larger ones.

There is the notion that the Suspension Clause is different from the Fourth, Fifth, and Sixth Amendments because it does not mention individuals and those amendments

---

[11] The text of the Suspension Clause also does not lend itself freely to extraterritorial application. The Clause permits suspension of the writ only in cases of "Rebellion or Invasion," neither of which is applicable to foreign military conflicts. *See Hamdi v. Rumsfeld*, 542 U.S. 507, 593–94 (2004) (Thomas, J., dissenting); *see also* J. Andrew Kent, *A Textual and Historical Case Against a Global Constitution*, 95 GEO. L.J. (forthcoming 2007) (manuscript at 59–60, available at http://ssrn.com/abstract=888602).

[12] James Madison's plan was to insert almost the entire Bill of Rights into the Constitution rather than wait for amendment. His proposed location of the Bill of Rights? Article I, Section 9 – next to the Suspension Clause. *See* Thomas Y. Davies, *Recovering the Original Fourth Amendment*, 98 MICH. L. REV. 547, 700–01 & n.437 (1999).

do (respectively, "people," "person," and "the accused"). *See* Dissent at 3. Why the dissent thinks this is significant eludes us. Is the point that if a provision does not mention individuals there is no constitutional right? That cannot be right. The First Amendment's guarantees of freedom of speech and free exercise of religion do not mention individuals; nor does the Eighth Amendment's prohibition on cruel and unusual punishment or the Seventh Amendment's guarantee of a civil jury. Of course it is fair to assume that these provisions apply to individuals, just as it is fair to assume that petitions for writs of habeas corpus are filed by individuals.

The dissent also looks to the Bill of Attainder and Ex Post Facto Clauses, both located next to the Suspension Clause in Article I, Section 9. We do not understand what the dissent is trying to make of this juxtaposition. The citation to *United States v. Lovett*, 328 U.S. 303 (1946), is particularly baffling. *Lovett* held only that the Bill of Attainder Clause was justiciable. The dissent's point cannot be that the Bill of Attainder Clause and the Ex Post Facto Clause do not protect individual rights. Numerous courts have held the opposite.[13] "The fact that the Suspension Clause abuts the prohibitions on bills of attainder and ex post facto laws, provisions well-accepted to protect individual liberty, further supports viewing the habeas privilege as *a core individual right.*" Amanda L. Tyler, *Is Suspension a Political Question?*, 59 Stan. L. Rev. 333, 374 & n.227 (2006) (emphasis added).[14]

Why is the dissent so fixated on how to characterize the Suspension Clause? The unstated assumption must be that the reasoning of our decisions and the Supreme Court's in denying constitutional rights to aliens outside the United States would not apply if a constitutional provision could be characterized as protecting something other than a "right." On this theory, for example, aliens outside the United States are entitled to the protection of the Separation of Powers because they have no individual rights under the Separation of Powers. Where the dissent gets this strange idea is a mystery, as is the reasoning behind it.

III.

Federal courts have no jurisdiction in these cases. In supplemental briefing after enactment of the DTA, the government asked us not only to decide the habeas jurisdiction question, but also to review the merits of the detainees' designation as enemy combatants by their Combatant Status Review Tribunals. *See* DTA §1005(e)(2).[15] The detainees objected to converting their habeas appeals to appeals from their Tribunals. In briefs filed after the DTA became law and after the Supreme Court decided *Hamdan*, they argued that we were without authority to do so.[16] Even if we have authority to convert

---

[13] *See South Carolina v. Katzenbach*, 383 U.S. 301, 323–24 (1966) ("[C]ourts have consistently regarded the Bill of Attainder Clause of Article I and the principle of the separation of powers only as protections for individual persons and private groups. . . .") (citing *United States v. Brown*, 381 U.S. 437 (1965); *Ex parte Garland*, 71 U.S. (4 Wall.) 333 (1866)); *see also Wilkinson v. Dotson*, 544 U.S. 74, 82 (2005); *Weaver v. Graham*, 450 U.S. 24, 28–29 (1981); *Nixon v. Adm'r of Gen. Servs.*, 433 U.S. 425, 468–69 (1977); *Shabazz v. Gabry*, 123 F.3d 909, 912 (6th Cir. 1997).

[14] *Accord* Jay S. Bybee, *Common Ground: Robert Jackson, Antonin Scalia, and a Power Theory of the First Amendment*, 75 Tul. L. Rev. 251, 318, 321 (2000) ("[W]e could easily describe [Article I,] Section 9 as a bill of rights for the people of the United States.").

[15] *See* Supplemental Br. of the Federal Parties Addressing the Detainee Treatment Act of 2005 53–54 ("This Court can and should convert the pending appeals into petitions for review under [DTA section] 1005(e)(2).").

[16] *See* The Guantanamo Detainees' Supplemental Br. Addressing the Effect of the Supreme Ct.'s Op. in *Hamdan v. Rumsfeld*, 126 S. Ct. 2749 (2006), on the Pending Appeals 8–9 ("The detainees in the pending petitions challenge the lawfulness of their detentions – not the subsequent CSRT decisions. . . ."); Corrected Supplemental Br. of Pet'rs Boumediene, et al., & Khalid Regarding Section 1005 of the Detainee Treatment Act of 2005 56–59 ("Nothing in the [DTA] authorizes the Court to 'convert' Petitioners' notices of appeal of the

the habeas appeals over the petitioners' objections, the record does not have sufficient information to perform the review the DTA allows. Our only recourse is to vacate the district courts' decisions and dismiss the cases for lack of jurisdiction.

So ordered.

ROGERS, *Circuit Judge*, dissenting: I can join neither the reasoning of the court nor its conclusion that the federal courts lack power to consider the detainees' petitions. While I agree that Congress intended to withdraw federal jurisdiction through the Military Commissions Act of 2006, Pub. L. No. 109–366, 120 Stat. 2600 ("MCA"), the court's holding that the MCA is consistent with the Suspension Clause of Article I, section 9, of the Constitution does not withstand analysis. By concluding that this court must reject "the detainees' claims to constitutional rights," Op. at 21, the court fundamentally misconstrues the nature of suspension: Far from conferring an individual right that might pertain only to persons substantially connected to the United States, *see United States v. Verdugo-Urquidez*, 494 U.S. 259, 271 (1990), the Suspension Clause is a limitation on the powers of Congress. Consequently, it is only by misreading the historical record and ignoring the Supreme Court's well-considered and binding dictum in *Rasul v. Bush*, 542 U.S. 466, 481–82 (2004), that the writ at common law would have extended to the detainees, that the court can conclude that neither this court nor the district courts have jurisdiction to consider the detainees' habeas claims.

A review of the text and operation of the Suspension Clause shows that, by nature, it operates to constrain the powers of Congress. Prior to the enactment of the MCA, the Supreme Court acknowledged that the detainees held at Guantanamo had a statutory right to habeas corpus. *Rasul*, 542 U.S. at 483–84. The MCA purports to withdraw that right but does so in a manner that offends the constitutional constraint on suspension. The Suspension Clause limits the removal of habeas corpus, at least as the writ was understood at common law, to times of rebellion or invasion unless Congress provides an adequate alternative remedy. The writ would have reached the detainees at common law, and Congress has neither provided an adequate alternative remedy, through the Detainee Treatment Act of 2005, Pub. L. No. 109–148, Div. A, tit. X, 119 Stat. 2680, 2739 ("DTA"), nor invoked the exception to the Clause by making the required findings to suspend the writ. The MCA is therefore void and does not deprive this court or the district courts of jurisdiction.

On the merits of the detainees' appeal in *Khalid v. Bush*, 355 F. Supp. 2d 311 (D.D.C. 2005) and the cross-appeals in *In re Guantanamo Detainee Cases*, 355 F. Supp. 2d 443 (D.D.C. 2005), I would affirm in part in *Guantanamo Detainee Cases* and reverse in *Khalid* and remand the cases to the district courts.

I.

Where a court has no jurisdiction it is powerless to act. *See, e.g., Marbury v. Madison*, 5 U. S. (1 Cranch) 13 7, 173–74 (1803). But a statute enacted by Congress purporting to deprive a court of jurisdiction binds that court only when Congress acts pursuant to the powers it derives from the Constitution. The court today concludes that the Suspension Clause is an individual right that cannot be invoked by the detainees. *See* Op. at 22. The

---

district court's judgment into original petitions for review of CSRT decisions under section 1005(e)(2) of the Act."); The Guantanamo Detainees' Corrected Second Supplemental Br. Addressing the Effect of the Detainee Treatment Act of 2005 on this Ct.'s Jurisdiction over the Pending Appeals 43–44 ("[T]his court should not convert these petitions into petitions for review under the DTA as the government suggests.").

text of the Suspension Clause and the structure of the Constitution belie this conclusion. The court further concludes that the detainees would have had no access to the writ of habeas corpus at common law. *See* Op. at 14–17. The historical record and the guidance of the Supreme Court disprove this conclusion.

In this Part, I address the nature of the Suspension Clause, the retroactive effect of Congress's recent enactment on habeas corpus – the MCA – and conclude with an assessment of the effect of the MCA in light of the dictates of the Constitution.

A.

The court holds that Congress may suspend habeas corpus as to the detainees because they have no individual rights under the Constitution. It is unclear where the court finds that the limit on suspension of the writ of habeas corpus is an individual entitlement. The Suspension Clause itself makes no reference to citizens or even persons. Instead, it directs that "[t]he Privilege of the Writ of Habeas Corpus shall not be suspended, unless when in Cases of Rebellion or Invasion the public Safety may require it. " U. S. CONST. art. I, §9, cl. 2. This mandate appears in the ninth section of Article I, which enumerates those actions expressly excluded from Congress's powers. Although the Clause does not specifically say so, it is settled that only Congress may do the suspending. *Ex parte Bollman*, 8 U.S. (4 Cranch) 75, 101 (1807); *see Hamdi v. Rumsfeld*, 542 U.S. 507, 562 (2004) (Scalia, J., dissenting); *Ex parte Merryman*, 17 F. Cas. 144, 151–152 (No. 9487) (Taney, Circuit Justice, C.C.D. Md. 1861); 2 JOSEPH STORY, COMMENTARIES ON THE CONSTITUTION OF THE UNITED STATES §1342 (5th ed. 1891). In this manner, by both its plain text and inclusion in section 9, the Suspension Clause differs from the Fourth Amendment, which establishes a "right of the people," the Fifth Amendment, which limits how a "person shall be held," and the Sixth Amendment, which provides rights to "the accused." These provisions confer rights to the persons listed.[1]

The other provisions of Article I, section 9, indicate how to read the Suspension Clause. The clause immediately following provides that "[n]o Bill of Attainder or ex post facto Law shall be passed."[2] The Supreme Court has construed the Attainder Clause as establishing a "category of Congressional actions which the Constitution barred." *United States v. Lovett*, 328 U.S. 303, 315 (1946). In *Lovett*, the Court dismissed the possibility that an Act of Congress in violation of the Attainder Clause was non-justiciable, remarking:

---

[1] The Suspension Clause is also distinct from the First Amendment, which has been interpreted as a guarantor of individual rights. *See, e.g., United States v. Robel*, 389 U.S. 258, 263 (1967); *Gitlow v. New York*, 268 U.S. 652, 666 (1925). The court cannot seriously maintain that the two provisions are alike while acknowledging that the First Amendment confers an individual right enforceable by the courts and simultaneously claiming that the Suspension Clause does not, *see* Op. at 13 n.5 (citing *Bollman*, 8 U.S. (4 Cranch) at 95); *see also In re Barry*, 42 F. 113, 122 (C.C.S.D.N.Y. 1844), *error dismissed sub nom. Barry v. Mercein*, 46 U.S. 103 (1847) ("The ninth section of the first article of the constitution, par. 2, declaring that 'the privilege of the writ of habeas corpus shall not be suspended unless, when in cases of rebellion or invasion, the public safety may require it does not purport to convey power or jurisdiction to the judiciary. It is in restraint of executive and legislative powers, and no further affects the judiciary than to impose on them the necessity, if the privilege of habeas corpus is suspended by any authority, to decide whether the exigency demanded by the constitution exists to sanction the act.").

[2] Suspensions and bills of attainder have a shared history. In England, suspensions occasionally named specific individuals and therefore amounted to bills of attainder. *See* Rex A. Collings, Jr., *Habeas Corpus for Convicts – Constitutional Right or Legislative Grace?*, 40 CAL. L. REV. 335, 339 (1952).

Our Constitution did not contemplate such a result. To quote Alexander Hamilton, *** a limited constitution *** [is] one which contains certain specified exceptions to the legislative authority; such, for instance, as that it shall pass no bills of attainder, no ex post facto laws, and the like. Limitations of this kind can be preserved in practice no other way than through the medium of the courts of justice; *whose duty it must be to declare all acts contrary to the manifest tenor of the Constitution void.* Without this, all the reservations of particular rights or privileges would amount to nothing.

Id. at 314 (quoting THE FEDERALIST No. 78) (emphasis added) (alteration and omissions in original). So too, in *Weaver v. Graham*, 450 U.S. 24, 28–29 & n.10 (1981), where the Court noted that the ban on *ex post facto* legislation "restricts governmental power by restraining arbitrary and potentially vindictive legislation" and acknowledged that the clause "confin[es] the legislature to penal decisions with prospective effect." *See also Marbury*, 5 U.S. (1 Cranch) at 179–80; *Foretich v. United States*, 351 F.3d 1198, 1216-26 (D.C. Cir. 2003). For like reasons, any act in violation of the Suspension Clause is void, *cf. Lovett*, 328 U.S. at 316, and cannot operate to divest a court of jurisdiction.[3]

The court dismisses the distinction between individual rights and limitations on Congress's powers. It chooses to make no affirmative argument of its own, instead hoping to rebut the sizable body of conflicting authorities.

The court appears to believe that the Suspension Clause is just like the constitutional amendments that form the Bill of Rights.[4] It is a truism, of course, that individual rights like those found in the first ten amendments work to limit Congress. However, individual rights are merely a subset of those matters that constrain the legislature. These two sets cannot be understood as coextensive unless the court is prepared to recognize such awkward individual rights as Commerce Clause rights, *see* U. S. CONST. art. I, §8, cl. 3, or the personal right not to have a bill raising revenue that originates in the Senate, *see* U.S. CONST. art. I, §7, cl. 1; *see also Schlesinger v. Reservists Comm. to Stop the War*, 418 U.S. 208, 224 (1974) (finding no individual right under the Ineligibility Clause).

That the Suspension Clause appears in Article I, section 9, is not happenstance. In Charles Pinckney's original proposal, suspension would have been part of the judiciary

---

[3] The court cites a number of cases for the proposition that the Attainder Clause confers an individual right instead of operating as a structural limitation on Congress. *See* Op. at 23 n.13. None of these cases makes the court's point. In *South Carolina v. Katzenbach*, 383 U.S. 301, 323–24 (1966), the Supreme Court held that it is not a bill of attainder for Congress to punish a state. This speaks to the definition of a bill of attainder and says nothing about the operation of the Attainder Clause. *Weaver v. Graham*, 450 U.S. 24, 30 (1981), says the opposite of what the court asserts. In *Weaver*, the Supreme Court emphasized that the *Ex Post Facto* Clause is not intended to protect individual rights but governs the operation of government institutions:

The presence or absence of an affirmative, enforceable right is not relevant, however, to the *ex post facto* prohibition, which forbids the imposition of punishment more severe than the punishment assigned by law when the act to be punished occurred. Critical to relief under the *Ex Post Facto* Clause is not an individual's right to less punishment, but the lack of fair notice and governmental restraint when the legislature increases punishment beyond what was prescribed when the crime was consummated. Thus, even if a statute merely alters penal provisions accorded by the grace of the legislature, it violates the Clause if it is both retrospective and more onerous than the law in effect on the date of the offense.

The Court also emphasized the structural nature of the limitations of Article I, section 9, in *Nixon v. Adm'r of Gen. Servs.*, 433 U.S. 425, 469 (1977) (noting that "the Bill of Attainder Clause [is]...one of the organizing principles of our system of government"). Unsurprisingly, the court cites no authority that would support its novel construction of section 9 by providing that certain individuals lack Attainder Clause or *Ex Post Facto* Clause rights.

[4] For this point, the court quotes, without context, from *H.P. Hood & Sons, Inc. v. Du Mond*, 336 U.S. 525 (1949), *see* Op. at 22. In that case, the Supreme Court emphasized that the Bill of Rights limited the powers of Congress and did not affect the powers of the individual states, *H.P. Hood & Sons*, 336 U.S. at 534, at least until certain amendments were incorporated after ratification of the Fourteenth Amendment. This says nothing about the distinction, relevant here, between individual rights and limitations on Congress.

provision. It was moved in September 1789 by the Committee on Style and Arrangement, which gathered the restrictions on Congress's power in one location. *See* WILLIAM F. DUKER, A CONSTITUTIONAL HISTORY OF HABEAS CORPUS 128–32 (1980); 2 THE RECORDS OF THE FEDERAL CONVENTION OF 1787, at 596 (Max Farrand ed., rev. ed. 1966). By the court's reasoning, the Framers placed the Suspension Clause in Article I merely because there were no similar individual rights to accompany it. It is implausible that the Framers would have viewed the Suspension Clause, as the court implies, as a budding Bill of Rights but would not have assigned the provision its own section of the Constitution, much as they did with the only crime specified in the document, treason, which appears alone in Article III, section 3. Instead, the court must treat the Suspension Clause's placement in Article I, section 9, as a conscious determination of a limit on Congress's powers. The Supreme Court has found similar meaning in the placement of constitutional clauses ever since *McCulloch v. Maryland,* 17 U.S. (4 Wheat.) 316, 419–21 (1819) (Necessary and Proper Clause); *see also,e.g., Skinner v. Mid-America Pipeline Co.,* 490 U.S. 212, 220–21 (1989) (Taxing Clause).

The court also alludes to the idea that the Suspension Clause cannot apply to foreign military conflicts because the exception extends only to cases of "Rebellion or Invasion." Op. at 21 n. 11. The Framers understood that the privilege of the writ was of such great significance that its suspension should be strictly limited to circumstances where the peace and security of the Nation were jeopardized. Only after considering alternative proposals authorizing suspension "on the most urgent occasions" or forbidding suspension outright did the Framers agree to a narrow exception upon a finding of rebellion or invasion. *See* 2 THE RECORDS OF THE FEDERAL CONVENTION OF 1787, *supra*, at 438. Indeed, it would be curious if the Framers were implicitly sanctioning Executive-ordered detention abroad without judicial review by limiting suspension – and by the court's reasoning therefore limiting habeas corpus – to domestic events. To the contrary, as Alexander Hamilton foresaw in *The Federalist No. 84,* invoking William Blackstone,

> To bereave a man of life (says he), or by violence to confiscate his estate, without accusation or trial, would be so gross and notorious an act of despotism, as must at once convey the alarm of tyranny throughout the whole nation; but confinement of the person, by secretly hurrying him to jail, where his sufferings are unknown or forgotten, is a less public, a less striking, and therefore *a more dangerous engine* of arbitrary government.

THE FEDERALIST NO. 84, at 468 (E.H. Scott ed. 1898) (quoting WILLIAM BLACKSTONE, 1 COMMENTARIES *131–32); *see also Ex parte Milligan,* 71 U.S. (4 Wall.) 2, 125 (1866).

. . .

C.

The question, then, is whether by attempting to eliminate all federal court jurisdiction to consider petitions for writs of habeas corpus, Congress has overstepped the boundary established by the Suspension Clause. The Supreme Court has stated on several occasions that "at the absolute minimum, the Suspension Clause protects the writ 'as it existed in 1789.'" *St. Cyr,* 533 U.S. at 301 (quoting *Felker v. Turpin,* 518 U.S. 651, 663–64 (1996)) (emphasis added). Therefore, at least insofar as habeas corpus exists and existed in 1789, Congress cannot suspend the writ without providing an adequate alternative except in the narrow exception specified in the Constitution.[5] This proscription applies

---

[5] It is unnecessary to resolve the question of whether the Constitution provides for an affirmative right to habeas corpus – either through the Suspension Clause, the Fifth Amendment guarantee of due process, or the Sixth Amendment – or presumed the continued vitality of this "writ antecedent to statute," *Williams v.*

equally to removing the writ itself and to removing all jurisdiction to issue the writ. *See United States v. Klein*, 80 U.S. (13 Wall.) 128 (1872). *See generally* ERWIN CHEMERINSKY, FEDERAL JURISDICTION §3.2 (4th ed. 2003).

1.

Assessing the state of the law in 1789 is no trivial feat, and the court's analysis today demonstrates how quickly a few missteps can obscure history. In conducting its historical review, the court emphasizes that no English cases predating 1789 award the relief that the detainees seek in their petitions. Op. at 15–17. "The short of the matter," the court concludes, is that "habeas corpus would not have been available in 1789 to aliens without presence or property within the United States." Op. at 17. But this misses the mark. There may well be no case at common law in which a court exercises jurisdiction over the habeas corpus claim of an alien from a friendly nation, who may himself be an enemy, who is captured abroad and held outside the sovereign territory of England but within the Crown's exclusive control without being charged with a crime or violation of the Laws of War. On the other hand, the court can point to no case where an English court has refused to exercise habeas jurisdiction because the enemy being held, while under the control of the Crown, was not within the Crown's dominions.[6] The paucity of direct precedent is a consequence of the unique confluence of events that defines the situation of these detainees and not a commentary on the reach of the writ at common law.

The question is whether by the process of inference from similar, if not identical, situations the reach of the writ at common law would have extended to the detainees' petitions. At common law, we know that "the reach of the writ depended not on formal notions of territorial sovereignty, but rather on the practical question of 'the exact extent and nature of the jurisdiction or dominion exercised in fact by the Crown.'" *Rasul*, 542 U.S. at 482 (quoting *Ex parte Mwenya*, [1960] 1 Q.B. 241, 303 (C.A.) (Lord Evershed, M.R.)). We also know that the writ extended not only to citizens of the realm, but to aliens, *see id.* at 481 & n.11, even in wartime, *see id.* at 474–75; *Case of Three Spanish Sailors*, 2 Black. W. 1324, 96 Eng. Rep. 775 (C.P. 1779); *Rex v. Schiever*, 2 Burr. 765, 97 Eng. Rep. 551 (K.B. 1759). A War of 1812-era case in which Chief Justice John Marshall granted a habeas writ to a British subject establishes that even conceded enemies of the United States could test in its courts detention that they claimed was unauthorized.

Kaiser, 323 U.S. 471, 484 n.2 (1945) (internal quotation marks omitted). Because the Supreme Court in *Rasul* held that the writ existed in 2004 and that there was, therefore, something to suspend, it is sufficient to assess whether the writ sought here existed in 1789. Given my conclusion, *see infra* Part C.1, it is also unnecessary to resolve the question of whether the Suspension Clause protects the writ of habeas corpus as it has developed since 1789. *Compare St. Cyr*, 533 U.S. at 304–05, and *LaGuerre v. Reno*, 164 F.3d 1035, 1038 (7th Cir. 1998), with *Felker*, 518 U.S. at 663–64, and Gerald L. Neuman, *Habeas Corpus, Executive Detention, and the Removal of Aliens*, 98 COLUM. L. REV. 961, 970 (1998). The court oddly chooses to ignore the issue by truncating its reference to *St. Cyr*, without comment, and omitting the qualifier "at the absolute minimum." *See* Op. at 14.

[6] The court's assertion that "extraterritorial detention was not unknown in Eighteenth Century England," Op. at 18 n.9, is of no moment. The court references the 1667 impeachment of the Earl of Clarendon, Lord High Chancellor of England. *See id.* at 16, 18 n.9. Clarendon was accused of sending enemies to faraway lands to deprive them of effective legal process. The court makes the unsupported inference that habeas corpus was therefore unavailable abroad. Nothing in the Clarendon affair suggests that habeas corpus was sought and refused. Instead, as remains the case today, legal process can be evaded when prisoners are detained without access to the courts. That the detainees at Guantanamo were able to procure next friends and attorneys to pursue their petitions whereas seventeenth-century Englishmen would have found this difficult, if not impossible, says nothing about the availability of the writ at common law. The court's obfuscation as to the distinction between impracticality and unavailability is further addressed *infra*.

See Gerald L. Neuman & Charles F. Hobson, *John Marshall and the Enemy Alien: A Case Missing from the Canon*, 9 Green Bag 2D 39 (2005) (reporting *United States v. Williams* (C.C.D.Va. Dec. 4, 1813)).

To draw the ultimate conclusion as to whether the writ at common law would have extended to aliens under the control (if not within the sovereign territory) of the Crown requires piecing together the considerable circumstantial evidence, a step that the court is unwilling to take. Analysis of one of these cases, the 1759 English case of *Rex v. Schiever*, shows just how small this final inference is. Barnard Schiever was the subject of a neutral nation (Sweden), who was detained by the Crown when England was at war with France. *Schiever*, 2 Burr. at 765, 97 Eng. Rep. at 551. He claimed that his classification as a "prisoner of war" was factually inaccurate, because he "was desirous of entering into the service of the merchants of England" until he was seized on the high seas by a French privateer, which in turn was captured by the British Navy. *Id.* In an affidavit, he swore that his French captor "detained him[] against his will and inclination . . . and treated him with so much severity[] that [his captor] would not suffer him to go on shore when in port . . . but closely confined him to duty [on board the ship]." *Id.* at 765–66, 97 Eng. Rep. at 551. The habeas court ultimately determined, on the basis of Schiever's own testimony, that he was properly categorized and thus lawfully detained. *Id.* at 766, 97 Eng. Rep. at 551–52.

The court discounts *Schiever* because, after England captured the French privateer while en route to Norway, it was carried into Liverpool, England, where Schiever was held in the town jail. *Id.*, 97 Eng. Rep. at 551. As such, the case did not involve "an alien outside the territory of the sovereign." Op. at 14–15. However, Schiever surely was not *voluntarily* brought into England, so his mere presence conferred no additional rights. As the Supreme Court observed in *Verdugo-Urquidez*, "involuntary [presence] is not the sort to indicate any substantial connection with our country." 494 U.S. at 271. Any gap between *Schiever* and the detainees' detention at Guantanamo Bay is thus exceedingly narrow.

This court need not make the final inference. It has already been made for us. In *Rasul*, the Supreme Court stated that "[a]pplication of the habeas statute to persons detained at the [Guantanamo] base is consistent with the historical reach of the writ of habeas corpus." 542 U. S. at 481. By reaching a contrary conclusion, the court ignores the settled principle that "carefully considered language of the Supreme Court, even if technically dictum, generally must be treated as authoritative." *Sierra Club v. EPA*, 322 F.3d 718, 724 (D.C. Cir. 2003) (quoting *United States v. Oakar*, 111 F.3d 146, 153 (D.C. Cir. 1997)) (internal quotation marks omitted). Even setting aside this principle, the court offers no convincing analysis to compel the contrary conclusion. The court makes three assertions: First, Lord Mansfield opinion in *Rex v. Cowle*, 2 Burr. 834, 97 Eng. Rep. 587 (K.B. 1759), disavows the right claimed by the detainees. Second, it would have been impractical for English courts to extend the writ extraterritorially. Third, *Johnson v. Eisentrager*, 339 U.S. 763 (1949), is controlling. None of these assertions withstands scrutiny.

In *Cowle*, Lord Mansfield wrote that "[t]here is no doubt as to the power of this Court; where the place is under the subjection of the Crown of England; the only question is, as to the propriety." 2 Burr. at 856, 97 Eng. Rep. at 599. He noted thereafter, by way of qualification, that the writ would not extend "[t]o foreign dominions, which belong to a prince who succeeds to the throne of England." *Id.*, 97 Eng. Rep. at 599–600. Through the use of ellipsis marks, the court excises the qualification and concludes that the writ does not extend "[t]o foreign dominions." Op. at 16. This masks two problems in its analysis. A "foreign dominion" is not a foreign country, as the court's reasoning implies, but rather "a country which at some time formed part of the dominions of a foreign state or potentate, but which by conquest or cession has become a part of the dominions of the Crown of England." *Ex parte Brown*, 5 B. & S. 280, 122 Eng. Rep. 835 (K.B. 1864). And the exception noted in Lord Mansfield's qualification has nothing to do with extraterritoriality: Instead, habeas from mainland courts was unnecessary for territories like Scotland that were controlled by princes in the line of succession because they had independent court systems. *See* WILLIAM BLACKSTONE, 1 COMMENTARIES *95-98; James E. Pfander, *The Limits of Habeas Jurisdiction and the Global War on Terror*, 91 CORNELL L. REV. 497, 512-13 (2006). In the modern-day parallel, where a suitable alternative for habeas exists, the writ need not extend. *See* 2 ROBERT CHAMBERS, A COURSE OF LECTURES ON THE ENGLISH LAW DELIVERED AT OXFORD 1767-1773, at 8 (Thomas M.Curley, ed., 1986) (quoting *Cowle* as indicating that, notwithstanding the power to issue the writ "in *Guernsey, Jersey, Minorca*, or the *plantations*," courts would not think it "proper to interpose" because "the most usual way is to complain to the *king in Council*, the supreme court of appeal from those provincial governments"); *see also infra* Part C.2. The relationship between England and principalities was the only instance where it was "found necessary to restrict the scope of the writ." 9 WILLIAM HOLDSWORTH, A HISTORY OF ENGLISH LAW 124 (1938). *Cowle*, by its plain language, then, must be read as recognizing that the writ of habeas corpus ran even to places that were "no part of the realm," where the Crown's other writs did not run, nor did its laws apply. 2 Burr. at 835-36, 853-55, 97 Eng. Rep. at 587-88, 598-99. The Supreme Court has adopted this logical reading. *See Rasul*, 542 U. S. at 481-82; *see also* Mitchell B. Malachowski, *From Gitmo with Love: Redefining Habeas Corpus Jurisdiction in the Wake of the Enemy Combatant Cases of 2004*, 52 NAVAL L. REV. 118, 122-23 (2005).[7]

The court next disposes of *Cowle* and the historical record by suggesting that the "power" to issue the writ acknowledged by Lord Mansfield can be explained by the Habeas Corpus Act of 1679, 31 Car. 2, c. 2. *See* Op. at 16. The Supreme Court has stated that the Habeas Corpus Act "enforces the common law," *Ex parte Watkins*, 28 U.S. (3 Pet.) 193, 202 (1730), thus hardly suggesting that the "power" recognized by Lord Mansfield was statutory and not included within the 1789 scope of the common-law writ. To the extent that the court makes the curious argument that the Habeas Corpus Act would have made it too impractical to produce prisoners if applied extraterritorially because it imposed fines on jailers who did not quickly produce the body, Op. at 16-17, the court cites no precedent that suggests that "practical problems" eviscerate "the precious safeguard of personal liberty [for which] there is no higher duty than to maintain it unimpaired," *Bowen v. Johnston*, 306 U. S. 19, 26 (1939). This line of reasoning employed by the court fails for two main reasons:

First, the Habeas Corpus Act of 1679 was expressly limited to those who "have beene committed for criminall or supposed criminall Matters." 31 Car. 2, c. 2, §1. Hence, the burden of expediency imposed by the Act could scarcely have prevented common-law

---

[7] The significance of a 1794 opinion by the U.S. Attorney General, *see* Op. at 15, which expresses the view that the writ should issue to the foreign commander of a foreign ship-of-war in U.S. ports, reasoning that the foreign ship has "no exemption from the jurisdiction of the country into which he comes," 1 Op. Att'y Gen. 47 (1794), is unclear. Nor is it clear what point the court is making by referencing *In re Ning Yi-Ching*, 56 T.L.R. 3 (K.B. Vacation Ct. 1939). In *Rasul*, the Supreme Court noted that *Ning Yi-Ching* "made quite clear that 'the remedy of habeas corpus was not confined to British subjects,' but would extend to 'any person . . . detained' within the reach of the writ," 542 U.S. at 483 n.13 (quoting *Ning Yi-Ching*, 56 T.L.R. at 5), and that the case does not support a "narrow view of the territorial reach of the writ," id. Here, the court provides a parenthetical quotation for *Ning Yi-Ching* that recalls a dissenting position from a prior case that was later repudiated. See *Rasul*, 542 U.S. at 483 n.14; *Mwenya*, [1960] 1 Q.B. at 295 (Lord Evershed, M.R.).

courts from exercising habeas jurisdiction in noncriminal matters such as the petitions in these appeals. Statutory habeas in English courts did not extend to non-criminal detention until the Habeas Corpus Act of 1816, 56 Geo. 3, c. 100, although courts continued to exercise their common-law powers in the interim. *See* 2 CHAMBERS, *supra*, at 11; 9 HOLDSWORTH, *supra*, at 121.

Second, there is ample evidence that the writ did issue to faraway lands. In *Ex parte Anderson*, 3 El. & El. 487, 121 Eng. Rep. 525 (Q.B. 1861), *superseded by statute*, 25 & 26 Vict., c. 20, §1, the Court of Queen's Bench exercised its common-law powers to issue a writ of habeas corpus to Quebec in Upper Canada after expressly acknowledging that it was "sensible of the inconvenience which may result from such a step." *Id.* at 494–95, 121 Eng. Rep. at 527–28; *see also Brown*, 5 B. & S. 280, 122 Eng. Rep. 835 (issuing a writ to the Isle of Man in the sea between England and Ireland). English common-law courts also recognized the power to issue habeas corpus in India, even to non-subjects, and did so notwithstanding competition from local courts, well before England recognized its sovereignty in India. *See* B.N. PANDEY, THE INTRODUCTION OF ENGLISH LAW INTO INDIA 112, 149, 151 (1967); *see also Rex v. Mitter*, Morton 210 (Sup. Ct., Calcutta 1781), *reprinted in* 1 THE INDIAN DECISIONS (OLD SERIES) 1008 (T.A. Venkasawmy Row ed., 1911); *Rex v. Hastings*, Morton 206, 208–09 (Sup. Ct., Calcutta 1775) (opinion of Chambers, J.), *reprinted in* 1 THE INDIAN DECISIONS, *supra*, at 1005, 1007; *id.* at 209 (opinion of Impey, C. J.); Kal Raustiala, *The Geography of Justice*, 73 FORDHAM L. REV. 2501, 2530 n.156 (2005).

Finally, the court reasons that *Eisentrager* requires the conclusion that there is no constitutional right to habeas for those in the detainees' posture. *See* Op. at 17–18. In *Eisentrager*, the detainees claimed that they were "entitled, as a constitutional right, to sue in some court of the United States for a writ of *habeas corpus*." 339 U.S. at 777. Thus *Eisentrager* presented a far different question than confronts this court.[8] The detainees do not here contend that the Constitution accords them a positive right to the writ but rather that the Suspension Clause restricts Congress's power to eliminate a preexisting statutory right. To answer that question does not entail looking to the extent of the detainees' ties to the United States but rather requires understanding the scope of the writ of habeas corpus at common law in 1789. The court's reliance on *Eisentrager* is misplaced.

2.

This brings me to the question of whether, absent the writ, Congress has provided an adequate alternative procedure for challenging detention. If it so chooses, Congress may replace the privilege of habeas corpus with a commensurate procedure without overreaching its constitutional ambit. However, as the Supreme Court has cautioned, if a subject of Executive detention "were subject to any substantial procedural hurdles which ma[k]e his remedy . . . less swift and imperative than federal habeas corpus, the gravest constitutional doubts would be engendered [under the Suspension Clause]." *Sanders v. United States*, 373 U.S. 1, 14 (1963).

The Supreme Court has, on three occasions, found a replacement to habeas corpus to be adequate. In *United States v. Hayman*, 342 U.S. 205 (1952), the Court reviewed 42 U.S.C. §2255, which extinguished the writ as to those convicted of federal crimes before Article III judges in exchange for recourse before the sentencing court. Prior to

---

[8] To the extent that the court relies on *Eisentrager* as proof of its historical theory, the Supreme Court rejected that approach in *Rasul*, *see* 542 U.S. at 475–79.

the enactment of section 2255, the writ was available in the jurisdiction of detention, not the jurisdiction of conviction. The Court concluded that this substitute was acceptable in part because the traditional habeas remedy remained available by statute where section 2255 proved "inadequate or ineffective." *Id.* at 223. The Court came to a similar conclusion in *Swain v. Pressley*, 430 U.S. 372 (1977), reviewing a statute with a similar "inadequate or ineffective" escape hatch, *id.* at 381 (reviewing D.C. CODE §23–110). In that case, the Court concluded that a procedure for hearing habeas in the District of Columbia's courts, as distinct from the federal courts, was an adequate alternative. Finally, in *Felker*, 518 U. S. at 663–64, the Court found no Suspension Clause violation in the restrictions on successive petitions for the writ under the Antiterrorism and Effective Death Penalty Act of 1996, Pub. L. No. 104–132, 110 Stat. 1217, concluding that these were "well within the compass of [the] evolutionary process" of the habeas corpus protocol for abuse of the writ and did not impose upon the writ itself.

These cases provide little cover for the government. As the Supreme Court has stated, "[a]t its historical core, the writ of habeas corpus has served as a means of reviewing the legality of Executive detention, and it is in that context that its protections have been strongest." *St. Cyr*, 533 U.S. at 301. With this in mind, the government is mistaken in contending that the combatant status review tribunals ("CSRTs") established by the DTA suitably test the legitimacy of Executive detention. Far from merely adjusting the mechanism for vindicating the habeas right, the DTA imposes a series of hurdles while saddling each Guantanamo detainee with an assortment of handicaps that make the obstacles insurmountable.

At the core of the Great Writ is the ability to "inquire into illegal detention with a view to an order releasing the petitioner." *Preiser v. Rodriguez*, 411 U.S. 475, 484 (1973) (internal quotation marks and alteration omitted). An examination of the CSRT procedure and this court's CSRT review powers reveals that these alternatives are neither adequate to test whether detention is unlawful nor directed toward releasing those who are unlawfully held.

"Petitioners in habeas corpus proceedings . . . are entitled to careful consideration and plenary processing of their claims including full opportunity for the presentation of the relevant facts." *Harris v. Nelson*, 394 U.S. 286, 298 (1969). The offerings of CSRTs fall far short of this mark. Under the common law, when a detainee files a habeas petition, the burden shifts to the government to justify the detention in its return of the writ. When not facing an imminent trial,[9] the detainee then must be afforded an opportunity to traverse the writ, explaining why the grounds for detention are inadequate in fact or in law. *See, e.g.*, 28 U.S.C. §§2243, 2248; *Bollman*, 8 U.S. (4 Cranch) at 125; *Ex parte Beeching*, 4 B. & C. 137, 107 Eng. Rep. 1010 (K.B. 1825); *Schiever*, 2 Burr. 765, 97 Eng. Rep. 551; *cf. Hamdi*, 542 U.S. at 537–38 (plurality opinion). A CSRT works quite differently. *See* Order Establishing Combatant Status Review Tribunal (July 7, 2004), *available* at http://www.defenselink.mil/news/Jul2004/d20040707review.pdf. The detainee bears the burden of coming forward with evidence explaining why he should *not* be detained. The detainee need not be informed of the basis for his detention (which may be classified), need not be allowed to introduce rebuttal evidence (which is sometimes deemed by the CSRT too impractical to acquire), and must proceed without the benefit of his own

---

[9] At common law, where criminal charges were pending, a prisoner filing a habeas writ would be remanded, although habeas incorporated a speedy-trial guarantee. *See, e.g., Ex parte Beeching*, 4 B. & C. 137, 107 Eng. Rep. 1010 (K.B. 1825); *Bushell's Case*, Vaugh. 135, 124 Eng. Rep. 1006, 1009-10 (C.P. 1670). *But see* MCA §3(a)(1), 120 Stat. at 2602 (codified at 10 U.S.C. §948b(d)(A)). Once there was "a judgment of conviction rendered by a court of general criminal jurisdiction," release under the writ was unavailable. *Hayman*, 342 U.S. at 210–11.

counsel.[10] Moreover, these proceedings occur before a board of military judges subject to command influence, *see Hamdan*, 126 S. Ct. at 2804, 2806 (Kennedy, J., concurring in part); *Weiss v. United States*, 510 U.S. 163, 179–80 (1994); *cf.* 10 U.S.C. §837(a). Insofar as each of these practices impedes the process of determining the true facts underlying the lawfulness of the challenged detention, they are inimical to the nature of habeas review.

This court's review of CSRT determinations, *see* DTA §1005(e)(2), 119 Stat. at 2742, is not designed to cure these inadequacies. This court may review only the record developed by the CSRT to assess whether the CSRT has complied with its own standards. Because a detainee still has no means to present evidence rebutting the government's case – even assuming the detainee could learn of its contents – assessing whether the government has more evidence in its favor than the detainee is hardly the proper antidote. The fact that this court also may consider whether the CSRT process "is consistent with the Constitution and laws of the United States," DTA §1005(e)(2)(C)(ii), 119 Stat. at 2742, does not obviate the need for habeas. Whereas a cognizable constitutional, statutory, or treaty violation could defeat the lawfulness of the government's cause for detention, the writ issues whenever the Executive lacks a lawful justification for continued detention. The provisions of DTA §1005(e)(2) cannot be reconciled with the purpose of habeas corpus, as they handcuff attempts to combat "the great engines of judicial despotism," THE FEDERALIST NO. 83, at 456 (Alexander Hamilton) (E.H. Scott ed. 1898).

Additionally, and more significant still, continued detention may be justified by a CSRT on the basis of evidence resulting from torture. Testimony procured by coercion is notoriously unreliable and unspeakably inhumane. *See generally* INTELLIGENCE SCIENCE BOARD, EDUCING INFORMATION: INTERROGATION: SCIENCE AND ART (2006), *available at* http://www.fas.org/irp/dni/educing.pdf. This basic point has long been recognized by the common law, which "has regarded torture and its fruits with abhorrence for over 500 years." *A. v. Sec'y of State*, [2006] 2 A.C. 221 ¶51 (H.L.) (appeal taken from Eng.) (Bingham, L.); *see also Hamdan*, 126 S. Ct. at 2786; *Jackson v. Denno*, 378 U.S. 368, 386 (1964); *Proceedings Against Felton*, 3 Howell's St. Tr. 367, 3 71 (162 8) (Eng.); JOHN H. LANGBEIN, TORTURE AND THE LAW OF PROOF 73 (1977) ("Already in the fifteenth and sixteenth centuries, . . . the celebrated Renaissance 'panegyrists' of English law were . . . extolling the absence of torture in England.") (footnote omitted). The DTA implicitly endorses holding detainees on the basis of such evidence by including an anti-torture provision that applies only to future CSRTs. DTA §1005(b)(2), 119 Stat. at 2741. Even for these future proceedings, however, the Secretary of Defense is required only to develop procedures to assess whether evidence obtained by torture is probative, not to require its exclusion. *Id.* §1005(b)(1), 119 Stat. at 2741.

Even if the CSRT protocol were capable of assessing whether a detainee was unlawfully held and entitled to be released, it is not an adequate substitute for the habeas writ because this remedy is not guaranteed. Upon concluding that detention is unjustified, a habeas court "can only direct [the prisoner] to be discharged." *Bollman*, 8 U.S. (4 Cranch) at 136; *see also* 2 STORY, *supra*, §1339. But neither the DTA nor the MCA require this, and a recent report studying CSRT records shows that when at least three detainees were found by CSRTs not to be enemy combatants, they were subjected to a second, and in one case a third, C SRT proceeding until they were finally found to be properly classified as enemy

---

[10] With a few possible exceptions, the Guantanamo detainees before the federal courts are unlikely to be fluent in English or to be familiar with legal procedures and, as their detentions far from home and cut off from their families have been lengthy, they are likely ill prepared to be able to obtain evidence to support their claims that they are not enemies of the United States.

combatants. Mark Denbeaux et al., No-Hearing Hearings: CSRT: The Modern Habeas Corpus?, at 37–39 (2006), http://law.shu.edu/news/final_no_hearing_hearings_report.pdf.

3.

Therefore, because Congress in enacting the MCA has revoked the privilege of the writ of habeas corpus where it would have issued under the common law in 1789, without providing an adequate alternative, the MCA is void unless Congress's action fits within the exception in the Suspension Clause: Congress may suspend the writ "when in Cases of Rebellion or Invasion the public Safety may require it." U. S. CONST. art. I, §9, cl. 2. However, Congress has not invoked this power.

Suspension has been an exceedingly rare event in the history of the United States. On only four occasions has Congress seen fit to suspend the writ. These examples follow a clear pattern: Each suspension has made specific reference to a state of "Rebellion" or "Invasion" and each suspension was limited to the duration of that necessity. In 1863, recognizing "the present rebellion," Congress authorized President Lincoln during the Civil War "whenever, in his judgment, the public safety may require it, . . . to suspend the writ of habeas corpus." Act of Mar. 3, 1863, ch. 81, §1, 12 Stat. 755, 755. As a result, no writ was to issue "so long as said suspension by the President shall remain in force, and said rebellion continue." *Id.* In the Ku Klux Klan Act of 1871, Congress agreed to authorize suspension whenever "the unlawful combinations named [in the statute] shall be organized and armed, and so numerous and powerful as to be able, by violence, to either overthrow or set at defiance the constituted authorities of such State, and of the United States within such State," finding that these circumstances "shall be deemed a rebellion against the government of the United States." Act of Apr. 20, 1871, ch. 22, §4, 17 Stat. 13, 14–15. Suspension was also authorized "when in cases of rebellion, insurrection, or invasion the public safety may require it " in two territories of the United States: the Philippines, Act of July 1, 1902, ch. 1369, §5, 32 Stat. 691, 692, and Hawaii, Hawaiian Organic Act, ch. 339, §67, 31 Stat. 141, 153 (1900); *see Duncan v. Kahanamoku*, 327 U.S. 304, 307–08 (1946). *See also* DUKER, *supra*, at 149, 178 n.190.

Because the MCA contains neither of these hallmarks of suspension, and because there is no indication that Congress sought to avail itself of the exception in the Suspension Clause, its attempt to revoke federal jurisdiction that the Supreme Court held to exist exceeds the powers of Congress. The MCA therefore has no effect on the jurisdiction of the federal courts to consider these petitions and their related appeals.

. . .

SUPREME COURT OF THE UNITED STATES

LAKHDAR BOUMEDIENE ET AL.

06–1195　　　　　　　　　　*v.*

GEORGE W. BUSH, PRESIDENT OF THE UNITED STATES, ET AL.

KHALED A. F. AL ODAH, NEXT FRIEND OF FAWZI KHALID ABDULLAH FAHAD AL ODAH, ET AL.

06–1196　　　　　　　　　　*v.*

UNITED STATES ET AL.

ON PETITIONS FOR WRITS OF CERTIORARI TO THE UNITED STATES COURT OF APPEALS FOR THE DISTRICT OF COLUMBIA CIRCUIT

Nos. 06–1195 and 06–1196.　Decided April 2, 2007

The petitions for writs of certiorari are denied.

Statement of JUSTICE STEVENS and JUSTICE KENNEDY respecting the denial of certiorari.

Despite the obvious importance of the issues raised in these cases, we are persuaded that traditional rules governing our decision of constitutional questions, see *Ashwander* v. *TVA*, 297 U. S. 288, 341 (1936) (Brandeis, J., concurring), and our practice of requiring the exhaustion of available remedies as a precondition to accepting jurisdiction over applications for the writ of habeas corpus, cf. *Ex parte Hawk*, 321 U. S. 114 (1944) (*per curiam*), make it appropriate to deny these petitions at this time. However, "[t]his Court has frequently recognized that the policy underlying the exhaustion-of-remedies doctrine does not require the exhaustion of inadequate remedies." *Marino* v. *Ragen*, 332 U. S. 561, 570, n. 12 (1947) (Rutledge, J., concurring). If petitioners later seek to establish that the Statement of Government has unreasonably delayed proceedings under the Detainee Treatment Act of 2005, Tit. X, 119 Stat. 2739, or some other and ongoing injury, alternative means exist for us to consider our jurisdiction over the allegations made by petitioners before the Court of Appeals. See 28 U. S. C. §§1651(a), 2241. Were the Government to take additional steps to prejudice the position of petitioners in seeking review in this Court, "courts of competent jurisdiction," including this Court, "should act promptly to ensure that the office and purposes of the writ of habeas corpus are not compromised." *Padilla* v. *Hanft*, 547 U. S. 1062, 1064 (2006) (KENNEDY, J., concurring in denial of certiorari). And as always, denial of certiorari does not constitute an expression of any opinion on the merits. See *Rasul* v. *Bush*, 542 U. S. 466, 480–481 (2004) (majority opinion of STEVENS, J.); *id.*, at 487 (KENNEDY, J., concurring in judgment).

---

* Justice Breyer, joined by Justice Souter, dissented. Justice Ginsburg joined the first part of the dissent. – *Eds*.

No. 06-1196

In the Supreme Court of the United States

KHALED A. F. AL ODAH, ET AL., PETITIONERS,

v.

UNITED STATES OF AMERICA, ET AL., RESPONDENTS.

ON PETITION FOR WRIT OF CERTIORARI TO
THE UNITED STATES COURT OF APPEALS
FOR THE DISTRICT OF COLUMBIA CIRCUIT

REPLY TO OPPOSITION TO
PETITION FOR REHEARING

DAVID J. CYNAMON	THOMAS B. WILNER
MATTHEW J. MACLEAN	COUNSEL OF RECORD
OSMAN HANDOO	NEIL H. KOSLOWE
PILLSBURY WINTHROP	AMANDA E. SHAFER
SHAW PITTMAN LLP	SHERI L. SHEPHERD
	SHEARMAN & STERLING LLP

GITANJALI GUTIERREZ	
J. WELLS DIXON	GEORGE BRENT MICKUM IV
SHAYANA KADIDAL	SPRIGGS & HOLLINGSWORTH
CENTER FOR	
CONSTITUTIONAL RIGHTS	

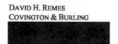

Counsel for Petitioners
Additional Counsel Listed on Inside Cover

JOSEPH MARGULIES	JOHN J. GIBBONS
MACARTHUR JUSTICE CENTER	LAWRENCE S. LUSTBERG
NORTHWESTERN UNIVERSITY	GIBBONS P.C.
LAW SCHOOL	

MARK S. SULLIVAN	BAHER AZMY
CHRISTOPHER G. KARAGHEUZOFF	SETON HALL LAW SCHOOL
JOSHUA COLANGELO-BRYAN	CENTER FOR SOCIAL JUSTICE
DORSEY & WHITNEY LLP	

DAVID H. REMES	MARC D. FALKOFF
COVINGTON & BURLING	COLLEGE OF LAW
	NORTHERN ILLINOIS
	UNIVERSITY

SCOTT SULLIVAN	ERWIN CHEMERINSKY
DEREK JINKS	DUKE LAW SCHOOL
UNIVERSITY OF TEXAS	
SCHOOL OF LAW	
RULE OF LAW IN WARTIME	
PROGRAM	

STEPHEN YAGMAN	CLIVE STAFFORD SMITH
	JUSTICE IN EXILE

. . .

---

* Redactions in this document have been added for privacy purposes. – *Eds*.

Appendix

DECLARATION OF STEPHEN ABRAHAM
Lieutenant Colonel, United States Army Reserve

I, Stephen Abraham, hereby declare as follows:

1.　　I am a lieutenant colonel in the United States Army Reserve, having been commissioned in 1981 as an officer in Intelligence Corps. I have served as an intelligence officer from 1982 to the present during periods of both reserve and active duty, including mobilization in 1990 ("Operation Desert Storm") and twice again following 9-11. In my civilian occupation, I am an attorney with the law firm Fink & Abraham LLP ███████████████████████

2.　　This declaration responds to certain statements in the Declaration of Rear Admiral (Retired) James M. McGarrah ("McGarrah Dec."), filed in *Bismullah v. Gates*, No. 06-1197 (D.C. Cir.). This declaration is limited to unclassified matters specifically related to the procedures employed by Office for the Administrative Review of the Detention of Enemy Combatants ("OARDEC") and the Combatant Status Review Tribunals ("CSRTs") rather than to any specific information gathered or used in a particular case, except as noted herein. The contents of this declaration are based solely on my personal observations and experiences as a member of OARDEC. Nothing in this declaration is intended to reflect or represent the official opinions of the Department of Defense or the Department of the Army.

3.　　From September 11, 2004 to March 9, 2005, I was on active duty and assigned to OARDEC. Rear Admiral McGarrah served as the Director of OARDEC during the entirety of my assignment.

4.　　While assigned to OARDEC, in addition to other duties, I worked as an agency liaison, responsible for coordinating with government agencies, including certain Department of Defense ("DoD") and non-DoD organizations, to gather or validate information relating to detainees for use in CSRTs. I also served as a member of a CSRT, and had the opportunity to observe and participate in the operation of the CSRT process.

5.　　As stated in the McGarrah Dec., the information comprising the Government Information and the Government

Evidence was not compiled personally by the CSRT Recorder, but by other individuals in OARDEC. The vast majority of the personnel assigned to OARDEC were reserve officers from the different branches of service (Army, Navy, Air Force, Marines) of varying grades and levels of general military experience. Few had any experience or training in the legal or intelligence fields.

6.   The Recorders of the tribunals were typically relatively junior officers with little training or experience in matters relating to the collection, processing, analyzing, and/or dissemination of intelligence material. In no instances known to me did any of the Recorders have any significant personal experience in the field of military intelligence. Similarly, I was unaware of any Recorder having any significant or relevant experience dealing with the agencies providing information to be used as a part of the CSRT process.

7.   The Recorders exercised little control over the process of accumulating information to be presented to the CSRT board members. Rather, the information was typically aggregated by individuals identified as case writers who, in most instances, had the same limited degree of knowledge and experience relating to the intelligence community and intelligence products. The case writers, and not the Recorders, were primarily responsible for accumulating documents, including assembling documents to be used in the drafting of an unclassified summary of the factual basis for the detainee's designation as an enemy combatant.

8.   The information used to prepare the files to be used by the Recorders frequently consisted of finished intelligence products of a generalized nature - often outdated, often "generic," rarely specifically relating to the individual subjects of the CSRTs or to the circumstances related to those individuals' status.

9.   Beyond "generic" information, the case writer would frequently rely upon information contained within the Joint Detainee Information Management System ("JDIMS"). The subset of that system available to the case writers was limited in terms of the scope of information, typically excluding information that was characterized as highly sensitive law enforcement information, highly classified information, or information not voluntarily released by the originating agency. In that regard, JDIMS did not constitute a complete repository, although this limitation was frequently not understood

by individuals with access to or who relied upon the system as a source of information. Other databases available to the case writer were similarly deficient. The case writers and Recorders did not have access to numerous information sources generally available within the intelligence community.

10.   As one of only a few intelligence-trained and suitably cleared officers, I served as a liaison while assigned to OARDEC, acting as a go-between for OARDEC and various intelligence organizations. In that capacity, I was tasked to review and/or obtain information relating to individual subjects of the CSRTs. More specifically, I was asked to confirm and represent in a statement to be relied upon by the CSRT board members that the organizations did not possess "exculpatory information" relating to the subject of the CSRT.

11.   During my trips to the participating organizations, I was allowed only limited access to information, typically prescreened and filtered. I was not permitted to see any information other than that specifically prepared in advance of my visit. I was not permitted to request that further searches be performed. I was given no assurances that the information provided for my examination represented a complete compilation of information or that any summary of information constituted an accurate distillation of the body of available information relating to the subject.

12.   I was specifically told on a number of occasions that the information provided to me was all that I would be shown, but I was never told that the information that was provided constituted all available information. On those occasions when I asked that a representative of the organization provide a written statement that there was no exculpatory evidence, the requests were summarily denied.

13.   At one point, following a review of information, I asked the Office of General Counsel of the intelligence organization that I was visiting for a statement that no exculpatory information had been withheld. I explained that I was tasked to review all available materials and to reach a conclusion regarding the non-existence of exculpatory information, and that I could not do so without knowing that I had seen all information.

14.   The request was denied, coupled with a refusal even to acknowledge whether there existed additional information

that I was not permitted to review. In short, based upon the selective review that I was permitted, I was left to "infer from the absence of exculpatory information in the materials I was allowed to review that no such information existed in materials I was not allowed to review.

15.   Following that exchange, I communicated to Rear Admiral McGarrah and the OARDEC Deputy Director the fundamental limitations imposed upon my review of the organization's files and my inability to state conclusively that no exculpatory information existed relating to the CSRT subjects. It was not possible for me to certify or validate the non-existence of exculpatory evidence as related to any individual undergoing the CSRT process.

16.   The content of intelligence products, including databases, made available to case writers, Recorders, or liaison officers, was often left entirely to the discretion of the organizations providing the information. What information was not included in the bodies of intelligence products was typically unknown to the case writers and Recorders, as was the basis for limiting the information. In other words, the person preparing materials for use by the CSRT board members did not know whether they had examined all available information or even why they possessed some pieces of information but not others.

17.   Although OARDEC personnel often received large amounts of information, they often had no context for determining whether the information was relevant or probative and no basis for determining what additional information would be necessary to establish a basis for determining the reasonableness of any matter to be offered to the CSRT board members. Often, information that was gathered was discarded by the case writer or the Recorder because it was considered to be ambiguous, confusing, or poorly written. Such a determination was frequently the result of the case writer or Recorder's lack of training or experience with the types of information provided. In my observation, the case writer or Recorder, without proper experience or a basis for giving context to information, often rejected some information arbitrarily while accepting other information without any articulable rationale.

18.   The case writer's summaries were reviewed for quality assurance, a process that principally focused on format

and grammar. The quality assurance review would not ordinarily check the accuracy of the information underlying the case writer's unclassified summary for the reason that the quality assurance reviewer typically had little more experience than the case writer and, again, no relevant or meaningful intelligence or legal experience, and therefore had no skills by which to critically assess the substantive portions of the summaries.

19.   Following the quality assurance process, the unclassified summary and the information assembled by the case writer in support of the summary would then be forwarded to the Recorder. It was very rare that a Recorder or a personal representative would seek additional information beyond that information provided by the case writer.

20.   It was not apparent to me how assignments to CSRT panels were made, nor was I personally involved in that process. Nevertheless, I discerned the determinations of who would be assigned to any particular position, whether as a member of a CSRT or to some other position, to be largely the product of ad hoc decisions by a relatively small group of individuals. All CSRT panel members were assigned to OARDEC and reported ultimately to Rear Admiral McGarrah. It was well known by the officers in OARDEC that any time a CSRT panel determined that a detainee was not properly classified as an enemy combatant, the panel members would have to explain their finding to the OARDEC Deputy Director. There would be intensive scrutiny of the finding by Rear Admiral McGarrah who would, in turn, have to explain the finding to his superiors, including the Under Secretary of the Navy.

21.   On one occasion, I was assigned to a CSRT panel with two other officers, an Air Force colonel and an Air Force major, the latter understood by me to be a judge advocate. We reviewed evidence presented to us regarding the recommended status of a detainee. All of us found the information presented to lack substance.

22.   What were purported to be specific statements of fact lacked even the most fundamental earmarks of objectively credible evidence. Statements allegedly made by percipient witnesses lacked detail. Reports presented generalized statements in indirect and passive forms without stating the

source of the information or providing a basis for establishing the reliability or the credibility of the source. Statements of interrogators presented to the panel offered inferences from which we were expected to draw conclusions favoring a finding of "enemy combatant" but that, upon even limited questioning from the panel, yielded the response from the Recorder, "We'll have to get back to you." The personal representative did not participate in any meaningful way.

23.   On the basis of the paucity and weakness of the information provided both during and after the CSRT hearing, we determined that there was no factual basis for concluding that the individual should be classified as an enemy combatant. Rear Admiral McGarrah and the Deputy Director immediately questioned the validity of our findings. They directed us to write out the specific questions that we had raised concerning the evidence to allow the Recorder an opportunity to provide further responses. We were then ordered to reopen the hearing to allow the Recorder to present further argument as to why the detainee should be classified as an enemy combatant. Ultimately, in the absence of any substantive response to the questions and no basis for concluding that additional information would be forthcoming, we did not change our determination that the detainee was not properly classified as an enemy combatant. OARDEC's response to the outcome was consistent with the few other instances in which a finding of "Not an Enemy Combatant" (NEC) had been reached by CSRT boards. In each of the meetings that I attended with OARDEC leadership following a finding of NEC, the focus of inquiry on the part of the leadership was "what went wrong."

24.   I was not assigned to another CSRT panel.

I hereby declare under the penalties of perjury based on my personal knowledge that the foregoing is true and accurate.

Stephen Abraham

Dated: June 15, 2007

U.S. Department of Justice
Office of the Solicitor General

Washington, D.C ▇▇▇

June 26, 2007

Honorable William K. Suter
Clerk
Supreme Court of the United States
Washington, D.C. ▇▇▇

<u>Khaled A.F. Al Odah</u> v. <u>United States</u>, No. 06-1196

Dear Mr. Suter:

On June 22, 2007, petitioners filed a reply to the government's brief in opposition to the petition for rehearing. The reply contained a declaration by Lt. Col. Stephen Abraham, United States Army Reserve. See Reply App. i-viii. That declaration, which was filed in _Bismullah v. Gates_, No. 06-1197 (D.C. Cir.; appeal pending), is not part of the record in this case. The Abraham declaration "responds to certain statements" (Reply App. i) in the declaration of Rear Adm. (Ret.) James M. McGarrah, United States Navy, which was filed in the _Bismullah_ case. In the event that the Court chooses to consider the Abraham declaration in connection with the petition for rehearing in this case, a copy of the McGarrah declaration is attached.

I would appreciate your circulating this letter and the attachment to the Members of the Court.

Sincerely,

Paul D. Clement
Solicitor General

cc: See Attached Service List

---

* Redactions on this page have been added for privacy purposes. – _Eds._

IN THE UNITED STATES COURT OF APPEALS
FOR THE DISTRICT OF COLUMBIA CIRCUIT

HAJI BISMULLAH, et al.,	)	
Petitioners,	)	
v.	)	No. 06-1197
	)	
ROBERT M. GATES,	)	
Secretary of Defense,	)	
Respondent.	)	
	)	
	)	
HUZAIFA PARHAT, et al.	)	
Petitioners,	)	
v.	)	No. 06-1397
	)	
ROBERT M. GATES,	)	
Secretary of Defense,	)	
Respondent.	)	
	)	

DECLARATION OF REAR ADMIRAL (Retired) JAMES M. McGARRAH

Pursuant to 28 U.S.C. § 1746, I, James M. McGarrah, hereby declare that to the best of my knowledge, information, and belief, the following is true, accurate, and correct:

1. I was the Director of the Office for the Administrative Review of the Detention of Enemy Combatants (OARDEC) from July 2004 until March 2006. I currently serve as a Special Assistant to the Deputy Assistant Secretary of Defense for Detainee Affairs. This declaration is intended to provide a general description of the overall Combatant Status Review Tribunal (CSRT) process during this period in which I served as the Director of OARDEC, and concurrently as the CSRT Convening Authority. CSRT Order, 7 July 2004, para f. This declaration is based on my personal knowledge as well as information obtained in my official capacity as Director of OARDEC and CSRT Convening Authority.

2. In July 2004, the Department of Defense established the CSRT process. This process was established to provide a formalized, standardized process to review the combatant status of all "foreign nationals held as enemy combatants in the control of the Department of Defense at the Guantanamo Bay Naval Base, Cuba." CSRT Order, 7 Jul 2004. OARDEC was established in July 2004, and charged with implementing this process, as well as the annual Administrative Review

Boards conducted for detainees at Guantanamo. As Director of OARDEC, I was appointed the CSRT Convening Authority by the Secretary of the Navy in July 2004. During my tenure as Director, we conducted 558 Combatant Status Review Tribunals (CSRTs). During that time frame, over 200 personnel (including active duty and reserve military, civilians and contractors) were assigned to OARDEC, and were involved in carrying out OARDEC's missions. The primary OARDEC mission during this period was preparing for and conducting these Tribunals, and involved the vast majority of these assigned personnel. Some of these personnel were assigned to work at Guantanamo Bay while others were assigned in the Washington, D.C. area.

3. The CSRT procedures provide that the CSRT "Tribunal is authorized to * * * request the production of such reasonably available information in the possession of the U.S. Government bearing on the issue of whether the detainee meets the criteria to be designated as an enemy combatant, including information generated in connection with the initial determination to hold the detainee as an enemy combatant and in any subsequent reviews of that determination, as well as any records, determinations, or reports generated in connection with such proceedings (cumulatively called hereinafter the 'Government Information')." CSRT Procedures, Enc. 1, § E(3). The CSRT Recorder is charged with, among other things, "obtain[ing] and examin[ing] the Government Information." CSRT Procedures, Enc. 2, § C(1). Additionally, "the Recorder has a duty to present to the CSRT such evidence in the Government Information as may be sufficient to support the detainee's classification as an enemy combatant, including the circumstances of how the detainee was taken into the custody of the U.S. or allied forces (the "Government Evidence")." CSRT Procedures, Enc. 2, § B(1).

4. Prior to September 1, 2004, the CSRT Recorder personally collected the Government Information. At that time, due to the other extensive responsibilities of the Recorder[1] and in order to provide greater efficiency in the collection of this information, additional individuals were assigned to assist the Recorder in gathering detainee information. Responsibilities of Recorder, CSRT Procedures, Enc. 2, § C(2). Accordingly, after September 1, 2004, the task of gathering and

---

1 Among other duties, the Recorder must attend and present evidence at CSRT hearings and prepare the records of those proceedings. *See* CSRT Procedures, Enc. 2, § C

analyzing the Government Information was performed by a specially-formed research, collection and coordination team (hereinafter referred to as "Team"). This Team, which was dedicated to the functions of obtaining, examining and analyzing detainee information, brought greater manpower resources to this important function. In addition, due to the location of the Team in the Washington, D.C. area in close proximity to other Government agencies, the interagency approval procedure used for clearance of the Government Evidence was much more efficient. *See supra* text accompanying Paragraph 10. The dedicated Team focused on the tasks of identifying relevant information on each detainee, including information that might suggest that the detainee should not be designated as an enemy combatant.

5. Members assigned to the Team each received approximately two weeks of training prior to assuming their data collection responsibilities, as well as additional instruction, as appropriate, during their tenures. The training included instruction on the CSRT process with specific emphasis on the Recorder's functions and responsibilities, operator training on the pertinent government databases, as well as cultural awareness and intelligence training to assist Team members in better understanding the potential significance of individual data elements. The Team was organized in three separate functions.

a. The first function, Case Writer, had primary responsibility for researching, reviewing and ultimately collecting information from government sources. The Case Writers would then use this information to draft an unclassified summary of the factual basis for the detainee's designation as an enemy combatant.

b. The second function, Quality Assurance (QA), reviewed the draft products from the Case Writers to ensure they were logical, consistent and grammatically correct.

c. The third function, Coordination, worked with the various government agencies whose information was to be used as Government Evidence, in order to receive clearance to use their information in the Tribunal, as well as to verify the accuracy of the Unclassified Summary.

6. Although the Team functioned as a data collection "staff" for the Recorders, each Recorder was held personally responsible for reviewing and verifying the information provided by the Team, for finalizing each package of unclassified and classified Government Evidence (to

include the Unclassified Summary), and for presenting this evidence to the tribunal. In reviewing and verifying the information received from the Team, the Recorder had access to the same information systems used by the Team, and could add information to be presented to the CSRT panel as Government Evidence or as material that might suggest that the detainee should not be designated as an enemy combatant; could decline to use as Government Evidence any material provided by the Team; and/or could submit requests for further information to obtain additional evidence from government entities. New information obtained by the Recorder in this manner would be treated as Government Information and, if appropriate, would be included in the Government Evidence presented to the CSRT panel. Throughout the CSRT process, the Recorder was responsible for making the final determination of what material would be presented to the CSRT as the Government Evidence. CSRT Procedures, Enc. 2, § B(1). In addition, both the Personal Representative and the Tribunal members had, and exercised, the ability to request additional information; the Recorder had the responsibility to respond to such requests.

7. The Team pursued leads found in government files relating to a detainee to identify other material that would qualify as Government Information. First, the Team conducted computer searches via a Defense Department database called the Joint Detainee Information Management System (JDIMS).

a. JDIMS is an information management tool developed and used primarily to support interrogations. Information stored on this database includes interrogation reports, intelligence messages, intelligence reports, analyst products, and periodic detainee assessments by DoD and other U.S. Government organizations, such as the U.S. Army Criminal Investigation Task Force (CITF). Only information classified at the SECRET level and below is placed into the JDIMS system. The information also must be in the possession and control of the Joint Intelligence Group (JIG), an element of Joint Task Force Guantanamo (JTF-GTMO). The JDIMS system is a repository of centralized information, but does not and could not hold all information that is in the possession of the United States Government regarding a particular detainee.

b. JIG personnel regularly use and rely on this database as a primary resource when conducting research about detainees and their interrelationships, when preparing for interrogations and when responding to official requests for information about detainees, as well as for other mission-critical functions. Accordingly, the JIG regularly populates the database with new detainee information developed or uncovered through research and interrogations, and that is assessed as pertinent to the detainee.

c. Because the JDIMS system represented one of the most complete repositories of information on each detainee, it was used as the starting point for gathering the material that would qualify as the Government Information. Additionally, this database permits the interrelationships between individuals and/or organizations to be searched and cross-referenced electronically. Ultimately, most of the data qualifying as Government Information were found through JDIMS. The Team also followed references that arose in these files – if a file revealed possible locations for more information, the Team pursued those leads.

8. The second database regularly searched by the Team was the database system called I2MS, used primarily by investigators from the Criminal Investigation Task Force (the investigatory arm for the Office of Military Commissions). This system holds information pertaining to individual detainees collected by CITF from both the law enforcement and intelligence communities, and would include files on the detainees developed by the authorities who captured the detainees and transferred them to Guantanamo, files relating to any subsequent reviews of the determination to continue to hold the detainee, and interrogation files. The Team also followed references that arose in these files – if a file revealed possible locations for more information, the Team pursued those leads.

9. Third, the Team reviewed paper files in the possession of JTF-GTMO, as well as other Department of Defense databases and files that might contain information on the detainee.

10. The Team also had the ability to submit requests for information to other organizations within the Department of Defense and to other federal agencies that might have information bearing on the issue of whether the detainee meets the criteria to be designated as an enemy combatant, that was not already in the JDIMS database. These requests included information above the classification level of SECRET.

a. In both the initial data search and in requests for additional information from other agencies, the Team's requests would be for any information bearing on the issue of whether the detainee meets the criteria to be designated as an enemy combatant, and also specifically asked those agencies to provide any information that might suggest the detainee should *not* be designated as an enemy combatant.

b. In some instances, the Team did not directly obtain copies of Government Information from certain intelligence agencies. Instead, upon request, certain agencies allowed properly cleared members of the Team to review the organization's information responsive to their request in order to satisfy the Team's request that the agencies produce reasonably available information under the CSRT procedure. The Team could use information the agency authorized for inclusion in the CSRT record to support an enemy combatant status. However, during their review, there were instances where the Team was not permitted to use certain documents as Government Evidence or to make copies of them, because release of these documents could reasonably be expected to cause harm to national security by revealing sensitive information such as sources or methods. These searches were broadly based on names and other available identifying information, and involved voluminous responsive documents, many of which were found not relevant to the determination of whether a detainee continued to meet the criteria for designation as an enemy combatant

c. In other instances, the Team would submit a request for information to law enforcement agencies; however, these agencies would not always provide the Team with information contained in certain files, due to the fact there was an ongoing investigation. In these cases, the law enforcement agencies would do a search of the information requested and provide the Team with documentation stating that none of the information withheld would support a determination that the detainee is not an enemy combatant.

d. The Team never encountered a situation where an agency objected to the use of information that suggested a detainee *should not* be designated an enemy combatant.

11. A file of information was gathered as a result of these inquiries, but it did not necessarily include all material that might be considered to meet the definition of "Government Information" in the CSRT procedures. CSRT Procedures, Enc. 1, § E(3).

a. First, material that might qualify as Government Information from government databases would be reviewed, but might not be collected in a distinct file if it was viewed as being not relevant or only marginally relevant.

b. Second, as explained in Paragraph 10, some material in the possession of intelligence agencies that would likely qualify as Government Information would be reviewed, but could not be collected or used as Government Evidence, because of the sensitivity of the material.

12. In some instances, all of the compiled Government Information referred to in Paragraph 11 above was included in the Government Evidence. In fact, however, the Recorder was required to present to the tribunal only "such evidence in the Government Information as may be *sufficient* to support the detainee's classification as an enemy combatant..." CSRT Procedures, Enc. 1, §H(4) (emphasis added). Therefore in many instances not all of the Government Information was included as Government Evidence. Three primary considerations were employed in selecting the Government Evidence from among this information.

a. First, with respect to information derived from intelligence agencies, those agencies needed to approve the use of their information as part of the Government Evidence before it could be presented to the CSRT, particularly if that information was going to be used in the unclassified portion of the CSRT. If the agency or organization declined to approve the use of information tending to show that the detainee was an enemy combatant, it was deemed "not reasonably available." Often, the primary reason that this information could not be used as Government Evidence is because release of these documents could reasonably be expected to cause harm to national security by revealing sensitive information such as sources or methods. Also, there was a concern about dissemination of this information beyond what was necessary. That said, the Team never encountered a situation where an agency objected to the use of information that suggested a detainee should not be designated an enemy combatant.

b. Second, information was often duplicative of other information. Material was frequently not presented to the CSRT as part of the Government Evidence because it would merely duplicate other information already included in the Government Evidence and therefore would be unnecessarily redundant.

c. Third, the Recorder might elect not to use certain information as Government Evidence if the Recorder determined that other data being used as Government Evidence appeared sufficient to support the detainee's classification as an enemy combatant. For example, if a detainee was alleged to be an enemy combatant based on six actions he was allegedly involved in and these six actions were supported by documents already in the Government Evidence, the Recorder could decide not to include documents about additional actions that the detainee took that would also suggest that the detainee is an enemy combatant. As a result, no Government Information excluded from the Government Evidence was taken into consideration by the CSRT in reaching a determination as to enemy combatant status.

13. The CSRT procedures specify that "[i]n the event the Government Information contains evidence to suggest that the detainee should not be designated as an enemy combatant, the Recorder shall also provide such evidence to the Tribunal." CSRT Procedures, Enc. 2, § B.1; *see* CSRT Procedures, Enc. 1, § H.4 (same).

a. The Team and Recorder ensured that, as they reviewed Government Information, *all* material that might suggest the detainee should not be designated as an enemy combatant was identified and included in the materials presented to the CSRT and included in the CSRT Record. Thus, the Team and Recorder did not exclude any such material even if it had been originally obtained from other intelligence agencies. They also did not exclude any such material based on any sort of sufficiency assessment. However, if certain information which suggested that the detainee should not be designated as an enemy combatant was duplicative, the Recorder might decide not to include that duplicative information in the Government Evidence.

b. There was one other circumstance where this type of material may be excluded from the Government Evidence—if it did not relate to a specific allegation being made against the detainee. For example, if the government had data that indicated the detainee had engaged in a certain specific combatant activity and also had evidence that he had not engaged in that specific activity, the Team and Recorder could elect to present no data about that specific activity at all. In short, if the Recorder decided not to demonstrate to the CSRT that a specific incident relating to the detainee occurred, the Recorder could decide not to submit evidence to the CSRT suggesting that this specific incident did not occur.

14. In addition to the Government Evidence, the following factual material was presented to the CSRT and made part of the CSRT record:

(a)   material submitted by the detainee or his Personal Representative;

(b)   testimony of the detainee or witnesses deemed relevant and reasonably available.

(c)   material obtained by the CSRT panel through its own requests for information.

15. After the CSRT deliberated and reached its conclusion, the CSRT determination was reviewed by the CSRT Legal Advisor and the CSRT Director. CSRT Procedures, Enc. 1, § I(7) & (8). If the CSRT concluded, based upon the evidence before it, that the detainee should no longer be classified as an enemy combatant, the CSRT Director would notify the intelligence agencies and provide them an opportunity to submit additional information relating to the detainee or to reconsider any of their prior decisions that had prevented the Recorder from using their material as Government Evidence at the CSRT. Additionally, if the CSRT Legal Advisor or CSRT Director returned the record to the CSRT for further proceedings, the Recorder would have the ability to supplement the material presented to the CSRT as Government Evidence.

16. Both the CSRT Order and CSRT Regulations specifically defined the record as including (among other things) "all the documentary evidence presented to the tribunal" (Government Evidence). CSRT Order, 7 July 2004, para g(3), and CSRT Procedures, Encl 1., para I(5). There was no requirement for OARDEC to compile a record of material comprising all of the records in government files that would qualify as Government Information. The Recorder was required only to prepare a "Record of Proceedings" which must include 1) a statement of the time and place of the hearing, persons present, and their qualifications; 2) the Tribunal Report Cover Sheet; 3) the classified and unclassified reports detailing the findings of fact upon which the Tribunal decision was based; 4) copies of all documentary *evidence presented to the tribunal* and summaries of all witness testimony; and 5) a dissenting member's summary report, if any. CSRT Procedures, Enc. 2, §C(8). However, OARDEC made an effort to retain the Government Information as referred to in Paragraph 11, compiled for each CSRT. It is my understanding that despite their efforts, some of these electronic files became corrupted following a technical change-over from one computer system to another in 2005. This has made it difficult to fully recreate the electronic files of Government Information compiled for each tribunal. I also understand that OARDEC is currently working to retrieve stored data from system archives to see if it is possible to recreate the files. As of this date,

OARDEC is uncertain whether this is possible.

I declare under penalty of perjury under the laws of the United States of America that the foregoing is true, accurate, and correct.

Dated: 31 May 2007

James M. McGarrah

James M. McGarrah
Rear Admiral, Civil Engineer Corps, U.S. Navy (Retired)
Special Assistant
Office of the Deputy Assistant Secretary of Defense,
Detainee Affairs

6/29/2007: GRANT OF CERTIORARI

(ORDER LIST: 551 U.S.)

FRIDAY, JUNE 29, 2007

APPEAL -- SUMMARY DISPOSITION

06-589   CHRISTIAN CIVIC LEAGUE OF MAINE V. FEC, ET AL.

The judgment is vacated and the case is remanded to the United States District Court for the District of Columbia for further consideration in light of *Federal Election Commission v. Wisconsin Right to Life, Inc.*, 551 U.S. ___ (2007).

CERTIORARI -- SUMMARY DISPOSITIONS

06-582   UNIVERSITY OF NOTRE DAME V. LASKOWSKI, JOAN, ET AL.

The petition for a writ of certiorari is granted. The judgment is vacated and the case is remanded to the United States Court of Appeals for the Seventh Circuit for further consideration in light of Hein v. Freedom From Religion Foundation, Inc., 551 U.S. ___ (2007).

CERTIORARI GRANTED

06-1195)   BOUMEDIENE, LAKHDAR, ET AL. V. BUSH PRESIDENT OF U.S., ET AL.
06-1196)   AL ODAH, KHALED A. F., ET AL. V UNITED STATES, ET AL.

The petitions for rehearing are granted. The orders entered April 2, 2007, denying the petitions for writs of certiorari are vacated. The petitions for writs of certiorari are granted. The cases are consolidated and a total of one hour is allotted for oral argument. As it would be of material assistance to consult any decision in *Bismullah, et al.*, v. *Gates*, No. 06-1197, and *Parhat, et al.*, v. *Gates*, No. 06-1397, currently pending in the United States Court of Appeals for the District of Columbia Circuit, supplemental briefing will be scheduled upon the issuance of any decision in those cases.

. . .

Case Update: April 2008

While the case was pending before the Supreme Court in March 2004, Shafiq Rasul, Asif Iqbal and three other petitioners were sent back to their home countries without conviction. In March 2007, after the D.C. Circuit had dismissed the remaining habeas petitions, David Hicks pled guilty to material support for terrorism. He was released from an Australian prison in late December 2007. The Supreme Court heard oral arguments from the remaining petitioners in Boumediene v. Bush and al-Odah v. U.S. as combined cases on December 5, 2007. Arguments focused on the adequacy of legal representation in the Combatant Status Review Tribunals, as well as on the questions of whether non-citizens have habeas corpus rights and whether the procedures provided in the MCA are an adequate substitute for habeas.

CHAPTER 2

Hamdi v. Rumsfeld

On April 28, 2004, hours after the Supreme Court heard oral arguments in *Hamdi v. Rumsfeld* and *Rumsfeld v. Padilla*, photographs of Iraqi detainees subjected to torture by American soldiers reached television screens around the world for the first time. The incommunicado detention of Yaser Esam Hamdi and the abuse represented in those photographs – which revealed images of naked detainees stacked in a pyramid, hooded with arms outstretched, crumpled on a cement floor and tied by a leash, and cowering before an attack dog – share a common origin. Both arose from the Bush administration's belief that in wartime the executive branch is virtually immune from legal restraint, either in the form of the Geneva Conventions or the checks and balances that serve as the cornerstone of our republic. In fact, the basic premise behind so many of the U.S. government's most controversial practices following September 11 – from the incommunicado and indefinite detention without charge of both U.S. citizens and non-citizens alike, to wiretapping communications without a warrant, to the torture of detainees, to the creation of kangaroo military commissions – is simply that the president by virtue of Article II of the Constitution enjoys unchecked and uncheckable authority that is impervious to judicial review or congressional oversight.

In the spring of 2002, Frank W. Dunham, Jr., decided to challenge this premise by filing a habeas corpus petition on behalf of Yaser Hamdi in Mr. Dunham's capacity as the federal public defender for the Eastern District of Virginia. Born in Baton Rouge, Louisiana, and raised in Saudi Arabia, Mr. Hamdi was 21 years old when he was seized in Afghanistan and detained – without criminal charge – by the United States government. Brought to the U.S. that April, he was initially held at the naval brig in Norfolk, Virginia, and detained as an "enemy combatant" – a person alleged by the military to be "affiliated" with the Taliban. Because he was not charged with a crime, however, Mr. Hamdi faced the real prospect of indefinite detention at the hands of the military without any chance to assert his innocence or to challenge the basis for his detention in a courtroom. Indeed, the government at the outset fought the appointment of any lawyer to represent him, and refused for two years to allow his lawyers to even meet with him on the ground that they might unwittingly convey messages to a terrorist organization.

In considering Mr. Hamdi's case, the Fourth Circuit Court of Appeals agreed with the government that the Constitution vests the president with the authority to detain individuals, including citizens, captured in armed conflict overseas and that any inquiry into the factual basis for such detentions would violate the separation of powers. When the case reached the Supreme Court, two basic issues were before the Justices: what authority exists to detain an American citizen as an enemy combatant, and was Mr. Hamdi entitled to challenge the factual basis for his detention?

With respect to the first question, the government argued not only that it enjoyed inherent power to detain Mr. Hamdi but also that Congress, by virtue of the Authorization for Use of Military Force (or "AUMF") passed one week after the September 11, 2001, attacks, had authorized the president to detain enemy combatants seized in Afghanistan.

A plurality of the Court, in an opinion authored by Justice Sandra Day O'Connor, concluded that Congress had authorized the detention of persons who were "part of or supporting forces hostile to the United States or coalition partners" and "engaged in an armed conflict against the United States" in Afghanistan. The plurality also held, however, that a citizen detainee is entitled to notice of the allegations underlying the detention, access to counsel and a fair hearing before a neutral tribunal. The opinion emphasized that Congress's authorization to detain was not a "blank check," and was subject to both judicial review and procedural due process.

Two elements of the Justices' opinions have implications far beyond the detention of Yaser Hamdi. First, while Justice O'Connor reasoned that the AUMF necessarily gave the president power to detain persons seized in the armed conflict in Afghanistan, her plurality opinion also concluded that the extent of congressional authorization is shaped by the laws and customs of armed conflict. A general authorization of military force, Justice O'Connor found, permits the detention of captured combatants, including American citizens, as a necessary part of battlefield operations. At the same time, detention practices that are inconsistent with "a clearly established principle of the law of war" fall outside the scope of such a resolution. Therefore, in the absence of specific statutory authorization, executive branch actions that violate bedrock principles of the laws of war, such as the core protections embodied in the Geneva Conventions, are unauthorized by Congress.

Second, eight members of the Court also rejected the premise behind much of the executive branch's unilateral, and often secret, infringement of civil liberties that followed the September 11 attacks. According to the plurality, limiting judicial review of the executive's enemy combatant determinations "cannot be mandated by any reasonable view of separation of powers, as this approach serves only to *condense* power into a single branch of government." Justices David Souter and Ruth Bader Ginsburg agreed that, "[i]n a government of separated powers, deciding finally on what is a reasonable degree of guaranteed liberty whether in peace or war (or some condition in between) is not well entrusted to the Executive Branch of Government." Meanwhile, Justices Antonin Scalia and John Paul Stevens maintained that the Constitution prohibited Mr. Hamdi's extrajudicial detention, and that "[i]f civil rights are to be curtailed during wartime, it must be done openly and democratically." In sum, eight members of the Court soundly rejected the idea that, in the context of civil liberties, the executive's actions in wartime are immune from judicial review or congressional oversight.

Three months after the Supreme Court's decision, Mr. Hamdi was released from a U.S. military prison and flown home to Saudi Arabia; he has since married and is now studying at a university. Less than six months later, Frank Dunham was admitted to the hospital with a diagnosis of brain cancer.

Shortly after the diagnosis, I called Mr. Hamdi in Saudi Arabia. I called him again in 2006 after Mr. Dunham passed away from his illness. I have no way of knowing whether those calls to Saudi Arabia were monitored, without a warrant or other judicial oversight, by the National Security Agency. But the Supreme Court's decision in *Hamdi* makes unmistakably clear that the Constitution does not permit the president, unilaterally, to abridge the rights of American citizens without oversight by the other two co-equal branches of government.

Geremy C. Kamens
Assistant Federal Public Defender
Alexandria, Virginia

**IN THE UNITED STATES DISTRICT COURT
FOR THE EASTERN DISTRICT OF VIRGINIA
NORFOLK DIVISION**

YASER ESAM HAMDI,   )
)
FRANK W. DUNHAM, JR., As Next)
Friend of Yaser Esam Hamdi,   )
)
     Petitioners,   )
)
)
v.   )   CASE NO. 2:02 CV 348
)
)
DONALD RUMSFELD   )
Secretary of Defense   )
The Pentagon   )
██████████████   )
)
COMMANDER W.R. PAULETTE,)
Norfolk Naval Brig   )
████████████████)
)
     Respondents.   )

---

* Redactions on this page have been added for privacy purposes. – *Eds.*

PETITION FOR WRIT OF HABEAS CORPUS

1. Petitioner Yaser Esam Hamdi, a citizen of the United States of America, is being held illegally, denied access to legal counsel, and denied access to the Court in violation of his constitutionally protected rights. Frank W. Dunham, Jr., on behalf of Mr. Hamdi as his Next Friend, requests that this Court issue a Writ of Habeas Corpus.

PARTIES

2. Petitioner Yaser Esam Hamdi is an American citizen presently incarcerated and unlawfully held by Respondents at the Norfolk Naval Station in Norfolk, Virginia. Mr. Hamdi was born in Baton Rouge, Louisiana, on September 26, 1980. *See* Exhibit A.

3. Petitioner Frank W. Dunham, Jr., is the Federal Public Defender for the Eastern District of Virginia. Mr. Dunham has requested permission to contact Mr. Hamdi. . . . . To date, Respondents have failed to allow Mr. Dunham or other attorneys from the Office of the Federal Public Defender to meet with or contact Mr. Hamdi. . . . .

4. On May 8, 2002, Mr. Hamdi's father, Isam Foud Amin Hamdi, spoke personally with Mr. Dunham and Larry W. Shelton, Supervisor of the Norfolk Division of the Federal Public Defender's Office. Mr. Hamdi's father asked the Federal Public Defender's Office to undertake the representation of his son in the federal courts for the Eastern District of Virginia. Mr. Hamdi's father also has requested this assistance through a legal representative. *See* Exhibit D. Because Mr. Hamdi has been denied access to both counsel and the courts of the United States, Mr. Dunham has filed this petition as Next Friend.

5. Respondent Paulette is a Commander in charge of the Norfolk Naval Brig. He is the custodian immediately responsible for the detention of Mr. Hamdi.

6. Respondent Rumsfeld is the United States Secretary of Defense and Respondent Paulette's superior.

JURISDICTION

7. Petitioners bring this action under 28 U.S.C. §§2241 and 2242, and invoke this Court's jurisdiction under 28 U.S.C. §§1331, 1350, 1651, 2201, and 2202; as well as under the Fifth and Fourteenth Amendments to the United States Constitution.

8. This Court is empowered under 28 U.S.C. §2241 to grant the Writ of Habeas Corpus, and to entertain the Petition filed by Frank W. Dunham, Jr., as Next Friend under 28 U.S.C. §2242.

VENUE

9. Venue is proper in the United States District Court for the Eastern District of Virginia because the Petitioner's custodian resides in this district and the Petitioner is being held unlawfully in this district. 28 U.S.C. §§1391(b); 1391(e).

STATEMENT OF FACTS

10. Mr. Hamdi is a citizen of the United States of America. When seized by the United States Government, Mr. Hamdi resided in Afghanistan.

Petioner's Seizure By The United States

11. In the wake of September 11, 2001, the United States initiated military action against the Taliban Government in Afghanistan. On September 18, 2001, a Joint Resolution of Congress authorized the President to use force against the "nations, organizations, or persons" that "planned, authorized, committed, or aided the terrorist attacks on September 11, 2001, or [that] harbored such organizations or persons." Joint Resolution 23, Authorization for Use of Military Force, Public Law 107–40, 115 Stat. 224 (Sept. 18, 2001) ("the Resolution")......The Resolution does not authorize the indefinite detention of persons seized on the field of battle.

12. In the course of the military campaign, and as part of their effort to overthrow the Taliban, the United States provided military assistance to the Northern Alliance, a loosely-knit coalition of military groups opposed to the Taliban Government.

13. In the course of its assistance to the Northern Alliance, the United States obtained access to individuals held by various factions of the Northern Alliance. On information and belief, Mr. Hamdi was captured or transferred into the custody of the United States in the Fall of 2001. Mr. Hamdi has been held in United States custody since that time without access to legal counsel or notice of any charges pending against him.

The Detention Order

14. On November 13, 2001, President George W. Bush issued a Military Order authorizing indefinite detention without due process of law. The Order authorizes Respondent Rumsfeld to detain "any individual who is *not a United States citizen*" that President George W. Bush has "reason to believe:"

i. is or was a member of the organization known as al Qaida;

ii. has engaged in, aided or abetted, or conspired to commit, acts of international terrorism, or acts in preparation therefor, that have caused, threaten to cause, or have as their aim to cause, injury to or adverse effects on the United States, its citizens, national security, foreign policy, or economy;
or

iii. has knowingly harbored one or more individuals described in subparagraphs (i) and (ii).

See Military Order of November 13, 2001, 66 Fed. Reg. 57,833 (Nov. 16, 2001)....
President George W. Bush must make this determination in writing. The Order was neither authorized nor directed by Congress, and is beyond the scope of the Joint Resolution of September 18, 2001.

15. On information and belief, President George W. Bush has never certified or determined in any manner, in writing or otherwise, that Mr. Hamdi is subject to this detention order.

16. By its own terms, the Military Order does not authorize the detention of United States citizens. Accordingly, Mr. Hamdi is not properly subject to this detention order.

Guantanamo Bay Naval Station

17. On or about January 11, 2002, the United States military began transporting prisoners captured in Afghanistan to Camp X-Ray at the United States Naval

Base in Guantanamo Bay, Cuba. Approximately 7,000 military and civilian people reside in Guantanamo Bay under the complete jurisdiction and control of the United States.

18. On or about January 11, 2002, the precise date unknown to counsel but known to Respondents, the United States military transferred Mr. Hamdi to Camp X-Ray, Guantanamo Bay, where he was held until April 2002.

19. While held in Guantanamo Bay, the United States military denied Mr. Hamdi access to legal representation or notice of the charges against him.

Norfolk Naval Brig

20. On or about April 6, 2002, Mr. Hamdi was tranferred to a military jail at the Norfolk Naval Station in Norfolk, Virginia.

21. To date, Mr. Hamdi has not been charged with an offense, nor has he been notified of any pending or contemplated charges. Mr. Hamdi has made no appearance before either a military or civilian tribunal of any sort, nor has he been provided counsel or the means to contact counsel. On information and belief, Mr. Hamdi has not been informed of his rights under the United States Constitution. As a result, Mr. Hamdi is entirely unable to assert his constitutional rights to counsel or protection from unlawful detention.

CLAIMS AS TO THE UNLAWFULNESS OF PETITIONER'S DETENTION

FIRST CLAIM FOR RELIEF
(DUE PROCESS —FIFTH AND FOURTEENTH AMENDMENTS
TO THE UNITED STATES CONSTITUTION)

22. Petitioners incorporate paragraphs 1-21 by reference.

23. As an American citizen, Mr. Hamdi enjoys the full protections of the Constitution. *See Reid v. Covert*, 354 U.S. 1, 32–33 (1957) ("[The view that] constitutional safeguards do not shield a citizen abroad when the Government exercises its power over him . . . is erroneous. The mere fact that [the defendants] had gone overseas . . . should not reduce the protection the Constitution gives them."); *see also Kinsella v. United States ex rel. Singleton*, 361 U.S. 234, 244–48 (1960) (refusing to permit military prosecution of citizen who was not a member of the United States armed forces).

24. By the actions described above, Respondents, acting under color of law, have violated and continue to violate the Fifth and Fourteenth Amendments to the United States Constitution. *See, e.g., Zadvydas v. Davis*, 533 U.S. 678, 690 (2001) ("Freedom from imprisonment – from government custody, detention, or other forms of physical restraint – lies at the heart of the liberty that the [Due Process] Clause protects. . . . And this Court has said that government detention violates that Clause unless the detention is ordered in a *criminal* proceeding with adequate constitutional protections. . . .").

SECOND CLAIM FOR RELIEF
(SUSPENSION OF THE WRIT)

25. Petitioners incorporate paragraphs 1-24 by reference.

26. To the extent the order of November 13, 2001, disallows any challenge to the legality of the Mr. Hamdi's detention by way of habeas corpus, the Order and its

enforcement constitute an unlawful Suspension of the Writ, in violation of Article I of the United States Constitution.

PRAYER FOR RELIEF

WHEREFORE, Petitioners pray for relief as follows:

1. Grant Petitioner Frank W. Dunham, Jr., Next Friend status, as Next Friend of Yaser Esam Hamdi;

2. Order Respondents to permit counsel to meet and confer with the Mr. Hamdi in private and unmonitored communications;

3. Order Respondents to cease all interrogations of Mr. Hamdi, direct or indirect, while this litigation is pending;

4. Order and declare that Mr. Hamdi is being held in violation of the Fifth and Fourteenth Amendments to the United States Constitution;

5. To the extent Respondents contest any material factual allegations in this Petition, schedule an evidentiary hearing, at which Petitioners may adduce proof in support of their allegations;

6. Order that Petitioner Yaser Esam Hamdi be released from Respondents' unlawful custody;

7. Such other relief as the Court may deem necessary and appropriate to protect Petitioner Yaser Esam Hamdi's rights under the United States Constitution.

Dated: May 9, 2002

Respectfully submitted,

Yaser Esam Hamdi, and Frank
W. Dunham, Jr., as Next Friend of
Yaser Esam Hamdi

By: FRANK W. DUNHAM, Jr.
Federal Public Defender
. . .
Larry W. Shelton
Supervisory Assistant Federal Public
Defender
. . .
Geremy C. Kamens
Assistant Federal Public Defender
. . .

STATE OF LOUISIANA
CERTIFICATE OF LIVE BIRTH

Birth No. 119   80 58 393

CHILD'S LAST NAME	FIRST NAME	SECOND NAME	DATE OF BIRTH
HAMDI	YASER	ESAM	SEP 26, 1980

SEX: BOY — Single ☒ Twin ☐ Triplet ☐ — 1st ☐ 2d ☐ 3d ☐

HOUR OF BIRTH: 4:05 P.M.

PLACE OF BIRTH (CITY, TOWN OR LOCATION): BATON ROUGE — PARISH OF BIRTH: EAST BATON ROUGE

NAME OF HOSPITAL OR INSTITUTION: WOMAN'S HOSPITAL — IS PLACE OF BIRTH INSIDE CITY LIMITS? Yes ☒ No ☐

USUAL RESIDENCE OF MOTHER (CITY, TOWN OR LOCATION): BATON ROUGE — PARISH: EAST BATON ROUGE — STATE: LOUISIANA — IS RESIDENCE INSIDE CITY LIMITS? Yes ☒ No ☐

FULL NAME OF FATHER: ESAM FOUAD HAMDI — CITY AND STATE OF BIRTH: MECCA, SAUDI ARABIA — AGE AT TIME OF THIS BIRTH: 25 — COLOR OR RACE OF FATHER: Arabian

FULL MAIDEN NAME OF MOTHER: NADIAH HUSSEN FATTAH — CITY AND STATE OF BIRTH: TAIF, SAUDI ARABIA — AGE AT TIME OF THIS BIRTH: 21 — COLOR OR RACE OF MOTHER: Arabian

I certify that the above stated information is true and correct to the best of my knowledge. SIGNATURE OF PARENT OR OTHER INFORMANT — Parent ☒ Other ☐ — DATE OF SIGNATURE: 9, 28, 1980

MOTHER'S MAILING ADDRESS: ▓▓▓▓▓

I certify that I attended this birth and that the child was born alive on the date stated above. SIGNATURE OF ATTENDANT: [signature], MD — M.D. ☒ Midwife ☐ Other ☐ — DATE OF SIGNATURE: 10/13/80

DATE ACCEPTED BY LOCAL REGISTRAR: OCT 2 1 1980 — SIGNATURE OF LOCAL REGISTRAR: Mary P. Couillard — DATE FILED BY STATE REGISTRAR: OCT 22 1980

CONFIDENTIAL INFORMATION FOR MEDICAL AND HEALTH USE ONLY

APR 13 1981

I CERTIFY THAT THE ABOVE IS A TRUE AND CORRECT COPY OF A CERTIFICATE OR DOCUMENT REGISTERED WITH THE DIVISION OF VITAL RECORDS OF THE STATE OF LOUISIANA, PURSUANT TO LSA—R.S. 40:32, ET SEQ.

[signature]
STATE HEALTH OFFICER

[signature]
STATE REGISTRAR

---

* Redactions in this exhibit have been added for privacy purposes. – Eds.

EXHIBIT D*

08-05-02 10:21 Dr NAJEEB AL NAUIMI.

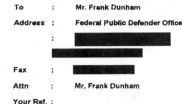

LAW OFFICES OF
DR NAJEEB AL NAUIMI

To	:	Mr. Frank Dunham	Copy to	:	
Address	:	Federal Public Defender Office	Address	:	
	:		Fax	:	
Fax	:		From	:	Dr. Najeeb Al Nauimi
Attn	:	Mr. Frank Dunham	Date	:	8th May 2002
Your Ref.	:		Ref.	:	

Dear Mr. Frank Dunham,

Let me introduce myself, I am a former minister of justice in Qatar. I also own a law firm through which I run my private practice. I have formed a committee of lawyers who are committed for the defence of the detainees in Guantanamo prison or other prisons arrested in the armed conflict. I have been referred to you by the council on American Islamic Relations. I write this behalf of Yasser Essam Al Hamdi, whose father has also approached me for assistance. You may be aware that Yasser Essam Hamdi is a detainee at Norfolk in the United States and he is not being given any access to lawyer.

It has been very interesting to learn about you who is helping out defenceless. I am also working with a similar interest. I have received a power of attorney from the father of Yasser Essam Hamdi to act on his behalf. I am interested to work with you in this case and do whatever you can to ensure that he is given a fair trial in the court. I would also personally like to meet with Yasser Essam Hamdi and be present at any trial he may have. You can access my Website to gain information on me, which is www.nn-law.com.

I will be able to provide you more information on Yasser Essam Hamdi and also I will arrange to deliver to you the documents you require to represent him after you have agreed to act on his behalf.

Looking forward to hear from you

Kind regards

Dr. Najeeb Al Nauimi

---

* Redactions in this exhibit have been added for privacy purposes. – *Eds.*

Kingdom of Saudi Arabia :
Ministry of Justice
Notarial Office - Khubar the Second

Ref. No : 10/5449
Date : 14/02/1423 A.H.
S. Folder No : 5449

Power of Attorney Deed

Praise to Allah Alone & Peace & Blessing Be on Our Prophet
Muhammed.

Attended before me I, Abdulla Mohd. .... , Notary Public of
Khubar the second,
ISAM FOUD AMIN HAMDI
Holding passport No : ▮▮▮ dated 02/06/1394 & Civil Registration No :
▮▮▮▮▮ after being identified by Ali Nassir Saleh, Civil Registry No :
▮▮▮▮▮ and acknowledge by saying "I appointed the advocate Dr.
Najib Mohd. Ahmed A. Al Nuaimi / Qatari National to act on my behalf
as my true legal attorney in all maters related to me and represent me in
all Law-suits filed before the American and International Courts of all
types and grades concerning apprehension of my son YASER ISAM
FOUD HAMDI during the Afghan war and his detention in Ghuantinamo
Camp and later transferred to the was prison located in the State of
Virgina in the USA - and work for his release and furnish him with all the
required assistance in the same whether before the said courts or before
the relevant international authorities and organizations to represent me
before all the Ministries, the concerned government and non government
departments and agencies related to the apprehension of my said son,
sign on all required documents and papers attend court session with the
powers to plea and defend my son with all kinds of pleadings and defence
- collect all rights all the rights give and compromise settlement, cancel
Law-suits and claims and waive the same and abondon litigation on them
- deny handwritings, stamps and signatures and appeal against them with
forgery or with any other method.

My said attorney has the right to submit evidences and request
appointment of expertise and deny them and attend before them submit
testimonies and decide opposition and appeal against their report findings
- withdraw judgements submit memos, pay fees, guarantees .. etc. receive
monies deposited in my name in the treasuries of the courts and other
different administrative bodies - and furthermore he is entitled to mandate
others in all of the above or part thereof.

Signature & Stamp

(1) Identifying Witness   **(2) Identifying Witness**
....

Mandator   **Notary Public**
....

UNITED STATES DISTRICT COURT
FOR THE EASTERN DISTRICT OF VIRGINIA
Norfolk Division

YASER ESAM HAMDI, and

FRANK W. DUNHAM, JR.,
As Next Friend of Yaser Esam Hamdi,

   Petitioners,

v.   ACTION NO. 2:02CV348

DONALD RUMSFELD, and

COMMANDER W.R. PAULETTE,

   Respondents.

ORDER

On May 20, 2002, the Court heard argument on the Respondents' Motion for Extension of Time to Respond to Petition for a Writ of Habeas Corpus [Document No. 7]. The Petitioners were represented by Frank W. Dunham, Jr., Esq., Larry W. Shelton, Esq. and Geremy C. Kamens, Esq. The Respondents were represented by Lawrence R. Leonard, Esq. The Official Court Reporter was Sharon Borden.

After a review of the memoranda and the applicable statutory and case law, the Court GRANTED the Respondents' Motion for Extension of Time for the reasons stated on the record. The Respondents are granted an extension of time until June 13, 2002 to respond to the Petition for Writ of Habeas Corpus, and the Petitioners can reply to the response by June 21, 2002.

Further, it is ORDERED that the Respondents allow an attorney from the Federal Public Defender's Office, with the appropriate governmental security clearance, the opportunity to meet with Yaser Esam Hamdi within the next five days without military personnel present. If an interpreter is necessary, one with the appropriate governmental security clearance will be allowed to attend the meeting.

The Clerk shall mail a copy of this Order to all counsel of record.

_____
UNITED STATES MAGISTRATE JUDGE

Norfolk, Virginia

May **20** , 2002

UNITED STATES DISTRICT COURT
EASTERN DISTRICT OF VIRGINIA
NORFOLK DIVISION

YASER ESAM HAMDI,

and

FRANK W. DUNHAM, JR., As Next
Friend of Yaser Esam Hamdi,

    Petitioners,

v.   Civil Action No. 2:02cv348

DONALD RUMSFELD,
Secretary of Defense,

and

COMMANDER W.R. PAULETTE,
Norfolk Naval Brig
Norfolk, Virginia,

    Respondents.

MEMORANDUM OF POINTS AND AUTHORITIES IN SUPPORT OF RESPONDENTS' OBJECTIONS TO MAGISTRATE JUDGE'S ORDER OF MAY 20, 2002 REGARDING ACCESS

INTRODUCTION

On May 20, 2002, the magistrate judge in this case entered an Order requiring the custodians of the Naval Brig at Naval Station Norfolk to act within five days to provide the federal Public Defender with private, unmonitored consultations with an enemy combatant who was seized in Afghanistan and is now held under the control of the United States military. See Order. . . . That extraordinary Order was erroneous for several reasons and must be vacated.[1]

First, the magistrate judge entered an order granting partial relief on this habeas petition without properly determining that the Court has jurisdiction to proceed. In fact, the Court lacks jurisdiction because the magistrate judge improperly permitted the Public Defender to proceed as next friend for the detainee. The Public Defender has not alleged any relationship whatsoever with the detainee. To the contrary, as underscored by his request for access, he has never met the detainee or communicated with him in any way. He thus cannot satisfy the demanding test for next friend standing established by the Supreme Court in Whitmore v. Arkansas, 495 U.S. 149 (1990). This Court therefore lacks jurisdiction.

---

[1] In filing this objection, respondents do not waive any arguments that may be raised in their answer to the petition, due on June 13, 2002. In particular, respondents note that Secretary of Defense Donald Rumsfeld is not properly named as a respondent. See, e.g., Chatman-Bey v. Thornburgh, 864 F.2d 804, 811 (D.C. Cir. 1988).

Second, the magistrate judge disregarded the "next-friend" nature of the petition by improperly appointing the Public Defender as counsel for the detainee. It is undisputed that the detainee himself is not "seeking relief" from this Court, 18 U.S.C. §3006A (2000), and thus he is not a party for whom counsel may be appointed under section 3006A. Rather, there is currently only one party petitioner in this case – the Public Defender himself as next friend for the detainee. Accordingly, the Public Defender could properly be appointed in this case only if he can be appointed as counsel for himself as next friend – an anomaly that neither the magistrate judge nor the parties have addressed. The too-hasty approach to standing and appointment of counsel reflected in these proceedings demonstrate that the magistrate judge has failed carefully to examine and distinguish between two critical issues that must be addressed before this case can proceed: (i) whether there is a party seeking to invoke the court's jurisdiction who has standing to do so, and (ii) whether that party can properly be represented at taxpayer expense by the Public Defender.

Third, even if those flaws could be remedied, the problem remains that magistrate judges are expressly forbidden by statute from granting injunctive relief. See 28 U.S.C. §636(b)(1)(A), (B) (2000). The Order was thus entirely ultra vires.

Thus, the fundamental question presented here is whether the magistrate judge improperly ordered relief without addressing a series of issues demonstrating that the Court in fact has no power to act and that the Public Defender had no statutory authority to proceed.

It bears emphasis that any petition such as this challenging the detention of an enemy combatant necessarily raises sensitive questions related to the proper role of the courts in reviewing actions taken under the President's authority as Commander in Chief. The United States is currently engaged in combat operations against the al Qaida terrorist network and remaining members of the Taliban in Afghanistan. Detention of enemy combatants is a critical part of that operation. Courts are usually loath to tread on such ground unless required to do so. In addition, in the context of the current conflict – in which al Qaida manuals have shown that terrorists are trained to pass messages upon capture through unwitting intermediaries[2] – an Order such as this mandating unmonitored access to an enemy combatant necessarily implicates important security concerns. Where such issues are at stake, it is vitally important that matters such as the standing of a purported next friend, the statutory authority of the Public Defender to proceed, and the authority of the magistrate judge to enter an order be carefully examined to ensure that this Court's jurisdiction has been properly invoked before relief is ordered.

BACKGROUND

A. The Conflict in Afghanistan and the Detainee's Capture

On September 11, 2001, the al Qaida terrorist organization launched a large-scale, coordinated attack on the United States and killed approximately 3,000 persons. In response, Congress passed a resolution, S.J. Res. 23, authorizing the President to use force against the "nations, organizations, or persons" that "planned, authorized, committed, or aided the terrorist attacks that occurred on September 11, 2001, or [that] harbored such organizations or persons." Authorization for Use of Military Force, Pub. L. No. 107–40,

---

[2] A copy of an al Qaida traning manual containing such instructions is available at www.usdoj.gov:80/ag/trainingmanual.htm.

115 Stat. 224 (2001). The President, acting under his authority as Commander in Chief, and with congressional support, dispatched the armed forces of the United States to Afghanistan to seek out and subdue the al Qaida terrorist network and the Taliban regime that had supported and protected that network.

In the course of operations in Afghanistan, U.S. and allied forces captured hundreds of enemy combatants. The detainee at issue in this case, Yaser Hamdi, was seized as an enemy combatant. As the petition filed by the Public Defender correctly states, the detainee was taken into custody by the U.S. military in Afghanistan. *See* Pet. ¶¶10, 13. The military has determined that he should continue to be detained as an enemy combatant under the laws of war, and he is currently being held at the Naval Station Brig at Norfolk.

The United States has formally notified the government of Saudi Arabia that the detainee is one of several Saudi nationals being held by the United States as combatants seized in the conflict in Afghanistan. As will be explained more fully in respondents' response to the Petition, the authority of the United States to seize and detain enemy combatants for the duration of an armed conflict is well settled.[3] The policy of the United States is that all detainees captured in Afghanistan have been and will continue to be treated humanely and consistent with the principles of the Geneva Convention. Consistent with that policy, the detainee has been permitted a visit from representatives of the International Committee of the Red Cross (ICRC) since his arrival at Norfolk, just as other detainees from the conflict in Afghanistan who are held elsewhere under the control of the U. S. military have been permitted such visits. In addition, the detainee is permitted to send mail, subject to screening.

B. The Petition for Habeas Corpus

On May 10, 2002, the federal Public Defender ("Public Defender") for the Eastern District of Virginia, Mr. Frank W. Dunham, Jr., filed a petition for habeas corpus naming as petitioners both the detainee (Yaser Esam Hamdi) and himself as next friend for the detainee. The petition sought as relief, among other things, that the Court "Order Respondents to permit counsel to meet and confer with the [sic] Mr. Hamdi in private and unmonitored communications." Pet. at 7.

The Public Defender concededly filed this pleading in the detainee's name without ever having had any communication with the detainee. See Pet. ¶¶4, 13, 21. The Public Defender had been in contact, however, with the detainee's father. See id. ¶4. Indeed, the Public Defender attached to the Petition a power of attorney from the detainee's father granting a lawyer in Qatar power to proceed on his behalf and a letter from this lawyer. That letter did not request that the Public Defender file an action on behalf of the detainee's father (or on behalf of the detainee). Instead, the lawyer stated that he was "interested to work with you [the Public Defender] in this case and do whatever you can to ensure that he [the detainee] is given a fair trial in the court." Letter of May 8, 2002 from Dr. Najeeb al Nauimi to Mr. Frank Dunham (attached as Ex. B). The Public Defender did not, on the basis of this letter, seek to have the detainee's father appointed as next friend.

---

[3] See, e.g., Ex parte Quirin, 317 U.S. 1, 31 (1942) (stating that "[u]nlawful combatants are . . . subject to capture and detention"); see generally L. Oppenheim, International Law 368–69 (H. Lauterpacht ed., 7th ed. 1952). It makes no difference that the detainee may be a U. S. citizen. See Quirin, 317 U.S. at 37–38 ("Citizenship in the United States of an enemy belligerent does not relieve him from the consequences of a belligerency which is unlawful. . . ."); In re Territo, 156 F.2d 142, 145 (9th Cir. 1946).

The Public Defender also sought to be appointed counsel for the detainee. After a statement from the detainee's father was filed stating that the detainee "has no assets whatsoever, with which he will be able to retain the services of a lawyer," Statement of Esam Fouad Hamdi (attached as Ex. C), the magistrate judge to whom the case had been assigned appointed the Public Defender counsel for the detainee. See Order of May 14, 2002. . . .

The magistrate judge initially scheduled respondents' answer to be due on Thursday, May 23, 2002. Upon respondents' motion for an extension of time, the magistrate judge held a hearing on Monday, May 20, 2002, and granted respondents an extension until June 13, 2002. At the same hearing, however, the Public Defender orally requested that he be given immediate access to the detainee. The magistrate judge granted relief upon this oral motion and entered an Order requiring the government to provide the Public Defender access for private, unmonitored consultations with the detainee within five days. See Order at 2. . . .

ARGUMENT

I. BECAUSE THE PUBLIC DEFENDER IS NOT A PROPER NEXT FRIEND, THE COURT LACKS JURISDICTION OVER THE CASE.

. . . Here, the magistrate judge erred in issuing a preliminary order requiring the United States to provide the Public Defender with access to the detainee without first properly considering whether the Public Defender had standing to bring the underlying habeas action. See Lujan v. Defenders of Wildlife, 504 U.S. 555, 561 (1992) ("The party invoking federal jurisdiction bears the burden of establishing the[] elements [of standing]"). Because the Public Defender clearly does not have standing to bring the underlying habeas action, the magistrate judge's order must be vacated.

Although the detainee's name is included in the caption of the habeas petition, it is undisputed that he did not himself file the habeas petition, and that he did not request that it be filed on his behalf. Rather, the Public Defender filed the underlying action after some contact with the detainee's father, and the Public Defender named himself – not the father – as next friend. It is therefore the Public Defender that bears the burden of demonstrating that he has standing to bring the action.

As a general rule, to establish standing the "complainant must allege an injury to himself that is 'distinct and palpable.'" Whitmore, 495 U.S. at 155 (emphasis added) (citations omitted). Here, it is undisputed that the Public Defender has not himself suffered any legal injury. Instead, the Public Defender is attempting to assert that he has standing to bring the action as the detainee's "next friend." Because the Public Defender cannot qualify for "next friend" status under the exacting standards established by the Supreme Court in Whitmore, however, this court has no jurisdiction over the underlying habeas action and the magistrate judge's order must be vacated.

As the Ninth Circuit has explained, "the putative next friend must show: (1) that the petitioner is unable to litigate his own cause due to mental incapacity, lack of access to court, or other similar disability; and (2) the next friend has some significant relationship with, and is truly dedicated to the best interests of, the petitioner." Massie ex rel. Kroll v. Woodford, 244 F.3d 1192, 1194 (9th Cir. 2001) (citing Whitmore, 495 U.S. at 164). . . . .

The Public Defender clearly does not meet the second prong of the Whitmore test. "The burden is on the 'next friend' clearly to establish the propriety of his status and thereby justify the jurisdiction of the court." Id. (emphasis added). As the Supreme Court has warned, "'next friend' standing is by no means granted automatically to whomever seeks to pursue an action on behalf of another." Id. at 163. Instead, the Public Defender must present "clear evidence" establishing the basis for satisfying both prongs of the Whitmore test. Brewer v. Lewis, 989 F.2d 1021, 1026 (9th Cir. 1993) (emphasis added). Far from meeting this standard, the Public Defender has not asserted that he has any relationship whatsoever with the detainee. He has utterly failed to allege, let alone present "clear evidence" of, any meaningful relationship between himself and the detainee. Indeed, the Public Defender acknowledges that he has never met or spoken with the detainee, and that he does not even know whether the detainee speaks English such that he could communicate with him. Hearing Transcript at 26 (May 20, 2002) ("Trans.")......

Close relatives, such as parents, siblings, and spouses, have been found to have a sufficient relationship to act as next friends. See, e.g., Vargas v. Lambert, 159 F.3d 1161, 1168 (9th Cir. 1998) (parent); Smith ex rel. Missouri Public Defender Comm'n v. Armontrout, 812 F.2d 1050 (8th Cir. 1987) (brother), cert. denied 483 U.S. 1033 (1987); In re Ferrens, 8 F. Cas. 1158, 1159 (S.D.N.Y. 1869) (wife). But more distant relatives and acquaintances generally do not have a sufficient relationship. See, e.g., Davis v. Austin, 492 F. Supp. 273 (N.D. Ga. 1980) (neither detainee's first cousin nor a minister who had counseled detainee could sue as next friend) (cited with approval in Whitmore, 495 U.S. at 164). The Public Defender here has not attempted to establish even that remote a connection with the detainee. Indeed, the Public Defender readily admitted before the magistrate judge that he has no idea whether the detainee actually desires to challenge his confinement by attempting to invoke the jurisdiction of the courts of the United States, or which claims he would want to press. Trans. 12 ("Mr. Hamdi might tell us . . . I don't want an infidel Christian lawyer representing me on a habeas corpus petition in the United States district court").

. . .

IV. THE IMPORTANCE OF THE ISSUES HERE UNDERSCORES THE NEED FOR CAREFUL AND ORDERLY CONSIDERATION OF MATTERS SUCH AS STANDING AND THE PUBLIC DEFENDER'S POWER TO PROCEED.

. . .

. . . At present, however, the combination of an improper next friend with an improper appointment of the Public Defender as counsel for an ineligible person has bootstrapped both the Court and the Public Defender into a position to proceed without any assessment of the central flaw in this case: namely, no party has been identified who (1) properly has standing to bring the habeas petition (and who seeks to do so), who is also (2) eligible for representation by the Public Defender. Each of those issues – and others – must be addressed in an orderly fashion before the Court exercises its jurisdiction to order relief.

Orderly inquiry into these issues is especially appropriate in a case where the Court is being asked to exercise its jurisdiction to review actions of the military taken under the President's power as Commander in Chief to direct wartime operations. Courts are normally circumspect in approaching such matters and will proceed only when required to do so. See, e.g., Dames & Moore v. Regan, 453 U.S. 654, 660–61 (1981); cf. Johnson v. Eisentrager, 339 U.S. 763 (1950) (describing inherent interference with conduct of war that habeas litigation by enemy prisoners entails). Here, at a minimum, respect for the important interests at stake in the case require a careful and orderly procedure to inquire into the authority of the Court to proceed before relief is ordered.

If these issues had been considered in the proper order, moreover, it also would have permitted respondents to explain additional consequences of the form of relief that was provided. There are substantial government interests in regulating any contemplated access to the detainee that at a minimum should be taken into consideration before the Court rules on the issue. For example, the military must have the ability to interrogate detainees for any intelligence about al Qaida, its assets, and its plans. Any contacts with outsiders can interfere with the success of the interrogation effort. By prematurely ordering unrestricted access to the detainee, the magistrate judge ensured that the impact that access would have on the interrogation effort could not even be considered in addressing whether access to the detainee could be ordered and if so under what conditions.

Similarly, the magistrate judge ordered that the Public Defender be provided private, unmonitored meetings with the detainee, instructing that access should be provided "without military personnel present." Order at 2. But that requirement ignores a significant security concern. It is well known that an al Qaida training manual uncovered by the United States provides instructions for passing concealed messages to their colleagues from behind bars after they have been captured – even through unwitting intermediaries. There is legitimate cause for concern that any combatants seized in Afghanistan, al Qaida or not, may have received similar training. This detainee in particular presents a specific concern to the United States related to force protection because he has been to the detention facility at Guantanamo Bay, he has seen the procedures used there for security, and thus is in a position to communicate valuable information to enemies of the United States. The Order here, directing immediate, unmonitored access ensured that the court did not even consider appropriate screening or monitoring procedures that will be necessary for addressing such critical security interests.

CONCLUSION

For the foregoing reasons, the Court should vacate the Order requiring access to the detainee and permit respondents to address the issues of standing and statutory authority of the Public Defender – in addition to any other issues – in an orderly fashion in their response to the Petition.

> Respectfully submitted,
> Paul J. McNulty
> United States Attorney
>
> By:

Paul D. Clement	Lawrence R. Leonard, ...
Deputy Solicitor General	Managing Assistant United States Attorney
Alice S. Fisher	...
Joan L. Larsen	
Patrick F. Philbin	
Deputy Assistant Attorneys General	

**IN THE UNITED STATES DISTRICT COURT
FOR THE EASTERN DISTRICT OF VIRGINIA
NORFOLK DIVISION**

YASER ESAM HAMDI, and
FRANK W. DUNHAM, JR.,
As Next Friend of Yaser Esam Hamdi,

    Petitioners,

v.   CIVIL ACTION NO. 2:02cv348

DONALD RUMSFELD, and
COMMANDER W.R. PAULETTE,

    Respondents.

ORDER

Currently before the Court is the matter of a petition for a writ of habeas corpus filed on behalf of the Petitioner, Yaser Esam Hamdi, who is currently being held incommunicado in the brig of the naval base in Norfolk, Virginia. On May 29, 2002, the Court heard arguments on the Motion of Frank W. Dunham, as appointed counsel and next friend for the Petitioner, to be allowed to meet with Hamdi,. As stated in open court, the Court hereby **ORDERS** the following:

. . .

On the matter of appointment of counsel, the Court **ORDERS** and confirms the appointment of Frank W. Dunham and the Federal Public Defenders Office as counsel for the Petitioner, Yaser Esam Hamdi.

The Court **ORDERS** that this case is properly filed by Frank Dunham as next friend. As the Supreme Court has long held, "Proceedings in habeas corpus are to be disposed of in a summary way. The interests of both the public and the petitioner require promptness; that if he is unlawfully restrained of his liberty it may be given to him as speedily as possible; that if not, all having anything to do with his restraint be advised thereof, and the mind of the public be put to rest, and also that if further action is to be taken in the matter it may be taken without delay." Storti v. Commonwealth of Massachusetts, 183 U.S. 138, 143 (1901). In this case, technical issues regarding who is best situated to be next friend will not be allowed to interfere with having the "mind of the public be put at rest" by a swift resolution of the substance of this petition.

. . .

Moreover, Hamdi is entitled to counsel and the attorneys for the government and the Public Defender have agreed to present an Agreed Order outlining the terms and conditions of such a meeting between Hamdi and his counsel. If no such Agreed Order is presented to the Court by 5:00 p.m. today, May 29, 2002, then it is **ORDERED** that the Respondents allow either Frank Dunham or Larry Shelton from the Federal Public Defender's Office, as long as they possess the appropriate governmental security clearance, the opportunity to meet with Yaser Esam Hamdi within seventy-two hours of the entry of this Order in open court, absent an intervening Court Order to the contrary, with the result that the meeting must be allowed to go forward as of 1:00 p.m. on Saturday, June 1, 2002. Furthermore, because it is represented to the Court that an interpreter will be needed for the attorney to communicate with Hamdi, an interpreter with the appropriate governmental security clearance will be allowed to attend the meeting. Finally, this meeting is to be private between Hamdi, the attorney, and the interpreter, without military personnel present, and without any listening or recording devices of any kind being employed in any way.

Hamdi must be allowed to meet with his attorney because of fundamental justice provided under the Constitution of the United States. Hamdi, who was held with the other detainees taken in Afghanistan in Guantanamo Bay, Cuba, is the only one of those detainees who was moved to the continental United States without pending charges, and therefore into the jurisdiction of the Eastern District of Virginia and held incommunicado. Had he remained in Cuba, no court of the United States seemingly would have jurisdiction over a habeas corpus petition. But because he is within this jurisdiction, and has had a petition for a writ of habeas corpus properly filed on his behalf, it is the business of this Court to determine whether or not his detention is legal. Perhaps in this case his detention is legal; but it is not for the military alone to make that judgment. The Respondents could not cite one case where a prisoner of any variety within the jurisdiction of a United States District Court, who was held incommunicado and indefinitely, and who had filed a petition for a writ of habeas corpus, was denied access to an attorney or the right to file such a petition. Until a higher court tells the undersigned differently, a person within this Court's jurisdiction with a petition for habeas corpus pending will at the very least be allowed to meet with his publicly appointed counsel so that both sides of the matter may be presented. Fair play and fundamental justice require nothing less.

Finally, the Magistrate Judge's other procedural actions in this case are appropriate to the situation, and therefore this Court confirms those actions to the extent they have not been rendered moot by the instant opinion, and vacates any portion of any prior orders of this Court contrary hereto.

The Clerk of the Court is **DIRECTED** to forward copies of this Order to all counsel of record, and to Yaser Esam Hamdi.

IT IS SO ORDERED.

> Robert G. Doumar
> UNITED STATES DISTRICT JUDGE

Norfolk, Virginia
May 29th, 2002

IN THE UNITED STATES COURT OF APPEALS
FOR THE FOURTH CIRCUIT

YASER ESAM HAMDI,	)	
	)	
FRANK W. DUNHAM, JR., As	)	
Next Friend of Yaser Esam Hamdi,	)	
	)	
Petitioners-Appellees,	)	
	)	No. 00-_____
v.	)	[E.D. Va. Civ. Action No. 2:02cv348]
	)	
DONALD RUMSFELD,	)	
Secretary of Defense,	)	
	)	
COMMANDER W.R. PAULETTE,	)	
Norfolk Naval Brig,	)	
	)	
Respondents-Appellants.	)	
	)	
	)	
YASSER ESAM HAMDI,	)	
	)	
CHRISTIAN A. PEREGRIM,	)	
	)	
Petitioners-Appellees,	)	
	)	No. 00-_____
v.	)	[E.D. Va. Civ. Action No. 2:02cv382]
	)	
UNITED STATES NAVY,	)	
	)	
Respondent-Appellant.	)	

EMERGENCY MOTION FOR STAY PENDING APPEAL

INTRODUCTION AND SUMMARY

Pursuant to Federal Rule of Appellate Procedure 8(a) and Fourth Circuit I.O.P. 8.1, respondents-appellants Donald Rumsfeld, et al. (respondents), respectfully request the Court to enter an emergency stay pending appeal of the district court's order of May 29, 2002. That order mandates that respondents – the Secretary of Defense and Commander of the Norfolk Naval Brig – grant the federal Public Defender with private, unmonitored access to an enemy combatant, Yaser Esam Hamdi, who was captured in Afghanistan and is being held by the United States military in connection with the armed conflict that is still being waged in Afghanistan. Unless stayed by this Court, that order will take effect on Saturday, June 1, 2002, at 1 p.m. For several reasons, an emergency stay of that order pending appeal is warranted.

First, the court consciously disregarded its lack of jurisdiction to act at all in this case. Although the Public Defender, who has no prior relationship with the detainee, plainly lacks next-friend standing under Whitmore v. Arkansas, 495 U.S. 149 (1990), the district court nonetheless ordered that the Public Defender be given next-friend status on the ground that "technical issues regarding who is best situated to be next friend will not be allowed to interfere with having the 'mind of the public be put at rest' by a swift resolution of the substance of this petition." Order of May 29, 2002 (Order), at 3.... But Whitmore itself teaches that jurisdictional limits on next-friend standing are by no means excusable "technicalities." In Whitmore, the Court admonished that the "the requirement of an Art. III 'case or controversy' is not merely a traditional 'rule of practice,' but rather is imposed directly by the Constitution. It is not for this Court to employ untethered notions of what might be good public policy to expand our jurisdiction in an appealing case." 495 U.S. at 161.

Second, the district court ignored settled principles of judicial restraint that caution against interfering with sensitive foreign policy or national security concerns. See, e.g., Dames & Moore v. Regan, 453 U.S. 654, 660–61 (1981); cf. Johnson v. Eisentrager, 339 U.S. 763 (1950) (describing inherent interference with conduct of war that habeas litigation by enemy prisoners entails). This case directly involves the President's core constitutional functions as Commander in Chief in wartime: the capture, detention, and treatment of the enemy and the collection and evaluation of intelligence vital to the national security. Yet, far from treading lightly, the district court brushed aside clear jurisdictional defects and took the extraordinary step of ordering the military to permit unmonitored access by the Public Defender to an enemy combatant during wartime, before even allowing the United States to answer the Public Defender's petition and explain why this enemy combatant is being lawfully detained, and why access to counsel is both unwarranted and antithetical to national security. More generally, the district court's order is based on the unprecedented creation of a generalized right of immediate access to counsel by enemy combatants who are being detained by the military during the midst of the very hostilities that led to their capture.

Third, the district court's access order could result in substantial and irreparable harm. A vital part of any military campaign in time of war – particularly one as complex and unpredictable as the current campaign against an unconventional, unprincipled, and savage enemy – is gathering reliable intelligence from enemies captured during the hostilities. The moment that counsel is inserted between captured, hostile combatants and military authorities engaged in intelligence gathering, the relationship of trust and dependency between detainees and the military that is key to such intelligence-gathering efforts may be destroyed, and critical, life-saving intelligence may be lost. In addition, members of the al Qaida network and its supporters are trained to pass concealed messages through unwitting intermediaries such as attorneys. At a bare minimum, before such interests are jeopardized, and access to counsel is permitted in any form, the court should wait until respondents file their return to the habeas petition showing why the detainee is being lawfully held without any need for further factual development.

Accordingly, respondents respectfully request that the Court (1) issue a stay of the district court's access order pending resolution of this appeal; (2) at a minimum, issue an interim stay pending complete consideration of the emergency stay motion; and (3) issue a decision regarding the stay requests by 1 p.m. on Saturday, June 1, 2002.

. . .

ARGUMENT

In deciding whether to grant a stay, the Court considers (1) the likelihood that the party seeking a stay will prevail on the merits of the appeal; (2) the likelihood of irreparable harm to the movant if the stay is denied; (3) the possibility of substantial harm to others resulting from the stay; and (4) the public interest in granting the stay. See Blackwelder Furniture Co. v. Seilig Mfg. Co., 550 F.2d 189, 193–194 (4th Cir. 1977); Long v. Robinson, 432 F.2d 977, 979 (4th Cir. 1970). Consideration of those factors here strongly supports granting respondents' stay request.[3]

I.   RESPONDENTS ARE LIKELY TO PREVAIL ON THE MERITS

The district court's access order is tainted by several fundamental legal errors, each of which requires that that order be set aside on appeal.

A.   The Court Lacked Jurisdiction To Enter Any Relief

. . .

1. Even if the district court properly concluded that the Public Defender had next-friend standing to initiate this action on behalf of the detainee, the court erred in confirming the appointment of the Public Defender as counsel for the detainee. Order at 2. The statute governing appointment of counsel, 18 U.S.C. §3006A(a)(2)(B), provides that "[w]henever *** the interests of justice so require, representation may be provided for any financially eligible person who *** is seeking relief under section 2241, 2254, or 2255 of title 28." (emphasis added). Here, because the petition in this case was not brought by an individual who is himself "seeking relief under section 2241," the district court's order appointing the Public Defender to act as counsel for the detainee is invalid. Indeed, in the typical case the fact that the individual is not seeking, or perhaps unable to seek, relief is what results in the filing of a next friend petition to begin with.

The only party seeking relief in this case is the Public Defender as purported next friend for the detainee. As In re Heidnik, 112 F.3d 105, 112 (3d Cir. 1997), illustrates, when counsel is appointed in such a putative next-friend situation, it is properly appointed only for the next friend. Here, that would make the Public Defender both the lawyer and the client. Nothing in Section 3006A suggests that Congress intended that bizarre result or, more generally, to authorize a Public Defender to launch his own next-friend litigation, at taxpayer expense, whenever he determines that another individual should be seeking habeas relief. And that is particularly true where, as here, there are other potential next friends, such as the detainee's father, who could serve as the client for the Public Defender – assuming, that is, that such clients would be financially eligible to qualify for appointment of counsel pursuant to Section 3006A.[7]

B.   The Court Erred In Ordering Access To Counsel Before The Government Has Filed Its Return

As the foregoing demonstrates, a series of significant legal errors led the district court to issue an order improperly granting relief – immediate access to counsel – before a number of defects in the case going to the very power of the court and the Public

---

[3] . . .

[7] Far from curing the threshold defects discussed above, the district court's decision to "consolidat[e]" the petition in this case with the second petition that was filed by Mr. Peregrim, which the court mistakenly characterized as a "pro se" petition, only casts further doubt on the process by which the court arrived at its access order. There is no basis to conclude that Mr. Peregrim would have standing. As the district court recognized in its May 24 Order, "[Mr.] Peregrim has not identified himself as a lawyer or next friend of [the detainee] and how or why he may be authorized to bring a writ of habeas corpus on behalf of [the detainee]." Mr. Peregrim also has made no showing of eligibility for appointment of counsel.

Defender to proceed could even be addressed. In fact, the court ordered preliminary relief that is inextricably bound up with the merits of the petition – indeed, it is part of the relief expressly sought on the merits of the petition. See Pet. at 7. Before ordering any such relief, the district court, at a minimum, should have waited until respondents filed their return showing why the detainee is being lawfully held based on incontrovertible or unreviewable factors.

The petition in this case raises substantial and urgent national security concerns and seeks review of actions and determinations the Constitution expressly commits to the President as Commander in Chief. Under such extraordinary circumstances, the need to follow appropriate habeas procedures and to allow respondents to file their return showing why the detainee is legally being held <u>before</u> awarding any form of relief is not only a matter of proper habeas procedure and prudence, but follows inexorably and compellingly from a proper respect for the constitutional separation of powers.

As respondents will fully address in their return, the United States military, in taking custody of this detainee in Afghanistan in connection with its military operations there, has determined that he is an enemy combatant who must be detained for the security of the United States and the success of its military objectives in the ongoing conflict. Moreover, the President, in the exercise of his commander-in-chief and foreign-affairs powers, has conclusively determined that all of the forces associated with the Taliban and al Qaida have the status of unlawful combatants. Consistent with the laws and customs of war, such unlawful combatants, including the detainee at issue here, may be detained at least for the duration of the hostilities. See <u>Eisentrager</u>, 339 U.S. at 786 ("This Court has characterized as 'well-established' the 'power of the military to exercise jurisdiction over members of the armed forces, those directly connected with such forces, or enemy belligerents, prisoners of war, or others charged with violating the laws of war.'") (citations omitted). The free-floating right of immediate access to counsel – even before the government has answered a habeas petition – created by the district court below has no footing in the laws of war, and has never been recognized by any court in the Constitution.

Moreover, because the Executive's determinations regarding the status of enemy forces involves a quintessential political question, and one uniquely assigned to the President by the Constitution, they are not subject to second-guessing by the courts. See, e.g., <u>Stewart</u> v. <u>Kahn</u>, 78 U.S. 493, 506 (1870) ("The measures to be taken in carrying on war *** are not defined [in the Constitution]. The decisions of all such questions rests wholly in the discretion of [the political branches]."); <u>United States</u> v. <u>The Three Friends</u>, 166 U.S. 1, 63 (1887) ("it belongs to the political department to determine when belligerency shall be recognized, and its action must be accepted"); <u>The Prize Cases</u>, 67 U.S. (2 Black) 635, 670 (1862) ("Whether the President *** has met with such armed hostile resistance, and a civil war of such alarming proportions as will compel him to accord to them the character of belligerents, is a question to be decided by him, and this Court must be governed by the decisions and acts of the political department").

Accordingly, respondents' return showing the detainee's status as an unlawful combatant captured in Afghanistan and the legal conclusions that flow from that status will likely be dispositive of the merits of the petition without the need for further inquiry, or any evidentiary inquiry, by the district court.[8] It was therefore error for the

---

[8] Indeed, a full-blown evidentiary hearing into a detainee's enemy combatant status itself could raise significant constitutional problems. See <u>Eisentrager</u>, 339 U.S. at 779 ("It would be difficult to devise a more effective fettering of a field commander than to allow the very enemies he is ordered to reduce to submission to call him to account in his own civil courts and divert his efforts and attention from the military offensive abroad to the legal defensive at home.").

district court to order immediate and unmonitored access to counsel for the detained unlawful combatant. That order substantially burdens the President's exercise of his commander-in-chief powers during a time of war and threatens to frustrate important national security interests without any showing that such access would assist, or indeed even be relevant to, the proper resolution of this case.

C. The Court Erred In Ordering Unmonitored Access To Counsel

The district court compounded its erroneous holdings regarding jurisdiction and the right to counsel by ordering that the improperly appointed Public Defender be provided unmonitored access to the detainee, "without military personnel present, and without any listening or recording devices of any kind being employed in any way. " Order at 4. The military has vital interests in regulating any contemplated access to the detainee that at a minimum must be carefully considered before the court could properly rule on access issues. But the district court, by issuing its premature and misguided access order, failed even to consider any of those important interests.

For example, it is well known that an al Qaida training manual provides instructions for passing concealed messages to fellow terrorists from behind bars after capture – even through unwitting intermediaries – and that al Qaida members and their supporters deploy techniques of stealth and secrecy, including codes and "hidden messages" to further their efforts. See Al Qaida Manual, www.usdoj.gov:80/ag/trainingmanual.htm. There is legitimate cause for concern that any combatants seized in Afghanistan, al Qaida or not, may have received similar training. Although the government does not doubt the integrity or professionalism of the Public Defender, there remains a substantial danger that even the most honorable of individuals might become the inadvertent, unknowing and unwitting conduit for the transmission of nefarious messages, even when there is good-faith belief that such communications are being made in pursuit of a client's representation. Moreover, this detainee in particular presents a specific concern to the United States related to force protection because he has been to the detention facility at Guantanamo Bay, he has seen the procedures used there for security and intelligence gathering, and thus is in a position to communicate valuable, highly sensitive information to enemies of the United States.

By directing immediate, unmonitored access before the government has filed its return to the petition demonstrating why the detainee is an enemy combatant being lawfully held during the pendency of the hostilities, the district court's access order ensures that such vital security interests will be entirely disregarded, regardless of the strength of the government's showing in its return, which as explained below, may obviate any need for an evidentiary hearing in this matter. Accordingly, at the very least, the district court's order of unmonitored access to counsel should be reversed.

II. THE BALANCE OF HARMS STRONGLY FAVORS A STAY

A. Irreparable Harm To The Movant

Respondents will suffer irreparable harm if the Court does not stay the district court's access order. In the context of the conflict that began with the savage September 11, 2001 attack by al Qaida on the United States, the order necessarily implicates important national security concerns. For example, the military must have the ability to interrogate detainees for any intelligence about al Qaida, its assets, its plans, and its supporters. A vital part of the interrogation process is establishing a relationship of trust and dependence between detainees and the military. It is generally only after such a relationship is established – a process that may take considerable time – that military officials are able to obtain reliable and useful intelligence information. Any contacts with outsiders may well interfere with the success of interrogation efforts. And, in particular, inserting counsel between detained enemy combatants and the military can irreparably harm the development of the type of relationship that is critical to the military's intelligence gathering mission, a mission that is directly related to combat activities that remain active and ongoing in Afghanistan. In addition, as discussed, members of Al Qaida and their supporters are trained to pass messages through unwitting intermediaries. In short, the district court's access order raises significant and unnecessary national security risks.

B.   Possibility Of Harm To Others

By contrast, maintaining the status quo pending review of the district court's order will not greatly harm the Public Defender, the enemy combatant, or anyone else. . . . . At most, even assuming that respondents' appeal is ultimately unsuccessful, the stay would merely result in some delay in enforcing the access order, but that is the normal cost of the appellate process and does not constitute a cognizable basis for denying respondents a stay.

C.   The Public Interest

The public interest strongly favors a stay. The Public Defender's habeas petition challenges the legality of detaining an enemy combatant. Such a petition necessarily raises sensitive questions related to the proper role of the courts in reviewing actions taken under the President's authority as Commander in Chief. . . . . Orderly treatment of those questions is especially appropriate because the Court is being asked to review the actions of the military undertaken under the President's power as Commander in Chief during wartime operations at a time when the lives of Americans and the security of America are at grave risk. Courts are wisely circumspect in such matters and will proceed only when required to do so. See, e.g., Dames & Moore, 453 U.S. at 660–661; Eisentrager, 339 U.S. 763 (1950).Thus, a limited stay to enable this Court to resolve the fundamental jurisdictional and other defects in the district court's access order is plainly in the public interest.

CONCLUSION

For the foregoing reasons, the Court should grant a stay pending appeal of the district court's order requiring respondents to provide the Public Defender with unmonitored access to the detainee as of Saturday, June 1, at 1 p.m.

Respectfully submitted,
Paul J. McNulty
United States Attorney

By:

Paul D. Clement
   Deputy Solicitor General
Alice S. Fisher
   Deputy Assistant Attorney General

Lawrence R. Leonard
Managing Assistant United States Attorney
. . .

**IN THE UNITED STATES DISTRICT COURT
FOR THE EASTERN DISTRICT OF VIRGINIA
NORFOLK DIVISION**

YASER ESAM HAMDI,	)
	)
ESAM FOUAD HAMDI, As Next Friend of Yaser Esam Hamdi,	)
	)
Petitioners,	)
	)
v.	) CASE NO. 2:02 cv 439
	)
DONALD RUMSFELD Secretary of Defense The Pentagon ▓▓▓▓▓▓	)
	)
COMMANDER W.R. PAULETTE, Norfolk Naval Brig ▓▓▓▓▓▓	)
	)
Respondents.	)

PETITION FOR WRIT OF HABEAS CORPUS

1. Petitioner Yaser Esam Hamdi, a citizen of the United States of America, is being held illegally, denied access to legal counsel, and denied access to the Court in violation of his constitutionally protected rights. Esam Fouad Hamdi, on behalf of his son, Yaser Esam Hamdi as his Next Friend, requests that this Court issue a Writ of Habeas Corpus.

. . .

3. Petitioner Esam Fouad Hamdi is the father of Yaser Esam Hamdi. Esam Fouad Hamdi has had no contact with his son since Respondents gained custody of Yaser Esam Hamdi in 2001.

. . .

PRAYER FOR RELIEF

WHEREFORE, Petitioners pray for relief as follows:

1. Grant Petitioner Esam Fouad Hamdi Next Friend status, as Next Friend of Yaser Esam Hamdi;

2. Appoint counsel to represent Yaser Esam Hamdi because he is indigent and has no funds with which to retain counsel in the United States;[1]

3. Order Respondents to cease all interrogations of Yaser Esam Hamdi, direct or indirect, while this litigation is pending;

---

* Redactions on this page have been added for privacy purposes. – *Eds.*
1 . . .

4. Order and declare that Yaser Esam Hamdi is being held in violation of the Fifth and Fourteenth Amendments to the United States Constitution;

5. To the extent Respondents contest any material factual allegations in this Petition, schedule an evidentiary hearing, at which Petitioners may adduce proof in support of their allegations;

6. Order that Petitioner Yaser Esam Hamdi be released from Respondents' unlawful custody;

7. Such other relief as the Court may deem necessary and appropriate to protect Petitioner Yaser Esam Hamdi's rights under the United States Constitution.

Dated: June 8th, 2002

                        Respectfully submitted,

                        Yaser Esam Hamdi, and Esam Fouad Hamdi,
                        as Next Friend of Yaser Esam Hamdi

                        Esam Fouad Hamdi
                                            . . .
            . . .

6/11/2002: DISTRICT COURT ORDER

IN THE UNITED STATES DISTRICT COURT
FOR THE EASTERN DISTRICT OF VIRGINIA
NORFOLK DIVISION

YASER ESAM HAMDI, and
ESAM FOUAD HAMDI,
As Next Friend of Yaser Esam Hamdi,

  Petitioners,

v.   CIVIL ACTION NO. 2:02cv439

DONALD RUMSFELD, and
COMMANDER W.R. PAULETTE,

  Respondents.

ORDER

Currently before the Court is the matter of a third petition for a writ of habeas corpus pursuant to 28 U.S.C. §2241, filed on behalf of the Petitioner, Yaser Esam Hamdi, who is currently being held incommunicado in the brig of the naval base in Norfolk, Virginia.

The instant petition has been filed by Hamdi's father, Esam Fouad Hamdi, as next friend. The Supreme Court in Whitmore v. Arkansas, 495 U.S. 149 (1990), established a two prong test for whether someone is a proper next friend for purposes of filing a habeas corpus petition on behalf of a person in custody. "First, a 'next friend' must provide an adequate explanation – such as inaccessibility, mental incompetence, or other disability – why the real party in interest cannot appear on his own behalf to prosecute the action." Id. at 163. The reason why the real party in interest cannot appear on his own behalf in this case is obvious – Yaser Esam Hamdi is being held incommunicado on a military installation within the Eastern District of Virginia. The second prong requires that "the 'next friend' must be truly dedicated to the best interests of the person on whose behalf he seeks to litigate the action" and that dedication is generally shown by the next friend having "some significant relationship with the real party in interest." Id. The Petitioner's father, who has attempted for some months to arrange for his son to meet with an attorney, clearly qualifies under this standard. Therefore, having found that the Petitioner's father, Esam Fouad Hamdi, is a proper next friend of the Petitioner, the Court hereby **ORDERS** the petition filed.

The instant petition is the third filed on behalf of Hamdi. The prior two cases (2:02cv348 and 2:02cv382) have been consolidated. . . . [T]he Court hereby **ORDERS** that those cases be consolidated with the instant case. It further appearing to the Court that the matters involved in this case are currently on appeal before the United States Court of Appeals for the Fourth Circuit, the Court **ORDERS** that this case be consolidated with those cases subject to the United States Court of Appeals for the Fourth Circuit allowing such consolidation.

Furthermore, it is appropriate to appoint counsel in this case, specifically the Federal Public Defender's Office. The petition includes an affidavit by Esam Fouad Hamdi that his son is without funds to retain his own counsel, and that the father is also unable to pay for an attorney for his son. The Court hereby finds that this affidavit is sufficient evidence of financial eligibility to warrant the appointment of counsel under 28 U.S.C. §3006A. As to the identity of counsel, Frank Dunham and/or Larry Shelton of the Federal Public Defenders Office have both been appointed counsel for Hamdi in the already pending consolidated case, and given their familiarity with this case and their eagerness to proceed as Hamdi's attorneys, this Court sees no reason to appoint another counsel.

Therefore, this Court **ORDERS** that the Federal Public Defenders Office, and/or Frank Dunham and/or Larry Shelton be appointed counsel for the Petitioner.

. . .

Furthermore, for the same reasons articulated in the May 29, 2002 Order, this Court hereby **ORDERS** that the Respondents allow either Frank Dunham or Larry Shelton from the Federal Public Defender's Office, as long as they possess the appropriate governmental security clearance, the opportunity to meet with Yaser Esam Hamdi within seventy-two hours of the entry of this Order or immediately following the elimination of any stay of this Order. Because it is represented to the Court that an interpreter will be needed for the attorney to communicate with Hamdi, an interpreter with the appropriate governmental security clearance will be allowed to attend the meeting. Finally, this meeting is to be private between Hamdi, the attorney, and the interpreter, without military personnel present, and without any listening or recording devices of any kind being employed in any way.

Finally, the Court **ORDERS** that this Order is stayed until 5:00 p.m. on Friday, June 14, 2002 to allow the Respondents an opportunity to appeal this Order, or if the United States Court of Appeals for the Fourth Circuit allows the consolidation of this matter with the other pending cases, until further Order of the Court of Appeals.

. . .

IT IS SO ORDERED.

Robert G. Doumar
UNITED STATES DISTRICT JUDGE

Norfolk, Virginia
June 11th, 2002

6/13/2002: FOURTH CIRCUIT ORDER

FILED: June 13, 2002

UNITED STATES COURT OF APPEALS
FOR THE FOURTH CIRCUIT

No. 02-6895
(CA-02-439-2)

YASER ESAM HAMDI; ESAM FOUAD HAMDI, as next
friend of Yaser Esam Hamdi,

Petitioners - Appellees,

versus

DONALD RUMSFELD; W. R. PAULETTE, Commander,

Respondents - Appellants.

O R D E R

Appellants filed an emergency motion for temporary stay pending consideration of their motion for stay pending appeal and an emergency motion for stay pending appeal.

The Court grants the emergency motion for temporary stay and stays the district court's order of June 11, 2002, pending this Court's ruling on appellants' motion for a stay pending appeal of that order.

. . .

Entered at the direction of Chief Judge Wilkinson with the concurrence of Judge Wilkins and Judge Traxler.

For the Court

/s/ Patricia S. Connor

Clerk

PUBLISHED

UNITED STATES COURT OF APPEALS
FOR THE FOURTH CIRCUIT

YASER ESAM HAMDI,
    Petitioner-Appellee,

and

CHRISTIAN A. PEREGRIM,
    Plaintiff,

FRANK WILLARD DUNHAM, JR., as
next friend of Yaser Esam Hamdi,
    Petitioner,

v.

DONALD RUMSFELD, Secretary of
Defense; W. R. PAULETTE,
Commander,
    Respondents-Appellants,

and

UNITED STATES NAVY,
    Defendant.

No. 02-6827

Appeal from the United States District Court
for the Eastern District of Virginia, at Norfolk.
Robert G. Doumar, Senior District Judge.
(CA-02-348-2, CA-02-382-2)

Argued: June 4, 2002

Decided: June 26, 2002

Before WILKINSON, Chief Judge, and WILKINS and
TRAXLER, Circuit Judges.

2   HAMDI v. RUMSFELD
_____

Reversed and remanded by published opinion. Chief Judge Wilkinson
wrote the opinion, in which Judge Wilkins and Judge Traxler joined.

_____

COUNSEL

ARGUED: Gregory George Garre, UNITED STATES DEPART-
MENT OF JUSTICE, Washington, D.C., for Appellants. Frank Wil-
lard Dunham, Jr., Federal Public Defender, OFFICE OF THE
FEDERAL PUBLIC DEFENDER, Norfolk, Virginia, for Appellee.
ON PLEADINGS: Paul D. Clement, Deputy Solicitor General, Alice
S. Fisher, Deputy Assistant Attorney General, Paul J. McNulty,
United States Attorney, Lawrence R. Leonard, Managing Assistant
United States Attorney, Norfolk, Virginia, for Appellants. Larry W.
Shelton, Supervisory Assistant Federal Public Defender, Geremy C.
Kamens, Assistant Federal Public Defender, OFFICE OF THE FED-
ERAL PUBLIC DEFENDER, Norfolk, Virginia, for Appellee.

_____

OPINION

WILKINSON, Chief Judge:

The Federal Public Defender for the Eastern District of Virginia and Christian Peregrim, a private citizen, filed petitions for a writ of habeas corpus as "next friend" of Yaser
Esam Hamdi, a detainee at the Norfolk Naval Station Brig who was captured as an alleged enemy combatant during ongoing military operations in Afghanistan. The district
court concluded that the Public Defender properly filed his case as next friend, and
ordered the government to allow him unmonitored access to Hamdi. Hamdi's father,
however, was ready, willing, and able to file, and in fact has filed, a petition as Hamdi's
next friend, and we believe it incumbent upon the Public Defender and Peregrim to
show a significant relationship with Hamdi in order to proceed. Because neither the
Public Defender nor Peregrim has any significant relationship whatever with Hamdi,
each fails to satisfy an important prerequisite for next friend standing. Accordingly, we
reverse the order of the district court and remand these cases with directions that they
be dismissed for want of subject matter jurisdiction.[1]

. . .

_____

[1] Here we decide the Public Defender's and Peregrim's cases only. (No. 02-6827). A separate habeas petition
that Hamdi's father filed as next friend after oral argument before this court remains pending. (No. 02-6895).
The court regards the filing by Hamdi's father as a valid next friend petition and has ordered that appeal to
be briefed and argued by the parties on the merits.

PUBLISHED

UNITED STATES COURT OF APPEALS
FOR THE FOURTH CIRCUIT

YASER ESAM HAMDI; ESAM FOUAD
HAMDI, as next friend of Yaser
Esam Hamdi,

Petitioners-Appellees,

v.

DONALD RUMSFELD; W. R. PAULETTE,
Commander,

Respondents-Appellants.

No. 02-6895

Appeal from the United States District Court
for the Eastern District of Virginia, at Norfolk.
Robert G. Doumar, Senior District Judge.
(CA-02-439-2)

Argued: June 25, 2002

Decided: July 12, 2002

Before WILKINSON, Chief Judge, and WILKINS and
TRAXLER, Circuit Judges.

Reversed and remanded by published opinion. Chief Judge Wilkinson
wrote the opinion, in which Judge Wilkins and Judge Traxler joined.

COUNSEL

ARGUED: Paul D. Clement, Deputy Solicitor General, UNITED
STATES DEPARTMENT OF JUSTICE, Washington, D.C., for
Appellants. Geremy Charles Kamens, Assistant Federal Public

Defender, Norfolk, Virginia, for Appellees. **ON BRIEF:** Paul J. McNulty, United States Attorney, Alice S. Fisher, Deputy Assistant Attorney General, Gregory G. Garre, Assistant to the Solicitor General, Lawrence R. Leonard, Managing Assistant United States Attorney, UNITED STATES DEPARTMENT OF JUSTICE, Washington, D.C., for Appellants. Frank W. Dunham, Jr., Federal Public Defender, Robert J. Wagner, Assistant Federal Public Defender, Larry W. Shelton, Assistant Federal Public Defender, Norfolk, Virginia, for Appellees.

OPINION

WILKINSON, Chief Judge.

Esam Fouad Hamdi has filed a petition for a writ of habeas corpus as next friend of his son, Yaser Esam Hamdi, a detainee at the Norfolk Naval Station Brig who was captured as an alleged enemy combatant during ongoing military operations in Afghanistan. In its order of June 11, 2002, the district court concluded that Hamdi's father properly filed his case as next friend, appointed the Federal Public Defender for the Eastern District of Virginia as counsel for the petitioners, and ordered the government to allow the Public Defender unmonitored access to Hamdi. Because the district court appointed counsel and ordered access to the detainee without adequately considering the implications of its actions and before allowing the United States even to respond, we reverse the court's June 11 order mandating access to counsel and remand the case for proceedings consistent with this opinion.

I.

. . .

Hamdi was initially transferred to Camp X-Ray at the Naval Base in Guantanamo Bay, Cuba. After it came to light that he was born in Louisiana and may not have renounced his American citizenship, Hamdi was brought to the Norfolk Naval Station Brig. His petition claims he was taken into custody in Afghanistan in the fall of 2001, transferred to Guantanamo Bay in January 2002, and transferred again to Norfolk in April 2002. Believing that Hamdi's detention is necessary for intelligence gathering efforts, the United States has determined that Hamdi should continue to be detained as an enemy combatant in accordance with the laws and customs of war.

On May 10, 2002, the Federal Public Defender for the Eastern District of Virginia, Frank Dunham, filed a habeas petition, naming as petitioners both Hamdi and himself as Hamdi's next friend. The Public Defender had been in contact with Hamdi's father, but the father had not sought to be appointed as next friend as of the time the Defender filed his petition. Subsequently, one Christian Peregrim, a private citizen from New Jersey, filed a separate habeas petition on Hamdi's behalf, naming the United States Navy as respondent. On May 29, the district court held a hearing, consolidated the Public Defender's petition with Peregrim's, and concluded that the Defender's case was "properly filed by Frank Dunham as next friend."

After directing the government to respond by June 13, the district court ordered that "Hamdi must be allowed to meet with his attorney because of fundamental justice provided under the Constitution." Further, the court ordered that the meeting be un-monitored and be allowed to take place as of June 1, twelve days before the government's answer was due.

On May 31, the United States filed a motion for stay pending appeal of the district court's access order. We stayed the court's order and heard oral argument four days later.

While these cases were under submission, Hamdi's father filed a separate petition for a writ of habeas corpus under 28 U.S.C. §§2241 & 2242, naming as petitioners both Hamdi and himself as next friend. This petition is presently before us. The father's petition asked, *inter alia*, that the district court: (1) "Grant Petitioner Esam Fouad Hamdi Next Friend status, as Next Friend of Yaser Esam Hamdi;" (2) "Appoint counsel to represent Yaser Esam Hamdi because he is indigent and has no funds with which to retain counsel in the United States;" (3) "Order Respondents to cease all interrogations of Yaser Esam Hamdi, direct or indirect, while this litigation is pending;" and (4) "Order that Petitioner Yaser Esam Hamdi be released from Respondents' unlawful custody." Unlike the Public Defender's petition, the father's petition did not specifically request that counsel be granted unmonitored access to Hamdi.

On June 11, before the government had been served with the father's petition, the district court determined that Hamdi's father could proceed as next friend. The court then ordered the government to answer by noon on June 17, and appointed the Public Defender as counsel for the detainee based on the father's affidavit stating that neither he nor his son was able to pay for an attorney. *See* 18 U.S.C. §3006A. Further, the court again ordered the government to allow the Defender unmonitored access to Hamdi "for the same reasons articulated in the May 29, 2002 Order." The court specified that this meeting was to be "private between Hamdi, the attorney, and the interpreter, without military personnel present, and without any listening or recording devices of any kind being employed in any way." And the court ordered that the meeting be allowed to take place by June 14, three days before the government's response was due. Finally, the court stayed its order to allow the government an opportunity to appeal.

On June 13, the United States filed a second motion for stay pending appeal. The following day, we stayed both the district court's June 11 order and all proceedings before that court regarding the detainee. We heard oral argument on the instant appeal on June 25.

We subsequently dismissed the habeas petitions filed by the Public Defender and Peregrim as Hamdi's next friend. Neither had a significant relationship with the detainee, *Hamdi v. Rumsfeld*, No. 02-6827, slip op. at 2 (4th Cir. June 26, 2002), and Hamdi's father plainly had a significant relationship with his son and had filed a valid next friend petition. *See id.* at 3 n.1. We therefore turn to the district court's June 11 order.[1]

II.

The order arises in the context of foreign relations and national security, where a court's deference to the political branches of our national government is considerable. It is the President who wields "delicate, plenary and exclusive power ... as the sole organ of the federal government in the field of international relations – a power which does not require as a basis for its exercise an act of Congress." *United States v. Curtiss-Wright Export Corp.*, 299 U.S. 304, 320 (1936). And where as here the President does act with statutory authorization from Congress, there is all the more reason for deference. *See*,

---

[1] For the same reasons stated in our previous opinion, *see Hamdi*, No. 02-6827, slip op. at 5 n.2, we are presented here with an appealable order.

e.g., *Youngstown Sheet & Tube Co. v. Sawyer*, 343 U.S. 579, 635–37 & n.2 (1952) (Jackson, J., concurring). Indeed, Articles I and II prominently assign to Congress and the President the shared responsibility for military affairs. *See* U.S. Const. art. I, §8; art. II, §2. In accordance with this constitutional text, the Supreme Court has shown great deference to the political branches when called upon to decide cases implicating sensitive matters of foreign policy, national security, or military affairs. *See, e.g., Dames & Moore v. Regan*, 453 U.S. 654, 660–61 (1981); *Curtiss-Wright*, 299 U.S. at 319–20; *United States v. The Three Friends*, 166 U.S. 1, 63 (1897); *Stewart v. Kahn*, 78 U.S. (11 Wall.) 493, 506 (1870); *The Prize Cases*, 67 U.S. (2 Black) 635, 670 (1862).

This deference extends to military designations of individuals as enemy combatants in times of active hostilities, as well as to their detention after capture on the field of battle. The authority to capture those who take up arms against America belongs to the Commander in Chief under Article II, Section 2. As far back as the Civil War, the Supreme Court deferred to the President's determination that those in rebellion had the status of belligerents. *See The Prize Cases*, 67 U.S. (2 Black) at 670. And in World War II, the Court stated in no uncertain terms that the President's wartime detention decisions are to be accorded great deference from the courts. *Ex parte Quirin*, 317 U.S. 1, 25 (1942). It was inattention to these cardinal principles of constitutional text and practice that led to the errors below.

III.

The district court's June 11 order directed the United States to provide the Public Defender unmonitored access to Hamdi. And petitioners contend that order represented an unexceptional exercise of a district court's discretion in a case challenging the legality of an American citizen's restraint. Petitioners' characterization, however, is incomplete. The court's order was not merely a garden-variety appointment of counsel in an ordinary criminal case. If it had been, the lower court's discretion would be almost plenary and hardly a subject for appeal, much less reversal. *See* 18 U.S.C. §3006A. But the June 11 order was different in kind. In the face of ongoing hostilities, the district court issued an order that failed to address the many serious questions raised by Hamdi's case.

For example, it has been the government's contention that Hamdi is an "enemy combatant" and as such "may be detained at least for the duration of the hostilities." The government has asserted that "enemy combatants who are captured and detained on the battlefield in a foreign land" have "no general right under the laws and customs of war, or the Constitution . . . to meet with counsel concerning their detention, much less to meet with counsel in private, without military authorities present." The Public Defender for his part has contended that "no evidence has been submitted to support" Hamdi's status as an enemy combatant and that "unlike aliens located outside the United States, Petitioner Hamdi [as an American citizen detained in the United States] is entitled to constitutional protections" including unmonitored access to counsel.

The district court's June 11 order purported to resolve these and many other questions without proper benefit of briefing and argument. Indeed the court directed that counsel have unmonitored access to Hamdi three days before the government's response was even due. There is little indication in the order (or elsewhere in the record for that matter) that the court gave proper weight to national security concerns. The peremptory nature of the proceedings stands in contrast to the significance of the issues before the court. The June 11 order does not consider what effect petitioner's unmonitored access to counsel might have upon the government's ongoing gathering of intelligence. The order does not ask to what extent federal courts are permitted to review military judgments of combatant status. Indeed, the order does not mention the term enemy combatant at all.

Instead, the June 11 order apparently assumes (1) that Hamdi is not an enemy combatant or (2) even if he might be such a person, he is nonetheless entitled not only to counsel but to immediate and unmonitored access thereto. Either ruling has sweeping implications for the posture of the judicial branch during a time of international conflict, and neither may rest on a procedurally flawed foundation that denied both petitioners and the government a chance to properly present their arguments, or to lay even a modest foundation for meaningful appellate review. The district court's order must be reversed and remanded for further proceedings.

IV.

A.

The government urges us not only to reverse and remand the June 11 order, but in the alternative to reach further and dismiss the instant petition in its entirety. In its brief before this court, the government asserts that "given the constitutionally limited role of the courts in reviewing military decisions, courts may not second-guess the military's determination that an individual is an enemy combatant and should be detained as such." The government thus submits that we may not review at all its designation of an American citizen as an enemy combatant – that its determinations on this score are the first and final word.

Any dismissal of the petition at this point would be as premature as the district court's June 11 order. In dismissing, we ourselves would be summarily embracing a sweeping proposition – namely that, with no meaningful judicial review, any American citizen alleged to be an enemy combatant could be detained indefinitely without charges or counsel on the government's say-so. Given the interlocutory nature of this appeal, a remand rather than an outright dismissal is appropriate.

If dismissal is thus not appropriate, deference to the political branches certainly is. It should be clear that circumspection is required if the judiciary is to maintain its proper posture of restraint. *The Prize Cases*, 67 U.S. at 670 ("[T]his Court must be governed by the decisions and acts of the political department of the Government to which this power was entrusted."). The federal courts have many strengths, but the conduct of combat operations has been left to others. *See, e.g., Quirin*, 317 U.S. at 25–26. The executive is best prepared to exercise the military judgment attending the capture of alleged combatants. The political branches are best positioned to comprehend this global war in its full context and it is the President who has been charged to use force against those "nations, organizations, or persons *he determines*" were responsible for the September 11 terrorist attacks. Authorization for Use of Military Force, 115 Stat. at 224 (emphasis added). The unconventional aspects of the present struggle do not make its stakes any less grave. Accordingly, any judicial inquiry into Hamdi's status as an alleged enemy combatant in Afghanistan must reflect a recognition that government has no more profound responsibility than the protection of Americans, both military and civilian, against additional unprovoked attack.

B.

The standards and procedures that should govern this case on remand are not for us to resolve in the first instance. It has long been established that if Hamdi is indeed an "enemy combatant" who was captured during hostilities in Afghanistan, the government's present detention of him is a lawful one. *See, e.g., Quirin*, 317 U.S. at 31, 37 (holding that both lawful and unlawful combatants, regardless of citizenship, "are subject to capture and detention as prisoners of war by opposing military forces"); *Duncan v. Kahanamoku*, 327 U.S. 304, 313–14 (1946) (same); *In re Territo*, 156 F.2d 142, 145 (9th Cir. 1946) (same). Separation of powers principles must, moreover, shape the standard for reviewing the government's designation of Hamdi as an enemy combatant. Any standard of inquiry must not present a risk of saddling military decision-making with the panoply of encumbrances associated with civil litigation.

As for procedures, we cannot blueprint them on this appeal. The government has sought to file as an *ex parte*, supplemental attachment to its brief before this court "a sealed declaration discussing the military's determination to detain petitioner Hamdi as an enemy combatant." The government explains that "[t]his declaration is not a matter of record, as it was not proffered in the district court because the proceedings there did not reach the point where the merits of the habeas petition were reached." The government further states that the declaration "specifically delineates the manner in which the military assesses and screens enemy combatants to determine who among them should be brought under Department of Defense control," and "describes how the military determined that petitioner Hamdi fit the eligibility requirements applied to enemy combatants for detention." This declaration is factual in nature. As such, it should come first before the district court, not the court of appeals.

The development of facts may pose special hazards of judicial involvement in military decision-making that argument of questions of pure law may not. For example, allowing alleged combatants to call American commanders to account in federal courtrooms would stand the warmaking powers of Articles I and II on their heads. Finally, the role that counsel should or should not play in resolving questions of law or fact is a matter of immense importance.[2]

V.

Upon remand, the district court must consider the most cautious procedures first, conscious of the prospect that the least drastic procedures may promptly resolve Hamdi's case and make more intrusive measures unnecessary. Our Constitution's commitment of the conduct of war to the political branches of American government requires the court's respect at every step. Because the district court appointed counsel and ordered access to the detainee without adequately considering the implications of its actions and before allowing the United States even to respond, we reverse the court's June 11 order mandating access to counsel and remand the case for proceedings consistent with this opinion.

REVERSED AND REMANDED

---

[2] Whether the financial eligibility requirements of 18 U.S.C. §3006A have been satisfied is likewise an issue we leave for remand.

IN THE UNITED STATES DISTRICT COURT
FOR THE EASTERN DISTRICT OF VIRGINIA
NORFOLK DIVISION

YASER ESAM HAMDI,

ESAM FOUAD HAMDI, As Next
Friend of Yaser Esam Hamdi,

Petitioners,

v.   Civil Action No. 2:02cv439

DONALD RUMSFELD,
Secretary of Defense,

COMMANDER W.R. PAULETTE,
Norfolk Naval Brig,

Respondents.

**RESPONDENTS' RESPONSE TO, AND MOTION TO DISMISS,
THE PETITION FOR A WRIT OF HABEAS CORPUS**

Respondents Donald Rumsfeld, Secretary of Defense, and Commander W.R. Paulette, Norfolk Naval Brig, by and through undersigned counsel, oppose and hereby move to dismiss the petition for a writ of habeas corpus in this case.

STATEMENT OF THE CASE

. . .

In the course of the military campaign – which remains active and ongoing – United States and allied forces have captured or taken control of numerous individuals. Consistent with the settled laws and customs of war, and with the practice followed in virtually every other major armed conflict in the nation's history, the United States military has determined that many of the individuals captured in Afghanistan should be detained as enemy combatants. See Declaration of Michael H. Mobbs (Mobbs Decl.) (attached hereto). Such detention serves the vital objective of preventing combatants from continuing to aid our enemies. In addition, detention of such combatants is critical to gathering intelligence in connection with the overall war effort, and especially with aiding military operations and preventing additional attacks on the United States or its allies.

The detainee in this case, Yaser Esam Hamdi, appears to be a Saudi national who, records indicate, was born in Louisiana. He was seized as an enemy combatant and taken into control of the United States military in Afghanistan, after the Taliban unit that he was with surrendered to Northern Alliance forces in late 2001. See Mobbs Decl. ¶¶3–4. Applying screening criteria established by the United States military to determine which detainees seized in Afghanistan should continue to be detained, United States military authorities determined that Hamdi should be detained as an enemy combatant.

Id. ¶6; see id. at ¶2, 7.[1] In Afghanistan, Hamdi told United States military authorities that he went to Afghanistan to train with and, if necessary, fight for the Taliban. Id. ¶5. Subsequent interviews with Hamdi also confirm his status as an enemy combatant. Indeed, Hamdi himself has stated that he laid down his assault rifle upon surrendering to Northern Alliance forces. Id. ¶9. Hamdi was transported by the United States military from Afghanistan to the Naval Base at Guantanamo Bay, Cuba, and was later transferred to the Naval Brig in Norfolk, Virginia. Id. ¶8.

. . .

On July 18, 2002, before issuance of the court of appeals' mandate in that appeal and before any order of the Fourth Circuit lifting the stay of "all proceedings" before this Court involving Hamdi, the Court ordered respondents, inter alia, to respond to the petition by noon on July 25, 2002. In addition, the Court ordered respondents to supply with their response answers to three issues not raised by the petition itself: (1) whether the detainee is being held "incommunicado" and, if he is not, "why *** he can have visitors but not one of them be a lawyer," Tr. of July 18, 2002 Hrg. at 5; (2) whether the detainee is being held in "solitary confinement" and, if so, "would due process apply to him" on the basis of being so held, id. at 6; and (3) "with whom is [the United States] fighting," and "how would [the war] ever end if there is no government or organization with one can deal," ibid. This motion to dismiss is filed in response to the Court's July 18 Order.[3]

ARGUMENT

THE PETITION SHOULD BE DISMISSED BECAUSE THE DETAINEE IS LAWFULLY DETAINED AS AN ENEMY COMBATANT

. . .

A. It Is Settled That The Military's Detention Of Enemy Combatants In Connection With Ongoing Hostilities, Including The Current Conflict, Is "Lawful"

The first claim raised by the petition in this case is that Hamdi is being detained in violation of the Constitution's due process guarantee. Pet. ¶¶21–23. That claim fails as a matter of law. The United States's authority to hold enemy combatants, including those with a claim to United States citizenship, is well-established and, indeed, in the wake of the recent appeal, is established law of the case in this action. Nothing in the Due Process Clause precludes such a detention. As the court of appeals has just held, "[i]t has long been established that if Hamdi is indeed an 'enemy combatant' who was captured during hostilities in Afghanistan, the government's present detention of him is a lawful one." Hamdi, 2002 WL 1483908, at *5 (emphasis added).

1. In so holding, the court of appeals drew upon a settled body of law recognizing that the United States military may seize and detain enemy combatants, or other belligerents, for the duration of a conflict. See Hamdi, 2002 WL 1483908, at *5. For

---

[1] The screening criteria themselves are classified. Respondents can provide the Court further information about the criteria in a classified filing that would be submitted ex parte and under seal. However, review of the screening criteria is not necessary to the resolution of the petition in this case, which, the for reasons explained below, fails as a matter of law.

3 . . .

example, in Ex parte Quirin, 317 U.S. 1, 30–31 (1942) (emphasis added and footnotes omitted), the Supreme Court stated:

> By universal agreement and practice, the law of war draws a distinction between the armed forces and the peaceful populations of belligerent nations and also between those who are lawful and unlawful combatants. Lawful combatants are subject to capture and detention as prisoners of war by opposing military forces. Unlawful combatants are likewise subject to capture and detention, but in addition they are subject to trial and punishment by military tribunals for acts which render their belligerency unlawful.

See id. at 31 n.8 (citing authorities); Duncan v. Kahanamoku 327 U.S. 304, 313–314 (1946); In re Territo, 156 F.2d 142, 145 (9th Cir. 1946); Ex parte Toscano, 208 F. 938, 940 (S.D. Cal. 1913).[4]

As the court of appeals recognized in this case, it also is settled that the military's authority to detain an enemy combatant is not diminished by a claim, or even a showing, of American citizenship. See Hamdi, 2002 WL 1483908, at *5 (parenthetical discussing Quirin, 317 U.S. at 31, 37); see also Quirin, 317 U.S. at 37 ("Citizenship in the United States of an enemy belligerent does not relieve him from the consequences of a belligerency which is unlawful"); Territo, 156 F.2d at 144 ("[I]t is immaterial to the legality of petitioner's detention as a prisoner of war by American military authorities whether petitioner is or is not a citizen of the United States of America."); Colepaugh v. Looney, 235 F.2d 429, 432 (10th Cir. 1956) ("[T]he petitioner's citizenship in the United States does not *** confer upon him any constitutional rights not accorded any other belligerent under the laws of war."), cert. denied 352 U.S. 1014 (1957). To be sure, the fact that such a combatant has American citizenship may enable him to proceed with a habeas action that could not be brought by an alien combatant (cf. Johnson v. Eisentrager, 339 U.S. 763 (1950)), but it does not affect the Executive's settled authority to detain him as an enemy combatant.

The United States military has captured and detained enemy combatants during the course of virtually every major conflict in the Nation's history, including recent conflicts such as the Gulf, Vietnam, and Korean wars. As the court of appeals has recognized, "[t]he unconventional aspects of the present struggle do not make its stakes any less grave," and they do not, as the court further held, diminish the military's settled authority to capture and detain enemy combatants in connection with that conflict. Hamdi, 2002 WL 1483908, at *5.[5]

2. As an enemy combatant, the military's "present detention" of Hamdi is "lawful," Hamdi, 2002 WL 1483908, at *5, even though he has not been "charged with an offense" or "provided counsel." Pet. ¶19. There is no obligation under the laws and customs of

---

[4] The practice of capturing and detaining enemy combatants is as old as war itself. See A. Rosas, The Legal Status of Prisoners of War 44–45 (1976). "The object of capture is to prevent the captured individual from serving the enemy. He is disarmed and from then on he must be removed as completely as practicable from the front, treated humanely, and in time exchanged, repatriated, or otherwise released." Territo, 156 F.2d at 146 (footnotes omitted). The capture and detention of enemy combatants also serves other vital military objectives, including the critical and age-old objective of obtaining intelligence from captured combatants to aid in the war effort. At the same time, once individuals are taken into control as enemy combatants, they are protected from harm or other reprisals, given medical care, and are treated humanely.

[5] As Quirin makes clear, the military's authority to capture and detain enemy combatants exists regardless of whether they are "lawful" or "unlawful" combatants under the laws and customs of war. Quirin, 317 U.S. at 30–31; see p. __ supra (quoting Quirin). In any event, the President has determined that al Qaida and the Taliban are unlawful combatants. See United States v. Lindh, 212 F. Supp.2d 541 2002 WL 1489373, at *8–*11 (E.D. Va. July 11, 2002). As noted above, Hamdi was captured as part of a Taliban unit. Mobbs Decl. ¶4.

war for captors to charge combatants with an offense (whether under the law of war or domestic law); indeed, a significant number, if not the vast majority, of those seized in war are never charged with any offense but instead are simply detained during the conflict. Similarly, there is no general right under the laws and customs of war for those detained as enemy combatants to be provided counsel. Even under the Third Geneva Convention – which does not afford protections to unlawful enemy combatants, such as the detainee here, see note 5, supra – prisoners of war have no right of access to counsel to challenge their detention. See, e.g., Geneva Convention Relative to the Treatment of Prisoners of War, Aug. 12, 1949, 6 U.S.T. 3317, 75 U.N.T.S. 135 (GPW), Article 105.[6]

The Constitution does not supply any different guarantee. The Sixth Amendment by its terms applies only in the case of "criminal prosecutions," U.S. Const. amend. VI, and therefore does not apply to the detention of any enemy combatant who – like most such combatants – has not been charged with any crime. Cf. Middendorf v. Henry, 425 U.S. 25, 38, (1976) ("[A] proceeding which may result in deprivation of liberty is nonetheless not a 'criminal proceeding' within the meaning of the Sixth Amendment if there are elements about it which sufficiently distinguish it from a traditional civilian criminal trial."). Similarly, the Self-Incrimination Clause of the Fifth Amendment is a "trial right of criminal defendants," and therefore also does not extend to this situation. United States v. Verdugo-Urquidez, 494 U.S. 259, 264 (1990) (emphasis added). The only possible remaining source of a right to charges or counsel is the Due Process Clause.

Any suggestion of a generalized due process right under the Fifth Amendment could not be squared with, inter alia, the historical unavailability of any right to prompt charges or counsel for those held as enemy combatants. Cf. Herrera v. Collins, 506 U.S. 390, 407–408 (1993); Medina v. California, 505 U.S. 437, 445–446 (1992); Moyer v. Peabody, 212 U.S. 78, 84 (1909); see also Colepaugh, 235 F.2d at 432; Ex parte Toscano, 208 F. at 943. As the Supreme Court stated in Quirin, 317 U.S. at 27–28, "[f]rom the very beginning of its history this Court has recognized and applied the law of war as including that part of the law of nations which prescribes, for the conduct of war, the status, rights and duties of enemy nations as well as of enemy individuals." Moreover, if the Court were to consider the creation of some entirely new right under the Fifth Amendment in this case, the Court would have to balance the creation of such a right against the government's own interests, including the President's plenary authority as Commander in Chief and the important national security interests implicated by allowing access to counsel to enemy combatants. See, e.g., Middendorf, 425 U.S. at 42–43; id. at 45–46; id. at 49–51 (Powell, J., joined by Blackmun, J., concurring). Accordingly, even the most general due process analysis would not support a claim that Hamdi's "present detention" is unlawful because he has not been charged or provided counsel.[7]

3. Similarly, nothing in 18 U.S.C. 4001 precludes Hamdi's detention as an enemy combatant. That provision – entitled "Limitation on detention; control of prisons" – states:

(a) No citizen shall be imprisoned or otherwise detained by the United States except pursuant to an Act of Congress.

---

[6] Article 105 of the GPW provides that a prisoner of war should be provided with counsel to defend against charges brought against him in a trial proceeding at least two weeks before the opening of such trial. But the availability of that general trial right only underscores that prisoners of war who do not face such charges are not entitled to counsel, or access to counsel, simply to challenge the fact of their wartime detention.

[7] In addition, the Supreme Court has rejected the argument that due process entitles state prisoners to counsel in seeking post-conviction relief, even in capital cases. See Pennsylvania v. Finley, 481 U.S. 551 (1987); Murray v. Giarratano, 492 U.S. 1 (1989) (plurality opinion); see also United States v. Gouveia, 467 U.S. 180 (1984) (no right to counsel during period of administrative detention).

(b) (1) The control and management of Federal penal and correctional institutions, except military or naval institutions, shall be vested in the Attorney General, who shall promulgate rules for the government thereof, and appoint all necessary officers and employees in accordance with the civil-service laws, the Classification Act, as amended, and the applicable regulations.

(2) The Attorney General may establish and conduct industries, farms, and other activities and classify the inmates, and provide for their rehabilitation, and reformation.

18 U.S.C. 4001. Although the petition does not mention Section 4001(a), petitioners raised it before the court of appeals and relied on it at oral argument before the Fourth Circuit. The court of appeals specifically inquired about Section 4001(a)'s application to this case, see Tr. of June 25, 2002 Arg. at 18–19, and yet reached the proper conclusion that Hamdi's "present detention" is "lawful" as long as he is properly classified as an enemy combatant. Hamdi, 2000 WL 1483908, at *5.

First, nothing in Section 4001 suggests that Congress sought to intrude upon the "long *** established" authority of the Executive to capture and detain enemy combatants in war time. Hamdi, 2000 WL 1483908, at *5; see id. at *3 ("The authority to capture those who take up arms against America belongs to the Commander in Chief under Article II, Section 2."). To the contrary, Section 4001 by its terms is addressed to the control of civilian prisons and related detentions. Indeed, subsection (b) explicitly addresses the "control and management of Federal penal and correctional institutions," and exempts from its coverage "military or naval institutions." 18 U.S.C. 4001(b). Subsection (a), the provision cited by petitioners in the court of appeals, cannot be read without reference to the immediately surrounding text. See Owasso Indep. Sch. Dist. v. Falvo, 122 S. Ct. 934, 939–940 (2002) (" 'It is a fundamental canon of statutory construction that the words of a statute must be read in their context and with a view to their place in the overall statutory scheme.'"); accord Tyler v. Cain, 533 U.S. 656, 662–663 (2001); Jones v. United States, 527 U.S. 373, 388 (1999). And, particularly when the provision is read as a whole, there is no basis for concluding that Section 4001 was in any way addressed to the military's detention of enemy combatants.

Second, even if Section 4001 were susceptible to a different interpretation, this Court's duty would be to adopt the facially reasonable – if not textually compelled – interpretation that Section 4001 is addressed to civilian rather than military detentions. As the Supreme Court has held, "where a statute is susceptible of two constructions, by one of which grave and doubtful constitutional questions arise and by the other of which such questions are avoided, our duty is to adopt the latter." Jones v. United States, 529 U.S. 848, 857 (2000); accord Edward J. DeBartolo Corp. v. Florida Gulf Coast Building & Constr. Trades Council, 485 U.S. 568, 575 (1988). The longstanding canon of constitutional avoidance independently forecloses any interpretation of Section 4001(a) that would extend it to interfere with the longstanding authority of the President as Commander in Chief and the armed forces to detain enemy combatants during war time. Petitioners' proposed reading of Section 4001(a) would directly interfere with the President's ability to detain an enemy combatant who claims citizenship. That situation arose in World War II, see Quirin, supra; Territo, supra, and has now arisen again. A Court should not infer that a provision that is explicitly addressed to civilian detentions meant to override that long-established and vital war time authority of the Executive.

Third, and in any event, the detention at issue is authorized by at least two different Acts of Congress. First, as the court of appeals specifically noted (Hamdi, 2000 WL 1483908, at *3, *5), the challenged Executive actions in this case fall within Congress's express statutory authorization to the President "to use force against those 'nations, organizations, or persons he determines' were responsible for the September 11 terrorist attacks." Hamdi, 2002 WL 1483908, at *5 (quoting 115 Stat. 224; emphasis added by court of appeals). Second, Congress has appropriated funding to the Department of Defense to pay for the expenses incurred in connection with "the maintenance, pay, and allowances of prisoners of war, other persons in the custody of the Army, Navy, or Air Force whose status is determined by the Secretary concerned to be similar to prisoners of war." 10 U.S.C. 956(5); see 10 U.S.C. 956(4) (appropriating funding for the "issue of authorized articles to prisoners and other persons in military custody"). By explicitly funding the detention of "prisoners of war" and persons – such as enemy combatants – "similar to prisoners of war" Congress has plainly authorized the military detention of such combatants. Therefore, Section 4001(a) does not in any way bar the military detention of enemy combatants such as Hamdi.

In sum, as long as Hamdi "is indeed an 'enemy combatant,'" then – as the Fourth Circuit already has established in this case – his "present detention" is "lawful." Hamdi, 2000 WL 1483908, at *5. Because the petition itself does not challenge the military's determination that Hamdi is an enemy combatant, but instead raises legal challenges that were considered and rejected, inter alia, by the Supreme Court in Quirin, petitioners' due process claims fails on its own terms. In any event, as explained in Part C, infra, even if the petition had challenged Hamdi's enemy combatant status (or if petitioners attempt to do so now), the military has properly determined that Hamdi is an enemy combatant and, as a matter of law, that determination satisfies any appropriate standard of review.

B. The President's Order Of November 13, 2001 Is Not Applicable To Hamdi And Has Not Resulted In Any Suspension Of The Writ

In addition to the alleged violation of due process, the only other claim raised by the petition is the legal claim that, to the extent that the President's Military Order of November 13, 2001 . . . forecloses judicial review of Hamdi's detention via habeas, "the Order and its enforcement constitute an unlawful suspension of the Writ." Pet. ¶25. That claim, too, fails as a matter of law. By its terms, the President's November 13, 2001 Order applies only to non-citizens whom the President determines "in writing" to be subject to his Order. See Military Order §2(a). The President has made no such written determination with respect to Hamdi, who is alleged to be an American citizen. Therefore, the President's Military Order has absolutely no application to Hamdi in his present situation. That is a sufficient basis to reject the petition's second claim as a matter of law. But in any event, the very fact of this habeas proceeding underscores that there has been no "Suspension of the Writ." Pet. ¶25. The writ of habeas corpus remains available to individuals, such as Hamdi, who are detained as enemy combatants to challenge the legality of their detention. Petitioners' challenges to Hamdi's detention as inconsistent with the Due Process Clause and 18 U.S.C. 4001(a) fail for the reasons explained above, but they involve a classic use of the writ to challenge the legality of detention, just as, for example, the Quirin petitioners employed the writ to raise a similar – and similarly unavailing – claims.

C. As A Matter Of Law, The Military Has Properly Determined That Hamdi Should Be Detained As An Enemy Combatant

Although the petition does not specifically challenge the military's determination that Hamdi is an enemy combatant, it is clear that such determination is proper and, as a matter of law, is entitled to be given effect by the courts under any appropriate standard of review.

1. The Fourth Circuit already has made clear in this case that the tremendous deference owed to the political branches in matters involving foreign relations and national security "extends to military designations of individuals as enemy combatants in times of active hostilities, as well as to their detention after capture on the field of battle." Hamdi, 2002 WL 1483908 at *3 (emphasis added). The court further emphasized that "the standard for reviewing the government's designation of Hamdi as an enemy combatant" is shaped by "[s]eparation of powers principles," and "must reflect a recognition that government has no more profound responsibility than the protection of Americans, both military and civilian, from additional unprovoked attack." Id. at *5.

Indeed, the Executive's determination that someone is an enemy combatant and should be detained as such is one of the most fundamental military judgments of all. See Hirota v. MacArthur, 338 U.S. 197, 215 (1949) ("[T]he capture and control of those who were responsible for the Pearl Harbor incident was a political question on which the President as Commander-in-Chief, and as spokesman for the nation in foreign affairs, had the final say.") (Douglas, J., concurring); cf. Ludecke v. Watkins, 335 U.S. 160, 170 (1948) (determinations with respect to how to treat enemy aliens "when the guns are silent but the peace of Peace has not come *** are matters of political judgment for which judges have neither technical competence nor official responsibility"); Eisentrager, 339 U.S. at 789 ("Certainly it is not the function of the Judiciary to entertain private litigation – even by a citizen – which challenges the legality, the wisdom, or the propriety of the Commander-in-Chief in sending our armed forces abroad or to any particular region."). And the Judiciary, as the Fourth Circuit has recognized, lacks institutional competence in making such military judgments. See Hamdi, 2002 WL 1483908 at *5 ("The executive is best prepared to exercise the military judgment attending the capture of alleged combatants."); see also Thomasson, 80 F.3d at 926 ("[T]he lack of competence on the part of the courts [with respect to military judgments] is marked) (quoting Rostker v. Goldberg, 453 U.S. 57, 65 (1981)); Tiffany, 931 F.2d at 278.

2. The sworn declaration appended hereto explaining the military's determination that Hamdi is an enemy combatant readily satisfies any constitutionally appropriate standard of judicial review in this extremely sensitive and important realm of Executive decisionmaking. Proper respect for separation of powers and the appropriate division of responsibilities between the judicial and executive branches may well limit the courts to the consideration of legal attacks on detention of the type considered in Quirin and Territo (and raised by petitioners here and discussed in Parts A and B, supra). At most, however, in light of fundamental separations of powers concerns, a court's proper role in a habeas proceeding such as this would be to confirm that there is a factual basis supporting the military's determination that the detainee is an enemy combatant. This return and the accompanying declaration more than satisfy that standard of review.

Indeed, in evaluating habeas challenges to analogous – but much less constitutionally sensitive – executive determinations, courts have refused to permit use of the writ to challenge the factual accuracy of such determinations, and instead call upon the Executive only to show "some evidence" supporting its determination. See, e.g., INS v. St. Cyr, 533 U.S. 289, 306 (2001)..... The focus of the inquiry is thus the Executive's determination, and the court's role is limited to confirming that there was a basis for that determination, and not to undertake a de novo determination for itself.

Moyer v. Peabody, 212 U.S. 78 (1909), is also instructive in this connection. There, the Court considered the due process challenge of a person who had been detained without probable cause for months by the governor of Colorado acting in his capacity of "commander in chief of the state forces" during a local "state of insurrection." Id. at 82. In rejecting that challenge, Justice Holmes, writing for a unanimous Court, explained: "So long as such arrests are made in good faith and in the honest belief that they are needed in order to head the insurrection off, the governor is the final judge and cannot be subjected to an action after he is out of office, on the ground that he had not reasonable ground for his belief." Id. at 85; see also United States v. Salerno, 481 U.S. 739, 748 (1987) .... [8]

The basic considerations underlying the limited scope of judicial review of the sorts of executive determinations underlying the foregoing cases are only magnified in a case such as this, involving a challenge to the military's determination that someone seized in the middle of active hostilities in a foreign land is an enemy combatant. And so too, at a bare minimum, the military's determination that an individual is an enemy combatant should be respected by the courts as long as the military shows some evidence for that determination. Any more demanding standard would disregard the compelling separations of powers concerns recognized by the court of appeals in this case and unnecessarily invite the "special hazards of judicial involvement in military decision-making" foreseen by the court of appeals. As the Fourth Circuit recognized, "allowing alleged combatants to call American commanders to account in federal courtrooms would stand the warmaking powers of Article I and II on their heads." Hamdi, 2000 WL 1483908, at *6. At the same time, applying a heightened standard would risk "a conflict between judicial and military opinion highly comforting to enemies of the United States." Eisentrager, 339 U.S. at 779.

Respondents here have provided a more than ample factual basis to support the military's determination that the detainee in this case is an enemy combatant. The Mobbs Declaration explains the relevant events surrounding Hamdi's capture and detention. In particular, the declaration explains that Hamdi went to Afghanistan to train with and, if necessary, fight for the Taliban; he remained with the Taliban after September 11, 2001, and after the United States military campaign began in Afghanistan in October 2001; and he was captured when his Taliban unit surrendered to – and, indeed, laid down arms to – Northern Alliances forces. Mobbs Decl. ¶¶3–5, 9.[9] The declaration further explains that the military determined that Hamdi should be detained as an enemy combatant

---

[8] Judicial deference to executive branch determinations is hardly unique. For example, in suits brought under the Administrative Procedure Act (APA), 5 U.S.C. 500 et seq., to challenge executive agency actions, the standard of judicial review is "a narrow, highly deferential one," see, e.g., Bagdonas v. Department of Treasury, 93 F.3d 422, 425 (7th Cir. 1996) (citing 5 U.S.C. S 706(2)(A)), bordering on a presumption that the action taken is valid, see Citizens to Preserve Overton Park. Inc. v. Volpe, 401 U.S. 402, 416 (1971), overruled on other grounds, 430 U.S. 99, 97 S. Ct. 980 (1977); accord Comsat Corp. v. National Science Foundation, 190 F.3d 269, 278 (4th Cir. 1999) (in APA cases, courts "defer to the agency's judgment, recognizing *** that federal judges – who have no constituency – have a duty to respect legitimate policy choices made by those who do *** [because] [o]ur Constitution vests such responsibilities in the political branches.") (citing Chevron U.S.A. Inc. v. Natural Resources Defense Council, Inc., 467 U.S. 837, 866 (1984)). The APA standard of review does not permit a reviewing court to "substitute [its] judgment for that of the agency." See, e.g., Heartwood, 230 F.3d 947, 953 (7th Cir. 2000) Instead, the court must affirm the action if the agency's "decision was supported by a 'rational basis.'" Bagdonas, 93 F.3d at 425–26. Although the standard of review appropriate with respect to the type of military determination at issue in this case is far more deferential than anything under the APA, the APA example underscores the typically hands-off approach of the Judiciary when it comes to reviewing executive decisionmaking.

[9] The fact that Hamdi was undisputably seized in the midst of hostile territory occupied by al Qaida and Taliban is itself significant. See Pet. ¶9 ("Hamdi resided in Afghanistan" when he was seized.); cf. Miller v. United States, 78 U.S. 268, 310–311 (1870) (In the context of determining rights to confiscated property, Court stated "[i]t is ever a presumption that inhabitants of an enemy's territory are enemies, even though they are not participants in the war, though they are subjects of neutral states, or even subjects or citizens of the government prosecuting the war against the state within which they reside."); Lamar, Executor v. Browne, 92 U.S. 187, 194 (1875) ("In war, all residents of enemy country are enemies.").

based on interrogations with Hamdi in which Hamdi himself stated that he went to Afghanistan to train with the Taliban and that he turned over his assault rifle to Northern Alliance forces. Id. ¶¶5, 9. The Mobbs Declaration amply supports the military's determination that Hamdi is an enemy combatant and, therefore, that Hamdi is being lawfully detained as such.

3. No further factual development or evidentiary proceedings are necessary to dispose of the petition. Under the deferential inquiry discussed above, a court's role is limited to evaluating whether the Executive has shown some factual basis for its decision. A court is not to review, or to second-guess, the particular facts relied upon the Executive in making its decision. In particular, in the context in which this case arises, there is no basis for a court to conduct evidentiary proceedings with respect to any of the particular facts or circumstances surrounding an individual's capture as an enemy combatant, effectively opening the door for "alleged enemy combatants to call American commanders to account in federal court rooms." Hamdi, 2000 WL 1483908, at *5. The Court's proper role does not permit it to call members of the United States military back from the front, or to somehow attempt to bring into the courtroom the Northern Alliance forces who accepted Hamdi's surrender. Nor would it be proper to call Hamdi himself to court and, thus, seriously jeopardize important national security interests related to intelligence gathering. There is no need for an attempt at recreation or de novo examination of the circumstances surrounding Hamdi's capture on a foreign battlefield. The relevant issue is whether the United States military had a factual basis for treating Hamdi as an enemy combatant. This return and the accompanying declaration readily demonstrate that the military had such a basis, and that is the end of the inquiry.

Similarly, because the exclusive focus is on whether the military had a factual basis for its determination, there is no need for an attorney to have access to a detained enemy combatant to see if the detainee disputes any of the facts relied upon by the military. That conclusion is bolstered further by the urgent national interests that would be jeopardized by allowing attorneys to have access to detained enemy combatants. First, such access would directly interfere with – and likely thwart – efforts of the United States military to gather and evaluate intelligence about the enemy, its assets, and its plans, and its supporters. Such intelligence is critical to the successful prosecution of any war effort and, in the present conflict, in all likelihood already has avoided additional harm to American lives or interests on the home front. Second, such access may enable detained enemy combatants to pass concealed messages to the enemy about military detention facilities, the security at such facilities, or other military operations – something that members (and presumably supporters) of al Qaida are trained to do. See Al Qaida Manual, www.usdoj.gov:80/ag/trainingmanual.htm.

Collecting and assessing intelligence is one of the most important duties of the Commander in Chief, especially in wartime. See United States v. Marchetti, 466 F.2d 1309, 1315 (4th Cir.) ("[g]athering intelligence information" is "within the President's constitutional responsibility for the security of the Nation as the Chief Executive and as Commander in Chief of our Armed forces"), cert. denied, 409 U.S. 1063 (1972); see also Snepp v. United States, 444 U.S. 507, 512 n.7 (1980) (per curiam) ("It is impossible for a government wisely to make critical decisions about foreign policy and national defense without the benefit of dependable foreign intelligence."). Especially when there is no need whatever for such access to dispose as a matter of law of a habeas petition such as this, a court should refuse to overstep the fundamental separation of powers principles discussed above and jeopardize vital national security interests in intelligence gathering.

D. Response To This Court's Own Queries Of July 18, 2002

On July 18, 2002, this Court ordered respondents to include in their response to the petition answers to three questions listed below that are not raised in the petition. See Tr. of July 18, 2002 Hrg. at 5–7; see id. at 7 (The answers to the Court's questions "will be provided in the answer that the government is to file to the petition."). That sua sponte request for information relevant to theories not raised by the petition is difficult to square with the restraint typically exercised by the courts in reviewing challenges, such as this case, arising "in the context of foreign relations and national security." Hamdi, 2000 WL 1483908, at *3; see id. at *6 ("Our Constitution's commitment of the conduct of war to the political branches of American government requires the court's respect at every step."). In addition, this Court's own queries cannot alter the claims presented by the petition giving rise to this case. In any event, as explained below, the answers to the Court's inquiries further confirm that Hamdi is being lawfully detained as an enemy combatant.

1. The Court inquired "why *** if [Hamdi] is possibly an American citizen, he can have visitors but not one of them be a lawyer." Tr. of July 18, 2002 Hrg. at 5. That query was addressed to press reports indicating "that all of the United States citizens who were being held or those people who may have had United States citizenship were not held incommunicado, according to press reports, and were having visitors." Ibid. A recent article in The Virginia Pilot reported on a panel discussion at a state bar association meeting. See C. Kahn, Federal Prosecutors Defend Handling of Terrorism Suspects, The Virginia Pilot (July 14, 2002). The comments to which the Court presumably referred appeared to have been directed to individuals held pursuant to criminal charges, material witness warrants, or immigration violations, and not those held as enemy combatants.[10]

Individuals who are detained by the military as enemy combatants, including Hamdi, are allowed only official contacts – i.e., government and military officials and representatives from the International Committee of the Red Cross. No other visitors are allowed. As discussed above, the military has generally determined that allowing other visitors – including lawyers – to have access to detained enemy combatants would jeopardize national security interests by interfering with ongoing intelligence gathering efforts and possibly allowing detainees to pass concealed messages about, inter alia, the security in the facilities where they have been detained. See p. 20, supra. Detained enemy combatants are permitted to send and receive mail to and from family members. Due to national and institutional security concerns, all mail is screened.

2. The Court inquired whether, if Hamdi is being held in "solitary confinement," "would due process apply to him." Tr. of July 18, 2002 Hrg. at 6. As discussed above, the Fourth Circuit has held that Hamdi's "present detention" is "lawful" as long as he is an enemy combatant. Hamdi, 2000 WL 1483908, at *5. Presently, Hamdi is not being held in solitary confinement, as that term is normally understood. He is, however, the only enemy combatant detained in the Norfolk Naval Brig and, pursuant to 10 U.S.C. 812, is not confined in "immediate association" with members of the United States armed forces. There is no factual dispute about this, but any legal challenge to the conditions of Hamdi's confinement would fail as a matter of law. The military's decision to separate Hamdi from any others at the Norfolk Naval Brig does not trigger any additional

---

[10] Although Mr. McNulty, United States Attorney for the Eastern District of Virginia, spoke at the state bar association meeting reported by the article, the comments to which the Court appears to have been referring were made by another Department of Justice official, as the article indicates.

layer of due process review. Determinations about the appropriate conditions of confinement for an individual properly held as an enemy combatant are committed to the military. Even if Hamdi were subject to the same due process protections applicable to typical prison inmates, however, no due process violation would result from separating him from the main prison population (or in limiting his visitation) when, as here, the reasons for those restrictions are related to obviously legitimate security and prison management concerns.[11] A fortiori, those types of conditions would not raise any different, or meritorious, due process claim with respect to the type of sensitive military detention at issue here.

3. Finally, the Court inquired about the unconventional aspects of the present conflict. See Tr. of July 18, 2002 Hrg. at 7 ("[W]ith whom is [the United States] fighting," and "how would [the war] ever end if there is no government or organization with one can deal."). The fighting in Afghanistan has focused on al Qiada and the Taliban, but, as Congress's Joint Resolution Authorizing the Use of Military Force underscores, the current conflict at a minimum involves the "nations, organizations, or persons he [i.e., the President] determines planned, authorized, committed, or aided the terrorist attacks that occurred on September 11, 2001, or harbored such organizations or persons." 115 Stat. 224. With respect to when the conflict will end, the key point is that there is no dispute that the United States is presently engaged in active hostilities. As a result, even if cessation of hostilities and the continued need to detain enemy combatants were matters for judicial inquiry, the concern that hostilities might persist indefinitely is clearly premature here.

More generally, the Supreme Court has expressly recognized that questions concerning the cessation of hostilities or the scope of armed conflict are committed to the political branches. See, e.g., Ludecke v. Watkins, 335 U.S. 160, 170 (1948) (Whether a state of "war" exists is a "matter[] of political judgment for which judges have neither technical competence nor official responsibility."); United States v. The Three Friends, 166 U.S. 1, 63 (1887) ("[I]t belongs to the political department to determine when belligerency shall be recognized, and its action must be accepted."); The Prize Cases, 67 U.S. (2 Black) 635, 670 (1862) ("Whether the President *** has met with such armed hostile resistance, and a civil war of such alarming proportions as will compel him to accord to them the character of belligerents, is a question to be decided by him, and this Court must be governed by the decisions and acts of the political department"). The unconventional nature of the war in which the Nation is currently engaged only heightens the need for judicial deference to the determination of the political branches with respect to such judgments.

In any event, as the Fourth Circuit has recognized – and as the savage attack of September 11 underscores – "[t]he unconventional aspects of the present struggle do not make its stakes any less grave." Hamdi, 2000 WL 1483908, at *5. Nor, as the Fourth

---

[11] Even in the civilian prison context, courts have afforded prison officials broad latitude to restrict visitation rights of both convicted inmates and pretrial detainees. See Block v. Rutherford, 468 U.S. 576, 585–589 (1984); Pell v. Procunier, 417 U.S. 817, 822–828 (1974). Even for pretrial detainees, who have not been convicted of any crime, prison officials are afforded great deference to impose restrictions, as long as they are reasonably related to a legitimate security concern. Bell v. Wolfish, 441 U.S. 520, 536–540 (1979). The same is true for segregation from other prisoners, as long as the segregation is not for punitive reasons, but merely for administrative or security concerns, as is true here. Higgs v. Carver, 286 F.3d 437, 438 (7th Cir. 2002) (pretrial detainees have no due process right to avoid administrative segregation), citing Bell v. Wolfish, 441 U.S. 520 (1979); Sandin v. Conner, 515 U.S. 472, 485 (1995) (30-day disciplinary segregation of convicted prisoner not subject to due process where it was not a "dramatic departure from the basic conditions of [the prisoner's] *** sentence").

Circuit's recent decision also makes clear, does the unconventional nature of the conflict in any way diminish the military's "established" authority lawfully to detain Hamdi as an enemy combatant. See ibid.

CONCLUSION

For the foregoing reasons, the petition for a writ of habeas corpus should be dismissed.

Respectfully submitted,
Paul J. McNulty
United States Attorney

By:

Paul D. Clement   Lawrence R. Leonard
   Deputy Solicitor General   Managing Assistant United States Attorney
Alice S. Fisher   . . .
   Deputy Assistant Attorney General

By:
Gregory G. Garre
Assistant to the Solicitor General
                              . . .

                 . . .

Declaration of Michael H. Mobbs
Special Advisor to the Under Secretary of Defense for Policy

Pursuant to 28 U.S.C. § 1746, I, Michael H. Mobbs, Special Advisor to the Under Secretary of Defense for Policy, hereby declare that, to the best of my knowledge, information and belief, and under the penalty of perjury, the following is true and correct:

1. I am a Special Advisor to the Under Secretary of Defense for Policy. In this position, I have been substantially involved with matters related to the detention of enemy combatants in the current war against the al Qaeda terrorists and those who support and harbor them (including the Taliban). I have been involved with detainee operations since mid-February 2002 and currently head the Under Secretary of Defense for Policy's Detainee Policy Group.

2. I am familiar with Department of Defense, U.S. Central Command and U.S. land forces commander policies and procedures applicable to the detention, control and transfer of al Qaeda or Taliban personnel in Afghanistan during the relevant period. Based upon my review of relevant records and reports, I am also familiar with the facts and circumstances related to the capture of Yaser Esam Hamdi and his detention by U.S. military forces.

3. Yaser Esam Hamdi traveled to Afghanistan in approximately July or August of 2001. He affiliated with a Taliban military unit and received weapons training. Hamdi remained with his Taliban unit following the attacks of September 11 and after the United States began military operations against the al Qaeda and Taliban on October 7, 2001.

4. In late 2001, Northern Alliance forces were engaged in battle with the Taliban. During this time, Hamdi's Taliban unit surrendered to Northern Alliance forces and he was transported with his unit from Konduz, Afghanistan to the prison in Mazar-e-Sharif, Afghanistan which was under the control of the Northern Alliance forces. Hamdi was directed to surrender his Kalishnikov assault rifle to Northern Alliance forces en route to Mazar-e-Sharif and did so. After a prison uprising, the Northern Alliance transferred Hamdi to a prison at Sheberghan, Afghanistan, which was also under the control of Northern Alliance forces.

5. While in the Northern Alliance prison at Sheberghan, Hamdi was interviewed by a U.S. interrogation team. He identified himself as a Saudi citizen who had been born in the United States and who entered Afghanistan the previous summer to train with and, if necessary, fight for the Taliban. Hamdi spoke English.

EXHIBIT

6. Al Qaeda and Taliban were and are hostile forces engaged in armed conflict with the armed forces of the United States and its Coalition partners. Accordingly, individuals associated with al Qaeda or Taliban were and continue to be enemy combatants. Based upon his interviews and in light of his association with the Taliban, Hamdi was considered by military forces to be an enemy combatant.

7. At the Sheberghan prison, Hamdi was determined by the U.S. military screening team to meet the criteria for enemy combatants over whom the United States was taking control. Based on an order of the U.S. land forces commander, a group of detainees, including Hamdi, was transferred from the Northern Alliance-controlled Sheberghan prison to the U.S. short-term detention facility in Kandahar. Hamdi was in-processed and screened by U.S. forces at the Kandahar facility.

8. In January 2002, a Detainee Review and Screening Team established by Commander, U.S. Central Command reviewed Hamdi's record and determined he met the criteria established by the Secretary of Defense for individuals over whom U.S. forces should take control and transfer to Guantanamo Bay.

9. A subsequent interview of Hamdi has confirmed the fact that he surrendered and gave his firearm to Northern Alliance forces which supports his classification as an enemy combatant.

MICHAEL H. MOBBS
Special Advisor to the
Under Secretary of Defense for Policy

Dated: ___24___ July 2002

IN THE UNITED STATES DISTRICT COURT
FOR THE EASTERN DISTRICT OF VIRGINIA
NORFOLK DIVISION

YASER ESAM HAMDI,	)	
	)	
ESAM FOUAD HAMDI, As Next	)	
Friend of Yaser Esam Hamdi,	)	
	)	
Petitioners,	)	
	)	
	)	
v.	)	CASE NO. 2:02CV439
	)	
	)	
DONALD RUMSFELD	)	
Secretary of Defense	)	
	)	
COMMANDER W.R. PAULETTE,	)	
Norfolk Naval Brig	)	
	)	
Respondents.	)	

PETITIONER'S TRAVERSE AND RESPONSE TO RESPONDENTS' MOTION TO DISMISS

Introduction

Respondents' arguments pose a grave threat to the constitutional rights of American citizens. Under the guise of the President's power to act as Commander in Chief of the armed forces, Respondents seek to strip from those they label as "enemy combatants" the protections ordinarily afforded to all citizens under the Bill of Rights of the Constitution. In Petitioner Hamdi's case, Respondents propose to do this on the basis of a sparse factual statement which raises more questions than it answers..... Respondents even contend that there is no need for "further factual development or evidentiary proceedings . . . to dispose of this case." (Resp. at 20).

Respondents' argument is no different from the "sweeping proposition" criticized by the Court of Appeals for the Fourth Circuit: "that, with no meaningful judicial review, any American citizen alleged to be an enemy combatant could be detained indefinitely without charges or counsel on the government's say-so." *Hamdi v. Rumsfeld*, No. 02-6895, 2002 WL 1483908, at * 5 (4th Cir. July 12, 2002). Here, Respondents rely upon the "say-so" of a lawyer, Michael H. Mobbs, who has no personal knowledge related to Petitioner Hamdi. And Respondents refuse to permit Petitioner Hamdi to reveal his account of his capture and detention. Aside from the inequity inherent in these circumstances, the position advanced by Respondents also would eliminate basic liberties required under the Constitution for all citizens: the right not to be detained indefinitely without due process, and the right not to be punished without due process.

The Mobbs Declaration is so inadequate on its face that this Court should grant a writ of habeas corpus on the basis of the record as its stands. Nonetheless, to the extent that the Court finds that the facts set forth in the Mobbs Declaration are sufficient to deny the issuance of a writ, Petitioner Hamdi must be permitted an opportunity to confront those facts and traverse them if he can.

As for the legal issues presented by this case, Respondents mischaracterize the breadth of Petitioner Hamdi's claims. Respondents contend that the underlying Petition raises a "challenge to the authority of the Commander in Chief and the military to detain

229

an enemy combatant captured in the theater of battle in a foreign land in connection
with an ongoing military campaign." (Resp. at 6). This hyperbole states a far broader
proposition than the issue presented by Petitioner Hamdi.

The claims asserted by Petitioner Hamdi-an individual that Respondents do not
dispute is an American citizen-pose no risk to the ability of the Executive Branch to
prosecute military actions overseas. Indeed, Petitioner Hamdi's claim that he cannot
be held indefinitely or punished without due process is not one that can be made by
enemy aliens overseas. *Johnson v. Eisentrager*, 339 U.S. 763 (1950). Nor does this claim
implicate Respondents' initial detention of Petitioner Hamdi in Afghanistan. Petitioner
Hamdi challenges only his current indefinite imprisonment in the United States Naval
Brig in Norfolk, Virginia. In other words, Petitioner Hamdi's claims have no practical
consequences for the conduct of the military overseas.

The relation between the Executive's conduct of military affairs and the continued indefinite detention of Petitioner Hamdi is relevant to the degree of deference to
be afforded the Executive branch by this Court. Respondents mistakenly contend that
deference to the President in his conduct of military affairs is unbridled, and that the
circumstances at issue have no bearing on the measure of deference given to Executive
conduct. But the deference invoked by Respondents is greatest when applied to the conduct of "military commanders engaged in day-to-day fighting in a theater of war," and
much less forgiving when the President purports to exercise his power as Commander
in Chief at home. *Youngstown Sheet & Tube Co. v. Sawyer*, 343 U.S. 579, 587 (1952).

Petitioner Hamdi is unable to object to Respondents' meager factual submission,
including statements allegedly obtained from Petitioner Hamdi himself, because Respondents refuse to permit access to his appointed counsel. Nonetheless, the record is
sufficient for this Court to: (1) conclude that Petitioner Hamdi must be released even
if Respondents' characterization of his status as an "enemy combatant" is entirely accurate; (2) order Respondents to provide additional factual material in support of their
decision to imprison Petitioner Hamdi.[1]

· · ·

Factual Conclusions

The Petition for Writ of Habeas Corpus alleges that Petitioner Hamdi is an American
citizen who was born in Baton Rouge, Louisiana, on September 26, 1980. (Pet'n ¶¶2,
9.) Respondents do not deny that Petitioner Hamdi is an American citizen.

A.   Afghanistan

1.   Petitioner Hamdi is Not a Member of al-Qaida, and is not a Terrorist

According to both the Petition and the Mobbs Declaration, Petitioner Hamdi was captured by the Northern Alliance and transferred into the custody of the United States in
the Fall of 2001 or late 2001, and "has been held in United States custody since that
time without access to legal counsel or notice of any charges pending against him."
(Pet'n ¶12.) In addition, according to the account of Petitioner Hamdi's conduct from

---

[1] Petitioner in no way concedes that Respondents' factual assertions are true. For example, information about
Petitioner Hamdi prior to his transfer to the custody of Respondents is based on the hearsay of unknown
members of the Northern Alliance.

the Mobbs Declaration, Petitioner Hamdi was with a unit of Taliban soldiers when he was captured. Mobbs ¶4. In other words, Respondents make no claim that Mr. Hamdi belonged to al-Qaida or any terrorist organization. Based on the record before it, the Court therefore can conclude that Petitioner Hamdi is not a member of al-Qaida, and is not a member of a terrorist organization.

2.   The War with the Taliban Is Over

The Court requested Respondents to explain "with whom is the belligerent action taken....And...how would it ever end?" July 18 Tr. at 6. To determine whether the armed conflict with the Taliban has concluded, the Court must "refer to some public act of the political departments of the government to fix the dates." *The Protector*, 79 U.S. 700, 702 (1871); see also *Ludecke v. Watkins*, 335 U.S. 160, 170 (1948); *The Prize Cases*, 67 U.S. 635, 670 (1862). On December 23, 2001, the United States recognized the newly installed government in Afghanistan. Amy Waldman, *New Leaders Set to Assume Power in Tranquil Kabul*, N.Y. Times, Dec. 22, 2001, at A1. The President also has recognized the change in regimes in both a Proclamation and a proposed regulation. *See* Amendment to the List of Proscribed Destinations in the International Traffic in Arms Regulations, 67 Fed. Reg. 44352 (July 2, 2002); Proclamation 7577 of July 17, 2002, 67 Fed. Reg. 47677 (July 19, 2002).

Most importantly, the President has terminated the national emergency declared to deal with the Taliban. *See* 64 Fed. Reg. 36759 (July 4, 1999). Pursuant to Executive Order 13268 of July 2, 2002, the President found that "the situation that gave rise to the declaration of a national emergency in Executive Order 13129 of July 4, 1999, with respect to the Taliban . . . has been significantly altered given the success of the military campaign in Afghanistan." 67 Fed. Reg. 44751. The President therefore "revoke[d] that order and terminate[d] the national emergency declared in that order with respect to the Taliban." *Id.*

The Executive branch has determined that the armed conflict with the Taliban has concluded. *Cf. Baker v. Carr*, 369 U.S. 186, 212 (1962) ("Similarly, recognition of belligerency abroad is an executive responsibility, but if the executive proclamations fall short of an explicit answer, a court may construe them....."). Consequently, even if the Court accepts the facts as reflected in the Mobbs Declaration, Petitioner Hamdi is entitled to immediate release.

B.   Detention in the Naval Brig in Norfolk

In January 2002, Respondents transported Petitioner Hamdi from Afghanistan to Guantanamo Bay, Cuba. (Pet'n ¶17.) In April 2002, Respondents moved Petitioner Hamdi again, this time to a military jail at the Norfolk Naval Station in Norfolk, Virgina. (Id. ¶19.) Respondents have not charged Petitioner Hamdi with any crime, and continue to deny him the means to contact counsel or challenge the legality of his detention. (Id.)

1.   Petitioner Hamdi's Transfer to Norfolk, Virginia, Is Consistent With Criminal Proceedings Rather than Detention of Enemy Combatants

Absent from Respondents' Response is any explanation as to why Petitioner was moved from Guantanamo Bay, Cuba, where he was initially housed with other persons taken into custody by the U.S. military in Afghanistan. If Respondents simply intended to detain and question Petitioner Hamdi for purposes of intelligence gathering,[3] as they claim, there would be no need to transfer Petitioner Hamdi to the United States. Indeed, Respondents make no mention of the screening procedure that led to Petitioner Hamdi's present incarceration in Norfolk, Virginia. That screening procedure, however, also led Respondents to bring John Walker Lindh to the Eastern District of Virginia. In the absence of any explanation from Respondents, the circumstances of this case are inconsistent with the mere detention of an alleged enemy combatant.

2. The Conditions of Petitioner Hamdi's Confinement Are Consistent With Criminal Proceedings Rather than Detention of Enemy Combatants

Regulations governing the detention of captured enemy combatants-indeed, all persons taken into custody by the United States Armed Forces-are set forth in a joint service regulation entitled *Enemy Prisoners of War, Retained Personnel, Civilian Internees and Other Detainees*. See Joint Service Regulation, *Enemy Prisoners of War, Retained Personnel, Civilian Internees and Other Detainees* (Oct. 1, 1997) ["EPW Regulations"].... This regulation implements codified and customary international law, including the Geneva Convention Relative to the Treatment of Prisoners of War, for the U.S. military. Petitioner Hamdi is not being treated in accordance with these regulations.

The EPW Regulations require that "[a]ll persons taken into custody by the U.S. forces will be provided the protections of the [1949 Geneva Convention Relative to the Treatment of Prisoners of War] until some other status is determined by competent authority. EPW Reg. 1–5(a)(2). Similarly, the EPW Regulations also provide: "In accordance with Article 5, GPW, if any doubt arises as to whether a person, having committed a belligerent act and been taken into custody by the U.S. Armed Forces, belongs to any of the categories enumerated in Article 4, GPW, such persons shall enjoy the protection of the present Convention until such time as their status has been determined by a competent tribunal." EPW Reg. 1–6(a). As noted, these regulations reflect Article 5 of the Geneva Convention related to prisoners of war. Article 5 of the Convention Relative to the Treatment of Prisoners of War (Third Geneva Convention), Aug. 12, 1949, 6 UST 3316, 75 UNTS 135 ("GPW"). Pursuant to these provisions, a captured enemy combatant cannot be treated as anything other than an Enemy Prisoner of War ("EPW") until such a tribunal has determined an alternative status.

Respondents contend that Petitioner Hamdi is not entitled to treatment as an EPW, but do not claim to have provided a tribunal as required before Respondents may deny prisoner of war status to Petitioner Hamdi. Nor have Respondents complied with other provisions set forth in the EPW Regulations. For example, EPW Reg. 3–2(b) prohibits internment of persons in "correctional facilities housing military or civilian prisoners," "except in extreme circumstances, in the best interests of the individual."[4] EPWs also are not to be separated from other prisoners belonging to the armed forces with which they were serving at the time of their capture except with their consent. *Id*. 3–4(b). Finally, EPWs must be quartered under conditions as favorable as those of the detaining power's forces in the same area. *Id*. 3–4(e). Respondents have not complied with these

---

[3] Respondents never explain in the Mobbs Declaration or elsewhere why Petitioner Hamdi is particularly significant for purposes of their interest in intelligence gathering.

[4] The EPW Regulations also require the roof of any internment facility to be marked with the letters "PW" denoting "Prisoner of War Camp," so as to be visible from the air. EPW Regs. 3–2(c).

regulations. Petitioner Hamdi is not contesting the conditions of his confinement; on the contrary, Respondents' failure to comply with the regulations that are applied to combatants indicates that Petitioner Hamdi is being held for potential prosecution, not as a combatant.

3. Petitioner Hamdi is being Punished

Petitioner Hamdi is being held in solitary confinement. He has been isolated from others similarly situated in Afghanistan and Guantanamo Bay, Cuba. He is prohibited from sharing a cell or communicating with other inmates at the Naval Brig. He is prohibited from having visitors with the exception of a representative of the International Committee of the Red Cross. He cannot make contact by telephone. He is prohibited from group prayer and group recreation. This "exclusion from human associations" constitutes solitary confinement, a "punishment of the most important and painful character." *See In re Medley*, 134 U.S. 160, 168–71 (1890).

Respondents have also steadfastly refused to explain when the armed conflict that purportedly authorizes the application of the laws of war to Petitioner Hamdi will end. The continuation of armed conflict with al-Qaida has no bearing on the propriety of Respondents' detention of Petitoner Hamdi, not only because Petitioner Hamdi has no connection to al-Qaida but also because the laws of war do not apply to the conflict between the United States and a non-state actor.[5] The conclusion of the conflict with the Taliban therefore constitutes the end of armed conflict for purposes of the authorization under international law to detain combatants. Respondents reticence to address this issue, moreover, illustrates Respondents' position that the duration of the Petitioner Hamdi's detention indeed may be unlimited.

Argument

I. Judicial Review Must Ensure Compliance with the Constitution While Affording Due Deference to the Executive

Brandishing the deference often afforded to the Executive's conduct of military affairs, Respondents contend that this Court need only "confirm that there is a factual basis supporting the military's determination that [Petitioner Hamdi] is an enemy combatant." Resp. at 16. Respondents' argument not only is inconsistent with the deference due the Executive branch in accordance with the separation of powers, it also implies the very unchecked power to imprison American citizens that was criticized by the Fourth Circuit. The judicial deference given to the Executive branch varies by the context in which the Executive purports to act. Here, the legality of Petitioner Hamdi's imprisonment cannot be determined simply by rubber-stamping Respondents' classification of Petitioner as an enemy combatant.

It is not contested that "[a]n important incident to the conduct of war is the adoption of measures by the military command not only to repel and defeat the enemy, but to seize and subject to disciplinary measures those enemies who in their attempt to

---

[5] Because al Qaida is not a nation state, the President has announced that the Geneva Conventions do not apply to the conflict with this terrorist organization.

thwart or impede our military effort have violated the law of war." *Ex parte Quirin*, 317 U.S. 1, 28–29 (1942). At the same time, the decision to detain an American citizen pursuant to this authority is undoubtedly reviewable by the Court. See *Hamdi v. Rumsfeld*, No. 02-6895, 2002 WL 1483908, at *5 (4th Cir. July 12, 2002); *see also Quirin*, 317 U.S. at 27–28 ("From the very beginning of its history this Court has recognized and applied the law of war as including that part of the law of nations which prescribes, for the conduct of war, the status, rights and duties of enemy nations as well as of enemy individuals.").[6]

"[T]he phrase 'war power' cannot be invoked as a talismanic incantation to support any exercise of . . . power which can be brought within its ambit. 'Even the war power does not remove constitutional limitations safeguarding essential liberties.'" *United States v. Robel*, 389 U.S. 258, 263–64 (1967); *cf. Baker v. Carr*, 369 U.S. 186, 211 (1962) ("Yet it is error to suppose that every case or controversy which touches foreign relations lies beyond judicial cognizance."). These comments reflect a longstanding suspicion of conduct by the Executive branch under the guise of national security that infringes upon constitutional rights. *Cf. Duncan v. Kahanamoku*, 327 U.S. 304, 319 (1946) ("In this country that fear [of military rule] has become part of our cultural and political institutions."). As the Supreme Court has explained, "[i]t is an unbending rule of law, that the exercise of military power, where the rights of the citizen are concerned, shall never be pushed beyond what the exigency requires." *Raymond v. Thomas*, 91 U.S. 712, 716 (1875).

Even when "martial law" is declared, the conduct of the Executive branch is subject to judicial review. *Sterling v. Constantin*, 287 U.S. 378, 401 (1932) ("What are the allowable limits of military discretion, and whether or not they have been overstepped in a particular case, are judicial questions."). Furthermore, as the Supreme Court explained in *Ex Parte Milligan*, 71 U.S. (4 Wall.) 2 (1866), the geography of the Executive branch's authority to infringe upon individual liberties under martial law is limited by necessity:

> Martial rule can never exist where the courts are open, and in the proper and unobstructed exercise of their jurisdiction. It is also confined to the locality of actual war. Because, during the late Rebellion it could have been enforced in Virginia, where the national authority was overturned and the courts driven out, it does not follow that it should obtain in Indiana, where that authority was never disputed, and justice was always administered. And so the case of a foreign invasion, martial rule may become a necessity in one state, when, in another, it would be "mere lawless violence."

---

[6] Respondents cite *Hirota v. MacArthur*, 338 U.S. 197 (1948) (Douglas, J., concurring), for the proposition that the propriety of the detention of combatants is a political question. Resp. at 15. Justice Douglas said nothing of the kind in *Hirota*. A dissenter in *Johnson v. Eisentrager*, 339 U.S. 763 (1950), Justice Douglas explained in *Hirota*:

> If an American General holds a prisoner, our process can reach him wherever he is. To that extent at least, the Constitution follows the flag. . . . It is our Constitution which he supports and defends. If there is evasion or violation of its obligations, it is no defense that he acts for another nation.
>
> I assume that we have no authority to review the judgment of an international tribunal. But if as a result of unlawful action, one of our Generals holds a prisoner in his custody, the writ of habeas corpus can effect a release from that custody.

338 U.S. at 204. The critical difference for the petitioners in *Hirota* was that the President had entered into an agreement with the Allied Powers to establish an International Military Tribunal. And because the President had "made arrangements with other nations for [the petitioners] trial, he act[ed] in a political role on a military matter." Justice Douglas thus concluded that "[h]is discretion cannot be reviewed by the judiciary." *Id*. at 209.

Id. at 127; *see also Duncan v. Kahanamoku*, 327 U.S. at 326 (Murphy, J., concurring) ("Tested by the *Milligan* rule, the military proceedings in issue plainly lacked constitutional sanction.").

Likewise, the deference afforded to the Executive branch's decision to detain an American citizen diminishes by the degree to which the detention is unrelated to foreign policy, national security, or military affairs. *See Ex parte Endo*, 323 U.S. 283, 302 (1944). Put differently, judicial deference to the Executive branch is greatest with respect to the conduct of "military commanders engaged in day-to-day fighting in a theater of war," and much less forgiving when the President purports to exercise his power as Commander in Chief at home. *Youngstown Sheet & Tube Co. v. Sawyer*, 343 U.S. 579, 587 (1952).

> [N]o doctrine that the Court could promulgate would seem to me more sinister and alarming than that a President whose conduct of foreign affairs is so largely uncontrolled, and often even is unknown, can vastly enlarge his mastery over the internal affairs of the country by his own commitment of the Nation's armed forces to some foreign venture.

Id. at 642 (Jackson, J., concurring). Even while World War II was in progress, the Supreme Court emphasized that "[w]hen the power to detain is derived from the power to protect the war effort against espionage and sabotage, detention which has no relationship to that objective is unauthorized." *Ex parte Endo*, 323 U.S. at 302. The Court therefore must examine the context of the Executive branch's exercise of its power in order to determine how much deference should be given to that exercise.

As noted by the court of appeals, "any judicial inquiry into Hamdi's status as an alleged enemy combatant in Afghanistan must reflect a recognition that government has no more profound responsibility than the protection of Americans, both military and civilian, against additional unprovoked attack." *Hamdi*, 2002 WL 1483908, at *5. This observation is consistent with an acknowledgment that issues related to national security "merit the most careful consideration." *United States v. U.S. District Court*, 407 U.S. 297, 319 (1972).

Because this case involves an American citizen, however, it has very few implications for the Executive branch's conduct of military affairs against our enemies. For example, Petitioner's claims have no relation to the treatment of enemy aliens, who are not entitled to constitutional protections. *Eisentrager*, 339 U.S. at 785. Similarly, Petitioner Hamdi has challenged his indefinite imprisonment by Respondents in this country, not the propriety of his temporary detention abroad. As explained below, these claims are constitutionally distinct and are drawn from different locations within the Constitution.

Respondents also liken this case to the deference afforded by courts in their review of an agency decision. In the administrative context, however, deference to administrative determinations is the result of a congressional delegation of authority to the agency. *Adams Fruit Co. v. Barrett*, 494 U.S. 638, 649 (1990). Congress has not, and could not, delegate the customary international lawmaking power to the military.

Even if the Court sought to apply principles from the administrative context, courts do not defer when Congress "has directly spoken to the precise question at issue." *Chevron U.S.A. v. Nat. Resources Def. Council*, 467 U.S. 837, 842 (1984). As explained below, it has. *See* 18 U.S.C. §4001(a).

Finally, deference is not warranted in the administrative context when a litigating position is "wholly unsupported by regulations, rulings, or administrative practice." *Smiley v. Citibank*, 517 U.S. 735, 741 (1996). Respondents' treatment of Petitioner

Hamdi, in fact, is unsupported by the ostensibly applicable regulations applied by all branches of the United States military. *See* EPW Regulations. These regulations have no provision for "unlawful combatants," or even "enemy combatants" for that matter. *Cf. Hamdi*, 2002 WL 1483908, at *4 ("Indeed, the order does not mention the term enemy combatant at all."). More importantly, these regulations provide that "all person detained by the United States Armed Forces receive prisoner of war protection regardless of whether they are entitled to prisoner of war status under the [Geneva Conventions]." Capt. Vaughn A. Ary, *Accounting for Prisoners of War: A Legal Review of the United States Armed Forces Identification and Reporting Procedures*, 1994 Army Lawyer 16, 17 (Aug. 1994) (citing EPW Regulations ¶1–5). Respondents' decision to depart from these regulations certainly does not support a finding that Respondents' classification decision is entitled to substantial deference.

The Court of Appeals for the Fourth Circuit declined to address the "standards and procedures that should govern this case." *Hamdi*, 2002 WL 1483908, at *5. The appellate court simply noted that caution is warranted given that this case arises "in the context of foreign relations and national security." *Id.* at *3. Indeed, Respondents' detention of Petitioner is "not to be set aside by the courts without a clear conviction that [it is] in conflict with the Constitution or laws of Congress constitutionally enacted." *Quirin*, 317 U.S. at 25. At the same time, however, the court of appeals warned that Respondents do not have the power to detain a citizen "indefinitely without charges or counsel on the government's say-so." *Hamdi*, 2002 WL 1483908, at *5. In sum, while the questions raised by the Petition require a degree of "deference to the political branches," that deference should not be allowed to prevent Petitioner from adducing evidence to establish a "clear conviction that [his imprisonment is] in conflict with the Constitution [and] laws of Congress constitutionally enacted." *Quirin*, 317 U.S. at 25.

II. Petitioner Hamdi's Constitutional Rights Outweigh The Government's Interest in Inteligence Gathering

A. Petitioner Hamdi's Citizenship Entitles Him To Assert Constitutional Protections

American citizenship distinguishes Petitioner Hamdi from others charged as "enemy combatants," and entitles him to assert constitutional protections against indefinite detention and punishment without due process. Respondents' allegation that Petitioner Hamdi fought on behalf of the Taliban is insufficient to strip Petitioner Hamdi of these significant protections. Likewise, Respondents' invocation of the customary laws of war does not mean that Petitioner Hamdi's imprisonment is consistent with the Constitution.[7]

---

[7] In a statement unnecessary to the holding of its July 12, 2002, opinion, the Court of Appeals for the Fourth Circuit observed that "[i]t has long been established that if Hamdi is indeed an 'enemy combatant' who was captured during hostilities in Afghanistan, the government's present detention of him is a lawful one." *Hamdi*, 2002 WL 1483908, at *5. Respondents wrongly contend that this conclusion is the law of the case. Resp. at 7. Statements or observations unrelated to the court of appeals' holding do not become law of the case. See *Kokkonen v. Guardian Life Ins. Co. of America*, 511 U.S. 375, 379 (1994) ("It is to the holdings of our cases, rather than their dicta that we must attend."); *California v. Rooney*, 483 U.S. 307, 312–14 (1987) (dismissing writ of certiorari as improvidently granted on ground that issue was not squarely before lower court); *Creek v. Village of Westhaven*, 144 F.3d 441, 445 (7th Cir. 1998) (noting that dicta does not become law of the case). In addition, because the political branches of the government have declared that the armed conflict with the Taliban has ended, and because Petitioner Hamdi is entitled to constitutional protections regardless of his status as an enemy combatant, the Fourth Circuit's dictum is inaccurate.

Unlike aliens, American citizens are entitled to the protections of the Constitution both in the United States and abroad. *See Reid v. Covert*, 354 U.S. 1, 32–33 (1957) ("[The view that] constitutional safeguards do not shield a citizen abroad when the Government exercises its power over him . . . is erroneous. The mere fact that [the defendants] had gone overseas . . . should not reduce the protection the Constitution gives them."); *see also Kinsella v. United States ex rel. Singleton*, 361 U.S. 234, 244–48 (1960) (refusing to permit military prosecution of citizen who was not a member of the United States armed forces). In *Eisentrager*, the Supreme Court explicitly distinguished the rights of citizens from those of enemy aliens, explaining that war "exposes the relative vulnerability of the alien's status." 339 U.S. at 772.[8] Specifically, the *Eisentrager* court rejected the application of Fifth Amendment rights to enemy aliens abroad. *Id*. at 782–85.

The Supreme Court in *Eisentrager* did not address the question whether a citizen fighting on behalf of a belligerent would be entitled to constitutional protections. But if status as an "enemy combatant" were sufficient in itself to eliminate protections ordinarily afforded under the Constitution, the *Eisentrager* court's discussion of citizenship would make little sense. In other words, if enemy combatants are by definition unprotected by the Constitution, the Supreme Court need not have addressed the issue of citizenship at all in order to reach the conclusion that the petitioners in *Eisentrager*, all of whom were unquestionably enemy combatants, could not assert rights under the Fifth Amendment.

In *Ex Parte Quirin*, of course, the Supreme Court stated that "[c]itizenship in the United States of an enemy belligerent does not relieve him from the consequences of a belligerency which is *unlawful because in violation of the law of war*." 317 U.S. at 37 (emphasis added). The petitioners in *Quirin* were accused of secretly entering the United States to engage in sabotage operations. As explained by the Court, these allegations charged a violation of the laws of war:

> The spy who secretly and without uniform passes the military lines of a belligerent in time of war, seeking to gather military information and communicate it to the enemy, or an enemy combatant who without uniform comes secretly through the lines for the purpose of waging war by destruction of life or property, are familiar examples of belligerents who are generally deemed not to be entitled to the status of prisoners of war, but to be offenders against the law of war subject to trial and punishment by military tribunals.

Id. at 31. Accordingly, the petitioners in *Quirin* were subject to trial by military tribunal. *See id*. at 28; 10 U.S.C. §821. But the fact that a citizen may be tried by a military tribunal for an offense in violation of the law of war has nothing to do with Petitioner Hamdi's challenge to his imprisonment. It does not mean that citizens accused as "enemy combatants" are indistinguishable from aliens who are so charged.

Moreover, Respondents do not assert that Petitioner Hamdi committed any offense against the law of war analogous to the petitioners in *Quirin*. Instead, Respondents claim that Petitioner Hamdi is not entitled to prisoner of war status because he "was captured as part of a Taliban unit." Resp. at 9 n.5. An individual who is not entitled to prisoner of war status, however, is not necessarily an "unlawful combatant." *See* Alan

---

[8] Even during wartime, however, "enemy aliens" within the United States are not for that reason necessarily divested of rights. See *Von Moltke v. Gillies*, 332 U.S. 708, 740 (1948) (Burton, J., dissenting) ("Her status as an enemy alien does not, in itself, affect her right to counsel or the informed character of her plea of guilty and her waiver of counsel"); *Ex parte Kawato*, 317 U.S. 69, 78 (1942) (holding that enemy aliens residing in the United States are not denied access to courts); *cf. Eisentrager*, 339 U.S. at 775 ("The resident enemy alien is constitutionally subject to summary arrest, internment and deportation whenever a 'declared war' exists.").

Rosas, The Legal Status of Prisoners of War 311 (1976) ("In legal literature the term 'unlawful' (or 'unprivileged') combatant is sometimes used with respect also to such individual members of armed forces, who have forfeited their right to be treated as prisoners of war. In order to assess the desirability of such terminology, one should consider separately the situation of a spy, a person guilty of war crimes in general, and a person who has carried a perfidious attack under civilian disguise (saboteur, etc.)"). By the same token, "lawful combatants are always entitled to prisoner of war status, while the reverse is not necessarily true." *Id*. at 305.

Whether or not Petitioner Hamdi is entitled to prisoner of war status, and whether or not he would be subject to the jurisdiction of a military tribunal, he is entitled to constitutional protections like any other citizen. *See Reid*, 354 U.S. at 32–33; *Kinsella*, 361 U.S. at 244–48; *Eisentrager*, 339 U.S. at 772. Respondents' position that Petitioner Hamdi has no greater rights than if he were an enemy alien is simply inconsistent with this precedent and the significance of citizenship under our laws.

The importance of citizenship in this context is also reflected in a congressional statute, 18 U.S.C. §4001(a). That statute provides that "[n]o citizen shall be imprisoned or otherwise detained by the United States except pursuant to an Act of Congress." §4001(a). The plain language of the statute prohibits the detention or imprisonment of citizens by the United States "except" by congressional legislation, and the other sub-paragraphs contained in the statute do not diminish the force of that language. See §§4001(b)(1) & (2).

Should the Court have any question as to the application of this statute to Respondents' conduct, the legislative history establishes that Congress sought to prohibit Respondents from engaging in the precise conduct challenged here. *See Chemehuevi Tribe of Indians v. Federal Power Comm.*, 420 U.S. 395, 405 (1975) (resorting to legislative history). In particular, Congress enacted §4001(a) in 1971 "to prohibit the establishment of emergency detention camps and to provide that no citizen of the United States shall be committed for detention or imprisonment *in any facility of the United States Government* except in conformity with the provisions of title 18." H.R. No. 92–116, at 1434 (1971) (emphasis added). Likewise, the purposes set out in the relevant House report explain that the enabling legislation is designed to: "(1) to restrict the imprisonment or other detention of citizens by the United States to situations in which statutory authority for their incarceration exists; and (2) to repeal the Emergency Detention Act of 1950 (Title II of the Internal Security Act of 1950) which both authorizes the establishment of detention camps and imposes certain conditions on their use." *Id*.

In an effort to avoid the plain language and intent of this statute, Respondents urge the Court not to construe it in a manner that would "interfere with the longstanding authority of the President as Commander in Chief and the armed forces to detain enemy combatants during war time." Resp. at 12. In fact, Respondents suggest that a broad reading of §4001(a) would implicate "grave and doubtful constitutional questions," and therefore that it should not be read to apply to "military detentions."

It is difficult to see how this statute would impose any serious obstacle to the Executive branch's conduct of military affairs. Indeed, a construction of the statute that authorized the indefinite detention of citizens by the military in the United States would appear to raise even more grave constitutional questions than those postulated by Respondents. *See Zadvydas v. Davis*, 533 U.S. 678, 689 (2001) (rejecting reading of alien detention statute that would permit indefinite incarceration). Nonetheless, to the extent that application of the statute would hinder the conduct of military operations against citizens abroad, Respondents' argument suggests only that Congress did not intend §4001(a) to apply outside the United States. *See EEOC v. Arabian Am. Oil Co.*, 499 U.S. 244, 248 (1991) ("It is a longstanding principle of American law 'that legislation of Congress, unless a contrary intent appears, is meant to apply only within the territorial jurisdiction of the United States.'"). Accordingly, by bringing Petitioner Hamdi to the United States, Respondents are the architects of the conflict between their imprisonment of Petitioner Hamdi and 18 U.S.C. §4001(a).

Respondents also urge that their incarceration of Petitioner Hamdi is consistent with §4001(a) because of the congressional authorization permitting the President "to use all necessary and appropriate force against those nations, organizations, or persons he determines planned, authorized, committed, or aided the terrorist attacks that occurred on September 11, 2001, or harbored such organizations or persons, in order to prevent any future acts of international terrorism against the United States..." Act of Sept. 18, 2001, Pub. L. No. 107–40, 115 Stat. 224 (2001). Similarly, Respondents suggest that Petitioner Hamdi's indefinite incarceration is authorized by a statute that appropriate funds related to the detention of prisoners of war. 10 U.S.C. §956. These arguments are without merit.

. . .

B. Petitioner Hamdi's Imprisonment Violates His Constitutional Right to Due Process of Law

Respondents maintain that as a result of the customary international legal authority to detain combatants, Petitioner Hamdi enjoys no constitutional protection against indefinite imprisonment. . . . . . This parsimonious approach to the Constitution ignores both text and precedent.

The Due Process Clause of the Fifth Amendment prohibits the Government from "depriving" any person of liberty "without due process of law." U.S. Const. amend. V. "[G]overnment detention violates that Clause unless the detention is ordered in a *criminal* proceeding with adequate procedural protections . . . or, in certain special and 'narrow' non-punitive 'circumstances.'" *Zadvydas v. Davis*, 533 U.S. 678, 690 (2001). Accordingly, "the serious constitutional problem" raised by Respondents' asserted power to impose "an indefinite, perhaps permanent, deprivation of human liberty without any such [Due Process] protection is obvious." *Id.* at 692.

Petitioner Hamdi does not assert that the Constitution prohibited his custody by Respondents at all times. *See Ex parte Endo*, 323 U.S. at 301 ("We do not mean to imply that detention in connection with no phase of the evacuation program would be lawful. . . . Some such power might indeed be necessary to the successful operation of the evacuation program."). The Petition therefore asserts no claim against unreasonable seizure under the Fourth Amendment. *See County of Riverside v. McLaughlin*, 500 U.S. 44, 47 (1991); *Gerstein v. Pugh*, 420 U.S. 103, 114 (1975); *Fisher v. Washington Metropolitan Area Transit Auth.*, 690 F.2d 1133, 1140 n.10 (4th Cir. 1982). To be sure, the Executive branch's temporary detention of citizens during an emergency may be consistent with the Constitution. *Compare Moyer v. Peabody*, 212 U.S. 78, 85 (1909), *with Youngstown Sheet & Tube Co. v. Sawyer*, 343 U.S. 579, 652 (1952) (Jackson, J., concurring) ("[E]mergency powers are consistent with free government only when their control is lodged elsewhere than in the Executive who exercises them.").

Whatever the case with respect to temporary detention, however, long term indefinite imprisonment poses a separate constitutional issue. *Moyer*, 212 U.S. at 85 (noting that case involving extended detention may "raise a different question" then temporary detention at issue); *see also Fisher*, 690 F.2d at 1140 n.10. That separate issue is presented by Respondents' indefinite imprisonment and punishment of Petitioner Hamdi. *Bell v. Wolfish*, 441 U.S. 520, 535 & n.16 (1978) (holding that Due Process prohibits "punishment" of pretrial detainees); *In re Medley*, 134 U.S. 160, 171 (1890) (finding that solitary confinement constituted punishment). Petitioner Hamdi therefore has asserted nothing "new . . . under the Fifth Amendment." (Resp. at 10).

Also familiar is the potential conflict between Petitioner Hamdi's constitutional liberties and Respondents' broad exercise of Executive power. As the Supreme Court explained in *United States v. Robel*, 389 U.S. 258 (1967), when the exercise of an "enumerated power[] clashes with those individual liberties protected by the Bill of Rights, it is [the Federal Judiciary's] 'delicate and difficult task' to determine whether the resulting restriction on freedom can be tolerated." *Id.* at 264; *see also United States District Court*, 407 U.S. at 299 (explaining that constitutionality of Executive branch's electronic surveillance for purposes of domestic security required "sensitivity both to the Government's right to protect itself from unlawful subversion and attack and to the citizen's right to be secure in his privacy against unreasonable Government intrusion"); *cf.* (Resp. at 10) ("the Court would have to balance the creation of such a right against the government's own interests"). At the same time, the Court should remain mindful that the "concept of 'national defense' cannot be deemed an end in itself, justifying any exercise of [executive] power designed to promote such a goal. Implicit in the term 'national defense' is the notion of defending those values and ideals which set this Nation apart. . . . It would indeed be ironic if, in the name of national defense, we would sanction the subversion of one of those liberties . . . which makes the defense of the Nation worthwhile." *Robel*, 389 U.S. at 264.

Respondents have offered almost no explanation for their continued detention of Petitioner Hamdi other than their assertion that his confinement may aid their intelligence gathering efforts. Such efforts are not sufficient to justify indefinite detention. *Cf. Youngstown Sheet & Tube*, 343 U.S. at 646 (Jackson, J., concurring) ("What the power of command may include I do not try to envision, but I think it is not a military prerogative, without support of law, to seize persons or property because they are important or even essential for the military and naval establishment."). Indeed, the Government's desire to "fortify its intelligence collage" simply does not outweigh the considerable constitutional interests of American citizens at issue here. *United States District Court*, 407 U.S. at 325 (Douglas, J., concurring).

Furthermore, the rights asserted by Petitioner Hamdi do not threaten to "unduly frustrate the efforts of Government" to act abroad. *United States District Court*, 407 U.S. at 315. As described above, the underlying claims reflect the fact that the context in which the Executive branch exercises its power affects the strength of the Executive's authority. *Youngstown Sheet & Tube Co.*, 343 U.S. at 587. The longer that Respondents imprison Petitioner Hamdi without due process, the weaker is their claim to the imposition of that authority, and the stronger is Petitioner Hamdi's challenge that his imprisonment violates the Constitution. At this point, affording respect to Petitioner Hamdi's constitutional claims is more intrinsic to the "concept of 'national defense'" than Respondents' claimed authority under international law.

· · ·

Conclusion

Wherefore, Petitioner Hamdi respectfully requests that the Court deny Respondents' Motion to Dismiss, and order other appropriate relief in accordance with 28 U.S.C. §2243.

Respectfully submitted,

FRANK W. DUNHAM
Federal Public Defender

By:
Larry W. Shelton
Supervisory Assistant Federal Public Defender

. . .

Geremy C. Kamens
Assistant Federal Public Defender

. . .

. . .

IN THE UNITED STATES DISTRICT COURT
FOR THE EASTERN DISTRICT OF VIRGINIA
NORFOLK DIVISION

YASER ESAM HAMDI,
ESAM FOUAD HAMDI, as
next friend of YASER
ESAM HAMDI,

    Petitioners,

v.

DONALD H. RUMSFELD,
Secretary of Defense, and
COMMANDER W. R.
PAULETTE, Norfolk Naval
Brig, Norfolk, Virginia,

    Respondents.

CIVIL ACTION
NO. 2:02cv439

TRANSCRIPT OF PROCEEDINGS

Norfolk, Virginia

August 13, 2002

Before: THE HONORABLE ROBERT G. DOUMAR
United States District Judge

[2] Appearances:

FEDERAL PUBLIC DEFENDER
By: FRANK W. DUNHAM, JR., ESQUIRE
      LARRY M. SHELTON, ESQUIRE
      GEREMY C. KAMENS, ESQUIRE
      Counsel for the Petitioners

DEPARTMENT OF JUSTICE
OFFICE OF THE SOLICITOR GENERAL
By: GREGORY GEORGE GARRE, ESQUIRE
      and
UNITED STATES ATTORNEY'S OFFICE
By: LAWRENCE R. LEONARD, ESQUIRE
      Counsel for the Respondents

[3] THE CLERK: Case number 2:02cv439, Yaser Esam Hamdi, et al. versus Donald H. Rumsfeld and Commander W. R. Paulette.

Mr. Dunham, is the petitioner ready to proceed?

MR. DUNHAM: We are, Your Honor.

THE CLERK: Mr. Garre, are the respondents ready?

MR. GARRE: Yes, we are, Your Honor.

THE COURT: This case does represent a balance that must be struck between the executive's authority in times of conflict and the procedural safeguards that our Constitution provides for U.S. citizens that are detained on United States soil.

This court recognizes, and the Fourth Circuit has made clear, that the government is entitled to considerable deference in detention decisions during hostilities; however, the Fourth Circuit in declining to dismiss the case also stated that it refused to summarily embrace the sweeping proposition that any American citizen alleged to be an enemy combatant could be detained indefinitely without charges or counsel on the government's say-so.

In addition, I had previously issued some orders trying to find certain information; however, on August the 8th the Court of Appeals held, in accordance with the principles set forth in an opinion of July the 12th the District Court shall consider the sufficiency of the Mobbs' Declaration as an independent matter before proceeding further.

[4] Interpreting this, it's clear that I can only interpret the Mobbs' Declaration to determine if it is sufficient. And that is what this proceeding is about. It's without the presence of Mr. Hamdi. It's without anyone talking to Mr. Hamdi. It's without Mr. Hamdi having a right to say anything. It is solely on the presentation of the executive that he is an unlawful enemy combatant, which they have alleged.

On that I will hear from Mr. Garre as to why he believes it is sufficient. And then I will hear from Mr. Dunham as to why he believes it's insufficient. And then I may question them both later.

All right, Mr. Garre.

MR. GARRE: Thank you, Your Honor.

Your Honor, the respondents' position is that the Mobbs' Declaration provides a factual basis for the military's determination that Mr. Hamdi is indeed an enemy combatant who was captured during the hostilities in Afghanistan and that the military's detention of Mr. Hamdi is therefore lawful. For those reasons we think the Court should grant the government's motion to dismiss the petition in this case.

Now, the Fourth Circuit's order asked the Court to inquire into the sufficiency of the Mobbs' Declaration. We think that the Mobbs' Declaration satisfies the limited standard of review that the Fourth Circuit recognized would [5] apply in this case consistent with the overarching separation of powers and principles which must inform proceedings such as this.

The Fourth Circuit's most recent decision in this case lays out what it calls cardinal principles that we think are particularly relevant to the inquiry that is now before the Court in this habeas petition. The habeas petition, of course, raises several purely legal issues with respect to whether or not Mr. Hamdi can be detained simply because he is an American citizen, whether or not the statute relied on by the petitioners, 18 U.S.C. 4001, presents a bar to Mr. Hamdi's detention. They raise certain other claims which in no way would require a court to consider even the sufficiency of the Mobbs' Declaration, to hear from Mr. Hamdi, to —

THE COURT: Do you think no one should even consider the sufficiency?

MR. GARRE: Excuse me, Your Honor?

THE COURT: Do you think no one should even consider the sufficiency?

MR. GARRE: We think the Court of Appeals has directed this court to consider that, and we think that's an appropriate inquiry under the Court's recent decision. I'm just trying to explain that there are several legal issues.

THE COURT: Let me ask you another question. Has the writ of habeas corpus been vacated?

[6] MR. GARRE: It hasn't.

THE COURT: Is this a habeas corpus petition?

MR. GARRE: Your Honor, they have filed a habeas corpus petition.

THE COURT: Do you maintain that they can't?

MR. GARRE: Yes, we do, Your Honor. We've made clear in this case —

THE COURT: Has the President done anything to eradicate the habeas corpus?

MR. GARRE: No, Your Honor. In one of the claims they made –

THE COURT: Did Congress do anything to eradicate the habeas corpus?

MR. GARRE: No, Your Honor. One of the claims they made was the writ was suspended in this case. As far as I can tell, they have abandoned –

THE COURT: If the writ wasn't suspended, then why would just the decision of the executive be final?

MR. GARRE: Your Honor, the reason why the courts have a very limited role in this type of proceeding is because, as the Fourth Circuit recently stated, under our constitutional system the executive is the branch which is in the best position to make the military determinations necessary to the capture and detention of enemy combatants.

THE COURT: So the Constitution does not apply to Mr. [7] Hamdi; is that correct?

MR. GARRE: Well, I think it applies to Mr. Hamdi as it did to the individual who was alleged to be an American citizen in the *Quirin* case. In that case the Supreme Court held – and I think it's fair to say that the Court of Appeals in this case recognized –

THE COURT: Mr. Hamdi wasn't a spy. In the *Quirin* case we had people who came ashore to destroy the or to sabotage the United States in time of war and were

not in uniform. They were unquestionably in the category of spies; isn't that correct?

MR. GARRE: That's correct in the *Quirin* case, Your Honor. This case involves the detention of the individual –

THE COURT: In the *Quirin* case did they have counsel?

MR. GARRE: Your Honor, that case involved military charges that were brought against the saboteurs that resulted in –

THE COURT: All I asked is did they have counsel?

MR. GARRE: As I understand it, they did for the limited purpose of the proceeding that resulted in –

THE COURT: Was counsel able to speak with them?

MR. GARRE: Yes, Your Honor.

THE COURT: Well, in –

MR. GARRE: But if I could –

THE COURT: Is there any case that you know of, any [8] habeas corpus petition that you've ever heard of, prior to this case where counsel could not speak to the person being held?

MR. GARRE: Your Honor, if I could answer that this way:

THE COURT: Just answer it. Have you ever heard of such a case? You can answer.

MR. GARRE: Neither side has pointed to authority directly on point, but if I could explain that, Your Honor, with respect –

THE COURT: I'm going to allow you to explain it.

MR. GARRE: Thank you.

THE COURT: But could you answer the question?

MR. GARRE: Yes.

THE COURT: The question is – the answer is what?

MR. GARRE: The answer is no. Neither side has pointed to an authority directly on point that –

THE COURT: I didn't ask Mr. Dunham. He may find some authority.

MR. GARRE: What the Fourth Circuit has said in this case, and I would direct the Court to that decision, is that if Mr. Hamdi is indeed an enemy combatant his detention, his present detention, is a lawful one. Now, during the argument in that case Chief Judge Wilkinson made an observation which is perfectly accurate. That's since time immemorial armies during warfare have captured and detained combatants in warfare. He [9] also made the following hypothetical, which I think is appropriate here.

THE COURT: Did this man – I didn't hear anything in the Mobbs' Declaration that indicated that he fought anyone. Is there anything in the Mobbs' Declaration – is there anything in here that says that Hamdi shot at anyone?

MR. GARRE: No, Your Honor.

THE COURT: Is there anything in here that said Hamdi ever fired a weapon?

MR. GARRE: Your Honor, what the Mobbs' Declaration says is that Hamdi –

THE COURT: Is there anything in the Mobbs' Declaration that says Hamdi ever fired a weapon?

MR. GARRE: Your Honor, the declaration does not say that. What it does say is that Mr. Hamdi surrendered with an enemy unit, surrendered his AK-47 to – along with an enemy Taliban unit in Afghanistan during the period of hostilities.

THE COURT: I have it in front of me, so we'll discuss it piece by piece. First, let's discuss the question of the person who made this declaration. It says he is a special advisor.

Was he appointed by the President with the consent of the Senate?

MR. GARRE: That is my understanding, Your Honor.

THE COURT: He was?

[10] MR. GARRE: That's my understanding.

THE COURT: He was appointed by the President with the consent of the Senate?

MR. GARRE: No, Your Honor. Actually, if I could clarify that, the Under Secretary –

THE COURT: So I could go on the computer and find out when the President appointed Mr. Mobbs with the consent of the Senate?

MR. GARRE: Your Honor, I apologize. I misunderstood your question. The Under Secretary of State for Policy –

THE COURT: I didn't ask you about the Under Secretary of State. I asked you about Mr. Mobbs.

MR. GARRE: Mr. Mobbs was not, Your Honor.

THE COURT: Was Mr. Mobbs a convening authority for general court-martial jurisdiction in the military?

MR. GARRE: I don't believe he was, Your Honor.

THE COURT: Was Mr. Mobbs – does it appear in here anywhere that Mr. Mobbs was a commissioned officer of the United States?

MR. GARRE: It doesn't appear in the affidavit, Your Honor. Mr. Mobbs has reviewed –

THE COURT: Is Mr. Mobbs an employee of the United States?

MR. GARRE: Your Honor –

THE COURT: Or is he just a special advisor hired to [11] make a statement?

MR. GARRE: With respect, Your Honor, the declaration states that Mr. Mobbs is an employee of the United States, that he's a special advisor.

THE COURT: No, it does not. It says he's a special advisor to the Under Secretary of Defense for Policy, doesn't it?

MR. GARRE: It does, Your Honor.

THE COURT: It doesn't say he's a GS anything, does it?

MR. GARRE: It does not say that, Your Honor. It does say he has been substantially involved in the detainee operations and is familiar with the detainee operations involving the hostilities in Afghanistan, and –

THE COURT: So he is what one would call normally an expert; is that correct?

MR. GARRE: I don't know that he's being offered as an expert in the evidentiary sense, Your Honor. What he does –

THE COURT: Well, if he was offered as an expert, at least the Court could then decide under *Daubert* whether to accept his testimony or not; isn't that correct?

MR. GARRE: I suppose that's correct, Your Honor, if we were in a normal civil evidentiary proceeding, which I don't think that we are.

[12] THE COURT: This isn't a normal evidentiary proceeding because this isn't a writ of habeas corpus? Habeas corpus isn't a normal proceeding?

MR. GARRE: Your Honor, this is a habeas proceeding. I don't think Your Honor referred to the rules governing experts who – Mr. Mobbs hasn't been submitted as an expert in accordance with the civil rules.

THE COURT: So he isn't –

MR. GARRE: What he has been submitted, Your Honor, is to provide a factual basis for the military's determination Mr. Hamdi is indeed a military combatant. He does that, Your Honor. He lays down the criteria and the considerations on which the military relied in making that determination. He explains that Mr. Hamdi surrendered with an enemy unit. He explained Mr. Hamdi laid down his AK-47 with that unit.

THE COURT: I don't find the same explanations you do. Let's read the Mobbs' Declaration. Let's go down it paragraph by paragraph, Mr. Garre.

MR. GARRE: Yes, Your Honor.

THE COURT: Not what you interpret the paragraph here, but what the paragraphs say, okay?

He says Mr. Hamdi traveled to Afghanistan, doesn't he?

MR. GARRE: He does say that, Your Honor.

THE COURT: He says in approximately July or August [13] of 2001.

MR. GARRE: He does say that, Your Honor.

THE COURT: He says that he remained affiliated with a Taliban unit. What does affiliation mean?

MR. GARRE: Well, I think what he also says is –

THE COURT: He didn't say he was a member. He said he was "affiliated".

MR. GARRE: I want to stick to the terms of the affidavit, as Your Honor mentioned. He says in paragraph nine Mr. Hamdi's confirmed the fact he surrendered and gave his firearm to the Northern Alliance forces.

THE COURT: So if he – any person who was in the area who has a firearm and gave it to the Northern Alliance forces – we'll get to paragraph nine in a minute. Can we stick with paragraph three right now?

MR. GARRE: Your Honor, I'd like to answer the Court's questions consistent with the declaration. With respect, I think it's relevant to refer to –

THE COURT: You say number nine should be read with number three?

MR. GARRE: Your Honor, I think we should read the declaration as a whole. The question before the Court is the sufficiency of the declaration, not the sufficiency of any single sentence.

THE COURT: I understand that, Mr. Garre. Thank you.

[14] All right. Now, let me ask you this question: They talk about the Northern Alliance. The Northern Alliance does contain certain units that were Taliban units; isn't that correct?

MR. GARRE: I don't know if that's factually correct.

THE COURT: So news accounts – well, it's not in this report. Should I consider that, news accounts of that.

MR. GARRE: Certainly the Court of Appeals asked this court to consider the sufficiency of the declaration. I want to make this clear.

THE COURT: I won't consider that because it was just in newspaper accounts, and I assume they could be incorrect.

MR. GARRE: That's fine, Your Honor. I want to be clear, though, what the declaration states.

THE COURT: What is the Taliban? What is the Taliban?

MR. GARRE: As the – the Taliban, they are, as the declaration states in paragraph six, "Al-Qaida and Taliban were and are hostile forces engaged in armed conflict with the armed forces of the United States and its Coalition partners. Accordingly, individuals associated with al-Qaida or Taliban – "

THE COURT: Stop at that point right now. So that's your definition of the Taliban; is that correct?

MR. GARRE: That's what the Mobbs' Declaration [15] states.

THE COURT: That's what this Mobbs' Declaration states?

MR. GARRE: Yes. If I could also –

THE COURT: Anybody who was in conflict with your Coalition partners is a hostile force?

MR. GARRE: Well, I think that that would be a reasonable supposition, but that's not what the declaration says. The declaration goes on to say individuals associated with al-Qaida or Taliban were and are enemy combatants based on his interviews –

THE COURT: Do you have any information in here that says – there is nothing in here that says Mr. Hamdi was an al-Qaida.

MR. GARRE: No. No, there isn't.

THE COURT: Why is it in here then?

MR. GARRE: Excuse me, Your Honor?

THE COURT: Why is that in this Mobbs' Declaration? If there is no evidence of any kind that Hamdi was an al-Qaida, why have you mentioned that members of those forces should be considered if he's considered in the same element?

MR. GARRE: Because the hostilities in Afghanistan have focused on the al-Qaida and Taliban forces and individuals over there. That's –

THE COURT: Oh. That's why it's there, not to [16] connect Mr. Hamdi, but it's to show –

MR. GARRE: I have never understood the petitioners in this case to dispute that the al-Qaida or the Taliban were enemies of the nation.

THE COURT: The problem with the Taliban is that these are all warlords, are they not?

MR. GARRE: I don't know that that's factually correct, Your Honor, but it would – that statement would conflict with at least the governmental authority that the Taliban –

THE COURT: So that all of these articles about various warlords in Afghanistan having certain units –

MR. GARRE: I think, Your Honor, you're getting to the unconventional nature of the conflict. I appreciate Your Honor's questions. There is no question that we're dealing with a foe which is unconventional, which doesn't follow the laws of the customs of war, which doesn't wear uniforms, and for those reasons, among others, aren't put into the category of traditional POWs. But the Fourth Circuit made clear –

THE COURT: I understand they're not put in the category of traditional POWs. Answer my question then. I realize that the Fourth Circuit has made some rules and regulations, and I shall follow those to the tee. Now, Mr. Garre, don't misunderstand me.

MR. GARRE: Thank you, Your Honor.

[17] THE COURT: You have no fear.

MR. GARRE: But I did want to – if Your Honor had a question, I did want to state that the Fourth Circuit made clear the unconventional aspects of this conflict don't make mistakes any less grave. And it's clear from the decision, I think, that the unconventional nature of this conflict didn't in any way suggest to the Court of Appeals the military's long established authority to capture and detain enemy combatants was any different in this case than a German soldier captured in the Battle of the Bulge or any other armed conflict with which this court is familiar.

THE COURT: All right. I tend to agree with that in combatants. Combatants should be treated as any person would be. In fact, there are some Army regulations pertaining to it which will have the force and effect of law; isn't that correct? Isn't that correct?

MR. GARRE: I think that there certainly are regulations that have the effect of some law. The regulations, the petitioners certainly haven't based any claims on, and the regulations –

THE COURT: I didn't ask you what the petitioners based any claims on. I'm asking you now about regulations made pursuant to the authority of the Army and Navy and joint regulations. Do they have the force and effect of law?

MR. GARRE: They certainly have some force as law. [18] There certainly would have to be legal debate about their effect and, more importantly, their application to this case.

THE COURT: We know, therefore, when any person who's taken into custody by the United States, that one gets his complete name, his rank, his serial number, his date of birth, his city of birth, his county of birth, his – the name and address of next of kin, the date of capture, the place of capture, the capturing unit, the circumstances of capture, and certain other information. But all of that you have; isn't that correct, sir?

MR. GARRE: Well, I think to answer both the Court's questions, first of all, the regulations in this case if the Court is referring to the regulations appended to the petitioners' traverse –

THE COURT: I'm talking any persons of war, retained personnel, civilian attorneys, and other detainees under – it's Army regulation 190-8, a joint regulation applying to all of the – it's the Navy regulation OPNAVIONST

3461.6, Air Force AFJI 31-304, and Marine Corps MCO 3461.1.

MR. GARRE: Yes, Your Honor. If I could make a couple points addressed to those regulations.

THE COURT: All I'm asking is that regulation is followed, isn't it?

MR. GARRE: Your Honor, I'd like to explain. I'd like to give you the answer.

[19] THE COURT: It isn't followed?

MR. GARRE: No, Your Honor. That's not correct.

THE COURT: So it was followed?

MR. GARRE: The regulations – if I could try to explain.

THE COURT: I will allow you to explain.

MR. GARRE: Thank you.

THE COURT: Mr. Garre, one of the things that you'll find out about me is you answer my questions, I'll allow you to explain for three hours if it's necessary, okay?

MR. GARRE: Okay.

THE COURT: But answer my questions.

MR. GARRE: Yes, Your Honor.

THE COURT: I realize that in this era of the last decade we want to make explanations, but I want answers and then explanations, okay?

MR. GARRE: Yes, Your Honor.

THE COURT: Let's go.

Then does this regulation require every person when they take a person into custody and he's supposedly in a combat situation –

MR. GARRE: That's not my understanding of the regulations. I haven't on that aspect of it –

THE COURT: Let me focus on another regulation then. This regulation says persons in the custody of the United [20] States Armed Forces who have not been classified as an EPW, GPW, RP, CI, shall be treated as EPWs until a legal status is ascertained by competent authority. Isn't that correct?

MR. GARRE: It is correct, Your Honor.

THE COURT: And under this regulation the competent authority would be a military tribunal if the matter is in issue; isn't that correct?

MR. GARRE: I don't think that's correct, Your Honor. I think that the competent authority would include the President of the United States, the Commander-in-Chief, and I think –

THE COURT: How about Mr. Mobbs? Is he a competent authority?

MR. GARRE: I mean, I don't think that that question arises –

THE COURT: As you offered it – looking at this declaration, it says Mobbs did this, Mobbs decided that.

MR. GARRE: Your Honor, I apologize. I am trying to answer your question, but sometimes it requires additional information. And if I could explain the application of these regulations.

THE COURT: We're dealing with the Mobbs' Declaration in relation to law.

MR. GARRE: Your Honor –

THE COURT: That's all I can deal with.

[21] MR. GARRE: Your Honor's asked for the government's explanation as to the application of regulations. And if I could explain.

THE COURT: That's all right. Go ahead. You can explain. The regulations don't apply to the United States Navy?

MR. GARRE: Your Honor, the regulations state that persons can be provided with certain protections until their legal status is confirmed. In this case the President has determined that –

THE COURT: That does not appear that the President has determined anything. It appears that Mr. Mobbs has. I'm looking at the Mobbs' Declaration.

MR. GARRE: But, Your Honor –

THE COURT: That's all I'm considering.

MR. GARRE: Your Honor, the President has determined that members of the Taliban and the al-Qaida do not meet the definitions of POWs and, therefore, fall into the status of unlawful combatants. The Mobbs' Declaration explains –

THE COURT: Stop a minute. Do you mean to tell me that all of the people that are serving in the new Afghanistan government that were Taliban or were unlawful enemy combatants of the United States and we put them in office? Is that what you're saying?

MR. GARRE: It's not what I'm saying, Your Honor, for [22] this reason –

THE COURT: Well, we better – what I'm having – the problem I'm having, Mr. Garre, is we can't have our cake and eat it too. Either it applies or it doesn't apply.

MR. GARRE: It does not apply, Your Honor. I've tried to give the Court the reasons why it doesn't apply. It's also a quad services regulation, which is not itself binding on the Department of Defense. And it's, of course, not the basis of any claim based on petitioners. The regulations purport to apply to prisoners of war, people whose status hasn't been determined otherwise. The President has made that determination that members of the al-Qaida and Taliban are not entitled to prisoner of war status. Judge Ellis discussed that determination in his recent decision. We think the Mobbs' Declaration –

THE COURT: I read Judge Ellis' decision. In that case it was interesting. One of the factors that he utilized was the fact that – I'm sure you're familiar with it – that Mr. Lindh did not properly attack the problem; isn't that correct?

MR. GARRE: I'm not sure if I understand what the Court's referring to.

THE COURT: Well, let's see if I can find that opinion. In his opinion he had several factors that he applied. One of them was the ability of Lindh to contest the [23] matter; isn't that correct?

MR. GARRE: Well, of course, Mr. Lindh was charged with a criminal offenses [sic] which invoked constitutional rights that do not apply in this proceeding.

THE COURT: So if Hamdi were charged with a criminal offense which would cause him to be, let's say, jailed for six months or more, he would be entitled to counsel; isn't that correct?

MR. GARRE: He would be entitled to the same protections that Mr. Lindh received, and that would include counsel, yes. We don't dispute that, the application of the Sixth Amendment in this case, but we've argued in our return that the Sixth Amendment has no application by its terms or by precedent to this type of proceeding.

Now, Mr. Lindh was involved in a criminal proceeding. He pleaded guilty to aiding the Taliban and to using a weapon with the Taliban, and admitted in open court to be a Taliban soldier. That's resulted in his imprisonment for 20 years. Mr. Hamdi is being detained as an enemy combatant in connection with the current hostilities. He hasn't been charged with any criminal offense or other offense. And his detention is necessary, as we've explained, because of the purposes that combatants have always been detained: One, to prevent them from going out continuing to give aid or fight with the enemy; and two, because of the important role that intelligence [24] gathering has in any war effort. The government – precisely because of the unconventional –

THE COURT: How long does it take to question a man: A year? Two years?

MR. GARRE: Your Honor, Chief Judge –

THE COURT: 10 years? A lifetime? How long?

MR. GARRE: Your Honor, Chief Judge Wilkinson put it this way at the last oral argument, and I think it's an excellent analogy: Intelligence gathering is like building a puzzle. You have to put the puzzles together. And oftentimes you don't realize with any given piece how it fits in together until there are subsequent developments or subsequent information comes to light.

We know it takes time. It takes time in the current war effort in particular because of the unconventional nature –

THE COURT: How much time, Mr. Garre? I agree with Judge Wilkinson, of course. How much time?

MR. GARRE: I can't answer that question today, and I don't think one would be able to answer that question –

THE COURT: Would you say 10 years or 20?

MR. GARRE: Your Honor, we would not be in anymore position to answer that today than we would be after 11 months after the attacks on Pearl Harbor with respect to how long a war would last, how long we need to gather intelligence. It's [25] not a novel situation for the government to be in to not be able to answer those questions.

THE COURT: As long as you're gathering intelligence you can keep this man in a locked cell with no windows – he's already been there four months, five months? He can't even have a piece of paper and a pencil to write on?

MR. GARRE: Well –

THE COURT: Isn't that what you said in – before Judge – in the Court, according to the newspaper article?

MR. GARRE: I'm not familiar with those statements, Your Honor. They would be incorrect. I don't believe we made those – that position.

THE COURT: Well, maybe –

MR. GARRE: Petitioners have made clear, and this is on page nine of their traverse, I think, that they're not challenging the conditions of Mr. Hamdi's confinement. I think what – the way the Fourth Circuit characterized it, and I think it's the helpful and the correct way to do it, and that's a question of the Court whether or not Mr. Hamdi's detention –

THE COURT: Don't you think this is of some concern that a person is being held in solitary confinement in a windowless room –

MR. GARRE: Your Honor –

THE COURT: – for four months? Is that – incommunicado?

[26] MR. GARRE: I don't know where the characterization to the windowless room comes –

THE COURT: It came from a newspaper article, Mr. McCray or somebody familiar with the case.

MR. GARRE: We stated in our return that Mr. Hamdi is not in solitary confinement in the traditional sense that term is used. He happens to be the only captured enemy combatant who's currently detained at the Norfolk facility. By other laws and regulations he is separated from military personnel who are detained there. Mr. Hamdi does receive daily visits from the commander of the brig. He is able to meet with the chaplain at the brig three or four times a week. He meets with the doctor once a week. So the notion –

THE COURT: He just can't meet with a lawyer?

MR. GARRE: Well, Your Honor, again, I think that Chief Judge Wilkinson put it aptly when he mentioned during the last argument that no one would suggest that the German soldier captured at the Battle of the Bulge would be able to come back and be entitled to a right to counsel, much less –

THE COURT: I don't have any question about that, but we're not dealing with a German soldier captured at the Battle of the Bulge. We're dealing with an individual who evidently, according to your statement, was picked up in a situation in which, in reading this, he had a weapon and he was with a Taliban unit; isn't that correct?

[27] MR. GARRE: He surrendered with a Taliban unit. It also says he went to Afghanistan –

THE COURT: What's interesting here is it says – let's look at this paragraph. It says Northern Alliance forces were engaged in battle with the Taliban.

I have no doubts Northern Alliance forces engaged in a battle with the Taliban. It doesn't say in a battle with the Taliban unit that this man was in. It says engaged in a battle with the Taliban. That's true. The whole world knows that. Mobbs doesn't have to say that. But what he didn't say was they were engaged in a battle with this unit.

MR. GARRE: Your Honor, I think if the Court's concern is to whether or not someone who –

THE COURT: My concern is what is stated in this declaration. You have quite rightly, according to the Fourth Circuit, not given me anything evidently. And –

MR. GARRE: With respect, that's not true, Your Honor. The Mobbs' Declaration explains in detail –

THE COURT: The only thing is the Mobbs' Declaration, and, accordingly, I'm going down it piece by piece.

You know, one of the things in early life I was taught, when you're reading a letter, like a letter of reference, one reads for what is there and what is not there. It is important to determine what is left out as well as what is put in.

[28] What is put in is Northern Alliance forces were engaged in battle with the Taliban. We know that. Hamdi's unit surrendered to Northern Alliance forces, not to any U.S. forces. He was transported with his unit from Konduz, Afghanistan to the prison in Mazar-e-Sharif, Afghanistan which was under the control of Northern Alliance forces.

It was – the next sentence is extremely interesting. Hamdi was directed to surrender his – I can't pronounce it – assault rifle to Northern Alliance forces en route to Mazar-e-Sharif and did so.

In other words, he had his weapon after he turned himself over to Northern Alliance forces, and kept it until later. Doesn't sound much like anybody was afraid of him, does it?

MR. GARRE: Your Honor, I would disagree with that. I think if Your Honor looks at other paragraphs of the declaration, I think it is important to read it as a whole.

THE COURT: The next sentence –

MR. GARRE: The battlefield interrogation team determined that Mr. Hamdi went to train with and, if necessary, fight with the Taliban.

THE COURT: Wait a minute.

MR. GARRE: That's in paragraph five.

THE COURT: Wait a minute. Can you go down to the next paragraph?

[29] MR. GARRE: It's the next paragraph, Your Honor, that Your Honor was reading from.

THE COURT: He identified himself as a Saudi citizen, okay?

MR. GARRE: Yes, Your Honor.

THE COURT: If he identified himself as a Saudi citizen, why was he separated from the remainder of his compatriots, whomever they may be, in Guantanamo?

MR. GARRE: He was separated first in Afghanistan because the battlefield interrogation team made the determination that he was an enemy combatant.

THE COURT: Doesn't say anything about that. Somebody made a determination.

MR. GARRE: I think it does, Your Honor. I think it says, in paragraph five, Hamdi was interviewed by a U.S. interrogation team while he was in prison in Sheberghan.

THE COURT: U.S. interrogation team?

MR. GARRE: Yes, Your Honor. A team consisting of military personnel on the ground.

THE COURT: It doesn't say that. It says a U.S. interrogation team.

MR. GARRE: Yes, Your Honor. That's what it says.

THE COURT: I assume 10 U.S. citizens could be an interrogation team, or two. It doesn't say it's any type of interrogation team. It just says a U.S. interrogation team.

[30] MR. GARRE: It's the military forces in Afghanistan comprise that team, and that team made a determination.

THE COURT: Where does it say that in there? Does it say it in there?

MR. GARRE: Your Honor, let me then refer the Court to paragraph eight if it has concerns about whether or not that was a military unit that made that determination.

In January 2002 a detainee review and screening team established by the commander of U.S. Central Command reviewed Hamdi's record and determined that he met the criteria established by the Secretary of Defense for individuals over whom the United States forces should take control and moved to Guantanamo Bay, Cuba. The detention –

THE COURT: So he was supposed to be moved to Guantanamo Bay. He met the criteria for going to Guantanamo Bay. I don't know what that was, but I assume he met that criteria.

MR. GARRE: That's correct, Your Honor. The declaration also makes clear that the military has determined, based on interviews with Mr. Hamdi, and in light of his association with the Taliban, that Hamdi was considered by military forces to be an enemy combatant. That's –

THE COURT: Wait a minute. Where does it say that?

MR. GARRE: It says that in paragraph six, Your Honor, the last sentence of paragraph six.

[31] THE COURT: Hamdi was considered by military forces to be an enemy combatant.

MR. GARRE: That's right. That ties right into paragraph five which refers to the U.S. interrogation team which was the military force, Your Honor.

THE COURT: It doesn't say that. It says some military force determined –

MR. GARRE: The declaration states military forces made that determination. Significantly, petitioners don't –

THE COURT: Was that the Northern Alliance military forces?

MR. GARRE: No, Your Honor. I think –

THE COURT: How would I know it wasn't?

MR. GARRE: The Northern Alliance forces –

THE COURT: It doesn't say in here it was the American military forces. It says military forces.

MR. GARRE: Your Honor –

THE COURT: Is the Northern Alliance a military force?

MR. GARRE: Your Honor, with respect –

THE COURT: You see, you won't give me any information except that information that's in this Mobbs' Declaration. You may be entirely correct, Mr. Garre. You may be absolutely correct. He may be the worst enemy any man ever had. But the problem is what you're saying is I must rely on [32] this and only this. If I'm to rely on only this, then I must pick it apart. Do you understand that, Mr. Garre?

MR. GARRE: I do understand that, Your Honor, and I think –

THE COURT: If you gave me the information, you know, then all of this probably could have been avoided.

MR. GARRE: Well –

THE COURT: It just doesn't make sense.

MR. GARRE: With respect, Your Honor, we think that the standard that governs the proceeding at this stage is that the military would be asked to come forward and to provide a factual basis for its determination that Mr. Hamdi is an enemy combatant. That standard has been applied in other habeas contexts which involve the review of executive determinations which are entitled to even less deference.

THE COURT: In this regulation that may or may not apply because it applies to almost all of the – it says this: A competent tribunal shall determine the status of any person not appearing to be entitled to prisoner of war status who has committed a belligerent act or is engaged in hostile activities in aid of enemy armed forces and who asserts that he or she is entitled to treatment as a prisoner of war or concerning whom any doubt of a like nature exists.

And I'm speaking of –

MR. GARRE: 1.6(b), Your Honor.

[33] THE COURT: That's correct.

MR. GARRE: That's right. That provision doesn't apply because it's directed to individuals who are being held as and are entitled to status of POWs. It refers to Article IV of the Geneva Convention, which is –

THE COURT: You mean he's not contesting, then, I assume, that he's not an illegal enemy combatant? He's not contesting that?

MR. GARRE: I think –

THE COURT: And his statements would indicate to you that he's not contesting that? I don't have the benefit of his statements because you don't want to provide those obviously. And you don't have to. I'm not saying you do.

MR. GARRE: Mr. Hamdi is being held like the other detainees captured in connection with the hostilities in Afghanistan, not as a POW. The President has determined, and Judge Ellis explained this in his recent decision in the Lindh case –

THE COURT: If Judge Ellis were here, then he already would have decided the case. Do I have anything to decide or do you want to say Judge Ellis has decided that Hamdi should be held? Why am I here? If that's the case, you know, we may not have any of these proceedings, need we?

MR. GARRE: With respect, Your Honor, we have made clear that the courts have a role in habeas proceedings of this [34] type. Now, part of those proceedings are going to involve the review of legal challenges. And those are the principal challenges raised by the habeas petition in this case. And if Your Honor would like, I would be happy to discuss those challenges.

Now, another part of that role is the role that the Fourth Circuit discussed in its recent decision. And that's a much more limited role involving a review of the executive's determination that an individual is an enemy combatant.

Now, the Court's limited role in that sphere follows from the separation of powers principle governing this determination and respect for the fact that the military, the Fourth Circuit has said, and the executive branch is in the best position to make these determinations, and that the Court, therefore, has a much more limited role. It doesn't mean it has no role. The Fourth Circuit suggested –

THE COURT: The interpretation, assuming that the President has made a determination, and I haven't seen that, but I assume that that will be provided at some point in time –

MR. GARRE: Well, Your Honor, with respect –

THE COURT: Don't misunderstand me. I haven't been provided that.

MR. GARRE: The relevant material set out in Judge Ellis' decision, which –

[35] THE COURT: He said the interpretation of the President was due deference, that Lindh failed to carry his burden of demonstrating to the contrary. So Lindh had a right to demonstrate to the contrary, did he not?

MR. GARRE: In the criminal proceeding, which is not applicable here.

THE COURT: Lindh had a right to demonstrate he was not an illegal enemy combatant, did he not?

MR. GARRE: Yes, he did, Your Honor. And Lindh was entitled to other rights that are afforded –

THE COURT: And he failed to do that? Did he fail to do it?

MR. GARRE: Yes, Your Honor.

The reference to the President's decision is contained in the February press release. I would be happy to provide the Court that, if it would like. Petitioners haven't relied on that.

THE COURT: What you're saying is I can look at press releases then?

MR. GARRE: I said I would be happy to provide it.

THE COURT: Should I look at press releases?

MR. GARRE: This issue –

THE COURT: All I want to know – I don't want to look at press releases for one side and not look at press releases for the other.

[36] MR. GARRE: Let me try to be clear on this. We think the Court can resolve this case on the papers that are before it and that it can and should grant the government's motion to dismiss.

THE COURT: What's worrying me is the Mobbs' Declaration. I don't know who Mobbs is or was or is he a hired expert or was he hired for the purpose of making this affidavit. He may have been a person that investigated it thoroughly. He may be the most knowledgeable person. He may be a historian and know all about the history of the East and Near East. He may know about all the warlords that have been going back and forth there for centuries.

MR. GARRE: With respect, Your Honor, the Court's role here is not to conduct a *Daubert* type inquiry under 702.

THE COURT: I'm not going to go into a *Daubert* inquiry. I want to go back to this –

MR. GARRE: The question for the Court is whether or not the Mobbs' Declaration provides a factual basis for the military's determination. It does so. It explains in detail Mr. Hamdi is a classic type of enemy combatant who was captured on a foreign battlefield, surrendered, and laid down his gun, his AK-47, with an enemy unit. We think that – there hasn't been a real dispute over whether or not someone who surrenders with an enemy unit –

THE COURT: Dispute with what? What is Hamdi [37] disputing? Only thing he disputed is some lawyer that is bound by the problem of not being able to talk to him, not see any statements he made, not see anything from him, but only to look at the Mobbs' Declaration and to attack it. Isn't that all that they can do?

MR. GARRE: That's correct, and that's consistent with the Fourth Circuit's recent decision –

THE COURT: That's consistent with the Court of Appeals. I understand that.

MR. GARRE: – and the long established authority it relied on. But it's still relevant, Your Honor, that the petitioners – that the Court still has to look at the claims made by the petitioners in this case.

THE COURT: But, you know – let's go back to paragraph three. As I said, Hamdi was affiliated with a Taliban military unit. It doesn't say Hamdi was a member of a Taliban military unit, does it?

MR. GARRE: It says affiliated, Your Honor. And it also says, again in paragraph five, that the interrogation team confirmed that Hamdi went to train with and, if necessary, fight for the Taliban. Persons who train with enemy units –

THE COURT: That's not in paragraph three. That's in the other paragraph.

MR. GARRE: That's true, Your Honor.

THE COURT: I'm trying to go down them number by [38] number. I realize it does make it a little hard for you, Mr. Garre, because I appreciate what you're doing.

Now, number –

MR. GARRE: Thank you, Your Honor.

THE COURT: In – it does not say what military unit he was with, does it? It doesn't say what unit. It just says it was a unit.

MR. GARRE: That's right, Your Honor.

THE COURT: Okay. So in paragraph 4 Mobbs states that Hamdi was captured by Northern Alliance forces in late 2001. Now, if he investigated the record, he would know exactly when he was captured, wouldn't he, because we know from the regulation that somebody determined the date of capture, place of capture, and so forth, correct?

MR. GARRE: Your Honor, I don't know whether or not that fact is correct, and I don't think the regulation referred to is applicable to Mr. Hamdi, but, to be clear, the military has –

THE COURT: Let me say this so we understand one another from the beginning:

MR. GARRE: Yes.

THE COURT: I think the regulation pertains to the United States Armed Services, okay? As such, when the United States Armed Services got Hamdi, they had to follow the regulation. I'm not holding anything else, but that's just no [39] ifs, ands, or buts, okay?

MR. GARRE: I understand the Court's position on that. I think that's incorrect.

THE COURT: That's not the issue before me.

MR. GARRE: But if I could be clear, the military has – and this was referred to in the Mobbs' Declaration reports and records. It has more information on Mr. Hamdi's capture, but it's in the military. Mr. Mobbs has reviewed the relevant information with respect to Mr. Hamdi, laid out the grounds and circumstances under which he was captured and detained and determined to be an enemy combatant. It's not for the Court to conduct a de novo proceeding.

THE COURT: I'm not trying to conduct a de novo proceeding. All I want is the papers. If I had seen the papers, we probably would have ended this a long time ago. Now I'm curious. I get more curious all the time.

MR. GARRE: But – and –

THE COURT: And, you see – you know, generally, generally – not to say that the government would – generally when people hide things you can generally assume if it were advantageous to them they wouldn't hide it, would they? Is that a fair assumption?

MR. GARRE: Your Honor, that may be a fair assumption in some circumstances, but, to be clear, that wouldn't apply here. The military has provided the basis on which it's [40] determined that Mr. Hamdi is an enemy combatant. Under the limited standard review that would govern here the military has come forward and provided a factual basis which would satisfy the Fourth Circuit's decision in this case and which would make clear that the present detention of Mr. Hamdi is lawful. It's not –

THE COURT: What concerned me, this statement indicates that Hamdi kept his weapon after he surrendered, for some time after. And what bothers me is that what is traded between these two sides, the Northern Alliance or group, obviously, of people that – well, I don't want to even go into it. In any event, I don't know what distinguishes a Northern Alliance unit from a Taliban unit. There is nothing to say what distinguishes the two.

MR. GARRE: Well, Your Honor –

THE COURT: I dare say it would be hard for us to figure it out, wouldn't it, Mr. Garre?

MR. GARRE: With respect, I would disagree. As the declaration states, the Northern Alliance forces were engaged in battle with the Taliban. And that – the Court doesn't need –

THE COURT: Doesn't say they were engaged with the Taliban that Mr. Hamdi was with. That's what's so interesting about this.

MR. GARRE: Your Honor, I think what's interesting [41] about this is that Mr. Hamdi associated with a Taliban unit, an enemy unit, an enemy of the United States. He surrendered his AK-47 rifle when he was captured by Northern Alliance forces, which we've explained in our papers were Coalition forces. The United States interrogation team on the battlefield – petitioners don't challenge – they make this very clear. Petitioners are not challenging the battlefield determination.

THE COURT: Who is not challenging?

MR. GARRE: Petitioners. The individuals here today. It's in their papers, the traverse which is before this court.

THE COURT: As far as I'm concerned, I'm only looking at the Mobbs' Declaration. I'm challenging everything in the Mobbs' Declaration. So understand that, Mr. Garre.

MR. GARRE: I appreciate that.

THE COURT: I don't know what Mr. Dunham does or doesn't do.

MR. GARRE: I appreciate that.

THE COURT: I'm going down this thing piece by piece. And if you think that I don't understand the utilization of words, you're sadly mistaken. I understand what the words mean and what they don't mean. And I think Mr. Mobbs understands the utilization of words. He is a "special advisor" as far as I can tell. I don't even know what GS rank he may have or doesn't have or whether he's just a consultant.

MR. GARRE: Your Honor, I don't know that either, but [42] what I do know is he has been substantially involved with the detainee operations that the United States military has been involved in with respect to the al-Qaida and the Taliban. That's in paragraph one of the declaration. I can read it to the Court.

THE COURT: You can read it. Go ahead.

MR. GARRE: In this position, I have been substantially involved with matters related to the detention of enemy combatants in the current war against the al-Qaida terrorists and those who support and harbor them, including the Taliban. I have been involved with the detainee operations since mid-February 2002 and currently head the Under Secretary of Defense for Policy's Detainee Policy Group.

I think that clearly puts Mr. Mobbs in the position of someone who would be familiar with the overarching –

THE COURT: My secretary is familiar with the Hamdi case. Should she decide it?

MR. GARRE: I think what the Fourth Circuit –

THE COURT: She's a special advisor. In fact, the secretaries have gotten new titles now.

MR. GARRE: With respect, Your Honor, the question was made – I think it was made not seriously, but –

THE COURT: I'm only reducing things to an absurdity for the purpose of emphasizing certain attributes of the Mobbs' Declaration.

[43] MR. GARRE: We don't think that there is anything absurd about the Mobbs' Declaration or anything absurd about the government's position in this case.

THE COURT: I didn't say it was. I merely said I reduce things to an absurdity to emphasize those things that are wrong. I'm not trying to say it's absurd. And I want to make that clear. And, Mr. Garre, you know I wasn't. So be –

MR. GARRE: No, Your Honor. I appreciate that the Court was not being serious in that, but it does illustrate an important point, which is that the military is in the best position to make these judgments.

THE COURT: I didn't say the military wasn't in the best position. All I'm saying is it doesn't show in this Mobbs' Declaration that a military tribunal has acted, that a convening authority, as required by the regulation, convened a special military panel of which one of which would be composed of a member of the Judge Advocate General Corps, whether it be in the Navy, the Army, or the Marine Corps.

MR. GARRE: Your Honor –

THE COURT: They would then make a decision if it was in doubt. What you're saying is it's not in doubt, there is no question about it, except I don't know of any battle this man engaged in, I don't know of any weapon he ever fired, I don't know of anything he did, other than to be present with a Taliban unit according to them. And I assume that's correct. [44] But if I begin to have doubts about this, then why wouldn't the military tribunal have acted in the eight or nine months since he's been captured?

MR. GARRE: Your Honor, I've tried to explain the government's position, that those regulations the Court referred to are not applicable in this case. I understand that the Court disagrees with the government on that, but I think the Court's characterization –

THE COURT: I feel that the regulations apply. I'm not saying they don't apply. That doesn't affect his status any. It may be that they would decide he's an unlawful enemy combatant.

MR. GARRE: It doesn't affect his status. It in no way affects the determinations –

THE COURT: What worries me is nobody, nobody, seems to care what Hamdi says.

MR. GARRE: Oh, to the contrary, Your Honor. And I think, again, the Mobbs' Declaration –

THE COURT: You've picked out statements that said – and I looked at that statement. You know, a long time ago, as I told you, they said that he stated that he entered Afghanistan to train with and, if necessary, fight for the Taliban, correct?

MR. GARRE: That's what it states, Your Honor, yes.

THE COURT: If necessary. If necessary might mean in [45] self-defense. It might mean a myriad of a number of things. I don't know what he said, in what context it was said.

MR. GARRE: Your Honor, I think that that's not relevant to argue the case. The view we've set out in our motion to dismiss, and so that I can try to be more clear with the Court, our position – the military has determined that someone who goes to Afghanistan to train with an enemy unit, someone who stayed in Afghanistan after September 11th and the attacks on this nation, someone who surrendered in Afghanistan to Northern Alliance forces and surrendered his AK-47 to those forces, is an enemy combatant if the military makes that determination, and that the Mobbs' Declaration provides the Court with the substantial factual basis –

THE COURT: The military does not have to make that regulation in accordance with their regulations; is that correct?

MR. GARRE: Your Honor, I explained why we think that regulation does not apply here.

THE COURT: Well, maybe you better explain it again because I want to make sure I understand what the government's position is on the inapplicability of the regulation.

MR. GARRE: Well, first, as I said, just as a technical matter it's a quad services regulation that isn't specifically binding on the Department of Defense, and second and more –

[46] THE COURT: Wait a minute. Do I understand that the Department of Defense is holding him prisoner and not the military? He isn't in the Navy brig?

MR. GARRE: Well –

THE COURT: What's this commander doing here, the poor fellow who you say is visiting him every day? What is he doing here as a defendant? You want only Rumsfeld as the defendant?

MR. GARRE: Rumsfeld and the commander of the brig, that's right, Your Honor. And the second –

THE COURT: I'm not sure Rumsfeld was a necessary party, but if you feel he's a necessary party –

MR. GARRE: Excuse me, Your Honor?

THE COURT: Do you feel Rumsfeld is a necessary party?

MR. GARRE: Certainly in the typical habeas cases Your Honor is well familiar, the custodian, immediate custodian – that's right. Perhaps we should have

moved for the dismissal of Mr. Rumsfeld. We, frankly, were focused on other jurisdictional issues at the outset of this investigation.

THE COURT: Looks like Rumsfeld made a decision. I dare say he doesn't know anymore about this case than he's read in the newspaper, do you?

MR. GARRE: With respect, Your Honor, I don't know [47] how to answer that question.

THE COURT: He may know more about it now.

MR. GARRE: The regulation – if I could try to answer the Court's question on the regulations, the regulations apply – this is in 15 General Protection Policy, U.S. policy relative to the treatment of EPW, CL, and RP, in the custody of U. S. Armed Forces is as follows: Now, the EPW doesn't refer to people like Mr. Hamdi. EPW refers to prisoner of war. The CI –

THE COURT: You know what's interesting to me, because you're depending upon prisoner of war in accordance with the regulation; is that correct?

MR. GARRE: Well, the regulations are –

THE COURT: You –

MR. GARRE: Yes.

THE COURT: The only prisoners of war are in accordance with the regulation?

MR. GARRE: The regulation is addressed – it states in the regulation to those that meets the –

THE COURT: Mr. Garre, I have to fight for it. Are you contending that the only prisoners of war are those who are prisoners in accordance with the prisoner of war designation in the regulation?

MR. GARRE: I'm not sure. I want to answer the Court's question, but I'm not sure I understand it. What I am [48] contending –

THE COURT: Maybe I'll repeat it again.

MR. GARRE: Okay.

THE COURT: Do you contend that the regulation defines prisoners of war and that only those people as such defined in the regulation are prisoners of war?

MR. GARRE: Yes.

THE COURT: All right.

MR. GARRE: In the definition as contained in the regulation.

THE COURT: So everybody else is not a prisoner of war. They're a prisoner of what?

MR. GARRE: They may be another detainee or they may be a combatant. Your Honor, this is spelled out in the regulations. It's consistent with the Geneva Convention.

THE COURT: Let me ask about the customs of war. Forget the regulation. He isn't a prisoner of war under the regulation so far as you're concerned, so let's deal with something else.

Are there any customs of war?

MR. GARRE: Well, is Your Honor referring to the Geneva Convention?

THE COURT: I'm not worried – I haven't raised the Geneva Convention. I didn't even say the Geneva Convention applies. As far as I know, Afghanistan didn't sign the Geneva [49] Convention. If we apply the Geneva Convention, we're in pretty bad shape. Let's go ahead. Because Hamdi is entitled to a lot of things if he were a prisoner of war under the Geneva Convention. I'm only talking to Army regulations – Navy regulations that pertain to people who may be custodians, okay?

Now, let's go into the customs of war. Customs of war. If you take a prisoner in battle and in the customs of war they were a prisoner of war, is that correct, not under the regulations?

MR. GARRE: I think, Your Honor –

THE COURT: I'm talking about customs of war.

MR. GARRE: The *Quirin* case resolved that where it talks about –

THE COURT: Who?

MR. GARRE: The *Quirin* case, the Supreme Court case, 317 U.S. 1.

THE COURT: They weren't – they were spies. They landed on foreign territory in – and not in uniforms but in civilian clothes.

MR. GARRE: That's true about the saboteurs.

THE COURT: They talk about combatants. They talk about belligerents.

MR. GARRE: You know, that raises an important point about why the determination has been made that members of the – or people like Mr. Hamdi, al-Qaida and Taliban [50] detainees, have not been determined to be prisoners of war under the Geneva Convention or customs of law, because they don't fight with uniforms, they don't follow the laws and customs of war.

THE COURT: Stop. Where does it say he didn't have a uniform in the Mobbs' Declaration?

MR. GARRE: I'm referring –

THE COURT: In the Mobbs' Declaration does it say –

MR. GARRE: It didn't say that, Your Honor.

THE COURT: In the Mobbs' Declaration where did it say he was not a member of an organized unit?

MR. GARRE: It does not say that. He surrendered and went to train to fight with the Taliban unit.

THE COURT: Am I to assume that it was commanded by someone if it's a unit, or can I not assume that? You see, the real problem, Mr. Garre, is when you're deciding something only, only, on a declaration, then, unfortunately, the declaration has to be very thorough.

MR. GARRE: I appreciate Your Honor's effort to –

THE COURT: I can't do a thing other than look at this declaration. And if I look at the declaration, then I find that there are certain omissions that seem substantial.

MR. GARRE: Your Honor, I appreciate your efforts to look at the Mobbs' Declaration. And I do think it's fair to say that any good lawyer, and particularly any good judge, [51] would be able to go through a declaration and find the sorts of things that Your Honor has pointed to today. What we do think – and if I could be clear about the government's position – is that the declaration has to be read as a whole, and the declaration in this case which explains the grounds and circumstances underlying Mr. Hamdi's capture, his surrender, the reasons why he went to Afghanistan, and the military's determination –

THE COURT: I don't have any doubts he had a firearm. I don't have any doubts he went to Afghanistan to be with the Taliban. I don't have any doubts of either of those things, Mr. Garre. If that is sufficient, if that is sufficient, alone, standing alone, to put him in a cell without windows for six months or 10 months or four months or whatever it is, then so be it. I have some real doubts about that.

Let me hear from Mr. Dunham.

MR. GARRE: Thank you, Your Honor.

THE COURT: Because that's really where we are.

Mr. Dunham.

MR. DUNHAM: Excuse me one second, Your Honor.

Your Honor, we have problems with the Mobbs' Declaration as being the be all and the end all of how this case should be decided. In fact, we believe that the writ of habeas corpus, you might as well just toss it out the window if somebody like Mr. Mobbs –

[52] THE COURT: I can't decide that, Mr. Dunham. The Court of Appeals has already ruled that the only thing I can consider before proceeding any further is whether the Mobbs' Declaration is sufficient. If the Mobbs' Declaration is sufficient, Mr. Dunham, then there is no writ of habeas corpus in this case.

MR. DUNHAM: That's correct, Your Honor.

THE COURT: That's what the Court of Appeals has held.

MR. DUNHAM: That's right. But what the Court of Appeals also held was that Mr. Hamdi was entitled to meaningful judicial review. They clearly said that in the opinion. And I do not believe that you can give meaningful judicial review on the basis of the Mobbs' Declaration alone because it raises more questions than it answers.

The Mobbs' Declaration, for example, it does not say that Mr. Hamdi was an unlawful combatant. I mean, we keep getting explanations for why the regulations don't apply to Mr. Hamdi. The reason why the quad military regulations that Your Honor has been talking about, they don't apply, Mr. Garre says, because Mr. Hamdi is an unlawful combatant.

Now, to me, that's a glaring omission from the Mobbs' Declaration. It doesn't say anything about unlawful. It says he was an enemy combatant. Now, that's not why – that doesn't square with the conditions under which he's being held. He's [53] being held in a military brig in Norfolk. He's being held in solitary confinement. He's being punished. He's not being held like an enemy soldier. Back in 1890 the –

THE COURT: At least he can bring a 1983 action against the person, I assume, or at least a constitutional action for lack of due process, but we're not concerned with the lack of due process here. We're concerned with the Mobbs' Declaration.

MR. DUNHAM: I think we are concerned with whether or not Mr. Hamdi is truly being held as an enemy combatant, because I think he's being held as something else. I think that the Court can infer from the fact that the government's not following its clearly printed regulations with how you should treat somebody like Mr. Hamdi as the fact that that's not why they're holding him.

Now, we look at the — we look — because the question is whether the Mobbs' Declaration is adequate to determine why Mr. Hamdi is being held.

THE COURT: Assuming the Mobbs' Declaration is inadequate, shouldn't the government be given an opportunity to have a convening authority convene the appropriate military tribunal?

MR. DUNHAM: Well, I will — first off, I believe the regulations — yes. I believe the appropriate tribunal, yes. Whether the word military goes in front of it or not I might [54] question.

THE COURT: The regulation says, doesn't it, that a convening authority, that is a general court-martial convening authority, which would indicate a flag officer in the Navy, would have to convene such a tribunal?

MR. DUNHAM: The President has determined in this particular situation that you don't use military tribunals for U. S. citizens. That's why they charged John Walker Lindh with a —

THE COURT: So he is not entitled, but that doesn't make any difference what the President has said if the regulation requires it, Mr. Dunham.

MR. DUNHAM: The regulation requires that the man be treated as a prisoner of war unless a military tribunal determines otherwise.

THE COURT: That's correct.

MR. DUNHAM: That regulation is not just some military regulation that doesn't bind the Department of Defense. That is our government's attempt to comply with the requirements of the Geneva Convention which requires precisely that before you treat somebody as an unlawful combatant you must have some type of process, such as — by an appropriate authority, such as a military tribunal, to treat somebody as an unlawful combatant.

Now, you can't separate that out from the fact that [55] Mr. Mobbs' Declaration — Mr. Mobbs tries to tell the Court that we are still engaged in hostility with the Taliban.

THE COURT: Well, the question there is the President has declared the national emergency with the Taliban over; is that correct?

MR. DUNHAM: That's correct.

THE COURT: Now we understand that. But the question, really, is that there was a reservation in that declaration, too, was there not?

MR. DUNHAM: That's correct, with regard to al-Qaida. It's not a declaration with regard to — they

haven't established in the Mobbs' Declaration that Mr. Hamdi falls into that exception.

THE COURT: Well, he's not a member of the al-Qaida. They just throw the words in there because it helps them. It looks good.

MR. DUNHAM: So the point I'm making is that Mr. Hamdi is currently being held as if he were an unlawful combatant without having been given any of the benefits of the regulations for that determination and without any statement in the Mobbs' Declaration that he is an unlawful combatant. If he is merely an enemy combatant and that's all he is, he should be released because the hostilities with the government of Afghanistan have ended. And under all the laws of war when the hostilities end the prisoners are released. That's [56] international law.

And we believe that if the government wants to stand here and say, Your Honor, we're not going to give you anything but the Mobbs' Declaration —

THE COURT: Well, that's what they said, isn't it?

MR. DUNHAM: — we will rise or fall on that declaration, well, I say that if they do that we should get our writ granted today and we should walk over to the brig and get Mr. Hamdi because that declaration doesn't justify his detention.

Now, I am — I do not understand — this is one of the things I do not understand. They talk about Judge Ellis' decision in the Walker Lindh case. They don't bother to tell this case — that in the Walker Lindh case Judge Ellis had access to statements by Mr. Hamdi, statements that they

have not provided to this court. Judge Ellis determined that those statements were exculpatory to Mr. Lindh on the enemy combatant theory, whether or not Lindh was an enemy combatant, and he released those statements to Walker Lindh's private attorneys. But for some reason this court can't have them. They're not even classified. I can't figure out — I mean, I can understand an argument — I can understand it. I don't agree with it.

THE COURT: That's unclassified?

MR. DUNHAM: It's unclassified. My declaration is in [57] the file to that effect.

THE COURT: I saw that. It said it was not classified. How did you find out they were not classified?

MR. DUNHAM: Well, because when they had the hearing as to whether or not they could see Hamdi — Hamdi must be the most popular guy I know because everybody wants to see him.

THE COURT: Well, that's good he's out there. At least according to at least the newspaper report — I haven't looked at his cell — he doesn't have a window in that cell.

MR. DUNHAM: But the —

THE COURT: That's according to the newspaper.

MR. DUNHAM: They wanted to see him. Of course, when they got these exculpatory statements they wanted to go see him because they thought he might be a good witness to call at their trial. Judge Ellis told them, well, you've got to check with Dunham, Dunham is Hamdi's lawyer, he'll get you in to see him. Well, big deal, I can't even see him. But the bottom line is that's what Judge Ellis told them.

THE COURT: They could have seen him because Walker Lindh was charged with something. Now, Hamdi is not charged with anything.

MR. DUNHAM: No, but he was –

THE COURT: Because if he was charged with something, you know, he'd have to be brought before a magistrate, and probable cause would have to be utilized within – according to [58] the Supreme Court of the United States, within 48 hours. So we know they can't charge him now with something.

MR. DUNHAM: That's correct.

THE COURT: So it's been – I would dare say that this length of time – we know the decisions of the Supreme Court. They even set down a time limit for charging someone after they've taken them into custody.

MR. DUNHAM: Well –

THE COURT: But maybe it doesn't apply to the military. Maybe they could charge him. I would doubt the Supreme Court would let them hold somebody eight months or more without charging someone with something.

MR. DUNHAM: The only point I'm making, Your Honor, is that the government has more information about this situation than they have chosen to provide to the Court or to counsel for Mr. Hamdi, and that, to me, it's a very risky proposition, if they seriously want to hold this man, to come in here with an affidavit or a declaration

that's as flawed as this Mobbs' Declaration is, omitting as many facts as it omits.

Just the colloquy between Your Honor and Mr. Garre shows the – a number of deficiencies in this document, including the very basic factors of the date on which he was captured. I mean, that could be very significant in deciding legal rights. I mean, this says late in 2001. What does late in 2001 mean? Does that mean October 1st, December 31st? Why [59] do we have to guess as to when he was captured? All of these things as to the regulation are supposed to be taken down, unless maybe he's an unlawful combatant and the regulation doesn't apply to him. Mr. Mobbs doesn't say he's an unlawful combatant. Because Mr. Mobbs doesn't say he's an unlawful combatant and you're limited to the Mobbs' Declaration, you have to assume that he's a lawful combatant. And, yet, we are confronted with a detention in Norfolk, which is another dog that doesn't bark.

THE COURT: If you had to say he was a lawful combatant, it's obvious that they're not complying with the requirements of the Geneva Convention. But the Geneva Convention really doesn't apply to him. They wouldn't be complying with the regulations, which the Geneva Convention requires him to stay with the people of his own –

MR. DUNHAM: The other dog that doesn't bark in the Mobbs' Declaration is it doesn't explain why he's moved to Norfolk. Why is he separated from his unit? Why is he flown to Dulles Airport?

THE COURT: I assume they say this does indicate something about intelligence.

MR. DUNHAM: Doesn't say anything about intelligence. Since May we have been hearing about the intelligence value of Mr. Hamdi. I can't see him because it will interfere with the intelligence gathering operation that's going on. But, yet, [60] Mobbs doesn't say anything about intelligence gathering.

THE COURT: Well, Mr. Dunham, you know, it does take time to process intelligence, does it not?

MR. DUNHAM: Well, just as Justice –

THE COURT: They can keep him in solitary long enough maybe they can promise to get him out of solitary if he tells them what they want to hear.

MR. DUNHAM: Just as Mr. Garre quoted during [sic] Chief Judge Wilkinson during oral argument, I would like to quote from Justice Douglas in a concurring opinion in the *United States v. United States District Court* where it says that the government's desire to fortify its intelligence collage does not justify the extension of the detention of an American citizen.

And just holding him for intelligence reasons doesn't square. But, more importantly, we're here to talk about the Mobbs' Declaration. And Mobbs doesn't say he's in the Norfolk brig for intelligence gathering purposes. In fact, what is curious to me, and I agree with Your Honor's observation completely, that sometimes a declaration like that, it speaks louder for the things it doesn't say than the things that it does say. And I can't help but scratch my head and say we're challenging – we filed this writ of habeas corpus because Mr. Hamdi was in the Navy brig in Norfolk and we thought he was going to be charged with a federal offense and they were just [61] holding him there. So we filed the petition for writ of habeas corpus. He's in the Navy brig. That's the detention we're challenging.

If that's the detention, Mr. Mobbs never chooses to discuss. He never says why he's there, why he's being held there, what terms or conditions he's being held under. And, yet, that is the detention that's before this court, not what happened on the battlefield in Afghanistan, not what happened when they moved him to Guantanamo. The detention we're hoping you're trying to focus on is why is he in the Navy brig in Norfolk. That's the question we ask. We have seen press reports, and I guess, you know, they have been alluded to, but we've seen press reports that talk about the fact that he was brought here to prosecute him. They brought him to Dulles Airport. They were going to bring him to the Eastern District of Virginia to Alexandria, but, oh, somebody in the Justice Department didn't want him, so they sent him down here to the Navy brig. Well, that's just press. Maybe you can't believe this. But you would think that Mr. Mobbs in explaining the detention of Mr. Hamdi in Norfolk would at least mention Norfolk somewhere in his declaration. He doesn't have a word about it. And, to me, that speaks louder than anything else.

Now, when they brought Mr. Hamdi to Norfolk they brought a bunch of other problems because they have to address 18 U.S.C. 4001(a). Now, Mr. Mobbs never explains in his [62] declaration why that general statute doesn't apply in this case.

THE COURT: Well, it certainly says that he has to have a trial, doesn't it?

MR. DUNHAM: It says he has to have a trial. It says in the – and the Supreme Court has talked about that statute. Granted, that they spoke of it in dicta, but in *Howe v. Smith* in the ABA report – the ABA has just come out with a report cautioning courts to handle these proceedings with care.

THE COURT: I read the – you-all gave me all this stuff. You keep me awake all night reading this stuff, Mr. Dunham, I tell you.

MR. DUNHAM: The ABA report quotes Justice Burger as saying 4001, the plain language of 4001(a) prescribes detention – proscribes detention for any kind of – of any kind – proscribes detention of any kind by the United States absent a congressional grant of authority to detain.

Now, Mr. Mobbs' Declaration does not explain – that wouldn't apply to Mr. Hamdi if he was in Afghanistan.

THE COURT: It wouldn't apply to Mr. Hamdi if he was in Guantanamo.

MR. DUNHAM: It wouldn't apply to Mr. Hamdi if he was in Guantanamo. But when they bring him to Norfolk it applies. Now, they had to know that when they brought him here. And the government's presumed to know what the law is. And there's got [63] to be some reason why they think it doesn't apply or why they don't have to honor that, and it ought to be in the Mobbs' Declaration because we're talking about his detention in Norfolk, not what happened elsewhere.

I mean, how can you question the sergeant on the battlefield when there is still smoke coming out of the barrels and he's wrapping up a gaggle of guys? You know, by the time you get removed from that situation, and there's been some sorting out, and there's been some reports, and there's been some screening, and there's been some determinations made, by the time you get to that point you've got a lot of information, and you ought to be willing to share it with the judge in a habeas corpus proceeding; otherwise, the whole proceeding is a sham. To say, oh, whoa, the courts are open for habeas corpus –

THE COURT: You'll have to argue that before the Court of Appeals, Mr. Dunham. As far as I'm concerned here today, the Court of Appeals has said I have to determine if the Mobbs' Declaration is sufficient. I realize that you consider the habeas should have certain rights, a person in this proceeding; however, we're concerned with the sufficiency of the Mobbs' Declaration.

MR. DUNHAM: I understand, Your Honor.

THE COURT: You can argue that. You can go to the Supreme Court, and they'll tell you you have a right to speak [64] to him.

MR. DUNHAM: Well, I think that –

THE COURT: I can't do anything about that. I am interested in the Mobbs' Declaration, Mr. Dunham.

MR. DUNHAM: I will point out –

THE COURT: It's interesting to me because in reading – I assume it was Mr. Saltzburg who was a professor at the University of Virginia before he was a professor at GW had a great deal to do with writing that brief. How it got filed here is interesting, but you-all filed it, and I took the time to read it. It is interesting because the Geneva Convention does say if there is a doubt about the status of an individual he should be before a competent tribunal, which is what the Army regulation or the Navy regulation – it's interesting here, also, that this was not an engagement in which any Americans were involved in any capture or in any battle, if there was a battle. We don't know if he was in any battle. May not have been in any battle at all.

MR. DUNHAM: There is nothing in the Mobbs' Declaration to indicate that he fought anyone.

THE COURT: That's correct. There is not – there is an indication that he had a weapon.

MR. DUNHAM: That's right. Indication he had a weapon.

THE COURT: The oddity is that one of the problems [65] that I see that's tantamount in anything is to understand what it is that is considered on each side. How do the Northern Alliance distinguish themselves from the Taliban? How can the Taliban distinguish themselves from the Northern Alliance? Are there distinguishing characteristics so that they know who they're shooting at if they're shooting at each other? And how is it that they change sides so often?

MR. DUNHAM: That –

THE COURT: All of those questions are questions that have been raised by the press and certain other people concerning – and it creates real problems in my mind. But you're quite correct, there is nothing in here that says he's an unlawful combatant. They never said that.

MR. DUNHAM: And there is nothing in there that says –

THE COURT: What worries me is there is nothing to say that he was ever involved with any U. S. people.

MR. DUNHAM: There is nothing to say that he was even – that he even fought anybody. Nobody provides us a definition of the term enemy combatant. It's thrown around by everybody.

THE COURT: Well, in *Quirin* they didn't battle anyone. They just came ashore prepared to do so. And, Mr. Dunham, you have to understand that, because in *Quirin* they were captured prior to the time when they had an opportunity to [66] battle. Here the thing that worries me is the "if necessary" he would fight. I didn't know why or what would be, in his opinion, necessary.

In any event, you continue. I've interrupted you, Mr. Dunham.

MR. DUNHAM: The enemy combatant designation in my view –

THE COURT: That makes him a prisoner of war is what you're saying?

MR. DUNHAM: That's right. The regulations talk about the fact that, hey, if you don't know what he is, before you can make him an unlawful you've got to give him a tribunal.

THE COURT: That's right.

MR. DUNHAM: Whether he's a civilian detainee or whatever he is, you can't treat him less than as a prisoner of war without giving him the benefit of that process, which hasn't been done here.

THE COURT: Now, what is the effect of the Geneva Convention to non-signers of the Convention?

MR. DUNHAM: Afghanistan is a signer of the Convention, and the Taliban was the lawful government of Afghanistan.

THE COURT: Well, now, that is a serious question, isn't it, Mr. Dunham?

MR. DUNHAM: Let me –

[67] THE COURT: The government that was recognized by the United States was not the Taliban; is that correct?

MR. DUNHAM: Well, when the conflict began the Taliban was the governing party of the – governing body of Afghanistan and was recognized internationally as the government of that country. We replaced that government in December of 2001 and installed a new government, which we have recognized and which we have gone so far to say we are at peace with, and which we have gone so far as to remove regulations on the books declaring a state of emergency with that government. And that government has members of the Taliban in it.

THE COURT: Well, it does. I know it does. And that creates a lot of problems because, knowing the history of the area, and realizing what warlords were doing, and realizing that pillage and plunder is a means of – economic means of success in the East and has been for centuries – it's nothing that's new to history. Any student of the Near Eastern history can tell you that pillage and plunder were constant utilizations by various leaders of one kind or another, sometimes under certain religious aspects or certain sets of certain religions in order to pillage and plunder. And these warlords would collect tribute. That's what it was all about.

MR. DUNHAM: That's why the Mobbs' Declaration is further inadequate, because it does not answer the very specific question that the Court asked when we were here last. [68] This court asked the question lastly, with whom is the war I would suggest that we're fighting? Is it with the government of Afghanistan?

Now, nobody answers that question. Mobbs certainly doesn't answer it. There are a myriad of public statements by the President that would allow this court to draw conclusion as to what – whether we're still at war with the government of Afghanistan or not. But I think that even if –

THE COURT: We're certainly not at war with the present government of Afghanistan, Mr. Dunham.

MR. DUNHAM: We threw out one government, and there is a new government.

THE COURT: To the victor belongs the spoils. That's what plunder is about, isn't it? Pillage and plunder. To the strong – the strong take over the weak.

MR. DUNHAM: But when you take over, the conflict is over. You don't keep holding –

THE COURT: Well, the conflict isn't over because the weak wants to reassemble and remove the strong, and maybe they will get strong again. That's what they have been doing for, what, 1,000 years, 2,000 years, 5,000 years?

MR. DUNHAM: Isn't that all internal to Afghanistan at that point?

THE COURT: No, it isn't.

MR. DUNHAM: What you have is in order for the United [69] States to hold somebody as an enemy combatant there has to be an international conflict in which the U. S. is involved.

THE COURT: Does it have to be an enemy of the United States? That's the question, Mr. Dunham. Or is it an enemy of some other – I mean, if you're the enemy of my enemy, are you my – if you're the enemy of my friend, are you my enemy? I guess you are.

MR. DUNHAM: You know, I can't get into that, but at least it would seem to me you have to do something, not just intend to do something, that you have to actually do something. And I'm not sure that the government has any – there is nothing in the Mobbs' Declaration that indicates that Mr. Hamdi did anything other than go to Afghanistan to fight, if necessary. And I think that the failure of the Mobbs' Declaration to say that Mr. Hamdi was an actual combatant, actually took place in combatant activities –

THE COURT: There is no indication that he actually –

MR. DUNHAM: Nothing in there.

THE COURT: And if there were, he probably would have been tried by now, had an opportunity to counsel, and do all those things, but he didn't, so they're not trying him for that. They just want to keep him there for intelligence purposes, I gather, but that doesn't – you're right, it doesn't say so in the Mobbs' Declaration, does it?

[70] MR. DUNHAM: No, Your Honor. I go back to the fact if we didn't have an international conflict with Afghanistan you wouldn't be able to have – to invoke the rules of war which the government invokes as its right to hold people as enemy combatants. In other words, the existence of a state of –

THE COURT: What you're really not getting to, Mr. Dunham, is anyone who is considered to be a terrorist, then, is an enemy combatant, so if you are a terrorist you're an enemy combatant, are you not, because that's who – that's what the regulation said against enemy – groups or individuals, so doesn't make much difference. If the man next door to you is an enemy combatant and they say he's an unlawful enemy combatant, maybe the military, the President, or Mr. Mobbs could figure out if he's an enemy combatant.

MR. DUNHAM: That's what's scary.

THE COURT: Maybe we could eliminate all these guns in the areas. Just say they're enemy combatants.

MR. DUNHAM: If you had a gun and you had an intent, you're an enemy combatant, you don't need a trial. We just lock you up forever. That's the concern here.

THE COURT: We're not going to lock anybody up forever in this country. This question here is really this man was in a fighting situation, Mr. Dunham. He was where the fight was. And that's a real problem.

[71] MR. DUNHAM: That's correct.

THE COURT: If he had a weapon where the fight was, they certainly have a right to corral him. What worried me more about this case than anything else is they were corralled not by U. S. forces. He was corralled by these groups of people who comprise what they call the "Northern Alliance", which is really a group of various leaders or what one would normally term sort of a lord of a certain area. You know, feudalism existed well into the century in the Ottoman Empire, so that there were these various sort of fiefdoms. And it was strong people that were able to create these fiefdoms. There isn't any question about it. And they fight one another constantly and have constantly. What worries me is he happened to be in one of these fiefdoms.

MR. DUNHAM: Well, what is the problem with all of that, of course, is that we have absolutely no detail with regard to the circumstances under which he was initially captured. And as Your Honor has pointed out, he was allowed to keep his weapon. That doesn't sound like much of a capture to me. It almost sounds like a potential changing of alliances or whatever. We don't know what happened. And I'm sure the U. S. government knows what happened, but they haven't chose to present it to the Court. And that's further part of the problem. They're asking the Court to deny the petition for writ of habeas corpus on basically guesswork. They're asking [72] the Court to guess and fill in the blanks in the Mobbs' Declaration without providing the information that would make the Court feel comfortable in acting.

For that reason we believe the declaration is not adequate. We recognize that the government probably should be granted time to submit additional information because of the way the Court of Appeals suggested the Court should proceed, but were we here for final argument on this case and there was to be – everybody had had a chance to put into the record the evidence they wanted to put into the record, I would submit that the current record is not adequate to justify the detention here.

THE COURT: Thank you, Mr. Dunham.

All right, Mr. Garre. You've heard Mr. Dunham's argument. Tell me what your reply is to his argument.

MR. GARRE: Thank you, Your Honor.

First, I want to be clear that the government's position is that someone who surrenders with an enemy unit and turns over his AK-47 to the forces that capture him is an enemy combatant, that that person doesn't need to actually fire his weapon at anyone, at his captors. He certainly doesn't have to fire his weapon at United States soldiers in Afghanistan in order to meet that definition.

THE COURT: He was there to fight. And that's correct. My problem was – I am having a little problem with [73] that, but I may – it may be sufficient. It may not be sufficient.

Mr. Garre, what is concerning me are certain things he said. There is nothing that Mr. Dunham raised, which are excellent points, and there is nothing in here to say he was an unlawful enemy combatant.

MR. GARRE: With respect, Your Honor, we think under the some evidence standard we have explained in our motion to dismiss that applies here, which is that the military has to provide a factual basis for its determination that Mr. Hamdi is an enemy combatant,

that this declaration meets that standard. And we think that although Mr. Dunham tries very hard –

THE COURT: You have to describe the standard. You offered it to the Fourth Circuit, but they said no.

MR. GARRE: Maybe I'm not making myself clear, Your Honor. In our motion to dismiss we explained that a court in this certain situation applying a factual inquiry into the government's designation could look only to whether or not the government – the executive has supplied some basis, some evidence of factual –

THE COURT: All they have to do is say he's an unlawful combatant, and that's the end of it. Is that it, Mr. Dunham?

MR. GARRE: That certainly wouldn't be a fair characterization.

[74] THE COURT: They said he was an enemy combatant. They haven't said he's unlawful.

MR. GARRE: The Mobbs' Declaration, it provides the grounds and circumstances. I think it's important to focus, as Your Honor did earlier –

THE COURT: Where does the Mobbs' Declaration show he was an unlawful combatant?

MR. GARRE: First, as we said, and this was at page eight, note five of our motion to dismiss, whether Mr. Hamdi is an unlawful or a lawful combatant, enemy combatant, is not relevant to the military's authority to hold him. The *Quirin* –

THE COURT: So number one, you can hold a prisoner of war. If he's a lawful combatant, then he's a prisoner of war; is that correct?

MR. GARRE: That certainly is correct, Your Honor. And the *Quirin* case makes that quite clear when it distinguishes between lawful and unlawful combatants and the authority of the captors in both situations to detain those persons whether they're regarded as lawful, unlawful. The Fourth Circuit decision in this case also makes clear if indeed Mr. Hamdi is an enemy combatant who was captured during the hostilities in Afghanistan then his present detention is lawful.

Now, the bulk of Mr. Dunham's submissions –

[75] THE COURT: The Court of Appeals has already ruled, so I don't have to do anything; is that correct?

MR. GARRE: No, Your Honor.

THE COURT: Is that your position? Is that your position?

MR. GARRE: No, Your Honor.

THE COURT: They will tell Mr. Dunham take it to the Supreme Court.

MR. GARRE: It's not. I think I wanted to make clear a number of the arguments Mr. Dunham was making here today are legal arguments that are rejected by, if not just simply flatly inconsistent with, the Court of Appeals ruling, which is well supported by other precedents that we cited in our motion to dismiss.

THE COURT: It's interesting to me, Mr. Garre, because I tried valiantly, valiantly, to find a case of any kind in any court in which a lawyer was not entitled to consult with his client. I must tell you this case sets the most interesting precedent in relation to that that has ever existed in Anglo-American jurisprudence since the days of the Star Chamber.

MR. GARRE: Well, with respect, Your Honor, we would disagree with that characterization. Again, to go back to the comment that Chief Judge Wilkinson made during the argument in the Court of Appeals case which recognizes since time [76] immemorial those captured in warfare have been detained without charges and without counsel –

THE COURT: I'm not questioning any capture in warfare, nor am I questioning that at all. Mr. Dunham has raised an interesting point, a very interesting point. He says a person was brought here ostensibly to be tried in this court, or in Alexandria at least, in the Eastern District of Virginia, for whatever they wanted to try him for, because he was an American citizen. He obviously is not being kept with the other combatants, which is required both by the regulation and the Geneva Convention – there is no question about that – which would require him to be kept with other people of similar import.

MR. GARRE: But, Your Honor –

THE COURT: He raised the point about why was he brought to the Navy brig in Norfolk.

MR. GARRE: The logic of that conclusion – the logic of that argument leads to the conclusion that can't – with respect, we don't think that can be right that the military can capture and detain combatants on the battlefield. Once it's done that during a period of active and ongoing hostilities it can't bring those combatants back to American soil as it did in the case of thousands of individuals during World War II, that the military – the law prevents the military from holding individuals at other facilities that might be safer for the [77] United States military or that might be more conducive to other aspects of the war effort.

THE COURT: What's unsafe about this fellow they have to keep him incommunicado, in solitary confinement, other than the fact that he happened to have been born in the United States? Is he being punished because he was born in the United States? Is that why he's – listen. I think it's punishment. The Supreme Court thinks isolation is punishment also. They've had decision after decision. Of course, you can keep people in isolation. You can give them some due process. They're entitled to some hearing. You put them in isolation because of disciplinary matters or there is an administration reason for keeping them in isolation or they may be trying to escape or many other things. You can keep them in isolation.

How long you can keep them in isolation, all of these factors begin to weigh. Does a court – shouldn't a court take notice of that? You say they didn't raise the questions of that. But is that –

MR. GARRE: They have, as I understand it – and I'm reading from their traverse, which says that they are not challenging the conditions of Mr. Hamdi's confinement. We don't think – and we've explained this in our return to Your Honor's questions about the alleged fact he was held in solitary confinement. As I tried to explain earlier, he's not being held in solitary confinement in the sense that that term [78] is traditionally used.

THE COURT: What is solitary confinement in your sense? Does it mean that you can speak with – solitary confinement, do you speak with your captor?

MR. GARRE: Well –

THE COURT: I mean, what is it? What do you say, he's not being kept –

MR. GARRE: Mr. Hamdi now is the only enemy combatant –

THE COURT: From a standpoint of something that's brought to the Court's attention, that concerns me in relation to the real problem of due process of a person in custody who is unable to communicate with the world.

MR. GARRE: The government's position, and we've stated this and tried to make it clear in a motion to dismiss, is that its detention of Mr. Hamdi as a captured enemy combatant is lawful whether Mr. Hamdi was in Afghanistan, whether Mr. Hamdi was in Guantanamo, or whether he's in the Norfolk Naval Brig. The military made the determination to move Mr. Hamdi to the naval brig. He happens to be the only enemy combatant at that facility.

THE COURT: So, therefore, he can be held –

MR. GARRE: He is not – as I said, he receives visits.

THE COURT: You have another one down in South [79] Carolina. Why did you move that fellow down to South Carolina and Hamdi here, so they couldn't talk to one another and thereby be some intelligence problem; is that correct?

MR. GARRE: Your Honor, I'm not in a factual position to answer that question. The military made that determination. It may have been based on the different facilities under –

THE COURT: Did the military make it or did the Department of Justice make it?

MR. GARRE: My understanding is the military made that determination. As I said, I'm not in a factual basis to provide anymore information on that, nor do I think it's relevant to the habeas proceeding in this case.

THE COURT: I must admit it is not really relevant to the habeas proceeding except that an individual is being held incommunicado for a number of months, and the Court is ever mindful of that, and then the intelligence one receives from that has been held – you know, one of the major problems – I don't want to go into that.

MR. GARRE: Your Honor, if I could address another statement that Mr. Dunham –

THE COURT: I think fundamental fairness to people says we are not treating you as an animal, we are treating you as a person, we don't have you in a cage, we allow you to communicate. People are social by nature, aren't they?

MR. GARRE: Mr. Hamdi, as I said earlier, receives [80] visits every day from the commanding officer. He meets several times a week with the chaplain at the facility. He meets with the doctor every week.

THE COURT: Is he a Christian or what is he?

MR. GARRE: Your Honor, I don't know the answer to that question.

THE COURT: Is the chaplain a Mohammed chaplain or Christian chaplain? Is he – I don't know what Hamdi is. All I know –

MR. GARRE: If the Court's concern is about personal contact, I think it's the fact of the contact that's significant.

THE COURT: So personal contact, he is able to meet with his interrogators every day?

MR. GARRE: Your Honor, I want the government's point to be clear that the lawfulness of the present detention in this case isn't dependent on any –

THE COURT: But it has to weigh on my mind. He's still a human being.

MR. GARRE: I think the authorities that we have set out in our motion to dismiss and the Court of Appeals recognized were to call it the long established authority of the military to detain captured combatants during the period of hostilities authorize the detention in this case. The Mobbs' Declaration provides what we think is the factual basis [81] necessary for –

THE COURT: Let me ask you, Mr. Garre. You probably know. You probably know. Was it a battle or was he just surrendered?

MR. GARRE: The declaration says what it says, which says that he surrendered and gave his firearm to the Northern Alliance forces. That's in paragraph nine. It says he went to Afghanistan to train and fight with the Taliban.

Mr. Dunham, if I understand his arguments today correctly, doesn't dispute, and he certainly did not dispute in the petition, he was in Afghanistan or that he surrendered to these forces or –

THE COURT: Doesn't make much sense.

MR. GARRE: His central position seems to be –

THE COURT: He's never talked with Hamdi, hasn't seen a statement by Hamdi. The only information he has about Hamdi is what you gave him, which is darn little.

MR. GARRE: His argument seems to be he can't be an enemy combatant because he wasn't shooting at United States forces or other forces.

THE COURT: That doesn't have anything to do with it. And I understand that. That doesn't have anything to do with whether he's an enemy combatant.

MR. GARRE: Another thing in the government's view that doesn't have anything to do with that determination is Mr. [82] Dunham's argument – suggestion that the war with the Taliban is over.

THE COURT: Let's talk about something else a minute, Mr. Garre.

Suppose I said that I felt that this was not sufficient and that he is an enemy combatant according to them, but he may or may not be. Then you'd have no trouble convening a military tribunal, as the treaty and as the regulations require, in short order, wouldn't you?

MR. GARRE: With respect, Your Honor, I tried to explain why we don't think those regulations are required. We think –

THE COURT: So you wouldn't do it if I gave you some time? Is that what you're telling me, Mr. Garre? If you tell me you wouldn't do it if I gave you some time, I won't waste your time.

MR. GARRE: Your Honor, I'm not in a position here to say what the military would or would not do. What I'm here to say is –

THE COURT: All you have to do is answer. Do you want some time or not, Mr. Garre? I'm going to give it to you on a platter. If you want it, you can take it. If you don't want it, tell me I don't want it.

MR. GARRE: We would ask the Court to find that the Mobbs' Declaration is sufficient and to grant the government's [83] motion to dismiss. If the Court is not prepared to do that, then we would ask for some time to consider whatever order it would be that the Court would issue as to how proceedings would proceed.

THE COURT: I'm not going to issue any order, Mr. – I may just say the Mobbs' Declaration is insufficient and give you the reasons for it. In that case, Mr. Garre, if that's what you want, you may find yourself in a position that's ridiculous. Do you understand that? I said – you can come back tomorrow. You better consult with somebody, Mr. Garre.

MR. GARRE: Yes, Your Honor.

THE COURT: Please consult with somebody, will you?

MR. GARRE: Your Honor, the government would be happy to consult, but I do want the government's position to be clear that the Mobbs' Declaration is sufficient.

THE COURT: I understand the government's position. I'm trying to offer you something nicely, Mr. Garre, but, if you don't want it, you don't have to take it. And all you have to say is, Judge, I don't want it. That's all you have to say. It's just that simple.

MR. GARRE: Your Honor, as I said, if the Court's conclusion is that the declaration is not sufficient, then the government would like some time to consider what the proper course would be at that point. But if, on the other hand, we, would – we have asked the Court to find that the Mobbs' [84] Declaration is sufficient and to grant the government's motion to dismiss.

THE COURT: I don't want to stop you from taking up an appeal, I guess – I certainly don't want to do that, Mr. Garre – if I decide it's insufficient. It appears that it has some great omissions.

MR. GARRE: I don't want to go back and go over ground we've already been through, but we do think –

THE COURT: He has raised some interesting points that I didn't raise. One is an unlawful combatant was not mentioned. And so –

MR. GARRE: If I could address that point. I think it's now relevant to the government's authority to detain Mr. Hamdi. We said that in page eight, note five, of our petition.

THE COURT: So you're no longer trying to maintain that he's an unlawful combatant insofar as the Mobbs' Declaration is concerned, correct?

MR. GARRE: The Mobbs' Declaration states that he was with a Taliban unit and surrendered and turned over his firearm. Now, the President has determined that those captured combatants who were with the Taliban or the al-Qaida are unlawful –

THE COURT: Show me that, where the President has determined anything.

MR. GARRE: I think that's laid out in Judge Ellis' [85] decision which we referred to.

THE COURT: I'm not worried about Judge Ellis' decision. He isn't here.

MR. GARRE: We referred to it in our legal papers.

THE COURT: Just so you understand, I'll tell you one more time. He's in Alexandria, okay? He's a very, very intelligent, well-reasoned judge. And I'm sure that his decisions have good basis for all of us.

MR. GARRE: The decision –

THE COURT: But he may have been presented with evidence that I have not been presented with.

MR. GARRE: There wouldn't be any evidence to that determination because he's relying on the President's determination –

THE COURT: How do you know? He had all kinds of information, didn't he?

MR. GARRE: It's laid out in the decision where he explains why the President – he explains the President made this determination. And he concludes that the Taliban falls, in his words –

THE COURT: Stop a minute. So he has made a decision? The President has made a decision that Hamdi is an unlawful enemy combatant?

MR. GARRE: No, Your Honor. The President has determined that the detainees who were captured as Taliban or [86] al-Qaida, because of their association with the Taliban or the al-Qaida, do not meet the criteria under Article IV of the Geneva Convention for prisoner of war status and, therefore, are unlawful combatants.

THE COURT: Certainly the President is entitled to great deference in relation to the determination of an enemy combatant. No question about that. Whether one meets the criteria set forth in the Geneva Convention is a matter of law; is that correct?

MR. GARRE: Well, we think it's a matter in which the President should have the final say, but Judge Ellis went further –

THE COURT: If the President said that the Geneva Convention says you don't need a military tribunal, then whatever is in the Geneva Convention can be ignored; is that correct?

MR. GARRE: We think that the President is the final say on that political question, and –

THE COURT: I'm not talking about a political question. I'm asking you about a question of law. Isn't it a question of law whether a treaty applies or does not apply?

MR. GARRE: It can be in the appropriate context, yes, but the question of whether or not detainees are considered prisoners of war or that they fall into a different status, that ultimate determination was made by the President [87] here, and we think – Judge Ellis went further and discussed the criteria. He said in his words that the Taliban falls far short of meeting the criteria for a POW. And more importantly –

THE COURT: They may indeed fall short, because he indicated that they had no command units and that they had no designation and so forth. But nobody has given me that information. You have said to me we're not giving you anything, Judge.

MR. GARRE: Your Honor, we have presented the Court –

THE COURT: That's what you told me in no uncertain terms, didn't you, Mr. Garre?

MR. GARRE: We presented the Court with the Mobbs' Declaration.

THE COURT: You said we don't have to submit anything, we have the Mobbs' Declaration, and we want to rise or fall on it; isn't that right, Mr. Garre?

MR. GARRE: The government has explained in its motion to dismiss that the Mobbs' Declaration is adequate, it provides more than adequate factual basis for the military's determination that Mr. Hamdi is an enemy combatant.

THE COURT: You didn't want to give me any of Mr. Hamdi's statements, did you?

MR. GARRE: Your Honor, we submitted the Court with [88] the Mobbs' Declaration. And we think under the governing standard –

THE COURT: I tell you, it's hard to get an answer out of you, isn't it?

Well, you didn't. So I'll put it that way. How is that? You filed a thing saying you weren't going to do it; isn't that correct? And then you went to the Court of Appeals, and they said I have to look at this before I can do anything else.

MR. GARRE: We respectfully asked for relief from this court's order because we did think the Mobbs' Declaration would be sufficient. Now, if the Court were to conclude otherwise, then, as I said earlier, the government would have to consider its options, but we do think that the Mobbs' Declaration is sufficient. And that goes back to the cardinal principles of the Fourth Circuit recognized in its decision.

THE COURT: The problem I have is I have no desire to have an enemy combatant get out of any prisoner of war status he may be in, whatever the status is, whether he's illegal or legal or whatever you want to call it; however, I do think that the process requires something other than a bare assertion by someone by the name of Mobbs that they have looked at some papers and, therefore, they have determined that he should be held incommunicado. Just think about the concept of that. Is that what we're fighting for?

[89] MR. GARRE: Your Honor, I think the authorities we've relied on, the Court of Appeals relied on, is the established – long established, in the Court of

Appeals' words, authority to capture and detain enemy combatants. The Court of Appeals recognized if Mr. Hamdi is indeed an enemy combatant captured in Afghanistan during the hostilities his present detention is a lawful one. This is –

THE COURT: Why, therefore, should we not see what the basis of this decision – why it was made? Why is it so fearful that we should see the facts upon which that decision was made?

MR. GARRE: Your Honor, I think that the Mobbs' Declaration does provide the central criteria on which that decision was made. It explains that Mr. Hamdi went to Afghanistan to train with and, if necessary, fight with the Taliban. It explains Mr. Hamdi surrendered to Northern Alliance forces, gave – turned over his AK-47 to those forces.

THE COURT: Does Hamdi agree with that? Did Hamdi agree with that?

MR. GARRE: Your Honor, paragraph nine states in a subsequent interview Hamdi has confirmed –

THE COURT: I understand what paragraph nine said. I asked you, did Hamdi agree with that?

MR. GARRE: The declaration says what it states, and that's what the government –

[90] THE COURT: That's just –

MR. GARRE: The declaration makes clear Hamdi's own statements confirmed the government's determination.

THE COURT: The declaration says – you know, I can – Mr. Garre, I've been around too long.

MR. GARRE: Your Honor –

THE COURT: I've heard too many people make explanations of what certain things are. You know, I don't know why we can't see the facts, but we can't.

I'll look at this declaration. I will take some time and go over it again with a view in mind to what you've said, Mr. Garre, concerning the President. I will take into consideration that Judge Ellis has made a particular decision. And I will take into consideration those things that Mr. Mobbs, whomever he may be – nothing in here to say he's even an employee of the United States, but maybe some consultant or another. And he may be an excellent person. I'm not in any way reflecting on him, other than the fact this declaration doesn't tell me very much about him. Just didn't. He may be the most knowledgeable person about the East that ever has come down the pike. He may have read all the history books on Afghanistan, on the Near East.

MR. GARRE: Your Honor, the declaration explains his substantial involvement with these operations in paragraph one.

THE COURT: Mr. Garre, it's being – I can be [91] familiar – I'm familiar with the operations of this court, and that doesn't mean that because I think someone is guilty that they're guilty. A jury decides that. I may disagree with a jury. I may come to an entirely different conclusion than a jury after listening to the same evidence. So people may see or hear things differently.

MR. GARRE: The declaration also explains the military authorities in Afghanistan interviewed Mr. Hamdi and made this determination.

That goes to another point the Court raised about ambiguity about Northern Alliance forces or the conflict and struggle in Afghanistan. That's precisely one of the reasons why courts should defer to the military in making these sorts of determinations.

THE COURT: I'm trying to defer to the military. I go to the military regulations. You don't want to do those. You don't want to follow them. And, yet, I said, okay, then give me some information why you don't want to follow regulations. And you said we don't think they apply because he's an unlawful. But it doesn't say he's unlawful in here, as Mr. Dunham has pointed out.

MR. GARRE: It does say he is being considered as an enemy combatant because of his association with the Taliban. The President has determined the Taliban –

THE COURT: If that means he's a member of the unit [92] or he just went there – he may have gone there to train with them. It may be sufficient. I don't know. I'll look at it, Mr. Garre.

MR. GARRE: Thank you, Your Honor.

THE COURT: You may sit.

Anything else you want to tell me that you haven't brought up? Anything else? Anything else?

MR. DUNHAM: I just have one brief point, Your Honor.

THE COURT: I'll give Mr. Garre an opportunity to answer your one brief point, Mr. Dunham. Go ahead.

MR. DUNHAM: Mr. Garre repeatedly says we're not challenging the conditions of his confinement. What we're challenging by writ of habeas corpus is the basis upon which he's being confined, and we're saying he's not being confined as an enemy combatant in the Norfolk brig. He's being confined as an unlawful combatant. That's how he's being treated.

And we point to the – we say that detention as an unlawful combatant is unlawful. We say that solitary confinement since 1890 – this is a case in 1890 where they said solitary confinement was punishment of the worst kind. Here is what this gentleman had. This gentleman had access to attendants, the jailers, physician, spiritual advisor of his own selection.

THE COURT: That was –

MR. DUNHAM: Members of his –

[93] THE COURT: Not even an Army chaplain? He gets to choose what kind of chaplain?

MR. DUNHAM: Right. Members of his family could visit him. And he had access to counsel. And, yet, they said that was punishment of the worst kind. That's in 1890. One would think –

THE COURT: What's the name of that case?

MR. DUNHAM: *In re: Medley.* It's cited in our brief.

One would thing in over a hundred years we would have a little more enlightened view of things than they had in 1890. But, nevertheless, our point is he's being detained unlawfully. That's the purpose of the writ of habeas corpus. He's being detained as an unlawful enemy combatant, or worse, he's being detained as somebody who they just don't like and so they slapped a label on him and they're going to hold him that way. We don't think it's permissible. We don't think it's allowed for all the reasons we've stated.

THE COURT: All right, Mr. Garre. You've heard his position on that. Do you want to reply?

MR. GARRE: Your Honor, I just would refer the Court to what is in our papers and that we've already stated, and what the Fourth Circuit said, that if Mr. Hamdi is indeed an enemy combatant captured during hostilities in Afghanistan his present detention is a lawful one.

THE COURT: Let me ask you a question. The military [94] can do anything they want with him if that's the case; is that correct, without any tribunal, without anything? They can do anything?

MR. GARRE: What the military has said is it's treating the detainees –

THE COURT: I didn't ask you what they were doing with them.

MR. GARRE: – humanely.

THE COURT: I'm asking you as a matter of law can they do anything with him they want? Under your theory of law can they?

MR. GARRE: I think that his present detention is lawful if he's an enemy combatant.

THE COURT: I didn't ask you about the present detention. I'm asking you as a matter of law if a person is an unlawful combatant can the military do anything they want with him? What restraints are there on the military if he's an unlawful combatant? What restraints? Any?

MR. GARRE: Your Honor, I think under the authorities that we've relied upon, that the authorities made clear that –

THE COURT: Any restraint the military has?

MR. GARRE: – the detention is lawful, that the military has made clear they're treating the detainees humanely and consistent with international law.

THE COURT: Can I beg you to answer my question? My [95] question is simple. As a matter of law – we're just talking about the law now, nothing else. Assuming that a man is an unlawful combatant, what restraints are there on the military in relation to treatment?

MR. GARRE: I think the same restraints, if there are restraints, that would apply to Mr. Hamdi would apply to the Guantanamo detainees. And they would be the ones that Judge Kollar-Kotelly referred to in her recent decision, which is –

THE COURT: Okay. Prisoner of war restraints would apply to Hamdi; is that correct?

MR. GARRE: No, Your Honor.

THE COURT: You're saying the same restraints. I'm asking you what restraints. You know, define it. Tell me, what is the restraint, any restraint, anything?

MR. GARRE: Your Honor, I would refer the Court to Judge Kollar-Kotelly's recent decision in the Guantanamo –

THE COURT: I didn't ask you about somebody else's case.

MR. GARRE: I'm trying to answer your question by doing that. With respect, Your Honor, she referred to –

THE COURT: Tell me what you contend they are. Then you can recite what authorities you have.

MR. GARRE: They would be the international processes that take place between nations or nations, states, can communicate with one another on the appropriate conditions for [96] detainees.

THE COURT: Who communicates on behalf of unlawful detainees?

MR. GARRE: Well –

THE COURT: Unlawful combatants? Who is –

MR. GARRE: Your Honor, there have been communications with governments of –

THE COURT: What governments?

MR. GARRE: For instance, in this case Mr. Hamdi has made requests, as I understand it, to the Ambassador to Saudi Arabia.

THE COURT: Are we at war with Saudi Arabia?

MR. GARRE: No, Your Honor.

THE COURT: Then that's not the government he's battling for, is it?

MR. GARRE: We're talking about a different question, not whether or not we're at war with a particular government.

THE COURT: So his only recourse, then, is the government of the country of which he was a citizen, correct?

MR. GARRE: I don't think that that's correct, Your Honor.

THE COURT: So he has to depend upon them to contact the President of the United States in order to determine what restraints may or may not be imposed?

MR. GARRE: This question is not new. It was [97] addressed by the Supreme Court in the *Eisentrager* case. And it was addressed by Judge Kollar-Kotelly recently in the Guantanamo Bay detainees case. It's not a new situation.

The petitioners in this case have never relied on any claim – and, again, the Court has to go back to the claims in the petition in this case and the Fourth Circuit decision in this case.

THE COURT: How can they go back in the petition when they can't even talk to Hamdi? How do you – what happens here, you know, the government doesn't want anyone to talk to him other than some chaplain – we don't even know if it's a chaplain of his own faith – a chaplain, his custodian, and interrogators? And that's it, correct?

MR. GARRE: Those are the individuals I identified. We think the Fourth Circuit was right –

THE COURT: I must tell you – have you ever read *In Re: Medley*? I don't know what it says.

What court is it out of, Mr. Dunham?

MR. DUNHAM: It's the Supreme Court, Your Honor.

MR. GARRE: As I understand it, that case is factually quite distinguishable arising under different contexts and raising different issues.

THE COURT: I'm sure. I haven't read it. I don't know. He will read it.

MR. GARRE: I think what is relevant – and, again, I [98] point the Court to what the Fourth Circuit said in this case about Mr. Hamdi's present detention is it's lawful if the military has properly made that determination. And we think that it has.

THE COURT: So the military –

MR. GARRE: For the reasons –

THE COURT: If they sat him in boiling oil and they made that determination, would that be lawful?

MR. GARRE: I'm sorry? I didn't hear the Court's question.

THE COURT: If the military decided to put him in boiling oil, would that be lawful?

MR. GARRE: Your Honor, I don't think anyone has suggested that that has happened or would happen.

THE COURT: So some restraint on the military. What is the restraint?

MR. GARRE: If you go back and look at the *Thomasson* case in the Fourth Circuit, they talk about the political checks in the military, talk about the separation of powers in this sphere, and the Constitution does grant –

THE COURT: I certainly don't want to interfere with the military. I very much – I no have no desire to. But I do have a desire to see people are treated as human beings. I have to see to that.

MR. GARRE: The President made clear the detainees [99] are being treated humanely.

THE COURT: I'm sure the detainees in Guantanamo from – I've seen newsreels, or whatever you call it on television these days, where they talk to each other, they have lots of things, which certainly Mr. Hamdi does not have obviously.

MR. GARRE: Thank you, Your Honor.

THE COURT: And he's being treated differently, and we don't know why. Do you know why?

MR. GARRE: Your Honor, I believe the military has stated when it brought Mr. Hamdi to Norfolk that he was taken from Guantanamo when a determination was made that he possibly may be an American citizen. It's conceivable that Mr. Hamdi could be moved to a different facility. It's conceivable that other enemy combatants could be brought to Norfolk. When Mr. Hamdi was brought there

he happened to be the only enemy combatant. And he is today.

THE COURT: Well, you may be right, Mr. Garre. You may absolutely be right under the – it's possible. It seems somewhat strange, but it's possible.

MR. GARRE: Thank you, Your Honor.

MR. DUNHAM: Your Honor, without testing the Court's patience, there is one other point, if I could just briefly make as a result of what was said. If I could just make it real quickly.

[100] That is this point that if he's an enemy combatant his detention is lawful is the product of the Fourth Circuit doing what it kind of said this court shouldn't do, which is reaching too far before the District Court got a chance to bite on it. It's purely dicta at this point. The Fourth Circuit only decided that I couldn't see Hamdi under the order that the Court originally – that was the decision in the case. The rest of the language is purely dicta.

THE COURT: You have to take that up with them, Mr. Dunham. They put it out, and they've said it, and they've held it. That's the decision of the Court of Appeals that they made. They made it based on whatever Mr. – I assume whatever they heard in argument. I don't know. Must have been on some record. If they did, that's it. I can't very well say anything else, but I can determine whether he's being held in accordance with the Army regulations and the Geneva Convention and whether the Mobbs' Declaration is sufficient. And that's as far as I can go. I can't go any further under the restraints given me by the Court of Appeals.

I'm going to follow those restraints, Mr. Dunham. Your only recourse is to go to a higher court, I'm afraid. I'm not higher than they are.

Okay. Anything else? Anything you want to add, Mr. Garre?

MR. GARRE: No, Your Honor.

[101] THE COURT: Are you through, Mr. Dunham?

MR. DUNHAM: Yes, we are.

THE COURT: You'll hear from me in a couple of days. Let me think about this.

Court is in recess.

(Proceedings were adjourned at 1:10 p.m.)

CERTIFICATION

I certify that the foregoing is a correct transcript from the record of proceedings in the above-entitled matter.

/s/ Penny Commander Wile
Penny Commander Wile, RMR, CRR

August 14, 2002
Date

**IN THE UNITED STATES DISTRICT COURT
FOR THE EASTERN DISTRICT OF VIRGINIA
NORFOLK DIVISION**

YASER ESAM HAMDI, and
ESAM FOUAD HAMDI,
As Next Friend of Yaser Esam Hamdi,

      Petitioners,

v.   **CIVIL ACTION NO. 2:02cv439**

DONALD RUMSFELD, and
COMMANDER W.R. PAULETTE,

      Respondents.

ORDER

This case appears to be the first in American jurisprudence where an American citizen has been held incommunicado and subjected to an indefinite detention in the continental United States without charges, without any findings by a military tribunal, and without access to a lawyer. Despite the fact that Yaser Esam Hamdi ("Hamdi") has not been charged with an offense nor provided access to counsel, the Respondents contend that his present detention is lawful because he has been classified as an enemy combatant. Respondents' Response to, and Motion to Dismiss, the Petition for a Writ of Habeas Corpus ("Resp. Brief"), at 9. In denying the Respondents' Motion to Dismiss, the Court of Appeals for the Fourth Circuit rejected the Respondents' contention that the government's determination of Hamdi's status was beyond judicial review stating, "[i]n dismissing . . . with no meaningful judicial review, any American citizen alleged to be an enemy combatant could be detained indefinitely without charges or counsel on the government's say-so." Hamdi v. Rumsfeld, 296 F.3d 278, 282 (4th Cir. July 12, 2002) (emphasis added).

In this Court's hearing on the matter on August 13, 2002, the Respondents conceded that their determination of Hamdi's status was subject to judicial review. However, the Respondents argued that the Mobbs Declaration that it attached to its Response, in and of itself with no further evidence of any kind, was a sufficient factual basis to provide this Court with information adequate to dismiss the writ of habeas corpus. For the reasons stated below, this Court finds the Mobbs Declaration insufficient and once again **ORDERS** the Respondents to submit to the Court the materials previously requested in its July 31, 2002, Order, together with the screening criteria utilized to determine the status of Hamdi with the name(s) and address(es) of the persons who made the determination. The Respondents' Motion for Relief from this Court's production order of July 31, 2002, filed August 5, 2002, is **DENIED.** This Court is highly cognizant of the Respondents' concerns regarding any national security implications of the requested materials. The Court reiterates that the materials are to be produced solely for in camera review, ex parte, by the Court, in order to insure that the documents will in no possible way affect national security. The Court **ORDERS** that the sealed documents be produced by 4:30 p.m. on Wednesday, August 21, 2002, to this Division of this Court for the Judge's in camera review.

. . .

Discussion

This case represents the delicate balance that must be struck between the Executive's authority in times of armed conflict and the procedural safeguards that our Constitution provides for American citizens detained in the United States. Due to the uncertainty regarding Hamdi's status whether he was an enemy combatant, was an unlawful enemy combatant, or just a bystander, the legal considerations are further complicated by the protections potentially afforded by the international law of war as expressed in the Geneva Convention Relative to the Treatment of Prisoners of War, Aug. 12, 1949. 6 U.S.T. 3316, 75 U.N.T.S. 135 ("GPW"), to which the United States is a signatory. Depending on Hamdi's status, the joint service regulations governing the detention of captured enemy combatants or others may also be implicated. See Joint Service Regulation, Enemy Prisoners of War, Retained Personnel, Civilian Internees and Other Detainees (Oct. 1, 1997)(hereinafter Joint Service Regulation). These regulations "provide[] policy, procedures, and responsibility for the administration, treatment, employment, and compensation of enemy prisoners of war (EPW), retained personnel (RP), civilian internees (CI) and other detainees (OD) in the custody of U.S. Armed Forces." Id. at 1. The exact legal force of these regulations is not now determined, but the regulation states that it "implements international law, both customary and codified, relating to EPW, RP, CI, and ODs which includes those persons held during military operations other than war." Id. It specifically lists the GPW as one of the relevant treaties in its determination of international law. Id. At the very least, the Joint Service Regulation illustrates the U.S. military's position regarding its obligations under the GPW. Any decision regarding the legal effect of the GPW or the Joint Regulations would be premature at this point in the proceedings as it is necessary to first develop a factual background by which Hamdi's classification may be evaluated.[2] Under the facts that the Court has before it at this time, the Respondents have not shown that the requirements of the GPW nor the Joint Service Regulations, which apply regardless of the treaty, have been complied with. In light of the cautious procedures that the Court of Appeals outlined for this Court to follow, any determination of these issues would be premature as it is necessary to first develop a factual background.

   The judiciary has traditionally shown "great deference to the political branches when called upon to decide cases implicating sensitive matters of foreign policy, national security, or military affairs." Hamdi v. Rumsfeld, at 2000 WL 1483908, at *3. The Supreme Court has made it clear that the President is afforded deference when exercising his authority as Commander in Chief. Ex parte Quirin, 317 U.S. 1, 28–29 (1942). Deference is proper because of the Executive's special competency, and constitutional responsibility, over the conduct of overseas military operations. Deference to the President is particularly appropriate when Congress has authorized the Executive to "use

---

[2] The Joint Service Regulations as well as the treaty indicate that where a detainee's status may be in doubt that a military tribunal, appointed by the general courts-martial convening authority, must determine whether the detainee is a Prisoner of War. See Joint Service Regulation 1–6(b)("A competent tribunal shall determine the status of any person not appearing to be entitled to prisoner of war status who has committed a belligerent act or has engaged in hostile activities in aid of enemy armed forces, and who asserts that he or she is entitled to treatment as a prisoner of war, or concerning whom any doubt of a like nature exists."); Joint Service Regulation Glossary ("Other Detainee-Persons in the custody of the U.S. Armed Forces who have not been classified as an EPW (article 4, GPW), RP (article 33, GPW), or CI (article 78, GC), shall be treated as EPWs until a legal status is ascertained by competent authority."); GPW Art. 5("Should any doubt arise as to whether persons, having committed a belligerent act and having fallen into the hands of the enemy, belong to any of the categories enumerated in Article 4, such persons shall enjoy the protection of the present Convention until such time as their status has been determined by a competent tribunal.")(the GPW does not allude to general courts-martial convening authority).

all necessary and appropriate force against those nations, organizations, or persons he determines planned, authorized, committed, or aided the terrorist attacks that occurred on September 11, 2001, or harbored such organizations or persons." Authorization for Use of Military Force, Pub.L. No. 107–40, 115 Stat. 224 (2001). This deference extends to military designations of individuals as enemy combatants. Hamdi v. Rumsfeld, 2000 WL 1483908, at *4.

While it is clear that the Executive is entitled to deference regarding military designations of individuals, it is equally clear that the judiciary is entitled to a meaningful judicial review of those designations when they substantially infringe on the individual liberties, guaranteed by the United States Constitution, of American citizens. The scope of "any judicial inquiry into Hamdi's status as an alleged enemy combatant in Afghanistan must reflect a recognition that government has no more profound responsibility than the protection of Americans, both military and civilian, against additional unprovoked attack." Id. at 5. The standard of judicial inquiry must also recognize that the "concept of 'national defense' cannot be deemed an end in itself, justifying any exercise of [executive] power designed to promote such a goal. Implicit in the term 'national defense' is the notion of defending those values and ideals which sets this Nation apart.... It would indeed by ironic if, in the name of national defense, we would sanction the subversion of one of those liberties... which makes the defense of the Nation worthwhile." United States v. Robel, 389 U.S. 258, 264 (1967).

The Due Process Clause of the Fifth Amendment prohibits the government from "depriving" any person of liberty "without due process of law." U.S. Const. Amend. V. While Petitioners concede that Hamdi's initial detention in a foreign land during a period of ongoing hostilities is not subject, for obvious reasons, to a due process challenge, Petitioners argue that the continuing indefinite imprisonment on U.S. soil, in solitary confinement, and without access to counsel violates the detainee's Fifth Amendment rights. Petitioners' Traverse and Response to Respondents' Motion to Dismiss ("Pet. Brief"), at 20. For its part, the Respondents argue that Hamdi's due process rights have not been violated because of the "historical unavailability of any right to prompt charges or counsel for those held as enemy combatants." Resp. Brief, at 10. When asked during the August 13, 2002, hearing what, if any, constitutional protections Hamdi was entitled to, counsel for the Respondents responded that the Constitution applied to the same extent as "it did to the individual who was alleged to be an American citizen in the Quirin case." August 13, 2002, Hr'g Tr. at 7. Upon further questioning by the court, the Respondents' counsel conceded that the individual in Ex parte Quirin that it referred to was afforded access to counsel and the opportunity to defend himself before a military tribunal. Id. It is apparent that the defendant in Quirin to whom the Respondents referred was provided with a significantly broader measure of due process than Hamdi has received thus far. This Court finds that Hamdi is entitled to due process of law as provided by the Fifth Amendment to the United States Constitution.

The question then becomes whether the Respondents' classification of Hamdi's combatant status has violated his due process rights under the Constitution. The Respondents contend that the Mobbs Declaration is sufficient, by itself, to allow this Court to conduct a meaningful judicial review to insure that the government has not violated any of Hamdi's rights and protections. While recognizing the deference due to the Executive's decisions regarding combatant status classifications, the Court finds that a meaningful judicial review must, at a minimum, determine:

(1) Whether the government's classification of the detainee's status was determined pursuant to appropriate authority to make such determinations.

(2) Whether the screening criteria used to make and maintain the classification of an American born detainee held in the continental United States met sufficient procedural requirements as to be consistent with the Fifth Amendment's prohibition against governmental deprivation of life, liberty, or property without due process of law.

(3) On what basis has the government determined that the continuing detention of Hamdi without charges and without access to counsel serves national security.

(4) Whether the Geneva Treaty or the Joint Services Regulations required a different process.[3]

An examination of the Mobbs Declaration reveals that it falls far short of even these minimal criteria for judicial review. The Respondents produced the Mobbs Declaration as attachment 1 to its brief filed on July 25, 2002. The document is two pages long and consists of nine numbered paragraphs. The declaration is signed by a Michael H. Mobbs and dated July 24, 2002. A thorough examination of the Mobbs Declaration reveals that it leads to more questions than it answers.

The declaration fails to address the nature and authority of Mr. Mobbs to review and make declarations on behalf of the Executive regarding Hamdi's classification. Paragraph 1 of the Mobbs Declaration states that Mr. Mobbs is a Special Adviser to the Undersecretary of Defense for Policy. Mobbs Decl. at 1. The declaration does not indicate what authority a "Special Advisor" has regarding classification decisions of enemy combatants. Indeed, the declaration does not indicate whether Mr. Mobbs was appointed by the President, is an officer of the United States, is a member of the military, or even a paid employee of the government. During the August 13, 2002, hearing, when asked to explain Mr. Mobbs' authority and role in Hamdi's classification as an enemy combatant, the Respondents' counsel was unable to do so. Tr. at 10. In a general way, the declaration never refers to Hamdi as an "illegal" enemy combatant. The term is used constantly in Respondents' Memorandum. Nor is there anything in the declaration about intelligence or the gathering of intelligence from Hamdi. There is a huge amount of this in legal arguments. There is nothing to indicate why he is treated differently than all the other captured Taliban. There is no reason given for Hamdi to be in solitary confinement, incommunicado for over four months and being held for some eight-to-ten months without any charges of any kind. This is clearly an unreasonable length of time to be held in order to bring criminal charges.[4] So obviously criminal charges are not contemplated.

In Paragraph 2 of the Mobbs Declaration, Mr. Mobbs claims a familiarity with the policies and procedures applicable to Hamdi's detention. He claims to have reviewed the relevant records and reports regarding Hamdi's detention and capture. Mobbs Decl. at 1. The declaration does not answer under whose authority and by what procedures Mr. Mobbs engaged in such a review. Nor does it explain whether Mr. Mobbs is responsible for supervising the classification decisions of others. These are important considerations for any meaningful judicial review because the Court must be able to determine whether the person(s) making the classification decision did so with the authority of the Executive and pursuant to the statutes, rules, and regulations pertaining to such matters.

---

[3] Counsel for the Respondents indicate that the armed services did not have to follow the Joint Service Regulations when first taking Hamdi in custody. August 13, 2002, Hr'g Tr. 30, 31.

[4] Confinement for 48 hours triggers the right to a preliminary hearing. Riverside v. McLaughlin, 500 U.S. 44 (1991).

The declaration is insufficient to determine whether the screening criteria used by the government in classifying Hamdi and in making the decision to transfer Hamdi to the Norfolk Naval Brig violated his Fifth Amendment rights to the due process of law or violated the law or regulations of the Country. In paragraph 3 of the declaration, Mr. Mobbs states that Hamdi was "affiliated with a Taliban military unit and received weapons training." Id. The declaration makes no effort to explain what "affiliated" means nor under what criteria this "affiliation" justified Hamdi's classification as an enemy combatant. The declaration is silent as to what level of "affiliation" is necessary to warrant enemy combatant status. These are crucial determinations for purposes of judicial review. It does not say where or by whom he received weapons training or the nature and extent thereof.[5] Indeed, a close inspection of the declaration reveals that Mr. Mobbs never claims that Hamdi was fighting for the Taliban, nor that he was a member of the Taliban. Without access to the screening criteria actually used by the government in its classification decision, this Court is unable to determine whether the government has paid adequate consideration to due process rights to which Hamdi is entitled under his present detention.

In Paragraph 4 of the Mobbs Declaration, it indicates that Northern Alliance forces were engaged in battle with the Taliban. It does not say that the Taliban unit to which Hamdi was "affiliated" was ever in any battle while Hamdi's was "affiliated." Id. Nor does it identify the unit. Nor does it indicate who commanded the unit or the type of garb or uniform Hamdi may have worn when taken by the Northern Alliance. It further indicates after Hamdi "surrendered" that he kept his weapon.[6] He only gave up the weapon prior to being placed in prison. All the while he was under the care, custody and control of Northern Alliance forces. Whether the forces he surrendered to was led by a "war lord" or the unidentified unit to which he was "affiliated" was led by a "war lord" or whether the war lords changed sides is not set forth.

In paragraph 5 of the declaration, the U.S. interrogation team interviewed Hamdi while he was under the "Northern Alliance" control. It says that Hamdi identified himself as a Saudi citizen who had been born in the United States.[7] Mr. Mobbs claims that during the interview, Hamdi admitted that he "entered Afghanistan the previous summer to train with and, *if necessary*, fight for the Taliban." Id. (emphasis added). The Court notes that the declaration does not quote from this alleged admission from Hamdi, but rather appears to be paraphrased. A possible inference from Hamdi's alleged statement was that he was not fighting for the Taliban when he was surrendered to the Northern Alliance forces. It does not indicate what the "if necessary" connotes. Does it mean in self defense or did a threatened force from the Taliban make it "necessary?"

Paragraph 6 of the Declaration states Hamdi was originally classified as an enemy combatant by "military forces" based upon his interviews and in light of his association with the Taliban. Id. at 2. The document is silent on whose military forces, i.e. U.S. military forces or Northern Alliance forces, who originally classified Hamdi as an enemy combatant. If it was Northern Alliance forces that originally classified him, then it is unclear how Northern Alliance forces differentiated themselves from Taliban forces during the conflict. Was there some garb of each that made identification easy to participants? Is any individual associated with or near the Taliban an "enemy combatant?"

---

[5] Did someone give him a weapon and say "here's the safety and there's the trigger?"

[6] This doesn't sound like he was expected to fight or escape.

[7] The regulation required such a team to determine the name, rank, date of birth, city and country of birth, name and address of next of kin, date of capture, place of capture, capturing unit, circumstances of capture, nation in whose armed services the individual is serving and much more information. Joint Services Regulation 1–7.

In paragraph 7, Mr. Mobbs states that Hamdi was determined to meet the "criteria" for enemy combatants by the U.S. military screening team at the Sheberghan prison. Id. There is no mention of the criteria used to make such a determination.

In paragraph 8, the declaration states that "a Detainee Review and Screening Team established by Commander, U.S. Central Command reviewed Hamdi's record and determined he met the criteria established by the Secretary of Defense for individuals over whom U.S. forces should take control and transfer to Guantanamo Bay." Id. It is unclear whether the Detainee Review and Screening Team's criteria at Kandahar was the same criteria used to make the determination regarding Hamdi's status as an enemy combatant at Sheberghan. It does not list the criteria used.

In paragraph 9, the declaration asserts that a "subsequent interview of Hamdi has confirmed the fact that he surrendered and gave his firearm to Northern Alliance forces which supports his classification as an enemy combatant." Id. at 2. Again, it appears that Mr. Mobbs is merely paraphrasing a statement supposedly made by Hamdi. Due to the ease with which such statements may be taken out of context, the Court is understandably suspicious of the Respondents' assertions regarding statements that Hamdi is alleged to have made. While it may be premature, and eventually unnecessary, for the Court to bring Hamdi before it to inquire about these statements, the Court finds that it must be provided with complete copies of any statements by Hamdi in order to appropriately conduct a judicial review of his classification. Petitioners' counsel asserted at the hearing that some of these statements were unclassified and provided by the government to counsel for John Phillip Walker Lindh in a companion case in this district.

Without access to the screening criteria and Hamdi's statements, it is impossible to evaluate whether Mr. Mobbs is correct in his assertion that Hamdi's classification as an enemy combatant is justified. The Mobbs Declaration is little more than the government's "say-so" regarding the validity of Hamdi's classification as an enemy combatant. If the Court were to accept the Mobbs Declaration as sufficient justification for detaining Hamdi in the present circumstances, then it would in effect be abdicating any semblance of the most minimal level of judicial review. In effect, this Court would be acting as little more than a rubber-stamp. While the Respondents may very well be correct that Hamdi is appropriately classified as an enemy combatant, the Court is unwilling on the sparse facts before it to find so at this time. Obviously, the Respondents have the information as the United States military generally follows their own regulations.[8]

We must protect the freedoms of even those who hate us, and that we may find objectionable. If we fail in this task, we become victims of the precedents we create. We have prided ourselves on being a nation of laws applying equally to all and not a nation of men who have few or no standards. The warlords of Afghanistan may have been in the business of pillage and plunder. We cannot descend to their standards without debasing ourselves. We must preserve the rights afforded to us by our Constitution and laws for without it we return to the chaos of a rule of men and not of laws. Our Constitution was the first to develop a government of checks and balances. The legislative, executive, and judicial branches each check each other. While the Executive may very well be correct that Hamdi is an enemy combatant whose rights have not been violated, the Court is unwilling, on the sparse facts before it to find so at this time on the basis of the Mobbs Declaration. Therefore it is necessary to obtain the additional facts requested.

The Clerk of the Court is **DIRECTED** to transmit this Order via facsimile and U.S. mail to all counsel or record and to mail a copy to Yaser Esam Hamdi.

---

[8] Disobedience of regulations generally results in discipline actions.

IT IS SO ORDERED.

/s/ Robert G. Doumar

UNITED STATES DISTRICT JUDGE

. . .

PUBLISHED

UNITED STATES COURT OF APPEALS
FOR THE FOURTH CIRCUIT

YASER ESAM HAMDI; ESAM FOUAD
HAMDI, as next friend of Yaser
Esam Hamdi,
      Petitioners-Appellees,

      v.

DONALD RUMSFELD; W. R. PAULETTE,
Commander,
      Respondents-Appellants.

CENTER FOR CONSTITUTIONAL RIGHTS;
RICHARD L. ABEL, Connell Professor
of Law, University of California at
Los Angeles; WILLIAM J. ACEVES,
Professor of Law, California
Western School of Law; BRUCE A.
ACKERMAN, Sterling Professor of
Law & Political Science, Yale
University; LEE A. ALBERT,
Professor of Law, University at
Buffalo Law School, The State
University of New York; BARBARA
BADER ALDAVE, Loran L. Stewart
Professor of Corporate Law,
University of Oregon School of
Law; ALICIA ALVAREZ, Clinical
Associate Professor of Law, DePaul
University School of Law; DIANE
MARIE AMANN, Professor of Law,
University of California, Davis,
School of Law; MICHELLE J.
ANDERSON, Associate Professor of

No. 02-7338

...

Appeal from the United States District Court
for the Eastern District of Virginia, at Norfolk.
Robert G. Doumar, Senior District Judge.
(CA-02-439-2)

Argued: October 28, 2002

Decided: January 8, 2003

Before WILKINSON, Chief Judge, and WILKINS and
TRAXLER, Circuit Judges.

Reversed and remanded with directions to dismiss by published opinion. Opinion by WILKINSON, Chief Judge, and WILKINS and
TRAXLER, Circuit Judges, in which all three concur.

COUNSEL

ARGUED: Paul Clement, Deputy Solicitor General, UNITED
STATES DEPARTMENT OF JUSTICE, Washington, D.C., for
Appellants. Frank Willard Dunham, Jr., Federal Public Defender,
Norfolk, Virginia, for Appellees. **ON BRIEF:** Paul J. McNulty,
United States Attorney, Gregory G. Garre, Assistant to the Solicitor
General, David B. Salmons, Assistant to the Solicitor General, Law-
rence R. Leonard, Managing Assistant United States Attorney,
UNITED STATES DEPARTMENT OF JUSTICE, Washington,
D.C., for Appellants. Larry W. Shelton, Assistant Federal Public
Defender, Geremy C. Kamens, Assistant Federal Public Defender,
Norfolk, Virginia, for Appellees. David B. Rivkin, Jr., Lee A. Casey,
Darin R. Bartram, BAKER & HOSTETLER, L.L.P., Washington,
D.C., for Amici Curiae Ruth Wedgwood, et al. Shayana Kadidal, Bar-
bara Olshansky, Michael Ratner, William Goodman, CENTER FOR
CONSTITUTIONAL RIGHTS, New York, New York, for Amici
Curiae Center for Constitutional Rights, et al. Steven D. Benjamin,
Richmond, Virginia; Donald G. Rehkopf, Jr., BRENNA & BRENNA,
Rochester, New York, for Amicus Curiae Association of Criminal

Defense Lawyers. Steven R. Shapiro, Lucas Guttentag, Arthur N.
Eisenberg, Robin Goldfaden, AMERICAN CIVIL LIBERTIES
UNION FOUNDATION, New York, New York; Rebecca K. Glen-
berg, AMERICAN CIVIL LIBERTIES UNION OF VIRGINIA,
Richmond, Virginia, for Amici Curiae ACLU, et al.

OPINION

WILKINSON, Chief Judge, and WILKINS and TRAXLER, Circuit Judges:

Yaser Esam Hamdi filed a petition under 28 U.S.C. §2241 challenging the lawfulness of his confinement in the Norfolk Naval Brig.[1] On this third and latest appeal, the United States challenges the district court's order requiring the production of various materials regarding Hamdi's status as an alleged enemy combatant. The district court certified for appeal the question of whether a declaration by a Special Advisor to the Under Secretary of Defense for Policy setting forth what the government contends were the circumstances of Hamdi's capture was sufficient by itself to justify his detention. Because it is undisputed that Hamdi was captured in a zone of active combat in a foreign theater of conflict, we hold that the submitted declaration is a sufficient basis upon which to conclude that the Commander in Chief has constitutionally detained Hamdi pursuant to the war powers entrusted to him by the United States Constitution. No further factual inquiry is necessary or proper, and we remand the case with directions to dismiss the petition.

I.

. . .

In keeping with our earlier instruction that the district court should proceed cautiously in reviewing military decisions reached during sanctioned military operations, we directed the district court to first "consider the sufficiency of the Mobbs declaration as an independent matter before proceeding further." Following this order, the district court held a hearing on August 13 to review the sufficiency of the Mobbs declaration.

During this hearing, the district court recognized that "the government is entitled to considerable deference in detention decisions during hostilities." The court also noted that it did not "have any doubts [Hamdi] had a firearm [or] any doubts he went to Afghanistan to be with the Taliban." Despite these observations, however, the court asserted that it was "challenging everything in the Mobbs' declaration" and that it intended to "pick it apart" "piece by piece." The court repeatedly referred to information it felt was missing from the declaration, asking "Is there anything in here that said Hamdi ever fired a weapon?" The court questioned whether Mr. Mobbs was even a government employee and intimated that the government was possibly hiding disadvantageous information from the court.

. . .

II.

Yaser Esam Hamdi is apparently an American citizen. He was also captured by allied forces in Afghanistan, a zone of active military operations. This dual status – that of American citizen and that of alleged enemy combatant – raises important questions about the role of the courts in times of war.

A.

The importance of limitations on judicial activities during wartime may be inferred from the allocation of powers under our constitutional scheme. "Congress and the President,

---

[1] The court expresses its appreciation to the Public Defender's Office for the Eastern District of Virginia, the United States Attorney's Office for the Eastern District of Virginia, and the Solicitor General's Office for the professionalism of their efforts throughout these expedited appeals.

like the courts, possess no power not derived from the Constitution." *Ex parte Quirin*, 317 U.S. 1, 25 (1942). Article I, section 8 grants Congress the power to "provide for the common Defence and general Welfare of the United States . . . To declare War, grant Letters of Marque and Reprisal, and make Rules concerning Captures on Land and Water; To raise and support armies . . . [and] To provide and maintain a navy." Article II, section 2 declares that "[t]he President shall be Commander in Chief of the Army and Navy of the United States, and of the Militia of the several States, when called into the actual Service of the United States."

The war powers thus invest "the President, as Commander in Chief, with the power to wage war which Congress has declared, and to carry into effect all laws passed by Congress for the conduct of war and for the government and regulation of the Armed Forces, and all laws defining and punishing offences against the law of nations, including those which pertain to the conduct of war." *Quirin*, 317 U.S. at 26. These powers include the authority to detain those captured in armed struggle. *Hamdi II*, 296 F.3d at 281–82.[3] These powers likewise extend to the executive's decision to deport or detain alien enemies during the duration of hostilities, see *Ludecke v. Watkins*, 335 U.S. 160, 173 (1948), and to confiscate or destroy enemy property, *see Juragua Iron Co. v. United States*, 212 U.S. 297, 306 (1909).

Article III contains nothing analogous to the specific powers of war so carefully enumerated in Articles I and II. "In accordance with this constitutional text, the Supreme Court has shown great deference to the political branches when called upon to decide cases implicating sensitive matters of foreign policy, national security, or military affairs." *Hamdi II*, 296 F.3d at 281.

The reasons for this deference are not difficult to discern. Through their departments and committees, the executive and legislative branches are organized to supervise the conduct of overseas conflict in a way that the judiciary simply is not. The Constitution's allocation of the warmaking powers reflects not only the expertise and experience lodged within the executive, but also the more fundamental truth that those branches most accountable to the people should be the ones to undertake the ultimate protection and to ask the ultimate sacrifice from them. Thus the Supreme Court has lauded "[t]he operation of a healthy deference to legislative and executive judgments in the area of military affairs." *Rostker v. Goldberg*, 453 U.S. 57, 66 (1981).

The deference that flows from the explicit enumeration of powers protects liberty as much as the explicit enumeration of rights. The Supreme Court has underscored this founding principle: "The ultimate purpose of this separation of powers is to protect the liberty and security of the governed." *Metro. Wash. Airports Auth. v. Citizens for the Abatement of Aircraft Noise, Inc.*, 501 U.S. 252, 272 (1991). Thus, the textual allocation of responsibilities and the textual enumeration of rights are not dichotomous, because the textual separation of powers promotes a more profound understanding of our rights. For the judicial branch to trespass upon the exercise of the warmaking powers would be an infringement of the right to self-determination and self-governance at a time when the care of the common defense is most critical. This right of the people is no less a right because it is possessed collectively.

These interests do not carry less weight because the conflict in which Hamdi was captured is waged less against nation-states than against scattered and unpatriated

---

[3] Persons captured during wartime are often referred to as "enemy combatants." While the designation of Hamdi as an "enemy combatant" has aroused controversy, the term is one that has been used by the Supreme Court many times. *See, e.g., Madsen v. Kinsella*, 343 U.S. 341, 355 (1952); *In re Yamashita*, 327 U.S. 1, 7 (1946); *Quirin*, 317 U.S. at 31.

forces. We have emphasized that the "unconventional aspects of the present struggle do not make its stakes any less grave." *Hamdi II*, 296 F.3d at 283. Nor does the nature of the present conflict render respect for the judgments of the political branches any less appropriate. We have noted that the "political branches are best positioned to comprehend this global war in its full context," *id.*, and neither the absence of set-piece battles nor the intervals of calm between terrorist assaults suffice to nullify the warmaking authority entrusted to the executive and legislative branches.

B.

Despite the clear allocation of war powers to the political branches, judicial deference to executive decisions made in the name of war is not unlimited. The Bill of Rights which Hamdi invokes in his petition is as much an instrument of mutual respect and tolerance as the Fourteenth Amendment is. It applies to American citizens regardless of race, color, or creed. And as we become a more diverse nation, the Bill of Rights may become even more a lens through which we recognize ourselves. To deprive any American citizen of its protections is not a step that any court would casually take.

Drawing on the Bill of Rights' historic guarantees, the judiciary plays its distinctive role in our constitutional structure when it reviews the detention of American citizens by their own government. Indeed, if due process means anything, it means that the courts must defend the "fundamental principles of liberty and justice which lie at the base of all our civil and political institutions." *Powell v. Alabama*, 287 U.S. 45, 67 (1932) (internal quotation marks omitted). The Constitution is suffused with concern about how the state will wield its awesome power of forcible restraint. And this preoccupation was not accidental. Our forbears recognized that the power to detain could easily become destructive "if exerted without check or control" by an unrestrained executive free to "imprison, dispatch, or exile any man that was obnoxious to the government, by an instant declaration that such is their will and pleasure." 4 W. Blackstone, *Commentaries on the Laws of England* 349–50 (Cooley ed. 1899) (quoted in *Duncan v. Louisiana*, 391 U.S. 145, 151 (1968)).

The duty of the judicial branch to protect our individual freedoms does not simply cease whenever our military forces are committed by the political branches to armed conflict. The Founders "foresaw that troublous times would arise, when rulers and people would . . . seek by sharp and decisive measures to accomplish ends deemed just and proper; and that the principles of constitutional liberty would be in peril, unless established by irrepealable law." *Ex Parte Milligan*, 71 U.S. (4 Wall.) 2, 120 (1866). While that recognition does not dispose of this case, it does indicate one thing: The detention of United States citizens must be subject to judicial review. *See Hamdi II*, 296 F.3d at 283.

It is significant, moreover, that the form of relief sought by Hamdi is a writ of habeas corpus. In war as in peace, habeas corpus provides one of the firmest bulwarks against unconstitutional detentions. As early as 1789, Congress reaffirmed the courts' common law authority to review detentions of federal prisoners, giving its explicit blessing to the judiciary's power to "grant writs of habeas corpus for the purpose of an inquiry into the cause of commitment" for federal detainees. Act of Sept. 24, 1789, ch. 20, §14, 1 Stat. 81–82. While the scope of habeas review has expanded and contracted over the succeeding centuries, its essential function of assuring that restraint accords with the rule of law, not the whim of authority, remains unchanged. Hamdi's petition falls squarely within the Great Writ's purview, since he is an American citizen challenging his summary detention for reasons of state necessity.

C.

As the foregoing discussion reveals, the tensions within this case are significant. Such circumstances should counsel caution on the part of any court. Given the concerns discussed in the preceding sections, any broad or categorical holdings on enemy combatant designations would be especially inappropriate. We have no occasion, for example, to address the designation as an enemy combatant of an American citizen captured on American soil or the role that counsel might play in such a proceeding. *See, e.g., Padilla v. Bush*, No. 02 Civ. 445 (MBM), 2002 WL 31718308 (S.D.N.Y Dec. 4, 2002).We shall, in fact, go no further in this case than the specific context before us – that of the undisputed detention of a citizen during a combat operation undertaken in a foreign country and a determination by the executive that the citizen was allied with enemy forces.

The safeguards that all Americans have come to expect in criminal prosecutions do not translate neatly to the arena of armed conflict. In fact, if deference to the executive is not exercised with respect to military judgments in the field, it is difficult to see where deference would ever obtain. For there is a "well-established power of the military to exercise jurisdiction over members of the armed forces, those directly connected with such forces, [and] enemy belligerents, prisoners of war, [and] others charged with violating the laws of war." *Duncan v. Kahanamoku*, 327 U.S. 304, 313–14 (1946) (footnotes omitted). As we emphasized in our prior decision, any judicial inquiry into Hamdi's status as an alleged enemy combatant in Afghanistan must reflect this deference as well as "a recognition that government has no more profound responsibility" than the protection of American citizens from further terrorist attacks. *Hamdi II*, 296 F.3d at 283.

In this regard, it is relevant that the detention of enemy combatants serves at least two vital purposes. First, detention prevents enemy combatants from rejoining the enemy and continuing to fight against America and its allies. "The object of capture is to prevent the captured individual from serving the enemy. He is disarmed and from then on he must be removed as completely as practicable from the front. . . ." *In re Territo*, 156 F.2d 142, 145 (9th Cir. 1946). In this respect, "captivity is neither a punishment nor an act of vengeance," but rather "a simple war measure." W. Winthrop, *Military Law and Precedents* 788 (2d ed. 1920). And the precautionary measure of disarming hostile forces for the duration of a conflict is routinely accomplished through detention rather than the initiation of criminal charges. To require otherwise would impose a singular burden upon our nation's conduct of war.

Second, detention in lieu of prosecution may relieve the burden on military commanders of litigating the circumstances of a capture halfway around the globe. This burden would not be inconsiderable and would run the risk of "saddling military decisionmaking with the panoply of encumbrances associated with civil litigation" during a period of armed conflict. *Hamdi II*, 296 F.3d at 283–84. As the Supreme Court has recognized, "[i]t would be difficult to devise more effective fettering of a field commander than to allow the very enemies he is ordered to reduce to submission to call him to account in his own civil courts and divert his efforts and attention from the military offensive abroad to the legal defensive at home." *Johnson v. Eisentrager*, 339 U.S. 763, 779, (1950).[4]

---

[4] The government has contended that appointment of counsel for enemy combatants in the absence of charges would interfere with a third detention interest, that of gathering intelligence, by establishing an adversary

The judiciary is not at liberty to eviscerate detention interests directly derived from the war powers of Articles I and II. As the nature of threats to America evolves, along with the means of carrying those threats out, the nature of enemy combatants may change also. In the face of such change, separation of powers doctrine does not deny the executive branch the essential tool of adaptability. To the contrary, the Supreme Court has said that "[i]n adopting this flexible understanding of separation of powers, we simply have recognized Madison's teaching that the greatest security against tyranny . . . lies not in a hermetic division among the Branches, but in a carefully crafted system of checked and balanced power within each Branch." *Mistretta v. United States*, 488 U.S. 361, 381 (1989). If anything, separation of powers bears renewed relevance to a struggle whose unforeseeable dangers may demand significant actions to protect untold thousands of American lives.

The designation of Hamdi as an enemy combatant thus bears the closest imaginable connection to the President's constitutional responsibilities during the actual conduct of hostilities. We therefore approach this case with sensitivity to both the fundamental liberty interest asserted by Hamdi and the extraordinary breadth of warmaking authority conferred by the Constitution and invoked by Congress and the executive branch.

III.

After the district court issued its August 16 production order, it granted respondent's motion for an interlocutory appeal of that order. The following question was certified for our review:

> Whether the Mobbs Declaration, standing alone, is sufficient as a matter of law to allow a meaningful judicial review of Yaser Esam Hamdi's classification as an enemy combatant?

As the Supreme Court has made clear, we are not limited to this single question. Rather, an appellate court may address any issue fairly included within the certified order, because "it is the *order* that is appealable, and not the controlling question identified by the district court." *Yamaha Motor Corp., U.S.A. v. Calhoun*, 516 U.S. 199, 205 (1996) (internal quotation marks omitted).

On this appeal, it is argued that Hamdi's detention is invalid even if the government's assertions were entirely accurate. If that were clearly the case, there would be no need for further discovery such as that detailed in the August 16 production order, because Hamdi's detention would be invalid for reasons beyond the scope of any factual dispute. Indeed, any inquiry into the August 16 production order or any discussion of the certified question would be unnecessary, because neither could suffice to justify a detention that, as a threshold matter, was otherwise unlawful. Moreover, the burden of the August 16 order would necessarily outweigh any benefits if, quite independent of the disputed factual issues, Hamdi were already entitled to relief. *See* Fed. R. Civ. Proc. 26(b)(1)–(2). For that reason, any purely legal challenges to Hamdi's detention are fairly includable within the scope of the certified order. *See Juzwin v. Asbestos Corp.*, 900 F.2d 686, 692 (3d Cir. 1990) (stating that, on §1292(b) review of an order denying a dispositive motion, an appellate court is "free to consider all grounds advanced in support of the grant of [the

---

relationship with the captor from the outset. *See Hamdi II*, 296 F.3d at 282 (expressing concern that the June 11 order of the district court "does not consider what effect petitioner's unmonitored access to counsel might have upon the government's ongoing gathering of intelligence"). That issue, however, is not presented in this appeal.

motion] and all grounds suggested for sustaining its denial" (internal quotation marks omitted)).

In this vein, Hamdi and amici have in fact pressed two purely legal grounds for relief: 18 U.S.C. §4001(a) and Article 5 of the Geneva Convention. We now address them both.[5]

A.

18 U.S.C. §4001 regulates the detentions of United States citizens..... Hamdi argues that there is no congressional sanction for his incarceration and that §4001(a) therefore prohibits his continued detention. We find this contention unpersuasive.

Even if Hamdi were right that §4001(a) requires Congressional authorization of his detention, Congress has, in the wake of the September 11 terrorist attacks, authorized the President to "use *all necessary and appropriate force* against those nations, organizations, or persons he determines planned, authorized, committed, or aided the terrorist attacks" or "harbored such organizations or persons." Authorization for Use of Military Force, Pub.L. No. 107–40, 115 Stat. 224 (Sept. 18, 2001) (emphasis added). As noted above, capturing and detaining enemy combatants is an inherent part of warfare; the "necessary and appropriate force" referenced in the congressional resolution necessarily includes the capture and detention of any and all hostile forces arrayed against our troops. Furthermore, Congress has specifically authorized the expenditure of funds for "the maintenance, pay, and allowances of prisoners of war [and] other persons in the custody of the [military] whose status is determined . . . to be similar to prisoners of war." 10 U.S.C. §956(5) (2002). It is difficult if not impossible to understand how Congress could make appropriations for the detention of persons "similar to prisoners of war" without also authorizing their detention in the first instance.

Any alternative construction of these enactments would be fraught with difficulty. As noted above, the detention of enemy combatants serves critical functions. Moreover, it has been clear since at least 1942 that "[c]itizenship in the United States of an enemy belligerent does not relieve him from the consequences of [his] belligerency." *Quirin*, 317 U.S. at 37. If Congress had intended to override this well-established precedent and provide American belligerents some immunity from capture and detention, it surely would have made its intentions explicit.

It is likewise significant that §4001(a) functioned principally to repeal the Emergency Detention Act. That statute had provided for the preventive "apprehension and detention" of individuals inside the United States "deemed likely to engage in espionage or sabotage" during "internal security emergencies." H.R. Rep. 92–116, at 2 (Apr. 6, 1971). Proponents of the repeal were concerned that the Emergency Detention Act might, inter alia, "permit[ ] a recurrence of the round ups which resulted in the detention of Americans of Japanese ancestry in 1941 and subsequently during World War II." *Id*. There is no indication that §4001(a) was intended to overrule the longstanding rule that an armed and hostile American citizen captured on the battlefield during wartime may be treated like the enemy combatant that he is. We therefore reject Hamdi's contention that §4001(a) bars his detention.

---

[5] We reject at the outset one other claim that Hamdi has advanced in abbreviated form. He asserts that our approval of his continued detention means that the writ of habeas corpus has been unconstitutionally suspended. *See* U.S. Const. art. I, §9. We find this unconvincing; the fact that we have not ordered the relief Hamdi requests is hardly equivalent to a suspension of the writ.

B.

Hamdi and amici also contend that Article 5 of the Geneva Convention applies to Hamdi's case and requires an initial formal determination of his status as an enemy belligerent "by a competent tribunal." Geneva Convention Relative to the Treatment of Prisoners of War, Aug. 12, 1949, art. 5, 6 U.S.T. 3316, 75 U.N.T.S. 135.

This argument falters also because the Geneva Convention is not self-executing. "Courts will only find a treaty to be self-executing if the document, as a whole, evidences an intent to provide a private right of action." *Goldstar (Panama) v. United States*, 967 F.2d 965, 968 (4th Cir.1992). The Geneva Convention evinces no such intent. Certainly there is no explicit provision for enforcement by any form of private petition. And what discussion there is of enforcement focuses entirely on the vindication by diplomatic means of treaty rights inhering in sovereign nations. If two warring parties disagree about what the Convention requires of them, Article 11 instructs them to arrange a "meeting of their representatives" with the aid of diplomats from other countries, "with a view to settling the disagreement." Geneva Convention, at art. 11. Similarly, Article 132 states that "any alleged violation of the Convention" is to be resolved by a joint transnational effort "in a manner to be decided between the interested Parties." *Id*. at art. 132; *cf. id*. at arts. 129–30 (instructing signatories to enact legislation providing for criminal sanction of "persons committing . . . grave breaches of the present Convention"). We therefore agree with other courts of appeals that the language in the Geneva Convention is not "self-executing" and does not "create private rights of action in the domestic courts of the signatory countries." *Huynh Thi Anh v. Levi*, 586 F.2d 625, 629 (6th Cir. 1978) (applying identical enforcement provisions from the Geneva Convention Relative to the Protection of Civilian Persons in Time of War, Feb. 2, 1956, 6 U.S.T. 3516, 75 U.N.T.S. 287); *see also Holmes v. Laird*, 459 F.2d 1211, 1222 (D.C.Cir.1972) (noting that "corrective machinery specified in the treaty itself is nonjudicial").

Hamdi provides no reason to conclude that 28 U.S.C. §2241 makes these diplomatically-focused rights enforceable by a private right of petition. Indeed, it would make little practical sense for §2241 to have done so, since we would have thereby imposed on the United States a mechanism of enforceability that might not find an analogue in any other nation. This is not to say, of course, that the Geneva Convention is meaningless. Rather, its values are vindicated by diplomatic means and reciprocity, as specifically contemplated by Article 132. There is a powerful and self-regulating national interest in observing the strictures of the Convention, because prisoners are taken by both sides of any conflict. This is the very essence of reciprocity and, as the drafters of the Convention apparently decided, the most appropriate basis for ensuring compliance. As the Court in *Eisentrager* observed about the predecessor to the current Geneva Convention, "the obvious scheme of the Agreement [is] that responsibility for observance and enforcement of these rights is upon political and military authorities." 339 U.S. at 789 n.14.

Even if Article 5 were somehow self-executing, there are questions about how it would apply to Hamdi's case. In particular, it is anything but clear that the "competent tribunal" which would determine Hamdi's status would be an Article III court. Every country has different tribunals, and there is no indication that the Geneva Convention was intended to impose a single adjudicatory paradigm upon its signatories. Moreover, Hamdi's argument begs the question of what kind of status determination is necessary under Article 5 and how extensive it should be. Hamdi and the amici make much of the distinction between lawful and unlawful combatants, noting correctly that lawful combatants are not subject to punishment for their participation in a conflict. But for the purposes of this case, it is a distinction without a difference, since the option to detain until the cessation of hostilities belongs to the executive in either case. It is true that unlawful combatants are entitled to a proceeding before a military tribunal before they may be punished for the acts which render their belligerency unlawful. *Quirin*, 317 U.S. at 31. But they are also subject to mere detention in precisely the same way that lawful prisoners of war are. *Id*. The fact that Hamdi might be an unlawful combatant in no way means that the executive is required to inflict every consequence of that status on him. The Geneva Convention certainly does not require such treatment.

For all these reasons, we hold that there is no purely legal barrier to Hamdi's detention. We now turn our attention to the question of whether the August 16 order was proper on its own terms.

IV.

As we will discuss below, we conclude that Hamdi's petition fails as a matter of law. It follows that the government should not be compelled to produce the materials described in the district court's August 16 order.

We also note that the order, if enforced, would present formidable practical difficulties. The district court indicated that its production request might well be only an initial step in testing the factual basis of Hamdi's enemy combatant status. The court plainly did not preclude making further production demands upon the government, even suggesting that it might "bring Hamdi before [the court] to inquire about [his] statements."

Although the district court did not have "any doubts [that Hamdi] had a firearm" or that "he went to Afghanistan to be with the Taliban," the court ordered the government to submit to the court for in camera, ex parte review: (1) "[c]opies of all Hamdi's statements, and the notes taken from any interviews with Hamdi, that relate to his reasons for going to Afghanistan, his activities while in Afghanistan, or his participation in the military forces of the Taliban or any other organization in that country"; (2) "[a] list of all the interrogators who have questioned Hamdi, including their names and addresses, and the dates of the interviews"; (3) "[c]opies of any statements by members of the Northern Alliance" regarding Hamdi's surrender; (4) "[a] list that includes the date of Hamdi's capture, and that gives all the dates and locations of his subsequent detention"; (5) "[t]he name and title of the individual within the United States Government who made the determination that Hamdi was an illegal enemy combatant"; (6) "[t]he name and title of the individual within the United States Government who made the decision to move Hamdi from Guantanamo Bay, Cuba to the Norfolk Naval Station"; and (7) "the screening criteria utilized to determine the status of Hamdi." The court's order allows the government to redact "intelligence matters" from its responses, but only to the extent that those intelligence matters are outside the scope of inquiry into Hamdi's legal status.

Hamdi argues vigorously that this order should be affirmed. Because of the alleged "breadth with which Respondents construe their authority to imprison American citizens whom they consider to be enemy combatants," Br. of the Petitioners/Appellees at 27, Hamdi argues we must allow the district court to subject the government's classification of him to a searching review. While the ordinary §2241 proceeding naturally contemplates the prospect of factual development, *see* 28 U.S.C. §§2243, 2246, such an observation only begs the basic question in this case – whether further factual exploration would bring an Article III court into conflict with the warmaking powers of Article

I and II. Here, the specific interests asserted by the government flow directly from the warmaking powers and are intimately connected to them. Whatever the general force of these interests (which we discussed extensively above), they are most directly implicated by captures in a zone of active combat operations.

A review of the court's August 16 order reveals the risk of "stand[ing] the warmaking powers of Articles I and II on their heads," *Hamdi II*, 296 F.3d at 284. The district court, for example, ordered the government to produce all Hamdi's statements and notes from interviews. Yet it is precisely such statements, relating to a detainee's activities in Afghanistan, that may contain the most sensitive and the most valuable information for our forces in the field. The risk created by this order is that judicial involvement would proceed, increment by increment, into an area where the political branches have been assigned by law a preeminent role.

The district court further ordered the government to produce a list of all interrogators who have questioned Hamdi, including their names and addresses and the dates of the interviews, copies of any statements by members of the Northern Alliance regarding Hamdi's surrender, and a list that includes the date of Hamdi's capture and all the dates and locations of his subsequent detention. Once again, however, litigation cannot be the driving force in effectuating and recording wartime detentions. The military has been charged by Congress and the executive with winning a war, not prevailing in a possible court case. Complicating the matter even further is the fact that Hamdi was originally captured by Northern Alliance forces, with whom American forces were generally allied. The district court's insistence that statements by Northern Alliance members be produced cannot help but place a strain on multilateral efforts during wartime. The court also expressed concern in its order that the Northern Alliance did not "identify the unit [to which Hamdi was affiliated]," "where or by whom [Hamdi] received weapons training or the nature and extent thereof," or "who commanded the unit or the type of garb or uniform Hamdi may have worn...." In demanding such detail, the district court would have the United States military instruct not only its own personnel, but also its allies, on precise observations they must make and record during a battlefield capture.

Viewed in their totality, the implications of the district court's August 16 production order could not be more serious. The factual inquiry upon which Hamdi would lead us, if it did not entail disclosure of sensitive intelligence, might require an excavation of facts buried under the rubble of war. The cost of such an inquiry in terms of the efficiency and morale of American forces cannot be disregarded. Some of those with knowledge of Hamdi's detention may have been slain or injured in battle. Others might have to be diverted from active and ongoing military duties of their own. The logistical effort to acquire evidence from far away battle zones might be substantial. And these efforts would profoundly unsettle the constitutional balance.

For the foregoing reasons, the court's August 16 production request cannot stand.

V.

The question remains, however, whether Hamdi's petition must be remanded for further proceedings or dismissed.

Hamdi's American citizenship has entitled him to file a petition for a writ of habeas corpus in a civilian court to challenge his detention, including the military's determination that he is an "enemy combatant" subject to detention during the ongoing hostilities. Thus, as with all habeas actions, we begin by examining the precise allegations presented to us by the respective parties. In this case, there are two allegations that are crucial to our analysis. First, Hamdi's petition alleges that he was a resident of and seized in Afghanistan, a country in which hostilities were authorized and ongoing at the time of the seizure, but that his continued detention in this country without the full panoply of constitutional protections is unlawful. Second, the Government's response asserts that Hamdi is being detained pursuant to the Commander-in-Chief's Article II war powers and that the circumstances underlying Hamdi's detention, as reflected primarily in the Mobbs declaration, establish that Hamdi's detention is lawful.

Generally speaking, in order to fulfill our responsibilities under Article III to review a petitioner's allegation that he is being detained by American authorities in violation of the rights afforded him under the United States Constitution, we must first determine the source of the authority for the executive to detain the individual. Once the source of the authority is identified, we then look at the justification given to determine whether it constitutes a legitimate exercise of that authority.

A.

Here the government has identified the source of the authority to detain Hamdi as originating in Article II, Section 2 of the Constitution, wherein the President is given the war power. We have already emphasized that the standard of review of enemy combatant detentions must be a deferential one when the detainee was captured abroad in a zone of combat operations. The President "is best prepared to exercise the military judgment attending the capture of alleged combatants." *Hamdi II*, 296 F.3d at 283. Thus, in *Quirin*, the Supreme Court stated in no uncertain terms that detentions "ordered by the President in the declared exercise of his powers as Commander in Chief of the Army in time of war and of grave public danger" should not "be set aside by the courts without the clear conviction that they are in conflict with the Constitution or laws of Congress constitutionally enacted." *Quirin*, 317 U.S. at 25.

This deferential posture, however, only comes into play after we ascertain that the challenged decision is one legitimately made pursuant to the war powers. It does not preclude us from determining in the first instance whether the factual assertions set forth by the government would, if accurate, provide a legally valid basis for Hamdi's detention under that power. Otherwise, we would be deferring to a decision made without any inquiry into whether such deference is due. For these reasons, it is appropriate, upon a citizen's presentation of a habeas petition alleging that he is being unlawfully detained by his own government, to ask that the government provide the legal authority upon which it relies for that detention and the basic facts relied upon to support a legitimate exercise of that authority. Indeed, in this case, the government has voluntarily submitted – and urged us to review – an affidavit from Michael Mobbs, Special Advisor to the Under Secretary of Defense for Policy, describing what the government contends were the circumstances leading to Hamdi's designation as an enemy combatant under Article II's war power.

The Mobbs affidavit consists of two pages and nine paragraphs in which Mobbs states that he was "substantially involved with matters related to the detention of enemy combatants in the current war against the al Qaeda terrorists and those who support and harbor them." In the affidavit, Mobbs avers that Hamdi entered Afghanistan in July or August of 2001 and affiliated with a Taliban military unit. Hamdi received weapons training from the Taliban and remained with his military unit until his surrender to Northern Alliance forces in late 2001. At the time of his capture, Hamdi was in possession of an AK-47 rifle. After his capture, Hamdi was transferred first from

Konduz, Afghanistan to the prison in Mazar-e-Sharif, and then to a prison in She-berghan, Afghanistan where he was questioned by a United States interrogation team. This interrogation team determined that Hamdi met "the criteria for enemy combatants over whom the United States was taking control." Hamdi was then transported to the U.S. short term detention facility in Kandahar, and then transferred again to Guantanamo Bay and eventually to the Norfolk Naval Brig. According to Mobbs, a subsequent interview with Hamdi confirmed the details of his capture and his status as an enemy combatant.

The district court approached the Mobbs declaration by examining it line by line, faulting it for not providing information about whether Hamdi had ever fired a weapon, the formal title of the Taliban military unit Hamdi was with when he surrendered, the exact composition of the U.S. interrogation team that interviewed Hamdi in Sheberghan, and even the distinguishing characteristics between a Northern Alliance miliary unit and a Taliban military unit. Concluding that the factual allegations were insufficient to support the government's assertion of the power to detain Hamdi under the war power, the court then ordered the production of the numerous additional materials outlined previously. We think this inquiry went far beyond the acceptable scope of review.

To be sure, a capable attorney could challenge the hearsay nature of the Mobbs declaration and probe each and every paragraph for incompleteness or inconsistency, as the district court attempted to do. The court's approach, however, had a signal flaw. We are not here dealing with a defendant who has been indicted on criminal charges in the exercise of the executive's law enforcement powers. We are dealing with the executive's assertion of its power to detain under the war powers of Article II. *See Eisentrager*, 339 U.S. at 793 (Black, J., dissenting) ("[I]t is no 'crime' to be a soldier."); *cf. In re Winship*, 397 U.S. 358, 363 (1970) (explaining that elevated burden of proof applies in criminal cases because of consequences of conviction, including social stigma). To transfer the instinctive skepticism, so laudable in the defense of criminal charges, to the review of executive branch decisions premised on military determinations made in the field carries the inordinate risk of a constitutionally problematic intrusion into the most basic responsibilities of a coordinate branch.

The murkiness and chaos that attend armed conflict mean military actions are hardly immune to mistake. Yet these characteristics of warfare have been with us through the centuries and have never been thought sufficient to justify active judicial supervision of combat operations overseas. To inquire, for example, whether Hamdi actually fired his weapon is to demand a clarity from battle that often is not there. The district court, after reviewing the Mobbs affidavit, did not "have any doubts [Hamdi] had a firearm [or] any doubts he went to Afghanistan to be with the Taliban." To delve further into Hamdi's status and capture would require us to step so far out of our role as judges that we would abandon the distinctive deference that animates this area of law.

For these reasons, and because Hamdi was indisputably seized in an active combat zone abroad, we will not require the government to fill what the district court regarded as gaps in the Mobbs affidavit. The factual averments in the affidavit, if accurate, are sufficient to confirm that Hamdi's detention conforms with a legitimate exercise of the war powers given the executive by Article II, Section 2 of the Constitution and, as discussed elsewhere, that it is consistent with the Constitution and laws of Congress. *See Quirin*, 317 U.S. at 25. Asking the executive to provide more detailed factual assertions would be to wade further into the conduct of war than we consider appropriate and is unnecessary to a meaningful judicial review of this question.

B.

We turn then to the question of whether, because he is an American citizen currently detained on American soil by the military, Hamdi can be heard in an Article III court to rebut the factual assertions that were submitted to support the "enemy combatant" designation. We hold that no evidentiary hearing or factual inquiry on our part is necessary or proper, because it is undisputed that Hamdi was captured in a zone of active combat operations in a foreign country and because any inquiry must be circumscribed to avoid encroachment into the military affairs entrusted to the executive branch.

In support of its contention that no further factual inquiry is appropriate, the government has argued that a "some evidence" standard should govern the adjudication of claims brought by habeas petitioners in areas where the executive has primary responsibility. That standard has indeed been employed in contexts less constitutionally sensitive than the present one, albeit in a procedural posture that renders those cases distinguishable. *See, e.g., INS v. St. Cyr,* 533 U.S. 289, 306 (2001) (describing historical practice under which, so long as "there was some evidence to support" a deportation order, habeas courts would not "review factual determinations made by the Executive"); *Eagles v. Samuels,* 329 U.S. 304, 312 (1946); *Fernandez v. Phillips,* 268 U.S. 311, 312 (1925). In each of these cases, the Court indicated that the role of the writ is not to correct "mere error" in the executive's exercise of a discretionary power, but rather to check the executive branch if it asserts a "power to act beyond the authority granted." *Eagles,* 329 U.S. at 311–12. Thus, the government asserts, the role of a habeas court is not to reconsider the executive's decision, but rather only to confirm that "there was some basis for the challenged executive determination." Br. for Respondents-Appellants at 29. Once that determination is made, the government further asserts, the detainee may not offer any rebuttal evidence and no further factual inquiry is allowed.

It is not necessary for us to decide whether the "some evidence" standard is the correct one to be applied in this case because we are persuaded for other reasons that a factual inquiry into the circumstances of Hamdi's capture would be inappropriate.

1.

As we have emphasized throughout these appeals, we cannot set aside executive decisions to detain enemy combatants "without the clear conviction that they are in conflict with the Constitution or laws of Congress constitutionally enacted." *Quirin,* 317 U.S. at 25, 63. We cannot stress too often the constitutional implications presented on the face of Hamdi's petition. The constitutional allocation of war powers affords the President extraordinarily broad authority as Commander in Chief and compels courts to assume a deferential posture in reviewing exercises of this authority. And, while the Constitution assigns courts the duty generally to review executive detentions that are alleged to be illegal, the Constitution does not specifically contemplate any role for courts in the conduct of war, or in foreign policy generally.

Indeed, Article III courts are ill-positioned to police the military's distinction between those in the arena of combat who should be detained and those who should not. Any evaluation of the accuracy of the executive branch's determination that a person is an enemy combatant, for example, would require courts to consider, first, what activities the detainee was engaged in during the period leading up to his seizure and, second, whether those activities rendered him a combatant or not. The first question is factual and, were we called upon to delve into it, would likely entail substantial efforts to acquire evidence from distant battle zones. *See Eisentrager,* 339 U.S. at 779. The second question may require fine judgments about whether a particular activity is linked to the war efforts of a hostile power – judgments the executive branch is most competent to make.

Hamdi's petition places him squarely within the zone of active combat and assures that he is indeed being held in accordance with the Constitution and Congressional authorization for use of military force in the wake of al Qaida's attack. *Quirin*, 317 U.S. at 25. Any effort to ascertain the facts concerning the petitioner's conduct while amongst the nation's enemies would entail an unacceptable risk of obstructing war efforts authorized by Congress and undertaken by the executive branch.

2.

Hamdi contends that, although international law and the laws of this country might generally allow for the detention of an individual captured on the battlefield, these laws must vary in his case because he is an American citizen now detained on American soil. As an American citizen, Hamdi would be entitled to the due process protections normally found in the criminal justice system, including the right to meet with counsel, if he had been charged with a crime. But as we have previously pointed out, Hamdi has not been charged with any crime. He is being held as an enemy combatant pursuant to the well-established laws and customs of war. Hamdi's citizenship rightfully entitles him to file this petition to challenge his detention, but the fact that he is a citizen does not affect the legality of his detention as an enemy combatant.

Indeed, this same issue arose in *Quirin*. In that case, petitioners were German agents who, after the declaration of war between the United States and the German Reich, were trained at a German sabotage school where they "were instructed in the use of explosives and in methods of secret writing." *Quirin*, 317 U.S. at 21. The petitioners then journeyed by submarine to the beaches of New York and Florida, carrying large quantities of explosives and other sabotage devices. All of them were apprehended by FBI agents, who subsequently learned of their mission to destroy war industries and facilities in the United States. All of the petitioners were born in Germany but had lived in the United States at some point. One petitioner claimed American citizenship by virtue of the naturalization of his parents during his youth. The Court, however, did not need to determine his citizenship because it held that the due process guarantees of the Fifth and Sixth Amendments were inapplicable in any event. It noted that "[c]itizenship in the United States of an enemy belligerent does not relieve him from the consequences of a belligerency which is unlawful." *Id.* at 37. The petitioner who alleged American citizenship was treated identically to the other German saboteurs.

The *Quirin* principle applies here. One who takes up arms against the United States in a foreign theater of war, regardless of his citizenship, may properly be designated an enemy combatant and treated as such. The privilege of citizenship entitles Hamdi to a limited judicial inquiry into his detention, but only to determine its legality under the war powers of the political branches. At least where it is undisputed that he was present in a zone of active combat operations, we are satisfied that the Constitution does not entitle him to a searching review of the factual determinations underlying his seizure there.

3.

Similarly, we reject Hamdi's argument that even if his initial detention in Afghanistan was lawful, his continuing detention on American soil is not. Specifically, Hamdi contends that his petition does not implicate military concerns because "the under-lying claims in this case are designed to test the legality of Hamdi's imprisonment in a naval brig in Norfolk, Virginia, not a military determination made overseas on the basis of caution rather than accuracy." Br. of the Petitioners/Appellees at 44. But the fact that Hamdi is presently being detained in the United States – as opposed to somewhere overseas – does not affect the legal implications of his status as an enemy combatant. For the same reason that courts are ill-positioned to review the military's distinction between those who should or should not be detained in an arena of combat, courts are not in the position to overturn the military's decision to detain those persons in one location or another. It is not clear why the United States should be precluded from exercising its discretion to move a detainee to a site within this country, nor do we see what purpose would be served by second guessing the military's decision with respect to the locus of detention.

4.

To conclude, we hold that, despite his status as an American citizen currently detained on American soil, Hamdi is not entitled to challenge the facts presented in the Mobbs declaration. Where, as here, a habeas petitioner has been designated an enemy combatant and it is undisputed that he was captured in an zone of active combat operations abroad, further judicial inquiry is unwarranted when the government has responded to the petition by setting forth factual assertions which would establish a legally valid basis for the petitioner's detention. Because these circumstances are present here, Hamdi is not entitled to habeas relief on this basis.

C.

Finally, we address Hamdi's contention that even if his detention was at one time lawful, it is no longer so because the relevant hostilities have reached an end. In his brief, Hamdi alleges that the government "confuses the international armed conflict that allegedly authorized Hamdi's detention in the first place with an on-going fight against individuals whom Respondents refuse to recognize as 'belligerents' under international law." *Id.* at 53–54. Whether the timing of a cessation of hostilities is justiciable is far from clear. *See Ludecke*, 335 U.S. at 169 ("Whether and when it would be open to this Court to find that a war though merely formally kept alive had in fact ended, is a question too fraught with gravity even to be adequately formulated when not compelled."). The executive branch is also in the best position to appraise the status of a conflict, and the cessation of hostilities would seem no less a matter of political competence than the initiation of them. *See United States v. The Three Friends*, 166 U.S. 1, 63 (1897) ("[I]t belongs to the political department to determine when belligerency shall be recognized, and its action must be accepted according to the terms and intention expressed."). In any case, we need not reach this issue here. The government notes that American troops are still on the ground in Afghanistan, dismantling the terrorist infrastructure in the very country where Hamdi was captured and engaging in reconstruction efforts which may prove dangerous in their own right. Because under the most circumscribed definition of conflict hostilities have not yet reached their end, this argument is without merit.

VI.

It is important to emphasize that we are not placing our imprimatur upon a new day of executive detentions. We earlier rejected the summary embrace of "a sweeping proposition – namely that, with no meaningful judicial review, any American citizen alleged to be an enemy combatant could be detained indefinitely without charges or counsel on the government's say-so." *Hamdi II*, 296 F.3d at 283. But, Hamdi is not "any American citizen alleged to be an enemy combatant" by the government; he is an American citizen captured and detained by American allied forces in a foreign theater of war during active hostilities and determined by the United States military to have been indeed allied with enemy forces.

Cases such as Hamdi's raise serious questions which the courts will continue to treat as such. The nation has fought since its founding for liberty without which security rings hollow and for security without which liberty cannot thrive. The judiciary was meant to respect the delicacy of the balance, and we have endeavored to do so.

The events of September 11 have left their indelible mark. It is not wrong even in the dry annals of judicial opinion to mourn those who lost their lives that terrible day. Yet we speak in the end not from sorrow or anger, but from the conviction that separation of powers takes on special significance when the nation itself comes under attack. Hamdi's status as a citizen, as important as that is, cannot displace our constitutional order or the place of the courts within the Framer's scheme. Judicial review does not disappear during wartime, but the review of battlefield captures in overseas conflicts is a highly deferential one. That is why, for reasons stated, the judgment must be reversed and the petition dismissed. It is so ordered.

PUBLISHED

UNITED STATES COURT OF APPEALS
FOR THE FOURTH CIRCUIT

YASER ESAM HAMDI; ESAM FOUAD
HAMDI, as next friend of Yaser
Esam Hamdi,
> *Petitioners-Appellees,*

v.

DONALD RUMSFELD; W. R. PAULETTE,
Commander,
> *Respondents-Appellants.*

RUTH WEDGWOOD, Professor of Law,
Yale University Law School, and
Edward B. Burling Professor of
International Law and Diplomacy,
Johns Hopkins University; SAMUEL
ESTREICHER, Professor of Law, New   No. 02-7338
York University School of Law;
RONALD ROTUNDA, George Mason
University Foundation Professor of
Law, George Mason University
School of Law; DOUGLAS W. KMIEC,
Dean & St. Thomas More Professor
of Law, Catholic University; DAVID
B. RIVKIN, JR.; LEE A. CASEY; DARIN
R. BARTRAM;
> *Amici Curiae in support of*
> *Appellants.*

CENTER FOR CONSTITUTIONAL RIGHTS;
RICHARD L. ABEL, Connell Professor
of Law, University of California at
Los Angeles; WILLIAM J. ACEVES,

. . .

HAMDI v. RUMSFELD   15

of Law; NATIONAL ASSOCIATION OF
CRIMINAL DEFENSE LAWYERS;
AMERICAN CIVIL LIBERTIES UNION
FOUNDATION; ACLU FOUNDATION OF
VIRGINIA,
> *Amici Curiae in support*
> *of Appellees.*

Filed: July 9, 2003

ORDER

---

* This document consists of an order denying rehearing followed by two concurrences and two dissents. Because the concurrences are primarily responses to the dissents, the reader might find it useful to read the dissents first. – *Eds.*

Appellees filed a petition for rehearing and suggestion for rehearing en banc.

The panel voted to deny panel rehearing.

A member of the Court requested a poll on the petition for rehearing en banc, and a majority of the judges in active service voted to deny rehearing en banc. Judges Luttig, Motz, King, and Gregory voted to grant rehearing en banc. Chief Judge Wilkins, and Judges Widener, Wilkinson, Niemeyer, Williams, Michael, Traxler, and Shedd voted to deny rehearing en banc.

Judge Wilkinson filed an opinion, concurring in the denial of rehearing en banc. Judge Traxler filed an opinion, concurring in the denial of rehearing en banc. Judge Luttig filed an opinion, dissenting from the denial of rehearing en banc. Judge Motz filed an opinion, dissenting from the denial of rehearing en banc.

The Court denies the petition for rehearing and suggestion for rehearing en banc. The mandate shall issue forthwith.

Entered at the direction of Judge Wilkinson for the Court.

WILKINSON, Circuit Judge, concurring in the denial of rehearing en banc:

I concur in the denial of the rehearing en banc. The panel opinion written by Chief Judge Wilkins, Judge Traxler, and myself has already properly resolved this case. *See Hamdi v. Rumsfeld*, 316 F.3d 450 (4th Cir. 2003). I thus offer only these few comments in response to the dissent of my good colleague Judge Motz.

. . .

My colleague's desire for more and more information signals not the end of a constitutionally intrusive inquiry, but the beginning. To start down this road of litigating what Hamdi was actually doing among the enemy or to what extent he was aiding the enemy is to bump right up against the war powers of Articles I and II. Judges are ill equipped to serve as final and ultimate arbiters of the degree to which litigation should be permitted to burden foreign military operations. The ingredients essential to military success – its planning, tactics, and intelligence – are beyond our ken, and the courtroom is a poor vantage point for the breadth of comprehension that is required to conduct a military campaign on foreign soil.

Because I think it both unreasonable and unfair to expect either judges or attorneys to discard a lifetime of honed instinct, I suspect that in time, if the course of the dissent is followed, the norms of the criminal justice process would come to govern the review of battlefield detentions in federal court. The prospect of such extended litigation would operate to inhibit our armed forces in taking the steps they need to win a war. The specter of hindsight in the courtroom would haunt decision-making in the field. At a minimum, if rules are to be prescribed for litigating something as sensitive as the soundness of battlefield detentions in Article III courts, then the prescription should come from Congress or the Executive – the branches of government charged by our Constitution with the conduct of foreign war. I cannot conceive of the courts on their own motion – without the considered input of the political branches – devising a set of procedures allowing prisoners of war to hold American commanders accountable in federal court. If any illustration of the difficulties and hazards of such a judicial enterprise were needed, the history of Hamdi's case should more than suffice.

. . .

In sum, this petition was properly dismissed.

TRAXLER, Circuit Judge, concurring in the denial of rehearing en banc:

In their dissents from the denial of rehearing, my colleagues have appreciated the nature and magnitude of the competing interests at stake here. However, because I believe that their opinions at times have unfairly and inaccurately characterized the panel opinion, I regrettably find myself drawn to offer a few comments in response.[1]

I.

Each of my dissenting colleagues argues that the panel erred in premising its decision on the "admission" that Yaser Esam Hamdi was captured within the boundaries of Afghanistan. Judge Luttig questions whether any such admission was made, at least in the petition, and Judge Luttig and Judge Motz both believe that any such admission should be ineffective because it was made by Hamdi's father, Esam Fouad Hamdi, acting as Yaser Esam Hamdi's "next friend," and not directly by Yaser Esam Hamdi.

A.

. . .

. . . Judge Luttig correctly observes that the habeas petition does not *explicitly* state that "Hamdi was captured in a zone of active combat in a foreign theater of conflict." *Id.* However, from this single pleading omission, Judge Luttig inexplicably leaps to the conclusion that the remaining petition allegations are ambiguous on the question (or, worse, that we should ignore them) and, even more inexplicably, to the belief that when responding to a dissent to a denial for rehearing en banc, the panel has somehow forfeited a right to point to any other pleading or representation filed or otherwise made *by the petitioner* that supports the observation, unremarkable when made, that Hamdi was indeed in Afghanistan when captured.

First, the petition's failure to affirmatively state that Hamdi was captured in a foreign combat zone did not and still does not compel me to ignore the other allegations that are present, nor does it cause me to consider that the place of Hamdi's capture is a matter of dispute. As Judge Wilkinson has pointed out, the petition alleges that "[w]hen seized by the United States Government, Mr. Hamdi resided in Afghanistan.". . .[3] Were this the only allegation made, I suppose I could speculate about whether Hamdi had traveled from his "reside[nce] in Afghanistan" to another country "when [and where he was] seized by the United States Government," but I need not do so. . . . Significantly, the one statement quoted above is not the only allegation made; the petition provides a great deal more information than that. It avers that, following the terrorist attacks on September 11, 2001, "the United States initiated military action against the Taliban Government in Afghanistan," and that, "in the course of the military campaign, . . . , the United States provided military assistance to the Northern Alliance." . . . As a result of this military assistance in Afghanistan, the petition states that

> the United States obtained access to individuals held by various factions of the Northern Alliance. On information and belief, Mr. Hamdi was captured or transferred into the custody of the United States in the Fall of 2001.

. . . It goes on to allege that "[o]n or about January 11, 2002, the United States military began transporting prisoners captured in Afghanistan to Camp X-Ray at the United

---

[1] Because Judge Wilkinson has already written eloquently, and primarily, in response to Judge Motz's dissent, I focus my comments chiefly on matters raised by Judge Luttig.

[3] According to later representations made by his father, Hamdi left "Saudi Arabia for Pakistan and then Afghanistan on July 15, 2001 to do relief work in those countries," and became "trapped in Afghanistan once the military campaign began.". . .

States Naval Base in Guantanamo Bay, Cuba," and that on or about that same date, "the United States military transferred Yaser Esam Hamdi to Camp X-Ray, Guantanamo Bay." . . .

When we authored the panel opinion, I did not consider these petition allegations to be ambiguous, nor do I today. A plain reading of the submission to us made clear that Esam Fouad Hamdi, as next friend to Yaser Esam Hamdi and as his father, based his claims in large part on the fact that Yaser was seized in Afghanistan in the course of the United States military operations within that country. His contention was that the United States military should release Yaser because he was not in Afghanistan to fight us or our allies and, therefore, was not *properly* being held as an "enemy combatant" by our military forces.

. . .

Additionally, as Judge Motz has observed in her dissent, we had been presented in the Joint Appendix with a letter written by Hamdi's father to United States Senator Patrick Leahy (which *petitioner* had submitted to the district court). In the letter, Hamdi's father stated that Yaser had "left our home in Saudi Arabia for Pakistan and then Afghanistan on July 15, 2001 to do relief work in those countries," "was trapped in Afghanistan once the military campaign began," and "was caught up in a local dragnet of non-Afghans in Mazar-e-Sharif in Afghanistan in November 2001" along with John Walker Lindh. . . . He was then "kept in [an] Afghanistan jail for 2–3 months prior to being moved to Guantanamo Bay where he stayed for 2 months before they confirmed that he [was] an American citizen, then they moved him to the Norfolk jail." . . . At no time was it ever hypothesized that Hamdi might not have been in Afghanistan when he was seized. Indeed, it was affirmatively represented that Hamdi was "caught at the same time Mr. John Walker Lindh was caught" in Afghanistan, but that he was "not [being] treated the same way," and was not properly determined to be "an enemy combatant." . . . . [6]

. . .

I cannot base a decision in so momentous a case on the theoretical possibility that the general allegations in the petition – that the United States obtained access to Hamdi and other prisoners in the custody of the Northern Alliance in Afghanistan and transferred these prisoners "captured in Afghanistan" to Guantanamo Bay – are wrong and do not apply to Hamdi's situation. Indeed, it would be ludicrous for us to somehow presume that they were not intended to be believed. Nor do I know of any precedent that would prompt us here to ignore the factual representations made by the petitioner and counsel in support of the petition. . . . .

. . .

IV.

Finally, while I fully recognize that we have not gone as far as Judge Luttig would have us go, I take umbrage at his charge that this panel, as a result of "decisional paralysis," has "retreated" from its constitutional duty to decide this case based upon the facts presented and, instead, has fabricated a fact to ease our task. Nothing could be further from the truth. The government makes no such charge, no doubt cognizant that, in accordance with time-honored principles of constitutional decision-making, we

---

[6] *See United States v. Lindh*, 227 F.Supp.2d 565 (E.D.Va. 2002); *United States v. Lindh*, 212 F.Supp.2d 541 (E.D.Va. 2002); *United States v. Lindh*, 198 F.Supp.2d 739 (E.D.Va. 2002).

have gone no further than necessary to resolve the delicate balance of constitutional interests before us.... Nor, for that matter, does the petitioner, who argues not that Yaser's presence in Afghanistan was a matter of dispute, but only that we should not as a legal matter rely upon the allegations of the petition and the representations of the petitioner for the premise that Yaser was in an active combat zone within that country.

. . .

LUTTIG, Circuit Judge, dissenting from denial of rehearing *en banc*:

As should be true under a rule of law, the reasoning underlying our resolution of the important issue presented by this appeal has implications beyond the particular dispute before us. In this instance, those implications are for no less commanding constitutional interests than the President's power to conduct war and the right of our citizens to be free from governmental restraint except upon lawful justification.

As my colleagues have recognized, the panel's opinion resolving the important issue presented by this suit is unpersuasive, because of its exclusive reliance upon a mistaken characterization of the circumstances of Hamdi's seizure as "undisputed," when those circumstances are neither conceded in fact, nor susceptible to concession in law, because Hamdi has not been permitted to speak for himself or even through counsel as to those circumstances. That the panel opinion is unpersuasive is borne out by no less significant a fact than that the panel itself, as evidenced by the two separate concurrences today, cannot even now agree as to either the proper interpretation or defense of its opinion.

Additionally, beyond the opinion's unpersuasiveness, its refusal to rest decision on the proffer made by the President of the United States, and its insistence instead upon resting decision on a putative concession by the detainee, has yielded reasoning that all but eviscerates the President's Article II power to determine who are and who are not enemies of the United States during times of war.

Because of the facial unpersuasiveness of the court's opinion, and because the opinion of law that resolves the issue raised in this appeal is of even greater constitutional importance than the result reached by that opinion, I would grant the requested rehearing *en banc*.....

I.

On the central question presented in this case, it is evident that the panel found itself simply unwilling to allow petitioner Hamdi to challenge the facts supporting his designation by the Executive as an enemy combatant, under any standard of review urged by those who appeared on behalf of Hamdi. However, the panel was equally unwilling either to adopt the "some evidence" standard and accept as sufficient under that standard the facts offered by the government as justification for Hamdi's seizure or to hold that the Judiciary is without all authority to review the President's designation of an individual as an enemy combatant, as alternatively urged by the government. Faced with this decisional paralysis, the panel retreated to ground that not only neither party attempted to defend, but that is transparently indefensible – holding that Hamdi cannot challenge, and the court cannot question, the facts proffered by the government in support of Hamdi's particular seizure and detention as an enemy combatant, for the asserted reason that Hamdi has *conceded* that he was seized in a foreign combat zone.

A.

In resting its decision on this factually and legally untenable ground, the panel reneged on the promises it hastily made to the parties at the litigation's inception.

It promised the citizen seized by the government "meaningful judicial review" of his claim that he was not an enemy combatant, pointedly refusing to "embrac[e] a sweeping proposition – namely that, with no meaningful judicial review, any American citizen alleged to be an enemy combatant could be detained indefinitely without charges or counsel on the government's say-so." *Hamdi v. Rumsfeld*, 296 F.3d 278, 283 (4th Cir. 2002) ("*Hamdi II*"). But it ultimately provided that citizen a review that actually entailed absolutely no judicial inquiry into the facts on the basis of which the government designated that citizen as an enemy combatant.

One could hardly be faulted for wondering why, as the panel held, more is "unnecessary to a meaningful judicial review" of a challenge to an Executive's enemy combatant designation than a concession of seizure in a foreign combat zone. Under even an exceedingly deferential standard of review, such, though it is relevant to, would hardly seem dispositive of whether one has been legitimately classified as an enemy combatant. The embedded journalist or even the unwitting tourist could be seized and detained in a foreign combat zone. Indeed, the likelihood that such could occur is far from infinitesimal where the theater is global, not circumscribed, and the engagement is an unconventional war against terrorists, not a conventional war against an identifiable nation state. But surely we would not conclude that that journalist or tourist (who could be expected to readily admit to his seizure in the foreign combat zone) had received meaningful judicial review of his claim that he was not an enemy combatant, if that claim received no judicial scrutiny at all merely because he stipulated that he was seized in that foreign combat zone. It is undoubtedly for these reasons that the Executive neither designated Hamdi an enemy combatant on the basis of his mere seizure in a foreign combat zone nor defends its designation in this court on such basis.

But as the panel disowned its promise to the detainee to provide him meaningful judicial review, so also did it disown its promise to the Executive to accord him the substantial deference to which he is constitutionally entitled for his wartime decisions as to who constitute enemies of the United States. The panel promised the Executive that the Judiciary would not sit in full review of his judgments as to who is an enemy combatant of the United States, but it adopted a rule that will henceforth do just that, cast the Judiciary as ultimate arbiter, in each and every instance, of whether the Executive has properly so classified a detainee.

. . .

That the government's victory is but thinly guised defeat could not be better confirmed than by the arguments that have already been made in opposition to, and in support of, the panel's opinion by the parties to this dispute. Thus, those appearing on behalf of Hamdi argue, to no surprise and in compelling understatement, that the panel fundamentally erred for the reason that, "it cannot fairly be stated that it is 'undisputed' that Hamdi was captured within a zone of active combat operations in a foreign country" "[b]ecause Hamdi was denied the opportunity to meet with counsel, and was refused the opportunity to dispute the facts put forth by [the government] – including assertions as to where he was captured and what the circumstances were at the time." Appellee's Petition for Rehearing and Suggestion for Rehearing in Banc, at 12–13. The obvious remedy for this error being, they reasonably claim, a remand for further factual development on the issue, with allowance for participation by Hamdi himself.

And the government, as expected, rejoins that "the type of evidentiary proceeding that appellees seek would raise precisely the same problems concerning judicial oversight of military operations overseas that the panel properly concluded is not only unwise, but unauthorized under our constitutional scheme." Answer for Respondents-Appellants to Petition for Rehearing and Suggestion for Rehearing en Banc, at 11.

A more Pyrrhic victory would be hard to conceive.

. . .

B.

These breaches perhaps could be excused if the panel had divined an unassailable narrower ground for decision than that foreshadowed by either of its bold promises. However, its decision cannot be excused on this basis, because the ground upon which the panel rested its decision is anything but unassailable. *For it simply is not "undisputed" that Hamdi was seized in a foreign combat zone.*

. . .

. . . [T]he next friend petition. . . . states that, "[w]hen seized by the United States Government, Mr.Hamdi *resided* in Afghanistan." J.A. 9 (emphasis added). Of course, it is a *non sequitur* to conclude from the representation that Hamdi *resided* in Afghanistan at the time of his seizure, that he was also *seized* in a foreign zone of active combat. In the end, it is obvious that the panel simply missed the critical import of this distinction between residency on one hand, and seizure or capture on the other, even though it recognized – at least in passing – the distinction between the two. As it said, though incorrectly as to the latter, "Hamdi's petition alleges that he was a resident of *and* seized in Afghanistan. . . ." *Hamdi III*, 316 F.3d at 471 (emphasis added).

Insistence that the distinction be drawn between acknowledgment of residency and concession of seizure in a combat zone is not to be clever. I have no reason to believe that Hamdi was not in a combat zone at the time of his seizure, and, to the extent relevant, I believe that he was. But, as a court of law, we cannot impute a concession of this circumstance of seizure from an innocuous acknowledgment of residency in a country in which combat was underway. Such is not credible.

. . .

C.

Sensing the vulnerability of the panel's opinion, the concurrences in the denial of rehearing *en banc* (Judges Wilkinson and Traxler) attempt to save the panel opinion by marshaling for the first time today additional support, beyond that relied upon by the panel, for the panel's conclusion that it has been conceded that Hamdi was seized in a foreign combat zone. . . .

I have previously expressed my concern about the trend in our court to attempt "to add to, subtract from, or recharacterize the facts recited and relied upon in a challenged panel opinion, or even to fine-tune, if not fundamentally reshape, the legal analysis undertaken by the original panel, *in the course of opinions respecting the denial of rehearing en banc.*" *Jones v. Buchanan*, 325 F.3d 520, 538–40 (4th Cir. 2003) (Luttig, J., dissenting) (citing cases). Without repeating in full the reasons for this concern here, such attempted modifications are unfair to the litigants, because the parties (and the public) are bound by the panel opinion as it was written and issued, and they may obtain further review only of the issued panel opinion, without regard to modifications suggested by a concurrence in denial of *en banc* rehearing. . . .

But putting this concern to one side, the very fact that the concurrences have felt need to offer up the additional support that they have is confirmation that the panel at least now senses the analytical softness of its opinion. There would otherwise be no reason to attempt to shore up that opinion with these additional materials, which the panel fully considered originally and rejected as not providing any support for its conclusion that the location of seizure was "undisputed."

. . .

II.

Because of the overarching importance of the opinion of law that resolves the issue presented by this appeal, because of the panel opinion's dismissiveness of the substantial interests at stake in this case for both citizen and government, and because of the analytical vulnerability of the court's opinion as it stands, I believe that both the United States and the petitioner would be served by reconsideration by our full court.

Upon reconsideration, we should decide the critical issue of the appropriate standard that is to govern the Judiciary's review of an individual's challenge to an Executive designation of enemy combatant status, the indecision of which by the panel I believe fails to serve the substantial interests of not only the parties but also the public in the resolution of this issue. Having decided the governing standard, we should decide the issue of whether that standard has been satisfied in this case by the government's proffer of the facts contained in the Michael H. Mobbs affidavit, the like indecision of which by the panel also, I believe, fails to serve the parties and the public.

. . .

DIANA GRIBBON MOTZ, Circuit Judge, dissenting from denial of rehearing en banc:

For more than a year, a United States citizen, Yaser Esam Hamdi, has been labeled an enemy combatant and held in solitary confinement in a Norfolk, Virginia naval brig. He has not been charged with a crime, let alone convicted of one. The Executive will not state when, if ever, he will be released. Nor has the Executive allowed Hamdi to appear in court, consult with counsel, or communicate in any way with the outside world.

Precedent dictates that we must tolerate some abrogation of constitutional rights if Hamdi is, in fact, an enemy combatant. However, a panel of this court has held that a short hearsay declaration by Mr. Michael Mobbs – an unelected, otherwise unknown, government "advisor," – "standing alone" (subject to no challenge by Hamdi or court-ordered verification) is "sufficient as a matter of law to allow meaningful judicial review" and approval of the Executive's designation of Hamdi as an enemy combatant. *See Hamdi v. Rumsfeld*, 316 F.3d 450 (4th Cir. 2003). I cannot agree.

To justify forfeiture of a citizen's constitutional rights, the Executive must establish enemy combatant status with more than hearsay. In holding to the contrary, the panel allows appropriate deference to the Executive's authority in matters of war to eradicate the Judiciary's own Constitutional role: protection of the individual freedoms guaranteed all citizens. With respect, I believe the panel has seriously erred, and I dissent from the court's refusal to rehear this case *en banc*.

I.

The panel's decision marks the first time in our history that a federal court has approved the elimination of protections afforded a citizen by the Constitution solely on the basis of the Executive's designation of that citizen as an enemy combatant, without testing the accuracy of the designation. Neither the Constitution nor controlling precedent sanction this holding.

The rights provided in the Constitution to each American citizen include the right to due process of law and to petition for a writ of habeas corpus. U.S. Const. amend. V; art. I, §9. Unquestionably, the availability of habeas relief extends to detention pursuant to the Executive's military authority. *See, e.g., Ex parte Milligan*, 71 U.S. (4 Wall.) 2, 120–21 (1866); *Duncan v. Kahanamoku*, 327 U.S. 304 (1946). Just as clearly, the responsibility for ensuring that individuals detained by the Executive receive the due process guarantees of the Constitution, including the right to petition for habeas corpus, rests with the courts. *See In re Yamashit*, 327 U.S. 1, 9 (1946). As the Supreme Court has explained, "the allowable limits of military discretion, and whether or not they have been overstepped in a particular case, are judicial questions," *Sterling v. Constantin*, 287 U.S. 378, 401 (1932); *see Duncan*, 327 U.S. at 322–23; and the "government must always be accountable to the judiciary for a man's imprisonment." *Fay v. Noia*, 372 U.S. 391, 402 (1963), *overruled on other grounds*, *Coleman v. Thompson*, 501 U.S. 722 (1991).

. . .

. . . [I]n *Quirin*, a German-born soldier, who claimed to be an American citizen, stipulated that after receiving payment by the German government and instruction by the "German High Command to destroy war industries and war facilities in the United States," he and six other German soldiers secretly landed in the United States during World War II with "a supply of explosives." *Id.* at 20–21. Only after finding that these "conceded facts" demonstrated "plainly" that the soldiers were within the "boundaries of the jurisdiction of military tribunals," did the Supreme Court reject their contention that they could not be tried by a military commission. *Id.* at 46. Critical to the case at hand, the Court first expressly rejected the Executive's argument that the soldiers, "must be denied access to the courts because they are enemy aliens who have entered our territory." *Id.* at 24–25. Instead, each of the soldiers was permitted, with the assistance of counsel, to file his *own* (not a next friend) petition for a writ of habeas corpus, which the courts reviewed to ensure that each soldier was in fact an enemy combatant. *Id.*

None of the few other Supreme Court cases addressing the rights of enemy combatants involved American citizens. But even when dealing with the claims of German and Japanese citizens detained by military authorities outside the United States during World War II, the Court has never suggested that an enemy combatant is without recourse to challenge that designation in court. On the contrary, the Court has held that a resident alien – who, the Court specifically noted, has far less status than those, like Hamdi, who enjoy the "high privilege" of citizenship – *can* challenge the Executive's designation of him as an enemy. *Johnson v. Eisentrager*, 339 U.S. 763, 770, 775 (1950) (internal quotation marks and citation omitted). As the Court explained: "*Courts will entertain his plea* for freedom from Executive custody only *to ascertain* the existence of a state of war and *whether he is an alien enemy.*" *Id.* at 775 (emphasis added); *see also id.* at 784–85; *Ludecke v. Watkins*, 335 U.S. 160, 171 n.17 (1948) (noting that "whether the person restrained is in fact an alien enemy . . . may also be reviewed by the courts"); *Yamashita*, 327 U.S. at 8 (noting that "[t]he courts may inquire whether the detention complained of is within the authority of those detaining the petitioner" and "the Executive branch of the government could not, unless there was a suspension of the writ, withdraw from the courts the duty and power" to inquire whether the "Constitution or laws of the United States withhold authority" from a military tribunal).

Moreover, the Supreme Court has upheld the Executive's designation of a person as an enemy alien or enemy combatant only when presented with *facts* supporting this designation – facts stipulated by the petitioner with the advice of counsel, as in *Quirin*, or facts proved by the prosecution at a military trial in which the petitioner was afforded counsel, as in *Yamashita*. In the case at hand, no facts have been presented to support the Executive's designation. The Executive has not permitted Hamdi to consult with counsel or challenge the allegations contained in the Mobbs declaration. And Hamdi has certainly not stipulated to anything. Denied the most basic procedural protections, Hamdi could not possibly mount a challenge to the Executive's designation of him as an enemy combatant. Yet in *Eisentrager*, *Ludecke*, and *Yamashita* the Supreme Court has explained that even aliens are entitled to precisely this right. Thus, far from supporting the panel's position, controlling precedent prohibits its approach.

II.

Without any acknowledgment of its break with precedent, the panel embarks on a perilous new course – approving the Executive's designation of enemy combatant status not on the basis of facts stipulated or proven, but solely on the basis of an unknown Executive advisor's declaration, which the panel itself concedes is subject to challenge as "incomplete[ ]" and "inconsisten[t]" hearsay. *Hamdi*, 316 F.3d at 473. My good colleagues' opinion, although well-intentioned and replete with compelling declarations of separation-of-powers principles with which no one would quarrel, utterly fails to set forth an adequate rationale for its breathtaking holding.

Indeed, the panel offers only a single justification for its unprecedented decision to permit the Executive to support its designation of Hamdi as an enemy combatant with pure hearsay: Hamdi's capture in a "zone of active combat" was assertedly "undisputed." *See Hamdi*, 316 F.3d at 459. . . .

This is a thin reed on which to rest abrogation of constitutional rights, and one that collapses entirely upon examination. For Hamdi has never been given the opportunity to dispute any facts. The "facts" as to the place of Hamdi's "capture" could only be "undisputed" by reliance on a facially innocuous statement in a petition filed by Hamdi's father, as his "next friend." Thus, the panel determines that a petition filed by a next friend on behalf of, but without access to or consultation with, the petitioner constitutes a binding admission by the petitioner that results in the forfeiture of the petitioner's constitutional rights. This holding flatly contravenes venerable Supreme Court precedent. The Court long ago held that "a next friend or guardian *ad litem* cannot, by admissions or stipulations, surrender the rights of" the represented party. *Kingsbury v. Buckner*, 134 U.S. 650, 680 (1890); *see also White v. Miller*, 158 U.S. 128, 146 (1895) (same); *Stolte v. Larkin*, 110 F.2d 226, 233 (8th Cir.1940) (collecting cases).[1]

---

[1] Judge Wilkinson contends in his concurrence to the order denying rehearing *en banc* that these cases do not apply to Hamdi because he is an enemy combatant who is not entitled to rights "enjoyed by ordinary civil or criminal litigants." *See ante* at 18 n.2. This reasoning is dizzyingly circular. The panel relied heavily on an admission of Hamdi's next friend (who had no opportunity to consult with Hamdi) to find Hamdi an enemy combatant. Now, Judge Wilkinson maintains that *because* Hamdi is an enemy combatant, *White* and *Kingsbury* do not apply, and Hamdi is bound by his next friend's assertedly critical admission. *Id.* Thus, Judge Wilkinson seeks to use the panel's conclusion (that Hamdi is an enemy combatant) to justify the panel's improper reliance on an admission of Hamdi's next friend, which provides the very basis for that conclusion. In sum, according to Judge Wilkinson, because Hamdi's next friend made a purportedly devastating admission, Hamdi forfeits all rights to challenge that admission, and ultimately all constitutional rights. Surely this does not constitute the "meaningful judicial review" that the panel promised. *See Hamdi*, 316 F.3d at 462, 473.

Nor does the district court opinion, *Hall v. Hague*, 34 F.R.D. 449 (D. Md. 1964), relied on by Judge Traxler in his concurrence, *ante* at 29, offer support for the panel's startling approach. In *Hall*, a district judge merely determined that the guardian *ad litem* of a minor could admit certain housekeeping matters prior to trial, on the understanding that "[a]t the trial, the judge will be able to tell if any unjustified admissions have been

Just as importantly, even if the statement in his father's petition that "[w]hen seized," Hamdi "resided in Afghanistan" . . . somehow translated into Hamdi's admission that he was captured "in a zone of active combat," *Hamdi*, 316 F.3d at 459, this should not render the Executive's designation of enemy combatant status irrebuttable. The ramifications of such a holding are chilling. Pursuant to the panel's decision, for example, any of the "embedded" American journalists covering the war in Iraq or any member of a humanitarian organization working in Afghanistan,[2] could be imprisoned indefinitely without being charged with a crime or provided access to counsel if the Executive designated that person an "enemy combatant." Indeed, under the panel's holding, any American citizen seized in a part of the world where American troops are present – *e.g.*, the former Yugoslavia, the Philippines, or Korea – could be imprisoned indefinitely without being charged with a crime or afforded legal counsel, if the Executive asserted that the area was a zone of active combat.[3] . . . .

Nor, as the panel implicitly acknowledges, does the two-page, nine paragraph Mobbs declaration by itself, provide such justification. The panel's assessment of the Mobbs declaration is entirely accurate; that declaration could indeed be easily and successfully "challenge[d]" as "hearsay," and "probe [d]" for "incompleteness or inconsistency." *Hamdi*, 316 F.3d at 473.[4] The declaration contains no indicia of reliability except for Mr. Mobbs' oath – which seems of minimal value given that Mr. Mobbs does not claim *any* personal knowledge of the facts surrounding Hamdi's capture and incarceration. . . . . Indeed, the declaration's statement that Northern Alliance troops initially captured Hamdi suggests that even the U.S. military does not have any first-hand knowledge of Hamdi's conduct or status in Afghanistan.

In sum, the record provides no credible evidence supporting the Executive's designation of Hamdi as an enemy combatant. . . . . Thus, although the panel steadfastly maintains that it engages in a "meaningful judicial review," *see Hamdi*, 316 F.3d at 462,

---

made and take appropriate action." *Id.* at 449–50 (internal quotation marks and citation omitted) (emphasis added). This is a long way from holding, as the panel does (ignoring *Kingsbury* and *White*), that a statement in a petition filed by Hamdi's next friend constitutes an admission by Hamdi providing the basis for denial of his constitutional rights and indefinite imprisonment, *without the benefit of any trial*. Indeed, Judge Traxler's assertion that "there is no reason to believe that [Hamdi's] rights are being bargained away or that a factual mistake is being made," in the next friend petition, *ante* at 29 n.7, ignores the obvious. How could there be any "reason to believe that rights are being bargained away or that a factual mistake is being made" when the only person who could offer such a reason or contest a factual mistake – Yaser Esam Hamdi – has never been given the chance to do so? By keeping Hamdi imprisoned incommunicado, the Executive has denied him this opportunity. Thus, we simply have no idea whether his "rights are being bargained away" or "a factual mistake is being made." It is precisely to avoid resolving an individual's fate on such uncertain grounds that the Supreme Court has held that a next friend petition "cannot be excepted to for insufficiency, nor can any admission . . . be binding." *White*, 158 U.S. at 146.

[2] I note that in a letter to Senator Patrick Leahy, contained in the record, but ignored by the panel, Hamdi's father, in fact, states that his son went to Afghanistan less than two months before September 11, 2001 to do "relief work," was "trapped in Afghanistan once that military campaign began," could not have received military training, and was never an enemy combatant. . . .

[3] I find puzzling the contention that the panel opinion "does not speak to the issue of whether an 'enemy combatant' may challenge the government's claim that the former Yugoslavia, the Philippines, or Korea is a zone of active military operations," *ante* at 36–37. First, no basis is provided for distinguishing between the "troops . . . still on the ground in Afghanistan," *Hamdi*, 316 F.3d at 476, and American troops "on the ground" in the former Yugoslavia, the Philippines, or Korea. Moreover, in suggesting that a person detained in one of those countries might be able to challenge the Executive's designation of that country as a zone of active military operations, the concurrence necessarily implies that the question of what constitutes such a zone is justiciable – a conclusion seemingly at odds not only with the panel opinion, *see* 316 F.3d at 476 (dismissing Hamdi's contention that hostilities in Afghanistan had ended), but also with the concurrence itself. *See ante* at 32 n.9.

[4] . . .

473, its rubberstamp of the Executive's unsupported designation lacks both the procedural and substantive content of such review.[5]

At the same time, I hasten to note that the total inadequacy of the Executive's proffer and the panel's review here does not provide license for a searching judicial inquiry into the factual circumstances of every detainee's capture, or require compliance with a production order as demanding as that called for by the district court.[6] Such an approach could hamper the Executive's ability to wage war, as the panel explains at length. *See Hamdi*, 316 F.3d at 469–473. But the possibility, no matter how real, that an improperly conducted judicial inquiry could impair the Executive's ability to wage war cannot, as the panel seems to believe, provide a justification for holding that the Executive can indefinitely detain an American citizen (even one captured in a zone of active hostilities) without producing any credible evidence that the citizen is an "enemy combatant." The Constitution gives Congress, not the Executive and not the courts, the power to suspend the writ of habeas corpus when the public safety requires it. U.S. Const. art. I, §9. Absent a suspension of the writ, the Constitution demands that we strike the proper balance between ensuring the Executive's ability to wage war effectively *and* protecting the individual rights guaranteed to all American citizens. *See Yamashita*, 327 U.S. at 8. Without such a balance, our system of ordered liberty will indeed ring hollow.

Thus, in contrast to the panel's holding, which effectively transforms the asserted "fact" of being captured in a zone of active hostilities into an *irrebuttable* presumption of "enemy combatant" status,[7] a court could regard such a "fact" as creating a *rebuttable* presumption, thereby shifting the burden to Hamdi (and others like him) to establish that he was *not* an "enemy combatant." The burden of persuasion would then be on Hamdi, with the aid of counsel, to proffer affirmative evidence of his "non-combatant" status. This would seem to be the course dictated by precedent.

. . .

III.

. . .

. . . [O]ne need not refer back to the time of the Framers to understand that courts must be vigilant in guarding Constitutional freedoms, perhaps never more so than in time of war. We must not forget the lesson of *Korematsu*, a case in which the Supreme Court sanctioned the military internment of thousands of American citizens of Japanese ancestry during World War II. *See* 323 U.S. at 219. In its deference to an Executive report

---

[5] Moreover, while I applaud the panel's attempt to confine its holding to the facts at hand, without effect on the rights of citizens captured on American territory, *see Hamdi*, 316 F.3d at 465, similar attempts to constrain judicial holdings have proved unavailing. As Justice Jackson recounted, despite the Supreme Court's careful efforts to limit the scope of its holding in *Hirabayashi v. United States*, 320 U.S. 81 (1943), to the specific facts of that case, *see id.* at 101–02, 105, the Court later determined that *Hirabayashi* dictated the holding in *Korematsu v. United States*, 323 U.S. 214, 218 (1944). *See id.* at 247 (Jackson, J., dissenting) ("The Court is now saying that in *Hirabayashi* we did decide the very things we there said we were not deciding."). I fear that the panel may also have opened the door to the indefinite detention, without access to a lawyer or the courts, of any American citizen, even one captured on American soil, who the Executive designates an "enemy combatant," as long as the Executive asserts that the area in which the citizen was detained was an "active combat zone," and the detainee, deprived of access to courts and counsel, cannot dispute this fact.

[6] Although I agree with the panel that the district court's production order required too much, the experienced district judge should be commended nonetheless. For, during wartime and in the face of opposition by representatives of a President enjoying record popular support, the district judge has courageously attempted to provide the meaningful judicial review that the Constitution mandates, however unpopular the case.

[7] . . .

that, like the Mobbs declaration, was filed by a member of the Executive associated with the military and which purported to explain the Executive's actions, the Court upheld the Executive's conviction of Korematsu for simply remaining in his home, in violation of the military internment order. *See id.* at 215–16.

Of course, history has long since rejected the *Korematsu* holding. Indeed, Congress itself has specifically repudiated *Korematsu*, recognizing that "a grave injustice was done to" those "of Japanese ancestry by th[e] actions . . . carried out without adequate security reasons and . . . motivated largely by racial prejudice, wartime hysteria, and a failure of political leadership." 50 App. U.S.C.A. §1989a(a) (West 1990). But in truth, here, as in *Korematsu*, the Executive has failed to proffer any real evidence to justify its action. When presented with no basis for reviewing the Executive's designation that an American citizen is an enemy combatant, other than the assurance of a Defense Department "advisor" that someone in the United States military made this determination, a court must demand more. *Cf. Korematsu*, 323 U.S. at 245, (Jackson, J., dissenting) ("So the Court, having no real evidence before it, has no choice but to accept General DeWitt's own unsworn, self-serving statement, untested by any cross-examination.").

. . .

Courts have no higher duty than protection of the individual freedoms guaranteed by our Constitution. This is especially true in time of war, when our carefully crafted system of checks and balances must accommodate the vital needs of national security while guarding the liberties the Constitution promises all citizens. *See id.* at 234 (Murphy, J., dissenting) ("Individuals must not be left impoverished of their constitutional rights on a plea of military necessity that has neither substance nor support."). I believe that our court has failed in this case to carry out this most important responsibility. I would require a greater showing from the Executive before I would permit an American citizen, held in the United States, to be imprisoned indefinitely, without ever being afforded the opportunity to appear in court, contest the allegations against him, or consult with a lawyer.

. . .

No. 03-6696

In The
Supreme Court of the United States

YASER ESAM HAMDI; ESAM FOUAD HAMDI,
as next friend of Yaser Esam Hamdi,

Petitioners,

v.

DONALD RUMSFELD, Secretary of Defense, et al.,

Respondents.

On Writ Of Certiorari To The United States Court Of Appeals For The Fourth Circuit

BRIEF FOR PETITIONERS

Of Counsel
KENNETH P. TROCCOLI
Assistant Federal Public
  Defender
FRANCES H. PRATT
Research and Writing
  Attorney

FRANK W. DUNHAM, JR.
Federal Public Defender
Counsel of Record

GEREMY C. KAMENS
Assistant Federal Public
  Defender

OFFICE OF THE FEDERAL
  PUBLIC DEFENDER

Counsel for Petitioner

COCKLE LAW BRIEF PRINTING CO.
OR CALL COLLECT

---

* Redactions on this page have been added for privacy purposes. – *Eds.*

QUESTIONS PRESENTED

I. Whether the Constitution permits Executive officials to detain an American citizen indefinitely in military custody in the United States, hold him essentially incommunicado and deny him access to counsel, with no opportunity to question the factual basis for his detention before any impartial tribunal, on the sole ground that he was seized abroad in a theater of the War on Terrorism and declared by the Executive to be an "enemy combatant"?

II. Whether the indefinite detention of an American citizen seized abroad but held in the United States solely on the assertion of Executive officials that he is an "enemy combatant" is permissible under applicable congressional statutes and treaty provisions?

III. Whether the separation of powers doctrine precludes a federal court from following ordinary statutory procedures and conducting an inquiry into the factual basis for the Executive branch's asserted justification for its indefinite detention of an American citizen seized abroad, detained in the United States, and declared by Executive officials to be an "enemy combatant"?

. . .

STATEMENT OF THE CASE

The United States military seized an American citizen, Yaser Esam Hamdi, almost two and a half years ago. For much of that time, it has detained him essentially incommunicado at Navy prisons in Virginia and South Carolina.[2] Hamdi is not a member of the U.S. military, has not been charged with a crime, and his detention is pursuant to no provision of the U.S. Code. While this matter was pending in the lower courts, Hamdi was not permitted access to counsel, has never appeared at any hearing related to his imprisonment, and was not permitted to submit his version of the events leading up to his seizure.[3]

. . .

SUMMARY OF ARGUMENT

"Executive power to detain an individual is the hallmark of the totalitarian state." *United States v. Montalvo-Murillo*, 495 U.S. 711, 723 (1990) (Stevens, J., dissenting). The Fourth Circuit's opinion uncaged that power by (1) denying Hamdi the protection of the Great Writ and refusing him a meaningful hearing to challenge his detention; (2) recognizing a nonexistent executive power to indefinitely detain citizens; and (3) implying authority to detain citizens that Congress has not granted.

Hamdi's habeas petition challenges his indefinite detention – not his initial seizure by the Northern Alliance or transfer to U.S. custody. Almost two years have elapsed

---

[2] Hamdi has been forbidden any contact with fellow prisoners and the outside world, with the exception of a visit by a representative of the International Red Cross and the infrequent exchange of censored letters with his family. On February 3, 2004, Hamdi was allowed to meet counsel for the first time. Restrictions imposed by the military on the conditions under which this meeting was permitted did not allow confidential communications.

[3] From his seizure through completion of litigation below, Hamdi was denied the ability to review the petition or any other materials related to this case.

since the petition was filed, and during that time Hamdi has been held not as a prisoner of war but in solitary confinement, indefinitely detained in the United States without charge, conviction, or a factual hearing of any kind. Although this is a case about process and executive power, not conditions of confinement, Hamdi's conditions of confinement amount to punishment, and therefore bear on the process due.

. . .

To distinguish Hamdi's case from the petitioner in *Padilla v. Rumsfeld*, 352 F.3d 695, 723 (2d Cir. 2003), *cert. granted*, 72 U.S.L.W. 3488 (U.S. Feb. 20, 2004) (No. 03-1027), a case involving a U.S. citizen seized by the military in New York City, the Fourth Circuit found it "crucial" to its decision that it was "undisputed that Hamdi was captured in a zone of active combat operations in a foreign country." . . . 316 F.3d at 471, 473. The Fourth Circuit therefore sought to limit the scope of its ruling by seizing upon a fact – the location of Hamdi's initial seizure – found nowhere in the Mobbs declaration. The Fourth Circuit found this fact to be "undisputed" even though Hamdi was held incommunicado throughout the proceedings below. The location of Hamdi's seizure thus could not fairly be characterized as "conceded in fact, nor susceptible to concession in law, because Hamdi ha[d] not been permitted to speak for himself or even through counsel as to those circumstances." . . . Hamdi IV, 337 F.3d at 357 (Luttig, J., dissenting from denial of reh'g).

. . .

Judicial review of executive detention is demanded by, not contrary to, the separation of powers. Indeed, "[a]t its historical core, the writ of habeas corpus has served as a means of reviewing the legality of Executive detention, and it is in that context that its protections have been strongest." *INS v. St. Cyr*, 533 U.S. 289, 301 (2001).

Moreover, the Fourth Circuit recognized and deferred to a non-existent unilateral executive power to indefinitely detain citizens. The Executive admittedly has plenary power in areas of actual fighting, and may detain citizens seized in those areas temporarily without specific statutory authority or judicial review. But this authority extends only as far as required by military necessity. Once the citizen is removed from areas of actual fighting, the Executive cannot detain the citizen indefinitely without statutory authorization. Congress has enacted criminal statutes, in fact, designed to provide precisely this authority – but these statutes have not been invoked here.

Ex parte Quirin, 317 U.S. 1 (1942), provides no precedent for unilateral executive detention of citizens. The military authority at issue in *Quirin* that the Court permitted to be exercised over a citizen was explicitly authorized by Congress. No such congressional authorization exists here. Further, *Quirin* pre-dates 18 U.S.C. §4001(a), a statute which specifically prohibits executive detention of citizens without congressional authorization. Nor does the law of war discussed in *Quirin* independently authorize the detention of citizens. The Executive's power is derived not from international law but from the Congress and the Constitution. *Brown v. United States*, 12 U.S. (8 Cranch) 110, 126 (1814). The authority to indefinitely detain Hamdi is sanctioned by neither.

Congress alone has the power to define and punish offenses against the law of nations and to define criminal conduct. Only Congress has the power to suspend the Great Writ. And historically it is Congress that has authorized the detention of both enemy aliens and citizens in the United States. Accordingly, only Congress can authorize the prolonged detention of citizens, as 18 U.S.C. §4001(a) makes clear.

. . .

ARGUMENT

I. HAMDI CANNOT BE IMPRISONED FOR TWO YEARS WITHOUT
    MEANINGFUL REVIEW BY HABEAS CORPUS, A HEARING, OR ACCESS
    TO COUNSEL

   A. The Fourth Circuit Denied Hamdi Meaningful Habeas Review

. . .

The Suspension Clause ensures that the Executive cannot discard the judicial process and imprison citizens at its pleasure. *See Ex parte Merryman*, 17 F. Cas. 144, 152–53 (C.C.D. Md. 1861) (No. 9,487) (Taney, C.J.); *cf. In re Yamashita*, 327 U.S. 1, 9 (1946). Well-acquainted with the danger posed by the government's power to effect detention, the Founders enshrined the suspension power in Article I and limited its exercise to cases of rebellion or invasion. U.S. Const. art. I, §9.

Habeas corpus remains the most basic protection against unbridled detention by the Executive. According to the congressional scheme, courts are required to "hear and determine the facts" related to a petitioner's detention, and petitioners are allowed to "deny any of the facts set forth in the return or allege any other material facts." 28 U.S.C. §§2243, 2246. Furthermore, 28 U.S.C. §2248 provides that even if the government's factual allegations are not challenged, district courts may reject them if they "find [] from the evidence that they are not true."

. . .

   B. The Due Process Clause Guarantees a Meaningful Hearing and Access
       to Counsel to Any Citizen Detained Indefinitely

      1. Hamdi Was Entitled to, But Denied, a Meaningful Hearing

Hamdi's detention is offensive to the most basic and unimpeachable rule of due process: that no citizen may be incarcerated at the will of the Executive without recourse to a timely proceeding before an independent tribunal to determine whether the Executive's asserted justifications for the detention have a basis in fact and a warrant in law. *See, e.g., Zadvydas v. Davis*, 533 U.S. 678, 690 (2001); *Demore v. Kim*, 123 U.S. 1708, 1732–33 (2003) (Souter, J., dissenting in part); *Addington v. Texas*, 441 U.S. 418, 425–27 (1979); *Gerstein v. Pugh*, 420 U.S. 103, 117–18 (1975); *Jackson v. Indiana*, 406 U.S. 715, 737–39 (1972); *Shaughnessy v. Mezei*, 345 U.S. 206, 218 (1953) (Jackson, J., dissenting).

Under the Fourth Circuit's ruling, the Executive's indefinite detention of a citizen under the war power need not be predicated on any judicial process whatsoever. In addition, as contemplated by the Fourth Circuit's ruling, any habeas proceeding to challenge this extra-judicial detention begins and ends with the submission of an affidavit based on third-hand hearsay that may not be questioned. Even in the context of the seizure of property, the submission of a one-sided affidavit in support of a seizure fails to satisfy due process. *See, e.g., North Georgia Finishing, Inc. v. Di-Chem, Inc.*, 419 U.S. 601, 607 (1975); *Fuentes v. Shevin*, 407 U.S. 67, 73–74, 82–83 (1972). The Fourth Circuit's holding that nothing more was required to support the indefinite incarceration of a citizen is untenable.

At bottom, the Due Process Clause embraces a requirement of fundamental fairness. *See In re Oliver*, 333 U.S. 257, 273–78 (1948); *see also Spencer v. Texas*, 385 U.S. 554, 563–64 (1967). A habeas proceeding that allows Respondents not only to define the entire factual record but also to hold Petitioner incommunicado so that he cannot participate is no proceeding at all.

The Fourth Circuit held that ordinary habeas procedures were not required on the ground that Hamdi is being held pursuant to "well-established laws and customs of war." . . . 316 F.3d at 475. Nonetheless, the Fourth Circuit refused to consider whether Respondents have actually complied with those laws in detaining Hamdi.

The government has acknowledged, and the conditions of confinement confirm, that Hamdi is not being held as an ordinary prisoner of war.[8] On the contrary, his prolonged indefinite solitary confinement amounts to punishment as a criminal serving an indeterminate sentence without a trial or due process. Before detaining him as anything but a prisoner of war, however, Article 5 of the Geneva Convention Relative to the Treatment of Prisoners of War, Aug. 12, 1949, 6 U.S.T. 3316, 75 U.N.T.S. 135 ("GPW"), and United States military regulations designed to implement the GPW, require that Hamdi's status be "determined by a competent tribunal" if any doubt arises whether he is entitled to prisoner of war status. *See* AR 190–8, §1–6(a).[9] At a minimum, such a hearing would have permitted Hamdi to assert that he was not a combatant at all. *See id.* §1–6(e)(10)(c).

. . .

2. Hamdi Was Entitled to, But Denied, Access to the Courts and to Counsel

The Fourth Circuit also fundamentally erred by denying Hamdi the opportunity to participate in the underlying habeas proceeding and by disposing of the case without allowing Hamdi to meet his counsel. Without these rights, Hamdi had no meaningful opportunity to challenge his detention.

The idea that citizens have a right to consult with an attorney in connection with the assertion of their legal rights breaks no new ground. *Powell v. Alabama*, 287 U.S. 45, 68–69 (1932). Moreover, a person held incommunicado and denied the opportunity to meet with a lawyer plainly has not been given the right to be heard. *See Mullane v. Central Hanover Bank & Trust Co.*, 339 U.S. 306, 314 (1950).

In the context of a habeas proceeding, the significance of these elementary principles is greatly magnified. This Court has repeatedly maintained that the Due Process Clause prohibits the government from impairing habeas petitioners' ability to challenge the legality of their incarceration. *See Ex parte Hull*, 312 U.S. 546, 549 (1941); *Johnson v. Avery*, 393 U.S. 483, 485 (1969); *Wolff v. McDonnell*, 418 U.S. 539, 579 (1974). Denying Hamdi the ability to respond to the asserted basis for his detention is flatly incompatible with a meaningful opportunity to be heard. *Cf. Simmons v. South Carolina*, 512 U.S. 154, 175 (1994) (O'Connor, J., concurring).

---

[8] Prisoners of war generally cannot be held in correctional facilities, A[rmy]R[egulation] 190–8, §3-2(b), separated from their fellow soldiers, *id.* §3–4(b), quartered under conditions less favorable than U.S. troops, *id.* §3–4(e), or restricted from receiving mail, *id.* §3–5(a).

[9] Even if Hamdi was fighting on behalf of the Taliban, a fact suggested but never stated by the Mobbs declaration, an emerging consensus of scholarship establishes that he should be entitled to treatment as a prisoner of war. *See* George H. Aldrich, *The Taliban, Al Qaeda, and the Determination of Illegal Combatants*, 96 Am. J. Int'l L. 891, 897–98 (2002); Lawrence Azubuike, *Status of Taliban and Al Qaeda Soldiers: Another Viewpoint*, 19 Conn. J. Int'l L. 127, 143–50 (2003); Manooher Mofidi and Amy E. Eckert, *"Unlawful Combatants" or "Prisoners of War": The Law and Politics of Labels*, 36 Cornell Int'l L.J. 59, 87–88 (2002); Jordan J. Paust, *War and Enemy Status After 9/11: Attacks on the Laws of War*, 28 Yale J. Int'l L. 325, 333–34 (2003); Evan Wallach, *Afghanistan, Quirin, and Uchiyama: Does the Sauce Suit the Gander*, 2003 Army Law. 18, 21–26 (2003). *But see* Ruth Wedgwood, *Al Qaeda, Terrorism, and Military Commissions*, 96 Am. J. Int'l L. 328, 335 (2002).

Similarly, the Fourth Circuit's refusal to allow Hamdi to have access to counsel is inconsistent with this Court's decisions ensuring the right to court access. *See Procunier v. Martinez*, 416 U.S. 396, 419, 421–22 (1974), *overruled on other grounds by Thornburgh v. Abbott*, 490 U.S. 401 (1989); *Bounds v. Smith*, 430 U.S. 817, 821–23 (1977); *Ex parte Hull*, 312 U.S. at 549. Indeed, Hamdi's "right to pursue a remedy through the writ would be meaningless if he had to do so alone." *Padilla v. Rumsfeld*, 352 F.3d 695, 732 (2d Cir. 2003) (Wesley, J., dissenting in part), *cert. granted*, 72 U.S.L.W. 3488 (U.S. Feb. 20, 2004) (No. 03-1027).

C. Indefinite Imprisonment in Solitary Confinement of a Citizen Alleged to Be an "Enemy Combatant" Violates Substantive Due Process

"[T]he Due Process Clause [also] contains a substantive component that bars certain arbitrary, wrongful government actions 'regardless of the fairness of the procedures used to implement them.'" *Zinermon v. Burch*, 494 U.S. 113, 125 (1990) (quoting *Daniels v. Williams*, 474 U.S. 327, 331 (1986)). This component of due process prohibits detention "unless the detention is ordered in a *criminal* proceeding with adequate procedural protections, . . . or, in certain special and 'narrow' non-punitive 'circumstances.'" *Zadvydas v. Davis*, 533 U.S. 678, 690 (2001) (citations omitted). Intrinsic to the lawfulness of punishment, in other words, is the principle that it may not be imposed outside of criminal proceedings. *International Union, UMW of Am. v. Bagwell*, 512 U.S. 821, 826 (1994); *Wong Wing v. United States*, 163 U.S. 228, 237 (1896).

Hamdi's indefinite incarceration in solitary confinement, to be sure, constitutes a criminal punishment, *see In re Medley*, 134 U.S. 160, 168–71 (1890), and apparently has been imposed because Respondents allege, but have not charged, that Hamdi has engaged in criminal conduct. *Cf.* U.S. Const. art. III, §3 (authorizing Congress to punish treasonous conduct); 18 U.S.C. §2381; 50 U.S.C. §1705(b); *United States v. Lindh*, 212 F. Supp. 2d 541, 545 (E.D. Va. 2002). Even if no further procedures were required to establish Hamdi's status as an "unlawful combatant," the extra-judicial indefinite incommunicado imprisonment of a citizen is contrary to basic values underlying American society. Because his detention is punitive, it cannot be imposed by executive fiat. *Kennedy v. Mendoza-Martinez*, 372 U.S. 144, 167–70 (1963).

II. THE FOURTH CIRCUIT MISAPPLIED THE SEPARATION OF POWERS DOCTRINE TO FRUSTRATE JUDICIAL REVIEW AND A STATUTORY PROHIBITION ON THE UNILATERAL INDEFINITE DETENTION OF CITIZENS BY THE EXECUTIVE

Driven by its interpretation of the separation of powers, the Fourth Circuit refused to permit "[a]ny evaluation of the accuracy of the executive branch's determination that a person is an enemy combatant." . . . 316 F.3d at 474. It thereby limited the power of Article III courts to review the factual basis for any wartime detention of a citizen by the Executive. This is a dangerous misconstruction of the division of powers among the branches of our government. Under its ruling, the Fourth Circuit ceded power to the Executive during wartime to define the conduct for which a citizen may be detained, judge whether that citizen has engaged in the proscribed conduct, and imprison that citizen indefinitely, thereby allowing the separation of powers doctrine to be used as a means to concentrate, not separate, power in a single branch.

It was "the central judgment of the Framers of the Constitution that, within our political scheme, the separation of governmental powers into three coordinate Branches is essential to the preservation of liberty," *Mistretta v. United States*, 488 U.S. 361, 380 (1989), an insight that finds repeated expression in the United States Reports.[10] Use of separation of powers doctrine to justify the indefinite deprivation of a citizen's liberty upon the essentially unilateral and unreviewable determination of the Executive stands that principle on its head.

According to the court of appeals, any citizen designated by the Executive as an "enemy combatant" and seized in a "zone of active combat" may be detained indefinitely without a charge that the citizen violated any act of Congress as long as "the factual assertions set forth by the government would, *if accurate*, provide a legally valid basis for [that citizen's] detention under [the war] power." . . . 316 F.3d at 472 (emphasis added). Although noting that factual circumstances submitted by the Executive may support the detention of citizens only "if accurate," the Fourth Circuit, in a quintessential Catch-22, also held that "[the citizen] is not entitled to challenge the facts presented," . . . 316 F.3d at 476, and that Article III courts likewise may not assess their accuracy, . . . 316 F.3d at 474–75. The Executive therefore has the first and final word as to whether the military may detain an American citizen. *Cf.* . . . 296 F.3d at 283.

The danger posed by the collection of power in one branch was of paramount importance to the Founders. *See, e.g., The Federalist No. 47*, at 324 (James Madison) (Jacob E. Cooke ed., 1961) ("The accumulation of all powers legislative, executive and judiciary in the same hands . . . may justly be pronounced the very definition of tyranny."). The constitutional protections against this danger therefore were specifically designed to withstand the opposing momentum caused by war and national crises. As this Court has recognized, "[t]hey knew – the history of the world told them – the nation they were founding, be its existence short or long, would be involved in war; how often or how long continued, human foresight could not tell; and that unlimited power, wherever lodged at such a time, was especially hazardous to freemen." *Ex parte Milligan*, 71 U.S. (4 Wall.) 2, 125 (1866); *accord Youngstown*, 343 U.S. at 650 (Jackson, J., concurring) ("They knew what emergencies were, knew the pressures they engender for authoritative action, knew, too, how they afford a ready pretext for usurpation. We may also suspect that they suspected that emergency powers would tend to kindle emergencies."). The Fourth Circuit's decision authorizes the accumulation of an awesome power of government, the power to indefinitely deprive a citizen of his liberty, in a single branch. That is precisely what the separation of powers was designed to prevent.

A.   The Separation of Powers Doctrine, the Suspension Clause, and Precedent Require Meaningful Judicial Review

1.   Judicial Review Is Essential to the Separation of Powers

Constitutional protections against illegitimate executive detention would mean little without the opportunity to secure judicial review of the basis upon which the Executive claims the power to detain. The Great Writ, in fact, was designed to guarantee precisely this type of review. *See Brown v. Allen*, 344 U.S. 443, 533 (1953) (Jackson, J., concurring) ("The historic purpose of the writ has been to relieve detention by executive authorities

---

[10] *See, e.g., Clinton v. City of New York*, 524 U.S. 417, 450 (1998) (Kennedy, J., concurring); *Clinton v. Jones*, 520 U.S. 681, 699–700 (1997); *Loving v. United States*, 517 U.S. 748, 756–57 (1996); *INS v. Chadha*, 462 U.S. 919, 949, 951–59 (1983); *United States v. Brown*, 381 U.S. 437, 442–43 (1965); *Youngstown Sheet & Tube Co. v. Sawyer*, 343 U.S. 579, 613–14, 629 (1952) (Frankfurter, J., & Douglas, J., concurring); *United Public Workers of Am. v. Mitchell*, 330 U.S. 75, 91 (1947); *O'Donoghue v. United States*, 289 U.S. 516, 530 (1933); *Union Pac. R.R. Co. v. United States*, 99 U.S. 700, 718 (1878)

without judicial trial."); *see also Swain v. Pressley*, 430 U.S. 372, 386 (1977) (Burger, C.J., concurring in part and concurring in judgment) ("A doctrine that allowed transfer of the historic habeas jurisdiction to an Art. I court could raise separation-of-powers questions, since the traditional Great Writ was largely a remedy against executive detention.").

The Fourth Circuit's refusal to permit "any inquiry," ... 316 F.3d at 473, into the factual circumstances related to Hamdi's indefinite detention is flatly contrary to this historic function and effectively eviscerates habeas corpus as "the fundamental instrument for safeguarding individual freedom against arbitrary and lawless" executive detention. *Harris v. Nelson*, 394 U.S. 286, 290–91 (1969). The lower court's ruling, in fact, guarantees a judicial rubber-stamp rather than an independent check on the Executive's power to engage in unauthorized detentions, a result plainly at odds with the separation of powers. *See United States v. Klein*, 80 U.S. (13 Wall.) 128, 145–47 (1871).

Moreover, the Suspension Clause prevents the drastic limitation of judicial review required by the Fourth Circuit. Only Congress has the power to suspend judicial review of detention, and even then only in the event of rebellion or invasion. U.S. Const. art. 1, §9, cl. 2. Independently of statutes designed to implement habeas review, the Suspension Clause preserves the right to habeas review, at the very least, as it existed in 1789 under the common law. *INS v. St. Cyr*, 533 U.S. 289, 301 (2001); *see also Developments in the Law – Federal Habeas Corpus*, 83 Harv. L. Rev. 1038, 1267 (1970).

And under that common law, the review of executive detentions was far greater than that allowed by the Fourth Circuit in this case. Executive detentions are characterized by the absence of prior judicial process, and in particular the absence of a trial by which a jury has assessed the detainee's guilt or innocence. *Cf. Duncan v. Louisiana*, 391 U.S. 145, 156 (1968) (noting that jury trial serves to protect against arbitrary government detention). Consequently, judicial review of the return in a habeas proceeding under the common law was least deferential in the context of executive detentions. *See* Rollin C. Hurd, *A Treatise on the Right of Personal Liberty and on the Writ of Habeas Corpus* 271 (Da Capo Press ed. 1972) (1876) (noting that in cases of noncriminal imprisonment, the exceptions to the general rule against controverting the return were "governed by a principle sufficiently comprehensive to include most ... cases"); Jonathan L. Hafetz, Note, *The Untold Story of Noncriminal Habeas Corpus and the 1996 Immigration Acts*, 107 Yale L.J. 2509, 2526 (1998) (stating that "at common law executive detentions ... triggered a broad scope of review on habeas").

Without muscular judicial review of executive detention, the Great Writ cannot fulfill its historic common law role as a "bulwark" against the threat of arbitrary government. *See The Federalist No. 84* (Alexander Hamilton). The Fourth Circuit's ruling not only failed to acknowledge that habeas review is an essential part of the separation of powers, but it also effectively eliminated meaningful judicial review of executive detention in violation of the Suspension Clause.

2. The Fourth Circuit's Refusal to Permit Review of the Basis for Hamdi's Detention Is Without Precedent

The Fourth Circuit concluded that "any inquiry" in the circumstances of Hamdi's detention "must be circumscribed to avoid encroachment into the military affairs entrusted to the executive branch." ... 316 F.3d at 473. But other than the decision below, no court has refused to engage in a factual inquiry in a citizen's habeas proceeding on the ground that such an inquiry would unconstitutionally encroach on the Executive's authority. In fact, the case law is entirely to the contrary.

The separation of powers doctrine did not, for example, preclude this Court from rejecting the government's argument that a habeas petitioner was a prisoner of war in

Ex parte Milligan, 71 U.S. (4 Wall.) 2, 131 (1866). Similarly, in *Camp v. Lockwood*, 1 U.S. (1 Dall.) 393, 396–97 (Pa. Ct. C.P. 1788), the court addressed and rejected the plaintiff's claim that "the proceeding against him was as an enemy, and not as a traitor."

The Fourth Circuit was also concerned that the "logistical effort to acquire evidence from far away battle zones . . . would profoundly unsettle the constitutional balance." . . . 316 F.3d at 471. But this Court has not hesitated to review the factual circumstances related to a military seizure overseas during wartime, including the government's claim that a citizen had a "design" to trade with the enemy. *Mitchell v. Harmony*, 54 U.S. (13 How.) 115, 133 (1851). The location of a seizure, in other words, has absolutely nothing to do with a court's ability to exercise judicial review. As this Court has noted without geographic reservation, "[w]hat are the allowable limits of military discretion, and whether or not they have been overstepped in a particular case, are judicial questions." *Sterling v. Constantin*, 287 U.S. 378, 400 (1932); *see also United States v. Lee*, 106 U.S. 196, 219–21 (1882).

Judicial authority to review the propriety of military seizures overseas during wartime has been repeatedly illustrated, in particular, in cases involving the law of prize. *See The Dashing Wave*, 72 U.S. (5 Wall.) 170 (1866); *The Springbok*, 72 U.S. (5 Wall.) 1 (1866); *United States v. Guillem*, 52 U.S. (11 How.) 47 (1850); *see also* C. John Colombos, *A Treatise on the Law of Prize* 49–107 (1926). Likewise, in the aftermath of the Civil War, courts regularly reviewed the entitlement of claimants under the Captured and Abandoned Property Act to recover compensation for property seized by the military in "zones of armed combat." *See, e.g., Briggs v. United States*, 143 U.S. 346 (1892); *Lamar v. Brown*, 92 U.S. 187, 194–95 (1875); *Mrs. Alexander's Cotton*, 69 U.S. (2 Wall.) 404 (1864). In sum, the separation of powers has never before precluded federal courts from reviewing the propriety of military seizures, even if overseas.

B. The Executive Has No Power to Authorize the Indefinite Detention of Citizens

The court of appeals found that "[b]ecause it is undisputed that Hamdi was captured in a zone of active combat in a foreign theater of conflict, . . . the [Mobbs] declaration is a sufficient basis upon which to conclude that the Commander in Chief has constitutionally detained Hamdi pursuant to the war powers entrusted to him by the United States Constitution." . . . 316 F.3d at 459. The Fourth Circuit's conclusion rests on at least two mistaken premises: (1) the Commander-in-Chief Clause empowers the President to detain citizens indefinitely; and (2) this Court's opinion in *Ex parte Quirin*, 317 U.S. 1 (1942), establishes the President's authority to detain "enemy combatants" under the law of war.[11] These premises are inconsistent with both the Constitution and precedent.

1. The Commander-in-Chief Clause Does Not Permit the Indefinite Detention of Citizens Outside of Areas of Actual Fighting

The Constitution gives the Executive no inherent power to detain citizens indefinitely during war or peace. While the Commander-in-Chief Clause necessarily entails plenary executive authority in areas of actual fighting, the power over citizens incident to this

---

[11] A third mistaken premise is that it is "undisputed" that Hamdi was seized in a "zone of active combat," when Hamdi was denied any voice in the entire proceeding, *see* . . . 337 F.3d at 357 (Luttig, J., dissenting from denial of reh'g), and Mobbs, the only person who did have a voice, never explicitly alleged that Hamdi was seized in such a location. This gap in the factual record on an issue evidently "crucial" to the Fourth Circuit's opinion, . . . 316 F.3d at 471, is the consequence of the denial of meaningful judicial review.

authority is only temporary. The Executive enjoys the authority to detain citizens seized in areas of actual fighting without specific statutory authority or judicial review for only a limited period of time as required by military necessity. Once the citizen is removed from the area of actual fighting, the Constitution requires statutory authorization to hold that citizen indefinitely.

Article II, Section 2, Clause 1 of the Constitution invests the President with the commander-in-chief power. This "power [is] purely military." *Fleming v. Page*, 50 U.S. (9 How.) 603, 615 (1850). It involves the power to deploy and direct the movement of troops in the field. *Id.*; *accord The Federalist No. 69*, at 465 (Alexander Hamilton) (Jacob E. Cooke ed., 1961) (commander-in-chief power "amount[s] to nothing more than the supreme command and direction of the military and naval forces"). The President's power as Commander in Chief "is not a military prerogative, without support of law, to seize persons or property because they are important or even essential for the military and naval establishment." *Youngstown Sheet & Tube Co. v. Sawyer*, 343 U.S. 579, 646 (1952) (Jackson, J., concurring).

. . .

Outside of the area of actual fighting, the Court often has had occasion to reject assertions of military authority over citizens. *See United States ex rel. Toth v. Quarles*, 350 U.S. 11, 23 (1955). Indeed, the scope of military authority permitted over citizens has been narrowly cabined to allow evacuation from an area in the face of an imminent invasion, jurisdiction incident to temporary military government, jurisdiction over members of the armed forces, and jurisdiction to conduct timely, congressionally authorized military prosecutions of citizens charged with violating the laws of war. *See Duncan*, 327 U.S. at 313–14; *see also Korematsu v. United States*, 323 U.S. 214 (1944); *Ex parte Quirin*, 317 U.S. 1 (1942).

Apart from these exceptions to civil jurisdiction, the Court has confined military authority over citizens solely to areas of actual fighting. In *Ex parte Milligan*, after acknowledging that occasions may arise in which "martial rule can be properly applied" to permit military rule over citizens, the Court explained that military authority to impose martial rule is "confined to the locality of actual war." 71 U.S. (4 Wall.) at 127. Similarly, in *Reid v. Covert*, Justice Black noted that "[i]n the face of an actively hostile enemy, military commanders necessarily have broad power over persons on the battlefront." 354 U.S. 1, 33 (1957) (plurality opinion). As in *Milligan*, however, Justice Black made clear that "[t]he exigencies which have required military rule on the battlefront are not present in areas where no conflict exists." *Id.* at 35; *see also Kinsella v. United States ex rel. Singleton*, 361 U.S. 234, 244–48 (1960) (refusing to permit military prosecution of civilian citizen accompanying military abroad). In sum, the principle that "the exercise of military power, where the rights of the citizen are concerned, shall never be pushed beyond what the exigency requires," is established under our system of government as "an unbending rule of law." *Raymond v. Thomas*, 91 U.S. 712, 716 (1875).

Lower courts, likewise, have rejected efforts by the Executive to assert authority over citizens in places where no war exists.[12] Indeed, during the War of 1812, Chancellor

---

[12] *See Ex parte Orozco*, 201 F. 106, 112 (W.D. Tex. 1912) (finding that "arrest upon the mere order of the President" by the military in time of peace is unlawful); *Ex parte Merryman*, 17 F. Cas. 144, 149 (C.C.D. Md. 1861) (No. 9,487) ("I can see no ground whatever for supposing that the president, in any emergency, or in any state of things, can authorize the suspension of the privileges of the writ of habeas corpus, or the arrest of a citizen, except in aid of the judicial power."); *Ex parte Randolph*, 20 F. Cas. 242, 254 (C.C.D. Va. 1833) (No. 11,558) (Marshall, Circuit Justice) (granting habeas relief to petitioner held in custody by an executive official and stating that executive officials "cannot act on other persons, or on other subjects, than those marked out in

Kent rejected military detention of a citizen in the United States even though the military accused him of providing aid to the British within enemy territory. In *In re Stacy*, 10 Johns. 328 (N.Y. Sup. Ct. 1813), petitioner Samuel Stacy, Jr., was seized by the military and imprisoned in the United States because he purportedly aided British troops "within the territory of the King of Great Britain." *Id*. at 329 (reporter's notes). Nonetheless, "[i]f ever a case called for the most prompt interposition of the court to enforce obedience to its process," Chancellor Kent wrote, "this is one. A military commander is here assuming criminal jurisdiction over a private citizen, is holding him in the closest confinement, and contemning the civil authority of the State." *Id*. at 334. The fact that Stacy purportedly assisted the British in enemy territory was irrelevant to the ruling.

. . .

Like the temporary seizure of the nation's steel mills, the indefinite detention of citizens by the Executive "cannot properly be sustained as an exercise of the President's military power as Commander in Chief of the Armed Forces." See *Youngstown Sheet & Tube Co. v. Sawyer*, 343 U.S. 579, 587 (1952). Hamdi is far from any location approximating a battlefield, and courthouses remain open near where he is imprisoned in South Carolina. His continued detention by the military therefore is indistinguishable from the "gross usurpation of power" rejected by this Court in *Ex parte Milligan*. *See* 71 U.S. (4 Wall.) 2, 127 (1866); *see also id*. at 141 (Chase, C.J., concurring).

. . .

3.   The Law of War[15] Does Not Authorize the Executive Branch to Detain Citizens Indefinitely

The Fourth Circuit also held that Hamdi "is being held as an enemy combatant pursuant to the well-established laws and customs of war." . . . 316 F.3d at 475. The law of war, however, cannot abrogate constitutional and statutory prohibitions against such a unilateral executive power.

Holding that the petitioners in *Quirin* were subject to military commissions, this Court noted that under international law, "[l]awful combatants are subject to capture and detention as prisoners of war by opposing military forces. Unlawful combatants are likewise subject to capture and detention, but in addition they are subject to trial and punishment by military tribunals for acts which render their belligerency unlawful." 317 U.S. at 31. Because "Congress ha[d] incorporated by reference, as within the jurisdiction of military commissions, all offenses which are defined as such by the law of war," international law was directly at issue in *Quirin*. *Id*. at 30.

The Fourth Circuit wrongly presumed that the authority to capture and detain combatants under the law of war amounts to a unilateral executive power to exercise military authority over citizens alleged to be combatants. Chief Justice Marshall

---

the power [granted by statute], nor can they proceed in a manner different from that it prescribes"); *Smith v. Shaw*, 12 Johns. 257, 266 (N.Y. Sup. Ct. 1815) ("If the defendant was justifiable in doing what he did, every citizen of the United States would, in time of war, be equally exposed to a like exercise of military power and authority."); *In re Stacy*, 10 Johns. 328, 334 (N.Y. Sup. Ct. 1813) (Kent, C.J.) (ordering issuance of attachment to enforce obedience to writ of habeas corpus issued in favor of citizen held in military camp as an alleged spy). Even in *In re Territo*, 156 F.2d 142 (9th Cir. 1946), where the court found, prior to the enactment of 18 U.S.C. §4001(a), that international law permitted detention of citizens as prisoners of war, the petitioner was afforded a hearing and access to counsel.

[15] The "law of war" is an old term for the body of customary and treaty-based international humanitarian law that describes internationally-accepted norms related to the waging of armed conflict. *See* William Winthrop, *Military Law and Precedents* 42 (reprint 2d ed. 1920).

rejected this argument in *Brown v. United States*, holding that "in executing the laws of war," the Executive could not "seize and the Courts condemn all property which, according to the modern law of nations, is subject to confiscation." 12 U.S. (8 Cranch) 110, 128, 129 (1814). The law of war does not independently provide the authority for government action without legislation. *Id.*; *accord Conrad v. Waples*, 96 U.S. 279, 285 (1877) ("[Congress] might, undoubtedly, have provided for the confiscation of the entire property, from its being within the enemy's country; but the legislature did not so enact."). In other words, the law of war is not an independent description of executive power. *Cf. Youngstown Sheet & Tube Co. v. Sawyer*, 343 U.S. 579, 604 (1952) (Frankfurter, J., concurring) ("[T]he fact that power exists in the Government does not vest it in the President."). The Court's analysis in *Brown* applies with equal force to the indefinite detention of Hamdi.

Unlike at the time that this Court decided *Brown*, however, a statute explicitly confirms that the Executive branch cannot independently authorize the indefinite detention of a citizen. 18 U.S.C. §4001(a) unambiguously "proscrib[es] detention of *any kind* by the United States, absent a congressional grant of authority to detain." *Howe v. Smith*, 452 U.S. 473, 479 n.3 (1981). To the extent that this statute conflicts with long-in-the-tooth customs of war, the thirty-three year old statute states the law. *See Breard v. Greene*, 523 U.S. 371, 376 (1998); *see also The Nereide*, 13 U.S. (9 Cranch) 388, 423 (1815) (Marshall, C.J.) (noting that the Court would be "bound by the law of nations" until Congress passed a contrary enactment).

The Fourth Circuit employed the law of war to sweep aside constitutional and statutory arguments against the unilateral executive detention of citizens. It is well-settled, however, that "the phrase 'war power' cannot be invoked as a talismanic incantation to support any exercise of . . . power which can be brought within its ambit." *United States v. Robel*, 389 U.S. 258, 263–64 (1967). Because the Executive's power "must stem either from an act of Congress or from the Constitution itself," *Youngstown*, 343 U.S. at 585, and the authority to indefinitely detain Hamdi is derived from neither source, his detention is illegal.

The fact that the Executive does not have the power to detain citizens indefinitely without congressional authorization does not leave our nation helpless in the circumstances presented in this case. The only other case that has arisen involving a citizen allegedly found on the opposite side of hostilities in Afghanistan is almost factually indistinguishable from this one. And Congress has already provided the statutory authority that the Executive used successfully to prosecute the other case. *See United States v. Lindh*, 227 F. Supp. 2d 565, 567–69 (E.D. Va. 2002).

C. Congress Possesses the Exclusive Power to Authorize Any Detention of a Citizen That Is More Than Temporary, But Has Not Done So Here

1. The Power to Authorize the Prolonged Detention of Citizens Rests Solely With Congress

A unilateral executive power to indefinitely detain citizens has the potential to jeopardize our democratic system. The structure and text of the Constitution, legislation dating back to the founding of this country, legal precedent, and the plain language of 18 U.S.C. §4001(a) all demonstrate that the authority to permit the prolonged detention of citizens is entirely entrusted to Congress.

First, the provision of the Constitution that addresses detention without judicial review, the power to suspend the writ of habeas corpus, is contained in Article I. U.S.

Const. art. I, §9, cl. 2. In one of the only overt references to individual rights in the main text of the Constitution, the Suspension Clause ensures judicial review of executive detention unless the Legislature suspends the Great Writ. *See Ex parte Bollman*, 8 U.S. (4 Cranch) 75, 101 (1807); *Ex parte Merryman*, 17 F. Cas. 144, 148 (C.C.D. Md. 1861) (No. 9,487). If the Executive branch possessed an equivalent power by which it could circumvent judicial review of detention on its own authority, the promise of the Suspension Clause would be forsaken.

Second, Congress is assigned the responsibility to define and punish offenses against the law of nations. U.S. Const. art. I, sec. 8, cl. 10; *see Ex parte Quirin*, 317 U.S. 1, 27 (1942). Likewise, it is Congress that must define criminal conduct. *See Liparota v. United States*, 471 U.S. 419, 424 (1985); *United States v. Hudson*, 11 U.S. (7 Cranch) 32, 34 (1812). The assignment of these powers to Congress demonstrates that the legislature, not the Executive, is peculiarly entrusted to specify prohibited conduct upon which a citizen may be subjected to indefinite detention. In other words, if the liberty protected by the Due Process Clause "is to be regulated, it must be pursuant to the law-making functions of the Congress." *Kent v. Dulles*, 357 U.S. 116, 129 (1958).

Third, outside of the context of criminal proceedings, Congress has been responsible for authorizing the detention of both enemy aliens and citizens in the United States. In this country's infancy, Congress passed the Alien Enemy Act of 1798, ch. 66, §1, 1 Stat. 577 (now codified at 50 U.S.C. §21), which authorizes the President to detain and deport enemy aliens found in the United States following a declaration of war. Moreover, in 1812, Congress enacted an "Act for the safe keeping and accommodation of prisoners of war," which permitted the President to arrange for "the safe keeping, support, and exchange of prisoners of war." Act of July 6, 1812, ch. 128, 2 Stat. 777 (repealed 1817). These statutes "afford[] a strong implication that [the President] did not possess those powers by virtue of [a] declaration of war," and that the detention of enemy aliens and prisoners of war in the United States requires statutory authorization. *Brown v. United States*, 12 U.S. (8 Cranch) 110, 126 (1814).

Similarly, during the Cold War, Congress enacted the Emergency Detention Act of 1950, Pub. L. No. 81–831, Title II, 64 Stat. 1019 (1950) (formerly codified at 50 U.S.C. §§811–826 (repealed)), which allowed the President during war or insurrection to detain people suspected of espionage or sabotage. Like the Alien Enemy Act of 1798 and the Safe Keeping and Accommodation of Prisoners of War Act of 1812, the Emergency Detention Act would have been unnecessary if the Constitution independently granted the President broad war powers to indefinitely detain citizens suspected of acting on behalf of our enemies.

Fourth, this Court on several occasions has indicated that congressional authorization is required for non-criminal detentions as well. In *Brown v. United States*, Chief Justice Marshall, writing for the Court, made clear that in the United States, the government can neither detain prisoners of war nor confiscate enemy property in the absence of congressional legislation. 12 U.S. (8 Cranch) at 126–29. This Court also has rejected the claim that the Executive possesses inherent power to authorize detention pending extradition. In *Valentine v. United States*, the Court stated that "the Constitution creates no executive prerogative to dispose of the liberty of the individual. Proceedings against him must be authorized by law." 299 U.S. 5, 9 (1936); *see also United States v. Moreland*, 258 U.S. 433, 443 (1922) (Brandeis, J., dissenting) (noting that "imprisonment . . . imposed under an executive order . . . was clearly void under the Constitution, whatever its character or incidents, its duration or the place of confinement").

Fifth, Congress has made it unmistakably clear that all detentions of citizens by the federal government must be pursuant to an act of Congress. "No citizen," Congress has stated, "shall be imprisoned or otherwise detained by the United States except pursuant to an Act of Congress." 18 U.S.C. §4001(a). By the enactment of section 4001(a) in 1971, Congress eliminated whatever doubt may have existed before that time that the Executive possessed independent authority to indefinitely detain U.S. citizens. In the absence of congressional authorization for the indefinite detention of Hamdi, his continued detention is illegal.

2.   Congress Has Not Authorized Hamdi's Indefinite Detention

In addition to holding that 18 U.S.C. §4001(a) was not "intended to overrule the long-standing rule" that an American citizen may be indefinitely detained as an "enemy combatant,"...316 F.3d at 468, the Fourth Circuit held in the alternative that the extraordinary detention of Hamdi was authorized by two congressional acts: a joint resolution known as the Authorization for the Use of Military Force, S.J. Res. 23, Pub. L. No. 107–40, 115 Stat. 224 (Sept. 18, 2001) ("AUMF"), and an appropriations provision set forth at 10 U.S.C. §956(5). Neither of these acts authorize the indefinite detention of citizens.

a.   The Authorization for the Use of Military Force Does Not Authorize Hamdi's Indefinite Detention

Passed only one week after the September 11, 2001 terrorist attacks, the AUMF grants the President the power to "use all necessary and appropriate force against those nations, organizations, or persons he determines planned, authorized, committed, or aided the terrorist attacks that occurred on September 11, 2001, or harbored such organizations or persons." AUMF §2(a). The concise terms of the joint resolution say little else except that it constitutes "specific statutory authorization" as required by the War Powers Resolution. *Id*. §2(b).

By its terms, therefore, the AUMF constitutes no greater authorization of power to the President than if Congress had issued a declaration of war. And a "declaration of war has only the effect of placing...two nations in a state of hostility, of producing a state of war, of giving those rights which war confers; but not of operating, by its own force, any of those results such as a transfer of property, which are usually produced by ulterior measures of government." *Brown*, 12 U.S. (8 Cranch) at 125–26. Indeed, the power to detain prisoners of war in the United States is not granted simply "by virtue of the declaration of war." *Id*.; *cf. Caldwell v. Parker*, 252 U.S. 376, 385 (1920) (declaration of war did not make soldiers exclusively subject to prosecution by court-martial).

Moreover, the text and history of section 4001(a) weigh against a finding that the AUMF permits the indefinite detention of citizens. Section 4001(a) prohibits detention "of any kind absent a congressional grant of authority to detain." *Howe v. Smith*, 452 U.S. 473, 479 n.3 (1981). By virtue of this statute, Congress specifically addressed the precise authority at issue and required that citizens not be imprisoned or otherwise detained by the United States "except pursuant to an Act of Congress." 18 U.S.C. §4001(a). The statute was enacted partly in response to the detention of Japanese-Americans in the United States during the Second World War. See H.R. Rep. No. 116, 92d Cong., 1st Sess. (1971), reprinted in 1971 U.S.C.C.A.N. 1435, 1436. Construing section 4001(a) to allow the Executive to detain citizens based solely on a declaration of war runs directly counter to this basis for its enactment.

Under these circumstances, no authorization to detain citizens can be implied from the AUMF. "It is one thing to draw an intention of Congress from general language...where Congress has not addressed itself to a specific situation," Justice Frankfurter noted in *Youngstown*, but "[i]t is quite impossible...when Congress did specifically address itself to a problem, as Congress did to that of seizure, to find secreted in the interstices of legislation the very grant of power which Congress consciously withheld." *Youngstown Sheet & Tube Co. v. Sawyer*, 343 U.S. 579, 609 (1952) (Frankfurter, J., concurring).

More specifically, this Court made clear in *Ex parte Endo* that statutory authorization for the detention of citizens requires that it be done in clear and unmistakable language:

> We must assume that the Chief Executive and members of Congress, as well as the courts, are sensitive to and respectful of the liberties of the citizen. In interpreting a wartime measure we must assume that their purpose was to allow for the greatest possible accommodation between those liberties and the exigencies of war. We must assume, when asked to find implied powers in a grant of legislative or executive authority, that the law makers intended to place no greater restraint on the citizen than was clearly and unmistakably indicated by the language they used.

323 U.S. 283, 300 (1944).[16]

The AUMF, of course, does not "use the language of detention." *Id*. Nor does it mention citizens, much less section 4001(a). Given its attention to invocation of the War Powers Resolution, "[i]t is unlikely – indeed inconceivable – that Congress would...at the same time[] leave unstated and to inference something so significant and unprecedented as authorization to detain American citizens under the Non-Detention Act [18 U.S.C. §4001(a)]." *Padilla v. Rumsfeld*, 352 F.3d 695, 723 (2d Cir. 2003), *cert. granted*, 72 U.S.L.W. 3488 (U.S. Feb. 20, 2004) (No. 03-1027). Because the AUMF does not specifically authorize the detention of citizens, it cannot represent a congressional sanction for Hamdi's detention.

b. 10 U.S.C. §956(5) Does Not Authorize Hamdi's Indefinite Detention

10 U.S.C. §956(5) provides that department of defense "[f]unds...may be used for...expenses incident to the maintenance, pay, and allowances of prisoners of war, other persons...whose status is determined...to be similar to prisoners of war, and persons detained...pursuant to Presidential proclamation." This run-of-the mill statute does not authorize the indefinite detention of citizens.

As an initial matter, the statutory language says nothing about citizens, much less the authority to detain, and therefore is far from the specific authorization required by section 4001(a). On the contrary, the statute simply permits the use of funds for expenses related to the maintenance of prisoners of war, other detainees, and those detained by Presidential proclamation. Just as the statute does not purport to authorize the President to detain people by proclamation, it does not constitute authorization for detention of any other kind.

---

[16] In fact, this Court's jurisprudence reveals a healthy skepticism applied to statutes cited to support congressional authorization of the exercise of military control over citizens. *See Duncan v. Kahanamoku*, 327 U.S. 304, 324 (1946) (holding that Congress did not intend to supplant the civilian court system when it authorized martial law in territory of Hawaii); *Raymond v. Thomas*, 91 U.S. 712, 715–16 (1875) (holding that a military order annulling a judicial order was unauthorized by Congress and therefore void); *Ex parte Milligan*, 71 U.S. (4 Wall.) 2, 135 (1866) (Chase, C.J., concurring) (concluding that Congress had not authorized Milligan's seizure).

In *Ex parte Endo*, this Court explained that authority for the detention of citizens cannot be construed from just such a general appropriation. 323 U.S. at 303 n.24; *see also Greene v. McElroy*, 360 U.S. 474, 505 n.30 (1959). In the absence of language that "plainly show[s] a purpose to bestow [that] precise authority," an appropriations provision does not constitute authority for the Executive to detain citizens. *Endo*, 323 U.S. at 303 n.24.

. . .

3. The Indefinite Detention of Hamdi Constitutes Impermissible Lawmaking by the Executive Branch

In this case, the Fourth Circuit's extraordinary deference to the Executive effectively approved secret lawmaking incident to the creation of undisclosed criteria for determining which citizens the Executive will detain indefinitely. The Mobbs declaration indicates that the Executive determined that any citizen "associated" with the former government of Afghanistan may be designated an "enemy combatant." The Executive also established undisclosed criteria to determine whether a citizen so designated would be subject to indefinite detention. By these acts, the Executive endeavored to make its own secret law.

This Court has rebuffed attempts by the Executive to encroach upon the law-making function of the Congress. *See, e.g., Youngstown Sheet & Tube Co. v. Sawyer*, 343 U.S. 579 (1952) (striking down as impermissible lawmaking an Executive Order directing the Secretary of Commerce to take possession of and operate steel mills). The power to make laws was entrusted by "[t]he Founders of this Nation . . . to the Congress alone in both good and bad times." *Id*. at 589. On this point, the Court has observed, "the Constitution is neither silent nor equivocal." *Id*. at 587.

. . .

Although "the powers of the three branches are not always neatly defined," *Clinton v. Jones*, 520 U.S. 681, 701 (1997), the power to authorize the indefinite detention of citizens by the federal government is, as we have demonstrated above, firmly entrusted to Congress. The court of appeals therefore erred by recognizing an illegitimate power of the Executive to make its own law.

CONCLUSION

For the above-stated reasons, Petitioners respectfully request that this Court reverse the ruling of the United States Court of Appeals for the Fourth Circuit.

. . .

No. 03-6696

In the Supreme Court of the United States

YASER ESAM HAMDI AND ESAM FOUAD HAMDI,
AS NEXT FRIEND OF YASER ESAM HAMDI, PETITIONERS

v.

DONALD RUMSFELD, SECRETARY OF DEFENSE, ET AL.

*ON WRIT OF CERTIORARI
TO THE UNITED STATES COURT OF APPEALS
FOR THE FOURTH CIRCUIT*

BRIEF FOR THE RESPONDENTS

THEODORE B. OLSON
*Solicitor General
Counsel of Record*

PAUL D. CLEMENT
Deputy Solicitor General

GREGORY G. GARRE
*Assistant to the Solicitor
General*

JOHN A. DRENNAN
Attorney

Department of Justice
████████████████

* Redaction on this page has been added for privacy purposes. – *Eds*.

QUESTION PRESENTED

Whether the court of appeals erred in holding that respondents have established the legality of the military's detention of Yaser Esam Hamdi, a presumed American citizen who was captured in Afghanistan during the combat operations in late 2001, and was determined by the military to be an enemy combatant who should be detained in connection with the ongoing hostilities in Afghanistan.

. . .

STATEMENT

. . .

4. On December 2, 2003, the Department of Defense announced that, as a matter of policy, it will permit an enemy combatant who is a presumed citizen and detained in the United States to have access to counsel after the military has determined that such access will not compromise national security and it has either completed intelligence collection from the detainee or determined that access to counsel would not interfere with such efforts. See <www.defenselink.mil/releases/2003/nr20031202-0717.html>. The Department of Defense also announced that Hamdi would be permitted access to counsel under that policy, subject to appropriate security constraints. *Ibid*. Hamdi has met with counsel for petitioners on February 2 and March 2, 2004, at the Charleston Naval Brig. The latter visit was unmonitored.

SUMMARY OF ARGUMENT

The court of appeals correctly concluded that Hamdi's wartime detention is lawful and that this next-friend habeas action therefore should be dismissed.

I. Petitioners' purely legal challenges to Hamdi's wartime detention are without merit. In our constitutional system, the responsibility for waging war is committed to the political branches. In time of war, the President, as Commander in Chief, has the authority to capture and detain enemy combatants for the duration of hostilities. That includes enemy combatants presumed to be United States citizens. *Ex parte Quirin*, 317 U.S. 1 (1942). The U.S. military took control of Hamdi and determined that he was an enemy combatant in Afghanistan while waging a military campaign launched by the President with the express statutory backing of Congress. The military's authority to hold such a captured enemy combatant in connection with ongoing hostilities is well-established.

Nothing in 18 U.S.C. 4001(a) affects the Executive's authority to detain enemy combatants in wartime. Moreover, Congress has authorized such detentions by, *inter alia*, expressly backing the President's use of "all necessary and appropriate force" in the current conflict. 115 Stat. 224. Nor is Hamdi's detention inconsistent with Article 5 of the [Geneva Convention Relative to the Treatment of Prisoners of War of August 12, 1949, 75 U.N.T.S. No. 972 (GPW)]. The GPW is not self-executing and therefore does not confer any private rights that may be enforced in a habeas action. In any event, Article 5 applies only when there is "doubt" as to whether a detainee is entitled to prisoner-of-war (POW) privileges under the GPW. No such doubt exists here because the President has conclusively determined that al Qaeda and Taliban detainees are *not* entitled to those privileges. Neither the GPW nor the military's own regulations provide for any review of the military's determination that an individual is an enemy combatant in the first place.

II. Petitioners' challenge to the military's determination that Hamdi is an enemy combatant is also without merit. An enemy combatant who is a presumed citizen and who is detained in this country is entitled to judicial review of his detention by way of habeas corpus. In such a proceeding, a habeas petitioner may raise legal challenges to the individual's detention, such as petitioners' arguments that the Commander in Chief does not have the authority to detain a captured enemy combatant who is an American citizen, or that such a detention is barred by 18 U.S.C. 4001(a). However, the scope of judicial review that is available concerning the military's determination that an individual is an enemy combatant is necessarily limited by the fundamental separation-of-powers concerns raised by a court's review or second-guessing of such a core military judgment in wartime.

Applying an appropriately deferential standard of review, the court of appeals correctly concluded that the record adequately demonstrates that Hamdi is indeed an enemy combatant. The sworn declaration accompanying the government's return explains that Hamdi surrendered with an enemy unit in a theater of combat operations while armed with an AK-47, and that he is therefore a prototypical enemy combatant. Moreover, petitioners have repeatedly acknowledged that Hamdi was in Afghanistan – an area of extensive combat operations – when he was captured. Taking account of petitioners' own admissions and arguments in determining whether the challenged exercise of executive authority is lawful is consistent with the settled rule of restraint that a court should go no further than necessary to decide a sensitive constitutional issue before it.

III. The necessarily limited scope of review that is available in a habeas proceeding in this extraordinary context is consistent both with the Constitution and federal habeas statutes. The habeas statutes do not require a court to conduct evidentiary proceedings when, as here, a court may determine on the record before it that there is no cause for granting the writ. *Walker* v. *Johnston*, 312 U.S. 275 (1941). Nor does the Constitution guarantee captured enemy combatants an automatic or immediate right of access to counsel in a habeas proceeding such as this. A captured enemy combatant who is being detained during the conflict – and has not been charged with any crime – has no right under the law of war to meet with counsel to plot a legal strategy to secure his release. The Due Process Clause – which is interpreted in the light of that long-settled rule – does not supply any different guarantee. Moreover, granting enemy combatants an automatic right of access to counsel would interfere with the military's compelling interest in gathering intelligence to further the war effort.

The Department of Defense has adopted a policy to allow enemy combatants who are presumed United States citizens and detained in this country access to counsel once the military has determined that such access will not interfere with intelligence gathering. In light of that policy, the fact that Hamdi now enjoys access to counsel under the policy, and the canon of constitutional avoidance, the Court may wish to reserve the counsel issue for another day. If the Court reaches the issue, however, it should affirm the court of appeals' conclusion that Hamdi was not entitled to immediate access to counsel in this habeas action.

IV. Any attempt at further factual development concerning the military's enemy-combatant determination would present formidable constitutional and practical difficulties. Attempting to recreate the scene of Hamdi's capture is inconsistent with the practical reality that the troops in Afghanistan are charged with winning a war and not preparing to defend their judgments in a U.S. courtroom. In addition, any fact-finding concerning Hamdi's capture could require locating the American soldiers who interviewed Hamdi in Afghanistan, not to mention the Northern Alliance forces to whom Hamdi surrendered. Such efforts would divert the military's attention from the ongoing conflict in Afghanistan, and it would be demoralizing for American troops to be called to account for their actions in a federal courtroom by the very enemies whom they have been ordered by the political branches to reduce to submission.

ARGUMENT

THE COURT OF APPEALS CORRECTLY HELD THAT HAMDI'S WARTIME DETENTION IS LAWFUL AND THAT THIS ACTION SHOULD BE DISMISSED

The next-friend habeas petition in this case challenges the authority of the Commander in Chief and the armed forces under his command to detain an enemy combatant who was undisputedly captured in an active combat zone in a foreign land in connection with a military campaign that is still ongoing. This case does not present the threshold jurisdictional obstacle in *Rasul* v. *Bush*, Nos. 03-334 & 03-343, because the detainee at issue is a presumed American citizen and is being held in the United States. The U.S. courts therefore have jurisdiction to consider this habeas action and, in particular, have authority to hear legal challenges to Hamdi's detention. As the court of appeals recognized, however, the nature of judicial review available with respect to the military's enemy-combatant determination is limited by the profound separation-of-powers concerns implicated by efforts to second-guess the factual basis for the exercise of the Commander in Chief's authority to detain a captured enemy combatant in wartime. Guided by those considerations, the court of appeals correctly held that the government has demonstrated the legality of Hamdi's detention.

I. PETITIONERS' LEGAL CHALLENGES TO HAMDI'S WARTIME DETENTION ARE WITHOUT MERIT

Petitioners challenge Hamdi's detention on the purely legal grounds that the Executive lacks authority to detain an enemy combatant who is a presumed United States citizen; that such a detention is barred by 18 U.S.C. 4001(a); and that Article 5 of the GPW entitles such a detainee to a tribunal. Those arguments should be rejected.

A. The Challenged Wartime Detention Falls Squarely Within The Commander In Chief's War Powers

The Constitution vests the political branches and, in particular, the Commander in Chief, with the power necessary to "provide for the common defense," U.S. Const. preamble, including the authority to vanquish the enemy and repel foreign attack in time of war. See *Ex parte Quirin*, 317 U.S. 1, 26 (1942) (listing the enumerated war powers). That power is fully engaged with respect to the armed conflict that the United States is now fighting against the al Qaeda terrorist network and its supporters in the mountains of Afghanistan and elsewhere; is supported by the statutory backing of Congress; and applies equally to an enemy combatant, like Hamdi, who is a presumed United States citizen.

    1. Article II, §2, Cl. 1 of the Constitution states that "[t]he President shall be Commander in Chief of the Army and Navy of the United States." As this Court observed in *Johnson* v. *Eisentrager*, 339 U.S. 763, 788 (1950), it is "of course" the case that the textual "grant of war power includes all that is necessary and proper for carrying [it] into execution." See also *Quirin*, 317 U.S. at 28 ("An important incident to the conduct of war is the adoption of measures by the military command *** to repel and defeat

the enemy."); *Fleming* v. *Page*, 50 U.S. (9 How.) 603, 615 (1850) (President has authority, *inter alia*, to "employ [the U.S. armed forces] in the manner he may deem most effectual to harass and conquer and subdue the enemy."); accord *Stewart* v. *Kahn*, 78 U.S. (11 Wall.) 493, 506 (1870). . . . [4]

It is well-settled that the President's war powers include the authority to capture and detain enemy combatants in wartime, at least for the duration of a conflict. See *Quirin*, 317 U.S. at 30–31 & n.8; see also *Duncan* v. *Kahanamoku*, 327 U.S. 304, 313–314 (1946); 2 L. Oppenheim, *International Law* 308–309 (H. Lauterpacht ed., 5th ed. 1935); William Winthrop, *Military Law and Precedents* 788 (2d ed. 1920). . . . Indeed, the practice of capturing and detaining enemy combatants in wartime not only is deeply rooted in this Nation's history, see Lt. Col. G. Lewis & Capt. J. Mewha, *History of Prisoner of War Utilization by the United States Army 1776–1945, Dep't of the Army Pamphlet No. 20-213* (1955), but as old as warfare itself, see Allan Rosas, *The Legal Status of Prisoners of War* 44–45 (1976).

In *Quirin*, the Court explained that the "universal agreement and practice" under "the law of war" holds that "[l]awful combatants are subject to capture and detention as prisoners of war by opposing military forces." 317 U.S. at 30–31. . . . As a matter of practice, moreover, the mere detention of opposing forces as enemy combatants or prisoners of war without military punishment has been the rule, and detention and prosecution of enemy combatants for specific war crimes the exception.

The U.S. military has captured and detained enemy combatants during the course of virtually every major conflict in the Nation's history, including more recent conflicts such as the Gulf, Vietnam, and Korean wars. During World War II, the United States detained hundreds of thousands of POWs in the United States (some of whom were, or claimed to be, American citizens) without trial or counsel. See Lewis & Mewha, *supra*, at 244. During the Civil War, the United States detained hundreds of thousands of confederate combatants – who remained United States citizens. *Id*. at 27–28. As the court of appeals recognized, the military's settled authority to detain captured enemy combatants in wartime applies squarely to the global armed conflict in which the United States is currently engaged, in which – as the September 11 attacks demonstrate – the stakes are no less grave. . . . .

The detention of captured enemy combatants serves vital military objectives. First, "detention prevents enemy combatants from rejoining the enemy and continuing to fight against America and its allies." J.A. 430; see *In re Territo*, 156 F.2d 142, 145 (9th Cir. 1946). Second, detention enables the military to gather vital intelligence from captured combatants concerning the capabilities, internal operations, and intentions of the enemy. See Howard S. Levie, *Prisoners of War in International Armed Conflict*, 59 Int'l Law Studies 108–109 (U.S. Naval War College 1977); . . . (Woolfolk Decl.). Such intelligence-gathering is especially critical in the current conflict because of the unconventional way

---

[4] The Framers appreciated the importance of giving the Executive unquestioned authority to defend against foreign attack. As Hamilton wrote in *The Federalist No. 70*, "[d]ecision, activity, secrecy, and dispatch" are characteristic of a unitary executive power and are "essential to the protection of the community against foreign attacks." Forty-five years later, Justice Story, in discussing the Commander-in-Chief Clause, reaffirmed that: "Of all the cases and concerns of government, the direction of war most peculiarly demands those qualities, which distinguish the exercise of power by a single hand. Unity of plan, promptitude, activity, and decision, are indispensable to success; and these can scarcely exist, except when a single magistrate is entrusted exclusively with the power." *Commentaries on the Constitution of the United States* §767, at 546–547 (Ronald D. Rotunda & John E. Nowak eds. 1987). Although petitioners object . . . to "[t]he danger posed by the collection of power in one branch," the Constitution leaves no doubt that there is only one Commander in Chief. Petitioners' reliance on separation-of-powers cases in which there was no such singular textual constitutional commitment of power is misplaced.

in which the enemy operates. See Part III.B, *infra*. The detention of captured combatants during an ongoing armed conflict " 'is neither a punishment nor an act of vengeance,' but rather a 'simple war measure.'" J.A. 431 (quoting Winthrop, *supra*, at 788).[5]

Petitioners repeatedly characterize Hamdi's detention as "indefinite." But the detention of enemy combatants during World War II was just as "indefinite" while that war was being fought. It is true that, given its unconventional nature, the current conflict is unlikely to end with a formal cease-fire agreement, but that does not mean that Hamdi will not be released. The military has made clear that it has no intention of holding captured enemy combatants any longer than necessary in light of the interests of national security, and scores of captured enemy combatants have been released by the United States or transferred to the custody of other governments. See 03-334 & 03-343 U.S. Br. 47–49.

2. The only claim raised in the habeas petition in this case and still being pressed by petitioners is that, "as an American citizen," Hamdi's detention as an enemy combatant violates the Due Process Clause. . . . . The court of appeals correctly rejected that purely legal argument. . . . .

The military's authority to detain enemy combatants in wartime is not diminished by a claim, or even a showing, of American citizenship. . . . . As this Court observed more than 50 years ago in *Quirin*, "[c]itizenship in the United States of an enemy belligerent does not relieve him from the consequences of a belligerency which is unlawful." 317 U.S. at 37. . . .

Petitioners suggest that a presumed United States citizen should be relieved of the consequences of his status as an enemy combatant when it comes to *detention*, as opposed to trial and *punishment* for a war crime. . . . . That is incorrect. *Quirin* involved a challenge to the "detention and trial of petitioners." 317 U.S. at 25; *id*. at 18–19. Moreover, if, as this Court held in *Quirin*, citizenship does not relieve an enemy combatant of the most severe consequences of violating the law of war – a military commission and punishment up to death – then citizenship does not relieve an enemy combatant of the normal and less drastic consequence of capture by opposing forces, *i.e.*, detention during the conflict. *Id*. at 37–38.

The *Quirin* Court's discussion of *Ex parte Milligan*, 71 U.S. (4 Wall.) 2 (1866), reinforces the conclusion that citizens, no less than aliens, who are "part of or associate[]" with the armed forces of the enemy" may be held accountable under the law of war for their status or actions as enemy belligerents. *Quirin*, 317 U.S. at 45. *Milligan* involved a citizen who was seized by the military and was convicted by a military commission on charges that he conspired against the Union in the Civil War. 71 U.S. (4 Wall.) at 6–7. He challenged the military's authority to proceed against him, arguing that he was not a member of the U.S. armed forces and was not "within the limits of any State whose citizens were engaged in rebellion against the United States, at any time during the war." *Id*. at 7. The Court found that Milligan was "in nowise connected with the military

---

[5] Petitioners assert . . . that Hamdi's detention is "criminal punishment." But, as discussed above, the detention of enemy combatants has not "historically been regarded as a punishment" and is not designed to "promote the traditional aims of punishment." *Kennedy* v. *Mendoza-Martinez*, 372 U.S. 144, 168–169 (1963). Hamdi is being held for the classic non-punitive purposes of wartime detention, and has not been charged with any war crime or domestic offense. In that respect, Hamdi's situation is unlike that of the so-called "American Taliban" to whom petitioners compare Hamdi. See Pet. Br. 40 (arguing that John Walker Lindh's case is "indistinguishable" from Hamdi's). Unlike Hamdi, Lindh was charged with criminal offenses based on his association with the Taliban and, after pleading guilty to aiding the Taliban and using a weapon with the Taliban, Lindh was sentenced to 20 years' imprisonment. See <www.cnn.com/2002/LAW/10/04/lindh.statement>. Because Hamdi is not serving any criminal punishment, he may be released after the current hostilities end or at any point that the military determines such release is appropriate.

service," and held that he therefore was not subject to punishment under the law of war. *Id.* at 121–122.

The presumed American in *Quirin*, Herman Haupt, argued that the law of war did not apply to him under the rationale of *Milligan*. In rejecting that claim, the *Quirin* Court emphasized that *Milligan*'s "statement as to the inapplicability of the law of war to Milligan's case" was limited to "the facts before it." 317 U.S. at 45. In particular, the *Quirin* Court stressed, "Milligan, not being a part of or associated with the armed forces of the enemy, was a non-belligerent, not subject to the law of war." *Ibid.* Haupt, unlike Milligan, associated with the forces of the enemy and therefore was an "enemy belligerent." *Id.* at 37. As a result, the *Quirin* Court held, Haupt was fully subject to the law of war even though he was a presumed American. *Ibid.* Hamdi, who surrendered in Afghanistan with a Taliban unit while armed with an AK-47, is, like Haupt, a prototypical enemy belligerent subject to the law of war. See Part II.B, *infra*.[6]

B. Hamdi's Detention Is Bolstered By, And By No Means Contrary To, The Actions Of Congress

1. Petitioners argue . . . that "Congress alone" has the power to authorize the detention of a captured enemy combatant who is a presumed American citizen. See also Pet. Br. 29–30, 41–42. That is incorrect. Especially in the case of foreign attack, the President's authority to wage war is not dependent on "any special legislative authority." *The Prize Cases*, 67 U.S. (2 Black) 635, 668 (1862). The Nation was viciously attacked on September 11, 2001; the President dispatched the armed forces with orders to destroy the organizations and individuals responsible for that attack; and, as Commander in Chief, the President may employ the armed forces "in the manner he may deem most effectual to harass and conquer and subdue the enemy." *Fleming*, 50 U.S. (9 How.) at 615; see p. 13, *supra*. That includes the authority to engage in the time-honored and humanitarian practice of *detaining* enemy combatants captured in connection with the conflict, as opposed to subjecting such combatants to the more harmful consequences of war.

Petitioners acknowledge . . . that the Executive has "plenary power" to capture and detain enemy combatants like Hamdi "in areas of actual fighting," but argue that once a "citizen is removed from the area of actual fighting," the Executive cannot detain the citizen without "statutory authorization." See Pet. Br. 29. That argument is misguided. This Court has long recognized that the commander-in-chief power "is not limited to victories in the field and the dispersion of the insurgent forces," but "carries with it inherently the power to guard against the immediate renewal of the conflict." *Stewart*, 78 U.S. at 507; see *In re Yamashita*, 327 U.S. 1, 12 (1946). One of the most conventional and humane ways of protecting against the "immediate renewal" of fighting in connection with an ongoing conflict is to detain captured combatants so that they may not rejoin the enemy.

Moreover, the general practice of the U.S. military – and the practice called for by the GPW (art. 19, 6 U.S.T. at 3334) – is to evacuate captured enemy combatants from the battlefield and to a secure location for detention. That protects both U.S. soldiers

---

[6] Petitioners rely . . . on other cases to support their claim that no citizen may be subject to military authority outside of an active battlefield. Those cases, however, involved the military trial of *civilians* for ordinary crimes, and not the wartime detention of an *enemy combatant* like Hamdi. See, *e.g.*, *United States ex rel. Toth* v. *Quarles*, 350 U.S. 11 (1955) (ex-serviceman charged with murder); *Reid* v. *Covert*, 354 U.S. 1 (1957) (plurality) (wife of serviceman charged with murder); *Kinsella* v. *United States ex rel. Singleton*, 361 U.S. 234 (1960) (wife of serviceman charged with murder); *Raymond* v. *Thomas*, 91 U.S. 712 (1875); cf. *In re Stacey*, 10 Johns. 328 (N.Y. Sup. Ct. 1813) (military commander "assum[ed] criminal jurisdiction over a private citizen").

and detainees. Once the military makes a determination that an individual is an enemy combatant who should be detained in connection with the conflict, the *place* where the combatant is detained in no way affects the legality of that determination, much less the circumstances that led to the determination in the first place.

2. In any event, Congress *has* affirmed the type of classic wartime detention at issue in this case. As explained above, immediately following the September 11 attacks, Congress not only recognized by statute that "the President has authority under the Constitution to take action to deter and prevent acts of international terrorism against the United States," but explicitly backed the President's use of "all necessary and appropriate force" in connection with the current conflict. 115 Stat. 224. As the court of appeals explained, "capturing and detaining enemy combatants is an inherent part of warfare; the 'necessary and appropriate force' referenced in the congressional resolution necessarily includes the capture and detention of any and all hostile forces arrayed against our troops." J.A. 435; see 03-1027 U.S. Br. 38–44, *Rumsfeld* v. *Padilla* (discussing authorization).

Capturing and detaining enemy combatants is a quintessential and necessary aspect of the *use* of military force, not to mention a customary and necessary means of *defeating* the enemy. See *Quirin*, 317 U.S. at 28–29 ("An important incident to the conduct of war is the adoption of measures by the military command not only to repel and defeat the enemy, but to seize and subject to disciplinary measures those enemies who in their attempt to thwart or impede our military effort have violated the law of war."). American troops are still engaged in active combat against al Qaeda and Taliban fighters in Afghanistan, and have just launched a new offensive against the enemy. . . . . The President's authority to use military force in Afghanistan and elsewhere in the global armed conflict against the al Qaeda terrorist network must include the authority to detain those enemy combatants who are captured during the conflict; otherwise, such combatants could rejoin the enemy and renew their belligerency against our forces.

Accordingly, far from being at odds with Congress's actions, the classic wartime detention at issue comes with the express statutory backing of Congress. And the President's constitutional authority in these matters therefore is at its apogee. See *Dames & Moore* v. *Regan*, 453 U.S. 654, 668 (1981); *Youngstown Sheet & Tube Co.* v. *Sawyer*, 343 U.S. 579, 637 (1952) (Jackson, J., concurring).

3. Although they did not raise the claim in their habeas petition, petitioners argue . . . that Hamdi's detention is barred by 18 U.S.C. 4001(a). The court of appeals properly rejected that argument. . . . . As the government has fully explained in *Padilla* (see 03-1027 U.S. Br. 44–49), Section 4001 does not intrude on the authority of the Executive to capture and detain enemy combatants in wartime. . . .

. . .

C.   Hamdi's Detention Is Consistent With Article 5 Of The GPW And The Military's Own Regulations

Although they did not raise the claim in their habeas petition, petitioners argue (Br. 17–18) that Hamdi's detention is barred by Article 5 of the GPW, 6 U.S.T. at 3322. That is incorrect. To begin with, the GPW supplies no basis for granting habeas relief because it is not self-executing. J.A. 436; see *Eisentrager*, 339 U.S. at 789 n.14; 03-334 & 03-343 U.S. Br. 39 (citing authorities). Moreover, as the court of appeals explained, the fact that the habeas statute permits an individual to challenge his detention based on a violation of a treaty, 28 U.S.C. 2241, does not mean that a habeas petitioner may challenge his detention based on an alleged violation of a non-self-executing treaty like the GPW, which does not confer any privately enforceable rights. . . . .

In any event, petitioners' Article 5 claim fails for the same reason as their claim that Hamdi's detention is inconsistent with the military's regulations concerning POWs and other detainees. Br. 17–18 (citing Army Regulation, *Enemy Prisoners of War, Retained Personnel, Civilian Internees and Other Detainees* (1997) (C.A. App. 91-128)). Both Article 5 and the military's regulations call for a military tribunal only when there is "doubt" as to an individual's "legal status" under the GPW to receive POW privileges, and not as to each and every captured combatant. See Reg. 1–5a(2) (C.A. App. 96) ("All persons taken into custody by the U.S. forces will be provided the protections" afforded POWs "until some other *legal* status is determined *by competent authority*.") (emphases added).[8] In the case of Hamdi and the other al Qaeda and Taliban detainees in the current conflict, there is no such doubt. The President – the highest "competent authority" on the subject – has conclusively determined that al Qaeda and Taliban detainees, including Hamdi, do not qualify for POW privileges under the GPW. . . . . [9]

Furthermore, neither Article 5 nor the military's regulations apply to the threshold determination whether an individual is in fact subject to capture and detention. As explained, they apply only to the determination whether a captured combatant is entitled to POW privileges under the GPW, which in turn is based on whether the combatant is a lawful or unlawful combatant. As the court of appeals explained, for purposes of this habeas petition, that is "a distinction without a difference, since the option to detain until the cessation of hostilities belongs to the executive in either case." J.A. 438; see *Quirin*, 327 U.S. at 30–31.

II. UNDER ANY CONSTITUTIONALLY APPROPRIATE STANDARD, THE RECORD DEMONSTRATES THAT HAMDI IS AN ENEMY COMBATANT

Petitioners also challenge the military's determination that Hamdi is an enemy combatant. The court of appeals properly rejected that argument and held that no further factual development is warranted.

A. The Executive's Determination That An Individual Is An Enemy Combatant Is Entitled To The Utmost Deference By A Court

As this Court has observed, "courts traditionally have been reluctant to intrude upon the authority of the Executive in military and national security affairs." *Department of the Navy* v. *Egan*, 484 U.S. 518, 530 (1988); see *Haig* v. *Agee*, 453 U.S. 280, 292 (1981)

---

[8] The commentary accompanying Article 5 states that it was added to address the concern "that decisions which might have the gravest consequences should not be left to a *single* person, who might often be of *subordinate* rank." Int'l Comm. of the Red Cross, Commentary III, *Geneva Convention Relative to the Treatment of Prisoners of War* 77 (Jean S. Pictet & Jean de Preux eds. 1960) (Commentary III) (emphases added). As discussed above, individuals, such as Hamdi, who have been taken into U.S. control in Afghanistan and ultimately designated for continued detention by the military are subjected to a detailed and multilayered screening process. Moreover, as discussed in the text below, the President himself has made the only determination that is legally relevant for purposes of Article 5–*i.e.*, that al Qaeda and Taliban detainees are not entitled to POW privileges under the GPW. See also No. 03-334 & 03-343 Br. for Amici Law Professors, Former Legal Advisers of the Department of State and Ambassadors et al. 20–24 (discussing Article 5 of GPW).

[9] The President's determination is based on the fact that al Qaeda and Taliban fighters systematically do not follow the law of war and therefore do not qualify as lawful combatants under Article 4 of the GPW, 6 U.S.T. at 3320, entitled to POW privileges. See Office of the White House Press Secretary, *Fact Sheet, Status of Detainees at Guantanamo* (Feb. 7, 2002) <www.whitehouse.gov/news/releases/2002/02/2002020713.html>; Dep't of Defense, *Briefing on Detainee Operations* (Feb. 13, 2004) <www.defenselink.mil/transcripts/2004/tr20040213-0443.html>; 03-34 & 03-343 U.S. Br. 45 n.18. The determination whether captured enemy combatants are entitled to POW privileges under the GPW is a quintessential matter that the Constitution (not to mention the GPW) leaves to the political branches and, in particular, the President.

("Matters intimately related to foreign policy and national security are rarely proper subjects for judicial intervention."). The customary deference that courts afford the Executive in matters of military affairs is especially warranted in this context.

A commander's wartime determination that an individual is an enemy combatant is a quintessentially military judgment, representing a core exercise of the Commander-in-Chief authority. See *Hirota* v. *MacArthur*, 338 U.S. 197, 215 (1949) ("[T]he capture and control of those who were responsible for the Pearl Harbor incident was a political question on which the President as Commander in Chief, and as spokesman for the nation in foreign affairs, had the final say.") (Douglas, J., concurring); cf. *Ludecke* v. *Watkins*, 335 U.S. 160, 170 (1948); *Eisentrager*, 339 U.S. at 789. In this case, that determination was made by U.S. armed forces in Afghanistan acting under the directives of the U.S. Land Forces Commander in Afghanistan..... As the court of appeals explained, "[t]he designation of Hamdi as an enemy combatant thus bears the closest imaginable connection to the President's constitutional responsibilities during the conduct of hostilities." J.A. 432.

Especially in the course of hostilities, the military through its operations and intelligence-gathering has an unmatched vantage point from which to learn about the enemy and make judgments as to whether those seized during a conflict are friend or foe. As the court of appeals stated, "[t]he executive is best prepared to exercise the military judgment attending the capture of alleged combatants," and "[t]he political branches are best positioned to comprehend this global war in its full context." J.A. 341; see also *Rostker* v. *Goldberg*, 453 U.S. 57, 65–66 (1981).... At the same time, the Executive – unlike the courts – is politically accountable for the decisions made in prosecuting war and in defending the Nation. See *Chicago & So. Air Lines, Inc.* v. *Waterman S.S Corp.*, 333 U.S. 103, 111 (1948)....

. . .

A court's review of a habeas petition filed on behalf of a captured enemy combatant in wartime is of the "most limited scope," and should focus on whether the military is authorized to detain an individual that it has determined is an enemy combatant. That is, the central question for a court is whether "the detention complained of" – here, the detention of a presumed American who the military has determined surrendered with an enemy unit in an active combat zone in a foreign land – "is within the authority of [the military]." 327 U.S. at 8. If such a classic wartime detention is authorized (and it is, for the reasons discussed above), the courts do not inquire whether the military authorities "have made a wrong decision on disputed facts." *Ibid*.

At most, however, in light of the fundamental separation-of-powers principles recognized by this Court's decisions and discussed above, a court's proper role in a habeas proceeding such as this would be to confirm that there is an adequate basis for the military's determination that an individual is an enemy combatant. In particular, the court can ensure that the Executive's articulated basis for detention is a lawful one and, for example, that the detained individual falls on the proper side of the line that divides this Court's decisions in *Milligan* and *Quirin*. The court of appeals appropriately exercised such a role in this case and thereby avoided embroiling the courts in a factual dispute about a battlefield capture halfway around the world.

B. The Record Demonstrates That Hamdi Is An Archetypal Battlefield Combatant

1. The record in this case amply supports the military's determination that Hamdi is an enemy combatant who may be detained by the military while our forces are still

engaged in combat. The Mobbs Declaration ... voluntarily submitted by respondents in support of their return explains the factual basis for the military's enemy-combatant determination that Hamdi is an enemy combatant. The declaration explains that Hamdi went to Afghanistan to train with and, if necessary, fight for the Taliban; stayed with the Taliban after the U.S. and coalition forces had launched the military campaign in Afghanistan; and surrendered with his Taliban unit to–and, indeed, laid down arms to–coalition forces.... (Mobbs Decl. ¶¶3–5, 9). It further explains that Hamdi's own statements confirm that he affiliated with an enemy unit and was armed when he surrendered.... (¶9)....[10]

An individual who surrenders while armed with an enemy unit in an active combat zone undeniably qualifies as an enemy combatant. Indeed, such a person is an archetypal battlefield combatant. Cf. *Quirin*, 317 U.S. at 38 ("Nor are petitioners any the less belligerents if, as they argue, they have not actually committed or attempted to commit any act of depredation *or entered the theatre or zone of active military operations*.") (emphasis added); Oppenheim, *supra*, at 223 (Citizens of even neutral states, "if they enter the armed forces of a belligerent, or do certain other things in his favour, *** acquire enemy character."); *id*. at 224 ("during the World War hundreds of subjects of neutral States, who were fighting in the ranks of the belligerents, were captured and retained as prisoners").

Indeed, even if Hamdi had not been armed when he surrendered, he still would qualify as an enemy combatant. It is settled under the law of war that the military's authority to detain individuals extends to non-combatants who enter the theater of battle with the enemy force, including clerks, laborers, and other "civil[ian] persons engaged in military duty or in immediate connection with an army." Winthrop, *supra*, at 789; see William E.S. Flory, *Prisoners of War* 35 (1942) ("The American orders of 1863 provided that persons who accompany an army may be made prisoners of war."); GPW art. 4(A)(4), 6 U.S.T. at 3320 ("[p]ersons who accompany the armed forces without actually being members thereof, such as civilian members of military aircraft crews, war correspondents, supply contractors, members of labour units or of services responsible for the welfare of the armed forces," may be detained); Hague Convention of 1907, art. 3, 36 Stat. 2277 ("The armed forces of the belligerent parties may consist of combatants and non combatants" who in "case of capture" may be detained as prisoners of war.); Ingrid Detter, *The Law of War* 135–136 (2d ed. 2000).

Even the district court, which stated bluntly that it was "challenging everything in the Mobbs Declaration," ... taking it "piece by piece," ... and trying to "pick it apart," ... declared that it did not have "any doubts [Hamdi] went to Afghanistan to be with the Taliban," ... that he "had a firearm," *ibid*., that he was "present with a Taliban unit," ... , and that "[h]e was there to fight," .... In other words, even the district court – which microscopically reviewed the wording of the Mobbs Declaration, see Gov't C.A. Br. 33–42 – recognized that the record established all that was necessary, and indeed much more, to show that Hamdi is an enemy combatant captured in connection with the ongoing hostilities in Afghanistan.

2. The record supports the military's enemy-combatant determination in another compelling respect: "it is undisputed that Hamdi was captured in a zone of active combat operations in a foreign country." J.A. 418, 448, 453; ....

The next-friend habeas petition in this case avers that Hamdi "resided in Afghanistan" when he was seized.... (Pet. ¶9). Hamdi's father, the next-friend who filed this action, reiterated that fact in a letter that petitioners placed into the record.... (Aug. 8, 2002 Letter from E. Hamdi to Sen. Leahy). Throughout this litigation,

---

[10] ...

petitioners have made clear that they are not challenging Hamdi's capture and detention in Afghanistan..... The certiorari petition itself acknowledges that Hamdi was
in Afghanistan when he was captured. See Pet. 5 ("[Hamdi] resided in Afghanistan in
the Fall of 2001."). And, as discussed, that fact is affirmed by the sworn declaration
submitted by respondents.....

Under the law of war, an individual's residence in hostile territory in a time of war
may have important legal effect. Indeed, in a traditional war between nation states, *all*
inhabitants of enemy territory have been presumed to be enemies. See *Miller* v. *United
States*, 78 U.S. (11 Wall.) 268, 310–311 (1870) ("It is ever a presumption that inhabitants
of an enemy's territory are enemies, even though they are not participants in the war,
though they are subjects of neutral states, or even subjects or citizens of the government
prosecuting the war against the state within which they reside."); *Lamar* v. *Browne*, 92
U.S. 187, 194 (1875) ("In war, all residents of enemy country are enemies."); *Juragua
Iron Co.* v. *United States*, 212 U.S. 297, 308 (1909) (Those who reside in enemy territory
"are adhering to the enemy so long as they remain within his territory."); *Brown* v. *Hiatts*,
82 U.S. (15 Wall.) 177, 184 (1872) ("[T]he inhabitants of the Confederate States *** and
of the loyal States *** became *** reciprocally enemies to each other [during the Civil
War]"); J.A. 481–483 (Traxler, J., concurring in the denial of rehearing) (citing authorities).

Even in a traditional war, the fact that an individual resides in enemy territory does
not mean that he necessarily is subject to capture, detention, or violence under the law
of war. But at a minimum, the Commander in Chief's constitutional authority to make
determinations about who is an enemy combatant is at its height when that authority
is exercised with respect to individuals who are present in a combat zone in a foreign
land, not to mention present with enemy forces. As Judge Traxler explained, courts are
"compelled, by the nature of war and by dint of the separation of powers *** to give
deference to the Executive to determine who within a hostile country is friend and who
is foe.".....

The unconventional nature of the current armed conflict only makes such deference
more appropriate. In a traditional war, the combatants of the belligerent nation would
wear distinctive insignia and follow the laws and customs of war. See *Quirin*, 317 U.S. at
35. The enemy in the current conflict purposely blurs the lines between combatants and
non-combatants by refusing to wear a uniform or distinctive insignia and attempting
to blend into the civilian population. Therefore, the armed forces should be entitled, if
anything, to more deference in this conflict than in a traditional conflict in determining
who among those present in a theater of active combat operations qualify as enemy
combatants.

Furthermore, the acknowledged fact that Hamdi was seized in Afghanistan means
that attempting to conduct any evidentiary proceedings concerning the military's enemy-
combatant determination would place the courts in an untenable position. Attempting
to reconstruct the scene of Hamdi's capture during the battle near Konduz, Afghanistan
in late 2001 would require, *inter alia*, locating and contacting American soldiers, Northern Alliance members, or other allied forces, many of whom may remain engaged
in active combat overseas. As discussed in Part IV below, any such evidentiary inquiry into the Executive's conduct of an ongoing war would raise grave constitutional
problems.

· · ·

Taking account of petitioners' own allegations and arguments in this case in determining the scope of the appropriate judicial review also conforms with the settled rule of

restraint that a court should go no further than necessary to decide an issue before it. As this Court long ago observed, "[t]he best teaching of this Court's experience admonishes us not to entertain constitutional questions in advance of the strictest necessity." *Parker* v. *Los Angeles County*, 338 U.S. 327, 333 (1949); see also *Spector Motor Service* v. *McLaughlin*, 323 U.S. 101, 105 (1944) ("'If there is one doctrine more deeply rooted than any other in the process of constitutional adjudication, it is that we ought not to pass on questions of constitutionality *** unless such adjudication is unavoidable'"). Such restraint is particularly appropriate in light of the extremely sensitive nature of the constitutional challenge here to the exercise of the Commander in Chief's wartime authority to detain enemy combatants.[11]

3. In this Court, petitioners have not contested that Hamdi was in Afghanistan, nor have they suggested that they challenge his detention in Afghanistan. Instead, they argue in a footnote (Br. 28 n.11) that the court of appeals erred in stating that it was "'undisputed' that Hamdi was seized in a 'zone of active combat.'" In other words, to this day petitioners still do not contest that Hamdi was in Afghanistan in late 2001 when he was captured; rather, they dispute only the narrower issue whether Hamdi was seized within "a zone of active combat" in Afghanistan. The Mobbs Declaration...(¶4), the Afghanistan Combat Zone Executive Order,[12] and contemporaneous accounts of the fierce fighting in Konduz, Afghanistan in late 2001, see Dep't of Defense, *News Transcript* (Nov. 15, 2001) <www.defenselink.mil/news/Nov2001/t11152001_t1115sd. html>; *Konduz Falls to Northern Alliance* (Nov. 26, 2001) <www.cnn.com/2001/ WORLD/asiapcf/central/11/26/ret.afghan.konduz/>; *Online Newshour: Military Moves* (Nov. 9, 2001) < www.pbs.org/newshour/bb/military/July-dec01/military_11-9.html>, all confirm that Hamdi was captured amidst an active combat zone. In any event, the question whether a particular area of foreign territory in which U.S. and coalition forces are heavily engaged in military operations is an active combat zone is precisely the type of issue that the Constitution leaves to the judgment of the military commanders who are fighting the war, and that is not appropriate for evidentiary proceedings or second-guessing in a federal courtroom far removed from the battlefield.

C.　The Challenged Wartime Detention At Issue Is Lawful Under A "Some Evidence" Standard

The government also has justified Hamdi's detention under a "some evidence" standard.... . The court of appeals concluded that it was "not necessary for [it] to decide whether the 'some evidence' standard is the correct one to be applied in this case," because it was persuaded for the reasons explained above that further factual development into the circumstances of Hamdi's capture was not necessary and would be

---

[11] ...

[12] As a practical matter, Afghanistan – a country that thousands of U.S. armed forces had entered for the purpose, *inter alia*, of ousting the Taliban regime – was an active combat zone in late 2001..... In any event, on December 12, 2001, the President issued the Afghanistan Combat Zone Executive Order, which designated, for purposes of 26 U.S.C. 112 (combat zone pay for members of the armed forces), "Afghanistan, including the air space above, as an area in which Armed Forces of the United States are and have been engaged in conflict." The order further designated "September 19, 2001, as the date of the commencement of combatant activities in such zone." See <www.whitehouse.gov/news/releases/2001/12/20011214-8.html.>. Numerous federal laws take effect based on the President's designation of an area as a "combat zone" pursuant to 26 U.S.C. 112(c)(2). See 26 U.S.C. 112 historical notes (listing combat zone orders). The fact that *Congress* defers to the Executive's designation of an area as a combat zone would make it all the more anomalous for a *court* to second-guess that classic executive wartime determination in this case.

inappropriate..... But the some evidence standard nonetheless provides an additional basis on which to affirm the court of appeals' judgment.

Under the some evidence standard, the focus is exclusively on the factual basis supplied by the Executive to support its own determination. See *Superintendent v. Hill*, 472 U.S. 445, 455–457 (1985) (explaining that the "some evidence" standard "does not require" a "weighing of the evidence," but rather calls for assessing "whether there is any evidence in the record that could support the conclusion" so as to ensure that the "record is not so devoid of evidence that the findings" are "without support or otherwise arbitrary"). This Court has applied the some evidence standard in evaluating habeas challenges to executive determinations in *less* constitutionally sensitive areas than the wartime detention of captured enemy combatants.[13]

To be sure, in the cases in which the some evidence standard has been applied, the challenged executive determination is typically based on an administrative record developed after an adversarial proceeding. However, the standard also offers an appropriate guidepost in the context of the judicial review of an Executive's enemy combatant determination in wartime in light of the constitutional imperative of ensuring that the courts do not become entangled in matters textually committed by the Constitution to the Commander in Chief. See Part IV, *infra*; J.A. 342 ("Separation of powers principles must *** shape the standard for reviewing the government's designation of Hamdi as an enemy combatant."). The some evidence standard offers a way to avoid such entanglement while also providing for judicial review of the military's enemy-combatant determination, because it focuses on the factors on which the Executive based the challenged determination.

While necessarily limited in scope, the some evidence standard offers a legal framework for assuring that the Executive is not detaining an individual arbitrarily....

III. THE NECESSARILY LIMITED SCOPE OF REVIEW IN THIS EXTRAORDINARY CONTEXT COMPORTS WITH THE CONSTITUTION AND THE FEDERAL HABEAS STATUTES

Petitioners argue that Hamdi is entitled to more "muscular judicial review"... of his wartime detention, a full-blown evidentiary proceeding, and immediate access to counsel..... The court of appeals correctly rejected those arguments and held that no further proceedings or access to counsel was required to establish the lawfulness of Hamdi's detention.

A. Neither The Suspension Clause, The Habeas Statutes, Nor The Common Law Requires Additional Proceedings

1. Petitioners argue... that Hamdi's detention and the limited scope of judicial review provided by the court of appeals violates the Suspension Clause. U.S. Const. Art. I, §9, Cl. 2. That argument is without merit. The court of appeals made clear that Hamdi was entitled to judicial review of his detention in this habeas proceeding, and the government has never contested that point..... As the court of appeals explained, "the fact that [it did] not order[] the relief Hamdi requests is hardly equivalent to a suspension of the writ.".... To the contrary, the court of appeals carefully considered and rejected petitioners' challenges to Hamdi's wartime detention. Furthermore, cases like *Quirin* and *Yamashita* demonstrate that appropriate limits on the scope of judicial review available

---

[13] ...

in a habeas proceeding in constitutionally sensitive areas are not tantamount to a "suspension of the writ." [15]

2. Petitioners argue . . . that the habeas statute entitles Hamdi to fact-finding in this case. That argument also should be rejected. The habeas statutes allow for presenting facts or taking evidence only when necessary to enable a court to resolve the legality of the challenged detention. As the Court observed in *Walker* v. *Johnston*, 312 U.S. 275, 284 (1941), "the court may find that no issue of fact is involved" after examining the petition and return, and may conclude "from undisputed facts or from incontrovertible facts" that, "as a matter of law, no cause for granting the writ exists." See, *e.g.*, *Eisentrager*, 339 U.S. at 778 (citing *Walker*); *Quirin*, 317 U.S. at 24 (same). The Court has similarly recognized that a habeas petition may be denied without production of the detainee. See *Braden* v. *30th Judicial Circuit Court*, 410 U.S. 484, 494 (1973) (observing that Congress has "codif[ied] in the habeas corpus statute" the Court's decision in *Walker* "whereby a petition for habeas corpus can in many instances be resolved without requiring the presence of the petitioner before the court that adjudicates his claim") (citing 28 U.S.C. 2243).

Thus, as the court of appeals observed, "[w]hile the ordinary §2241 proceeding naturally contemplates the prospect of factual development, 28 U.S.C. §§2243, 2246, such an observation only begs the basic question in this case – whether further factual exploration" is necessary and appropriate in light of the extraordinary constitutional interests at stake. . . . . As explained in Part II above, the court of appeals properly concluded that the habeas petition in this case could be disposed of on the current record without "further factual exploration." . . . .

3. Petitioners suggest . . . that the habeas proceeding in this case was imcompatible with the "common law role" of the Great Writ. They are mistaken. As a historical matter, the writ generally was not extended to enemy combatants. See R.J. Sharpe, *The Law of Habeas Corpus* 112 (1976) (Under the writ's common law tradition, "a prisoner of war has no standing to apply for the writ of habeas corpus."); see also, *e.g.*, *Moxon* v. *The Fanny*, 17 F. Cas. 942 (D. Pa. 1793) (No. 9895) ("The courts of England *** will not even grant a habeas corpus in the case of a prisoner of war ***. Although our judiciary is somewhat differently arranged, I see not, in this respect, that they should not be equally cautious."); *Ex parte Graber*, 247 F. 882, 886–887 (N.D. Ala. 1918) (consistent with the practices of England and Canada, executive's decision to detain an enemy combatant is unreviewable); *Ex parte Liebmann*, 85 K.B. 210, 214 (1915) ("It is *** settled law that no writ of habeas corpus will be granted in the case of a prisoner of war."). Hamdi, whose wartime detention has been carefully reviewed by the courts, has received much more process in this habeas proceeding than a captured enemy combatant would have received at common law.

B. Hamdi Was Not Entitled To Any Automatic Or Immediate Access To Counsel

Petitioners argue . . . that Hamdi has "a right to consult with an attorney in connection with the assertion of [his] legal rights," and that he was deprived of due process because

---

[15] In *St. Cyr*, 533 U.S. at 301 (internal quotation marks omitted), this Court observed that, at a minimum, "the Suspension Clause protects the writ as it existed in 1789." Generally speaking, one of the purposes of the common law writ was to require the Executive to state why it was holding an individual, and not for a court to review the factual basis for the Executive's decision. See, *e.g.*, Clarke D. Forsythe, *The Historical Origins of Broad Federal Habeas Review Reconsidered*, 70 Notre Dame L. Rev. 1079, 1094 (1995) ("At common law, the allegations in the 'return' were deemed conclusive and could not be controverted by the prisoner."); Dallin H. Oaks, *Legal History in the High Court-Habeas Corpus*, 64 Mich. L. Rev. 451, 453 (1966). Moreover, as explained below, at common law habeas corpus generally was unavailable for captured enemy combatants.

he was not granted access to a lawyer immediately upon the filing of this habeas action. That argument should be rejected. Indeed, the notion of requiring the military to afford captured enemy combatants with an attorney to help plot a legal strategy to gain their release by a court is antithetical to the very object of war.[16]

1. There is no right under the law of war for an enemy combatant to meet with counsel to contest his wartime detention. Even lawful enemy combatants who are entitled to POW privileges under the GPW – which does not include the detainees in the current conflict, see note 9, *supra* – are not entitled to counsel to challenge their detention. Rather, Article 105 of the GPW provides only that a POW may be afforded counsel in the event that formal *charges* are initiated against him in a prosecution, underscoring that POWs who have not been charged with specific war crimes enjoy no right to counsel to challenge their detention. 6 U.S.T. at 3317; see also Winthrop, *supra*, at 165 (even with respect to military commissions, "the admission of counsel for the accused in military cases, is not a right but a privilege only").

The enemy combatants in *Quirin* were charged with violations of the law of war and of the Articles of War – offenses punishable by death – and tried before a military commission. 317 U.S. at 22–23. Accordingly, they were provided counsel by the military to aid in preparing a response to those charges. Hamdi, by contrast, has not been charged with any offense and has not been subjected to any military trial or punishment. Rather, as discussed, he is simply being detained during the conflict as a simple war measure. The vast majority of combatants seized in a war are, like Hamdi, never charged with an offense but instead are detained to prevent them from rejoining the fighting.

2. Nor was Hamdi entitled to access to counsel to challenge his detention under the Due Process Clause of the Fifth Amendment.[17]

a. Recognizing such a generalized right to counsel under the Fifth Amendment could not be squared with the fact that captured enemy combatants have not been guaranteed a right to counsel in similar circumstances. As this Court stated in *Quirin*, 317 U.S. at 27–28, "[f]rom the very beginning of its history this Court has recognized and applied the law of war as including that part of the law of nations which prescribes, for the conduct of war, the status, rights and duties of enemy nations as well as of enemy individuals." That is consistent with the analysis that this Court applies in determining the scope of the Due Process Clause in other contexts. See *Herrera* v. *Collins*, 506 U.S. 390, 407–408 (1993) (examining "[h]istorical practice" in assessing scope of "Fourteenth Amendment's guarantee of due process"); *Medina* v. *California*, 505 U.S. 437, 445–446 (1992); *Moyer* [v. *Peabody*], 212 U.S. [78,] 84 [(1909)]. Because the automatic right of access to counsel that petitioners seek has no foundation in any tradition or practice, the Fifth Amendment could not possibly confer such a right.

b. Moreover, as the court of appeals recognized, any process that Hamdi is due in this proceeding must take its form from the constitutional and national security limitations on a habeas proceeding in this sensitive context. See . . . *Moyer*, 212 U.S. at 84

---

[16] Even the district court – which ordered that Hamdi be given immediate access to counsel – acknowledged that an enemy combatant who was captured during the Battle of the Bulge would not have been entitled to counsel to challenge his detention in Germany or, as was the case for thousands of captured combatants in World War II, in this country. . . . . The unconventional nature of the present conflict – in which America has been attacked by the enemy on a scale greater than the attack on Pearl Harbor – does not warrant any different result.

[17] The Sixth Amendment applies only in the case of "criminal prosecutions," U.S. Const. Amend. VI, and therefore does not apply to the detention of any captured enemy combatant who – like the vast majority of such combatants – has not been charged with any domestic crime. Similarly, the Self-Incrimination Clause of the Fifth Amendment is a "trial right of criminal defendants," and therefore also does not apply to this situation. *United States* v. *Verdugo-Urquidez*, 494 U.S. 259, 264 (1990).

("[W]hat is due process of law depends on circumstances. It varies with the subject-matter and the necessities of the situation."). Under any constitutionally appropriate standard of review (see Part II, *supra*), there is no cause for a detained enemy combatant to enjoy a generalized right to counsel to challenge the Executive's core Article II judgment that he is an enemy combatant. That is certainly true in this case, where, as the court of appeals correctly held, the record adequately demonstrates the lawfulness of Hamdi's wartime detention.

. . .

c. In addition, any due process analysis would have to account for the Executive's compelling interest – especially during the initial stages of an individual's detention – in preventing a captured enemy combatant from enjoying access to counsel or others. As explained in detail in the Woolfolk Declaration . . . , to a degree perhaps greater than in any prior armed conflict in which the United States has been engaged, "[t]he security of this nation and its citizens is wholly dependent upon the U.S. Government's ability to gather, analyze, and disseminate timely and effective intelligence." J.A. 347[19] The military has found that a critical source of such intelligence is enemy combatants who are captured in connection with the conflict. . . . . With respect to Hamdi, the military determined that "Hamdi's background and experience, particularly in the Middle East, Afghanistan, and Pakistan, suggest considerable knowledge of Taliban and al Qaeda training and operations." . . . .

The military has learned that creating a relationship of trust and dependency between a questioner and a detainee is of "paramount importance" to successful intelligence gathering. . . . . The formation of such a relationship takes time and varies from one detainee to another, but when such a relationship is formed, critical intelligence may be – and has been – gathered. . . . . The intelligence collected to date from captured enemy combatants has proven vital to the strategic military operations that are ongoing in Afghanistan (such as in learning the routes that the enemy uses to travel through difficult terrain) as well as in understanding the manner in which the enemy operates (including how it communicates, recruits members, and obtains funding). See *Guantanamo Detainees*, *supra*.

This critical source of information would be gravely threatened if this Court held that the moment a next-friend habeas petition is filed on behalf of a captured enemy combatant, a right of access to counsel automatically attaches with respect to the detainee. As Colonel Woolfolk stressed in this case, "[d]isruption of the interrogation environment, such as through access to a detainee by counsel, undermines this interrogation dynamic" and, "[s]hould this occur, a critical resource may be lost, resulting in a direct threat to national security." . . . . Colonel Woolfolk further explained that, during the proceedings below, the military had determined that granting Hamdi access to counsel would have "disrupt[ed] the secure interrogation environment that the United States has labored to create" with respect to Hamdi, and would "thwart any opportunity to develop intelligence through this detainee." . . . .

d. Although a captured enemy combatant has no absolute right to counsel to challenge his detention, the Department of Defense has adopted a policy of providing enemy combatants who are presumed United States citizens and detained in this country access to counsel once the military has determined that such access would not interfere with ongoing intelligence-gathering with respect to the detainee. In Hamdi's case, the military determined in December 2003 that such access would be appropriate.

---

[19] . . .

Especially in light of the military's adoption of that policy, the compelling national security interests in permitting the military to engage in such intelligence gathering, and the ordinary canon of constitutional-avoidance, the Court should reject petitioners' argument that Hamdi was entitled to an absolute and immediate right to counsel to challenge his detention. Such access, automatic and as of right, would defeat one of the critical purposes of detaining the enemy.[20]

In this extraordinarily sensitive national security context, the Court should be wary of adopting a means of testing the validity of an enemy combatant's detention that defeats one of the important military functions served by that detention, even when, as here, the Executive has supplied the factual basis for the detention and a court has determined that it is lawful. Rather, the appropriate constitutional balance would allow an immediate opportunity to bring legal challenges to detention in a habeas proceeding such as this, and would afford access to counsel at the point that the commanders who are responsible for gathering intelligence in wartime – as well as defending the Nation from additional attacks and defeating the enemy in an ongoing conflict reach a judgment that such access would not interfere with those vital efforts. Declining to resolve the counsel issue in this case would not foreclose the possibility of entertaining a later challenge to the delay in granting access to counsel.

In any event, particularly in light of the fact that Hamdi now has access to counsel, the Court should avoid any ruling in this case that would attempt to place a particular time limit on the military's efforts to gather intelligence from a captured combatant. Holding that the military must grant a detained enemy combatant access to counsel within a specified period of time could in many cases prove just as damaging in terms of the loss of potential intelligence as holding that a detainee must be granted counsel as soon as he is placed in military custody.[21]

3. Although they did not press the argument below..., petitioners argue...that denying Hamdi access to counsel is inconsistent with decisions of this Court indicating that prison inmates have a "right to court access." But that line of cases arose in the distinctly different context of inmates who had been committed to the criminal justice system to serve sentences of imprisonment....

...[22]

IV. THE ALTERNATIVE PROCEEDING ENVISIONED BY THE DISTRICT COURT AND PETITIONERS IS CONSTITUTIONALLY INTOLERABLE

The type of proceeding ordered by the district court and urged by petitioners is fraught with constitutional problems.

---

[20] ...

[21] There is another compelling interest in preventing enemy combatants from enjoying access to counsel before the military determines that such access would not undermine national security. Such access may enable detained enemy combatants to pass concealed messages through unwitting counsel to the enemy which could compromise the war effort – something that members (and presumably supporters) of al Qaeda are trained to do.....

[22] Hamdi is no longer strictly inaccessible because, since December 2003, he has been permitted to meet with counsel. Nonetheless, the court of appeals' judgment was based on the premise that this was a proper next-friend action..... In addition, the fact that Hamdi now has access to counsel in no way alters the court of appeals' conclusion that the record in this case is sufficient to support the conclusion that Hamdi's detention is lawful. However, if Hamdi were to file a new direct habeas petition raising new arguments that could not have been brought in this action, the courts could entertain that petition subject to the customary restraints on duplicative litigation and the constitutional considerations discussed above.

1. The district court proceedings offer a glimpse as to what a habeas proceeding might be like under the alternative legal regime urged by petitioners..... After the government explains the factual basis for its enemy combatant determination, a habeas petitioner would – as any "capable attorney" could do – "challenge the hearsay nature of the [military's] declaration and probe each and every paragraph for incompleteness or inconsistency.".... The district court sought to do that at the August 13, 2002 hearing where it "challeng[ed] everything in the Mobbs Declaration.".... Petitioners repeat many of the same challenges.....[23] As the court of appeals explained, however, "[t]o transfer the instinctive skepticism, so laudable in the defense of criminal charges, to the review of executive branch decisions premised on military determinations made in the field carries the inordinate risk of a constitutionally problematic intrusion into the most basic responsibilities of a coordinate branch."....

2. The standard of review applied by the district court and requested by petitioners...also inevitably would invite discovery into the military's decisionmaking in connection with ongoing military operations. The district court below issued an unprecedented production order requiring the military to produce "for in camera review by the Court" materials including:

- "Copies of all Hamdi's statements, and the notes taken from any interviews with Hamdi";
- "A list of all the interrogators who have questioned Hamdi, including their names and addresses"; and
- "Copies of any statements by members of the Northern Alliance regarding [Hamdi]."

.... What is more, as the court of appeals observed, "[t]he district court indicated that its production order might well be only an initial step in testing the factual basis of Hamdi's enemy combatant status.".... The district court's request for the names and addresses of soldiers who interviewed Hamdi suggests that it viewed them as potential witnesses in a full-blown evidentiary proceeding.

Attempting to compile such materials would directly intrude into the military's conduct of an ongoing campaign. As the court of appeals explained:

> The factual inquiry upon which Hamdi would lead us, if it did not entail disclosure of sensitive intelligence, might require an excavation of facts buried under the rubble of war. The cost of such an inquiry in terms of the efficiency and morale of American forces cannot be disregarded. Some of those with knowledge of Hamdi's detention may have been slain or injured in battle. Others might have to be diverted from active and ongoing military duties of their own. The logistical effort to acquire evidence from far away battle zones might be substantial. And these efforts would profoundly unsettle the constitutional balance.

J.A. 442; see also J.A. 461–464 (Wilkinson, J., concurring in the denial of rehearing) ("This desire to have the courts wade further and further into the supervision of armed warfare ignores the undertow of judicial process, the capacity of litigation to draw us into the review of military judgments step by step.").

---

[23] An enemy combatant, armed with court-appointed counsel, would have every incentive to challenge the military's version of events and to encourage an attorney to do so on his behalf. Indeed, members of al Qaeda, and presumably their supporters, are trained to deceive authorities about their identities and their role in the organization. See <www.usdoj.gov/ag/manualpart1_1.pdf.> (reproducing al Qaeda training manual).

Any effort by a court to recreate the scenes of Hamdi's capture and detention are complicated by two particular factors in this case. First, Hamdi was captured half-way around the globe in Afghanistan, a country in which thousands of U.S. armed forces are today engaged in active combat operations against al Qaeda and Taliban fighters. Second, Hamdi initially surrendered with his Taliban unit to Northern Alliance forces. See . . . (Mobbs Decl. ¶4). It is not uncommon for the U.S. military to take control of enemy combatants who have been captured by or who surrender to coalition forces. But the fact that only Northern Alliance forces were present at the moment of Hamdi's surrender would further complicate any judicial effort to recreate Hamdi's battlefield capture in a habeas proceeding.

This Court itself has recognized the grave practical and constitutional concerns that would arise from enmeshing the courts in such inquiries while the Nation is at war. In *Eisentrager*, the Court observed that habeas proceedings delving into the military's treatment of enemy combatants abroad "would hamper the war effort and bring aid and comfort to the enemy." 339 U.S. at 779. Indeed, the Court explained, "[i]t would be difficult to devise more effective fettering of a field commander than to allow the very enemies he is ordered to reduce to submission to call him to account in his own civil courts and divert his efforts and attention from the military offensive abroad to the legal defensive at home." *Ibid*. "Nor is it unlikely," the Court continued, "that the result of such enemy litigiousness would be a conflict between judicial and military opinion highly comforting to enemies of the United States." *Ibid*.

. . .

CONCLUSION

The judgment of the court of appeals should be affirmed.

. . .

SUPREME COURT OF THE UNITED STATES

No. 03–6696

YASER ESAM HAMDI AND ESAM FOUAD HAMDI, AS NEXT FRIEND OF YASER ESAM HAMDI, PETITIONERS *v.* DONALD H. RUMSFELD, SECRETARY OF DEFENSE, ET AL.

ON WRIT OF CERTIORARI TO THE UNITED STATES COURT OF APPEALS FOR THE FOURTH CIRCUIT

[June 28, 2004]

JUSTICE O'CONNOR announced the judgment of the Court and delivered an opinion, in which THE CHIEF JUSTICE, JUSTICE KENNEDY, and JUSTICE BREYER join.

At this difficult time in our Nation's history, we are called upon to consider the legality of the Government's detention of a United States citizen on United States soil as an "enemy combatant" and to address the process that is constitutionally owed to one who seeks to challenge his classification as such. The United States Court of Appeals for the Fourth Circuit held that petitioner's detention was legally authorized and that he was entitled to no further opportunity to challenge his enemy-combatant label. We now vacate and remand. We hold that although Congress authorized the detention of combatants in the narrow circumstances alleged here, due process demands that a citizen held in the United States as an enemy combatant be given a meaningful opportunity to contest the factual basis for that detention before a neutral decisionmaker.

I

On September 11, 2001, the al Qaeda terrorist network used hijacked commercial airliners to attack prominent targets in the United States. Approximately 3,000 people were killed in those attacks. One week later, in response to these "acts of treacherous violence," Congress passed a resolution authorizing the President to "use all necessary and appropriate force against those nations, organizations, or persons he determines planned, authorized, committed, or aided the terrorist attacks" or "harbored such organizations or persons, in order to prevent any future acts of international terrorism against the United States by such nations, organizations or persons." Authorization for Use of Military Force ("the AUMF"), 115 Stat. 224. Soon thereafter, the President ordered United States Armed Forces to Afghanistan, with a mission to subdue al Qaeda and quell the Taliban regime that was known to support it.

This case arises out of the detention of a man whom the Government alleges took up arms with the Taliban during this conflict. His name is Yaser Esam Hamdi. Born in Louisiana in 1980, Hamdi moved with his family to Saudi Arabia as a child. By 2001, the parties agree, he resided in Afghanistan. At some point that year, he was seized by members of the Northern Alliance, a coalition of military groups opposed to the Taliban government, and eventually was turned over to the United States military. The

Government asserts that it initially detained and interrogated Hamdi in Afghanistan before transferring him to the United States Naval Base in Guantanamo Bay in January 2002. In April 2002, upon learning that Hamdi is an American citizen, authorities transferred him to a naval brig in Norfolk, Virginia, where he remained until a recent transfer to a brig in Charleston, South Carolina. The Government contends that Hamdi is an "enemy combatant," and that this status justifies holding him in the United States indefinitely – without formal charges or proceedings – unless and until it makes the determination that access to counsel or further process is warranted.

In June 2002, Hamdi's father, Esam Fouad Hamdi, filed the present petition for a writ of habeas corpus under 28 U.S.C. §2241 in the Eastern District of Virginia, naming as petitioners his son and himself as next friend. The elder Hamdi alleges in the petition that he has had no contact with his son since the Government took custody of him in 2001, and that the Government has held his son "without access to legal counsel or notice of any charges pending against him." App. 103, 104. The petition contends that Hamdi's detention was not legally authorized. *Id.*, at 105. It argues that, "[a]s an American citizen, . . . Hamdi enjoys the full protections of the Constitution," and that Hamdi's detention in the United States without charges, access to an impartial tribunal, or assistance of counsel "violated and continue[s] to violate the Fifth and Fourteenth Amendments to the United States Constitution." *Id.*, at 107. The habeas petition asks that the court, among other things, (1) appoint counsel for Hamdi; (2) order respondents to cease interrogating him; (3) declare that he is being held in violation of the Fifth and Fourteenth Amendments; (4) "[t]o the extent Respondents contest any material factual allegations in this Petition, schedule an evidentiary hearing, at which Petitioners may adduce proof in support of their allegations"; and (5) order that Hamdi be released from his "unlawful custody." *Id.*, at 108–109. Although his habeas petition provides no details with regard to the factual circumstances surrounding his son's capture and detention, Hamdi's father has asserted in documents found elsewhere in the record that his son went to Afghanistan to do "relief work," and that he had been in that country less than two months before September 11, 2001, and could not have received military training. *Id.*, at 188–189. The 20-year-old was traveling on his own for the first time, his father says, and "[b]ecause of his lack of experience, he was trapped in Afghanistan once that military campaign began." *Id.*, at 188–189.

The District Court found that Hamdi's father was a proper next friend, appointed the federal public defender as counsel for the petitioners, and ordered that counsel be given access to Hamdi. *Id.*, at 113–116. The United States Court of Appeals for the Fourth Circuit reversed that order, holding that the District Court had failed to extend appropriate deference to the Government's security and intelligence interests. 296 F.3d 278, 279, 283 (2002). It directed the District Court to consider "the most cautious procedures first," *id.*, at 284, and to conduct a deferential inquiry into Hamdi's status, *id.*, at 283. It opined that "if Hamdi is indeed an 'enemy combatant' who was captured during hostilities in Afghanistan, the government's present detention of him is a lawful one." *Ibid.*

On remand, the Government filed a response and a motion to dismiss the petition. It attached to its response a declaration from one Michael Mobbs (hereinafter "Mobbs Declaration"), who identified himself as Special Advisor to the Under Secretary of Defense for Policy. Mobbs indicated that in this position, he has been "substantially involved with matters related to the detention of enemy combatants in the current war against the al Qaeda terrorists and those who support and harbor them (including the Taliban)." App. 148. He expressed his "familiar[ity]" with Department of Defense and United States military policies and procedures applicable to the detention, control, and transfer of al Qaeda and Taliban personnel, and declared that "[b]ased upon my review of relevant records and reports, I am also familiar with the facts and circumstances related to the capture of . . . Hamdi and his detention by U.S. military forces." *Ibid.*

Mobbs then set forth what remains the sole evidentiary support that the Government has provided to the courts for Hamdi's detention. The declaration states that Hamdi "traveled to Afghanistan" in July or August 2001, and that he thereafter "affiliated with a Taliban military unit and received weapons training." *Ibid.* It asserts that Hamdi "remained with his Taliban unit following the attacks of September 11" and that, during the time when Northern Alliance forces were "engaged in battle with the Taliban," "Hamdi's Taliban unit surrendered" to those forces, after which he "surrender[ed] his Kalishnikov assault rifle" to them. *Id.,* at 148–149. The Mobbs Declaration also states that, because al Qaeda and the Taliban "were and are hostile forces engaged in armed conflict with the armed forces of the United States," "individuals associated with" those groups "were and continue to be enemy combatants." *Id.,* at 149. Mobbs states that Hamdi was labeled an enemy combatant "[b]ased upon his interviews and in light of his association with the Taliban." *Ibid.* According to the declaration, a series of "U.S. military screening team[s]" determined that Hamdi met "the criteria for enemy combatants," and "a subsequent interview of Hamdi has confirmed that he surrendered and gave his firearm to Northern Alliance forces, which supports his classification as an enemy combatant." *Id.,* at 149–150.

After the Government submitted this declaration, the Fourth Circuit directed the District Court to proceed in accordance with its earlier ruling and, specifically, to "'consider the sufficiency of the Mobbs Declaration as an independent matter before proceeding further.'" 316 F.3d at 450, 462 (2003). The District Court found that the Mobbs Declaration fell "far short" of supporting Hamdi's detention. App. 292. It criticized the generic and hearsay nature of the affidavit, calling it "little more than the government's 'say-so.'" *Id.,* at 298. It ordered the Government to turn over numerous materials for *in camera* review, including copies of all of Hamdi's statements and the notes taken from interviews with him that related to his reasons for going to Afghanistan and his activities therein; a list of all interrogators who had questioned Hamdi and their names and addresses; statements by members of the Northern Alliance regarding Hamdi's surrender and capture; a list of the dates and locations of his capture and subsequent detentions; and the names and titles of the United States Government officials who made the determinations that Hamdi was an enemy combatant and that he should be moved to a naval brig. *Id.,* at 185–186. The court indicated that all of these materials were necessary for "meaningful judicial review" of whether Hamdi's detention was legally authorized and whether Hamdi had received sufficient process to satisfy the Due Process Clause of the Constitution and relevant treaties or military regulations. *Id.,* at 291–292.

The Government sought to appeal the production order, and the District Court certified the question of whether the Mobbs Declaration, "'standing alone, is sufficient as a matter of law to allow meaningful judicial review of [Hamdi's] classification as an enemy combatant.'" 316 F.3d, at 462. The Fourth Circuit reversed, but did not squarely answer the certified question. It instead stressed that, because it was "undisputed that Hamdi was captured in a zone of active combat in a foreign theater of conflict," no factual inquiry or evidentiary hearing allowing Hamdi to be heard or to rebut the Government's assertions was necessary or proper. *Id.,* at 459. Concluding that the factual averments in the Mobbs Declaration, "if accurate," provided a sufficient basis upon which to conclude that the President had constitutionally detained Hamdi pursuant to the President's war powers, it ordered the habeas petition dismissed. *Id.,* at 473. The Fourth Circuit emphasized that the "vital purposes" of the detention of uncharged enemy combatants – preventing those combatants from rejoining the enemy while relieving the military of the burden of litigating the circumstances of wartime captures halfway around the globe – were interests "directly derived from the war powers of Articles I and II." *Id.*, at 465–466. In that court's view, because "Article III contains nothing analogous to the specific powers of war so carefully enumerated in Articles I and II," *id.*, at 463, separation of powers principles prohibited a federal court from "delv[ing] further into Hamdi's status and capture," *id.*, at 473. Accordingly, the District Court's more vigorous inquiry "went far beyond the acceptable scope of review." *Ibid.*

On the more global question of whether legal authorization exists for the detention of citizen enemy combatants at all, the Fourth Circuit rejected Hamdi's arguments that 18 U.S.C. §4001(a) and Article 5 of the Geneva Convention rendered any such detentions unlawful. The court expressed doubt as to Hamdi's argument that §4001(a), which provides that "[n]o citizen shall be imprisoned or otherwise detained by the United States except pursuant to an Act of Congress," required express congressional authorization of detentions of this sort. But it held that, in any event, such authorization was found in the post-September 11 Authorization for Use of Military Force. 316 F.3d, at 467. Because "capturing and detaining enemy combatants is an inherent part of warfare," the court held, "the 'necessary and appropriate force' referenced in the congressional resolution necessarily includes the capture and detention of any and all hostile forces arrayed against our troops." *Ibid.*; see also *id.*, at 467–468 (noting that Congress, in 10 U.S.C. §956(5), had specifically authorized the expenditure of funds for keeping prisoners of war and persons whose status was determined "to be similar to prisoners of war," and concluding that this appropriation measure also demonstrated that Congress had "authorized [these individuals'] detention in the first instance"). The court likewise rejected Hamdi's Geneva Convention claim, concluding that the convention is not self-executing and that, even if it were, it would not preclude the Executive from detaining Hamdi until the cessation of hostilities. 316 F.3d, at 468–469.

Finally, the Fourth Circuit rejected Hamdi's contention that its legal analyses with regard to the authorization for the detention scheme and the process to which he was constitutionally entitled should be altered by the fact that he is an American citizen detained on American soil. Relying on *Ex parte Quirin*, 317 U.S. 1 (1942), the court emphasized that "[o]ne who takes up arms against the United States in a foreign theater of war, regardless of his citizenship, may properly be designated an enemy combatant and treated as such." 316 F.3d, at 475. "The privilege of citizenship," the court held, "entitles Hamdi to a limited judicial inquiry into his detention, but only to determine its legality under the war powers of the political branches. At least where it is undisputed that he was present in a zone of active combat operations, we are satisfied that the Constitution does not entitle him to a searching review of the factual determinations underlying his seizure there." *Ibid.*

The Fourth Circuit denied rehearing en banc, 337 F.3d 335 (2003), and we granted certiorari. 540 U.S._ (2004). We now vacate the judgment below and remand.

II

The threshold question before us is whether the Executive has the authority to detain citizens who qualify as "enemy combatants." There is some debate as to the proper scope of this term, and the Government has never provided any court with the full criteria that it uses in classifying individuals as such. It has made clear, however, that, for purposes of this case, the "enemy combatant" that it is seeking to detain is an individual who, it alleges, was "'part of or supporting forces hostile to the United States or coalition partners'" in Afghanistan and who "'engaged in an armed conflict against the United States'" there. Brief for Respondents 3. We therefore answer only the narrow question before us: whether the detention of citizens falling within that definition is authorized.

The Government maintains that no explicit congressional authorization is required, because the Executive possesses plenary authority to detain pursuant to Article II of the Constitution. We do not reach the question whether Article II provides such authority, however, because we agree with the Government's alternative position, that Congress has in fact authorized Hamdi's detention, through the AUMF.

Our analysis on that point, set forth below, substantially overlaps with our analysis of Hamdi's principal argument for the illegality of his detention. He posits that his detention is forbidden by 18 U.S.C. §4001(a). Section 4001(a) states that "[n]o citizen shall be imprisoned or otherwise detained by the United States except pursuant to an Act of Congress." Congress passed §4001(a) in 1971 as part of a bill to repeal the Emergency Detention Act of 1950, 50 U.S.C. §811 *et seq.*, which provided procedures for executive detention, during times of emergency, of individuals deemed likely to engage in espionage or sabotage. Congress was particularly concerned about the possibility that the Act could be used to reprise the Japanese internment camps of World War II. H.R. Rep. No. 92-116 (1971); *id.*, at 4 ("The concentration camp implications of the legislation render it abhorrent"). The Government again presses two alternative positions. First, it argues that §4001(a), in light of its legislative history and its location in Title 18, applies only to "the control of civilian prisons and related detentions," not to military detentions. Brief for Respondents 21. Second, it maintains that §4001(a) is satisfied, because Hamdi is being detained "pursuant to an Act of Congress" – the AUMF. *Id.*, at 21–22. Again, because we conclude that the Government's second assertion is correct, we do not address the first. In other words, for the reasons that follow, we conclude that the AUMF is explicit congressional authorization for the detention of individuals in the narrow category we describe (assuming, without deciding, that such authorization is required), and that the AUMF satisfied §4001(a)'s requirement that a detention be "pursuant to an Act of Congress" (assuming, without deciding, that §4001(a) applies to military detentions).

The AUMF authorizes the President to use "all necessary and appropriate force" against "nations, organizations, or persons" associated with the September 11, 2001, terrorist attacks. 115 Stat. 224. There can be no doubt that individuals who fought against the United States in Afghanistan as part of the Taliban, an organization known to have supported the al Qaeda terrorist network responsible for those attacks, are individuals Congress sought to target in passing the AUMF. We conclude that detention of individuals falling into the limited category we are considering, for the duration of the particular conflict in which they were captured, is so fundamental and accepted an incident to war as to be an exercise of the "necessary and appropriate force" Congress has authorized the President to use.

The capture and detention of lawful combatants and the capture, detention, and trial of unlawful combatants, by "universal agreement and practice," are "important incident[s] of war." *Ex parte Quirin*, 317 U.S., at 28. The purpose of detention is to prevent captured individuals from returning to the field of battle and taking up arms once again. Naqvi, Doubtful Prisoner-of-War Status, 84 Int'l Rev. Red Cross 571, 572 (2002) ("[C]aptivity in war is 'neither revenge, nor punishment, but solely protective custody, the only purpose of which is to prevent the prisoners of war from further participation in the war'") (quoting decision of Nuremberg Military Tribunal, reprinted in 41 Am. J. Int'l L. 172, 229 (1947)); W. Winthrop, Military Law and Precedents 788 (rev. 2d ed. 1920) ("The time has long passed when 'no quarter' was the rule on the battlefield. . . . It is now recognized that 'Captivity is neither a punishment nor an act of vengeance,' but 'merely a temporary detention which is devoid of all penal character.'...'A prisoner of war is no convict; his imprisonment is a simple war measure.'" (citations omitted); cf. *In re Territo*, 156 F.2d 142, 145 (1946) ("The object of capture is to prevent the captured individual from serving the enemy. He is disarmed and from then on must be removed as completely as practicable from the front, treated humanely, and in time exchanged, repatriated, or otherwise released" (footnotes omitted)).

There is no bar to this Nation's holding one of its own citizens as an enemy combatant. In *Quirin*, one of the detainees, Haupt, alleged that he was a naturalized United States citizen. 317 U.S., at 20. We held that "[c]itizens who associate themselves with the military arm of the enemy government, and with its aid, guidance and direction enter this country bent on hostile acts, are enemy belligerents within the meaning of...the law of war." *Id.*, at 37–38. While Haupt was tried for violations of the law of war, nothing in *Quirin* suggests that his citizenship would have precluded his mere detention for the duration of the relevant hostilities. See *id.*, at 30–31. See also Lieber Code, ¶153, Instructions for the Government of Armies of the United States in the Field, Gen. Order No. 100 (1863), reprinted in 2 Lieber, Miscellaneous Writings, p. 273 (contemplating, in code binding the Union Army during the Civil War, that "captured rebels" would be treated "as prisoners of war"). Nor can we see any reason for drawing such a line here. A citizen, no less than an alien, can be "part of or supporting forces hostile to the United States or coalition partners" and "engaged in an armed conflict against the United States," Brief for Respondents 3; such a citizen, if released, would pose the same threat of returning to the front during the ongoing conflict.

In light of these principles, it is of no moment that the AUMF does not use specific language of detention. Because detention to prevent a combatant's return to the battlefield is a fundamental incident of waging war, in permitting the use of "necessary and appropriate force," Congress has clearly and unmistakably authorized detention in the narrow circumstances considered here.

Hamdi objects, nevertheless, that Congress has not authorized the *indefinite* detention to which he is now subject. The Government responds that "the detention of enemy combatants during World War II was just as 'indefinite' while that war was being fought." *Id.*, at 16. We take Hamdi's objection to be not to the lack of certainty regarding the date on which the conflict will end, but to the substantial prospect of perpetual detention. We recognize that the national security underpinnings of the "war on terror," although crucially important, are broad and malleable. As the Government concedes, "given its unconventional nature, the current conflict is unlikely to end with a formal cease-fire agreement." *Ibid.* The prospect Hamdi raises is therefore not far-fetched. If the Government does not consider this unconventional war won for two generations, and if it maintains during that time that Hamdi might, if released, rejoin forces fighting against the United States, then the position it has taken throughout the litigation of this case suggests that Hamdi's detention could last for the rest of his life.

It is a clearly established principle of the law of war that detention may last no longer than active hostilities. See Article 118 of the Geneva Convention (III) Relative to the Treatment of Prisoners of War, Aug. 12, 1949, [1955] 6 U.S.T. 3316, 3406, T.I.A.S. No. 3364 ("Prisoners of war shall be released and repatriated without delay after the cessation of active hostilities"). See also Article 20 of the Hague Convention (II) on Laws and Customs of War on Land, July 29, 1899, 32 Stat. 1817 (as soon as possible after "conclusion of peace"); Hague Convention (IV), *supra*, Oct. 18, 1907, 36 Stat. 2301("conclusion of peace" (Art. 20)); Geneva Convention, *supra*, July 27, 1929, 47 Stat.2055 (repatriation should be accomplished with the least possible delay after conclusion of peace (Art. 75)); Praust, Judicial Power to Determine the Status and Rights of Persons Detained without

Trial, 44 Harv. Int'l L.J. 503, 510–511 (2003) (prisoners of war "can be detained during an armed conflict, but the detaining country must release and repatriate them 'without delay after the cessation of active hostilities,' unless they are being lawfully prosecuted or have been lawfully convicted of crimes and are serving sentences" (citing Arts. 118, 85, 99, 119, 129, Geneva Convention (III), 6 T. I.A. S., at 3384, 3392, 3406, 3418)).

Hamdi contends that the AUMF does not authorize indefinite or perpetual detention. Certainly, we agree that indefinite detention for the purpose of interrogation is not authorized. Further, we understand Congress' grant of authority for the use of "necessary and appropriate force" to include the authority to detain for the duration of the relevant conflict, and our understanding is based on longstanding law-of-war principles. If the practical circumstances of a given conflict are entirely unlike those of the conflicts that informed the development of the law of war, that understanding may unravel. But that is not the situation we face as of this date. Active combat operations against Taliban fighters apparently are ongoing in Afghanistan. See, *e.g.*, Constable, U.S. Launches New Operation in Afghanistan, Washington Post, Mar. 14, 2004, p. A22 (reporting that 13,500 United States troops remain in Afghanistan, including several thousand new arrivals); J. Abizaid, Dept. of Defense, Gen. Abizaid Central Command Operations Update Briefing, Apr. 30, 2004, http://www.defenselink.mil/transcripts/2004/tr20040430-1402.html (as visited June 8, 2004, and available in the Clerk of Court's case file) (media briefing describing ongoing operations in Afghanistan involving 20,000 United States troops). The United States may detain, for the duration of these hostilities, individuals legitimately determined to be Taliban combatants who "engaged in an armed conflict against the United States." If the record establishes that United States troops are still involved in active combat in Afghanistan, those detentions are part of the exercise of "necessary and appropriate force," and therefore are authorized by the AUMF.

Ex parte Milligan, 4 Wall. 2, 125 (1866), does not undermine our holding about the Government's authority to seize enemy combatants, as we define that term today. In that case, the Court made repeated reference to the fact that its inquiry into whether the military tribunal had jurisdiction to try and punish Milligan turned in large part on the fact that Milligan was not a prisoner of war, but a resident of Indiana arrested while at home there. *Id.*, at 118, 131. That fact was central to its conclusion. Had Milligan been captured while he was assisting Confederate soldiers by carrying a rifle against Union troops on a Confederate battlefield, the holding of the Court might well have been different. The Court's repeated explanations that Milligan was not a prisoner of war suggest that had these different circumstances been present he could have been detained under military authority for the duration of the conflict, whether or not he was a citizen.[1]

Moreover, as JUSTICE SCALIA acknowledges, the Court in *Ex parte Quirin*, 317 U.S. 1 (1942), dismissed the language of *Milligan* that the petitioners had suggested prevented them from being subject to military process. *Post*, at 17–18 (dissenting opinion). Clear in this rejection was a disavowal of the New York State cases cited in *Milligan*, 4 Wall., at 128–129, on which JUSTICE SCALIA relies. *See id.*, at 128–129. Both *Smith* v. *Shaw*, 12 Johns. *257 (N.Y. 1815), and *M'Connell* v. *Hampton*, 12 Johns. *234 (N.Y. 1815), were civil suits for false imprisonment. Even accepting that these cases once could have been viewed as standing for the sweeping proposition for which JUSTICE SCALIA cites them – that the military does not have authority to try an American citizen accused of spying

---

[1] Here the basis asserted for detention by the military is that Hamdi was carrying a weapon against American troops on a foreign battlefield; that is, that he was an enemy combatant. The legal category of enemy combatant has not been elaborated upon in great detail. The permissible bounds of the category will be defined by the lower courts as subsequent cases are presented to them.

against his country during wartime – *Quirin* makes undeniably clear that this is not the law today. Haupt, like the citizens in *Smith* and *M'Connell*, was accused of being a spy. The Court in *Quirin* found him "subject to trial and punishment by [a] military tribunal[ ]" for those acts, and held that his citizenship did not change this result. 317 U.S., at 31, 37–38.

Quirin was a unanimous opinion. It both postdates and clarifies *Milligan*, providing us with the most apposite precedent that we have on the question of whether citizens may be detained in such circumstances. Brushing aside such precedent – particularly when doing so gives rise to a host of new questions never dealt with by this Court – is unjustified and unwise.

To the extent that JUSTICE SCALIA accepts the precedential value of *Quirin*, he argues that it cannot guide our inquiry here because "[i]n *Quirin* it was uncontested that the petitioners were members of enemy forces," while Hamdi challenges his classification as an enemy combatant. *Post*, at 19. But it is unclear why, in the paradigm outlined by JUSTICE SCALIA, such a concession should have any relevance. JUSTICE SCALIA envisions a system in which the only options are congressional suspension of the writ of habeas corpus or prosecution for treason or some other crime. *Post*, at 2660. He does not explain how his historical analysis supports the addition of a third option – detention under some other process after concession of enemy-combatant status – or why a concession should carry any different effect than proof of enemy-combatant status in a proceeding that comports with due process. To be clear, our opinion only finds legislative authority to detain under the AUMF once it is sufficiently clear that the individual is, in fact, an enemy combatant; whether that is established by concession or by some other process that verifies this fact with sufficient certainty seems beside the point.

Further, JUSTICE SCALIA largely ignores the context of this case: a United States citizen captured in a *foreign* combat zone. JUSTICE SCALIA refers to only one case involving this factual scenario – a case in which a United States citizen-POW (a member of the Italian army) from World War II was seized on the battlefield in Sicily and then held in the United States. The court in that case held that the military detention of that United States citizen was lawful. See *In re Territo*, 156 F.2d, at 148.

JUSTICE SCALIA's treatment of that case – in a footnote – suffers from the same defect as does his treatment of *Quirin*: Because JUSTICE SCALIA finds the fact of battlefield capture irrelevant, his distinction based on the fact that the petitioner "conceded" enemy combatant status is beside the point. See *supra*, at 2668. JUSTICE SCALIA can point to no case or other authority for the proposition that those captured on a foreign battlefield (whether detained there or in U.S. territory) cannot be detained outside the criminal process.

Moreover, JUSTICE SCALIA presumably would come to a different result if Hamdi had been kept in Afghanistan or even Guantanamo Bay. See *post*, at 25 (SCALIA, J., dissenting). This creates a perverse incentive. Military authorities faced with the stark choice of submitting to the full-blown criminal process or releasing a suspected enemy combatant captured on the battlefield will simply keep citizen-detainees abroad. Indeed, the Government transferred Hamdi from Guantanamo Bay to the United States naval brig only after it learned that he might be an American citizen. It is not at all clear why that should make a determinative constitutional difference.

III

Even in cases in which the detention of enemy combatants is legally authorized, there remains the question of what process is constitutionally due to a citizen who disputes his enemy-combatant status. Hamdi argues that he is owed a meaningful and timely hearing and that "extra-judicial detention [that] begins and ends with the submission of an affidavit based on third-hand hearsay" does not comport with the Fifth and Fourteenth Amendments. Brief for Petitioners 16. The Government counters that any more process than was provided below would be both unworkable and "constitutionally intolerable." Brief for Respondents 46. Our resolution of this dispute requires a careful examination both of the writ of habeas corpus, which Hamdi now seeks to employ as a mechanism of judicial review, and of the Due Process Clause, which informs the procedural contours of that mechanism in this instance.

A

Though they reach radically different conclusions on the process that ought to attend the present proceeding, the parties begin on common ground. All agree that, absent suspension, the writ of habeas corpus remains available to every individual detained within the United States. U.S. Const., Art. I, §9, cl. 2 ("The Privilege of the Writ of Habeas Corpus shall not be suspended, unless when in Cases of Rebellion or Invasion the public Safety may require it"). Only in the rarest of circumstances has Congress seen fit to suspend the writ. See, *e.g.*, Act of Mar. 3, 1863, ch. 81, §1, 12 Stat. 755; Act of April 20, 1871, ch. 22, §4, 17 Stat. 14. At all other times, it has remained a critical check on the Executive, ensuring that it does not detain individuals except in accordance with law. See *INS* v. *St. Cyr*, 533 U.S. 289, 301 (2001). All agree suspension of the writ has not occurred here. Thus, it is undisputed that Hamdi was properly before an Article III court to challenge his detention under 28 U.S.C. §2241. Brief for Respondents 12. Further, all agree that §2241 and its companion provisions provide at least a skeletal outline of the procedures to be afforded a petitioner in federal habeas review. Most notably, §2243 provides that "the person detained may, under oath, deny any of the facts set forth in the return or allege any other material facts," and §2246 allows the taking of evidence in habeas proceedings by deposition, affidavit, or interrogatories.

The simple outline of §2241 makes clear both that Congress envisioned that habeas petitioners would have some opportunity to present and rebut facts and that courts in cases like this retain some ability to vary the ways in which they do so as mandated by due process. The Government recognizes the basic procedural protections required by the habeas statute, *Id.*, at 37–38, but asks us to hold that, given both the flexibility of the habeas mechanism and the circumstances presented in this case, the presentation of the Mobbs Declaration to the habeas court completed the required factual development. It suggests two separate reasons for its position that no further process is due.

B

First, the Government urges the adoption of the Fourth Circuit's holding below – that because it is "undisputed" that Hamdi's seizure took place in a combat zone, the habeas determination can be made purely as a matter of law, with no further hearing or factfinding necessary. This argument is easily rejected. As the dissenters from the denial of rehearing en banc noted, the circumstances surrounding Hamdi's seizure cannot in any way be characterized as "undisputed," as "those circumstances are neither conceded in fact, nor susceptible to concession in law, because Hamdi has not been permitted to speak for himself or even through counsel as to those circumstances." 337 F.3d 335, 357 (2003) (Luttig, J., dissenting from denial of rehearing en banc); see also *id.*, at 371– 372 (Motz, J., dissenting from denial of rehearing en banc). Further, the "facts" that constitute the alleged concession are insufficient to support Hamdi's detention. Under the definition of enemy combatant that we accept today as falling within the scope of Congress' authorization, Hamdi would need to be "part of or supporting forces hostile to the United States or coalition partners" and "engaged in an armed conflict against the United States" to justify his detention in the United States for the duration of the relevant conflict. Brief for Respondents 3. The habeas petition states only that "[w]hen seized by the United States Government, Mr. Hamdi resided in Afghanistan." App. 104. An assertion that one *resided* in a country in which combat operations are taking place is not a concession that one was "*captured* in a zone of active combat operations in a foreign theater of war," 316 F.3d, at 459 (emphasis added), and certainly is not a concession that one was "part of or supporting forces hostile to the United States or coalition partners" and "engaged in an armed conflict against the United States." Accordingly, we reject any argument that Hamdi has made concessions that eliminate any right to further process.

C

The Government's second argument requires closer consideration. This is the argument that further factual exploration is unwarranted and inappropriate in light of the extraordinary constitutional interests at stake. Under the Government's most extreme rendition of this argument, "[r]espect for separation of powers and the limited institutional capabilities of courts in matters of military decision-making in connection with an ongoing conflict" ought to eliminate entirely any individual process, restricting the courts to investigating only whether legal authorization exists for the broader detention scheme. Brief for Respondents 26. At most, the Government argues, courts should review its determination that a citizen is an enemy combatant under a very deferential "some evidence" standard. *Id.*, at 34 ("Under the some evidence standard, the focus is exclusively on the factual basis supplied by the Executive to support its own determination") (citing *Superintendent, Mass. Correctional Institution at Walpole v. Hill*, 472 U.S. 445, 455–457 (1985) (explaining that the some evidence standard "does not require" a "weighing of the evidence," but rather calls for assessing "whether there is any evidence in the record that could support the conclusion")). Under this review, a court would assume the accuracy of the Government's articulated basis for Hamdi's detention, as set forth in the Mobbs Declaration, and assess only whether that articulated basis was a legitimate one. Brief for Respondents 36; see also 316 F. 3d, at 473–474 (declining to address whether the "some evidence" standard should govern the adjudication of such claims, but noting that "[t]he factual averments in the [Mobbs] affidavit, if accurate, are sufficient to confirm" the legality of Hamdi's detention).

In response, Hamdi emphasizes that this Court consistently has recognized that an individual challenging his detention may not be held at the will of the Executive without recourse to some proceeding before a neutral tribunal to determine whether the Executive's asserted justifications for that detention have basis in fact and warrant in law. See, *e.g.*, *Zadvydas v. Davis*, 533 U.S. 678, 690 (2001); *Addington v. Texas*, 441 U.S. 418, 425–427 (1979). He argues that the Fourth Circuit inappropriately "ceded power to the Executive during wartime to define the conduct for which a citizen may be detained, judge whether that citizen has engaged in the proscribed conduct, and imprison that citizen indefinitely," Brief for Petitioners 21, and that due process demands that he receive a hearing in which he may challenge the Mobbs Declaration and adduce his own counter evidence. The District Court, agreeing with Hamdi, apparently believed that the appropriate process would approach the process that accompanies a criminal trial. It therefore disapproved of the hearsay nature of the Mobbs Declaration and anticipated quite extensive discovery of various military affairs. Anything less, it concluded, would not be "meaningful judicial review." App. 291.

Both of these positions highlight legitimate concerns. And both emphasize the tension that often exists between the autonomy that the Government asserts is necessary in order to pursue effectively a particular goal and the process that a citizen contends he is due before he is deprived of a constitutional right. The ordinary mechanism that we use for balancing such serious competing interests, and for determining the procedures that are necessary to ensure that a citizen is not "deprived of life, liberty, or property, without due process of law," U.S. Const., Amdt. 5, is the test that we articulated in *Mathews* v. *Eldridge*, 424 U.S. 319 (1976). See, *e.g., Heller* v. *Doe*, 509 U.S. 312, 330–331 (1993); *Zinermon* v. *Burch*, 494 U.S. 113, 127–28 (1990); *United States* v. *Salerno*, 481 U.S. 739, 746 (1987); *Schall* v. *Martin*, 467 U.S. 253, 274–275 (1984); *Addington* v. *Texas*, *supra*, at 425. *Mathews* dictates that the process due in any given instance is determined by weighing "the private interest that will be affected by the official action" against the Government's asserted interest, "including the function involved" and the burdens the Government would face in providing greater process. 424 U.S., at 335. The *Mathews* calculus then contemplates a judicious balancing of these concerns, through an analysis of "the risk of an erroneous deprivation" of the private interest if the process were reduced and the " probable value, if any, of additional or substitute safeguards." *Ibid.* We take each of these steps in turn.

1

It is beyond question that substantial interests lie on both sides of the scale in this case. Hamdi's "private interest . . . affected by the official action," *ibid.*, is the most elemental of liberty interests – the interest in being free from physical detention by one's own government. *Foucha* v. *Louisiana*, 504 U.S. 71, 80 (1992) ("Freedom from bodily restraint has always been at the core of the liberty protected by the Due Process Clause from arbitrary governmental action"); see also *Parham* v. *J. R.*, 442 U.S. 584, 600 (1979) (noting the "substantial liberty interest in not being confined unnecessarily"). "In our society liberty is the norm," and detention without trial "is the carefully limited exception." *Salerno, supra*, at 755. "We have always been careful not to 'minimize the importance and fundamental nature' of the individual's right to liberty," *Foucha, supra*, at 80 (quoting *Salerno, supra*, at 750), and we will not do so today.

Nor is the weight on this side of the *Mathews* scale offset by the circumstances of war or the accusation of treasonous behavior, for "[i]t is clear that commitment for *any* purpose constitutes a significant deprivation of liberty that requires due process protection," *Jones* v. *United States*, 463 U.S. 354, 361 (1983) (emphasis added; internal quotation marks omitted), and at this stage in the *Mathews* calculus, we consider the interest of the *erroneously* detained individual. *Carey* v. *Piphus*, 435 U.S. 247, 259 (1978) ("Procedural due process rules are meant to protect persons not from the deprivation, but from the mistaken or unjustified deprivation of life, liberty, or property"); see also *id.*, at 266 (noting "the importance to organized society that procedural due process be observed," and emphasizing that "the right to procedural due process is 'absolute' in the sense that it does not depend upon the merits of a claimant's substantive assertions"). Indeed, as *amicus* briefs from media and relief organizations emphasize, the risk of erroneous deprivation of a citizen's liberty in the absence of sufficient process here is very real. See Brief for AmeriCares et al. as *Amici Curiae* 13–22 (noting ways in which "[t]he nature of humanitarian relief work and journalism present a significant risk of mistaken military detentions"). Moreover, as critical as the Government's interest may be in detaining those who actually pose an immediate threat to the national security of the United States during ongoing international conflict, history and common sense teach us that an unchecked system of detention carries the potential to become a means for oppression and abuse of others who do not present that sort of threat. See *Ex parte Milligan*, 4 Wall., at 125 ("[The Founders] knew – the history of the world told them – the nation they were founding, be its existence short or long, would be involved in war; how often or how long continued, human foresight could not tell; and that unlimited power, wherever lodged at such a time, was especially hazardous to freemen"). Because we live in a society in which "[m]ere public intolerance or animosity cannot constitutionally justify the deprivation of a person's physical liberty," *O'Connor* v. *Donaldson*, 422 U.S. 563, 575 (1975), our starting point for the *Mathews* v. *Eldridge* analysis is unaltered by the allegations surrounding the particular detainee or the organizations with which he is alleged to have associated. We reaffirm today the fundamental nature of a citizen's right to be free from involuntary confinement by his own government without due process of law, and we weigh the opposing governmental interests against the curtailment of liberty that such confinement entails.

2

On the other side of the scale are the weighty and sensitive governmental interests in ensuring that those who have in fact fought with the enemy during a war do not return to battle against the United States. As discussed above, *supra*, at 10, the law of war and the realities of combat may render such detentions both necessary and appropriate, and our due process analysis need not blink at those realities. Without doubt, our Constitution recognizes that core strategic matters of warmaking belong in the hands of those who are best positioned and most politically accountable for making them. *Department of Navy* v. *Egan*, 484 U.S. 518, 530 (1988) (noting the reluctance of the courts "to intrude upon the authority of the Executive in military and national security affairs"); *Youngstown Sheet & Tube Co.* v. *Sawyer*, 343 U.S. 579, 587 (1952) (acknowledging "broad powers in military commanders engaged in day-to-day fighting in a theater of war").

The Government also argues at some length that its interests in reducing the process available to alleged enemy combatants are heightened by the practical difficulties that would accompany a system of trial-like process. In its view, military officers who are engaged in the serious work of waging battle would be unnecessarily and dangerously distracted by litigation half a world away, and discovery into military operations would both intrude on the sensitive secrets of national defense and result in a futile search for evidence buried under the rubble of war. Brief for Respondents 46–49. To the extent that these burdens are triggered by heightened procedures, they are properly taken into account in our due process analysis.

3

Striking the proper constitutional balance here is of great importance to the Nation during this period of ongoing combat. But it is equally vital that our calculus not give short shrift to the values that this country holds dear or to the privilege that is American citizenship. It is during our most challenging and uncertain moments that our Nation's commitment to due process is most severely tested; and it is in those times that we must preserve our commitment at home to the principles for which we fight abroad. See *Kennedy* v. *Mendoza-Martinez*, 372 U.S. 144, 164–165 (1963) ("The imperative necessity for safeguarding these rights to procedural due process under the gravest of emergencies has existed throughout our constitutional history, for it is then, under the pressing exigencies of crisis, that there is the greatest temptation to dispense with guarantees which, it is feared, will inhibit government action"); see also *United States* v. *Robel*, 389 U.S. 258, 264 (1967) ("It would indeed be ironic if, in the name of national defense, we would sanction the subversion of one of those liberties ... which makes the defense of the Nation worthwhile").

With due recognition of these competing concerns, we believe that neither the process proposed by the Government nor the process apparently envisioned by the District Court below strikes the proper constitutional balance when a United States citizen is detained in the United States as an enemy combatant. That is, "the risk of erroneous deprivation" of a detainee's liberty interest is unacceptably high under the Government's proposed rule, while some of the "additional or substitute procedural safeguards" suggested by the District Court are unwarranted in light of their limited "probable value" and the burdens they may impose on the military in such cases. *Mathews*, 424 U.S., at 335.

We therefore hold that a citizen-detainee seeking to challenge his classification as an enemy combatant must receive notice of the factual basis for his classification, and a fair opportunity to rebut the Government's factual assertions before a neutral decisionmaker. See *Cleveland Bd. of Ed.* v. *Loudermill*, 470 U.S. 532, 542 (1985) ("An essential principle of due process is that a deprivation of life, liberty, or property 'be preceded by notice and opportunity for hearing appropriate to the nature of the case'") (quoting *Mullane* v. *Central Hanover Bank & Trust Co.*, 339 U.S. 306, 313 (1950)); *Concrete Pipe & Products of Cal., Inc.* v. *Construction Laborers Pension Trust for Southern Cal.*, 508 U.S. 602, 617 (1993) ("due process requires a 'neutral and detached judge in the first instance'") (quoting *Ward* v. *Monroeville*, 409 U.S. 57, 61–62 (1972)). "For more than a century the central meaning of procedural due process has been clear: 'Parties whose rights are to be affected are entitled to be heard; and in order that they may enjoy that right they must first be notified.' It is equally fundamental that the right to notice and an opportunity to be heard 'must be granted at a meaningful time and in a meaningful manner.'" *Fuentes* v. *Shevin*, 407 U.S. 67, 80 (1972) (quoting *Baldwin* v. *Hale*, 1 Wall. 223, 233 (1864); *Armstrong* v. *Manzo*, 380 U.S. 545, 552 (1965) (other citations omitted)). These essential constitutional promises may not be eroded.

At the same time, the exigencies of the circumstances may demand that, aside from these core elements, enemy combatant proceedings may be tailored to alleviate their uncommon potential to burden the Executive at a time of ongoing military conflict. Hearsay, for example, may need to be accepted as the most reliable available evidence from the Government in such a proceeding. Likewise, the Constitution would not be offended by a presumption in favor of the Government's evidence, so long as that presumption remained a rebuttable one and fair opportunity for rebuttal were provided. Thus, once the Government puts forth credible evidence that the habeas petitioner meets the enemy-combatant criteria, the onus could shift to the petitioner to rebut that evidence with more persuasive evidence that he falls outside the criteria. A burden-shifting scheme of this sort would meet the goal of ensuring that the errant tourist, embedded journalist, or local aid worker has a chance to prove military error while giving due regard to the Executive once it has put forth meaningful support for its conclusion that the detainee is in fact an enemy combatant. In the words of *Mathews*, process of this sort would sufficiently address the "risk of erroneous deprivation" of a detainee's liberty interest while eliminating certain procedures that have questionable additional value in light of the burden on the Government. 424 U.S., at 335.[2]

---

[2] Because we hold that Hamdi is constitutionally entitled to the process described above, we need not address at this time whether any treaty guarantees him similar access to a tribunal for a determination of his status.

We think it unlikely that this basic process will have the dire impact on the central functions of warmaking that the Government forecasts. The parties agree that initial captures on the battlefield need not receive the process we have discussed here; that process is due only when the determination is made to *continue* to hold those who have been seized. The Government has made clear in its briefing that documentation regarding battlefield detainees already is kept in the ordinary course of military affairs. Brief for Respondents 3–4. Any factfinding imposition created by requiring a knowledgeable affiant to summarize these records to an independent tribunal is a minimal one. Likewise, arguments that military officers ought not have to wage war under the threat of litigation lose much of their steam when factual disputes at enemy-combatant hearings are limited to the alleged combatant's acts. This focus meddles little, if at all, in the strategy or conduct of war, inquiring only into the appropriateness of continuing to detain an individual claimed to have taken up arms against the United States. While we accord the greatest respect and consideration to the judgments of military authorities in matters relating to the actual prosecution of a war, and recognize that the scope of that discretion necessarily is wide, it does not infringe on the core role of the military for the courts to exercise their own time-honored and constitutionally mandated roles of reviewing and resolving claims like those presented here. Cf. *Korematsu* v. *United States*, 323 U.S. 214, 233–234 (1944) (Murphy, J., dissenting) ("[L]ike other claims conflicting with the asserted constitutional rights of the individual, the military claim must subject itself to the judicial process of having its reasonableness determined and its conflicts with other interests reconciled"); *Sterling* v. *Constantin*, 287 U.S. 378, 401 (1932) ("What are the allowable limits of military discretion, and whether or not they have been overstepped in a particular case, are judicial questions").

In sum, while the full protections that accompany challenges to detentions in other settings may prove unworkable and inappropriate in the enemy-combatant setting, the threats to military operations posed by a basic system of independent review are not so weighty as to trump a citizen's core rights to challenge meaningfully the Government's case and to be heard by an impartial adjudicator.

D

In so holding, we necessarily reject the Government's assertion that separation of powers principles mandate a heavily circumscribed role for the courts in such circumstances. Indeed, the position that the courts must forgo any examination of the individual case and focus exclusively on the legality of the broader detention scheme cannot be mandated by any reasonable view of separation of powers, as this approach serves only to *condense* power into a single branch of government. We have long since made clear that a state of war is not a blank check for the President when it comes to the rights of the Nation's citizens. *Youngstown Sheet & Tube*, 343 U.S., at 587. Whatever power the United States Constitution envisions for the Executive in its exchanges with other nations or with enemy organizations in times of conflict, it most assuredly envisions a role for all three branches when individual liberties are at stake. *Mistretta* v. *United States*, 488 U.S. 361, 380 (1989) (it was "the central judgment of the Framers of the Constitution that, within our political scheme, the separation of governmental powers into three coordinate Branches is essential to the preservation of liberty"); *Home Building & Loan Assn.* v. *Blaisdell*, 290 U.S. 398, 426 (1934) (The war power "is a power to wage war successfully, and thus it permits the harnessing of the entire energies of the people in a supreme cooperative effort to preserve the nation. But even the war power does not remove constitutional limitations safeguarding essential liberties"). Likewise, we have made clear that, unless Congress acts to suspend it, the Great Writ of habeas corpus allows the Judicial Branch to play a necessary role in maintaining this delicate balance of governance, serving as an important judicial check on the Executive's discretion in the realm of detentions. See *St. Cyr*, 533 U.S., at 301 ("At its historical core, the writ of habeas corpus has served as a means of reviewing the legality of Executive detention, and it is in that context that its protections have been strongest"). Thus, while we do not question that our due process assessment must pay keen attention to the particular burdens faced by the Executive in the context of military action, it would turn our system of checks and balances on its head to suggest that a citizen could not make his way to court with a challenge to the factual basis for his detention by his government, simply because the Executive opposes making available such a challenge. Absent suspension of the writ by Congress, a citizen detained as an enemy combatant is entitled to this process.

Because we conclude that due process demands some system for a citizen detainee to refute his classification, the proposed "some evidence" standard is inadequate. Any process in which the Executive's factual assertions go wholly unchallenged or are simply presumed correct without any opportunity for the alleged combatant to demonstrate otherwise falls constitutionally short. As the Government itself has recognized, we have utilized the "some evidence" standard in the past as a standard of review, not as a standard of proof. Brief for Respondents 35. That is, it primarily has been employed by courts in examining an administrative record developed after an adversarial proceeding – one with process at least of the sort that we today hold is constitutionally mandated in the citizen enemy-combatant setting. See, *e.g.*, *St. Cyr, supra; Hill*, 472 U.S., at 455–457. This standard therefore is ill suited to the situation in which a habeas petitioner has received no prior proceedings before any tribunal and had no prior opportunity to rebut the Executive's factual assertions before a neutral decisionmaker.

Today we are faced only with such a case. Aside from unspecified "screening" processes, Brief for Respondents 3–4, and military interrogations in which the Government suggests Hamdi could have contested his classification, Tr. of Oral Arg. 40, 42, Hamdi has received no process. An interrogation by one's captor, however effective an intelligence-gathering tool, hardly constitutes a constitutionally adequate factfinding before a neutral decisionmaker. Compare Brief for Respondents 42–43 (discussing the "secure interrogation environment," and noting that military interrogations require a controlled "interrogation dynamic" and "a relationship of trust and dependency" and are "a critical source" of "timely and effective intelligence") with *Concrete Pipe*, 508 U.S., at 617–618 ("one is entitled as a matter of due process of law to an adjudicator who is not in a situation which would offer a possible temptation to the average man as a judge . . . which might lead him not to hold the balance nice, clear and true" (internal quotation marks omitted)). That even purportedly fair adjudicators "are disqualified by their interest in the controversy to be decided is, of course, the general rule." *Tumey* v. *Ohio*, 273 U.S. 510, 522 (1927). Plainly, the "process" Hamdi has received is not that to which he is entitled under the Due Process Clause.

There remains the possibility that the standards we have articulated could be met by an appropriately authorized and properly constituted military tribunal. Indeed, it is notable that military regulations already provide for such process in related instances, dictating that tribunals be made available to determine the status of enemy detainees who assert prisoner-of-war status under the Geneva Convention. See Enemy Prisoners of War, Retained Personnel, Civilian Internees and Other Detainees, Army Regulation 190–8, §1–6 (1997). In the absence of such process, however, a court that receives a petition for a writ of habeas corpus from an alleged enemy combatant must itself ensure that the minimum requirements of due process are achieved. Both courts below recognized as much, focusing their energies on the question of whether Hamdi was due an opportunity to rebut the Government's case against him. The Government, too, proceeded on this assumption, presenting its affidavit and then seeking that it be evaluated under a deferential standard of review based on burdens that it alleged would accompany any greater process. As we have discussed, a habeas court in a case such as this may accept affidavit evidence like that contained in the Mobbs Declaration, so long as it also permits the alleged combatant to present his own factual case to rebut the Government's return. We anticipate that a District Court would proceed with the caution that we have indicated is necessary in this setting, engaging in a factfinding process that is both prudent and incremental. We have no reason to doubt that courts faced with these sensitive matters will pay proper heed both to the matters of national security that might arise in an individual case and to the constitutional limitations safeguarding essential liberties that remain vibrant even in times of security concerns.

IV

Hamdi asks us to hold that the Fourth Circuit also erred by denying him immediate access to counsel upon his detention and by disposing of the case without permitting him to meet with an attorney. Brief for Petitioners 19. Since our grant of certiorari in this case, Hamdi has been appointed counsel, with whom he has met for consultation purposes on several occasions, and with whom he is now being granted unmonitored meetings. He unquestionably has the right to access to counsel in connection with the proceedings on remand. No further consideration of this issue is necessary at this stage of the case.

* * *

The judgment of the United States Court of Appeals for the Fourth Circuit is vacated, and the case is remanded for further proceedings.

It is so ordered.

. . .

JUSTICE SOUTER, with whom JUSTICE GINSBURG joins, concurring in part, dissenting in part, and concurring in the judgment.

According to Yaser Hamdi's petition for writ of habeas corpus, brought on his behalf by his father, the Government of the United States is detaining him, an American citizen on American soil, with the explanation that he was seized on the field of battle in Afghanistan, having been on the enemy side. It is undisputed that the Government has not charged him with espionage, treason, or any other crime under domestic law. It is likewise undisputed that for one year and nine months, on the basis of an Executive designation of Hamdi as an "enemy combatant," the Government denied him the right to send or receive any communication beyond the prison where he was held and, in particular, denied him access to counsel to represent him.[1] The Government asserts a right to hold Hamdi under these conditions indefinitely, that is, until the Government determines that the United States is no longer threatened by the terrorism exemplified in the attacks of September 11, 2001.

In these proceedings on Hamdi's petition, he seeks to challenge the facts claimed by the Government as the basis for holding him as an enemy combatant. And in this Court he presses the distinct argument that the Government's claim, even if true, would

---

[1] The Government has since February 2004 permitted Hamdi to consult with counsel as a matter of policy, but does not concede that it has an obligation to allow this. Brief for Respondents 9, 39–46.

not implicate any authority for holding him that would satisfy 18 U.S.C. §4001(a) (Non-Detention Act), which bars imprisonment or detention of a citizen "except pursuant to an Act of Congress."

The Government responds that Hamdi's incommunicado imprisonment as an enemy combatant seized on the field of battle falls within the President's power as Commander in Chief under the laws and usages of war, and is in any event authorized by two statutes. Accordingly, the Government contends that Hamdi has no basis for any challenge by petition for habeas except to his own status as an enemy combatant; and even that challenge may go no further than to enquire whether "some evidence" supports Hamdi's designation, see Brief for Respondents 34–36; if there is "some evidence," Hamdi should remain locked up at the discretion of the Executive. At the argument of this case, in fact, the Government went further and suggested that as long as a prisoner could challenge his enemy combatant designation when responding to interrogation during incommunicado detention he was accorded sufficient process to support his designation as an enemy combatant. See Tr. of Oral Arg. 40; *id.*, at 42 ("[H]e has an opportunity to explain it in his own words" "[d]uring interrogation"). Since on either view judicial enquiry so limited would be virtually worthless as a way to contest detention, the Government's concession of jurisdiction to hear Hamdi's habeas claim is more theoretical than practical, leaving the assertion of Executive authority close to unconditional.

The plurality rejects any such limit on the exercise of habeas jurisdiction and so far I agree with its opinion. The plurality does, however, accept the Government's position that if Hamdi's designation as an enemy combatant is correct, his detention (at least as to some period) is authorized by an Act of Congress as required by §4001(a), that is, by the Authorization for Use of Military Force, 115 Stat. 224 (hereinafter Force Resolution). *Ante*, at 9–14. Here, I disagree and respectfully dissent. The Government has failed to demonstrate that the Force Resolution authorizes the detention complained of here even on the facts the Government claims. If the Government raises nothing further than the record now shows, the Non-Detention Act entitles Hamdi to be released.

I

The Government's first response to Hamdi's claim that holding him violates §4001(a), prohibiting detention of citizens "except pursuant to an Act of Congress," is that the statute does not even apply to military wartime detentions, being beyond the sphere of domestic criminal law. Next, the Government says that even if that statute does apply, two Acts of Congress provide the authority §4001(a) demands: a general authorization to the Department of Defense to pay for detaining "prisoners of war" and "similar" persons, 10 U.S.C. §956(5), and the Force Resolution, passed after the attacks of 2001. At the same time, the Government argues that in detaining Hamdi in the manner described, the President is in any event acting as Commander in Chief under Article II of the Constitution, which brings with it the right to invoke authority under the accepted customary rules for waging war. On the record in front of us, the Government has not made out a case on any theory.

II

The threshold issue is how broadly or narrowly to read the Non-Detention Act, the tone of which is severe: "No citizen shall be imprisoned or otherwise detained by the United States except pursuant to an Act of Congress." Should the severity of the Act be relieved when the Government's stated factual justification for incommunicado detention is a war on terrorism, so that the Government may be said to act "pursuant" to congressional terms that fall short of explicit authority to imprison individuals? With one possible though important qualification, see *infra*, at 10–11, the answer has to be no. For a number of reasons, the prohibition within §4001(a) has to be read broadly to accord the statute a long reach and to impose a burden of justification on the Government.

First, the circumstances in which the Act was adopted point the way to this interpretation. The provision superseded a cold-war statute, the Emergency Detention Act of 1950 (formerly 50 U.S.C. §811 *et seq.* (1970 ed.)), which had authorized the Attorney General, in time of emergency, to detain anyone reasonably thought likely to engage in espionage or sabotage. That statute was repealed in 1971 out of fear that it could authorize a repetition of the World War II internment of citizens of Japanese ancestry; Congress meant to preclude another episode like the one described in *Korematsu* v. *United States*, 323 U.S. 214 (1944). See H. R. Rep. No. 92-116, pp. 2, 4–5 (1971). While Congress might simply have struck the 1950 statute, in considering the repealer the point was made that the existing statute provided some express procedural protection, without which the Executive would seem to be subject to no statutory limits protecting individual liberty. See *id.*, at 5 (mere repeal "might leave citizens subject to arbitrary executive action, with no clear demarcation of the limits of executive authority"); 117 Cong. Rec. 31544 (1971) (Emergency Detention Act "remains as the only existing barrier against the future exercise of executive power which resulted in" the Japanese internment); cf. *id.*, at 31548 (in the absence of further procedural provisions, even §4001(a) "will virtually leave us stripped naked against the great power... which the President has"). It was in these circumstances that a proposed limit on Executive action was expanded to the inclusive scope of §4001(a) as enacted.

The fact that Congress intended to guard against a repetition of the World War II internments when it repealed the 1950 statute and gave us §4001(a) provides a powerful reason to think that §4001(a) was meant to require clear congressional authorization before any citizen can be placed in a cell. It is not merely that the legislative history shows that §4001(a) was thought necessary in anticipation of times just like the present, in which the safety of the country is threatened. To appreciate what is most significant, one must only recall that the internments of the 1940's were accomplished by Executive action. Although an Act of Congress ratified and confirmed an Executive order authorizing the military to exclude individuals from defined areas and to accommodate those it might remove, see *Ex parte Endo*, 323 U.S. 283, 285–288 (1944), the statute said nothing whatever about the detention of those who might be removed, *id.*, at 300–301; internment camps were creatures of the Executive, and confinement in them rested on assertion of Executive authority, see *id.*, at 287–293. When, therefore, Congress repealed the 1950 Act and adopted §4001(a) for the purpose of avoiding another *Korematsu*, it intended to preclude reliance on vague congressional authority (for example, providing "accommodations" for those subject to removal) as authority for detention or imprisonment at the discretion of the Executive (maintaining detention camps of American citizens, for example). In requiring that any Executive detention be "pursuant to an Act of Congress," then, Congress necessarily meant to require a congressional enactment that clearly authorized detention or imprisonment.

Second, when Congress passed §4001(a) it was acting in light of an interpretive regime that subjected enactments limiting liberty in wartime to the requirement of a clear statement and it presumably intended §4001(a) to be read accordingly. This need for clarity was unmistakably expressed in *Ex parte Endo, supra*, decided the same day as *Korematsu*. *Endo* began with a petition for habeas corpus by an interned citizen claiming to be loyal and law-abiding and thus "unlawfully detained." 323 U.S., at 294. The petitioner was held entitled to habeas relief in an opinion that set out this principle for scrutinizing wartime statutes in derogation of customary liberty:

> "In interpreting a wartime measure we must assume that [its] purpose was to allow for the greatest possible accommodation between . . . liberties and the exigencies of war. We must assume, when asked to find implied powers in a grant of legislative or executive authority, that the law makers intended to place no greater restraint on the citizen than was clearly and unmistakably indicated by the language they used." *Id.*, at 300.

Congress's understanding of the need for clear authority before citizens are kept detained is itself therefore clear, and §4001(a) must be read to have teeth in its demand for congressional authorization.

Finally, even if history had spared us the cautionary example of the internments in World War II, even if there had been no *Korematsu*, and *Endo* had set out no principle of statutory interpretation, there would be a compelling reason to read §4001(a) to demand manifest authority to detain before detention is authorized. The defining character of American constitutional government is its constant tension between security and liberty, serving both by partial helpings of each. In a government of separated powers, deciding finally on what is a reasonable degree of guaranteed liberty whether in peace or war (or some condition in between) is not well entrusted to the Executive Branch of Government, whose particular responsibility is to maintain security. For reasons of inescapable human nature, the branch of the Government asked to counter a serious threat is not the branch on which to rest the Nation's entire reliance in striking the balance between the will to win and the cost in liberty on the way to victory; the responsibility for security will naturally amplify the claim that security legitimately raises. A reasonable balance is more likely to be reached on the judgment of a different branch, just as Madison said in remarking that "the constant aim is to divide and arrange the several offices in such a manner as that each may be a check on the other – that the private interest of every individual may be a sentinel over the public rights." The Federalist No. 51, p. 349 (J. Cooke ed. 1961). Hence the need for an assessment by Congress before citizens are subject to lockup, and likewise the need for a clearly expressed congressional resolution of the competing claims.

III

Under this principle of reading §4001(a) robustly to require a clear statement of authorization to detain, none of the Government's arguments suffices to justify Hamdi's detention.

A

First, there is the argument that §4001(a) does not even apply to wartime military detentions, a position resting on the placement of §4001(a) in Title 18 of the United States Code, the gathering of federal criminal law. The text of the statute does not, however, so limit its reach, and the legislative history of the provision shows its placement in Title 18 was not meant to render the statute more restricted than its terms. The draft of what is now §4001(a) as contained in the original bill prohibited only imprisonment unauthorized by Title 18. See H.R. Rep. No. 92-116, at 4. In response to the Department of Justice's objection that the original draft seemed to assume wrongly that all provisions for the detention of convicted persons would be contained in Title 18, the provision was amended by replacing a reference to that title with the reference to an "Act of Congress." *Id.*, at 3. The Committee on the Judiciary, discussing this change, stated that "[limiting] detention of citizens . . . to situations in which . . . an Act of Congres[s] exists" would "assure that no detention camps can be established without at least the acquiescence of the Congress." *Id.*, at 5. See also *supra*, at 4–6. This understanding, that the amended bill would sweep beyond imprisonment for crime and apply to Executive detention in furtherance of wartime security, was emphasized in an extended debate. Representative Ichord, chairman of the House Internal Security Committee and an opponent of the bill, feared that the redrafted statute would "deprive the President of his emergency powers and his most effective means of coping with sabotage and espionage agents in war-related crises." 117 Cong. Rec., at 31542. Representative Railsback, the bill's sponsor, spoke of the bill in absolute terms: "[I]n order to prohibit arbitrary executive action, [the bill] assures that no detention of citizens can be undertaken by the Executive without the prior consent of Congress." *Id.*, at 31551. This legislative history indicates that Congress was aware that §4001(a) would limit the Executive's power to detain citizens in wartime to protect national security, and it is fair to say that the prohibition was thus intended to extend not only to the exercise of power to vindicate the interests underlying domestic criminal law, but to statutorily unauthorized detention by the Executive for reasons of security in wartime, just as Hamdi claims.[2]

B

Next, there is the Government's claim, accepted by the plurality, that the terms of the Force Resolution are adequate to authorize detention of an enemy combatant under the circumstances described,[3] a claim the Government fails to support sufficiently to satisfy §4001(a) as read to require a clear statement of authority to detain. Since the Force Resolution was adopted one week after the attacks of September 11, 2001, it naturally speaks with some generality, but its focus is clear, and that is on the use of military power. It is fairly read to authorize the use of armies and weapons, whether against other armies or individual terrorists. But, like the statute discussed in *Endo*, it never so much as uses the word detention, and there is no reason to think Congress might have perceived any need to augment Executive power to deal with dangerous citizens within the United States, given the well-stocked statutory arsenal of defined criminal offenses covering the gamut of actions that a citizen sympathetic to terrorists might commit. See, *e.g.*, 18 U.S.C. §2339A (material support for various terrorist acts); §2339B (material support to a foreign terrorist organization); §2332a (use of a weapon of mass destruction, including conspiracy and attempt); §2332b(a)(1) (acts of terrorism "transcending national boundaries," including threats, conspiracy, and attempt); 18 U.S.C. §2339C (Supp. 2004) (financing of certain terrorist acts); see also 18 U.S.C. §3142(e) (pretrial detention). See generally Brief for Janet Reno et al. as *Amici Curiae*

---

[2] Nor is it possible to distinguish between civilian and military authority to detain based on the congressional object of avoiding another *Korematsu* v. *United States*, 323 U.S. 214 (1944). See Brief for Respondents 21 (arguing that military detentions are exempt). Although a civilian agency authorized by Executive order ran the detention camps, the relocation and detention of American citizens was ordered by the military under authority of the President as Commander in Chief. See *Ex parte Endo*, 323 U.S. 283, 285–288 (1944). The World War II internment was thus ordered under the same Presidential power invoked here and the intent to bar a repetition goes to the action taken and authority claimed here.

[3] As noted, *supra*, at 3, the Government argues that a required Act of Congress is to be found in a statutory authorization to spend money appropriated for the care of prisoners of war and of other, similar prisoners, 10 U.S.C. §956(5). It is enough to say that this statute is an authorization to spend money if there are prisoners, not an authorization to imprison anyone to provide the occasion for spending money.

in *Rumsfeld* v. *Padilla*, O.T.2003, No. 03-1027, pp. 14–19, and n. 17 (listing the tools available to the Executive to fight terrorism even without the power the Government claims here); Brief for Louis Henkin et al. as *Amici Curiae* in *Rumsfeld* v. *Padilla*, O. T.2003, No. 03-1027, p. 23, n. 27.[4]

C

Even so, there is one argument for treating the Force Resolution as sufficiently clear to authorize detention of a citizen consistently with §4001(a). Assuming the argument to be sound, however, the Government is in no position to claim its advantage.

Because the Force Resolution authorizes the use of military force in acts of war by the United States, the argument goes, it is reasonably clear that the military and its Commander in Chief are authorized to deal with enemy belligerents according to the treaties and customs known collectively as the laws of war. Brief for Respondents 20–22; see *ante*, at 9–14 (accepting this argument). Accordingly, the United States may detain captured enemies, and *Ex parte Quirin*, 317 U.S. 1 (1942), may perhaps be claimed for the proposition that the American citizenship of such a captive does not as such limit the Government's power to deal with him under the usages of war. *Id.*, at 31, 37–38. Thus, the Government here repeatedly argues that Hamdi's detention amounts to nothing more than customary detention of a captive taken on the field of battle: if the usages of war are fairly authorized by the Force Resolution, Hamdi's detention is authorized for purposes of §4001(a).

There is no need, however, to address the merits of such an argument in all possible circumstances. For now it is enough to recognize that the Government's stated legal position in its campaign against the Taliban (among whom Hamdi was allegedly captured) is apparently at odds with its claim here to be acting in accordance with customary law of war and hence to be within the terms of the Force Resolution in its detention of Hamdi. In a statement of its legal position cited in its brief, the Government says that "the Geneva Convention applies to the Taliban detainees." Office of the White House Press Secretary, Fact Sheet, Status of Detainees at Guantanamo (Feb. 7, 2002), www.whitehouse.gov/news/releases/2002/ 02/20020207-13.html (as visited June 18, 2004, and available in Clerk of Court's case file) (hereinafter White House Press Release) (cited in Brief for Respondents 24, n. 9). Hamdi presumably is such a detainee, since according to the Government's own account, he was taken bearing arms on the Taliban side of a field of battle in Afghanistan. He would therefore seem to qualify for treatment as a prisoner of war under the Third Geneva Convention, to which the United States is a party. Article 4 of the Geneva Convention (III) Relative to the Treatment of Prisoners of War, Aug. 12, 1949, [1955] 6 U.S.T. 3316, 3320, T.I.A.S. No. 3364.

By holding him incommunicado, however, the Government obviously has not been treating him as a prisoner of war, and in fact the Government claims that no Taliban detainee is entitled to prisoner of war status. See Brief for Respondents 24; White House Press Release. This treatment appears to be a violation of the Geneva Convention provision that even in cases of doubt, captives are entitled to be treated as prisoners of war "until such time as their status has been determined by a competent tribunal." Art. 5, 6 U.S.T., at 3324. The Government answers that the President's determination that

---

[4] Even a brief examination of the reported cases in which the Government has chosen to proceed criminally against those who aided the Taliban shows the Government has found no shortage of offenses to allege. See *United States* v. *Lindh*, 212 F. Supp. 2d 541, 547 (ED Va. 2002); *United States* v. *Khan*, 309 F. Supp. 2d 789, 796 (ED Va. 2004).

Taliban detainees do not qualify as prisoners of war is conclusive as to Hamdi's status and removes any doubt that would trigger application of the Convention's tribunal requirement. See Brief for Respondents 24. But reliance on this categorical pronouncement to settle doubt is apparently at odds with the military regulation, Enemy Prisoners of War, Retained Personnel, Civilian Internees and Other Detainees, Army Reg. 190–8, §§1–5, 1–6 (1997), adopted to implement the Geneva Convention, and setting out a detailed procedure for a military tribunal to determine an individual's status. See, *e.g.*, *id.*, §1–6 ("A competent tribunal shall be composed of three commissioned officers"; a "written record shall be made of proceedings"; "[p]roceedings shall be open" with certain exceptions; "[p]ersons whose status is to be determined shall be advised of their rights at the beginning of their hearings," "allowed to attend all open sessions," "allowed to call witnesses if reasonably available, and to question those witnesses called by the Tribunal," and to "have a right to testify"; and a tribunal shall determine status by a "[p]reponderance of evidence"). One of the types of doubt these tribunals are meant to settle is whether a given individual may be, as Hamdi says he is, an "[i]nnocent civilian who should be immediately returned to his home or released." *Id.*, 1–6*e*(10)(*c*). The regulation, jointly promulgated by the Headquarters of the Departments of the Army, Navy, Air Force, and Marine Corps, provides that "[p]ersons who have been determined by a competent tribunal not to be entitled to prisoner of war status may not be executed, imprisoned, or otherwise penalized without further proceedings to determine what acts they have committed and what penalty should be imposed." *Id.*, §1–6*g*. The regulation also incorporates the Geneva Convention's presumption that in cases of doubt, "persons shall enjoy the protection of the . . . Convention until such time as their status has been determined by a competent tribunal." *Id.*, §1–6*a*. Thus, there is reason to question whether the United States is acting in accordance with the laws of war it claims as authority.

Whether, or to what degree, the Government is in fact violating the Geneva Convention and is thus acting outside the customary usages of war are not matters I can resolve at this point. What I can say, though, is that the Government has not made out its claim that in detaining Hamdi in the manner described, it is acting in accord with the laws of war authorized to be applied against citizens by the Force Resolution. I conclude accordingly that the Government has failed to support the position that the Force Resolution authorizes the described detention of Hamdi for purposes of §4001(a).

It is worth adding a further reason for requiring the Government to bear the burden of clearly justifying its claim to be exercising recognized war powers before declaring §4001(a) satisfied. Thirty-eight days after adopting the Force Resolution, Congress passed the statute entitled Uniting and Strengthening America by Providing Appropriate Tools Required to Intercept and Obstruct Terrorism Act of 2001 (USA PATRIOT ACT), 115 Stat. 272; that Act authorized the detention of alien terrorists for no more than seven days in the absence of criminal charges or deportation proceedings, 8 U.S.C. §1226a(a)(5)(2000 ed., Supp. I). It is very difficult to believe that the same Congress that carefully circumscribed Executive power over alien terrorists on home soil would not have meant to require the Government to justify clearly its detention of an American citizen held on home soil incommunicado.

D

Since the Government has given no reason either to deflect the application of §4001(a) or to hold it to be satisfied, I need to go no further; the Government hints of a constitutional challenge to the statute, but it presents none here. I will, however, stray across the line between statutory and constitutional territory just far enough to note the weakness of the Government's mixed claim of inherent, extrastatutory authority under a combination of Article II of the Constitution and the usages of war. It is in fact in this connection that the Government developed its argument that the exercise of war powers justifies the detention, and what I have just said about its inadequacy applies here as well. Beyond that, it is instructive to recall Justice Jackson's observation that the President is not Commander in Chief of the country, only of the military. *Youngstown Sheet & Tube Co.* v. *Sawyer*, 343 U.S. 579, 643–644 (1952) (concurring opinion); see also *id.*, at 637–638. (Presidential authority is "at its lowest ebb" where the President acts contrary to congressional will).

There may be room for one qualification to Justice Jackson's statement, however: in a moment of genuine emergency, when the Government must act with no time for deliberation, the Executive may be able to detain a citizen if there is reason to fear he is an imminent threat to the safety of the Nation and its people (though I doubt there is any want of statutory authority, see *supra*, at 9–10). This case, however, does not present that question, because an emergency power of necessity must at least be limited by the emergency; Hamdi has been locked up for over two years. Cf. *Ex parte Milligan*, 4 Wall. 2, 127 (1866) (martial law justified only by "actual and present" necessity as in a genuine invasion that closes civilian courts).

Whether insisting on the careful scrutiny of emergency claims or on a vigorous reading of §4001(a), we are heirs to a tradition given voice 800 years ago by Magna Carta, which, on the barons' insistence, confined executive power by "the law of the land."

IV

Because I find Hamdi's detention forbidden by §4001(a) and unauthorized by the Force Resolution, I would not reach any questions of what process he may be due in litigating disputed issues in a proceeding under the habeas statute or prior to the habeas enquiry itself. For me, it suffices that the Government has failed to justify holding him in the absence of a further Act of Congress, criminal charges, a showing that the detention conforms to the laws of war, or a demonstration that §4001(a) is unconstitutional. I would therefore vacate the judgment of the Court of Appeals and remand for proceedings consistent with this view.

Since this disposition does not command a majority of the Court, however, the need to give practical effect to the conclusions of eight members of the Court rejecting the Government's position calls for me to join with the plurality in ordering remand on terms closest to those I would impose. See *Screws* v. *United States*, 325 U.S. 91, 134 (Rutledge, J., concurring in result). Although I think litigation of Hamdi's status as an enemy combatant is unnecessary, the terms of the plurality's remand will allow Hamdi to offer evidence that he is not an enemy combatant, and he should at the least have the benefit of that opportunity.

It should go without saying that in joining with the plurality to produce a judgment, I do not adopt the plurality's resolution of constitutional issues that I would not reach. It is not that I could disagree with the plurality's determinations (given the plurality's view of the Force Resolution) that someone in Hamdi's position is entitled at a minimum to notice of the Government's claimed factual basis for holding him, and to a fair chance to rebut it before a neutral decision maker, see *ante*, at 26; nor, of course, could I disagree with the plurality's affirmation of Hamdi's right to counsel, see *ante*, at 32–33. On the other hand, I do not mean to imply agreement that the Government could claim an evidentiary presumption casting the burden of rebuttal on Hamdi, see *ante*, at 27, or that an opportunity to litigate before a military tribunal might obviate or truncate enquiry by a court on habeas, see *ante*, at 31–32.

Subject to these qualifications, I join with the plurality in a judgment of the Court vacating the Fourth Circuit's judgment and remanding the case.

. . .

JUSTICE SCALIA, with whom JUSTICE STEVENS joins, dissenting.

Petitioner, a presumed American citizen, has been imprisoned without charge or hearing in the Norfolk and Charleston Naval Brigs for more than two years, on the allegation that he is an enemy combatant who bore arms against his country for the Taliban. His father claims to the contrary, that he is an inexperienced aid worker caught in the wrong place at the wrong time. This case brings into conflict the competing demands of national security and our citizens' constitutional right to personal liberty. Although I share the Court's evident unease as it seeks to reconcile the two, I do not agree with its resolution.

Where the Government accuses a citizen of waging war against it, our constitutional tradition has been to prosecute him in federal court for treason or some other crime. Where the exigencies of war prevent that, the Constitution's Suspension Clause, Art. I, §9, cl. 2, allows Congress to relax the usual protections temporarily. Absent suspension, however, the Executive's assertion of military exigency has not been thought sufficient to permit detention without charge. No one contends that the congressional Authorization for Use of Military Force, on which the Government relies to justify its actions here, is an implementation of the Suspension Clause. Accordingly, I would reverse the decision below.

I

The very core of liberty secured by our Anglo-Saxon system of separated powers has been freedom from indefinite imprisonment at the will of the Executive. Blackstone stated this principle clearly:

> "Of great importance to the public is the preservation of this personal liberty: for if once it were left in the power of any, the highest, magistrate to imprison arbitrarily whomever he or his officers thought proper . . . there would soon be an end of all other rights and immunities. . . . To bereave a man of life, or by violence to confiscate his estate, without accusation or trial, would be so gross and notorious an act of despotism, as must at once convey the alarm of tyranny throughout the whole kingdom. But confinement of the person, by secretly hurrying him to gaol, where his sufferings are unknown or forgotten; is a less public, a less striking, and therefore a more dangerous engine of arbitrary government. . . .

> "To make imprisonment lawful, it must either be, by process from the courts of judicature, or by warrant from some legal officer, having authority to commit to prison; which warrant must be in writing, under the hand and seal of the magistrate, and express the causes of the commitment, in order to be examined into (if necessary) upon a *habeas corpus*. If there be no cause expressed, the gaoler is not bound to detain the prisoner. For the law judges in this respect, . . . that it is unreasonable to send a prisoner, and not to signify withal the crimes alleged against him." 1 W. Blackstone, Commentaries on the Laws of England 132–133 (1765) (hereinafter Blackstone).

These words were well known to the Founders. Hamilton quoted from this very passage in The Federalist No. 84, p. 444 (G. Carey & J. McClellan eds. 2001). The two ideas central to Blackstone's understanding – due process as the right secured, and habeas corpus as the instrument by which due process could be insisted upon by a citizen illegally imprisoned – found expression in the Constitution's Due Process and Suspension Clauses. See Amdt. 5; Art. I, §9, cl. 2.

The gist of the Due Process Clause, as understood at the founding and since, was to force the Government to follow those common-law procedures traditionally deemed necessary before depriving a person of life, liberty, or property. When a citizen was deprived of liberty because of alleged criminal conduct, those procedures typically required committal by a magistrate followed by indictment and trial. See, *e.g.*, 2 & 3 Phil. & M., c. 10 (1555); 3 J. Story, Commentaries on the Constitution of the United States §1783, p. 661 (1833) (hereinafter Story) (equating "due process of law" with "due presentment or indictment, and being brought in to answer thereto by due process of the common law"). The Due Process Clause "in effect affirms the right of trial according to the process and proceedings of the common law." *Ibid*. See also T. Cooley, General Principles of Constitutional Law 224 (1880) ("When life and liberty are in question, there must in every instance be judicial proceedings; and that requirement implies an accusation, a hearing before an impartial tribunal, with proper jurisdiction, and a conviction and judgment before the punishment can be inflicted" (internal quotation marks omitted)).

To be sure, certain types of permissible *non* criminal detention – that is, those not dependent upon the contention that the citizen had committed a criminal act – did not require the protections of criminal procedure. However, these fell into a limited number of well-recognized exceptions – civil commitment of the mentally ill, for example, and temporary detention in quarantine of the infectious. See *Opinion on the Writ of Habeas Corpus*, 97 Eng. Rep. 29, 36–37 (H.L. 1758) (Wilmot, J.). It is unthinkable that the Executive could render otherwise criminal grounds for detention noncriminal merely by disclaiming an intent to prosecute, or by asserting that it was incapacitating dangerous offenders rather than punishing wrongdoing. Cf. *Kansas* v. *Hendricks*, 521 U.S. 346, 358 (1997) ("A finding of dangerousness, standing alone, is ordinarily not a sufficient ground upon which to justify indefinite involuntary commitment").

These due process rights have historically been vindicated by the writ of habeas corpus. In England before the founding, the writ developed into a tool for challenging executive confinement. It was not always effective. For example, in *Darnel's Case*, 3 How. St. Tr. 1 (K. B. 1627), King Charles I detained without charge several individuals for failing to assist England's war against France and Spain. The prisoners sought writs of habeas corpus, arguing that without specific charges, "imprisonment shall not continue on for a time, but for ever; and the subjects of this kingdom may be restrained of their liberties perpetually." *Id.*, at 8. The Attorney General replied that the Crown's interest in protecting the realm justified imprisonment in "a matter of state . . . not ripe nor timely" for the ordinary process of accusation and trial. *Id.*, at 37. The court denied relief, producing widespread outrage, and Parliament responded with the Petition of Right, accepted by the King in 1628, which expressly prohibited imprisonment without formal charges, see 3 Car. 1, c. 1, §§5, 10.

The struggle between subject and Crown continued, and culminated in the Habeas Corpus Act of 1679, 31 Car. 2, c. 2, described by Blackstone as a "second *magna charta*, and stable bulwark of our liberties." 1 Blackstone 133. The Act governed all persons "committed or detained . . . for any crime." §3. In cases other than felony or treason plainly expressed in the warrant of commitment, the Act required release upon appropriate sureties (unless the commitment was for a nonbailable offense). *Ibid*. Where the commitment was for felony or high treason, the Act did not require immediate release, but instead required the Crown to commence criminal proceedings within a specified time. §7. If the prisoner was not "indicted some Time in the next Term," the judge was "required . . . to set at Liberty the Prisoner upon Bail" unless the King was unable to produce his witnesses. *Ibid.* Able or no, if the prisoner was not brought to trial by the *next* succeeding term, the Act provided that "he shall be discharged from his Imprisonment." *Ibid.* English courts sat four terms per year, see 3 Blackstone 275–277, so the practical effect of this provision was that imprisonment without indictment or trial for felony or high treason under §7 would not exceed approximately three to six months.

The writ of habeas corpus was preserved in the Constitution – the only common-law writ to be explicitly mentioned. See Art. I, §9, cl. 2. Hamilton lauded "the establishment of the writ of *habeas corpus*" in his Federalist defense as a means to protect against "the practice of arbitrary imprisonments . . . in all ages, [one of] the favourite and most formidable instruments of tyranny." The Federalist No. 84, *supra*, at 444. Indeed, availability of the writ under the new Constitution (along with the requirement of trial by jury in criminal cases, see Art. III, §2, cl. 3) was his basis for arguing that additional, explicit procedural protections were unnecessary. See The Federalist No. 83, at 433.

II

The allegations here, of course, are no ordinary accusations of criminal activity. Yaser Esam Hamdi has been imprisoned because the Government believes he participated in the waging of war against the United States. The relevant question, then, is whether there is a different, special procedure for imprisonment of a citizen accused of wrongdoing *by aiding the enemy in wartime.*

A

JUSTICE O'CONNOR, writing for a plurality of this Court, asserts that captured enemy combatants (other than those suspected of war crimes) have traditionally been detained until the cessation of hostilities and then released. *Ante*, at 10–11. That is probably an accurate description of wartime practice with respect to enemy *aliens*. The tradition with respect to American citizens, however, has been quite different. Citizens aiding the enemy have been treated as traitors subject to the criminal process.

As early as 1350, England's Statute of Treasons made it a crime to "levy War against our Lord the King in his Realm, or be adherent to the King's Enemies in his Realm, giving to them Aid and Comfort, in the Realm, or elsewhere." 25 Edw. 3, Stat. 5, c. 2. In his 1762 Discourse on High Treason, Sir Michael Foster explained:

> "With regard to Natural-born Subjects there can be no Doubt. They owe Allegiance to the Crown at all Times and in all Places.
> .   .   .   .   .
> "The joining with Rebels in an Act of Rebellion, or with Enemies in Acts of Hostility, will make a Man a Traitor: in the one Case within the Clause of Levying War, in the other within that of Adhering to the King's enemies.
> .   .   .   .   .
> "States in Actual Hostility with Us, though no War be solemnly Declared, are Enemies within the meaning of the Act. And therefore in an Indictment on the Clause of Adhering to the King's Enemies, it is sufficient to Aver that the Prince or State Adhered to *is an Enemy*, without shewing any War Proclaimed. . . . And if the Subject of a Foreign Prince in Amity with Us, invadeth the Kingdom without Commission from his Sovereign, He is an Enemy. And a Subject of *England* adhering to Him is a Traitor within this Clause of the Act." A Report of Some Proceedings on the Commission . . . for the Trial of the Rebels in the Year 1746 in the County of Surry, and of Other Crown Cases, Introduction, §1, p. 183; Ch. 2, §8, p. 216; §12, p. 219.

Subjects accused of levying war against the King were routinely prosecuted for treason. *E.g., Harding's Case*, 2 Ventris 315, 86 Eng. Rep. 461 (K. B. 1690); *Trial of Parkyns*, 13 How. St. Tr. 63 (K. B. 1696); *Trial of Vaughan*, 13 How. St. Tr. 485 (K. B. 1696); *Trial of Downie*, 24 How. St. Tr. 1 (1794). The Founders inherited the understanding that a citizen's levying war against the Government was to be punished criminally. The Constitution provides: "Treason against the United States, shall consist only in levying War against them, or in adhering to their Enemies, giving them Aid and Comfort"; and establishes a heightened proof requirement (two witnesses) in order to "convic[t]" of that offense. Art. III, §3, cl. 1.

In more recent times, too, citizens have been charged and tried in Article III courts for acts of war against the United States, even when their noncitizen co-conspirators were not. For example, two American citizens alleged to have participated during World War I in a spying conspiracy on behalf of Germany were tried in federal court. See *United States* v. *Fricke*, 259 F. 673 (SDNY 1919); *United States* v. *Robinson*, 259 F. 685 (SDNY 1919). A German member of the same conspiracy was subjected to military process. See *United States ex rel. Wessels* v. *McDonald*, 265 F. 754 (EDNY 1920). During World War II, the famous German saboteurs of *Ex parte Quirin*, 317 U.S. 1 (1942), received military process, but the citizens who associated with them (with the exception of one citizen-saboteur, discussed below) were punished under the criminal process. See *Haupt* v. *United States*, 330 U.S. 631 (1947); L. Fisher, Nazi Saboteurs on Trial 80–84 (2003); see also *Cramer* v. *United States*, 325 U.S. 1 (1945).

The modern treason statute is 18 U.S.C. §2381; it basically tracks the language of the constitutional provision. Other provisions of Title 18 criminalize various acts of warmaking and adherence to the enemy. See, *e.g.*, §32 (destruction of aircraft or aircraft facilities), §2332a (use of weapons of mass destruction), §2332b (acts of terrorism transcending national boundaries), §2339A (providing material support to terrorists), §2339B (providing material support to certain terrorist organizations), §2382 (misprision of treason), §2383 (rebellion or insurrection), §2384 (seditious conspiracy), §2390 (enlistment to serve in armed hostility against the United States). See also 31 CFR §595.204 (2003) (prohibiting the "making or receiving of any contribution of funds, goods, or services" to terrorists); 50 U.S.C. §1705(b) (criminalizing violations of 31 CFR §595.204). The only citizen other than Hamdi known to be imprisoned in connection with military hostilities in Afghanistan against the United States *was* subjected to criminal process and convicted upon a guilty plea. See *United States* v. *Lindh*, 212 F.Supp. 2d 541 (ED Va. 2002) (denying motions for dismissal); Seelye, N.Y. Times, Oct. 5, 2002, p. A1, col. 5.

B

There are times when military exigency renders resort to the traditional criminal process impracticable. English law accommodated such exigencies by allowing legislative suspension of the writ of habeas corpus for brief periods. Blackstone explained:

> "And yet sometimes, when the state is in real danger, even this [*i.e.*, executive detention] may be a necessary measure. But the happiness of our constitution is, that it is not left to the executive power to determine when the danger of the state is so great, as to render this measure expedient. For the parliament only, or legislative power, whenever it sees proper, can authorize the crown, by suspending the *habeas corpus* act for a short and limited time, to imprison suspected persons without giving any reason for so doing.... In like manner this experiment ought only to be tried in case of extreme emergency; and in these the nation parts with it[s] liberty for a while, in order to preserve it for ever." 1 Blackstone 132.

Where the Executive has not pursued the usual course of charge, committal, and conviction, it has historically secured the Legislature's explicit approval of a suspension. In England, Parliament on numerous occasions passed temporary suspensions in times of threatened invasion or rebellion. *E.g.*, 1 W. & M., c. 7 (1688) (threatened return of James II); 7 & 8 Will. 3, c. 11 (1696) (same); 17 Geo. 2, c. 6 (1744) (threatened French invasion); 19 Geo. 2, c. 1 (1746) (threatened rebellion in Scotland); 17 Geo. 3, c. 9 (1777) (the American Revolution). Not long after Massachusetts had adopted a clause in its constitution explicitly providing for habeas corpus, see Mass. Const. pt. 2, ch. 6, art. VII (1780), reprinted in 3 Federal and State Constitutions, Colonial Charters and Other Organic Laws 1888, 1910 (F. Thorpe ed. 1909), it suspended the writ in order to deal with Shay's Rebellion, see Act for Suspending the Privilege of the Writ of Habeas Corpus, ch. 10, 1786 Mass. Acts 510.

Our Federal Constitution contains a provision explicitly permitting suspension, but limiting the situations in which it may be invoked: "The privilege of the Writ of Habeas Corpus shall not be suspended, unless when in Cases of Rebellion or Invasion the public Safety may require it." Art. I, §9, cl. 2. Although this provision does not state that suspension must be effected by, or authorized by, a legislative act, it has been so understood, consistent with English practice and the Clause's placement in Article I. See *Ex parte Bollman*, 4 Cranch 75, 101 (1807); *Ex parte Merryman*, 17 F. Cas. 144, 151-152 (CD Md. 1861) (Taney, C. J., rejecting Lincoln's unauthorized suspension); 3 Story §1336, at 208–209.

The Suspension Clause was by design a safety valve, the Constitution's only "express provision for exercise of extraordinary authority because of a crisis," *Youngstown Sheet & Tube Co.* v. *Sawyer*, 343 U.S. 579, 650 (1952) (Jackson, J., concurring). Very early in the Nation's history, President Jefferson unsuccessfully sought a suspension of habeas corpus to deal with Aaron Burr's conspiracy to overthrow the Government. See 16 Annals of Congress 402–425 (1807). During the Civil War, Congress passed its first Act authorizing Executive suspension of the writ of habeas corpus, see Act of Mar. 3, 1863, 12 Stat. 755, to the relief of those many who thought President Lincoln's unauthorized proclamations of suspension (*e.g.*, Proclamation No. 1, 13 Stat. 730 (1862)) unconstitutional. Later Presidential proclamations of suspension relied upon the congressional authorization, *e.g.*, Proclamation No. 7, 13 Stat. 734 (1863). During Reconstruction, Congress passed the Ku Klux Klan Act, which included a provision authorizing suspension of the writ, invoked by President Grant in quelling a rebellion in nine South Carolina counties. See Act of Apr. 20, 1871, ch. 22, §4, 17 Stat. 14; A Proclamation [of Oct. 17, 1871], 7 Compilation of the Messages and Papers of the Presidents 136–138 (J. Richardson ed. 1899) (hereinafter Messages and Papers); *id.*, at 138–139.

Two later Acts of Congress provided broad suspension authority to governors of U.S. possessions. The Philippine Civil Government Act of 1902 provided that the Governor of the Philippines could suspend the writ in case of rebellion, insurrection, or invasion. Act of July 1, 1902, ch. 1369, §5, 32 Stat. 691. In 1905 the writ was suspended for nine months by proclamation of the Governor. See *Fisher* v. *Baker*, 203 U.S. 174, 179–181 (1906). The Hawaiian Organic Act of 1900 likewise provided that the Governor of Hawaii could suspend the writ in case of rebellion or invasion (or threat thereof). Ch. 339, §67, 31 Stat. 153.

III

Of course the extensive historical evidence of criminal convictions and habeas suspensions does not *necessarily* refute the Government's position in this case. When the writ is suspended, the Government is entirely free from judicial oversight. It does not claim such total liberation here, but argues that it need only produce what it calls "some evidence" to satisfy a habeas court that a detained individual is an enemy combatant. See Brief for Respondents 34. Even if suspension of the writ on the one hand, and committal for criminal charges on the other hand, have been the only *traditional* means of dealing with citizens who levied war against their own country, it is theoretically possible that the Constitution does not *require* a choice between these alternatives.

I believe, however, that substantial evidence does refute that possibility. First, the text of the 1679 Habeas Corpus Act makes clear that indefinite imprisonment on reasonable suspicion is not an available option of treatment for those accused of aiding the enemy, absent a suspension of the writ. In the United States, this Act was read as "enforc[ing] the common law," *Ex parte Watkins*, 3 Pet. 193, 202 (1830), and shaped the early understanding of the scope of the writ. As noted above, see *supra*, at 5, §7 of the Act specifically addressed those committed for high treason, and provided a remedy if they were not *indicted and tried* by the second succeeding court term. That remedy was *not* a bobtailed judicial inquiry into whether there were reasonable grounds to believe the prisoner had taken up arms against the King. Rather, if the prisoner was not indicted and tried within the prescribed time, "he shall be discharged from his Imprisonment." 31 Car. 2, c. 2, §7. The Act does not contain any exception for wartime. That omission is conspicuous, since §7 explicitly addresses the offense of "High Treason," which often involved offenses of a military nature. See cases cited *supra*, at 7.

Writings from the founding generation also suggest that, without exception, the only constitutional alternatives are to charge the crime or suspend the writ. In 1788, Thomas Jefferson wrote to James Madison questioning the need for a Suspension Clause in cases of rebellion in the proposed Constitution. His letter illustrates the constraints under which the Founders understood themselves to operate:

> "Why suspend the Hab. corp. in insurrections and rebellions? The parties who may be arrested may be charged instantly with a well defined crime. Of course the judge will remand them. If the publick safety requires that the government should have a man imprisoned on less probable testimony in those than in other emergencies; let him be taken and tried, retaken and retried, while the necessity continues, only giving him redress against the government for damages." 13 Papers of Thomas Jefferson 442 (July 31, 1788) (J. Boyd ed.1956).

A similar view was reflected in the 1807 House debates over suspension during the armed uprising that came to be known as Burr's conspiracy:

> "With regard to those persons who may be implicated in the conspiracy, if the writ of habeas corpus be not suspended, what will be the consequence? When apprehended, they will be brought before a court of justice, who will decide whether there is any evidence that will justify their commitment for farther prosecution. From the communication of the Executive, it appeared there was sufficient evidence to authorize their commitment. Several months would elapse before their final trial, which would give time to collect evidence, and if this shall be sufficient, they will not fail to receive the punishment merited by their crimes, and inflicted by the laws of their country." 16 Annals of Congress, at 405 (remarks of Rep. Burwell).

The absence of military authority to imprison citizens indefinitely in wartime – whether or not a probability of treason had been established by means less than jury trial – was confirmed by three cases decided during and immediately after the War of 1812. In the first, *In re Stacy*, 10 Johns. *328 (N.Y. 1813), a citizen was taken into military custody on suspicion that he was "carrying provisions and giving information to the enemy." *Id.*, at *330 (emphasis deleted). Stacy petitioned for a writ of habeas corpus, and, after the defendant custodian attempted to avoid complying, Chief Justice Kent ordered attachment against him. Kent noted that the military was "without any color of authority in any military tribunal to try a citizen for that crime" and that it was "holding him in the closest confinement, and contemning the civil authority of the state." *Id.*, at *333–*334.

Two other cases, later cited with approval by this Court in *Ex parte Milligan*, 4 Wall. 2, 128–129 (1866), upheld verdicts for false imprisonment against military officers. In *Smith* v. *Shaw*, 12 Johns. *257 (N.Y. 1815), the court affirmed an award of damages for detention of a citizen on suspicion that he was, among other things, "an enemy's spy in time of war." *Id.*, at *265. The court held that "[n]one of the offences charged against *Shaw* were cognizable by a court-martial, except that which related to his being a spy; and if he was an *American* citizen, he could not be charged with such an offence. He might be amenable to the civil authority for treason; but could not be punished, under martial law, as a spy." *Ibid.* "If the defendant was justifiable in doing what he did, every citizen of the *United States* would, in time of war, be equally exposed to a like exercise of military power and authority." *Id.*, at *266. Finally, in *M'Connell* v. *Hampton*, 12 Johns. *234 (N.Y. 1815), a jury awarded $9,000 for false imprisonment after a military officer confined a citizen on charges of treason; the judges on appeal did not question the verdict but found the damages excessive, in part because "it does not appear that [the defendant]... knew [the plaintiff] was a citizen." *Id.*, at *238 (Spencer, J.). See generally Wuerth, The President's Power to Detain "Enemy Combatants": Modern Lessons from Mr. Madison's Forgotten War, 98 Nw. U.L.Rev. (forthcoming 2004) (available in Clerk of Court's case file).

President Lincoln, when he purported to suspend habeas corpus without congressional authorization during the Civil War, apparently did not doubt that suspension was required if the prisoner was to be held without criminal trial. In his famous message to Congress on July 4, 1861, he argued only that he could suspend the writ, not that even without suspension, his imprisonment of citizens without criminal trial was permitted. See Special Session Message, 6 Messages and Papers 20–31.

Further evidence comes from this Court's decision in *Ex parte Milligan, supra*. There, the Court issued the writ to an American citizen who had been tried by military commission for offenses that included conspiring to overthrow the Government, seize munitions, and liberate prisoners of war. *Id.*, at 6–7. The Court rejected in no uncertain terms the Government's assertion that military jurisdiction was proper "under the 'laws and usages of war,'" *id.*, at 121:

> "It can serve no useful purpose to inquire what those laws and usages are, whence they originated, where found, and on whom they operate; they can never be applied to citizens in states which have upheld the authority of the government, and where the courts are open and their process unobstructed." *Ibid.*[1]

Milligan is not exactly this case, of course, since the petitioner was threatened with death, not merely imprisonment. But the reasoning and conclusion of *Milligan* logically cover the present case. The Government justifies imprisonment of Hamdi on principles of the law of war and admits that, absent the war, it would have no such authority. But

---

[1] As I shall discuss presently, see *infra*, at 17–19, the Court purported to limit this language in *Ex parte Quirin*, 317 U.S. 1, 45 (1942). Whatever *Quirin's* effect on *Milligan's* precedential value, however, it cannot undermine its value as an indicator of original meaning. Cf. *Reid* v. *Covert*, 354 U.S. 1, 30 (1957) (plurality opinion) (*Milligan* remains "one of the great landmarks in this Court's history").

if the law of war cannot be applied to citizens where courts are open, then Hamdi's imprisonment without criminal trial is no less unlawful than Milligan's trial by military tribunal.

Milligan responded to the argument, repeated by the Government in this case, that it is dangerous to leave suspected traitors at large in time of war:

> "If it was dangerous, in the distracted condition of affairs, to leave Milligan unrestrained of his liberty, because he 'conspired against the government, afforded aid and comfort to rebels, and incited the people to insurrection,' the *law* said arrest him, confine him closely, render him powerless to do further mischief; and then present his case to the grand jury of the district, with proofs of his guilt, and, if indicted, try him according to the course of the common law. If this had been done, the Constitution would have been vindicated, the law of 1863 enforced, and the securities for personal liberty preserved and defended." *Id.*, at 122.

Thus, criminal process was viewed as the primary means – and the only means absent congressional action suspending the writ – not only to punish traitors, but to incapacitate them.

The proposition that the Executive lacks indefinite wartime detention authority over citizens is consistent with the Founders' general mistrust of military power permanently at the Executive's disposal. In the Founders' view, the "blessings of liberty" were threatened by "those military establishments which must gradually poison its very fountain." The Federalist No. 45, p. 238 (J. Madison). No fewer than 10 issues of the Federalist were devoted in whole or part to allaying fears of oppression from the proposed Constitution's authorization of standing armies in peacetime. Many safeguards in the Constitution reflect these concerns. Congress's authority "[t]o raise and support Armies" was hedged with the proviso that "no Appropriation of Money to that Use shall be for a longer Term than two Years." U.S. Const., Art. I, §8, cl. 12. Except for the actual command of military forces, all authorization for their maintenance and all explicit authorization for their use is placed in the control of Congress under Article I, rather than the President under Article II. As Hamilton explained, the President's military authority would be "much inferior" to that of the British King:

> "It would amount to nothing more than the supreme command and direction of the military and naval forces, as first general and admiral of the confederacy: while that of the British king extends to the *declaring* of war, and to the *raising* and *regulating* of fleets and armies; all which, by the constitution under consideration, would appertain to the legislature." The Federalist No. 69, p. 357.

A view of the Constitution that gives the Executive authority to use military force rather than the force of law against citizens on American soil flies in the face of the mistrust that engendered these provisions.

IV

The Government argues that our more recent jurisprudence ratifies its indefinite imprisonment of a citizen within the territorial jurisdiction of federal courts. It places primary reliance upon *Ex parte Quirin*, 317 U.S. 1 (1942), a World War II case upholding the trial by military commission of eight German saboteurs, one of whom, Hans Haupt, was a U.S. citizen. The case was not this Court's finest hour. The Court upheld the commission and denied relief in a brief *per curiam* issued the day after oral argument concluded, see *id.*, at 18–19, unnumbered note; a week later the Government carried out the commission's death sentence upon six saboteurs, including Haupt. The Court eventually explained its reasoning in a written opinion issued several months later.

Only three paragraphs of the Court's lengthy opinion dealt with the particular circumstances of Haupt's case. See *id.*, at 37–38, 45–46. The Government argued that Haupt, like the other petitioners, could be tried by military commission under the laws of war. In agreeing with that contention, *Quirin* purported to interpret the language of *Milligan* quoted above (the law of war "can never be applied to citizens in states which have upheld the authority of the government, and where the courts are open and their process unobstructed") in the following manner:

> "Elsewhere in its opinion . . . the Court was at pains to point out that Milligan, a citizen twenty years resident in Indiana, who had never been a resident of any of the states in rebellion, was not an enemy belligerent either entitled to the status of a prisoner of war or subject to the penalties imposed upon unlawful belligerents. We construe the Court's statement as to the inapplicability of the law of war to Milligan's case as having particular reference to the facts before it. From them the Court concluded that Milligan, not being a part of or associated with the armed forces of the enemy, was a non-belligerent, not subject to the law of war. . . ." 317 U.S., at 45.

In my view this seeks to revise *Milligan* rather than describe it. *Milligan* had involved (among other issues) two separate questions: (1) whether the military trial of Milligan was justified by the laws of war, and if not (2) whether the President's suspension of the writ, pursuant to congressional authorization, prevented the issuance of habeas corpus. The Court's categorical language about the law of war's inapplicability to citizens where the courts are open (with no exception mentioned for citizens who were prisoners of war) was contained in its discussion of the first point. See 4 Wall., at 121. The factors pertaining to whether Milligan could reasonably be considered a belligerent and prisoner of war, while mentioned earlier in the opinion, see *id.*, at 118, were made relevant and brought to bear in the Court's later discussion, see *id.*, at 131, of whether Milligan came within the statutory provision that effectively made an exception to Congress's authorized suspension of the writ for (as the Court described it) "all parties, not prisoners of war, resident in their respective jurisdictions, . . . who were citizens of states in which the administration of the laws in the Federal tribunals was unimpaired," *id.*, at 116. *Milligan* thus understood was in accord with the traditional law of habeas corpus I have described: Though treason often occurred in wartime, there was, absent provision for special treatment in a congressional suspension of the writ, no exception to the right to trial by jury for citizens who could be called "belligerents" or "prisoners of war."[2]

But even if *Quirin* gave a correct description of *Milligan*, or made an irrevocable revision of it, *Quirin* would still not justify denial of the writ here. In *Quirin* it was uncontested that the petitioners were members of enemy forces. They were "*admitted* enemy invaders," 317 U.S., at 47 (emphasis added), and it was "undisputed" that they had landed in the United States in service of German forces, *id.*, at 20. The specific holding of the Court was only that, "upon the *conceded* facts," the petitioners were "plainly within [the] boundaries" of military jurisdiction, *id.*, at 46 (emphasis added).[3]

---

[2] Without bothering to respond to this analysis, the plurality states that *Milligan* "turned in large part" upon the defendant's lack of prisoner-of-war status, and that the *Milligan* Court explicitly and repeatedly *said* so. See *ante*, at 14. Neither is true. To the extent, however, that prisoner-of-war status was relevant in *Milligan*, it was only because prisoners of war *received different statutory treatment* under the conditional suspension then in effect.

[3] The only two Court of Appeals cases from World War II cited by the Government in which citizens were detained without trial likewise involved petitioners who were conceded to have been members of enemy

But where those jurisdictional facts are *not* conceded – where the petitioner insists that he is *not* a belligerent – *Quirin* left the pre-existing law in place: Absent suspension of the writ, a citizen held where the courts are open is entitled either to criminal trial or to a judicial decree requiring his release.[4]

V

It follows from what I have said that Hamdi is entitled to a habeas decree requiring his release unless (1) criminal proceedings are promptly brought, or (2) Congress has suspended the writ of habeas corpus. A suspension of the writ could, of course, lay down conditions for continued detention, similar to those that today's opinion prescribes under the Due Process Clause. Cf. Act of Mar. 3, 1863, 12 Stat. 755. But there is a world of difference between the people's representatives' determining the need for that suspension (and prescribing the conditions for it), and this Court's doing so.

The plurality finds justification for Hamdi's imprisonment in the Authorization for Use of Military Force, 115 Stat. 224, which provides:

> "That the President is authorized to use all necessary and appropriate force against those nations, organizations, or persons he determines planned, authorized, committed, or aided the terrorist attacks that occurred on September 11, 2001, or harbored such organizations or persons, in order to prevent any future acts of international terrorism against the United States by such nations, organizations or persons." §2(a).

---

forces. See *In re Territo*, 156 F.2d 142, 143–145 (CA9 1946); *Colepaugh v. Looney*, 235 F.2d 429, 432 (CA10 1956). The plurality complains that *Territo* is the only case I have identified in which "a United States citizen [was] captured in a *foreign* combat zone," *ante*, at 16. Indeed it is; such cases must surely be rare. But given the constitutional tradition I have described, the burden is not upon me to find cases in which the writ was *granted* to citizens in this country *who had been captured on foreign battlefields;* it is upon those who would carve out an exception for such citizens (as the plurality's complaint suggests it would) to find a single case (other than one where enemy status was admitted) in which habeas was *denied*.

[4] The plurality's assertion that *Quirin* somehow "clarifies" *Milligan*, *ante*, at 15 , is simply false. As I discuss *supra*, at 17–19, the *Quirin* Court propounded a mistaken understanding of *Milligan*; but nonetheless its holding was limited to "the case presented by the present record," and to "*the conceded facts*," and thus avoided conflict with the earlier case. See 317 U.S., at 45–46 (emphasis added). The plurality, ignoring this expressed limitation, thinks it "beside the point" whether belligerency is conceded or found "by some other process" (not necessarily a jury trial) "that verifies this fact with sufficient certainty." *Ante*, at 16. But the whole point of the procedural guarantees in the Bill of Rights is to limit the methods by which the Government can determine facts that the citizen disputes and on which the citizen's liberty depends. The plurality's claim that *Quirin*'s one-paragraph discussion of *Milligan* provides a "[c]lear...disavowal" of two false imprisonment cases from the War of 1812, *ante*, at 15, thus defies logic; unlike the plaintiffs in those cases, Haupt was concededly a member of an enemy force.

The Government also cites *Moyer v. Peabody*, 212 U.S. 78 (1909), a suit for damages against the Governor of Colorado, for violation of due process in detaining the alleged ringleader of a rebellion quelled by the state militia after the Governor's declaration of a state of insurrection and (he contended) suspension of the writ "as incident thereto." *Ex parte Moyer*, 35 Colo. 154, 157, 91 P. 738, 740 (1905). But the holding of *Moyer v. Peabody* (even assuming it is transferable from state-militia detention after state suspension to federal standing-army detention without suspension) is simply that "[s]o long as such arrests [were] made in good faith and in the honest belief that they [were] needed in order to head the insurrection off," 212 U.S., at 85, an action in damages could not lie. This "good-faith" analysis is a forebear of our modern doctrine of qualified immunity. Cf. *Scheuer v. Rhodes*, 416 U.S. 232, 247–248 (1974) (understanding *Moyer* in this way). Moreover, the detention at issue in *Moyer* lasted about two and a half months, see 212 U.S., at 85, roughly the length of time permissible under the 1679 Habeas Corpus Act, see *supra*, at 4–5.

In addition to *Moyer v. Peabody*, JUSTICE THOMAS relies upon *Luther v. Borden*, 7 How. 1 (1849), a case in which the state legislature had imposed martial law–a step even more drastic than suspension of the writ. See *post*, at 13–14 (dissenting opinion). But martial law has not been imposed here, and in any case is limited to "the theatre of active military operations, where war really prevails," and where therefore the courts are closed. *Ex parte Milligan*, 4 Wall. 2, 127 (1866); see also *id.*, at 129–130 (distinguishing *Luther*).

This is not remotely a congressional suspension of the writ, and no one claims that it is. Contrary to the plurality's view, I do not think this statute even authorizes detention of a citizen with the clarity necessary to satisfy the interpretive canon that statutes should be construed so as to avoid grave constitutional concerns, see *Edward J. DeBartolo Corp. v. Florida Gulf Coast Building & Constr. Trades Council*, 485 U.S. 568, 575 (1988); with the clarity necessary to comport with cases such as *Ex parte Endo*, 323 U.S. 283, 300 (1944), and *Duncan* v. *Kahanamoku*, 327 U.S. 304, 314–316, 324 (1946); or with the clarity necessary to overcome the statutory prescription that "[n]o citizen shall be imprisoned or otherwise detained by the United States except pursuant to an Act of Congress." 18 U.S.C. §4001(a).[5] But even if it did, I would not permit it to overcome Hamdi's entitlement to habeas corpus relief. The Suspension Clause of the Constitution, which carefully circumscribes the conditions under which the writ can be withheld, would be a sham if it could be evaded by congressional prescription of requirements *other than the common-law requirement of committal for criminal prosecution* that render the writ, though available, unavailing. If the Suspension Clause does not guarantee the citizen that he will either be tried or released, unless the conditions for suspending the writ exist and the grave action of suspending the writ has been taken; if it merely guarantees the citizen that he will not be detained unless Congress by ordinary legislation says he can be detained; it guarantees him very little indeed.

It should not be thought, however, that the plurality's evisceration of the Suspension Clause augments, principally, the power of Congress. As usual, the major effect of its constitutional improvisation is to increase the power of the Court. Having found a congressional authorization for detention of citizens where none clearly exists; and having discarded the categorical procedural protection of the Suspension Clause; the plurality then proceeds, under the guise of the Due Process Clause, to prescribe what procedural protections *it* thinks appropriate. It "weigh[s] the private interest . . . against the Government's asserted interest," *ante*, at 22 (internal quotation marks omitted), and – just as though writing a new Constitution – comes up with an unheard-of system in which the citizen rather than the Government bears the burden of proof, testimony is by hearsay rather than live witnesses, and the presiding officer may well be a "neutral" military officer rather than judge and jury. See *ante*, at 26–27. It claims authority to engage in this sort of "judicious balancing" from *Mathews* v. *Eldridge*, 424 U.S. 319 (1976), a case involving . . . *the withdrawal of disability benefits!* Whatever the merits of this technique when newly recognized property rights are at issue (and even there they are questionable), it has no place where the Constitution and the common law already supply an answer.

---

[5] The plurality rejects any need for "specific language of detention" on the ground that detention of alleged combatants is a "fundamental incident of waging war." *Ante*, at 2641. Its authorities do not support that holding in the context of the present case. Some are irrelevant because they do not address the detention of *American citizens*. *E.g.*, Naqvi, Doubtful Prisoner-of-War Status, 84 Int'l Rev. Red Cross 571, 572 (2002). The plurality's assertion that detentions of citizen and alien combatants are equally authorized has no basis in law or common sense. Citizens and noncitizens, even if equally dangerous, are not similarly situated. See, *e.g.*, *Milligan*, *supra*; *Johnson* v. *Eisentrager*, 339 U.S. 763 (1950); Rev. Stat. 4067, 50 U.S.C. §21 (Alien Enemy Act). That captivity may be consistent with the principles of international law does not prove that it also complies with the restrictions that the Constitution places on the American Government's treatment of its own citizens. Of the authorities cited by the plurality that do deal with detention of citizens, *Quirin* and *Territo* have already been discussed and rejected. See *supra*, at 19–20, and n. 3. The remaining authorities pertain to U.S. detention of citizens during the Civil War, and are irrelevant for two reasons: (1) the Lieber Code was issued following a congressional authorization of suspension of the writ, see Instructions for the Government of Armies of the United States in the Field, Gen. Order No. 100 (1863), reprinted in 2 Lieber, Miscellaneous Writings, p. 246; Act of Mar. 3, 1863, 12 Stat. 755, §§1, 2; and (2) citizens of the Confederacy, while citizens of the United States, were also regarded as citizens of a hostile power.

Having distorted the Suspension Clause, the plurality finishes up by transmogrifying the Great Writ – disposing of the present habeas petition by remanding for the District Court to "engag[e] in a factfinding process that is both prudent and incremental," *ante*, at 32. "In the absence of [the Executive's prior provision of procedures that satisfy due process], ... a court that receives a petition for a writ of habeas corpus from an alleged enemy combatant must itself ensure that the minimum requirements of due process are achieved." *Ante*, at 31–32. This judicial remediation of executive default is unheard of. The role of habeas corpus is to determine the legality of executive detention, not to supply the omitted process necessary to make it legal. See *Preiser v. Rodriguez*, 411 U.S. 475, 484 (1973) ("[T]he essence of habeas corpus is an attack by a person in custody upon the legality of that custody, and ... the traditional function of the writ is to secure release from illegal custody"); 1 Blackstone 132–133. It is not the habeas court's function to make illegal detention legal by supplying a process that the Government could have provided, but chose not to. If Hamdi is being imprisoned in violation of the Constitution (because without due process of law), then his habeas petition should be granted; the Executive may then hand him over to the criminal authorities, whose detention for the purpose of prosecution will be lawful, or else must release him.

There is a certain harmony of approach in the plurality's making up for Congress's failure to invoke the Suspension Clause and its making up for the Executive's failure to apply what it says are needed procedures – an approach that reflects what might be called a Mr. Fix-it Mentality. The plurality seems to view it as its mission to Make Everything Come Out Right, rather than merely to decree the consequences, as far as individual rights are concerned, of the other two branches' actions and omissions. Has the Legislature failed to suspend the writ in the current dire emergency? Well, we will remedy that failure by prescribing the reasonable conditions that a suspension should have included. And has the Executive failed to live up to those reasonable conditions? Well, we will ourselves make that failure good, so that this dangerous fellow (if he is dangerous) need not be set free. The problem with this approach is not only that it steps out of the courts' modest and limited role in a democratic society; but that by repeatedly doing what it thinks the political branches ought to do it encourages their lassitude and saps the vitality of government by the people.

VI

Several limitations give my views in this matter a relatively narrow compass. They apply only to citizens, accused of being enemy combatants, who are detained within the territorial jurisdiction of a federal court. This is not likely to be a numerous group; currently we know of only two, Hamdi and Jose Padilla. Where the citizen is captured outside and held outside the United States, the constitutional requirements may be different. Cf. *Johnson v. Eisentrager*, 339 U.S. 763, 769–771 (1950); *Reid v. Covert*, 354 U.S. 1, 74–75 (1957) (Harlan, J., concurring in result); *Rasul v. Bush*, *ante*, at 15–17 (SCALIA, J., dissenting). Moreover, even within the United States, the accused citizen-enemy combatant may lawfully be detained once prosecution is in progress or in contemplation. See, *e.g.*, *County of Riverside v. McLaughlin*, 500 U.S. 44 (1991) (brief detention pending judicial determination after warrantless arrest); *United States v. Salerno*, 481 U.S. 739 (1987) (pretrial detention under the Bail Reform Act). The Government has been notably successful in securing conviction, and hence long-term custody or execution, of those who have waged war against the state.

I frankly do not know whether these tools are sufficient to meet the Government's security needs, including the need to obtain intelligence through interrogation. It is far beyond my competence, or the Court's competence, to determine that. But it is not beyond Congress's. If the situation demands it, the Executive can ask Congress to authorize suspension of the writ – which can be made subject to whatever conditions Congress deems appropriate, including even the procedural novelties invented by the plurality today. To be sure, suspension is limited by the Constitution to cases of rebellion or invasion. But whether the attacks of September 11, 2001, constitute an "invasion," and whether those attacks still justify suspension several years later, are questions for Congress rather than this Court. See 3 Story §1336, at 208–209.[6] If civil rights are to be curtailed during wartime, it must be done openly and democratically, as the Constitution requires, rather than by silent erosion through an opinion of this Court.

* * *

The Founders well understood the difficult tradeoff between safety and freedom. "Safety from external danger," Hamilton declared,

> "is the most powerful director of national conduct. Even the ardent love of liberty will, after a time, give way to its dictates. The violent destruction of life and property incident to war; the continual effort and alarm attendant on a state of continual danger, will compel nations the most attached to liberty, to resort for repose and security to institutions which have a tendency to destroy their civil and political rights. To be more safe, they, at length, become willing to run the risk of being less free." The Federalist No. 8, p. 33.

The Founders warned us about the risk, and equipped us with a Constitution designed to deal with it.

Many think it not only inevitable but entirely proper that liberty give way to security in times of national crisis – that, at the extremes of military exigency, *inter arma silent leges*. Whatever the general merits of the view that war silences law or modulates its voice, that view has no place in the interpretation and application of a Constitution designed precisely to confront war and, in a manner that accords with democratic principles, to accommodate it. Because the Court has proceeded to meet the current emergency in a manner the Constitution does not envision, I respectfully dissent.

· · ·

JUSTICE THOMAS, dissenting.

The Executive Branch, acting pursuant to the powers vested in the President by the Constitution and with explicit congressional approval, has determined that Yaser Hamdi is an enemy combatant and should be detained. This detention falls squarely within the Federal Government's war powers, and we lack the expertise and capacity to second-guess that decision. As such, petitioners' habeas challenge should fail, and there is no reason to remand the case. The plurality reaches a contrary conclusion by failing adequately to consider basic principles of the constitutional structure as it relates to national security and foreign affairs and by using the balancing scheme of *Mathews* v. *Eldridge*, 424 U.S. 319 (1976). I do not think that the Federal Government's war powers can be balanced away by this Court. Arguably, Congress could provide for additional procedural protections, but until it does, we have no right to insist upon them. But even if I were to agree with the general approach the plurality takes, I could not accept the particulars. The plurality utterly fails to account for the Government's compelling

---

[6] JUSTICE THOMAS worries that the constitutional conditions for suspension of the writ will not exist "during many...emergencies during which...detention authority might be necessary," *post*, at 16. It is difficult to imagine situations in which security is so seriously threatened as to justify indefinite imprisonment without trial, and yet the constitutional conditions of rebellion or invasion are not met.

interests and for our own institutional inability to weigh competing concerns correctly. I respectfully dissent.

I

"It is 'obvious and unarguable' that no governmental interest is more compelling than the security of the Nation." *Haig* v. *Agee*, 453 U.S. 280, 307 (1981) (quoting *Aptheker* v. *Secretary of State*, 378 U.S. 500, 509 (1964)). The national security, after all, is the primary responsibility and purpose of the Federal Government. See, *e.g.*, *Youngstown Sheet & Tube Co.* v. *Sawyer*, 343 U.S. 579, 662 (1952) (Clark, J., concurring in judgment); The Federalist No. 23, pp. 146–147 (J. Cooke ed. 1961) (A. Hamilton) ("The principle purposes to be answered by Union are these – The common defence of the members – the preservation of the public peace as well against internal convulsions as external attacks"). But because the Founders understood that they could not foresee the myriad potential threats to national security that might later arise, they chose to create a Federal Government that necessarily possesses sufficient power to handle any threat to the security of the Nation. The power to protect the Nation

> "ought to exist without limitation... *[b]ecause it is impossible to foresee or define the extent and variety of national exigencies, or the correspondent extent & variety of the means which may be necessary to satisfy them.* The circumstances that endanger the safety of nations are infinite; and for this reason no constitutional shackles can wisely be imposed on the power to which the care of it is committed." *Id.*, at 147.

See also The Federalist Nos. 34 and 41.

The Founders intended that the President have primary responsibility – along with the necessary power – to protect the national security and to conduct the Nation's foreign relations. They did so principally because the structural advantages of a unitary Executive are essential in these domains. "Energy in the executive is a leading character in the definition of good government. It is essential to the protection of the community against foreign attacks." The Federalist No. 70, p. 471 (A. Hamilton). The principle "ingredien[t]" for "energy in the executive" is "unity." *Id.*, at 472. This is because "[d]ecision, activity, secrecy, and dispatch will generally characterise the proceedings of one man, in a much more eminent degree, than the proceedings of any greater number." *Ibid.*

These structural advantages are most important in the national-security and foreign-affairs contexts. "Of all the cares or concerns of government, the direction of war most peculiarly demands those qualities which distinguish the exercise of power by a single hand." The Federalist No. 74, p. 500 (A. Hamilton). Also for these reasons, John Marshall explained that "[t]he President is the sole organ of the nation in its external relations, and its sole representative with foreign nations." 10 Annals of Cong. 613 (1800); see *id.*, at 613–614. To this end, the Constitution vests in the President "[t]he executive Power," Art. II, §1, provides that he "shall be Commander in Chief of the" armed forces, §2, and places in him the power to recognize foreign governments, §3.

This Court has long recognized these features and has accordingly held that the President has *constitutional* authority to protect the national security and that this authority carries with it broad discretion.

> "If a war be made by invasion of a foreign nation, the President is not only authorized but bound to resist force by force. He does not initiate the war, but is bound to accept the challenge without waiting for any special legislative authority.... Whether the President

in fulfilling his duties, as Commander in-chief, in suppressing an insurrection, has met with such armed hostile resistance . . . is a question to be decided *by him.*" *Prize Cases*, 2 Black 635, 668 (1863).

The Court has acknowledged that the President has the authority to "employ [the Nation's Armed Forces] in the manner he may deem most effectual to harass and conquer and subdue the enemy." *Fleming* v. *Page*, 9 How. 603, 615 (1850). With respect to foreign affairs as well, the Court has recognized the President's independent authority and need to be free from interference. See, *e.g.*, *United States* v. *Curtiss-Wright Export Corp.*, 299 U.S. 304, 320 (1936) (explaining that the President "has his confidential sources of information. He has his agents in the form of diplomatic, consular and other officials. Secrecy in respect of information gathered by them may be highly necessary, and the premature disclosure of it productive of harmful results"); *Chicago & Southern Air Lines, Inc.* v. *Waterman S.S. Corp.*, 333 U.S. 103, 111 (1948).

Congress, to be sure, has a substantial and essential role in both foreign affairs and national security. But it is crucial to recognize that *judicial* interference in these domains destroys the purpose of vesting primary responsibility in a unitary Executive. I cannot improve on Justice Jackson's words, speaking for the Court:

> "The President, both as Commander-in-Chief and as the Nation's organ for foreign affairs, has available intelligence services whose reports are not and ought not to be published to the world. It would be intolerable that courts, without the relevant information, should review and perhaps nullify actions of the Executive taken on information properly held secret. Nor can courts sit *in camera* in order to be taken into executive confidences. But even if courts could require full disclosure, the very nature of executive decisions as to foreign policy is political, not judicial. Such decisions are wholly confided by our Constitution to the political departments of the government, Executive and Legislative. They are delicate, complex, and involve large elements of prophecy. They are and should be undertaken only by those directly responsible to the people whose welfare they advance or imperil. They are decisions of a kind for which the Judiciary has neither aptitude, facilities nor responsibility and which has long been held to belong in the domain of political power not subject to judicial intrusion or inquiry." *Ibid.*

Several points, made forcefully by Justice Jackson, are worth emphasizing. First, with respect to certain decisions relating to national security and foreign affairs, the courts simply lack the relevant information and expertise to second-guess determinations made by the President based on information properly withheld. Second, even if the courts could compel the Executive to produce the necessary information, such decisions are simply not amenable to judicial determination because "[t]hey are delicate, complex, and involve large elements of prophecy." *Ibid.* Third, the Court in *Chicago & Southern Air Lines* and elsewhere has correctly recognized the primacy of the political branches in the foreign-affairs and national-security contexts.

For these institutional reasons and because "Congress cannot anticipate and legislate with regard to every possible action the President may find it necessary to take or every possible situation in which he might act," it should come as no surprise that "[s]uch failure of Congress . . . does not, 'especially . . . in the areas of foreign policy and national security,' imply 'congressional disapproval' of action taken by the Executive." *Dames & Moore* v. *Regan*, 453 U.S. 654, 678 (1981) (quoting *Agee*, 453 U.S., at 291). Rather, in these domains, the fact that Congress has provided the President with broad authorities does not imply – and the Judicial Branch should not infer – that Congress intended to deprive him of particular powers not specifically enumerated. See *Dames & Moore*, 453 U.S., at 678. As far as the courts are concerned, "the enactment of legislation closely related to the question of the President's authority in a particular case which evinces legislative intent to accord the President broad discretion may be considered to 'invite' 'measures on independent presidential responsibility.'" *Ibid.* (quoting *Youngstown*, 343 U.S., at 637 (Jackson, J., concurring)).

Finally, and again for the same reasons, where "the President acts pursuant to an express or implied authorization from Congress, he exercises not only his powers but also those delegated by Congress[, and i]n such a case the executive action 'would be supported by the strongest of presumptions and the widest latitude of judicial interpretation, and the burden of persuasion would rest heavily upon any who might attack it.'" *Dames & Moore, supra*, at 668 (quoting *Youngstown, supra*, at 637 (Jackson, J., concurring)). That is why the Court has explained, in a case analogous to this one, that "the detention[,] ordered by the President in the declared exercise of his powers as Commander in Chief of the Army in time of war and of grave public danger[, is] not to be set aside by the courts without the clear conviction that [it is] in conflict with the Constitution or laws of Congress constitutionally enacted." *Ex parte Quirin*, 317 U.S. 1, 25 (1942). See also *Ex parte Milligan*, 4 Wall. 2, 133 (1866) (Chase, C. J., concurring in judgment) (stating that a sentence imposed by a military commission "must not be set aside except upon the clearest conviction that it cannot be reconciled with the Constitution and the constitutional legislation of Congress"). This deference extends to the President's determination of all the factual predicates necessary to conclude that a given action is appropriate. See *Quirin, supra*, at 25 ("We are not here concerned with any question of the guilt or innocence of petitioners"). See also *Hirabayashi* v. *United States*, 320 U.S. 81, 93 (1943); *Prize Cases*, 2 Black, at 670; *Martin* v. *Mott*, 12 Wheat. 19, 29–30 (1827).

To be sure, the Court has at times held, in specific circumstances, that the military acted beyond its warmaking authority. But these cases are distinguishable in important ways. In *Ex parte Endo*, 323 U.S. 283 (1944), the Court held unlawful the detention of an admittedly law-abiding and loyal American of Japanese ancestry. It did so because the Government's asserted reason for the detention had nothing to do with the congressional and executive authorities upon which the Government relied. Those authorities permitted detention for the purpose of preventing espionage and sabotage and thus could not be pressed into service for detaining a loyal citizen. See *id.*, at 301–302. Further, the Court "stress[ed] the silence . . . of the [relevant] Act *and the Executive Orders.*" *Id.*, at 301 (emphasis added); see also *id.*, at 301–304. The Court sensibly held that the Government could not detain a loyal citizen pursuant to executive and congressional authorities that could not conceivably be implicated given the Government's factual allegations. And in *Youngstown*, Justice Jackson emphasized that "Congress ha[d] not left seizure of private property an open field but ha[d] covered it by three statutory policies inconsistent with th[e] seizure." 343 U.S., at 639 (concurring opinion). See also *Milligan, supra*, at 134 (Chase, C. J., concurring in judgment) (noting that the Government failed to comply with statute directly on point).

I acknowledge that the question whether Hamdi's executive detention is lawful is a question properly resolved by the Judicial Branch, though the question comes to the Court with the strongest presumptions in favor of the Government. The plurality agrees that Hamdi's detention is lawful if he is an enemy combatant. But the question whether Hamdi is actually an enemy combatant is "of a kind for which the Judiciary has neither aptitude, facilities nor responsibility and which has long been held to belong in the domain of political power not subject to judicial intrusion or inquiry." *Chicago & Southern Air Lines*, 333 U.S., at 111. That is, although it is appropriate for the Court to determine the judicial question whether the President has the asserted authority, see, *e.g., Ex parte Endo, supra,* we lack the information and expertise to question whether Hamdi is actually an enemy combatant, a question the resolution of which is committed to other branches.[1] In the words of then-Judge Scalia:

> "In Old Testament days, when judges ruled the people of Israel and led them into battle, a court professing the belief that it could order a halt to a military operation in foreign lands might not have been a startling phenomenon. But in modern times, and in a country where such governmental functions have been committed to elected delegates of the people, such an assertion of jurisdiction is extraordinary. The [C]ourt's decision today reflects a willingness to extend judicial power into areas where we do not know, and have no way of finding out, what serious harm we may be doing." *Ramirez de Arellano* v. *Weinberger,* 745 F. 2d 1500, 1550–1551 (CADC 1984) (en banc) (dissenting opinion) (footnote omitted).

See also *id.,* at 1551, n. 1 (noting that "[e]ven the ancient Israelites eventually realized the shortcomings of judicial commanders-in-chief"). The decision whether someone is an enemy combatant is, no doubt, "delicate, complex, and involv[es] large elements of prophecy," *Chicago & Southern Air Lines, supra,* at 111, which, incidentally might in part explain why "the Government has never provided any court with the full criteria that it uses in classifying individuals as such," *ante,* at 8. See also *infra,* at 18–20 (discussing other military decisions).

II

"The war power of the national government is 'the power to wage war successfully.'" *Lichter* v. *United States,* 334 U.S. 742, 767, n. 9 (1948) (quoting Hughes, War Powers Under the Constitution, 42 A.B.A. Rep. 232, 238). It follows that this power "is not limited to victories in the field, but carries with it the inherent power to guard against the immediate renewal of the conflict," *In re Yamashita,* 327 U.S. 1, 12 (1946); see also *Stewart* v. *Kahn,* 11 Wall. 493, 507 (1871), and quite obviously includes the ability to detain those (even United States citizens) who fight against our troops or those of our allies, see, *e.g., Quirin,* 317 U.S., at 28–29, 30–31; *id.,* at 37–39; *Duncan* v. *Kahanamoku,* 327 U.S. 304, 313–314 (1946); W. Winthrop, Military Law and Precedents 788 (2d ed. 1920); W. Whiting, War Powers Under the Constitution of the United States 167 (43d ed. 1871); *id.,* at 44–46 (noting that Civil War "rebels" may be treated as foreign belligerents); see also *ante,* at 10–12.

Although the President very well may have inherent authority to detain those arrayed against our troops, I agree with the plurality that we need not decide that question because Congress has authorized the President to do so. See *ante,* at 2639. The Authorization for Use of Military Force (AUMF), 115 Stat. 224, authorizes the President to "use all necessary and appropriate force against those nations, organizations, or persons he determines planned, authorized, committed, or aided the terrorist attacks" of September 11, 2001. Indeed, the Court has previously concluded that language materially identical to the AUMF authorizes the Executive to "make the ordinary use of the soldiers . . .; that he may kill persons who resist and, of course, that he may use the milder measure of seizing [and detaining] the bodies of those whom he considers to stand in the way of restoring peace." *Moyer* v. *Peabody,* 212 U.S. 78, 84 (1909).

---

[1] Although I have emphasized national-security concerns, the President's foreign-affairs responsibilities are also squarely implicated by this case. The Government avers that Northern Alliance forces captured Hamdi, and the District Court demanded that the Government turn over information relating to statements made by members of the Northern Alliance. See 316 F. 3d 450, 462 (CA4 2003).

The plurality, however, qualifies its recognition of the President's authority to detain enemy combatants in the war on terrorism in ways that are at odds with our precedent. Thus, the plurality relies primarily on Article 118 of the Geneva Convention (III) Relative to the Treatment of Prisoners of War, Aug. 12, 1949, [1955] 6 U.S.T. 3406, T.I.A.S. No. 3364, for the proposition that "[i]t is a clearly established principle of the law of war that detention may last no longer than active hostilities." *Ante*, at 12–13. It then appears to limit the President's authority to detain by requiring that the record establis[h] that United States troops are still involved in active combat in Afghanistan because, in that case, detention would be "part of the exercise of 'necessary and appropriate force.'" *Ante*, at 14. But I do not believe that we may diminish the Federal Government's war powers by reference to a treaty and certainly not to a treaty that does not apply. See n. 6, *infra*. Further, we are bound by the political branches' determination that the United States is at war. See, *e.g.*, *Ludecke* v. *Watkins*, 335 U.S. 160, 167–170 (1948); *Prize Cases*, 2 Black, at 670; *Mott*, 12 Wheat., at 30. And, in any case, the power to detain does not end with the cessation of formal hostilities. See, *e.g.*, *Madsen* v. *Kinsella*, 343 U.S. 341, 360 (1952); *Johnson* v. *Eisentrager*, 339 U.S. 763, 786 (1950); cf. *Moyer*, *supra*, at 85.

Accordingly, the President's action here is "supported by the strongest of presumptions and the widest latitude of judicial interpretation." *Dames & Moore*, 453 U.S., at 668 (internal quotation marks omitted).[2] The question becomes whether the Federal Government (rather than the President acting alone) has power to detain Hamdi as an enemy combatant. More precisely, we must determine whether the Government may detain Hamdi given the procedures that were used.

III

I agree with the plurality that the Federal Government has power to detain those that the Executive Branch determines to be enemy combatants. See *ante*, at 10. But I do not think that the plurality has adequately explained the breadth of the President's authority to detain enemy combatants, an authority that includes making virtually conclusive factual findings. In my view, the structural considerations discussed above, as recognized in our precedent, demonstrate that we lack the capacity and responsibility to second-guess this determination.

This makes complete sense once the process that is due Hamdi is made clear. As an initial matter, it is possible that the Due Process Clause requires only "that our Government must proceed according to the 'law of the land' – that is, according to written constitutional and statutory provisions." *In re Winship*, 397 U.S. 358, 382 (1970) (Black, J., dissenting). I need not go this far today because the Court has already explained the nature of due process in this context.

In a case strikingly similar to this one, the Court addressed a Governor's authority to detain for an extended period a person the executive believed to be responsible, in part, for a local insurrection. Justice Holmes wrote for a unanimous Court:

> "When it comes to a decision by the head of the State upon a matter involving its life, the ordinary rights of individuals must yield to what *he deems* the necessities of the moment. Public danger warrants the substitution of executive process for judicial process. This was admitted with regard to killing men in the actual clash of arms, and we think it

---

[2] It could be argued that the habeas statutes are evidence of congressional intent that enemy combatants are entitled to challenge the factual basis for the Government's determination. See, *e.g.*, 28 U.S.C. §§2243, 2246. But factual development is needed only to the extent necessary to resolve the legal challenge to the detention. See, *e.g.*, *Walker* v. *Johnston*, 312 U.S. 275, 284 (1941).

obvious, although it was disputed, that the same is true of temporary detention to prevent apprehended harm." *Moyer*, 212 U.S., at 85 (citation omitted; emphasis added).

The Court answered Moyer's claim that he had been denied due process by emphasizing that

"it is familiar that what is due process of law depends on circumstances. It varies with the subject-matter and the necessities of the situation. Thus summary proceedings suffice for taxes, and executive decisions for exclusion from the country.... Such arrests are not necessarily for punishment, but are by way of precaution to prevent the exercise of hostile power." *Id.*, at 84–85 (citations omitted).

In this context, due process requires nothing more than a good-faith executive determination.[3] To be clear: The Court has held that an executive, acting pursuant to statutory and constitutional authority may, consistent with the Due Process Clause, unilaterally decide to detain an individual if the executive deems this necessary for the public safety *even if he is mistaken.*

Moyer is not an exceptional case. In *Luther* v. *Borden*, 7 How. 1 (1849), the Court discussed the President's constitutional and statutory authority, in response to a request from a state legislature or executive, "'to call forth such number of the militia of any other State or States, as may be applied for, as he may judge sufficient to suppress [an] insurrection.'" *Id.*, at 43 (quoting Act of Feb. 28, 1795). The Court explained that courts could not review the President's decision to recognize one of the competing legislatures or executives. See 7 How., at 43. If a court could second-guess this determination, "it would become the duty of the court (provided it came to the conclusion that the President had decided incorrectly) to discharge those who were arrested or detained by the troops in the service of the United States." *Ibid.* "If the judicial power extends so far," the Court concluded, "the guarantee contained in the Constitution of the United States [referring to Art. IV, §4] is a guarantee of anarchy, and not of order." *Ibid.* The Court clearly contemplated that the President had authority to detain as he deemed necessary, and such detentions evidently comported with the Due Process Clause as long as the President correctly decided to call forth the militia, a question the Court said it could not review.

The Court also addressed the natural concern that placing "this power in the President is dangerous to liberty, and may be abused." *Id.*, at 44. The Court noted that "[a]ll power may be abused if placed in unworthy hands," and explained that "it would be difficult . . . to point out any other hands in which this power would be more safe, and at the same time equally effectual." *Ibid.* Putting that aside, the Court emphasized that this power "is conferred upon him by the Constitution and laws of the United States, and must therefore be respected and enforced in its judicial tribunals." *Ibid.* Finally, the Court explained that if the President abused this power "it would be in the power of Congress to apply the proper remedy. But the courts must administer the law as they find it." *Id.*, at 45.

Almost 140 years later, in *United States* v. *Salerno*, 481 U.S. 739, 748 (1987), the Court explained that the Due Process Clause "lays down [no] categorical imperative." The Court continued:

"We have repeatedly held that the Government's regulatory interest in community safety can, in appropriate circumstances, outweigh an individual's liberty interest. For example,

---

[3] Indeed, it is not even clear that the Court required good faith. See *Moyer*, 212 U.S., at 85, ("It is not alleged that [the Governor's] judgment was not honest, if that be material, or that [Moyer] was detained after fears of the insurrection were at an end").

in times of war or insurrection, when society's interest is at its peak, the Government may detain individuals whom the Government believes to be dangerous." *Ibid.*

The Court cited *Ludecke* v. *Watkins*, 335 U.S. 160 (1948), for this latter proposition even though *Ludecke* actually involved detention of enemy aliens. See also *Selective Draft Law Cases*, 245 U.S. 366 (1918); *Jacobson* v. *Massachusetts*, 197 U.S. 11, 27–29 (1905) (upholding legislated mass vaccinations and approving of forced quarantines of Americans even if they show no signs of illness); cf. *Kansas* v. *Hendricks*, 521 U.S. 346 (1997); *Juragua Iron Co.* v. *United States*, 212 U.S. 297 (1909).

The Government's asserted authority to detain an individual that the President has determined to be an enemy combatant, at least while hostilities continue, comports with the Due Process Clause. As these cases also show, the Executive's decision that a detention is necessary to protect the public need not and should not be subjected to judicial second-guessing. Indeed, at least in the context of enemy-combatant determinations, this would defeat the unity, secrecy, and dispatch that the Founders believed to be so important to the warmaking function. See Part I, *supra.*

I therefore cannot agree with JUSTICE SCALIA's conclusion that the Government must choose between using standard criminal processes and suspending the writ. See *ante*, at 14–16, 17–20 (dissenting opinion). JUSTICE SCALIA relies heavily upon *Ex parte Milligan*, 4 Wall. 2 (1866), see *ante*, at 14–16, 17–20, and three cases decided by New York state courts in the wake of the War of 1812, see *ante*, at 13–14. I admit that *Milligan* supports his position. But because the Executive Branch there, unlike here, did not follow a specific statutory mechanism provided by Congress, the Court did not need to reach the broader question of Congress' power, and its discussion on this point was arguably dicta, see 4 Wall., at 122, as four Justices believed, see *id.*, at 132, 134–136 (Chase, C. J., joined by Wayne, Swayne, and Miller, JJ., concurring in judgment).

More importantly, the Court referred frequently and pervasively to the criminal nature of the proceedings instituted against Milligan. In fact, this feature serves to distinguish the state cases as well. See *In re Stacy*, 10 Johns. *328, *334 (N.Y. 1813) ("a military commander is here assuming *criminal jurisdiction* over a private citizen" (emphasis added)); *Smith* v. *Shaw*, 12 Johns. *257, *265 (N.Y.1815) (Shaw "might be amenable to the civil authority for treason; but could not *be punished*, under martial law, as a spy" (emphasis added)); *M'Connell* v. *Hampton*, 12 Johns. *234 (N.Y. 1815) (same for treason).

Although I do acknowledge that the reasoning of these cases might apply beyond criminal punishment, the punishment-nonpunishment distinction harmonizes all of the precedent. And, subsequent cases have at least implicitly distinguished *Milligan* in just this way. See, *e.g.*, *Moyer*, 212 U.S., at 84–85 ("Such arrests are not necessarily for punishment, but are by way of precaution"). Finally, *Quirin* overruled *Milligan* to the extent that those cases are inconsistent. See *Quirin*, 317 U.S., at 45 (limiting *Milligan* to its facts). Because the Government does not detain Hamdi in order to punish him, as the plurality acknowledges, see *ante*, at 10–11, *Milligan* and the New York cases do not control.

JUSTICE SCALIA also finds support in a letter Thomas Jefferson wrote to James Madison. See *ante*, at 12. I agree that this provides some evidence for his position. But I think this plainly insufficient to rebut the authorities upon which I have relied. In any event, I do not believe that JUSTICE SCALIA's evidence leads to the necessary "clear conviction that [the detention is] in conflict with the Constitution or laws of Congress constitutionally enacted," *Quirin*, *supra*, at 25, to justify nullifying the President's wartime action.

Finally, JUSTICE SCALIA's position raises an additional concern. JUSTICE SCALIA apparently does not disagree that the Federal Government has all power necessary to protect the Nation. If criminal processes do not suffice, however, JUSTICE SCALIA would require Congress to suspend the writ. See *ante*, at 26. But the fact that the writ may not be suspended "unless when in Cases of Rebellion or Invasion the public Safety may require it," Art. I, §9, cl. 2, poses two related problems. First, this condition might not obtain here or during many other emergencies during which this detention authority might be necessary. Congress would then have to choose between acting unconstitutionally[4] and depriving the President of the tools he needs to protect the Nation. Second, I do not see how suspension would make constitutional otherwise unconstitutional detentions ordered by the President. It simply removes a remedy. JUSTICE SCALIA's position might therefore require one or both of the political branches to act unconstitutionally in order to protect the Nation. But the power to protect the Nation must be the power to do so lawfully.

Accordingly, I conclude that the Government's detention of Hamdi as an enemy combatant does not violate the Constitution. By detaining Hamdi, the President, in the prosecution of a war and authorized by Congress, has acted well within his authority. Hamdi thereby received all the process to which he was due under the circumstances. I therefore believe that this is no occasion to balance the competing interests, as the plurality unconvincingly attempts to do.

IV

Although I do not agree with the plurality that the balancing approach of *Mathews* v. *Eldridge*, 424 U.S. 319 (1976), is the appropriate analytical tool with which to analyze this case,[5] I cannot help but explain that the plurality misapplies its chosen framework, one that if applied correctly would probably lead to the result I have reached. The plurality devotes two paragraphs to its discussion of the Government's interest, though much of those two paragraphs explain why the Government's concerns are misplaced. See *ante*, at 24–25. But: "It is 'obvious and unarguable' that no governmental interest is more compelling than the security of the Nation." *Agee*, 453 U.S., at 307 (quoting *Aptheker*, 378 U.S., at 509). In *Moyer*, the Court recognized the paramount importance of the Governor's interest in the tranquility of a Colorado town. At issue here is the far more significant interest of the security of the Nation. The Government seeks to further that interest by detaining an enemy soldier not only to prevent him from rejoining the ongoing fight. Rather, as the Government explains, detention can serve to gather critical intelligence regarding the intentions and capabilities of our adversaries, a function that the Government avers has become all the more important in the war on terrorism. See Brief for Respondents 15; App. 347–351.

Additional process, the Government explains, will destroy the intelligence gathering function. Brief for Respondents 43–45. It also does seem quite likely that, under the process envisioned by the plurality, various military officials will have to take time to litigate this matter. And though the plurality does not say so, a meaningful ability to challenge the Government's factual allegations will probably require the Government to divulge highly classified information to the purported enemy combatant, who might then upon release return to the fight armed with our most closely held secrets.

The plurality manages to avoid these problems by discounting or entirely ignoring them. After spending a few sentences putatively describing the Government's interests, the plurality simply assures the Government that the alleged burdens "are properly taken

---

[4] I agree with JUSTICE SCALIA that this Court could not review Congress' decision to suspend the writ. See *ante*, at 26.

[5] Evidently, neither do the parties, who do not cite *Mathews* even once.

into account in our due process analysis." *Ante*, at 25. The plurality also announces that "the risk of erroneous deprivation of a detainee's liberty interest is unacceptably high under the Government's proposed rule." *Ante*, at 26 (internal quotation marks omitted). But there is no particular reason to believe that the federal courts have the relevant information and expertise to make this judgment. And for the reasons discussed in Part I, *supra*, there is every reason to think that courts cannot and should not make these decisions.

The plurality next opines that "[w]e think it unlikely that this basic process will have the dire impact on the central functions of warmaking that the Government forecasts." *Ante*, at 27. Apparently by limiting hearings "to the alleged combatant's acts," such hearings "meddl[e] little, if at all, in the strategy or conduct of war." *Ante*, at 28. Of course, the meaning of the combatant's acts may become clear only after quite invasive and extensive inquiry. And again, the federal courts are simply not situated to make these judgments.

Ultimately, the plurality's dismissive treatment of the Government's asserted interests arises from its apparent belief that enemy-combatant determinations are not part of "the actual prosecution of a war," *ibid.*, or one of the "central functions of warmaking," *ante*, at 27. This seems wrong: Taking *and holding* enemy combatants is a quintessential aspect of the prosecution of war. See, *e.g.*, *ante*, at 10–11; *Quirin*, 317 U.S., at 28. Moreover, this highlights serious difficulties in applying the plurality's balancing approach here. First, in the war context, we know neither the strength of the Government's interests nor the costs of imposing additional process.

Second, it is at least difficult to explain why the result should be different for other military operations that the plurality would ostensibly recognize as "central functions of warmaking." As the plurality recounts:

> "Parties whose rights are to be affected are entitled to be heard; and in order that they may enjoy that right they must first be notified. It is equally fundamental that the right to notice and an opportunity to be heard must be granted at a meaningful time and in a meaningful manner." *Ante*, at 26 (internal quotation marks omitted).

See also *ibid.* ("notice" of the Government's factual assertions and "a fair opportunity to rebut [those] assertions before a neutral decisionmaker" are essential elements of due process). Because a decision to bomb a particular target might extinguish *life* interests, the plurality's analysis seems to require notice to potential targets. To take one more example, in November 2002, a Central Intelligence Agency (CIA) Predator drone fired a Hellfire missile at a vehicle in Yemen carrying an al Qaeda leader, a citizen of the United States, and four others. See Priest, CIA Killed U.S. Citizen In Yemen Missile Strike, Washington Post, Nov. 8, 2002, p. A1. It is not clear whether the CIA knew that an American was in the vehicle. But the plurality's due process would seem to require notice and opportunity to respond here as well. Cf. *Tennessee v. Garner*, 471 U.S. 1 (1985). I offer these examples not because I think the plurality would demand additional process in these situations but because it clearly would not. The result here should be the same.

I realize that many military operations are, in some sense, necessary. But many, if not most, are merely expedient, and I see no principled distinction between the military operation the plurality condemns today (the holding of an enemy combatant based on the process given Hamdi) from a variety of other military operations. In truth, I doubt that there is any sensible, bright-line distinction. It could be argued that bombings and missile strikes are an inherent part of war, and as long as our forces do not violate the laws of war, it is of no constitutional moment that civilians might be killed. But this does not serve to distinguish this case because it is also consistent with the laws of war to detain enemy combatants exactly as the Government has detained Hamdi.[6] This, in fact, bolsters my argument in Part III to the extent that the laws of war show that the power to detain is part of a sovereign's war powers.

Undeniably, Hamdi has been deprived of a serious interest, one actually protected by the Due Process Clause. Against this, however, is the Government's overriding interest in protecting the Nation. If a deprivation of liberty can be justified by the need to protect a town, the protection of the Nation, *a fortiori*, justifies it.

I acknowledge that under the plurality's approach, it might, at times, be appropriate to give detainees access to counsel and notice of the factual basis for the Government's determination. See *ante*, at 25–27. But properly accounting for the Government's interests also requires concluding that access to counsel and to the factual basis would not always be warranted. Though common sense suffices, the Government thoroughly explains that counsel would often destroy the intelligence gathering function. See Brief for Respondents 42–43. See also App. 347–351 (affidavit of Col. D. Woolfolk). Equally obvious is the Government's interest in not fighting the war in its own courts, see, *e.g.*, *Johnson* v. *Eisentrager*, 339 U.S., at 779, and protecting classified information, see, *e.g.*, *Department of Navy* v. *Egan*, 484 U.S. 518 (1988) (President's "authority to classify and control access to information bearing on national security and to determine" who gets access "flows primarily from [the Commander-in-Chief Clause] and exists quite apart from any explicit congressional grant"); *Agee*, 453 U.S., at 307 (upholding revocation of former CIA employee's passport in large part by reference to the Government's need "to protect the secrecy of [its] foreign intelligence operations").[7]

* * *

For these reasons, I would affirm the judgment of the Court of Appeals.

---

[6] Hamdi's detention comports with the laws of war, including the Geneva Convention (III) Relative to the Treatment of Prisoners of War, Aug. 12, 1949, [1955] 6 U.S.T. 3406, T.I.A.S. No. 3364. See Brief for Respondents 22–24.

[7] These observations cast still more doubt on the appropriateness and usefulness of *Mathews* v. *Eldridge*, 424 U.S. 319 (1976), in this context. It is, for example, difficult to see how the plurality can insist that Hamdi unquestionably has the right to access to counsel in connection with the proceedings on remand, when new information could become available to the Government showing that such access would pose a grave risk to national security. In that event, would the Government need to hold a hearing before depriving Hamdi of his newly acquired right to counsel even if that hearing would itself pose a grave threat?

IN THE UNITED STATES DISTRICT COURT
FOR THE EASTERN DISTRICT OF VIRGINIA
NORFOLK DIVISION

FILED

SEP 2 4 2004

CLERK, U.S. DISTRICT COURT
NORFOLK, VA

YASER ESAM HAMDI,

    Petitioner,

v.

    CASE NO. 2:02CV439

DONALD RUMSFELD
Secretary of Defense
The Pentagon

COMMANDER C.T. HANFT,
Commander, Consolidated Naval Brig

    Respondents.

MOTION TO STAY PROCEEDINGS

    Yaser Esam Hamdi, by counsel, hereby moves the Court to stay the pending proceedings until further action is requested by either party. The United States is simultaneously moving in the Court of Appeals for the Fourth Circuit to stay the issuance of the mandate in this case until October 1, 2004. In support of this motion, Mr. Hamdi states the following:

1.   On June 11, 2002, a Petition for Habeas Corpus was filed on behalf of Yaser Esam Hamdi in the Norfolk division of the Eastern District of Virginia;

2.   On June 28, 2004, the United States Supreme Court issued an opinion in this case that contemplates additional proceedings;

3.   As a result of negotiations, the parties have entered into an Agreement that sets out the terms under which Mr. Hamdi is to be released from custody, and the Agreement is attached as Exhibit A to this Motion;

---

* Redactions on this page have been added for privacy purposes. – *Eds*.

4.   Wherefore, Yaser Hamdi respectfully requests that the Court stay further action in this case pending a request by either party for assistance so that the parties may carry out the terms of the Agreement;

5.   The United States has no objection to this Motion.

Respectfully submitted,

YASER ESAM HAMDI

By counsel

for

FRANK W. DUNHAM, JR.
FEDERAL PUBLIC DEFENDER
EASTERN DISTRICT OF
VIRGINIA

Agreement

The United States of America, by and through its representative, and Yaser Esam Hamdi ("Hamdi"), and Hamdi's attorneys Frank W. Dunham, Jr. and Geremy C. Kamens (collectively "the parties") hereby agree as follows:

WHEREAS the United States captured Hamdi in Afghanistan and is detaining him at a naval brig in Charleston, South Carolina as an enemy combatant;

WHEREAS the United States maintains that Hamdi was affiliated with a Taliban military unit and is an enemy combatant for the reasons set forth in the Declaration of Michael Mobbs dated July 24, 2002;

WHEREAS Hamdi was born in Baton Rouge, Louisiana;

WHEREAS the question whether Hamdi has performed an expatriating act under Section 349(a) of the Immigration and Nationality Act, as amended (8 U.S.C. § 1481(a), hereinafter "Section 349(a)"), has not been adjudicated;

WHEREAS Hamdi considers himself to be a citizen of the Kingdom of Saudi Arabia;

WHEREAS Hamdi maintains that he never affiliated with or joined a Taliban military unit, never was an enemy combatant, that is, never was part of or supported forces hostile to the United States and, never engaged in armed conflict against the United States; and he also maintains he was never a member of nor affiliated with al Qaeda;

WHEREAS, in order to implement this Agreement, the United States has agreed and agrees to take all reasonable steps to secure whatever travel documents Hamdi may need to travel from the United States to the Kingdom of Saudi Arabia;

NOW THEREFORE, the parties have agreed to the release of Hamdi from United States custody in accordance with the following terms and conditions:

1. The United States agrees to release Hamdi from United States custody at the naval brig in Charleston, South Carolina (or any other brig or jail in which he is detained) after obtaining all necessary travel documents and country clearances for him to travel to the Kingdom of Saudi Arabia, but in any event no later than September 30, 2004. If, for reasons beyond the control of the Government of the United States, Hamdi cannot be transported to the Kingdom of Saudi Arabia on or before September 30, 2004, the United States shall not be in breach of this Agreement, provided Hamdi is transported to the Kingdom of Saudi Arabia as soon thereafter as it is within the power of the United States to do so. However, Hamdi may, in such event, seek relief concerning his conditions of confinement from the United States District Court in the Eastern District of Virginia while awaiting transport.

2. The United States agrees to transport Hamdi in civilian clothes and unhooded directly from the United States to the Kingdom of Saudi Arabia without unreasonable delay in route and without travel to Guantanamo Bay, Cuba; or to permit the Kingdom of Saudi Arabia to transport Hamdi to the Kingdom of Saudi Arabia, subject to security and logistical arrangements deemed appropriate by the United States.

3. Although the United States expressly retains the authority to share any information concerning Hamdi with the Saudi government, the United States agrees to make no request that Hamdi be detained by the Kingdom of Saudi Arabia based on information as to Hamdi's conduct known to the United States as of the official date of this Agreement. In the event the United States shares information with the Kingdom of Saudi Arabia pursuant to this paragraph, or if it is asked for guidance or information concerning Hamdi by the Kingdom of Saudi Arabia, it shall advise that considerations of United States national security do not require his detention in light of the terms of this Agreement.

4. Hamdi agrees that he will not engage in, assist in or conspire to commit any combatant activities or act in preparation thereof against the United States or its citizens, or against allies of the United States or citizens of such allies; and that he will not engage in, assist in or conspire to commit any acts of terrorism or knowingly harbor anyone who does.

5. In particular, Hamdi agrees not to aid, assist or in any way affiliate with the Taliban or any member of al Qaeda or any terrorist organization or terrorist so designated by the United States. (A list of designated terrorist organizations and designated terrorists shall be provided to Hamdi upon his request.)

6. Hamdi agrees to notify officials of the Kingdom of Saudi Arabia and the U.S. Embassy in Riyadh, Saudi Arabia, immediately if (a) he is solicited to engage in, assist in, or conspire to commit any combatant activities or to harbor anyone who does, (b) he comes into contact with any person known to him to be, or designated by the United States as, a terrorist, a terrorist organization, or a member affiliate of such terrorist organization, or (c) he becomes aware of any planned or executed acts of terrorism.

7. Hamdi hereby renounces terrorism and violent jihad.

8. Hamdi agrees to appear before a diplomatic or consular officer of the United States at the United States Embassy in Riyadh, Saudi Arabia, formally to renounce any claim that he may have to United States nationality pursuant to Section 349(a)(5). This provision is without prejudice to the right of the United States to determine that Hamdi lost United States nationality at an earlier time. Hamdi further agrees to so appear within seven (7) days of arriving in the Kingdom of Saudi Arabia pursuant to paragraphs 1 and 2 of this Agreement.

9. Hamdi agrees to remain and reside in the Kingdom of Saudi Arabia for a period of five (5) years from the official date of this Agreement without travel outside the Kingdom of Saudi Arabia.

10. Hamdi agrees never to travel to Afghanistan, Iraq, Israel, Pakistan, Syria, the West Bank, or the Gaza Strip. He further agrees not to travel to the United States for ten (10) years and, after that time, to receive the express permission of the Secretary of Defense or his designee and the Secretary of the Department of Homeland Security or his designee prior to initiating travel to the United States (in addition to applying for any and all necessary visas or travel documents).

11. For fifteen (15) years from the official date of this Agreement, Hamdi agrees to report to the United States Embassy (or any official of the Kingdom of Saudi Arabia so designated by the United States) any intent or plans to travel outside the Kingdom of Saudi Arabia at least thirty (30) days in advance of such proposed travel.

12. Hamdi agrees that if he does not fulfill any of the conditions of this Agreement, he may be detained immediately insofar as consistent with the law of armed conflict.

13. Except in case of breach of this Agreement by the United States, Hamdi hereby releases, waives, forfeits, relinquishes and forever discharges the United States, its departments, agencies, officers, employees, instrumentalities and agents, in their individual or official capacities, from any and all claims for any violation of United States, foreign, or international law arising from acts or omissions occurring prior to the official date of this Agreement, and from any and all challenges to the terms and conditions imposed by this Agreement. In the case of a breach of this Agreement by the United States, the United States agrees, as to any claim by Hamdi not barred by the applicable statute of limitations or laches as of the official date of this Agreement, to waive any defense based on the statute of limitations or laches.

14. Any and all disagreements or disputes arising under or relating to this Agreement shall be adjudicated in the U.S. District Court for the Eastern District of Virginia under United States law without reference to any conflict of law provisions.

15. The official date of this Agreement is the date on which it shall have been signed by all parties to the Agreement.

16. The parties agree to move jointly to stay all proceedings in the pending habeas case until September 30, 2004.

17. This Agreement constitutes the full and complete Agreement between the parties. Any modification to the Agreement must be in writing and signed by all parties to the Agreement.

18. Simultaneously with the execution of this Agreement, counsel for all parties will sign, and counsel for Hamdi shall retain, a Stipulation of Dismissal, in the form appended hereto as Exhibit

A ["the dismissal stipulation"] dismissing the action captioned as Yaser Esam Hamdi, Petitioner, versus Donald Rumsfeld, et al, Respondents, Case No. 2:02CV439 (E.D. Va.) with prejudice. Upon notification of counsel for Hamdi in writing of a date certain upon which Hamdi will be transported to Saudi Arabia, counsel for Petitioner Hamdi shall remit the dismissal stipulation to counsel for the United States. Immediately before release of Hamdi by the United States, whether upon arrival in Saudi Arabia or prior thereto, Hamdi shall notify his counsel that he is about to be released from United States custody in accordance with this Agreement and that he has returned to the Kingdom of Saudi Arabia or is about to be returned to the Kingdom of Saudi Arabia outside United States custody. Upon delivery of that notice to Hamdi's counsel, and upon release of Hamdi from United States custody, counsel for the United States may then cause the Stipulation of Dismissal to be filed.

Petitioner's Signature: I hereby agree that I have consulted with my attorney and fully understand all rights with respect to this Agreement. I have read this Agreement and Exhibit A and have carefully reviewed every provision therein with my attorneys. I understand all the terms contained in this Agreement, including Exhibit A, and its effect on my claim to United States citizenship. I understand this Agreement and voluntarily agree to it.

Date: 9/15/2004

_____
Yaser Esam Hamdi
Petitioner

Petitioner's Counsel Signature: We are counsel for the Petitioner in this case. We have fully explained to the Petitioner his rights with respect to this Agreement. We have carefully reviewed every provision of this Agreement, including Exhibit A, with the Petitioner and have explained its effect on his claim to United States citizenship. To our knowledge, the Petitioner's decision to enter into this Agreement is an informed and voluntary one.

Date: 9/15/04

_____
Frank W. Dunham, Jr.

Date: 9/15/04

_____
Jeremy C. Kamens

For the United States of America:

Date: 9-17-04

_____
Ryan Henry, Principal Deputy Under
Secretary of Defense for Policy

10/12/2004: DISMISSAL STIPULATION*

FOR THE EASTERN DISTRICT OF VIRGINIA
NORFOLK DIVISION

FILED

OCT 1 2 2004

CLERK, U.S. DISTRICT COURT
NORFOLK, VA

YASER ESAM HAMDI,)
)
Petitioner,)
)
v.)   CASE NO. 2:02CV439
)
DONALD RUMSFELD)
Secretary of Defense)
The Pentagon)
Arlington, Va.,)
)
COMMANDER C.T. HANFT,)
Commander, Consolidated Naval Brig)
[REDACTED])
)
)
Respondents.)

STIPULATION OF DISMISSAL

Petitioner Yaser Esam Hamdi, and Respondents, by undersigned counsel for all parties,

stipulate that, pursuant to Rule 41(a)(1)(ii) of the Federal Rules of Civil Procedure, the above-

captioned action is hereby dismissed in its entirety with prejudice as settled, and without costs,

attorney's fees or expenses as against any party.

Dated: October 11, 2004   Respectfully submitted,

Respondents: Petitioner:
Donald Rumsfeld   Yaser Esam Hamdi
Commander C.T. Hanft   By counsel
By Counsel

_____   _____
                                        Frank W. Dunham, Jr., Esq.
                                        Federal Public Defender
Lawrence R. Leonard   Geremy C. Kamens
Managing Assistant United States   Assistant Federal Public Defender
Attorney   [REDACTED]

---

* Redactions on this page have been added for privacy purposes. – *Eds*.

PART TWO. MILITARY COMMISSIONS

CHAPTER 3

Hamdan v. Rumsfeld

According to his affidavit submitted to the U.S. District Court in Seattle at the outset of his case against the secretary of defense and the president of the United States, Salim Ahmed Hamdan was born in a village in the Hadhramout region of Yemen "in approximately 1969." At about age 20, he moved to Sa'ana, the capital of Yemen, where he worked odd jobs, including driving a taxi on a part-time basis. He was an orphan, without siblings, with the rough equivalent of a fourth-grade education, renting a mattress in a crowded boardinghouse and hoping to find the kind of regular employment that might eventually allow him to marry and start a family.

Though not particularly religious, Mr. Hamdan was approached in 1996 by someone "seeking men to aid Muslims struggling against the communists in Tajikistan." Mr. Hamdan signed on to that project, traveling first to Pakistan, then to Afghanistan, where he met with others making their way north to Tajikistan. However, Tajik troops at the border prevented the group from entering the country and "the weather in the mountains was bad," so Mr. Hamdan "turned around and left for Kabul." His intention was to return to Yemen, but he was persuaded by one of his associates to remain in Afghanistan to work as a driver. The same person who first approached Mr. Hamdan took him to a farm outside Jalalabad and introduced him to the owner, Osama bin Laden. Mr. bin Laden offered him a job driving "workers from the local village to work [at the farm] and back again." After about seven months, he would occasionally drive Mr. bin Laden to various places as well. Mr. Hamdan was to remain a driver for Mr. bin Laden until the American invasion of Afghanistan in the fall of 2001. Between 1996 and 2001, he returned to Yemen twice, once in 1998 to get married and again in 2000 to participate in the hajj.

By 2001, Mr. Hamdan's wife and young daughter were living in Kandahar, in southern Afghanistan. When the fighting drew near there in the fall of 2001, Mr. Hamdan left Mr. bin Laden in Kabul and returned to Kandahar in order to try to evacuate his family. He borrowed a car and drove his family to the border with Pakistan. He left them there with the intention of returning the vehicle and selling his household furnishings in order to finance a return trip for himself and his family to Yemen. But he never made it. On the way to Kandahar, he was seized at a roadblock set up by indigenous forces loyal to the former king of Afghanistan, Zahir Shah. He was then sold for a $5,000 bounty to U.S. military personnel.

Mr. Hamdan was held for several months in Afghanistan before being transported to the Guantanamo Bay Naval Station in May 2002. He denies that he is a member of al Qaeda and denies ever planning or engaging in hostile acts against the United States or its allies. In July 2003, after more than a year at Guantanamo, he was designated by the president as eligible for trial by military commission. That December, he was placed in solitary confinement ("pre-commission segregation" in the government's terminology) and a military lawyer, Lt. Commander Charles Swift of the U.S. Navy, was detailed as his defense counsel.

Though no charges had been preferred against Mr. Hamdan, Lt. Cmdr. Swift was told that his job was to facilitate the negotiation of a guilty plea and that his continued access to the prisoner was contingent on making progress toward that end. To his great credit and that of the JAG Corps which he served with such distinction, Lt. Cmdr. Swift was not prepared to accept these rules of engagement. He promptly demanded charges and a speedy trial in conformity with the Uniform Code of Military Justice (or "UCMJ"). After he was told in February 2004 that the UCMJ did not apply, Lt. Cmdr. Swift – consulting closely with Georgetown Law Professor Neal Katyal – approached my law firm, Perkins Coie, to ask if we would assist them in representing Mr. Hamdan in a legal challenge to the military commission to be filed in U.S. federal court. Perkins Coie quickly agreed to do so.

The case challenged the aggressive assertion of executive authority in setting up military tribunals far from any battlefield or zone of military occupation. There could be no necessity-based justification for such tribunals in a place like Guantanamo, and it seemed clear to us that the proposed military commissions were simply an inferior brand of justice to be meted out to non-citizens in a manner inconsistent with our legal tradition. Indeed, the rules promulgated for the commissions allowed for the exclusion of defendants from their own trials, the introduction of evidence that would never be disclosed to the defendants and the admission of evidence extracted by coercion. In our view, such practices are incompatible with fundamental principles of due process and have no place in an American court of law.

Our position in the litigation was simply this: if Mr. Hamdan is a war criminal, then charge him with a war crime and try him in a court martial in a manner consistent with the UCMJ and the Third Geneva Convention Relative to the of Prisoners of War.

We faced a series of extraordinary procedural hurdles that had to be cleared in order to get rulings on the merits. Among other things, the commission rules were literally being written, and changed, as our case proceeded. Curiously, the changes in the rules or in Mr. Hamdan's conditions of confinement often seemed to come right before a court was expected to consider the merits of our arguments (for example, Mr. Hamdan was released from solitary confinement immediately prior to oral argument at the district court) or right after a significant filing by our side (for example, rule changes were announced while our petition for certiorari was pending). And while we thought that the jurisdictional issue had been resolved by *Rasul*, shortly after the Supreme Court granted certiorari in our case Congress passed, and the president signed, the Detainee Treatment Act of 2005 (or "DTA"). The government then immediately moved for the dismissal of Mr. Hamdan's petition, arguing that the statute stripped federal courts of jurisdiction over pending as well as future cases filed by Guantanamo detainees. The Court decided to hear oral argument on the jurisdictional question as well as on the merits in March 2006. We would be arguing to a Court composed of eight Justices, as Chief Justice Roberts had recused himself because he had been part of the D.C. Circuit panel that had previously ruled against Mr. Hamdan.

Our primary arguments were that the DTA did not apply retroactively to strip habeas jurisdiction over pending cases; that if it did provide a clear statement eliminating habeas jurisdiction, then it violated the Suspension Clause of the U.S. Constitution; that the military commission violated the provision of the UCMJ which requires any military commission established by the president to comply with the laws of war; that the commission also violated the UCMJ provision which requires that commission procedures not be "contrary to or inconsistent with" the UCMJ; that conspiracy is not a violation of the laws of war; and that the commission violated the Third Geneva Convention in several respects.

The Supreme Court announced its decision on June 28, 2006, the last day of the 2006 term. The decision was 5-3 in Mr. Hamdan's favor, reversing and vacating the circuit court's decision, and remanding for further proceedings. The Court began by accepting our argument that, as a matter of statutory construction, the DTA did not apply retroactively to strip jurisdiction over pending cases such as Mr. Hamdan's. It rejected the government's argument that the Authorization for the Use of Military Force, passed shortly after the 9/11 attacks, provided statutory authorization for the military commissions and held that the structure and procedures of the military commission violated both the UCMJ and the Geneva Conventions.

In addition, the Court held that, regardless of whether Mr. Hamdan was a POW entitled to all the protections of the Geneva Conventions he was at least entitled to the protections of Common Article 3, which applies even in the so-called "War on Terror." The military commission violated that provision because it is not a "regularly constituted court." Moreover, a plurality of four Justices held that conspiracy is not an offense against the laws of war.

Hamdan stands as an important decision on the limits of executive authority within our constitutional system. While many aspects of the ruling are significant, the Court's holding that Common Article 3 applies and must be respected is particularly noteworthy because, among other things, the provision prohibits "humiliating and degrading treatment" and "outrages to personal dignity." Such standards clearly have broad application to many aspects of U.S. detainee policy outside the question of prosecution for alleged war crimes. Indeed, from my perspective, this aspect of the *Hamdan* decision radically called into question the legality of much of the Bush administration's policy in the War on Terror. The reports of abuse and mistreatment emerging from Guantanamo and Abu Ghraib, for example, or the president's admission in September 2006 that "alternative interrogation techniques" were employed against prisoners at CIA "black sites," raise profound and very troubling questions in this regard.

Indeed, it seems that the Bush administration was similarly concerned, as it quickly mobilized to attempt a legislative override of *Hamdan*. The result was the Military Commissions Act of 2006 (or "MCA"), signed into law in October 2006. The MCA purports to provide the congressional authorization for military commissions that was lacking in the initial commission convened to try Salim Hamdan. Among other things, the statute defines new offenses triable by commission (including conspiracy), allows for the introduction of testimony obtained through coercion, reverses the presumption against the admissibility of hearsay evidence and purports to strip all American courts of jurisdiction over any cases filed by alleged alien illegal combatants, even resident aliens residing lawfully in the United States. The MCA recites that its provisions fully comply with the Geneva Conventions but at the same time prohibits any defendant from invoking rights based on the Conventions in any American court. It purports to invest the president with what is fundamentally a judicial function – the responsibility to "interpret the meaning and application" of the Geneva Conventions. Meanwhile, it amends the U.S. War Crimes Act, eliminating certain violations of Common Article 3 as war crimes under U.S. law and retroactively exculpating any individuals who may have engaged in such violations at any time since the War Crimes Act was last amended in the 1990s. As of this writing, Mr. Hamdan's victory in the Supreme Court in June of 2006 has not made much difference for him personally, as he remains incarcerated at Guantanamo Bay and has been recharged under the MCA with the crimes of conspiracy and providing material support for terrorism. His case has been dismissed from federal court pursuant to the jurisdiction-stripping provision of the MCA and the matter is currently on appeal. But regardless of the ultimate outcome for Mr. Hamdan personally, his case stands as an important reaffirmation of the principle that, even in times of grave threat to our national security, in the words of the Supreme Court, "the Executive is bound to comply with the Rule of Law that prevails in this jurisdiction."

Joseph M. McMillan
Perkins Coie LLP
Co-counsel for Salim Hamdan
February 2007

7/03/2003: PRESIDENT'S DETERMINATION THAT HAMDAN IS SUBJECT TO ORDER AUTHORIZING MILITARY COMMISSIONS*

DefenseLink News Release: President Determines Enemy Combatants Subject to His Military Order

 U.S. Department of Defense
Office of the Assistant Secretary of Defense (Public Affairs)
News Release

On the Web:
http://www.defenselink.mil/releases/release.aspx?releaseid=5511
Media contact: ▮▮▮▮▮▮▮▮▮▮▮▮

Public contact:
http://www.defenselink.mil/faq/comment.html
▮▮▮▮▮▮▮▮▮▮▮

IMMEDIATE RELEASE

No. 485-03
July 03, 2003

President Determines Enemy Combatants Subject to His Military Order

The President determined that six enemy combatants currently detained by the United States are subject to his Military Order of November 13, 2001. Today's action is the next step in the process that may lead to military commissions. The President determined that there is reason to believe that each of these enemy combatants was a member of al Qaida or was otherwise involved in terrorism directed against the United States.

Military Commissions have historically been used to try violations of the law of armed conflict and related offenses. Offenses that may be charged include those listed in the *Crimes and Elements for Trials by Military Commission* (Department of Defense Military Commission Instruction No. 2).

Many considerations are used in selecting cases – relevant factors include: 1) the quality of evidence, 2) the completeness of intelligence gathering and, 3) our desire to bring closure to individual cases. There is evidence that the individuals designated by the President may have attended terrorist training camps and may have been involved in such activities as: financing al-Qaida, providing protection for Usama bin Laden, and recruiting future terrorists.

The Department of Defense is prepared to conduct full and fair trials if and when the Appointing Authority approves charges on an individual subject to the President's military order.

Since no charges against any of the detainees have been approved, their names will not be released.

---

* Redactions on this page have been added for privacy purposes. – *Eds.*

DEPARTMENT OF DEFENSE
OFFICE OF GENERAL COUNSEL

12 Feb 04

MEMORANDUM FOR THE APPOINTING AUTHORITY

FROM: Detailed Defense Counsel

TO: Appointing Authority

THRU: Prosecution in the case of U.S. v. Hamdan

SUBJ: UNITED STATES v. HAMDAN

1.   On 15 December 2003 the defense received from the Chief Prosecutor a letter requesting the Chief Defense Counsel detail defense counsel in the subject case to begin preparations for trial. Pursuant to this letter a deadline of 9 January 2004 was imposed in when the defense was to respond to the prosecutor concerning Mr. Hamdan's willingness to enter into a pretrial agreement.

2.   Following notification from the defense on 9 January 2004, that the defense had been unable to meet with Mr. Hamdan due to the absence of qualified interpreter, the original deadline was rescinded and a second deadline of 12 February 2004 was imposed.

3.   The defense met with Mr. Hamdan on 30 January through 1 February 2004, and again on 7 through 9 February 2004. After extensive consultation, Mr. Hamdan is unwilling to enter into pretrial negotiations until such time as he is lawfully charged before a Military Commission.

4.   As a consequence of his pending trial, Mr. Hamdan has moved out of detention in Camp Delta with his fellow detainees into Camp Echo, where he is being held in what is deemed by Joint Task Force Guantanamo as "pre-commission segregation." Pre-commission segregation has materially altered the conditions of Mr. Hamdan's confinement. He is held in what amounts to solitary confinement, is unable to exercise in daylight and has no contact with any other detainee. Consequently the defense considers that based on the conditions of Mr. Hamdan's confinement, and the legal actions to date, Mr. Hamdan is being held in pretrial confinement rather than war time detention.

5.   Mr. Hamdan, pursuant to Article 10 of the Uniform Code of Military Justice (UCMJ) Mr. Hamdan demands to be informed of the specific charges against him or to be released from pre-commission segregation into general detention. Article 10, UCMJ holds "when any person subject to this chapter is placed in arrest or confinement prior to trial, immediate steps shall be taken to inform him of the specific wrong of which he is accused and to try him or to dismiss the charges and release him." Military order of 15 November 2001 relies in part on UCMJ Articles 21 and 36. Article 36 allows the President to prescribe rules for military courts-martial and military commissions, so far as they are not inconsistent with "this chapter" (Uniform Code of Military Justice), consequently Article 10 as a general provision of the Uniform Code of Military Justice is applicable to military commissions and the protections granted there-under should be afforded to a detainee in pre-commission segregation.

C. D. SWIFT
LCDR, JAGC, U.S. NAVY
Detailed Defense Counsel

---

* Redaction on this page has been added for privacy purposes. – *Eds*.

398

2/23/2004: MEMO FROM THE LEGAL ADVISOR TO THE APPOINTING AUTHORITY*

FOR OFFICIAL USE ONLY

**DEPARTMENT OF DEFENSE
OFFICE OF GENERAL COUNSEL**
███████████████████████

February 23, 2004

MEMORANDUM FOR Lieutenant Commander C.D. Swift, USN, Detailed Defense Counsel for Salem Ahmed Hamdan

SUBJECT: In the Case of Salem Ahmed Hamdan: Question Regarding the Application of Article 10, UCMJ

    I am in receipt of your February 12, 2004 memorandum requesting a determination that Article 10, UCMJ, applies to the Department of Defense detention of Salem Ahmed Hamdan. The Department of Defense is detaining Mr. Hamdan as an unlawful enemy combatant. Article 10, UCMJ, does not apply to Mr. Hamdan's detention.

Thomas L. Hemingway
Brig Gen, USAF
Legal Advisor to the Appointing Authority
Office of Military Commissions

cc: Chief Defense Counsel

- 36

FOR OFFICIAL USE ONLY

---

* Redaction on this page has been added for privacy purposes. – *Eds.*

```
_____ FILED      _____ ENTERED
_____ LODGED_____ RECEIVED

        APR 0 6 2004   MR
          AT SEATTLE
     CLERK U.S. DISTRICT COURT
   WESTERN DISTRICT OF WASHINGTON
   BY _____                DEPUTY
```

UNITED STATES DISTRICT COURT
WESTERN DISTRICT OF WASHINGTON
AT SEATTLE

Lieutenant Commander CHARLES SWIFT, a
resident of the State of Washington, as next
friend for SALIM AHMED HAMDAN,
    Military Commission Detainee,
    Camp Echo,
    Guantanamo Bay Naval Base,
    Guantanamo Bay, Cuba,

        Petitioner,

    v.

DONALD H. RUMSFELD, United States
Secretary of Defense; JOHN D
ALTENBURG, Jr., Appointing Authority for
Military Commissions, Department of Defense;
Brigadier General THOMAS L.
HEMINGWAY, Legal Advisor to the
Appointing Authority for Military
Commissions; Brigadier General JAY HOOD,
Commander Joint Task Force, Guantanamo,
Camp Echo, Guantanamo Bay, Cuba;
GEORGE W. BUSH, President of the United
States,

        Respondents.

CV04 - 0777L

PETITION FOR WRIT OF
MANDAMUS PURSUANT TO 28 U.S.C.
§ 1361 OR, IN THE ALTERNATIVE,
WRIT OF HABEAS CORPUS

04-CV-00777-PET

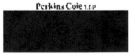

Perkins Coie LLP

PETITION FOR WRIT OF MANDAMUS PURSUANT
TO 28 U.S.C. § 1361 OR, IN THE ALTERNATIVE,
WRIT OF HABEAS CORPUS – 1
[42439-0001.SL040950.008]

---

* Redactions throughout this document have been added for privacy purposes. – *Eds.*

**PETITION FOR WRIT OF MANDAMUS
PURSUANT TO 28 U.S.C § 1361 OR, IN THE ALTERNATIVE,
WRIT OF HABEAS CORPUS**

COMES NOW, Petitioner Charles Swift, Lieutenant Commander, Judge Advocate

Generals Corps, United States Navy, by and through the undersigned counsel and, acting as

"next friend" to and on behalf of Salim Ahmad Hamdan, files this Petition for Writ of

Mandamus pursuant to 28 U.S.C § 1361 or, in the alternative, for a Writ of Habeas Corpus.

Salim Ahmad Hamdan ("Mr. Hamdan") is one of six persons identified for trial by Military

Commission. He is currently being held incommunicado in pre-trial custody by United

States Military Authorities, including Respondents herein, at Naval Base Guantanamo Bay

("Guantanamo"). The incarceration of Mr. Hamdan under these circumstances violates the

U.S. Constitution, U.S. law, and U.S. treaty obligations.

On November 13, 2001, President George W. Bush ("Respondent President Bush")

issued a Military Order that authorized the use of military tribunals to try noncitizens

accused of terrorism and other war crimes. *See* President George W. Bush's Military Order,

Nov. 13, 2001, attached as Exhibit B to the Declaration of Lieutenant Commander Charles

Swift ("Swift Decl."), filed herewith. In that same month, Afghan paramilitary forces

captured Mr. Hamdan while he was attempting to flee with his wife and child from the

ongoing military conflict in Afghanistan. Subsequently Mr. Hamdan was turned over to

United States forces and eventually transferred to Guantanamo. On July 3, 2003,

Respondent President Bush found that there was "reason to believe" that Mr. Hamdan was

PETITION FOR WRIT OF MANDAMUS PURSUANT
TO 28 U.S.C. § 1361 OR, IN THE ALTERNATIVE,
WRIT OF HABEAS CORPUS - 1
[43439-0001/SL040950.008]

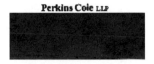

Perkins Coie LLP

eligible for trial by military commission pursuant to his Military Order of November 13,

2001. *See* Press Briefing of Senior Department of Defense ("DOD") Official and Senior

Military Officer, July 3, 2004, attached as Exhibit A to the Swift Decl.

    In early December 2003, in preparation for trial by military commission,

Mr. Hamdan was placed in Camp Echo, *"our facility where we hold the pre-commission*

detainees." Press Briefing of Army Major General Geoffrey D. Miller, Feb. 13, 2004, at 30,

attached as Exhibit C to the Swift Decl. (emphasis added). Conditions in Camp Echo are

tantamount to solitary confinement, in that Mr. Hamdan is held in isolation from all other

prisoners and permitted no visitors except Lieutenant Commander Swift. Yet as of the date

of this Petition, DOD still has not set a trial date or even advised Mr. Hamdan regarding the

nature of the charges on which he is to be tried.

    Lieutenant Commander Swift is under orders to serve as Defense Counsel within the

Office of Military Commissions in the Office of the General Counsel of the United States

Department of Defense, as established pursuant to the Military Order. *See* Official Change

of Duty Orders for Lieutenant Commander Swift, Sept. 2003, attached as Exhibit F to the

Swift Decl. On December 18, 2003, Lieutenant Commander Swift was assigned to serve as

Mr. Hamdan's appointed military defense counsel and he continues to serve in that capacity

as of the date of this Petition. Lieutenant Commander Swift is under legal and military

obligation to zealously represent Mr. Hamdan's interests and as such is a proper "next

friend" for the purpose of this Petition. Lieutenant Commander Swift is legally domiciled in

the Western District of Washington State and is entitled to seek relief in this Court.

Perkins Coie LLP

On January 30, 2004, Mr. Hamdan first met with his detailed defense counsel, Lieutenant Commander Swift. On February 12, 2004, Lieutenant Commander Swift submitted on behalf of Mr. Hamdan, under Article 10 of the Uniform Code of Military Justice ("UCMJ"), a demand for charges and a speedy trial. *See* Memorandum for the Appointing Authority, Feb. 12, 2004, attached as Exhibit D to the Swift Decl. On February 23, 2004, the appointing authority responded by summarily denying Mr. Hamdan's right to a speedy trial. *See* Appointing Authority Opinion Letter, Feb. 23, 2004, attached as Exhibit E to the Swift Decl.

Denial of a speedy trial in Mr. Hamdan's case and his consequential prolonged detention in solitary confinement risks long-term psychological injury to Mr. Hamdan, and threatens to impair materially his ability to assist in the preparation of his own defense should charges ever be brought.

Lieutenant Commander Swift, as next friend to Mr. Hamdan, seeks a Writ of Mandamus or, in the alternative, a Writ of Habeas Corpus ordering Mr. Hamdan's release from pre-commission segregation and prohibiting further prosecution of his case before military commission for Respondent's failure to provide him a speedy trial as required by the UCMJ, military regulations including the Military Order, and the Geneva Conventions of 1949.

Furthermore, on behalf of Mr. Hamdan, Lieutenant Commander Swift seeks a Writ of Mandamus or a Writ of Habeas Corpus that prohibits the Respondents from using a military commission to try Mr. Hamdan, and that prohibits the indefinite detention of

Perkins Coie LLP

Mr. Hamdan for an unscheduled trial before such a commission, when such a commission will be held far beyond the theater of military operations and at a time when Congress has not declared war. Absent relief from this Court, such a commission would act without the necessary congressional approval, and would exist pursuant to a unilateral executive order that purports to suspend the right of the accused to seek habeas review before Article III courts. Indeed, it would also disregard fundamental precepts of equal protection by making only noncitizens subject to these military commissions. A military commission so constituted is an unprecedented, unconstitutional, and dangerously unchecked expansion of executive authority. As such, the President's unilateral Military Order violates separation of powers and equal protection principles of the U.S. Constitution, and constitutes an illegal suspension of the writ of habeas corpus in violation of the suspension clause, U.S. Const. Art. I § 9, cl. 2, and therefore is an illegal and invalid basis for Mr. Hamdan's continued pre-commission segregation.

     As part of these alternative grounds of relief, therefore, Lieutenant Commander Swift also challenges the attempt by Respondent President Bush to oust Article III courts of habeas corpus jurisdiction over prosecutions of individuals apprehended in the course of conducting military operations that occur within territories or leased properties of the United States, solely by labeling such persons as "enemy combatants" under the terms of the Military Order. Particularly because the duration of the war on terrorism is potentially never-ending, and where Respondents have incarcerated Mr. Hamdan without advising him of his status or even the charges on which he presumably will be tried at a place and time

Perkins Coie LLP

undisclosed, it is essential that the U.S. Constitution protect the accused against otherwise

open-ended and unrestrained executive power, by assuring that an Article III court is

permitted to exercise its time-honored civilian review of the military justice system that the

United States Supreme Court has recognized to be essential since *In re Grimley*, 137 U.S.

147 (1890), and *Ex Parte Milligan*, 71 U.S. 2 (1866).[1]

Lieutenant Commander Swift also seeks, on behalf of Mr. Hamdan, a Writ of

Mandamus or a Writ of Habeas Corpus to prohibit the use of a military commission to

detain or prosecute Mr. Hamdan because he is not within the jurisdiction of a military

commission. Mr. Hamdan does not meet the criteria set out in the Military Order for

identifying specific individuals who are subject to its terms. Such individuals include

members of an organization recognized as a "terrorist" organization by the United States,

combatants actively engaged in acts of war or violence against the United States, and those

people who have participated in plans to kill or injure American citizens or to damage

American property. Mr. Hamdan is not a member of a terrorist organization, he was not a

combatant in Afghanistan at the time of his apprehension, he never has taken up arms

---

[1] Though this action may be understood as one seeking a writ of prohibition barring the trial of Petitioner by military commission, as opposed to a writ of mandamus compelling a federal officer to perform a nondiscretionary duty, the distinction between the two is of no moment. *See Calderon v. U.S. Dist. Court for Northern Dist. of Cal.*, 134 F.3d 981, 983 n.3 (9th Cir. 1998) ("The writ of prohibition is the 'fraternal twin' of its more familiar sibling, the writ of mandamus. . . . [and t]he two are evaluated under an identical standard." (citations omitted)). Because nearly all of the relevant precedents speak in terms of mandamus, this petition follows the more traditional nomenclature.

PETITION FOR WRIT OF MANDAMUS PURSUANT
TO 28 U.S.C. § 1361 OR, IN THE ALTERNATIVE,
WRIT OF HABEAS CORPUS - 5
[43439-0001/SI.040950.008]

Perkins Coie LLP

against the United States, and he never has participated in any plan to kill or injure Americans or to damage American property.

I.   JURISDICTION

1.   This action arises under the Constitution, laws, and treaties of the United States, including Articles I, II, III, and VI, and Amendments 5 and 14 of the U.S. Constitution, 28 U.S.C. §§ 1361, 1391, 2241 and 2242, 5 U.S.C. § 702, the All Writs Act, 28 U.S.C. § 1651, 42 U.S.C. § 1981, and the Geneva Conventions.

2.   This Court has subject-matter jurisdiction under 28 U.S.C. §§ 1361 and 1391, as well as 28 U.S.C. § 1331, and may grant relief pursuant to those statutes as well as 28 U.S.C. § 2241, 5 U.S.C. § 702, and the All Writs Act, 28 U.S.C. § 1651. Indeed, three of the five independent grounds for habeas jurisdiction in 28 U.S.C. § 2241(c) are met in this case, subsections (1), (3), and (4). Counsel for Respondent President Bush has observed that such judicial review is available. *See* Alberto R. Gonzales, Editorial, *Martial Justice, Full and Fair*, N.Y. Times, Nov. 30, 2001, at A27 (stating that the Military Order "preserves judicial review in civilian courts" because it permits those arrested "by a military commission . . . to challenge the lawfulness of the commission's jurisdiction through a habeas corpus action in a federal court"). Furthermore, Paragraph (a)12 of Article 2 of the UCMJ, 10 U.S.C. § 802(a)(12), grants jurisdiction over a petition for judicial review filed by or on behalf of parties incarcerated at Guantanamo.

3.   This Court has personal jurisdiction over the parties. Lieutenant Commander Swift is a legal resident of the Western District of Washington. Respondents have substantial contacts with the State of Washington and its residents, and are officers or employees of the United States, or an agency thereof, acting in their official capacity or

Perkins Coie LLP

under color of legal authority throughout the United States, including the Western District of Washington.

II.   VENUE

4.   Venue is proper in the Western District of Washington for this mandamus action pursuant to 28 U.S.C. § 1391(e) as Lieutenant Commander Swift is a legal resident of the Western District, and Respondents are officers or employees of the United States, or an agency thereof, acting in their official capacity or under color of legal authority throughout the United States, including the Western District of Washington. Lieutenant Commander Swift, as next friend and representative of Mr. Hamdan's interests, is the appropriate person to choose a forum in this case as Mr. Hamdan is without the ability to initiate proceedings on his own behalf. Additionally, the Western District is also an appropriate venue to consider a Writ of Habeas Corpus under 28 U.S.C. §§ 1331 and 2241. *See Braden v. 30th Judicial Circuit Court of Ky.*, 410 U.S. 484, 493-500 (1973); *Gherebi v. Bush*, 352 F.3d 1278, 1304-05 (9th Cir. 2003); *Padilla ex rel. Newman v. Bush*, 233 F. Supp. 2d 564, 587 (S.D.N.Y. 2002), *rev'd in part, Padilla v. Rumsfeld*, 352 F.3d 695 (2003), *cert. granted*, 124 S. Ct. 1353 (U.S. Feb. 20, 2004).

III.   PARTIES

5.   Petitioner Lieutenant Commander Swift is a resident of the Western District of Washington, having resided in the Western District immediately prior to going on active duty as a member of the United States Military. He continues to maintain his voter registration address in the Western District of Washington State, and has done so since 1990.

6.   Mr. Hamdan is a native and citizen of Yemen. He was first taken into United States Military custody in November 2001 and has remained in the custody of the United

States Government continuously since that date. Mr. Hamdan has no known family members within the United States or its territories.

7.   Respondent Brigadier General Jay Hood is the Commander of Joint Task Force Guantanamo and is responsible for all matters concerning persons detained as enemy combatants in Guantanamo. General Hood's predecessor, Brigadier General Jeffrey Miller, ordered the placement of Mr. Hamdan in pre-trial segregation in Camp Echo where Mr. Hamdan currently is confined.

8.   Respondent Donald H. Rumsfeld is the Secretary of Defense of the United States, serving at the pleasure of Respondent President Bush, and is ultimately responsible for the administration of the United States Military, including the Office of Military Commissions. As such, Mr. Rumsfeld has full custodial authority over Mr. Hamdan's continued detention and his announced prosecution.

9.   Respondent John D. Altenburg, Jr., is the Appointing Authority for Military Commissions and exercises his authority over the entire military commission process, including over Mr. Hamdan and Lieutenant Commander Swift.

10.   Respondent Brigadier General Thomas L. Hemingway is the Legal Advisor to the Appointing Authority.

11.   Respondent George W. Bush is the President of the United States of America and Commander-in-Chief of the United States Military and the person who decreed the Military Order pursuant to which all Respondents have acted.

IV.   STATEMENT OF FACTS

12.   In the wake of the terrorist acts of September 11, 2001, the United States, at the direction of Respondent President Bush, initiated a military campaign against the Taliban, the organization then in governing power in Afghanistan. On September 18, 2001,

Perkins Coie LLP

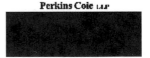

Congress passed a "Use-of-Force" Resolution that authorized Respondent President Bush to use force against "nations, organizations, or persons" that "planned, authorized, committed, or aided the terrorist attacks on September 11, 2001, or [that] harbored such organizations or persons." Joint Resolution 23, Authorization for Use of Military Force, Pub. L. No. 107-40, 115 Stat. 224 (2001) ("Use-of-Force Resolution").

13.   In the course of the ensuing military campaign in Afghanistan that was conducted under the Use-of-Force Resolution, and as part of its effort to overthrow the Taliban, the United States provided military assistance to the Northern Alliance, a loosely knit coalition of Afghani and other military groups opposed to the Taliban government.

14.   In October or November 2001, while working as a civilian driver in Afghanistan, Mr. Hamdan was seized by soldiers loyal to the former king of Afghanistan, Zahir Shah. Those soldiers were searching for Arabs to sell to American forces then engaged in military action against the Taliban. *See* Affidavit of Salim Ahmed Hamdan at 10, attached as Exhibit B to the Declaration of Charles P. Schmitz, Ph.D., filed herewith.[2] Mr. Hamdan was delivered by the Afghani soldiers to the American forces.

15.   Prior to his capture, Mr. Hamdan had been living and working in Afghanistan since 1996 or 1997. He initially had traveled to Afghanistan from his native Yemen in 1996

---

[2] Both the original Arabic Hamdan Affidavit and its English translation are being filed under seal in a manner consistent with the Classified Information Procedures Act, 18 U.S.C. app. 3 § 1 *et seq.* ("CIPA"). Lieutenant Commander Swift adopts this procedure and hereby provides notice pursuant to CIPA § 5 in an abundance of caution. However, he does not believe that any of the information contained in this Petition, its attachments, or the supporting memorandum of law, contains any classified or protected material. In Lieutenant Commander Swift's view, any contention by Respondents that the material is protected would be without merit, as the Appointing Authority of DOD has given his permission to disclose publicly all facts alleged herein, and many other facts alleged herein have been publicly disclosed by Respondents themselves. *See, e.g.,* Press Briefing of Senior DOD Official and Senior Military Officer, Ex. A to the Swift Decl.; Press Briefing of Army Major General Geoffrey D. Miller, Ex. C to the Swift Decl.; Press Interviews attached as Exhibit G to the Swift Decl.

with the intention of entering Tajikistan, but his efforts to do so were unsuccessful.

Mr. Hamdan subsequently accepted a job in Afghanistan as a driver on a farm owned by an individual he came to know as Osama Bin Laden. The job entailed driving Afghani workers back and forth between a local village and the farm. After several months working in that capacity, Mr. Hamdan occasionally was asked to drive Osama Bin Laden to various locations as part of his employment. *See id.* at 9.

16.   During the period that he was employed by Osama Bin Laden as a civilian driver, Mr. Hamdan returned to Yemen twice for entirely personal reasons unrelated to his employment. The first occasion was in 1998 to be married, and the second occasion was in 2000 to attend the wedding of his brother-in-law and to participate in the Hajj, the annual pilgrimage to Mecca, which is a sacred holy event for persons of the Muslim faith such as Mr. Hamdan. In February of 2001, Mr. Hamdan returned to Afghanistan with his wife and daughter to continue working as a civilian driver. He was still working as a driver in October 2001 when American military action against the Taliban began. *See id.*

17.   When Mr. Hamdan learned that Northern Alliance forces were attacking Kandahar, where his wife and two-year-old daughter then were residing, he borrowed a car for the purpose of evacuating them to Pakistan, with the intention of eventually returning with them to Yemen. Mr. Hamdan was able to drive his wife and daughter to Pakistan. Mr. Hamdan then drove back to Afghanistan to return the car to its owner and to sell his personal belongings in order to finance his family's return to Yemen. It was on this return trip to Afghanistan that Mr. Hamdan was seized by Afghan paramilitary forces and subsequently delivered into the custody of United States Military forces. *See id.* at 9-10.

18.   Since his capture in Afghanistan and his surrender to the United States, Mr. Hamdan continuously has been in the physical custody of the United States Military.

PETITION FOR WRIT OF MANDAMUS PURSUANT
TO 28 U.S.C. § 1361 OR, IN THE ALTERNATIVE,
WRIT OF HABEAS CORPUS - 10
[43439-0001/SL040950.008]

Perkins Coie LLP

He has been detained by Respondents now for more than two years. He currently is being detained unlawfully in pre-commission segregation at Camp Echo, a separate confinement facility apart from the Camp Delta detention center located in Guantanamo. Mr. Hamdan is under the direct control of Respondents and their agents.

19.   Mr. Hamdan is not, and never has been, an enemy alien or unlawful combatant of the United States. He never has been a member of Al Qaida or any other organization recognized as a terrorist group by the United States. He never has taken up arms against the United States, or knowingly participated in any way in any plan to kill or injure Americans, or to damage American property, and he has not knowingly assisted anyone in such efforts. Furthermore, Mr. Hamdan did not plan, authorize, commit, or aid in the terrorist attacks against the United States that occurred on September 11, 2001, and he has not "harbored" anyone who had done so. *See id.* at 12.

20.   Nevertheless, acting under the Military Order, in July 2003, approximately 20 months after Mr. Hamdan's apprehension or arrest, Respondent President Bush decreed Mr. Hamdan one of six "enemy combatants" eligible to be tried before a military commission. *See* Military Order, Ex. B to the Swift Decl.; Press Briefing of Senior DOD Official and Senior Military Officer, Ex. A to the Swift Decl.; Press Briefing of Army Major General Geoffrey D. Miller, Ex. C to the Swift Decl.; Press Interviews, Ex. G to the Swift Decl. Pursuant to Respondent President Bush's unilateral determination, Mr. Hamdan was placed in pre-commission segregation in early December 2003. Pre-commission segregation entailed placing Mr. Hamdan in solitary confinement and restricting his access to sunlight as well as limiting his physical activity and exercise. *See* Press Briefing of Army Major General Geoffrey D. Miller, Ex. C to the Swift Decl.

21.   On December 18, 2003, the Chief Defense Counsel for Military Commissions detailed Lieutenant Commander Swift to serve as Mr. Hamdan's appointed military defense counsel. *See* Appointment Letter, Dec. 18, 2003, attached as Exhibit H to the Swift Decl. Prior to that date, Mr. Hamdan was unrepresented by counsel and had no access to legal representation.

22.   Lieutenant Commander Swift met with Mr. Hamdan at Guantanamo for the first time during the last weekend of January 2004. He subsequently met with Mr. Hamdan during the first and last weekends of February 2004 and during the third weekend of March 2004. During these meetings, Mr. Hamdan authorized Lieutenant Commander Swift, in writing, to serve as next friend for the purposes of bringing this Petition. *See* Next Friend Authorization attached as Exhibit I to the Swift Decl.

23.   On February 12, 2004, Lieutenant Commander Swift, acting on behalf of Mr. Hamdan, informed the Appointing Authority via the assigned Prosecutor that, pursuant to the UCMJ, Mr. Hamdan "demands to be informed of the specific charges against him or to be released from pre-commission segregation into general detention." Memorandum for the Appointing Authority at 33, Ex. D to the Swift Decl.

24.   On February 23, 2004, the Legal Advisor to the Appointing Authority responded to Lieutenant Commander Swift's Memorandum with an Opinion Letter that asserted that the UCMJ does <u>not</u> apply to Mr. Hamdan's detention. This assertion was not supported by any legal argument or any citation to authority. *See* Appointing Authority Opinion Letter, Ex. E to the Swift Decl. For all practical purposes, Mr. Hamdan's demand that charges be brought, that he be informed of such charges, and that trial on such charges occur were ignored as if Mr. Hamdan had no rights at all.

Perkins Coie LLP

25.   The logical result of Respondents' conduct to date with regard to Mr. Hamdan is he could serve a potential life sentence without ever being charged with a crime and without being afforded a chance to prove his innocence. Absent relief from this Court, Mr. Hamdan may remain in custody without charges being filed or trial being afforded for the indefinite future, without any recourse to judicial review or any other check or balance on the power of the Executive Branch to keep Mr. Hamdan incarcerated under conditions of its unilateral choosing. The status quo also threatens to coerce unlawfully an admission of wrongdoing from Mr. Hamdan. Indeed, Respondents have informed Mr. Hamdan that he shall remain in custody until such time as he wishes to plead guilty to some unspecified crime against the United States in a manner satisfactory to Respondents, and that his appointed defense counsel is not authorized to mount any legal defense to either his detention or the circumstances of his incarceration, but rather is available only to assist Mr. Hamdan in pleading guilty to some unspecified offense. The treatment of Mr. Hamdan to date and the potential for further abuse strike at the heart of the Constitution's Founders' fears about trial delay – a fear recognized in more modern times by the drafters of the UCMJ.

26.   Mr. Hamdan's transfer into pre-commission segregation at Camp Echo sets him apart from the approximately 600 individuals who have been detained at Camp Delta, Guantanamo, in that Mr. Hamdan is being detained for trial.

27.   Mr. Hamdan's current conditions of confinement place him at significant risk for future psychiatric deterioration, possibly including the development of irreversible psychiatric difficulties. *See* Declaration of Dr. Daryl Matthews ("Matthews Decl."), filed herewith, at 4, ¶ 14.

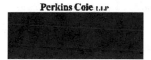

Perkins Coie LLP

28.   Mr. Hamdan's current conditions of confinement in conjunction with the restrictions imposed on his legal representation by DOD make him particularly susceptible to mental coercion and false confession in conjunction with his trial before a potential military commission. *See id.*; Target Letter, Dec. 15, 2003, at ¶ 3 attached as Exhibit J to the Swift Decl.[3]

29.   Mr. Hamdan's current conditions of confinement also may cause mental deterioration to the point of significant impairment of his ability to assess his legal situation and to assist in his own defense. *See* Matthews Decl. at 4, ¶ 15.

30.   Mr. Hamdan's array of pre-isolation stressors place him at particularly high risk, as does the psychological stress of the uncertainty he faces due to the lack of charges against him and the nature and duration of his future confinement. *See id.*

V.   EXHAUSTION OF REMEDIES

31.   Lieutenant Commander Swift, acting on behalf of Mr. Hamdan, communicated his legal challenge to the pre-commission detention of Mr. Hamdan to the Appointing Authority, but was rebuked without recitation to any legal reasoning or legal citation. *See* Appointing Authority Opinion Letter, Ex. E to the Swift Decl. (denying speedy trial claim and applicability of UCMJ). There is no military commission in existence today in which a legal challenge may be raised, and until charges are brought against Mr. Hamdan, no military commission will exist in which he can seek relief. Accordingly, Lieutenant Commander Swift has exhausted any remedies that would be an alternative to this Petition. Because the injury to Mr. Hamdan arises from the Executive Branch's unlawful assertion of

---

[3] In an abundance of caution, Petitioner also has filed the Target Letter under seal pursuant to CIPA § 5.

Perkins Coie LLP

authority, and because he is not being held in a state but rather within a territory or leased property of the United States, only the federal courts can provide a remedy in this case.

VI.   CLAIMS FOR RELIEF

COUNT ONE

DENIAL OF A SPEEDY TRIAL IN VIOLATION OF ARTICLE 10 OF THE UNIFORM CODE OF MILITARY JUSTICE

32.   Lieutenant Commander Swift re-alleges and incorporates by reference paragraphs 1 though 31 above.

33.   The Military Order pursuant to which Mr. Hamdan has been detained for trial purports to be based, in part, on congressional authorization embodied in selected provisions of the UCMJ. In promulgating the Military Order, Respondent President Bush relied, in part, on his authority under 10 U.S.C. § 836, which allows the Executive Branch to prescribe rules for military commissions, so long as they are not inconsistent with the UCMJ. *See* Military Order at 15, Ex. B to the Swift Decl. However, Article 10 of the UCMJ, 10 U.S.C. § 810, provides that any arrest or confinement of an accused must be terminated unless charges promptly are brought and made known to the accused, and speedy trial afforded for a determination of guilt on such charges:

> When any person subject to this chapter is placed in arrest or confinement prior to trial, immediate steps shall be taken to inform him of the specific wrong of which he is accused and to try him or dismiss the charges and release him.

10 U.S.C. § 810.

34.   Mr. Hamdan is a person subject to the UCMJ by virtue of Respondent President Bush's Military Order, as well as by virtue of Article 2 of the UCMJ, 10 U.S.C. § 802(a)(12), which provides that "persons within an area leased by or otherwise reserved or

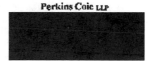

Perkins Coie LLP

acquired for the use of the United States" and under the control of any of the various branches of the military are subject to the UCMJ.

35.   Courts have recognized that delays of the type imposed on Mr. Hamdan are intolerable in the absence of extraordinary or compelling circumstances, and Respondents have provided no reason whatsoever for their indefinite delay in charging Mr. Hamdan. Because Respondents did not take "immediate steps . . . to inform" Mr. Hamdan "of the specific wrong of which he is accused," they now have a clear and nondiscretionary duty under the UCMJ to "release him" from his pre-commission confinement.

COUNT TWO

VIOLATION OF ARTICLE 103 OF THE THIRD GENEVA CONVENTION AND UNITED STATES GOVERNMENT REGULATIONS

36.   Lieutenant Commander Swift re-alleges and incorporates by reference paragraphs 1 through 35 above.

37.   The lengthy pre-trial confinement of Mr. Hamdan violates Article 103 of the 1949 Geneva Convention, as well as United States Government regulations. Article 103 of the Geneva Convention Relative to the Treatment of Prisoners of War, Aug. 12, 1949, 6 U.S.T. 3316, 3394, 75 U.N.T.S. 135, provides that

> [j]udicial investigations relating to a prisoner of war shall be conducted as rapidly as circumstances permit and so that his trial shall take place as soon as possible. A prisoner of war shall not be confined while awaiting trial unless a member of the armed forces of the Detaining Power would be so confined if he were accused of a similar offence, or if it is essential to do so in the interests of national security. *In no circumstances shall this confinement exceed three months.*

(Emphasis added.) Additionally, Article 5 of the Geneva Convention states:

[S]hould any doubt arise as to whether persons . . . belong to any of the categories [entitled to protection as a POW under the Convention], such persons shall enjoy the protection of the present Convention until such time as their status has been determined by a competent tribunal.

38.   Likewise, Army Regulation 190-8, Enemy Prisoners of War, Retained Personnel, Civilian Internees and Other Detainees § 1-6(a) (1997), at 70, attached as Exhibit K to the Swift Decl, requires that United States military forces abide by the provisions of Article 5 of the Geneva Convention. Finally, Department of the Navy, NWP 1-14M: The Commander's Handbook on the Law of Naval Operations 11.7 (1995), at 77, attached as Exhibit L to the Swift Decl., states that "individuals captured as spies or as illegal combatants have the right to assert their claim of entitlement to prisoner-of-war status before a judicial tribunal and to have the question adjudicated."

39.   Again, defendants have a clear nondiscretionary duty to release Mr. Hamdan under the Geneva Convention and under the United States Government's own regulations because he has been detained in pre-commission segregation for more than three months.

COUNT THREE

VIOLATION OF COMMON ARTICLE 3 OF THE GENEVA CONVENTIONS

40.   Lieutenant Commander Swift re-alleges and incorporates by reference paragraphs 1 through 39 above.

41.   Even the few individuals who lack Article 5 and Article 103 protections of the Third Geneva Convention are entitled to the protection of Common Article 3 of that treaty. Common Article 3 prohibits the contracting parties from "the passing of sentences . . . without previous judgment pronounced by a regularly constituted court, affording all the judicial guarantees which are recognized as indispensable by civilized people."

Perkins Coie LLP

42.   In this case, the lengthy pre-trial confinement of Mr. Hamdan without charge, and without process to contest his guilt, amounts to an arbitrary and illegally imposed sentence that is incompatible with fundamental guarantees of due process recognized by all civilized people.

COUNT FOUR

CONSTITUTIONAL VIOLATION:
ESTABLISHMENT OF MILITARY COMMISSIONS IN VIOLATION OF SEPARATION OF POWERS

43.   Lieutenant Commander Swift re-alleges and incorporates by reference paragraphs 1 though 42 above.

44.   Mr. Hamdan's detention is unlawful because he is being detained to face charges before a military commission that is itself the product of unconstitutional Executive Branch action. Respondent President Bush's Military Order providing for the establishment of military commissions is ultra vires and void, because it is an unconstitutional exercise of legislative and judicial power by the Executive Branch. The Constitution vests "All legislative Powers" in Congress, and requires, at a bare minimum, that unlawful conduct be defined in advance, either by positive legislation, or by reference to a recognized body of international law.

45.   Article I of the Constitution grants Congress, not the Executive, the power "To define and punish . . . Offences against the Law of Nations" and "To constitute Tribunals inferior to the Supreme Court." Accordingly, absent circumstances so exigent as to demonstrably rule out resort to Congress, that lawmaking body and not the Chief Executive must be the authorizing agent of the military commissions and the body that defines the offenses for which an accused will be answerable before such commissions.

Perkins Coie LLP

Neither the Use-of-Force Resolution nor any other act of Congress grants to the Executive Branch under the circumstances presented here the authority to establish military commissions, or to define the offenses that will be subject to their exclusive jurisdiction.

46.   In addition to enabling the unlawful exercise of legislative powers, the Military Order also purports to suspend the Writ of Habeas Corpus and to circumscribe the jurisdiction of the federal courts in violation of Art. I § 9 and Art. III § 2 of the Constitution, by denying to persons held subject to the Military Order any access, remedy, or proceeding before "any court of the United States." Military Order at § 7, Ex. B to the Swift Decl. To allow the Chief Executive to proceed in this manner to dismantle the jurisdiction of the federal courts, redesigning the very architecture of American justice, is to succumb to an executive unilateralism decried by both our Founders and twentieth-century courts, and all who came between. *See, e.g., Youngstown Sheet & Tube Co. v. Sawyer*, 343 U.S. 579 (1952). Respondents are under a clear and nondiscretionary duty to obey the Constitution and its foundational command of the separation of powers.

COUNT FIVE

CONSTITUTIONAL VIOLATION:
TRIAL BEFORE MILITARY COMMISSIONS IN VIOLATION OF
EQUAL PROTECTION

47.   Lieutenant Commander Swift re-alleges and incorporates by reference paragraphs 1 through 46 above.

48.   Mr. Hamdan is being detained under the authority of a Military Order that violates Mr. Hamdan's right to equal protection of the laws of the United States. Mr. Hamdan may only be held for trial by a military commission by dint of his noncitizenship. The Military Order, by its terms, applies only to noncitizens. The Military

Order is, to the best of Petitioner's understanding, the first of its kind to make this

citizen/alien distinction. It runs afoul of the very purpose of the Equal Protection Clause of

the United States Constitution. The Framers of the Clause understood that discrimination

against aliens was pervasive and problematic and therefore intentionally extended the reach

of the Clause to "persons" rather than confining it to "citizens." Foremost in their minds was

the language of *Dred Scott v. Sandford*, 60 U.S. (19 How.) 393, 449 (1856), which had been

utilized to limit due process guarantees by framing them as nothing more than the

"privileges of the citizen."

49.   The Military Order reverts back to an antebellum concept of fundamental

rights, one in which aliens are singled out for lesser forms of justice than other citizens.

While the government is given considerable latitude in areas such as immigration, under the

Constitution there is little or no room for government by approximation when it puts people

on one side or the other of a crude line that differentiates between individuals who are given

access to the fundamental protections of civilian justice (including indictment, a jury trial

presided over by a judge not answerable to the prosecutor, and access to an appeal before a

commission independent of the prosecuting authority) and those afforded only a distinctly

less protective and inferior brand of adjudication.[4] If the Executive Branch ever may take

such a step—shunting aliens into a procedure from which all U.S. citizens are spared—he

may do so only upon a convincing showing of necessity that matches the claim of threat to

the fact of alienage. This singling out of aliens for such fundamental disfavor might be

---

[4] The Military Commission rules thus violate notions of procedural due process and Article III protections, not simply in the ways indicated above, but also in matters such as access to exculpatory evidence and the right to confront witnesses. Were a trial of Mr. Hamdan ever to take place before a military commission, Petitioner expects that those matters would become the subject of collateral attack.

justified in rare circumstances, but it is hard to imagine—and, absent explicit congressional

action, impossible to assume that such circumstances are present today.

COUNT SIX

DETENTION IN VIOLATION OF 42 U.S.C. § 1981

50.   Lieutenant Commander Swift re-alleges and incorporates by reference

paragraphs 1 through 49 above.

51.   Mr. Hamdan is being detained under the authority of the Military Order

which contravenes 42 U.S.C. § 1981. That fundamental statutory provision guarantees

equal rights for all persons to give evidence, to receive equal benefit of all laws and

proceedings for the security of persons, and to receive like punishment. Mr. Hamdan is

being unlawfully detained for purposes of trial by military commission because he is a

noncitizen—a citizen who committed the very same acts as Mr. Hamdan could not be

detained under the Military Order and held for trial before a military commission.

COUNT SEVEN

CONSTITUTIONAL AND STATUTORY VIOLATION: INVESTING MILITARY COMMISSIONS WITH SUBJECT-MATTER JURISDICTION CONTRARY TO THE RECOGNIZED LAWS OF WAR

52.   Lieutenant Commander Swift re-alleges and incorporates by reference

paragraphs 1 through 51 above.

53.   In the Military Order, the Respondent President Bush purports to derive his

authority, in part, from provisions of the UCMJ that he claims authorize the use of military

commissions in accordance with the laws of war.

54.   The jurisdiction of military commissions is strictly limited to (1) violations of

the laws of war, or (2) other crimes occurring during or in the immediate aftermath of a declared war while United States forces occupy, and hence must adequately police, territory

captured from the enemy. As a plurality of the Supreme Court held in *Reid v. Covert,* 354

U.S. 1, 21 (1957),

> [t]he jurisdiction of military tribunals is a very limited and
> extraordinary jurisdiction derived from the cryptic language in Art. I,
> § 8 [granting Congress the power to "define and punish. . . Offences
> against the Law of Nations"], and, at most, was intended to be only a
> narrow exception to the normal and preferred method of trial in courts
> of law. Every extension of military jurisdiction is an encroachment
> on the jurisdiction of the civil courts, and, more important, acts as a
> deprivation of the right to jury trial and of other treasured
> constitutional protections.

55.   In the present case, by identifying as individuals subject to its terms anyone

who "is or was a member of the organization known as al Qaida," the Military Order

unlawfully invests military commissions with jurisdiction far exceeding that recognized

under the customary laws of war and the UCMJ.

56.   Moreover, there is no indication that Mr. Hamdan has committed any offense

as to which a military commission might have jurisdiction to try him. Thus, even if

Respondent President Bush is deemed to have been granted congressional authorization to

establish military commissions, he has unlawfully exceeded that authorization by expanding

the jurisdiction of the commissions beyond all legitimate bounds. Such conduct violates

both the UCMJ and the Separation of Powers mandated by the U.S. Constitution.

COUNT EIGHT

THE APPOINTING AUTHORITY, AND ANY MILITARY COMMISSION THAT MAY BE ESTABLISHED, LACKS PERSONAL JURISDICTION OVER MR. HAMDAN

57.   Lieutenant Commander Swift re-alleges and incorporates by reference

paragraphs 1 through 56 above.

PETITION FOR WRIT OF MANDAMUS PURSUANT
TO 28 U.S.C. § 1361 OR, IN THE ALTERNATIVE,
WRIT OF HABEAS CORPUS - 22
[43439-0001/SL040950.008]

Perkins Coie LLP

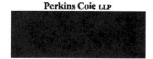

58.   Before a military commission can lawfully assert jurisdiction or detain

Mr. Hamdan, the Military Order requires Respondent President Bush to have reason to

believe that Mr. Hamdan:

(i)   is or was a member of the organization known as al Qaida;

(ii)   has engaged in, aided or abetted, or conspired to commit, acts of
        international terrorism, or acts in preparation therefore, that have
        caused, threaten to cause, or have as their aim to cause, injury to
        or adverse effects on the United States, its citizens, national
        security, foreign policy, or economy; or

(iii)   has knowingly harbored one or more individuals described [in
        the categories above].

Military Order at § 2(a)(1), Ex. B to the Swift Decl.

59.   Mr. Hamdan meets none of the criteria set forth in the Military Order to

identify individuals subject to its terms. Respondents have come forward with no evidence

to justify detention of Mr. Hamdan pursuant to the Military Order, and have adopted a

process and procedure whereby they never will be required to do so and, absent relief from

this Court, whereby Mr. Hamdan never can compel them to do so.

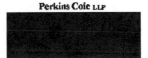

Perkins Coie LLP

PRAYER FOR RELIEF

WHEREFORE, Petitioner prays that this Court grant the following relief:

1.   Grant Petitioner Lieutenant Commander Charles Swift "next friend" status as next friend of Salim Ahmed Hamdan;

2.   Award the Writ of Mandamus or issue an Order directing the respondents to show cause why the writ should not be granted.

3.   If an Order to show cause is issued, to include as part of the Order a prompt schedule to receive briefing from the parties, including a Response from Respondents, and a Reply from Petitioner, on the issues raised in this Petition, followed by a hearing before this Court on any contested factual or legal issues, and production of the body of Mr. Hamdan as appropriate;

4.   After notice and hearing, determine that Mr. Hamdan has been denied a speedy trial; that his incarceration violates the Constitution, laws, treaties and regulations of the United States; that the Military Order is unconstitutional; and that Respondents have no jurisdiction over Mr. Hamdan.

5.   After notice and hearing, issue a Writ of Mandamus that directs Respondents to obey their clear, nondiscretionary duty to follow the Constitution, laws, regulations, and treaties of the United States, and therefore to release Mr. Hamdan from Camp Echo and from further solitary confinement;

6.   After notice and hearing, issue a Writ of Mandamus that orders Respondents not to use the Military Order of November 13, 2001 to detain or bring charges against Mr. Hamdan or anyone else in a Military Commission because that Order violates the U.S. Constitution, U.S. law, and U.S. treaty obligations, both facially and as applied to Mr. Hamdan, and is therefore ultra vires and illegal;

PETITION FOR WRIT OF MANDAMUS PURSUANT
TO 28 U.S.C. § 1361 OR, IN THE ALTERNATIVE,
WRIT OF HABEAS CORPUS - 24
[43439-0001/SL040950.008]

Perkins Coie LLP

7.   Order Respondents promptly to justify as lawful any continued detention of Mr. Hamdan;

8.   Enter an Order that the Court shall retain jurisdiction over this matter to permit Mr. Hamdan to respond to arguments advanced by Respondents on matters related to his continued detention;

9.   In the absence of adequate justification, order Mr. Hamdan's release; and

10.   Grant such other and further relief on behalf of Petitioner and against Respondents as this Court deems just and proper, including but not limited to, as an alternative to a Writ of Mandamus, a Writ of Habeas Corpus.

Perkins Coie LLP

1
2
3
4
5
6
7
8
9
10
11
12
13
14
15
16
17
18
19
20
21
22
23
24
25
26
27
28
29
30
31
32
33
34
35
36
37
38
39
40
41
42
43
44
45
46
47

DATED: April 6, 2004.

NEAL KATYAL

By _____

Neal Katyal, ▮▮▮▮▮▮▮
▮▮▮▮▮▮▮▮▮▮▮▮▮▮

Attorney for Petitioner
Pro Hac Vice Application Pending

LIEUTENANT COMMANDER
CHARLES SWIFT

By _____

Lieutenant Commander Charles Swift,
▮▮▮▮▮▮▮

Next Friend of Salim Ahmed Hamdan
Pro Hac Vice Application Pending

PERKINS COIE LLP

By _____

Harry H. Schneider, Jr., ▮▮▮▮▮▮▮
Joseph M. McMillan, ▮▮▮▮▮▮▮
David R. East, ▮▮▮▮▮▮▮
Charles C. Sipos, ▮▮▮▮▮▮▮

Attorneys for Petitioner

PETITION FOR WRIT OF MANDAMUS PURSUANT
TO 28 U.S.C. § 1361 OR, IN THE ALTERNATIVE,
WRIT OF HABEAS CORPUS - 26
[43439-0001/SL040950.005]

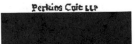
Perkins Coie LLP

UNITED STATES OF AMERICA	)
	)
v.	)
	) **CHARGE:**
SALIM AHMED HAMDAN	) **CONSPIRACY**
a/k/a Salim Ahmad Hamdan	)
a/k/a Salem Ahmed Salem Hamdan	)
a/k/a Saqr al Jadawy	)
a/k/a Saqr al Jaddawi	)
a/k/a Khalid bin Abdallah	)
a/k/a Khalid wl'd Abdallah	)

Salim Ahmed Hamdan (a/k/a Salim Ahmad Hamdan, a/k/a Salem Ahmed Salem Hamdan, a/k/a Saqr al Jadawy, a/k/a Saqr al Jaddawi, a/k/a Khalid bin Abdallah, a/k/a Khalid wl'd Abdallah) is a person subject to trial by Military Commission. At all times material to the charge:

JURISDICTION

1. Jurisdiction for this Military Commission is based on the President's determination of July 3, 2003 that Salim Ahmed Hamdan (a/k/a Salim Ahmad Hamdan, a/k/a Salem Ahmed Salem Hamdan, a/k/a Saqr al Jadawy, a/k/a Saqr al Jaddawi, a/k/a Khalid bin Abdallah, a/k/a Khalid wl'd Abdallah, hereinafter "Hamdan") is subject to his Military Order of November 13, 2001.

2. Hamdan's charged conduct is triable by a military commission.

GENERAL ALLEGATIONS

3. Al Qaida ("the Base"), was founded by Usama bin Laden and others around 1989 for the purpose of opposing certain governments and officials with force and violence.

4. Usama bin Laden is recognized as the *emir* (prince or leader) of al Qaida.

5. A purpose or goal of al Qaida, as stated by Usama bin Laden and other al Qaida leaders, is to support violent attacks against property and nationals (both military and civilian) of the United States and other countries for the purpose of, *inter alia*, forcing the United States to withdraw its forces from the Arabian Peninsula and in retaliation for U.S. support of Israel.

6. Al Qaida operations and activities are directed by a *shura* (consultation) council composed of committees, including: political committee; military committee; security committee; finance committee; media committee; and religious/legal committee.

7. Between 1989 and 2001, al Qaida established training camps, guest houses, and business operations in Afghanistan, Pakistan and other countries for the purpose of supporting violent attacks against property and nationals (both military and civilian) of the United States and other countries.

8. In August 1996, Usama bin Laden issued a public *"Declaration of Jihad Against the Americans,"* in which he called for the murder of U.S. military personnel serving on the Arabian Peninsula.

9. In February of 1998, Usama bin Laden, Ayman al Zawahari and others under the banner of the "International Islamic Front for Jihad on the Jews and Crusaders," issued a *fatwa* (purported religious ruling) requiring all Muslims able to do so to kill Americans – whether civilian or military – anywhere they can be found and to "plunder their money."

10. On or about May 29, 1998, Usama bin Laden issued a statement entitled "The Nuclear Bomb of Islam," under the banner of the "International Islamic Front for Fighting Jews and Crusaders," in which he stated that "it is the duty of the Muslims to prepare as much force as possible to terrorize enemies of God."

11. Since 1989, members and associates of al Qaida, known and unknown, have carried out numerous terrorist attacks, including, but not limited to: the attacks against the American Embassies in Kenya and Tanzania in August 1998; the attack against the USS COLE in October 2000; and the attacks on the United States on September 11, 2001.

CHARGE: CONSPIRACY

12. Salim Ahmed Hamdan (a/k/a Salim Ahmad Hamdan, a/k/a Salem Ahmed Salem Hamdan, a/k/a Saqr al Jadawy, a/k/a Saqr al Jaddawi, Khalid bin Abdallah, a/k/a Khalid wl'd Abdallah, hereinafter "Hamdan"), in Afghanistan, Pakistan, Yemen and other countries, from on or about February 1996 to on or about November 24, 2001, willfully and knowingly joined an enterprise of persons who shared a common criminal purpose and conspired and agreed with Usama bin Laden, Saif al Adel, Dr. Ayman al Zawahari (a/k/a "the Doctor"), Muhammad Atef (a/k/a Abu Hafs al Masri), and other members and associates of the al Qaida organization, known and unknown, to commit the following offenses triable by military commission: attacking civilians; attacking civilian objects; murder by an unprivileged belligerent; destruction of property by an unprivileged belligerent; and terrorism.

13. In furtherance of this enterprise and conspiracy, Hamdan and other members or associates of al Qaida committed the following overt acts:

a. In 1996, Hamdan met with Usama bin Laden in Qandahar, Afghanistan and ultimately became a bodyguard and personal driver for Usama bin Laden. Hamdan served in this capacity until his capture in November of 2001. Based on his contact with Usama bin Laden and members or associates of al Qaida during this period, Hamdan believed that Usama bin Laden and his associates were involved in the attacks on the U.S Embassies in Kenya and Tanzania in August 1998, the attack on the USS COLE in October 2000, and the attacks on the United States on September 11. 2001.

b. From 1996 through 2001, Hamdan:

    1) delivered weapons, ammunition or other supplies to al Qaida members and associates;

2) picked up weapons at Taliban warehouses for al Qaida use and delivered them directly to Saif al Adel, the head of al Qaida's security committee, in Qandahar, Afghanistan;

3) purchased or ensured that Toyota Hi Lux trucks were available for use by the Usama bin Laden bodyguard unit tasked with protecting and providing physical security for Usama bin Laden; and

4) served as a driver for Usama bin Laden and other high ranking al Qaida members and associates. At the time of the al Qaida sponsored attacks on the U.S Embassies in Tanzania and Kenya in August of 1998, and the attacks on the United States on September 11, 2001, Hamdan served as a driver in a convoy of three to nine vehicles in which Usama bin Laden and others were transported to various areas in Afghanistan. Such convoys were utilized to ensure the safety of Usama bin Laden and the others. Bodyguards in these convoys were armed with Kalishnikov rifles, rocket propelled grenades, hand-held radios and handguns.

c. On divers occasions between 1996 and November of 2001, Hamdan drove or accompanied Usama bin Laden to various al Qaida-sponsored training camps, press conferences, or lectures. During these trips, Usama bin Laden would give speeches in which he would encourage others to conduct "martyr missions" (meaning an attack wherein one would kill himself as well as the targets of the attack) against the Americans, to engage in war against the Americans, and to drive the "infidels" out of the Arabian Peninsula.

d. Between 1996 and November of 2001, Hamdan, on divers occasions received training on rifles, handguns and machine guns at the al Qaida-sponsored al Farouq camp in Afghanistan.

Judge Lasnik

UNITED STATES DISTRICT COURT
WESTERN DISTRICT OF WASHINGTON
AT SEATTLE

Lieutenant Commander CHARLES SWIFT, as next friend for SALIM AHMED HAMDAN, Military Commission Detainee, Camp Echo, Guantanamo Bay Naval Base, Guantanamo, Cuba,
 	
     Petitioner,
 	
    v.
 	
DONALD H. RUMSFELD, United States Secretary of Defense; JOHN D. ALTENBURG, Jr., Appointing Authority for Military Commissions, Department of Defense; Brigadier General THOMAS L. HEMINGWAY, Legal Advisor to the Appointing Authority for Military Commissions; Brigadier General JAY HOOD, Commander Joint Task Force, Guantanamo, Camp Echo, Guantanamo Bay, Cuba; GEORGE W. BUSH, President of the United States,
 	
     Respondents.
	NO. C04-0777RSL
	
	NOTICE OF MOTION AND RESPONDENTS' CROSS-MOTION TO DISMISS; CONSOLIDATED RETURN TO PETITION AND MEMORANDUM OF LAW IN SUPPORT OF CROSS-MOTION TO DISMISS
	
	(Note on Motion Calendar for:
	 September 3, 2004)

Respondents respectfully request, pursuant to Rule 12(b)(1) and (b)(6), of the Federal Rules of Civil Procedure, that this Court deny the petition for writ of mandamus or, in the alternative, writ of habeas corpus ("petition"), grant respondents' cross-motion to dismiss, and enter a judgment of dismissal in favor of respondents This cross-motion is made and based on the accompanying memorandum, the pleadings and papers filed herein, and such oral

NOTICE OF MOTION AND RESPONDENTS' CROSS-MOTION TO DISMISS;
CONSOLIDATED RETURN TO PETITION AND MEMORANDUM OF LAW
IN SUPPORT OF CROSS-MOTION TO DISMISS - 1
(C04-0777RSL)

---

* Redactions on this page and the following have been added for privacy purposes. – *Eds.*

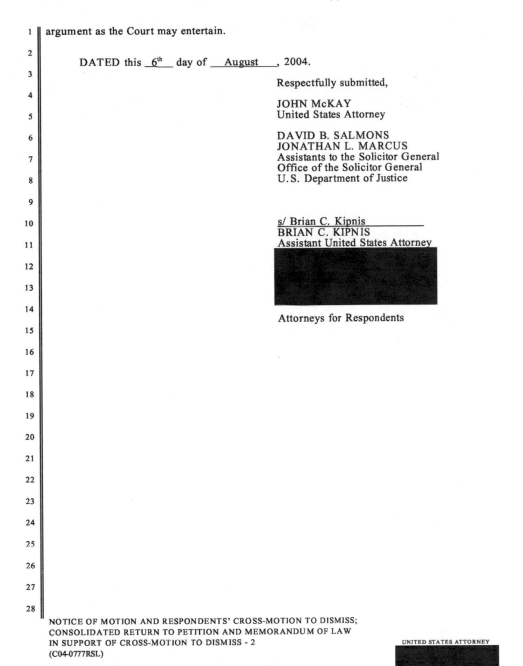

1   argument as the Court may entertain.

2

         DATED this _6ᵗʰ_ day of ___August___, 2004.

3

                          Respectfully submitted,

4

                          JOHN McKAY

5   United States Attorney

6   DAVID B. SALMONS
                          JONATHAN L. MARCUS

7   Assistants to the Solicitor General
                          Office of the Solicitor General

8   U.S. Department of Justice

9

10   s/ Brian C. Kipnis
                          BRIAN C. KIPNIS

11   Assistant United States Attorney

12

13

14

                          Attorneys for Respondents

15

16

17

18

19

20

21

22

23

24

25

26

27

28

NOTICE OF MOTION AND RESPONDENTS' CROSS-MOTION TO DISMISS;
CONSOLIDATED RETURN TO PETITION AND MEMORANDUM OF LAW
IN SUPPORT OF CROSS-MOTION TO DISMISS - 2
(C04-0777RSL)

UNITED STATES ATTORNEY

MEMORANDUM OF POINTS AND AUTHORITIES

INTRODUCTION

Respondents, through undersigned counsel, oppose and hereby move to dismiss the petition for writ of mandamus or habeas corpus ("petition") filed in this case.

    The petition raises statutory, constitutional, and treaty-based challenges to the President's authority to subject Salim Ahmed Hamdan to trial by military commission and to confine him in connection with the commission proceedings. The petition also challenges the President's authority to detain Hamdan as an enemy combatant and seeks Hamdan's release.

As explained in our Motion to Dismiss or Transfer dated July 16, 2004, this Court lacks jurisdiction over the petition for two separate reasons. First, the petitioner, Charles Swift, does not have standing to bring this action as a next friend to Hamdan, because Swift has failed to show that Hamdan was unable to bring the action in his own name. Second, this Court lacks jurisdiction under the habeas statute, because none of the respondents resides in this District. Although petitioner has styled his petition as a request for a writ of mandamus or, in the alternative, habeas corpus, his petition – which challenges the legality of his custody pursuant to the military commission proceedings and the legality of his detention as an enemy combatant – is the exclusive province of habeas corpus. Even if mandamus were an appropriate vehicle in these circumstances, this Court would remain an improper forum, because neither Hamdan, the real party in interest, nor Swift, the nominal party, resides in this District.

In the event this Court declines to dismiss the petition for lack of jurisdiction or to transfer the case to the District of Columbia, the Court should not consider the petition at this time, because the military commission proceedings against Hamdan are ongoing. Indeed, both the government and Hamdan have proposed that the trial begin in December. The law is clear that the federal courts will not intercede in military process, but rather, will wait until such process is complete before considering challenges to the jurisdiction of the Military Commission.

Petitioner's claims lack merit in any event. Military commissions have a long historical pedigree, and the Supreme Court has repeatedly approved their use for wartime trials of enemy combatants such as Hamdan. See Ex parte Quirin, 317 U.S. 1 (1942); Yamashita v. Styer, 327 U.S. 1 (1946). Petitioner's claims – regardless of how they are styled[1] – must therefore be dismissed.

STATEMENT OF FACTS

1. On September 11, 2001, the United States endured a foreign enemy attack more savage, deadly, and destructive than any sustained by the Nation on any one day in its history. That morning, agents of the al Qaida terrorist network hijacked four commercial airliners loaded with passengers and jet fuel and flew the planes as missiles towards targets in the Nation's financial center and its seat of government. Two of the planes struck the World Trade Center office towers in New York City just as the business day began, and a third hit the headquarters of the Department of Defense at the Pentagon. The fourth was brought down in Pennsylvania by its passengers before it could reach its target, presumed to be the United States Capitol or the White House. The September 11 attacks killed approximately 3,000 persons, exceeding the loss of life inflicted at Pearl Harbor. The attacks also caused injury to thousands more persons, destroyed hundreds of millions of dollars in property, and exacted a heavy toll on the Nation's infrastructure and economy.

The President, acting as Commander in Chief, took immediate action to defend the country and prevent additional attacks. Congress swiftly enacted its support of the President's use of "all necessary and appropriate force against those nations, organizations, or persons he determines planned, authorized, committed, or aided the terrorist attacks that occurred on September 11, 2001." Authorization for Use of Military Force,

---

[1] ...

Pub. L. No. 107-40, 115 Stat. 224 (2001) (AUMF). Congress emphasized that the forces responsible for the September 11 attacks "continue to pose an unusual and extraordinary threat to the national security," and that "the President has authority under the Constitution to take action to deter and prevent acts of international terrorism against the United States." Ibid.

The President ordered the armed forces of the United States to Afghanistan to subdue the al Qaida terrorist network and the Taliban regime that supported it. In the course of those ongoing operations, United States and coalition forces have removed the Taliban from power, have eliminated the "primary source of support to the terrorists who viciously attacked our Nation on September 11, 2001," and have "seriously degraded" al Qaida's training capabilities. Office of the White House Press Secretary, Letter from the President to the Speaker of the House of Representatives and the President Pro Tempore of the Senate (Sept. 19, 2003) (<www.whitehouse.gov/news/releases/2003/09/20030919-1.html>). Al Qaida and the Taliban nonetheless remain a significant threat to United States and coalition forces. Moreover, Usama bin Laden has continued his call to al Qaida and its supporters to maintain their war against the United States, and the United States and other nations have been subject to attacks throughout the world. See, e. g., Tape urges Muslim fight against U.S. (Feb. 2, 2003) (<www.cnn.com/2003/ALLPOLITICS/02/11/powell.binladen/index.html>). See also Qaeda Tapes Taunt U.S., France (Feb. 24, 2004) (<www.cbsnews.com/stories/2004/01/04/terror/main591217.shtml>).

2. In the context of both the removal of the Taliban from power and in the broader efforts to dismantle the al Qaida terrorist network and its supporters, the United States, consistent with the Nation's settled historical practice in times of war, has seized and detained numerous persons fighting for and associated with the enemy during the course of the ongoing military campaign. Individuals taken into U. S. control in connection with the ongoing hostilities undergo a multi-step screening process to determine if their detention is necessary. Only a small fraction of those captured in connection with the current conflict and subjected to the screening process have been designated for detention at Guantanamo. Upon their arrival at Guantanamo, detainees are subject to an additional assessment by military commanders regarding the need for their detention. The military is currently detaining approximately 600 aliens at Guantanamo.

3. Equally consistent with historical practice, the President has ordered the establishment of military commissions to try a subset of those detainees for violations of the laws of war and other applicable laws. In doing so, the President expressly relied on "the authority vested in me *** as Commander in Chief of the Armed Forces of the United States by the Constitution and the laws of the United States of America, including the [AUMF] and sections 821[2] and 836[3] of title 10, United States Code." Detention, Treatment, and Trial of Certain Non-Citizens in the War Against Terrorism, 66 Fed. Reg. 57833 (Nov. 13, 2001) (hereinafter "Military Order").

The President made several findings that undergird the Military Order. He found, inter alia, that "[i]nternational terrorists, including members of al Qaida, have carried out attacks on United States diplomatic and military personnel and facilities abroad and on citizens and property within the United States on a scale that has created a state of armed conflict that requires the use of the United States Armed Forces," §1(a); that such terrorists "possess both the capability and the intention to undertake further terrorist attacks against the United States that, if not detected and prevented, will cause

---

[2] . . .

[3] . . .

mass deaths, mass injuries, and massive destruction of property, and may place at risk the continuity of the operations of the United States Government," §1(c); that, in order "to protect the United States and its citizens, and for the effective conduct of military operations and prevention of terrorist attacks, it is necessary for individuals subject to" the Military Order to "be detained, and, when tried, *** be tried for violations of the laws of war and other applicable laws by military tribunals," §1(e); and that "[g]iven the danger to the safety of the United States and the nature of international terrorism *** it is not practicable to apply in military commissions under this order the principles of law and the rules of evidence generally recognized in the trial of criminal cases in the United States district courts," §1(f).

. . .

The Order authorizes the Secretary of Defense to issue orders and regulations governing the Military Commissions, "which shall at a minimum provide for," among other things, "a full and fair trial, with the military commission sitting as the triers of both fact and law," id. §4(c)(2); "admission of such evidence as would *** have probative value to a reasonable person," id. §4(c)(3); "conviction only upon the concurrence of two-thirds of the members of the commission present at the time of the vote, a majority being present," id. §4(c)(6); and "submission of the record of the trial, including any conviction or sentence, for review and final decision by" the President or the Secretary of Defense if so designated by the President," id. §4(c)(8).

The Secretary of Defense, acting pursuant to the Military Order, established the Appointing Authority for Military Commissions.[4] See Department of Defense Directive No. 5105.70, Feb. 10, 2004. The Appointing Authority has many responsibilities, including to appoint military commissions to try individuals subject to the Military Order; designate a judge advocate of any United States Armed Force to serve as a Presiding Officer over each military commission; approve and refer charges against such individuals; approve plea agreements; decide interlocutory questions certified by the Presiding Officer; ensure military commission proceedings are open to the maximum extent practicable; and order that investigative or other resources be made available to Defense Counsel and the Accused to the extent necessary for a full and fair trial. Id. §4.

The military commissions that the Appointing Authority establishes have jurisdiction over individuals subject to the Military Order who are "alleged to have committed an offense in a charge that has been referred to the Commission by the Appointing Authority." Military Commission Order No. 1, 32 C.F.R. §9.3(a) (2003). That charge must allege "violations of the laws of war" or "other offenses triable by military commission." Id. §9.3(b). An individual so charged (the "Accused") is assigned defense counsel (one or more military officers who are judge advocates of any United States armed force) to conduct his defense before the Commission. Id. §9.4(c)(2). The Accused may choose to replace the detailed defense counsel with another military officer who is a judge advocate, provided that such officer is available. Id. §9.4(c)(2)(iii)(A). The Accused may also retain a civilian attorney of choice at no expense to the United States government, ibid., provided that such attorney meets certain criteria, id. §9.4(c)(2)(iii)(B).

Under the procedures the Secretary established for the commissions, the Accused must, inter alia, (1) receive a copy of the charges in English and, if appropriate, in another language that the Accused understands, "sufficiently in advance of trial to prepare a defense"; (2) be presumed innocent until proven guilty; and (3) be found not guilty

---

[4] The Secretary designated John D. Altenburg, Jr., a respondent in this action, to serve as the Appointing Authority.

unless the offense is proved beyond a reasonable doubt. Id. §§9.5(a), (b),(c). The prosecution must provide the defense "with access to evidence [it] intends to introduce at trial" and to "evidence known to the prosecution that tends to exculpate the Accused." Id. §9.5(e). The Accused is permitted but not required to testify at trial, and the Commission may not draw an adverse inference from a decision not to testify. Id. §9.5(f). The Accused also "may obtain witnesses and documents for [his] defense, to the extent necessary and reasonably available as determined by the Presiding Officer," id. §9.5(h), and may present evidence at trial and cross-examine prosecution witnesses, id. §9.5(i). In addition, once a Commission's finding on a charge becomes final, "the Accused shall not again by tried" for that charge. Id. §9.5(p).

The Secretary of Defense has directed the commissions to provide for a "full and fair trial"; to "[p]roceed impartially and expeditiously"; and to "[h]old open proceedings except where otherwise decided by the Appointing Authority or the Presiding Officer[.]" Id. §§9.6(b)(1),(2),(3). Proceedings may be closed in order to (1) protect classified information; (2) prevent unauthorized disclosure of protected information; (3) protect the physical safety of participants, including witnesses; and (4) protect intelligence and law enforcement sources and methods. Id. §9.6(b)(3). In no circumstance, however, may the detailed defense counsel be excluded from a proceeding, ibid., and in no circumstance may the Commission admit into evidence information not presented to detailed defense counsel, id. §9.6(d)(5)(ii)(C).

Once a trial is completed (including sentencing in the event of a guilty verdict), the Presiding Officer must "transmit the authenticated record of trial to the Appointing Authority," id. at §9.6(h)(1), which "shall promptly perform an administrative review of the record of trial," id. §9.6(h)(3). If the Appointing Authority determines that the commission proceedings are "administratively complete," the Appointing Authority must transmit the record of trial to the Review Panel, which consists of three military officers,[5] at least one of whom has experience as a judge. Id. 9.6(h)(4). The Review Panel must return the case to the Appointing Authority for further proceedings when a majority of that panel "has formed a definite and firm conviction that a material error of law occurred." Military Commission Instruction No. 9, §4(C)(1)(a). On the other hand, if a majority of the panel finds no such error, it must forward the case to the Secretary with a written opinion recommending that (1) each finding of guilt "be approved, disapproved, or changed to a finding of Guilty to a lesser-included offense" and (2) the sentence imposed "be approved, mitigated, commuted, deferred, or suspended." Id. §4(C)(1)(b). "An authenticated finding of Not Guilty," however, "shall not be changed to a finding of Guilty." 32 C.F.R. §9.6(h)(2).

The Secretary must review the trial record and the Review Panel's recommendation and "either return the case for further proceedings or *** forward it to the President with a recommendation as to disposition," if the President has not designated him the final decision-maker. Military Commission Instruction No. 9. §5. In the absence of such a designation, the President makes the final decision, and may approve or disapprove the commission's findings or "change a finding of Guilty to a finding of Guilty to a lesser-included offense, or mitigate, commute, defer, or suspend the sentence imposed or any portion thereof." Id. §6.

4. Pursuant to the Military Order, on July 3, 2003, the President designated Salim Ahmed Hamdan, a Guantanamo detainee on whose behalf this petition has been filed, for trial by military commission, upon determining that there is reason to believe that Hamdan was a member of al Qaida or otherwise involved in terrorism against the

---

[5] These officers may include civilians commissioned pursuant to 10 U.S. C. §603.

United States. July, 2003 Background Briefing on Military Commissions..., at 1. As a result of this designation, on December 18, 2003, the Department of Defense (DOD) assigned Lieutenant Commander Charles Swift, the named petitioner, to meet with and defend Hamdan before a military commission. Dec. 18, 2003 Memorandum Detailing Defense Counsel.... That same month, Hamdan, who had been housed with other enemy combatants at Guantanamo, was moved to a different facility at Guantanamo, Camp Echo, where he has his own cell in which he may have private discussions with his lawyers. Feb. 13, 2004 Briefing on Detainee Operations at Guantanamo Bay..., at 10.

5. On April 6, 2004, Swift filed this petition as an alleged next-friend of Hamdan challenging Hamdan's pre-trial confinement, prospective trial, and continued detention on multiple statutory, constitutional, and treaty-based grounds..... The petition requests, among other things, an order mandating Hamdan's release from confinement in Camp Echo, enjoining respondents from enforcing the Military Order of November 13, 2001, compelling respondents to justify Hamdan's continued detention as an enemy combatant, and mandating Hamdan's release from U.S. custody in the absence of adequate justification.....

6. On July 9, 2004, the prosecutor charged Hamdan with conspiring with Usama Bin Laden, Dr. Ayman al Zawahari (a/k/a "the Doctor"), and others members and associates of al Qaida from on or about February 1996 to on or about November 24, 2001, to commit offenses triable by military commission – namely, attacking civilians, attacking civilian objects, murder by an unprivileged belligerent, destruction of property by an unprivileged belligerent, and terrorism. Charge ¶12...; see 32 C.F.R. §§11.6(a)(2), (a)(3), (b)(2), (b)(3), (b)(4). The charge alleges that "[b]etween 1989 and 2001, al Qaida established training camps, guest houses, and business operations in Afghanistan, Pakistan and other countries for the purpose of supporting violent attacks against property and nationals (both military and civilian) of the United States and other countries." Id. ¶7. It also alleges that "[i]n February of 1998, Usama Bin Laden, Ayman al Zawahiri and others under the banner of the 'International Islamic Front for Jihad on the Jews and Crusaders,' issued a fatwa (purported religious ruling) requiring all Muslims able to do so to kill Americans – whether civilian or military – anywhere they can be found and to 'plunder their money.'" Id. ¶9. It further alleges that "[s]ince 1989, members and associates of al Qaida *** have carried out numerous terrorist attacks, including, but not limited to: the attacks against the American Embassies in Kenya and Tanzania in August 1998; the attack against the USS COLE in October 2000; and the attacks on the United States on September 11, 2001." Id. ¶11.

As for Hamdan's role in the conspiracy, the charge asserts that "[i]n 1996, Hamdan met with Usama bin Laden in Qandahar, Afghanistan, and ultimately became a bodyguard and personal driver for Usama bin Laden," serving in that capacity "until his capture in November of 2001." Id. ¶13(a). The charge further alleges that, in furtherance of al Qaida's objectives, Hamdan from 1996 through 2001 "delivered weapons, ammunition or other supplies to al Qaida members and associates," id. ¶13(a); "picked up weapons at Taliban warehouses for al Qaida use and delivered them directly to Saif al Adel, the head of al Qaida's security committee, in Qandahar, Afghanistan," id. ¶13(b)(1); "purchased or ensured that Toyota Hi Lux trucks were available for use by the Usama bin Laden bodyguard unit tasked with protecting and providing physical security" for bin Laden, id. ¶13(b)(2); "served as a driver in a convoy of three to nine vehicles in which Usama bin Laden and others were transported to various areas in Afghanistan" at the time of the 1998 embassy attacks and the September 11 attacks, id. ¶13(b)(4); "drove or accompanied Usama bin Laden to various al Qaida sponsored training camps, press conferences, or lectures," id. ¶13(c); and "received training on rifles, handguns and machine guns at the al Qaida-sponsored al Farouq camp in Afghanistan," id. ¶13(d).

The Appointing Authority approved and referred the charge to a Military Commission on July 13, 2004. . . . . The charge is noncapital, so Hamdan faces a maximum sentence of life imprisonment. Both the government and Hamdan have proposed that his Commission trial begin in December. Hamdan is scheduled to appear before the Commission on August 23, 2004, for preliminary matters.[6]

ARGUMENT

Since the founding of this nation, the military has used military commissions during wartime to try violations against the laws of war. Nearly ninety years ago, Congress recognized this historic practice and approved its continuing use. And nearly sixty years ago, the Supreme Court upheld the use of military commissions during World War II against a series of challenges, including cases involving a presumed American citizen, captured in the United States, Ex parte Quirin, 317 U.S. 1 (1942); the Japanese military governor of the Phillippines, Yamashita v. Styer, 327 U. S. 1 (1946); German nationals who alleged that they worked for civilian agencies of the German government in China, Johnson v. Eisentrager, 339 U. S. 763 (1950); and the spouse of a serviceman posted in occupied Germany, Madsen v. Kinsella, 343 U.S. 341 (1952). Despite the fact that both Congress and the Judiciary have blessed the Executive's use of military commissions during wartime, despite the fact that the statutory framework today is identical in all material respects to that which existed during the prior legal challenges, and despite the fact that the President has inherent power as Commander in Chief to establish military commissions in the war against al Qaida and the Taliban, petitioner contends that Hamdan's detention pursuant to the Military Order violates federal statutes, the Constitution, and the Geneva Conventions. As discussed in more detail below, these claims cannot be heard at this time and lack merit in any event.[7]

I. THIS COURT SHOULD ABSTAIN UNTIL THE MILITARY PROCEEDINGS ARE COMPLETED AND HAMDAN HAS EXHAUSTED HIS MILITARY REMEDIES

Petitioner asks this Court to intercede in the midst of an ongoing military process designed to determine whether Hamdan has committed violations of the laws of war and other offenses triable by military commission. This Court should reject this invitation. Petitioner cannot cite any example of a federal court enjoining a military commission – or a military tribunal of any sort – convened during wartime from trying someone whom the Executive Branch has determined is affiliated with enemy forces. That is because the law is clear that federal courts generally will not consider challenges to military process, jurisdictional or otherwise, until that process has run its course.

---

[6] Before his trial, Hamdan will have the opportunity to challenge his status as an enemy combatant before a Combatant Status Review Tribunal. See July 7, 2004 Order Establishing Combatant Status Review Tribunal, available at www.defenselink.mil/news/Jul/2004/d20040707review.pdf. That Tribunal will only confirm whether Hamdan is properly classified as an enemy combatant, not whether he committed the offense approved and referred for trial by the Military Commission.

[7] These claims cannot be heard for the additional reasons that petitioner lacks standing to serve as Hamdan's next-friend or as a third party, this Court lacks habeas jurisdiction, a mandamus petition is not appropriate given the nature of petitioner's claims, and this Court is not a proper venue even if mandamus were a proper vehicle. . . . .

The leading case governing the role of the federal courts in addressing challenges to military process is Schlesinger v. Councilman, 420 U.S. 738 (1975). There, the Supreme Court rejected an Army captain's attempt to enjoin his impending court-martial on charges that he wrongfully possessed, transferred, and sold marijuana. Councilman contended that the military court lacked jurisdiction because the charges were not "service connected," but the Court held that such a contention did not constitute a sufficient basis to intervene in the military proceedings.

At the outset, the Court recognized that "'military law *** is a jurisprudence which exists separate and apart from the law which governs in our federal judicial establishment.'" Id. at 746 (quoting Burns v. Wilson, 346 U.S. 137, 140 (1953)). In determining the proper role for federal courts presented with challenges to military proceedings, the Court found instructive the federal approach to ongoing state court proceedings. The Court observed that "considerations of comity [and] the necessity of respect for coordinate judicial systems have led this Court to preclude equitable intervention in pending state criminal proceedings unless the harm sought to be averted is both great and immediate, of a kind that cannot be eliminated by *** defense against a single criminal prosecution." Id. at 756 (internal quotation marks omitted). The Court further observed that this abstention doctrine is "similar" to "the requirement of the exhaustion of administrative remedies," which is predicated on "the special competence of agencies *** to develop the facts, to apply the law in which they are peculiarly expert, and to correct their own errors." Ibid. "These considerations[,]" the Court concluded, "apply in equal measure to the balance governing the propriety of equitable intervention in pending court-martial proceedings." Id. at 757.

The Court further explained that principles of abstention and exhaustion have special salience in the military context: As the Court observed, "there is here something more that, in our view, counsels strongly against the exercise of equity power even where, under the administrative exhaustion rule, intervention might be appropriate." Ibid (emphasis added). The Court identified that "something" as "the unique military exigencies" that set the military apart from civilian society and that relate to its "primary business *** to fight or be ready to fight wars should the occasion arise." Ibid. Based on these "strong considerations," id. at 761, the Court held that "when a serviceman charged with crimes by military authorities can show no harm other than that attendant to resolution of his case in the military court system, the federal district courts must refrain from intervention, by way of injunction or otherwise." Id. at 758.

The Court rejected Councilman's contention that the threat of being deprived of his liberty by a court lacking jurisdiction constituted "irreparable harm" justifying federal court intervention. The Court explained that "'(c)ertain types of injury, in particular, the cost, anxiety, and inconvenience of having to defend against a single criminal prosecution, (can) not by themselves be considered "irreparable" in the special legal sense of that term.'" Id. at 755 (quoting Younger v. Harris, 401 U.S. 37, 46 (1971)) (parentheses in Councilman).

The principles that led the Councilman Court to reject federal court intervention in ongoing military proceedings apply with even greater force here, where the President in his capacity as Commander in Chief, and with the approval of Congress,[8] established the military commissions challenged herein upon finding that they are "necessary" for

---

[8] As discussed in greater detail below, the Supreme Court has repeatedly held that one of the provisions that President Bush expressly invoked in establishing the military commissions, 10 U.S.C. §821, constitutes congressional authorization for the President to convene military commissions during wartime to try violations of the laws of war. And the Supreme Court recently made clear in Hamdi v. Rumsfeld, 124 S. Ct. 2633, 2640 (2004) (plurality opinion); id. at 2679 (Thomas, J., dissenting), that the AUMF triggered the exercise

"the effective conduct of military operations and prevention of terrorist attacks." Military Order §1(e). Given that the Military Order applies to enemy combatants who are captured during the ongoing war with al Qaida and its supporters, the traditional deference courts pay the military justice system is at the pinnacle. The Executive Branch, not this court, bears the responsibility for protecting the nation from foreign attack and is in the best position to determine appropriate procedures for trying enemy combatants charged with violations of the laws of war consistent with national security and the need to provide a full and fair trial. See id. §§1(f); 4(c)(2). The Executive Branch has exercised that authority in this war by establishing military commissions and an elaborate set of procedures governing their use, including multiple levels of review. See Statement of Facts Part 3, supra. In these circumstances, this Court should await the outcome of Hamdan's military prosecution before considering his legal challenges.[9]

. . .

II.   HAMDAN'S DETENTION DOES NOT VIOLATE 10 U.S.C. §810

Petitioner argues . . . that Hamdan's present confinement at Camp Echo violates his alleged right to a speedy trial under Article 10 of the Uniform Code of Military Justice (UCMJ), 10 U. S. C. §810. Petitioner's claim lacks merit for at least three reasons. First, the President has designated Hamdan for trial by a military commission for violation of the laws of war, so provisions of the UCMJ governing courts-martial do not apply to him. . . . . Second, as an enemy combatant who is subject to detention for the duration of the ongoing armed conflict, see Hamdi, 124 S. Ct. at 2641–2642 (plurality opinion); id. at 2681–2682 (Thomas, J., dissenting), Hamdan has no legal basis on which to raise a speedy trial claim related to the nature or length of his detention. That is because he has no legal entitlement to a particular form of detention (e.g., to stay at Camp Delta) even assuming he were not subject to trial. Third, even if Article 10 were applicable to him, Hamdan would not be entitled to any relief, because he has failed to show that the military did not act with "reasonable diligence" in bringing and approving charges against him, much less that he has been prejudiced by the alleged delay.

A.   The Provisions Of The UCMJ Applicable To Courts-Martial Do Not Apply To Hamdan, Whom The President Has Designated For Trial Before A Military Commission.

Petitioner argues . . . that because the UCMJ extends courts-martial jurisdiction over "persons within an area leased by *** the United States," 10 U.S.C.§802(a)(12), it follows

---

of the President's traditional war powers, including, under 10 U.S.C. §821, the power to convene military commissions.

[9] If a United States servicemen does not have access to the federal courts pending his court-martial, surely a nonresident alien captured during wartime should have no greater access pending his military trial. Cf. Johnson v. Eisentrager, 339 U. S. 763, 783 (1950) (refusing to read Fifth Amendment in manner that would put enemy aliens "in more protected position than our soldiers."). The exigencies presented by fighting a war with a ruthless enemy are undoubtedly greater than the exigencies related to the need to maintain discipline in the armed forces and relied on by Councilman.

The fact that the Supreme Court in Ex parte Quirin, 317 U. S. 1 (1942), considered the saboteurs' claims before the military commission proceedings were complete does not support departure from abstention principles here. Quirin was decided over 30 years before Councilman and well before the abstention doctrine underlying Councilman had been established. See Younger v. Harris, 401 U.S. 37 (1971). Moreover, in Quirin, the petitioners included a presumed American citizen and, unlike Hamdan, were facing the prospect of imminent execution.

that all of the substantive and procedural rules set out in the UCMJ, including Article 10, are automatically applicable to him. There is a crucial flaw in his logic. The rules set out in the UCMJ apply to courts-martial, not commissions. Pursuant to the Military Order, the President designated Hamdan as eligible for trial before a military commission. See Order §2(b). While the UCMJ recognizes the jurisdiction of military commissions to try violations of the laws of war, see Article 21 ("The provisions of this chapter conferring jurisdiction upon courts-martial do not deprive military commissions *** of concurrent jurisdiction with respect to offenders or offenses that by statute or by the law of war may be tried by military commissions"), it does not purport to subject such commissions to its comprehensive set of rules governing courts-martial. Indeed, the Supreme Court has repeatedly recognized that while Congress has prescribed in detailed fashion the jurisdiction and procedures governing courts-martial, it has taken a hands-off approach with respect to wartime military commissions, by recognizing and approving their use but not regulating their procedures.

In Yamashita v. Styer, 327 U. S. 1 (1946), the Supreme Court expressly rejected the contention that a military commission convened to try General Yamashita, an enemy combatant, was subject to the procedures in the Articles of War (the precursor to the UCMJ) governing courts-martial. The Court explained that, by Article 15 of the Articles of War (now Article 21 of the UCMJ), Congress "recogniz[ed] military commissions in order to preserve their traditional jurisdiction over enemy combatants unimpaired by the Articles," and "gave sanction *** to any use of the military commission contemplated by the common law of war." Id. at 19. Although the Court relied in part on the fact that General Yamashita did not fall within the categories of persons made subject to the jurisdiction of courts-martial by the Articles of War, the Court also based its holding on the fact that "the military commission before which he was tried, though sanctioned, and its jurisdiction saved, by Article 15, was not convened by virtue of the Articles of War, but pursuant to the common law of war," Ibid. (emphasis added). Moreover, the Court in Madsen v. Kinsella, 343 U.S. 341 (1952), subsequently rejected any suggestion that the Articles of War would apply to the trial by commission of a person subject to court-martial, upholding the trial by military commission of a U. S. citizen subject to the jurisdiction of courts-martial, notwithstanding that the commission trial was not conducted in strict accordance with the specific Articles of War governing courts-martial.[14]

The Madsen Court characterized the unique nature and purpose of military commissions:

> Since our nation's earliest days, such commissions have been constitutionally recognized agencies for meeting many urgent governmental responsibilities related to war. They have been called our commonlaw war courts. They have taken many forms and borne many names. Neither their procedure nor their jurisdiction has been prescribed by statute. It has been adapted in each instance to the need that called it forth.

Id. at 346–348 (footnotes omitted) (emphasis added). The Court went on to hold that, "[i]n the absence of attempts by Congress to limit the President's power, it appears that,

---

[14] In Reid v. Covert, 354 U. S. 1 (1957), a plurality of the Supreme Court ruled that a U.S.-citizen civilian spouse of a serviceman could not be subjected to the jurisdiction of a court-martial during peacetime. The Reid plurality concluded that Madsen was not controlling because Madsen involved a trial in occupied enemy territory, where "the Army commander can establish military or civilian commissions as an arm of the occupation to try everyone in the occupied area." 354 U. S. at 35 n.63. Madsen remains good law today, and the Supreme Court has limited Reid to its facts. See United States v. Verdugo Urquidez, 494 U. S. 259, 270 (1990).

as Commander-in-Chief of the Army and Navy of the United States, he may, in time of war, establish and prescribe the jurisdiction and procedure of military commissions, and of tribunals in the nature of such commissions, in territory occupied by Armed Forces of the United States." Id. at 348. The Court explained that, in contrast to Congress' active regulation of "the jurisdiction and procedure of United States courts-martial," id. at 349, Congress had shown "evident restraint" with respect to making rules for military commissions, ibid. The Court further explained that Article 15 (now UCMJ Article 21) reflected Congress' intent to allow the Executive Branch to exercise its discretion as to what form of tribunal to employ during wartime. Id. at 353.

When the President established military commissions to try unlawful combatants in the ongoing armed conflict with al Qaida and the Taliban and set out the procedures that will govern them, he exercised the very discretion that the Madsen Court held was implicit in his powers as Commander in Chief and was left unrestricted by Congress. See 32 C.F.R. Parts 9–17 (2004). Because, as Madsen explained, Congress did not purport to apply the numerous CMJ provisions regulating courts-martial to the common law military commissions, Article 10 of the UCMJ, which sets out a speedy trial standard for courts-martial, is inapplicable to Hamdan.

Petitioner contends nevertheless ... that because the President expressly invoked the UCMJ in establishing the military commissions, he must afford Hamdan all of the procedural protections set forth in the UCMJ. The latter proposition does not follow from the former. The President invoked the provisions of the UCMJ that recognize his authority to use military commissions to try violations of the laws of war, Article 21, and to create a set of procedures to govern them, Article 36. Reliance on that authority, which the Supreme Court has construed to set military commissions apart from courts-martial and the UCMJ rules that govern them, could not logically trigger application of the entire UCMJ. Indeed, that is essentially the argument the Court rejected in Yamashita and Madsen. In any event, that enemy combatants facing military commissions do not receive the protection of Article 10 is not "contrary to or inconsistent with" the UCMJ, 10 U.S.C. §836(a), because, as Congress recognized in taking a hands-off approach, military commissions convened during wartime to try violations of the laws of war must deal with military exigencies in administering justice. Because of the unique context in which the commissions operate, and the need for flexibility that context presents, it is not "contrary to or inconsistent with" the UCMJ for the commissions to try enemy combatants for violations of the laws of war without adhering to the speedy trial rules that apply to courts-martial.[15]

B. Even Assuming Hamdan has Standing to Assert A Violation of Article 10, His Claim Fails as a Matter of Law.

Even assuming speedy trial concepts under Article 10 applied to Hamdan's confinement, petitioner has not established any violation. In order to prevail on an Article 10 claim, petitioner must establish that the government has failed to proceed against Hamdan

---

[15] Even assuming that Article 10 does apply to the military commissions, Hamdan cannot claim its protection, at least insofar as he seeks release from his present confinement. That is because the military has determined that Hamdan is an enemy combatant. As such, he may be detained for the duration of hostilities. Hamdi, 124 S. Ct. at 2641 (plurality opinion); id. at 2679 (Thomas, J. dissenting) (suggesting enemy combatant can be detained past cessation of formal hostilities). In light of his combatant status, Hamdan has no legal right to seek release from a particular form of confinement based on the length of time he has been held without a trial, even assuming that the speedy trial standards applied and that the military was not complying with them.

with "reasonable diligence." United States v. Cooper, 58 M.J. 54, 58 (C.A.A.F. 2003). All that petitioner states on this score is that "the Government did not need over two years to gather evidence.".... That conclusory statement is patently insufficient. To begin with, to the extent there is any relevant time period for an individual lawfully detained as an enemy combatant, the Article 10 clock would not begin to run until the detainee is "ordered into arrest or confinement" pursuant to a charge. 10 U. S. C. §810; see Cooper, 58 M.J. at 58 (Article 10 triggered "when a servicemember is placed in pretrial confinement"). Thus, any speedy trial clock here would not have begun to run until December 2003, when Hamdan was placed in Camp Echo to facilitate his ability to meet with counsel in connection with the impending charges.

Moreover, the amount of time that has elapsed, standing alone, does not suggest, much less establish, the absence of reasonable diligence. As the military courts have made clear, "[t]here is no 'magic number' of days in pretrial confinement which would give rise to a presumption of an Article 10, UCMJ, speedy trial violation." United States v. Goode, 54 M.J. 836 (N-M Ct. Crim. App. 2001); United States v. Kossman, 38 M.J. 258 (C.M.A. 1993) ("Pointedly, however, the drafters of Article 10 made no provision as to hours or days in which a case must be prosecuted because there are perfectly reasonable exigencies that arise in individual cases which just do not fit under a set time limit.") (internal quotation marks omitted). In the Goode case, the court held that a defendant who spent 337 days in pretrial confinement failed to make out an Article 10 or constitutional speedy trial violation. Id. at 838–840. Here, the government has charged Hamdan with participating in a foreign-based, far-reaching conspiracy spanning five and a half years. See Charge ¶¶12–13.... The breadth and complexity of the charge as well as the fact that it was brought during the ongoing war against al Qaida and its supporters refutes petitioner's unsupported assertion that the government is engaged in "foot dragging.".... See Barker v. Wingo, 407 U. S. 514, 531 (1972) ("[T]he delay that can be tolerated for an ordinary street crime is considerably less than for a serious, complex conspiracy charge.").

Petitioner's claim also founders on his failure to show prejudice from the alleged delay. See Barker, 407 U. S. at 533–534 (identifying four factors relevant to constitutional speedy trial claim, including prejudice to the defendant, and holding that defendant was minimally prejudiced by delay of more than five years); MacDonald, 435 U. S. at 858 (constitutional speedy trial right protects against three types of injury, but "the most serious" is impairment of the defense caused by delay); Cooper, 58 M.J. at 61 (directing military courts to consider Barker factors in evaluating Article 10 claim). Petitioner's contention that his defense will be based on testimony "that grows more stale with each passing day" falls well short of the mark. Such "[g]eneralized assertions of the loss of memory, witnesses, or evidence are insufficient to establish actual prejudice." United States v. Manning, 56 F. 3d 1188, 1194 (9th Cir. 1995). Likewise, petitioner's assertion... that Hamdan's present confinement "creates a genuine risk of psychological injury," that could impair his ability to assist in his own defense is precisely the kind of speculative claim that cannot form the basis for a finding of prejudice.[16] See ibid. (rejecting prejudice claim that embraces "pure conjecture"). Petitioner's speedy trial claim must therefore be dismissed.

---

[16] The vague and generalized nature of petitioner's claims only serve to highlight the premature status of this proceeding. See Part I (Argument), supra. Because "resolution of a speedy trial claim necessitates a careful assessment of the particular facts of the case," the claim – if it can be considered in federal court at all – is "best considered only after the relevant facts have been developed at trial " MacDonald, 435 U. S. at 858.

III.   HAMDAN'S CONFINEMENT PRIOR TO TRIAL DOES NOT VIOLATE THE GENEVA CONVENTIONS

Petitioner contends . . . that Hamdan's confinement in Camp Echo prior to his trial violates Article 103 of the Geneva Convention Relative to the Treatment of Prisoners of War (GPW), 6 U.S.T. 3316 (1955),[17] and Common Article 3[18] of the same treaty. Because the Geneva Conventions (1) are not self-executing, (2) do not apply to this conflict, and (3) do not afford a basis for relief even if they were self-executing and applied to this conflict, petitioner's claim lacks merit.

   B.   The Geneva Conventions Are Not Self-Executing.

Petitioner's reliance on provisions of the 1949 Geneva Conventions fails at the outset, because, as the Conventions' text and legislative history conclusively show, and as a solid majority of courts have held, those Conventions are not self-executing. Indeed, the GPW contains many provisions that, when considered together, demonstrate that the contracting parties understood that violations of the treaty would be enforced through diplomatic means. As the Fourth Circuit recently explained:

> [W]hat discussion there is [in the text of the GPW] of enforcement focuses entirely on the vindication by diplomatic means of treaty rights inhering in sovereign nations. If two warring parties disagree about what the Convention requires of them, Article 11 instructs them to arrange a "meeting of their representatives" with the aid of diplomats from other countries, "with a view to settling the disagreement." Geneva Convention, at art. 11. Similarly, Article 132 states that "any alleged violation of the Convention" is to be resolved by a joint transnational effort "in a manner to be decided between the interested Parties." Id. at art. 132; cf. id. at arts. 129–30 (instructing signatories to enact legislation providing for criminal sanction for "persons committing *** grave breaches of the present Convention"). We therefore agree with other courts of appeals that the language in the Geneva Convention is not "self-executing" and does not "create private rights of action in the domestic courts of the signatory countries." Huynh Thi Anh v. Levi, 586 F.2d 625, 629 (6th Cir. 1978) (applying identical enforcement provisions from the Geneva Convention Relative to the Protection of Civilian Persons in Time of War, Feb. 2, 1956, 6 U.S.T. 3516); see also Holmes v. Laird, 459 F.2d 1211, 1222 (D.C. Cir. 1972) (noting that "corrective machinery specified in the treaty itself is nonjudicial").

---

[17] That Article provides, in relevant part:

> Judicial investigations relating to a prisoner of war shall be conducted as rapidly as circumstances permit and so that his trial shall take place as soon as possible. A prisoner of war shall not be confined while awaiting trial unless a member of the armed forces of the Detaining Power would be so confined if he were accused of a similar offense, or if it is essential to do so in the interests of national security. In no circumstances shall this confinement exceed three months.

GPW art. 103.

[18] That Article provides, in relevant part:

> In the case of armed conflict not of an international character occurring in the territory of one of the High Contracting Parties, each party to the conflict shall be bound to apply, as a minimum, the following provisions:
> 1. Persons taking no active part in the hostilities, including members of armed forces who have laid down their arms and those placed hors de combat by sickness, wounds, detention, or any other cause, shall in all circumstances be treated humanely, without any adverse distinction founded on race, colour, religion or faith, sex, birth or wealth, or any other similar criteria.
>   To this end the following acts are and shall remain prohibited at any time and in any place whatsoever with respect to the above-mentioned persons:
> (d) The passing of sentences and the carrying out of executions without previous judgment pronounced by a regularly constituted court affording all the judicial guarantees which are recognized as indispensable by civilized peoples.

GPW art. 3.

Hamdi v. Rumsfeld, 316 F.3d 450, 468–469 (4ᵗʰ Cir. 2003), vacated on other grounds, 124 S. Ct. 2686 (2004); see also Al Odah v. United States, 321 F.3d 1134, 1147 (D.C. Cir. 2003) (Randolph, J., concurring), overruled on other grounds, Rasul v. Bush, 124 S. Ct. 2686 (2004); Tel-Oren v. Libyan Arab Republic, 726 F.2d 774, 808–810 (D.C. Cir. 1984) (Bork, J., concurring); Handel v. Artukovic, 601 F. Supp. 1421, 1424–1426 (C.D. Cal. 1985).[19]

The Fourth Circuit alluded to the fact that there was one area in which the contracting parties sought to go beyond diplomacy to enforce violations of the treaty: "grave breaches," which the parties pledged to punish themselves by enacting domestic criminal legislation. See Article 129 (GPW) ("The High Contracting Parties undertake to enact any legislation necessary to provide effective penal sanctions for persons committing, or ordering to be committed, any of the grave breaches of the present Convention defined in [Article 130]."); Article 130 ("Grave breaches to which the preceding Article relates shall be those involving any of the following acts, if committed against person or property protected by the Convention: *** wilfully depriving a prisoner of war of the rights of fair and regular trial prescribed in this Convention. ").[20] Congress responded by enacting the War Crimes Act of 1996, 18 U. S.C. §2441. That Act provides a means for remedying grave breaches, but obviously does not create any privately enforceable rights. The Executive Branch, through its ability to bring prosecutions, remains responsible for ensuring adherence to the treaty. In light of this clear textual framework for enforcing the treaty, there is no sound basis on which to conclude that the treaty provided prisoners of war, let alone unlawful combatants such as Hamdan, with private rights of action.

Contrary to petitioner's claim . . . , the legislative history does not suggest otherwise. In fact, the Senate Report on which petitioner relies makes clear that the GPW is not self-executing. In a section titled "Provisions Relating To Execution Of The Conventions," the Report states that "[t]he parties agree, moreover, to enact legislation necessary to provide effective penal sanctions for persons committing violations of the contentions enumerated as grave breaches[.]" S. Exec. Rep. No. 84-9 (1955), at 7. The Report celebrates

---

[19] Article 11 provides in full:

In cases where they deem it advisable in the interest of protected persons, particularly in cases of disagreement between the Parties to the conflict as to the application or interpretation of the provisions of the present Convention, the Protecting Powers shall lend their good offices with a view to settling the disagreement.

For this purpose, each of the Protecting Powers may, either at the invitation of one Party or on its own initiative, propose to the Parties to the conflict a meeting of their representatives, and in particular of the authorities responsible for prisoners of war, possibly on neutral territory suitably chosen. The Parties to the conflict shall be bound to give effect to the proposals made to them for this purpose. The Protecting Powers may, if necessary, propose for approval by the Parties to the conflict a person belonging to a neutral Power, or delegated by the International Committee of the Red Cross, who shall be invited to take part in such a meeting.

Article 132 provides in full:

At the request of a Party to the conflict, an enquiry shall be instituted, in a manner to be decided between the interested Parties, concerning any alleged violation of the Convention. If agreement has not been reached concerning the procedure for the enquiry, the Parties should agree on the choice of an umpire who will decide upon the procedure to be followed. Once the violation has been established, the Parties to the conflict shall put an end to it and shall repress it with the least possible delay.

[20] The other Articles of the GPW governing execution of the Convention reinforce the conclusion that the treaty is not self-executing. They call for the contracting parties to permit representatives of the Protecting Powers (neutral nations) and the International Committee of the Red Cross to visit prisoners of war (Art. 126); to inculcate the principles of the Convention in their countries' populace (Art. 127); and to communicate with one another "through the Swiss Federal Council and, during hostilities, through the Protecting Powers, the official translations of the present Convention, as well as the laws and regulations which they may adopt to ensure the application thereof," (Art. 128) (emphasis added). See also Art. 8 ("The present Convention shall be applied with the cooperation and under the scrutiny of the Protecting Powers [neutral nations] whose duty it is to safeguard the interests of the Parties to the conflict.").

this provision as "an advance over the 1929 [Geneva] instruments which contained no corresponding provisions." Ibid.

Significantly, the Supreme Court interpreted the 1929 Geneva Convention in Johnson v. Eisentrager, 339 U. S. 763 (1950), and held that it was not self-executing. The Court ruled there that the German prisoners of war who were challenging the jurisdiction of the military commission which convicted them "could not" invoke the Geneva Convention because

> It is *** the obvious scheme of the Agreement that responsibility for observance and enforcement of these rights is upon political and military authorities. Rights of alien enemies are vindicated under it only through protests and intervention of protecting powers as the rights of our citizens against foreign governments are vindicated only by Presidential intervention.

Id. at 789 & n. 14. The Senate that ratified the 1949 GPW was operating against the backdrop of Eisentrager, yet in discussing the "advance[s]" over the 1929 treaty, it never so much as suggested that alleged violations of the updated GPW could be enforced through private actions. To the contrary, the one "advance" contemplated and remarked upon was the enactment of criminal legislation to address "grave breaches." S. Exec. Rep. No. 84-9 (1955), at 7, 27 ("the grave breaches provisions cannot be regarded as self-executing"). Moreover, in addressing how future compliance with the treaty would be achieved, the Senate Report did not mention legal claims or judicial machinery, but instead observed that "the weight of world opinion," would "exercise a salutary restraint on otherwise unbridled actions." Id at 32.

Given that it is apparent on the face of the treaty and from the legislative history that the parties contemplated the need for enacting legislation, the Fourth Circuit's conclusion in Hamdi that the GPW is not self-executing is undoubtedly correct. Petitioner's claim . . . that this Court is "bound" by the Ninth Circuit's decision in In re Territo, 156 F.2d 142 (9th Cir. 1946), is wrong on several counts.[21] First, that case, which involved an American citizen's challenge to his confinement as a prisoner of war, did not involve the GPW, but rather, its 1929 precursor. Second, the Territo court did not hold that the 1929 treaty was self-executing, nor did it have occasion to decide the question, because the prisoner did not claim on appeal that his detention violated the Geneva Convention; he claimed the treaty was not applicable. Id. at 145. Finally, even if the Territo court had held the 1929 Convention self-executing, Eisentrager expressly rejected that notion four years later. 339 U.S. at 789 n.14.

---

[21] Petitioner's reliance on United States v. Noriega, 808 F. Supp. 791 (S.D. Fla. 1992), United States v. Lindh, 212 F. Supp. 2d 541 (E. D. Va. 2002), and Padilla ex rel. Newman v. Bush, 233 F. Supp.2d 564 (S.D.N.Y. 2002), rev'd in part, 352 F.3d 695 (2d Cir. 2003), rev'd sub nom. Rumsfeld v. Padilla, 124 S. Ct. 2711 (2004), is likewise misplaced. Padilla did not address whether the GPW authorizes private rights of action, see id. at 590. Lindh permitted the assertion of the GPW "as a defense to criminal prosecution"; however, the Fourth Circuit in Hamdi subsequently held the GPW to be non-self-executing. Hamdi, 316F. 3d at 468. As for Noriega, the district court discussed the GPW in an advisory opinion. 808 F. Supp. at 793, 799 (acknowledging that issue was not presented "in the context of a live controversy"). Moreover, Noriega's discussion does not apply to GPW Articles 3 and 103, the two provisions on which petitioner relies. That is because the court viewed the GPW Articles at issue as self-executing on the theory that the "grave breaches" cited in the GPW and expressly requiring implementing legislation did not refer to those Articles. Id. at 797 n. 8. In contrast, violations of Articles 3 and 103, if proven, would constitute grave breaches of the GPW, see Art. 130 (willful deprivation of POW's right to fair trial), which under the plain terms of the treaty cannot be enforced without implementing legislation, and which, as contemplated by the Treaty, are to be remedied by the possibility of criminal sanction, not private rights of action.

B.   The Geneva Conventions Do Not Apply to the United States' Armed
     Conflict Against Al Qaida Under the Terms of Common Article 2.

The Geneva Conventions do not apply to every conceivable armed conflict. Article 2
of the GPW provides for only three circumstances in which the Geneva Conventions
"apply": (a) in "all cases of declared war or of any other armed conflict which may
arise between two or more of the High Contracting Parties," art. 2(1); (b) in 'all cases
of partial or total occupation of the territory of a High Contracting Party," art.2(2);
or (c) when a non-signatory "Power[] in conflict" "accepts and applies the provisions
[of GC]," art.2(3). Because the armed conflict between the United States and al Qaida
satisfies none of these situations, the Geneva Conventions do not apply to al Qaida
fighters such as Hamdan.

The President has found that the armed conflict between the United States and
al Qaida does not come within Article 2 of the GPW. See Memorandum for the Vice
President, et al. From President, Re: Humane Treatment of al Qaeda and Taliban Detainees at 1 (Feb. 7, 2002), available at www.library.law.pace.edu/government/detainee_
memos.html. The President's determination is undoubtedly correct as a matter of law.
The U.S.-al Qaida armed conflict is not one "between two or more of the High Contracting Parties" within the meaning of article 2(1). Al Qaida has not signed or ratified
the GPW. Nor could it. Al Qaida is not a State. Rather, it is a terrorist organization
composed of members from many nations, with ongoing military operations in many
nations. As a non-State entity, it cannot be a "High Contracting Party" to the Convention. In addition, the U.S.-al Qaida armed conflict has not resulted in the "occupation
of the territory of a High Contracting Party" within the meaning of article 2(2). As a
non-State actor, al Qaida has no territory that could be occupied within the meaning
of article 2(2). Nor is it a "Power in conflict" that can "accept[] and appl[y]" the Convention within the meaning of article 2(3). See, e.g., G.I.A.D. Draper, The Red Cross
Conventions 16 (1958) (arguing that "in the context of Article 2, para. 3, 'Powers' means
States capable then and there of becoming Contracting Parties to these Conventions
either by ratification or by accession"); 2B Final Record of the Diplomatic Conference
of Geneva of 1949, at 108 (explaining that article 2(3) would impose an "obligation to
recognize that the Convention be applied to the non-Contracting adverse State, in so
far as the latter accepted and applied the provisions thereof" (emphasis added) ("Final
Record"); 4 Pictet, Commentary, at 23 (using "non-Contracting State" interchangeably
with "non-Contracting Power" and "non-Contracting Party"). In any event, far from embracing the Convention or any other provision of the law of armed conflict, al Qaida
has consistently acted in flagrant defiance of the law of armed conflict.

In sum, the Geneva Conventions are inapplicable to the United States' armed conflict with al Qaida, and for this reason as well Hamdan cannot claim their protections.

C.   GPW 103 and Common Article 3 are Facially Inapplicable to Hamdan.

Even assuming Hamdan could claim protection under the Conventions, his claims
would still fail as a matter of law

1. GPW Article 103 does not apply to Hamdan. That Article provides, in relevant
part:

> Judicial investigations relating to a prisoner of war shall be conducted as rapidly as cir-
> cumstances permit and so that his trial shall take place as soon as practicable. A prisoner
> of war shall not be confined while awaiting trial unless a member of the armed forces

of the Detaining Power would be so confined if he were accused of a similar offence, or if it is essential to do so in the interests of national security. In no circumstances shall this confinement exceed three months.

GPW art. 103 (emphasis added). The problem for Hamdan is that he is not a "prisoner of war" eligible for Article 103's protection. GPW Article 4 makes clear that prisoners of war "carry[] arms openly" and "conduct[] their operations in accordance with the laws and customs of war." Those, like Hamdan, who fail to adhere to those conditions are not entitled to prisoner of war status and its attendant benefits when captured. See S. Exec. Rep. No. 84-9, at 5 ("extension of [the treaty's] protection to 'partisans' does not embrace that type of partisan who performs the role of farmer by day, guerilla by night"). The President has determined that Hamdan is subject to the Military Order. See Ex. A to 4/5/04 Swift Decl. As a member of al Qaida or otherwise involved in terrorism against the United States, Hamdan by definition does not observe the criteria necessary to qualify as a prisoner of war. See Padilla, 233 F. Supp.2d at 593 (citing the "obvious conclusion" that "when the President designated Padilla an 'enemy combatant,' he necessarily meant that Padilla was an unlawful combatant, acting as an associate of a terrorist organization whose operations do not meet the *** criteria necessary to confer lawful combatant status on its members and adherents").

Petitioner nevertheless argues ... that Hamdan is entitled to Article 103's protection because doubt has arisen as to his status as an unlawful combatant and that, in the face of this doubt, GPW Article 5[22] and various United States military regulations require that he receive full prisoner of war protection until a competent tribunal has determined his status. Pet.'s Mem. 34 (citing GPW, 6 U. S.T. at 3324 (art. 5); Army Regulation 190–8 §1–6(A) (1997), at 70; Dep't of the Navy, NWP 1–14M 11.7 (1995), at 77). But petitioner never explains why doubt has arisen as to his status. He acknowledges that he was closely affiliated with Usama bin Laden for a lengthy period of time, and he does not claim, much less present evidence, that he followed a responsible commander, bore a fixed, distinctive sign, carried arms openly, or observed the laws of war. See GPW art. 4(A)(2). Because both the President and a federal court, see Padilla, supra, have determined that al Qaida is not entitled to protection as prisoners of war, there can be no doubt about his unlawful combatant status.

2. Hamdan's Common Article 3 claim fares no better. Article 3, which prohibits "the passing of sentences and the carrying out of executions without previous judgment" applies only "[i]n the case of armed conflict not of an international character occurring in the territory of one of the High Contracting Parties." The United States' war against al Qaida, however, is a conflict of "an international character," and it is not limited to the territory of "one of the High Contracting Parties." (Emphasis added.) Al Qaida operates in many countries and our armed conflict with al Qaida terrorists extends not only to Afghanistan but to Pakistan, countries in Europe and southeast Asia, and the United States itself. See Memorandum for Alberto R. Gonzales, Counsel to the President, and William J. Haynes II, General Counsel, Department of Defense, from Jay S. Bybee, Assistant Attorney General, Office of Legal Counsel, Re: Application of Treaties and Laws to al Qaeda and Taliban detainees, at 5–9 (Jan. 22, 2002),

---

[22] That provision provides in relevant part that

Should any doubt arise as to whether persons, having committed a belligerent act and having fallen into the hands of the enemy, belong to any of the categories enumerated in Article 4, such persons shall enjoy the protection of the present Convention until such time as their status has been determined by a competent tribunal.

GPW art. 5.

available at www.library.law.pace.edu/government/detainee_memos.html. Thus, by its own terms, Article 3 does not apply to the conflict pursuant to which Hamdan remains confined.

Even if the protections in common Article 3 did apply, Hamdan's treatment would not violate that article. He has not been "sentenced *** without previous judgment." To the contrary, the proceedings against Hamdan are in their preliminary stages. Hamdan was charged with an offense on July 9, 2004, and that charge was approved and referred by the Appointing Authority on July 13, 2004. The parties have proposed December dates for his trial by military commission. At his trial, Hamdan will enjoy, inter alia, the presumption of innocence, the assistance of counsel, and the opportunity to cross-examine prosecution witnesses, and the government will have to prove his guilt beyond a reasonable doubt. See Statement of Facts Part 3, supra. And any finding of guilt will be reviewed by a review panel, the Secretary of Defense, and the President, if the President does not designate the Secretary as the final decision-maker. This process is undoubtedly consistent with the protections set out in Common Article 3.

Moreover, Hamdan's confinement pending his military trial does not constitute the "passing of [a] sentence[] *** without previous judgment." GPW Art. 3(1)(d). Hamdan is not being confined in Camp Echo as a punishment for the offense he is alleged to have committed. Rather, by virtue of being designated as eligible for trial before a military commission, Hamdan was assigned petitioner as his counsel to assist him with the legal proceedings. In order to facilitate contacts between the military commission designees and their counsel without jeopardizing security at Guantanamo, the military established a separate facility at Camp Echo to house Hamdan and the other designees. Confining Hamdan for substantial security reasons to facilitate his access to counsel pending his wartime trial does not constitute "punishment." To the contrary, it is well established that the wartime detention of an enemy combatant is a legitimate war measure, not punishment. Hamdi, 124 S. Ct. at 2640 ("The purpose of detention is to prevent captured individuals from returning to the field of battle and taking up arms once again.") (plurality opinion).

IV.   PETITIONER'S EQUAL PROTECTION CLAIMS ARE MERITLESS

Petitioner advances the novel argument . . . that the Military Order violates the equal protection component of the Fifth Amendment and 42 U. S. C. §1981, because it applies to non-citizens only. Like the other claims the petition raises, there are numerous reasons why it lacks merit. First, as the Supreme Court held in United States v. Verdugo Urquidez, 494 U. S. 259 (1990), and Johnson v. Eisentrager, 339 U. S. 763 (1950), Hamdan, as an alien with no voluntary connection to the United States, has no Fifth Amendment rights. Second, even apart from those decisions, Hamdan's equal protection claim would fail because Hamdan is not a member of a suspect class and, even if he were, courts have historically shown extraordinary deference to the federal government regarding its policies toward aliens, deference that reaches its apex when applied to decisions of the President during wartime that implicate national security and sensitive foreign policy matters. Third, and related to the first point, the military order does not discriminate against Hamdan in its allocation of fundamental rights, because Hamdan has no fundamental right to avoid trial by a military commission. Finally, Hamdan's statutory claim fails because the statute is facially inapplicable to federal action, and, in any event offers no greater protection than the Constitution.

A. The Equal Protection Component Of The Fifth Amendment Does Not
    Extend To Hamdan.

As a non-resident alien with no voluntary contacts with the United States, Hamdan cannot invoke the Constitution of the United States. In fact, the Supreme Court has already expressly rejected the claim that the equal protection component of the Fifth Amendment applies to non-resident aliens such as Hamdan. In United States v. Verdugo-Urquidez, a nonresident alien whose Mexican residence was searched by federal agents, contended not only that the search violated his Fourth Amendment rights, but also that it violated the equal protection component of the Fifth Amendment by treating him differently from citizens with respect to the Fourth Amendment. 494 U.S. at 273. The Court flatly rejected this contention, explaining that "[n]ot only are history and case law against [Verdugo-Urquidez], but as pointed out in Johnson v. Eisentrager, 339 U. S. 763 *** (1950), the result of accepting this claim would have significant and deleterious consequences for the United States in conducting activities beyond its boundaries." Verdugo-Urquidez, 494 U. S. at 273. The Court also rejected Verdugo-Urquidez's reliance on a series of cases, including Plyler v. Doe, 457 U.S. 202 (1982), extending some constitutional protection to aliens. Verdugo-Urquidez, 494 U.S. at 271. The Court explained that those cases "establish only that aliens receive constitutional protections when they have come within the territory of the United States and developed substantial connections with this country." Ibid. Because Verdugo-Urquidez "is an alien who has had no previous significant voluntary connection with the United States," the Court held that those cases "avail him not." Ibid.

Petitioner's equal protection argument does not cite or discuss Verdugo-Urquidez or Eisentrager. But those decisions make clear that Hamdan, as a non-resident alien with no voluntary, substantial contacts with the United States, see ibid. ("lawful but involuntary" presence does not constitute "substantial connection"), cannot assert an equal protection claim. Verdugo-Urquidez reiterated Eisentrager's "emphatic" rejection of the extension of Fifth Amendment protections to nonresident aliens such as Hamdan. 494 U. S. at 269. The Eisentrager defendants, like Hamdan, challenged their trial before a military commission on Fifth Amendment grounds. The Fifth Amendment, the Court explained, does not "confer[] rights upon all persons, whatever their nationality, wherever they are located and whatever their offenses[.]" Id. at 783. If it were otherwise "enemy elements *** could require the American judiciary to assure them freedoms of speech, press, and assembly as in the First Amendment, right to bear arms as in the Second, security against 'unreasonable searches and seizures as in the Fourth, as well as rights to jury trial as in the Fifth and Sixth Amendments." Id. at 784. Had the Bill of Rights been meant to apply so broadly, the Court explained, "it could scarcely have failed to excite contemporary comment," yet "[n]ot one word can be cited," and "[n]o decision of th[e] Court supports such a view." Id at 784–785; see Zadvydas v. Davis, 533 U.S. 678, 693 (2001) (deeming it "well established" that due process protections "are unavailable to aliens outside of our geographic borders"); United States v. Curtiss-Wright Export Corp., 299 U. S. 304, 318 (1936) ("Neither the Constitution nor the laws passed in pursuance of it have any force in foreign territory unless in respect of our own citizens[.]").[23] Verdugo-Urquidez and Eisentrager thus bar petitioner's equal protection claim.[24]

---

[23] ...

[24] The Court's recent decision in Rasul v. Bush, 124 S. Ct. 2686 (2004), in no way affects Eisentrager's and Verdugo-Urquidez's rulings that non-resident aliens are not entitled to Fifth Amendment protections. Rasul only decided the question whether U.S. courts have statutory jurisdiction over petitions for writs of habeas

B.   Even If Hamdan Could Invoke The Fifth Amendment, His Claim
     Lacks Merit.

Even assuming contrary to Verdugo-Urquidez and Eisentrager that Hamdan could raise a claim under the Fifth Amendment's equal protection component, that claim lacks merit. The President found that in order "[t]o protect the United States and its citizens," it was "necessary" to establish military commissions to try non-citizens captured during the ongoing armed conflict for violations of the laws of war. Military Order §1(e). If this politically sensitive determination is reviewable at all, it is subject to the utmost deference, because it constitutes an exercise of the President's war powers vis-a-vis aliens and implicates pressing national security and foreign policy concerns. As the Supreme Court has repeatedly observed,

> [A]ny policy toward aliens is vitally and intricately interwoven with contemporaneous policies in regard to the conduct of foreign relations, the war power, and the maintenance of a republican form of government. Such matters are so exclusively entrusted to the political branches of government as to be largely immune from judicial inquiry or interference.

Matthews v. Diaz, 426 U. S. 67, 81 n.17 (1976) (quoting Harisiades v. Shaughnessy, 342 U. S. 580, 588–589 (1952)). Petitioner offers no basis for disturbing the President's judgment here.

1.   Heightened Scrutiny Applies Only to State Actions
     That Affect Resident Aliens.

Petitioner asserts . . . that aliens are a suspect class, citing In re Griffiths, 413 U.S. 717, 721–722 (1973), and Graham v. Richardson, 403 U.S. 365, 372 (1971), for this proposition. Those cases, however, stand for a substantially narrower point: that lawful, resident aliens are a suspect class for equal protection purposes, and that policies that differentiate between that group and other similarly situated persons are subject to "close judicial scrutiny." Graham, 403 U.S. at 372. Nothing in either case suggests that the Supreme Court meant to include aliens differently situated from Griffiths and Richardson, who were lawfully admitted resident aliens. See, e. g. , Griffiths, 413 U.S. at 722 (according protection to resident aliens on the premise that "like citizens, [they] pay taxes, support the economy, serve in the Armed Forces, and contribute in myriad other ways to our society"); Verdugo-Urquidez, 494 U. S. at 273 (rejecting nonresident alien's reliance on Graham).

That the President's order applies to lawful, resident aliens as well as non-resident aliens makes no difference. As a nonresident alien, Hamdan has no standing to allege an equal protection violation on behalf of that distinct group. See Lujan v. Defenders of Wildlife, 504 U.S. 555, 560 (1992) ("[T]he plaintiff must have suffered an 'injury in

---

corpus filed by aliens located outside U.S. territory. See 124 S. Ct. at 2695 ("Eisentrager plainly does not preclude the exercise of §2241 jurisdiction over petitioners' claims."). Rasul said nothing about the possession of constitutional rights by non-resident aliens. Its footnote stating that "petitioners' allegations *** unquestionably describe 'custody in violation of the Constitution or laws or treaties of the United States,'" id. at 2698 n.15, is dictum which cannot be construed to overrule prior holdings of the Court and which, in any event, does not specify that the allegations make out a constitutional violation, as opposed to some other form of violation. In any event, to the extent non-resident aliens held in Guantanamo enjoy any constitutional rights, they clearly would enjoy less rights than citizens detained under similar circumstances. Cf. The Insular Cases (discussed in Verdugo-Urquidez, 494 U.S. at 268).

fact' – an invasion of a legally protected interest which is *** concrete and particularized."); see also Sabri v. United States, 124 S. Ct. 1941, 1948–1949 (2004) (" [W]e have recognized the validity of facial attacks alleging overbreadth *** in relatively few settings, and generally, on the strength of specific reasons weighty enough to overcome our well-founded reticence."). As a representative of the broader unprotected class of aliens, Hamdan's challenge would be subject to rational basis review. See, e. g., Dandridge v. Williams, 397 U.S. 471, 485 (1970); United States v. Carolene Products, 304 U.S. 144, 152 (1938). Under that standard, the Military Order must be upheld as long as a court can identify any rational basis for it. Carolene Products, 304 U.S. at 152. Given that the "[e]xecutive power over enemy aliens *** has been deemed throughout our history, essential to war-time security," Eisentrager, 339 U.S. at 774, it cannot seriously be argued that the President's action, taken in response to attacks executed by a foreign-based terrorist organization, lacks a rational basis.

Moreover, courts have only applied heightened scrutiny to policies regarding aliens that are promulgated by states, as opposed to the federal government. Griffiths and Graham, the two cases on which petitioner principally relies, dealt respectively with Connecticut's bar admission rules and Arizona and Pennsylvania's distribution of welfare benefits. In these and other cases involving state action, the Court has made it clear that federal policies regarding aliens are entitled to a much higher degree of deference. See, e. g., Graham, 413 U. S. at 379–80; Plyler, 457 U. S. at 225.

Indeed, cases considering federal policies that differentiate against aliens are marked by the Court's extreme deference towards the political branches. In Mathews v. Diaz, 426 U. S. 67 (1976), the Court expressly distinguished state and federal actions for purposes of equal protection doctrine relating to aliens, id. at 84–85, explaining that the relationship between the United States and aliens "has been committed to the political branches of the Federal Government," id. at 81. The Court went on to apply great deference in upholding a federal law that differentiated against aliens for purposes of determining eligibility for Medicare benefits. A host of other cases echo Mathews judicial deference toward federal policies governing aliens. See, e. g., Fiallo v. Bell, 430 U.S. 787, 792 (1977); Shaughnessy v. United States ex rel. Mezei, 345 U.S. 206, 210 (1953); Harisiades v. Shaughnessy, 342 U.S. 580, 588–589 (1952). The concern motivating the Court's deference – that regulation of aliens is committed to the political branches of the federal government – is magnified in this case, where the President's Military Order not only regulates aliens, but does so in order to prosecute the war against international terrorism effectively. See, e. g., Dep't of the Navy v. Egan, 484 U.S. 518, 530 (1988) ("courts traditionally have been reluctant to intrude upon the authority of the Executive in military and national security affairs"). Accordingly, the heightened scrutiny that would apply to state actions differentiating against lawful resident aliens does not apply to the President's exercise of his war powers.

2. The Military Order Does Not Discriminate In The Allocation Of Fundamental Rights.

Petitioner's final equal protection argument . . . is that the Military Order violates the Fifth Amendment because it discriminates in the allocation of fundamental rights. The Court's jurisprudence makes clear, however, that heightened scrutiny is applied only to the differential allocation of constitutionally guaranteed rights. See San Antonio Independent School Dist. v. Rodriguez, 411 U.S. 1, 32–33 (1973). Because it is well established that enemy combatants – the only individuals subject to trial by military commission – possess no constitutional right to be tried for their war crimes in front of an Article III court, see Ex parte Quirin, 317 U. S. 1 (1942) (citizen and alien enemy combatants alike are subject to trial by military commission); Yamashita v. Styer, 327 U.S. 1 (1946) (alien enemy combatant), the line of cases on which petitioner relies . . . is inapposite. Thus, while the Military Order would survive the most exacting scrutiny, it need only have a rational basis, as it undoubtedly does

C.   The President's Order Does Not Violate 42 U. S. C. §1981.

Petitioner's argument . . . that the Military Order violates 42 U. S.C. §1981 is equally mer-itless. Petitioner relies on a 1974 Ninth Circuit case holding that Section 1981 applied to federal action, Bowers v. Campbell, 505 F.2d 1155, but that case was decided before the law was amended in 1991. The 1991 amendment provides that "[t]he rights protected by this section are protected against impairment by nongovernmental discrimination and impairment under color of State law." 42 U. S. C. §1981(c) (emphasis added). This amendment renders Section 1981 facially inapplicable to federal action. For this rea-son, every federal court of appeals that has considered the issue since the law was amended has held that federal actions cannot give rise to claims under Section 1981. See Davis-Warren Auctioneers, J.V. v. F.D.I.C., 215 F.3d 1159, 1161 (10ᵗʰ Cir. 2000); Davis v. United States Dep't of Justice, 204 F.3d 723, 725–726 (7ᵗʰ Cir. 2000); Lee v. Hughes, 145 F.3d 1272, 1277 (11ᵗʰ Cir. 1998). Petitioner cites a single post-amendment district court case to the contrary, La Compania Ocho, Inc. v. United States Forest Serv., 874 F. Supp. 1242 (D. N.M. 1995), but that case was overruled by Davis-Warren.

Even if Section 1981 did apply to the federal government, the Supreme Court has held (in the context of state action, of course) that the section is co-extensive with the Equal Protection Clause. See Grutter v. Bollinger, 539 U.S. 306, 343 (2003); General Bldg. Contractors Ass'n, Inc. v. Pennsylvania, 458 U.S. 375, 389–391 (1982). Petitioner's Section 1981 claim thus would fail for the same reasons that doom his constitutional equal protection challenge.

V.   THE MILITARY COMMISSION THAT WILL TRY HAMDAN DOES NOT VIOLATE SEPARATION OF POWERS

When he issued the Military Order, the President invoked not only his authority as Com-mander in Chief, but also the authority granted him by Congress in the Authorization for Use of Military Force (AUMF) and the authority Congress recognized he had in Sections 821 and 836 of Title 10 of the United States Code. In Hamdi, the Court made clear that the AUMF authorizes the President to exercise "against individuals Congress sought to target in passing the AUMF" his traditional war powers, including "the cap-ture, detention, and trial of enemy combatants." 124 S. Ct. at 2640 (plurality opinion) (citing Ex parte Quirin, 317 U.S. at 28); id. at 2679 (Thomas, J., dissenting) ("Congress has authorized the President" to "detain those arrayed against our troops"). As someone charged with, inter alia, delivering weapons, ammunition and other supplies to al Qaida members and associates, Hamdan, like Hamdi, falls squarely within the cross-hair of the AUMF.

Not only has Congress authorized the President generally to exercise his war powers against Hamdan, but it has specifically recognized and approved the President's exercise of his authority to convene military commissions to try persons such as Hamdan who are charged with committing offenses cognizable under the common law of war. Indeed, as the Supreme Court held in both Ex parte Quirin and Yamashita, Congress has done so through the very provisions of the Uniform Code of Military Justice that the President cited in the Military Order.

Congress' longstanding decision both to recognize and approve the exercise of the President's wartime authority to convene military commissions to try violations of the laws of war reflects Congress' understanding that military exigencies require providing the President flexibility rather than detailed procedures in dealing with enemy fighters. That decision is entitled to just as much deference as Congress' decision to legislate detailed rules for the military's use of courts-martial. As Justice Jackson has explained, "[w]hen the President acts pursuant to an express or implied authorization of Congress, his authority is at its maximum, for it includes all that he possesses in his own right plus all that Congress can delegate." Youngstown Sheet & Tube Co. v. Sawyer, 343 U.S. 579, 635–636 (1952) (Jackson, J., concurring). In these circumstances, the President's action is "'supported by the strongest presumptions and the widest latitude of judicial interpretation, and the burden of persuasion would rest heavily upon any who might attack it.'" Dames & Moore v. Regan, 453 U. S. 654, 674 (1981) (quoting Youngstown, 343 U.S. at 637 (Jackson, J., concurring)). Hamdan could not possibly meet his burden, because he does not have any constitutional rights and even if he did, the Supreme Court has already squarely rejected the arguments he advances here.

A.   Hamdan Cannot Invoke Structural Protections Of Our Constitution.

Hamdan has no standing to claim a separation-of-powers violation. As a non-resident alien with no voluntary connections to the United States, Hamdan possesses no constitutional rights. See Part IV(A), supra. He thus may allege neither infringements of individual rights expressly recognized by the Constitution nor infringements of rights derived from the structural protections built into the Constitution.

B.   Congress Has Authorized The Military Commission Which Will Try Hamdan.

The whole premise of petitioner's separation-of-powers argument, that "the tribunals at issue here were created solely by virtue of an Executive order, without congressional authorization" . . . , is without foundation. When the President issued the Military Order establishing military commissions to try individuals such as Hamdan for violations of the laws of war and other offenses triable by military commission, he expressly relied not only on his powers as Commander in Chief,[25] but also on, inter alia, 10 U.S.C. §821. That section, which is entitled "Jurisdiction of courts-martial not exclusive," states that "[t]he provisions of this chapter conferring jurisdiction upon courts-martial do not deprive military commissions *** of concurrent jurisdiction with respect to offenders or offenses that by statute or by the law of war may be tried by military commissions." 10 U. S.C. §821 (emphasis added). That language originated in Article 15 of the Articles of War, which was enacted in 1916. See Act of August 29, 1916, 39 Stat. 619, 653. At that time, Congress had decided to extend the jurisdiction of courts-martial to all offenses against the laws of war. The main proponent of Article 15 testified that, in light of the extension of courts-martial jurisdiction, it was important to make clear that the military commissions' "common law of war jurisdiction was not ousted." S. Rep. No. 63-229, at

---

[25] As we discuss below, the President could have relied on his Commander-in-Chief powers alone, but this Court need not resolve that question because the Supreme Court has squarely held that the federal law on which the President relied constitutes congressional authorization for military commissions.

53 (1914) (testimony of Judge Advocate General Crowder before the House Committee on Military Affairs); see also S. Rep. No. 64–130, at 40 (1916) (the military commission "is our common-law war court" that "has no statutory existence").

When the Supreme Court addressed challenges to the many military commissions convened during and after World War II, it agreed with General Crowder's view about the place military commissions occupied in our legal system, construing Article 15 as congressional recognition and approval of the common-law role military commissions play during wartime in punishing violations of the laws of war.[26] In Ex Parte Quirin, 317 U.S. 1 (1942), the Court expressly held that Article 15 – whose language is identical to today's Section 821 – "authorized trial of offenses against the laws of war before such commissions." Id. at 29 (emphasis added); id. at 28 ("By the Articles of War, and especially Article 15, Congress has explicitly provided, so far as it may constitutionally do so, that military commissions shall have jurisdiction to try offenders or offenses against the law of war ***"). The Quirin Court held not only that Congress had authorized the President to use military commissions, but also that Congress did not purport to codify violations of the laws of war over which the commissions could exercise jurisdiction. Rather, "Congress has incorporated by reference, as within the jurisdiction of military commissions, all offenses which are defined as such by the laws of war." Id. at 30; id. at 35 (relying on the "long course of practical administrative construction by [the] military authorities"). Applying these principles, the Court approved the military commission's exercise of jurisdiction over the Nazi saboteurs for alleged offenses against the common law of war.

Recognizing that Quirin undoes his entire separation-of-powers argument, petitioner attempts to distinguish it on various grounds, none of which has any merit. Petitioner contends that Quirin is different because the charges there "were explicitly authorized by Congress," Pet.'s Mem. 48. That argument ignores the very holding of the decision and the Court's application of that holding to the first charge leveled against the saboteurs, which alleged "[v]iolation of the [common] law of war," 317 U. S. at 23, not an offense prescribed by Congress.[27] The Court explained that the whole point of Article 15 was congressional recognition and approval of the military's enforcement of a body of common law governing the rules of warfare that Congress did not purport to codify:

> Congress has incorporated by reference, as within the jurisdiction of military commissions, all offenses which are defined as such by the law of war ***, and which may constitutionally be included within that jurisdiction. Congress had the choice of crystallizing in permanent form and in minute detail every offense against the law of war, or of adopting the system of common law applied by military tribunals so far as it should be recognized and deemed applicable by the courts. It chose the latter course.

Id. at 30 (citation omitted).

The Quirin Court went on to assess whether the saboteurs had been charged with "an offense against the law of war cognizable before a military tribunal." Id. at 29. In doing so, the Court did not look to federal statutes, but rather, to other cases tried before military commissions, id. at 31 nn.9 & 10 (discussing cases of confederate soldiers and officers convicted for hostile actions in civilian dress or other disguises, including

---

[26] ...

[27] Petitioner emphasizes . . . that charges 2 and 3 were explicitly authorized by Congress, but the Quirin Court upheld the military commission's authority to try petitioners based solely on charge 1. The fact that the Court limited its analysis to the charge that relied on the common law, rather than on the statutory charges, demonstrates the degree to which petitioner misreads Quirin.

attempts to derail a train and to set fire to New York City); contemporary secondary sources on military and international law, id. at 31; and the Rules of Land Warfare promulgated by the War Department for the guidance of the Army,[28] id. at 33–34. After canvassing these sources, the Court concluded that the Nazi saboteurs were properly charged with a violation of the law of war because, "[b]y a long course of practical administrative construction by its military authorities, our Government has likewise recognized that those who during time of war pass surreptitiously from enemy territory into our own, discarding their uniforms upon entry, for the commission of hostile acts involving destruction of life or property, have the status of unlawful combatants punishable as such by military commission." Id. at 35 (emphasis added). Contrary to petitioner's argument, the Court never implied, much less stated, that the alleged violation of the law of war was cognizable because it was defined by Congress or because it resembled a statutory offense.

Given the total absence of evidence in Quirin that the Court approved the first charge based on explicit statutory authorization, petitioner looks outside Quirin to the statement in Madsen, that "'the military commission's conviction of saboteurs *** was upheld on charges of violating the law of war as defined by statute'." Pet's Mem. 49 (emphasis in Mem.). A review of the pages in Quirin which Madsen cited indicates that what the Madsen Court meant was nothing more than what the Quirin Court held, namely, that Congress, via Article 15, acted to define the law of war as incorporating the body of common law applied by military commissions. See Quirin, 317 U.S. at 38 (the "Act of Congress [Article 15], by incorporating the law of war, punishes" violation of common law of war) (emphasis added); id. at 28 ("Congress *** has thus exercised its authority to define and punish offenses against the law of nations by sanctioning, within constitutional limitations, the jurisdiction of military commissions to try persons for offenses which, according to the rules and precepts of the law of nations, and more particularly the law of war, are cognizable by such tribunals.") (emphasis added).

Respondents' reading of Quirin is confirmed by Yamashita v. Styer, 327 U. S. 1 (1946), which is not discussed in petitioner's separation-of-powers argument. In Yamashita, the Court characterized Quirin as holding that

> [Congress] had not attempted to codify the law of war or to mark its precise boundaries. Instead, by Article 15 it had incorporated, by reference, as within the preexisting jurisdiction of military commissions created by appropriate military command, all offenses which are defined as such by the law of war, and which may constitutionally be included within that jurisdiction. It thus adopted the system of military common law applied by military tribunals so far as it should be recognized and deemed applicable by the courts, and as further defined and supplemented by the Hague Convention, to which the United States and the Axis powers were parties.

327 U. S. at 11 (emphasis added). Petitioner's revisionist take on Quirin thus cannot be reconciled with the Yamashita Court's own interpretation and application of Quirin four years later.

Under Quirin, there can be no doubt that Hamdan is charged with an offense that alleges a violation of the laws of war. He is charged with conspiring with an international terrorist organization that has carried out numerous attacks – including the

---

[28] The Court cited provisions of the Rules of Land Warfare identifying persons subject to military trial for violations of the laws of war, including "'persons who take up arms and commit hostilities' without having the means of identification prescribed for belligerents." Id. at 34 (quoting Paragraph 348). The Court observed that "the specified violations [in the Rules] are intended to be only illustrative of the applicable principles of the common law of war, not "an exclusive enumeration." Ibid.

September 11 attacks – that violate every precept of the laws of war.[29] Indeed, those attacks targeted civilians and were carried out by enemy forces disguised as civilians who did not carry arms openly. See id. at 34. And the particular offenses Hamdan is charged with conspiring to commit – attacking civilians, attacking civilian objects, murder by an unprivileged belligerent, destruction of property by an unprivileged belligerent, and terrorism – implicate the most basic protections of the laws of war. See 32 C.F.R. §§11.6(a)(2) and (a)(3); §§11.6(b)(2), (b)(3), and (b)(4); Yamashita, 327 U.S. at 17 ("Obviously charges of violations of the law of war triable before a military tribunal need not be stated with the precision of a common law indictment.").

Both the military's own field manual and the 1907 Hague Convention – two sources on which the Quirin Court heavily relied – confirm that the charge against Hamdan constitutes an offense against the customary laws of war. The Field Manual declares that "[c]ustomary international law prohibits the launching of attacks *** against either the civilian population as such or individual civilians" and that "[t]he attack or bombardment, by whatever means, of towns, villages, dwellings, or buildings which are undefended is prohibited." Dep't of the Army, Field Manual 27-10, The Law of Land Warfare ¶¶39–40; see also Hague Convention No. IV of October 18, 1907, 36 Stat. 2295, art. 23 (stating that "it is especially forbidden" both "[t]o kill or wound an enemy who [has] laid down his arms, or [has] no longer means of defense," and "[t]o destroy or seize the enemy's property, unless such destruction or seizure be imperatively demanded by the necessities of war."). The manual further provides that individuals "who take up arms and commit hostile acts without having complied with the conditions prescribed by the laws of war for recognition as belligerents" are not entitled to combatant immunity for their hostile acts, but rather "may be tried and sentenced to execution or imprisonment." Id. ¶80. See also Yamashita, 327 U.S. at 14 (recognizing as violation of the law of war "deliberate plan and purpose to massacre and exterminate a large part of the civilian population *** and to devastate and destroy public, private and religious property"); GPW art. 4 (extending POW protections only to lawful belligerents). Under these common law sources, the charge against Hamdan – implicating him in al Qaida's attacks on the United States – "plainly alleges violation of the law of war."[30] Quirin, 317 U.S. at 36.

Petitioner's attempt...to distinguish Quirin on the basis of the declaration of war there is equally unavailing. Congress authorized the President to "use all necessary and appropriate force against those nations, organizations, or persons he determines planned, authorized, committed or aided the terrorist attacks that occurred on

---

[29] The President, the Congress, and NATO have all recognized al Qaida's attacks as an act of war. See Military Order, §1(a); AUMF, 115 Stat. 224; and Statement of NATO Secy. Gen. (Oct. 2, 2001) (available at http://usinfo.state.gov.topical/pol/terror/01100205.htm). In any event, whether there exists a state of armed conflict to which the laws of war apply is a political question for the President, not the courts. See The Prize Cases, 67 U. S. (2 Black) 635, 670 (1862); Eisentrager, 339 U.S. at 789; Ludecke v. Watkins, 335 U.S. 160, 170 (1948).

[30] Petitioner...misplaces reliance on Ex parte Milligan, 71 U.S. (4 Wall.) 2 (1866). To begin with, Milligan, which involved the military prosecution of an American citizen, was not a separation-of-powers case, for the Court held there that the government as a whole had no power to subject Milligan to military jurisdiction. Id. at 122. Moreover, Quirin "construe[d]" the "inapplicability of the law of war to Milligan's case as having particular reference to the facts," namely, that Milligan, as a person neither "a part of or associated with the armed forces of the enemy, was a non-belligerent." 317 U. S. at 19; see also Duncan v. Kahanamoku, 327 U. S. 304 (1946) (military tribunal cannot try persons for embezzling stock or brawling with soldiers). Finally, when addressing the application of the laws of war to the current armed conflict, a majority of the Supreme Court embraced Quirin, not Milligan, as the controlling precedent. Hamdi, 124 S. Ct. at 2643 (plurality opinion) ("Quirin was a unanimous opinion. It both postdates and clarifies Milligan[.]"); ibid. (rejecting a reading of Quirin that would limit application of its principles to cases where enemy combatant status is conceded); id.at 2682 (Thomas, J.) ("Quirin overruled Milligan to the extent those cases are inconsistent.").

September 11, 2001, *** in order to prevent any future acts of international terrorism against the United States[.]" Authorization for Use of Military Force (AUMF), Pub. L. No. 107-40, 115 Stat. 224 (2001). In Hamdi, a plurality of the Court ruled that this authorization triggered the exercise of the President's traditional war powers, in particular, the power to detain enemy combatants.[31] The Court explained that "detention of individuals [that Congress sought to target in passing the AUMF] ***, for the duration of the particular conflict in which they were captured, is so fundamental and accepted an incident to war as to be an exercise of the 'necessary and appropriate force' Congress has authorized the President to use." 124 S. Ct. at 2640 (plurality opinion). That ruling applies with equal force to the President's power to punish war criminals. Indeed, the Hamdi Court justified its own conception of the President's war powers by expressly relying on Quirin for the proposition that "[t]he capture and detention of lawful combatants and the capture, detention, and trial of unlawful combatants, by 'universal agreement and practice,' are 'important incident[s] of war. '" Hamdi, 124 S. Ct. at 2640 (quoting Quirin, 317 U. S. at 28) (emphasis added). Because al Qaida is the central target of the AUMF, Congress has clearly authorized the President to exercise his war powers by subjecting to military trial individuals such as Hamdan who are charged with conspiring to achieve its goals.[32]

The absence of a formal declaration of war is likewise immaterial to application of the substantive prohibitions of the UCMJ. It is well settled that the UCMJ applies to armed conflicts that the United States has prosecuted without a formal declaration of war. See, e.g., United States v. Anderson, 38 C.M.R. 386, 386 (C.M.A. 1968) ("The current military involvement of the United States in Vietnam undoubtedly constitutes a 'time of war' in that area, within the meaning of Article 43"); United States v. Bancroft, 11 C.M.R. 3, 5 (C.M.A. 1953) ("a finding that this is a time of war, within the meaning of the language of the Code, is compelled by the very nature of the present conflict" in Korea). The cases that petitioner cites to the contrary, United States v. Averette, 41 C.M.R. 363, 365 (C.M.A. 1970), and Zamora v. Woodson, 42 C.M.R. 5 (C.M.A. 1970), hold that a formal declaration of war is necessary only before the UCMJ is applied to civilians, and are thus inapplicable to Hamdan, an alien captured in Afghanistan in the ongoing armed conflict and determined by the military to be an enemy combatant.

Finally, contrary to petitioner's contention, Quirin has not been eroded by subsequent legal developments. Hamdi reconfirms Quirin. 124 S. Ct. at 2643 (plurality opinion); id. at 2682 (Thomas, J., dissenting). Petitioner cites the codification of the UCMJ, but Congress expressly stated that the codification preserved the holding of Quirin. See S. Rep. No. 486, 81st Cong, 1st Sess. 13 (1949); H.R. Rep. No. 491, 81st Cong, 1st Sess. 17 (1949). As for the Geneva Conventions, as discussed above in Part III, they are not self-executing, do not apply, and, in any event, approve the military trial of unlawful combatants, see, e. g., S. Exec. Rep. No. 84-9, at 5 ("guerilla[s] *** remain subject to trial and punishment as unlawful belligerents"). And the War Crimes Act of 1996 and Expanded War Crimes Act of 1997 were intended to supplement rather than replace

---

[31] The plurality's ruling on this important point enjoys majority support, given Justice Thomas's position in dissent. See Hamdi, 124 S. Ct. at 2679 (Thomas, J., dissenting) ("Although the President very well may have inherent authority to detain those arrayed against our troops, I agree with the plurality that we need not decide that question because Congress has authorized the President to do so.").

[32] The Hamdi Court's ruling reflects the longstanding principle that the President's prerogative to invoke the laws of war in a time of armed conflict, including in respect to the punishment of war criminals, in no way turns on a formal declaration. See, e. g., The Prize Cases, 67 U.S. (2 Black) 635, 668, 670 (1862); J. Ely, War and Responsibility 25 (1993) (the suggestion "that congressional combat authorizations must actually be labeled 'declarations of war'" is "manifestly out of accord with the specific intent of the founders").

the jurisdiction of military commissions over war crimes. Indeed, Congress could not have been clearer on this score. The War Crimes Act itself says nothing about altering the traditional jurisdiction of military commissions. That is not surprising, given that "[t]he enactment of H. R. 3680 [the War Crimes Act of 1996] is not intended to affect in any way the jurisdiction of any court-martial, military commission, or other military tribunal under any article of the Uniform Code of Military Justice or under the law of war or the law of nations." H. Rep. No. 698, 104th Cong. 2d Sess. 12 (1996).[33] Because Congress clearly did not intend to "occup[y] the field" (Pet.'s Mem. 72) previously occupied by military commissions, the subject matter jurisdiction of those commissions today is no narrower than it was during World War II. To the contrary, that jurisdiction remains broad enough to cover violations of the laws of armed conflict as defined by both historical and contemporary standards.[34]

B. The President Has The Inherent Authority To Create
     Military Commissions.

Even if the legislative provisions the President expressly invoked did not constitute the congressional authorization that the Supreme Court has held they constitute, see Hamdi (construing AUMF), supra; Quirin (construing precursor to 10 U.S.C. §821), the military commissions would still be constitutional. That is because the President's authority to create military commissions is inherent in his position as Commander-in-Chief. U.S. Const. Art. II §2.

The Executive Branch's war power has always included the unilateral authority to create military commissions, because that authority is necessary to effectuate the war power. As the Court explained in Eisentrager, "[t]he first of the enumerated powers of the President is that he shall be Commander-in-Chief of the Army and Navy of the United States. And, of course, grant of war power includes all that is necessary and proper for carrying these powers into execution." 339 U. S. at 788 (citation omitted). That war power includes "the power *** to punish those enemies who violated the law of war." Hirota, 338 U.S. at 208 (Douglas, J,. concurring) (citations omitted). And "punishment of war criminals" is an essential "part of the prosecution of the war," because it is "directed to a dilution of enemy power and [to] retribution for wrongs done." Id. at 208; see also Yamashita, 327 U. S. at 11 ("An important incident to the conduct of war is the adoption of measures by the military commander, not only to repel and defeat the enemy, but to seize and subject to disciplinary measures those enemies who *** have violated the law of war."). Indeed, the laws of war exist to impose limits on belligerent conduct; as leader of the armed forces, the President must have the authority to enforce those limits to protect the nation.

The Executive Branch's unilateral authority to create military commissions not only necessarily inheres in the powers granted the President by the Constitution, but is also borne out by historical practice. In 1780, during the Revolutionary War, General

---

[33] Military commissions may, of course, try persons for violations of the laws of war even if the underlying conduct could also be construed to violate criminal statutes. One of the Nazi saboteurs in Quirin was an American citizen who could have been charged with treason, but that fact did not negate his eligibility for trial by commission. 317 U. S. at 38. See also Colepaugh v. Looney, 235 F.2d 429, 432–433 (10th Cir. 1956) ("an accused has no constitutional right to choose the offense or the tribunal in which he will be tried").

[34] The Supreme Court has repeatedly held that the repeal by implication of an earlier statute is disfavored. See, e. g., Rodriguez v. United States, 480 U.S. 522, 524 (1987). Given that Congress made clear its intent not to repeal 10 U. S. C. §821, the War Crimes Act cannot be read to displace the traditional jurisdiction of military commissions to try violations of the common law of war.

Washington as Commander in Chief of the Continental Army appointed a "Board of General Officers" to try the British Major Andre as a spy, see Quirin, 317 U.S. at 31 n. 9, when there was no court-martial authority to try him. See George B. Davis, A Treatise on the Military Law of the United States 308 n.1 (1913). General Andrew Jackson similarly convened military trials in 1818 to try two English subjects for inciting the Creek Indians to war with the United States. See William Winthrop, Military Law and Precedents 464, 832 (2d ed. 1920). In the Mexican American War, General Winfield Scott appointed tribunals called "council[s] of war" to try offenses under the laws of war and tribunals called "military commission[s]" to serve essentially as occupation courts administering justice for occupied territory. See id. at 832–33; Davis, supra at 308. And after the outbreak of the Civil War, military commissions were convened to try offenses against the laws of war, see Davis, supra, at 308 n.2; Winthrop, supra at 833.

The Court has never called into question the validity of that historical practice. To the contrary, in Ex parte Vallindigham, 68 U.S. 243 (1863), the Court, in the course of concluding that it did not have jurisdiction to review the proceedings before a military commission, explained that military jurisdiction can be "derived from the common law of war." Id. at 249. And the three seminal military commission cases, Milligan, Quirin, and Yamashita, are all consistent with the position that the President does not require statutory authorization to establish military commissions to try violations of the laws of war. As mentioned above, Milligan is not a separation-of-powers case, and has been narrowly confined to its facts. In Quirin, the Court, in light of its reliance on congressional authorization, simply found it "unnecessary" to decide whether the President had unilateral authority. Finally, in Yamashita, although the same statutes that were dispositive in Quirin on the question of congressional authorization were still in force (as they are now), the Court strongly suggested that the President has inherent authority to convene military commissions. The Court observed that the Articles of War "recognized the 'military commission' appointed by military command, as it had previously existed in United States Army practice, as an appropriate tribunal for the trial and punishment of offenses against the law of war." Yamashita, 327 U. S. at 5 (emphasis added). The Court further explained that "'[a] military commission is our commonlaw war court. It has no statutory existence, though it is recognized by statute law. '" Id. at 20 n.7 (quoting General Crowder). The logical implication is that even without Article 15 or any other statute, the President can create commissions on the basis of his inherent authority as Commander-in-Chief. See also Madsen, 343 U.S. at 346–347 ("Since our nation's earliest days, [military] commissions have been constitutionally recognized agencies for meeting many urgent governmental responsibilities related to war. They have taken many forms and borne many names. Neither their procedure nor their jurisdiction has been prescribed by statute.").

CONCLUSION

For the reasons stated above, respondents respectfully request that the petition be denied, that their cross-motion to dismiss be granted, and that a judgment of dismissal be entered in favor of respondents.

DATED this 6th day of August, 2004.

. . .

UNITED STATES DISTRICT COURT
WESTERN DISTRICT OF WASHINGTON
AT SEATTLE

CHARLES SWIFT, as next friend for SALIM AHMED HAMDAN, Petitioner, v. DONALD H. RUMSFELD, *et al.*, Respondents.	Case No. C04-0777L **ORDER TRANSFERRING CASE TO DISTRICT COURT FOR THE DISTRICT OF COLUMBIA**

. . .

III. CONCLUSION

This Court must accept the guidance of the two higher appellate courts, both of which have expressed a clear preference for consolidating all Guantanamo Bay detainee habeas corpus challenges and related claims within one district only – the District of Columbia District Court. For the foregoing reasons, the Court GRANTS IN PART Respondents' motion (Dkt. # 34). The Court STRIKES the deadlines for Petitioner's reply and TRANS-FERS this case to the United States District Court for the District of Columbia.[3]

DATED this 9th day of August, 2004.

_____

Robert S. Lasnik
United States District Judge

_____

[3] . . .

11/08/2004: DISTRICT COURT DECISION*

**UNITED STATES DISTRICT COURT
FOR THE DISTRICT OF COLUMBIA**

SALIM AHMED HAMDAN,   :
                    :

      Plaintiff,   :
                    :

    v.   :   Civil Action No. 04-1519 (JR)
                    :

DONALD H. RUMSFELD,   :
                    :

      Defendant.   :

MEMORANDUM OPINION

Salim Ahmed Hamdan petitions for a writ of habeas corpus, challenging the lawfulness of the Secretary of Defense's plan to try him for alleged war crimes before a military commission convened under special orders issued by the President of the United States, rather than before a court-martial convened under the Uniform Code of Military Justice. The government moves to dismiss. Because Hamdan has not been determined by a competent tribunal to be an offender triable under the law of war, 10 U.S.C. §821, and because in any event the procedures established for the Military Commission by the President's order are "contrary to or inconsistent" with those applicable to courts-martial, 10 U.S.C. §836, Hamdan's petition will be **granted** in part. The government's motion will be **denied**. The reasons for these rulings are set forth below.

. . .

ANALYSIS

. . .

2. No proper determination has been made that Hamdan is an offender triable by military tribunal under the law of war.

    a.   The President may establish military commissions only for offenders or offenses triable by military tribunal under the law of war.

The major premise of the government's argument that the President has untrammeled power to establish military tribunals is that his authority emanates from Article II of the Constitution and is inherent in his role as commander-in-chief. None of the principal cases on which the government relies, Ex parte Quirin, 317 U.S. 1 (1942), Application of Yamashita, 327 U.S. 1 (1946), and Madsen v. Kinsella, 343 U.S. 341 (1952), has so held. In Quirin the Supreme Court located the power in Article I, §8, emphasizing the President's executive power as commander-in-chief "to wage war which Congress has declared, and to carry into effect all laws passed by Congress for the conduct of war and for the government and regulation of the Armed Forces, and all laws defining and punishing offences against the law of nations, including those which pertain to the conduct of

---

* The petition filed in the District Court for the District of Columbia on Sept. 2, 2004, is identical to that filed in the Western District of Washington. – *Eds.*

war." Quirin, 317 U.S. at 10 (emphasis added). Quirin stands for the proposition that the authority to appoint military commissions is found, not in the inherent power of the presidency, but in the Articles of War (a predecessor of the Uniform Code of Military Justice) by which Congress provided rules for the government of the army. Id. Thus, Congress provided for the trial by courts-martial of members of the armed forces and specific classes of persons associated with or serving with the army, id., and "the Articles [of War] also recognize the 'military commission' appointed by military command as an appropriate tribunal for the trial and punishment of offenses against the law of war not ordinarily tried by court martial." Id. The President's authority to prescribe procedures for military commissions was conferred by Articles 38 and 46 of the Articles of War. Id. The Quirin Court sustained the President's order creating a military commission, because "[b]y his Order creating the . . . Commission [the President] has undertaken to exercise the authority conferred upon him by Congress. . . ." Id. at 11.

This sentence continues with the words ". . . and also such authority as the Constitution itself gives the Commander in Chief, to direct the performance of those functions which may constitutionally be performed by the military arm of the nation in time of war." Id. at 11. That dangling idea is not explained – in Quirin or in later cases. The Court expressly found it unnecessary in Quirin "to determine to what extent the President as Commander in Chief has constitutional power to create military commissions without the support of Congressional legislation. For here Congress has authorized trial of offenses against the law of war before such commissions." Id.

In Yamashita, the Supreme Court noted that it had "had occasion [in Quirin] to consider at length the sources and nature of the authority to create military commissions for the trial of enemy combatants for offenses against the law of war," Yamashita, at 327 U.S. at 7, and noted:

> [W]e there pointed out that Congress, in the exercise of the power conferred upon it by Article I, §8 Cl. 10 of the Constitution to 'define and punish . . . Offenses against the Law of Nations . . . ,' of which the law of war is a part, had by the Articles of War [citation omitted] recognized the 'military commission' appointed by military command as it had previously existed in United States Army practice, as an appropriate tribunal for the trial and punishment of offenses against the law of war.

Id. at 7 (emphasis added). Further on, the Court noted:

> We further pointed out that Congress, by sanctioning trial of enemy combatants for violations of the law of war by military commission, had not attempted to codify the law of war or to mark its precise boundaries. Instead, by Article 15 it had incorporated, by reference, as within the preexisting jurisdiction of military commissions created by appropriate military command, all offenses which are defined as such by the law of war, and which may constitutionally be included within that jurisdiction. It thus adopted the system of military common law applied by military tribunals so far as it should be recognized and deemed applicable by the courts, and as further defined and supplemented by the Hague Convention, to which the United States and the Axis powers were parties."

Id. at 7–8 (emphasis added). And again:

> Congress, in the exercise of its constitutional power to define and punish offenses against the law of nations, of which the law of war is a part, has recognized the 'military commission' appointed by military command, as it had previously existed in United States Army practice, as an appropriate tribunal for the trial and punishment of offenses against the law of war.

Id. at 16 (emphasis added). Yamashita concluded that, by giving "sanction... to any use of the military commission contemplated by the common law of war," Congress "preserve[d] their traditional jurisdiction over enemy combatants unimpaired by the Articles [of War]...." Id. at 20.

What was then Article 15 of the Articles of War is now Article 21 of the Uniform Code of Military Justice, 10 U.S.C. §821. It provides:

> The provisions of this chapter conferring jurisdiction upon courts-martial do not deprive military commissions, provost courts, or other military tribunals of concurrent jurisdiction with respect to offenders or offenses that by statute or by the law of war may be tried by military commissions, provost courts, or other military tribunals.

Quirin and Yamashita make it clear that Article 21 represents Congressional approval of the historical, traditional, non-statutory military commission. The language of that approval, however, does not extend past "offenders or offenses that by statute or by the law of war may be tried by military commissions...." 10 U.S.C. §821.

Any additional jurisdiction for military commissions would have to come from some inherent executive authority that Quirin, Yamashita, and Madsen neither define nor directly support. If the President does have inherent power in this area, it is quite limited. Congress has the power to amend those limits and could do so tomorrow. Were the President to act outside the limits now set for military commissions by Article 21, however, his actions would fall into the most restricted category of cases identified by Justice Jackson in his concurring opinion in Youngstown Sheet & Tube Co. v. Sawyer, 343 U.S. 579, 637 (1952), in which "the President takes measures incompatible with the expressed or implied will of Congress," and in which the President's power is "at its lowest ebb."[5]

> b.   The law of war includes the Third Geneva Convention, which requires trial by court-martial as long as Hamdan's POW status is in doubt.

> "From the very beginning of its history this Court has recognized and applied the law of war as including that part of the law of nations which prescribes, for the conduct of war, the status, rights and duties of enemy nations as well as of enemy individuals."

This language is from Quirin, 317 U.S. at 27–28. The United States has ratified the Geneva Convention Relative to the Treatment of Prisoners of War of August 12, 1949, 6 U.S.T. 3316, 74 U.N.T.S. 135 (the Third Geneva Convention). Afghanistan is a party to the Geneva Conventions.[6] The Third Geneva Convention is acknowledged to be part of the law of war, 10/25/04 Tr. at 55; Military Commission Instruction No. 2, §(5)(G) (Apr. 30, 2003); 32 C.F.R. §11.5(g), http://www.defenselink.mil/news/May2003/d20030430milcominstno2.pdf. It is applicable by its terms in "all cases of declared war or of any other armed conflict which may arise between two or more of the High Contracting Parties, even if the state of war is not recognized by one of them." Third Geneva Convention, art. 2. That language covers the hostilities in Afghanistan that were ongoing in late 2001, when Hamdan was captured there. If Hamdan is entitled to the protections accorded prisoners of war under the Third Geneva Convention, one need look no farther than Article 102 for the rule that requires his habeas petition to be granted:

> A prisoner of war can be validly sentenced only if the sentence has been pronounced by the same courts according to the same procedure as in the case of members of

---

[5] For further development of this argument, see Brief Amici Curiae of Sixteen Law Professors at 9–13.

[6] See International Committee of the Red Cross, Treaty Database, at http://www.icrc.org/ihl.

the armed forces of the Detaining Power, and if, furthermore, the provisions of the present Chapter have been observed.[7]

The Military Commission is not such a court. Its procedures are not such procedures.

The government does not dispute the proposition that prisoners of war may not be tried by military tribunal. Its position is that Hamdan is not entitled to the protections of the Third Geneva Convention at all, and certainly not to prisoner-of-war status, and that in any event the protections of the Third Geneva Convention are not enforceable by way of habeas corpus.

(1) The government's first argument that the Third Geneva Convention does not protect Hamdan asserts that Hamdan was captured, not in the course of a conflict between the United States and Afghanistan, but in the course of a "separate" conflict with al Qaeda. That argument is rejected. The government apparently bases the argument on a Presidential "finding" that it claims is "not reviewable." See Motion to Dismiss at 33, Hicks v. Bush (D.D.C. No. 02-00299) (October 14, 2004). The finding is set forth in Memorandum from the President, to the Vice President et al., Humane Treatment of al Qaeda and Taliban Detainees(February 7, 2002), http://www.library.law.pace.edu/research/020207_bushmemo.pdf, stating that the Third Geneva Convention applies to the Taliban detainees, but not to the al Qaeda detainees captured in Afghanistan, because al Qaeda is not a state party to the Geneva Conventions. Notwithstanding the President's view that the United States was engaged in two separate conflicts in Afghanistan (the common public understanding is to the contrary, see Joan Fitzpatrick, Jurisdiction of Military Commissions and the Ambiguous War on Terrorism, 96 Am. J. Int'l. L. 345, 349 (2002) (conflict in Afghanistan was international armed conflict in which Taliban and al Qaeda joined forces against U.S. and its Afghan allies)), the government's attempt to separate the Taliban from al Qaeda for Geneva Convention purposes finds no support in the structure of the Conventions themselves, which are triggered by the place of the conflict, and not by what particular faction a fighter is associated with. See Amicus Brief of General David M. Brahms (ret.), Admiral Lee F. Gunn (ret.), Admiral John D. Hutson (ret.), General Richard O'Meara (ret.) (Generals and Admirals Amicus Brief) at 17 (citing Memorandum from William H. Taft IV, Legal Adviser, Dep't of State, to Counsel to the President ¶3 (Feb. 2, 2002), http://www.fas.org/sgp/othergov/taft.pdf). Thus at some level – whether as a prisoner-of-war entitled to the full panoply of Convention protections or only under the more limited protections afforded by Common Article 3, see infra note 13 – the Third Geneva Convention applies to all persons detained in Afghanistan during the hostilities there.

(2) The government next argues that, even if the Third Geneva Convention might theoretically apply to anyone captured in the Afghanistan theater, members of al Qaeda such as Hamdan are not entitled to POW status because they do not satisfy the test established by Article 4(2) of the Third Geneva Convention – they do not carry arms openly and operate under the laws and customs of war. Gov't Resp. at 35. See also The White House, Statement by the Press Secretary on the Geneva Convention (May 7, 2003), http://www.whitehouse.gov/news/releases/2003/05/20030507-18.html. We know this, the government argues, because the President himself has determined that Hamdan was a member of al Qaeda or otherwise involved in terrorism against the United States. Id. Presidential determinations in this area, the government argues, are due "extraordinary deference." 10/25/04 Tr. at 38. Moreover (as the court was advised for the first time at oral argument on October 25, 2004) a Combatant Status Review Tribunal (CSRT) found,

---

[7] ...

after a hearing on October 3, 2004, that Hamdan has the status of an enemy combatant "as either a member of or affiliated with Al Qaeda." 10/25/04 Tr. at 12.

Article 5 of the Third Geneva Convention provides:

> **Should any doubt arise as to whether persons, having committed a belligerent act and having fallen into the hands of the enemy, belong to any of the categories enumerated in Article 4 such persons shall enjoy the protection of the present Convention until such time as their status has been determined by a competent tribunal.**

This provision has been implemented and confirmed by Army Regulation 190–8, Enemy Prisoners of War, Retained Personnel, Civilian Internees and Other Detainees, http://www.army.mil/usapa/epubs/pdf/r190_8.pdf., Hamdan has asserted his entitlement to POW status, and the Army's regulations provide that whenever a detainee makes such a claim his status is "in doubt." Army Regulation 190–8, §1–6(a); Hamdi, 124 S. Ct. at 2658 (Souter, J., concurring). The Army's regulation is in keeping with general international understandings of the meaning of Article 5. See generally Generals and Admirals Amicus Brief at 18–22.

Thus the government's position that no doubt has arisen as to Hamdan's status does not withstand scrutiny, and neither does the government's position that, if a hearing is required by Army regulations, "it was provided," 10/25/04 Tr. at 40. There is nothing in this record to suggest that a competent tribunal has determined that Hamdan is not a prisoner-of-war under the Geneva Conventions. Hamdan has appeared before the Combatant Status Review Tribunal, but the CSRT was not established to address detainees' status under the Geneva Conventions. It was established to comply with the Supreme Court's mandate in Hamdi, supra, to decide "whether the detainee is properly detained as an enemy combatant" for purposes of continued detention. Memorandum From Deputy Secretary of Defense, to Secretary of the Navy, Order Establishing Combatant Status Review Tribunal 3 (July 7, 2003), http://www.defenselink.mil/news/Jul2004/d20040707review.pdf; see also Memorandum From Secretary of the Navy, Implementation of Combatant Status Review Tribunal Procedures for Enemy Combatants Detained at Guantanamo Bay Naval Base, Cuba (July 29, 2004), http://www.defenselink.mil/news/Jul2004/d20040730comb.pdf.

The government's legal position is that the CSRT determination that Hamdan was a member of or affiliated with al Qaeda is also determinative of Hamdan's prisoner-of-war status, since the President has already determined that detained al Qaeda members are not prisoners-of-war under the Geneva Conventions, see 10/25/04 Tr. at 37. The President is not a "tribunal," however. The government must convene a competent tribunal (or address a competent tribunal already convened) and seek a specific determination as to Hamdan's status under the Geneva Conventions. Until or unless such a tribunal decides otherwise, Hamdan has, and must be accorded, the full protections of a prisoner-of-war.

(3) The government's next argument, that Common Article 3 does not apply because it was meant to cover local and not international conflicts, is also rejected.[8] It is universally agreed, and is demonstrable in the Convention language itself, in the context in which it was adopted, and by the generally accepted law of nations, that Common Article 3 embodies "international human norms," Mehinovic v. Vuckovic, 198 F. Supp. 2d 1322, 1351 (N.D. Ga. 2002), and that it sets forth the "most fundamental requirements of the law of war." Kadic v. Karadzic, 70 F.3d at 232, 243 (2d Cir. 1995). The International Court of Justice has stated it plainly: "There is no doubt that, in the event of international

---

[8] Article 3 of the Third Geneva Convention is called "Common Article 3" because it is common to all four of the 1949 Geneva Conventions. . . . .

armed conflicts . . . [the rules articulated in Common Article 3] . . . constitute a minimum yardstick, in addition to the more elaborate rules which are also to apply to international conflicts; and they are rules which, in the Court's opinion, reflect what the court in 1949 called 'elementary considerations of humanity.'" Nicaragua v. United States, 1986 I.C.J. 14, 114 (Judgment of June 27). The court went on to say that, "[b]ecause the minimum rules applicable to international and non-international conflicts are identical, there is no need to address the question whether . . . [the actions alleged to be violative of Common Article 3] must be looked at in the context of the rules which operate for one or the other category of conflict."[9] Id.

The government has asserted a position starkly different from the positions and behavior of the United States in previous conflicts, one that can only weaken the United States' own ability to demand application of the Geneva Conventions to Americans captured during armed conflicts abroad. *Amici* remind us of the capture of U.S. Warrant Officer Michael Durant in 1993 by forces loyal to a Somali warlord. The United States demanded assurances that Durant would be treated consistently with protections afforded by the Convention, even though, if the Convention were applied as narrowly as the government now seeks to apply it to Hamdan, "Durant's captors would not be bound to follow the convention because they were not a 'state'". Neil McDonald & Scott Sullivan, Rational Interpretation in Irrational Times: The Third Geneva Convention and "War On Terror", 44 Harv. Int'l. L.J. 301, 310 (2003). Examples of the way other governments have already begun to cite the United States' Guantanamo policy to justify their own repressive policies are set forth in Lawyers Committee for Human Rights, Assessing the New Normal: Liberty and Security for the Post-September 11 United States, at 77–80 (2003).

(4) The government's putative trump card is that Hamdan's rights under the Geneva Conventions, if any, and whatever they are, are not enforceable by this Court – that, in effect, Hamdan has failed to state a claim upon which relief can be granted – because the Third Geneva Convention is not "self-executing" and does not give rise to a private cause of action.

As an initial matter, it should be noted Hamdan has not asserted a "private right of action" under the Third Geneva Convention. The Convention is implicated in this case by operation of the statute that limits trials by military tribunal to "offenders . . . triable under the law of war." 10 U.S.C. §821. The government's argument thus amounts to the assertion that no federal court has the authority to determine whether the Third Geneva Convention has been violated, or, if it has, to grant relief from the violation.

Treaties made under the authority of the United States are the supreme law of the land. U.S. Const. art. VI, cl. 2. United States courts are bound to give effect to international law and to international agreements of the United States unless such agreements are "non-self-executing." The Paquete Habana, 175 U.S. 677, 708 (1900); Restatement (Third) of the Foreign Relations Law of the United States §111. A treaty is "non-self-executing" if it manifests an intention that it not become effective as domestic law without enactment of implementing legislation; or if the Senate in consenting to the treaty requires implementing legislation; or if implementing legislation is constitutionally required. Id. at §111(4). The controlling law in this Circuit on the subject of whether or not treaties are self-executing is Diggs v. Richardson, 555 F.2d 848 (D.C. Cir. 1976), a suit to prohibit the importation of seal furs from Namibia, brought by a citizen plaintiff who sought to compel United States government compliance with a United Nations Security Council resolution calling on member states to have no dealings with South

---

[9] See also Brief Amici of Sixteen Law Professors at 33 n.32.

Africa. The decision in that case instructs a court interpreting a treaty to look to the intent of the signatory parties as manifested by the language of the treaty and, if the language is uncertain, then to look to the circumstances surrounding execution of the treaty. Id. at 851. Diggs relies on the Head Money Cases, 112 U.S. 580 (1884), which established the proposition that a "treaty is a law of the land as an act of congress is, whenever its provisions prescribe a rule by which the rights of the private citizen or subject may be determined." Id. At 598. The Court in Diggs concluded that the provisions of the Security Council resolution were not addressed to the judicial branch of government, that they did not by their terms confer rights on individuals, and that instead the resolution clearly called upon governments to take action. Diggs, 555 F.2d at 851.

The Geneva Conventions, of course, are all about prescribing rules by which the rights of individuals may be determined. Moreover, as petitioner and several of the *amici* have pointed out, see, e.g., Pet'r's Mem. Supp. of Pet. at 39 n.11, it is quite clear from the legislative history of the ratification of the Geneva Conventions that Congress carefully considered what further legislation, if any, was deemed "required to give effect to the provisions contained in the four conventions," S. Rep. No. 84–9, at 30 (1955), and found that only four provisions required implementing legislation. Articles 5 and 102, which are dispositive of Hamdan's case, supra, were not among them. What did require implementing legislation were Articles 129 and 130, providing for additional criminal penalties to be imposed upon those who engaged in "grave" violations of the Conventions, such as torture, medical experiments, or "wilful" denial of Convention protections, none of which is involved here. Third Geneva Convention, art. 130. Judge Bork must have had those provisions in mind, together with Congress' response in enacting the War Crimes Act, 18 U.S.C. §2441, when he found that the Third Geneva Convention was not self-executing because it required "implementing legislation." Tel-Oren v. Libyan Arab Republic, et al., 726 F.2d 774, 809 (D.C. Cir. 1984) (Bork, J., concurring). That opinion is one of three written by a three-judge panel, none of which was joined by any other member of the panel. It is not Circuit precedent and it is, I respectfully suggest, erroneous. "Some provisions of an international agreement may be self-executing and others non-self-executing." Restatement (Third) of Foreign Relations Law of the United States §111 cmt. h.[10]

* * *

Because the Geneva Conventions were written to protect individuals, because the Executive Branch of our government has implemented the Geneva Conventions for fifty years without questioning the absence of implementing legislation, because Congress clearly understood that the Conventions did not require implementing legislation except in a few specific areas, and because nothing in the Third Geneva Convention itself manifests the contracting parties' intention that it not become effective as domestic law without the enactment of implementing legislation, I conclude that, insofar as it is pertinent here, the Third Geneva Convention is a self-executing treaty.[11] I further conclude

---

[10] The observation in Al-Odah v. United States, 321 F.3d 1134, 1147 (D.c. cir.2003), that the Third Geneva Convention is not self-executing merely relies on the reasons stated by Judge Bork in Tel-Oren, 726 F.2d at 809. Since that observation was not essential to the outcome in Al-Odah,, and since in any event Al-Odah was reversed by the Supreme Court, I am not bound by it.

[11] Hamdan is a citizen of Yemen. The government has refused permission for Yemeni diplomats to visit Hamdan at Guantanamo Bay. Decl. of Lieutenant Commander Charles Swift at 4 (May 3, 2004). It ill behooves the government to argue that enforcement of the Geneva Convention is only to be had through diplomatic channels.

that it is at least a matter of some doubt as to whether or not Hamdan is entitled to the protections of the Third Geneva Convention as a prisoner of war and that accordingly he must be given those protections unless and until the "competent tribunal" referred to in Article 5 concludes otherwise. It follows from those conclusions that Hamdan may not be tried for the war crimes he is charged with except by a court-martial duly convened under the Uniform Code of Military Justice.

b.   Abstention is appropriate with respect to Hamdan's rights
under Common Article 3.

There is an argument that, even if Hamdan does not have prisoner-of-war status, Common Article 3 would be violated by trying him for his alleged war crimes in this Military Commission. Abstention is appropriate, and perhaps required, on that question, because, unlike Article 102, which unmistakably mandates trial of POW's only by general court-martial and thus implicates the jurisdiction of the Military Commission, the Common Article 3 requirement of trial before a "regularly constituted court affording all the judicial guarantees which are recognized as indispensable by civilized peoples" has no fixed, term-of-art meaning. A substantial number of rights and procedures conferred by the UCMJ are missing from the Military Commission's rules. See infra note 12; Generals and Admirals Amicus Brief at 24. I am aware of no authority that defines the word "guarantees" in Common Article 3 to mean that all of these rights must be guaranteed in advance of trial. Only Hamdan's right to be present at every phase of his trial and to see all the evidence admitted against him is of immediate pretrial concern. That right is addressed in the next section of this opinion.

3.   In at least one critical respect, the procedures of the Military Commission are fatally contrary to or inconsistent with those of the Uniform Code of Military Justice.

In most respects, the procedures established for the Military Commission at Guantanamo under the President's order define a trial forum that looks appropriate and even reassuring when seen through the lens of American jurisprudence. The rules laid down by Military Commission Order No. 1, 32 C.F.R. §9.3, provide that the defendant shall have appointed military counsel, that he may within reason choose to replace "detailed" counsel with another military officer who is a judge advocate if such officer is available, that he may retain a civilian attorney if he can afford it, that he must receive a copy of the charges in a language that he understands, that he will be presumed innocent until proven guilty, that proof of guilt must be beyond a reasonable doubt, that he must be provided with the evidence the prosecution intends to introduce at trial and with any exculpatory evidence known to the prosecution, with important exceptions discussed below, that he is not required to testify at trial and that the Commission may not draw an adverse inference from his silence, that he may obtain witnesses and documents for his defense to the extent necessary and reasonably available, that he may present evidence at trial and cross-examine prosecution witnesses, and that he may not be placed in jeopardy twice for any charge as to which a finding has become final. Id. at §§9.4 and 9.5.

The Military Commission is remarkably different from a court-martial, however, in two important respects. The first has to do with the structure of the reviewing authority after trial; the second, with the power of the appointing authority or the presiding officer to exclude the accused from hearings and deny him access to evidence presented against him.[12]

Petitioner's challenge to the first difference is unsuccessful. It is true that the President has made himself, or the Secretary of Defense acting at his direction, the final reviewing authority, whereas under the Uniform Code of Military Justice there would be two levels of independent review by members of the Third Branch of government – an appeal to the Court of Appeals for the Armed Forces, whose active bench consists of five civilian judges, and possible review by the Supreme Court on writ of certiorari. The President has, however, established a Review Panel that will review the trial record and make a recommendation to the Secretary of Defense, or, if the panel finds an error of law, return the case for further proceedings. The President has appointed to that panel some of the most distinguished civilian lawyers in the country (who may receive temporary commissions to fulfill the requirement that they be "officers," see Military Commission Order No. 1(6)(H); 32 C.F.R. §9.6(h)).[13] And, as for the President's naming himself or the Secretary of Defense as the final reviewing authority, that, after all, is what a military commission is. If Hamdan is triable by any military tribunal, the fact that final review of a finding of guilt would reside in the President or his designee is not "contrary to or inconsistent with" the UCMJ.

---

[12] A great many other differences are identified and discussed in David Glazier, Kangaroo Court or Competent Tribunal? Judging the 21st Century Military Commission, 89 Va. L. Rev. 2005, 2015–2020 (2003). Differences include (not an exhaustive list):

Article 16 requires that every court-martial consist of a military judge and no less than five members, as opposed to the Military Commission rules that require only three members. Military Commission Order No. 1 (4) (A); Article 10 of the UCMJ provides a speedy trial right, while the Military Commission rules provide none. Article 13 states that pre-trial detention should not be more rigorous than required to ensure defendant's presence, while the Commission rules contain no such provision and, in fact, Hamdan was held in solitary confinement in Camp Echo for over 10 months. Article 30 states that charges shall be signed by one with personal knowledge of them or who has investigated them. The Military Commission rules include no such requirement. Article 31 provides that the accused must be informed before interrogation of the nature of the accusation, his right not to make any statement, and that statements he makes may be used in proceedings against him, and further provides that statements taken from the accused in violation of these requirements may not be received in evidence at a military proceeding. The Military Commission rules provide that the accused may not be forced to testify at his own trial, but the rule does not "preclude admission of evidence of prior statements or conduct of the Accused." Military Commission Order No. 1(5) (F). Article 33 states that the accused will receive notice of the charges against him within eight days of being arrested or confined unless written reason is given why this is not practicable. The Military Commission rules include no such requirement, and in fact, Hamdan, after being moved to Camp Echo for pre-commission detainment, was not notified of the charges against him for over 6 months. Article 38 provides the accused with certain rights before charges brought against him may be "referred" for trial, which include the right to counsel and the right to present evidence on his behalf. The Military Commission rules provide for no pre-trial referral process at all. Article 41 gives each side one peremptory challenge, while the Military Commission rules provide for none. Article 42 requires all trial participants to take an oath to perform their duties faithfully. The Military Commission rules allow witnesses to testify without taking an oath. Military Commission Order No. 1(6) (D). Article 52 requires three-fourths concurrence to impose a life sentence. The Military Commission rules only require two-thirds concurrence of the members to impose such a sentence. Military Commission Order No. 1 (6) (F). Article 26 provides that military judges do not vote on guilt or innocence. Under the Military Commission rules, the Presiding Officer is a voting member of the trial panel. Military Commission Order No. 1 (4) (A).

[13] Griffin B. Bell, a former United States Circuit Judge and Attorney General; William T. Coleman, Jr., a former Secretary of Transportation; Edward George Biester, Jr., a former Congressman, former Pennsylvania Attorney General, and current Pennsylvania Judge; and Frank J. Williams, Chief Justice of the Rhode Island Supreme Court. See Dep't of Defense, Military Commission Biographies, http://www.defenselink.mil/news/Aug2004/commissions_biographies.html.

The second difference between the procedures adopted for the Military Commission and those applicable in a court-martial convened under the Uniform Code of Military Justice is far more troubling. That difference lies in the treatment of information that is classified; information that is otherwise "protected"; or information that might implicate the physical safety of participants, including witnesses, or the integrity of intelligence and law enforcement sources and methods, or "other national security interests." See Military Commission Order No. 1(6)(B)(3); 32 C.F.R. §9.6(b). Under the Secretary of Defense's regulations, the Military Commission must "[h]old open proceedings except where otherwise decided by the Appointing Authority or the Presiding Officer." Id. Detailed military defense counsel may not be excluded from proceedings, nor may evidence be received that has not been presented to detailed defense counsel, Military Commission Order No. 1 (6)(B)(3), (6)(D)(5); 32 C.F.R. §§9.6(b)(3), (d)(5). The accused himself may be excluded from proceedings, however, and evidence may be adduced that he will never see (because his lawyer will be forbidden to disclose it to him). See id.

Thus, for example, testimony may be received from a confidential informant, and Hamdan will not be permitted to hear the testimony, see the witness's face, or learn his name. If the government has information developed by interrogation of witnesses in Afghanistan or elsewhere, it can offer such evidence in transcript form, or even as summaries of transcripts. See Military Commission Order No. 1(6)(D); 32 C.F.R. §9.6(d). The Presiding Officer or the Appointing Authority may receive it in evidence if it meets the "reasonably probative" standard but forbid it to be shown to Hamdan. See id. As counsel for Hamdan put it at oral argument, portions of Mr. Hamdan's trial can be conducted "outside his presence. He can be excluded, not for his conduct, [but] because the government doesn't want him to know what's in it. They make a great big deal out of I can be there, but anybody who's practiced trial law, especially criminal law, knows that where you get your cross examination questions from is turning to your client and saying, 'Did that really happen? Is that what happened?' I'm not permitted to do that." 10/25/04 Tr. at 97.

It is obvious beyond the need for citation that such a dramatic deviation from the confrontation clause could not be countenanced in any American court, particularly after Justice Scalia's extensive opinion in his decision this year in Crawford v. Washington, 124 S.Ct. 1354 (2004). It is also apparent that the right to trial "in one's presence" is established as a matter of international humanitarian and human rights law.[14] But it is unnecessary to consider whether Hamdan can rely on any American constitutional notions of fairness, or whether the nature of these proceedings really is, as counsel asserts, akin to the Star Chamber, 10/25/04 Tr. at 97 (and violative of Common Article 3), because – at least in this critical respect – the rules of the Military Commission are fatally "contrary to or inconsistent with" the statutory requirements for courts-martial convened under the Uniform Code of Military Justice, and thus unlawful.

In a general court-martial conducted under the UCMJ, the accused has the right to be present during sessions of the court:

---

[14] International Covenant on Civil and Political Rights, Dec. 19, 1966, 999 U.N.T.S. 171, art. 14(d)(3); Protocol Additional to the Geneva Conventions of 12 August 1949, and relating to the Protection of Victims of International Armed Conflicts, June 8, 1977, 1125 U.N.T.S. 3, art. 75.4(e). "This includes, at a minimum, all hearings in which the prosecutor participates. E.g., Eur.Ct.H.Rts., Belziuk v. Poland, App. No. 00023103/93, Judgment of 25 March 1998, para. 39." Brief Amici Curiae of Louise Doswald-Beck et al. at 32–33 n.137. In this country, as Justice Scalia noted in Crawford v. Washington, 124 S. Ct. at 1363, the right to be present was held three years after the adoption of the Sixth Amendment to be a rule of common law "founded on natural justice" (quoting from State v. Webb, 2 N.C. 104 (1794)).

> When the members of a court-martial deliberate or vote, only the members may be present. All other proceedings, including any other consultation of the members of the court with counsel or the military judge, shall be made a part of the record and shall be in the presence of the accused, the defense counsel, the trial counsel, and, in cases in which a military judge has been detailed to the court, the military judge.

UCMJ Article 39(b), 10 U.S.C. §839(b) (emphasis added).

Article 36 of the Uniform Code of Military Justice, 10 U.S.C. §836(a), provides:

> Pretrial, trial, and post-trial procedures, including modes of proof, for cases arising under this chapter triable in courts-martial, military commissions and other military tribunals, and procedures for courts of inquiry, may be prescribed by the President by regulations which shall, so far as he considers practicable, apply the principles of law and the rules of evidence generally recognized in the trial of criminal cases in the United States district courts, but which may not be contrary to or inconsistent with this chapter. (Emphasis added.)

The government argues for procedural "flexibility" in military commission proceedings, asserting that

> construing Article 36 rigidly to mean that there can be no deviation from the UCMJ...would have resulted in having virtually all of the UCMJ provisions apply to the military commissions, which would clearly be in conflict with historical practice, as recognized by the Supreme Court, in both Yamashita and Madsen, and also inconsistent with Congress' intent, as reflected in Articles 21 and 36, and other provisions of the UCMJ that specifically mention commissions when a particular rule applies to them.

10/25/04 Tr. 26–27. But the language of Article 36 does not require rigid adherence to all of the UCMJ's rules for courts-martial. It proscribes only procedures and modes of proof that are "contrary to or inconsistent with" the UCMJ.[15]

As for the government's reliance on Yamashita and Madsen: Yamashita offers support for the government's position only if developments between 1946 and 2004 are ignored. In 1946, the Supreme Court held that Article 38 of the Articles of War (the predecessor of Article 36 of the UCMJ) did not provide to enemy combatants in military tribunals the procedural protections (in that case, restrictions on the use of depositions) available in courts-martial under the Articles of War. Yamashita, 327 U.S. at 18–20. The Court's holding depended upon the fact that General Yamashita, an enemy combatant, was not subject to trial by courts-martial under then Article 2 of the Articles of War (the predecessor to Article 2 of the UCMJ), which conferred courts-martial jurisdiction only over U.S. military personnel and those affiliated with them. Id. at 19–20. The Court held that Congress intended to grant court-martial protections within tribunals only to those persons who could be tried under the laws of war in either courts-martial or tribunals. See id. The UCMJ and the 1949 Geneva Conventions had not come into effect in 1946. Article 2 of the UCMJ is now broader than Article 2 of the Articles of War. See generally Library of Congress, Index and Legislative History of the UCMJ (1950), http://www.loc.gov/rr/frd/Military_ Law/index_legHistory.html. It has been expanded to include as persons subject to court-martial, both prisoners of war, 10 U.S.C. §802(a)(9), and "persons within an area leased by or otherwise reserved or acquired for the use of

---

[15] In *Kangaroo Court or Competent Tribunal?*, supra note 14 at 2020–22, the author suggests that one possible reading of this provision would require consistency only with those nine UCMJ articles (of 158 total) that expressly refer to or recite their applicability to military commissions. A review of the articles that contain such references or recitals, however, see id. at 2014 n 23, demonstrates the implausibility of such a reading.

the United States which is under the control of the Secretary concerned and which is outside the United States and outside the Commonwealth of Puerto Rico, Guam, and the Virgin Islands." Id. §802(a)(12). One or both of those new categories undoubtedly applies to petitioner. For this reason, Yamashita's holding now arguably gives more support to petitioner's case than to the government's.[16]

Madsen follows Yamashita in its general characterization of military commissions as "our commonlaw war courts" and states that "[n]either their procedure nor their jurisdiction has been prescribed by statute." Madsen, 343 U.S. at 346–47. It does not appear that any procedural issue was actually raised in Madsen, however, nor were the Geneva Conventions addressed in any way in that case. Madsen was an American citizen, the dependent wife of an Armed Forces member, charged with murdering her husband in the American Zone of Occupied Germany in 1947 and tried there by the United States Court of the Allied High Commission for Germany. Her argument, which the Court rejected, was simply that the jurisdiction of military commissions over civilian offenders and non-military offenses was automatically ended by amendments to the Articles of War enacted in 1916 that extended the jurisdiction of courts-martial to persons accompanying United States forces outside the territorial jurisdiction of the United States. Id. at 351–52.

Even though Madsen presented no procedural issue, the Supreme Court did generally review the procedures applicable to Madsen's trial. A comparison between those procedures and the rules of the Guantanamo Military Commission is not favorable to the government's position here. In Madsen, United States Military Government Ordinance No. 2 (the analogue of the Military Commission Order in this case) provided, under "rights of accused":

> Every person accused before a military government court shall be entitled…to be present at his trial, to give evidence and to examine or cross-examine any witness; but the court may proceed in the absence of the accused if the accused has applied for and been granted permission to be absent, or if the accused is believed to be a fugitive from justice.

Id. at 358 n.24. There was no provision for the exclusion of the accused if classified information was to be introduced.

The government's best argument, drawing on language found in both Yamashita and Madsen, is that a "commonlaw war court" has been "adapted in each instance to the need that called it forth," 343 U.S. at 347–48 (citing Yamishita, 327 U.S. at 18–23). Neither the President in his findings and determinations nor the government in its briefs has explained what "need" calls forth the abandonment of the right Hamdan would have under the UCMJ to be present at every stage of his trial and to confront and cross-examine all witnesses and challenge all evidence brought against him. Presumably the problems of dealing with classified or "protected" information underlie the President's blanket finding that using the regular rules is "not practicable." The military has not found it impracticable to deal with classified material in courts-martial, however. An extensive and elaborate process for dealing with classified material has evolved in the Military Rules of Evidence. Mil. R. Evid. 505; see 10/25/04 Tr. 131–32. Alternatives to full

---

[16] Yamashita has been undercut by history in another important respect. The Supreme Court found the guarantee of trial by court-martial for prisoners of war in the 1929 Geneva Convention inapplicable to General Yamashita because it construed that provision as applicable only to prosecutions for acts committed while in the status of prisoner of war. The Third Geneva Convention, adopted after and in light of Yamashita, made it clear that the court-martial trial provision applies as well to offenses committed by combatants while combatants. Third Geneva Convention, art. 85. See also, Glazier, supra note 12 at 2079–80.

disclosure are provided, Mil. R. Evid. 505(i)(4)(D). Ultimately, to be sure, the government has a choice to make, if the presiding military judge determines that alternatives may not be used and the government objects to disclosure of information. At that point, the conflict between the government's need to protect classified information and the defendant's right to be present becomes irreconcilable, and the only available options are to strike or preclude the testimony of a witness, or declare a mistrial, or find against the government on any issue as to which the evidence is relevant and material to the defense, or dismiss the charges (with or without prejudice), Mil. R. Evid. 505(i)(4)(E). The point is that the rules of the Military Commission resolve that conflict, not in favor of the defendant, but in favor of the government.

Unlike the other procedural problems with the Commission's rules that are discussed elsewhere in this opinion, this one is neither remote nor speculative: Counsel made the unrefuted assertion at oral argument that Hamdan has already been excluded from the *voir dire* process and that "the government's already indicated that for two days of his trial, he won't be there. And they'll put on the evidence at that point." 10/25/04 Tr. 132. Counsel's appropriate concern is not only for the established right of his client to be present at his trial, but also for the adequacy of the defense he can provide to his client. The relationship between the right to be present and the adequacy of defense is recognized by military courts, which have interpreted Article 39 of the UCMJ in the light of Confrontation Clause jurisprudence. The leading Supreme Court case is Maryland v. Craig, 497 U.S. 836 (1990) (one-way television viewing of witness in child abuse case permissible under rule of necessity), which noted that the "central concern of the Confrontation Clause is to ensure the reliability of the evidence against a criminal defendant by subjecting it to rigorous testing in the context of an adversary proceeding before the trier of fact" and that the "elements of confrontation" – "physical presence, oath, cross-examination, and observation of demeanor by the trier of fact," serve among other things to enhance the accuracy of fact-finding by "reducing the risk that a witness will wrongfully implicate an innocent person." Id. at 846 (internal citations omitted).

Following Craig in a military case involving child abuse, the Court of Appeals for the Armed Forces found that a military judge had misapplied the Supreme Court's holding when he excluded the defendant from the courtroom during a general court-martial:

> There [in Craig], the witness was outside the courtroom and the defendant was present. Here, the witness was in the courtroom and appellant was excluded. While appellant could observe J's testimony, he could not observe the reactions of the court members or the military judge, and they could not observe his demeanor. He could not communicate with his counsel except through the bailiff, who was not a member of the defense team. We hold that this procedure violated the Sixth Amendment, Article 39, and RCM 804. While Craig and [United States v. Williams, 37 M.J. 289 (C.M.A.1993)] permit restricting an accused's face-to-face confrontation of a witness, they do not authorize expelling an accused from the courtroom.

United States v. Dalton, 45 M.J. 212, 219 (C.A.A.F.1996); see also United States v. Longstreath, 45 M.J. 366 (C.A.A.F.1996) (defendant separated from witness by television but present in courtroom).[17]

A tribunal set up to try, possibly convict, and punish a person accused of crime that is configured in advance to permit the introduction of evidence and the testimony of witnesses out of the presence of the accused is indeed substantively different from a regularly convened court-martial. If such a tribunal is not a "regularly constituted

---

17 ...

court affording all the judicial guarantees which are recognized as indispensable by civilized peoples," it is violative of Common Article 3. That is a question on which I have determined to abstain. In the meantime, however, I cannot stretch the meaning of the Military Commission's rule enough to find it consistent with the UCMJ's right to be present. 10 U.S.C. §839. A provision that permits the exclusion of the accused from his trial for reasons other than his disruptive behavior or his voluntary absence is indeed directly contrary to the UCMJ's right to be present. I must accordingly find on the basis of the statute that, so long as it operates under such a rule, the Military Commission cannot try Hamdan.

4.   Hamdan's detention claim appears to be moot, and his speedy trial and equal protection claims need not be ruled upon at this time.

Until a few days before the oral argument on Hamdan's petition, his most urgent and striking claim was that he had been unlawfully and inhumanely held in isolation since December 2003 and that such treatment was affecting his mental and psychological health as well as his ability to assist in the preparation of his defense. Late on the Friday afternoon before the oral argument held on Monday, October 25, 2004, the government filed its "notice of a change in circumstances," advising the court that Hamdan had been moved back to Camp Delta – a separate wing of Camp Delta, to be sure, but nevertheless an open-air part of Camp Delta where pre-commission detainees can communicate with each other, exercise, and practice their religion. 10/25/04 Tr. at 11–12. That change in status may not exactly moot Hamdan's claim about his confinement in isolation, which the government is capable of repeating and which has evaded review. The treatment Hamdan may or may not be afforded in the future, however, is not susceptible to review on a writ of habeas corpus.

The second most urgent and most important claim in Hamdan's original petition was his claim of entitlement to the protection of the Uniform Code of Military Justice's speedy trial rule and his assertion that he had been detained more than the maximum 90 days permitted by Article 103 of the Third Geneva Convention. These concerns were more urgent before Hamdan was transferred out of Camp Echo and back to Camp Delta and before the Supreme Court made it clear, in <u>Hamdi</u>, that, whether or not Hamdan has been charged with a crime, he may be detained for the duration of the hostilities in Afghanistan if he has been appropriately determined to be an enemy combatant.[18] The UCMJ's speedy trial requirements establish no specific number of days that will require dismissal of a suit. Article 103 of the Third Geneva Convention does bar pretrial detention exceeding 90 days, but it provides no mechanism or guidance for dealing with violations. The record does not permit a careful analysis of speedy trial issues under the test for the correlative Sixth Amendment right by <u>Barker v. Wingo</u>, 407 U.S. 514 (1972). It is well established in any event that the critical element of prejudice is best evaluated post-trial. <u>U.S. v MacDonald</u>, 435 U.S. 850, 858–9 (1978).

It is also unnecessary for me to decide whether, by virtue of his detention at Guantanamo Bay, Hamdan has any rights at all under the United States Constitution or under 42 U.S.C. §1981.[19]

---

[18] Hamdan does not currently challenge his detention as an enemy combatant in proceedings before this Court.

[19] The Supreme Court's recent decision in <u>Rasul</u> does little to clarify the Constitutional status of Guantanamo Bay but may contain some hint that non-citizens held at Guantanamo Bay have some Constitutional protection. See <u>Rasul</u>, 124 S.Ct. at 2698 n.15.

CONCLUSION

It is now clear, by virtue of the Supreme Court's decision in <u>Hamdi</u>, that the detentions of enemy combatants at Guantanamo Bay are not unlawful per se. The granting (in part) of Hamdan's petition for habeas corpus accordingly brings only limited relief. The order that accompanies this opinion provides: (1) that, unless and until a competent tribunal determines that Hamdan is not entitled to POW status, he may be tried for the offenses with which he is charged only by court-martial under the Uniform Code of Military Justice; (2) that, unless and until the Military Commission's rule permitting Hamdan's exclusion from commission sessions and the withholding of evidence from him is amended so that it is consistent with and not contrary to UCMJ Article 39, Hamdan's trial before the Military Commission would be unlawful; and (3) that Hamdan must be released from the pre-Commission detention wing of Camp Delta and returned to the general population of detainees, unless some reason other than the pending charges against him requires different treatment. Hamdan's remaining claims are in abeyance.

JAMES ROBERTSON
United States District Judge

November 8, 2004

**UNITED STATES DISTRICT COURT
FOR THE DISTRICT OF COLUMBIA**

SALIM AHMED HAMDAN,　　　　　:
　　　　　　　　　　　　　　　:
　　　　　Plaintiff,　　　　　:
　　　　　　　　　　　　　　　:
　　v.　　　　　　　　　　　　: Civil Action No. 04-1519 (JR)
　　　　　　　　　　　　　　　:
DONALD H. RUMSFELD,　　　　　:
　　　　　　　　　　　　　　　:
　　　　　Defendant.　　　　　:

ORDER

For the reasons set forth in the accompanying memorandum opinion it is

ORDERED that the petition of Salim Ahmed Hamdan for habeas corpus [1-1] is **granted in part**. It is

FURTHER ORDERED that the cross-motion to dismiss of Donald H. Rumsfeld [1-84] is **denied**. It is

FURTHER ORDERED that, unless and until a competent tribunal determines that petitioner is not entitled to the protections afforded prisoners-of-war under Article 4 of the Geneva Convention Relative to the Treatment of Prisoners of War of August 12, 1949, he may not be tried by Military Commission for the offenses with which he is charged. It is

FURTHER ORDERED that, unless and until the rules for Military Commissions (Department of Defense Military Commission Order No. 1) are amended so that they are consistent with and not contrary to Uniform Code of Military Justice Article 39, 10 U.S.C. § 839, petitioner may not be tried by Military Commission for the offenses with which he is charged. It is

FURTHER ORDERED that petitioner be released from the other than the pending charges against him requires different treatment. And it is

FURTHER ORDERED that petitioner's remaining claims are **in abeyance,** the Court having abstained from deciding them.

　　　　　　　　　　　　　　JAMES ROBERTSON
　　　　　　　　　　　United States District Judge

United States Court of Appeals

FOR THE DISTRICT OF COLUMBIA CIRCUIT

Argued April 7, 2005   Decided July 15, 2005
Reissued July 18, 2005

No. 04-5393

SALIM AHMED HAMDAN,
APPELLEE

v.

DONALD H. RUMSFELD, UNITED STATES SECRETARY OF
DEFENSE, ET AL.,
APPELLANTS

Appeal from the United States District Court
for the District of Columbia
(04cv01519)

Peter D. Keisler, Assistant Attorney General, U.S. Department of Justice, argued the cause for appellants. With him on the briefs were *Paul D. Clement*, Acting Solicitor General, *Gregory G. Katsas*, Deputy Assistant Attorney General, *Kenneth L. Wainstein*, U.S. Attorney, *Douglas N. Letter, Robert M. Loeb, August Flentje, Sharon Swingle, Eric Miller* and *Stephan E. Oestreicher, Jr.*, Attorneys.

. . .

Neal K. Katyal and *Charles Swift*, pro hac vice, argued the cause for appellee. With them on the briefs were *Benjamin S. Sharp, Kelly A. Cameron, Harry H. Schneider, Jr., Joseph M. McMillan, David R. East*, and *Charles C. Sipos*.

. . .

Before: RANDOLPH and ROBERTS, *Circuit Judges*, and WILLIAMS, *Senior Circuit Judge*.

Opinion for the Court filed by *Circuit Judge* RANDOLPH.

Concurring opinion filed by *Senior Circuit Judge* WILLIAMS.

RANDOLPH, *Circuit Judge*:

. . .

II.

In an argument distinct from his claims about the Geneva Convention, which we will discuss next, Hamdan maintains that the President violated the separation of powers inherent in the Constitution when he established military commissions. The argument is that Article I, §8, of the Constitution gives Congress the power "to constitute Tribunals inferior to the supreme Court," that Congress has not established military commissions, and that the President has no inherent authority to do so under Article II. *See* Neal K. Katyal & Laurence H. Tribe, *Waging War, Deciding Guilt: Trying the Military Tribunals*, 111 Yale L.J. 1259, 1284–85 (2002).

There is doubt that this separation-of-powers claim properly may serve as a basis for a court order halting a trial before a military commission, *see United States v. Cisneros*, 169 F.3d 763, 768–69 (D.C. Cir.1999), and there is doubt that someone in Hamdan's position is entitled to assert such a constitutional claim, *see People's Mojahedin Org. v. Dep't of State*, 182 F.3d 17, 22 (D.C. Cir. 1999); *32 County Sovereignty Comm. v. Dep't of State*, 292 F.3d 797, 799 (D.C. Cir. 2002). In any event, on the merits there is little to Hamdan's argument.

The President's Military Order of November 13, 2001, stated that any person subject to the order, including members of al Qaeda, "shall, when tried, be tried by a military commission for any and all offenses triable by [a] military commission that such individual is alleged to have committed. . . ." 66 Fed. Reg. at 57,834. The President relied on four sources of authority: his authority as Commander in Chief of the Armed Forces, U.S. Const., art. II, §2; Congress's joint resolution authorizing the use of force; 10 U.S.C. §821; and 10 U.S.C. §836. The last three are, of course, actions of Congress.

In the joint resolution, passed in response to the attacks of September 11, 2001, Congress authorized the President "to use all necessary and appropriate force against those nations, organizations, or persons he determines planned, authorized, committed, or aided" the attacks and recognized the President's "authority under the Constitution to take action to deter and prevent acts of international terrorism against the United States." Authorization for Use of Military Force, Pub. L. No. 107–40, 115 Stat. 224, 224 (2001). *In re Yamashita*, 327 U.S. 1 (1946), which dealt with the validity of a military commission, held that an "important incident to the conduct of war is the adoption of measures by the military commander, not only to repel and defeat the enemy, but to seize and subject to disciplinary measures those enemies who, in their attempt to thwart or impede our military effort, have violated the law of war." *Id.* at 11. "The trial and punishment of enemy combatants," the Court further held, is thus part of the "conduct of war." *Id.* We think it no answer to say, as Hamdan does, that this case is different because Congress did not formally declare war. It has been suggested that only wars between sovereign nations would qualify for such a declaration. *See* John M. Bickers, *Military Commissions are Constitutionally Sound: A Response to Professors Katyal and Tribe*, 34 Tex. Tech. L. Rev. 899, 918 (2003). Even so, the joint resolution "went as far toward a declaration of war as it might, and as far or further than Congress went in the Civil War, the Philippine Insurrection, the Boxer Rebellion, the Punitive Expedition against Pancho Villa, the Korean War, the Vietnam War, the invasion of Panama, the Gulf War, and numerous other conflicts." *Id.* at 917. The plurality in *Hamdi v. Rumsfeld*, in suggesting that a military commission could determine whether an American citizen was an enemy combatant in the current conflict, drew no distinction of the sort Hamdan urges upon us. 124 S. Ct. at 2640–42.

Ex parte Quirin also stands solidly against Hamdan's argument. The Court held that Congress had authorized military commissions through Article 15 of the Articles of War. 317 U.S. at 28–29; *accord In re Yamashita*, 327 U.S. at 19–20. The modern version of Article 15 is 10 U.S.C. §821, which the President invoked when he issued his military order. Section 821 states that court-martial jurisdiction does not "deprive military commissions...of concurrent jurisdiction with respect to offenders or offenses that by statute or by the law of war may be tried by military commissions." Congress also authorized the President, in another provision the military order cited, to establish procedures for military commissions. 10 U.S.C. §836(a). Given these provisions and *Quirin* and *Yamashita*, it is impossible to see any basis for Hamdan's claim that Congress has not authorized military commissions. *See* Curtis A. Bradley & Jack L. Goldsmith, *Congressional Authorization and the War on Terrorism*, 118 HARV. L. REV. 2048, 2129–31 (2005). He attempts to distinguish *Quirin* and *Yamashita* on the ground that the military commissions there were in "war zones" while Guantanamo is far removed from the battlefield. We are left to wonder why this should matter and, in any event, the distinction does not hold: the military commission in *Quirin* sat in Washington, D.C., in the Department of Justice building; the military commission in *Yamashita* sat in the Phillipines after Japan had surrendered.

We therefore hold that through the joint resolution and the two statutes just mentioned, Congress authorized the military commission that will try Hamdan.

III.

This brings us to Hamdan's argument, accepted by the district court, that the Geneva Convention Relative to the Treatment of Prisoners of War, Aug. 12, 1949, 6 U.S.T. 3316 ("1949 Geneva Convention"), ratified in 1955, may be enforced in federal court.

"Treaties made, or which shall be made, under the Authority of the United States, shall be the supreme Law of the Land." U.S. CONST., art. VI, cl. 2. Even so, this country has traditionally negotiated treaties with the understanding that they do not create judicially enforceable individual rights. *See Holmes v. Laird*, 459 F.2d 1211, 1220, 1222 (D.C. Cir. 1972); *Canadian Transport Co. v. United States*, 663 F.2d 1081, 1092 (D.C. Cir. 1980). As a general matter, a "treaty is primarily a compact between independent nations," and "depends for the enforcement of its provisions on the interest and honor of the governments which are parties to it." *Head Money Cases*, 112 U.S. 580, 598 (1884). If a treaty is violated, this "becomes the subject of international negotiations and reclamation," not the subject of a lawsuit. *Id.*; *see Charlton v. Kelly*, 229 U.S. 447, 474 (1913); *Whitney v. Robertson*, 124 U.S. 190, 194–95 (1888); *Foster v. Neilson*, 27 U.S. (2 Pet.) 253, 306, 314 (1829), *overruled on other grounds, United States v. Percheman*, 32 U.S. (7 Pet.) 51 (1883).

Thus, "[i]nternational agreements, even those directly benefitting private persons, generally do not create private rights or provide for a private cause of action in domestic courts." RESTATEMENT (THIRD) OF THE FOREIGN RELATIONS LAW OF THE UNITED STATES §907 cmt. a, at 395 (1987). The district court nevertheless concluded that the 1949 Geneva Convention conferred individual rights enforceable in federal court. We believe the court's conclusion disregards the principles just mentioned and is contrary to the Convention itself. To explain why, we must consider the Supreme Court's treatment of the Geneva Convention of 1929 in *Johnson v. Eisentrager*, 339 U.S. 763 (1950), and this court's decision in *Holmes v. Laird*, neither of which the district court mentioned.

In *Eisentrager*, German nationals, convicted by a military commission in China of violating the laws of war and imprisoned in Germany, sought writs of habeas corpus in federal district court on the ground that the military commission violated their rights under the Constitution and their rights under the 1929 Geneva Convention. 339 U.S. at 767. The Supreme Court, speaking through Justice Jackson, wrote in an alternative holding that the Convention was not judicially enforceable: the Convention specifies rights of prisoners of war, but "responsibility for observance and enforcement of these rights is upon political and military authorities." *Id.* at 789 n.14. We relied on this holding in *Holmes v. Laird*, 459 F.2d at 1222, to deny enforcement of the individual rights provisions contained in the NATO Status of Forces Agreement, an international treaty.

This aspect of *Eisentrager* is still good law and demands our adherence. *Rasul v. Bush*, 124 S. Ct. 2686 (2004), decided a different and "narrow" question: whether federal courts had jurisdiction under 28 U.S.C. §2241 "to consider challenges to the legality of the detention of foreign nationals" at Guantanamo Bay. *Id.* at 2690. The Court's decision in *Rasul* had nothing to say about enforcing any Geneva Convention. Its holding that federal courts had habeas corpus jurisdiction had no effect on *Eisentrager*'s interpretation of the 1929 Geneva Convention. That interpretation, we believe, leads to the conclusion that the 1949 Geneva Convention cannot be judicially enforced.

Although the government relied heavily on *Eisentrager* in making its argument to this effect, Hamdan chose to ignore the decision in his brief. Nevertheless, we have compared the 1949 Convention to the 1929 Convention. There are differences, but none of them renders *Eisentrager*'s conclusion about the 1929 Convention inapplicable to the 1949 Convention. Common Article 1 of the 1949 Convention states that parties to the Convention "undertake to respect and to ensure respect for the present Convention in all circumstances." The comparable provision in the 1929 version stated that the "Convention shall be respected . . . in all circumstances." Geneva Convention of 1929, art. 82. The revision imposed upon signatory nations the duty not only of complying themselves but also of making sure other signatories complied. Nothing in the revision altered the method by which a nation would enforce compliance. Article 8 of the 1949 Convention states that its provisions are to be "applied with the cooperation and under the scrutiny of the Protecting Powers. . . ." This too was a feature of the 1929 Convention. *See* Geneva Convention of 1929, art. 86. But Article 11 of the 1949 Convention increased the role of the protecting power, typically the International Red Cross, when disputes arose: "[I]n cases of disagreement between the Parties to the conflict as to the application or interpretation of the provisions of the present Convention, the Protecting Powers shall lend their good offices with a view to settling the disagreement." Here again there is no suggestion of judicial enforcement. The same is true with respect to the other method set forth in the 1949 Convention for settling disagreements. Article 132 provides that "at the request of a Party to the conflict, an enquiry shall be instituted, in a manner to be decided between the interested Parties, concerning any alleged violation of the Convention." If no agreement is reached about the procedure for the "enquiry," Article 132 further provides that "the Parties should agree on the choice of an umpire who will decide upon the procedure to be followed."

Hamdan points out that the 1949 Geneva Convention protects individual rights. But so did the 1929 Geneva Convention, as the Court recognized in *Eisentrager*. The NATO Status of Forces Agreement, at issue in *Holmes v. Laird*, also protected individual rights, but we held that the treaty was not judicially enforceable. 459 F.2d at 1222.

Eisentrager also answers Hamdan's argument that the habeas corpus statute, 28 U.S.C. §2241, permits courts to enforce the "treaty-based individual rights" set forth in the Geneva Convention. The 1929 Convention specified individual rights but as we have discussed, the Supreme Court ruled that these rights were to be enforced by means other than the writ of habeas corpus. The Supreme Court's *Rasul* decision did give district courts jurisdiction over habeas corpus petitions filed on behalf of Guantanamo detainees such as Hamdan. But *Rasul* did not render the Geneva Convention judicially enforceable. That a court has jurisdiction over a claim does not mean the claim is valid. *See Bell v. Hood*, 327 U.S. 678, 682–83 (1946). The availability of habeas may obviate a petitioner's need to rely on a private right of action, *see Wang v. Ashcroft*, 320 F.3d 130, 140–41 & n.16 (2d Cir. 2003), but it does not render a treaty judicially enforceable.

We therefore hold that the 1949 Geneva Convention does not confer upon Hamdan a right to enforce its provisions in court. *See Huynh Thi Anh v. Levi*, 586 F.2d 625, 629 (6th Cir. 1978).

IV.

Even if the 1949 Geneva Convention could be enforced in court, this would not assist Hamdan. He contends that a military commission trial would violate his rights under Article 102, which provides that a "prisoner of war can be validly sentenced only if the sentence has been pronounced by the same courts according to the same procedure as in the case of members of the armed forces of the Detaining Power." One problem for Hamdan is that he does not fit the Article 4 definition of a "prisoner of war" entitled to the protection of the Convention. He does not purport to be a member of a group who displayed "a fixed distinctive sign recognizable at a distance" and who conducted "their operations in accordance with the laws and customs of war." *See* 1949 Convention, arts. 4A(2)(b), (c) & (d). If Hamdan were to claim prisoner of war status under Article 4A(4) as a person who accompanied the armed forces without actually being [a] member[ ] thereof," he might raise that claim before the military commission under Army Regulation 190–8. *See* Section VII of this opinion, *infra*. (We note that Hamdan has not specifically made such a claim before this court.)

Another problem for Hamdan is that the 1949 Convention does not apply to al Qaeda and its members. The Convention appears to contemplate only two types of armed conflicts. The first is an international conflict. Under Common Article 2, the provisions of the Convention apply to "all cases of declared war or of any other armed conflict which may arise between two or more of the High Contracting Parties, even if the state of war is not recognized by one of them." Needless to say, al Qaeda is not a state and it was not a "High Contracting Party." There is an exception, set forth in the last paragraph of Common Article 2, when one of the "Powers" in a conflict is not a signatory but the other is. Then the signatory nation is bound to adhere to the Convention so long as the opposing Power "accepts and applies the provisions thereof." Even if al Qaeda could be considered a Power, which we doubt, no one claims that al Qaeda has accepted and applied the provisions of the Convention.

The second type of conflict, covered by Common Article 3, is a civil war – that is, an "armed conflict not of an international character occurring in the territory of one of the High Contracting Parties. . . ." In that situation, Common Article 3 prohibits "the passing of sentences and the carrying out of executions without previous judgment pronounced by a regularly constituted court affording all the judicial guarantees which are recognized as indispensable by a civilized people." Hamdan assumes that if Common Article 3 applies, a military commission could not try him. We will make the same assumption *arguendo*, which leaves the question whether Common Article 3 applies. Afghanistan is a "High Contracting Party." Hamdan was captured during hostilities there. But is the war against terrorism in general and the war against al Qaeda in particular, an "armed conflict not of an international character"? *See* INT'L COMM. RED CROSS, COMMENTARY: III GENEVA CONVENTION RELATIVE TO THE TREATMENT OF PRISONERS OF WAR 37 (1960) (Common Article 3 applies only to armed conflicts confined to "a single country"). President Bush determined, in a memorandum to the Vice President and others on February 7, 2002, that it did not fit that description because the conflict was "international in scope." The district court disagreed with the President's view of Common Article 3, apparently because the court thought we were not engaged in a separate conflict with al Qaeda, distinct from the conflict with the Taliban. *Hamdan v. Rumsfeld*, 344 F.Supp.2d 152, 161 (D.D.C. 2004). We have difficulty understanding the court's rationale. Hamdan was captured in Afghanistan in November 2001, but the conflict with al Qaeda arose before then, in other regions, including this country on September 11, 2001. Under the Constitution, the President "has a degree of independent authority to act" in foreign affairs, *Am. Ins. Ass'n v. Garamendi*, 539 U.S. 396, 414 (2003), and, for this reason and others, his construction and application of treaty provisions is entitled to "great weight." *United States v. Stuart*, 489 U.S. 353, 369 (1989); *Sumitomo Shoji America, Inc. v. Avagliano*, 457 U.S. 176, 185 (1982); *Kolovrat v. Oregon*, 366 U.S. 187, 194 (1961). While the district court determined that the actions in Afghanistan constituted a single conflict, the President's decision to treat our conflict with the Taliban separately from our conflict with al Qaeda is the sort of political-military decision constitutionally committed to him. *See Japan Whaling Ass'n v. Am. Cetacean Soc'y*, 478 U.S. 221, 230 (1986). To the extent there is ambiguity about the meaning of Common Article 3 as applied to al Qaeda and its members, the President's reasonable view of the provision must therefore prevail.

V.

Suppose we are mistaken about Common Article 3. Suppose it does cover Hamdan. Even then we would abstain from testing the military commission against the requirement in Common Article 3(1)(d) that sentences must be pronounced "by a regularly constituted court affording all the judicial guarantees which are recognized as indispensable by civilized peoples." *See Councilman*, 420 U.S. at 759; *New* [*v. Cohen*], 129 F.3d 639, 644 [(D.C. Cir. 1997)]; *supra* Part I. Unlike his arguments that the military commission lacked jurisdiction, his argument here is that the commission's procedures – particularly its alleged failure to require his presence at all stages of the proceedings – fall short of what Common Article 3 requires. The issue thus raised is not *whether* the commission may try him, but rather *how* the commission may try him. That is by no stretch a jurisdictional argument. No one would say that a criminal defendant's contention that a district court will not allow him to confront the witnesses against him raises a jurisdictional objection. Hamdan's claim therefore falls outside the recognized exception to the *Councilman* doctrine. Accordingly, comity would dictate that we defer to the ongoing military proceedings. If Hamdan were convicted, and if Common Article 3 covered him, he could contest his conviction in federal court after he exhausted his military remedies.

VI.

After determining that the 1949 Geneva Convention provided Hamdan a basis for judicial relief, the district court went on to consider the legitimacy of a military commission in the event Hamdan should eventually appear before one. In the district court's view, the principal constraint on the President's power to utilize such commissions is found in Article 36 of the Uniform Code of Military Justice, 10 U.S.C. §836, which provides:

> Pretrial, trial, and post-trial procedures, including modes of proof, for cases arising under this chapter triable in courts-martial, military commissions and other military tribunals...may be prescribed by the President by regulations which shall, so far as he considers practicable, apply the principles of law and the rules of evidence generally recognized in the trial of criminal cases in the United States district courts, *but which may not be contrary to or inconsistent with this chapter.*

(Emphasis added.) The district court interpreted the final qualifying clause to mean that military commissions must comply in all respects with the requirements of the Uniform Code of Military Justice (UCMJ). This was an error.

Throughout its Articles, the UCMJ takes care to distinguish between "courts-martial" and "military commissions." *See, e.g.*, 10 U.S.C. §821 (noting that "provisions of this chapter conferring jurisdiction upon courts-martial do not deprive military commissions...of concurrent jurisdiction"). The terms are not used interchangeably, and the majority of the UCMJ's procedural requirements refer only to courts-martial. The district court's approach would obliterate this distinction. A far more sensible reading is that in establishing military commissions, the President may not adopt procedures that are "contrary to or inconsistent with" the UCMJ's provisions governing military commissions. In particular, Article 39 requires that sessions of a "trial by *court-martial*...shall be conducted in the presence of the accused." Hamdan's trial before a *military commission* does not violate Article 36 if it omits this procedural guarantee.

The Supreme Court's opinion in *Madsen v. Kinsella*, 343 U.S. 341 (1952), provides further support for this reading of the UCMJ. There, the Court spoke of the place of military commissions in our history, referring to them as "our commonlaw war courts.... Neither their procedure nor their jurisdiction has been prescribed by statute." *Id.* at 346–48. The Court issued its opinion two years after enactment of the UCMJ, and it is difficult, if not impossible, to square the Court's language in *Madsen* with the sweeping effect with which the district court would invest Article 36. The UCMJ thus imposes only minimal restrictions upon the form and function of military commissions, *see, e.g.*, 10 U.S.C. §§828, 847(a)(1), 849(d), and Hamdan does not allege that the regulations establishing the present commission violate any of the pertinent provisions.

VII.

Although we have considered all of Hamdan's remaining contentions, the only one requiring further discussion is his claim that even if the Geneva Convention is not judicially enforceable, Army Regulation 190–8 provides a basis for relief. This regulation, which contains many subsections, "implements international law, both customary and codified, relating to [enemy prisoners of war], [retained personnel], [civilian internees], and [other detainees] which includes those persons held during military operations other than war." AR 190–8 §1-1(b). The regulation lists the Geneva Convention among the "principal treaties relevant to this regulation." §1-1(b)(3); *see Hamdi*, 124 S. Ct. at 2658 (Souter, J., concurring) (describing AR 190–8 as "implementing the Geneva Convention"). One subsection, §1–5(a)(2), requires that prisoners receive the protections of the Convention "until some other legal status is determined by competent *authority*." (Emphasis added.) The President found that Hamdan was not a prisoner of war under the Convention. Nothing in the regulations, and nothing Hamdan argues, suggests that the President is not a "competent authority" for these purposes.

Hamdan claims that AR 190–8 entitles him to have a "competent tribunal" determine his status. But we believe the military commission is such a tribunal. The regulations specify that such a "competent tribunal" shall be composed of three commissioned officers, one of whom must be field-grade. AR 190–8 §1.6(c). A field-grade officer is an officer above the rank of captain and below the rank of brigadier general – a major, a lieutenant colonel, or a colonel. The President's order requires military commissions to be composed of between three and seven commissioned officers. 32 C.F.R. §9.4(a)(2), (3). The commission before which Hamdan is to be tried consists of three colonels. Brief for Appellants at 7. We therefore see no reason why Hamdan could not assert his claim to prisoner of war status before the military commission at the time of his trial and thereby receive the judgment of a "competent tribunal" within the meaning of Army Regulation 190–8.

* * *

For the reasons stated above, the judgment of the district court is reversed.

So ordered.

WILLIAMS, *Senior Circuit Judge*, concurring.

I concur in all aspects of the court's opinion except for the conclusion that Common Article 3 does not apply to the United States's conduct toward al Qaeda personnel captured in the conflict in Afghanistan. Maj. Op. 15–16. Because I agree that the Geneva Convention is not enforceable in courts of the United States, and that any claims under Common Article 3 should be deferred until proceedings against Hamdan are finished, I fully agree with the court's judgment.

* * *

There is, I believe, a fundamental logic to the Convention's provisions on its application. Article 2 (¶1) covers armed conflicts between two or more contracting parties. Article 2 (¶3) makes clear that in a multi-party conflict, where any two or more signatories are on opposite sides, those parties "are bound by [the Convention] in their mutual relations" – but not (by implication) vis-à-vis any non-signatory. And as the court points out, Maj. Op. at 14, under Article 2 (¶3) even a non-signatory "Power" is entitled to the benefits of the Convention, as against a signatory adversary, if it "accepts and applies" its provisions.

Non-state actors cannot sign an international treaty. Nor is such an actor even a "Power" that would be eligible under Article 2 (¶3) to secure protection by complying with the Convention's requirements. Common Article 3 fills the gap, providing some minimal protection for such non-eligibles in an "armed conflict not of an international character occurring in the territory of one of the High Contracting Parties." The gap being filled is the non-eligible party's failure to be a nation. Thus the words "not of an international character" are sensibly understood to refer to a conflict between a signatory nation and a non-state actor. The most obvious form of such a conflict is a civil war. But given the Convention's structure, the logical reading of "international character" is one that matches the basic derivation of the word "international," i.e., *between nations*. Thus, I think the context compels the view that a conflict between a signatory and a non-state actor is a conflict "not of an international character." In such a conflict, the signatory is bound to Common Article 3's modest requirements of "humane [ ]" treatment and "the judicial guarantees which are recognized as indispensable by civilized peoples."

I assume that our conflicts with the Taliban and al Qaeda are distinct, and I agree with the court that in reading the Convention we owe the President's construction "great weight." Maj. Op. at 15. But I believe the Convention's language and structure compel the view that Common Article 3 covers the conflict with al Qaeda.

No. 05-184

IN THE
Supreme Court of the United States

SALIM AHMED HAMDAN,
Petitioner,

v.

DONALD RUMSFELD, ET AL.,
Respondents.

**On Writ of Certiorari to the
United States Court of Appeals
for the District of Columbia Circuit**

**BRIEF FOR PETITIONER
SALIM AHMED HAMDAN**

Lt. Cdr. Charles Swift
Office of Military
Commissions

Neal Katyal
(Counsel of Record)

Thomas C. Goldstein
Amy Howe
Kevin K. Russell
GOLDSTEIN & HOWE, P.C.

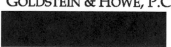

Harry H. Schneider, Jr.
Joseph M. McMillan
Charles C. Sipos
PERKINS COIE LLP

January 6, 2006

QUESTIONS PRESENTED

* Redactions on this page have been added for privacy purposes. – *Eds*.

1. Whether the military commission established by the President to try Petitioner and others similarly situated for alleged war crimes in the "war on terror" is duly authorized under Congress's Authorization for the Use of Military Force (AUMF), Pub. L. No. 107-40, 115 Stat. 224; the Uniform Code of Military Justice (UCMJ); or the inherent powers of the President?

2. Whether Petitioner and others similarly situated can obtain judicial enforcement from an Article III court of rights protected under the 1949 Geneva Convention in an action for a writ of habeas corpus challenging the legality of their detention by the Executive branch?

. . .

SUMMARY OF ARGUMENT

This case involves a critical question regarding the allocation of power among Congress, the President and the federal courts in the ongoing "war on terror." The President has claimed the unilateral authority to try suspected terrorists wholly outside the traditional civilian and military judicial systems, for crimes defined by the President alone, under procedures lacking basic protections, before "judges" who are his chosen subordinates. He has further asserted the power to disregard treaty obligations that Congress has ratified and the federal courts repeatedly have enforced, obligations that protect not only Hamdan but also American servicemembers. Such assertions reach far beyond any war power ever conferred upon the Executive, even during declared wars. The court of appeals' limitless approval of this unprecedented arrogation of power must be reversed.

I. In this case, the President seeks not to revive, but to invent, a new form of military jurisdiction. While military commissions have served an important role in times of war, their use has been strictly limited in light of their inherent threat to liberty and the separation of powers. Accordingly, this Court has never before recognized the legitimacy of a commission except to the extent it has been specifically authorized by Congress. And even in the few cases where this Court has found congressional authorization, this Court has always construed the commissions' jurisdiction as limited by the treaties and traditions constituting the law of war, absent express statutory provisions to the contrary.

In this case, the commissions established by the President transgress *both* boundaries. 10 U.S.C. 821 clearly provides that commissions at most may try "offenders or offenses that by statute or by the law of war may be tried by military commissions." Likewise, the AUMF only permits the use of "necessary and appropriate force." To construe that phrase as authorizing commissions that try offenses, much less offenses unrecognized by the law of war, in a forum far removed in time and distance from any battlefield, and without important procedural safeguards, would provide to the President an almost limitless authority that Congress could not have intended and that threatens our divided government. If in the interest of "national security," this Court concludes that the President has such authority, it will be hard pressed to limit, in any principled manner, the President's assertion of similarly unprecedented powers in other areas of civil society, so long as they purport to serve that same objective. Indeed, it is not hard to imagine a future President invoking this case as precedent, and asserting the need to subject American citizens to military commissions for any offense somehow connected to the "war on terror."

To avoid such dangers, even when Congress has authorized commissions, this Court has always construed that authority to be limited to trying offenders and offenses subject to commission trial under the law of war. It should adopt the same approach in this case and conclude that, even if some form of commission has been authorized, the commission created by the President here is unlawful. First, the commission fails to provide procedural protections required by statute, and long deemed essential to the legitimacy of military tribunals enforcing the law of war. Under 10 U.S.C. 836(a), Congress prohibited the use of procedures in commission trials that are "contrary to or inconsistent with" the UCMJ. Despite this express restriction, the government acknowledges that the commission procedures do not afford essential UCMJ protections, including the right to be present during the proceedings (§839(b)). Second, Petitioner is not an offender subject to commission trial under the law of war. To the extent the government argues that petitioner is triable by commission because the conflict with al Qaeda is subject to the law of war, it must also acknowledge that he is entitled to the protection of the law of war, including the provisions of the Geneva Convention that prohibit commission trials.

Moreover, the law of war does not, in fact, extend to the offense with which Hamdan has been charged. Hamdan's single count of conspiracy has never constituted an offense against the law of war. Nor has the law of war ever been extended to acts of terrorism when they occur outside of a traditional battlefield in a declared war between nation-states. Instead, such crimes have long been tried, with nearly uniform success by the government, in civilian courts. If the American people have lost faith in their judicial institutions and have determined to abandon that tradition, that step must be taken clearly and deliberately by Congress, not through an assertion of unilateral power by the President.

II. The judgment below must be reversed for a further, independent reason. This is the first commission since ratification of the GPW in 1955. Hamdan – apprehended on the field of battle in a war between the United States and the government of Afghanistan, both signatories to that treaty is entitled to its protections, which form an essential component of the law of war. Under the GPW, until a "competent tribunal" determines that Hamdan is not a POW, he is entitled to its protections. One such protection is the right to be tried before the same tribunal as American servicemembers charged with the same offense. The government does not dispute that this requires trial before a court-martial, with all the attendant procedural protections afforded American servicemembers that commissions deny.

The court of appeals erred further in concluding that Common Article 3 of the GPW does not protect Hamdan. That Article is a minimum baseline that applies to all conflicts. In the end, the President cannot claim that the criminal offenses of the laws of war apply to the war on terror, and at the same time deny the accused the right to invoke any of the protections of the laws of war.

Finally, the court of appeals erred in concluding that rights protected by the GPW could not be judicially enforced. In this case, the rights at issue are part of the laws of war, and thereby constrain any authorization of a commission. Moreover, they have been codified in statutes and regulations, which are independently enforceable in habeas and mandamus actions.

III. Hamdan does not challenge the President's power to use troops or his power to temporarily detain true enemy combatants. *See Hamdi v. Rumsfeld*, 542 U.S. 507 (2004). He challenges the *further* assertion of power to subject detainees to *ad hoc* trials. Unlike forward-looking detentions – which implicate war powers and where courts lack comparative expertise – tribunals that look retrospectively at guilt intrude on areas where civilian courts have competence and protect our Constitution's checks and balances. *E.g., In re Yamashita*, 327 U.S. 1 (1946); *Quirin*, 317 U.S. 1; *United States v. Grimley*, 137 U.S. 147 (1890); *Ex parte Milligan*, 71 U.S. 2 (1866).

Nor does Hamdan challenge the government's right to try him for offenses proscribed by law in a civilian court or court-martial, under protections long considered fundamental to the legitimacy of *any* American court. And Hamdan does not challenge the authority of *Congress* to alter the traditional jurisdiction of civilian and military courts, subject to constitutional constraints. But in the absence of such a decision by the legislative branch, the President may not displace the jurisdiction of those regularly constituted courts and disclaim the treaty obligations to which Congress has committed the nation.

This is the rare case where invalidating the government's action preserves the status quo, a carefully crafted equilibrium in place for many decades. Our fundamental principles of separation of powers have survived many dire threats to this nation's security – from capture of the nation's capital by enemy forces, to Civil War, to the threat of nuclear annihilation during the Cold War – and those principles must not be abandoned now.

ARGUMENT

I. PETITIONER'S COMMISSION IS NOT AUTHORIZED

A. Military Commissions Play A Limited Role in the Nation's Constitutional Structure and Tradition

This Court has repeatedly recognized that "the Framers harbored a deep distrust of executive military power and military tribunals." *Loving v. United States*, 517 U.S. 748, 760 (1996); *Toth v. Quarles*, 350 U.S. 11, 22 (1955) ("Free countries of the world have tried to restrict military tribunals to the narrowest jurisdiction deemed absolutely essential to maintaining discipline among troops in active service."). The traditions of this country favor civilian courts and courts-martial, not commissions, for the prosecution of war crimes.

Civilian Criminal Trials. Since the Founding, Congress has used civilian trials to address violence against Americans from stateless organizations, beginning with piracy and continuing to the present. 18 U.S.C. pt. 1, ch. 113B. In the aftermath of September 11, Congress enacted legislation to ensure the adequacy of civilian law enforcement agencies and the criminal justice system to respond to the modern threat of terrorism. USA PATRIOT Act, 115 Stat. 272 (Oct. 26, 2001). Congress also revised criminal statutes for offenses triable in federal court. *E.g.*, 18 U.S.C. 1993, 2331, 2339C, 2339D. Federal criminal laws have helped convict numerous terrorists, including those involved in the 1993 World Trade Center and the 1995 Oklahoma City bombings. These federal charges are available to try Petitioner and others. Accused 'dirty bomber' Jose Padilla has now been indicted on criminal charges in a federal civilian court.

Courts-Martial. Military courts have played an important but limited role. The traditional military court is the court-martial, a body that has long had jurisdiction to try service-members. In the 20th century, Congress gave courts-martial jurisdiction over violations of the laws of war. 10 U.S.C. 818.

Military Commissions. The jurisdiction of commissions has always been strictly confined. They have been permitted only as courts of necessity, convened temporarily by commanders in zones of active military operations and used to try war crimes or enforce justice in occupied territory when no other courts were open or had jurisdiction. 2 WINTHROP, MILITARY LAW & PRECEDENTS 831 (2d ed. 1920).

Commissions were thus used on the battlefields of the Mexican-American war, but only "until Congress could be stimulated to legislate on the subject." 2 MEMOIRS OF

Lieut.-General Scott 392–93 (1864). They were used again during the Civil War, but subject to the "general rule" that they be used "only for cases which cannot be tried by a court-martial or by a proper civil tribunal." 1 The War of Rebellion 242 (2d Series 1894); Lieber Code, Gen. Order No. 100, *in* The Laws of Armed Conflict 3 (1988) (stating that commissions can only try offenses with no "jurisdiction conferred by statute on courts-martial"); *In re Egan*, 8 F. Cas. 367 (C.C.N.D.N.Y 1866) (No. 4303) (Nelson, J.) (invalidating commission because "all authorities agree that it can be indulged only in case of necessity.... This necessity must be shown affirmatively by the party assuming to exercise this extraordinary and irregular power."); *Madsen v. Kinsella*, 343 U.S. 341, 348, 355 (1952) (upholding commissions used overseas as a temporary court system in occupied territory).

Petitioner's commission does not fall within any of these traditional uses of commissions. Among other things, it was convened at Guantanamo Bay, which is neither a zone of combat nor occupied territory. Even *Quirin*, which marked the absolute outer bounds of the commissions used in World War II, recognized that war crimes tribunals have been exceptionally limited by constitutional tradition, specific legislation, and the laws of war. Here, however, the President has given the commission a jurisdiction that far exceeds any ever previously exercised.

B. Military Tribunals Must Be Strictly Limited

Concerns over the justice system and role of the military during the rule of King George III were grievances leading to the founding of this Nation. *See* DECLARATION OF INDEPENDENCE para. 11, 14, 20, 21 (U.S. 1776) (charging that the Crown had "affected to render the Military independent of and superior to the civil power"; "depriv[ed] us, in many cases, of the benefits of Trial by Jury"; "made Judges dependent on his Will alone"; and "transport[ed] us beyond Seas to be tried for pretended offences."). This Court has recognized that commissions, which concentrate judicial functions into Executive hands in times of war when civil liberties are most imperiled, are fundamentally at odds with divided government and so must be used only out of great necessity. *Milligan*, 71 U.S. at 124 ("Martial law, established on such a basis [for military convenience], destroys every guarantee of the Constitution, and effectually renders the 'military independent of and superior to the civil power.'").

Accordingly, "the jurisdiction of military tribunals is a very limited and extraordinary jurisdiction derived from the cryptic language in Art. I, §8, and, at most, was intended to be only a narrow exception to the normal and preferred method of trial in courts of law. Every extension of military jurisdiction is an encroachment on the jurisdiction of the civil courts," *Reid v. Covert*, 354 U.S. 1, 21 (1957). While *Reid* commanded a plurality, a majority soon extended it to noncapital crimes when "critical areas of occupation" were not involved. *Kinsella v. Singleton*, 361 U.S. 234, 244 (1960).

In order to guard against the unauthorized extension of the jurisdiction of military tribunals, this Court repeatedly reviews challenges to their jurisdiction and strikes down those that transgress statutory and constitutional limits. *See, e.g., Milligan*, 71 U.S. at 120–27 (commission may not try civilian charged with conspiracy and other violations when civilian courts remain open); *Duncan v. Kahanamoku*, 327 U.S. 304, 313, 324 (1946) (invalidating commission when civilian court able to function). Indeed, as the court of appeals acknowledged, *Quirin* provides "a compelling historical precedent for the power of civilian courts to entertain challenges that seek to interrupt the processes of military commissions." . . . .

C.   Congress Must Authorize Military Commissions

The Constitution vests Congress with the power to create commissions and define their limits. Article II establishes the President's title as "Commander in Chief," but Article I, §8 specifically grants Congress the power to "constitute Tribunals inferior to the supreme Court," "define and punish... Offences against the Law of Nations," "declare War," "make Rules for the Government and Regulation of the land and naval Forces" and "disciplin[e] the Militia."

Citing this language, *Quirin* and *Yamashita* held that the authority to establish commissions rests with Congress:

> *Ex parte Quirin* ... pointed out that Congress, in the exercise of the power conferred upon it by Article I, §8, Cl. 10 of the Constitution to "define and punish... Offenses against the Law of Nations...," of which the law of war is a part, had by the Articles of War [ ] recognized the "military commission" appointed by military command, as it had previously existed in United States Army practice, as an appropriate tribunal for the trial and punishment of offenses against the law of war.

Yamashita, 327 U.S. at 7 (citation omitted); *see also Quirin*, 317 U.S. at 28–29; *Toth*, 350 U.S. at 14 ("this assertion of military authority over civilians cannot rest on the President's power as commander-in-chief"); Federalist No. 47, at 301 (Rossiter ed. 1961) (J. Madison); *Wiener v. United States*, 357 U.S. 349, 355 (1958); *Harisiades v. Shaughnessy*, 342 U.S. 580, 588 (1952).[1]

"There are powerful reasons for construing constitutional silence on [a] profoundly important issue as equivalent to an express prohibition." *Clinton v. New York*, 524 U.S. 417, 439 (1998). While the use of force requires unity and dispatch, the process of justice requires more than a military judiciary serving at the pleasure of the President. Here, the President exercises "legislative, executive and judicial powers with respect to those subject to military trials. Such blending of functions in one branch of the Government is the objectionable thing which the draftsmen of the Constitution endeavored to prevent by providing for the separation of governmental powers." *Reid*, 354 U.S. at 39 (plurality).

D.   Congress Has Not Authorized Petitioner's Commission

The court of appeals held that Congress had authorized the commission in the AUMF and two long-standing UCMJ provisions, 10 U.S.C. 821, 836(a)..... None of these provisions authorize a commission; nor do they authorize the President to employ tribunals unfettered by tradition or the law of war. To whatever extent Congress *may* lawfully create commissions, none of the three statutes invoked by the President may be read to do so.

Sections 821 and 836(a). The court of appeals erred in holding that these provisions authorized this commission. At most, the provisions acknowledge that the President may, on occasion, be authorized to establish commissions, but *restrict* how the President may implement that authority.

---

[1] *Milligan* split 5-4 on whether *Congress* could create commissions, *see* 71 U.S. at 136–37 (Chase, C.J.), but was unanimous that the President could not do so himself. *Id.* at 120 ("The Constitution of the United States is a law for rulers and people, equally in war and in peace, and covers with the shield of its protection all classes of men, at all times, and under all circumstances. No doctrine, involving more pernicious consequences, was ever invented by the wit of man than that any of its provisions can be suspended during any of the great exigencies of government.")

10 U.S.C 821 makes clear that the UCMJ does not itself deprive an otherwise valid commission of its traditional jurisdiction. Unlike other contemporaneous provisions, such as 10 U.S.C. §§818, 904, 906, it does not confer any jurisdiction. Before §821 is read to authorize a tribunal to mete out death sentences and life imprisonment, particularly one that lacks traditional constraints on executive authority and protections traditionally conferred upon the accused, a clear legislative statement is necessary.[2]

To the extent this provision can be read to sanction the use of commissions, it necessarily limits that authority to the trial of "offenders or offenses that by statute or by the law of war may be tried by military commissions." 10 U.S.C. 821. That is precisely how this Court interpreted similar statutory language. See *Quirin*, 317 U.S. at 28–29; *Amicus Br. of the Brennan Center for Justice & William Eskridge*, at 15–23.

Nor is §836(a) authority for the commission. It simply authorizes the President to issue regulations for the conduct of military trials. It does not authorize their establishment or define their jurisdiction. To the contrary, the provision specifically withholds from the President the power to define offenses triable by commissions, giving him instead only the authority to establish the "procedures" by which the offenses defined elsewhere may be tried. *Id.* And even then, the authorization is limited, precluding procedures "contrary to or inconsistent with this chapter." *Id.*

The AUMF. The AUMF authorizes the President to "use all necessary and appropriate force against those nations, organizations, or persons he determines planned, authorized, committed, or aided the terrorist attacks that occurred on September 11, 2001, or harbored such organizations or persons, in order to prevent any future acts of international terrorism against the United States by such nations, organizations or persons." 115 Stat. 224. Determined not to provide the President "a blank check,"[3] Congress reserved from the President the full range of powers that accompany a Declaration of War.[4]

The object of the AUMF was to authorize military action.[5] It said nothing about criminal punishment. In *Quirin*, even the Declaration of War was not enough to authorize a commission; the Court relied instead on other statutes. . . . If commissions qualify as a "use [of] force," then those words permit any action the President believes related to terrorism, however tangential. Indeed, the President has, in this case and elsewhere, claimed precisely such unlimited powers under his broad reading of the AUMF.

A plurality of this Court recently rejected the idea that "a state of war" can be "a blank check for the President," *Hamdi*, 542 U.S. at 536. It reached that conclusion in

---

[2] . . .

[3] 147 Cong. Rec. H5655 (2001) (statement of Rep. Smith); *id.* at H5663 (AUMF "not a carte blanche for the use of force") (Rep. Schakowsky); S9949 ("It was not the intent of Congress to give the President unbridled authority . . . to wage war against terrorism") (Sen. Byrd); S9951 (similar) (Sen. Levin); H5654 (Rep. Smith); S9416 ("[W]ords in earlier drafts of this joint resolution, which might have been interpreted to grant a broader authority to use military force, were deleted") (Sen. Levin); S9417 (AUMF "does not give the President a blanket approval to take military action . . . It is not an open-ended authorization to use force in circumstances beyond those we face today.") (Sen. Kerry); H5671 (AUMF "not unlimited") (Rep. Udall); H5675 (AUMF "narrow") (Rep. Jackson); S9417 ("does not contain a broad grant of powers") (Sen. Feingold).

[4] 147 CONG. REC. H5638, H5680 (2001) ("By not declaring war, the resolution preserves our precious civil liberties"; "declarations of war trigger broad statutes that . . . authorize the President to apprehend 'alien enemies.'") (Rep. Conyers); S9418 ("If this is indeed to be a war, then the President should seek a declaration of war.") (Sen. Feingold); H5646 ("We do not make a formal declaration of war today.") (Rep. Hoyer); H5662 (Rep. Davis); H5673 ("I would have strong reservations about a resolution authorizing the use of force in an open ended manner . . . This is not that resolution.") (Rep. Wu); H5653 ("We need a declaration of war" to "[g]ive the President the tools, the absolute flexibility he needs") (Rep. Barr).

[5] *See* 147 CONG. REC. H5646 (2001) ("[W]e authorize the President to use all necessary and appropriate military force") (Rep. Schiff); H5644 (Rep. Roukema); H5666 (Rep. Cardin); H5672 (Rep. Portman).

the far less onerous context of detention. *Id.* at 518 (citing sources for the proposition that "[c]aptivity in war is 'neither revenge, nor punishment'" and "'merely a temporary detention which is devoid of all penal character'"); *id.* (referring to "mere detention"); *id.* at 523 (stating that *Quirin* is "the most apposite precedent that we have on the question of whether citizens may be *detained* in such circumstances") (emphasis added). *But see id.* at 518 (describing history that "[t]he capture and detention of lawful combatants and the capture, detention, and trial of unlawful combatants, by 'universal agreement and practice,' are 'important incident[s] of war,' *Ex parte Quirin*, 317 U.S. at 28," but avoiding discussion of what body today must try unlawful combatants).[6] It is wholly consistent with wartime precedent to interpret the AUMF as authority for one thing (detention) but not another (trial and punishment). "Congress in drafting laws may decide that the Nation may be 'at war' for one purpose and 'at peace' for another"; the "attitude of a free society toward the jurisdiction of military tribunals – our reluctance to give them authority to try people for nonmilitary offenses – has a long history." *Lee v. Madigan*, 358 U.S. 228, 230–32 (1959).

Even if "force" were stretched to mean something it does not, the AUMF only authorizes "necessary and appropriate" force. The government has not shown that resurrecting a tribunal eschewed in Korea and Vietnam (and which four years after the September 11 attacks has not even completed one trial) is somehow necessary or appropriate, let alone both. The *Hamdi* plurality held that "detention of individual ... is so fundamental and accepted an incident to war as to be an exercise of the 'necessary and appropriate force' Congress has authorized the President to use."[7] But the AUMF's language does not give the President unchecked authority to determine what is "necessary and appropriate."[8]

The Court has never considered an expansion of military jurisdiction that displaces traditional tribunals to be a "necessary" aspect of military operations. *Reid* rejected a similar argument by *both* the President and Congress regarding the Constitution's "Necessary and Proper" Clause, calling it a "latitudinarian interpretation ... at war with the well-established purpose of the Founders to keep the military strictly within its proper sphere, subordinate to civil authority." 354 U.S. at 30; *Amicus Br. of General Brahms et al.*

Finally, assuming that "force" includes military tribunals, the AUMF only permits action necessary "to prevent" terrorism. Compare Br. Opp. at 22 (commission serves retributivist purpose). In light of Respondents' separate claim of power to detain Hamdan indefinitely as an enemy combatant, the burden can only be met if his trial serves general deterrence.[9] Terrorists fear being killed by our Armed Forces and intelligence

---

[6] Justice Thomas' dissent was carefully confined to detention, mentioning the term or its derivation at least forty-six times. *See Hamdi*, 542 U.S. at 578–98 (Thomas, J., dissenting). Justice Thomas found *punishment* to stand on entirely different footing, isolating *Milligan*: "More importantly, the Court referred frequently and pervasively to the criminal nature of the proceedings instituted against Milligan ... the punishment-nonpunishment distinction harmonizes all of the precedent." *Id.* at 593 (citations omitted). Commissions, in contrast, "implicate ... the two primary objectives of criminal punishment: retribution or deterrence" and "affix culpability for prior criminal conduct." *Kansas v. Hendricks*, 521 U.S. 346, 361–62 (1997); *Hamdi*, 542 U.S. at 556–57 (Scalia, J., dissenting).

[7] 542 U.S. at 518. The decision looked to the GPW to provide guidance on what types of force were "necessary and appropriate." *Id.* at 521.

[8] The AUMF is narrower than previous congressional authorizations of force. Shortly after passage of the AUMF, Congress passed the Iraq Force Resolution, which authorized the President to "use the Armed Forces of the United States as *he determines* to be necessary and appropriate." 116 Stat. 1498 (2002) (emphasis added). . . . .

[9] The AUMF does not appear to contemplate general deterrence. Congress adopted the AUMF in lieu of a proposed White House Resolution that would have given the President the power "to deter and pre-empt any

community. If they cannot deter a terrorist, it is far-fetched to think that a prosecution of Hamdan at Guantanamo five years after his supposed crime would do so. Nor is it credible to suggest that a commission is "necessary" to "prevent" terrorism. After all, if Hamdan's prosecution promotes deterrence, it can take place in an Article III court or a court-martial. Both are authorized, available, and could have taken place years ago.

It is the Court's "duty 'to give effect, if possible, to every clause and word of a statute.'" *United States v. Menasche*, 348 U.S. 528, 538–39 (1955) (citation omitted). Congress passed a resolution circumscribed in scope, purpose, and effect; its words do not authorize commissions. This Court has never found that the laws of war supplant open civil and military courts when only "force" was authorized. Nor have other Presidents claimed as much. Here, the conflict in which the commission has been convened (the so called "war on terror") is not even tethered to a specific nation-state, location, or time period. Even if a limited authorization for military action such as the AUMF is sufficient to authorize a traditional commission to try traditional war crimes, that is not at all what the President has undertaken in this case.

E. This Court Should Enforce the Jurisdictional Limits of Military Commissions

Even if this Court were to conclude that the President possesses some inherent authority to convene military commissions, or that Congress has implicitly authorized their use, that authority must be strictly confined to safeguard liberty and our constitutional division of authority between the executive, legislative, and judicial branches. This Court has thus long construed authorizations for commissions to allow the President at most to employ them in accordance with their traditional use.

Accordingly, *Duncan* refused to read the "Organic Act," establishing the territorial Hawaiian government, to permit military courts to supplant civilian ones in World War II:

> [The Founders rejected placing] in the hands of one man the power to make, interpret and enforce the laws.... We believe that when Congress passed the Hawaiian Organic Act and authorized the establishment of "martial law" it had in mind and did not wish to exceed the boundaries between military and civilian power . . . which had become part of our political philosophy and institutions prior to the time Congress passed the Organic Act. The phrase "martial law" as employed in that act, therefore, . . . was not intended to authorize the supplanting of courts by military tribunals.

327 U.S. at 322, 324. Although Hawaii was "under fire" and a "battle field," *id.* at 344 (Burton, J., dissenting), the Court embraced *Milligan*'s strict confinement of military tribunals, just four years after *Quirin*.

To hold otherwise would pose grave risks to liberty and the careful balance of legislative, executive and judicial power established under our Constitutional system:

---

future acts of terrorism." 147 Cong. Rec. S9951 (2001). Congress instead used the circumscribed "prevent" instead of broader "deter" language. Otherwise, the President could order assassinations of foreign leaders and a "little old lady in Switzerland," *In re Guantanamo Detainee Cases*, 355 F. Supp. 2d 443, 475 (2005), tangentially connected to terrorism. Furthermore, there is no evidence that legislators thought commissions "necessary and appropriate." If anything, they expressed a desire to use civilian trials. *E.g.*, 147 Cong. Rec. H5680 (Rep. Conyers).

With the known hostility of the American People to any interference by the military with the regular administration of justice in the civil courts, no such intention should be ascribed to Congress in the absence of clear and direct language to that effect.

Coleman v. Tennessee, 97 U.S. 509, 514 (1878); *see also Sterling v. Constantin*, 287 U.S. 378, 401 (1932) ("[T]he allowable limits of military discretion, and whether or not they have been overstepped in a particular case, are judicial questions."); *Lincoln v. United States*, 197 U.S. 419, 427–28 (1905) (Holmes, J.) (rejecting claim that the "President's order" to tax goods "was a lawful exercise of the war power" because the statute "was not a power in blank for any military occasion").

F. Petitioner's Commission, By Ignoring Statutory and Common Law Constraints, Exceeds Any Possible Authorization Provided By Congress

The commissions created by the President fail to provide essential protections long afforded under the law of war and mandated in the UCMJ and Geneva Conventions.

1. *The Commission Violates Specific Statutory Restrictions*

Evading the procedures used in courts-martial has never been an acceptable rationale justifying the use of military commissions. The court of appeals radically extended this Court's jurisprudence by permitting wide-ranging procedural deviations once the Executive labels his tribunal a "commission." That has never been the law.

a. Commissions from the days of General Scott, *supra*, have applied court-martial procedure. General Order 1 in the Civil War likewise required them to "be constituted in a similar manner and their proceedings be conducted according to the same general rules as courts-martial *in order to prevent abuses which might otherwise arise*." War of the Rebellion, *supra*, at 248 (emphasis added). Even with these safeguards, *Milligan* found commissions impermissible.[10]

10 U.S.C. 836(a) codifies the longstanding requirement of consistency between commissions and courts-martial; it precludes the President from employing procedures in commissions that are "contrary to or inconsistent with" the UCMJ. It states that if Hamdan is merely "triable" in a court-martial, the UCMJ cannot be set aside. A commission that circumvents the procedural requirements of the UCMJ "exceeds the President's authority." *United States v. Douglas*, 1 M.J. 354, 356 (C.M.A. 1976). Because Hamdan's commission concededly does not conform to the procedures applied in courts-martial,

---

[10] Historical practice, legal commentary, and military regulations all confirm that commissions follow court-martial rules. *E.g.*, Winthrop, *supra*, at 841–42 ("[A]s a general rule and as the only quite safe and satisfactory course for the rendering of justice to both parties, a military commission will–like a court-martial–... ordinarily and properly be governed, upon all important questions, by the established rules and principles of law and evidence."); Rollin Ives, Treatise on Military Law 284 (1879) ("The forms of procedure... are the same as before courts-martial."); Manual for Courts Martial, prmbl. Pt. 2(b)(2) (2000) ("military commissions... shall be guided by the appropriate principles of law and rules of procedures and evidence prescribed for courts-martial.").

For instance, JAG review invalidated a commission under Article of War 65. The Article prohibited the convening officer to charge, but its text only referenced courts-martial. 4 Stat. 417 (1830). Nevertheless, the Judge Advocate General agreed that the Article had been violated and disapproved the proceedings. Joseph Holt to Gen. John Pope (Nov. 3, 1863), *quoted in* Chomsky, *The United States-Dakota War Trials*, 43 Stan. L. Rev. 13, 43 (1990). *See also* Mem., Procedural Law Applied by Military Commissions (National Archives, Legal Division Gen. D. MacArthur) ("If the conduct of military commissions in the past is to be a guide, the same rules for procedure and rules of evidence governing General Courts Martial would prevail."), *quoted in* Evan Wallach, *Afghanistan, Quirin, and Uchiyama: Does the Sauce Suit the Gander?*, 2003 Army Law. 18, 31 n. 118.

it is unlawful. *See Amicus Br. of Military Law Historians; Amicus Br. of National Institute for Military Justice.*

10 U.S.C. 821 confirms this conclusion. Its drafter, General Crowder, stated it "just saves to these war courts . . . a concurrent jurisdiction with courts-martial . . . Both classes of courts have the same procedure." S. Rep. 64-130, at 40–41. Congress' use of the term "concurrent" jurisdiction *limits* commissions. The Court has held, for example, that the Tucker Act's grant of "concurrent jurisdiction" to district courts limits those courts.[11] Otherwise, litigants would "forum-sho[p]." *Hanna v. Plumer*, 380 U.S. 460, 468 (1965). Just as rule parity prevents litigants from forum-shopping their Tucker Act claims, parity here prevents the "abuses which might otherwise arise." Civil War Order 1, *supra*.

b. The commission's procedures are avowedly "contrary to or inconsistent with" the procedural protections afforded by the UCMJ and by historical practice. 10 U.S.C. 836(a). For example, the proceedings can "exclude the Accused." Mil. Order No. 1 §6(B)(3). As the district court concluded, this rule, which has already been used to bar Hamdan's presence, is fatally inconsistent with 10 U.S.C. 839(b).[12] Pet. App. 47a. That provision protects the fundamental rights to be present throughout trial and to confront witnesses. Under §839(b), except for voting and deliberation, "[a]ll other proceedings . . . shall be in the presence of the accused." *See United States v. Dean*, 13 M.J. 676, 678 (A.F.C.M.R. 1982) ("The accused must be present at all stages of his trial"); *United States v. Daulton*, 45 M.J. 212, 219 (C.M.A. 1996) (witness testimony). In fact, JAG review in the Civil War led to the dismissal of a commission for violation of this right. See *infra* p. 24; *Amicus Br. of American Jewish Congress et al.*[13]

Apart from §839, the common law (which binds military commissions) requires the accused to be present. *See Diaz v. United States*, 223 U.S. 442, 455 (1912) ("[O]ur courts, with substantial accord, have regarded [the right to be present] as extending to every stage of the trial . . . *and as being scarcely less important to the accused than the right of trial itself*.") (emphasis added); *Lewis v. United States*, 146 U.S. 370, 372, 375 (1892) (right of presence at *voir dire* is of "peculiar sacredness" required by "the dictates of humanity"); *Dean*, 13 M.J. at 678; *Daulton*, 45 M.J. at 219. Customary international law also guarantees an accused the right to be "tried in his presence." Prot. I, Geneva

---

[11] *United States v. Sherwood*, 312 U.S, 584, 591 (1941) (the Act "did no more than authorize the District Court to sit as a court of claims"); *Bates Mfg. Co. v. United States*, 303 U.S. 567, 571 (1938); *United States v. Jones*, 131 U.S. 1, 19 (1889) ("We cannot yield to the suggestion that any broader jurisdiction as to subject matter is given to the Circuit and District Courts than that which is given to the Court of Claims. It is clearly the same jurisdiction-'concurrent jurisdiction' only."); *DeCecco v. United States*, 485 F.2d 372, 374 (1st Cir. 1973); *Warren v. United States*, 94 F.2d 597 (2d Cir. 1938) (because claims court could not hear suits for treaty violations, neither could district court); *Hans v. Louisiana*, 134 U.S. 1, 18 (1890) ("concurrent jurisdiction" in federal question statute shows Congress "did not intend to invest its courts with any new and strange jurisdictions").

[12] Several commission procedures are contrary to the UCMJ on their face. Commission rules do not permit independent review, contrary to §§867 and 867a. The final decision lies with the President. Mil. Order No. 1 §6(H)(6). Similarly, §6(D)(1), permitting admission of evidence so long as it has "probative value to a reasonable person," conflicts with §836(a), which requires the rules of evidence generally to conform to those in the District Courts. The commission rule permits, for example, testimony obtained by torture. *See Amicus Br. of Human Rights First.*

  The panel also relied on *Madsen*, but the UCMJ took effect after Madsen's trial. 343 U.S. at 345 n.6. And Madsen did not challenge commission procedures. *Id.* at 342. Strikingly, her commission guaranteed her "the rights . . . [t]o be present" and "cross-examine any witness." *Id.* at 358 n.24.

[13] After Hamdan filed his Certiorari Petition, the Government made some semantic changes to commission procedures. Pet. Br. App. 46a, 59a. Yet both old and new rules permit Hamdan's exclusion if "protected" – a category far broader than "classified" – information is considered. *Compare* 32 C.F.R. §9.6(b), *with* §6(D)(5)(b). The Government offers no authority to suggest that its new iteration of rules is consistent with the UCMJ.

Conventions relating to Protection of Int'l Armed Conflict, art. 75(4)(e) (1977) (Protocol I).

Similarly, this Court has held that "a criminal trial is not just unless one can confront his accusers." *Coy v. Iowa*, 487 U.S. 1012, 1018 n.2 (1988). Although the right to confront witnesses is reflected in the Sixth Amendment, it has a genesis in natural law and has been recognized as essential in military courts and international law. *Crawford v. Washington*, 541 U.S. 36, 49 (2004) ("'It is a rule of the common law, founded on natural justice, that no man shall be prejudiced by evidence which he had not the liberty to cross examine.'") (quoting *State v. Webb*, 2 N.C. 103 (1794)); *Mattox v. United States*, 156 U.S. 237, 243 (1895); *Daulton*, 45 M.J. at 219; Protocol I, art. 75(4)(g) (guaranteeing accused's right "to examine, or have examined, the witnesses against him"). Our Government, in fact, took the position during World War II that conducting a commission without the participation of the accused was a punishable violation of the laws of war. Wallach, *supra*, at 45–47.

In the face of this precedent, the Government has offered no authority that permits a commission to be convened without rights of presence and confrontation. Nor have they offered anything to suggest that Congress has authorized a commission whose own procedures violate the laws of war.

c. Yet the panel below held that the President is free to dispense with virtually the entire UCMJ except in the rare instances where the words "military commission" explicitly appear. Pet. App. 15a. This holding reads out of existence the express language of §836(a) and yields absurd results. Only three procedural rules in the UCMJ mention "military commissions": §828 (requiring a court reporter); §849(d) (permitting deposition testimony), and §850(a) (permitting admission of prior sworn statements). The remaining places where the words appear are jurisdictional or refer to non-procedural rules. *See, e.g.*, §§821, 847–48, 904, 906. The panel concluded that Congress deliberately placed constraints through §836(a), but limited those constraints to court reporters, depositions and affidavits.[14] The UCMJ's text and stated purpose belie such a notion, for it "covers both the substantive and the procedural law governing military justice," S. Rep. No. 81-486, at 1 (1949) ("Purpose of the Bill").

In effect, the panel replaced the UCMJ with the old Articles of War from *Yamashita*. Article 2 of those Articles did not extend procedural protections to persons facing commissions. *Yamashita*, 327 U.S. at 19–20. But as the district court held, the UCMJ supplanted *Yamashita*. Over the Army JAG's objection, it broadened Article 2 to include both "prisoners of war" and "persons within an area leased by or otherwise reserved or acquired for the use of the United States." §802(a)(9), (10), (12); Pet. App. 42a–43a; Statement of Gen. Green, Sen. Armed Serv. Comm., May 9, 1949, at 266.

d. The President's commission also flouts other statutory commands. To take two examples, 10 U.S.C. 3037(c) provides:

> The Judge Advocate General . . . shall receive, revise, and have recorded the proceedings of courts of inquiry and military commissions.

---

[14] It would be highly peculiar for Congress to choose to regulate depositions and court reporters if it was Congress' intent to leave commissions otherwise deregulated. In the face of the clear language of §836(a), the far more plausible explanation is that Congress' omission of the words "military commissions" from certain procedural rules in the UCMJ reflected the historical understanding of symmetry in procedure.

Indeed, the UCMJ fails to mention "courts-martial" in numerous sections, yet it is clear that those provisions nonetheless apply. *See, e.g.*, §§807, 813, 830. For example, 10 U.S.C. 855 forbids a court-martial from punishing through "flogging" or "branding."

"The Judge Advocate General adds integrity to the system of military justice by serving as a reviewing authority." Louis Fisher, Military Tribunals And Presidential Power 124 (2005). In the Civil War, JAG review led to invalidation of many commissions, including for denial of the right to be present.[15] Hamdan *has already been denied* this basic right. . . . . But the Military Order cuts the presidentially appointed and Senate-confirmed JAG out entirely.

Moreover, Congress has prohibited having non-citizens subject "to different punishments, pains, or penalties, on account of such person being an alien." 18 U.S.C. 242. This statute forbids "being subjected to different punishments, pains or penalties by reason of alienage . . . than are prescribed for the punishment of citizens." *United States v. Classic*, 313 U.S. 299, 326 (1941). No past commission, including *Quirin* itself, excluded citizens by design.[16]

2.   *Petitioner Is Not An Offender Triable By Commission*

As discussed in Part II, *infra*, because Petitioner was captured on the battlefields of Afghanistan and claims POW protection, the law of war requires that he be afforded the protections provided to an American servicemember. Because Congress has not authorized the President to employ commissions that contravene the law of war, this commission lacks jurisdiction to try Petitioner.

This case is thus unlike *Quirin*, where the saboteurs (who shed their uniforms and admitted arriving with explosives) did not contest their unlawful combatant status. *See* 317 U.S. at 46 (commission appropriate "upon the conceded facts"); *Ex parte Endo*, 323 U.S. 283, 302 (1944) (detention not authorized "in case of those whose loyalty was not conceded or established"). But, as here, "where those jurisdictional facts are *not* conceded-where the petitioner insists that he is *not* a belligerent-*Quirin* left the pre-existing law in place." *Hamdi*, 542 U.S. at 571–72 (Scalia, J., dissenting).

This case is far closer to that pre-existing law of *Milligan* than it is to *Quirin*. Respondents call Milligan a "civilian," but the Government told the Court then that he was an unlawful belligerent who "conspired with and armed others."[17] Respondents'

---

[15]

> [Judge Advocate General Holt] repeatedly overturned the decisions of trials by military commission (as well as courts-martial) for what can only be called legal technicalities . . . Holt reviewed the sentence of Mary Clemmens . . . [stating]: "Further, it is stated that the Commission was duly sworn – but does not add 'in the presence of the accused.' Nor does the Record show that the accused had any opportunity of challenge afforded her. These are particulars, in which it has always been held that the proceedings of a Military Commission should be assimilated to those of a Court Martial. And as these defects would be fatal in the latter case, they must be held to be so in the present instance."

> Mark Neely, The Fate Of Liberty 162–63 (1991) (quoting Holt's opinion).

[16] A separate statute, 42 U.S.C. 1981, contains a similar ban. Yet the Military Order funnels non-citizens, and only non-citizens, through this separate and unequal system. This discrimination explains why Congress cannot easily reverse the panel, and highlights the role of this Court. "[N]othing opens the door to arbitrary action so effectively as to allow those officials to pick and choose only a few to whom they will apply legislation and thus to escape the political retribution that might be visited upon them if larger numbers were affected." *Ry. Express Agency v. New York*, 336 U.S. 106, 112 (1949) (Jackson, J., concurring); *Cruzan v. Dir., Mo. Dep't of Health*, 497 U.S. 261, 300 (1990) (Scalia, J., concurring).

These difficulties are exacerbated because judicial decisions that transfer unintended powers to the President, like the opinion below, are difficult to correct when no trials have concluded and a bicameral supermajority is required. *See* U.S. Const., art. I §7, cl. 2 (veto override); White House, Statement of Policy, July 21, 2005 (stating that the AUMF provides all the authority the President needs and recommending veto of a bill governing detention and trial of enemy combatants).

[17] Lambdin Milligan was charged with: 1. 'Conspiracy against the Government of the United States;' 2. 'Affording aid and comfort to rebels against the authority of the United States;' 3. 'Inciting insurrection;' 4. 'Disloyal practices;' and 5. 'Violation of the laws of war' 71 U.S. at 6. The Government claimed

attempt to downplay *Milligan* is also undermined by post-*Quirin* reliance on it in *Duncan*, 327 U.S. at 322, and *Reid*, 354 U.S. at 30 (plurality) (*Milligan* remains "one of the great landmarks in this Court's history").

Finally, this commission takes place outside of occupied territory or a zone of war, deviations from practice that Congress would not have anticipated and that this Court has not approved. *Milligan*, 71 U.S. at 127 ("confined to the locality of actual war."). Geographic limitations on jurisdiction ensure that commissions are used out of necessity, not to avoid procedural protections.[18] *Reid*, for example, forbade military trial of dependents outside of conquered territory, in spite of Article 15 and treaties authorizing them. The Court would not indulge "[t]he concept that the Bill of Rights and other constitutional protections against arbitrary government are inoperative when they become inconvenient" because it would "destroy the benefit of a written Constitution and undermine the basis of our Government." 354 U.S. at 14. *Madsen* was "not controlling" because it "concerned trials in enemy territory which had been conquered and held by force of arms," *id.* at 35 n.63. The government argued that "present threats to peace" and "world tension" justified expanding the "battlefront" concept. *Id.* Yet the "exigencies which have required military rule on the battlefront are not present in areas where no conflict exists," *id.*

Respondents have had many opportunities to provide facts showing that Hamdan resembles the *Quirin* saboteurs. At every turn, including in their Return, they have failed. Their recitation of "facts" to show jurisdiction, many for the first time upon

---

that "These crimes of the petitioner were committed within … a State which had been and was then threatened with invasion, having arsenals which the petitioner plotted to seize … where … the petitioner conspired with and armed others." *Id.* at 17 (reprinting United States' argument) (emphasis added). *See also id.* at 130 (majority op.); *id.* at 132 (Chase, C.J., concurring); *Hamdi*, 542 U.S. at 566 (Scalia, J., dissenting).

The assertions in Hamdan's charge, by contrast, fail even to allege that he committed a crime during war. Conspicuously absent is any statement of when the supposed violation occurred. For a commission to have jurisdiction, it must be established that the crime was committed in a war.

Unlike Mr. Milligan, Petitioner has not even been charged with, let alone convicted of, conspiring to seize arsenals and release POWs. Even still, *Milligan* unanimously read Congress's silence to constitute lack of authorization. See *Milligan*, 71 U.S. at 122 ("Why was he not delivered to the Circuit Court of Indiana to be proceeded against according to law? No reason of necessity could be urged against it; because Congress had declared penalties against the offences charged, provided for their punishment, and directed that court to hear and determine them.").

Furthermore, the charges in *Quirin* were statutorily authorized to be tried by commission. Charges 2 and 3 were violations of Articles of War 81 and 82, now codified as 10 U.S.C. 904 and 906, which explicitly authorized commission trial. In discussing the first, law of war, charge, the Court looked to Article 82 317 U.S. at 41. And that first charge may have been pendant to charges 2 and 3. In fact, the government's formal specifications of the first charge tracked the statutory language of Articles 81 and 82. Katyal & Tribe, *Waging War, Deciding Guilt: Trying the Military Tribunals*, 111 YALE L.J. 1259, 1282–83 (2002). *Madsen* also observed that in *Quirin*, the "conviction of saboteurs … was upheld on charges of violating the law of war *as defined by statute*." 343 U.S. at 355 n.22 (emphasis added).

18 *See* EDGAR DUDLE, MILITARY LAW 313 (3d ed. 1910) (commissions only in battle zones); *Eisentrager*, 339 U.S. at 780 (the "grave grounds for challenging military jurisdiction" in *Quirin* included that the trial was not "in a zone of active military operations"); *Madsen*, 343 U.S. at 348 (limiting holding to "territory occupied by Armed Forces"); *Caldwell*, 252 U.S. at 387 (the phrase "'except in time of war,'" doubtfully does anything "more than to recognize the right of the military authorities, in time of war, within the areas affected by military operations or … where civil authority was either totally suspended or obstructed, to deal with the crimes specified–a doubt which … would demonstrate … the entire absence of jurisdiction in the military tribunals."); *Reid*, 354 U.S. at 40 ("Throughout history many transgressions by the military have been called 'slight' and have been justified as 'reasonable' in light of the 'uniqueness' of the times," but "[w]e should not break faith with this nation's tradition of keeping military power subservient to civilian authority").

In *Quirin*, Attorney General Biddle stressed that the Eastern seaboard "was declared to be under the control of the Army." Pet. Br. App. 93a. The Court agreed. 317 U.S. at 22 n.1. *See also Yamashita*, 327 U.S. at 66 n.31; U.S. Br., *Yamashita*, at 42 ("Our army recaptured the Philippines by force of arms and has 'occupied' these Islands since within the meaning of the Regulations" governing the Trials of War Criminals).

appellate review, is too little, too late. To permit the President, on his say-so, to place anyone before this *ad hoc* commission is to countenance an unprecedented expansion of Executive authority.

G. The Commission Lacks Jurisdiction Because Petitioner Has Not Been Charged With An Offense Triable By Commission Under the Law of War

Although Congress has authorized the President to promulgate *procedures* for trials within the jurisdiction of commissions, 10 U.S.C. 836(a), it withheld the power to define the offenses subject to such trial. Rather, 10 U.S.C. 821 ordains that, at most, the jurisdiction of commissions would be defined by the law of war. This jurisdictional limitation is the defining feature of military tribunals and the most important protection against the threat to liberty and our constitutional separation of powers posed by the existence of military trials. *Milligan*, 71 U.S. at 127.

Quirin recognized that a court must examine if "it is within the constitutional power of the National Government to place petitioners upon trial before a military commission for the offenses with which they are charged." 317 U.S. at 29. The Court "*must therefore first inquire* whether any of the acts charged is an offense against the law of war cognizable before a military tribunal." *Id.* (emphasis added). The sole charge in this case, conspiracy, is not such an offense.

The charge fails to state a violation of the law of war for two reasons: 1) "conspiracy" is not an offense recognized by the laws of war; and 2) while acts of stateless terrorism are justifiably subject to severe punishment under civilian criminal law, they do not constitute war crimes falling within the jurisdiction of a military commission.

1. *Conspiracy Is Not a Violation of the Laws of War*

Neither the 1907 Hague Convention Respecting the Laws and Customs of War on Land, nor the Geneva Conventions of 1929 or 1949, make any mention of conspiracy as an offense against the law of war.[19] The failure of the 1949 Geneva Conventions to identify conspiracy is particularly significant, since those treaties require signatories to punish so-called "grave breaches" of the Conventions by criminal prosecutions. *See, e.g.*, GPW, art. 129. To fulfill this obligation, Congress passed the War Crimes Act of 1996 and the Expanded War Crimes Act of 1997, codified at 18 U.S.C. 2441. The Acts define a "war crime" as any "grave breach" of the Geneva Conventions, or violation of select provisions of the 1907 Hague Convention or the Landmine Protocol.

Thus, Congress no longer relies on the "common law of war" to define war crimes (as it did in World War II); it now has "crystalliz[ed]," *Quirin*, 317 U.S. at 30, and occupied the field with legislation identifying such crimes. Reflecting the universal disregard of conspiracy in international law, conspiracy is not on that large congressional list of offenses.

---

[19] In construing "longstanding law-of-war principles" in *Hamdi*, 542 U.S. at 521, the plurality relied primarily on provisions from the Hague and Geneva Conventions. *See also* Int'l Comm. of Red Cross, *Commentary: III Geneva Convention Relative to the Treatment of Prisoners of War* 471 (Pictet ed. 1960) ("ICRC Commentary") ("In actual fact, since the codification of 1949, there are no customary rules which are not included in either the Hague Conventions or in the new [1949 Geneva] Conventions. The points for which no provision is made are precisely those on which there is a lack of agreement.") In this context, the GPW's judicial enforceability is irrelevant. It codifies customary laws of war which bind the commission: "the customary rules become fully applicable in the case of a prisoner whose country of origin, or the Power on which he depends, is not a party to the international instruments governing the laws of war." *Id.*

Likewise, the statutes and treaties establishing the major tribunals punishing war crimes in Rwanda and Yugoslavia, as well as the International Criminal Court, do not regard conspiracy as a war crime. The absence of conspiracy as a stand-alone crime is deliberate – conspiracy is seen as an abusive tool of prosecutors and rejected throughout the world. *See Amicus Br. of Specialists in Conspiracy*, at 6–18, 21–25. Customary international law evidences the same refusal. The Nuremburg judges, for example, ruled that there was no offense of conspiracy to commit war crimes or crimes against humanity. They rejected broad language in the London Charter suggesting such offenses.[20] And conspiracy doctrines have never been thought appropriate for war crimes charges against low-level offenders such as Hamdan.

In short, there is no stand-alone war crime of conspiracy that permits Petitioner's trial.[21] Accordingly, the commission lacks jurisdiction because Hamdan has not been charged with an offense that a commission may try.

2.   *The Law of War Does Not Subject Offenses From the "War on Terror" to Trial by Military Commission*

As Petitioner's charge demonstrates, the President is attempting to use commissions as an alternative forum for the trial of criminal charges that historically have been tried in civilian courts. But if the Nation has lost confidence in the ability of its judicial system to adjudicate such claims, and has determined to shift the responsibility for the definition of offenses (and their trial and punishment) to the military, that decision must be made by Congress, not the President, and it must also be made with unmistakable clarity. No such decision is evident in the UCMJ or AUMF.

In using these commissions in the "war on terror," the President has expanded not only their traditionally limited jurisdiction, but also his own powers, both to "define and punish . . . Offenses against the Law of Nations" (a power vested in Congress in Art. I, §8) and to adjudicate offenses (the province of the judiciary). The court of appeals ratified this maneuver, permitting the President to sweep aside not only the civilian, but also military, justice systems in circumstances untethered to armed conflict as traditionally understood. In *Hamdi*, for example, the Court could apply the laws of war to limit Executive detention because the conflict in Afghanistan is recognizable as a war.

---

[20] The court confined conspiracy to crimes against peace (aggressive war), and only against very high-level German officials who were directly involved in specific acts of aggression. "The International Military Tribunal ultimately interpreted the [conspiracy] concept very narrowly, and adopted a construction of the Charter under which conspiracies to commit 'war crimes' or 'crimes against humanity' were ruled entirely outside the jurisdiction of the Tribunal." Telford Taylor, Final Report to the Secretary of the Army on the Nuremberg War Crimes Trials 70 (1949). As Assistant Attorney General Herbert Wechsler, head of the Criminal Division, stated, "it is an error to designate as conspiracy the crime itself, the more so since the common-law conception of the criminality of an unexecuted plan is not universally accepted in civilized law." *See The American Road to Nuremburg*, 84, 87 (Dec. 29, 1944 Mem.) (Smith ed. 1982).

[21] Indeed, Respondents' "definition" of conspiracy is woefully lacking. For example, it eliminates the most important element of conspiracy: agreement. Under Mil. Comm. Instr. No. 2, §6(C)(6)(a)(1), a defendant need only "join[] an enterprise of persons who shar[e] a common criminal purpose." Furthermore, even under broad domestic standards, conspiracy is a specific intent crime. *See Clark v. La. State Penitentiary*, 694 F.2d 75 (5th Cir. 1982). Yet Hamdan's charge does not allege specific intent.

Domestic criminal law recognizes an offense of conspiracy because of its strong checks on prosecutorial and judicial abuse-indictment by a grand jury, jury trial, confrontation, access to exculpatory evidence, and so on. These procedural rights are preconditions before conspiracy is available.

The "war on terror" – which the Executive claims is a "separate conflict" under which Hamdan's commission is convened – is potentially unlimited in scope, duration, and all other criteria which traditionally separate a state of war from a state of peace. Thus, allowing any offense that could be associated with the "war on terror" to be tried by commission would permit thousands of civilian court prosecutions for terrorism to be transferred to commissions. Indeed, nothing prevents the President from extending his Military Order to American citizens. The careful jurisprudence and procedures of Article III courts, and those of courts-martial, would all be sacrificed for presidential flexibility. *See* Danny Hakim, *After Convictions, the Undoing of a U.S. Terror Prosecution*, N.Y. Times, Oct. 7, 2004, at A1 (describing Article III checks on prosecutorial abuse, particularly withholding exculpatory information, in terrorism cases). This case is the litmus test for such authority.

Quirin, decided in the context of a traditional war with conceded enemy belligerents, provides no precedent for such sweeping Executive authority. It even assumed "there are acts regarded in other countries, or by some writers on international law, as offenses against the law of war which would not be triable by military tribunal here, either because they are not recognized by our courts as violations of the law of war or because they are of that class of offenses constitutionally triable only by a jury." 317 U.S. at 29.

One way in which this Court has confined commissions is by insisting on a Declared War or closure of civilian courts. In this case, Congress has not issued a Declaration against al Qaeda, nor has it in any other way expressed its intent to authorize and extend the laws of war to punishment in that conflict through commissions. "To apply the laws of armed conflict and thereby displace domestic and international criminal and human rights law below that threshold would be to do violence to human rights and civil liberties that protect us all." Official Statement (Rona), ICRC, *http://www.icrc.org/Web/Eng/siteeng0.nsf/iwpList488/3C2914F52152E565C1256E 60005C84CO* (2004).

In every instance in which this Court has approved a commission, Congress had explicitly declared war against a nation-state. In *Quirin*, for example, the Declaration prominently figured: "The Constitution thus invests the President as Commander in Chief with the power to wage war which Congress has declared," 317 U.S. at 26.[22] The power was directly traced to the declared war, *id.* at 26–28, in the same way that the same Court, six years later, relied on the Declaration to invoke the Alien Enemy Act of 1798, *Ludecke v. Watkins*, 335 U.S. 160 (1948). Similarly, *Yamashita* permitted commissions

---

[22] E.g., 317 U.S. at 21 ("After the declaration of war between the United States and the German Reich, petitioners received training at a sabotage school"); *id.* at 26. Moreover, the meaning of Article 15 changed when the UCMJ was codified. Congress deleted the words "in time of war" from another provision, Article of War 78, to make clear that *that* provision, evidently in contrast to such others as Article 15, permitted a court-martial to impose death for trespass in circumstances "amounting to a state of belligerency, but where a formal state of war does not exist." H.R. 2498 Hrg. H. Cmte. Armed Serv., 81st Cong. 1229 (1949).

It is not only the power inherent to Declarations, but their specific language, that authorizes commissions. In World War II, Congress stated:

[T]he state of war between the United States and the Government of Germany . . . is hereby formally declared; and the President is hereby authorized and directed to employ the *entire* naval and military forces of the United States *and the resources of the Government to carry on war* against the Government of Germany; and, to bring the conflict to a successful termination, *all of the resources of the country* are hereby pledged by the Congress.

Jt. Res. Dec. 11, 1941, 55 Stat. 796, 796 (emphasis added); Edwin Corwin, Total War and the Constitution 120 (1947). Other Declarations were similar. Jt. Res. Dec. 8, 1941, 55 Stat. 795 (Japan); Jt. Res. Dec. 7, 1917, 40 Stat. 429 (Austria-Hungary); Jt. Res. Apr. 6, 1917, 40 Stat. 1 (Germany).

"so long as a state of war exists-*from* its *declaration* until peace is proclaimed." 327 U.S. at 11–12 (emphasis added); *see also Madsen*, 343 U.S. at 346 n.9 (authorization from Declare War power); *Eisentrager*, 339 U.S. at 775 ("whenever a 'declared war' exists."). A Declaration puts government officials and defendants on notice that ordinary civilian processes must give way.[23]

The laws of war also govern other extreme circumstances where war is not declared but the conflict ends civilian law. *The Prize Cases*, 67 U.S. 635, 667 (1863) (using "common law" test of whether war exists by examining if "the regular course of justice is interrupted by revolt, rebellion, or insurrection, so that the courts of justice cannot be kept open"); *id.* at 682 (finding war had not begun and returning seized property). *Milligan* followed that test, 71 U.S. at 120, even though the Government told the Court that Lambdin Milligan was an unlawful combatant who "plotted to seize" arsenals and "conspired with and armed others." *Id.* at 17.[24]

At the very most, Congress has authorized commissions to enforce the laws of war. But Hamdan's commission has not been constituted to try crimes from the Afghan conflict. *Compare* Pet. App. 12a, 18a, *with Hamdi*, 542 U.S. at 521 (the "United States may detain, for the *duration of these* hostilities, individuals legitimately determined to be *Taliban* combatants 'who engaged in an armed conflict against the United States'") (plurality) (emphasis added). This case presents the question *Hamdi* left open, that "[i]f the practical circumstances of a given conflict are entirely unlike those of the conflicts that informed the development of the law of war, that understanding may unravel." *Id.*; *see also id.* at 551–52 (Souter, J., concurring in part).

Whether Hamdan's commission is authorized is not answered by the World War II cases either, since those operated in a traditional war between nation-states. That conflict was obviously governed by the laws of war, and the defendants fell within commission jurisdiction as enemy aliens.[25] Al Qaeda, however, is not a nation-state, and an

---

[23] *See Youngstown*, 343 U.S. at 634 (Jackson, J., concurring); *id.* at 613 (Frankfurter, J., concurring); *N.Y. Times v. U.S.* 403 U.S. 713, 722 (1971) ("[T]he war power stems from a declaration of war") (Douglas, J., concurring); WILLIAM H. REHNQUIST, ALL THE LAWS BUT ONE 218 (2000); Leslie Gelb & Anne-Marie Slaughter, *Declare War*, ATLANTIC MONTHLY, Nov. 2005 (founders insisted on a declaration of war because it maximizes "political accountability"); J. Gregory Sidak, *War, Liberty, and Enemy Aliens*, 67 N.Y.U.L. REV. 1402 (1992) (formal declaration of war needed).

Our courts have strictly policed military jurisdiction by insisting on declared war. In cases involving soldiers, who are always within military jurisdiction, courts are permissive. *E.g.*, *United States v. Bancroft*, 3 U.S.C.M.A. 3 (1953). But when such jurisdiction is contested, as it is here, courts consistently require a Declaration. *United States v. Averette*, 19 U.S.C.M.A. 363, 365 (1970) (finding that Vietnam conflict was not a time of war because general usage does "not serve as a shortcut for a formal declaration of war, at least in the sensitive area of subjecting civilians to military jurisdiction"); *Cole v. Laird*, 468 F.2d 829, 831 n.2 (5th Cir. 1972) (civilians are subject to court-martial in "a formally-declared, global war"); *Robb v. United States*, 456 F.2d 768, 771 (Ct. Cl. 1972) ("the phrase 'in time of war' . . . refers to a state of war formally declared by Congress despite the fact that the conflict in Vietnam is a war in the popular sense of the word"); *Willenbring v. Neurauter*, 48 M.J. 152, 157 (C.A.A.F. 1998).

[24] Even for seizure of wagons and mules during the Mexican-American War, the Court required that "danger must be immediate and impending; or the necessity urgent." *Mitchell v. Harmony*, 54 U.S. 115, 134 (1851). *See also Lee*, 358 U.S. at 233 ("The views of Blackstone on military jurisdiction became deeply imbedded in our thinking: 'The necessity of order and discipline in an army is the only thing which can give it countenance; and therefore it ought not to be permitted in time of peace, when the king's courts are open for all persons to receive justice according to the laws of the land.'"); *Duncan*, 327 U.S. at 326 (Murphy, J., concurring); *id.* at 335–37 (Stone, C.J., concurring).

[25] *E.g.*, *Eisentrager*, 339 U.S. at 772 ("[i]n war, the subjects of each country were enemies to each other") (citation omitted). *Quirin* found that notwithstanding Haupt's U.S. citizenship, his joining of the German military made him an enemy under the "Hague Convention and the laws of war." 317 U.S. at 38. Haupt's relatives were tried by civilian courts because they had not joined the German military and were not "enemies."

accused's enemy status cannot be determined by citizenship. With a declaration of war, the laws of war apply in full; otherwise, they apply only where Congress has authorized their extension.[26] Even staunch defenders of Executive power concede that the Declare War Clause's "primary function was to trigger the international laws of war".[27]

The panel somehow reached the conclusion that Hamdan could be tried for a violation of the laws of war, even though it also found that the conflict with al Qaeda was not governed by the canonical statement of the laws of war – the GPW. But if the laws of war do not apply, there is nothing to charge. As Colin Powell warned, a finding that the Geneva Conventions do not apply "undermines the President's Military Order by removing an important legal basis for trying the detainees before Military Commissions." Sec. of State Mem., Jan. 2002, at *http://msnbc.msn.com/id/4999363*. In other words, if the GPW does not apply, then the laws of war do not apply; if the laws of war do not apply, then a commission has no jurisdiction. The panel took the untenable view that Petitioner lacks rights under treaties and statutes, but is subject to their penalties. *See Milligan*, 71 U.S. at 131 ("If he cannot enjoy the immunities attaching to the character of a prisoner of war, how can he be subject to their pains and penalties?").

If the UCMJ were stretched to give the President the sole discretion to decide when the laws of war applied and when they did not, it would become an unconstitutional delegation. *See Clinton*, 524 U.S. at 449–53 (Kennedy, J., concurring); *Am. Textile Mfrs. Inst. v. Donovan*, 452 U.S. 490, 545 (1981) (Rehnquist, J., dissenting); *Cal. Bankers v. Schultz*, 416 U.S. 21, 91–93 (1974) (Brennan, J., dissenting*); Panama Ref. Co. v. Ryan*, 293 U.S. 388 (1935); *A.L.A. Schechter Poultry v. United States*, 295 U.S. 495 (1935). Such an interpretation would give the President the ability to set up tribunals at will, define offenses as war crimes, and try cases before military judges that serve at his pleasure. Katyal & Tribe, *supra*, at 1290.

For this commission to be lawful, Respondents must show that the laws of war permit *this* offender and *this* charge in *this* conflict to be tried in a commission with *these* procedures. *Quirin* does not provide an adequate precedent, for the Court stated it had "no occasion now to define with meticulous care the ultimate boundaries of the jurisdiction of military tribunals" and "hold[s] only that those particular acts constitute an offense against the law of war which the Constitution authorizes to be tried by military commission." 317 U.S. at 45–46. Even with those limits, *Quirin* has been severely criticized. *Hamdi*, 542 U.S. at 572 n.4 (Scalia, J., dissenting) ("the *Quirin* Court propounded a mistaken understanding of *Milligan*"); *id.* at 592 (Thomas, J., dissenting);

---

[26] *See Bas v. Tingy*, 4 U.S. 37, 43 (1800) (Chase, J.) ("Congress is empowered to declare a general war, or Congress may wage a limited war; limited in place, in objects, and in time. If a general war is declared, its extent and operations are only restricted and regulated by the jus belli, forming a part of the law of nations; but if a partial war is waged, its extent and operation depend on our municipal laws."); *id.* at 40 (Washington, J.) (similar); *Talbot v. Seeman*, 5 U.S. 1, 28 (1801) ("congress may authorize general hostilities, in which case the general laws of war apply to our situation; or partial hostilities, in which case the laws of war, so far as they actually apply to our situation, must be noticed.") (Marshall, C.J.); *Brown v. United States*, 12 U.S. 110, 129 (1814) (rejecting Presidential authority to confiscate enemy property without explicit statute during declared war); *Little v. Barreme*, 6 U.S. 170 (1804) (same reasoning applied to the taking of ships on the high seas).

[27] John Yoo, The *Continuation of Politics by Other Means: The Original Understanding of War Powers*, 84 CAL. L. REV. 167, 242–43 (1996) (citations omitted). *See also id.* at 245 (Declaration notifies citizens and enemies); *id.* at 248 (distinguishing between partial and complete war); Eugene Rostow, *Great Cases Make Bad Law: The War Powers Act*, 50 TEX. L. REV. 833, 850 (1972) ("the term 'declare war' in the Constitution referred to the . . . sharp distinction between the law of war and the law of peace"); *id.* at 834–35, 856 (same); Eugene Rostow, *Once More Unto the Breach: The War Powers Resolution Revisited*, 21 VAL. L. REV. 1, 6 (1986) ("All international uses of force are not 'war' in the legal sense of the word, however bloody and extended the conflicts may be . . . A 'declaration of war' transforms the relationship between the belligerents"); *id.* at 51 (*Milligan* and *Covert* are among "the finest justifications of our claim to be a nation under law").

Amicus Br. of Quirin *Historians*. It is not a stable foundation for a dramatic expansion of Executive power that will become a permanent fixture in our law.

In the end, even if the "war on terror" is truly a war in which commissions can prosecute war criminals, the laws of war define their jurisdiction. Hamdan's commission falls well outside these parameters. The laws of war do not permit the charge, courts-martial and civilian courts are open, and the tribunal flouts court-martial rules and the laws of war themselves. Such a commission cannot be tolerated in a Republic such as ours, dedicated to the rule of law and the division of power, rather than its concentration in Executive hands.

II. PETITIONER'S COMMISSION VIOLATES THE THIRD GENEVA CONVENTION

Article 5 of the GPW requires a hearing to determine POW status "[s]hould any doubt arise." Until a "competent tribunal" decides otherwise, those captured "shall enjoy" its protections. "*Id.* Hamdan was apprehended in a theater of military operations and asserts a right to GPW protection. . . . . It is undisputed that no such Article 5 hearing has occurred. Thus, as the district court correctly concluded, Hamdan is entitled to presumptive POW status. One right POWs hold is the Article 102 right to be tried by "the same courts, according to the same procedure as in the case of members of the armed forces of the Detaining Power." As such, even if Hamdan's commission is otherwise consistent with federal law, the Geneva Conventions bar his trial.

The district court's invalidation of the commission on this ground precisely tracks the views of our military. In 1951, the Manual for Courts Martial was revised because GPW ratification "will alter to a material extent the procedures heretofore applied by military commissions." Pet. Br. App. 34a. Under GPW Articles 85 and 102, "unless we are willing to try our own personnel who commit war crimes by military commission under a more summary procedure than that provided for courts-martial and under civil law rules of evidence – we will have to try enemy prisoners of war accused of war crimes under the same procedure as that prescribed for courts-martial." *Id.* Respondents have no authority to depart from this longstanding rule, which was designed to outlaw a spoils system of victor's justice.

A.   The GPW Is Enforceable Without Its Self-Execution

The court of appeals did not reject Hamdan's GPW claim on the merits, but rather because the "Convention does not confer upon Hamdan a right to enforce its provisions in court." . . . . That conclusion is in error.

As an initial matter, the court of appeals was wrong in concluding that the rights to which petitioner lays claim are embodied solely in the GPW. To the contrary, the United States has implemented its obligations under the GPW by statute[28] and regulation,[29]

---

[28] *See* National Defense Authorization Act, §1091(b)(4), Pub. L. No. 108-375, 118 Stat. 1811, 2069 (2004) ("It is the policy of the United States to . . . ensure that, in a case in which there is doubt as to whether a detainee is entitled to prisoner of war status under the Geneva Conventions, such detainee receives the protections accorded to prisoners of war until the detainee's status is determined by a competent tribunal."); *id .* §1092(a) (directing Secretary of Defense to implement procedures to ensure that detainees are treated "in a humane manner consistent with the international obligations and laws of the United States and the policies set forth in section 1091(b)"); *id.* §1092(b)(3) (requiring "[p]roviding all detainees with information, in their own language, of the applicable protections afforded under the Geneva Conventions").

[29] *See* AR 190–8 §1–5(a)(2) ("All persons taken into custody by U.S. forces will be provided with the protections of the GPW until some other legal status is determined by competent legal authority."); *id.* §1–6 ("A competent

both of which are subject to enforcement through a mandamus or habeas corpus petition. *Miguel v. McCarl*, 291 U.S. 442, 451 (1934) ("[W]here the proper construction of a statute is clear, the duty of an officer called upon to act under it is ministerial in its nature and may be compelled by mandamus"); 28 U.S.C. 2241(c).[30]

Second, the GPW is part of the law of war and limits the jurisdiction of commissions, see 10 U.S.C. 821, a limitation this Court has repeatedly enforced.[31] Thus, for example, in *Quirin*, this Court carefully considered the petitioners' status to discern whether they were, in fact, unlawful belligerents triable by commission. 317 U.S. at 36–37. The Government has acknowledged that the laws of war now include the GPW. . . . . As explained above, under GPW Article 102, Hamdan is not an "offender" triable by commission because a member of the U.S. armed forces is not subject to commission trial. Likewise, as explained above, "conspiracy" is not an "offense" recognized by the laws of war and thus is not triable in a commission.

Respondents' reliance on §821 runs against the longstanding canon that "an act of Congress ought never to be construed to violate the law of nations if any other possible construction remains," *Murray v. Schooner Charming Betsy*, 6 U.S. (2 Cranch) 64, 118 (1804); *see also MacLeod v. United States*, 229 U.S. 416, 427 (1913) (interpreting a presidential order during Spanish-American War so that it is "consistent with the principles of international law"); *Cross v. Harrison*, 57 U.S. 164, 190 (1853) (adopting "the law of arms"); *Prize Cases*, 67 U.S. at 665 (addressing whether the President had "a right to institute a blockade . . . on the principles of international law"); *Brown*, 12 U.S. at 125–28; *id.* at 153 (Story, J., dissenting) ("when the legislative authority . . . has declared war in its

---

tribunal shall determine the status of any person not appearing to be entitled to prisoner of war status . . . who asserts that he or she is entitled to treatment as a prisoner of war, or concerning whom any doubt of a like nature exists"); *id.* §3–7 ("Judicial proceedings against [POWs] will be by courts-martial or by civil courts. When [POWs] are tried by courts-martial, pretrial, trial, and post-trial procedures will be according to the UCMJ and the U.S. Manual for Courts-Martial. [POWs] will not be tried by a civil court for committing an offense unless a member of the U.S. Armed Forces would be so tried.").

These regulations have long been included in military manuals, further evidencing GPW implementation. *See, e.g.,* Army Field Manual (FM) 27-10, *The Law of Land Warfare,* ch. 3 §I ¶71 (1956) ("[Article 5] applies to any person not appearing to be entitled to prisoner-of-war status . . . who asserts that he is entitled to treatment as a prisoner of war"); Judge Advocate General's School, *Operational Law Handbook* 22 (2003) ("regardless of the nature of the conflict, all enemy personnel should initially be accorded the protections of the GPW Convention").

[30] AR 190–8, as "authorized War Department regulations[,] have the force of law." *Standard Oil Co. v. Johnson,* 316 U.S. 481, 484 (1942). *See also Vitarelli v. Seaton,* 359 U.S. 535, 540 (1959) ("[T]he Secretary . . . was bound by the regulations which he himself had promulgated for dealing with such cases, even though without such regulations he could have discharged petitioner summarily"); *Service v. Dulles,* 354 U.S. 363, 388–89 (1957) (same); *Paul v. United States,* 371 U.S. 245, 255 (1963) (same); *Nixon v. Sec'y of the Navy,* 422 F.2d 934, 937 (2d Cir. 1970) ("[t]he Navy is bound by its own validly promulgated regulations, and the district courts [on mandamus] are free to entertain suits by servicemen requesting compliance with such rules"); *United States v. Heffner,* 420 F.2d 809, 811 (4th Cir. 1969); *Hammond v. Lenfest,* 398 F.2d 705, 715 (2d Cir. 1968) ("a validly promulgated regulation binds the government [even when] the government action is essentially discretionary in nature.").

[31] *Quirin* interpreted the predecessor of §821 to "incorporat[e] the law of war." 317 U.S. at 38. So, too, *Yamashita* found that the predecessor statute adopted rules "further defined and supplemented by the Hague Convention," 327 U.S. at 8. *See also* H. Armed Servs. Comm. Hrng., 81st Cong., at 959 (1949) ("'law of war' is set out in various treaties like the Geneva convention and supplements to that.") (Col. Dinsmore).

10 U.S.C. 821 was enacted under Congress' Article I "define and punish" power. To read that Clause to permit tribunals whose procedures violate international law is contrary to its purpose. *See* Dickinson, *The Law of Nations as Part of the National Law of the United States,* 101 U. Pa. L. Rev. 26, 36 (1952). "[T]o pretend to define the law of nations which depend[] on the authority of all the Civilized Nations of the World[] would have a look of arrogance that would make us ridiculous." 2 Records of the Federal Convention of 1787, at 615 (Farrand ed. 1911) (James Wilson).

most unlimited manner, the executive . . . cannot lawfully transcend the rules of warfare established among civilized nations. He cannot lawfully exercise powers or authorize proceedings which the civilized world repudiates and disclaims."); *Amicus Br. of Urban Morgan Institute* at 3–14. The *Hamdi* plurality followed this tradition by interpreting the AUMF in light of "longstanding law-of-war principles," including the GPW. 542 U.S. at 519–21.[32]

Third, Congress has specifically authorized courts to determine whether Petitioner's detention is "in violation of the Constitution or laws *or treaties* of the United States." 28 U.S.C. 2241(c)(3) (emphasis added). In accordance with that language, this Court has repeatedly entertained habeas corpus actions to enforce treaty-based rights.[33]

Likewise, treaty rights have long been enforced through petitions for mandamus. For example, *Jordan v. Tashiro*, 278 U.S. 123, 128–30 (1928), permitted such a petition to protect Japanese nationals' rights under a 1911 treaty. The Court articulated a fundamental canon of treaty interpretation: "where a treaty fairly admits of two constructions, one restricting the rights that may be claimed under it and the other enlarging them, the more liberal construction is to be preferred." *Id.* at 127. Notably, the Court went on to state: "The principle of liberal construction of treaties would be nullified if a grant of enumerated privileges were held not to include the use of the usual methods and instrumentalities of their exercise." *Id.* at 130. Of course, the "usual methods and instrumentalities" for enforcing rights include lawsuits. So long as the GPW is in effect in domestic law (and there is no dispute that it is), and so long as the GPW protects individual rights (and the Government admits that it does), then it is judicially enforceable, and Hamdan can rely on the habeas statute or common-law mandamus to supply the form of action. *See Rasul*, 542 U.S. at 483; *Factor*, 290 U.S. at 286; *Chew Heong*, 112 U.S. at 560; *Jordan*, 278 U.S. at 128–30.

The panel's decision in this case "amounts to the assertion that no federal court has the authority to determine whether the Third Geneva Convention has been violated, or,

---

[32] Moreover, under the last-in-time rule, when a treaty is subsequent to congressional action, the treaty controls. *Reid*, 354 U.S. at 18 n.34 (plurality). *Cook v. United States*, 288 U.S. 102, 119 (1933), found that a 1924 treaty trumped a 1922 statute, even though Congress reenacted the statute in 1930. Statutes enacted after a treaty do not trump the treaty without a clear statement. *Id.* at 120. Therefore, the Geneva Conventions, ratified in 1955, control this case and overcome any contrary implication from §821.

[33] *Factor v. Laubenheimer*, 290 U.S. 276 (1933); *Mali v. Keeper of the Common Jail*, 120 U.S. 1, 17 (1887) ("we see no reason why [petitioner] may not enforce his rights under the treaty by writ of *habeas corpus* in any proper court of the United States"); *United States v. Rauscher*, 119 U.S. 407 (1886); *Chew Heong v. United States*, 112 U.S. 536, 560 (1884) (granting relief to habeas petitioner to re-enter the United States as established by treaty); *Medellin v. Dretke*, 125 S. Ct. 2088, 2104 (2005) (O'Connor, J., dissenting) ("This Court has repeatedly enforced treaty-based rights of individual foreigners, allowing them to assert claims arising from various treaties. These treaties . . . do not share any special magic words. Their rights-conferring language is arguably no clearer than the Vienna Convention's is, and they do not specify judicial enforcement.") (citing cases).

    For example, *Wang v. Ashcroft*, 320 F.3d 130 (2d Cir. 2003), enforced a treaty based on implementing regulations. It did so despite the statute's language that "nothing in this section shall be construed as providing any court jurisdiction to consider or review claims under the Convention or this section." *Id.* at 140 (quoting 8 U.S.C. 1252). Such language "does not speak with sufficient clarity to exclude [treaty] claims from §2241 jurisdiction"; to conclude otherwise would raise constitutional concerns under *St. Cyr.* "'[A]t the absolute minimum, the Suspension Clause protects the writ as it existed in 1789.' " *Id.* at 143 (citation omitted). Other courts have reached the same conclusion. *St. Fort v. Ashcroft*, 329 F.3d 191, 202 (1st Cir. 2003); *Singh v. Ashcroft*, 351 F.3d 435, 441 (9th Cir. 2003).

    Moreover, one theory holds that "a treaty that is ratified but not self-executing need not be implemented in order for a party to have a habeas cause of action under that treaty." *Ogbudimkpa v. Ashcroft*, 342 F.3d 207, 218 n.22 (3d Cir. 2003).

if it has, to grant relief from the violation." . . . . The Court should reject that claim, which strips the judiciary of its time-honored role as enforcer of treaty-based rights.

B.   The GPW Provisions Are Directly Enforceable

Hamdan's rights are separately enforceable under the Supremacy Clause because the GPW is self-executing. A treaty is self-executing when "no domestic legislation is required to give the Convention the force of law in the United States." *Trans World Airlines, Inc. v. Franklin Mint Corp.*, 466 U.S. 243, 252 (1984). Treaties that "by their terms confer rights upon individual citizens," *Diggs v. Richardson*, 555 F.2d 848, 851 (D.C. Cir. 1976), are generally self-executing, unless a contrary intention is manifest. RESTATEMENT (THIRD) OF FOREIGN REL. LAW §111 Rptr.'s n.5 (1987) ("RESTATEMENT").

"To ascertain whether [a provision] confers a right on individuals, we first look to the treaty's text as we would with a statute's." *Medellin v. Dretke*, 125 S. Ct. 2088, 2103 (2005) (O'Connor, J., dissenting); *id.* (stating that under *Foster v. Neilson*, 27 U.S. 253 (1829), "[b]ecause the [Vienna] Convention is self-executing, . . . its guarantees are susceptible to judicial enforcement just as the provisions of a statute would be."). The GPW's text plainly confers individual rights; it does not merely regulate relations among states. Nothing in the relevant GPW provisions (particularly Arts. 3, 5, and 102) calls for legislation. Congress knew "that very tittle in the way of new legislative enactments will be required to give effect to the provisions." Ratifying Report, *supra*, at 30. The Committee identified only four areas where additional legislation would be required, none at issue here. *Id.* at 30–31. Of course, "[s]ome provisions of an international agreement may be self-executing and others non-self-executing." RESTATEMENT, §111 cmt. h. . . .

The Government no longer contends that the GPW is not self-executing. Instead, it argues that the GPW does not contemplate judicial enforcement. The Court of Appeals accepted this argument by selectively quoting an 1884 case. Pet. App. 7a (quoting *Head Money Cases*, 112 U.S. 580, 598 (1884)). But the panel ignored language in the same opinion explaining when treaty provisions *are* judicially enforceable:

> But a treaty may also contain provisions which confer certain rights upon the citizens or subjects of one of the nations residing in the territorial limits of the other, which partake of the nature of municipal law, and which are capable of enforcement as between private parties in the courts of the country. . . . A treaty, then, is a law of the land as an act of congress is, whenever its provisions prescribe a rule by which the rights of the private citizen or subject may be determined. And when such rights are of a nature to be enforced in a court of justice, that court resorts to the treaty for a rule of decision for the case before it as it would to a statute.

112 U.S. at 598–99. Indeed, this Court has repeatedly enforced treaty rights for two centuries without stopping to inquire whether a "private right of action" was created.[34]

---

[34] *See, Amicus Br. of Louis Henkin et al.* (*Henkin Br.*); *Kolovrat v. Oregon*, 366 U.S. 187 (1961) (treaty-based rights of non-resident aliens enforced to prevent state action in taking of property); *Jordan, supra*; *Asakura v. City of Seattle*, 265 U.S. 332, 341 (1924) (affirming injunctive relief against ordinance that violated a treaty; "[the treaty] operates of itself without the aid of any legislation, state or national; and it will be applied and given authoritative effect by the courts."); *United States v. Percheman*, 32 U.S. (7 Pet.) 51, 88–89 (1833) (land grants confirmed by treaty are judicially enforceable); *Owings v. Norwood's Lessee*, 9 U.S. 344, 348 (1809) ("Whenever a right grows out of, or is protected by, a treaty . . . whoever may have this right, it is to be protected"); *United States v. Schooner Peggy*, 5 U.S. 103, 110 (1801) ("[W]here a treaty is the law of the land, and as such affects the rights of parties litigating in court, that treaty as much binds those rights, and is as much to be regarded by the court, as an act of congress.").

In this case, the panel admitted that the GPW protects individual rights. . . . . However, it concluded that dicta in a footnote of *Eisentrager*, 339 U.S. at 789 n.14, about the 1929 Geneva Convention bound its decision. The panel's use of that footnote was gravely flawed. First, *Eisentrager* concerned jurisdiction, and that holding has been superseded by *Rasul*. The footnote merely reflected the Court's consideration of whether, apart from the habeas statute, the 1929 treaty provided a basis for jurisdiction.

Second, the GPW drafters thought the 1929 treaty failed to adequately protect POWs and wrote a completely different instrument. See *supra* p.2. A major innovation of the GPW is Article 5, which creates a presumption in favor of protection and the right to a status determination – an Article that was completely absent from the 1929 treaty:

> This amendment was based on the view that decisions which might have the gravest consequences should not be made by a single person. . . . . *The matter should be taken to a court* . . .

ICRC Commentary, *supra*, at 77 (emphasis added). Article 5 thus illustrates that the GPW did not rely entirely on diplomatic enforcement. *See also id.* at 90–91 ("It was not until the Conventions of 1949 . . . that the existence of 'rights' conferred on prisoners of war was affirmed."); *id.* at 23 ("the Conventions have been drawn up first and foremost to protect individuals, and not to serve State interests."); Geoffrey Best, *War and Law Since 1945*, at 80–114 (1994).

Eisentrager itself reflects the weakness of the 1929 Convention. It held that no rights were at issue in the case because the 1929 treaty did *not* "appl[y] to a trial for war crimes." 339 U.S. at 790. The GPW specifically *reversed* that interpretation, which originated in *Yamashita*, 327 U.S. at 22. *See* GPW art. 85; ICRC Commentary, *supra*, at 413.

Finally, the fact that the GPW prescribes a role for neutrals or "Protecting Powers" in disputes does not remotely support the inference that diplomacy was intended as the *only* method of enforcement. Rather, its very first Article requires signatories to do all within their power "to respect and to ensure respect for the present Convention in all circumstances." Art. 1. *See* ICRC Commentary, at 17–18 ("it is not merely an engagement concluded on a basis of reciprocity" but "a series of unilateral engagements"; "it is for the Government to supervise the execution of the orders it gives" and "must of necessity prepare . . . the legal, material or other means of ensuring the faithful enforcement").

In this country, the mechanism for "ensur[ing] respect" for treaty rights includes the independent judiciary. Indeed, the GPW drafters understood that enforcement would be promoted by a combination of factors, including

> pressure of public opinion, pressure by Powers party to the Convention but not involved in the conflict, the fear of the members of the Government in power of being subsequently disavowed or even punished, and *court decisions*. . . . The individual is considered in his own right. The State is not the only subject of law. . . .

Id. at 86 (emphasis added).

Finally, the presence of diplomatic enforcement provisions has not precluded judicial enforcement. For example, in *Chew Heong*, the Court granted habeas corpus to protect a Chinese national's treaty rights, even though the treaty provided for diplomatic remedies and not for judicial enforcement. 112 U.S. at 542, 549–56. *See also Shanks v. Dupont*, 28 U.S. 242 (1830); *Louis Henkin Br.*, *supra*, at 24–28.

C. The Geneva Conventions Protect Petitioner

The court of appeals concluded that Hamdan was chargeable under the law of war but not protected by it. The propositions are backwards. The laws of war do not apply in the allegedly separate "war on terror" in which Hamdan's commission has been convened, but they do protect those *captured* in the conflict in *Afghanistan*, including Hamdan. GPW Article 2 provides, in pertinent part:

> [T]he present Convention shall apply to all cases of declared war or of any other armed conflict which may arise between two or more of the High Contracting Parties. . . . The Convention shall also apply to all cases of partial or total occupation of the territory of a High Contracting Party.

Afghanistan and the United States are High Parties. Yet Respondents claim that Hamdan is not protected because the "war against terror" is a separate conflict. This position ignores the undisputed facts of Hamdan's capture, is inconsistent with Article 2, and departs from American practice.

First, even if absolute deference is shown to the Executive with respect to its distinction between the Taliban and al Qaeda, and even if al Qaeda fighters are not protected by the GPW, Hamdan *denies* he is a member of al Qaeda. The Government cannot rely on an unproven allegation to deny Hamdan GPW protections pending an Article 5 hearing. This is the clear import not only of the Article, but also of federal statutes and regulations, *supra* pp. 37–41.[35]

Second, it is undisputed that Hamdan was captured in a conflict that meets the conditions of Article 2. The alleged "separate conflicts" against al Qaeda and the Taliban were fought on the same territory, at the same time, with the same forces, under the same congressional resolution.[36] As the State Department Legal Advisor explained:

> [The suggestion that there is] a distinction between our conflict with al Qaeda and our conflict with the Taliban does not conform to the structure of the Conventions. The Conventions call for a decision whether they apply to the conflict in Afghanistan. If they do, their provisions are applicable to all persons involved in that conflict – al Qaeda, Taliban, Northern Alliance, U.S. troops, civilians, etc. If the Conventions do not apply to the conflict, no one involved in it will enjoy the benefit of their protection as a matter of law.

William Taft IV Memorandum, Legal Advisor, State Dep't ¶3 (2/2/02), at *http://www.fas.org/sgp/othergov/taft.pdf.*

---

[35] "Doubt" triggering the Article 5 presumption of POW status arises from Hamdan's denial of al Qaeda membership, the circumstances surrounding his capture (*i.e.*, seizure by a local militia and delivery to U.S. forces in exchange for a bounty), and the sufficient but not necessary assertion of protected status under the GPW. *E.g.,* . . . Jan McGirk, *Pakistani Writes of His US Ordeal*, Boston Globe, Nov. 17, 2002, at A30 ("Pakistani intelligence sources said Northern Alliance commanders could receive $5000 for each Taliban prisoner and 20,000 for a Qaeda fighter. As a result, bounty hunters rounded up any men who came near the battlegrounds and forced them to confess"). In addition, Hamdan has strong claims to protection under GPW Art. 4A(4) and 4A(1). *See Amicus Br. of Ryan Goodman, Derek Jinks & Anne-Marie Slaughter* at 6–16 (*Goodman/Jinks/Slaughter Br.*).

    A negative Article 5 finding would merely protect Hamdan under similar rights in the Fourth Convention. "Every person in enemy hands must have some status under international law: he is either a prisoner of war and, as such, covered by the Third Convention, a civilian covered by the Fourth Convention . . . *There is no* intermediate status; nobody in enemy hands can be outside the law." ICRC Commentary, *IV Geneva Convention Relative to the Protection of Civilian Persons* 50–51 (1960) (emphasis added).

[36] Respondent Rumsfeld stated that "the Taliban . . . were tied tightly at the waist to al Qaeda. They behaved like them, they worked with them, they functioned with them," at *http://www.defenselink.mil/news/Jan2002/t01282002-t0127sd2.html.*

This is consistent with the practice of the U.S. military in every major conflict since World War II. For example, in Vietnam, with its high incidence of irregular warfare, the military accorded POW status to both regular North Vietnamese Army and Viet Cong fighters. Even guerillas were given Article 5 hearings.[37] There was no gap.

Accordingly, under GPW Article 102, those committing offenses in the Afghan conflict may be tried by courts-martial for war crimes, not by commissions.

Third, the panel's deference to the President's determination that Hamdan was captured in a separate conflict is unwarranted. *See Amicus Br. of Retired Generals and Admirals*. The panel relied on *Japan Whaling Ass'n v. Am. Cetacean Soc'y*, 478 U.S. 221 (1986), but that case *rejected* a contention that the political question doctrine barred judicial resolution of an issue affecting foreign policy: "[T]he courts have the authority to construe treaties and executive agreements." *Id.* at 230. While the Executive's interpretation is "of weight," it is settled that "the construction of a treaty by the political department of the government" is "not conclusive upon courts called upon to construe it." *Factor*, 290 U.S. at 295. This Court has declined to adopt Executive interpretations many times. *See, e.g., Perkins v. Elg*, 307 U.S. 325, 335–42 (1939); *Johnson v. Browne*, 205 U.S. 309, 319–21 (1907); *De Lima v. Bidwell*, 182 U.S. 1, 181, 194 (1901).

In short, Respondents' contention that no individual assessment of Hamdan's status is required, and that he can be denied POW status by presidential fiat, is irreconcilable with text of Article 5, defeats its purpose, and departs from past American practice. This undermines "respect for the present Convention" (GPW art. 1) and compromises our ability to insist on GPW observance when American personnel fall into enemy hands. The Court should reject that position, and consistent with longstanding tradition, adopt the treaty interpretation that faithfully enforces the protections the United States has promised to others and expects for its own forces. *Factor*, 290 U.S. at 293.[38]

D.   Common Article 3 Protects Hamdan

The commission is also invalid because it violates GPW Article 3, which prohibits "the passing of sentences and the carrying out of executions without previous judgment pronounced by a regularly constituted court affording all the judicial guarantees which are recognized as indispensable by civilized peoples" in "the case of armed conflict not of an international character occurring in the territory of one of the High Contracting Parties." .... This provision sets forth the "most fundamental requirements of the law of war." *Kadic v. Karadzic*, 70 F.3d 232, 243 (2d Cir. 1995). Additional Protocol I, *supra*, which binds the United States as customary international law, separately requires a "regularly constituted court."

Even if Hamdan does not qualify as a POW under GPW Article 4, he is nonetheless protected by these provisions. The commission clearly does not comply with them

---

[37] 60 Documents on Prisoners of War 722–31, 748–51 (Levie ed. 1979). Irregular fighters were given POW status unless caught in an act of "'terrorism, sabotage or spying," and if denied POW status, they were given protections of the Fourth Geneva Convention. Elsea, Cong. Rsch. Serv., *Treatment of "Battlefield Detainees" in the War on Terrorism* 29 (2002).

[38] The panel also reached the extraordinary conclusion that Hamdan could raise his POW status claim in his commission. . . . . This acknowledges that "doubt" concerning Hamdan's status exists, and such doubt precludes a commission trial in the first place. It would condone an unprecedented procedural laxity, including a 4-year delay, in implementing a solemn treaty obligation. The commission also does not meet AR 190–8, and his status determination cannot take place in a tribunal trying him for war crimes. Finally, even if the commission could serve as an Article 5 tribunal, it has not been convened to do so. Instead, the Executive contends that it has no obligation to provide a status determination and claims no court has the authority to say otherwise.

because it is not a "regularly constituted court." As the ICRC's definitive recent work explains, a "court is regularly constituted if it has been established and organised in accordance with the laws and procedures already in force in a country." INT'L CTE. RED CROSS, 1 CUSTOMARY INT'L HUMANITARIAN LAW 355 (2005). The "court must be able to perform its functions independently of any other branch of the government, especially the executive." *Id.* at 356.

Instead, the commission is an *ad hoc* tribunal fatally compromised by command influence, lack of independence and impartiality, and lack of competence to adjudicate the complex issues of domestic and international law. . . . . The rules for trial change arbitrarily – and even changed after the Petition for Certiorari was filed. It is not regularly constituted; its defects cannot be cured without a complete structural overhaul and fixed rules. *See, Amicus Br. of Madeleine Albright et al.* at 4–19.

Commission procedures also fail to provide adequate "judicial guarantees" in many ways, including admitting evidence extracted under duress and denying the fundamental rights of confrontation and presence. These flaws are not theoretical; they have already had practical consequence, as Hamdan's exclusion from *voir dire* reveals.

The divided panel nonetheless held that Article 3 does not apply because the conflict against al Qaeda is "international," and Article 3 only applies to internal conflicts. Even were that true, Article 3 extends to all conflicts as a matter of customary international law. And as Judge Williams recognized: "the logical reading of 'international character' is one that matches the basic derivation of the word 'international,' i.e., *between nations*." . . . . *Kadic* and other cases establish that Article 3 binds all conflicts, and *all* parties, as a minimum standard of conduct. *E.g., Prosecutor v. Delalic*, Judgement, IT-96-21-A ¶143 (ICTY App. 2001) (Common Article 3 principles "are so fundamental that they are regarded as governing both internal and international conflicts"); *Nicaragua v. United States*, 1986 I.C.J. 14, 114 (Article 3 is "a minimum yardstick" for international conflict); *Goodman/links/Slaughter Br.* at 17–27; *Amicus Br. of City Bar of New York.*

As an alternative holding, the panel found abstention appropriate on Common Article 3. But abstention on this claim is improper for the same reasons the panel gave in rejecting abstention earlier in its opinion. The panel approved of the *Quirin* defendants' pre-conviction challenge to the tribunal's lawfulness and jurisdiction. The animating concerns of *Councilman* abstention "do not exist in Hamdan's case and we are thus left with nothing to detract from *Quirin*'s precedential value." . . . .

For reasons developed already in this Court, this is not a typical abstention case because the lawfulness of the tribunal is at stake. Cert. Reply Br., at 1–6; C.A. Br. 25–30. If the commission is not a "regularly constituted court" under Common Article 3, it is not authorized under Section 821. The commission is not a regular trial applying regular procedures, like courts martial or Article III trials. Rather, it lacks speedy trial rights and Hamdan can languish for many years (indeed, forever) before a final decision is rendered. C.A. Br. 10–13. The commission lacks competence, expertise, and impartiality. *Id.* at 13–20. And because, unlike courts-martial, the President makes the final decision in Hamdan's case, abstention is futile; the President has already stated his views on the questions presented. *Id.*

Unlike other settings, the abstention question here is integrally bound up with the merits. *See Amicus Br. of Arthur Miller.* On every other issue in this case, Respondents claim court-martial rules are irrelevant; yet here they seek to reap its favorable benefits such as *Councilman* abstention.

As the panel recognized, there are rights at the periphery of Common Article 3 that may necessitate trial before federal review. . . . . But the simple matters of whether the commission is a "regularly constituted court," and can deny fundamental rights (including the right to be present, trial by an impartial body, and trial without risk of testimony obtained by torture) are surely not among them. A commission that does not comply with such rules violates the laws of war and is improperly constituted. Waiting for a trial accomplishes nothing, except to put Petitioner in a state of limbo as to trial strategy and his fate that may persist for years. *See Amicus Br. of Prof. Richard Rosen et al.* at 6–24. Again, in contrast to all other American criminal processes, there is no incentive whatsoever to reach final decision under this scheme. In this rare setting, abstention does more harm to the rule of law than does reaching the merits.

* * *

This Court has long understood that, in all of American law, there is "no graver question" than the fundamental one presented here. *Milligan*, 71 U.S. (4 Wall.) at 118. Given the myriad ways in which Hamdan's trial would run afoul of constitutional, statutory, and treaty-based rights, Petitioner's entitlement to the modest relief sought is manifest.

CONCLUSION

The Court of Appeals' judgment should be reversed and Hamdan's Petition should be granted.

. . .

No. 05-184

In the Supreme Court of the United States

SALIM AHMED HAMDAN, PETITIONER

v.

DONALD H. RUMSFELD, SECRETARY OF DEFENSE,
ET AL.

*ON WRIT OF CERTIORARI
TO THE UNITED STATES COURT OF APPEALS
FOR THE DISTRICT OF COLUMBIA CIRCUIT*

**RESPONDENTS' MOTION TO DISMISS
FOR LACK OF JURISDICTION**

PAUL D. CLEMENT
*Solicitor General
Counsel of Record*

PETER D. KEISLER
Assistant Attorney General

GREGORY G. GARRE
Deputy Solicitor General

GREGORY G. KATSAS
*Deputy Assistant Attorney
General*

JONATHAN L. MARCUS
*Assistant to the Solicitor
General*

DOUGLAS N. LETTER
ROBERT M. LOEB
ERIC D. MILLER
Attorneys

Department of Justice

. . .

* Redaction on this page has been added for privacy purposes. – *Eds*.

STATEMENT

. . .

5. Congress enacted the Detainee Treatment Act of 2005, Pub. L. No. 109–148, Div. A, Tit. X, 119 Stat. 2739, which was signed into law on December 30, 2005. Section 1005(e)(1) of the Act amends the habeas corpus statute, 28 U.S.C. 2241, by adding the following new subsection:

(e) Except as provided in section 1005 of the Detainee Treatment Act of 2005, no court, justice, or judge shall have jurisdiction to hear or consider –

(1) an application for a writ of habeas corpus filed by or on behalf of an alien detained by the Department of Defense at Guantanamo Bay, Cuba; or

(2) any other action against the United States or its agents relating to any aspect of the detention by the Department of Defense of an alien at Guantanamo Bay, Cuba, who –

(A) is currently in military custody; or

(B) has been determined by the United States Court of Appeals for the District of Columbia Circuit in accordance with the procedures set forth in section 1005(e) of the Detainee Treatment Act of 2005 to have been properly detained as an enemy combatant.

Section 1005 further provides that the District of Columbia Circuit has "exclusive jurisdiction" to review the final decisions of Combatant Status Review Tribunals (CSRTs) (DTA §1005(e)(2)(A), 119 Stat. 2742) and military commissions (§1005(e)(3)(A), 119 Stat. 2743). The review procedure that the Act establishes for military commission decisions "shall be as of right" for those aliens sentenced in "a capital case" or "to a term of imprisonment of 10 years or more" and "shall be at the discretion of the [District of Columbia Circuit]" in "any other case." §1005(e)(3)(B), 119 Stat. 2743. The Act limits the jurisdiction that Section 1005(e)(3) vests in the District of Columbia Circuit to appeals "brought by or on behalf of an alien" who was detained at Guantanamo Bay "at the time of the [military commission] proceedings" and "for whom a final decision has been rendered." §1005(e)(3)(C), 119 Stat. 2743. The Act further confines the District of Columbia Circuit's jurisdiction to consideration of "whether the final decision was consistent with the standards and procedures specified in [Military Commission Order No. 1, dated August 31, 2005 (or any successor military order)]," and "to the extent the Constitution and laws of the United States are applicable, whether the use of such standards and procedures to reach the final decision is consistent with the Constitution and laws of the United States." §1005(e)(3)(D), 119 Stat. 2743.

The Act provides that Section 1005 "shall take effect on the date of the enactment of this Act." DTA §1005(h)(1), 119 Stat. 2743. It further specifies that the exclusive statutory procedures that the Act establishes for review of CSRT and military commission decisions "shall apply with respect to any claim whose review is governed by" those procedures and "that is pending on or after the date of the enactment of this Act." §1005(h)(2), 119 Stat. 2743.

ARGUMENT

UNDER WELL-SETTLED PRINCIPLES, CONGRESS'S DECISION TO REMOVE JURISDICTION OVER THIS ACTION AND OTHERS LIKE IT MUST BE GIVEN IMMEDIATE EFFECT

Section 1005(e)(1) of the Act – which Congress explicitly made effective on the date of its enactment – amends the habeas corpus statute to provide that "no court, justice, or judge shall have jurisdiction to hear or consider" a habeas corpus petition or "any other action against the United States or its agents relating to any aspect of the detention by the Department of Defense" filed by an alien in military custody at Guantanamo Bay. DTA §1005(e)(1), 119 Stat. 2742. This action plainly falls within that provision because it was filed against executive officers on behalf of an alien held at Guantanamo Bay and relates to the alien's detention.[3] As such, the courts – including this Court – lack jurisdiction to "hear or consider" this action.

1. Petitioner suggests that Congress did not intend the Act to remove this Court's jurisdiction to hear this action. See 05-790 Pet. for an Extraordinary Writ at 6–7. That contention is contradicted not only by the plain terms of the Act, but also by this Court's precedents.

It is well settled that statutes that remove jurisdiction apply to pending cases and or-dinarily should be given immediate effect. More than a century ago, this Court held that an Act of Congress repealed its jurisdiction to review a circuit court decision denying a habeas corpus petition filed by a Mississippi resident, McCardle, who sought release from "custody by military authority for trial before a military commission." *Ex parte Mc-Cardle*, 74 U.S. (7 Wall.) 506, 508 (1868).[4] Although the Court had asserted jurisdiction over the matter and heard oral argument before the law was passed, the Court nonethe-less concluded that, after the law was enacted, it could not "proceed at all" with the case and dismissed the appeal for "want of jurisdiction." *Id.* at 515. As the Court explained, "[j]urisdiction is power to declare the law, and when it ceases to exist, the only function remaining to the court is that of announcing the fact and dismissing the cause." *Id.* at 514. Moreover, the Court continued, application of the new law to a pending matter flowed from "the general rule" that "when an act of the legislature is repealed, it must be considered, except as to transactions past and closed, as if it never existed." *Ibid.* (citation omitted).

This Court has "regularly" applied that rule to "intervening statutes conferring or ousting jurisdiction, whether or not jurisdiction lay when the underlying conduct oc-curred or when the suit was filed." *Landgraf* v. *USI Film Prods.*, 511 U.S. 244, 274 (1994); see *ibid.* (describing "consistent practice") (internal quotation marks and bracket omit-ted); accord *id.* at 292 (Scalia, J., concurring in the judgment) (noting "consistent prac-tice of giving immediate effect to statutes that alter a court's jurisdiction"). The Court reaffirmed that rule just two terms ago. *Republic of Austria* v. *Altmann*, 541 U.S. 677, 693 (2004) (noting that in *Landgraf*, "we sanctioned the application to all pending and fu-ture cases of 'intervening' statutes that merely 'confe[r] or ous[t] jurisdiction'") (quoting *Landgraf*, 511 U.S. at 274). As the Court has explained, "jurisdictional statutes 'speak to the power of the court rather than to the rights or obligations of the parties.'" *Landgraf*,

---

3 ...

4 The 1868 Act provided "[t]hat so much of the act approved February [5, 1867], *** as authorizes an appeal from the judgment of the circuit court to the Supreme Court of the United States, or the exercise of any such jurisdiction by said Supreme Court on appeals which have been or may hereafter be taken, be, and the same is hereby repealed." Act of Mar. 27, 1868, ch. 34, §2, 15 Stat. 44.

511 U.S. at 274 (quoting *Republic Nat'l Bank* v. *United States*, 506 U.S. 80, 100 (1992) (Thomas, J., concurring)). In addition, such statutes "usually 'take[] away no substantive right but simply change[] the tribunal that is to hear the case.'" *Ibid.* (quoting *Hallowell* v. *Commons*, 239 U.S. 506, 508–509 (1916)). See *Hughes Aircraft Co.* v. *United States ex rel. Schumer*, 520 U.S. 939, 951 (1997).

Because statutes removing jurisdiction presumptively apply to pending cases, Congress must expressly reserve pending cases to preserve the federal courts' jurisdiction over them. As the Court put it in *Bruner* v. *United States*, 343 U.S. 112 (1952), the "rule" that "has been adhered to consistently by this Court" is "that, when a law conferring jurisdiction is repealed without any reservation as to pending cases, all cases fall with the law." *Id.* at 116–117 & n.8 (citing *McCardle* and other cases). That is true no matter how far the pending litigation has progressed. *Bruner* involved a statute that was enacted after the Court had granted certiorari in the case and repealed federal district court jurisdiction over certain Tucker Act claims. The Court held that, "[a]bsent such a reservation [as to pending cases]," the district court lacked jurisdiction over the plaintiff's claim "even though the District Court had jurisdiction *** when petitioner's action was brought." *Id.* at 115. Accordingly, the Court concluded that the case should be dismissed for want of jurisdiction. *Id.* at 117.

. . .

Congress "expects its statutes to be read in conformity with this Court's precedents." *United States* v. *Wells*, 519 U.S. 482, 495 (1997); see *North Star Steel Co.* v. *Thomas*, 515 U.S. 29, 34 (1995). Accordingly, because the relevant provision of the Detainee Treatment Act does not contain any reservation saving pending cases, "all cases fall with the law." *Bruner*, 343 U.S. at 116–117. That conclusion is underscored by the fact that the Act explicitly provides – without reservation – that it "shall take effect on the date of the enactment." DTA §1005(h)(1), 119 Stat. 2743. Because subject-matter jurisdiction must subsist throughout the litigation, that language effects an immediate elimination of jurisdiction.[6]

In addition, Congress not only declined to include a reservation saving pending cases, but it expressly provided that the exclusive procedures established by the Act for review of challenges to completed CSRTs and military commission trials apply to cases "pending on or after" the Act's enactment. §1005(h)(2), 119 Stat. 2743. Thus, Congress made clear that the federal courts no longer have jurisdiction over actions filed on behalf of Guantanamo detainees, and it reinforced that result by providing that, without regard to whether an action is "pending on or after" the date of enactment, the exclusive review procedures in Section 1005(e)(2) and (3) provide the only avenue for judicial relief.[7]

---

[6] Whether Section 1005(h)(1) is construed to eliminate this Court's appellate jurisdiction or the district court's jurisdiction over the action (or both), it is appropriate to dismiss the petition for want of jurisdiction. See, *e.g.*, [*Insurance Co.* v.] *Ritchie*, 72 U.S. (5 Wall.) [541,] . . . 544–545 [(1867)]. In the alternative, the Court could vacate and remand with instructions to the lower courts to dismiss the action. See, *e.g.*, *Gallardo* [v. *Santini Fertilizer Co.*], 275 U.S. [62,] . . . 63–64 [(1927)].

[7] Relying on legislative history, petitioner contends (05-790 Pet. for Extraordinary Relief 6–7) that Congress did not intend to "interfere with *this* case." Because the statute's jurisdiction-ousting provision unambiguously applies to pending cases, there is no need to "turn to the more controversial realm of legislative history." *Lamie* v. *United States Trustee*, 540 U.S. 526, 536 (2004). In any event, legislative history supports the conclusion that Congress was aware that the Act's jurisdiction-ousting rule would extend to pending cases, including this case. See, *e.g.*, 151 Cong. Rec. S14,263 (daily ed. Dec. 21, 2005) (statement of co-sponsor Sen. Kyl) ("The courts' rule of construction for these types of statutes is that legislation ousting the courts of jurisdiction is applied to pending cases. It has to. We're not just changing the law governing the action. We are eliminating the forum in which that action can be heard."); *id.* at S14,264 (statement of Sen. Kyl) ("[T]he court should dismiss Hamdan for want of jurisdiction. That is what they did in Ex Parte McCardle. *** I think that a

3. . . .

. . .

. . .

The Act clearly evinces Congress's intent in the wake of this Court's decision in *Rasul v. Bush*, 542 U.S. 466 (2004), strictly to limit the judicial review available to aliens detained at Guantanamo during the ongoing conflict. Reading the statute to permit pending cases to survive would be manifestly at odds with that intent because it would permit hundreds of pending cases – collectively involving the large majority of Guantanamo detainees and countless challenges to the operation of Guantanamo – to proceed.[10] In addition, such a reading would produce an absurd result because it would require many of those cases to be carved up in order to allow them to proceed under the exclusive review procedure in the District of Columbia Circuit (for claims "governed by" the CSRT review procedure) and general habeas review (for all other claims). That would only further complicate the detainee litigation by creating a hodgepodge of claims arising in the same case pending in separate courts, would do nothing to address hundreds of detainee cases now pending in district court, and cannot possibly be what Congress intended.

. . .

* * * * *

This Court should dismiss the writ for want of jurisdiction or remand the case with instructions to dismiss. At a minimum, this Court should dismiss the writ as improvidently granted. By establishing an exclusive review procedure for military commission challenges, Congress has made plain its judgment that judicial review of military commission proceedings should occur only after those proceedings have been completed.

CONCLUSION

The writ of certiorari should be dismissed for want of jurisdiction or, at a minimum, the writ should be dismissed as improvidently granted.

. . .

---

majority of the court would do the right thing – to send Hamdan back to the military commission, and then allow him to appeal pursuant to section [1005]."). And the statements of Senator Levin or others quoted by petitioner can in no way alter the effect of the text duly enacted by Congress.

[10] Habeas petitions have been filed on behalf of a purported 600 detainees. Because more than 100 of those appear to be duplicate filings, and other filings identify names that cannot be matched with actual detainees, the precise number of detainees with cases pending is unknown, although the number is well over 300. Moreover, a petition was filed (a "John Does 1-570" action) purporting (erroneously, for a number of reasons) to seek relief on behalf of every Guantanamo detainee who has not already filed an action. Petition for Writ of Habeas Corpus, *John Does 1-570* v. *Bush*, No. 1:05CV00313 (CKK) (D.D.C. Feb. 10, 2005). These actions collectively have consumed enormous resources and disrupted the operation of Guantanamo during time of war.

No. 05-184

IN THE
Supreme Court of the United States

SALIM AHMED HAMDAN,
Petitioner,

v.

DONALD RUMSFELD, ET AL.,
Respondents.

**On Writ of Certiorari to the
United States Court of Appeals
for the District of Columbia Circuit**

PETITIONER'S OPPOSITION TO RESPONDENTS' MOTION TO DISMISS

Lt. Cdr. Charles Swift
Office of Military
 Commissions

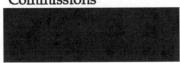

Thomas C. Goldstein
Amy Howe
Kevin K. Russell
GOLDSTEIN & HOWE, P.C.

January 31, 2006

Neal Katyal
(Counsel of Record)

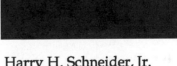

Harry H. Schneider, Jr.
Joseph M. McMillan
Charles C. Sipos
PERKINS COIE LLP

. . .

---

* Redactions on this page have been added for privacy purposes. – *Eds.*

ARGUMENT

. . .

III. TO THE EXTENT THAT THE DTA DEPRIVES THIS COURT OF JURISDICTION, IT IS UNCONSTITUTIONAL

To read the DTA as the government proposes would render it unconstitutional. Even "[t]he fact that this Court would be required to *answer* the difficult question of what the Suspension Clause protects is in and of itself a reason to avoid answering the constitutional questions that would be raised by concluding that review was barred entirely." *St. Cyr*, 533 U.S. at 301 n.13.[32]

A. Congress Did Not Constitutionally Suspend Hamdan's Right To Petition For Habeas Corpus

The DTA cannot deprive Hamdan of his constitutional right to habeas corpus. "Habeas corpus is . . . a writ antecedent to statute, . . . throwing its root deep into the genius of our common law. . . . The writ appeared in English law several centuries ago [and] became an integral part of our common-law heritage by the time the Colonies achieved independence." *Rasul*, 542 U.S. at 473–74 (citations omitted).

Our Founders took care to ensure that the availability of habeas was not dependent upon executive or legislative grace. *See, e.g., St. Cyr*, 533 U.S. 304 n.24 (noting Suspension Clause protects against loss of right to pursue habeas claim by "either the inaction or the action of Congress"). Thus, the Constitution's right to habeas relief exists even in the absence of statutory authorization, and may be suspended only by explicit congressional action and only under limited conditions. *See Johnson v. Eisentrager*, 39 U.S. 763, 767–68 (1950) (assuming that, in the absence of statutory right of habeas, petitioners could bring claim directly under Constitution to the extent their claims fell within the scope of habeas protected by the Suspension Clause); *Rasul*, 542 U.S. at 473–78. Because Congress has not invoked its Suspension power, and because any such attempt in these circumstances would be invalid, the district court retains jurisdiction to consider Hamdan's habeas petition even if Congress has withdrawn access to habeas previously authorized by statute.

1. If Congress intends to implement its Suspension Clause power, it must do so with unmistakable clarity. *See St. Cyr*, 533 U.S. at 298–99. Nothing here meets that requirement.[33]

Congress has only suspended the writ four times; in each, Congress invoked its Suspension power, each time using the verb "suspend." *See Natl. Security Ctr. Br.* 26–30. Simply withdrawing a statutory basis for habeas is not a sufficient indication of Congress' intent. *Cf. St. Cyr*, 533 U.S. at 298–300.

---

[32] It might be argued that the government's reading of the DTA is preferable because it allows courts to avoid adjudicating the legality of commissions. Such reasoning is foreclosed by the many cases that require clear statements for jurisdictional repeals, even where constitutional challenges to *statutes* are at issue. *See St. Cyr*, 533 U.S. at 299. It is also in tension with *Quirin* – and for good reason. Petitioner is not a plaintiff seeking money damages. He is a defendant in a proceeding where the government seeks to deprive him of all the liberty he has for the rest of his life. The remedy for an Executive that seeks to avoid adjudication of a particular constitutional question is to forgo the prosecution in the specific tribunal. *See United States v. Nixon*, 418 U.S. 683, 694–96 (1974).

[33] "No one contends that the congressional Authorization for Use of Military Force . . . is an implementation of the Suspension Clause." *Hamdi*, 542 U.S. at 554 (Scalia, J. dissenting).

2. The DTA should not be read as an attempted exercise of the Suspension Clause power for the additional reason that any such attempt clearly would be invalid. Congress lacks *carte blanche* power to suspend the writ at will, even in times of open war. Instead, the Constitution permits a suspension only when in "Cases of Rebellion or Invasion the public Safety may require it." U.S. CONST. art. I, §9, cl. 2. In enacting the DTA, Congress made no such finding.

In addition, even during actual "Rebellion or Invasion," this Court has required that congressional suspension be limited in scope and duration in ways that the DTA is not. First, Congress must tailor its suspension geographically to jurisdictions in rebellion or facing imminent invasion. Thus, in *Ex parte Milligan*, this Court considered the Act of March 3d, 1863, which suspended habeas in rebelling territories. Because Milligan was a resident of Indiana, a State not in rebellion, his right to habeas was protected. 71 U.S. 2, 126 (1866).[34] Like Indiana, "Guantanamo Bay . . . is . . . far removed from any hostilities." *Rasul*, 542 U.S. at 487 (Kennedy, J., concurring). Thus, the DTA could not, even if intended to do so, constitutionally suspend petitioner's right to a writ of habeas corpus.

Moreover, Congress may suspend the writ only for a limited time. *See* U.S. CONST., art. I, §9, cl. 2. The DTA, however, has no terminal date and indefinitely denies statutory access to habeas corpus.

3. The scope of the right protected from suspension is defined by the historic purposes and applications of the writ. *See St. Cyr*, 533 U.S. at 300–01. "Consistent with the historic purpose of the writ, this Court has recognized the federal courts' power to review applications for habeas relief in a wide variety of cases involving Executive detention, in wartime as well as in times of peace," including petitions of "admitted enemy aliens convicted of war crimes during a declared war and held in the United States, *Ex parte Quirin* . . . and its insular possessions, *In re Yamashita*." *Rasul*, 542 U.S. at 474 (citations omitted).[35]

Thus, *In re Yamashita* entertained a habeas petition similar to Hamdan's, asking whether there was legal authority for the establishment of a commission and whether the petitioner fell within its jurisdiction. 327 U.S. 1, 9–18 (1946).[36] Although the petitioner

---

[34] The Court reached this conclusion even though Congress had authorized a broader suspension. *See* Act of Mar. 3, 1863, 12 Stat. 755 (authorizing the President to "suspend the privilege of the writ of habeas corpus in any case throughout the United States, or any part thereof").

[35] It makes no constitutional difference that petitioner is a non-citizen accused of being an enemy of the United States. Aliens have been able to file habeas petitions to challenge detention at least since the 17th century. *See St. Cyr*, 533 U.S. at 305–06 (from founding, habeas "jurisdiction was regularly invoked on behalf of noncitizens"); *id.* at 301–02 (collecting cases); see also *Amicus Br. for the Bar Human Rights Committee of the Bar of England and Wales and the Commonwealth Lawyers Association (Commonwealth Lawyers Br.)* at 5. Both the Habeas Corpus Act of 1641, 16 Car. 1, and the Habeas Corpus Act of 1679, 31 Car. 2, granted "any person" the right to file a petition. *See generally Amicus Br. of Legal Historians, Rasul v. Bush*, No. 03-334 (original conception of habeas permitted challenges by enemy aliens).

Moreover, the Great Writ has long been available to challenge the military's treatment of alleged enemies. *See Rasul*, 542 U.S at 474–75. For example, English courts heard habeas claims from alleged foreign enemy combatants challenging their status in the Eighteenth Century. *See, e.g., Three Spanish Sailors' Case*, 96 Eng. Rep. 775, 776 (C.P. 1779) (Spanish sailors challenging detention as alleged prisoners of war); *Rex v. Schiever*, 97 Eng. Rep. 51 (K.B. 1759) (Swedish sailor captured aboard enemy ship); *Commonwealth Lawyers Br.* 6–8 & n.9 (collecting cases). Similarly, U.S. courts heard enemy aliens' habeas petitions from the War of 1812, *Lockington v. Smith*, 15 F. Cas. 758 (C.C.D. Pa. 1817), through the Second World War, *Quirin* 317 U.S. at 1.

[36] The writ has traditionally been available to challenge the jurisdiction of a committing tribunal, including a military commission. *E.g., Quirin*, 317 U.S. at 19; *Milligan*, 71 U.S. at 118; Paul M. Bator, *Finality in Criminal Law and Federal Habeas Corpus for State Prisoners*, 76 HARV. L. REV. 441, 475 (1963) ("The classical function of the writ of habeas corpus was to assure the liberty of subjects against detention by the executive or the military."); *St. Cyr*, 533 U.S. at 302 n.19 ("impressment into the British Navy").

was able to rely on the statutory provisions authorizing habeas, this Court explained that the result would have been no different had there been no statutory habeas, as Congress and the Executive "could not, unless there was suspension of the writ, withdraw from the courts the duty and power to make such inquiry into the authority of the commission as may be made by habeas corpus." *Id.* at 9. *See also Quirin*, 317 U.S. at 25 ("neither the [Presidential Proclamation subjecting enemy aliens to commissions] nor the fact that they are enemy aliens forecloses consideration by the courts of petitioners' contentions that the Constitution and laws of the United States constitutionally enacted forbid their trial by military commission.").

Eisentrager does not support a different result. The petitioners in that case were captured, held, and tried by a commission sitting in China and "at no relevant time and in no stage of [their] captivity, ha[d] been within [U.S.] territorial jurisdiction." 339 U.S. at 768.[37] The qualification was essential, for the writ has long been extended to alleged enemy aliens held or tried within English and U.S. territory. *E.g., Rasul*, 542 U.S. at 482 ("As Lord Mansfield wrote in 1759, . . . there was 'no doubt' as to the court's power to issue writs of habeas corpus if the territory was 'under the subjection of the Crown.'") (citation omitted); *id.* at 480–82 & nn.11–14 (collecting cases); 3 W. BLACKSTONE, COMMENTARIES ON THE LAWS OF ENGLAND 131 (1766) (observing that "[t]his is a high prerogative writ, . . . running into all parts of the king's dominions . . . wherever that restraint may be inflicted.").

Thus, *Eisentrager* acknowledged that the judiciary retained the obligation to inquire into the "jurisdictional elements" of the detention of an enemy alien with a sufficient connection to U.S. territory. 339 U.S. at 775. In these and other habeas cases, the Court explained, "it was the alien's presence within its territorial jurisdiction that gave the Judiciary power to act," *id.* at 771, for "their presence in the country implied protection," *id.* at 777–78.

Moreover, Hamdan's standing to seek the writ is even greater than that of petitioners in *Quirin, Yamashita*, and *Eisentrager*, all cases involving *admitted* enemy aliens. Hamdan is a citizen of Yemen, a nation *not* at war with the U.S., and he *denies* ever engaging in hostilities directed at the U.S. In *Eisentrager*, this Court stated that it would entertain habeas petitions from aliens to at least (1) "ascertain the existence of a state of war," and (2) ascertain "whether [petitioner] is an enemy alien." 339 U.S. at 775. Both questions are at issue in this case, as Hamdan challenges whether the AUMF truly declared a general "war on terrorism," and disputes that he is an enemy of this country.

---

[37] Thus, the Court explained that each Petitioner

> (a) [was] an enemy alien; (b) [had] *never been or resided in* the United States; (c) was captured *outside* of our territory and there held in military custody . . . ; (d) was tried and convicted by a Military Commission sitting *outside* the United States; (e) for offenses against laws of war committed *outside* the United States; (f) and [was] at all times imprisoned *outside* the United States.

339 U.S. at 777 (emphasis added). It was based on this lack of connection to territory within U.S control that the Court distinguished *Quirin* and *Yamashita. Id.* at 779–80. The Court explained that a nexus with a territory under U.S. control, like the Philippines then or Guantanamo now, was sufficient to invoke the right to habeas. *Id.* at 780. Moreover, the *Eisentrager* Petitioners did *not* invoke 28 U.S.C. §2241(c)(3), violation of the Constitution and laws of the United States, so the Court had no occasion to reach the specific issue. *See Odah* Amicus Br., at 11–13.

As this Court concluded in *Rasul*, individuals detained in Guantanamo Bay are within the "territorial jurisdiction" of the United States. 542 U.S. at 480. *See also id.* at 487 (Kennedy, J., concurring in judgment) ("Guantanamo Bay is in every practical respect a United States territory, and it is one far removed from any hostilities."). Hamdan's petition thus falls within "the historical reach of the writ of habeas corpus," *id.* at 481, and within the protection of the Suspension Clause under *Eisentrager.*

While the majority in *Rasul* held that the *Eisentrager* considerations required interpreting the habeas statute to encompass the petitioners' claims – and therefore did not reach any constitutional question – the same considerations lead inexorably to the conclusion that the petitioners in that case, and in this one, are also entitled to bring habeas claims directly under the Constitution. *See id.* at 486–88 (Kennedy, J., concurring in judgment) (rejecting majority's distinction between statutory and constitutional right to habeas and, applying *Eisentrager* constitutional analysis, concluding that habeas was available to the petitioners).

In this case, there has been no attempted suspension of the Great Writ. The courts retain the "duty and power" to hear Hamdan's claims. *Yamashita*, 327 U.S. at 9.

Nor can the government establish any other compelling reason why, contrary to this historical tradition, the protection of the Suspension Clause should not extend to the limited challenges raised by Hamdan. Hamdan does not ask the courts to second guess the factual determinations of a tribunal, but rather to exercise the quintessential legal (not military) judgment of whether the commissions are lawfully constituted and whether he falls within their jurisdiction, determinations this Court has repeatedly made even in the midst of a declared war without ever suggesting that doing so would impermissibly interfere "in the conduct of military affairs." *Rasul*, 542 U.S. at 487 (Kennedy, J., concurring in judgment). *See Quirin*, 317 U.S. at 24–48; *Yamashita*, 327 U.S. at 9–25; *see also Hamdi*, 542 U.S. at 534 (plurality) (rejecting view that limited judicial review "will have the dire impact on the central functions of warmaking that the Government forecasts"). Nor does Hamdan's petition challenge the military's authority to detain temporarily combatants in a zone of hostilities in light of military necessities. To the contrary, Hamdan challenges a proceeding that metes out retrospective punishment, not one that disables combatants in an ongoing conflict. These factors "suggest[] a weaker case of military necessity and much greater alignment with the traditional function of habeas corpus." *Rasul*, 542 U.S. at 488 (Kennedy, J., concurring in judgment).

4. Had Congress provided an adequate substitute to habeas, this would be a different case. *See St. Cyr*, 533 U.S. at 305. But the limited judicial review in the DTA is wholly inadequate. *See supra* pp. 1–2, 13–15; *Commonwealth Lawyers Br.* 6–15 (expeditious review has historically been, and remains, at the core of the habeas writ); *In re Bonner*, 151 U.S. 242, 259 (1894) (holding that when a "prisoner is ordered to be confined in [a facility] where the law does not allow the court to send him for a single hour . . . [t]o deny the writ of habeas corpus in such a case is a virtual suspension of it").

B.   The DTA Violates Equal Protection Guarantees

If the DTA precludes petitioner from pursuing his present claims for relief, it is only because he is an alien (rather than a citizen) being detained by the Department of Defense (rather than the Central Intelligence Agency, Department of Justice, or any other agency) at a facility in Guantanamo Bay (rather than in a brig in Norfolk, Virginia or any other place). Legislation that deprives individuals of access to the protections of the Great Writ based on such an arbitrary collage of distinctions – and at the exclusive discretion of the Executive – violates the Fifth Amendment.

The Fifth Amendment protects aliens within U.S. territory as well as U.S. citizens. *See, e.g.*, *Wong Wing v. United States*, 163 U.S. 228 (1896); *Mathews v. Diaz*, 426 U.S. 67, 77 (1976) (all "aliens within the *jurisdiction* of the United States" are protected) (emphasis added); *Galvan v. Press*, 347 U.S. 522, 530 (1954). As *Rasul*, 542 U.S. at 480, noted, "the

United States exercises 'complete jurisdiction and control' over the Guantanamo Bay Naval Base." Accordingly, Hamdan is protected by the Fifth Amendment.

Legislation that enacts substantial discriminatory barriers to the exercise of fundamental rights is subject to strict scrutiny. *See, e.g., Clark v. Jeter*, 486 U.S. 456, 461 (1988). Access to courts is such a fundamental right. *See Tennessee v. Lane*, 541 U.S. 509, 522–23 (2004); *Griffin v. Illinois*, 351 U.S. 12 (1956); *Douglas v. California*, 372 U.S. 353 (1963). The right of access to habeas is particularly fundamental, and is indeed so important to our constitutional tradition that it is singled out for constitutional protection. U.S. Const. art. I, §9, cl. 2.[38]

In any event, the DTA fails even rational-basis scrutiny. It withdraws habeas only from non-citizens detained by the military in Guantanamo, while preserving the writ for individuals identically situated in everything but citizenship, custodian, or location of detention. There is no rational basis for withdrawing habeas rights only from those held by the Defense Department. Likewise there is no rational justification for withdrawing habeas access from only those aliens housed in Guantanamo Bay, but not those held elsewhere.

"[T]his Court has consistently recognized that where there is in fact discrimination against individual interests, the constitutional guarantee of equal protection of the laws is not inapplicable simply because the discrimination is based upon some group characteristic such as geographic location." *San Antonio Indep. Sch. Dist. v. Rodriguez*, 411 U.S. 1, 92 (1973) (Marshall, J., dissenting). The government has offered no justification for the distinctions drawn by the DTA and none is apparent. The discrimination here is surely more corrosive than, for example, conditioning access to habeas on a filing fee. *Smith v. Bennett*, 365 U.S. 708 (1961). It offends the very essence of equal justice under law. It is targeted at a population who cannot vote, and concerns not government benefits, but the touchstone issue of who can come into court to protect his liberty.[39]

CONCLUSION

There is no reason to read into the DTA a clear statement that is not there; rather, there is every reason not to do so, and to hold that the DTA has no effect on this Court's jurisdiction.[40] Accordingly, the Motion to Dismiss should be denied. In the event that

---

[38] *Carafas v. LaVallee*, 391 U.S. 234, 238 (1968) (declaring that the right to habeas corpus is "shaped to guarantee the most fundamental of all rights"); *Coolidge v. New Hampshire*, 403 U.S. 443, 454 n.4 (1971) (listing the right to the writ of habeas corpus among rights that are "to be regarded as of the very essence of constitutional liberty") (citation omitted).

[39] The government's reading of the DTA raises several other constitutional problems as well. The Article III Exceptions Clause violation is discussed *supra* pp. 24–26. It would also run afoul of the Bill of Attainder Clause. U.S. CONST., art. I, sec. 9, cl. 9. A law is an unlawful attainder if (1) it applies to easily ascertainable members of a group, and (2) inflicts punishment. *United States v. Lovett*, 328 U.S. 303, 315 (1946). The Act, as read by respondents, satisfies both prongs. The DTA's plain language applies only to "alien[s] detained by the Department of Defense at Guantanamo." §1005(e)(1). And the Act constitutes punishment under respondents' interpretation. The extended detention, and in Hamdan's case the denial of his right to challenge the jurisdiction and legality of the commission itself, is at least as punitive as the denial of the right to engage in a particular profession. *See Ex parte Garland*, 4 Wall. 333 (1867) (denial of right to practice law is an attainder); *cf*. 151 Cong. Rec. S12664 ("If you want to give terrorists habeas corpus rights as if they were American citizens, that they are not part of an outfit trying to wage war on us, fine, vote against me.") (Nov. 10, 2005) (remarks of Sen. Graham).

[40] The DTA is a sober reminder that a sense of proportion is essential in assessing the merits of petitioner's claims and that Congress stands ready to react to this Court's rulings. All that is at stake in this case is the default rule about the legality of military commissions without further congressional action. If this Court rules for petitioner, Congress can then authorize commissions or some other trial system. The government's representations should not mislead the Court into thinking that more is at stake in ruling for Petitioner than

the Court sees any merit to the Motion, petitioner respectfully requests that any ruling on it be deferred until after the oral argument. *Cf. Oregon v. Guzek*, No. 04-928 (Order of Nov. 23, 2005).

. . .

---

actually is *Cf.* U.S. Br., *Rasul v. Bush*, Nos. 03-334, at 12–13 ("Exercising jurisdiction over claims filed on behalf of aliens held at Guantanamo would . . . require U.S. soldiers to divert their attention from the combat operations overseas . . . [and] intrude on Congress's ability to delineate the subject-matter jurisdiction of the federal courts.").

In the Supreme Court of the United States

SALIM AHMED HAMDAN, PETITIONER

v.

DONALD H. RUMSFELD, SECRETARY OF DEFENSE,
ET AL.

*ON WRIT OF CERTIORARI TO THE
UNITED STATES COURT OF APPEALS
FOR THE DISTRICT OF COLUMBIA CIRCUIT*

PAUL D. CLEMENT
*Solicitor General
Counsel of Record*

PETER D. KEISLER
Assistant Attorney General

GREGORY G. GARRE
Deputy Solicitor General

GREGORY G. KATSAS
*Deputy Assistant Attorney
General*

JONATHAN L. MARCUS
KANNON K. SHANMUGAM
*Assistants to the Solicitor
General*

DOUGLAS N. LETTER
ROBERT M. LOEB
ERIC D. MILLER
*Attorneys
Department of Justice*

▬▬▬▬▬▬▬▬▬▬▬▬▬▬▬▬▬

---

* Redaction on this page has been added for privacy purposes. – *Eds*.

QUESTIONS PRESENTED

1. Whether the Detainee Treatment Act of 2005 divests this Court of jurisdiction over this case.

2. Whether federal courts should abstain from interfering with ongoing military commission proceedings.

3. Whether the President has constitutional or statutory authority to establish military commissions.

4. Whether the Geneva Convention Relative to the Treatment of Prisoners of War creates judicially enforceable rights.

5. Whether the President permissibly determined that the Geneva Convention does not cover, or afford prisoner-of-war status to, al Qaeda combatants.

6. Whether the federal regulations governing military commissions must conform to provisions in the Uniform Code of Military Justice that apply by their terms only to courts-martial.

. . .

SUMMARY OF ARGUMENT

I. Petitioner's pre-trial challenge to his military commission is jurisdictionally foreclosed by the Detainee Treatment Act of 2005 and fatally premature. The DTA removes jurisdiction over a broad class of actions by Guantanamo detainees, including this action, and establishes an exclusive review mechanism for challenging the *final* decisions of CSRTs or military commissions in the District of Columbia Circuit. The DTA establishes a statutory rule of abstention that eliminates all jurisdiction over petitioner's pre-trial complaints about his military commission. The DTA thus reinforces the military abstention doctrine of *Schlesinger* v. *Councilman*, 420 U.S. 738 (1975), and makes clear that dismissal of this action is warranted. Abstention is especially appropriate here because the armed conflict against al Qaeda remains ongoing and because Congress itself has determined that post-conviction judicial review is appropriate and sufficient.

II. The President had ample authority to convene the military commission against petitioner. Indeed, the DTA itself conclusively demonstrates that Congress is aware that the President has convened military commissions in the current conflict and that Congress recognizes his authority to do so. That recognition is well-founded. As the President found in his Military Order establishing military commissions, the AUMF and two provisions of the UCMJ, 10 U.S.C. 821, 836, recognize the President's authority to convene military commissions. The AUMF authorized the President "to use all necessary and appropriate force" against al Qaeda and its supporters. As a plurality of this Court recognized in *Hamdi* v. *Rumsfeld*, 542 U.S. 507 (2004), the AUMF thus authorized the President to exercise his full war powers in connection with the conflict against al Qaeda, including the authority necessary for "the capture, detention, *and trial* of unlawful combatants." *Id.* at 518 (emphasis added). Like the detention of captured enemy combatants, the trial of such combatants by military commission "is so fundamental and accepted an incident to war as to be an exercise of the 'necessary and appropriate' force Congress has authorized the President to use." *Ibid.*

Article 21 of the UCMJ, 10 U.S.C. 821, provides that the extension of court-martial jurisdiction "do[es] not deprive military commissions[] *** of concurrent jurisdiction with respect to offenders or offenses that by statute or by the law of war may be tried by military commissions." In *Ex parte Quirin*, 317 U.S. 1 (1942), this Court construed the materially identical statutory precursor to Article 21 to authorize the President to convene military commissions to try offenses against the law of war. Article 36 of the UCMJ, 10 U.S.C. 836, authorizes the President to prescribe rules for military commissions, and to depart from the "principles of law and the rules of evidence" applicable in ordinary criminal trials when "he considers" those rules not "practicable." Article 36 thus recognizes both the President's authority to structure the military commission and his need for flexibility in doing so. And, of course, the DTA makes clear that Congress has ratified the use of military commissions in this context.

Even if Congress's support for the President's Military Order were not so clear, the President has the inherent authority to convene military commissions to try and punish captured enemy combatants in wartime – even in the absence of any statutory authorization. Indeed, military commissions have been convened by the President in numerous conflicts since the founding and have often been used during wartime without congressional authorization. The President's authority in this realm not only provides an independent basis for rejecting petitioner's challenge, but strongly counsels against reading the UCMJ to restrict the Commander in Chief's ability in wartime to hold enemy fighters accountable for violating the law of war.

Nor is there any basis for concluding that the President lacks the authority to convene a military commission against *petitioner*. The Geneva Convention does not preclude the trial of petitioner by military commission. As a threshold matter, the Convention does not create private rights enforceable in domestic courts and thus is of no assistance to petitioner in this action. The longstanding presumption is that treaties or international agreements do not create judicially enforceable individual rights. In *Johnson* v. *Eisentrager*, 339 U.S. 763 (1950), this Court concluded that a previous version of the Geneva Convention did not confer privately enforceable rights and that enforcement of the treaty is instead a matter of State-to-State relations. Nothing in the text or history of the current version of the Convention suggests that the President or the Senate intended to take the radical step of creating judicially enforceable rights. Nor do any of the provisions of domestic law on which petitioner relies, including the habeas statute, transform the Convention into a judicially enforceable international instrument.

Even if the Convention were judicially enforceable, it still would not aid petitioner. The President has determined that members and affiliates of al Qaeda, such as petitioner, are not covered by the Geneva Convention. That determination represents a core exercise of the President's Commander-in-Chief and foreign affairs powers during wartime and is entitled to be given effect by the courts. Moreover, the President's determination is supported by the plain text of the Geneva Convention articles defining the treaty's scope. Furthermore, petitioner clearly does not satisfy the relevant requirements in the Convention for POW status, which is determined by reference to the characteristics of the belligerent force (in this case, al Qaeda), not the individual. And a CSRT has rejected petitioner's claim that he is a non-combatant, determining instead that petitioner (an admitted personal assistant to bin Laden) was an enemy combatant affiliated with al Qaeda.

The nature of the offense with which petitioner has been charged – conspiracy – also is no bar to proceeding against him by military commission. Conspiracy has been prosecuted as a war crime throughout our Nation's history, and that long-standing practice defeats petitioner's claim.

III. Petitioner's pre-trial objections to the military commission's procedures are equally meritless. The rules established by the UCMJ for courts-martial do not govern military commissions. The UCMJ does not purport to establish a comprehensive set of rules for military commissions. Instead, it takes pains to distinguish "military commissions" or "military tribunals" from the comprehensively regulated "courts-martial," and, reflecting Congress's traditional hands-off approach to military commissions (in contrast to courts-martial), imposes only a handful of requirements on those commissions. Article 3 of the Geneva Convention does not entitle petitioner to additional procedures either. Like the rest of the Geneva Convention, Article 3 is not individually enforceable. In any event, the President has determined that Article 3 does not apply to the conflict with al Qaeda, and the text and history of Article 3 confirms the correctness of that determination.

ARGUMENT

Since the founding of this Nation, the United States has used military commissions during armed conflicts to try violations of the law of war. Ninety years ago, in revising the Articles of War, Congress recognized that historic practice and approved its continuing use. And this Court upheld the use of military commissions during and after World War II in cases involving a presumed American citizen Nazi saboteur captured in the United States, *Ex parte Quirin*, 317 U.S. 1 (1942); the Japanese military governor of the Phillippines, *In re Yamashita*, 327 U.S. 1 (1946); German nationals who claimed that they worked for civilian agencies of the German government in China, *Johnson* v. *Eisentrager*, 339 U.S. 763 (1950); and even the wife of an American serviceman posted in occupied Germany, *Madsen* v. *Kinsella*, 343 U.S. 341 (1952).

Facing an enemy today characterized by its systematic disregard for the law of war and for the lives of innocent civilians, such as the victims of the September 11 attacks, Congress authorized the President to use his traditional war powers "to prevent any future acts of international terrorism against the United States" by al Qaeda and its supporters. AUMF §2(a), 115 Stat. 224. Soon after, and in express reliance on that authorization and on provisions of the UCMJ, the President ordered the establishment of military commissions to try violations of the law of war in the ongoing armed conflict with al Qaeda. What is more, Congress recently ratified the President's decision to convene such military commissions in the DTA, which establishes an exclusive review mechanism in the District of Columbia Circuit for challenges to the final decisions of military commissions. That is self-evidently not the legislation Congress would have enacted if it viewed the commissions as *ultra vires* or defective in ways that demanded pre-trial correction. The only plausible conclusion is that Congress has interposed no objection to the President's decision to convene military commissions in the current conflict, including the commission at issue in this case.

Neither petitioner nor his amici have provided any basis for the Court to disregard the time-honored practice of trying and punishing captured enemy combatants by military commissions, as reflected in this Court's decisions recognizing the validity of military commissions in prior conflicts and the various statutes in which Congress has expressed its approval of the President's decision to use military commissions both more generally and in the current conflict specifically.

I. THIS PRE-TRIAL CHALLENGE TO PETITIONER'S MILITARY COMMISSION IS JURISDICTIONALLY FORECLOSED AND FATALLY PREMATURE

First and foremost, as explained at length in respondents' motion to dismiss, the DTA immediately eliminates jurisdiction over this action and establishes an exclusive review mechanism in the District of Columbia Circuit for challenges to "final decisions" rendered by military commissions. See §1005(e)(3)(A), (C) and (D), 119 Stat. 2743. The

DTA thus amounts to a statutory rule of abstention that precludes review of ongoing military proceedings and requires detainees to await an adverse decision before seeking judicial review. The plain terms of the statute require the dismissal of petitioner's pre-trial challenge for lack of jurisdiction.

Second, even if the DTA did not apply to this case, abstention would be appropriate under the established judge-made rule that civilian courts should await the final outcome of on-going military proceedings before entertaining an attack on those proceedings. See *Schlesinger* v. *Councilman*, 420 U.S. 738 (1975). In *Councilman*, this Court explained that the need for protection against judicial interference with the "primary business of armies and navies to fight or be ready to fight wars" "counsels strongly against the exercise of equity power" to intervene in an ongoing court-martial. *Id.* at 757 (citation omitted). The Court held that even a case with relatively limited potential for interference with military action – the prosecution of a serviceman for possession and sale of marijuana – implicated "unique military exigencies" of "powerful" and "contemporary vitality." *Ibid.* These exigencies, the Court held, should generally preclude a court from entertaining "habeas petitions by military prisoners unless all available military remedies have been exhausted." *Id.* at 758.

. . .

II. THE PRESIDENT HAS AMPLE AUTHORITY TO CONVENE MILITARY COMMISSIONS TO TRY AND PUNISH AL QAEDA COMBATANTS SUCH AS PETITIONER

Petitioner's central submission is that the President lacked the authority to establish military commissions to try and punish captured enemy combatants in the ongoing armed conflict against al Qaeda. That contention is refuted by Congress's actions, this Court's precedents, and the war powers vested in the President by the Constitution.

A. Congress Has Authorized The Use Of Military Commissions In The Armed Conflict With Al Qaeda

1. Congress's most recent action in this area – the Detainee Treatment Act of 2005 – alone defeats petitioner's claim that the military commissions are not authorized. In the DTA, Congress expressly recognized and ratified the latest Military Order governing the use of military commissions in the specific context of the current conflict and established an exclusive mechanism for individuals such as petitioner to obtain judicial review of final decisions issued by military commissions. See §1005(e)(3)(A) and (C), 119 Stat. 2743. The DTA also delineates restrictions on judicial review of military commissions, differentiating the review available based on the length of the sentence a defendant receives. See §1005(e)(3)(B) and (D), 119 Stat. 2743. Petitioner's contention that the military commissions are not authorized by Congress is irreconcilable with the DTA. The DTA reflects Congress's judgment that the current military commissions are neither *ultra vires* nor too deficient to be allowed to proceed to render a final decision. In any event, as the court of appeals correctly concluded based on pre-DTA enactments, Congress has independently authorized the use of military commissions in the current conflict.

2. a. In the AUMF, Congress authorized the use of military commissions in the ongoing conflict against al Qaeda. Congress recognized that "the President has authority under the Constitution to take action to deter and prevent acts of international terrorism against the United States," AUMF preamble, 115 Stat. 224, and authorized the President

"to use all necessary and appropriate force against those nations, *organizations*, or *persons* he determines planned, authorized, committed, or aided the terrorist attacks that occurred on September 11, 2001, *** in order to prevent any future acts of international terrorism against the United States," AUMF §2a, 115 Stat. 224 (emphasis added).

In *Hamdi* v. *Rumsfeld*, 542 U.S. 507 (2004), a plurality of this Court concluded that the AUMF authorized the President to exercise his traditional war powers, and it relied on *Quirin* for the proposition that "the capture, detention, *and trial* of unlawful combatants, by 'universal agreement and practice,' are 'important incident[s] of war.'" *Id.* at 518 (quoting *Quirin*, 317 U.S. at 28, 30) (emphasis added). Likewise, in *Yamashita*, the Court explained that an "important incident to the conduct of war is the adoption of measures by the military commander, not only to repel and defeat the enemy, but to seize and subject to disciplinary measures those enemies who, in their attempt to thwart or impede our military effort, have violated the law of war." 327 U.S. at 11; see *Hirota*, 338 U.S. at 208 (Douglas, J., concurring) (noting that the Article II power includes the power "to punish those enemies who violated the law of war," which "is a part of the prosecution of war"). Because "[t]he trial and punishment of enemy combatants" (*Yamashita*, 327 U.S. at 11) is a fundamental incident of war, it follows that, in authorizing the President "to use all necessary and appropriate force" against al Qaeda, the AUMF authorized the use of military commissions against enemy combatants, such as petitioner.

b. Congress has not only authorized the President to exercise his traditional war powers in the specific context of the armed conflict with al Qaeda; it has also specifically recognized his ongoing authority to invoke military commissions when he deems them necessary. Article 21 of the UCMJ, 10 U.S.C. 821, states that "[t]he provisions [of the UCMJ] conferring jurisdiction upon courts-martial do not deprive military commissions *** of concurrent jurisdiction with respect to offenders or offenses that by the law of war may be tried by military commissions." That language originated in, and is identical in all material respects to, Article 15 of the Articles of War, which were enacted during World War I. See Act of Aug. 29, 1916, ch. 418, §3, 39 Stat. 650 (Articles of War). In the Articles of War, Congress extended the jurisdiction of courts-martial to offenses and offenders that had traditionally fallen within the jurisdiction of military commissions, while preserving the institution and jurisdiction of the commissions. See *Madsen*, 343 U.S. at 349–355. The main proponent of Article 15 testified that, as Congress was extending the jurisdiction of courts-martial, it was vital to make clear that the military commissions' "common law of war jurisdiction was not ousted." S. Rep. No. 229, 63d Cong., 2d Sess. 53, 98–99 (1914) (testimony of Judge Advocate General Crowder).

Moreover, this Court has construed Article 15 as having "*authorized* trial of offenses against the laws of war before such commissions." *Quirin*, 317 U.S. at 29 (emphasis added). Although the language of this authorization in Article 15 seems indirect, that simply recognizes that Congress was adding its imprimatur to a practice with a long history which did not depend on express statutory authorization. When Congress enacted Article 21 of the UCMJ, it merely recodified Article 15 of the Articles of War. See S. Rep. No. 486, 81st Cong., 1st Sess. 13 (1949) (explaining that Article 21 of the UCMJ "preserve[s]" Article 15 of the Articles of War, which "has been construed by the Supreme Court"); H.R. Rep. No. 491, 81st Cong., 1st Sess. 17 (1949) (same). Consequently, this Court's interpretation of Article 15 controls the interpretation of Article 21. See, *e.g.*, *Lorillard* v. *Pons*, 434 U.S. 575, 580–581 (1978).

c. Article 36 of the UCMJ, 10 U.S.C. 836, provides even further statutory recognition of the President's authority to use military commissions. It authorizes the President to establish procedures "for cases arising under this chapter triable in *** military commissions." That provision also grants the President broad discretion in establishing the rules for proceedings before military commissions, expressly providing that the President may adopt rules that depart from "the principles of law and the rules of evidence generally recognized in the trial of criminal cases in the United States district courts," when "he considers" application of those rules to be not "practicable."

3. Petitioner's attempts to undermine the obvious import of those congressional enactments are unavailing. The fact that Congress has not issued a formal declaration of war against al Qaeda is irrelevant. The President's prerogative to invoke the law of war in a time of armed conflict, including with respect to the trial and punishment of war criminals, in no way turns on the existence of such a declaration. See, *e.g., The Prize Cases*, 67 U.S. (2 Black) 635, 668, 670 (1862). The Court in *Hamdi* rejected a similar contention and found that the AUMF was sufficient to confirm Congress's support for the President's exercise of his war powers. See 542 U.S. at 518 (plurality opinion); *id.* at 587 (Thomas, J., dissenting).

In addition, none of the UCMJ provisions that recognize the President's authority to convene military commissions requires a formal declaration of war, and it is settled that the UCMJ applies to armed conflicts that the United States has prosecuted without a formal declaration of war. See, *e.g., United States* v. *Anderson*, 38 C.M.R. 386, 387 (C.M.A. 1968) (Vietnam); *United States* v. *Bancroft*, 11 C.M.R. 3, 5–6 (C.M.A. 1953) (Korea).[1] The case on which petitioner relies (Br. 32–33 n.23) for the contrary proposition, *United States* v. *Averette*, 41 C.M.R. 363 (C.M.A. 1970), is inapposite. That case interpreted the phrase "in time of war" as used in *Article 2* of the UCMJ as applied to a civilian accompanying the U.S. Armed Forces who was subjected to a court-martial. *Id.* at 365–366. The UCMJ provisions discussed above authorizing military commissions do not contain the limiting phrase "in time of war," and petitioner is not a civilian like the defendant in *Averette*, but a confirmed enemy combatant.

Petitioner also errs in arguing . . . that the use of military commissions is not "necessary" to prevent terrorism and therefore unauthorized by the AUMF. This Court has recognized that courts are not competent to second-guess judgments of the political branches regarding the extent of force necessary to prosecute a war. See, *e.g., The Prize Cases*, 67 U.S. (2 Black) at 670 (stating that the President "must determine what degree of force the crisis demands"). In any event, this Court has also recognized the general principle, in *Quirin, Yamashita*, and other cases, that trying unlawful combatants for violating the law of war is a fundamental part of the conduct of the war itself. The punishment of persons who have violated the law of war is an appropriate and time-honored means of deterring or incapacitating them from doing so again, and of discouraging others from doing so in the future.[2]

---

[1] See also Curtis A. Bradley & Jack L. Goldsmith, *Congressional Authorization and the War on Terrorism*, 118 Harv. L. Rev. 2047, 2129 (2005) (noting that military commissions were used in connection with the Civil War and conflicts with Indian tribes).

[2] Petitioner suggests . . . that the President's Military Order establishing military commissions violates two federal statutes. First, he points to 10 U.S.C. 3037(c), which directs the Judge Advocate General (JAG) of the Army to "receive, revise, and have recorded the proceedings of courts of inquiry and military commissions." That statute, phrased as a directive to the JAG, does not create privately enforceable rights. But in any event, Section 3037(c), like analogous provisions for other branches of the armed services, see 10 U.S.C. 5148(d) (Navy); 10 U.S.C. 8037(c) (Air Force), does not apply to military commissions convened by the President, but only commissions convened by a particular service. Second, petitioner points to 18 U.S.C. 242, a criminal statute that prohibits various forms of discriminatory conduct against aliens. But that statute is facially inapplicable because petitioner is not a "person in any State, Territory, Commonwealth, Possession, or District" within its meaning. See DTA §1005(g), 119 Stat. 2743 (expressly providing that Guantanamo Bay is outside the United States). Moreover, that statute does not purport to regulate the conduct of the United States toward aliens, which is addressed in detail by immigration statutes that routinely treat aliens differently, cf. *Harisiades* v. *Shaughnessy*, 342 U.S. 580, 588–589 (1952) (noting virtually plenary authority over aliens),

B. The Constitution Authorizes The President To Establish Military Commissions To Try Al Qaeda Combatants

Congress's multiple authorizations of the President's use of military commissions in the ongoing conflict with al Qaeda obviate the need to consider the President's inherent authority to act in the absence of such authorization. See *Hamdi*, 542 U.S. at 518 (plurality opinion); *id.* at 587 (Thomas, J., dissenting). Nevertheless, the President undoubtedly possesses that authority, as history, Congress's enactments, and this Court's precedents make clear.

As this Court has noted, "[t]he first of the enumerated powers of the President is that he shall be Commander-in-Chief of the Army and Navy of the United States." *Eisentrager*, 339 U.S. at 788. The President's war power under Article II, Section 2, of the Constitution includes the inherent authority to create military commissions even in the absence of any statutory authorization, because that authority is a necessary and longstanding component of his war powers. See *ibid.* (noting that, "of course, grant of war power includes all that is necessary and proper for carrying these powers into execution"). The war power thus includes "the power *** to punish those enemies who violated the law of war," because that power is "part of the prosecution of the war" and "a furtherance of the hostilities directed to a dilution of enemy power and involving retribution for wrongs done." *Hirota*, 338 U.S. at 208 (Douglas, J., concurring) (citation omitted); see *Yamashita*, 327 U.S. at 11; *Quirin*, 317 U.S. at 28, 30.

When the Constitution was written and ratified, it was well recognized that one of the powers inherent in military command was the authority to institute tribunals for punishing enemy violations of the law of war. For example, during the Revolutionary War, George Washington, as commander in chief of the Continental Army, appointed a "Board of General Officers" to try the British Major John Andre as a spy. See *Quirin*, 317 U.S. at 31 n.9. At the time, there was no provision in the American Articles of War for court-martial proceedings to try an enemy for the offense of spying. See George B. Davis, *A Treatise on the Military Law of the United States* 308 n.1 (1913). At a minimum, in investing the President with the authority to be Commander in Chief, the framers surely intended to give the President the same authority that General Washington possessed during the Revolutionary War to convene military tribunals to punish offenses against the law of war.

The well-established executive practice of using military commissions confirms this conclusion. Throughout our Nation's history, Presidents have exercised their inherent commander-in-chief authority to establish military commissions without any specific authorization from Congress. See Winthrop, *supra*, at 831 ("In general, *** [Congress] has left it to the President, and the military commanders representing him, to employ the commission, as occasion may require, for the investigation and punishment of violations of the laws of war."). For example, during the Mexican-American War in the 1840s, tribunals called "council[s] of war" were convened to try offenses under the law of war; other tribunals, called "military commission[s]," were created to administer justice in occupied areas. See, *e.g.*, Davis, *supra*, at 308; Winthrop, *supra*, at 832–833. Likewise, during the Civil War, military commissions were convened to try offenses against the law of war, despite the lack of statutory authorization. See Davis, *supra*, at 308 n.2; Winthrop, *supra*, at 833.[3]

---

much less in the context of the President's treatment of captured enemy combatants during active hostilities. In any event, this argument has been forfeited because it was not presented to the court of appeals.

[3] In 1863, Congress did endorse the use of military commissions to try members of the military for certain offenses committed during time of war. See Act of Mar. 3, 1863, ch. 75, §30, 12 Stat. 736. That statute, however,

As this Court has repeatedly explained, "'traditional ways of conducting government . . . give meaning' to the Constitution." *Mistretta* v. *United States*, 488 U.S. 361, 401 (1989) (citation omitted), and "[t]he construction placed upon the Constitution *** by the men who were contemporary with its formation" is "almost conclusive," *United States* v. *Curtiss-Wright Export Corp.*, 299 U.S. 304, 328 (1936) (citation omitted); accord *Quirin*, 317 U.S. at 41–42. The historical practice of the President's use of military commissions in time of armed conflict therefore strongly (if not conclusively) confirms the existence of that war power.

The President's inherent authority to establish military commissions is reflected in the actions of Congress and the courts in this context. The elliptical manner in which Congress acknowledged military commissions and left them undisturbed in Article 21 of the UCMJ – as opposed to authorizing them directly in plain terms of affirmative authorization – acknowledges that congressional authorization was not necessary and was not present during most of the first 125 years during which the executive employed such commissions. Likewise, as this Court explained in *Quirin*, "the detention and trial of petitioners – ordered by the President in the declared exercise of his powers as Commander in Chief of the Army in time of war and of grave public danger are not to be set aside by the courts without the clear conviction that they are in conflict with the Constitution or laws of Congress." 317 U.S. at 25. Petitioner has not come remotely close to making the necessary showing that Congress intended to *limit* the President's inherent authority to establish military commissions in this context.[4]

C. Al Qaeda's Wholesale Disregard For The Law Of War Does Not Exempt It From Punishment For Violations Of The Law Of War

Petitioner contends . . . that the law of war does not apply to the current conflict with al Qaeda, a foreign terrorist organization that engages in systematic violations of the law of war to accomplish its ideological and political goals. That contention is seriously mistaken.

The Constitution vests in the President the authority to determine whether a state of armed conflict exists against an enemy to which the law of war applies. See *The Prize Cases*, 67 U.S. (2 Black) at 670 ("Whether the President in fulfilling his duties, as Commander-in-chief, in suppressing an insurrection, has met with such armed hostile resistance, and a civil war of such alarming proportions as will compel him to accord to them the character of belligerents, is a question to be decided *by him*, and this Court must be governed by the decisions and acts of the political department of the Government to which this power was entrusted."); see also *Eisentrager*, 339 U.S. at 789 ("Certainly it is not the function of the Judiciary to entertain private litigation – even by a citizen – which challenges the legality, the wisdom, or the propriety of the Commander-in-Chief in sending our armed forces abroad or to any particular region."); *Ludecke* v. *Watkins*, 335 U.S. 160, 170 (1948) (explaining that whether a "state of war" exists is a "matter[]

---

did not purport to establish military commissions; instead, it acknowledged their existence as a matter of inherent executive authority (and sanctioned their use as alternatives to courts-martial in some cases). See *Ex parte Vallandigham*, 68 U.S. (1 Wall.) 243, 249 (1864) ("In the armies of the United States, *** cases which do not come within the *** jurisdiction conferred by statute or court-martial, are tried by *military commissions*.").

[4] Petitioner states . . . that *Quirin* held that the "authority to establish commissions rests with Congress." *Quirin*, however, expressly declined to settle questions about the relative powers of the political branches over military commissions in a case in which both the President and Congress (through Article 15 of the Articles of War) had sanctioned their use.

of political judgment for which judges have neither technical competence nor official responsibility"); *The Three Friends*, 166 U.S. 1, 63 (1897) (noting that "it belongs to the political department to determine when belligerency shall be recognized, and its action must be accepted").

The President's determination that "members of al Qaida *** have carried out attacks *** on a scale that has created a state of armed conflict," Military Order §1(a), is thus conclusive in establishing the applicability of the law of war to the conflict. Moreover, Congress itself determined that the law of war was applicable to al Qaeda when it authorized the President to use all "necessary and appropriate force" against the "nations, organizations, or persons he determines" were responsible for the September 11 attacks or those who "aided" them. AUMF §2a, 115 Stat. 224. There is no basis for this Court to invalidate the judgments made by both political branches that the law of war applies to al Qaeda.

In any event, those judgments were correct. It is well established that the law of war fully applies to armed conflicts involving groups or entities other than traditional nation-states. See *The Prize Cases*, 67 U.S. (2 Black) at 666 (noting that "it is not necessary to constitute war, that both parties should be acknowledged as independent nations or sovereign states"); Ingrid Detter, *The Law of War* 134 (2d ed. 2000) (observing that "non-recognition of groups, fronts or entities has not affected their status as belligerents nor the ensuing status of their soldiers as combatants"). Any contrary conclusion in this case would blink reality in view of the fact that al Qaeda has repeatedly declared itself an enemy of the United States, and has inflicted damage on a scale that exceeds previous attacks on our soil by nation-states, and in a manner that, by any commonsense understanding, constitutes an act of war. There is no doubt that al Qaeda's attacks against American civilians and military targets (including an attack on the headquarters of the Nation's Department of Defense) have triggered a right to deploy military forces abroad to defend the United States by combating al Qaeda.

Petitioner identifies several purported distinctions between this conflict and other wars, but none of them is material. For example, petitioner asserts . . . that the conflict with al Qaeda is "potentially unlimited in scope [and] duration." That assertion, however, underestimates this Nation's capabilities and resolve and was no less true of World War II from the perspective of 1941. Moreover, the fact that the endpoint of the conflict with al Qaeda is not immediately in sight supports holding its combatants accountable for their war crimes in a manner that promotes, rather than compromises, other efforts to prosecute the war and bring the conflict to an end.

Petitioner suggests . . . that, if the Geneva Convention does not apply to al Qaeda, the law of war does not apply either. That suggestion is baseless. There is no field preemption under the Geneva Convention. The Convention seeks to *regulate* the conduct of warfare to which it applies with respect to nation-states that have entered the Convention and agreed to abide by its terms, but it does not purport to apply to every armed conflict that might arise or to crowd out the common law of war. Instead, as explained below, the Convention applies only to those conflicts identified in Articles 2 and 3. If an armed conflict, therefore, does not fall within the Convention, the Convention simply does not regulate it. Nothing in the Convention prohibits a belligerent party from applying the law of war to a conflict to which the Convention does not apply.[5]

---

[5] Cf. Geneva Convention art. 142, 6 U.S.T. at 3424, 75 U.N.T.S. at 242 (noting that a denunciation of the Convention by a High Contracting Party "shall have effect only in respect of the denouncing Power" and "shall in no way impair the obligations which the Parties to the conflict shall remain bound to fulfil by virtue of the principles of the law of nations, as they result from the usages established among civilized peoples, from the laws of humanity and the dictates of the public conscience").

D. Petitioner's Case-Specific And Treaty-Based Objections To His Military Commission Lack Merit

Because the President clearly has the constitutional and statutory authority to convene military commissions to try al Qaeda combatants, and because the law of war clearly applies to the ongoing armed conflict with al Qaeda, petitioner is reduced to arguing that *his* particular military commission is not authorized. Petitioner's various arguments in this respect are no more availing than his broad-based attacks.

1. Military commissions may be and long have been convened outside the zone of combat

Petitioner contends (Br. 10, 26–27 n.18) that his commission is invalid because it is located outside a zone of combat or occupied territory. That contention is unsound. The commission in *Quirin* was held in Washington, D.C., while the commission in *Yamashita* was held in the Philippines, which was a U.S. territory at the time. Moreover, although military commissions authorized to administer civil law generally (*i.e.*, to maintain law and order) are naturally convened in the territory being occupied, there is no requirement that commissions established for the much narrower purpose of prosecuting violations of the law of war must be confined to a war zone. *Quirin* plainly did not impose such a requirement; the UCMJ was enacted against the backdrop of *Quirin*; and such a requirement would only invite unnecessary risks for all involved. Cf. 1949 Convention art. 23, 6 U.S.T. at 3336, 75 U.N.T.S. at 154 (providing that "[n]o prisoner of war may at any time be *** detained in areas where he may be exposed to the fire of the combat zone").

2. The offense of conspiracy may be and long has been tried before a military commission

Petitioner contends... that conspiracy, the offense with which he has been charged, is not a cognizable offense under the law of war. That is not so. Individuals have been tried before military commissions for conspiracy to commit war crimes throughout this Nation's history. The *Quirin* saboteurs were charged with conspiracy, see 317 U.S. at 23, as was another Nazi saboteur whose convictions were subsequently upheld, see *Colepaugh* v. *Looney*, 235 F.2d 429 (10th Cir. 1956), cert. denied, 352 U.S. 1014 (1957). See generally Winthrop, *supra*, at 839 & n.5 (listing conspiracy offenses prosecuted by military commissions); Charles Roscoe Howland, *Digest of Opinions of the Judge Advocates General of the Army* 1071 (1912) (noting that conspiracy "to violate the laws of war by destroying life or property in aid of the enemy" was an offense against the law of war that was "punished by military commissions" throughout the Civil War). That long-standing practice suffices to defeat petitioner's claim.

Petitioner argues that Congress covered the field of war crimes in enacting the War Crimes Act of 1996 (18 U.S.C. 2441) and the Expanded War Crimes Act of 1997 (Act of Nov. 26, 1997, Pub. L. No. 105–118, §583, 111 Stat. 2436). But those Acts were intended to *supplement* the jurisdiction of military commissions over war crimes. See, *e.g.*, H.R. Rep. No. 698, 104th Cong., 2d Sess. 12 (1996) ("The enactment of [the War Crimes Act of 1996] is not intended to affect in any way the jurisdiction of any court-martial, military commission, or other military tribunal under any article of the [UCMJ] or under the law of war or the law of nations."). The Acts therefore say nothing about altering the preexisting jurisdiction of military commissions. See, *e.g.*, *Cook County* v. *United States ex rel. Chandler*, 538 U.S. 119, 132 (2003) (noting "the cardinal rule... that repeals by implication are not favored") (citation omitted).

3. As a non-citizen enemy combatant, petitioner may be tried before a military commission

Notwithstanding his capture in a foreign combat zone, the CSRT's determination that he is an enemy combatant, and this Court's decisions in *Quirin* and *Hamdi*, petitioner invokes *Ex parte Milligan*, 71 U.S. (4 Wall.) 2 (1866), to contend . . . that his military commission is not authorized because he is a civilian. *Milligan* is wholly inapposite. *Milligan* involved the military prosecution of an American citizen "in civil life, in nowise connected with the military service." 71 U.S. at 121–122. In *Quirin*, this Court "construe[d]" the "inapplicability of the law of war to [defendant's] case as having particular reference to the facts": namely, that the defendant in *Milligan*, as a person who was not "a part of or associated with the armed forces of the enemy," was a "non-belligerent." 317 U.S. at 45. And in *Hamdi*, a majority of this Court rejected a far more plausible invocation of *Milligan*, by an American citizen, and reaffirmed *Quirin*. See 542 U.S. at 523 (plurality opinion) ("*Quirin* was a unanimous opinion. It both postdates and clarifies *Milligan*, providing us with the most apposite precedent that we have."); *id.* at 593 (Thomas, J., dissenting) ("*Quirin* overruled *Milligan* to the extent that those cases are inconsistent.").[6]

Petitioner contends that he should be considered a non-belligerent like the defendant in *Milligan*, rather than an enemy combatant like the defendants in *Quirin*, because he contests his combatant status. But the *Hamdi* plurality refused to limit *Quirin* to cases in which enemy-combatant status was conceded, noting that the AUMF authorizes the United States to detain even *citizen* enemy combatants captured in a foreign combat zone and concluding that "whether [enemy-combatant status] is established by concession or by some other process that verifies this fact with sufficient certainty seems beside the point." 542 U.S. at 523. Petitioner is an *alien* enemy combatant captured abroad. Because a CSRT found that petitioner had the status of an enemy combatant (as either a member or an affiliate of al Qaeda), . . . petitioner squarely falls within the four corners of the AUMF and is properly subject to military jurisdiction under *Hamdi* and *Quirin*.[7]

4. Petitioner's treaty-based objections lack merit

Petitioner argues . . . that subjecting him to a military commission would violate the Geneva Convention. For several reasons, that argument is mistaken.

a. The Geneva Convention does not give rise to judicially enforceable rights

i. As the court of appeals held, the Geneva Convention is not individually enforceable. . . . . The long-established presumption is that treaties and other international agreements do not create judicially enforceable rights. As the Court has observed: "A treaty

---

[6] Petitioner seeks (Br. 26 n.17) to distinguish *Quirin* on the ground that two of the four charges (Counts 2 and 3) were statutorily authorized to be tried by military commission. But *Quirin* upheld the commission's authority to try the individuals based *solely* on the common-law-of-war charge (Count 1). Indeed, *Quirin* noted that, through Article 15 of the Articles of War, Congress had recognized the military's ability to enforce common-law rules of warfare which Congress had chosen not to codify in detail. 317 U.S. at 30.

[7] Petitioner claims . . . that respondents did not establish his enemy-combatant status until this case was on appeal. That is incorrect. The military determined that petitioner was an enemy combatant through a careful screening process that resulted in his transfer to Guantanamo. In addition, the government informed the district court of the CSRT's determination. . . . . Notwithstanding petitioner's argument to the court of appeals that the CSRT's determination was "not part of the Record," . . . the court of appeals noted the determination (and relied on it). . . . Petitioner nevertheless inexplicably refuses to acknowledge the CSRT's determination that he is an enemy combatant. If petitioner disagrees with that determination, he may challenge it pursuant to the exclusive review procedures established by the DTA, see §1005(e)(2), 119 Stat. 2742, but there is no basis for this Court to ignore that determination in deciding this case.

is primarily a compact between independent nations. It depends for the enforcement of its provisions on the interest and the honor of the governments which are parties to it." *Head Money Cases*, 112 U.S. 580, 598 (1884). When a violation of a treaty nonetheless occurs, it "becomes the subject of international negotiations and reclamations," not of judicial redress. *Ibid.*; see *Charlton* v. *Kelly*, 229 U.S. 447, 474 (1913); *Whitney* v. *Robertson*, 124 U.S. 190, 194–195 (1888); *Foster* v. *Neilson*, 27 U.S. (2 Pet.) 253, 306 (1829); see generally U.S. Br. at 11–16, *Bustillo* v. *Johnson*, No. 05-51 (to be argued March 29, 2006).

To be sure, treaties can, and on occasion do, create judicially enforceable private rights. But since such treaties are the exception, rather than the rule, there is a presumption that a treaty will be enforced through political and diplomatic channels, rather than through the courts. *United States* v. *Emuegbunam*, 268 F.3d 377, 389–390 (6th Cir. 2001), cert. denied, 535 U.S. 977 (2002); *United States* v. *De La Pava*, 268 F.3d 157, 164 (2d Cir. 2001); *United States* v. *Jimenez-Nava*, 243 F.3d 192, 195–196 (5th Cir.), cert. denied, 533 U.S. 962 (2001); *United States* v. *Li*, 206 F.3d 56, 61 (1st Cir.), cert. denied, 531 U.S. 956 (2000). That background principle applies even when a treaty benefits private individuals. See 2 Restatement (Third) of the Foreign Relations Law of the United States §907 cmt. a, at 395 (1987) ("International agreements, even those directly benefitting private persons, generally do not create private rights or provide for a private right of action in domestic courts."). And it applies wholly apart from whether the treaty is self-executing (*i.e.*, whether the treaty requires implementing legislation to be given effect). See 1 *id.* §111 cmt. h, at 47; Carlos Manuel Vazquez, *The Four Doctrines of Self-Executing Treaties*, 89 Am. J. Int'l L. 695, 721 (1995).

In *Eisentrager*, this Court held that captured Nazi combatants challenging the jurisdiction of a military tribunal could not invoke the 1929 version of the Geneva Convention because the Convention was not judicially enforceable. 339 U.S. at 789. Like the current version of the Convention, the 1929 version contained various provisions that protected individual rights. See, *e.g.*, Convention Relative to the Treatment of Prisoners of War, July 27, 1929, arts. 2, 3, 16, 42, 47 Stat. 2021, 2031, 2036, 2045, 118 L.N.T.S. 343, 357, 363, 373 (1929 Convention). The Court explained, however, that the Convention's protections, like those of most treaties, "are vindicated under it only through protests and intervention of protecting powers." *Eisentrager*, 339 U.S. at 789 n.14. Although petitioner seeks . . . to characterize this analysis as dictum, it was an alternative holding that formed the basis for the Court's rejection of the respondents' claims that the military commission violated their rights under the Convention.[8]

To be sure, the current version of the Geneva Convention does differ in some respects from the 1929 version. But, as the court of appeals concluded, none of the differences is material. . . . . To the contrary, the plain terms of the current version of the Convention confirm that, as with the 1929 version, vindication of the treaty is a matter for State-to-State diplomatic relations, not for the domestic courts. When the President signed and the Senate ratified the current version of the Convention, there was no indication that they viewed that version as effecting a change in the essential character of the treaty by permitting captured enemy forces to challenge alleged treaty violations in the courts.

Article 1 of the 1949 version of the Convention clarified that it was the duty of every party to the Convention not only to adhere to the Convention itself, but also to ensure

---

[8] Petitioner suggests that the alternative holding of *Eisentrager* was undone by *Rasul* v. *Bush*, 542 U.S. 466 (2004). In *Rasul*, however, the Court considered only the "narrow" question of whether statutory habeas jurisdiction existed, *id.* at 470; it did not address the enforceability of the Geneva Convention or any aspect of *Eisentrager*'s alternative holding on the merits. As the court of appeals concluded, therefore, "[t]his aspect of *Eisentrager* is still good law" and demands our adherence." . . . .

compliance by every other party. Compare 1949 Convention art. 1, 6 U.S.T. at 3318, 75 U.N.T.S. at 136 ("[The parties] undertake to respect and to ensure respect for the present Convention in all circumstances."), with 1929 Convention art. 82, 47 Stat. 2059, 118 L.N.T.S. at 391 ("[The] Convention shall be respected *** in all circumstances."). It does not follow from the fact that the Convention established a duty for *peer nations* to ensure enforcement through political and diplomatic channels, however, that the Convention created a right to enforcement by *individuals* through the domestic courts.

Article 8 of the 1949 version provides that the Convention is to be "applied with the cooperation and under the scrutiny of the Protecting Powers." 6 U.S.T. at 3324, 75 U.N.T.S. at 142.[9] Reliance on "protecting powers" was also a feature of the 1929 version. See 1929 Convention art. 86, 47 Stat. 2060, 118 L.N.T.S. at 393. Article 11 of the 1949 version, however, clarified and increased the role of the protecting powers in resolving disagreements. See 1949 Convention art. 11, 6 U.S.T. at 3326, 75 U.N.T.S. at 144 ("[I]n cases of disagreement between the Parties to the conflict as to the application or interpretation of the provisions of the present Convention, the Protecting Powers shall lend their good offices with a view to settling the disagreement."). Article 11 thus created a primary method for resolving disputes relating to application and interpretation of the Convention. See Howard S. Levie, *Prisoners of War in International Armed Conflict*, 59 Int'l L. Stud. 1, 87 (1978).

Article 132 of the 1949 version created another method for resolving disputes. It states that, "[at] the request of a Party to the conflict, an enquiry shall be instituted, in a manner to be decided between the interested Parties, concerning any alleged violation of the Convention." 6 U.S.T. at 3420, 75 U.N.T.S. at 238. Article 132 further states that if "agreement has not been reached concerning the procedure for the enquiry, the Parties should agree on the choice of an umpire who will decide upon the procedure to be followed." *Ibid.* The 1929 version, by contrast, did not provide for the use of an "umpire" to settle disputes. See 1929 Convention art. 87, 47 Stat. 2061, 118 L.N.T.S. at 393. The 1949 version of the Convention thus creates specific additional mechanisms for ensuring enforcement – none of which remotely resembles a legal action brought by a detainee in the courts of the detaining nation.[10] Those enforcement provisions therefore only reinforce the Court's holding in *Eisentrager*.

As this Court noted in *Eisentrager*, a contrary construction of the Geneva Convention would severely encumber the President's authority as Commander in Chief. See 339 U.S. at 779. Indeed, petitioner's argument suggests that the hundreds of thousands of POWs held by the United States in this country during World War II were entitled to enforce the 1929 version of the Convention through private legal actions in our courts. The Executive Branch's construction of the Convention avoids such absurd consequences and is entitled to "great weight." See, *e.g.*, *United States* v. *Stuart*, 489 U.S. 353, 369 (1989); *Sumitomo Shoji Am., Inc.* v. *Avagliano*, 457 U.S. 176, 184–185 (1982).

ii. Petitioner contends . . . that, even if the Geneva Convention does not *itself* create judicially enforceable rights, it is has been made enforceable by a variety of provisions of domestic law. That argument lacks merit.

Petitioner asserts (Br. 37 n.28) that the Convention has been made enforceable by a "policy" statement made by Congress in the Ronald W. Reagan National Defense

---

[9] In recent times, the role of the "protecting power" has been performed by the International Committee of the Red Cross. In 1949, it was typically performed by a neutral State.

[10] Notably, the negotiators of the 1949 version of the Convention considered, but ultimately rejected, a proposal to confer jurisdiction on the International Court of Justice to interpret or apply the Convention. International Committee of the Red Cross, *Commentary to the Geneva Convention Relative to the Treatment of Prisoners of War* 126–127 (1960) (ICRC Commentary).

Authorization Act for Fiscal Year 2005 (NDAA), Pub. L. No. 108–375, 118 Stat. 1811. Such "sense of Congress" statements, however, create no enforceable federal rights. See, *e.g.*, *Yang* v. *California Dep't of Soc. Servs.*, 183 F.3d 953, 958–961 (9th Cir. 1999); *Monahan* v. *Dorchester Counseling Ctr., Inc.*, 961 F.2d 987, 994–995 (1st Cir. 1992). Moreover, the policy statement at issue simply reaffirms the acknowledged obligations *of the United States* under the Geneva Convention; it says nothing about the availability of a cause of action for individuals in the domestic courts in the event there is a violation of those obligations. See NDAA §1091(b)(4), 118 Stat. 2069.

Petitioner next relies (Br. 38 n.29) on Army regulations concerning the implementation of the Geneva Convention by Army personnel. By their own terms, however, those regulations do not extend any substantive rights; instead, they merely establish internal policies. See, *e.g.*, U.S. Dep't of the Army et al., Regulation 190–8, *Enemy Prisoners of War, Retained Personnel, Civilian Internees and Other Detainees* para. 1-1(a) (Nov. 1, 1997) (Army Regulation 190–8). And, of course, it would be quite remarkable to construe an Army regulation to create rights for enemy combatants that can be enforced in *civilian* courts. In any event, the CSRT determined that petitioner is a combatant, thus resolving the only "POW" claim petitioner raised below. As the court of appeals noted, moreover, petitioner may advance his POW claim at trial before the military commission. . . . .

Petitioner asserts . . . that his Geneva Convention claim is enforceable through 10 U.S.C. 821, which recognizes the jurisdiction of military commissions over "offenders or offenses that by statute or by the law of war may be tried by military commissions." That provision, however, was originally included in the Articles of War in 1916; it therefore could not "implement" or "execute" a treaty that was ratified only in 1956. Moreover, as we have explained, that provision by its terms provides authority, rather than restricting it. It was not intended to limit the President's authority to use military commissions in any manner, but rather to *preserve* his longstanding authority to place before military commissions persons who, like petitioner, are charged with offenses against the law of war. In any event, a statutory reference to the "law of war," without more, especially in an authorizing provision, cannot render judicially enforceable a treaty that does not by its terms create judicially enforceable rights. Cf. *Sosa* v. *Alvarez-Machain*, 542 U.S. 692, 714 (2004) (holding that statute referring to the "law of nations" was jurisdictional and did not create cause of action).[11]

Finally, petitioner argues . . . that the habeas corpus statute, 28 U.S.C. 2241, renders the Geneva Convention enforceable. As the court of appeals recognized, however, that argument is squarely foreclosed by *Eisentrager*, which rejected a habeas action brought by prisoners seeking to enforce the Convention. . . . . Like the federal-question statute, 28 U.S.C. 1331, the habeas statute merely confers jurisdiction and does not create any substantive rights. See, *e.g.*, *Bowrin* v. *INS*, 194 F.3d 483, 489 (4th Cir. 1999); *Jimenez* v. *Aristeguieta*, 311 F.2d 547, 557 n.6 (5th Cir. 1962), cert. denied, 373 U.S. 914 (1963). Although the habeas statute refers to "treaties," that reference does not render all treaties judicially enforceable any more than the federal-question statute's reference to "treaties" does.[12] Unsurprisingly, every court of appeals to have considered the question has

---

[11] Petitioner's reliance . . . on the canon of construction that "an act of Congress ought never to be construed to violate the law of nations if any other possible construction remains," *Murray* v. *Schooner Charming Betsy*, 6 U.S. (2 Cranch) 64, 118 (1804), is also misplaced. Petitioner's military commission has been established in accordance with the law of nations. In any event, this Court has never applied the *Charming Betsy* canon to invalidate a presidential action that was taken in express reliance on a federal statute and involves the exercise of the President's core authority as Commander in Chief.

[12] *Wildenhus's Case*, 120 U.S. 1 (1887), is not to the contrary. In that case, the Court affirmed the denial of a writ of habeas corpus involving a claim based on a consular treaty between the United States and Belgium.

rejected the argument that the habeas statute allows for enforcement of treaties that do not themselves create judicially enforceable rights. See *Poindexter* v. *Nash*, 333 F.3d 372 (2d Cir. 2003), cert. denied, 540 U.S. 1210 (2004); *Wesson* v. *United States Penitentiary Beaumont*, 305 F.3d 343 (5th Cir. 2002), cert. denied, 537 U.S. 1241 (2003); *Hain* v. *Gibson*, 287 F.3d 1224 (10th Cir. 2002), cert. denied, 537 U.S. 1173 (2003); *United States ex rel. Perez* v. *Warden*, 286 F.3d 1059 (8th Cir.), cert. denied, 537 U.S. 869 (2002). Petitioner has provided no basis for this Court to depart from that settled understanding.[13]

b. *Petitioner has no valid claim under the Convention in any event*

i. Even if the Geneva Convention were judicially enforceable, it is inapplicable to the ongoing conflict with al Qaeda and thus does not assist petitioner. The President has determined that the Geneva Convention does not "apply to our conflict with al Qaeda in Afghanistan or elsewhere throughout the world because, among other reasons, al Qaeda is not a High Contracting Party to [the Convention]." .... The President further determined that, "because [the Convention] does not apply to our conflict with al Qaeda, al Qaeda detainees also do not qualify as prisoners of war." .... The President's determination represents a classic exercise of his war powers and his authority over foreign affairs more generally, see *Curtiss-Wright*, 299 U.S. at 320; was made in accordance with Congress's resolution authorizing the use of force; and is binding on the courts, see *Banco Nacional de Cuba* v. *Sabbatino*, 376 U.S. 398, 410 (1964); *Chicago & S. Air Lines, Inc.* v. *Waterman S.S. Corp.*, 333 U.S. 103, 111 (1948).

The decision whether the Geneva Convention applies to a terrorist network like al Qaeda is akin to the decision whether a foreign government has sufficient control over an area to merit recognition or whether a foreign state has ratified a treaty. In each case, the decision is solely for the Executive. See *Doe* v. *Braden*, 57 U.S. (16 How.) 635, 657 (1853) (noting that "it would be impossible for the executive department of the government to conduct our foreign relations with any advantage to the country, and fulfill the duties which the Constitution has imposed upon it, if every court in the country was authorized to inquire and decide whether the person who ratified the treaty on behalf of a foreign nation had the power, by its constitution and laws, to make the engagements into which he entered").

Even if some judicial review of the President's determination were appropriate, moreover, the standard of review would surely be extraordinarily deferential to the President. And, under any standard, the President's determination is manifestly correct. Article 2 provides that the Convention is applicable to "all cases of declared war or of

---

The Court did not purport to hold that treaty rights are privately enforceable in habeas, and *Wildenhus's Case* sheds no light on the question whether the Geneva Convention, a treaty that implicates the President's core Commander-in-Chief powers, may be privately enforced in habeas. The other cases on which petitioner relies are similarly unavailing. In *Ogbudimkpa* v. *Ashcroft*, 342F.3d 207 (2003), the Third Circuit expressly declined to consider an argument similar to that advanced by petitioner. See *id.* at 218 n.22. In *Wang* v. *Ashcroft*, 320 F.3d 130 (2003), the Second Circuit allowed a habeas petitioner to enforce rights created not by a treaty, but by statute. See *id.* at 140–141.

[13] Moreover, in enacting the DTA, Congress has removed any basis for arguing that the habeas statute provides a mechanism for enforcing the Geneva Convention. Congress has replaced habeas jurisdiction with an exclusive review mechanism that, in contrast to the habeas statute it displaced, omits treaty-based challenges. See DTA §1005(e)(2)(C)(ii) and (3)(D)(ii), 119 Stat. 2742, 2743. That action would preclude claims even under treaties that, unlike the Geneva Convention, give rise to judicially enforceable individual rights, and is clearly inconsistent with any notion that Congress acted to make the Geneva Convention applicable to al Qaeda, let alone in any judicially enforceable manner. Likewise, the system of judicial review that Congress established presupposes that CSRTs will obviate any treaty-based claim to an essentially duplicative Article 5 tribunal. See DTA §1005(e)(2), 119 Stat. 2742.

any other armed conflict which may arise between two or more of the High Contracting Parties" or of armed conflict between a High Contracting Party and a "Power[] in conflict" that is not a High Contracting Party insofar as it "accepts and applies the provisions" of the Convention. 6 U.S.T. at 3318, 75 U.N.T.S. at 136. Al Qaeda indisputably is *not* a "High Contracting Party" that has ratified the Geneva Convention. Nor can al Qaeda qualify as a "Power[] in conflict" that could benefit from the Convention. The term "Power" refers to States that would be capable of ratifying treaties such as the Convention – something that a terrorist organization like al Qaeda cannot do.[14] And even if al Qaeda could be thought of as a "Power" within the meaning of the Convention, it has not "accept[ed] and applie[d] the provisions" of the Convention, but has instead openly flouted them by acting in flagrant defiance of the law of armed conflict. As a result, al Qaeda and its members are not entitled to the Convention's protections. A contrary interpretation would discourage States from joining and honoring the Convention.[15]

Petitioner observes . . . that he was captured in Afghanistan and that Afghanistan, unlike al Qaeda, is a party to the Geneva Convention. But the Convention does not apply based on where a particular conflict occurs, or a particular combatant is captured. Instead, Article 2 specifies that the Convention "shall apply to all cases of declared war or of any other armed conflict which may arise *between two or more of the High Contracting Parties*." 6 U.S.T. at 3318, 75 U.N.T.S. at 136 (emphasis added). Because the United States and Afghanistan are both "High Contracting Parties," the President determined that the Convention could potentially apply to Afghanistan's Taliban regime. . . . . It does not follow, however, that the Convention would cover al Qaeda combatants who happen to be located in Afghanistan, because the conflict between the United States and al Qaeda is discrete and different from the conflict between the United States and the Taliban (and because al Qaeda is not a "High Contracting Party" or "Power" for purposes of Article 2). For the reasons discussed above, the question whether there is one conflict or two is precisely the kind of foreign-policy judgment that is committed to the President's discretion.

ii. Even if this Court were to conclude (notwithstanding the President's determination) that the Convention is applicable to al Qaeda, petitioner's trial by military commission would not violate the substantive terms of the Convention. Petitioner relies . . . on Article 102 of the Convention, which provides that "[a] prisoner of war can be validly sentenced only if the sentence has been pronounced by the same courts according to the same procedure as in the case of members of the armed forces of the Detaining Power." 6 U.S.T. at 3394, 75 U.N.T.S. at 212.

---

[14] See, *e.g.*, G.I.A.D. Draper, *The Red Cross Conventions* 16 (1958) (arguing that "in the context of Article 2, para. 3, 'Powers' means States capable then and there of becoming Contracting Parties to these Conventions either by ratification or by accession"); 2B Final Record of the Diplomatic Conference of Geneva of 1949, at 108 (explaining that Article 2, para. 3, would impose an "obligation to recognize that the Convention be applied to the non-Contracting adverse State, in so far as the latter accepted and applied the provisions thereof").

[15] The conclusion that the Convention does not apply to conflicts with a terrorist network like al Qaeda is underscored by the fact that the United States has refused to ratify protocols that would extend the Geneva Convention to other types of conflicts and combatants. See Protocol Additional to the Geneva Conventions of 12 August 1949, and Relating to the Protection of Victims of International Armed Conflicts (Protocol I), June 8, 1977, 1125 U.N.T.S. 3; Protocol Additional to the Geneva Conventions of 12 August 1949, and Relating to the Protection of Victims of Non-International Armed Conflicts (Protocol II), June 8, 1977, 1125 U.N.T.S. 609. In transmitting those protocols to Congress, President Reagan expressed concern, *inter alia*, that one of the protocols would "grant combatant status to irregular forces even if they do not satisfy the traditional requirements to distinguish themselves from the civilian population and otherwise comply with the laws of war" and would thereby "endanger civilians among whom terrorists and other irregulars attempt to conceal themselves." S. Treaty Doc. No. 2, 100th Cong., 1st Sess. iv (1987).

Article 102, however, applies only to a "prisoner of war." And petitioner does not qualify as a POW for purposes of Article 102 because he does not meet the requirements set out in Article 4 for POW status. The relevant subsection, Article 4(A)(2), provides that members of militias or volunteer corps are eligible for POW status only if the *group* in question displays "a fixed distinctive sign," "carr[ies] arms openly," and "conduct[s] [its] operations in accordance with the laws and customs of war." 6 U.S.T. at 3320, 75 U.N.T.S. at 138. "[T]he widely accepted view" is that, "if the group does not meet the first three criteria *** [an] individual member cannot qualify for privileged status as a POW." W. Thomas Mallison & Sally V. Mallison, *The Juridical Status of Irregular Combatants Under the International Humanitarian Law of Armed Conflict*, 9 Case W. Res. J. Int'l L. 39, 62 (1977); see, *e.g.*, *United States* v. *Lindh*, 212 F. Supp. 2d 541, 552 n.16, 558 n.39 (E.D. Va. 2002) (noting that "[w]hat matters for determination of lawful combatant status is not whether Lindh personally violated the laws and customs of war, but whether the Taliban did so," and that "there is no plausible claim of lawful combatant immunity in connection with al Qaeda membership").[16] A1 Qaeda does not remotely satisfy those criteria.[17]

Petitioner contends (Br. 36–37, 45 n.35) that his assertion of POW status is itself sufficient to establish "doubt" as to whether he is a POW, and that he must be treated as a POW until a tribunal constituted under Article 5 of the Convention eliminates that doubt. In relevant part, Article 5 provides that, "[s]hould any doubt arise as to whether persons, having committed a belligerent act and having fallen into the hands of the enemy, belong to any of the categories enumerated in Article 4, such persons shall enjoy the protection of the present Convention until such time as their status has been determined by a competent tribunal." 6 U.S.T. at 3324, 75 U.N.T.S. at 142. In this case, however, the CSRT process, which clearly discharges any obligation under Article 5, has removed any conceivable doubt by confirming prior military determinations and finding that petitioner is an enemy combatant who is a member or affiliate of al Qaeda. . . . .[18]

---

[16] In previous conflicts, the United States has made group status determinations concerning captured enemy combatants. See, *e.g.*, Levie, *supra*, at 61 (World War II).

[17] Petitioner suggests for the first time (Br. 45 n.35) that, even if he does not constitute a POW under Article 4(A)(2) because al Qaeda does not satisfy the specified criteria, he is a POW under Article 4(A)(1) because he is a "[m]ember of the armed forces of a Party to the conflict" or a "member of [the] militia[] or volunteer corps forming part of such armed forces," or a POW under Article 4(A)(4) because he is a "person who accompan[ies] the armed forces without actually being [a] member[ ]." 6 U.S.T. at 3320, 75 U.N.T.S. at 138. Those claims have been forfeited because they were not raised in the court of appeals. Moreover, the Article 4(A)(1) claim assumes facts that contradict the factual assertions he has previously made, . . . and the Article 4(A)(4) claim is refuted by the CSRT finding that petitioner is an enemy combatant. Petitioner's claims fail for the additional reason that the concept of "armed forces" in Article 4(A)(1) and (A)(4) appears to presuppose that the criteria set out in Article 4(A)(2) are satisfied. See ICRC Commentary 62–63.

[18] The CSRT was patterned after the "competent tribunal" described in Geneva Convention Article 5 and Army Regulation 190–8 (cited favorably in *Hamdi*, 542 U.S. at 538 (plurality opinion)), but provides more process. See 151 Cong. Rec. S12,754 (daily ed. Nov. 14, 2005) (statement of Sen. Graham) (observing that the CSRT system "is Geneva Convention article 5 tribunals on steroids"). In proceedings before the CSRT, petitioner was entitled to call reasonably available witnesses, to question other witnesses, to testify or otherwise address the tribunal, and not to testify if he so chose. Petitioner was additionally entitled to a decision, by the preponderance of the evidence, by commissioned officers sworn to execute their duties impartially, and to review by the Staff Judge Advocate for legal sufficiency. See Memorandum from Gordon England, Secretary of the Navy, Regarding the Implementation of CSRT Procedures for Enemy Combatants Detained at Guantanamo (July 29, 2004) <http://www.defenselink.mil/news/Ju12004/d20040730comb.pdf>. In addition, unlike an Article 5 or Army Regulation 190–8 tribunal, the CSRT guaranteed petitioner the rights to have a personal representative for assistance in preparing his case, to receive an unclassified summary of the evidence before the hearing, and to introduce relevant documentary evidence.

E.   Petitioner Does Not Enjoy The Protections Of Our Constitution

Petitioner's argument that the President lacks the authority to convene a military commission to try and punish him for his alleged war crimes fails for the many independent reasons discussed above. Because that argument is predicated on the proposition . . . that the Constitution places structural limits on the President's authority to convene military commissions, however, it fails for an additional, even more fundamental reason. As an alien enemy combatant detained outside the United States, petitioner does not enjoy the protections of our Constitution. See Reply Br. in Support of Mot. to Dismiss for Lack of Jurisdiction 18–20.

III. PETITIONER'S PROCEDURAL OBJECTIONS TO HIS MILITARY COMMISSION ARE UNFOUNDED

A.   The Procedures Established For Petitioner's Military Commission Do Not Contravene The UCMJ

Petitioner argues . . . that the UCMJ requires that any military commission proceeding must conform to the rules for courts-martial.[19] He relies on Article 36(a) of the UCMJ, 10 U.S.C. 836(a), which authorizes the President to promulgate regulations establishing procedures for military commissions and states that such regulations "shall, so far as [the President] considers practicable, apply the principles of law and the rules of evidence generally recognized in the trial of criminal cases in the United States district courts, but *** may not be contrary to or inconsistent with this chapter." In petitioner's view, Article 36(a) necessarily implies that the rules the President chooses to promulgate for military commissions must be consistent with the rules set out in other provisions of the UCMJ for courts-martial. That is manifestly incorrect.

Petitioner's theory rests on a fundamental misunderstanding of the UCMJ. The UCMJ is directed almost exclusively to establishing the rules for courts-martial. The UCMJ does not purport to establish comprehensive procedures for military commissions, which are preserved by the UCMJ as "our common-law war courts" with a distinct tradition that dates from the earliest days of the Republic. The UCMJ takes pains to distinguish between "military commissions" or "military tribunals," on the one hand, and "courts-martial," on the other, using these distinct terms to connote discrete, rather than equivalent, types of tribunals. In fact, only nine of the statute's 158 articles even mention military commissions and specify particular safeguards that must be provided in military commissions as well as in the more comprehensively regulated courts-martial. See 10 U.S.C. 821, 828, 836, 847–850, 904, 906. If military commissions must replicate all of the procedures employed in courts-martial, it is not at all clear why Congress bothered to preserve them.

Madsen confirms that the UCMJ provisions governing courts-martial do not extend to military commissions. In *Madsen*, the Court upheld the trial by military commission of a person who was also subject to court-martial jurisdiction under the Articles of War. In doing so, the Court made clear that the Articles of War did not apply to a trial by military commission. The Court described military commissions as "our common-law war courts" and observed that "[n]either their procedure nor their jurisdiction has

---

[19] As a preliminary matter, it is not appropriate to consider objections to the procedures governing the military commissions before the commission has even applied them to petitioner. The DTA expressly authorizes detainees to raise such challenges following a final adverse decision. See §1005(e)(3), 119 Stat. 2743.

been prescribed by statute." 343 U.S. at 346–347. Rather, the Court noted, the military commission "has been adapted in each instance to the need that called it forth." *Id.* at 347–348. The Court further explained that, in contrast to its active regulation of "the jurisdiction and procedure of United States courts-martial," Congress had shown "evident restraint" with respect to the regulation of military commissions. *Id.* at 349. The Court concluded that, "[i]n the absence of attempts by Congress to limit the President's power," the President "may, in time of war, establish and prescribe the jurisdiction and procedure of military commissions." *Id.* at 348; see *Quirin*, 317 U.S. at 30 (noting that Congress rejected option of "crystallizing in permanent form and in minute detail every offense" triable by commissions and instead "adopt[ed] the system of common law applied by the military tribunals").[20]

Petitioner suggests (Br. 19–20 n.10) that regulations and historical practice "confirm that commissions follow courtmartial rules." He quotes a portion of the preamble to the Manual for Courts Martial, which states that "military commissions *** shall be guided by the appropriate principles of law and rules of procedure and evidence prescribed for courts-martial." See Manual for Courts-Martial, pt. 1, para. 2(b)(2), at I.1 (2005). That captures roughly half the common sense of the matter. Of course, military commissions, which tend to be an episodic response to particular conflicts, borrow from the permanent procedures for courts-martial where appropriate. But as the omitted introductory clause of the sentence petitioner quotes makes clear, the President may tailor those procedures to the current exigency, and so the procedures are "[s]ubject to *** any regulations prescribed by the President or by other competent authority." *Ibid.*[21]

More generally, petitioner's assertion that military commissions historically have been *required* to follow rules for courts-martial is incorrect. It is settled that military commissions "will not be rendered illegal by the omission of details required upon trials by court-martial" (and that the rules for commissions may by regulation depart from those of courts-martial). Winthrop, *supra*, at 841. Thus, while military tribunals "should observe, as nearly as may be consistently with their purpose," the rules of procedure of courts-martial, conformance to those rules "is not obligatory," and military commissions were "not bound by the Articles of War." William E. Birkhimer, *Military Government and Martial Law* 533–535 (3d ed. 1914); see Richard S. Hartigan, *Lieber's Code and the Law of War* 47–48 (1983). The *Quirin* precedent illustrates these points. See Louis Fisher, Congressional Research Service, *Military Tribunals: The Quirin Precedent* 8 (Mar. 26, 2002) <http:// www.fas.org/irp/crs/RL31340.pdf> (*Quirin* commission "adopted a three-and-a-half page" statement of rules with language providing that "[t]he commission

---

[20] Although *Madsen* interpreted the Articles of War (notwithstanding the fact that UCMJ had already been enacted, see 343 U.S. at 345 n.6), the relevant provisions of the UCMJ are identical in all material respects to their counterparts in the Articles of War. Compare Articles of War arts. 15 and 38, 39 Stat. 653, 656, with UCMJ arts. 21 and 36, 10 U.S.C. 821, 836.

[21] Petitioner asserts . . . that, during World War II, the United States took the position that "conducting a commission without the participation of the accused was a punishable violation of the laws of war." Petitioner may personally be present at every stage of the trial before his military commission, however, except if he engages in disruptive conduct or the prosecution introduces classified or otherwise protected information. 32 C.F.R. 9.5(k); Military Commission Order No. 1, §6(B)(3) and (D)(5)(b). Those exceptions, moreover, are surely permissible. See Charter of the International Tribunal, Aug. 8, 1945, art. 12, 59 Stat. 1548, 82 U.N.T.S. 290 (authorizing trial of defendant in his absence "in the interests of justice"). International tribunals, like domestic courts, permit trial proceedings in the defendant's absence if he engages in disruptive conduct. See, *e.g.*, International Criminal Tribunal for Former Yugoslavia R.P. & Evid. 80. Equally compelling reasons support the rule permitting the exclusion of the defendant when the prosecution is introducing classified or otherwise protected information for which no adequate substitute is available and whose admission will not deprive the defendant of a full and fair trial. . . . . And there is certainly no basis to presume, before the trial has even commenced, that the trial will not be conducted in good faith and according to law.

could *** discard procedures from the Articles of War or the *Manual for Courts-Martial* whenever it wanted to.").

Congress enacted the UCMJ against the backdrop of this historical practice and understanding regarding the commonlaw role of the military commission. See *Uniform Code of Military Justice: Hearings Before the Subcomm. No. 1 of the House Comm. on Armed Services on H.R. 2498*, 81st Cong., 1st Sess. 1017 (1949) (statement of Robert Smart, Professional Staff Member of Subcommittee) ("We are not prescribing rules of procedure for military commissions here. This only pertains to courts martial."). The UCMJ predominantly addresses only courts-martial, with an eye toward providing a particular form of process to members of the United States armed forces. It would defeat the plain language, structure, and history of the UCMJ to read into the numerous provisions that on their face regulate only courts-martial an intent to regulate, much less all but eliminate, military commissions.[22]

B. Article 3 of the Geneva Convention Does Not Apply To Petitioner's Military Commission

Finally, petitioner argues . . . that the procedures governing his military commission do not comport with the requirements of Article 3 of the Geneva Convention.[23] As a preliminary matter, that contention fails because the Geneva Convention is not judicially enforceable. In any event, Article 3 by its plain terms does not apply to the ongoing conflict with al Qaeda. Article 3 applies only "[i]n the case of armed conflict *not of an international character* occurring in the territory of *one* of the High Contracting Parties" (emphasis added). As the President determined, because the conflict between the United States and al Qaeda has taken place and is ongoing in several countries, the conflict is "of an international character," and Article 3 is thus inapplicable. . . . . Once again, the President's determination is dispositive or, at a minimum, entitled to great weight. . . . .

The International Committee of the Red Cross (ICRC) commentary for the Geneva Convention confirms the President's determination. The commentary explains that the article "applies to non-international conflicts only." ICRC, *Commentary to the Geneva Convention Relative to the Treatment of Prisoners of War* 34 (1960). "Speaking generally, it must be recognized that the conflicts referred to in Article 3 are armed conflicts, *** which are in many respects similar to an international war, but take place *within the confines of a single country.*" *Id.* at 37 (emphasis added).[24]

---

[22] Petitioner further contends (Br. 21 n.12) that the military commission's rule permitting the admission of evidence if it has "probative value to a reasonable person" conflicts with Article 36(a) of the UCMJ, 10 U.S.C. 836(a), because that article embraces the Federal Rules of Evidence. But Article 36(a) expressly authorizes the President to depart from those rules if "he considers" their application not "practicable." Pursuant to that authority, the President has made a finding that "it is not practicable to apply in military commissions" the Federal Rules of Evidence because of "the danger to the safety of the United States and the nature of international terrorism." Military Order §1(f). In addition, the military commission's evidentiary standard is the same one commonly used by international tribunals. See, *e.g.*, ICTY R.P. & Evid. 89(C).

[23] Article 3 is sometimes known as "Common Article 3" because it is contained in other Geneva Conventions (on which petitioner does not rely) besides the Geneva Convention Relative to the Treatment of Prisoners of War. See Geneva Convention for the Amelioration of the Conditions of the Wounded and Sick in Armed Forces in the Field, Aug. 12, 1949, art. 3, 6 U.S.T. 3114, 75 U.N.T.S. 31; Geneva Convention for the Amelioration of the Conditions of the Wounded and Sick and Shipwrecked Members of Armed Forces at Sea, Aug. 12, 1949, art. 3, 6 U.S.T. 3217, 75 U.N.T.S. 85, Geneva Convention Relative to the Protection of Civilian Persons in Time of War, Aug. 12, 1949, art. 3, 6 U.S.T. 3516, 75 U.N.T.S. 287.

[24] Judge Williams's contrary view . . . not only conflicts with the text of Article 3 and the ICRC Commentary, but also with the provision's drafting history. The ICRC's draft version provided that Article 3 would apply to armed conflicts "not of an international character, *** which may occur in the territory of one *or more* of

Petitioner relies on *Kadic* v. *Karadzic*, 70 F.3d 232 (2d Cir. 1995), which held that Article 3 "binds parties to internal conflicts" even if they are not States. *Id.* at 243. That case, however, did not consider the applicability of Article 3 to a conflict that is *not* internal to a single State, such as that between the United States and al Qaeda. As the court of appeals explained in this case, such a conflict may reasonably be described as being "of an international character" and therefore outside the scope of Article 3.....[25]

In any event, petitioner's military commission complies with Article 3. In relevant part, Article 3 prohibits "[t]he passing of sentences and the carrying out of executions without previous judgment pronounced by a regularly constituted court affording all the judicial guarantees which are recognized as indispensable by civilized peoples." 6 U.S.T. at 3320, 75 U.N.T.S. at 138. Petitioner's military commission, governed by the extensive procedural protections set out in 32 C.F.R. Part 9, and subject to judicial review under the DTA, readily meets this standard. And the longstanding statutory recognition of the military commission as a legitimate body to try violations of the law of war and the repeated use of commissions throughout this Nation's history further refute petitioner's contention that the commission is not a regularly constituted court, as well as refuting his broader contention that use of a military commission is not authorized.

CONCLUSION

The writ of certiorari should be dismissed for lack of jurisdiction. In the alternative, the judgment of the court of appeals should be affirmed.

. . .

---

the High Contracting Parties." ICRC Commentary 31 (emphasis added). The fact that the final text excluded the phrase "or more" confirms that Article 3 does not extend beyond civil wars and domestic insurgency movements wholly internal to a single State.

[25] Petitioner also claims . . . that certain international tribunals have held that the standards set out in Article 3 apply in all conflicts as customary international law. That disregards the text of Article 3. And, in any event, such customary international law cannot override a controlling executive act, such as the President's Military Order in this case. See *The Paquete Habana*, 175 U.S. 677, 700 (1900) (holding that customary international law applies where there is "no controlling executive or legislative act or judicial decision").

No. 05-184

IN THE

Supreme Court of the United States

SALIM AHMED HAMDAN,
Petitioner,

v.

DONALD RUMSFELD ET AL.,
Respondents.

**On Writ of Certiorari to the
United States Court of Appeals
for the District of Columbia Circuit**

REPLY BRIEF FOR THE PETITIONER

Lt. Cdr. Charles Swift
Office of Military
Commissions

Neal Katyal
(Counsel of Record)

Thomas C. Goldstein
Amy Howe
Kevin K. Russell
GOLDSTEIN & HOWE, P.C.

Harry H. Schneider, Jr.
Joseph M. McMillan
Charles C. Sipos
PERKINS COIE LLP

March 2006

. . .

---

* Redactions on this page have been added for privacy purposes. – *Eds.*

REPLY BRIEF FOR PETITIONER

Reduced to its essence, the government's argument is that the federal judiciary has no real power to review actions taken by the President in the name of fighting terrorism. The Court should reject that proposition, as it did two years ago in *Hamdi v. Rumsfeld*, 542 U.S. 507 (2004), and *Rasul v. Bush*, 542 U.S. 466 (2004), and earlier in *Youngstown Sheet & Tube Co. v. Sawyer*, 343 U.S. 579 (1952), and *Ex parte Milligan*, 71 U.S. 2 (1866).[1] Here, the President seeks not merely to detain temporarily but to dispense life imprisonment and death through a judicial system of his own design. Anyone, anytime, may be swept into this system and forced to endure years of waiting before their cases are even heard.

This jerrybuilt tribunal is not, the President claims, constrained by the Constitution . . . , the statutory rules for courts-martial . . . , or even the most rudimentary protections of the laws of war. . . . Instead, when we are in "this context" . . . – a state of being determined by the President . . . – the governing rule is that he alone has the final say. The President's assertion of absolute dominion over human subjects and trial and punishment cannot be reconciled with the constitutional checks vested in Congress by Article I, and in the courts by Article III.[2]

"[T]he Framers harbored a deep distrust of executive military power and military tribunals." *Loving v. United States*, 517 U.S. 748, 760 (1996). The President cannot avoid that constitutional heritage through the legerdemain of titling an adjudicatory body a "commission," in an attempt to claim the power, *inter alia*, to admit testimony obtained by torture,[3] eliminate the right to be present . . . , and charge offenses that do not violate the laws of war, all in a conflict of indefinite geographic scope and duration.

In fact, the President already has broad power to detain and try Hamdan – but not in the lawless, autocratic, ever-shifting way he seeks to do here. The President can charge Hamdan with a violation of the laws of war stemming from the U.S. conflict with Afghanistan. Those laws of war apply to Hamdan because he was captured in that conflict, and they also vest him with rights under the GPW. (Such war-crimes charges can be brought in a court martial, 10 U.S.C. 818; a civilian court, 18 U.S.C. 2241; or a properly constituted military commission.) Likewise, the President can charge Hamdan with a violation enumerated in Common Article 3, under which Hamdan is protected because it sets a minimal baseline for even stateless conflicts. But Hamdan is *not* being prosecuted under that Article, *nor* is he being prosecuted for a crime occurring from the Afghani conflict. Instead, this case arises from a charge, concocted for an undefined "separate" conflict, unknown to the laws of war and to the long history of commissions.

The longstanding restrictions on commissions are not such disposable niceties. Rather, they are time-tested barriers to the dangerous seepage of martial law into our civilian order. To fail to enforce these limits would be to allow a dangerous and unprecedented expansion of Executive authority whose legal premise must be that the fight against terrorism justifies a reallocation of constitutional power. There would be no principled way to prevent that precedent from becoming the edifice upon which any

---

[1] *See United States v. Bollman*, 24 F. Cas. 1189 (C.C.D.D.C. 1807) (pre-trial habeas case, wherein Chief Judge Cranch stated: "[W]hen wars, and rumors of wars, plots, conspiracies and treasons excite alarm, it is the duty of a court to be peculiarly watchful lest the public feeling should reach the seat of justice . . . although we may thereby bring one criminal to punishment, we may furnish the means by which an hundred innocent persons may suffer. The constitution was made for times of commotion.").

[2] The government stresses the "protections" afforded to Hamdan in Pentagon Military Order No. 1, but it fails to mention that the Order specifies that the protections are neither "enforceable" nor "rights." Pet. 2.

[3] The Pentagon recently confirmed, as *Amicus Br. Human Rights First et al.* warned, commission rules "allow for" "evidence gained through torture." Carol Rosenberg, *Hearings May Consider Torture*, MIAMI HER., Mar. 2, 2006.

number of actions could be grounded, even against U.S. citizens, from surveillance to indefinite detention, on the mere allegation that they are affiliates in that "war." If fighting terrorism requires such a basic shift in our legal order, it is for Congress, not the Executive, to say so; and Congress must say so in the most explicit of terms.

. . .

II. Hamdan's Commission Is Unauthorized

The inescapable fact is that the conflict with al Qaeda is not equivalent to the only war in which this Court approved commissions. Congress has not declared war; the laws of war have not been extended to these nonstate, nonterritorial actors; the conflict is in its fifth year; and Congress stands ready to act. So far, Congress has only authorized "force," conditioning even that grant by requiring it to be "necessary and appropriate" to promote specific (not general) deterrence. Pet. Br. 14–18; *Amicus Br. of Generals Brahms and Cullen* (Brahms Br.) 10–29. The Court need not decide whether these differences with World War II are sufficient to prohibit *all* commissions since *Hamdan's* commission is impermissible. Only if the Court rejected this limited position would it be necessary to confront the broader question of whether commissions as a whole are authorized today.

1.   *The DTA Did Not "expressly recogniz[e] and ratif[y]" Hamdan's Commission.* . . . .

Citing neither the DTA itself nor precedent, the government claims that the DTA ratified the commissions. But the statute is in fact silent on that question; it conspicuously avoids referring to the President's November 13 Order. The Act concerned only the federal courts, and not a single word of its text, or even the *post hoc* colloquy and briefing by Senators Graham and Kyl, suggest otherwise.[6] The DTA did establish a procedure to challenge the latest DOD Order – hardly a ratifying action. Instead, the DTA explicitly stated in §1005(e)(3)(D) and §1005(f) that it would not even take a position on whether the Constitution and laws apply. It is unthinkable that the momentous decision to approve the first military commissions in a half-century would have been made without a single word to that effect – particularly when two of the co-sponsors for over a month (and many other Senators) said the opposite.[7] *See Gooding v. United States*, 416 U.S. 430, 457–58 (1974) ("congressional silence . . . is not easy to interpret [and] it would be unusual for such a significant change as that proposed . . . to have entirely escaped notice").

. . .

2.   *Hamdan's Commission Transgresses Statutory Limits.* . . . .

a. The Laws of War Do Not Apply to this Stateless, Nonterritorial Conflict. The government acknowledges that Hamdan is not a traditional war-crimes defendant. It does not allege that he is a soldier in a nation's armed forces, as in *Quirin* and *Yamashita*, nor does it allege his membership in a rebel group in civil war, as in *Milligan*.

---

[6] Senator Graham and Kyl's *amicus* brief suggests that their December 21 colloquy took place on the Senate floor. . . . A C-SPAN recording of the Senate debate on the Conference Report, however, shows that the colloquy was inserted in the Record after the fact. The recording is at http://www.hamdanvrumsfeld.com/C-Span-12-21-05-T3.mpg, and counsel has verified it with individuals present in the chamber at the time.

[7] . . .

It alleges, instead, that Hamdan conspired with a terrorist group to commit crimes that have, heretofore, been the subject of criminal trials in civil courts (with near-uniform government success).

It is true that Hamdan came into U.S. custody after being captured by bounty hunters in a country in a state of war. But the government does *not* charge him with any offense arising from that conflict. Instead, it asserts that Hamdan conspired with al Qaeda. . . . . The place of apprehension has no relevance to Hamdan's charge. Indeed, the charge would be no different, and the government could still insist on its right to try him before a commission, if he had been arrested by the police in a Chicago airport instead of turned over to the U.S. military in Afghanistan.

By the same token, nothing in the government's argument turns on the fact that petitioner is a non-citizen. Petitioner is subject to trial by commission because he is alleged to belong to a terrorist group. The government has repeatedly insisted that in this context, citizenship makes no difference, and it has asserted the President's right to declare any person (citizen or non-citizen) captured anywhere (Chicago or Afghanistan) to be an "enemy combatant" because of an association with al Qaeda. *See* Govt. Br., *Hamdi*, *supra*, at 24–36; Govt. Br., *Rumsfeld v. Padilla*, 542 U.S. 426 (2004), at 31–32. And while the President has not yet exercised his asserted power to try Americans by commission, the government leaves no doubt that accepting its arguments in this case would confirm the President's power to do so in the future.

Such are the necessary consequences of an uncritical extension of the laws of war to the "war on terror" by simple analogy. The undefined, unlimited, and potentially unending nature of the conflict eliminates pragmatic restraints on military authority that traditionally limit the risk that ordinary Americans and other innocent individuals will be denied civilian trials and relegated to truncated proceedings affording no guarantee of independence or fairness. In the war on terror, there are no uniforms, battle lines or even a general geographic area bounding the conflict and the universe of potential alleged combatants. Because of the nebulous nature of the conflict, many millions could be plausibly accused of being an unlawful combatant. Indeed, the cases that have reached this Court illustrate this point, ranging from persons captured by bounty hunters in Afghanistan to U.S. citizens in Illinois. The government has further acknowledged that it holds in Guantanamo citizens from dozens of nations, ranging from Yemen to Australia.

The laws of war, by contrast, were written with the understanding that 1) there was a physical state to have recourse against (or a rebel group with territory) and 2) there would be an end to the conflict. As this Court has held, the laws of war are to mitigate the harms of war. *See The Prize Cases*, 67 U.S. 635, 667 (1863).[10] Yet the government's claim means that the laws of war do not impose a *single* restriction on the United States' treatment of al Qaeda. This startling result, totally at odds with the entire body of law

---

[10] The government's citation to the *Prize Cases* . . . distorts its meaning by omitting the sentences preceding and following its quotation: "The parties belligerent in a public war are independent *nations*. But it is not necessary to constitute war, that both parties should be acknowledged as independent nations or sovereign States. A war may exist where one of the belligerents, *claims sovereign rights* as against the other." 67 U.S. at 666 (emphasis added). The government also omits the territorial limitation: "When the party in rebellion occupy and hold in a hostile manner a *certain portion of territory* . . . have organized armies; have commenced hostilities against their former sovereign, the world acknowledges them as belligerents, and the contest a war." *Id.* at 666–67 (emphasis added). In those areas, civilian courts are closed. *Id.* at 667. *See also id.* at 690–93 (Nelson, J., dissenting). The Court's deference language was confined to circumstances where such conditions were present. None exists here. Similar problems infect the government's use . . . of INGRID DETTER, THE LAW OF WAR 134 (2d ed. 2000) – as her cited cases make clear.

it purportedly describes, illustrates the fundamental deficiencies with the government's position. Indeed, *Hamdi* limited its holding to the war in Afghanistan, and warned that its understanding of the laws of war may "unravel" if a conflict was sufficiently different. 542 U.S. at 521 (plurality). The government's position here forces that unraveling.

The government's reliance on past law-of-war commissions ignores a key fact: none has been applied to stateless, territory-less actors like al Qaeda.[11] Many groups assert engagement in war, but nations reject such claims.[12]

. . .

b. The Conspiracy Charge Does Not State a Violation. Commissions can only try violations of the laws of war, not domestic offenses. *Quirin* requires the Court to "*first* inquire whether any of the acts charged is an offense against the law of war cognizable before a military tribunal." 317 U.S. at 29 (emphasis added). Conspiracy is not such an offense.[14]

The government rests its argument on the law of conspiracy that it claims existed in 1942. . . . . Whatever the law of conspiracy was then, developments since that time, from Nuremberg and Tokyo to the Rome Statute, have long superceded it. Conspiracy Br. 13–18; 1 THE TOKYO JUDGMENT 31–33 (Roling & Ruter eds. 1977). These iconic treatments *reject* conspiracy as a triable war crime.[15]

Moreover, no federal court, before or after Nuremberg, has ever found, or even implied, that conspiracy is an offense against the laws of war. With good reason. A single nation's practice cannot define the meaning of the laws of war. Conspiracy Br. 6.[16] Federal courts, including *Quirin* itself, have studiously avoided even hinting at recognizing conspiracy. *Id.* at 22–24.[17] Unlike defendants in past commissions,

---

[11] The only potentially contrary example is the Modocs, but that precedent cuts the other way. The Attorney General stated that because the Modocs were a sovereign nation "recognized as independent communities for treaty-making purposes . . . they may properly . . . be held subject to those rules of warfare." 14 Op. A.G. 249, 253 (1873). Al Qaeda, according to the government . . . , cannot negotiate treaties as a sovereign, and cannot be encompassed by the full laws of war.

[12] *E.g., U.K. Reservation to A.P. I of GPW* (1998) ("the term 'armed conflict' . . . is not constituted by the commission of ordinary crimes including acts of terrorism whether concerted or in isolation")

[14] Pet. Br. 28–30; *Amicus Br. of Conspiracy Specialists* (Conspiracy Br.); C.A. *Amicus Br. of Profs. Danner & Martinez,* at *http:// www.law.georgetown.edu/faculty/nkk/documents/dannermartinezamicus.pdf.*

[15] The government misperceives the significance of the War Crimes Act. It relies on language in the 1996 House Report stating that the 1996 Act did not affect commission jurisdiction. . . . . Hamdan has never argued otherwise or suggested a "'repea[l] by implication.'" *Id.* (citation omitted). The 1996 Act did not purport to define "war crimes," only the 1997 amendments did – as this Court invited Congress to do in *Quirin.* . . . . That is to say, one year after the 1996 Act and the government's legislative history, *Congress for the first time defined and codified an exhaustive list* of war crimes. The list did *not* include conspiracy. Pub. L. No. 105–118, §583, 111 Stat. 2436 (1997). A new report, H.R. Rep. No. 105–204 (1997), accompanied that revolutionary change. It repeated some language from the 1996 report, but it *omitted* the commission-jurisdiction disclaimer. Its only reference to commissions was to those pages from the 1996 Report that express doubt about their legality, finding *Quirin* to create "uncertainty." *Id.* at 9 & n.10 (citing H.R. Rep. No. 104-698, at 6 (1996)).

[16] "The test bringing these offenses within the common law of war has been their almost universal acceptance as crimes by the nations of the world. . . . By definition, the law of war must be a concept which changes with the practice of war and the customs of nations. It is neither formalized nor static." *United States v. Schultz,* 1 C.M.A. 512, 522 (1952).

[17] Those who aided the saboteurs were tried by civilian courts, not commissions. *See* MICHAEL DOBBS, SABOTEURS 267 (2004). *Colepaugh v. Looney,* 235 F.2d 429 (10th Cir. 1956), affirmed a 1945 conviction based on a *statutory* charge. Although the trial took place before the judgments at Nuremberg and Tokyo, *Colepaugh* did not approve the conspiracy charge. Rather, it found a direct violation by shedding military dress and carrying concealed sidearms and false identification, while lurking about military fortifications. *Id.* at 432. *Colepaugh* also contradicts the government's DTA argument by stating that removal of federal jurisdiction would "subvert the rule of law to the rule of man." *Id.* at 431.

Hamdan is charged only with conspiracy, so the issue cannot be sidestepped as it was in past federal cases. The authority *vel non* for the conspiracy charge against Hamdan is of pressing moment because *all* of the current commission defendants (10 of 10) face the charge of conspiracy, and 7 of those 10 face *only* that charge. *See http://www.defenselink.mil/news/Nov2004/charge_sheets.html.*

The government's citation to Winthrop . . . backfires. Winthrop's discussion is of *occupation courts trying ordinary domestic offenses* (such as robbery, battery, and conspiracy). W. Winthrop, Military Law and Precedents 839 & n.5 (1920). For commissions trying "violations of the laws of war," Winthrop lists over 25 offenses. Conspiracy is not one of them. *Id.* at 839–40.[18]

. . .

c. The Government's Efforts to Distinguish Milligan Fail. The government claims that Milligan was not "a part of or associated with the armed forces of the enemy," Govt. Br. 29 (quoting *Quirin*). Milligan was *convicted* of trying to arm the rebels and free prisoners of war. If Milligan could not be tried for those acts by commission, then neither could Hamdan be so tried for conspiracy. The government's claim that *Milligan* turned on citizenship was rejected in *Quirin*, 317 U.S. at 37–38, the decision that the government asserts clarifies *Milligan*. . . . .[20] Without indicia showing someone to be an unlawful combatant (*e.g.*, the burying of uniforms or a concession), in a conflict governed by the laws of war, law-of-war commission jurisdiction is foreclosed.[21]

d. Commissions Must Comply With the UCMJ. The government asserts that (1) Hamdan's reading requires identical procedures for courts-martial and commissions, thus "eliminating" commissions, and (2) commission history discloses unlimited Executive authority. Both are wrong.

The government does not address, much less justify, the result those arguments produce: that Congress has sanctioned a process that excludes an accused from his own trial, and that this Court is powerless to halt that process. The government also avoids meaningful discussion of the fact that this commission has *already* denied Hamdan the right to be present. No authority permits the government to exclude involuntarily a nondisruptive defendant from his criminal trial. *Diaz v. United States*, 223 U.S. 442, 455 (1912).[22]

---

[18] Winthrop corrected some loose language in C. Howland, Digest of Opinions of the Judge Advocates General of the Army 1071 (1912). Howland's mention of conspiracy cited a number of commission cases, but those cases (which are kept in the National Archives) do not reveal a single conspiracy charge (and certainly not the approval of one) in them.

[20] The government also misportrays the *Hamdi* plurality. . . . . *Hamdi* concerned a person picked up on an Afghani battlefield carrying a gun in a war between two nations, not an unarmed individual crossing the border while attempting to save his pregnant wife, picked up by a bounty hunter, and alleged to be part of a stateless, territory-less group.

[21] Hamdan was never charged with being a "personal assistant," or "terrorist training," . . . nor was he charged with a "desire" to destroy the U.S. *Amicus Br. Former Attorneys General et al.* 13 n.3. in fact, the indictment ascribes no *mens rea* to Hamdan at all – not even that he knowingly delivered weapons. The charge, unlike the unsupported insinuations in the government's brief, never states that the delivery of weapons or Hamdan's training was related to *any* conflict with the U.S., as opposed to the internal Afghani and Tajiki conflicts. . . . .

[22] Exclusion of disruptive defendants is not at issue; such defendants are deemed to "consent" to exclusion. Nuremberg's rules permitted exclusion for disruption and when a defendant could not be found. *See* 2 Trial of the Major War Criminals Before the I.M.T. 484 (1995) (exclusion "unjust" unless defendant disruptive); *id.* at 26–28; *id.* R. Pro. 5. Like *Quirin* and *Madsen*, there was no exclusion for classified or unclassified (protected) evidence – and certainly not for someone the government claims it can detain indefinitely and thereby prevent any potential leak.

Enforcing the plain language of §836(a) does not require identical procedures for courts-martial and commissions. The Code does not establish a comprehensive procedural regime, rather it sets statutory minimums for any military court. *Amicus Br. Am. Jewish Cmte.* 16–18. To that end, the UCMJ contains fewer than 50 procedural sections. The full rules for courts-martial, by contrast, are found in the 867-page Manual for Courts Martial (M.C.M.). Hamdan does not contend that every M.C.M. rule applies to commissions,[23] only that commissions must be consistent with the UCMJ.[23] It is implausible that Congress would have expressly made the Code's procedures applicable to commissions in §836(a), only to have that moderate constraint subject to Executive waiver. *Cf. Loving*, 517 U.S. at 772 (delegation under §836 is "set within boundaries the President may not exceed").

The government has no answer to Judge Robertson's conclusion that the modification of UCMJ Article 2 extends UCMJ protections to Hamdan. . . . . This change nullified that aspect of *Yamashita*. . . . .[24] And the government's historical claims are inaccurate; commissions have been exceptional in their personal jurisdiction, not their procedure. *See Madsen v. Kinsella*, 343 U.S. 341, 353 n.20 (1952) (Gen. Crowder was motivated to propose Article 15 because "'no civil court'" or court-martial could try American soldiers for homicide of Cubans). The government's argument is also contradicted by a more complete reading of its sources.[25] *See* S. Rep. No. 64-130, at 41 (1916) ("Both classes of courts have the same procedure.") (Gen. Crowder).[26]

Ignoring 4 of 5 authorities in footnote 10 of Petitioner's Brief, the government . . . claims that this footnote's quotation of the M.C.M. is "roughly half the common sense of the matter" and points to the M.C.M.'s mention of the President's regulatory authority. The omitted clause is irrelevant; Petitioner has never claimed that the President cannot depart from the M.C.M. (as opposed to the UCMJ). And the government itself tellingly omits from its "sense of the matter" the first part of the same sentence: "*Subject to any applicable rule of international law* or to any regulations prescribed by the President or by other competent authority, military commissions and provost courts shall be guided by the appropriate principles of law and rules of procedures and evidence prescribed

---

[23] M.C.M. rights may exceed the UCMJ baseline. *United States v. Davis*, 47 M.J. 484, 486 (C.A.A.F. 1998). Even here, commission and M.C.M. rules may differ, where neither is inconsistent with the UCMJ. *Compare, e.g.*, Mil. Order No. 1 §5(M) (minimal procedures during sentencing) and R.C.M. 1001(c) (detailed procedures) *with* 10 U.S.C. 856 (not barring either rule).

[24] The only detailed opinion read §836(a)'s predecessor to apply procedural limits to commissions. *In re Yamashita*, 327 U.S. 1, 71–72 (1946) (Rutledge, J., dissenting). The majority did *not* dispute that reading, relying instead on the old Article 2. *Id* at 19–20. *Madsen* did not question it either, as no procedural challenge was raised. Pet. Br. 21 n.12. Madsen's commission guaranteed the right to be present, *id.* , and incorporated Federal Rules of Evidence and aspects of the M.C.M. *See* U.S. Military Govt. Courts for Germany, No. 31, 14 Fed. Reg. 129 (1949).

[25] *Compare* Govt. Br. 46–47 (citing Birkhimer), *with* W. Birkhimer, Military Government and Martial Law 541 (1914) ("[R]egarding the martial-law tribunal: 'It should proceed . . . upon sworn evidence *given in the presence of the accused*.'") (emphasis added); *compare* Govt. Br. 46 (citing Winthrop) *with* Winthrop at 842 (commissions "will ordinarily and properly be governed, upon all important questions, by the established rules and principles of law and evidence. Where essential . . . to the doing of justice, these rules and principles will be liberally construed and applied."). ICTY permits exclusion only for disruptive conduct, ICTY R.P. & Evid. 80(B).

[26] The government selectively quotes the UCMJ legislative history. . . . . This history does not, and could not, say that the UCMJ leaves commissions unregulated – a reading that would contradict the UCMJ's plain text. Mr. Larkin stated that the provision applied to commissions. *UCMJ: Hearings H.R. 2498*, 81st Cong., 1st Sess. 1017 (1949). *See also id.* (Vice-Chair Rivers); *id.* at 846, 976, 1061. The government's quote follows a colloquy about a different subsection, §836(b), which required M.C.M. rules to be reported to Congress. It merely confirms that M.C.M. rules do not bind commissions. It does not dispel §836(a)'s text or Crowder's authoritative statement that both tribunals have the "same procedure."

for courts-martial." M.C.M., Pt. 1, Para. 2(B)(2) (2005) (emphasis added). As Petitioner's opening brief made clear, the military's own view has been that the GPW *strictly limits* the President's ability to depart from court-martial rules. . . . .

Finally, the commission violates 10 U.S.C. 3037, which does not limit itself to presidential commissions, and which Hamdan can invoke to show lack of authorization.

Each of the above distinguishes this case from *Quirin* and eliminates the need to consider the extravagant claim of "inherent" presidential power, or to examine whether the President could establish a different form of commission.[27]

III. Hamdan's Commission Violates the GPW

Hamdan's commission is improperly constituted and lacks personal jurisdiction under the laws of war because he is entitled to the minimal guarantees of Common Article 3, and, as a presumptive POW, parity under GPW article 102.

. . .

3. Hamdan's Commission Violates Common Article 3. Common Article 3 requires "a regularly constituted court affording all the judicial guarantees which are recognized as indispensable by civilized peoples" when "armed conflict not of an international character occur[s] in the territory of one of the High Contracting Parties." As Judge Williams concluded, its plain text applies to Hamdan. . . . .

The government seizes on the word "one," but that word merely means that the Article applies whenever the territory of a Party is involved. The text, history, and structure of Article 3 reject the notion that "one" is a ceiling. It does not say the Article applies *only* to conflicts in one country. Rather, it provides a "minimum yardstick" for all conflicts.[38]

In any event, Common Article 3's minimal guarantees are binding as customary international law in all conflicts. *Goodman/Jinks/Slaughter Br.* 18–25. Congress explicitly implemented it, rendering the government's reliance on *The Paquete Habana*, 175 U.S. 677 (1900), misplaced. *See, e.g.,* 1996 War Crimes Act, 18 U.S.C. 2441(c)(3)

---

[27] The government's sweeping claim of inherent power is contradicted by the text of the Constitution, . . . ; precedent, *e.g., Hamdi*, 542 U.S. at 536 (plurality); *Toth v. Quarles*, 350 U.S. 11,14 (1955); *Yamashita*, 327 U.S. at 7; *Quirin*, 317 U.S. at 28; and history, *Amicus Br. of Jack Rakove et al.*

  Quirin itself appears confined to *statutorily defined* offenses against the laws of war. The government is correct that *Quirin* reached only Count 1 . . . even though its brief earlier suggests *Quirin* reached the conspiracy offense . . . . The Court approved only the first specification of Count 1, which mirrored an offense triable by commission by explicit statute. . . . . *Quirin* acknowledged other offenses *may* be triable by commission "*so far as* it should be recognized and deemed applicable by the *courts*." 317 U.S. at 30 (emphasis added). Such ambiguity is not a stable edifice. Pet. Br. 36; *Amici Br. of Richard Epstein et al.*

[38] *E.g.,* Pet. Br. 49; *Amicus Br. of Assoc. of New York Bar* 8–11. The Article's plain text does not say one "nation," but one "Part[y]." The government's reading therefore requires conflicts spilling into neighboring nations to receive Article 3 protection when the neighboring nations are *not* parties to the Geneva Convention, but strips a conflict of Article 3 protection when the neighboring nations ratified the Convention. This is nonsensical.

  The government mentions an ICRC draft, Govt. Br. 49 n.24, but that was a draft of Article 2. ICRC Commentary, *supra,* at 31. That draft was rejected because it brought full GPW protection to non-international conflicts – not for any other reason. *Id.* at 34–35. The new Article 3 was premised on the view that it was "equally applicable to civil and to international wars" so "its observance does not depend upon preliminary discussions on the nature of the conflict." *Id.* at 35. Absolutely nothing in the commentary states that the conflict must be within a single country. This may "generally" be the case, but "the scope of application of the article must be as wide as possible." *Id.* at 36, 37. The government's source is explicit: "Representing, as it does, the minimum which must be applied in the least determinate of conflicts, its terms must *a fortiori* be respected in the case of international conflicts proper, when all the provisions of the Convention are applicable. For 'the greater obligation includes the lesser,'" *id.* at 38; *see also id.* at 16. Otherwise, a party to a civil war could evade Article 3 by crossing a border. *Goodman/Jinks/Slaughter Br.* 22–23.

(criminalizing "conduct . . . which constitutes a violation of common Article 3"). Instead of a "controlling Executive Act" to abrogate Article 3, the Executive implemented it and recognizes its universality.[39] Finally, the President has never been able to break with customary international law when customary law is the basis for the President's action in the first place. Since the President claims the power to enforce laws of war through commissions, it cannot be that the President can then disregard those laws when they forbid the tribunal. To hold otherwise writes the "blank check" that *Hamdi* rejected.

The government has no answer to the ICRC's lengthy analysis of Common Article 3's requirements, such as its clear proviso that the court be independent of the Executive and not an *ad hoc* tribunal created, appointed, and overseen by him. . . . . The argument that a commission is "regularly constituted" because one existed a half-century ago stretches "regularly" past any breaking point. ICRC, IV Geneva Commentary 340 (1960) ("'[R]egularly constituted' . . . wording definitely excludes all special tribunals. It is the ordinary military courts . . . which will be competent."). Separately, the commission does not provide the requisite minimal guarantees, as its "protections" are not enforceable and permit denial of the right to be present at trial and introduction of testimony obtained by torture. *N.Y. Bar Br. 11–21; Amicus Br. of 422 Current and Former Members of the United Kingdom et al. 16–25; Goodman/Jinks/Slaughter Br. 25–27.*

CONCLUSION

The judgment below should be reversed.

. . .

---

[39] *E.g.*, U.S. Dept. of Army, Law of War Handbook 144 (2005) ("This expanded view of Common Article 3 is consistent not only with U.S. Policy (which extends its application even into non-conflict operations other than war through DODD 5100.77), but also with the original understanding of its scope as expressed in the official commentary.").

SUPREME COURT OF THE UNITED STATES

No. 05–184

SALIM AHMED HAMDAN, PETITIONER *v.* DONALD H. RUMSFELD, SECRETARY OF DEFENSE, ET AL.

ON WRIT OF CERTIORARI TO THE UNITED STATES COURT OF APPEALS FOR THE DISTRICT OF COLUMBIA CIRCUIT

[June 29, 2006]

JUSTICE STEVENS announced the judgment of the Court and delivered the opinion of the Court with respect to Parts I through IV, Parts VI through VI–D–iii, Part VI–D–v, and Part VII, and an opinion with respect to Parts V and VI–D–iv, in which JUSTICE SOUTER, JUSTICE GINSBURG, and JUSTICE BREYER join.

Petitioner Salim Ahmed Hamdan, a Yemeni national, is in custody at an American prison in Guantanamo Bay, Cuba. In November 2001, during hostilities between the United States and the Taliban (which then governed Afghanistan), Hamdan was captured by militia forces and turned over to the U.S. military. In June 2002, he was transported to Guantanamo Bay. Over a year later, the President deemed him eligible for trial by military commission for then-unspecified crimes. After another year had passed, Hamdan was charged with one count of conspiracy "to commit... offenses triable by military commission." ....

Hamdan filed petitions for writs of habeas corpus and mandamus to challenge the Executive Branch's intended means of prosecuting this charge. He concedes that a court-martial constituted in accordance with the Uniform Code of Military Justice (UCMJ), 10 U.S.C. §801 *et seq.* (2000 ed. and Supp. III), would have authority to try him. His objection is that the military commission the President has convened lacks such authority, for two principal reasons: First, neither congressional Act nor the common law of war supports trial by this commission for the crime of conspiracy – an offense that, Hamdan says, is not a violation of the law of war. Second, Hamdan contends, the procedures that the President has adopted to try him violate the most basic tenets of military and international law, including the principle that a defendant must be permitted to see and hear the evidence against him.

The District Court granted Hamdan's request for a writ of habeas corpus. 344 F. Supp. 2d 152 (DC 2004). The Court of Appeals for the District of Columbia Circuit reversed. 415 F. 3d 33 (2005). Recognizing, as we did over a half-century ago, that trial by military commission is an extraordinary measure raising important questions about the balance of powers in our constitutional structure, *Ex parte Quirin*, 317 U.S. 1, 19 (1942), we granted certiorari. 546 U.S.__ (2005).

For the reasons that follow, we conclude that the military commission convened to try Hamdan lacks power to proceed because its structure and procedures violate both the UCMJ and the Geneva Conventions. Four of us also conclude, see Part V, *infra*, that the offense with which Hamdan has been charged is not an "offens[e] that by . . . the law of war may be tried by military commissions." 10 U.S.C. §821.

I

On September 11, 2001, agents of the al Qaeda terrorist organization hijacked commercial airplanes and attacked the World Trade Center in New York City and the national headquarters of the Department of Defense in Arlington, Virginia. Americans will never forget the devastation wrought by these acts. Nearly 3,000 civilians were killed.

Congress responded by adopting a Joint Resolution authorizing the President to "use all necessary and appropriate force against those nations, organizations, or persons he determines planned, authorized, committed, or aided the terrorist attacks . . . in order to prevent any future acts of international terrorism against the United States by such nations, organizations or persons." Authorization for Use of Military Force (AUMF), 115 Stat. 224, note following 50 U.S.C. §1541 (2000 ed., Supp. III). Acting pursuant to the AUMF, and having determined that the Taliban regime had supported al Qaeda, the President ordered the Armed Forces of the United States to invade Afghanistan. In the ensuing hostilities, hundreds of individuals, Hamdan among them, were captured and eventually detained at Guantanamo Bay.

On November 13, 2001, while the United States was still engaged in active combat with the Taliban, the President issued a comprehensive military order intended to govern the "Detention, Treatment, and Trial of Certain Non-Citizens in the War Against Terrorism," 66 Fed. Reg. 57833 (hereinafter November 13 Order or Order). Those subject to the November 13 Order include any noncitizen for whom the President determines "there is reason to believe" that he or she (1) "is or was" a member of al Qaeda or (2) has engaged or participated in terrorist activities aimed at or harmful to the United States. *Id.*, at 57834. Any such individual "shall, when tried, be tried by military commission for any and all offenses triable by military commission that such individual is alleged to have committed, and may be punished in accordance with the penalties provided under applicable law, including imprisonment or death." *Ibid.* The November 13 Order vested in the Secretary of Defense the power to appoint military commissions to try individuals subject to the Order, but that power has since been delegated to John D. Altenberg, Jr., a retired Army major general and longtime military lawyer who has been designated "Appointing Authority for Military Commissions."

On July 3, 2003, the President announced his determination that Hamdan and five other detainees at Guantanamo Bay were subject to the November 13 Order and thus triable by military commission. In December 2003, military counsel was appointed to represent Hamdan. Two months later, counsel filed demands for charges and for a speedy trial pursuant to Article 10 of the UCMJ, 10 U.S.C. §810. On February 23, 2004, the legal adviser to the Appointing Authority denied the applications, ruling that Hamdan was not entitled to any of the protections of the UCMJ. Not until July 13, 2004, after Hamdan had commenced this action in the United States District Court for the Western District of Washington, did the Government finally charge him with the offense for which, a year earlier, he had been deemed eligible for trial by military commission.

The charging document, which is unsigned, contains 13 numbered paragraphs. The first two paragraphs recite the asserted bases for the military commission's jurisdiction – namely, the November 13 Order and the President's July 3, 2003, declaration that Hamdan is eligible for trial by military commission. The next nine paragraphs, collectively entitled "General Allegations," describe al Qaeda's activities from its inception in 1989 through 2001 and identify Osama bin Laden as the group's leader. Hamdan is not mentioned in these paragraphs.

Only the final two paragraphs, entitled "Charge: Conspiracy," contain allegations against Hamdan. Paragraph 12 charges that "from on or about February 1996 to on or about November 24, 2001," Hamdan "willfully and knowingly joined an enterprise of persons who shared a common criminal purpose and conspired and agreed with [named members of al Qaeda] to commit the following offenses triable by military commission: attacking civilians; attacking civilian objects; murder by an unprivileged belligerent; and terrorism." . . . . There is no allegation that Hamdan had any command responsibilities, played a leadership role, or participated in the planning of any activity.

Paragraph 13 lists four "overt acts" that Hamdan is alleged to have committed sometime between 1996 and November 2001 in furtherance of the "enterprise and conspiracy": (1) he acted as Osama bin Laden's "bodyguard and personal driver," "believ[ing]" all the while that bin Laden "and his associates were involved in" terrorist acts prior to and including the attacks of September 11, 2001; (2) he arranged for transportation of, and actually transported, weapons used by al Qaeda members and by bin Laden's bodyguards (Hamdan among them); (3) he "drove or accompanied [O]sama bin Laden to various al Qaida-sponsored training camps, press conferences, or lectures," at which bin Laden encouraged attacks against Americans; and (4) he received weapons training at al Qaeda-sponsored camps. . . . .

After this formal charge was filed, the United States District Court for the Western District of Washington transferred Hamdan's habeas and mandamus petitions to the United States District Court for the District of Columbia. Meanwhile, a Combatant Status Review Tribunal (CSRT) convened pursuant to a military order issued on July 7, 2004, decided that Hamdan's continued detention at Guantanamo Bay was warranted because he was an "enemy combatant."[1] Separately, proceedings before the military commission commenced.

On November 8, 2004, however, the District Court granted Hamdan's petition for habeas corpus and stayed the commission's proceedings. It concluded that the President's authority to establish military commissions extends only to "offenders or offenses triable by military [commission] under the law of war," 344 F. Supp. 2d, at 158; that the law of war includes the Geneva Convention (III) Relative to the Treatment of Prisoners of War, Aug. 12, 1949, [1955] 6 U.S.T. 3316, T.I.A.S. No. 3364 (Third Geneva Convention); that Hamdan is entitled to the full protections of the Third Geneva Convention until adjudged, in compliance with that treaty, not to be a prisoner of war; and that, whether or not Hamdan is properly classified as a prisoner of war, the military commission convened to try him was established in violation of both the UCMJ and Common Article 3 of the Third Geneva Convention because it had the power to convict based on evidence the accused would never see or hear. 344 F. Supp. 2d, at 158–172.

The Court of Appeals for the District of Columbia Circuit reversed. Like the District Court, the Court of Appeals declined the Government's invitation to abstain from considering Hamdan's challenge. Cf. *Schlesinger* v. *Councilman*, 420 U.S. 738 (1975). On the merits, the panel rejected the District Court's further conclusion that Hamdan was entitled to relief under the Third Geneva Convention. All three judges agreed that the

---

[1] An "enemy combatant" is defined by the military order as "an individual who was part of or supporting Taliban or al Qaeda forces, or associated forces that are engaged in hostilities against the United States or its coalition partners." Memorandum from Deputy Secretary of Defense Paul Wolfowitz re: Order Establishing Combatant Status Review Tribunal §a (Jul. 7, 2004), available at http://www.defense link.mil/news/Jul2004 /d20040707review.pdf (all Internet materials as visited June 26, 2006, and available in Clerk of Court's case file).

Geneva Conventions were not "judicially enforceable," 415 F. 3d, at 38, and two thought that the Conventions did not in any event apply to Hamdan, *id.*, at 40–42; but see *id.*, at 44 (Williams, J., concurring). In other portions of its opinion, the court concluded that our decision in *Quirin* foreclosed any separation-of-powers objection to the military commission's jurisdiction, and held that Hamdan's trial before the contemplated commission would violate neither the UCMJ nor U.S. Armed Forces regulations intended to implement the Geneva Conventions. 415 F. 3d, at 38, 42–43.

On November 7, 2005, we granted certiorari to decide whether the military commission convened to try Hamdan has authority to do so, and whether Hamdan may rely on the Geneva Conventions in these proceedings.

II

On February 13, 2006, the Government filed a motion to dismiss the writ of certiorari. The ground cited for dismissal was the recently enacted Detainee Treatment Act of 2005 (DTA), Pub. L. 109–148, 119 Stat. 2739. We postponed our ruling on that motion pending argument on the merits, 546 U.S.__ (2006), and now deny it.

. . .

The Government argues that §§1005(e)(1) and 1005(h) had the immediate effect, upon enactment, of repealing federal jurisdiction not just over detainee habeas actions yet to be filed but also over any such actions then pending in any federal court – including this Court. Accordingly, it argues, we lack jurisdiction to review the Court of Appeals' decision below.

Hamdan objects to this theory on both constitutional and statutory grounds. Principal among his constitutional arguments is that the Government's preferred reading raises grave questions about Congress' authority to impinge upon this Court's appellate jurisdiction, particularly in habeas cases. Support for this argument is drawn from *Ex parte Yerger*, 8 Wall. 85 (1869), in which, having explained that "the denial to this court of appellate jurisdiction" to consider an original writ of habeas corpus would "greatly weaken the efficacy of the writ," *id.*, at 102–103, we held that Congress would not be presumed to have effected such denial absent an unmistakably clear statement to the contrary. See *id.*, at 104–105; see also *Felker* v. *Turpin*, 518 U.S. 651 (1996); *Durousseau* v. *United States*, 6 Cranch 307, 314 (1810) (opinion for the Court by Marshall, C.J.) (The "appellate powers of this court" are not created by statute but are "given by the constitution"); *United States* v. *Klein*, 13 Wall. 128 (1872). Cf. *Ex parte McCardle*, 7 Wall. 506, 514 (1869) (holding that Congress had validly foreclosed one avenue of appellate review where its repeal of habeas jurisdiction, reproduced in the margin,[4] could not have been "a plainer instance of positive exception"). Hamdan also suggests that, if the Government's reading is correct, Congress has unconstitutionally suspended the writ of habeas corpus.

We find it unnecessary to reach either of these arguments. Ordinary principles of statutory construction suffice to rebut the Government's theory – at least insofar as this case, which was pending at the time the DTA was enacted, is concerned.

---

[4] "'*And be it further enacted*, That so much of the act approved February 5, 1867, entitled "An act to amend an act to establish the judicial courts of the United States, approved September 24, 1789," as authorized an appeal from the judgment of the Circuit Court to the Supreme Court of the United States, or the exercise of any such jurisdiction by said Supreme Court, on appeals which have been, or may hereafter be taken, be, and the same is hereby repealed.'" 7 Wall., at 508.

The Government acknowledges that only paragraphs (2) and (3) of subsection (e) are expressly made applicable to pending cases, see §1005(h)(2), 119 Stat. 2743–2744, but argues that the omission of paragraph (1) from the scope of that express statement is of no moment. This is so, we are told, because Congress' failure to expressly reserve federal courts' jurisdiction over pending cases erects a presumption against jurisdiction, and that presumption is rebutted by neither the text nor the legislative history of the DTA.

The first part of this argument is not entirely without support in our precedents. We have in the past "applied intervening statutes conferring or ousting jurisdiction, whether or not jurisdiction lay when the underlying conduct occurred or when the suit was filed." *Landgraf* v. *USI Film Products*, 511 U.S. 244, 274 (1994) (citing *Bruner* v. *United States*, 343 U.S. 112 (1952); *Hallowell* v. *Commons*, 239 U.S. 506 (1916)); see *Republic of Austria* v. *Altmann*, 541 U.S. 677, 693 (2004). But the "presumption" that these cases have applied is more accurately viewed as the nonapplication of another presumption – viz., the presumption against retroactivity – in certain limited circumstances.[5] If a statutory provision "would operate retroactively" as applied to cases pending at the time the provision was enacted, then "our traditional presumption teaches that it does not govern absent clear congressional intent favoring such a result." *Landgraf*, 511 U.S., at 280. We have explained, however, that, unlike other intervening changes in the law, a jurisdiction-conferring or jurisdiction – stripping statute usually "takes away no substantive right but simply changes the tribunal that is to hear the case." *Hallowell*, 239 U.S., at 508. If that is truly all the statute does, no retroactivity problem arises because the change in the law does not "impair rights a party possessed when he acted, increase a party's liability for past conduct, or impose new duties with respect to transactions already completed." *Landgraf*, 511 U.S., at 280.[6] And if a new rule has no retroactive effect, the presumption against retroactivity will not prevent its application to a case that was already pending when the new rule was enacted.

That does not mean, however, that all jurisdiction-stripping provisions – or even all such provisions that truly lack retroactive effect – must apply to cases pending at the time of their enactment.[7] "[N]ormal rules of construction," including a contextual reading of the statutory language, may dictate otherwise. *Lindh* v. *Murphy*, 521 U.S. 320, 326 (1997).[8] A familiar principle of statutory construction, relevant both in *Lindh* and

---

[5] See *Hughes Aircraft Co.* v. *United States ex rel. Schumer*, 520 U.S. 939, 951 (1997) ("The fact that courts often apply newly enacted jurisdiction-allocating statutes to pending cases merely evidences certain limited circumstances failing to meet the conditions for our generally applicable presumption against retroactivity . . .").

[6] Cf. *Hughes Aircraft*, 520 U.S., at 951 ("Statutes merely addressing *which* court shall have jurisdiction to entertain a particular cause of action can fairly be said merely to regulate the secondary conduct of litigation and not the underlying primary conduct of the parties" (emphasis in original)).

[7] In his insistence to the contrary, JUSTICE SCALIA reads too much into *Bruner* v. *United States*, 343 U.S. 112 (1952), *Hallowell* v. *Commons*, 239 U.S. 506 (1916), and *Insurance Co.* v. *Ritchie*, 5 Wall. 541 (1867). . . . . None of those cases says that the absence of an express provision reserving jurisdiction over pending cases trumps or renders irrelevant any other indications of congressional intent. Indeed, *Bruner* itself relied on such other indications – including a negative inference drawn from the statutory text, cf. *infra*, at 13 – to support its conclusion that jurisdiction was not available. The Court observed that (1) Congress had been put on notice by prior lower court cases addressing the Tucker Act that it ought to specifically reserve jurisdiction over pending cases, see 343 U.S., at 115, and (2) in contrast to the congressional silence concerning reservation of jurisdiction, reservation *had* been made of "'any rights or liabilities' existing at the effective date of the Act" repealed by another provision of the Act, *ibid.*, n. 7.

[8] The question in *Lindh* was whether new limitations on the availability of habeas relief imposed by the Antiterrorism and Effective Death Penalty Act of 1996 (AEDPA), 110 Stat. 1214, applied to habeas actions pending on the date of AEDPA's enactment. We held that they did not. At the outset, we rejected the State's argument that, in the absence of a clear congressional statement to the contrary, a "procedural" rule must apply to pending cases. 521 U.S., at 326.

here, is that a negative inference may be drawn from the exclusion of language from one statutory provision that is included in other provisions of the same statute. See *id.*, at 330; see also, *e.g.*, *Russello* v. *United States*, 464 U.S. 16, 23 (1983) ("'[W]here Congress includes particular language in one section of a statute but omits it in another section of the same Act, it is generally presumed that Congress acts intentionally and purposely in the disparate inclusion or exclusion'"). The Court in *Lindh* relied on this reasoning to conclude that certain limitations on the availability of habeas relief imposed by AEDPA applied only to cases filed after that statute's effective date. Congress' failure to identify the temporal reach of those limitations, which governed noncapital cases, stood in contrast to its express command in the same legislation that new rules governing habeas petitions in capital cases "apply to cases pending on or after the date of enactment." §107(c), 110 Stat. 1226; see *Lindh*, 521 U.S., at 329–330. That contrast, combined with the fact that the amendments at issue "affect[ed] substantive entitlement to relief," *id.*, at 327, warranted drawing a negative inference.

A like inference follows *a fortiori* from *Lindh* in this case. "If . . . Congress was reasonably concerned to ensure that [§§1005(e)(2) and (3)] be applied to pending cases, it should have been just as concerned about [§1005(e)(1)], unless it had the different intent that the latter [section] not be applied to the general run of pending cases." *Id.*, at 329. If anything, the evidence of deliberate omission is stronger here than it was in *Lindh*. In *Lindh*, the provisions to be contrasted had been drafted separately but were later "joined together and . . . considered simultaneously when the language raising the implication was inserted." *Id.*, at 330. We observed that Congress' tandem review and approval of the two sets of provisions strengthened the presumption that the relevant omission was deliberate. *Id.*, at 331; see also *Field* v. *Mans*, 516 U.S. 59, 75 (1995) ("The more apparently deliberate the contrast, the stronger the inference, as applied, for example, to contrasting statutory sections originally enacted simultaneously in relevant respects"). Here, Congress not only considered the respective temporal reaches of paragraphs (1), (2), and (3) of subsection (e) together at every stage, but omitted paragraph (1) from its directive that paragraphs (2) and (3) apply to pending cases only after having *rejected* earlier proposed versions of the statute that would have included what is now paragraph (1) within the scope of that directive. Compare DTA §1005(h)(2), 119 Stat. 2743–2744, with 151 Cong. Rec. S12655 (Nov. 10, 2005) (S. Amdt. 2515); see *id.*, at S14257–S14258 (Dec. 21, 2005) (discussing similar language proposed in both the House and the Senate).[9] Congress' rejection of the very language that would have achieved the result the Government urges here weighs heavily against the Government's interpretation. See *Doe* v. *Chao*, 540 U.S. 614, 621–623 (2004).[10]

. . .

---

[9] That paragraph (1), along with paragraphs (2) and (3), is to "take effect on the date of enactment," DTA §1005(h)(1), 119 Stat. 2743, is not dispositive; "'a 'statement that a statute will become effective on a certain date does not even arguably suggest that it has any application to conduct that occurred at an earlier date.'" *INS* v. *St. Cyr*, 533 U.S. 289, 317 (2001) (quoting *Landgraf* v. *USI Film Products*, 511 U.S. 244, 257 (1994)). Certainly, the "effective date" provision cannot bear the weight JUSTICE SCALIA would place on it. See *post*, at 5, and n. 1. Congress deemed that provision insufficient, standing alone, to render subsections (e)(2) and (e)(3) applicable to pending cases; hence its adoption of subsection (h)(2). JUSTICE SCALIA seeks to avoid reducing subsection (h)(2) to a mere redundancy – a consequence he seems to acknowledge must otherwise follow from his interpretation – by speculating that Congress had special reasons, not also relevant to subsection (e)(1), to worry that subsections (e)(2) and (e)(3) would be ruled inapplicable to pending cases. As we explain *infra*, at 2768, and n. 12, that attempt fails.

[10] . . .

Finally, we cannot leave unaddressed JUSTICE SCALIA's contentions that the "meaning of §1005(e)(1) is entirely clear," *post*, at 6, and that "the *plain import* of a statute repealing jurisdiction is to eliminate the power to consider and render judgment – in an already pending case no less than in a case yet to be filed," *post*, at 3 (emphasis in original). Only by treating the *Bruner* rule as an inflexible trump (a thing it has never been, see n. 7, *supra*) and ignoring both the rest of §1005's text and its drafting history can one conclude as much. Congress here expressly provided that subsections (e)(2) and (e)(3) applied to pending cases. It chose not to so provide – after having been presented with the option – for subsection (e)(1). The omission is an integral part of the statutory scheme that muddies whatever "plain meaning" may be discerned from blinkered study of subsection (e)(1) alone. The dissent's speculation about what Congress might have intended by the omission not only is counterfactual, cf. n. 10, *supra* (recounting legislative history), but rests on both a misconstruction of the DTA and an erroneous view our precedents, see *supra*, at 17, and n. 12.

For these reasons, we deny the Government's motion to dismiss.[15]

III

Relying on our decision in *Councilman*, 420 U.S. 738, the Government argues that, even if we have statutory jurisdiction, we should apply the "judge-made rule that civilian courts should await the final outcome of on-going military proceedings before entertaining an attack on those proceedings." Brief for Respondents 12. Like the District Court and the Court of Appeals before us, we reject this argument.

In *Councilman*, an army officer on active duty was referred to a court-martial for trial on charges that he violated the UCMJ by selling, transferring, and possessing marijuana. 420 U.S., at 739–740. Objecting that the alleged offenses were not "'service connected,'" *id.*, at 740, the officer filed suit in Federal District Court to enjoin the proceedings. He neither questioned the lawfulness of courts-martial or their procedures nor disputed that, as a serviceman, he was subject to court-martial jurisdiction. His sole argument was that the subject matter of his case did not fall within the scope of court-martial authority. See *id.*, at 741, 759. The District Court granted his request for injunctive relief, and the Court of Appeals affirmed.

We granted certiorari and reversed. *Id.*, at 761. We did not reach the merits of whether the marijuana charges were sufficiently "service connected" to place them within the subject-matter jurisdiction of a court-martial. Instead, we concluded that, as a matter of comity, federal courts should normally abstain from intervening in pending court-martial proceedings against members of the Armed Forces,[16] and further that

---

[15] Because we conclude that §1005(e)(1) does not strip federal courts' jurisdiction over cases pending on the date of the DTA's enactment, we do not decide whether, if it were otherwise, this Court would nonetheless retain jurisdiction to hear Hamdan's appeal. Cf. *supra*, at 10. Nor do we decide the manner in which the canon of constitutional avoidance should affect subsequent interpretation of the DTA. See, *e.g.*, *St. Cyr*, 533 U.S., at 300 (a construction of a statute "that would entirely preclude review of a pure question of law by any court would give rise to substantial constitutional questions").

[16] *Councilman* distinguished service personnel from civilians, whose challenges to ongoing military proceedings are cognizable in federal court. See, *e.g.*, *United States ex rel. Toth* v. *Quarles*, 350 U.S. 11 (1955). As we explained in *Councilman*, abstention is not appropriate in cases in which individuals raise "'substantial arguments denying the right of the military to try them at all,'" and in which the legal challenge "turn[s] on the status of the persons as to whom the military asserted its power." 420 U.S., at 759 (quoting *Noyd* v. *Bond*, 395 U.S. 683, 696, n. 8 (1969)). In other words, we do not apply *Councilman* abstention when there is a substantial question whether a military tribunal has personal jurisdiction over the defendant. Because

there was nothing in the particular circumstances of the officer's case to displace that general rule. See *id.,* at 740, 758.

Councilman identifies two considerations of comity that together favor abstention pending completion of ongoing court-martial proceedings against service personnel. See *New v. Cohen,* 129 F. 3d 639, 643 (CADC1997); see also 415 F. 3d, at 36–37 (discussing *Councilman* and *New*). First, military discipline and, therefore, the efficient operation of the Armed Forces are best served if the military justice system acts without regular interference from civilian courts. See *Councilman,* 420 U.S., at 752. Second, federal courts should respect the balance that Congress struck between military preparedness and fairness to individual service members when it created "an integrated system of military courts and review procedures, a critical element of which is the Court of Military Appeals, consisting of civilian judges 'completely removed from all military influence or persuasion....'" *Id.,* at 758 (quoting H. R. Rep. No. 491, 81st Cong., 1st Sess., p. 7 (1949)). Just as abstention in the face of ongoing state criminal proceedings is justified by our expectation that state courts will enforce federal rights, so abstention in the face of ongoing court-martial proceedings is justified by our expectation that the military court system established by Congress – with its substantial procedural protections and provision for appellate review by independent civilian judges – "will vindicate servicemen's constitutional rights," 420 U.S., at 758. See *id.,* at 755–758.[17]

The same cannot be said here; indeed, neither of the comity considerations identified in *Councilman* weighs in favor of abstention in this case. First, Hamdan is not a member of our Nation's Armed Forces, so concerns about military discipline do not apply. Second, the tribunal convened to try Hamdan is not part of the integrated system of military courts, complete with independent review panels, that Congress has established. Unlike the officer in *Councilman,* Hamdan has no right to appeal any conviction to the civilian judges of the Court of Military Appeals (now called the United States Court of Appeals for the Armed Forces, see Pub. L. 103-337, 108 Stat. 2831). Instead, under Dept. of Defense Military Commission Order No. 1 (Commission Order No. 1), which was issued by the President on March 21, 2002, and amended most recently on August 31, 2005, and which governs the procedures for Hamdan's commission, any conviction would be reviewed by a panel consisting of three military officers designated by the Secretary of Defense. Commission Order No. 1 §6(H)(4). Commission Order No. 1 provides that appeal of a review panel's decision may be had only to the Secretary of Defense himself, §6(H)(5), and then, finally, to the President, §6(H)(6).[18]

We have no doubt that the various individuals assigned review power under Commission Order No. 1 would strive to act impartially and ensure that Hamdan receive all protections to which he is entitled. Nonetheless, these review bodies clearly lack the structural insulation from military influence that characterizes the Court of Appeals for

---

we conclude that abstention is inappropriate for a more basic reason, we need not consider whether the jurisdictional exception recognized in *Councilman* applies here.

[17] See also *Noyd,* 395 U.S., at 694–696 (noting that the Court of Military Appeals consisted of "disinterested civilian judges," and concluding that there was no reason for the Court to address an Air Force Captain's argument that he was entitled to remain free from confinement pending appeal of his conviction by court-martial "when the highest military court stands ready to consider petitioner's arguments"). Cf. *Parisi* v. *Davidson,* 405 U.S. 34, 41–43 (1972) ("Under accepted principles of comity, the court should stay its hand only if the relief the petitioner seeks . . . would also be available to him with reasonable promptness and certainty through the machinery of the military judicial system in its processing of the court-martial charge").

[18] If he chooses, the President may delegate this ultimate decisionmaking authority to the Secretary of Defense. See §6(H)(6).

the Armed Forces, and thus bear insufficient conceptual similarity to state courts to warrant invocation of abstention principles.[19]

In sum, neither of the two comity considerations underlying our decision to abstain in *Councilman* applies to the circumstances of this case. Instead, this Court's decision in *Quirin* is the most relevant precedent. In *Quirin*, seven German saboteurs were captured upon arrival by submarine in New York and Florida. 317 U.S., at 21. The President convened a military commission to try the saboteurs, who then filed habeas corpus petitions in the United States District Court for the District of Columbia challenging their trial by commission. We granted the saboteurs' petition for certiorari to the Court of Appeals before judgment. See *id.*, at 19. Far from abstaining pending the conclusion of military proceedings, which were ongoing, we convened a special Term to hear the case and expedited our review. That course of action was warranted, we explained, "[i]n view of the public importance of the questions raised by [the cases] and of the duty which rests on the courts, in time of war as well as in time of peace, to preserve unimpaired the constitutional safeguards of civil liberty, and because in our opinion the public interest required that we consider and decide those questions without any avoidable delay." *Ibid.*

As the Court of Appeals here recognized, *Quirin* "provides a compelling historical precedent for the power of civilian courts to entertain challenges that seek to interrupt the processes of military commissions." 415 F. 3d, at 36.[20] The circumstances of this case, like those in *Quirin*, simply do not implicate the "obligations of comity" that, under appropriate circumstances, justify abstention. *Quackenbush* v. *Allstate Ins. Co.*, 517 U.S. 706, 733 (1996) (KENNEDY, J., concurring).

Finally, the Government has identified no other "important countervailing interest" that would permit federal courts to depart from their general "duty to exercise the jurisdiction that is conferred upon them by Congress." *Id.*, at 716 (majority opinion). To the contrary, Hamdan and the Government both have a compelling interest in knowing in advance whether Hamdan may be tried by a military commission that arguably is without any basis in law and operates free from many of the procedural rules prescribed

---

[19] JUSTICE SCALIA chides us for failing to include the District of Columbia Circuit's review powers under the DTA in our description of the review mechanism erected by Commission Order No. 1. See *post*, at 22. Whether or not the limited review permitted under the DTA may be treated as akin to the plenary review exercised by the Court of Appeals for the Armed Forces, petitioner here is not afforded a right to such review. See *infra*, at 52; §1005(e)(3), 119 Stat. 2743.

[20] Having correctly declined to abstain from addressing Hamdan's challenge to the lawfulness of the military commission convened to try him, the Court of Appeals suggested that *Councilman* abstention nonetheless applied to bar its consideration of one of Hamdan's arguments – namely, that his commission violated Article 3 of the Third Geneva Convention, 6 U.S.T. 3316, 3318. See Part VI, *infra*. Although the Court of Appeals rejected the Article 3 argument on the merits, it also stated that, because the challenge was not "jurisdictional," it did not fall within the exception that *Schlesinger* v. *Councilman*, 420 U.S. 738 (1975), recognized for defendants who raise substantial arguments that a military tribunal lacks personal jurisdiction over them. See 415 F. 3d, at 42.

In reaching this conclusion, the Court of Appeals conflated two distinct inquiries: (1) whether Hamdan has raised a substantial argument that the military commission lacks authority to try him; and, more fundamentally, (2) whether the comity considerations underlying *Councilman* apply to trigger the abstention principle in the first place. As the Court of Appeals acknowledged at the beginning of its opinion, the first question warrants consideration only if the answer to the second is yes. See 415 F. 3d, at 36–37. Since, as the Court of Appeals properly concluded, the answer to the second question is in fact no, there is no need to consider any exception.

At any rate, it appears that the exception would apply here. As discussed in Part VI, *infra*, Hamdan raises a substantial argument that, because the military commission that has been convened to try him is not a "'regularly constituted court'" under the Geneva Conventions, it is ultra vires and thus lacks jurisdiction over him. Brief for Petitioner 5.

by Congress for courts-martial – rules intended to safeguard the accused and ensure the reliability of any conviction. While we certainly do not foreclose the possibility that abstention may be appropriate in some cases seeking review of ongoing military commission proceedings (such as military commissions convened on the battlefield), the foregoing discussion makes clear that, under our precedent, abstention is not justified here. We therefore proceed to consider the merits of Hamdan's challenge.

IV

The military commission, a tribunal neither mentioned in the Constitution nor created by statute, was born of military necessity. See W. Winthrop, Military Law and Precedents 831 (rev. 2d ed. 1920) (hereinafter Winthrop). Though foreshadowed in some respects by earlier tribunals like the Board of General Officers that General Washington convened to try British Major John André for spying during the Revolutionary War, the commission "as such" was inaugurated in 1847. *Id.*, at 832; G. Davis, A Treatise on the Military Law of the United States 308 (2d ed. 1909) (hereinafter Davis). As commander of occupied Mexican territory, and having available to him no other tribunal, General Winfield Scott that year ordered the establishment of both "*'military commissions'*" to try ordinary crimes committed in the occupied territory and a *"council of war"* to try offenses against the law of war. Winthrop 832 (emphases in original).

When the exigencies of war next gave rise to a need for use of military commissions, during the Civil War, the dual system favored by General Scott was not adopted. Instead, a single tribunal often took jurisdiction over ordinary crimes, war crimes, and breaches of military orders alike. As further discussed below, each aspect of that seemingly broad jurisdiction was in fact supported by a separate military exigency. Generally, though, the need for military commissions during this period – as during the Mexican War – was driven largely by the then very limited jurisdiction of courts-martial: "The *occasion* for the military commission arises principally from the fact that the jurisdiction of the court-martial proper, in our law, is restricted by statute almost exclusively to members of the military force and to certain specific offences defined in a written code." *Id.*, at 831 (emphasis in original).

Exigency alone, of course, will not justify the establishment and use of penal tribunals not contemplated by Article I, §8 and Article III, §1 of the Constitution unless some other part of that document authorizes a response to the felt need. See *Ex parte Milligan*, 4 Wall. 2, 121 (1866) ("Certainly no part of the judicial power of the country was conferred on [military commissions]"); *Ex parte Vallandigham*, 1 Wall. 243, 251 (1864); see also *Quirin*, 317 U.S., at 25 ("Congress and the President, like the courts, possess no power not derived from the Constitution"). And that authority, if it exists, can derive only from the powers granted jointly to the President and Congress in time of war. See *id.*, at 26–29; *In re Yamashita*, 327 U.S. 1, 11 (1946).

The Constitution makes the President the "Commander in Chief" of the Armed Forces, Art. II, §2, cl. 1, but vests in Congress the powers to "declare War... and make Rules concerning Captures on Land and Water," Art. I, §8, cl. 11, to "raise and support Armies," *id.*, cl. 12, to "define and punish... Offences against the Law of Nations," *id.*, cl. 10, and "To make Rules for the Government and Regulation of the land and naval Forces," *id.*, cl. 14. The interplay between these powers was described by Chief Justice Chase in the seminal case of *Ex parte Milligan:*

"The power to make the necessary laws is in Congress; the power to execute in the President. Both powers imply many subordinate and auxiliary powers. Each includes all authorities essential to its due exercise. But neither can the President, in war more than in peace, intrude upon the proper authority of Congress, nor Congress upon the proper authority of the President.... Congress cannot direct the conduct of campaigns, nor can the President, or any commander under him, without the sanction of Congress, institute tribunals for the trial and punishment of offences, either of soldiers or civilians, unless in cases of a controlling necessity, which justifies what it compels, or at least insures acts of indemnity from the justice of the legislature." 4 Wall., at 139–140.[21]

Whether Chief Justice Chase was correct in suggesting that the President may constitutionally convene military commissions "without the sanction of Congress" in cases of "controlling necessity" is a question this Court has not answered definitively, and need not answer today. For we held in *Quirin* that Congress had, through Article of War 15, sanctioned the use of military commissions in such circumstances. 317 U.S., at 28 ("By the Articles of War, and especially Article 15, Congress has explicitly provided, so far as it may constitutionally do so, that military tribunals shall have jurisdiction to try offenders or offenses against the law of war in appropriate cases"). Article 21 of the UCMJ, the language of which is substantially identical to the old Article 15 and was preserved by Congress after World War II,[22] reads as follows:

> "Jurisdiction of courts-martial not exclusive.
> "The provisions of this code conferring jurisdiction upon courts-martial shall not be construed as depriving military commissions, provost courts, or other military tribunals of concurrent jurisdiction in respect of offenders or offenses that by statute or by the law of war may be tried by such military commissions, provost courts, or other military tribunals." 64 Stat. 115.

We have no occasion to revisit *Quirin*'s controversial characterization of Article of War 15 as congressional authorization for military commissions. Cf. Brief for Legal Scholars and Historians as *Amici Curiae* 12–15. Contrary to the Government's assertion, however, even *Quirin* did not view the authorization as a sweeping mandate for the President to "invoke military commissions when he deems them necessary." Brief for Respondents 17. Rather, the *Quirin* Court recognized that Congress had simply preserved what power, under the Constitution and the common law of war, the President had had before 1916 to convene military commissions – with the express condition that the President and those under his command comply with the law of war. See 317 U.S., at 28–29.[23] That much is evidenced by the Court's inquiry, *following* its conclusion that Congress had authorized military commissions, into whether the law of war had indeed been complied with in that case. See *ibid*.

The Government would have us dispense with the inquiry that the *Quirin* Court undertook and find in either the AUMF or the DTA specific, overriding authorization for the very commission that has been convened to try Hamdan. Neither of these congressional

---

[21] See also Winthrop 831 ("[I]n general, it is those provisions of the Constitution which empower Congress to 'declare war' and 'raise armies,' and which, in authorizing the initiation of *war*, authorize the employment of all necessary and proper agencies for its due prosecution, from which this tribunal derives its original sanction" (emphasis in original)).

[22] Article 15 was first adopted as part of the Articles of War in 1916. See Act of Aug. 29, 1916, ch. 418, §3, Art. 15, 39 Stat. 652. When the Articles of War were codified and re-enacted as the UCMJ in 1950, Congress determined to retain Article 15 because it had been "construed by the Supreme Court (*Ex Parte Quirin*, 317 U.S. 1 (1942))." S. Rep. No. 486, 81st Cong., 1st Sess., 13 (1949).

[23] Whether or not the President has independent power, absent congressional authorization, to convene military commissions, he may not disregard limitations that Congress has, in proper exercise of its own war powers, placed on his powers. See *Youngstown Sheet & Tube Co.* v. *Sawyer*, 343 U.S. 579, 637 (1952) (Jackson, J., concurring). The Government does not argue otherwise.

Acts, however, expands the President's authority to convene military commissions. First, while we assume that the AUMF activated the President's war powers, see *Hamdi* v. *Rumsfeld*, 542 U.S. 507 (2004) (plurality opinion), and that those powers include the authority to convene military commissions in appropriate circumstances, see *id.*, at 518; *Quirin*, 317 U.S., at 28–29; see also *Yamashita*, 327 U.S., at 11, there is nothing in the text or legislative history of the AUMF even hinting that Congress intended to expand or alter the authorization set forth in Article 21 of the UCMJ. Cf. *Yerger*, 8 Wall., at 105 ("Repeals by implication are not favored").[24]

Likewise, the DTA cannot be read to authorize this commission. Although the DTA, unlike either Article 21 or the AUMF, was enacted after the President had convened Hamdan's commission, it contains no language authorizing that tribunal or any other at Guantanamo Bay. The DTA obviously "recognize[s]" the existence of the Guantanamo Bay commissions in the weakest sense, Brief for Respondents 15, because it references some of the military orders governing them and creates limited judicial review of their "final decision[s]," DTA §1005(e)(3), 119 Stat. 2743. But the statute also pointedly reserves judgment on whether "the Constitution and laws of the United States are applicable" in reviewing such decisions and whether, if they are, the "standards and procedures" used to try Hamdan and other detainees actually violate the "Constitution and laws." *Ibid.*

Together, the UCMJ, the AUMF, and the DTA at most acknowledge a general Presidential authority to convene military commissions in circumstances where justified under the "Constitution and laws," including the law of war. Absent a more specific congressional authorization, the task of this Court is, as it was in *Quirin*, to decide whether Hamdan's military commission is so justified. It is to that inquiry we now turn.

V

The common law governing military commissions may be gleaned from past practice and what sparse legal precedent exists. Commissions historically have been used in three situations. See Bradley & Goldsmith, Congressional Authorization and the War on Terrorism, 118 Harv. L. Rev. 2048, 2132–2133 (2005); Winthrop 831–846; Hearings on H.R. 2498 before the Subcommittee of the House Committee on Armed Services, 81st Cong., 1st Sess., 975 (1949). First, they have substituted for civilian courts at times and in places where martial law has been declared. Their use in these circumstances has raised constitutional questions, see *Duncan* v. *Kahanamoku*, 327 U.S. 304 (1946); *Milligan*, 4 Wall., at 121–122, but is well recognized.[25] See Winthrop 822, 836–839.

---

[24] On this point, it is noteworthy that the Court in *Ex parte Quirin*, 317 U.S. 1 (1942), looked beyond Congress' declaration of war and accompanying authorization for use of force during World War II, and relied instead on Article of War 15 to find that Congress had authorized the use of military commissions in some circumstances. See *id.*, at 26–29. JUSTICE THOMAS' assertion that we commit "error" in reading Article 21 of the UCMJ to place limitations upon the President's use of military commissions, see *post*, at 5 (dissenting opinion), ignores the reasoning in *Quirin*.

[25] The justification for, and limitations on, these commissions were summarized in *Milligan:*

"If, in foreign invasion or civil war, the courts are actually closed, and it is impossible to administer criminal justice according to law, *then*, on the theatre of active military operations, where war really prevails, there is a necessity to furnish a substitute for the civil authority, thus overthrown, to preserve the safety of the army and society; and as no power is left but the military, it is allowed to govern by martial rule until the laws can have their free course. As necessity creates the rule, so it limits its duration; for, if this government is continued *after* the courts are reinstated, it is a gross usurpation of power. Martial rule can never exist where the courts are open, and in the proper and unobstructed exercise of their jurisdiction. It is also confined to the locality of actual war." 4 Wall., at 127 (emphases in original).

Second, commissions have been established to try civilians "as part of a temporary military government over occupied enemy territory or territory regained from an enemy where civilian government cannot and does not function." *Duncan*, 327 U.S., at 314; see *Milligan*, 4 Wall., at 141–142 (Chase, C. J., concurring in judgment) (distinguishing "MARTIAL LAW PROPER" from "MILITARY GOVERNMENT" in occupied territory). Illustrative of this second kind of commission is the one that was established, with jurisdiction to apply the German Criminal Code, in occupied Germany following the end of World War II. See *Madsen v. Kinsella*, 343 U.S. 341, 356 (1952).[26]

The third type of commission, convened as an "incident to the conduct of war" when there is a need "to seize and subject to disciplinary measures those enemies who in their attempt to thwart or impede our military effort have violated the law of war," *Quirin*, 317 U.S., at 28–29, has been described as "utterly different" from the other two. Bickers, Military Commissions are Constitutionally Sound: A Response to Professors Katyal and Tribe, 34 Tex. Tech. L. Rev. 899, 902 (2002–2003).[27] Not only is its jurisdiction limited to offenses cognizable during time of war, but its role is primarily a factfinding one – to determine, typically on the battlefield itself, whether the defendant has violated the law of war. The last time the U.S. Armed Forces used the law-of-war military commission was during World War II. In *Quirin*, this Court sanctioned President Roosevelt's use of such a tribunal to try Nazi saboteurs captured on American soil during the War. 317 U.S. 1. And in *Yamashita*, we held that a military commission had jurisdiction to try a Japanese commander for failing to prevent troops under his command from committing atrocities in the Philippines. 327 U.S. 1.

Quirin is the model the Government invokes most frequently to defend the commission convened to try Hamdan. That is both appropriate and unsurprising. Since Guantanamo Bay is neither enemy-occupied territory nor under martial law, the law-of-war commission is the only model available. At the same time, no more robust model of executive power exists; *Quirin* represents the high-water mark of military power to try enemy combatants for war crimes.

The classic treatise penned by Colonel William Winthrop, whom we have called "the 'Blackstone of Military Law,'" *Reid v. Covert*, 354 U.S. 1, 19, n. 38 (1957) (plurality opinion), describes at least four preconditions for exercise of jurisdiction by a tribunal of the type convened to try Hamdan. First, "[a] military commission, (except where otherwise authorized by statute), can legally assume jurisdiction only of offenses committed within the field of the command of the convening commander." Winthrop 836. The "field of command" in these circumstances means the "theatre of war." *Ibid*. Second, the offense charged "must have been committed within the period of the war."[28]

---

[26] The limitations on these occupied territory or military government commissions are tailored to the tribunals' purpose and the exigencies that necessitate their use. They may be employed "pending the establishment of civil government," *Madsen*, 343 U.S., at 354–355, which may in some cases extend beyond the "cessation of hostilities," *id.*, at 348.

[27] So much may not be evident on cold review of the Civil War trials often cited as precedent for this kind of tribunal because the commissions established during that conflict operated as both martial law or military government tribunals and law-of-war commissions. Hence, "military commanders began the practice [during the Civil War] of using the same name, the same rules, and often the same tribunals" to try both ordinary crimes and war crimes. Bickers, 34 Tex. Tech. L. Rev., at 908. "For the first time, accused horse thieves and alleged saboteurs found themselves subject to trial by the same military commission." *Id.*, at 909. The Civil War precedents must therefore be considered with caution; as we recognized in *Quirin*, 317 U.S., at 29, and as further discussed below, commissions convened during time of war but under neither martial law nor military government may try only offenses against the law of war.

[28] If the commission is established pursuant to martial law or military government, its jurisdiction extends to offenses committed within "the exercise of military government or martial law." Winthrop 837.

Id., at 837. No jurisdiction exists to try offenses "committed either before or after the war." *Ibid.* Third, a military commission not established pursuant to martial law or an occupation may try only "[i]ndividuals of the enemy's army who have been guilty of illegitimate warfare or other offences in violation of the laws of war" and members of one's own army "who, in time of war, become chargeable with crimes or offences not cognizable, or triable, by the criminal courts or under the Articles of war." *Id.*, at 838. Finally, a law-of-war commission has jurisdiction to try only two kinds of offense: "Violations of the laws and usages of war cognizable by military tribunals only," and "[b]reaches of military orders or regulations for which offenders are not legally triable by court-martial under the Articles of war." *Id.*, at 839.[29]

All parties agree that Colonel Winthrop's treatise accurately describes the common law governing military commissions, and that the jurisdictional limitations he identifies were incorporated in Article of War 15 and, later, Article 21 of the UCMJ. It also is undisputed that Hamdan's commission lacks jurisdiction to try him unless the charge "properly set[s] forth, not only the details of the act charged, but the circumstances conferring *jurisdiction.*" *Id.*, at 842 (emphasis in original). The question is whether the preconditions designed to ensure that a military necessity exists to justify the use of this extraordinary tribunal have been satisfied here.

The charge against Hamdan, described in detail in Part I, *supra*, alleges a conspiracy extending over a number of years, from 1996 to November 2001.[30] All but two months of that more than 5-year-long period preceded the attacks of September 11, 2001, and the enactment of the AUMF – the Act of Congress on which the Government relies for exercise of its war powers and thus for its authority to convene military commissions.[31] Neither the purported agreement with Osama bin Laden and others to commit war

---

[29] Winthrop adds as a fifth, albeit not-always-complied-with, criterion that "the *trial* must be had within the theatre of war . . . ; that, if held elsewhere, and where the civil courts are open and available, the proceedings and sentence will be *coram non judice.*" *Id.*, at 836. The Government does not assert that Guantanamo Bay is a theater of war, but instead suggests that neither Washington, D. C., in 1942 nor the Philippines in 1945 qualified as a "war zone" either. Brief for Respondents 27; cf. *Quirin*, 317 U.S. 1; *In re Yamashita*, 327 U.S. 1 (1946).

[30] The elements of this conspiracy charge have been defined not by Congress but by the President. See Military Commission Instruction No. 2, 32 CFR §11.6 (2005).

[31] JUSTICE THOMAS would treat Osama bin Laden's 1996 declaration of jihad against Americans as the inception of the war. See *post*, at 7–10 (dissenting opinion). But even the Government does not go so far; although the United States had for some time prior to the attacks of September 11, 2001, been aggressively pursuing al Qaeda, neither in the charging document nor in submissions before this Court has the Government asserted that the President's *war powers* were activated prior to September 11, 2001. Cf. Brief for Respondents 25 (describing the events of September 11, 2001, as "an act of war" that "triggered a right to deploy military forces abroad to defend the United States by combating al Qaeda"). JUSTICE THOMAS' further argument that the AUMF is "backward looking" and therefore authorizes *trial by military commission* of crimes that occurred prior to the inception of war is insupportable. See *post*, at 8, n. 3. If nothing else, Article 21 of the UCMJ requires that the President comply with the law of war in his use of military commissions. As explained in the text, the law of war permits trial only of offenses "committed within the period of the war." Winthrop 837; see also *Quirin*, 317 U.S., at 28–29 (observing that law-of-war military commissions may be used to try "those enemies *who in their attempt to thwart or impede our military effort* have violated the law of war" (emphasis added)). The sources that JUSTICE THOMAS relies on to suggest otherwise simply do not support his position. Colonel Green's short exegesis on military commissions cites Howland for the proposition that "[o]ffenses committed before a *formal declaration of war* or *before the declaration of martial law* may be tried by military commission." The Military Commission, 42 Am. J. Int'l L. 832, 848 (1948) (emphases added) (cited *post*, at 9–10). Assuming that to be true, nothing in our analysis turns on the admitted absence of either a formal declaration of war or a declaration of martial law. Our focus instead is on the September 11, 2001 attacks that the Government characterizes as the relevant "act[s] of war," and on the measure that authorized the President's deployment of military force – the AUMF. Because we do not question the Government's position that the war commenced with the events of September 11, 2001, the *Prize Cases*, 2 Black 635 (1863) (cited *post*, at 2, 7, 8, and 10 (THOMAS, J., dissenting)), are not germane to the analysis.

crimes, nor a single overt act, is alleged to have occurred in a theater of war or on any specified date after September 11, 2001. None of the overt acts that Hamdan is alleged to have committed violates the law of war.

These facts alone cast doubt on the legality of the charge and, hence, the commission; as Winthrop makes plain, the offense alleged must have been committed both in a theater of war and *during*, not before, the relevant conflict. But the deficiencies in the time and place allegations also underscore – indeed are symptomatic of – the most serious defect of this charge: The offense it alleges is not triable by law-of-war military commission. See *Yamashita*, 327 U.S., at 13 ("Neither congressional action nor the military orders constituting the commission authorized it to place petitioner on trial unless the charge proffered against him is of a violation of the law of war").[32]

Finally, JUSTICE THOMAS' assertion that Julius Otto Kuehn's trial by military commission "for conspiring with Japanese officials to betray the United States fleet to the Imperial Japanese Government prior to its attack on Pearl Harbor" stands as authoritative precedent for Hamdan's trial by commission, *post*, at 9, misses the mark in three critical respects. First, Kuehn was tried for the *federal espionage crimes* under what were then 50 U.S.C. §§31, 32, and 34, *not* with common-law violations of the law of war. See Hearings before the Joint Committee on the Investigation of the Pearl Harbor Attack, 79th Cong., 1st Sess., pt. 30, pp. 3067–3069 (1946). Second, he was tried by *martial law* commission (a kind of commission JUSTICE THOMAS acknowledges is not relevant to the analysis here, and whose jurisdiction extends to offenses committed within "the exercise of . . . martial law," Winthrop 837, see *supra*, n. 28), *not* a commission established exclusively to try violations of the law of war. See *ibid.* Third, the martial law commissions established to try crimes in Hawaii were ultimately declared illegal by this Court. See *Duncan* v. *Kahanamoku*, 327 U.S. 304, 324 (1946) ("The phrase 'martial law' as employed in [the Hawaiian Organic Act], while intended to authorize the military to act vigorously for the maintenance of an orderly civil government and for the defense of the Islands against actual or threatened rebellion or invasion, was not intended to authorize the supplanting of courts by military tribunals").

[32] JUSTICE THOMAS adopts the remarkable view, not advocated by the Government, that the charging document in this case actually includes more than one charge: Conspiracy *and* several other ill-defined crimes, like "joining an organization" that has a criminal purpose, "'[b]eing a guerilla,'" and aiding the enemy. See *post*, at 16–21, and n. 9. There are innumerable problems with this approach.

First, the crimes JUSTICE THOMAS identifies were not actually charged. It is one thing to observe that charges before a military commission "'need not be stated with the precision of a common law indictment,'" *post*, at 15, n. 7 (citation omitted); it is quite another to say that a crime *not charged* may nonetheless be read into an indictment. Second, the Government plainly had available to it the tools and the time it needed to charge petitioner with the various crimes JUSTICE THOMAS refers to, if it believed they were supported by the allegations. As JUSTICE THOMAS himself observes, see *post*, at 21, the crime of aiding the enemy may, in circumstances where the accused owes allegiance to the party whose enemy he is alleged to have aided, be triable by military commission pursuant to Article 104 of the UCMJ, 10 U.S.C. §904. Indeed, the Government has charged detainees under this provision when it has seen fit to do so. See Brief for David Hicks as *Amicus Curiae* 7.

Third, the cases JUSTICE THOMAS relies on to show that Hamdan may be guilty of violations of the law of war not actually charged do not support his argument. JUSTICE THOMAS begins by blurring the distinction between those categories of "offender" who may be tried by military commission (*e.g.*, jayhawkers and the like) with the "offenses" that may be so tried. Even when it comes to "'being a guerilla,'" cf. *post*, at 18, n. 9 (citation omitted), a label alone does not render a person susceptible to execution or other criminal punishment; the charge of "'being a guerilla'" invariably is accompanied by the allegation that the defendant "'took up arms'" as such. This is because, as explained by Judge Advocate General Holt in a decision upholding the charge of "'being a guerilla'" as one recognized by "the universal usage of the times," the charge is simply shorthand (akin to "being a spy") for "the perpetration of a succession of similar acts" of violence. Record Books of the Judge Advocate General Office, R. 3, 590. The sources cited by JUSTICE THOMAS confirm as much. See cases cited *post*, at 18, n. 9.

Likewise, the suggestion that the Nuremberg precedents support Hamdan's conviction for the (uncharged) crime of joining a criminal organization must fail. Cf. *post*, at 19–21. The convictions of certain high-level Nazi officials for "membership in a criminal organization" were secured pursuant to specific provisions of the Charter of the International Military Tribunal that permitted indictment of individual organization members following convictions of the organizations themselves. See Arts. 9 and 10, in 1 Trial of the Major War Criminals Before the International Military Tribunal 12 (1947). The initial plan to use organizations' convictions as predicates for mass individual trials ultimately was abandoned. See T. Taylor, Anatomy of the Nuremberg Trials: A Personal Memoir 584–585, 638 (1992).

There is no suggestion that Congress has, in exercise of its constitutional authority to "define and punish . . . Offences against the Law of Nations," U.S. Const., Art. I, §8, cl. 10, positively identified "conspiracy" as a war crime.[33] As we explained in *Quirin*, that is not necessarily fatal to the Government's claim of authority to try the alleged offense by military commission; Congress, through Article 21 of the UCMJ, has "incorporated by reference" the common law of war, which may render triable by military commission certain offenses not defined by statute. 317 U.S., at 30. When, however, neither the elements of the offense nor the range of permissible punishments is defined by statute or treaty, the precedent must be plain and unambiguous. To demand any less would be to risk concentrating in military hands a degree of adjudicative and punitive power in excess of that contemplated either by statute or by the Constitution. Cf. *Loving* v. *United States*, 517 U.S. 748, 771 (1996) (acknowledging that Congress "may not delegate the power to make laws"); *Reid*, 354 U.S., at 23–24 ("The Founders envisioned the army as a necessary institution, but one dangerous to liberty if not confined within its essential bounds"); The Federalist No. 47, p. 324 (J. Cooke ed. 1961) (J. Madison) ("The accumulation of all powers legislative, executive and judiciary in the same hands . . . may justly be pronounced the very definition of tyranny").[34]

This high standard was met in *Quirin;* the violation there alleged was, by "universal agreement and practice" both in this country and internationally, recognized as an offense against the law of war. 317 U.S., at 30; see *id.*, at 35–36 ("This precept of the law of war has been so recognized in practice both here and abroad, and has so generally been accepted as valid by authorities on international law that we think it must be regarded as a rule or principle of the law of war recognized by this Government by its enactment of the Fifteenth Article of War" (footnote omitted)). Although the picture arguably was less clear in *Yamashita*, compare 327 U.S., at 16 (stating that the provisions of the Fourth Hague Convention of 1907, 36 Stat. 2306, "plainly" required the defendant to control the troops under his command), with 327 U.S., at 35 (Murphy, J., dissenting), the disagreement between the majority and the dissenters in that case concerned whether the historic and textual evidence constituted clear precedent – not whether clear precedent was required to justify trial by law-of-war military commission.

At a minimum, the Government must make a substantial showing that the crime for which it seeks to try a defendant by military commission is acknowledged to be an offense against the law of war. That burden is far from satisfied here. The crime of "conspiracy" has rarely if ever been tried as such in this country by any law-of-war military commission not exercising some other form of jurisdiction,[35] and does not

---

[33] Cf. 10 U.S.C. §904 (making triable by military commission the crime of aiding the enemy); §906 (same for spying); War Crimes Act of 1996, 18 U.S.C. §2441 (2000 ed. and Supp. III) (listing war crimes); Foreign Operations, Export Financing, and Related Appropriations Act, 1998, §583, 111 Stat. 2436 (same).

[34] While the common law necessarily is "evolutionary in nature," *post*, at 13 (THOMAS, J., dissenting), even in jurisdictions where common law crimes are still part of the penal framework, an act does not become a crime without its foundations having been firmly established in precedent. See, *e.g.*,*R.v. Rimmington*, [2006] 2 All E. R. 257, 275–279 (House of Lords); *id.*, at 279 (while "some degree of vagueness is inevitable and development of the law is a recognised feature of common law courts, . . . the law-making function of the courts must remain within reasonable limits"); see also *Rogers* v. *Tennessee*, 532 U.S. 451, 472–478 (2001) (SCALIA, J., dissenting). The caution that must be exercised in the incremental development of common-law crimes by the judiciary is, for the reasons explained in the text, all the more critical when reviewing developments that stem from military action.

[35] The 19th-century trial of the "Lincoln conspirators," even if properly classified as a trial by law-of-war commission, cf. W. Rehnquist, All the Laws But One: Civil Liberties in Wartime 165–167 (1998) (analyzing the conspiracy charges in light of ordinary criminal law principles at the time), is at best an equivocal exception. Although the charge against the defendants in that case accused them of "combining, confederating, and conspiring together" to murder the President, they were also charged (as we read the indictment, cf. *post*, at

appear in either the Geneva Conventions or the Hague Conventions – the major treaties on the law of war.[36] Winthrop explains that under the common law governing military commissions, it is not enough to intend to violate the law of war and commit overt acts in furtherance of that intention unless the overt acts either are themselves offenses against the law of war or constitute steps sufficiently substantial to qualify as an attempt. See Winthrop 841 ("[T]he jurisdiction of the military commission should be restricted to cases of offence consisting in *overt acts*, *i.e.*, in unlawful commissions or actual attempts to commit, and not in intentions merely" (emphasis in original)).

The Government cites three sources that it says show otherwise. First, it points out that the Nazi saboteurs in *Quirin* were charged with conspiracy. See Brief for Respondents 27. Second, it observes that Winthrop at one point in his treatise identifies conspiracy as an offense "prosecuted by military commissions." *Ibid.* (citing Winthrop 839, and n. 5). Finally, it notes that another military historian, Charles Roscoe Howland, lists conspiracy "'to violate the laws of war by destroying life or property in aid of the enemy'" as an offense that was tried as a violation of the law of war during the Civil War. Brief for Respondents 27–28 (citing C. Howland, Digest of Opinions of the Judge Advocates General of the Army 1071 (1912) (hereinafter Howland)). On close analysis, however, these sources at best lend little support to the Government's position and at worst undermine it. By any measure, they fail to satisfy the high standard of clarity required to justify the use of a military commission.

That the defendants in *Quirin* were charged with conspiracy is not persuasive, since the Court declined to address whether the offense actually qualified as a violation of the law of war – let alone one triable by military commission. The *Quirin* defendants were charged with the following offenses:

"[I.] Violation of the law of war.

"[II.] Violation of Article 81 of the Articles of War, defining the offense of relieving or attempting to relieve, or corresponding with or giving intelligence to, the enemy.

"[III.] Violation of Article 82, defining the offense of spying.

"[IV.] Conspiracy to commit the offenses alleged in charges [I, II, and III]." 317 U.S., at 23.

The Government, defending its charge, argued that the conspiracy alleged "constitute[d] an additional violation of the law of war." *Id.*, at 15. The saboteurs disagreed; they maintained that "[t]he charge of conspiracy can not stand if the other charges fall." *Id.*, at 8. The Court, however, declined to resolve the dispute. It concluded, first, that the specification supporting Charge I adequately alleged a "violation of the law of war" that was not "merely colorable or without foundation." *Id.*, at 36. The facts the Court deemed sufficient for this purpose were that the defendants, admitted enemy combatants, entered upon U.S. territory in time of war without uniform "for the purpose of destroying

---

23, n. 14 (THOMAS, J., dissenting)) with "maliciously, unlawfully, and traitorously murdering the said Abraham Lincoln." H. R. Doc. No. 314, 55th Cong., 1st Sess., 696 (1899). Moreover, the Attorney General who wrote the opinion defending the trial by military commission treated the charge as if it alleged the substantive offense of assassination. See 11 Op. Atty. Gen. 297 (1865) (analyzing the propriety of trying by military commission "the offence of having assassinated the President"); see also *Mudd* v. *Caldera*, 134 F. Supp. 2d 138, 140 (DC 2001).

[36] By contrast, the Geneva Conventions do extend liability for substantive war crimes to those who "orde[r]" their commission, see Third Geneva Convention, Art. 129, 6 U. S. T., at 3418, and this Court has read the Fourth Hague Convention of 1907 to impose "command responsibility" on military commanders for acts of their subordinates, see *Yamashita*, 327 U.S., at 15–16.

property used or useful in prosecuting the war." That act was "a hostile and warlike" one. *Id.*, at 36, 37. The Court was careful in its decision to identify an overt, "complete" act. Responding to the argument that the saboteurs had "not actually committed or attempted to commit any act of depredation or entered the theatre or zone of active military operations" and therefore had not violated the law of war, the Court responded that they had actually "passed our military and naval lines and defenses or went behind those lines, in civilian dress and with hostile purpose." *Id.*, at 38. "The offense was complete when with that purpose they entered – or, having so entered, they remained upon – our territory in time of war without uniform or other appropriate means of identification." *Ibid.*

Turning to the other charges alleged, the Court explained that "[s]ince the first specification of Charge I sets forth a violation of the law of war, we have no occasion to pass on the adequacy of the second specification of Charge I, or to construe the 81st and 82nd Articles of War for the purpose of ascertaining whether the specifications under Charges II and III allege violations of those Articles or whether if so construed they are constitutional." *Id.*, at 46. No mention was made at all of Charge IV – the conspiracy charge.

If anything, *Quirin* supports Hamdan's argument that conspiracy is not a violation of the law of war. Not only did the Court pointedly omit any discussion of the conspiracy charge, but its analysis of Charge I placed special emphasis on the *completion* of an offense; it took seriously the saboteurs' argument that there can be no violation of a law of war – at least not one triable by military commission – without the actual commission of or attempt to commit a "hostile and warlike act." *Id.*, at 37–38.

That limitation makes eminent sense when one considers the necessity from whence this kind of military commission grew: The need to dispense swift justice, often in the form of execution, to illegal belligerents captured on the battlefield. See S. Rep. No. 130, 64th Cong., 1st Sess., p. 40 (1916) (testimony of Brig. Gen. Enoch H. Crowder) (observing that Article of War 15 preserves the power of "the military commander *in the field in time of war*" to use military commissions (emphasis added)). The same urgency would not have been felt vis-à-vis enemies who had done little more than agree to violate the laws of war. Cf. 31 Op. Atty. Gen. 356, 357, 361 (1918) (opining that a German spy could not be tried by military commission because, having been apprehended before entering "any camp, fortification or other military premises of the United States," he had "committed [his offenses] outside of the field of military operations"). The *Quirin* Court acknowledged as much when it described the President's authority to use law-of-war military commissions as the power to "seize and subject to disciplinary measures those enemies *who in their attempt to thwart or impede our military effort* have violated the law of war." 317 U.S., at 28–29 (emphasis added).

Winthrop and Howland are only superficially more helpful to the Government. Howland, granted, lists "conspiracy by two or more to violate the laws of war by destroying life or property in aid of the enemy" as one of over 20 "offenses against the laws and usages of war" "passed upon and punished by military commissions." Howland 1071. But while the records of cases that Howland cites following his list of offenses against the law of war support inclusion of the other offenses mentioned, they provide no support for the inclusion of conspiracy as a violation of the law of war. See *ibid.* (citing Record Books of the Judge Advocate General Office, R. 2, 144; R. 3, 401, 589, 649; R. 4, 320; R. 5, 36, 590; R. 6, 20; R. 7, 413; R. 8, 529; R. 9, 149, 202, 225, 481, 524, 535; R. 10, 567; R. 11, 473, 513; R. 13, 125, 675; R. 16, 446; R. 21, 101, 280). Winthrop, apparently recognizing as much, excludes conspiracy of any kind from his own list of offenses against the law of war. See Winthrop 839–840.

Winthrop does, unsurprisingly, include "criminal conspiracies" in his list of "[c]rimes and statutory offenses cognizable by State or U.S. courts" and triable by martial law or military government commission. See *id.*, at 839. And, in a footnote, he cites several Civil War examples of "conspiracies of this class, *or of the first and second classes combined.*" *Id.*, at 839, n. 5 (emphasis added). The Government relies on this footnote for its contention that conspiracy was triable both as an ordinary crime (a crime of the "first class") and, independently, as a war crime (a crime of the "second class"). But the footnote will not support the weight the Government places on it.

As we have seen, the military commissions convened during the Civil War functioned at once as martial law or military government tribunals and as law-of-war commissions. See n. 27, *supra.* Accordingly, they regularly tried war crimes and ordinary crimes together. Indeed, as Howland observes, "[n]ot infrequently the crime, as charged and found, was a combination of the two species of offenses." Howland 1071; see also Davis 310, n. 2; Winthrop 842. The example he gives is "'murder in violation of the laws of war.'" Howland 1071–1072. Winthrop's conspiracy "of the first and second classes combined" is, like Howland's example, best understood as a species of compound offense of the type tried by the hybrid military commissions of the Civil War. It is not a stand-alone offense against the law of war. Winthrop confirms this understanding later in his discussion, when he emphasizes that "*overt acts*" constituting war crimes are the only proper subject at least of those military tribunals not convened to stand in for local courts. Winthrop 841, and nn. 22, 23 (emphasis in original) (citing W. Finlason, Martial Law 130 (1867)).

Justice Thomas cites as evidence that conspiracy is a recognized violation of the law of war the Civil War indictment against Henry Wirz, which charged the defendant with "'[m]aliciously, willfully, and traitorously ... combining, confederating, and conspiring [with others] to injure the health and destroy the lives of soldiers in the military service of the United States ... to the end that the armies of the United States might be weakened and impaired, in violation of the laws and customs of war.'" *Post*, at 24–25 (dissenting opinion) (quoting H. R. Doc. No. 314, 55th Cong., 3d Sess., 785 (1865); emphasis deleted). As shown by the specification supporting that charge, however, Wirz was alleged to have *personally committed* a number of atrocities against his victims, including torture, injection of prisoners with poison, and use of "ferocious and bloodthirsty dogs" to "seize, tear, mangle, and maim the bodies and limbs" of prisoners, many of whom died as a result. *Id.*, at 789–790. Crucially, Judge Advocate General Holt determined that one of Wirz's alleged co-conspirators, R.B. Winder, should *not* be tried by military commission because there was as yet insufficient evidence of his own personal involvement in the atrocities: "[I]n the case of R.B. Winder, *while the evidence at the trial of Wirz was deemed by the court to implicate him in the conspiracy* against the lives of all Federal prisoners in rebel hands, *no such specific overt acts of violation of the laws of war* are as yet fixed upon him as to make it expedient to prefer formal charges and bring him to trial." *Id.*, at 783 (emphases added).[37]

---

[37] The other examples Justice Thomas offers are no more availing. The Civil War indictment against Robert Louden, cited *post*, at 25, alleged a conspiracy, but not one in violation of the law of war. See War Dept., General Court Martial Order No. 41, p. 20 (1864). A separate charge of "'[t]ransgression of the laws and customs of war'" made no mention of conspiracy. *Id.*, at 17. The charge against Lenger Grenfel and others for conspiring to release rebel prisoners held in Chicago only supports the observation, made in the text, that the Civil War tribunals often charged hybrid crimes mixing elements of crimes ordinarily triable in civilian courts (like treason) and violations of the law of war. Judge Advocate General Holt, in recommending that Grenfel's death sentence be upheld (it was in fact commuted by Presidential decree, see H. R. Doc. No. 314,

Finally, international sources confirm that the crime charged here is not a recognized violation of the law of war.[38] As observed above, see *supra*, at 40, none of the major treaties governing the law of war identifies conspiracy as a violation thereof. And the only "conspiracy" crimes that have been recognized by international war crimes tribunals (whose jurisdiction often extends beyond war crimes proper to crimes against humanity and crimes against the peace) are conspiracy to commit genocide and common plan to wage aggressive war, which is a crime against the peace and requires for its commission actual participation in a "concrete plan to wage war." 1 Trial of the Major War Criminals Before the International Military Tribunal: Nuremberg, 14 November 1945-1 October 1946, p. 225 (1947). The International Military Tribunal at Nuremberg, over the prosecution's objections, pointedly refused to recognize as a violation of the law of war conspiracy to commit war crimes, see, *e.g.*, 22 *id.*, at 469,[39] and convicted only Hitler's most senior associates of conspiracy to wage aggressive war, see S. Pomorski, Conspiracy and Criminal Organization, in the Nuremberg Trial and International Law 213, 233–235 (G. Ginsburgs & V. Kudriavtsev eds. 1990). As one prominent figure from the Nuremberg trials has explained, members of the Tribunal objected to recognition of conspiracy as a violation of the law of war on the ground that "[t]he Anglo-American concept of conspiracy was not part of European legal systems and arguably not an element of the internationally recognized laws of war." T. Taylor, Anatomy of the Nuremberg Trials: A Personal Memoir 36 (1992); see also *id.*, at 550 (observing that Francis Biddle, who as Attorney General prosecuted the defendants in *Quirin*, thought the French judge had made a "'persuasive argument that conspiracy in the truest sense is not known to international law'").[40]

In sum, the sources that the Government and Justice Thomas rely upon to show that conspiracy to violate the law of war is itself a violation of the law of war in fact demonstrate quite the opposite. Far from making the requisite substantial showing, the Government has failed even to offer a "merely colorable" case for inclusion of conspiracy among those offenses cognizable by law-of-war military commission. Cf. *Quirin*, 317 U.S., at 36. Because the charge does not support the commission's jurisdiction, the commission lacks authority to try Hamdan.

---

at 725), explained that the accused "united himself with traitors and malefactors for the overthrow of our Republic in the interest of slavery." *Id.*, at 689.

[38] The Court in *Quirin* "assume[d] that there are acts regarded in other countries, or by some writers on international law, as offenses against the law of war which would not be triable by military tribunal here, either because they are not recognized by our courts as violations of the law of war or because they are of that class of offenses constitutionally triable only by a jury." 317 U.S., at 29. We need not test the validity of that assumption here because the international sources only corroborate the domestic ones.

[39] Accordingly, the Tribunal determined to "disregard the charges . . . that the defendants conspired to commit War Crimes and Crimes against Humanity." 22 Trial of the Major War Criminals Before the International Military Tribunal 469 (1947); see also *ibid.* ("[T]he Charter does not define as a separate crime any conspiracy except the one to commit acts of aggressive war").

[40] See also 15 United Nations War Crimes Commissions, Law Reports of Trials of War Criminals 90–91 (1949) (observing that, although a few individuals were charged with conspiracy under European domestic criminal codes following World War II, "the United States Military Tribunals" established at that time did not "recognis[e] as a separate offence conspiracy to commit war crimes or crimes against humanity"). The International Criminal Tribunal for the former Yugoslavia (ICTY), drawing on the Nuremberg precedents, has adopted a "joint criminal enterprise" theory of liability, but that is a species of liability for the substantive offense (akin to aiding and abetting), not a crime on its own. See *Prosecutor* v. *Tadić*, Judgment, Case No. IT-94-1-A (ICTY App. Chamber, July 15, 1999); see also *Prosecutor* v. *Milutinović*, Decision on Dragoljub Ojdanić's Motion Challenging Jurisdiction – Joint Criminal Enterprise, Case No. IT-99-37-AR72, ¶26 (ICTY App. Chamber, May 21, 2003) (stating that "[c]riminal liability pursuant to a joint criminal enterprise is not a liability for . . . conspiring to commit crimes").

The charge's shortcomings are not merely formal, but are indicative of a broader inability on the Executive's part here to satisfy the most basic precondition – at least in the absence of specific congressional authorization – for establishment of military commissions: military necessity. Hamdan's tribunal was appointed not by a military commander in the field of battle, but by a retired major general stationed away from any active hostilities. Cf. *Rasul* v. *Bush*, 542 U.S., at 487 (KENNEDY, J., concurring in judgment) (observing that "Guantanamo Bay is . . . far removed from any hostilities"). Hamdan is charged not with an overt act for which he was caught redhanded in a theater of war and which military efficiency demands be tried expeditiously, but with an *agreement* the inception of which long predated the attacks of September 11, 2001 and the AUMF. That may well be a crime,[41] but it is not an offense that "by the law of war may be tried by military commissio[n]." 10 U.S.C. §821. None of the overt acts alleged to have been committed in furtherance of the agreement is itself a war crime, or even necessarily occurred during time of, or in a theater of, war. Any urgent need for imposition or execution of judgment is utterly belied by the record; Hamdan was arrested in November 2001 and he was not charged until mid-2004. These simply are not the circumstances in which, by any stretch of the historical evidence or this Court's precedents, a military commission established by Executive Order under the authority of Article 21 of the UCMJ may lawfully try a person and subject him to punishment.

VI

Whether or not the Government has charged Hamdan with an offense against the law of war cognizable by military commission, the commission lacks power to proceed. The UCMJ conditions the President's use of military commissions on compliance not only with the American common law of war, but also with the rest of the UCMJ itself, insofar as applicable, and with the "rules and precepts of the law of nations," *Quirin*, 317 U.S., at 28 – including, *inter alia*, the four Geneva Conventions signed in 1949. See *Yamashita*, 327 U.S., at 20–21, 23–24. The procedures that the Government has decreed will govern Hamdan's trial by commission violate these laws.

A

The commission's procedures are set forth in Commission Order No. 1, which was amended most recently on August 31, 2005 – after Hamdan's trial had already begun. Every commission established pursuant to Commission Order No. 1 must have a presiding officer and at least three other members, all of whom must be commissioned officers. §4(A)(1). The presiding officer's job is to rule on questions of law and other evidentiary and interlocutory issues; the other members make findings and, if applicable, sentencing decisions. §4(A)(5). The accused is entitled to appointed military counsel and may hire civilian counsel at his own expense so long as such counsel is a U.S. citizen with security clearance "at the level SECRET or higher." §§4(C)(2)–(3).

---

[41] JUSTICE THOMAS' suggestion that our conclusion precludes the Government from bringing to justice those who conspire to commit acts of terrorism is therefore wide of the mark. See *post*, at 8, n. 3; 28–30. That conspiracy is not a violation of the law of war triable by military commission does not mean the Government may not, for example, prosecute by court-martial or in federal court those caught "plotting terrorist atrocities like the bombing of the Khobar Towers." *Post*, at 29.

The accused also is entitled to a copy of the charge(s) against him, both in English and his own language (if different), to a presumption of innocence, and to certain other rights typically afforded criminal defendants in civilian courts and courts-martial. See §§5(A)–(P). These rights are subject, however, to one glaring condition: The accused and his civilian counsel may be excluded from, and precluded from ever learning what evidence was presented during, any part of the proceeding that either the Appointing Authority or the presiding officer decides to "close." Grounds for such closure "include the protection of information classified or classifiable . . . ; information protected by law or rule from unauthorized disclosure; the physical safety of participants in Commission proceedings, including prospective witnesses; intelligence and law enforcement sources, methods, or activities; and other national security interests." §6(B)(3).[42] Appointed military defense counsel must be privy to these closed sessions, but may, at the presiding officer's discretion, be forbidden to reveal to his or her client what took place therein. *Ibid.*

Another striking feature of the rules governing Hamdan's commission is that they permit the admission of *any* evidence that, in the opinion of the presiding officer, "would have probative value to a reasonable person." §6(D)(1). Under this test, not only is testimonial hearsay and evidence obtained through coercion fully admissible, but neither live testimony nor witnesses' written statements need be sworn. See §§6(D)(2)(b), (3). Moreover, the accused and his civilian counsel may be denied access to evidence in the form of "protected information" (which includes classified information as well as "information protected by law or rule from unauthorized disclosure" and "information concerning other national security interests," §§6(B)(3), 6(D)(5)(a)(v)), so long as the presiding officer concludes that the evidence is "probative" under §6(D)(1) and that its admission without the accused's knowledge would not "result in the denial of a full and fair trial." §6(D)(5)(b).[43] Finally, a presiding officer's determination that evidence "would not have probative value to a reasonable person" may be overridden by a majority of the other commission members. §6(D)(1).

Once all the evidence is in, the commission members (not including the presiding officer) must vote on the accused's guilt. A two-thirds vote will suffice for both a verdict of guilty and for imposition of any sentence not including death (the imposition of which requires a unanimous vote). §6(F). Any appeal is taken to a three-member review panel composed of military officers and designated by the Secretary of Defense, only one member of which need have experience as a judge. §6(H)(4). The review panel is directed to "disregard any variance from procedures specified in this Order or elsewhere that would not materially have affected the outcome of the trial before the Commission." *Ibid.* Once the panel makes its recommendation to the Secretary of Defense, the Secretary can either remand for further proceedings or forward the record to the President with his recommendation as to final disposition. §6(H)(5). The President then, unless he has delegated the task to the Secretary, makes the "final decision." §6(H)(6). He may change the commission's findings or sentence only in a manner favorable to the accused. *Ibid.*

---

[42] The accused also may be excluded from the proceedings if he "engages in disruptive conduct." §5(K).

[43] As the District Court observed, this section apparently permits reception of testimony from a confidential informant in circumstances where "Hamdan will not be permitted to hear the testimony, see the witness's face, or learn his name. If the government has information developed by interrogation of witnesses in Afghanistan or elsewhere, it can offer such evidence in transcript form, or even as summaries of transcripts." 344 F. Supp. 2d 152, 168 (DC 2004).

B

Hamdan raises both general and particular objections to the procedures set forth in Commission Order No. 1. His general objection is that the procedures' admitted deviation from those governing courts-martial itself renders the commission illegal. Chief among his particular objections are that he may, under the Commission Order, be convicted based on evidence he has not seen or heard, and that any evidence admitted against him need not comply with the admissibility or relevance rules typically applicable in criminal trials and court-martial proceedings.

The Government objects to our consideration of any procedural challenge at this stage on the grounds that (1) the abstention doctrine espoused in *Councilman*, 420 U.S. 738, precludes pre-enforcement review of procedural rules, (2) Hamdan will be able to raise any such challenge following a "final decision" under the DTA, and (3) "there is . . . no basis to presume, before the trial has even commenced, that the trial will not be conducted in good faith and according to law." Brief for Respondents 45–46, nn. 20–21. The first of these contentions was disposed of in Part III, *supra*, and neither of the latter two is sound.

First, because Hamdan apparently is not subject to the death penalty (at least as matters now stand) and may receive a sentence shorter than 10 years' imprisonment, he has no automatic right to review of the commission's "final decision"[44] before a federal court under the DTA. See §1005(e)(3), 119 Stat. 2743. Second, contrary to the Government's assertion, there *is* a "basis to presume" that the procedures employed during Hamdan's trial will violate the law: The procedures are described with particularity in Commission Order No. 1, and implementation of some of them has already occurred. One of Hamdan's complaints is that he will be, and *indeed already has been*, excluded from his own trial. See Reply Brief for Petitioner 12; App. to Pet. for Cert. 45a. Under these circumstances, review of the procedures in advance of a "final decision – the timing of which is left entirely to the discretion of the President under the DTA – is appropriate. We turn, then, to consider the merits of Hamdan's procedural challenge.

C

In part because the difference between military commissions and courts-martial originally was a difference of jurisdiction alone, and in part to protect against abuse and ensure evenhandedness under the pressures of war, the procedures governing trials by military commission historically have been the same as those governing courts-martial. See, *e.g.*, 1 The War of the Rebellion 248 (2d series 1894) (General Order 1 issued during the Civil War required military commissions to "be constituted in a similar manner and their proceedings be conducted according to the same general rules as courts-martial in order to prevent abuses which might otherwise arise"). Accounts of commentators from Winthrop through General Crowder – who drafted Article of War 15 and whose views have been deemed "authoritative" by this Court, *Madsen*, 343 U.S., at 353 – confirm as much.[45] As recently as the Korean and Vietnam wars, during which use of military commissions was contemplated but never made, the principle of procedural parity was

---

[44] Any decision of the commission is not "final" until the President renders it so. See Commission Order No. 1 §6(H)(6).

[45] See Winthrop 835, and n. 81 ("military commissions are constituted and composed, and their proceedings are conducted, similarly to general courts-martial"); *id.*, at 841–842; S. Rep. No. 130, 64th Cong., 1st Sess., 40 (1916) (testimony of Gen. Crowder) ("Both classes of courts have the same procedure"); see also, *e.g.*, H. Coppée, Field Manual of Courts-Martial, p. 104 (1863) ("[Military] commissions are appointed by the same

espoused as a background assumption. See Paust, Antiterrorism Military Commissions: Courting Illegality, 23 Mich. J. Int'l L. 1, 3–5 (2001–2002).

There is a glaring historical exception to this general rule. The procedures and evidentiary rules used to try General Yamashita near the end of World War II deviated in significant respects from those then governing courts-martial. See 327 U.S. 1. The force of that precedent, however, has been seriously undermined by post-World War II developments.

Yamashita, from late 1944 until September 1945, was Commanding General of the Fourteenth Army Group of the Imperial Japanese Army, which had exercised control over the Philippine Islands. On September 3, 1945, after American forces regained control of the Philippines, Yamashita surrendered. Three weeks later, he was charged with violations of the law of war. A few weeks after that, he was arraigned before a military commission convened in the Philippines. He pleaded not guilty, and his trial lasted for two months. On December 7, 1945, Yamashita was convicted and sentenced to hang. See *id.*, at 5; *id.*, at 31–34 (Murphy, J., dissenting). This Court upheld the denial of his petition for a writ of habeas corpus.

The procedures and rules of evidence employed during Yamashita's trial departed so far from those used in courts-martial that they generated an unusually long and vociferous critique from two Members of this Court. See *id.*, at 41–81 (Rutledge, J., joined by Murphy, J., dissenting).[46] Among the dissenters' primary concerns was that the commission had free rein to consider all evidence "which in the commission's opinion 'would be of assistance in proving or disproving the charge,' without any of the usual modes of authentication." *Id.*, at 49 (Rutledge, J.).

The majority, however, did not pass on the merits of Yamashita's procedural challenges because it concluded that his status disentitled him to any protection under the Articles of War (specifically, those set forth in Article 38, which would become Article 36 of the UCMJ) or the Geneva Convention of 1929, 47 Stat. 2021 (1929 Geneva Convention). The Court explained that Yamashita was neither a "person made subject to the Articles of War by Article 2" thereof, 327 U.S., at 20, nor a protected prisoner of war being tried for crimes committed during his detention, *id.*, at 21.

At least partially in response to subsequent criticism of General Yamashita's trial, the UCMJ's codification of the Articles of War after World War II expanded the category of persons subject thereto to include defendants in Yamashita's (and Hamdan's) position,[47] and the Third Geneva Convention of 1949 extended prisoner-of-war protections

---

authorities as those which may order courts-martial. They are constituted in a manner similar to such courts, and their proceedings are conducted in exactly the same way, as to form, examination of witnesses, etc.").

[46] The dissenters' views are summarized in the following passage:

"It is outside our basic scheme to condemn men without giving reasonable opportunity for preparing defense; in capital or other serious crimes to convict on 'official documents . . . ; affidavits; . . . documents or translations thereof; diaries . . . , photographs, motion picture films, and . . . newspapers' or on hearsay, once, twice or thrice removed, more particularly when the documentary evidence or some of it is prepared *ex parte* by the prosecuting authority and includes not only opinion but conclusions of guilt. Nor in such cases do we deny the rights of confrontation of witnesses and cross-examination." *Yamashita*, 327 U.S., at 44 (footnotes omitted).

[47] Article 2 of the UCMJ now reads:

"(a) The following persons are subject to [the UCMJ]:

"(9) Prisoners of war in custody of the armed forces.

"(12) Subject to any treaty or agreement to which the United States is or may be a party or to any accepted rule of international law, persons within an area leased by or otherwise reserved or acquired for the use of the United States which is under the control of the Secretary concerned and which is outside the United States and outside the Commonwealth of Puerto Rico, Guam, and the Virgin Islands." 10 U.S.C. §802(a).

Guantanamo Bay is such a leased area. See *Rasul* v. *Bush*, 542 U.S. 466, 471 (2004).

to individuals tried for crimes committed before their capture. See 3 Int'l Comm. of Red Cross,[48] Commentary: Geneva Convention Relative to the Treatment of Prisoners of War 413 (1960) (hereinafter GCIII Commentary) (explaining that Article 85, which extends the Convention's protections to "[p]risoners of war prosecuted under the laws of the Detaining Power for acts committed prior to capture," was adopted in response to judicial interpretations of the 1929 Convention, including this Court's decision in *Yamashita*). The most notorious exception to the principle of uniformity, then, has been stripped of its precedential value.

The uniformity principle is not an inflexible one; it does not preclude all departures from the procedures dictated for use by courts-martial. But any departure must be tailored to the exigency that necessitates it. See Winthrop 835, n. 81. That understanding is reflected in Article 36 of the UCMJ, which provides:

> "(a) The procedure, including modes of proof, in cases before courts-martial, courts of inquiry, military commissions, and other military tribunals may be prescribed by the President by regulations which shall, so far as he considers practicable, apply the principles of law and the rules of evidence generally recognized in the trial of criminal cases in the United States district courts, but which may not be contrary to or inconsistent with this chapter.

> "(b) All rules and regulations made under this article shall be uniform insofar as practicable and shall be reported to Congress." 70A Stat. 50.

Article 36 places two restrictions on the President's power to promulgate rules of procedure for courts-martial and military commissions alike. First, no procedural rule he adopts may be "contrary to or inconsistent with" the UCMJ – however practical it may seem. Second, the rules adopted must be "uniform insofar as practicable." That is, the rules applied to military commissions must be the same as those applied to courts-martial unless such uniformity proves impracticable.

Hamdan argues that Commission Order No. 1 violates both of these restrictions; he maintains that the procedures described in the Commission Order are inconsistent with the UCMJ and that the Government has offered no explanation for their deviation from the procedures governing courts-martial, which are set forth in the Manual for Courts-Martial, United States (2005 ed.) (Manual for Courts-Martial). Among the inconsistencies Hamdan identifies is that between §6 of the Commission Order, which permits exclusion of the accused from proceedings and denial of his access to evidence in certain circumstances, and the UCMJ's requirement that "[a]ll ... proceedings" other than votes and deliberations by courts-martial "shall be made a part of the record and shall be in the presence of the accused." 10 U.S.C.A. §839(c) (Supp. 2006). Hamdan also observes that the Commission Order dispenses with virtually all evidentiary rules applicable in courts-martial.

The Government has three responses. First, it argues, only 9 of the UCMJ's 158 Articles – the ones that expressly mention "military commissions"[49] – actually apply to

---

[48] The International Committee of the Red Cross is referred to by name in several provisions of the 1949 Geneva Conventions and is the body that drafted and published the official commentary to the Conventions. Though not binding law, the commentary is, as the parties recognize, relevant in interpreting the Conventions' provisions.

[49] Aside from Articles 21 and 36, discussed at length in the text, the other seven Articles that expressly reference military commissions are: (1) 28 (requiring appointment of reporters and interpreters); (2) 47 (making it a crime to refuse to appear or testify "before a court-martial, military commission, court of inquiry, or any other military court or board"); (3) 48 (allowing a "court-martial, provost court, or military commission"

commissions, and Commission Order No. 1 sets forth no procedure that is "contrary to or inconsistent with" those 9 provisions. Second, the Government contends, military commissions would be of no use if the President were hamstrung by those provisions of the UCMJ that govern courts-martial. Finally, the President's determination that "the danger to the safety of the United States and the nature of international terrorism" renders it impracticable "to apply in military commissions . . . the principles of law and rules of evidence generally recognized in the trial of criminal cases in the United States district courts," November 13 Order §1(f), is, in the Government's view, explanation enough for any deviation from court-martial procedures. See Brief for Respondents 43–47, and n. 22.

Hamdan has the better of this argument. Without reaching the question whether any provision of Commission Order No. 1 is strictly "contrary to or inconsistent with" other provisions of the UCMJ, we conclude that the "practicability" determination the President has made is insufficient to justify variances from the procedures governing courts-martial. Subsection (b) of Article 36 was added after World War II, and requires a different showing of impracticability from the one required by subsection (a). Subsection (a) requires that the rules the President promulgates for courts-martial, provost courts, and military commissions alike conform to those that govern procedures in *Article III courts*, "so far as *he considers* practicable." 10 U.S.C. §836(a) (emphasis added). Subsection (b), by contrast, demands that the rules applied in courts-martial, provost courts, and military commissions – whether or not they conform with the Federal Rules of Evidence – be "uniform *insofar as practicable*." §836(b) (emphasis added). Under the latter provision, then, the rules set forth in the Manual for Courts-Martial must apply to military commissions unless impracticable.[50]

The President here has determined, pursuant to subsection (a), that it is impracticable to apply the rules and principles of law that govern "the trial of criminal cases in the United States district courts," §836(a), to Hamdan's commission. We assume that complete deference is owed that determination. The President has not, however, made a similar official determination that it is impracticable to apply the rules for courts-martial.[51] And even if subsection (b)'s requirements may be satisfied without such an official determination, the requirements of that subsection are not satisfied here.

Nothing in the record before us demonstrates that it would be impracticable to apply court-martial rules in this case. There is no suggestion, for example, of any logistical

---

to punish a person for contempt); (4) 49(d) (permitting admission into evidence of a "duly authenticated deposition taken upon reasonable notice to the other parties" *only* if "admissible under the rules of evidence" and *only* if the witness is otherwise unavailable); (5) 50 (permitting admission into evidence of records of courts of inquiry "if otherwise admissible under the rules of evidence," and if certain other requirements are met); (6) 104 (providing that a person accused of aiding the enemy may be sentenced to death or other punishment by military commission or court-martial); and (7) 106 (mandating the death penalty for spies convicted before military commission or court-martial).

[50] JUSTICE THOMAS relies on the legislative history of the UCMJ to argue that Congress' adoption of Article 36(b) in the wake of World War II was "motivated" solely by a desire for "uniformity across the separate branches of the armed services." *Post*, at 35. But even if Congress was concerned with ensuring uniformity across service branches, that does not mean it did not also intend to codify the longstanding practice of procedural parity between courts-martial and other military tribunals. Indeed, the suggestion that Congress did *not* intend uniformity across tribunal types is belied by the textual proximity of subsection (a) (which requires that the rules governing criminal trials in federal district courts apply, absent the President's determination of impracticability, to courts-martial, provost courts, and *military commissions* alike) and subsection (b) (which imposes the uniformity requirement).

[51] We may assume that such a determination would be entitled to a measure of deference. For the reasons given by JUSTICE KENNEDY, see *post*, at 5 (opinion concurring in part), however, the level of deference accorded to a determination made under subsection (b) presumably would not be as high as that accorded to a determination under subsection (a).

difficulty in securing properly sworn and authenticated evidence or in applying the usual principles of relevance and admissibility. Assuming *arguendo* that the reasons articulated in the President's Article 36(a) determination ought to be considered in evaluating the impracticability of applying court-martial rules, the only reason offered in support of that determination is the danger posed by international terrorism.[52] Without for one moment underestimating that danger, it is not evident to us why it should require, in the case of Hamdan's trial, any variance from the rules that govern courts-martial.

The absence of any showing of impracticability is particularly disturbing when considered in light of the clear and admitted failure to apply one of the most fundamental protections afforded not just by the Manual for Courts-Martial but also by the UCMJ itself: the right to be present. See 10 U.S.C.A. §839(c) (Supp.2006). Whether or not that departure technically is "contrary to or inconsistent with" the terms of the UCMJ, 10 U.S.C. §836(a), the jettisoning of so basic a right cannot lightly be excused as "practicable."

Under the circumstances, then, the rules applicable in courts-martial must apply. Since it is undisputed that Commission Order No. 1 deviates in many significant respects from those rules, it necessarily violates Article 36(b).

The Government's objection that requiring compliance with the court-martial rules imposes an undue burden both ignores the plain meaning of Article 36(b) and misunderstands the purpose and the history of military commissions. The military commission was not born of a desire to dispense a more summary form of justice than is afforded by courts-martial; it developed, rather, as a tribunal of necessity to be employed when courts-martial lacked jurisdiction over either the accused or the subject matter. See Winthrop 831. Exigency lent the commission its legitimacy, but did not further justify the wholesale jettisoning of procedural protections. That history explains why the military commission's procedures typically have been the ones used by courts-martial. That the jurisdiction of the two tribunals today may sometimes overlap, see *Madsen*, 343 U.S., at 354, does not detract from the force of this history;[53] Article 21 did not transform the military commission from a tribunal of true exigency into a more convenient adjudicatory tool. Article 36, confirming as much, strikes a careful balance between uniform procedure and the need to accommodate exigencies that may sometimes arise in a theater of war. That Article not having been complied with here, the rules specified for Hamdan's trial are illegal.[54]

---

[52] JUSTICE THOMAS looks not to the President's official Article 36(a) determination, but instead to press statements made by the Secretary of Defense and the Under Secretary of Defense for Policy. See *post*, at 36–38 (dissenting opinion). We have not heretofore, in evaluating the legality of Executive action, deferred to comments made by such officials to the media. Moreover, the only additional reason the comments provide – aside from the general danger posed by international terrorism – for departures from court-martial procedures is the need to protect classified information. As we explain in the text, and as JUSTICE KENNEDY elaborates in his separate opinion, the structural and procedural defects of Hamdan's commission extend far beyond rules preventing access to classified information.

[53] JUSTICE THOMAS relies extensively on *Madsen* for the proposition that the President has free rein to set the procedures that govern military commissions. See *post*, at 30, 31, 33, n. 16, 34 and 45. That reliance is misplaced. Not only did *Madsen* not involve a law-of-war military commission, but (1) the petitioner there did not challenge the procedures used to try her, (2) the UCMJ, with its new Article 36(b), did not become effective until May 31, 1951, *after* the petitioner's trial, see 343 U.S., at 345, n. 6, and (3) the procedures used to try the petitioner actually afforded *more* protection than those used in courts-martial, see *id.*, at 358–360; see also *id.*, at 358 ("[T]he Military Government Courts for Germany ... have had a less military character than that of courts-martial").

[54] Prior to the enactment of Article 36(b), it may well have been the case that a deviation from the rules governing courts-martial would not have rendered the military commission "'*illegal.*'" *Post*, at 30–31, n. 16 (THOMAS, J., dissenting) (quoting Winthrop 841). Article 36(b), however, imposes a statutory command that must be heeded.

D

The procedures adopted to try Hamdan also violate the Geneva Conventions. The Court of Appeals dismissed Hamdan's Geneva Convention challenge on three independent grounds: (1) the Geneva Conventions are not judicially enforceable; (2) Hamdan in any event is not entitled to their protections; and (3) even if he is entitled to their protections, *Councilman* abstention is appropriate. Judge Williams, concurring, rejected the second ground but agreed with the majority respecting the first and the last. As we explained in Part III, *supra*, the abstention rule applied in *Councilman*, 420 U.S. 738, is not applicable here.[55] And for the reasons that follow, we hold that neither of the other grounds the Court of Appeals gave for its decision is persuasive.

i

The Court of Appeals relied on *Johnson* v. *Eisentrager*, 339 U.S. 763 (1950), to hold that Hamdan could not invoke the Geneva Conventions to challenge the Government's plan to prosecute him in accordance with Commission Order No. 1. *Eisentrager* involved a challenge by 21 German nationals to their 1945 convictions for war crimes by a military tribunal convened in Nanking, China, and to their subsequent imprisonment in occupied Germany. The petitioners argued, *inter alia*, that the 1929 Geneva Convention rendered illegal some of the procedures employed during their trials, which they said deviated impermissibly from the procedures used by courts-martial to try American soldiers. See *id.*, at 789. We rejected that claim on the merits because the petitioners (unlike Hamdan here) had failed to identify any prejudicial disparity "between the Commission that tried [them] and those that would try an offending soldier of the American forces of like rank," and in any event could claim no protection, under the 1929 Convention, during trials for crimes that occurred before their confinement as prisoners of war. *Id.*, at 790.[56]

Buried in a footnote of the opinion, however, is this curious statement suggesting that the Court lacked power even to consider the merits of the Geneva Convention argument:

> "We are not holding that these prisoners have no right which the military authorities are bound to respect. The United States, by the Geneva Convention of July 27, 1929, 47 Stat. 2021, concluded with forty-six other countries, including the German Reich, an agreement upon the treatment to be accorded captives. These prisoners claim to be and are entitled to its protection. It is, however, the obvious scheme of the Agreement that responsibility for observance and enforcement of these rights is upon political and military authorities. Rights of alien enemies are vindicated under it only through protests and intervention of protecting powers as the rights of our citizens against foreign governments are vindicated only by Presidential intervention." *Id.*, at 789, n. 14.

The Court of Appeals, on the strength of this footnote, held that "the 1949 Geneva Convention does not confer upon Hamdan a right to enforce its provisions in court." 415 F. 3d, at 40.

Whatever else might be said about the *Eisentrager* footnote, it does not control this case. We may assume that "the obvious scheme" of the 1949 Conventions is identical

---

[55] JUSTICE THOMAS makes the different argument that Hamdan's Geneva Convention challenge is not yet "ripe" because he has yet to be sentenced. See *post*, at 43–45. This is really just a species of the abstention argument we have already rejected. See Part III, *supra*. The text of the Geneva Conventions does not direct an accused to wait until sentence is imposed to challenge the legality of the tribunal that is to try him.

[56] As explained in Part VI-C, *supra*, that is no longer true under the 1949 Conventions.

in all relevant respects to that of the 1929 Convention,[57] and even that that scheme would, absent some other provision of law, preclude Hamdan's invocation of the Convention's provisions as an independent source of law binding the Government's actions and furnishing petitioner with any enforceable right.[58] For, regardless of the nature of the rights conferred on Hamdan, cf. *United States* v. *Rauscher*, 119 U.S. 407 (1886), they are, as the Government does not dispute, part of the law of war. See *Hamdi*, 542 U.S., at 520–521 (plurality opinion). And compliance with the law of war is the condition upon which the authority set forth in Article 21 is granted.

ii

For the Court of Appeals, acknowledgment of that condition was no bar to Hamdan's trial by commission. As an alternative to its holding that Hamdan could not invoke the Geneva Conventions at all, the Court of Appeals concluded that the Conventions did not in any event apply to the armed conflict during which Hamdan was captured. The court accepted the Executive's assertions that Hamdan was captured in connection with the United States' war with al Qaeda and that that war is distinct from the war with the Taliban in Afghanistan. It further reasoned that the war with al Qaeda evades the reach of the Geneva Conventions. See 415 F. 3d, at 41–42. We, like Judge Williams, disagree with the latter conclusion.

The conflict with al Qaeda is not, according to the Government, a conflict to which the full protections afforded detainees under the 1949 Geneva Conventions apply because Article 2 of those Conventions (which appears in all four Conventions) renders the full protections applicable only to "all cases of declared war or of any other armed conflict which may arise between two or more of the High Contracting Parties." 6 U.S.T., at 3318.[59] Since Hamdan was captured and detained incident to the conflict with al Qaeda and not the conflict with the Taliban, and since al Qaeda, unlike Afghanistan, is not a "High Contracting Party" – *i.e.*, a signatory of the Conventions, the protections of those Conventions are not, it is argued, applicable to Hamdan.[60]

We need not decide the merits of this argument because there is at least one provision of the Geneva Conventions that applies here even if the relevant conflict is not one between signatories.[61] Article 3, often referred to as Common Article 3 because,

---

[57] But see, *e.g.*, 4 Int'l Comm. of Red Cross, Commentary: Geneva Convention Relative to the Protection of Civilian Persons in Time of War 21 (1958) (hereinafter GCIV Commentary) (the 1949 Geneva Conventions were written "first and foremost to protect individuals, and not to serve State interests"), GCIII Commentary 91 ("It was not . . . until the Conventions of 1949 . . . that the existence of 'rights' conferred in prisoners of war was affirmed").

[58] But see generally Brief for Louis Henkin et al. as *Amici Curiae;* 1 Int'l Comm. for the Red Cross, Commentary: Geneva Convention for the Amelioration of the Condition of the Wounded and Sick in Armed Forces in the Field 84 (1952) ("It should be possible in States which are parties to the Convention . . . for the rules of the Convention to be evoked before an appropriate national court by the protected person who has suffered a violation"); GCII Commentary 92; GCIV Commentary 79.

[59] For convenience's sake, we use citations to the Third Geneva Convention only.

[60] The President has stated that the conflict with the Taliban is a conflict to which the Geneva Conventions apply. See White House Memorandum, Humane Treatment of Taliban and al Qaeda Detainees 2 (Feb. 7, 2002), available at http://www.justicescholars.org/pegc/archive/White_House/bush_memo_20020207_ed.pdf (hereinafter White House Memorandum).

[61] Hamdan observes that Article 5 of the Third Geneva Convention requires that if there be "any doubt" whether he is entitled to prisoner-of-war protections, he must be afforded those protections until his status is determined by a "competent tribunal." 6 U.S.T., at 3324. See also Headquarters Depts. of Army, Navy, Air Force, and Marine Corps, Army Regulation 190–8, Enemy Prisoners of War, Retained Personnel, Civilian Internees and Other Detainees (1997), App. 116. Because we hold that Hamdan may not, in any event, be tried by the military commission the President has convened pursuant to the November 13 Order and Commission Order

like Article 2, it appears in all four Geneva Conventions, provides that in a "conflict not of an international character occurring in the territory of one of the High Contracting Parties, each Party[62] to the conflict shall be bound to apply, as a minimum," certain provisions protecting "[p]ersons taking no active part in the hostilities, including members of armed forces who have laid down their arms and those placed *hors de combat* by . . . detention." *Id.*, at 3318. One such provision prohibits "the passing of sentences and the carrying out of executions without previous judgment pronounced by a regularly constituted court affording all the judicial guarantees which are recognized as indispensable by civilized peoples." *Ibid.*

The Court of Appeals thought, and the Government asserts, that Common Article 3 does not apply to Hamdan because the conflict with al Qaeda, being "'international in scope,'" does not qualify as a "'conflict not of an international character.'" 415 F. 3d, at 41. That reasoning is erroneous. The term "conflict not of an international character" is used here in contradistinction to a conflict between nations. So much is demonstrated by the "fundamental logic [of] the Convention's provisions on its application." *Id.*, at 44 (Williams, J., concurring). Common Article 2 provides that "the present Convention shall apply to all cases of declared war or of any other armed conflict which may arise between two or more of the High Contracting Parties." 6 U.S.T., at 3318 (Art. 2, ¶1). High Contracting Parties (signatories) also must abide by all terms of the Conventions vis-à-vis one another even if one party to the conflict is a nonsignatory "Power," and must so abide vis-à-vis the nonsignatory if "the latter accepts and applies" those terms. *Ibid.* (Art. 2, ¶3). Common Article 3, by contrast, affords some minimal protection, falling short of full protection under the Conventions, to individuals associated with neither a signatory nor even a nonsignatory "Power" who are involved in a conflict "in the territory of" a signatory. The latter kind of conflict is distinguishable from the conflict described in Common Article 2 chiefly because it does not involve a clash between nations (whether signatories or not). In context, then, the phrase "not of an international character" bears its literal meaning. See, *e.g.*, J. Bentham, Introduction to the Principles of Morals and Legislation 6, 296 (J. Burns & H. Hart eds. 1970) (using the term "international law" as a "new though not inexpressive appellation" meaning "betwixt nation and nation"; defining "international" to include "mutual transactions between sovereigns as such"); Commentary on the Additional Protocols to the Geneva Conventions of 12 August 1949, p. 1351 (1987) ("[A] non-international armed conflict is distinct from an international armed conflict because of the legal status of the entities opposing each other").

Although the official commentaries accompanying Common Article 3 indicate that an important purpose of the provision was to furnish minimal protection to rebels involved in one kind of "conflict not of an international character," *i.e.*, a civil war, see GCIII Commentary 36–37, the commentaries also make clear "that the scope of the Article must be as wide as possible," *id.*, at 36.[63] In fact, limiting language that would have rendered Common Article 3 applicable "especially [to] cases of civil war, colonial

---

No. 1, the question whether his potential status as a prisoner of war independently renders illegal his trial by military commission may be reserved.

[62] The term "Party" here has the broadest possible meaning; a Party need neither be a signatory of the Convention nor "even represent a legal entity capable of undertaking international obligations." GCIII Commentary 37.

[63] See also GCIII Commentary 35 (Common Article 3 "has the merit of being simple and clear. . . . Its observance does not depend upon preliminary discussions on the nature of the conflict"); GCIV Commentary 51 ("[N]obody in enemy hands can be outside the law"); U.S. Army Judge Advocate General's Legal Center and School, Dept. of the Army, Law of War Handbook 144 (2004) (Common Article 3 "serves as a 'minimum yardstick of protection in all conflicts, not just internal armed conflicts'" (quoting *Nicaragua* v. *United States*, 1986 I.C.J. 14, ¶218, 25 I. L. M. 1023)); *Prosecutor* v. *Tadić*, Case No. IT-94-1, Decision on the Defence Motion for Interlocutory Appeal on Jurisdiction, ¶102 (ICTY App. Chamber, Oct. 2, 1995) (stating that "the character of the conflict is irrelevant" in deciding whether Common Article 3 applies).

conflicts, or wars of religion," was omitted from the final version of the Article, which coupled broader scope of application with a narrower range of rights than did earlier proposed iterations. See GCIII Commentary 42–43.

iii

Common Article 3, then, is applicable here and, as indicated above, requires that Hamdan be tried by a "regularly constituted court affording all the judicial guarantees which are recognized as indispensable by civilized peoples." 6 U.S.T., at 3320 (Art. 3, ¶1(d)). While the term "regularly constituted court" is not specifically defined in either Common Article 3 or its accompanying commentary, other sources disclose its core meaning. The commentary accompanying a provision of the Fourth Geneva Convention, for example, defines "'regularly constituted'" tribunals to include "ordinary military courts" and "definitely exclud[e] all special tribunals." GCIV Commentary 340 (defining the term "properly constituted" in Article 66, which the commentary treats as identical to "regularly constituted");[64] see also *Yamashita*, 327 U.S., at 44 (Rutledge, J., dissenting) (describing military commission as a court "specially constituted for a particular trial"). And one of the Red Cross' own treatises defines "regularly constituted court" as used in Common Article 3 to mean "established and organized in accordance with the laws and procedures already in force in a country." Int'l Comm. of Red Cross, 1 Customary International Humanitarian Law 355 (2005); see also GCIV Commentary 340 (observing that "ordinary military courts" will "be set up in accordance with the recognized principles governing the administration of justice").

The Government offers only a cursory defense of Hamdan's military commission in light of Common Article 3. See Brief for Respondents 49–50. As JUSTICE KENNEDY explains, that defense fails because "[t]he regular military courts in our system are the courts-martial established by congressional statutes." *Post*, at 8 (opinion concurring in part). At a minimum, a military commission "can be 'regularly constituted' by the standards of our military justice system only if some practical need explains deviations from court-martial practice." *Post*, at 10. As we have explained, see Part VI-C, *supra*, no such need has been demonstrated here.[65]

iv

Inextricably intertwined with the question of regular constitution is the evaluation of the procedures governing the tribunal and whether they afford "all the judicial guarantees which are recognized as indispensable by civilized peoples." 6 U.S.T., at 3320 (Art. 3, ¶1(d)). Like the phrase "regularly constituted court," this phrase is not defined in the text of the Geneva Conventions. But it must be understood to incorporate at least the barest of those trial protections that have been recognized by customary international law. Many of these are described in Article 75 of Protocol I to the Geneva Conventions of 1949, adopted in 1977 (Protocol I). Although the United States declined to ratify Protocol I, its objections were not to Article 75 thereof. Indeed, it appears that the Government "regard[s] the provisions of Article 75 as an articulation of safeguards to which all persons in the hands of an enemy are entitled." Taft, The Law of Armed Conflict After 9/11: Some Salient Features, 28 Yale J. Int'l L. 319, 322 (2003). Among the

---

[64] The commentary's assumption that the terms "properly constituted" and "regularly constituted" are interchangeable is beyond reproach; the French version of Article 66, which is equally authoritative, uses the term "réguliérement constitués" in place of "properly constituted."

[65] Further evidence of this tribunal's irregular constitution is the fact that its rules and procedures are subject to change midtrial, at the whim of the Executive. See Commission Order No. 1, §11 (providing that the Secretary of Defense may change the governing rules "from time to time").

rights set forth in Article 75 is the "right to be tried in [one's] presence." Protocol I, Art. 75(4)(e).[66]

We agree with JUSTICE KENNEDY that the procedures adopted to try Hamdan deviate from those governing courts-martial in ways not justified by any "evident practical need," *post*, at 11, and for that reason, at least, fail to afford the requisite guarantees. See *post*, at 8, 11–17. We add only that, as noted in Part VI-A, *supra*, various provisions of Commission Order No. 1 dispense with the principles, articulated in Article 75 and indisputably part of the customary international law, that an accused must, absent disruptive conduct or consent, be present for his trial and must be privy to the evidence against him. See §§6(B)(3), (D).[67] That the Government has a compelling interest in denying Hamdan access to certain sensitive information is not doubted. Cf. *post*, at 47–48 (THOMAS, J., dissenting). But, at least absent express statutory provision to the contrary, information used to convict a person of a crime must be disclosed to him.

v

Common Article 3 obviously tolerates a great degree of flexibility in trying individuals captured during armed conflict; its requirements are general ones, crafted to accommodate a wide variety of legal systems. But *requirements* they are nonetheless. The commission that the President has convened to try Hamdan does not meet those requirements.

VII

We have assumed, as we must, that the allegations made in the Government's charge against Hamdan are true. We have assumed, moreover, the truth of the message implicit in that charge – viz., that Hamdan is a dangerous individual whose beliefs, if acted upon, would cause great harm and even death to innocent civilians, and who would act upon those beliefs if given the opportunity. It bears emphasizing that Hamdan does not challenge, and we do not today address, the Government's power to detain him for the duration of active hostilities in order to prevent such harm. But in undertaking to try

---

[66] Other international instruments to which the United States is a signatory include the same basic protections set forth in Article 75. See, *e.g.*, International Covenant on Civil and Political Rights, Art. 14, ¶3(*d*), Mar. 23, 1976, 999 U.N.T.S. 171 (setting forth the right of an accused "[t]o be tried in his presence, and to defend himself in person or through legal assistance of his own choosing"). Following World War II, several defendants were tried and convicted by military commission for violations of the law of war in their failure to afford captives fair trials before imposition and execution of sentence. In two such trials, the prosecutors argued that the defendants' failure to apprise accused individuals of all evidence against them constituted violations of the law of war. See 5 U.N. War Crimes Commission 30 (trial of Sergeant-Major Shigeru Ohashi), 75 (trial of General Tanaka Hisakasu).

[67] The Government offers no defense of these procedures other than to observe that the defendant may not be barred from access to evidence if such action would deprive him of a "full and fair trial." Commission Order No. 1, §6(D)(5)(b). But the Government suggests no circumstances in which it would be "fair" to convict the accused based on evidence he has not seen or heard. Cf. *Crawford* v. *Washington*, 541 U.S. 36, 49 (2004) ("'It is a rule of the common law, founded on natural justice, that no man shall be prejudiced by evidence which he had not the liberty to cross examine'" (quoting *State* v. *Webb*, 2 N.C. 103, 104 (Super. L. & Eq. 1794) *(per curiam)*); *Diaz* v. *United States*, 223 U.S. 442, 455 (1912) (describing the right to be present as "scarcely less important to the accused than the right of trial itself"); *Lewis* v. *United States*, 146 U.S. 370, 372 (1892) (exclusion of defendant from part of proceedings is "contrary to the dictates of humanity" (internal quotation marks omitted)); *Joint Anti-Fascist Refugee Comm.* v. *McGrath*, 341 U.S. 123, 170, n. 17, 171 (1951) (Frankfurter, J., concurring) ("[t]he plea that evidence of guilt must be secret is abhorrent to free men" (internal quotation marks omitted)). More fundamentally, the legality of a tribunal under Common Article 3 cannot be established by bare assurances that, whatever the character of the court or the procedures it follows, individual adjudicators will act fairly.

Hamdan and subject him to criminal punishment, the Executive is bound to comply with the Rule of Law that prevails in this jurisdiction.

The judgment of the Court of Appeals is reversed, and the case is remanded for further proceedings.

It is so ordered.

THE CHIEF JUSTICE took no part in the consideration or decision of this case.

. . .

JUSTICE BREYER, with whom JUSTICE KENNEDY, JUSTICE SOUTER, and JUSTICE GINSBURG join, concurring.

The dissenters say that today's decision would "sorely hamper the President's ability to confront and defeat a new and deadly enemy." *Post*, at 29 (opinion of THOMAS, J.). They suggest that it undermines our Nation's ability to "preven[t] future attacks" of the grievous sort that we have already suffered. *Post*, at 48. That claim leads me to state briefly what I believe the majority sets forth both explicitly and implicitly at greater length. The Court's conclusion ultimately rests upon a single ground: Congress has not issued the Executive a "blank check." Cf. *Hamdi* v. *Rumsfeld*, 542 U.S. 507, 536 (2004) (plurality opinion). Indeed, Congress has denied the President the legislative authority to create military commissions of the kind at issue here. Nothing prevents the President from returning to Congress to seek the authority he believes necessary.

Where, as here, no emergency prevents consultation with Congress, judicial insistence upon that consultation does not weaken our Nation's ability to deal with danger. To the contrary, that insistence strengthens the Nation's ability to determine – through democratic means – how best to do so. The Constitution places its faith in those democratic means. Our Court today simply does the same.

. . .

JUSTICE KENNEDY, with whom JUSTICE SOUTER, JUSTICE GINSBURG, and JUSTICE BREYER join as to Parts I and II, concurring in part.

Military Commission Order No. 1, which governs the military commission established to try petitioner Salim Hamdan for war crimes, exceeds limits that certain statutes, duly enacted by Congress, have placed on the President's authority to convene military courts. This is not a case, then, where the Executive can assert some unilateral authority to fill a void left by congressional inaction. It is a case where Congress, in the proper exercise of its powers as an independent branch of government, and as part of a long tradition of legislative involvement in matters of military justice, has considered the subject of military tribunals and set limits on the President's authority. Where a statute provides the conditions for the exercise of governmental power, its requirements are the result of a deliberative and reflective process engaging both of the political branches. Respect for laws derived from the customary operation of the Executive and Legislative Branches gives some assurance of stability in time of crisis. The Constitution is best preserved by reliance on standards tested over time and insulated from the pressures of the moment.

These principles seem vindicated here, for a case that may be of extraordinary importance is resolved by ordinary rules. The rules of most relevance here are those pertaining to the authority of Congress and the interpretation of its enactments.

It seems appropriate to recite these rather fundamental points because the Court refers, as it should in its exposition of the case, to the requirement of the Geneva Conventions of 1949 that military tribunals be "regularly constituted" *ante*, at 69 – a requirement that controls here, if for no other reason, because Congress requires that military commissions like the ones at issue conform to the "law of war," 10 U.S.C. §821. Whatever the substance and content of the term "regularly constituted" as interpreted in this and any later cases, there seems little doubt that it relies upon the importance of standards deliberated upon and chosen in advance of crisis, under a system where the single power of the Executive is checked by other constitutional mechanisms. All of which returns us to the point of beginning – that domestic statutes control this case. If Congress, after due consideration, deems it appropriate to change the controlling statutes, in conformance with the Constitution and other laws, it has the power and prerogative to do so.

I join the Court's opinion, save Parts V and VI-D-iv. To state my reasons for this reservation, and to show my agreement with the remainder of the Court's analysis by identifying particular deficiencies in the military commissions at issue, this separate opinion seems appropriate.

I

Trial by military commission raises separation-of-powers concerns of the highest order. Located within a single branch, these courts carry the risk that offenses will be defined, prosecuted, and adjudicated by executive officials without independent review. Cf. *Loving* v. *United States*, 517 U.S. 748, 756–758, 760 (1996). Concentration of power puts personal liberty in peril of arbitrary action by officials, an incursion the Constitution's three-part system is designed to avoid. It is imperative, then, that when military tribunals are established, full and proper authority exists for the Presidential directive.

The proper framework for assessing whether Executive actions are authorized is the three-part scheme used by Justice Jackson in his opinion in *Youngstown Sheet & Tube Co.* v. *Sawyer*, 343 U.S. 579 (1952). "When the President acts pursuant to an express or implied authorization of Congress, his authority is at its maximum, for it includes all that he possesses in his own right plus all that Congress can delegate." *Id.*, at 635. "When the President acts in absence of either a congressional grant or denial of authority, he can only rely upon his own independent powers, but there is a zone of twilight in which he and Congress may have concurrent authority, or in which its distribution is uncertain." *Id.*, at 637. And "[w]hen the President takes measures incompatible with the expressed or implied will of Congress, his power is at its lowest ebb." *Ibid.*

In this case, as the Court observes, the President has acted in a field with a history of congressional participation and regulation. *Ante*, at 28–30, 55–57. In the Uniform Code of Military Justice (UCMJ), 10 U.S.C. §801 *et seq.*, which Congress enacted, building on earlier statutes, in 1950, see Act of May 5, 1950, ch. 169, 64 Stat. 107, and later amended, see, *e.g.*, Military Justice Act of 1968, 82 Stat. 1335, Congress has set forth governing principles for military courts. The UCMJ as a whole establishes an intricate system of military justice. It authorizes courts-martial in various forms, 10 U.S.C. §§816–820 (2000 ed. and Supp. III); it regulates the organization and procedure of those courts, *e.g.*, §§822–835, 851–854; it defines offenses, §§877–934, and rights for the accused, *e.g.*, §§827(b)–(c), 831, 844, 846, 855 (2000 ed.); and it provides mechanisms for appellate review, §§859–876b (2000 ed. and Supp. III). As explained below, the statute further recognizes that special military commissions may be convened to try war crimes. See *infra*, at 5–6; §821 (2000 ed.). While these laws provide authority for certain forms of military courts, they also impose limitations, at least two of which control this case. If the President has exceeded these limits, this becomes a case of conflict between Presidential and congressional action – a case within Justice Jackson's third category, not the second or first.

One limit on the President's authority is contained in §836 of the UCMJ. That section provides:

> "(a) Pretrial, trial, and post-trial procedures, including modes of proof, for cases arising under this chapter triable in courts-martial, military commissions and other military tribunals, and procedures for courts of inquiry, may be prescribed by the President by regulations which shall, so far as he considers practicable, apply the principles of law and the rules of evidence generally recognized in the trial of criminal cases in the United States district courts, but which may not be contrary to or inconsistent with this chapter.

> "(b) All rules and regulations made under this article shall be uniform insofar as practicable." 10 U.S.C. §836 (2000 ed.).

In this provision the statute allows the President to implement and build on the UCMJ's framework by adopting procedural regulations, subject to three requirements: (1) Procedures for military courts must conform to district-court rules insofar as the President "considers practicable"; (2) the procedures may not be contrary to or inconsistent with the provisions of the UCMJ; and (3) "insofar as practicable" all rules and regulations under §836 must be uniform, a requirement, as the Court points out, that indicates the rules must be the same for military commissions as for courts-martial unless such uniformity is impracticable, *ante*, at 57, 59, and n. 50.

As the Court further instructs, even assuming the first and second requirements of §836 are satisfied here – a matter of some dispute, see *ante*, at 57–59 – the third requires us to compare the military-commission procedures with those for courts-martial and determine, to the extent there are deviations, whether greater uniformity would be practicable. *Ante*, at 59–62. Although we can assume the President's practicability judgments are entitled to some deference, the Court observes that Congress' choice of language in the uniformity provision of 10 U.S.C. §836(b) contrasts with the language of §836(a). This difference suggests, at the least, a lower degree of deference for §836(b) determinations. *Ante*, at 59–60. The rules for military courts may depart from federal-court rules whenever the President "considers" conformity impracticable, §836(a); but the statute requires procedural uniformity across different military courts "insofar as [uniformity is] practicable," §836(b), not insofar as the President considers it to be so. The Court is right to conclude this is of relevance to our decision. Further, as the Court is also correct to conclude, *ante*, at 60, the term "practicable" cannot be construed to permit deviations based on mere convenience or expedience. "Practicable" means "feasible," that is, "possible to practice or perform" or "capable of being put into practice, done, or accomplished." Webster's Third New International Dictionary 1780 (1961). Congress' chosen language, then, is best understood to allow the selection of procedures based on logistical constraints, the accommodation of witnesses, the security of the proceedings, and the like. Insofar as the "[p]retrial, trial, and post-trial procedures" for the military commissions at issue deviate from court-martial practice, the deviations must be explained by some such practical need.

In addition to §836, a second UCMJ provision, 10 U.S.C. §821, requires us to compare the commissions at issue to courts-martial. This provision states:

> "The provisions of this chapter conferring jurisdiction upon courts-martial do not deprive military commissions, provost courts, or other military tribunals of concurrent jurisdiction with respect to offenders or offenses that by statute or by the law of war may be tried by military commissions, provost courts, or other military tribunals."

In §821 Congress has addressed the possibility that special military commissions – criminal courts other than courts-martial – may at times be convened. At the same time, however, the President's authority to convene military commissions is limited: It extends only to "offenders or offenses" that "by statute or by the law of war may be tried by" such military commissions. *Ibid.;* see also *ante,* at 28–29. The Government does not claim to base the charges against Hamdan on a statute; instead it invokes the law of war. That law, as the Court explained in *Ex parte Quirin,* 317 U.S. 1 (1942), derives from "rules and precepts of the law of nations"; it is the body of international law governing armed conflict. *Id.,* at 28. If the military commission at issue is illegal under the law of war, then an offender cannot be tried "by the law of war" before that commission.

The Court is correct to concentrate on one provision of the law of war that is applicable to our Nation's armed conflict with al Qaeda in Afghanistan and, as a result, to the use of a military commission to try Hamdan. *Ante,* at 65–70; see also 415 F. 3d 33, 44 (CADC 2005) (Williams, J., concurring). That provision is Common Article 3 of the four Geneva Conventions of 1949. It prohibits, as relevant here, "[t]he passing of sentences and the carrying out of executions without previous judgment pronounced by a regularly constituted court affording all the judicial guarantees which are recognized as indispensable by civilized peoples." See, *e.g.,* Article 3 of the Geneva Convention (III) Relative to the Treatment of Prisoners of War, Aug. 12, 1949, [1955] 6 U.S.T. 3316, 3318, T.I.A.S. No. 3364. The provision is part of a treaty the United States has ratified and thus accepted as binding law. See *id.,* at 3316. By Act of Congress, moreover, violations of Common Article 3 are considered "war crimes," punishable as federal offenses, when committed by or against United States nationals and military personnel. See 18 U.S.C. §2441. There should be no doubt, then, that Common Article 3 is part of the law of war as that term is used in §821.

The dissent by JUSTICE THOMAS argues that Common Article 3 nonetheless is irrelevant to this case because in *Johnson* v. *Eisentrager,* 339 U.S. 763 (1950), it was said to be the "obvious scheme" of the 1929 Geneva Convention that "[r]ights of alien enemies are vindicated under it only through protests and intervention of protecting powers," *i.e.,* signatory states, *id.,* at 789, n. 14. As the Court explains, *ante,* at 63–65, this language from *Eisentrager* is not controlling here. Even assuming the *Eisentrager* analysis has some bearing upon the analysis of the broader 1949 Conventions and that, in consequence, rights are vindicated "under [those Conventions]" only through protests and intervention, 339 U.S., at 789, n. 14, Common Article 3 is nonetheless relevant to the question of authorization under §821. Common Article 3 is part of the law of war that Congress has directed the President to follow in establishing military commissions. *Ante,* at 66–67. Consistent with that view, the *Eisentrager* Court itself considered on the merits claims that "procedural irregularities" under the 1929 Convention "deprive[d] the Military Commission of jurisdiction." 339 U.S., at 789, 790.

In another military commission case, *In re Yamashita,* 327 U.S. 1 (1946), the Court likewise considered on the merits – without any caveat about remedies under the Convention – a claim that an alleged violation of the 1929 Convention "establish[ed] want of authority in the commission to proceed with the trial." *Id.,* at 23, 24. That is the precise inquiry we are asked to perform here.

Assuming the President has authority to establish a special military commission to try Hamdan, the commission must satisfy Common Article 3's requirement of a "regularly constituted court affording all the judicial guarantees which are recognized as indispensable by civilized peoples," 6 U.S.T., at 3318. The terms of this general standard are yet to be elaborated and further defined, but Congress has required compliance with it by referring to the "law of war" in §821. The Court correctly concludes that the military commission here does not comply with this provision.

Common Article 3's standard of a "regularly constituted court affording all the judicial guarantees which are recognized as indispensable by civilized peoples," *ibid.*, supports, at the least, a uniformity principle similar to that codified in §836(b). The concept of a "regularly constituted court" providing "indispensable" judicial guarantees requires consideration of the system of justice under which the commission is established, though no doubt certain minimum standards are applicable. See *ante*, at 69–70; 1 Int'l Committee of the Red Cross, Customary International Humanitarian Law 355 (2005) (explaining that courts are "regularly constituted" under Common Article 3 if they are "established and organised in accordance with the laws and procedures already in force in a country").

The regular military courts in our system are the courts-martial established by congressional statutes. Acts of Congress confer on those courts the jurisdiction to try "any person" subject to war crimes prosecution. 10 U.S.C. §818. As the Court explains, moreover, while special military commissions have been convened in previous armed conflicts – a practice recognized in §821 – those military commissions generally have adopted the structure and procedure of courts-martial. See, *e.g.*, 1 The War of the Rebellion: A Compilation of the Official Records of the Union and Confederate Armies 248 (2d series 1894) (Civil War general order requiring that military commissions "be constituted in a similar manner and their proceedings be conducted according to the same general rules as courts-martial in order to prevent abuses which might otherwise arise"); W. Winthrop, Military Law and Precedents 835, n. 81 (rev. 2d ed. 1920) ("[M]ilitary commissions are constituted and composed, and their proceedings are conducted, similarly to general courts-martial"); 1 United Nations War Crimes Commission, Law Reports of Trials of War Criminals 116–117 (1947) (reprint 1997) (hereinafter Law Reports) (discussing post-World War II regulations requiring that military commissions "hav[e] regard for" rules of procedure and evidence applicable in general courts-martial); see also *ante*, at 53–57; *post*, at 31, n. 15 (THOMAS, J., dissenting). Today, moreover, §836(b) – which took effect after the military trials in the World War II cases invoked by the dissent, see *Madsen* v. *Kinsella*, 343 U.S. 341, 344–345, and n. 6 (1952); *Yamashita, supra*, at 5; *Quirin*, 317 U.S., at 23 – codifies this presumption of uniformity at least as to "[p]retrial, trial, and post-trial procedures." Absent more concrete statutory guidance, this historical and statutory background – which suggests that some practical need must justify deviations from the court-martial model – informs the understanding of which military courts are "regularly constituted" under United States law.

In addition, whether or not the possibility, contemplated by the regulations here, of midtrial procedural changes could by itself render a military commission impermissibly irregular, *ante*, at 70, n. 65; see also Military Commission Order No. 1, §11 (Aug. 31, 2005), . . . (hereinafter MCO), an acceptable degree of independence from the Executive is necessary to render a commission "regularly constituted" by the standards of our Nation's system of justice. And any suggestion of Executive power to interfere with an ongoing judicial process raises concerns about the proceedings' fairness. Again, however, courts-martial provide the relevant benchmark. Subject to constitutional limitations, see *Ex parte Milligan*, 4 Wall. 2, (1866), Congress has the power and responsibility to determine the necessity for military courts, and to provide the jurisdiction and procedures applicable to them. The guidance Congress has provided with respect to courts-martial indicates the level of independence and procedural rigor that Congress has deemed necessary, at least as a general matter, in the military context.

At a minimum a military commission like the one at issue – a commission specially convened by the President to try specific persons without express congressional authorization – can be "regularly constituted" by the standards of our military justice system only if some practical need explains deviations from court-martial practice. In this regard the standard of Common Article 3, applied here in conformity with §821, parallels the practicability standard of §836(b). Section 836, however, is limited by its terms to matters properly characterized as procedural – that is, "[p]retrial, trial, and post-trial procedures" – while Common Article 3 permits broader consideration of matters of structure, organization, and mechanisms to promote the tribunal's insulation from command influence. Thus the combined effect of the two statutes discussed here – §§836 and 821 – is that considerations of practicability must support departures from court-martial practice. Relevant concerns, as noted earlier, relate to logistical constraints, accommodation of witnesses, security of the proceedings, and the like, not mere expedience or convenience. This determination, of course, must be made with due regard for the constitutional principle that congressional statutes can be controlling, including the congressional direction that the law of war has a bearing on the determination.

These principles provide the framework for an analysis of the specific military commission at issue here.

II

In assessing the validity of Hamdan's military commission the precise circumstances of this case bear emphasis. The allegations against Hamdan are undoubtedly serious. Captured in Afghanistan during our Nation's armed conflict with the Taliban and al Qaeda – a conflict that continues as we speak – Hamdan stands accused of overt acts in furtherance of a conspiracy to commit terrorism: delivering weapons and ammunition to al Qaeda, acquiring trucks for use by Osama bin Laden's bodyguards, providing security services to bin Laden, and receiving weapons training at a terrorist camp..... Nevertheless, the circumstances of Hamdan's trial present no exigency requiring special speed or precluding careful consideration of evidence. For roughly four years, Hamdan has been detained at a permanent United States military base in Guantanamo Bay, Cuba. And regardless of the outcome of the criminal proceedings at issue, the Government claims authority to continue to detain him based on his status as an enemy combatant.

Against this background, the Court is correct to conclude that the military commission the President has convened to try Hamdan is unauthorized. *Ante*, at 62, 69–70, 72. The following analysis, which expands on the Court's discussion, explains my reasons for reaching this conclusion.

To begin with, the structure and composition of the military commission deviate from conventional court-martial standards. Although these deviations raise questions about the fairness of the trial, no evident practical need explains them.

Under the UCMJ, courts-martial are organized by a "convening authority" – either a commanding officer, the Secretary of Defense, the Secretary concerned, or the President. 10 U.S.C. §§822–824 (2000 ed. and Supp. III). The convening authority refers charges for trial, Manual for Courts-Martial, United States, Rule for Courts-Martial 401 (2005 ed.) (hereinafter R.C.M.), and selects the court-martial members who vote on the guilt or innocence of the accused and determine the sentence, 10 U.S.C. §§825(d)(2), 851–852 (2000 ed.); R.C.M. 503(a). Paralleling this structure, under Military Commission Order No. 1 an "'Appointing Authority'" – either the Secretary of Defense or the Secretary's "designee" – establishes commissions subject to the order, MCO No. 1, §2, approves and refers charges to be tried by those commissions, §4(B)(2)(a), and appoints commission members who vote on the conviction and sentence, §§4(A)(1–3). In addition the Appointing Authority determines the number of commission members (at least three), oversees the chief prosecutor, provides "investigative or other resources" to the defense insofar as he or she "deems necessary for a full and fair trial," approves or rejects plea agreements, approves or disapproves communications with news media by prosecution or defense counsel (a function shared by the General Counsel of the Department of Defense), and issues supplementary commission regulations (subject to approval by the General Counsel of the Department of Defense, unless the Appointing Authority is the Secretary of Defense). See MCO No. 1, §§4(A)(2), 5(H), 6(A)(4), 7(A); Military Commission Instruction No. 3, §5(C) (July 15, 2005) (hereinafter MCI), available at www. defenselink.mil/news/Aug2005/d20050811MC13.pdf; MCI No. 4, §5(C) (Sept. 16, 2005), available at www. defenselink.mil/news/Oct2005/d20051003MCI4.pdf MCI No. 6, §3(B)(3) (April 15, 2004), available at www.defenselink.mil/news/Apr2004/d20040420ins6.pdf (all Internet materials as visited June 27, 2006, and available in Clerk of Court's case file).

Against the background of these significant powers for the Appointing Authority, which in certain respects at least conform to ordinary court-martial standards, the regulations governing the commissions at issue make several noteworthy departures. At a general court-martial – the only type authorized to impose penalties of more than one year's incarceration or to adjudicate offenses against the law of war, R.C.M. 201(f); 10 U.S.C. §§818–820 (2000 ed. and Supp. III) – the presiding officer who rules on legal issues must be a military judge. R.C.M. 501(a)(1), 801(a)(4)–(5); 10 U.S.C. §816(1) (2000 ed., Supp. III); see also R.C.M. 201(f)(2)(B)(ii) (likewise requiring a military judge for certain other courts-martial); 10 U.S.C. §819 (2000 ed. and Supp. III) (same). A military judge is an officer who is a member of a state or federal bar and has been specially certified for judicial duties by the Judge Advocate General for the officer's Armed Service. R.C.M. 502(c); 10 U.S.C. §826(b). To protect their independence, military judges at general courts-martial are "assigned and directly responsible to the Judge Advocate General or the Judge Advocate General's designee." R.C.M. 502(c). They must be detailed to the court, in accordance with applicable regulations, "by a person assigned as a military judge and directly responsible to the Judge Advocate General or the Judge Advocate General's designee." R.C.M. 503(b); see also 10 U.S.C. §826(c); see generally *Weiss* v. *United States*, 510 U.S. 163, 179–181 (1994) (discussing provisions that "insulat[e] military judges from the effects of command influence" and thus "preserve judicial impartiality"). Here, by contrast, the Appointing Authority selects the presiding officer, MCO No. 1, §§4(A)(1), (A)(4); and that officer need only be a judge advocate, that is, a military lawyer, §4(A)(4).

The Appointing Authority, moreover, exercises supervisory powers that continue during trial. Any interlocutory question "the disposition of which would effect a termination of proceedings with respect to a charge" is subject to decision not by the presiding officer, but by the Appointing Authority. §4(A)(5)(e) (stating that the presiding officer "shall certify" such questions to the Appointing Authority). Other interlocutory questions may be certified to the Appointing Authority as the presiding officer "deems appropriate." *Ibid.* While in some circumstances the Government may appeal certain rulings at a court-martial – including "an order or ruling that terminates the proceedings with respect to a charge or specification," R.C.M. 908(a); see also 10 U.S.C. §862(a) – the appeals go to a body called the Court of Criminal Appeals, not to the convening authority. R.C.M. 908; 10 U.S.C. §862(b); see also R.C.M. 1107 (requiring the convening authority to approve or disapprove the findings and sentence of a court-martial but providing for such action only after entry of sentence and restricting actions that increase penalties); 10 U.S.C. §860 (same); cf. §837(a) (barring command influence on court-martial actions). The Court of Criminal Appeals functions as the military's intermediate appeals court; it is established by the Judge Advocate General for each Armed Service and composed of appellate military judges. R.C.M. 1203; 10 U.S.C. §866. This is another means in which, by structure and tradition, the court-martial process is insulated from those who have an interest in the outcome of the proceedings.

Finally, in addition to these powers with respect to the presiding officer, the Appointing Authority has greater flexibility in appointing commission members. While a general court-martial requires, absent a contrary election by the accused, at least five members, R.C.M. 501(a)(1); 10 U.S.C. §816(1) (2000 ed. and Supp. III), the Appointing Authority here is free, as noted earlier, to select as few as three. MCO No. 1, §4(A)(2). This difference may affect the deliberative process and the prosecution's burden of persuasion.

As compared to the role of the convening authority in a court-martial, the greater powers of the Appointing Authority here – including even the resolution of dispositive issues in the middle of the trial – raise concerns that the commission's decisionmaking may not be neutral. If the differences are supported by some practical need beyond the goal of constant and ongoing supervision, that need is neither apparent from the record nor established by the Government's submissions.

It is no answer that, at the end of the day, the Detainee Treatment Act of 2005 (DTA), 119 Stat. 2739, affords military-commission defendants the opportunity for judicial review in federal court. As the Court is correct to observe, the scope of that review is limited, DTA §1005(e)(3)(D), *id.*, at 2743; see also *ante*, at 8–9, and the review is not automatic if the defendant's sentence is under 10 years, §1005(e)(3)(B), *ibid.* Also, provisions for review of legal issues after trial cannot correct for structural defects, such as the role of the Appointing Authority, that can cast doubt on the factfinding process and the presiding judge's exercise of discretion during trial. Before military-commission defendants may obtain judicial review, furthermore, they must navigate a military review process that again raises fairness concerns. At the outset, the Appointing Authority (unless the Appointing Authority is the Secretary of Defense) performs an "administrative review" of undefined scope, ordering any "supplementary proceedings" deemed necessary. MCO No. 1 §6(H)(3). After that the case is referred to a three-member Review Panel composed of officers selected by the Secretary of Defense. §6(H)(4); MCI No. 9, §4(B) (Oct. 11, 2005), available at www.defenselink.mil/news/Oct2005/d20051014MCI9.pdf. Though the Review Panel may return the case for further proceedings only if a majority "form[s] a definite and firm conviction that a material error of law occurred," MCO No. 1, §6(H)(4); MCI No. 9, §4(C)(1)(a), only one member must have "experience as a judge," MCO No. 1, §6(H)(4); nothing in the regulations requires that other panel members have legal training. By comparison to the review of court-martial judgments performed by such independent bodies as the Judge Advocate General, the Court of Criminal Appeals, and the Court of Appeals for the Armed Forces, 10 U.S.C. §§862, 864, 866, 867, 869, the review process here lacks structural protections designed to help ensure impartiality.

These structural differences between the military commissions and courts-martial – the concentration of functions, including legal decisionmaking, in a single executive official; the less rigorous standards for composition of the tribunal; and the creation of special review procedures in place of institutions created and regulated by Congress – remove safeguards that are important to the fairness of the proceedings and the independence of the court. Congress has prescribed these guarantees for courts-martial; and no evident practical need explains the departures here. For these reasons the commission cannot be considered regularly constituted under United States law and thus does not satisfy Congress' requirement that military commissions conform to the law of war.

Apart from these structural issues, moreover, the basic procedures for the commissions deviate from procedures for courts-martial, in violation of §836(b). As the Court explains, *ante*, at 51, 61, the Military Commission Order abandons the detailed Military Rules of Evidence, which are modeled on the Federal Rules of Evidence in conformity with §836(a)'s requirement of presumptive compliance with district-court rules.

Instead, the order imposes just one evidentiary rule: "Evidence shall be admitted if . . . the evidence would have probative value to a reasonable person," MCO No. 1, §6(D)(1). Although it is true some military commissions applied an amorphous evidence standard in the past, see, *e.g.*, 1 Law Reports 117–118 (discussing World War II military commission orders); Exec. Order No. 9185, 7 Fed. Reg. 5103 (1942) (order convening military commission to try Nazi saboteurs), the evidentiary rules for those commissions were adopted before Congress enacted the uniformity requirement of 10 U.S.C. §836(b) as part of the UCMJ, see Act of May 5, 1950, ch. 169, 64 Stat. 107, 120, 149. And while some flexibility may be necessary to permit trial of battlefield captives like Hamdan, military statutes and rules already provide for introduction of deposition testimony for absent witnesses, 10 U.S.C. §849(d); R.C.M. 702, and use of classified information, Military Rule Evid. 505. Indeed, the deposition-testimony provision specifically mentions military commissions and thus is one of the provisions the Government concedes must be followed by the commission at issue. See *ante*, at 58. That provision authorizes admission of deposition testimony only if the witness is absent for specified reasons, §849(d) – a requirement that makes no sense if military commissions may consider all probative evidence. Whether or not this conflict renders the rules at issue "contrary to or inconsistent with" the UCMJ under §836(a), it creates a uniformity problem under §836(b).

The rule here could permit admission of multiple hearsay and other forms of evidence generally prohibited on grounds of unreliability. Indeed, the commission regulations specifically contemplate admission of unsworn written statements, MCO No. 1, §6(D)(3); and they make no provision for exclusion of coerced declarations save those "established to have been made as a result of torture," MCI No. 10, §3(A) (Mar. 24, 2006), available at www. defenselink.mil/news/Mar2006/d20060327MCI10.pdf; cf. Military Rule Evid. 304(c)(3) (generally barring use of statements obtained "through the use of coercion, unlawful influence, or unlawful inducement"); 10 U.S.C. §831(d) (same). Besides, even if evidence is deemed nonprobative by the presiding officer at Hamdan's trial, the military-commission members still may view it. In another departure from court-martial practice the military commission members may object to the presiding officer's evidence rulings and determine themselves, by majority vote, whether to admit the evidence. MCO No. 1, §6(D)(1); cf. R.C.M. 801(a)(4), (c)(1) (providing that the military judge at a court-martial determines all questions of law).

As the Court explains, the Government has made no demonstration of practical need for these special rules and procedures, either in this particular case or as to the military commissions in general, *ante*, at 59–61; nor is any such need self-evident. For all the Government's regulations and submissions reveal, it would be feasible for most, if not all, of the conventional military evidence rules and procedures to be followed.

In sum, as presently structured, Hamdan's military commission exceeds the bounds Congress has placed on the President's authority in §§836 and 821 of the UCMJ. Because Congress has prescribed these limits, Congress can change them, requiring a new analysis consistent with the Constitution and other governing laws. At this time, however, we must apply the standards Congress has provided. By those standards the military commission is deficient.

III

In light of the conclusion that the military commission here is unauthorized under the UCMJ, I see no need to consider several further issues addressed in the plurality opinion by JUSTICE STEVENS and the dissent by JUSTICE THOMAS.

First, I would not decide whether Common Article 3's standard – a "regularly consti-tuted court affording all the judicial guarantees which are recognized as indispensable by civilized peoples," 6 U.S.T., at 3320 (¶(1)(d)) – necessarily requires that the accused have the right to be present at all stages of a criminal trial. As JUSTICE STEVENS explains, Military Commission Order No. 1 authorizes exclusion of the accused from the proceed-ings if the presiding officer determines that, among other things, protection of classified information so requires. See §§6(B)(3), (D)(5); *ante*, at 50. JUSTICE STEVENS observes that these regulations create the possibility of a conviction and sentence based on evidence Hamdan has not seen or heard – a possibility the plurality is correct to consider trou-bling. *Ante*, at 71–72, n. 67 (collecting cases); see also *In re Oliver*, 333 U.S. 257, 277 (1948) (finding "no support for sustaining petitioner's conviction of contempt of court upon testimony given in petitioner's absence").

As the dissent by JUSTICE THOMAS points out, however, the regulations bar the pre-siding officer from admitting secret evidence if doing so would deprive the accused of a "full and fair trial." MCO No. 1, §6(D)(5)(b); see also *post*, at 47. This fairness deter-mination, moreover, is unambiguously subject to judicial review under the DTA. See §1005(e)(3)(D)(i), 119 Stat. 2743 (allowing review of compliance with the "standards and procedures" in Military Commission Order No. 1). The evidentiary proceedings at Hamdan's trial have yet to commence, and it remains to be seen whether he will suffer any prejudicial exclusion.

There should be reluctance, furthermore, to reach unnecessarily the question whether, as the plurality seems to conclude, *ante*, at 70, Article 75 of Protocol I to the Geneva Conventions is binding law notwithstanding the earlier decision by our Govern-ment not to accede to the Protocol. For all these reasons, and without detracting from the importance of the right of presence, I would rely on other deficiencies noted here and in the opinion by the Court – deficiencies that relate to the structure and proce-dure of the commission and that inevitably will affect the proceedings – as the basis for finding the military commissions lack authorization under 10 U.S.C. §836 and fail to be regularly constituted under Common Article 3 and §821.

I likewise see no need to address the validity of the conspiracy charge against Hamdan – an issue addressed at length in Part V of JUSTICE STEVENS' opinion and in Part II-C of JUSTICE THOMAS' dissent. See *ante*, at 36–49; *post*, at 12–28. In light of the con-clusion that the military commissions at issue are unauthorized Congress may choose to provide further guidance in this area. Congress, not the Court, is the branch in the better position to undertake the "sensitive task of establishing a principle not incon-sistent with the national interest or international justice." *Banco Nacional de Cuba* v. *Sabbatino*, 376 U.S. 398, 428 (1964).

Finally, for the same reason, I express no view on the merits of other limitations on military commissions described as elements of the common law of war in Part V of JUSTICE STEVENS' opinion. See *ante*, at 31–36, 48–49; *post*, at 6–12.

With these observations I join the Court's opinion with the exception of Parts V and VI-D-iv.

. . .

JUSTICE SCALIA, with whom JUSTICE THOMAS and JUSTICE ALITO join, dissenting.

On December 30, 2005, Congress enacted the Detainee Treatment Act (DTA). It unambiguously provides that, as of that date, "no court, justice, or judge" shall have jurisdiction to consider the habeas application of a Guantanamo Bay detainee. Notwithstanding this plain directive, the Court today concludes that, on what it calls the statute's *most natural* reading, *every* "court, justice, or judge" before whom such a habeas application was pending on December 30 has jurisdiction to hear, consider, and render judgment on it. This conclusion is patently erroneous. And even if it were not, the jurisdiction supposedly retained should, in an exercise of sound equitable discretion, not be exercised.

I

A

The DTA provides: "[N]o court, justice, or judge shall have jurisdiction to hear or consider an application for a writ of habeas corpus filed by or on behalf of an alien detained by the Department of Defense at Guantanamo Bay, Cuba." §1005(e)(1), 119 Stat. 2742 (internal division omitted). This provision "t[ook] effect on the date of the enactment of this Act," §1005(h)(1), *id.*, at 2743, which was December 30, 2005. As of that date, then, *no* court had jurisdiction to "hear or consider" the merits of petitioner's habeas application. This repeal of jurisdiction is simply not ambiguous as between pending and future cases. It prohibits *any* exercise of jurisdiction, and it became effective as to *all* cases last December 30. It is also perfectly clear that the phrase "no court, *justice*, or judge" includes this Court and its Members, and that by exercising our appellate jurisdiction in this case we are "hear[ing] or consider[ing] . . . an application for a writ of habeas corpus."

An ancient and unbroken line of authority attests that statutes ousting jurisdiction unambiguously apply to cases pending at their effective date. For example, in *Bruner* v. *United States*, 343 U.S. 112 (1952), we granted certiorari to consider whether the Tucker Act's provision denying district court jurisdiction over suits by "officers" of the United States barred a suit by an *employee* of the United States. After we granted certiorari, Congress amended the Tucker Act by adding suits by "'employees'" to the provision barring jurisdiction over suits by officers. *Id.*, at 114. This statute narrowing the jurisdiction of the district courts "became effective" while the case was pending before us, *ibid.*, and made no explicit reference to pending cases. Because the statute "did not reserve jurisdiction over pending cases," *id.*, at 115, we held that it clearly ousted jurisdiction over them. Summarizing centuries of practice, we said: "This rule – that, when a law conferring jurisdiction is repealed without any reservation as to pending cases, all cases fall with the law – has been adhered to consistently by this Court." *Id.*, at 116–117. See also *Landgraf* v. *USI Film Products*, 511 U.S. 244, 274 (1994) (opinion for the Court by STEVENS, J.) ("We have regularly applied intervening statutes conferring or ousting jurisdiction, whether or not jurisdiction lay when the underlying conduct occurred or when the suit was filed").

This venerable rule that statutes ousting jurisdiction terminate jurisdiction in pending cases is not, as today's opinion for the Court would have it, a judge-made "presumption against jurisdiction," *ante*, at 11, that we have invented to resolve an ambiguity in the statutes. It is simple recognition of the reality that the *plain import* of a statute repealing jurisdiction is to eliminate the power to consider and render judgment – in an already pending case no less than in a case yet to be filed.

> "Without jurisdiction the court cannot proceed at all in any cause. Jurisdiction is power to declare the law, and when it ceases to exist, the only function remaining to the court is that of announcing the fact and dismissing the cause. *And this is not less clear upon authority than upon principle.*" *Ex parte McCardle*, 7 Wall. 506, 514 (1869) (emphasis added).

To alter this plain meaning, our cases have required an explicit reservation of pending cases in the jurisdiction-repealing statute. For example, *Bruner*, as mentioned, looked to whether Congress made "any reservation as to pending cases." 343 U.S., at 116–117; see also *id.*, at 115 ("Congress made no provision for cases pending at the effective date of the Act withdrawing jurisdiction and, for this reason, Courts of Appeals ordered pending cases terminated for want of jurisdiction"). Likewise, in *Hallowell* v. *Commons*, 239 U.S. 506 (1916), Justice Holmes relied on the fact that the jurisdiction-ousting provision "made no exception for pending litigation, but purported to be universal," *id.*, at 508. And in *Insurance Co.* v. *Ritchie*, 5 Wall. 541 (1867), we again relied on the fact that the jurisdictional repeal was made "without any saving of such causes as that before us," *id.*, at 544. As in *Bruner*, *Hallowell*, and *Ritchie*, the DTA's directive that "no court, justice, or judge shall have jurisdiction," §1005(e)(1), 119 Stat. 2742, is made "without any reservation as to pending cases" and "purport[s] to be universal." What we stated in an earlier case remains true here: "[W]hen, if it had been the intention to confine the operation of [the jurisdictional repeal] . . . to cases not pending, it would have been so easy to have said so, we must presume that Congress meant the language employed should have its usual and ordinary signification, and that the old law should be unconditionally repealed." *Railroad Co.* v. *Grant*, 98 U.S. 398, 403 (1879).

The Court claims that I "rea[d] too much into" the *Bruner* line of cases, *ante*, at 12, n. 7, and that "the *Bruner* rule" has never been "an inflexible trump," *ante*, at 19. But the Court sorely misdescribes *Bruner* – as if it were a kind of early-day *Lindh* v. *Murphy*, 521 U.S. 320 (1997), resolving statutory ambiguity by oblique negative inference. On the contrary, as described above, *Bruner* stated its holding as an unqualified "rule," which "has been adhered to consistently by this Court." 343 U.S., at 116–117. Though *Bruner* referred to an express savings clause elsewhere in the statute, *id.*, at 115, n. 7, it disavowed any reliance on such oblique indicators to vary the plain meaning, quoting *Ritchie* at length: "'It is quite possible that this effect of the [jurisdiction-stripping statute] was not contemplated by Congress. . . . [B]ut when terms are unambiguous we may not speculate on probabilities of intention.'" 343 U.S., at 116 (quoting 5 Wall., at 544–545).

The Court also attempts to evade the *Bruner* line of cases by asserting that "the 'presumption' [of application to pending cases] that these cases have applied is more accurately viewed as the nonapplication of another presumption – viz., the presumption against retroactivity – in certain limited circumstances." *Ante*, at 11. I have already explained that what the Court calls a "presumption" is simply the acknowledgment of the unambiguous meaning of such provisions. But even taking it to be what the Court says, the effect upon the present case would be the same. *Prospective* applications of a statute are "effective" upon the statute's effective date; that is what an effective-date provision like §1005(h)(1) *means*.[1] "'[S]hall take effect upon enactment' is presumed

---

[1] The Court apparently believes that the effective-date provision means nothing at all. "That paragraph (1), along with paragraphs (2) and (3), is to 'take effect on the date of enactment,' DTA §1005(h)(1), 119 Stat. 2743, is not dispositive," says the Court, *ante*, at 14, n. 9. The Court's authority for this conclusion is its quote from

to mean 'shall have prospective effect upon enactment,' and that presumption is too strong to be overcome by any negative inference [drawn from other provisions of the statute]." *Landgraf*, 511 U.S., at 288 (Scalia, J., concurring in judgments). The Court's "nonapplication of . . . the presumption against retroactivity" to §1005(e)(1) is thus just another way of stating that the statute takes immediate effect in pending cases.

Though the Court resists the *Bruner* rule, it cannot cite a *single case* in the history of Anglo-American law (before today) in which a jurisdiction-stripping provision was denied immediate effect in pending cases, absent an explicit statutory reservation. By contrast, the cases granting such immediate effect are legion, and they repeatedly rely on the plain language of the jurisdictional repeal as an "inflexible trump," *ante*, at 19, by requiring an express reservation to save pending cases. See, *e.g.*, *Bruner*, *supra*, at 115; *Kline* v. *Burke Constr. Co.*, 260 U.S. 226, 234 (1922); *Hallowell*, 239 U.S., at 508; *Gwin* v. *United States*, 184 U.S. 669, 675 (1902); *Gurnee* v. *Patrick County*, 137 U.S. 141, 144 (1890); *Sherman* v. *Grinnell*, 123 U.S. 679, 680 (1887); *Railroad Co.* v. *Grant*, *supra*, at 403, *Assessors* v. *Osbornes*, 9 Wall. 567, 575 (1870); *Ex parte McCardle*, 7 Wall., at 514; *Ritchie*, *supra*, at 544; *Norris* v. *Crocker*, 13 How. 429, 440 (1852); *Yeaton* v. *United States*, 5 Cranch 281 (1809) (Marshall, C. J.), discussed in *Gwin*, *supra*, at 675; *King* v. *Justices of the Peace of London*, 3 Burr. 1456, 1457, 97 Eng. Rep. 924, 925 (K.B.1764). Cf. *National Exchange Bank of Baltimore* v. *Peters*, 144 U.S. 570, 572 (1892).

B

Disregarding the plain meaning of §1005(e)(1) and the requirement of explicit exception set forth in the foregoing cases, the Court instead favors "a negative inference . . . from the exclusion of language from one statutory provision that is included in other provisions of the same statute," *ante*, at 13. Specifically, it appeals to the fact that §1005(e)(2) and (e)(3) are explicitly made applicable to pending cases (by §1005(h)(2)). A negative inference of the sort the Court relies upon might clarify the meaning of an ambiguous provision, but since the meaning of §1005(e)(1) is entirely clear, the omitted language in that context would have been redundant.

Even if §1005(e)(1) were at all ambiguous in its application to pending cases, the "negative inference" from §1005(h)(2) touted by the Court would have no force. The numerous cases in the *Bruner* line would at least create a powerful default "presumption against jurisdiction," *ante*, at 11. The negative inference urged by the Court would be a particularly awkward and indirect way of rebutting such a longstanding and consistent practice. This is especially true since the negative inference that might be drawn from §1005(h)(2)'s specification that certain provisions *shall* apply to pending cases is matched by a negative inference in the opposite direction that might be drawn from §1005(b)(2), which provides that certain provisions shall *not* apply to pending cases.

The Court's reliance on our opinion in *Lindh* v. *Murphy*, 521 U.S. 320 (1997), is utterly misplaced. *Lindh* involved two provisions of the Antiterrorism and Effective

---

INS v. *St. Cyr*, 533 U.S. 289, 317 (2001), to the effect that "a statement that a statute will become effective on a certain date does not even arguably suggest that it has any application to conduct *that occurred at an earlier date*." *Ante*, at 14, n. 9 (emphasis added, internal quotation marks omitted). But this quote merely restates the obvious: An effective-date provision does not render a statute applicable to "conduct that occurred at an *earlier* date," but of course it renders the statute applicable to conduct that occurs *on the effective date and all future dates* – such as the Court's exercise of jurisdiction here. The Court seems to suggest that, because the effective-date provision does not authorize retroactive application, it also fails to authorize prospective application (and is thus useless verbiage). This cannot be true.

Death Penalty Act of 1996 (AEDPA): a set of amendments to chapter 153 of the federal habeas statute that redefined the scope of collateral review by federal habeas courts; and a provision creating a new chapter 154 in the habeas statute specially to govern federal collateral review of state capital cases. See 521 U.S., at 326–327. The latter provision explicitly rendered the new chapter 154 applicable to cases pending at the time of AEDPA's enactment; the former made no specific reference to pending cases. *Id.*, at 327. In *Lindh*, we drew a negative inference from chapter 154's explicit reference to pending cases, to conclude that the chapter 153 amendments did *not* apply in pending cases. It was essential to our reasoning, however, that both provisions appeared to be *identically difficult* to classify under our retroactivity cases. First, we noted that, after *Landgraf*, there was reason for Congress to suppose that an explicit statement was required to render the amendments to chapter 154 applicable in pending cases, because the new chapter 154 "will have substantive as well as purely procedural effects." 521 U.S., at 327. The next step – and the critical step – in our reasoning was that Congress had *identical* reason to suppose that an explicit statement would be required to apply the chapter 153 amendments to pending cases, but did not provide it. *Id.*, at 329. The negative inference of *Lindh* rested on the fact that "[n]othing . . . but a different intent explain [ed] the different treatment." *Ibid.*

Here, by contrast, there is ample reason for the different treatment. The exclusive-review provisions of the DTA, unlike both §1005(e)(1) and the AEDPA amendments in *Lindh*, confer *new* jurisdiction (in the D.C. Circuit) where there was none before. For better or for worse, our recent cases have contrasted jurisdiction-*creating* provisions with jurisdiction-*ousting* provisions, retaining the venerable rule that the latter are not retroactive even when applied in pending cases, but strongly indicating that the former are typically retroactive. For example, we stated in *Hughes Aircraft Co.* v. *United States ex rel. Schumer*, 520 U.S. 939, 951 (1997), that a statute "that *creates* jurisdiction where none previously existed" is "as much subject to our presumption against retroactivity as any other." See also *Republic of Austria* v. *Altmann*, 541 U.S. 677, 695, (2004) (opinion for the Court by STEVENS, J.); *id.*, at 722 (KENNEDY, J., dissenting). The Court gives our retroactivity jurisprudence a dazzling clarity in asserting that "subsections (e)(2) and (e)(3) 'confer' jurisdiction in a manner that cannot conceivably give rise to retroactivity questions under our precedents."[2] *Ante*, at 17–18. This statement rises to the level

---

[2] A comparison with *Lindh* v. *Murphy*, 521 U.S. 320 (1997), shows this not to be true. Subsections (e)(2) and (e)(3) of §1005 resemble the provisions of AEDPA at issue in *Lindh* (whose retroactivity as applied to pending cases the *Lindh* majority did not rule upon, see 521 U.S., at 326), in that they "g[o] beyond 'mere' procedure," *id.*, at 327. They impose novel and unprecedented disabilities on the Executive Branch in its conduct of military affairs. Subsection (e)(2) imposes judicial review on the Combatant Status Review Tribunals (CSRTs), whose implementing order did not subject them to review by Article III courts. See Memorandum from Deputy Secretary of Defense Paul Wolfowitz re: Order Establishing Combatant Status Review Tribunals, at 3 §*h* (July 7, 2004), available at http://www.defenselink.mil/news/Jul2004/d20040707review.pdf (all Internet materials as visited June 27, 2006, and available in Clerk of Court's case file). Subsection (e)(3) authorizes the D.C. Circuit to review "the validity of any final decision rendered pursuant to Military Commission Order No. 1," §1005(e)(3)(A), 119 Stat. 2743. Historically, federal courts have *never* reviewed the validity of the final decision of any military commission; their jurisdiction has been restricted to considering the commission's "lawful *authority* to hear, decide and condemn," *In re Yamashita*, 327 U.S. 1, 8 (1946) (emphasis added). See also *Johnson* v. *Eisentrager*, 339 U.S. 763, 786–787 (1950). Thus, contrary to the Court's suggestion, *ante*, at 17, subsections (e)(2) and (e)(3) confer new jurisdiction: They impose judicial oversight on a traditionally unreviewable exercise of military authority by the Commander in Chief. They arguably "spea[k] not just to the power of a particular court but to . . . substantive rights . . . as well," *Hughes Aircraft Co.* v. *United States ex rel. Shumer*, 520 U.S. 939, 951(1997) – namely, the unreviewable powers of the President. Our recent cases had reiterated that the Executive is protected by the presumption against retroactivity in such comparatively trivial contexts as suits for tax refunds and increased pay, see *Landgraf* v. *USI Film Products*, 511 U.S. 244, 271, n. 25 (1994).

of sarcasm when one considers its author's description of the governing test of our retroactivity jurisprudence:

> "The conclusion that a particular rule operates 'retroactively' comes at the end of a process of judgment concerning the nature and extent of the change in the law and the degree of connection between the operation of the new rule and a relevant past event. Any test of retroactivity will leave room for disagreement in hard cases, and is unlikely to classify the enormous variety of legal changes with perfect philosophical clarity. However, retroactivity is a matter on which judges tend to have 'sound … instinct[s],' … and familiar considerations of fair notice, reasonable reliance, and settled expectations offer sound guidance." *Landgraf*, 511 U.S., at 270 (opinion for the Court by STEVENS, J.).

The only "familiar consideration," "reasonable reliance," and "settled expectation" I am aware of pertaining to the present case is the rule of *Bruner* – applicable to §1005(e)(1), but not to §1005(e)(2) and (3) – which the Court stubbornly disregards. It is utterly beyond question that §1005(e)(2)'s and (3)'s application to pending cases (without explicit specification) was not as clear as §1005(e)(1)'s. That is alone enough to explain the difference in treatment.

Another obvious reason for the specification was to stave off any Suspension Clause problems raised by the immediately effective ouster of jurisdiction brought about by subsection (e)(1). That is to say, specification of the immediate effectiveness of subsections (e)(2) and (e)(3) (which, unlike subsection (e)(1), would not fall within the *Bruner* rule and would not *automatically* be deemed applicable in pending cases) could reasonably have been thought essential to be sure of replacing the habeas jurisdiction that subsection (e)(1) eliminated in pending cases with an adequate substitute. See *infra*, at 16–18.

These considerations by no means prove that an explicit statement would be *required* to render subsections (e)(2) and (e)(3) applicable in pending cases. But they surely gave Congress ample reason to *doubt* that their application in pending cases would unfold as naturally as the Court glibly assumes. In any event, even if it were true that subsections (e)(2) and (e)(3) "'confer' jurisdiction in a manner that cannot conceivably give rise to retroactivity questions," *ante*, at 17–18, this would merely establish that subsection (h)(2)'s reference to pending cases was wholly superfluous when applied to subsections (e)(2) and (c)(3), just as it would have been for subsection (e)(1). *Lindh's* negative inference makes sense only when Congress would have perceived "the wisdom of being explicit" with respect to the immediate application of *both* of two statutory provisions, 521 U.S., at 328, but chose to be explicit only for one of them – not when it would have perceived *no need* to be explicit for both, but enacted a redundancy only for one.

In short, it is simply untrue that Congress "'should have been just as concerned about'" specifying the application of §1005(e)(1) to pending cases, *ante*, at 14 (quoting *Lindh*, 521 U.S., at 329). In fact, the negative-inference approach of *Lindh* is particularly inappropriate in this case, because the negative inference from §1005(h)(2) would tend to defeat the purpose of the very provisions that *are* explicitly rendered applicable in pending cases, §1005(e)(2) and (3). Those provisions purport to vest "exclusive" jurisdiction in the D.C. Circuit to consider the claims raised by petitioners here. See *infra*, at 16–18. By drawing a negative inference *à la Lindh*, the Court supplants this exclusive-review mechanism with a dual-review mechanism for petitioners who were expeditious enough to file applications challenging the CSRTs or military commissions before December 30, 2005. Whatever the force of *Lindh's* negative inference in other cases, it surely should not apply here to defeat the purpose of the very provision from which the negative inference is drawn.

. . .

D

A final but powerful indication of the fact that the Court has made a mess of this statute is the nature of the consequences that ensue. Though this case concerns a habeas application challenging a trial by military commission, DTA §1005(e)(1) strips the courts of jurisdiction to hear or consider *any* "application for a writ of habeas corpus filed by or on behalf of an alien detained by the Department of Defense at Guantanamo Bay, Cuba." The vast majority of pending petitions, no doubt, do not relate to military commissions at all, but to more commonly challenged aspects of "detention" such as the terms and conditions of confinement. See *Rasul* v. *Bush*, 542 U.S. 466, 498 (2004) (SCALIA, J., dissenting). The Solicitor General represents that "[h]abeas petitions have been filed on behalf of a purported 600 [Guantanamo Bay] detainees," including one that "seek[s] relief on behalf of every Guantanamo detainee who has not already filed an action," Respondents' Motion to Dismiss for Lack of Jurisdiction 20, n. 10 (hereinafter Motion to Dismiss). The Court's interpretation transforms a provision abolishing jurisdiction over *all* Guantanamo-related habeas petitions into a provision that retains jurisdiction over cases sufficiently numerous to keep the courts busy for years to come.

II

Because I would hold that §1005(e)(1) unambiguously terminates the jurisdiction of all courts to "hear or consider" pending habeas applications, I must confront petitioner's arguments that the provision, so interpreted, violates the Suspension Clause. This claim is easily dispatched. We stated in *Johnson* v. *Eisentrager*, 339 U.S. 763, 768 (1950):

> "We are cited to no instance where a court, in this or any other country where the writ is known, has issued it on behalf of an alien enemy who, at no relevant time and in no stage of his captivity, has been within its territorial jurisdiction. Nothing in the text of the Constitution extends such a right, nor does anything in our statutes."

Notwithstanding the ill-considered dicta in the Court's opinion in *Rasul*, 542 U.S., at 480–481, it is clear that Guantanamo Bay, Cuba, is outside the sovereign "territorial jurisdiction" of the United States. See *id.*, at 500–505 (SCALIA, J., dissenting). Petitioner, an enemy alien detained abroad, has no rights under the Suspension Clause.

But even if petitioner were fully protected by the Clause, the DTA would create no suspension problem. This Court has repeatedly acknowledged that "the substitution of a collateral remedy which is neither inadequate nor ineffective to test the legality of a person's detention does not constitute a suspension of the writ of habeas corpus." *Swain* v. *Pressley*, 430 U.S. 372, 381 (1977); see also *INS* v. *St. Cyr*, 533 U.S. 289, 314, n. 38 (2001) ("Congress could, without raising any constitutional questions, provide an adequate substitute through the courts of appeals").

Petitioner has made no showing that the postdecision exclusive review by the D.C. Circuit provided in §1005(e)(3) is inadequate to test the legality of his trial by military commission. His principal argument is that the exclusive-review provisions are inadequate because they foreclose review of the claims he raises here. Though petitioner's brief does not parse the statutory language, his argument evidently rests on an erroneously narrow reading of DTA §1005(e)(3)(D)(ii), 119 Stat. 2743. That provision grants the D.C. Circuit authority to review, "to the extent the Constitution and laws of the United States are applicable, whether the use of such standards and procedures to reach the final decision is consistent with the Constitution and laws of the United States." In the quoted text, the phrase "such standards and procedures" refers to "the standards and procedures specified in the military order referred to in subparagraph (A)," namely "Military Commission Order No. 1, dated August 31, 2005 (or any successor military order)." DTA §1005(e)(3)(D)(i), (e)(3)(A), *ibid*. This Military Commission Order (Order No. 1) is the Department of Defense's fundamental implementing order for the President's order authorizing trials by military commission. Order No. 1 establishes commissions, §2; delineates their jurisdiction, §3; provides for their officers, §4(A); provides for their prosecution and defense counsel, §4(B), (C); lays out all their procedures, both pretrial and trial, §5(A)–(P), §6(A)–(G); and provides for posttrial military review through the Secretary of Defense and the President, §6(H). In short, the "standards and procedures specified in" Order No. 1 include *every aspect* of the military commissions, including the fact of their existence and every respect in which they differ from courts-martial. Petitioner's claims that the President lacks legal authority to try him before a military commission constitute claims that "the use of such standards and procedures," as specified in Order No. 1, is "[in]consistent with the Constitution and laws of the United States," DTA §1005(e)(3)(D)(ii), 119 Stat. 2743. The D.C. Circuit thus retains jurisdiction to consider these claims on postdecision review, and the Government does not dispute that the DTA leaves unaffected our certiorari jurisdiction under 28 U.S.C. §1254(1) to review the D.C. Circuit's decisions. Motion to Dismiss 16, n. 8. Thus, the DTA merely *defers* our jurisdiction to consider petitioner's claims; it does not eliminate that jurisdiction. It constitutes neither an "inadequate" nor an "ineffective" substitute for petitioner's pending habeas application.[7]

Though it does not squarely address the issue, the Court hints ominously that "the Government's preferred reading" would "rais[e] grave questions about Congress' authority to impinge upon this Court's appellate jurisdiction, particularly in habeas cases." *Ante*, at 10–11 (citing *Ex parte Yerger*, 8 Wall. 85 (1869); *Felker* v. *Turpin*, 518 U.S. 651 (1996); *Durousseau* v. *United States*, 6 Cranch 307 (1810); *United States* v. *Klein*, 13 Wall. 128 (1872); and *Ex parte McCardle*, 7 Wall. 506). It is not clear how there could be any such lurking questions, in light of the aptly named "*Exceptions* Clause" of Article III, §2, which, in making our appellate jurisdiction subject to "such Exceptions, and under such Regulations as the Congress shall make," explicitly permits exactly what Congress has done here. But any doubt our prior cases might have created on this score is surely chimerical in *this* case. As just noted, the exclusive-review provisions provide a substitute for habeas review adequate to satisfy the Suspension Clause, which *forbids* the suspension of the writ of habeas corpus. *A fortiori* they provide a substitute adequate to satisfy any implied substantive limitations, whether real or imaginary, upon the Exceptions Clause, which *authorizes* such exceptions as §1005(e)(1).

---

[7] Petitioner also urges that he could be subject to indefinite delay if military officials and the President are deliberately dilatory in reviewing the decision of his commission. In reviewing the constitutionality of legislation, we generally presume that the Executive will implement its provisions in good faith. And it is unclear in any event that delay would inflict any injury on petitioner, who (after an adverse determination by his CSRT, see 344 F. Supp. 2d 152, 161 (DC 2004)) is *already* subject to indefinite detention under our decision in *Hamdi* v. *Rumsfeld*, 542 U.S. 507 (2004). Moreover, the mere possibility of delay does not render an alternative remedy "inadequate [o]r ineffective to test the legality" of a military commission trial. *Swain* v. *Pressley*, 430 U.S. 372, 381 (1977). In an analogous context, we discounted the notion that postponement of relief until postconviction review inflicted any cognizable injury on a serviceman charged before a military court-martial. *Schlesinger* v. *Councilman*, 420 U.S. 738, 754–755 (1975); see also *Younger* v. *Harris*, 401 U.S. 37, 46 (1971).

III

Even if Congress had not clearly and constitutionally eliminated jurisdiction over this case, neither this Court nor the lower courts ought to exercise it. Traditionally, equitable principles govern both the exercise of habeas jurisdiction and the granting of the injunctive relief sought by petitioner. See *Schlesinger* v. *Councilman*, 420 U.S. 738, 754 (1975); *Weinberger* v. *Romero-Barcelo*, 456 U.S. 305, 311 (1982). In light of Congress's provision of an alternate avenue for petitioner's claims in §1005(e)(3), those equitable principles counsel that we abstain from exercising jurisdiction in this case.

In requesting abstention, the Government relies principally on *Councilman*, in which we abstained from considering a serviceman's claim that his charge for marijuana possession was not sufficiently "service-connected" to trigger the subject-matter jurisdiction of the military courts-martial. See 420 U.S., at 740, 758. Admittedly, *Councilman* does not squarely control petitioner's case, but it provides the closest analogue in our jurisprudence. As the Court describes, *ante*, at 21, *Councilman* "identifie[d] two considerations of comity that together favor[ed] abstention pending completion of ongoing court-martial proceedings against service personnel." But the Court errs in finding these considerations inapplicable to this case. Both of them, and a third consideration not emphasized in *Councilman*, all cut in favor of abstention here.

First, the Court observes that *Councilman* rested in part on the fact that "military discipline and, therefore, the efficient operation of the Armed Forces are best served if the military justice system acts without regular interference from civilian courts," and concludes that "Hamdan is not a member of our Nation's Armed Forces, so concerns about military discipline do not apply." *Ante*, at 22. This is true enough. But for some reason, the Court fails to make any inquiry into whether military commission trials might involve *other* "military necessities" or "unique military exigencies," 420 U.S., at 757, comparable in gravity to those at stake in *Councilman*. To put this in context: The charge against the respondent in *Councilman* was the off-base possession and sale of marijuana while he was stationed in Fort Sill, Oklahoma, see *id.*, at 739–740. The charge against the petitioner here is joining and actively abetting the murderous conspiracy that slaughtered thousands of innocent American civilians without warning on September 11, 2001. While *Councilman* held that the prosecution of the former charge involved "military necessities" counseling against our interference, the Court *does not even ponder the same question* for the latter charge.

The reason for the Court's "blinkered study" of this question, *ante*, at 19, is not hard to fathom. The principal opinion on the merits makes clear that it does not believe that the trials by military commission involve any "military necessity" *at all:* "The charge's shortcomings ... are indicative of a broader inability on the Executive's part here to satisfy the most basic precondition ... for establishment of military commissions: military necessity." *Ante*, at 48. This is quite at odds with the views on this subject expressed by our political branches. Because of "military necessity," a joint session of Congress authorized the President to "use all necessary and appropriate force," including military commissions, "against those nations, organizations, or persons [such as petitioner] he determines planned, authorized, committed, or aided the terrorist attacks that occurred on September 11, 2001." Authorization for Use of Military Force, §2(a), 115 Stat. 224, note following 50 U.S.C. §1541 (2000 ed., Supp. III). In keeping with this authority, the President has determined that "[t]o protect the United States and its citizens, and for the effective conduct of military operations and prevention of terrorist attacks, it is necessary for individuals subject to this order ... to be detained, and, when tried, to be tried for violations of the laws of war and other applicable laws by military tribunals."

Military Order of Nov. 13, 2001, 3 CFR §918(e) (2002). It is not clear where the Court derives the authority – or the audacity – to contradict this determination. If "military necessities" relating to "duty" and "discipline" required abstention in *Councilman, supra,* at 757, military necessities relating to the disabling, deterrence, and punishment of the mass-murdering terrorists of September 11 require abstention all the more here.

The Court further seeks to distinguish *Councilman* on the ground that "the tribunal convened to try Hamdan is not part of the integrated system of military courts, complete with independent review panels, that Congress has established." *Ante,* at 22. To be sure, *Councilman* emphasized that "Congress created an integrated system of military courts and review procedures, a critical element of which is the Court of Military Appeals consisting of civilian judges completely removed from all military influence or persuasion, who would gain over time thorough familiarity with military problems." 420 U.S., at 758 (internal quotation marks and footnote omitted). The Court contrasts this "integrated system" insulated from military influence with the review scheme established by Order No. 1, which "provides that appeal of a review panel's decision may be had only to the Secretary of Defense himself, §6(H)(5), and then, finally, to the President, §6(H)(6)." *Ante,* at 23.

Even if we were to accept the Court's extraordinary assumption that the President "lack[s] the structural insulation from military influence that characterizes the Court of Appeals for the Armed Forces," *ante,* at 23,[8] the Court's description of the review scheme here is anachronistic. As of December 30, 2005, the "fina[l]" review of decisions by military commissions is now conducted by the D.C. Circuit pursuant to §1005(e)(3) of the DTA, and by this Court under 28 U.S.C. §1254(1). This provision for review by Article III courts creates, if anything, a review scheme *more* insulated from Executive control than that in *Councilman.*[9] At the time we decided *Councilman,* Congress had not "conferred on any Art[icle] III court jurisdiction directly to review court-martial determinations." 420 U.S., at 746. The final arbiter of direct appeals was the Court of Military Appeals (now the Court of Appeals for the Armed Forces), an Article I court whose members possessed neither life tenure, nor salary protection, nor the constitutional protection from removal provided to federal judges in Article III, §1. See 10 U.S.C. §867(a)(2) (1970 ed.).

Moreover, a third consideration counsels strongly in favor of abstention in this case. *Councilman* reasoned that the "considerations of comity, the necessity of respect for coordinate judicial systems" that motivated our decision in *Younger* v. *Harris,* 401 U.S. 37 (1971), were inapplicable to courts-martial, because "the particular demands

---

[8] The very purpose of Article II's creation of a *civilian* Commander in Chief in the President of the United States was to generate "structural insulation from military influence." See The Federalist No. 28 (A.Hamilton); *id.,* No. 69 (same). We do not live under a military junta. It is a disservice to both those in the Armed Forces and the President to suggest that the President is subject to the undue control of the military.

[9] In rejecting our analysis, the Court observes that appeals to the D.C. Circuit under subsection (e)(3) are discretionary, rather than as of right, when the military commission imposes a sentence less than 10 years' imprisonment, see *ante,* at 23, n. 19, 52–53; §1005(e)(3)(B), 119 Stat. 2743. The relevance of this observation to the abstention question is unfathomable. The fact that Article III review is discretionary does not mean that it lacks "structural insulation from military influence," *ante,* at 23, and its discretionary nature presents no obstacle to the courts' future review these cases.

The Court might more cogently have relied on the discretionary nature of review to argue that the statute provides an inadequate substitute for habeas review under the Suspension Clause. See *supra,* at 16–18. But this argument would have no force, even if *all* appeals to the D.C. Circuit were discretionary. The exercise of habeas jurisdiction has traditionally been entirely a matter of the court's equitable discretion, see *Withrow* v. *Williams,* 507 U.S. 680, 715–718 (1993) (SCALIA, J., concurring in part and dissenting in part), so the fact that habeas jurisdiction is replaced by discretionary appellate review does not render the substitution "inadequate." *Swain,* 430 U.S., at 381.

of federalism are not implicated." 420 U.S., at 756, 757. Though military commissions likewise do not implicate "the particular demands of federalism," considerations of *interbranch* comity at the federal level weigh heavily against our exercise of equity jurisdiction in this case. Here, apparently for the first time in history, see Motion to Dismiss 6, a District Court enjoined ongoing military commission proceedings, which had been deemed "necessary" by the President "[t]o protect the United States and its citizens, and for the effective conduct of military operations and prevention of terrorist attacks." Military Order of Nov. 13, 3 CFR §918(e). Such an order brings the Judicial Branch into direct conflict with the Executive in an area where the Executive's competence is maximal and ours is virtually nonexistent. We should exercise our equitable discretion to *avoid* such conflict. Instead, the Court rushes headlong to meet it. Elsewhere, we have deferred exercising habeas jurisdiction until state courts have "the first opportunity to review" a petitioner's claim, merely to "reduc[e] friction between the state and federal court systems." *O'Sullivan* v. *Boerckel*, 526 U.S. 838, 844, 845 (1999). The "friction" created today between this Court and the Executive Branch is many times more serious.

In the face of such concerns, the Court relies heavily on *Ex parte Quirin*, 317 U.S. 1 (1942): "Far from abstaining pending the conclusion of military proceedings, which were ongoing, [in *Quirin*] we convened a special Term to hear the case and expedited our review." *Ante*, at 24. It is likely that the Government in *Quirin*, unlike here, preferred a hasty resolution of the case in this Court, so that it could swiftly execute the sentences imposed, see *Hamdi* v. *Rumsfeld*, 542 U.S. 507, 569 (2004) (SCALIA, J., dissenting). But the Court's reliance on *Quirin* suffers from a more fundamental defect: Once again, it ignores the DTA, which creates an avenue for the consideration of petitioner's claims that did not exist at the time of *Quirin*. Collateral application for habeas review was the *only* vehicle available. And there was no compelling reason to postpone consideration of the *Quirin* application until the termination of military proceedings, because the only cognizable claims presented were general challenges to the authority of the commissions that would not be affected by the specific proceedings. See *supra*, at 8–9, n. 2. In the DTA, by contrast, Congress has expanded the scope of Article III review and has channeled it exclusively through a single, postverdict appeal to Article III courts. Because Congress has created a novel unitary scheme of Article III review of military commissions that was absent in 1942, *Quirin* is no longer governing precedent.

I would abstain from exercising our equity jurisdiction, as the Government requests.

* * *

For the foregoing reasons, I dissent.

. . .

JUSTICE THOMAS, with whom JUSTICE SCALIA joins, and with whom JUSTICE ALITO joins in all but Parts I, II-C-1, and III-B-2, dissenting.

For the reasons set forth in JUSTICE SCALIA's dissent, it is clear that this Court lacks jurisdiction to entertain petitioner's claims, see *ante*, at 1–11. The Court having concluded otherwise, it is appropriate to respond to the Court's resolution of the merits of petitioner's claims because its opinion openly flouts our well-established duty to respect the Executive's judgment in matters of military operations and foreign affairs. The Court's evident belief that *it* is qualified to pass on the "[m]ilitary necessity," *ante*, at 48, of the Commander in Chief's decision to employ a particular form of force against our enemies is so antithetical to our constitutional structure that it simply cannot go unanswered. I respectfully dissent.

I

Our review of petitioner's claims arises in the context of the President's wartime exercise of his commander-in-chief authority in conjunction with the complete support of Congress. Accordingly, it is important to take measure of the respective roles the Constitution assigns to the three branches of our Government in the conduct of war.

As I explained in *Hamdi* v. *Rumsfeld*, 542 U.S. 507 (2004), the structural advantages attendant to the Executive Branch – namely, the decisiveness, "'activity, secrecy, and dispatch'" that flow from the Executive's "'unity,'" *id.*, at 581 (dissenting opinion) (quoting The Federalist No. 70, p. 472 (J. Cooke ed. 1961) (A. Hamilton)) – led the Founders to conclude that the "President ha[s] primary responsibility – along with the necessary power – to protect the national security and to conduct the Nation's foreign relations." 542 U.S., at 580. Consistent with this conclusion, the Constitution vests in the President "[t]he executive Power," Art. II, §1, provides that he "shall be Commander in Chief" of the Armed Forces, §2, and places in him the power to recognize foreign governments, §3. This Court has observed that these provisions confer upon the President broad constitutional authority to protect the Nation's security in the manner he deems fit. See, *e.g.*, *Prize Cases*, 2 Black 635, 668 (1863) ("If a war be made by invasion of a foreign nation, the President is not only authorized but bound to resist force by force ... without waiting for any special legislative authority"); *Fleming* v. *Page*, 9 How. 603, 615 (1850) (acknowledging that the President has the authority to "employ [the Nation's Armed Forces] in the manner he may deem most effectual to harass and conquer and subdue the enemy").

Congress, to be sure, has a substantial and essential role in both foreign affairs and national security. But "Congress cannot anticipate and legislate with regard to every possible action the President may find it necessary to take or every possible situation in which he might act," and "[s]uch failure of Congress ... does not, 'especially ... in the areas of foreign policy and national security,' imply 'congressional disapproval' of action taken by the Executive." *Dames & Moore* v. *Regan*, 453 U.S. 654, 678 (1981) (quoting *Haig* v. *Agee*, 453 U.S. 280, 291 (1981)). Rather, in these domains, the fact that Congress has provided the President with broad authorities does not imply – and the Judicial Branch should not infer – that Congress intended to deprive him of particular powers not specifically enumerated. See *Dames & Moore*, 453 U.S., at 678 ("[T]he enactment of legislation closely related to the question of the President's authority in a particular case which evinces legislative intent to accord the President broad discretion may be considered to invite measures on independent presidential responsibility" (internal quotation marks omitted)).

When "the President acts pursuant to an express or implied authorization from Congress," his actions are "'supported by the strongest of presumptions and the widest latitude of judicial interpretation, and the burden of persuasion ... rest[s] heavily upon any who might attack it.'" *Id.*, at 668 (quoting *Youngstown Sheet & Tube Co.* v. *Sawyer*, 343 U.S. 579, 637 (1952) (Jackson, J., concurring)). Accordingly, in the very context that we address today, this Court has concluded that "the detention and trial of petitioners – ordered by the President in the declared exercise of his powers as Commander in Chief of the Army in time of war and of grave public danger – are not to be set aside by the courts without the clear conviction that they are in conflict with the Constitution or laws of Congress constitutionally enacted." *Ex parte Quirin*, 317 U.S. 1, 25 (1942).

Under this framework, the President's decision to try Hamdan before a military commission for his involvement with al Qaeda is entitled to a heavy measure of deference. In the present conflict, Congress has authorized the President "to use all necessary and appropriate force against those nations, organizations, or persons *he determines* planned, authorized, committed, or aided the terrorist attacks that occurred on September 11, 2001 ... in order to prevent any future acts of international terrorism against the United States by such nations, organizations or persons." Authorization for Use of Military Force (AUMF) 115 Stat. 224, note following 50 U.S.C. §1541 (2000 ed., Supp. III) (emphasis added). As a plurality of the Court observed in *Hamdi*, the "capture, detention, and *trial* of unlawful combatants, by 'universal agreement and practice,' are 'important incident[s] of war,'" *Hamdi*, 542 U.S., at 518 (quoting *Quirin, supra*, at 28, 30; emphasis added), and are therefore "an exercise of the 'necessary and appropriate force' Congress has authorized the President to use." *Hamdi*, 542 U.S., at 518; *id.*, at 587 (THOMAS, J., dissenting). *Hamdi's* observation that military commissions are included within the AUMF's authorization is supported by this Court's previous recognition that "[a]n important incident to the conduct of war is the adoption of measures by the military commander, not only to repel and defeat the enemy, but to seize and subject to disciplinary measures those enemies who, in their attempt to thwart or impede our military effort, have violated the law of war." *In re Yamashita*, 327 U.S. 1, 11 (1946); see also *Quirin, supra*, at 28–29; *Madsen* v. *Kinsella*, 343 U.S. 341, 354, n. 20 (1952) ("'[T]he military commission ... is an institution of the greatest importance in the period of war and should be preserved'" (quoting S. Rep. No. 229, 63d Cong., 2d Sess., 53 (1914) (testimony of Gen. Crowder))).

Although the Court concedes the legitimacy of the President's use of military commissions in certain circumstances, *ante*, at 28, it suggests that the AUMF has no bearing on the scope of the President's power to utilize military commissions in the present conflict, *ante*, at 29–30. Instead, the Court determines the scope of this power based exclusively on Article 21 of the Uniform Code of Military Justice (UCMJ), 10 U.S.C. §821, the successor to Article 15 of the Articles of War, which *Quirin* held "authorized trial of offenses against the law of war before [military] commissions." 317 U.S., at 29. As I shall discuss below, Article 21 alone supports the use of commissions here. Nothing in the language of Article 21, however, suggests that it outlines the entire reach of congressional authorization of military commissions in all conflicts – quite the contrary, the language of Article 21 presupposes the existence of military commissions under an independent basis of authorization.[1] Indeed, consistent with *Hamdi's* conclusion that the AUMF itself authorizes the trial of unlawful combatants, the original sanction for military commissions historically derived from congressional authorization of "the initiation of war" with its attendant authorization of "the employment of all necessary and proper agencies for its due prosecution." W. Winthrop, Military Law and Precedents 831 (2d ed.1920) (hereinafter Winthrop). Accordingly, congressional authorization for military commissions pertaining to the instant conflict derives not only from Article 21 of the UCMJ, but also from the more recent, and broader, authorization contained in the AUMF.[2]

I note the Court's error respecting the AUMF not because it is necessary to my resolution of this case – Hamdan's military commission can plainly be sustained solely

---

[1] As previously noted, Article 15 of the Articles of War was the predecessor of Article 21 of the UCMJ. Article 21 provides as follows: "The provisions of this chapter conferring jurisdiction upon courts-martial do not deprive military commissions, provost courts, or other military tribunals of concurrent jurisdiction with respect to offenders or offenses that by statute or by the law of war may be tried by military commissions, provost courts, or other military tribunals." 10 U.S.C. §821.

[2] Although the President very well may have inherent authority to try unlawful combatants for violations of the law of war before military commissions, we need not decide that question because Congress has authorized the President to do so. Cf. *Hamdi* v. *Rumsfeld*, 542 U.S. 507, 587 (2004) (THOMAS, J., dissenting) (same conclusion respecting detention of unlawful combatants).

under Article 21 – but to emphasize the complete congressional sanction of the President's exercise of his commander-in-chief authority to conduct the present war. In such circumstances, as previously noted, our duty to defer to the Executive's military and foreign policy judgment is at its zenith; it does not countenance the kind of second-guessing the Court repeatedly engages in today. Military and foreign policy judgments

> "'are and should be undertaken only by those directly responsible to the people whose welfare they advance or imperil. They are decisions of a kind for which the Judiciary has neither aptitude, facilities nor responsibility and which has long been held to belong in the domain of political power not subject to judicial intrusion or inquiry.'" *Hamdi*, *supra*, at 582–583 (THOMAS, J., dissenting) (quoting *Chicago & Southern Air Lines, Inc.* v. *Waterman S.S. Corp.*, 333 U.S. 103, 111 (1948)).

It is within this framework that the lawfulness of Hamdan's commission should be examined.

II

The plurality accurately describes some aspects of the history of military commissions and the prerequisites for their use. Thus, I do not dispute that military commissions have historically been "used in three [different] situations," *ante*, at 31–32, and that the only situation relevant to the instant case is the use of military commissions "'to seize and subject to disciplinary measures those enemies who . . . have violated the law of war,'" *ante*, at 32 (quoting *Quirin, supra*, at 28–29). Similarly, I agree with the plurality that Winthrop's treatise sets forth the four relevant considerations for determining the scope of a military commission's jurisdiction, considerations relating to the (1) time and (2) place of the offense, (3) the status of the offender, and (4) the nature of the offense charged. Winthrop 836–840. The Executive has easily satisfied these considerations here. The plurality's contrary conclusion rests upon an incomplete accounting and an unfaithful application of those considerations.

A

The first two considerations are that a law-of-war military commission may only assume jurisdiction of "offences committed within the field of the command of the convening commander," and that such offenses "must have been committed within the period of the war." See *id.*, at 836, 837; *ante*, at 33. Here, as evidenced by Hamdan's charging document, the Executive has determined that the theater of the present conflict includes "Afghanistan, Pakistan and other countries" where al Qaeda has established training camps, App. to Pet. for Cert. 64a, and that the duration of that conflict dates back (at least) to Usama bin Laden's August 1996 *Declaration of Jihad Against the Americans*," *ibid*. Under the Executive's description of the conflict, then, every aspect of the charge, which alleges overt acts in "Afghanistan, Pakistan, Yemen and other countries" taking place from 1996 to 2001, satisfies the temporal and geographic prerequisites for the exercise of law-of-war military commission jurisdiction. *Id.*, at 65a–67a. And these judgments pertaining to the scope of the theater and duration of the present conflict are committed solely to the President in the exercise of his commander-in-chief authority. See *Prize Cases*, 2 Black, at 670 (concluding that the President's commander-in-chief judgment about the nature of a particular conflict was "a question to be decided *by him*, and this Court must be governed by the decisions and acts of the political department of the Government to which this power was entrusted").

Nevertheless, the plurality concludes that the legality of the charge against Hamdan is doubtful because "Hamdan is charged not with an overt act for which he was caught redhanded in a theater of war . . . but with an *agreement* the inception of which long predated . . . the [relevant armed conflict]." *Ante*, at 48 (emphasis in original). The plurality's willingness to second-guess the Executive's judgments in this context, based upon little more than its unsupported assertions, constitutes an unprecedented departure from the traditionally limited role of the courts with respect to war and an unwarranted intrusion on executive authority. And even if such second-guessing were appropriate, the plurality's attempt to do so is unpersuasive.

As an initial matter, the plurality relies upon the date of the AUMF's enactment to determine the beginning point for the "period of the war," Winthrop 836, thereby suggesting that petitioner's commission does not have jurisdiction to try him for offenses committed prior to the AUMF's enactment. *Ante*, at 34–36, 48. But this suggestion betrays the plurality's unfamiliarity with the realities of warfare and its willful blindness to our precedents. The starting point of the present conflict (or indeed any conflict) is not determined by congressional enactment, but rather by the initiation of hostilities. See *Prize Cases*, *supra*, at 668 (recognizing that war may be initiated by "invasion of a foreign nation," and that such initiation, and the President's response, usually *precedes* congressional action). Thus, Congress' enactment of the AUMF did not mark the beginning of this Nation's conflict with al Qaeda, but instead authorized the President to use force in the midst of an ongoing conflict. Moreover, while the President's "war powers" may not have been activated until the AUMF was passed, *ante*, 35, n. 31, the date of such activation has never been used to determine the scope of a military commission's jurisdiction.[3] Instead, the traditional rule is that "[o]ffenses committed before a formal declaration of war or before the declaration of martial law may be tried by military commission." Green, The Military Commission, 42 Am. J. Int'l L. 832, 848 (1948) (hereinafter Green); see also C. Howland, Digest of Opinions of the Judge-Advocates General of the Army 1067 (1912) (hereinafter Howland) ("A military commission . . . exercising . . . jurisdiction . . . under the laws of war . . . may take cognizance of offenses committed, during the war, *before* the initiation of the military government or martial law" (emphasis in original));[4] cf. *Yamashita*, 327 U.S., at 13 ("The extent to which the power to prosecute violations of the law of war shall be exercised before peace is declared rests, not with the courts, but with the political branch of the Government"). Consistent with this principle, on facts virtually identical to those here, a military commission tried Julius Otto Kuehn for conspiring with Japanese officials to

---

[3] Even if the formal declaration of war were generally the determinative act in ascertaining the temporal reach of the jurisdiction of a military commission, the AUMF itself is inconsistent with the plurality's suggestion that such a rule is appropriate in this case. See *ante*, at 34–36, 48. The text of the AUMF is backward looking, authorizing the use of "all necessary and appropriate force against those nations, organizations, or persons he determines planned, authorized, committed, or aided the terrorist attacks that occurred on September 11, 2001." Thus, the President's decision to try Hamdan by military commission – a use of force authorized by the AUMF – for Hamdan's involvement with al Qaeda prior to September 11, 2001, fits comfortably within the framework of the AUMF. In fact, bringing the September 11 conspirators to justice is the *primary point* of the AUMF. By contrast, on the plurality's logic, the AUMF would not grant the President the authority to try Usama bin Laden himself for his involvement in the events of September 11, 2001.

[4] The plurality suggests these authorities are inapplicable because nothing in its "analysis turns on the admitted absence of either a formal declaration of war or a declaration of martial law. Our focus instead is on the . . . AUMF." *Ante*, at 35, n. 31. The difference identified by the plurality is purely semantic. Both Green and Howland confirm that the date of the enactment that establishes a legal basis for forming military commissions – whether it be a declaration of war, a declaration of martial law, *or* an authorization to use military force – does not limit the jurisdiction of military commissions to offenses committed after that date.

betray the United States Fleet to the Imperial Japanese Government prior to its attack on Pearl Harbor. Green 848.[5]

Moreover, the President's determination that the present conflict dates at least to 1996 is supported by overwhelming evidence. According to the State Department, al Qaeda *declared war* on the United States as early as August 1996. See Dept. of State Fact Sheet: Usama bin Ladin (Aug. 21, 1998); Dept. of State Fact Sheet: The Charges against International Terrorist Usama Bin Laden (Dec. 20, 2000); cf. *Prize Cases*, 2 Black, at 668 (recognizing that a state of war exists even if "the declaration of it be *unilateral*" (emphasis in original)). In February 1998, al Qaeda leadership issued another statement ordering the indiscriminate – and, even under the laws of war as applied to legitimate nation-states, plainly illegal – killing of American civilians and military personnel alike. See Jihad Against Jews and Crusaders: World Islamic Front Statement 2 (Feb. 23, 1998), in Y. Alexander & M. Swetnam, Usama bin Laden's al-Qaida: Profile of a Terrorist Network, App. 1B (2001) ("The ruling to kill the Americans and their allies – civilians and military – is an individual duty for every Muslim who can do it in any country in which it is possible to do it"). This was not mere rhetoric; even before September 11, 2001, al Qaeda was involved in the bombing of the World Trade Center in New York City in 1993, the bombing of the Khobar Towers in Saudi Arabia in 1996, the bombing of the U.S. Embassies in Kenya and Tanzania in 1998, and the attack on the U.S.S. *Cole* in Yemen in 2000. See *id.*, at 1. In response to these incidents, the United States "attack[ed] facilities belonging to Usama bin Ladin's network" as early as 1998. Dept. of State Fact Sheet: Usama bin Ladin (Aug. 21, 1998). Based on the foregoing, the President's judgment – that the present conflict substantially predates the AUMF, extending at least as far back as al Qaeda's 1996 declaration of war on our Nation, and that the theater of war extends at least as far as the localities of al Qaeda's principal bases of operations – is beyond judicial reproach. And the plurality's unsupportable contrary determination merely confirms that "'the Judiciary has neither aptitude, facilities nor responsibility'" for making military or foreign affairs judgments. *Hamdi*, 542 U.S., at 585 (THOMAS, J., dissenting) (quoting *Chicago & Southern Air Lines*, 333 U.S., at 111).

B

The third consideration identified by Winthrop's treatise for the exercise of military commission jurisdiction pertains to the persons triable before such a commission, see *ante*, at 33; Winthrop 838. Law-of-war military commissions have jurisdiction over

---

[5] The plurality attempts to evade the import of this historical example by observing that Kuehn was tried before a martial law commission for a violation of federal espionage statutes. *Ibid.* As an initial matter, the fact that Kuehn was tried before a martial law commission for an offense committed prior to the establishment of martial law provides strong support for the President's contention that he may try Hamdan for offenses committed prior to the enactment of the AUMF. Here the AUMF serves the same function as the declaration of martial law in Hawaii in 1941, establishing legal authority for the constitution of military commissions. Moreover, Kuehn was not tried and punished "by statute, but by the laws and usages of war." *United States v. Bernard Julius Otto Kuehn*, Board of Review 5 (Office of the Military Governor, Hawaii 1942). Indeed, in upholding the imposition of the death penalty, a sentence "not authorized by the Espionage statutes," *ibid.*, Kuehn's Board of Review explained that "[t]he fact that persons may be tried and punished . . . by a military commission for committing acts defined as offenses by . . . federal statutes does not mean that such persons are being tried for violations of such . . . statutes; they are, instead, being tried for acts made offenses only by orders of the . . . commanding general." *Id.*, at 6. Lastly, the import of this example is not undermined by *Duncan v. Kahanamoku*, 327 U.S. 304 (1946). The question before the Court in that case involved only whether "loyal civilians in loyal territory should have their daily conduct governed by military orders," *id.*, at 319; it did "not involve the well-established power of the military to exercise jurisdiction over . . . enemy belligerents," *id.*, at 313.

"'individuals of the enemy's army who have been guilty of illegitimate warfare or other offences in violation of the laws of war,'" *ante*, at 33–34 (quoting Winthrop 838). They also have jurisdiction over "[i]rregular armed bodies or persons not forming part of the organized forces of a belligerent" "who would not be likely to respect the laws of war." *Id.*, at 783, 784. Indeed, according to Winthrop, such persons are not "within the protection of the laws of war" and were "liable to be shot, imprisoned, or banished, either summarily where their guilt was clear or upon trial and conviction by military commission." *Id.*, at 784. This consideration is easily satisfied here, as Hamdan is an unlawful combatant charged with joining and conspiring with a terrorist network dedicated to flouting the laws of war. 344 F. Supp. 2d 152, 161 (DC 2004)....

C

The fourth consideration relevant to the jurisdiction of law-of-war military commissions relates to the nature of the offense charged. As relevant here, such commissions have jurisdiction to try "'[v]iolations of the laws and usages of war cognizable by military tribunals only,'" *ante*, at 34 (quoting Winthrop 839). In contrast to the preceding considerations, this Court's precedents establish that judicial review of "whether any of the acts charged is an offense against the law of war cognizable before a military tribunal" is appropriate. *Quirin*, 317 U.S., at 29. However, "charges of violations of the law of war triable before a military tribunal need not be stated with the precision of a common law indictment." *Yamashita*, 327 U.S., at 17. And whether an offense is a violation of the law of war cognizable before a military commission must be determined pursuant to "the system of common law applied by military tribunals." *Quirin, supra*, at 30; *Yamashita, supra*, at 8.

The common law of war as it pertains to offenses triable by military commission is derived from the "experience of our wars" and our wartime tribunals, Winthrop 839, and "the laws and usages of war as understood and practiced by the civilized nations of the world," 11 Op. Atty. Gen. 297, 310 (1865). Moreover, the common law of war is marked by two important features. First, as with the common law generally, it is flexible and evolutionary in nature, building upon the experience of the past and taking account of the exigencies of the present. Thus, "[t]he law of war, like every other code of laws, declares what shall not be done, and does not say what may be done. The legitimate use of the great power of war, or rather the prohibitions upon the use of that power, increase or diminish as the necessity of the case demands." *Id.*, at 300. Accordingly, this Court has recognized that the "jurisdiction" of "our common-law war courts" has not been "prescribed by statute," but rather "has been adapted in each instance to the need that called it forth." *Madsen*, 343 U.S., at 346–348. Second, the common law of war affords a measure of respect for the judgment of military commanders. Thus, "[t]he commander of an army in time of war has the same power to organize military tribunals and execute their judgments that he has to set his squadrons in the field and fight battles. His authority in each case is from the law and usage of war." 11 Op. Atty. Gen., at 305. In recognition of these principles, Congress has generally "'left it to the President, and the military commanders representing him, to employ the commission, *as occasion may require*, for the investigation and punishment of violations of the law of war.'" *Madsen, supra*, at 347, n. 9 (quoting Winthrop 831; emphasis added).

In one key respect, the plurality departs from the proper framework for evaluating the adequacy of the charge against Hamdan under the laws of war. The plurality holds that where, as here, "neither the elements of the offense nor the range of permissible punishments is defined by statute or treaty, the precedent [establishing whether an offense is triable by military commission] must be plain and unambiguous." *Ante*, at 38. This is a pure contrivance, and a bad one at that. It is contrary to the presumption we acknowledged in *Quirin*, namely, that the actions of military commissions are "not to be set aside by the courts without the *clear conviction* that they are" unlawful, 317 U.S., at 25 (emphasis added). It is also contrary to *Yamashita*, which recognized the legitimacy of that military commission notwithstanding a substantial disagreement pertaining to whether Yamashita had been charged with a violation of the law of war. Compare 327 U.S., at 17 (noting that the allegations were "adequat[e]" and "need not be stated with . . . precision"), with *id.*, at 35 (Murphy, J., dissenting) (arguing that the charge was inadequate). Nor does it find support from the separation of powers authority cited by the plurality. Indeed, Madison's praise of the separation of powers in The Federalist No. 47, quoted *ante*, at 38–39, if it has any relevance at all, merely highlights the illegitimacy of today's judicial intrusion onto core executive prerogatives in the waging of war, where executive competence is at its zenith and judicial competence at its nadir.

The plurality's newly minted clear-statement rule is also fundamentally inconsistent with the nature of the common law which, by definition, evolves and develops over time and does not, in all cases, "say what may be done." 11 Op. Atty. Gen., at 300. Similarly, it is inconsistent with the nature of warfare, which also evolves and changes over time, and for which a flexible, evolutionary common-law system is uniquely appropriate.[6] Though the charge against Hamdan easily satisfies even the plurality's manufactured rule, see *supra*, at 16–28, the plurality's inflexible approach has dangerous implications for the Executive's ability to discharge his duties as Commander in Chief in future cases. We should undertake to determine whether an unlawful combatant has been charged with an offense against the law of war with an understanding that the common law of war is flexible, responsive to the exigencies of the present conflict, and deferential to the judgment of military commanders.

1

Under either the correct, flexible approach to evaluating the adequacy of Hamdan's charge, or under the plurality's new, clear-statement approach, Hamdan has been charged with conduct constituting two distinct violations of the law of war cognizable before a military commission: membership in a war-criminal enterprise and conspiracy to commit war crimes. The charging section of the indictment alleges both that Hamdan "willfully and knowingly joined an enterprise of persons who shared a common criminal purpose," App. to Pet. for Cert. 65a, and that he "conspired and agreed with [al Qaeda] to commit . . . offenses triable by military commission," *ibid*.[7]

---

[6] Indeed, respecting the present conflict, the President has found that "the war against terrorism ushers in a new paradigm, one in which groups with broad, international reach commit horrific acts against innocent civilians, sometimes with the direct support of states. Our Nation recognizes that this new paradigm – ushered in not by us, but by terrorists – requires new thinking in the law of war." App. 34–35. Under the Court's approach, the President's ability to address this "new paradigm" of inflicting death and mayhem would be completely frozen by rules developed in the context of conventional warfare.

[7] It is true that both of these separate offenses are charged under a single heading entitled "CHARGE: CONSPIRACY," . . . . But that does not mean that they must be treated as a single crime, when the law of war treats them as separate crimes. As we acknowledged in *In re Yamashita*, 327 U.S. 1 (1946), "charges of violations of the law of war triable before a military tribunal need not be stated with the precision of a common law indictment." *Id.*, at 17; cf. W. Birkhimer, Military Government and Martial Law 536 (3d ed.1914) (hereinafter Birkhimer) ("[I]t would be extremely absurd to expect the same precision in a charge brought

The common law of war establishes that Hamdan's willful and knowing member-ship in al Qaeda is a war crime chargeable before a military commission. Hamdan, a confirmed enemy combatant and member or affiliate of al Qaeda, has been charged with willfully and knowingly joining a group (al Qaeda) whose purpose is "to support violent attacks against property and nationals (both military and civilian) of the United States." *Id.*, at 64a; 344 F. Supp. 2d, at 161. Moreover, the allegations specify that Ham-dan joined and maintained his relationship with al Qaeda even though he "believed that Usama bin Laden and his associates were involved in the attacks on the U.S. Embassies in Kenya and Tazania in August 1998, the attack on the USS COLE in October 2000, and the attacks on the United States on September 11, 2001." . . . . These allegations, against a confirmed unlawful combatant, are alone sufficient to sustain the jurisdiction of Hamdan's military commission.

For well over a century it has been established that "to unite with banditti, jayhawk-ers, guerillas, or any other unauthorized marauders is a high offence against the laws of war; *the offence is complete when the band is organized or joined. The atrocities committed by such a band do not constitute the offence, but make the reasons, and sufficient reasons they are, why such banditti are denounced by the laws of war.*" 11 Op. Atty. Gen., at 312 (emphasis added).[8] In other words, unlawful combatants, such as Hamdan, violate the law of war merely by joining an organization, such as al Qaeda, whose principal pur-pose is the "killing [and] disabling . . . of peaceable citizens or soldiers." Winthrop 784; see also 11 Op. Atty. Gen., at 314 ("A bushwhacker, a jayhawker, a bandit, a war rebel, an assassin, being public enemies, may be tried, condemned, and executed as offenders against the laws of war"). This conclusion is unsurprising, as it is a "cardinal princi-ple of the law of war . . . that the civilian population must enjoy complete immunity." 4 International Committee of Red Cross, Commentary: Geneva Convention Relative to the Protection of Civilian Persons in Time of War 3 (J. Pictet ed.1958). "Numerous instances of trials, for 'Violation of the laws of war,' of offenders of this description,

---

before a court-martial as is required to support a conviction before a justice of the peace" (internal quotation marks omitted)).

Nevertheless, the plurality contends that Hamdan was "not actually charged," *ante*, at 37, n. 32 (emphasis deleted), with being a member in a war criminal organization. But that position is demonstrably wrong. Hamdan's charging document expressly *charges* that he "willfully and knowingly joined an enterprise of persons who shared a common criminal purpose." . . . . Moreover, the plurality's contention that we may only look to the label affixed to the charge to determine if the charging document alleges an offense triable by military commission is flatly inconsistent with its treatment of the Civil War cases – where it accepts as valid charges that did not appear in the heading or title of the charging document, or even the listed charge itself, but only in the supporting specification. See, *e.g., ante*, at 45–46 (discussing the military commission trial of Wirz). For example, in the Wirz case, Wirz was charged with conspiring to violate the laws of war, and that charge was supported with allegations that he personally committed a number of atrocities. The plurality concludes that military commission jurisdiction was appropriate in that case not based upon the charge of conspiracy, but rather based upon the allegations of various atrocities in the specification which were *not* separately charged. *Ante*, at 45. Just as these atrocities, not separately charged, were independent violations of the law of war supporting Wirz's trial by military commission, so too here Hamdan's membership in al Qaeda and his provision of various forms of assistance to al Qaeda's top leadership are independent violations of the law of war supporting his trial by military commission.

[8] These observations respecting the law of war were made by the Attorney General in defense of the military commission trial of the Lincoln conspirators'. As the foregoing quoted portion of that opinion makes clear, the Attorney General did not, as the Court maintains, "trea[t] the charge as if it alleged the substantive offense of assassination." *Ante*, at 40, n. 35. Rather, he explained that the conspirators "high offence against the laws of war" was "complete" when their band was "organized or joined," and did not depend upon "atrocities com-mitted by such a band." 11 Op. Atty. Gen. 297, 312 (1865). Moreover, the Attorney General's conclusions specifically refute the plurality's unsupported suggestion that I have blurred the line between "those cate-gories of 'offender' who may be tried by military commission . . . with the 'offenses' that may be so tried." *Ante*, at 37, n. 32.

are published in the General Orders of the years 1862 to 1866." Winthrop 784, and n. 57.[9]

Accordingly, on this basis alone, "the allegations of [Hamdan's] charge, tested by any reasonable standard, adequately allege a violation of the law of war." *Yamashita*, 327 U.S., at 17.

The conclusion that membership in an organization whose purpose is to violate the laws of war is an offense triable by military commission is confirmed by the experience of the military tribunals convened by the United States at Nuremberg. Pursuant to Article 10 of the Charter of the International Military Tribunal (IMT), the United States convened military tribunals "to bring individuals to trial for membership" in "a group or organization...declared criminal by the [IMT]." 1 Trials of War Criminals Before the Nuernberg Military Tribunals, p. XII (hereinafter Trials). The IMT designated various components of four Nazi groups – the Leadership Corps, Gestapo, SD, and SS – as criminal organizations. 22 IMT, Trial of the Major War Criminals 505, 511, 517 (1948); see also T. Taylor, The Anatomy of the Nuremberg Trials: A Personal Memoir 584–585 (1992). "[A] member of [such] an organization [could] be...convicted of the crime of membership and be punished for that crime by death." 22 IMT, at 499. Under this authority, the United States Military Tribunal at Nuremberg convicted numerous individuals for the act of knowing and voluntary membership in these organizations. For example, in Military Tribunal Case No. 1, *United States* v. *Brandt*, Karl Brandt, Karl Gebhardt, Rudolf Brandt, Joachim Mrugowsky, Wolfram Sievers, Viktor Brack, and Waldemar Hoven, were convicted and sentenced to death for the crime of, *inter alia*, membership in an organization declared criminal by the IMT; Karl Genzken and Fritz Fischer were sentenced to life imprisonment for the same; and Helmut Poppendick was convicted of no other offense than membership in a criminal organization and sentenced to a

---

[9] The General Orders establishing the jurisdiction for military commissions during the Civil War provided that such offenses were violations of the laws of war cognizable before military commissions. See H. R. Doc. No. 65, 55th Cong., 3d Sess., 164 (1894) ("[P]ersons charged with the violation of the laws of war as spies, bridge-burners, marauders, &c., will...be held for trial under such charges"); *id.*, at 234 ("[T]here are numerous rebels...that...furnish the enemy with arms, provisions, clothing, horses and means of transportation; [such] insurgents are banding together in several of the interior counties for the purpose of assisting the enemy to rob, to maraud and to lay waste to the country. *All such persons are by the laws of war in every civilized country liable to capital punishment*" (emphasis added)). Numerous trials were held under this authority. See, *e.g.*, U.S. War Dept., General Court-Martial Order No. 51, p. 1 (1866) (hereinafter G.C.M.O.). (indictment in the military commission trial of James Harvey Wells charged "[b]eing a guerrilla" and specified that he "willfully...[took] up arms as a guerrilla marauder, and did join, belong to, act and co-operate with guerrillas"); G.C.M.O. No. 108, Head-Quarters Dept. of Kentucky, p. 1 (1865) (indictment in the military commission trial of Henry C. Magruder charged "[b]eing a guerrilla" and specified that he "unlawfully, and of his own wrong, [took] up arms as a guerrilla marauder, and did join, belong to, act, and co-operate with a band of guerrillas"); G.C.M.O. No. 41, p. 1 (1864) (indictment in the military commission trial of John West Wilson charged that Wilson "did take up arms as an insurgent and guerrilla against the laws and authorities of the United States, and did join and co-operate with an armed band of insurgents and guerrillas who were engaged in plundering the property of peaceable citizens...in violation of the laws and customs of war"); G.C.M.O. No. 153, p. 1 (1864) (indictment in the military commission trial of Simeon B. Kight charged that defendant was "a guerrilla, and has been engaged in an unwarrantable and barbarous system of warfare against citizens and soldiers of the United States"); G.C.M.O. No. 93, pp. 3–4 (1864) (indictment in the military commission trial of Francis H. Norvel charged "[b]eing a guerrilla" and specified that he "unlawfully and by his own wrong, [took] up arms as an outlaw, guerrilla, and bushwhacker, against the lawfully constituted authorities of the United States government"); *id.*, at 9 (indictment in the military commission trial of James A. Powell charged "[t]ransgression of the laws and customs of war" and specified that he "[took] up arms in insurrection as a military insurgent, and did join himself to and, in arms, consort with...a rebel enemy of the United States, and the leader of a band of insurgents and armed rebels"); *id.*, at 10–11 (indictment in the military commission trial of Joseph Overstreet charged "[b]eing a guerrilla" and specified that he "did join, belong to, consort and co-operate with a band of guerrillas, insurgents, outlaws, and public robbers").

10-year term of imprisonment. 2 Trials 180-300. This Court denied habeas relief, 333 U.S. 836 (1948), and the executions were carried out at Landsberg prison on June 2, 1948. 2 Trials 330.

Moreover, the Government has alleged that Hamdan was not only a member of al Qaeda while it was carrying out terrorist attacks on civilian targets in the United States and abroad, but also that Hamdan aided and assisted al Qaeda's top leadership by supplying weapons, transportation, and other services. . . . . These allegations further confirm that Hamdan is triable before a law-of-war military commission for his involvement with al Qaeda. See H. R. Doc. No. 65, 55th Cong., 3d Sess., 234 (1894) ("[T]here are numerous rebels . . . that . . . furnish the enemy with arms, provisions, clothing, horses and means of transportation; [such] insurgents are banding together in several of the interior counties for the purpose of assisting the enemy to rob, to maruad and to lay waste to the country. *All such persons are by the laws of war in every civilized country liable to capital punishment*" (emphasis added)); Winthrop 840 (including in the list of offenses triable by law-of-war military commissions "dealing with . . . enemies, or furnishing them with money, arms, provisions, medicines, &c").[10] Undoubtedly, the conclusion that such conduct violates the law of war led to the enactment of Article 104 of the UCMJ, which provides that "[a]ny person who . . . aids, or attempts to aid, the enemy with arms, ammunition, supplies, money, or other things . . . shall suffer death or such other punishment as a court-martial or military commission may direct." 10 U.S.C. §904.

2

Separate and apart from the offense of joining a contingent of "uncivilized combatants who [are] not . . . likely to respect the laws of war," Winthrop 784, Hamdan has been charged with "conspir[ing] and agree[ing] with . . . the al Qaida organization . . . to commit . . . offenses triable by military commission," App. to Pet. for Cert. 65a. Those offenses include "attacking civilians; attacking civilian objects; murder by an unprivileged belligerent; and terrorism." *Ibid.* This, too, alleges a violation of the law of war triable by military commission.

"[T]he experience of our wars," Winthrop 839, is rife with evidence that establishes beyond any doubt that conspiracy to violate the laws of war is itself an offense cognizable before a law-of-war military commission. World War II provides the most recent examples of the use of American military commissions to try offenses pertaining to violations of the laws of war. In that conflict, the orders establishing the jurisdiction of military commissions in various theaters of operation provided that conspiracy to violate the laws of war was a cognizable offense. See Letter, General Headquarters, United States Army Forces, Pacific (Sept. 24, 1945), Record in *Yamashita* v. *Styer*, O.T. 1945, No. 672, pp. 14, 16 . . . (Order respecting the "Regulations Governing the Trial of War Criminals" provided that "participation in a common plan or conspiracy to accomplish" various offenses against the law of war was cognizable before military commissions); 1 United Nations War Crimes Commission, Law Reports of Trials of War Criminals 114–115 (1997) (hereinafter U.N. Commission) (recounting that the orders establishing World War II military commissions in the Pacific and China included "participation in a

---

[10] Even if the plurality were correct that a membership offense must be accompanied by allegations that the "defendant 'took up arms,'" *ante*, at 37, n. 32, that requirement has easily been satisfied here. Not only has Hamdan been charged with providing assistance to top al Qaeda leadership (itself an offense triable by military commission), he has also been charged with receiving weapons training at an al Qaeda camp. . . . .

common plan or conspiracy" pertaining to certain violations of the laws of war as an offense triable by military commission). Indeed, those orders authorized trial by military commission of participation in a conspiracy to commit "murder ... or other inhumane acts ... against any civilian population," *id.*, at 114, which is precisely the offense Hamdan has been charged with here. And conspiracy to violate the laws of war was charged in the highest profile case tried before a World War II military commission, see *Quirin*, 317 U.S., at 23, and on numerous other occasions. See, *e.g.*, *Colepaugh* v. *Looney*, 235 F. 2d 429, 431 (CA10 1956); Green 848 (describing the conspiracy trial of Julius Otto Kuehn).

To support its contrary conclusion, *ante*, at 35–36, the plurality attempts to evade the import of *Quirin* (and the other World War II authorities) by resting upon this Court's failure to address the sufficiency of the conspiracy charge in the *Quirin* case, *ante*, at 41–43. But the common law of war cannot be ascertained from this Court's failure to pass upon an issue, or indeed to even mention the issue in its opinion;[11] rather, it is ascertained by the practice and usage of war. Winthrop 839; *supra*, at 11–12.

The Civil War experience provides further support for the President's conclusion that conspiracy to violate the laws of war is an offense cognizable before law-of-war military commissions. Indeed, in the highest profile case to be tried before a military commission relating to that war, namely, the trial of the men involved in the assassination of President Lincoln, the charge provided that those men had "combin[ed], confederat[ed], and conspir[ed] ... to kill and murder" President Lincoln. G.C.M.O. No. 356 (1865), reprinted in H. R. Doc. No. 314, 55th Cong., 3d Sess., 696 (1899) (hereinafter G.C.M.O. No. 356).[12]

In addition to the foregoing high-profile example, Winthrop's treatise enumerates numerous Civil War military commission trials for conspiracy to violate the law of war. Winthrop 839, n. 5. The plurality attempts to explain these examples away by suggesting that the conspiracies listed by Winthrop are best understood as "a species of compound offense," namely, violations both of the law of war and ordinary criminal laws, rather than "stand-alone offense[s] against the law of war." *Ante*, at 44–45 (citing, as an example, murder in violation of the laws of war). But the fact that, for example, conspiracy to commit murder can at the same time violate ordinary criminal laws and the law of war, so that it is "a combination of the two species of offenses," Howland 1071, does not establish that a military commission would not have jurisdiction to try that crime solely on the basis that it was a violation of the law of war. Rather, if anything, and

---

[11] The plurality recounts the respective claims of the parties in *Quirin* pertaining to this issue and cites the United States Reports. *Ante*, at 41–42. But the claims of the parties are not included in the opinion of the Court, but rather in the sections of the Reports entitled "Argument for Petitioners," and "Argument for Respondent." See 317 U.S., at 6–17.

[12] The plurality concludes that military commission jurisdiction was appropriate in the case of the Lincoln conspirators because they were charged with "'maliciously, unlawfully, and traitorously murdering the said Abraham Lincoln,'" *ante*, at 40, n. 35. But the sole charge filed in that case alleged conspiracy, and the allegations pertaining to "maliciously, unlawfully, and traitorously murdering the said Abraham Lincoln" were not charged or labeled as separate offenses, but rather as overt acts "in pursuance of and in prosecuting said malicious, unlawful, and traitorous *conspiracy*." G.C.M.O. No. 356, at ___ emphasis added). While the plurality contends the murder of President Lincoln was charged as a distinct separate offense, the foregoing quoted language of the charging document unequivocally establishes otherwise. Moreover, though I agree that the allegations pertaining to these overt acts provided an independent basis for the military commission's jurisdiction in that case, that merely confirms the propriety of examining all the acts alleged – whether or not they are labeled as separate offenses – to determine if a defendant has been charged with a violation of the law of war. As I have already explained, Hamdan has been charged with violating the law of war not only by participating in a conspiracy to violate the law of war, but also by joining a war criminal enterprise and by supplying provisions and assistance to that enterprise's top leadership.

consistent with the principle that the common law of war is flexible and affords some level of deference to the judgments of military commanders, it establishes that military commissions would have the discretion to try the offense as (1) one against the law of war, or (2) one against the ordinary criminal laws, or (3) both.

In any event, the plurality's effort to avoid the import of Winthrop's footnote through the smokescreen of its "compound offense" theory, *ante*, at 44–45, cannot be reconciled with the particular charges that sustained military commission jurisdiction in the cases that Winthrop cites. For example, in the military commission trial of Henry Wirtz, Charge I provided that he had been

> "[m]aliciously, willfully, and traitorously . . . *combining, confederating, and conspiring*, together [with various other named and unnamed co-conspirators], to injure the health and destroy the lives of soldiers in the military service of the United States, then held and being prisoners of war within the lines of the so-called Confederate States, and in the military prisons thereof, to the end that the armies of the United States might be weakened and impaired, *in violation of the laws and customs of war*." G.C.M.O. No. 607 (1865), reprinted in H. R. Doc. No. 314, at 785 (emphasis added).

Likewise, in the military commission trial of Lenger Grenfel, Charge I accused Grenfel of "*[c]onspiring, in violation of the laws of war*, to release rebel prisoners of war confined by authority of the United States at Camp Douglas, near Chicago, Ill." G.C.M.O. No. 452 (1865), reprinted in H. R. Doc. No. 314, at 724 (emphasis added)[13]; see also G.C.M.O. No. 41, at 20 (1864) (indictment in the military commission trial of Robert Louden charged "[c]onspiring with the rebel enemies of the United States to embarrass and impede the military authorities in the suppression of the existing rebellion, by the burning and destruction of steamboats and means of transportation on the Mississippi river"). These examples provide incontrovertible support for the President's conclusion that the common law of war permits military commission trials for conspiracy to violate the law of war. And they specifically contradict the plurality's conclusion to the contrary, thereby easily satisfying its requirement that the Government "make a substantial showing that the crime for which it seeks to try a defendant by military commission is acknowledged to be an offense against the law of war." *Ante*, at 39–40.[14]

---

[13] The plurality's attempt to undermine the significance of these cases is unpersuasive. The plurality suggests the Wirz case is not relevant because the specification supporting his conspiracy charge alleged that he "*personally committed* a number of atrocities." *Ante*, at 45. But this does not establish that conspiracy to violate the laws of war, the very crime with which Wirz was charged, is not itself a violation of the law of war. Rather, at best, it establishes that in addition to conspiracy Wirz violated the laws of war by committing various atrocities, just as Hamdan violated the laws of war not only by conspiring to do so, but also by joining al Qaeda and providing provisions and services to its top leadership. Moreover, the fact that Wirz was charged with overt acts that are more severe than the overt acts with which Hamdan has been charged does not establish that conspiracy is not an offense cognizable before military commission; rather it merely establishes that Wirz's offenses may have been comparably worse than Hamdan's offenses.

    The plurality's claim that the charge against Lenger Grenfel supports its compound offense theory is similarly unsupportable. The plurality does not, and cannot, dispute that Grenfel was charged with conspiring to violate the laws of war by releasing rebel prisoners – a charge that bears no relation to a crime "ordinarily triable in civilian courts." *Ante*, at 46, n. 37. Tellingly, the plurality does not reference or discuss this charge, but instead refers to the conclusion of Judge Advocate Holt that Grenfel also "'united himself with traitors and malefactors for the overthrow of our Republic in the interest of slavery.'" *Ibid.* (quoting H. R. Doc. No. 314, at 689). But Judge Advocate Holt's observation provides no support for the plurality's conclusion, as it does not discuss the charges that sustained military commission jurisdiction, much less suggest that such charges were not violations of the law of war.

[14] The plurality contends that international practice – including the practice of the IMT at Nuremberg – supports its conclusion that conspiracy is not an offense triable by military commission because "'[t]he Anglo-American concept of conspiracy was not part of European legal systems and arguably not an element of the

The plurality further contends, in reliance upon Winthrop, that conspiracy is not an offense cognizable before a law-of-war military commission because "it is not enough to intend to violate the law of war and commit overt acts in furtherance of that intention unless the overt acts either are themselves offenses against the law of war or constitute steps sufficiently substantial to qualify as an attempt." *Ibid*. But Winthrop does not support the plurality's conclusion. The passage in Winthrop cited by the plurality states only that "the jurisdiction of the military commission should be restricted to cases of offence consisting in *overt acts,i.e*. in unlawful commissions or actual attempts to commit, and not in intentions merely." Winthrop 841 (emphasis in original). This passage would be helpful to the plurality if its subject were "conspiracy," rather than the "jurisdiction of the military commission." Winthrop is not speaking here of the requirements for a conspiracy charge, but of the requirements for *all* charges. Intentions do not suffice. An unlawful act – such as committing the crime of conspiracy – is necessary. Winthrop says nothing to exclude either conspiracy or membership in a criminal enterprise, both of which go beyond "intentions merely" and "consis[t] of *overt acts, i.e*. . . . unlawful commissions or actual attempts to commit," and both of which are *expressly* recognized by Winthrop as crimes against the law of war triable by military commissions. *Id.*, at 784; *id.*, at 839, and n. 5, 840. Indeed, the commission of an *"overt ac[t]"* is the traditional requirement for the completion of the crime of conspiracy, and the charge against Hamdan alleges numerous such overt acts. . . . . The plurality's approach, unsupported by Winthrop, requires that any overt act to further a conspiracy must *itself* be a completed war crime *distinct from conspiracy* – which merely begs the question the plurality sets out to answer, namely, whether conspiracy itself may constitute a violation of the law of war. And, even the plurality's unsupported standard is satisfied here. Hamdan has been charged with the overt acts of providing protection, transportation, weapons, and other services to the enemy, *id.*, . . . acts which in and of themselves are violations of the laws of war. See *supra*, at 20–21; Winthrop 839–840.

3

Ultimately, the plurality's determination that Hamdan has not been charged with an offense triable before a military commission rests not upon any historical example or authority, but upon the plurality's raw judgment of the "inability on the Executive's part here to satisfy the most basic precondition . . . for establishment of military commissions: military necessity." *Ante*, at 48. This judgment starkly confirms that the plurality has appointed itself the ultimate arbiter of what is quintessentially a policy and military judgment, namely, the appropriate military measures to take against those who "aided

---

internationally recognized laws of war.'" *Ante*, at 47 (quoting T. Taylor, Anatomy of the Nuremberg Trials: A Personal Memoir 36 (1992)). But while the IMT did not criminalize all conspiracies to violate the law of war, it did criminalize "participation in a common plan or conspiracy" to wage aggressive war. See 1 Trials, pp. XI–XII. Moreover, the World War II military tribunals of several European nations recognized conspiracy to violate the laws of war as an offense triable before military commissions. See 15 U.N. Commission 90–91 (noting that the French Military Tribunal at Marseilles found Henri Georges Stadelhofer "guilty of the crime of *association de malfaiteurs*," namely of "having formed with various members of the German Gestapo an association with the aim of preparing or committing crimes against persons or property, without justification under the laws and usages of war"); 11 *id.*, at 98 (noting that the Netherlands' military tribunals were authorized to try conspiracy to violate the laws of war). Thus, the European legal systems' approach to domestic conspiracy law has not prevented European nations from recognizing conspiracy offenses as violations of the law of war. This is unsurprising, as the law of war is derived not from domestic law but from the wartime practices of civilized nations, including the United States, which has consistently recognized that conspiracy to violate the laws of war is an offense triable by military commission.

the terrorist attacks that occurred on September 11, 2001." AUMF §2(a), 115 Stat. 224. The plurality's suggestion that Hamdan's commission is illegitimate because it is not dispensing swift justice on the battlefield is unsupportable. *Ante*, at 43. Even a cursory review of the authorities confirms that law-of-war military commissions have wide-ranging jurisdiction to try offenses against the law of war in exigent and nonexigent circumstances alike. See, *e.g.*, Winthrop 839–840; see also *Yamashita*, 327 U.S., at 5 (military commission trial after the cessation of hostilities in the Philippines); *Quirin*, 317 U.S. 1 (military commission trial in Washington, D.C.). Traditionally, retributive justice for heinous war crimes is as much a "military necessity" as the "demands" of "military efficiency" touted by the plurality, and swift military retribution is precisely what Congress authorized the President to impose on the September 11 attackers in the AUMF.

Today a plurality of this Court would hold that conspiracy to massacre innocent civilians does not violate the laws of war. This determination is unsustainable. The judgment of the political branches that Hamdan, and others like him, must be held accountable before military commissions for their involvement with and membership in an unlawful organization dedicated to inflicting massive civilian casualties is supported by virtually every relevant authority, including all of the authorities invoked by the plurality today. It is also supported by the nature of the present conflict. We are not engaged in a traditional battle with a nation-state, but with a worldwide, hydra-headed enemy, who lurks in the shadows conspiring to reproduce the atrocities of September 11, 2001, and who has boasted of sending suicide bombers into civilian gatherings, has proudly distributed videotapes of beheadings of civilian workers, and has tortured and dismembered captured American soldiers. But according to the plurality, when our Armed Forces capture those who are plotting terrorist atrocities like the bombing of the Khobar Towers, the bombing of the U.S.S. *Cole*, and the attacks of September 11 – even if their plots are advanced to the very brink of fulfillment – our military cannot charge those criminals with any offense against the laws of war. Instead, our troops must catch the terrorists "redhanded," *ante*, at 48, in the midst of *the attack itself*, in order to bring them to justice. Not only is this conclusion fundamentally inconsistent with the cardinal principal of the law of war, namely protecting non-combatants, but it would sorely hamper the President's ability to confront and defeat a new and deadly enemy.

After seeing the plurality overturn longstanding precedents in order to seize juris-diction over this case, *ante*, at 2–4 (SCALIA, J., dissenting), and after seeing them disregard the clear prudential counsel that they abstain in these circumstances from using equi-table powers, *ante*, at 19–24, it is no surprise to see them go on to overrule one after another of the President's judgments pertaining to the conduct of an ongoing war. Those Justices who today disregard the commander-in-chief's wartime decisions, only 10 days ago deferred to the judgment of the Corps of Engineers with regard to a matter much more within the competence of lawyers, upholding that agency's wildly implausible con-clusion that a storm drain is a tributary of the waters of the United States. See *Rapanos* v. *United States*, 547 U.S. __(2006). It goes without saying that there is much more at stake here than storm drains. The plurality's willingness to second-guess the determina-tion of the political branches that these conspirators must be brought to justice is both unprecedented and dangerous.

III

The Court holds that even if "the Government has charged Hamdan with an offense against the law of war cognizable by military commission, the commission lacks power to proceed" because of its failure to comply with the terms of the UCMJ and the four Geneva Conventions signed in 1949. *Ante*, at 49. This position is untenable.

A

As with the jurisdiction of military commissions, the procedure of such commissions "has [not] been prescribed by statute," but "has been adapted in each instance to the need that called it forth." *Madsen*, 343 U.S., at 347–348. Indeed, this Court has concluded that "[i]n the absence of attempts by Congress to limit the President's power, it appears that, as Commander in Chief of the Army and Navy of the United States, he may, in time of war, establish and prescribe the jurisdiction and procedure of military commissions." *Id.*, at 348. This conclusion is consistent with this Court's understanding that military commissions are "our common-law war courts." *Id.*, at 346–347.[15] As such, "[s]hould the conduct of those who compose martial-law tribunals become [a] matter of judicial determination subsequently before the civil courts, those courts will give great weight to the opinions of the officers as to what the customs of war in any case justify and render necessary." Birkhimer 534.

The Court nevertheless concludes that at least one provision of the UCMJ amounts to an attempt by Congress to limit the President's power. This conclusion is not only contrary to the text and structure of the UCMJ, but it is also inconsistent with precedent of this Court. Consistent with *Madsen*'s conclusion pertaining to the common-law nature of military commissions and the President's discretion to prescribe their procedures, Article 36 of the UCMJ authorizes the President to establish procedures for military commissions "which shall, *so far as he considers practicable*, apply the principles of law and the rules of evidence generally recognized in the trial of criminal cases in the United States district courts, but which may not be contrary to or inconsistent with this chapter." 10 U.S.C. §836(a) (emphasis added). Far from constraining the President's authority, Article 36 recognizes the President's prerogative to depart from the procedures applicable in criminal cases whenever *he alone* does not deem such procedures "practicable." While the procedural regulations promulgated by the Executive must not be "contrary to" the UCMJ, only a few provisions of the UCMJ mention "military commissions," see *ante*, at 58, n. 49, and there is no suggestion that the procedures to be employed by Hamdan's commission implicate any of those provisions.

---

[15] Though it does not constitute a basis for any holding of the Court, the Court maintains that, as a "general rule," "the procedures governing trials by military commission historically have been the same as those governing courts-martial." *Ante*, at 54, 53. While it is undoubtedly true that military commissions have invariably employed most of the procedures employed by courts-martial, that is not a requirement. See Winthrop 841 ("[M]ilitary commissions . . . are commonly conducted according to the rules and forms governing courts-martial. These war-courts are indeed more summary in their action than are the courts held under the Articles of war, and . . . their proceedings . . . will not be rendered *illegal* by the omission of details required upon trials by courts-martial" (emphasis in original; footnotes omitted)); 1 U.N. Commission 116–117 ("The [World War II] Mediterranean Regulations (No. 8) provide that Military Commissions shall conduct their proceedings as may be deemed necessary for full and fair trial, having regard for, *but not being bound by*, the rules of procedure prescribed for General Courts Martial" (emphasis added)); *id.*, at 117 ("In the [World War II] European directive it is stated . . . that Military Commissions shall have power to make, as occasion requires, such rules for the conduct of their proceedings consistent with the powers of such Commissions, and with the rules of procedure . . . as are deemed necessary for a full and fair trial of the accused, having regard for, without being bound by, the rules of procedure and evidence prescribed for General Courts Martial"). Moreover, such a requirement would conflict with the settled understanding of the flexible and responsive nature of military commissions and the President's wartime authority to employ such tribunals as he sees fit. See Birkhimer 537–538 ("[M]ilitary commissions may so vary their procedure as to adapt it to any situation, and may extend their powers to any necessary degree. . . . The military commander decides upon the character of the military tribunal which is suited to the occasion . . . and his decision is final").

Notwithstanding the foregoing, the Court concludes that Article 36(b) of the UCMJ, 10 U.S.C. §836(b), which provides that "'[a]ll rules and regulations made under this article shall be uniform insofar as practicable,'" *ante*, at 59, requires the President to employ the same rules and procedures in military commissions as are employed by courts-martial *"insofar as practicable." Ante*, at 59. The Court further concludes that Hamdan's commission is unlawful because the President has not explained why it is not practicable to apply the same rules and procedures to Hamdan's commission as would be applied in a trial by court martial. *Ante*, at 60.

This interpretation of §836(b) is unconvincing. As an initial matter, the Court fails to account for our cases interpreting the predecessor to Article 21 of the UCMJ – Article 15 of the Articles of War – which provides crucial context that bears directly on the proper interpretation of Article 36(b). Article 15 of the Articles of War provided that:

> "The provisions of these articles conferring jurisdiction upon courts-martial shall not be construed as depriving military commissions, provost courts, or other military tribunals of concurrent jurisdiction in respect of offenders or offences that by statute or by the law of war may be triable by such military commissions, provost courts, or other military tribunals."

In *Yamashita*, this Court concluded that Article 15 of the Articles of War preserved the President's unfettered authority to prescribe military commission procedure. The Court explained, "[b]y thus recognizing military commissions in order to preserve their traditional jurisdiction over enemy combatants unimpaired by the Articles, Congress gave sanction . . . to *any use* of the military commission contemplated by the common law of war." 327 U.S., at 20 (emphasis added)[16]; see also *Quirin*, 317 U.S., at 28; *Madsen*, 343 U.S., at 355. In reaching this conclusion, this Court treated as authoritative the congressional testimony of Judge Advocate General Crowder, who testified that Article 15 of the Articles of War was enacted to preserve the military commission as "'our common-law war court.'" *Yamashita, supra*, at 19, n. 7. And this Court recognized that Article 15's preservation of military commissions as common-law war courts preserved the President's commander-in-chief authority to both "establish" military commissions and to "prescribe [their] procedure[s]." *Madsen*, 343 U.S., at 348; *id.*, at 348–349 (explaining that Congress had "refrain[ed] from legislating" in the area of military commission procedures, in "contras[t] with its traditional readiness to . . . prescrib[e], with particularity, the jurisdiction and procedure of United States courts-martial"); cf. Green 834 ("The military commission exercising jurisdiction under common law authority is usually appointed by a superior military commander and is limited in its procedure only by the will of that commander. Like any other common law court, in the absence of directive of superior authority to the contrary, the military commission is free to formulate its own rules of procedure").

Given these precedents, the Court's conclusion that Article 36(b) requires the President to apply the same rules and procedures to military commissions as are applicable to

---

[16] The Court suggests that Congress' amendment to Article 2 of the UCMJ, providing that the UCMJ applies to "persons within an area leased by or otherwise reserved or acquired for the use of the United States," 10 U.S.C. §802(a)(12), deprives *Yamashita*'s conclusion respecting the President's authority to promulgate military commission procedures of its "precedential value." *Ante*, at 56. But this merely begs the question of the scope and content of the remaining provisions of the UCMJ. Nothing in the additions to Article 2, or any other provision of the UCMJ, suggests that Congress has disturbed this Court's unequivocal interpretation of Article 21 as preserving the common-law status of military commissions and the corresponding authority of the President to set their procedures pursuant to his commander-in-chief powers. See *Quirin*, 317 U.S., at 28; *Yamashita*, 327 U.S., at 20; *Madsen v. Kinsella*, 343 U.S. 341, 355 (1952).

courts-martial is unsustainable. When Congress codified Article 15 of the Articles of War in Article 21 of the UCMJ it was "presumed to be aware of . . . and to adopt" this Court's interpretation of that provision as preserving the common-law status of military commissions, inclusive of the President's unfettered authority to prescribe their procedures. *Lorillard* v. *Pons*, 434 U.S. 575, 580 (1978). The Court's conclusion that Article 36(b) repudiates this settled meaning of Article 21 is not based upon a specific textual reference to military commissions, but rather on a one-sentence subsection providing that "[a]ll rules and regulations made under this article shall be uniform insofar as practicable." 10 U.S.C. §836(b). This is little more than an impermissible repeal by implication. See *Branch* v. *Smith*, 538 U.S. 254, 273 (2003). ("We have repeatedly stated . . . that absent a clearly expressed congressional intention, repeals by implication are not favored" (citation and internal quotation marks omitted)). Moreover, the Court's conclusion is flatly contrary to its duty not to set aside Hamdan's commission "without the *clear* conviction that [it is] in conflict with the . . . laws of Congress constitutionally enacted." *Quirin*, *supra*, at 25 (emphasis added).

Nothing in the text of Article 36(b) supports the Court's sweeping conclusion that it represents an unprecedented congressional effort to change the nature of military commissions from common-law war courts to tribunals that must presumptively function like courts-martial. And such an interpretation would be strange indeed. The vision of uniformity that motivated the adoption of the UCMJ, embodied specifically in Article 36(b), is nothing more than uniformity across the separate branches of the armed services. See ch. 169, 64 Stat. 107 (preamble to the UCMJ explaining that the UCMJ is an act "[t]o unify, consolidate, revise, and codify the Articles of War, the Articles for the Government of the Navy, and the disciplinary laws of the Coast Guard"). There is no indication that the UCMJ was intended to require uniformity in procedure between courts-martial and military commissions, tribunals that the UCMJ itself recognizes are different. To the contrary, the UCMJ expressly recognizes that different tribunals will be constituted in different manners and employ different procedures. See 10 U.S.C. §866 (providing for three different types of courts-martial – general, special, and summary – constituted in different manners and employing different procedures). Thus, Article 36(b) is best understood as establishing that, so far as practicable, the rules and regulations governing tribunals convened by the Navy must be uniform with the rules and regulations governing tribunals convened by the Army. But, consistent with this Court's prior interpretations of Article 21 and over a century of historical practice, it cannot be understood to require the President to conform the procedures employed by military commissions to those employed by courts-martial.[17]

Even if Article 36(b) could be construed to require procedural uniformity among the various tribunals contemplated by the UCMJ, Hamdan would not be entitled to relief. Under the Court's reading, the President is entitled to prescribe different rules for military commissions than for courts-martial when he determines that it is not

---

[17] It bears noting that while the Court does not hesitate to cite legislative history that supports its view of certain statutory provisions, see *ante*, at 14–15, and n. 10, it makes no citation of the legislative history pertaining to Article 36(b), which contradicts its interpretation of that provision. Indeed, if it were authoritative, the *only* legislative history relating to Article 36(b) would confirm the obvious – Article 36(b)'s uniformity requirement pertains to uniformity between the three branches of the Armed Forces, and no more. When that subsection was introduced as an amendment to Article 36, its author explained that it would leave the three branches "enough leeway to provide a different provision where it is absolutely necessary" because "there are some differences in the services." Hearings on H.R. 2498 before the Subcommittee No. 1 of the House Committee on Armed Services, 81st Cong., 1st Sess., 1015 (1949). A further statement explained that "there might be some slight differences that would pertain as to the Navy in contrast to the Army, but at least [Article 36(b)] is an expression of the congressional intent that we want it to be as uniform as possible." *Ibid.*

"practicable" to prescribe uniform rules. The Court does not resolve the level of deference such determinations would be owed, however, because, in its view, "[t]he President has not ... [determined] that it is impracticable to apply the rules for courts-martial." *Ante*, at 60. This is simply not the case. On the same day that the President issued Military Commission Order No. 1, the Secretary of Defense explained that "the president decided to establish military commissions because he wanted the option of a process that is different from those processes which we already have, namely the federal court system ... and the military court system," Dept. of Defense News Briefing on Military Commissions (Mar. 21, 2002) (remarks of Donald Rumsfeld), available at http://www.dod.gov/transcrips/2002/t03212002_t0321sd.html (as visited June 26, 2006, and available in Clerk of Court's case file) (hereinafter News Briefing), and that "[t]he commissions are intended to be different ... because the [P]resident recognized that there had to be differences to deal with the unusual situation we face and that a different approach was needed." *Ibid.* The President reached this conclusion because

> "we're in the middle of a war, and ... had to design a procedure that would allow us to pursue justice for these individuals while at the same time prosecuting the war most effectively. And that means setting rules that would allow us to preserve our intelligence secrets, develop more information about terrorist activities that might be planned for the future so that we can take action to prevent terrorist attacks against the United States.... [T]here was a constant balancing of the requirements of our war policy and the importance of providing justice for individuals ... and *each* deviation from the standard kinds of rules that we have in our criminal courts was motivated by the desire to strike the balance between individual justice and the broader war policy." *Ibid.* (remarks of Douglas J. Feith, Under Secretary of Defense for Policy (emphasis added)).

The Court provides no explanation why the President's determination that employing court-martial procedures in the military commissions established pursuant to Military Commission Order No. 1 would hamper our war effort is in any way inadequate to satisfy its newly minted "practicability" requirement. On the contrary, this determination is precisely the kind for which the "Judiciary has neither aptitude, facilities nor responsibility and which has long been held to belong in the domain of political power not subject to judicial intrusion or inquiry.'" *Chicago & Southern Air Lines, Inc.* v. *Waterman S.S. Corp.*, 333 U.S. 103, 111 (1948). And, in the context of the present conflict, it is exactly the kind of determination Congress countenanced when it authorized the President to use all necessary and appropriate force against our enemies. Accordingly, the President's determination is sufficient to satisfy any practicability requirement imposed by Article 36(b).

The plurality further contends that Hamdan's commission is unlawful because it fails to provide him the right to be present at his trial, as recognized in 10 U.S.C.A. §839(c) (Supp. 2006). *Ante*, at 61. But §839(c) applies to courts-martial, not military commissions. It provides:

> "When the members of a court-martial deliberate or vote, only the members may be present. All other proceedings, including any other consultation of the members of the court with counsel or the military judge, shall be made a part of the record and shall be in the presence of the accused, the defense counsel, the trial counsel, and, in cases in which a military judge has been detailed to the court, the military judge."

In context, "all other proceedings" plainly refers exclusively to "other proceedings" pertaining to a court-martial.[18] This is confirmed by the provision's subsequent reference

---

[18] In addition to being foreclosed by the text of the provision, the Court's suggestion that 10 U.S.C.A. §839(c) (Supp. 2006) applies to military commissions is untenable because it would require, in military commission

to "members of the *court*" and to "cases in which a military judge has been detailed to the *court*." It is also confirmed by the other provisions of §839, which refer only to courts-martial. See §§839(a)(1)–(4) ("[A]ny time after the service of charges which have been referred for trial to a court-martial composed of a military judge and members, the military judge may . . . call the court into session without the presence of the members for the purpose of," hearing motions, issuing rulings, holding arraignments, receiving pleas, and performing various procedural functions). See also §839(b) ("Proceedings under subsection (a) shall be conducted in the presence of the accused"). Section 839(c) simply does not address the procedural requirements of military commissions.

B

The Court contends that Hamdan's military commission is also unlawful because it violates Common Article 3 of the Geneva Conventions, see *ante*, at 65–72. Furthermore, Hamdan contends that his commission is unlawful because it violates various provisions of the Third Geneva Convention. These contentions are untenable.

1

As an initial matter, and as the Court of Appeals concluded, both of Hamdan's Geneva Convention claims are foreclosed by *Johnson* v. *Eisentrager*, 339 U.S. 763 (1950). In that case the respondents claimed, *inter alia*, that their military commission lacked jurisdiction because it failed to provide them with certain procedural safeguards that they argued were required under the Geneva Conventions. *Id.*, at 789–790. While this Court rejected the underlying merits of the respondents' Geneva Convention claims, *id.*, at 790, it also held, in the alternative, that the respondents could "not assert . . . that anything in the Geneva Convention makes them immune from prosecution or punishment for war crimes," *id.*, at 789. The Court explained:

> "We are not holding that these prisoners have no right which the military authorities are bound to respect. The United States, by the Geneva Convention of July 27, 1929, 47 Stat. 2021, concluded with forty-six other countries, including the German Reich, an agreement upon the treatment to be accorded captives. These prisoners claim to be and are entitled to its protection. It is, however, the obvious scheme of the Agreement that responsibility for observance and enforcement of these rights is upon political and military authorities. Rights of alien enemies are vindicated under it only through protests and intervention of protecting powers as the rights of our citizens against foreign governments are vindicated only by Presidential intervention." *Id.*, at 789, n. 14.

This alternative holding is no less binding than if it were the exclusive basis for the Court's decision. See *Massachusetts* v. *United States*, 333 U.S. 611, 623 (1948). While the Court attempts to cast *Eisentrager*'s unqualified, alternative holding as footnote dictum, *ante*, at 63-34, it does not dispute the correctness of its conclusion, namely, that the provisions of the 1929 Geneva Convention were not judicially enforceable because that Convention contemplated that diplomatic measures by political and military authorities were the exclusive mechanisms for such enforcement. Nor does the Court suggest that the 1949 Geneva Conventions departed from this framework. See *ante*, at 64 ("We may assume that 'the obvious scheme' of the 1949 Conventions is identical in all relevant respects to that of the 1929 Convention").

---

proceedings, that the accused be present when the members of the commission voted on his guilt or innocence.

Instead, the Court concludes that petitioner may seek judicial enforcement of the provisions of the Geneva Conventions because "they are . . . part of the law of war. And compliance with the law of war is the condition upon which the authority set forth in Article 21 is granted." *Ante*, at 65 (citation omitted). But Article 21 authorizes the use of military commissions; it does not purport to render judicially enforceable aspects of the law of war that are not so enforceable of their own accord. See *Quirin*, 317 U.S., at 28 (by enacting Article 21, "Congress has explicitly provided, so far as it may constitutionally do so, that military tribunals shall have jurisdiction to try offenders or offenses against the law of war"). The Court cannot escape *Eisentrager's* holding merely by observing that Article 21 mentions the law of war; indeed, though *Eisentrager* did not specifically consider the Court's novel interpretation of Article 21, *Eisentrager* involved a challenge to the legality of a World War II military commission, which, like all such commissions, found its authorization in Article 15 of the Articles of War, the predecessor to Article 21 of the UCMJ. Thus, the Court's interpretation of Article 21 is foreclosed by *Eisentrager*.

In any event, the Court's argument is too clever by half. The judicial nonenforceability of the Geneva Conventions derives from the fact that those Conventions have exclusive enforcement mechanisms, see *Eisentrager, supra*, at 789, n. 14, and this, too, is part of the law of war. The Court's position thus rests on the assumption that Article 21's reference to the "laws of war" selectively incorporates only those aspects of the Geneva Conventions that the Court finds convenient, namely, the substantive requirements of Common Article 3, and not those aspects of the Conventions that the Court, for whatever reason, disfavors, namely the Conventions' exclusive diplomatic enforcement scheme. The Court provides no account of why the *partial* incorporation of the Geneva Conventions should extend only so far – and no further – because none is available beyond its evident preference to adjudicate those matters that the law of war, through the Geneva Conventions, consigns exclusively to the political branches.

Even if the Court were correct that Article 21 of the UCMJ renders judicially enforceable aspects of the law of war that are not so enforceable by their own terms, Article 21 simply cannot be interpreted to render judicially enforceable the particular provision of the law of war at issue here, namely Common Article 3 of the Geneva Conventions. As relevant, Article 21 provides that "[t]he provisions of this chapter conferring jurisdiction upon courts-martial do not deprive military commissions . . . of concurrent jurisdiction with respect to *offenders or offenses* that by statute *or by the law of war* may be tried by military commissions." 10 U.S.C. §821 (emphasis added). Thus, to the extent Article 21 can be interpreted as authorizing judicial enforcement of aspects of the law of war that are not otherwise judicially enforceable, that authorization only extends to provisions of the law of war that relate to whether a particular "offender" or a particular "offense" is triable by military commission. Common Article 3 of the Geneva Conventions, the sole provision of the Geneva Conventions relevant to the Court's holding, relates to neither. Rather, it relates exclusively to the particulars of the tribunal itself, namely, whether it is "regularly constituted" and whether it "afford[s] all the judicial guarantees which are recognized as indispensable by civilized peoples." Third Geneva Convention, Art. 3, ¶1(*d*), Relative to the Treatment of Prisoners of War, Aug. 12, 1949, [1955] 6 U.S.T. 3316, 3320, T. I. A. S No. 3364.

2

In addition to being foreclosed by *Eisentrager*, Hamdan's claim under Common Article 3 of the Geneva Conventions is meritless. Common Article 3 applies to "armed conflict not of an international character occurring in the territory of one of the High Contracting Parties." 6 U.S.T., at 3318. "Pursuant to [his] authority as Commander in

Chief and Chief Executive of the United States," the President has "accept[ed] the legal conclusion of the Department of Justice . . . that common Article 3 of Geneva does not apply to . . . al Qaeda . . . detainees, because, among other reasons, the relevant conflicts are international in scope and common Article 3 applies only to 'armed conflict not of an international character.'" App. 35. Under this Court's precedents, "the meaning attributed to treaty provisions by the Government agencies charged with their negotiation and enforcement is entitled to great weight." *Sumitomo Shoji America, Inc. v. Avagliano*, 457 U.S. 176, 184–185 (1982); *United States v. Stuart*, 489 U.S. 353, 369 (1989). Our duty to defer to the President's understanding of the provision at issue here is only heightened by the fact that he is acting pursuant to his constitutional authority as Commander in Chief and by the fact that the subject matter of Common Article 3 calls for a judgment about the nature and character of an armed conflict. See generally *United States v. Curtiss-Wright Export Corp.*, 299 U.S. 304, 320 (1936).

The President's interpretation of Common Article 3 is reasonable and should be sustained. The conflict with al Qaeda is international in character in the sense that it is occurring in various nations around the globe. Thus, it is also "occurring in the territory of" more than "one of the High Contracting Parties." The Court does not dispute the President's judgments respecting the nature of our conflict with al Qaeda, nor does it suggest that the President's interpretation of Common Article 3 is implausible or foreclosed by the text of the treaty. Indeed, the Court concedes that Common Article 3 is principally concerned with "furnish[ing] minimal protection to rebels involved in . . . a civil war," *ante*, at 68, precisely the type of conflict the President's interpretation envisions to be subject to Common Article 3. Instead, the Court, without acknowledging its duty to defer to the President, adopts its own, admittedly plausible, reading of Common Article 3. But where, as here, an ambiguous treaty provision ("not of an international character") is susceptible of two plausible, and reasonable, interpretations, our precedents require us to defer to the Executive's interpretation.

3

But even if Common Article 3 were judicially enforceable and applicable to the present conflict, petitioner would not be entitled to relief. As an initial matter, any claim petitioner has under Common Article 3 is not ripe. The only relevant "acts" that "are and shall remain prohibited" under Common Article 3 are "the *passing of sentences* and the *carrying out of executions* without previous judgment pronounced by a regularly constituted court affording all the judicial guarantees which are recognized as indispensable by civilized peoples." Art. 3, ¶1(*d*), 6 U.S.T., at 1318, 1320 (emphases added). As its terms make clear, Common Article 3 is only violated, as relevant here, by the act of "passing of sentenc[e]," and thus Hamdan will only have a claim *if* his military commission convicts him and imposes a sentence. Accordingly, as Hamdan's claim is "contingent [upon] future events that may not occur as anticipated, or indeed may not occur at all," it is not ripe for adjudication. *Texas v. United States*, 523 U.S. 296, 300 (1998) (internal quotation marks omitted).[19] Indeed, even if we assume he will be convicted and sentenced, whether his trial will be conducted in a manner so as to deprive him

---

[19] The Court does not dispute the conclusion that Common Article 3 cannot be violated unless and until Hamdan is convicted and sentenced. Instead, it contends that "the Geneva Conventions d[o] not direct an accused to wait until sentence is imposed to challenge the legality of the tribunal that is to try him." *Ante*, at 62, n. 55. But the Geneva Contentions do not direct defendants to enforce their rights through litigation, but through the Conventions' exclusive diplomatic enforcement provisions. Moreover, neither the Court's observation respecting the Geneva Conventions nor its reference to the equitable doctrine of abstention bears on the *constitutional* prohibition on adjudicating unripe claims.

of "the judicial guarantees which are recognized as indispensable by civilized peoples" is entirely speculative. And premature adjudication of Hamdan's claim is especially inappropriate here because "reaching the merits of the dispute would force us to decide whether an action taken by one of the other two branches of the Federal Government was unconstitutional." *Raines* v. *Byrd*, 521 U.S. 811, 819–820 (1997).

In any event, Hamdan's military commission complies with the requirements of Common Article 3. It is plainly "regularly constituted" because such commissions have been employed throughout our history to try unlawful combatants for crimes against the law of war. This Court has recounted that history as follows:

> "'By a practice dating from 1847 and renewed and firmly established during the Civil War, military commissions have become adopted as authorized tribunals in this country in time of war. . . . Their competency has been recognized not only in acts of Congress, but in executive proclamations, in rulings of the courts, and in the opinions of the Attorneys General.'" *Madsen*, 343 U.S., at 346, n. 8.

Hamdan's commission has been constituted in accordance with these historical precedents. As I have previously explained, the procedures to be employed by that commission, and the Executive's authority to alter those procedures, are consistent with the practice of previous American military commissions. See *supra*, at 30–34, and n. 15.

The Court concludes Hamdan's commission fails to satisfy the requirements of Common Article 3 not because it differs from the practice of previous military commissions but because it "deviate[s] from [the procedures] governing courts-martial." *Ante*, at 71. But there is neither a statutory nor historical requirement that military commissions conform to the structure and practice of courts-martial. A military commission is a different tribunal, serving a different function, and thus operates pursuant to different procedures. The 150-year pedigree of the military commission is itself sufficient to establish that such tribunals are "regularly constituted court [s]." Art. 3, ¶1(*d*), 6 U.S.T., at 3320.

Similarly, the procedures to be employed by Hamdan's commission afford "all the judicial guarantees which are recognized as indispensable by civilized peoples." Neither the Court nor petitioner disputes the Government's description of those procedures.

> "Petitioner is entitled to appointed military legal counsel, 32 C.F.R. 9.4(c)(2), and may retain a civilian attorney (which he has done), 32 C.F.R. 9.4(c)(2)(iii)(B). Petitioner is entitled to the presumption of innocence, 32 C.F.R. 9.5(b), proof beyond a reasonable doubt, 32 C.F.R. 9.5(c), and the right to remain silent, 32 C.F.R. 9.5(f). He may confront witnesses against him, 32 C.F.R. 9.5(i), and may subpoena his own witnesses, if reasonably available, 32 C.F.R. 9.5(h). Petitioner may personally be present at every stage of the trial unless he engages in disruptive conduct or the prosecution introduces classified or otherwise protected information for which no adequate substitute is available and whose admission will not deprive him of a full and fair trial, 32 C.F.R. 9.5(k); Military Commission Order No. 1 (Dep't of Defense Aug. 31, 2005) §6(B)(3) and (D)(5)(b). If petitioner is found guilty, the judgment will be reviewed by a review panel, the Secretary of Defense, and the President, if he does not designate the Secretary as the final decision-maker. 32 C.F.R. 9.6(h). The final judgment is subject to review in the Court of Appeals for the District of Columbia Circuit and ultimately in this Court. See DTA §1005(e)(3), 119 Stat. 2743; 28 U.S.C. 1254(1)." Brief for Respondents 4.

Notwithstanding these provisions, which in my judgment easily satisfy the nebulous standards of Common Article 3,[20] the plurality concludes that Hamdan's commission

---

[20] Notably, a prosecutor before the *Quirin* military commission has described these procedures as "a substantial improvement over those in effect during World War II," further observing that "[t]hey go a long way toward

is unlawful because of the possibility that Hamdan will be barred from proceedings and denied access to evidence that may be used to convict him. *Ante*, at 70–72. But, under the commissions' rules, the Government may not impose such bar or denial on Hamdan if it would render his trial unfair, a question that is clearly within the scope of the appellate review contemplated by regulation and statute.

Moreover, while the Executive is surely not required to offer a particularized defense of these procedures prior to their application, the procedures themselves make clear that Hamdan would only be excluded (other than for disruption) if it were necessary to protect classified (or classifiable) intelligence, Dept. of Defense, Military Commission Order No. 1, §6(B)(3) (Aug. 31, 2005), including the sources and methods for gathering such intelligence. The Government has explained that "we want to make sure that these proceedings, which are going on in the middle of the war, do not interfere with our war effort and . . . because of the way we would be able to handle interrogations and intelligence information, may actually assist us in promoting our war aims." News Briefing (remarks of Douglas J. Feith, Under Secretary of Defense for Policy). And this Court has concluded, in the very context of a threat to reveal our Nation's intelligence gathering sources and methods, that "[i]t is 'obvious and unarguable' that no governmental interest is more compelling than the security of the Nation," *Haig*, 453 U.S., at 307 (quoting *Aptheker* v. *Secretary of State*, 378 U.S. 500, 509 (1964)), and that "[m]easures to protect the secrecy of our Government's foreign intelligence operations plainly serve these interests," *Haig, supra*, at 307. See also *Snepp* v. *United States*, 444 U.S. 507, 509, n. 3 (1980) *(per curiam)* ("The Government has a compelling interest in protecting both the secrecy of information important to our national security and the appearance of confidentiality so essential to the effective operation of our foreign intelligence service"); *Curtiss-Wright*, 299 U.S., at 320. This interest is surely compelling here. According to the Government, "[b]ecause al Qaeda operates as a clandestine force relying on sleeper agents to mount surprise attacks, one of the most critical fronts in the current war involves gathering intelligence about future terrorist attacks and how the terrorist network operates – identifying where its operatives are, how it plans attacks, who directs operations, and how they communicate." Brief for United States in No. 03-4792, *United States* v. *Moussaoui* (CA4), p. 9. We should not rule out the possibility that this compelling interest can be protected, while at the same time affording Hamdan (and others like him) a fair trial.

In these circumstances, "civilized peoples" would take into account the context of military commission trials against unlawful combatants in the war on terrorism, including the need to keep certain information secret in the interest of preventing future attacks on our Nation and its foreign installations so long as it did not deprive the accused of a fair trial. Accordingly, the President's understanding of the requirements of Common Article 3 is entitled to "great weight." See *supra*, at 43.

4

In addition to Common Article 3, which applies to conflicts "not of an international character," Hamdan also claims that he is entitled to the protections of the Third Geneva Convention, which applies to conflicts between two or more High Contracting Parties. There is no merit to Hamdan's claim.

Article 2 of the Convention provides that "the present Convention shall apply to all cases of declared war or of any other armed conflict which may arise between two or

---

assuring that the trials will be full and fair." National Institute of Military Justice, Procedures for Trials by Military Commissions of Certain Non-United States Citizens in the War Against Terrorism, p. x (2002) (hereinafter Procedures for Trials) (foreword by Lloyd N. Cutler).

more of the High Contracting Parties." 6 U.S.T., at 1318. "Pursuant to [his] authority as Commander in Chief and Chief Executive of the United States," the President has determined that the Convention is inapplicable here, explaining that "none of the provisions of Geneva apply to our conflict with al Qaeda in Afghanistan or elsewhere throughout the world, because, among other reasons, al Qaeda is not a High Contracting Party." . . . . The President's findings about the nature of the present conflict with respect to members of al Qaeda operating in Afghanistan represents a core exercise of his commander-in-chief authority that this Court is bound to respect. See *Prize Cases*, 2 Black, at 670.

* * *

For these reasons, I would affirm the judgment of the Court of Appeals.

. . .

JUSTICE ALITO, with whom JUSTICE SCALIA and JUSTICE THOMAS join in Parts I–III, dissenting.

For the reasons set out in JUSTICE SCALIA's dissent, which I join, I would hold that we lack jurisdiction. On the merits, I join JUSTICE THOMAS' dissent with the exception of Parts I, II-C-1, and III-B-2, which concern matters that I find unnecessary to reach. I add the following comments to provide a further explanation of my reasons for disagreeing with the holding of the Court.

I

The holding of the Court, as I understand it, rests on the following reasoning. A military commission is lawful only if it is authorized by 10 U.S.C. §821; this provision permits the use of a commission to try "offenders or offenses" that "by statute or by the law of war may be tried by" such a commission; because no statute provides that an offender such as petitioner or an offense such as the one with which he is charged may be tried by a military commission, he may be tried by military commission only if the trial is authorized by "the law of war"; the Geneva Conventions are part of the law of war; and Common Article 3 of the Conventions prohibits petitioner's trial because the commission before which he would be tried is not "a regularly constituted court," Third Geneva Convention, Art. 3, ¶1(*d*), Relative to the Treatment of Prisoners of War, Aug. 12, 1949, [1955] 6 U.S.T. 3316, 3320, T. I. A. S. No. 3364. I disagree with this holding because petitioner's commission is "a regularly constituted court."

Common Article 3 provides as follows:

"In the case of armed conflict not of an international character occurring in the territory of one of the High Contracting Parties, each Party to the conflict shall be bound to apply, as a minimum, the following provisions:

"(1) . . . [T]he following acts are and shall remain prohibited . . . :

"(d) [T]he passing of sentences and the carrying out of executions without previous judgment pronounced by *a regularly constituted court* affording all the judicial guarantees which are recognized as indispensable by civilized peoples." *Id.*, at 3318–3320 (emphasis added).

Common Article 3 thus imposes three requirements. Sentences may be imposed only by (1) a "court" (2) that is "regularly constituted" and (3) that affords "all the judicial guarantees which are recognized as indispensable by civilized peoples." *Id.*, at 3320.

I see no need here to comment extensively on the meaning of the first and third requirements. The first requirement is largely self-explanatory, and, with respect to the third, I note only that on its face it imposes a uniform international standard that does not vary from signatory to signatory.

The second element ("regularly constituted") is the one on which the Court relies, and I interpret this element to require that the court be appointed or established in accordance with the appointing country's domestic law. I agree with the Court, see *ante*, at 69, n. 64, that, as used in Common Article 3, the term "regularly" is synonymous with "properly." The term "constitute" means "appoint," "set up," or "establish," Webster's Third New International Dictionary 486 (1961), and therefore "regularly constituted" means properly appointed, set up, or established. Our cases repeatedly use the phrases "regularly constituted" and "properly constituted" in this sense. See, *e.g.*, *Hamdi* v. *Rumsfeld*, 542 U.S. 507, 538 (2004) (plurality opinion of O'Connor, J.); *Nguyen* v. *United States*, 539 U.S. 69, 83 (2003); *Ryder* v. *United States*, 515 U.S. 177, 187 (1995); *Williams* v. *Bruffy*, 96 U.S. 176, 185 (1878).

In order to determine whether a court has been properly appointed, set up, or established, it is necessary to refer to a body of law that governs such matters. I interpret Common Article 3 as looking to the domestic law of the appointing country because I am not aware of any international law standard regarding the way in which such a court must be appointed, set up, or established, and because different countries with different government structures handle this matter differently. Accordingly, "a regularly constituted court" is a court that has been appointed, set up, or established in accordance with the domestic law of the appointing country.

II

In contrast to this interpretation, the opinions supporting the judgment today hold that the military commission before which petitioner would be tried is not "a regularly constituted court" (a) because "no evident practical need explains" why its "structure and composition . . . deviate from conventional court-martial standards," *ante*, at 11 (KENNEDY, J., concurring in part); see also *ante*, at 69–70 (Opinion of the Court); and (b) because, contrary to 10 U.S.C. §836(b), the procedures specified for use in the proceeding before the military commission impermissibly differ from those provided under the Uniform Code of Military Justice (UCMJ) for use by courts-martial, *ante*, at 52–62 (Opinion of the Court); *ante*, at 16–18 (KENNEDY, J., concurring in part). I do not believe that either of these grounds is sound.

A

I see no basis for the Court's holding that a military commission cannot be regarded as "a regularly constituted court" unless it is similar in structure and composition to a regular military court or unless there is an "evident practical need" for the divergence. There is no reason why a court that differs in structure or composition from an ordinary military court must be viewed as having been improperly constituted. Tribunals that vary significantly in structure, composition, and procedures may all be "regularly" or "properly" constituted. Consider, for example, a municipal court, a state trial court of general jurisdiction, an Article I federal trial court, a federal district court, and an international court, such as the International Criminal Tribunal for the Former Yugoslavia. Although these courts are "differently constituted" and differ substantially in many other respects, they are all "regularly constituted."

If Common Article 3 had been meant to require trial before a country's military courts or courts that are similar in structure and composition, the drafters almost certainly would have used language that expresses that thought more directly. Other provisions of the Convention Relative to the Treatment of Prisoners of War refer expressly to the ordinary military courts and expressly prescribe the "uniformity principle" that JUSTICE KENNEDY sees in Common Article 3, see *ante*, at 8–9. Article 84 provides that "[a] prisoner of war shall be tried only by a military court, unless the existing laws of the Detaining Power expressly permit the civil courts to try a member of the armed forces of the Detaining Power in respect of the particular offence alleged to have been committed by the prisoner of war." 6 U.S.T., at 3382. Article 87 states that "[p]risoners of war may not be sentenced by the military authorities and courts of the Detaining Power to any penalties except those provided for in respect of members of the armed forces of the said Power who have committed the same acts." *Id.*, at 3384. Similarly, Article 66 of the Geneva Convention Relative to the Treatment of Civilian Persons in Time of War – a provision to which the Court looks for guidance in interpreting Common Article 3, see *ante* at 69 – expressly provides that civilians charged with committing crimes in occupied territory may be handed over by the occupying power "to its properly constituted, non-political military courts, on condition that the said courts sit in the occupied country." 6 U.S.T. 3516, 3558–3560, T.I.A.S. No. 3365. If Common Article 3 had been meant to incorporate a "uniformity principle," it presumably would have used language like that employed in the provisions noted above. For these reasons, I cannot agree with the Court's conclusion that the military commission at issue here is not a "regularly constituted court" because its structure and composition differ from those of a court-martial.

Contrary to the suggestion of the Court, see *ante*, at 69, the commentary on Article 66 of Fourth Geneva Convention does not undermine this conclusion. As noted, Article 66 permits an occupying power to try civilians in its "properly constituted, non-political military courts," 6 U.S.T., at 3558. The commentary on this provision states:

> "The courts are to be 'regularly constituted'. This wording definitely excludes all special tribunals. It is the ordinary military courts of the Occupying Power which will be competent." 4 Int'l Comm. of Red Cross, Commentary: Geneva Convention Relative to the Protection of Civilian Persons in Time of War 340 (1958) (hereinafter GCIV Commentary).

The Court states that this commentary "defines "'regularly constituted'" tribunals to include 'ordinary military courts' and 'definitely exclud[e] all special tribunals.'" *Ante*, at 69 (alteration in original). This much is clear from the commentary itself. Yet the mere statement that a military court *is* a regularly constituted tribunal is of no help in addressing petitioner's claim that his commission *is not* such a tribunal. As for the commentary's mention of "special tribunals," it is doubtful whether we should take this gloss on Article 66 – which forbids an *occupying power* from trying *civilians* in courts set up specially for that purpose – to tell us much about the very different context addressed by Common Article 3.

But even if Common Article 3 recognizes this prohibition on "special tribunals," that prohibition does not cover petitioner's tribunal. If "special" means anything in contradistinction to "regular," it would be in the sense of "special" as "relating to a single thing," and "regular" as "uniform in course, practice, or occurrence." Webster's Third New International Dictionary 2186, 1913. Insofar as respondents propose to conduct the tribunals according to the procedures of Military Commission Order No. 1 and orders promulgated thereunder – and nobody has suggested respondents intend otherwise – then it seems that petitioner's tribunal, like the hundreds of others respondents propose to conduct, is very much regular and not at all special.

B

I also disagree with the Court's conclusion that petitioner's military commission is "illegal," *ante*, at 62, because its procedures allegedly do not comply with 10 U.S.C. §836. Even if §836(b), unlike Common Article 3, does impose at least a limited uniformity requirement amongst the tribunals contemplated by the UCMJ, but see *ante*, at 35 (THOMAS, J., dissenting), and even if it is assumed for the sake of argument that some of the procedures specified in Military Commission Order No. 1 impermissibly deviate from court-martial procedures, it does not follow that the military commissions created by that order are not "regularly constituted" or that trying petitioner before such a commission would be inconsistent with the law of war. If Congress enacted a statute requiring the federal district courts to follow a procedure that is unconstitutional, the statute would be invalid, but the district courts would not. Likewise, if some of the procedures that may be used in military commission proceedings are improper, the appropriate remedy is to proscribe the use of those particular procedures, not to outlaw the commissions. I see no justification for striking down the entire commission structure simply because it is possible that petitioner's trial might involve the use of some procedure that is improper.

III

Returning to the three elements of Common Article 3 – (1) a court, (2) that is appointed, set up, and established in compliance with domestic law, and (3) that respects universally recognized fundamental rights – I conclude that all of these elements are satisfied in this case.

A

First, the commissions qualify as courts.

Second, the commissions were appointed, set up, and established pursuant to an order of the President, just like the commission in *Ex parte Quirin*, 317 U.S. 1 (1942), and the Court acknowledges that *Quirin* recognized that the statutory predecessor of 10 U.S.C. §821 "preserved" the President's power "to convene military commissions," *ante*, at 29. Although JUSTICE KENNEDY concludes that "an acceptable degree of independence from the Executive is necessary to render a commission 'regularly constituted' by the standards of our Nation's system of justice," *ante* at 9–10, he offers no support for this proposition (which in any event seems to be more about fairness or integrity than regularity). The commission in *Quirin* was certainly no more independent from the Executive than the commissions at issue here, and 10 U.S.C. §§821 and 836 do not speak to this issue.[1]

Finally, the commission procedures, taken as a whole, and including the availability of review by a United States Court of Appeals and by this Court, do not provide a basis for deeming the commissions to be illegitimate. The Court questions the following two procedural rules: the rule allowing the Secretary of Defense to change the governing

---

[1] Section 821 looks to the "law of war," not separation of powers issues. And §836, as JUSTICE KENNEDY notes, concerns procedures, not structure, see *ante*, at 10.

rules "'from time to time'" (which does not rule out midtrial changes), see *ante*, at 70, n. 65 (Opinion of the Court); *ante*, at 9–10 (KENNEDY, J., concurring in part), and the rule that permits the admission of any evidence that would have "'probative value to a reasonable person'" (which departs from our legal system's usual rules of evidence), see *ante*, at 51, 60 (Opinion of the Court); *ante*, at 16–18 (KENNEDY, J., concurring in part).[2] Neither of these two rules undermines the legitimacy of the commissions.

Surely the entire commission structure cannot be stricken merely because it is possible that the governing rules might be changed during the course of one or more proceedings. *If* a change is made and applied during the course of an ongoing proceeding and *if* the accused is found guilty, the validity of that procedure can be considered in the review proceeding for that case. After all, not every midtrial change will be prejudicial. A midtrial change might amend the governing rules in a way that is inconsequential or actually favorable to the accused.

As for the standard for the admission of evidence at commission proceedings, the Court does not suggest that this rule violates the international standard incorporated into Common Article 3 ("the judicial guarantees which are recognized as indispensable by civilized peoples," 6 U.S.T., at 3320). Rules of evidence differ from country to country, and much of the world does not follow aspects of our evidence rules, such as the general prohibition against the admission of hearsay. See, *e.g.*, Blumenthal, Shedding Some Light on Calls for Hearsay Reform: Civil Law Hearsay Rules in Historical and Modern Perspective, 13 Pace Int'l L. Rev. 93, 96–101 (2001). If a particular accused claims to have been unfairly prejudiced by the admission of particular evidence, that claim can be reviewed in the review proceeding for that case. It makes no sense to strike down the entire commission structure based on speculation that some evidence might be improperly admitted in some future case.

In sum, I believe that Common Article 3 is satisfied here because the military commissions (1) qualify as courts, (2) that were appointed and established in accordance with domestic law, and (3) any procedural improprieties that might occur in particular cases can be reviewed in those cases.

B

The commentary on Common Article 3 supports this interpretation. The commentary on Common Article 3, ¶1(d), in its entirety states:

> "[A]lthough [sentences and executions without a proper trial] were common practice until quite recently, they are nevertheless shocking to the civilized mind.... Sentences and executions without previous trial are too open to error. 'Summary justice' may be effective on account of the fear it arouses..., but it adds too many further innocent victims to all the other innocent victims of the conflict. All civilized nations surround the administration of justice with safeguards aimed at eliminating the possibility of judicial errors. The Convention has rightly proclaimed that it is essential to do this even in time of war. *We must be very clear about one point: it is only 'summary' justice which it is intended to prohibit.* No sort of immunity is given to anyone under this provision. There is nothing in it to prevent a person presumed to be guilty from being arrested and

---

[2] The plurality, but not JUSTICE KENNEDY, suggests that the commission rules are improper insofar as they allow a defendant to be denied access to evidence under some circumstances. See, *ante*, at 70–72. But here too, if this procedure is used in a particular case and the accused is convicted, the validity of this procedure can be challenged in the review proceeding in that case. In that context, both the asserted need for the procedure and its impact on the accused can be analyzed in concrete terms.

so placed in a position where he can do no further harm; and it leaves intact the right of the State to prosecute, sentence and punish according to the law." GCIV Commentary 39 (emphasis added).

It seems clear that the commissions at issue here meet this standard. Whatever else may be said about the system that was created by Military Commission Order No. 1 and augmented by the Detainee Treatment Act, §1005(e)(1), 119 Stat. 2742, this system – which features formal trial procedures, multiple levels of administrative review, and the opportunity for review by a United States Court of Appeals and by this Court – does not dispense "summary justice."

* * *

For these reasons, I respectfully dissent.

IN THE UNITED STATES DISTRICT COURT
FOR THE DISTRICT OF COLUMBIA

Hicks (Rasul) v. Bush	)	Case No. 02-CV-0299 (CKK)
Al Odah v. United States	)	Case No. 02-CV-0828 (CKK)
Habib v. Bush	)	Case No. 02-CV-1130 (CKK)
Kurnaz v. Bush	)	Case No. 04-CV-1135 (ESH)
Khadr v. Bush	)	Case No. 04-CV-1136 (JDB)
Begg v. Bush	)	Case No. 04-CV-1137 (RMC)
El-Banna v. Bush	)	Case No. 04-CV-1144 (RWR)
Gherebi v. Bush	)	Case No. 04-CV-1164 (RBW)
Anam v. Bush	)	Case No. 04-CV-1194 (HHK)
Almurbati v. Bush	)	Case No. 04-CV-1227 (RBW)
Abdah v. Bush	)	Case No. 04-CV-1254 (HHK)
Hamdan v. Bush	)	Case No. 04-CV-1519 (JR)
Al-Qosi v. Bush	)	Case No. 04-CV-1937 (PLF)
Paracha v. Bush	)	Case No. 04-CV-2022 (PLF)
Al-Marri v. Bush	)	Case No. 04-CV-2035 (GK)
Zemiri v. Bush	)	Case No. 04-CV-2046 (CKK)
Deghayes v. Bush	)	Case No. 04-CV-2215 (RMC)
Mustapha v. Bush	)	Case No. 05-CV-0022 (JR)
Abdullah v. Bush	)	Case No. 05-CV-0023 (RWR)
Al-Mohammed v. Bush	)	Case No. 05-CV-0247 (HHK)

---

* This document was construed by the court as a motion to dismiss the petition based on the Military Commissions Act of 2006. – *Eds*.

† Redactions on the last page of this document have been added for privacy purposes. – *Eds*.

El-Mashad v. Bush	)	Case No. 05-CV-0270 (JR)
Al-Adahi v. Bush	)	Case No. 05-CV-0280 (GK)
Al-Joudi v. Bush	)	Case No. 05-CV-0301 (GK)
Doe 1-570 v. Bush	)	Case No. 05-CV-0313 (CKK)
Al-Wazan v. Bush	)	Case No. 05-CV-0329 (PLF)
Al-Anazi v. Bush	)	Case No. 05-CV-0345 (JDB)
Alhami v. Bush	)	Case No. 05-CV-0359 (GK)
Ameziane v. Bush	)	Case No. 05-CV-0392 (ESH)
Batarfi v. Bush	)	Case No. 05-CV-0409 (EGS)
Sliti v. Bush	)	Case No. 05-CV-0429 (RJL)
Kabir v. Bush	)	Case No. 05-CV-0431 (RJL)
Qayed v. Bush	)	Case No. 05-CV-0454 (RMU)
Al-Shihry v. Bush	)	Case No. 05-CV-0490 (PLF)
Aziz v. Bush	)	Case No. 05-CV-0492 (JR)
Al-Oshan v. Bush	)	Case No. 05-CV-0520 (RMU)
Tumani v. Bush	)	Case No. 05-CV-0526 (RMU)
Al-Oshan v. Bush	)	Case No. 05-CV-0533 (RJL)
Salahi v. Bush	)	Case No. 05-CV-0569 (JR)
Mammar v. Bush	)	Case No. 05-CV-0573 (RJL)
Al-Sharekh v. Bush	)	Case No. 05-CV-0583 (RJL)
Magram v. Bush	)	Case No. 05-CV-0584 (CKK)
Al Rashaidan v. Bush	)	Case No. 05-CV-0586 (RWR)
Mokit v. Bush	)	Case No. 05-CV-0621 (PLF)

Al Daini v. Bush	)	Case No. 05-CV-0634 (RWR)
Errachidi v. Bush	)	Case No. 05-CV-0640 (EGS)
Ahmed v. Bush	)	Case No. 05-CV-0665 (RWR)
Battayav v. Bush	)	Case No. 05-CV-0714 (RBW)
Adem v. Bush	)	Case No. 05-CV-0723 (RWR)
Aboassy v. Bush	)	Case No. 05-CV-0748 (RMC)
Hamlily v. Bush	)	Case No. 05-CV-0763 (JDB)
Imran v. Bush	)	Case No. 05-CV-0764 (CKK)
Al Habashi v. Bush	)	Case No. 05-CV-0765 (EGS)
Al Hamamy v. Bush	)	Case No. 05-CV-0766 (RJL)
Hamoodah v. Bush	)	Case No. 05-CV-0795 (RJL)
Khiali-Gul v. Bush	)	Case No. 05-CV-0877 (JR)
Rahmattullah v. Bush	)	Case No. 05-CV-0878 (CKK)
Mohammad v. Bush	)	Case No. 05-CV-0879 (RBW)
Rahman v. Bush	)	Case No. 05-CV-0882 (GK)
Bostan v. Bush	)	Case No. 05-CV-0883 (RBW)
Muhibullah v. Bush	)	Case No. 05-CV-0884 (RMC)
Mohammad v. Bush	)	Case No. 05-CV-0885 (GK)
Wahab v. Bush	)	Case No. 05-CV-0886 (EGS)
Chaman v. Bush	)	Case No. 05-CV-0887 (RWR)
Gul v. Bush	)	Case No. 05-CV-0888 (CKK)
Basardh v. Bush	)	Case No. 05-CV-0889 (ESH)
Nasrullah v. Bush	)	Case No. 05-CV-0891 (RBW)

Shaaban v. Bush	)	Case No. 05-CV-0892 (CKK)
Sohail v. Bush	)	Case No. 05-CV-0993 (RMU)
Tohirjanovich v. Bush	)	Case No. 05-CV-0994 (JDB)
Al Karim v. Bush	)	Case No. 05-CV-0998 (RMU)
Al-Khalaqi v. Bush	)	Case No. 05-CV-0999 (RBW)
Sarajuddin v. Bush	)	Case No. 05-CV-1000 (PLF)
Kahn v. Bush	)	Case No. 05-CV-1001 (ESH)
Mohammed v. Bush	)	Case No. 05-CV-1002 (EGS)
Mangut v. Bush	)	Case No. 05-CV-1008 (JDB)
Hamad v. Bush	)	Case No. 05-CV-1009 (JDB)
Khan v. Bush	)	Case No. 05-CV-1010 (RJL)
Zuhoor v. Bush	)	Case No. 05-CV-1011 (JR)
Al-Hela v. Bush	)	Case No. 05-CV-1048 (RMU)
Mousovi v. Bush	)	Case No. 05-CV-1124 (RMC)
Khalifh v. Bush	)	Case No. 05-CV-1189 (JR)
Zalita v. Bush	)	Case No. 05-CV-1220 (RMU)
Ahmed v. Bush	)	Case No. 05-CV-1234 (EGS)
Aminullah v. Bush	)	Case No. 05-CV-1237 (ESH)
Ghalib v. Bush	)	Case No. 05-CV-1238 (CKK)
Al Khaiy v. Bush	)	Case No. 05-CV-1239 (RJL)
Bukhari v. Bush	)	Case No. 05-CV-1241 (RMC)
Pirzai v. Bush	)	Case No. 05-CV-1242 (RCL)
Peerzai v. Bush	)	Case No. 05-CV-1243 (RCL)

Alsawam v. Bush	)	Case No. 05-CV-1244 (CKK)
Mohammadi v. Bush	)	Case No. 05-CV-1246 (RWR)
Al Ginco v. Bush	)	Case No. 05-CV-1310 (RJL)
Ullah v. Bush	)	Case No. 05-CV-1311 (RCL)
Al Bihani v. Bush	)	Case No. 05-CV-1312 (RJL)
Mohammed v. Bush	)	Case No. 05-CV-1347 (GK)
Saib v. Bush	)	Case No. 05-CV-1353 (RMC)
Hatim v. Bush	)	Case No. 05-CV-1429 (RMU)
Al-Subaiy v. Bush	)	Case No. 05-CV-1453 (RMU)
Dhiab v. Bush	)	Case No. 05-CV-1457 (GK)
Ahmed Doe v. Bush	)	Case No. 05-CV-1458 (ESH)
Sadkhan v. Bush	)	Case No. 05-CV-1487 (RMC)
Faizullah v. Bush	)	Case No. 05-CV-1489 (RMU)
Faraj v. Bush	)	Case No. 05-CV-1490 (PLF)
Khan v. Bush	)	Case No. 05-CV-1491 (JR)
Ahmad v. Bush	)	Case No. 05-CV-1492 (RCL)
Amon v. Bush	)	Case No. 05-CV-1493 (RBW)
Al Wirghi v. Bush	)	Case No. 05-CV-1497 (RCL)
Nabil v. Bush	)	Case No. 05-CV-1504 (RMC)
Al Hawary v. Bush	)	Case No. 05-CV-1505 (RMC)
Shafiiq v. Bush	)	Case No. 05-CV-1506 (RMC)
Kiyemba v. Bush	)	Case No. 05-CV-1509 (RMU)
Idris v. Bush	)	Case No. 05-CV-1555 (JR)

Attash v. Bush	)	Case No. 05-CV-1592 (RCL)
Al Razak v. Bush	)	Case No. 05-CV-1601 (GK)
Mamet v. Bush	)	Case No. 05-CV-1602 (ESH)
Rabbani v. Bush	)	Case No. 05-CV-1607 (RMU)
Zahir v. Bush	)	Case No. 05-CV-1623 (RWR)
Akhtiar v. Bush	)	Case No. 05-CV-1635 (PLF)
Ghanem v. Bush	)	Case No. 05-CV-1638 (CKK)
Albkri v. Bush	)	Case No. 05-CV-1639 (RBW)
Al-Badah v. Bush	)	Case No. 05-CV-1641 (CKK)
Almerfedi v. Bush	)	Case No. 05-CV-1645 (PLF)
Zaid v. Bush	)	Case No. 05-CV-1646 (JDB)
Al-Bahooth v. Bush	)	Case No. 05-CV-1666 (ESH)
Al-Siba'i v. Bush	)	Case No. 05-CV-1667 (RBW)
Al-Uwaidah v. Bush	)	Case No. 05-CV-1668 (GK)
Al-Jutaili v. Bush	)	Case No. 05-CV-1669 (TFH)
Ali Ahmed v. Bush	)	Case No. 05-CV-1678 (GK)
Khandan v. Bush	)	Case No. 05-CV-1697 (RBW)
Kabir (Sadar Doe) v. Bush	)	Case No. 05-CV-1704 (JR)
Al-Rubaish v. Bush	)	Case No. 05-CV-1714 (RWR)
Qasim v. Bush	)	Case No. 05-CV-1779 (JDB)
Sameur v. Bush	)	Case No. 05-CV-1806 (CKK)
Al-Harbi v. Bush	)	Case No. 05-CV-1857 (CKK)
Aziz v. Bush	)	Case No. 05-CV-1864 (HHK)

Hamoud v. Bush	)	Case No. 05-CV-1894 (RWR)
Al-Qahtani v. Bush	)	Case No. 05-CV-1971 (RMC)
Alkhemisi v. Bush	)	Case No. 05-CV-1983 (RMU)
Gamil v. Bush	)	Case No. 05-CV-2010 (JR)
Al-Shabany v. Bush	)	Case No. 05-CV-2029 (JDB)
Othman v. Bush	)	Case No. 05-CV-2088 (RWR)
Ali Al Jayfi v. Bush	)	Case No. 05-CV-2104 (RBW)
Jamolivich v. Bush	)	Case No. 05-CV-2112 (RBW)
Al-Mudafari v. Bush	)	Case No. 05-CV-2185 (JR)
Al-Mithali v. Bush	)	Case No. 05-CV-2186 (ESH)
Al-Asadi v. Bush	)	Case No. 05-CV-2197 (HHK)
Alhag v. Bush	)	Case No. 05-CV-2199 (HHK)
Nakheelan v. Bush	)	Case No. 05-CV-2201 (ESH)
Al Subaie v. Bush	)	Case No. 05-CV-2216 (RCL)
Ghazy v. Bush	)	Case No. 05-CV-2223 (RJL)
Al-Shimrani v. Bush	)	Case No. 05-CV-2249 (RMC)
Amin v. Bush	)	Case No. 05-CV-2336 (PLF)
Al Sharbi v. Bush	)	Case No. 05-CV-2348 (EGS)
Ben Bacha v. Bush	)	Case No. 05-CV-2349 (RMC)
Zadran v. Bush	)	Case No. 05-CV-2367 (RWR)
Alsaaei v. Bush	)	Case No. 05-CV-2369 (RWR)
Razakah v. Bush	)	Case No. 05-CV-2370 (EGS)
Al Darbi v. Bush	)	Case No. 05-CV-2371 (RCL)

Haleem v. Bush	)	Case No. 05-CV-2376 (RBW)
Al-Ghizzawi v. Bush	)	Case No. 05-CV-2378 (JDB)
Awad v. Bush	)	Case No. 05-CV-2379 (JR)
Al-Baidany v. Bush	)	Case No. 05-CV-2380 (CKK)
Al Rammi v. Bush	)	Case No. 05-CV-2381 (JDB)
Said v. Bush	)	Case No. 05-CV-2384 (RWR)
Al Halmandy v. Bush	)	Case No. 05-CV-2385 (RMU)
Mohammon v. Bush	)	Case No. 05-CV-2386 (RBW)
Al-Quhtani v. Bush	)	Case No. 05-CV-2387 (RMC)
Thabid v. Bush	)	Case No. 05-CV-2398 (ESH)
Rimi v. Bush	)	Case No. 05-CV-2427 (RJL)
Almjrd v. Bush	)	Case No. 05-CV-2444 (RMC)
Al Salami v. Bush	)	Case No. 05-CV-2452 (PLF)
Al Shareef v. Bush	)	Case No. 05-CV-2458 (RWR)
Khan v. Bush	)	Case No. 05-CV-2466 (RCL)
Hussein v. Bush	)	Case No. 05-CV-2467 (PLF)
Al-Delebany v. Bush	)	Case No. 05-CV-2477 (RMU)
Al-Harbi v. Bush	)	Case No. 05-CV-2479 (HHK)
Feghoul v. Bush	)	Case No. 06-CV-0618 (RWR)
Rumi v. Bush	)	Case No. 06-CV-0619 (RJL)
Ba Odah v. Bush	)	Case No. 06-CV-1668 (HHK)
Iqbal v. Bush	)	Case No. 06-CV-1674 (RMC)
Wasim v. Bush	)	Case No. 06-CV-1675 (RBW)

Naseer v. Bush	)	Case No. 06-CV-1676 (RJL)
Naseem v. Bush	)	Case No. 06-CV-1677 (RCL)
Khan v. Bush	)	Case No. 06-CV-1678 (RCL)
Matin v. Bush	)	Case No. 06-CV-1679 (RMU)
Rahmattullah v. Bush	)	Case No. 06-CV-1681 (JDB)
Ismatullah v. Bush	)	Case No. 06-CV-1682 (RJL)
Yaakoobi v. Bush	)	Case No. 06-CV-1683 (RWR)
Taher v. Bush	)	Case No. 06-CV-1684 (GK)
Akhouzada v. Bush	)	Case No. 06-CV-1685 (JDB)
Azeemullah v. Bush	)	Case No. 06-CV-1686 (CKK)
Toukh v. Bush	)	Case No. 06-CV-1687(ESH)
Naseer v. Bush	)	Case No. 06-CV-1689 (RMU)
Khan v. Bush	)	Case No. 06-CV-1690 (RBW)
Hamdullah v. Bush	)	Case No. 06-CV-1691 (GK)
Al-Shibh v. Bush	)	Case No. 06-CV-1725 (EGS)

NOTICE OF MILITARY COMMISSIONS ACT OF 2006

Respondents hereby give notice that on October 17, 2006, the President signed into law

the Military Commissions Act of 2006, Pub. L. No. 109-___ (copy attached) ("MCA"). The

MCA, among other things, amends 28 U.S.C. § 2241 to provide that "no court, justice, or judge

shall have jurisdiction" to consider either (1) *habeas* petitions "filed by or on behalf of an alien

detained by the United States who has been determined by the United States to have been

properly detained as an enemy combatant or is awaiting such determination," or (2) "any other

action against the United States or its agents relating to any aspect of the detention, transfer,

treatment, trial, or conditions of confinement of an alien who is or was detained by the United

States" as an enemy combatant, except as provided in section 1005(e)(2) and (e)(3) of the

Detainee Treatment Act of 2005, Pub. L. No. 109-148, tit. X, 119 Stat. 2680 (10 U.S.C. § 801

note).[1] *See* MCA § 7(a) (located on pages 36-37 of attachment). Further, the new amendment

to § 2241 takes effect on the date of enactment and applies specifically *"to all cases, without*

exception, pending on or after the date of the enactment of this Act which relate to any aspect of

the detention, transfer, treatment, trial, or conditions of detention of an alien detained by the

United States since September 11, 2001." *Id.* § 7(b) (emphasis added).[2]

Dated: October 18, 2006   Respectfully submitted,

                                                     PETER D. KEISLER
                                                     Assistant Attorney General

                                                     DOUGLAS N. LETTER
                                                     Terrorism Litigation Counsel

---

[1] Section 1005(e)(2) of the Detainee Treatment Act provides that the United States Court of Appeals for the District of Columbia Circuit "shall have exclusive jurisdiction to determine the validity of any final decision of a Combatant Status Review Tribunal that an alien is properly detained as an enemy combatant," and it further specifies the scope and intensiveness of that review. *See* Pub. L. No. 109-148, § 1005(e)(2). Similarly, § 1005(e)(3) of the Detainee Treatment Act, as amended by the MCA, provides that the Court of Appeals for the District of Columbia Circuit "shall have exclusive jurisdiction to determine the validity of any final decision rendered by a military commission." *Id.* § 1005(e)(3).

[2] Counsel for detainees in certain of the pending Guantanamo detainee appeals, *Boumediene v. Bush*, No. 05-5062 (D.C. Cir.), and *Al Odah v. United States*, No. 05-5064 (D.C. Cir.), have requested the Court of Appeals to permit supplemental briefing regarding the effect of the MCA.

/s/ Terry M. Henry

JOSEPH H. HUNT
VINCENT M. GARVEY
TERRY M. HENRY
JAMES J. SCHWARTZ
PREEYA M. NORONHA
ROBERT J. KATERBERG
ANDREW I. WARDEN
NICHOLAS J. PATTERSON
EDWARD H. WHITE
Attorneys
United States Department of Justice
Civil Division, Federal Programs Branch

Attorneys for Respondents

**UNITED STATES DISTRICT COURT
FOR THE DISTRICT OF COLUMBIA**

SALIM AHMED HAMDAN,	:	
	:	
Plaintiff,	:	
	:	
v.	:	Civil Action No. 04-1519 (JR)
	:	
DONALD H. RUMSFELD,	:	
	:	
Defendant.	:	

MEMORANDUM

The government seeks dismissal of the petition of Salim Ahmed Hamdan for a writ of habeas corpus for lack of subject matter jurisdiction, relying upon the jurisdiction-stripping provisions of the Military Commissions Act of 2006, Pub. L. No. 109-366, 120 Stat. 2600 (MCA).... Petitioner resists, arguing that the MCA did not remove our jurisdiction over pending Guantanamo habeas petitions, and alternatively that, if it did, it was an unconstitutional suspension of the writ of habeas corpus....

Background

Salim Ahmed Hamdan, a Yemeni national, was taken into United States military custody in Afghanistan in November 2001. He was transported to the Defense Department's detention facility at Guantanamo Bay in June 2002. In July 2003, the President declared him eligible for trial by military commission. On April 6, 2004, Hamdan petitioned for mandamus or habeas corpus in the United States District Court for the Western District of Washington. On July 13, 2004, after having been held for about two years and eight months without formal charges, Hamdan was finally charged at Guantanamo Bay with a single count of conspiracy. In August 2004, his habeas petition was transferred to this court.

On November 8, 2004, I granted Hamdan's petition for a writ of habeas corpus after finding that he could not be tried lawfully before a military commission that had not been approved by Congress, Hamdan v. Rumsfeld, 344 F. Supp. 2d 152 (D.D.C. 2004). That decision was reversed by a panel of the D.C. Circuit on July 15, 2005, 415 F.3d 33, in a decision that was itself reversed a year later by the Supreme Court, Hamdan v. Rumsfeld, 126 S. Ct. 2749 (2006), four justices noting that "[n]othing prevents the President from returning to Congress to seek the authority he believes necessary" to lawfully try enemy combatants, Id. at 2799, (Breyer, J., concurring).[1] On September 22, 2006, the Court of Appeals remanded the case to me "for further proceedings." The remand order contained no instructions, nor was it clear what proceedings, if any, would be possible – for by that time, the President had indeed "return[ed] to Congress," and he had asked Congress to strip the federal courts of their jurisdiction to hear any habeas petitions of the Guantanamo detainees.

---

[1] Four justices also concluded that conspiracy is not an offense that may be tried by a military commission. Id. at 2779.

On September 29, 2006 Congress enacted, and on October 17, 2006, the President signed, the Military Commissions Act. The day after the MCA became law, the government filed, in each of the 181 Guantanamo habeas cases pending in this Court, a Notice of Military Commissions Act of 2006..., highlighting the jurisdiction-stripping and retroactivity provisions of the Act. The government focused on section 7 of the Act, which amends the federal habeas statute by removing the jurisdiction of any "court, judge, or justice" over habeas petitions and all other actions filed by aliens who are either detained as enemy combatants or are "awaiting such determination." MCA §7(a). I construed that notice as a motion to dismiss for lack of subject matter jurisdiction and called for a response from Hamdan....[2]

Analysis

The Military Commissions Act and the briefs of the parties present three questions: (1) As a matter of statutory interpretation and construction, did Congress actually succeed in removing our statutory habeas jurisdiction over the detainee habeas cases? (2) If so, is the Military Commissions Act a constitutionally valid "suspension" of the writ of habeas corpus within the meaning of the Suspension Clause, U.S. Const. art. I §9 cl. 2? (3) If not, and if a "constitutional" writ of habeas corpus survives the Military Commissions Act, does Hamdan have a right to seek such a writ? The answers to these questions are "yes" to number (1) and "no" to numbers (2) and (3).

1. The MCA reflects clear congressional intent to limit the statutory habeas jurisdiction of the federal courts.

It has been clear since Ex Parte Yerger, 75 U.S. 85 (1869) (habeas petition by a prisoner facing trial by military commission), that statutory language will be interpreted as stripping courts of their habeas jurisdiction only when the intent of Congress is abundantly clear. "Implications from statutory text or legislative history are not sufficient to repeal habeas jurisdiction; instead, Congress must articulate specific and unambiguous statutory directives to effect a repeal." INS v. St. Cyr, 533 U.S. 289, 299 (2001). In the instant case, it appears to be conceded that Congress's intent to remove jurisdiction over future habeas petitions filed by aspecified class of individuals was clear enough. Hamdan's submission, however, is that the MCA lacks the requisite clarity to support its retroactive operation – stripping the courts of their jurisdiction over previously filed habeas cases.

. . .

Relying on what he calls "[o]rdinary principles of statutory construction,"... and quoting Hamdan, 126 S. Ct. at 2765–69, Hamdan argues that the retroactivity provision of §7(b) does not clearly apply to the habeas jurisdiction-stripping provision of §7(a), because, while the language of §7(b) tracks much of the language in §7(a) describing cases other than habeas petitions, it does not explicitly refer to habeas petitions. The argument is unsuccessful.

---

[2] I did not issue similar orders in the 14 other Guantanamo habeas cases on my own docket, in deference to the continuing pendency before the Court of Appeals of two cases in which that court has asked for supplemental briefing on the effect of the Military Commissions Act, Boumediene, et al. v. Bush, 450 F. Supp. 2d 25 (D.D.C. 2006) (appeal pending); Al Odah, et al. v. United States, 346 F. Supp. 2d 1 (D.D.C. 2004) (appeal pending). Hamdan's successful certiorari petition in the Supreme Court, however, sets his case apart from the others. Unlike the petitioners in those other cases, moreover, Hamdan moved for a briefing schedule on the subject of jurisdiction...even before the government filed its notice.

Section 7(b) instructs that "the amendment made by subsection (a)" is effective immediately, and that it applies both retroactively and prospectively. New subsections (e)(1) and (e)(2) both amend the habeas statute and therefore together comprise "the amendment made by subsection (a)." Section 7(b), then, means that all of §7(a), and not just the part encompassed in new subsection (e)(2), applies retroactively.

Application of the retroactivity clause in §7(b) to new subsection (e)(1) is also compelled by the framework of the statute. The references in section 7 are to one large category of cases: those cases that relate to any aspect of the detention, transfer, treatment, trial, or conditions of detention of certain aliens. In §7(a), Congress divided this broad category into two subcategories – (1) habeas petitions and (2) "any other action[s] against the United States . . . relating to any aspect of the detention . . ." – and removed jurisdiction over both types of cases. "Other," as used in this subsection, logically describes cases other than the habeas petitions referenced in the previous subsection and confirms the inclusion of habeas proceedings within the broader category encompassing "all cases . . . pending on or after the date of enactment of this Act which relate to any aspect of the detention, transfer, treatment, trial, or conditions of detention of an alien detained by the United States since September 11, 2001." Section 7(b) applies "without exception" to the broad category of cases encompassing both subcategories addressed in new subsections (e)(1) and (e)(2); this language is "so clear that it could sustain only one interpretation." Lindh v. Murphy, 521 U.S. 320, 329 n.4 (1997). Habeas petitions are thus clearly within the ambit of §7(b).

2. The MCA is not a constitutionally valid suspension of the writ of habeas corpus.

Congress unquestionably has the power to establish and to define the jurisdiction of the lower federal courts. U.S. Const. art. III, §§1, 2. But it does not necessarily follow, from the fact that Congress has repealed its statutory grant of habeas jurisdiction, that Congress has also "suspended" the writ. Some historical background will be helpful in explaining why this is so.

The history of habeas corpus – the "symbol and guardian of individual liberty," Peyton v. Rowe, 391 U.S. 54, 59 (1968) – is well established. What we now know as the "Great Writ" originated as the "prerogative writ of the Crown";[3] its purpose at first was to bring people into court rather than out of imprisonment. Alan Clarke, Habeas Corpus: The Historical Debate, 14 N.Y.L. Sch. J. Hum. Rts. 375, 378 (1998), citing S.A. DeSmith, The Prerogative Writs, 11 Cambridge L.J. 40 (1951); William F. Duker, A Constitutional History of Habeas Corpus 17 (1980). By the year 1230, the writ's utility for that purpose was a well-known aspect of English common law. Clarke, supra.

The transformation of the writ to a guardian of liberty dates to the 14th century, when the Norman Conquest overlaid a centralized court system on top of the existing courts. It was during this period that prisoners began to initiate habeas proceedings to challenge the legality of their detention. Id. The first such use was by detained members of the privileged classes who raised habeas claims in superior central courts to challenge their convictions in inferior courts; central courts would grant such writs to assert the primacy of their jurisdiction. Id. Thus, oddly enough, the original use of the writ by prisoners challenging convictions or detentions had more to do with jurisdictional

---

[3] Standing alone, the phrase "habeas corpus" refers to the common law writ of habeas corpus ad subjiciendum, or the "Great Writ." Preiser v. Rodriguez, 411 U.S. 475, 484–85 and n.2 (1973) citing Ex parte Bollman, 8 U.S. (4 Cranch) 75, 95 (1807).

disputes between courts than concerns over liberty. Id.; Gerald L. Neuman, Habeas Corpus, Executive Detention, and the Removal of Aliens, 98 Colum. L. Rev. 961, 970–71 (1998).

As the power of the common law courts expanded in the 15th century, so too did the availability and meaning of habeas corpus. The writ became a favorite tool of both Parliament and the judiciary in battling the monarch's assertion of unbridled power. Clarke, supra at 380. By 1670, habeas corpus was "the most usual remedy by which a man is restored again to his liberty, if he have been against law deprived of it." Bushell's Case, Vaughan 135, 136, 124 Eng. Rep. 1006, 1007. The growing significance of the writ is reflected in the Habeas Corpus Act of 1679, described by Blackstone as "a second *magna charta*, a stable bulwark of our liberties." 1 Blackstone 133.

Notwithstanding the cherished status of habeas corpus, its suspension in England was not uncommon. The writ was suspended in 1688 and 1696 because of conspiracies against the king, again during the American revolution, and at other points during the 18th century. Rex A. Collings, Jr., Habeas Corpus for Convicts – Constitutional Right or Legislative Grace?, 40 Cal. L. Rev. 335, 339 (1952).

Colonists in America were well aware of the growing significance of the Great Writ, and many asserted a common law right to habeas corpus in the period leading up to the adoption of the Constitution. Massachusetts, New Hampshire, and Georgia adopted constitutional provisions guaranteeing the writ or prohibiting its suspension under most circumstances. Max Rosenn, The Great Writ – A Reflection of Societal Change, 44 Ohio St. L.J. 337, 338 n.14 (1983). Several delegates to the Constitutional Convention sought to include a guarantee of habeas corpus in the federal Constitution, Erwin Chemerinsky, Thinking about Habeas Corpus, 37 Case W. Res. L. Rev. 748, 752, and the language that emerged from the Constitutional Convention, forbidding the suspension of habeas unless necessary in the face of "rebellion or invasion," U.S. Const. art. I, §9, cl. 2, was a compromise. Habeas corpus nevertheless enjoys powerful and unique constitutional stature as the only common law writ explicitly referenced in the Constitution. The first session of Congress also evinced appreciation for the writ: in section 14 of the Judiciary Act of 1789, Congress affirmatively gave the power to issue writs of habeas corpus to the newly created federal courts. Act of Sept. 24, 1789, ch. 20, §14, 1 Stat 73, 81. It is that statute, amended several times over the last 217 years, that the MCA has amended once again: this time to take away jurisdiction.[4]

Article I, section 9, clause 2 of the Constitution provides, "The Privilege of the Writ of *Habeas Corpus* shall not be suspended, unless when in Cases of Rebellion or Invasion the public Safety may require it." "Although [the Suspension Clause] does not state that suspension must be effected by, or authorized by, a legislative act, it has been so understood, consistent with English practice and the Clause's placement in Article I." Hamdi v. Rumsfeld, 542 U.S. 507, 562 (2004) (Scalia, J., dissenting), citing Ex parte Bollman, 8 U.S. at 101; Ex parte Merryman, 17 F. Cas. 144, 151–152 (CD Md. 1861) (Taney, C. J., rejecting Lincoln's unauthorized suspension); 3 Story §1336, at 208–209.[5]

Congress has authorized executive suspension of the writ only four times. See Duker, supra at 149, 178 n.190. All such suspensions were accompanied by clear statements

---

[4] The MCA may not have been Congress's last word on the statutory habeas rights of detainees such as Hamdan. On December 5, 2006, Senators Specter and Leahy introduced the Habeas Corpus Restoration Act of 2006, S. 4081, 109th Cong. (2006), which would grant statutory habeas rights to those whose rights were repealed by the MCA.

[5] In his dissent in Hamdi, Justice Scalia also makes reference to President Jefferson's unsuccessful attempt to suspend the writ in response to the Aaron Burr conspiracy. Hamdi, 542 U.S. at 563 (Scalia, J. dissenting), citing 16 Annals of Congress 402–425 (1807).

expressing congressional intent to suspend the writ and limiting the suspension to periods during which the predicate conditions (rebellion or invasion) existed. Id. The first such instance was during the Civil War, when the status and availability of habeas corpus were at the center of an epic struggle. In 1861, without congressional authorization, President Lincoln gave the Commanding General of the Army permission to suspend the writ in response to rioting between Philadelphia and Washington as Union troops moved down the coast. A. Lincoln, Letter to Commanding General Winfield Scott, (April 27, 1861), reprinted in Abraham Lincoln: Speeches and Writings, 1859–1865, at 237 (D. Fehrenbacher ed. 1989). John Merryman was subsequently arrested for interfering with troop movements and challenged the executive suspension of the writ. Chief Justice Taney, riding circuit, heard the case and ruled in Merryman's favor, holding that only Congress may suspend the writ. Ex parte Merryman, 17 F. Cas. at 151–152. Lincoln ignored Taney's order, but Congress eventually authorized executive suspension, mooting the question of whether or not Lincoln's initial suspension was unconstitutional and avoiding a Supreme Court test. Act of Mar. 3, 1863, 12 Stat. 755. Thereafter, Lincoln's suspensions explicitly relied upon the congressional grant of authority. See, e.g., Proclamation No. 7, 13 Stat. 734 (1863).

After the Civil War, Congress next authorized executive suspension of the writ in its Ku Klux Klan Act, which allowed President Grant to suspend the writ while rebellions were raging in several South Carolina counties. Duker, supra at 178 n.190. Congress's last two authorizations for executive suspension of the writ were in 1902, when it granted suspension power to the President and the governor during a rebellion in the Phillipines,[6] and in 1941, after the attack on Pearl Harbor, when Congress authorized the governor of Hawaii to temporarily suspend the writ in that territory.[7] All four congressionally authorized executive suspensions occurred during times of indisputable, and congressionally declared, rebellion or invasion.

The Supreme Court has never decided whether an Act of Congress alone has effectively "suspended" the writ. In two relatively recent cases involving the Antiterrorism and Effective Death Penalty Act of 1996 (AEDPA) and the Illegal Immigration Reform and Immigrant Responsibility Act of 1996 (IIRIRA), indeed, the Court has carefully avoided saying exactly what the Suspension Clause protects. In Felker v. Turpin, 518 U.S. 651 (1996), the Court, per Rehnquist, C.J., "assume[d], for purposes of decision here, that the Suspension Clause of the Constitution refers to the writ as it exists today, rather than as it existed in 1789," but held that the restrictions placed by the AEDPA upon second and successive statutory habeas petitions by prisoners were "well within the compass of [the writ's] evolutionary process, and . . . do not amount to a 'suspension' of the writ contrary to Article I, §9." 518 U.S. at 663–64. In INS v. St. Cyr, 533 U.S. 299 (2001), the Court rejected the government's argument that the AEDPA and the IIRIRA had effectively stripped the federal courts of jurisdiction to decide questions of law. Acknowledging that the scope of the writ has expanded significantly since the Founding, the Court noted that, "at the absolute minimum, the Suspension Clause protects the writ 'as it existed in 1789,'" id. at 1788 (quoting Felker). And the Court went on to observe:

> The fact that this Court would be required to answer the difficult question of what the Suspension Clause protects is in and of itself a reason to avoid answering the constitutional questions that would be raised by concluding that review was barred entirely. Cf. Neuman, Habeas Corpus, Executive Detention, and the Removal of Aliens, 98

---

[6] Act of July 1, 1902, ch. 1369, 32 Stat. 691.
[7] See Duncan v. Kahanamoku, 327 U.S. 304, 307–308 (1946).

Colum. L.Rev. 961, 980 (1998) (noting that "reconstructing habeas corpus law...[for purposes of a Suspension Clause analysis] would be a difficult enterprise, given fragmentary documentation, state-by-state disuniformity, and uncertainty about how state practices should be transferred to new national institutions").[8]

Id. at n.13. Whether the Suspension Clause protects only the "writ antecedent to statute," Williams v. Kaiser, 323 U.S. 471, 484 (1945), or "the writ as it exists today," Felker, 518 U.S. at 663, its protection is absolute in the absence of "invasion" or "rebellion." Neither rebellion nor invasion was occurring at the time the MCA was enacted. Indeed, Congress itself must not have thought that it was "suspending" the writ with the enactment of the MCA, since it made no findings of the predicate conditions, as it did when it approved Lincoln's suspension in the Civil War and each of the subsequent suspensions in Mississippi, the Phillipines, and Hawaii. Thus, the Great Writ has survived the Military Commissions Act. If and to the extent that the MCA operates to make the writ unavailable to a person who is constitutionally entitled to it, it must be unconstitutional.

3. Hamdan is not entitled to the constitutional writ that survives the MCA. The jurisdiction of federal courts over the habeas petitions of detainees at Guantanamo Bay rested upon the grant of jurisdiction in the habeas statute and upon the United States' exercise of "complete jurisdiction and control" over the Navy base in Cuba. Rasul, 542 U.S. 466, 471, 481 (2004). Because the habeas statute drew no distinction between citizens and aliens, moreover, the Court found "little reason to think that Congress intended the geographical coverage of the statute to vary depending on the detainee's citizenship. Aliens held at the base, no less than American citizens, are entitled to invoke the federal courts' authority under §2241." Id. at 481. My original assumption of jurisdiction of Hamdan's habeas petition depended entirely upon Rasul and upon §2241, 344 F. Supp. 2d at 156. Now that the MCA has amended §2241 so that it no longer serves as the basis for my jurisdiction, I must inquire whetherHamdan or any other alien is constitutionally entitled to the writ.

It has long been the practice of judges to ascertain the "meaning of the term habeas corpus [by reference to] the common law." Ex parte Bollman, 8 U.S. at 93–94 (1807). Petitioner cites at least two English common law cases in which "aliens detained by the Executive at wartime" brought habeas petitions challenging their designation as enemies. [78 at 20], citing Case of the Three Spanish Sailors, 96 Eng. Rep. 775, 776 (C.P. 1779); Rex v. Schiever, 97 Eng. Rep. 551 (K. B. 1759). In dicta, the majority in Rasul cited several other examples of pre-1789 habeas petitions brought by aliens detained within the sovereign territory or elsewhere within the sovereign's control. Rasul, 542 U.S. at 481 n.11.[9] Unfortunately, those cases do not so easily resolve the issue when the statutory

---

[8] In both Felker and St. Cyr, the Court was quick to point out that neither the AEDPA nor the IIRIRA purported to repeal its own original jurisdiction of habeas cases, which was expressly granted by the Judiciary Act of 1789, Felker, 518 U.S. at 660–61, quoted in St. Cyr, 533 U.S. at 298–99. The jurisdiction-stripping language of the MCA, of course, does purport to repeal the habeas jurisdiction of Supreme Court justices ("No court, justice or judge...." MCA §7(a)).

[9] The court supplied the following list of English and American habeas proceedings prior to 1789 and shortly thereafter: King v Schiever, 2 Burr. 765, 97 Eng. Rep. 551 (K. B. 1759); Sommersett v Stewart, 20 How. St. Tr. 1, 79–82 (K. B. 1772); Case of the Hottentot Venus, 13 East 195, 104 Eng. Rep. 344 (K. B. 1810)); United States v. Villato, 2 Dall. 370, 2 U.S. 370, 1 L. Ed. 419 (CC Pa. 1797); Ex parte D'Olivera, 7 F. Cas. 853, F. Cas. No. 3967 (CC Mass 1813) (Story, J., on circuit); Wilson v. Izard, 30 F. Cas. 131, F. Cas. No. 17810 (CC NY 1815) (Livingston, J., on circuit).

grant of habeas has been withdrawn. In each of them, habeas relief was either (1) denied, in an opinion that failed to distinguish between jurisdictional and substantive grounds for the dismissal;[10] (2) denied to a prisoner of war without connections to the country in which the writ was sought;[11] or (3) granted to an alien with a significant relationship to the country in which the writ was sought.[12] Not one of the cases mentioned in Rasul held that an alien captured abroad and detained outside the United States – or in "territory over which the United States exercises exclusive jurisdiction and control," Rasul, 542 U.S. at 475 – had a common law or constitutionally protected right to the writ of habeas corpus.[13]

The petitioner in Sommersett v. Stewart was not an enemy alien but a slave challenging his enslavement. Unlike Hamdan, James Sommersett was temporarily residing in England, and the asserted unlawfulness of his confinement stemmed from the arguable illegality of slavery in England. 98 Eng. Rep. 499 (K. B. 1772). In the Case of the Hottentot Venus, Saartje Baartman – a South African exhibited in a cage in Piccadilly, England – was a non-enemy foreigner from the British Protectorate of South Africa who could invoke the protection of the Crown by right. 104 Eng. Rep. 344 (K. B. 1810) .

In American habeas actions, alien petitioners have had access to the writ largely because they resided, lawfully or unlawfully, on American soil. See, e.g., The Japanese Immigrant Case, 189 U.S. 86, 101 (1903) (alien, while alleged to have entered the country unlawfully, nevertheless had made himself "a part of its population"); Yick Wo v. Hopkins, 118 U.S. 356 (1886) (petitioner had been a legal resident of the United States for over twenty years). Hamdan has been a prisoner of the United States for five years. He has lived nearly all of that time within the plenary and exclusive jurisdiction of the United States, but he has not become a part of the population enough to separate himself from the common law tradition generally barring non-resident enemy aliens from accessing courts in wartime. See Ex parte Kawato, 317 U.S. 69, 72–75 (1942) (describing common law rule). His detention in Guantanamo, in other words, has not meaningfully "increase[d] his identity with our society." Eisentrager v. Johnson, 339 U.S. 763, 770 (1950).

It is the Eisentrager case that appears to provide the controlling authority on the availability of constitutional habeas to enemy aliens.[14] In that case, petitioners were Germans living in China in the aftermath of World War II. Id. at 765. After trial before a United States Military Commission in China, they were convicted of war crimes and sent to occupied Germany to serve their sentences. Id. at 766. The Supreme Court

---

[10] See, e.g., Case of the Three Spanish Sailors, 96 Eng. Rep. 775, 776 (C.P. 1779); Rex v. Shiever, 97 Eng. Rep. 551 (K. B. 1759). Note, too, that petitioners in both of these cases were held within English sovereign territory, unlike petitioner Hamdan.

[11] Rex v. Schiever falls under this category as well: "[petitioner] is the King's prisoner of war, and we have nothing to do in that case, nor can we grant an habeas corpus to remove prisoners of war." 96 Eng. Rep. 1249 (K. B. 1759).

[12] See, e.g., U.S. v. Villato, 2 U.S. 370, 28 F. Cas. 377, 1 L. Ed. 419 (No. 16,622) (Pa. 1797) (petitioner, though Spanish-born, had traveled from New Orleans to Philadelphia and attempted to become a citizen before the offense that precipitated his detention).

[13] Note that even INS v. St Cyr, heavily relied upon by petitioner Hamdan and filled with language extolling the importance of habeas corpus in challenging executive detention, contains this limited description of the rights herein asserted: "[i]n England prior to 1789, in the Colonies, and in this Nation during the formative years of our Government, the writ of habeas corpus was available to nonenemy aliens as well as to citizens," 533 U.S. at 301.

[14] Eisentrager was unimportant to the statutory habeas question presented the last time Hamdan was here, as the Supreme Court had made plain in Rasul, 542 U.S. at 475–76, and was not dispositive on the questions presented in the earlier Hamdan case, 126 S.Ct. at 2794.

held that they had no constitutional entitlement to habeas relief in U.S. Courts because "at no relevant time were [they] within any territory over which the United States is sovereign, and the scenes of their offense, their capture, their trial, and their punishment were all beyond the territorial jurisdiction of any court of the United States." Id. at 778.

Hamdan contends that several of the differences between the Guantanamo petitioners and the Eisentrager petitioners are constitutionally significant. First, he notes that the Eisentrager petitioners admitted that they were enemy aliens, whereas petitioner Hamdan has always objected to his classification as an unlawful enemy combatant.... Here, however, as in Eisentrager (where petitioners amended their petitions to assert that they had really been civilian employees) Hamdan's "exact affiliation is ... for our purposes, immaterial." Eisentrager, 339 U.S. at 765. Second, Hamdan claims that, unlike the Eisentrager petitioners, he has never been afforded access to a proper tribunal. That observation is obviously true, thus far, but Hamdan is to face a military commission newly designed, because of his efforts, by a Congress that finally stepped up to its responsibility, acting according to guidelines laid down by the Supreme Court. It is difficult to see how continued habeas jurisdiction could make further improvements in his tribunal. Third, Hamdan argues that, after several years in a territory within "the complete jurisdiction and control" of the United States, his relationship with the United States is more extensive than those of petitioners in Eisentrager. See Rasul, 542 U.S. at 480. This third distinction merits further consideration.

Hamdan's lengthy detention beyond American borders but within the jurisdictional authority of the United States is historically unique. Nevertheless, as the government argues in its reply brief, his connection to the United States lacks the geographical and volitional predicates necessary to claim a constitutional right to habeas corpus.... Petitioner has never entered the United States and accordingly does not enjoy the "implied protection" that accompanies presence on American soil. Eisentrager, 339 U.S. at 777–79. Guantanamo Bay, although under the control of the United States military, remains under "the ultimate sovereignty of the Republic of Cuba." Rasul, U.S. 542 at 471. Presence within the exclusive jurisdiction and control of the United States was enough for the Court to conclude in Rasul that the broad scope of the habeas statute covered Guantanamo Bay detainees, but the detention facility lies outside the sovereign realm, and only U.S. citizens in such locations may claim entitlement to a constitutionally guaranteed writ. United States v. Curtiss-Wright Export Corp., 299 U.S. 304, 318 (1936). There is no dispute, moreover, that Hamdan's presence within the exclusive jurisdiction of the United States has been involuntary. Presence within the United States that is "lawful but involuntary [ ] is not of the sort to indicate any substantial connection with our country" that would justify the invocation of a constitutional right to habeas corpus, United States v. Verdugo-Urquidez, 494 U.S. 259, 271 (1990).[15]

Conclusion

Congress's removal of jurisdiction from the federal courts was not a suspension of habeas corpus within the meaning of the Suspension Clause (or, to the extent that it was, it was plainly unconstitutional, in the absence of rebellion or invasion), but Hamdan's

---

[15] My ruling does not address whether and to what extent enemy aliens may invoke other constitutional rights; I find only that the Suspension Clause does not guarantee the right to petition for habeas corpus to non-resident enemy aliens captured and detained outside the United States.

statutory access to the writ is blocked by the jurisdiction-stripping language of the Military Commissions Act, and he has no constitutional entitlement to habeas corpus.[16] Hamdan's habeas petition must accordingly be dismissed for want of subject matter jurisdiction.

JAMES ROBERTSON
United States District Judge

---

[16] Having been divested of jurisdiction over Hamdan's habeas petition, I do not reach his other arguments that the MCA is unconstitutional – because it does not provide an adequate substitute for habeas review, because it violates the principle of separation of powers by instructing the courts to ignore the Supreme Court's ruling that the Geneva Conventions afford judicially enforceable protections to petitioner Hamdan, because it is an unlawful Bill of Attainder, and because it violates Equal Protection.

UNITED STATES OF AMERICA	)	Decision and Order --
	)	Motion to Dismiss for
v.	)	Lack of Jurisdiction
	)	
SALIM AHMED HAMDAN	)	

The Defense has moved this Military Commission to dismiss all charges and specifications against the accused on the basis that the Commission lacks Jurisdiction over him. The Government opposes the motion. Both parties have filed written briefs and attached various documents to their briefs without objection. These documents attached to the motions have been admitted without objection by either side. The Commission heard oral argument in open court on 4 June 2007.

The Court finds that the following facts are true:

1. Mr. Hamdan (hereinafter "the accused") was captured in Afghanistan in November of 2001 and thereafter came into the custody of the United States. The accused has been held by the United States, either in Afghanistan or in Guantanamo Bay, since that time.

2. On February 7, 2002 the President issued a Memorandum entitled "Humane Treatment of al Qaeda and Taliban Detainees" in which he concluded that "Taliban detainees are unlawful combatants and therefore do not qualify as Prisoners of War under Article 4" of the Geneva Conventions.

3. On 7 July 2004, the Deputy Secretary of Defense published an Order Establishing Combatant Status Review Tribunals (CSRT). This Order defined "enemy combatant" as "an individual who was part of or supporting Taliban or al Qaeda forces, or associated forces that are engaged in hostilities against the United States or its coalition partners. This includes any person who has committed a belligerent act or has directly supported hostilities in aid of enemy armed forces."

4. The Order directed that a Tribunal be held for each detainee to determine whether he was an "enemy combatant" using that definition. The Tribunals were also directed to determine whether 'the detainee is properly detained as an enemy combatant."

5. On 2 October, 2004, the accused appeared before a CSRT at Guantanamo Bay and participated in such a hearing. The Tribunal received evidence and determined that he was a part of or associated with Al-Qaeda forces, and was properly detained as an "enemy combatant." The CSRT was not charged with determining, and therefore did not determine that the accused is an "alien unlawful enemy combatant."

6. Charges under the MCA were referred against this accused on 10 May 2007, alleging that he is subject to the jurisdiction of this tribunal as an "alien unlawful enemy combatant".

7. The accused challenges the jurisdiction of the Court on the basis that the Government cannot show, nor has it determined in a competent tribunal, that the accused is subject to the jurisdiction of the Commission. He claims, therefore that he is entitled to the protections that are accorded to a Prisoner of War until such a determination is made.

SUMMARY OF THE LAW

1. On 17 October, 2006, the Military Commissions Act (MCA) became law. The MCA limits the jurisdiction of Military Commissions to offenses made punishable by that Act or the law of war when committed by "an alien unlawful enemy combatant". 10 USC §948d(a). RMC 201(b)(1) is in accord.

2. The MCA defines "unlawful enemy combatant" to mean "(i) a person who has engaged in hostilities or who has purposefully and materially supported hostilities against the United States or its co-belligerents who is not a lawful enemy combatant (including a person who is part of the Taliban, al Qaeda, or associated forces); or "(ii) a person who, before, on, or after the date of the enactment of the Military Commissions Act of 2006, has been determined to be an unlawful enemy combatant by a Combatant Status Review Tribunal or another competent tribunal established under the authority of the President or the Secretary of the United States." 10 USC §948a(1).

3. The MCA makes a CSRT determination, whenever made, that a detainee is an "alien unlawful enemy combatant" dispositive of that issue for purposes of determining whether a detainee is subject to the jurisdiction of a Military Commission. Such a determination must be made by a CSRT or another competent tribunal established by the President or the Secretary of Defense. 10 USC §948d(c).

4. A Military commission is a court of limited jurisdiction. RMC 201(a)(1).

5. The burden is on the Government to show by a preponderance of the evidence that the accused is subject to the Jurisdiction of this Tribunal. RMC 905(c)(1);(2)(B).

DISCUSSION AND DECISION

The Government invites the Court to find that the 2004 determination that the accused is an "enemy combatant', coupled with the President's 2002 determination that members of al-Qaeda or the Taliban are unlawful combatants, amount to a finding that the accused is subject to the jurisdiction of this court. The Court declines to do so for the following reasons:

1. The 2004 CSRT determination that the accused is an "enemy combatant" was made for the purposes of determining whether or not he was properly detained, and not for the purpose of determining whether he was subject to trial by military commission.

2. The CSRT finding was made using a different standard than the one the MCA establishes for determining unlawful enemy combatant status. The definition of "enemy combatant" used by the 2004 CSRT is less exacting than the definition of "unlawful enemy combatant" prescribed in the MCA. The CSRT could have found a civilian not taking an active part in hostilities, but "part of" or "supporting" Taliban or al Qaeda forces engaged in hostilities to be an "enemy combatant". Yet the MCA limits this Court's jurisdiction to those who actually "engaged in hostilities or who . . . purposefully and materially supported hostilities." The CSRT did not apply this definition, and its finding therefore does not support the jurisdiction of this Tribunal.

3. The CSRT finding preceded the MCA by two years. The accused's participation in the CSRT may well have been much different had he realized its finding would be used to impose criminal jurisdiction upon him before a Military Commission.

4. The President's determination applied to members of al-Qaeda as a group, and did not represent an individualized determination that this accused supported or engaged in hostilities.

The MCA offers another route to a finding of jurisdiction: a finding by a CSRT "before, on, or after" the enactment of the MCA, that an accused is an alien unlawful enemy combatant. The October 2004 CSRT finding was before the enactment of the MCA, but it found only that the accused was an enemy combatant.

There may well be evidence in the Government's possession that could readily support a determination that the accused is subject to the jurisdiction of this Court. The Government may be able to easily demonstrate that jurisdiction by reopening the 2004 CSRT, or by organizing a different one, and directing it to clearly decide the accused's status. He is either entitled to the protections accorded to a Prisoner of War, or he is an alien unlawful enemy combatant subject to the jurisdiction of a Military Commission, or he may have some other status. The Government having failed to determine, by means of a competent tribunal, that the accused is an "unlawful enemy combatant" using the definition established by Congress, it has not shown, by a preponderance of the evidence, that the accused is subject to the jurisdiction of this Commission.

The Defense Motion to Dismiss all Charges and Specifications, for lack of jurisdiction, is GRANTED, without prejudice.

So Ordered this 4th day of June, 2007.

Keith J. Allred
Captain, JAGC, US Navy
Military Judge

Case Update: April 2008

In October 2007, the Supreme Court refused to hear Hamdan's appeal to his detention. His appeal in the Fourth Circuit is stayed pending the Supreme Court's decision in Boumediene and al-Odah. While charges against him in the military commission had been dismissed, they were later re-instated.

Hamdan is scheduled for a pretrial hearing in April 2008. His attorneys have moved to dismiss the case based on alleged political interference and a lack of impartiality in the convening authority which chooses the jury. Air Force Col. Morris Davis, former chief military prosecutor at Guantanamo, has said that he will testify in Hamdan's behalf.

In March, a military judge authorized Hamdan's lawyers to ask questions of high value detainees, including Khalid Sheik Mohammed. Defense attorneys wish to question these detainees as to the extent of Hamdan's knowledge of the Sept. 11th plot. The Pentagon had argued that such contact poses a national security risk.

Hamdan is scheduled for a military commission during the summer of 2008.

PART THREE. U.S. CAPTURES

CHAPTER 4

Padilla v. Bush

On May 8, 2002, Jose Padilla stepped off an airplane at Chicago's O'Hare International Airport. He was returning from a four-year journey of studying Islam and living abroad. As he stepped off that airplane, carrying a United States passport, he thought his trip was almost over. He was sadly and terribly mistaken. His physical journey would soon end, after a brief stop in New York, in a naval brig near Charleston, South Carolina. His lawyers were about to embark on a constitutional journey through federal courts up and down the Eastern Seaboard, including two trips to the United States Supreme Court. At the stops along the way, Mr. Padilla's legal team would test the limits of the powers of the Office of the President of the United States.

After clearing immigration in Chicago, Mr. Padilla was pulled aside by customs officials. He was taken to a conference room were he was questioned by FBI agents for hours. At the end of that interrogation, he was read his *Miranda* rights, arrested on a material witness warrant issued by the Federal District Court for the Southern District of New York, and then moved from Chicago to New York City.

The affidavit in support of the warrant was based on two sources of information – Abu Zubaydah (the individual described in the warrant application as "Confidential Source" or "CS-1") and Binyam Mohammed (described as "Subject-1"). It would later be learned that they had provided unreliable information under torture.

Relying on this same information, President Bush signed an order on June 9, 2002, transferring Mr. Padilla to military custody as an enemy combatant. Mr. Padilla was shortly thereafter transferred from New York to the brig in South Carolina. Not since before King John of England signed the Magna Carta in 1215 had an executive exercised such absolute authority over the liberty of an individual citizen. This reach of executive authority has no equal in American history. When President Lincoln suspended the writ of habeas corpus at the beginning of the Civil War, he knew that his action was of questionable legality. Lincoln sought and obtained congressional authorization for his actions as soon as Congress met. President Bush sought no such authorization. Even the shameful and disavowed internment of American citizens of Japanese descent during World War II was based to some degree on congressional action.

The government rationalized its removal of Mr. Padilla, an American citizen, from any form of constitutional process by claiming that their actions prevented him from setting off a dirty bomb. The simple fact is that there had never been a dirty bomb plot. Even under torture, Zubaydah had told his interrogators that any discussion of a dirty bomb had been considered a joke and rejected. Despite this knowledge, Attorney General John Ashcroft went on national television to announce that a dirty bomb plot had been prevented by Mr. Padilla's arrest and subsequent transfer to military custody.

Soon after Mr. Padilla had been transferred to the military, his attorneys filed a petition for a writ of habeas corpus seeking his return to civilian custody. The government moved to dismiss the petition on the ground that it should have been filed in South Carolina and that the court in New York lacked jurisdiction. The government also argued that the president had the authority to detain Mr. Padilla under the Authorization for Use of Military Force, by which Congress had authorized the president to use all necessary and appropriate means to capture those responsible for the attacks on September 11, 2001.

The critical questions in front of Judge Michael B. Mukasey – then chief judge of the United States District Court for the Southern District of New York and presently the attorney general of the United States – fell into several broad categories. Did the president have the authority under the Constitution or any act of Congress to order the indefinite military detention of an American citizen, seized on American soil? Did the court in the Southern District of New York have jurisdiction to hear the petition filed on Mr. Padilla's behalf? And finally, did Mr. Padilla have the right to have access to his attorneys?

In a series of decisions, Judge Mukasey found that the president did have the power to order the military detention of an American citizen if there was a factual basis to believe that the citizen had acted as soldier for an enemy of the United States. He also held that Mr. Padilla's military detention had begun New York, giving the court jurisdiction to hear the petition. Finally, Judge Mukasey found that the Due Process Clause of the Constitution required that Mr. Padilla be permitted access to his lawyers.

The case proceeded to the United States Court of Appeals for the Second Circuit, which held by a unanimous vote that the court in New York had jurisdiction to hear the petition and, by a vote of three to two, that the president lacked the power to order the detention of a citizen seized on American soil. The court ordered that Mr. Padilla either be indicted for some crime under traditional criminal process or released.

The government then sought review by the Supreme Court, which agreed to hear the issues of jurisdiction and presidential authority. In a five-to-four decision, the Court determined that the petition should have been filed in South Carolina and ordered that it be dismissed (leaving open the option for it to be re-filed). Over a strenuous dissent, the Court did not reach the issue of the president's authority to order the military detention of an American citizen.

A new petition seeking Mr. Padilla's release or criminal process was filed in South Carolina. District Court Judge Henry Floyd issued an opinion upholding the basic right of a citizen to be free unless he has been charged and convicted of a crime, which was later overturned by the Fourth Circuit Court of Appeals.

It was clear form the Supreme Court's previous five-to-four decision, and from Justice Scalia's dissent in *Hamdi v. Rumsfeld*, that the government had little chance of winning on the ultimate issue if the case were to go back to the Supreme Court. To avoid the Court's review of the issue of presidential authority, the government sought to moot Mr. Padilla's appeal by filing a civilian criminal indictment against him in Miami, Florida. He was indicted and subsequently convicted as a low-level member of a conspiracy to commit acts of violence overseas. None of the original charges against him, such as those alleging a dirty bomb plot, were alleged in the Florida indictment.

The rules required the Fourth Circuit to permit Mr. Padilla's transfer from military custody in South Carolina to civilian custody in Florida. Judge David Luttig, the author of the original Fourth Circuit opinion, denied the application for transfer and issued a heated opinion which questioned both the validity of the government's actions against Mr. Padilla and the seeming manipulation of the courts.

The Supreme Court ultimately granted Mr. Padilla's transfer to Florida and declined to hear the case on the merits.

On April 16, 2007, the Honorable Marcia G. Cooke of the United States District Court for the Southern District of Florida, sitting in Miami, ordered her courtroom deputy to bring in the first potential jurors in the trial of Jose Padilla and two co-defendants. At that moment, the constitutional balance of the United States had been restored. The constitutional significance of the trial of the United States v. Jose Padilla is not who won or lost but rather that the trial occurred.

Andrew Patel

5/08/2002: MATERIAL WITNESS WARRANT

CR 12 (Rev. 3/82)   WARRANT FOR ARREST

United States District Court	DISTRICT **SOUTHERN DISTRICT OF NEW YORK**
UNITED STATES OF AMERICA v. JOSE PADILLA, a/k/a "Abdullah Al Muhajir"	DOCKET NO. **02 Misc.** / MAG.'S CASE NO. **02 Mag.** NAME AND ADDRESS OF INDIVIDUAL TO BE ARRESTED JOSE PADILLA, a/k/a "Abdullah Al Muhajir"
WARRANT ISSUED ON THE BASIS OF: ☐ Order of Court ☐ Indictment ☐ Information ☒ Complaint	
TO: UNITED STATES MARSHAL OR ANY OTHER AUTHORIZED OFFICER	DISTRICT OF ARREST CITY

YOU ARE HEREBY COMMANDED to arrest the above-named person and bring that person before the nearest available magistrate to answer to the charge(s) listed below.

DESCRIPTION OF CHARGES (Being Investigated)

1. Conspiracy to kill U.S. Nationals (18 U.S.C. § 2332(b));
2. Bombing and bombing conspiracy (18 U.S.C.§ 844); and
3. Conspiracy to Use Weapons Of Mass Destruction (18 U.S.C. § 2332a)

IN VIOLATION OF	UNITED STATES CODE TITLE 18	SECTION 3144 (Material Witness)
BAIL FIXED BY COURT	OTHER CONDITIONS OF RELEASE	
ORDERED BY HON. MICHAEL B. MUKASEY	SIGNATURE (JUDGE/MAGISTRATE)	DATE 5/8/02
CLERK OF COURT JAMES M. PARKISON	(BY) DEPUTY CLERK	DATE ISSUED

RETURN

This warrant was received and executed with the arrest of the above-named person.

DATE RECEIVED	NAME AND TITLE OF ARRESTING OFFICER	SIGNATURE OF ARRESTING OFFICER
DATE EXECUTED		

United States Judge or Judge of a State Court of Record

UNITED STATES DISTRICT COURT
SOUTHERN DISTRICT OF NEW YORK
- - - - - - - - - - - - - - - - -x
                                    :
IN RE THE APPLICATION OF THE   :
                                    :
UNITED STATES FOR A MATERIAL   :   SEALED AFFIDAVIT
                                    :
WITNESS WARRANT, PURSUANT TO   :   02 Misc.   —
                                    :
18 U.S.C. § 3144, FOR   :
                                    :
JOSE PADILLA,   :
                                    :
a/k/a "Abdullah Al Muhajir"   :
                                    :
- - - - - - - - - - - - - - - - -x

COUNTY OF NEW YORK   )
STATE OF NEW YORK   ) ss.:
SOUTHERN DISTRICT OF NEW YORK)

     JOE ENNIS, being duly sworn, deposes and says:

     1.   I am a Special Agent with the Federal Bureau of Investigation ("FBI") and have been so employed for approximately three years. I am a member of the Joint Terrorist Task Force (JTTF), which is a task force comprised of members of the FBI and the New York City Police Department (NYPD). I make this affirmation in support of the Government's application for a material witness warrant, pursuant to Title 18, United States Code, Section 3144, for JOSE PADILLA, a/k/a "Abdullah Al Muhajir" (hereinafter PADILLA or "the Witness"). This application seeks PADILLA's detention so that he may be produced for testimony before a grand jury in the Southern District of New York.

Background

     2.   Grand juries in the Southern District of New York have been investigating plans and conspiracies by members and associates of Al Qaeda who have conducted terrorist attacks against the United States and U.S. interests, including the 1998 bombings of the U.S. embassies in Nairobi, Kenya and Dar es Salaam, Tanzania; the October 2000 attack in Yemen of the U.S.S. Cole; and,

the September 11th terrorist attacks on World Trade Center in New York and the Pentagon in Virginia. In addition, the Grand Jury is investigating plans or conspiracies to conduct similar attacks in the future, including any plans by Al Qaeda for bombings and/or other terrorist attacks in the United States and/or against U.S. interests abroad.

Materiality of Testimony

3.   For the reasons set forth in the paragraphs that follow, I believe that the testimony of JOSE PADILLA, a/k/a "Abdullah Al Muhajir" ("PADILLA") will be material to the grand jury's investigations, described above. The information in the following paragraphs is based upon my participation in the investigation, my conversations with other law enforcement officers, and my review of documents and reports prepared by other law enforcement officers. Where statements are reported, they are reported in substance and in part.

Information Provided By CS-1

4.   On or about April 22nd and 23rd, 2002, a Confidential Source ("CS-1") provided information to law enforcement officers and others while CS-1 was being detained in a foreign country.[1] I

---

[1]   Based on information developed by the Government, CS-1 has been involved with Al Qaeda for several years, and is believed to have been involved in the terrorist activities of Al Qaeda. In addition to the specific interviews referenced above, CS-1 has been interviewed on other prior occasions. It is believed that CS-1 has not been completely candid about his association with Al Qaeda, and his own terrorist activities, during these interviews with U.S. personnel. Much of the information provided by CS-1 about other individuals during earlier interviews has, however, been corroborated and has proven accurate and reliable. Some of the information provided by CS-1 about other individuals during earlier interviews remains uncorroborated, and may be part of an effort by CS-1 to mislead or confuse U.S. law enforcement. In addition, at the time of the interviews referenced above, CS-1 was being treated with various types of medication.

have reviewed a number of reports prepared based on those interviews, and have spoken with other law enforcement officers regarding those interviews. Based on my review of the reports of those interviews and on my conversations with other law enforcement officers, I learned that CS-1 provided the following information, in substance and in part, during those interviews:

a.   CS-1 provided information concerning two individuals, one of whom he initially referred to as a "South American." CS-1 later identified the "South American" as "Abdullah Al Muhajir" and provided a name for the other individual (who will hereinafter be referred to as "SUBJECT-1"). On or about April 23rd, CS-1 was shown two photographs. One of the photographs was taken from the U.S. passport of JOSE PADILLA, which was recovered from PADILLA's person, and was identified by CS-1 as the individual he knew as "Abdullah Al Muhajir." The other photograph was taken from a fake passport recovered from SUBJECT-1 and was identified by CS-1 as the individual he had previously named and described as the second individual in the company of the "South American."

b.   CS-1 further stated that PADILLA and SUBJECT-1 had previously approached CS-1 and asked for his opinion on their plan to build an explosive device which would combine "uranium" or other nuclear or radioactive material with an "ordinary" explosive device (hereinafter referred to as a "dirty bomb"), and detonate the dirty bomb in the United States. CS-1 stated that he told PADILLA and SUBJECT-1 that he did not think that the plan would work, but SUBJECT-1 indicated to CS-1 that he did think that the plan would work. CS-1 stated that he did not believe that PADILLA and SUBJECT-1 were members of Al Qaeda.

c.   CS-1 further stated that he believed that the plan articulated by PADILLA and SUBJECT-1 was still in the idea phase of the plan, and that PADILLA and SUBJECT-1 did not discuss any specific time at which they hoped to execute the plan. CS-1 further stated that PADILLA and SUBJECT-1 did not yet have any radioactive material, but that the two men mentioned trying to steal radioactive material from an unnamed university because security would be less stringent at a university. CS-I further stated that PADILLA and SUBJECT-1 had consulted an unidentified website on the procedure for assembling a dirty bomb.

d.   CS-1 further stated that he was not aware of any associates of PADILLA and SUBJECT-1 in the United States, but stated that PADILLA seemed very familiar with the Washington, D.C. area.

e.   CS-1 further stated that PADILLA and SUBJECT-1 asked CS-1 to put them in contact with another individual known to CS-1 as a member of Al Qaeda (hereinafter referred to as "SUBJECT-2"). CS-1 expressed his opinion to PADILLA and SUBJECT-1 that SUBJECT-2 would be interested in working with them because: (1) they are not Arab, and would therefore draw less attention, (2) they have passports which would not draw attention and would allow them to travel freely, and (3) they are willing to do work.

f.   CS-1 further stated that SUBJECT-1 was willing to become a martyr, but that PADILLA was not.

Information Provided By SUBJECT-1

5.   In or about early April 2002, SUBJECT-1 was also interviewed in connection with this investigation. SUBJECT-1 had been previously detained in Pakistan by the Pakistani authorities, while trying to board a flight, on suspicions that his non-U.S. passport was fraudulent (which it was). I have reviewed reports prepared based on this interview, and have spoken with other law enforcement officers regarding this interview. Based on my review of the reports of this interview and on my conversations with other law enforcement officers, I learned that SUBJECT-1 provided the following information, in substance and in part, during this interview: —

a.   SUBJECT-1 stated that he went to Pakistan in November 2001 for training in Afghanistan.

b.   SUBJECT-1 further stated that he and PADILLA met with CS-1 in Afghanistan in 2001 and traveled to Pakistan at the behest of CS-1 to receive training in "wiring explosives."

c.   SUBJECT-1 further stated that while in Pakistan he and PADILLA researched the construction of a uranium-enhanced explosive device, which would be detonated within the United States.   SUBJECT-1 further stated that he and PADILLA discussed this plan with CS-1, and that CS-1 referred them to other members of Al Qaeda for further discussion of this operation.

d.   SUBJECT-1 further stated that the Al Qaeda officials held at least two separate meetings with PADILLA, but that SUBJECT-1 was not a party to those conversations.   SUBJECT-1 stated that, although he was not a party to those conversations, he nevertheless believed that during those conversations the Al Qaeda officials directed PADILLA to return to the United States to conduct reconnaissance on behalf of Al Qaeda within the United States.[2]

Need for Material Witness Warrant and Detention

6.   For the following reasons, it has become impracticable to secure the presence of PADILLA by subpoena:

a.   PADILLA is currently on a flight from Pakistan to Chicago, and is being surveilled during that flight by several law enforcement officers.   That flight is scheduled to land in Chicago at approximately 2:00 p.m. today EST.

b.   Although PADILLA is a U.S. Citizen, he has in the past demonstrated his willingness to travel extensively throughout the world, including but not limited to Pakistan and

---

[2]   In a separate interview, SUBJECT-1's wife told law enforcement authorities that SUBJECT-1 would often become emotional and cry when he discussed his willingness to die for his God.

Afghanistan. Moreover, there is considerable incentive for PADILLA to flee, if he is not detained, once he learns that he has been implicated in the plot to detonate a dirty bomb by CS-1 and SUBJECT-1. Thus, there is no assurance that he would appear before the grand jury as directed.

    c. Based on the facts set forth above, it appears that PADILLA may have information relevant to the grand jury's investigation.

    7. I believe, based on the facts set forth above, that there is no condition or combination of conditions that would reasonably assure the appearance of PADILLA. Even assuming that there are conditions that might assure his appearance, however, I respectfully submit that the Court should detain PADILLA a reasonable period of time, to wit, until seven days after his initial appearance in New York on the material witness warrant. The limited detention is permissible under Section 3144, and would insure that the grand jury will receive PADILLA's testimony.

    WHEREFORE your deponent prays that the Court issue a material witness warrant for JOSE PADILLA, a/k/a "Abdullah Al Muhajir", and that he be imprisoned or bailed, as the case may be.

    WHEREFORE deponent also prays that the Material Witness Warrant and this Affidavit in Support of the Material Witness Warrant be placed under seal and that these documents not be unsealed until further Order of this Court.

            [signature]

            JOE ENNIS
            Special Agent
            Federal Bureau of Investigation

Sworn to before me this
8th day of May, 2002

[signature]

UNITED STATES DISTRICT JUDGE

A 51

THE WHITE HOUSE
WASHINGTON
FOR OFFICIAL USE ONLY

TO THE SECRETARY OF DEFENSE:

Based on the information available to me from all sources,

REDACTED

In accordance with the Constitution and consistent with the laws of the United States, including the Authorization for Use of Military Force Joint Resolution (Public Law 107-40);

I, GEORGE W. BUSH, as President of the United States and Commander in Chief of the U.S. armed forces, hereby DETERMINE for the United States of America that:

(1) Jose Padilla, who is under the control of the Department of Justice and who is a U.S. citizen, is, and at the time he entered the United States in May 2002 was, an enemy combatant;

(2) Mr. Padilla is closely associated with al Qaeda, an international terrorist organization with which the United States is at war;

(3) Mr. Padilla engaged in conduct that constituted hostile and war-like acts, including conduct in preparation for acts of international terrorism that had the aim to cause injury to or adverse effects on the United States;

(4) Mr. Padilla possesses intelligence, including intelligence about personnel and activities of al Qaeda, that, if communicated to the U.S., would aid U.S. efforts to prevent attacks by al Qaeda on the United States or its armed forces, other governmental personnel, or citizens;

(5) Mr. Padilla represents a continuing, present and grave danger to the national security of the United States, and detention of Mr. Padilla is necessary to prevent him from aiding al Qaeda in its efforts to attack the United States or its armed forces, other governmental personnel, or citizens;

(6) it is in the interest of the United States that the Secretary of Defense detain Mr. Padilla as an enemy combatant; and

(7) it is.   **REDACTED**   consistent with U.S. law and the laws of war for the Secretary of Defense to detain Mr. Padilla as an enemy combatant.

Accordingly, you are directed to receive Mr. Padilla from the Department of Justice and to detain him as an enemy combatant.

DATE _June 9, 2002_

White House Office-controlled Document

UNITED STATES DISTRICT COURT
SOUTHERN DISTRICT OF NEW YORK
---X

JOSE PADILLA,   :

DONNA R. NEWMAN, As Next   :
Friend of Jose Padilla
                                               :   02 Civ. 4445 (MBM)
            Petitioners,   :

                                               :
        -against-
                                               :

GEORGE W. BUSH   :
Ex officio Commander-in-Chief of US
Armed Forces   :
White House
██████████████████████   :

                                               :

DONALD RUMSFELD
Secretary of Defense
The Pentagon   :
████████████████   :

JOHN ASHCROFT   :
Attorney General
U.S. Department of Justice   :
████████████████████████   :

                                               :

COMMANDER M. A. MARR   :
Consolidated Naval Brig
████████████████   :
                                               :

            Respondents,   :
---X

AMENDED PETITION FOR WRIT OF HABEAS CORPUS

---

* Redactions on this page have been added for privacy purposes. – *Eds.*

1. Jose Padilla, a citizen of the United States of America, is being held illegally, denied access to legal counsel, and denied access to any Court for the determination of the legality of his detention in violation of his rights under the Constitution of the United States of America. Donna R. Newman, Esq., on behalf of Mr. Padilla as his Next Friend, respectfully requests that this Court issue a Writ of Habeas Corpus.

2. A Petition for Writ of Habeas Corpus was previously filed with this Court. This amended Petition is submitted pursuant to 28 U.S.C. §2242 and Rule 15 of the Federal Rules of Civil Procedure.

PARTIES

3. Petitioner Jose Padilla is an American Citizen presently incarcerated and unlawfully held by Respondents at the Consolidated Naval Brig in Charleston, South Carolina.

4. Petitioner Donna R. Newman is an attorney duly admitted to practice law in the Southern District of New York. On or about May 15, 2002, Petitioner Donna R. Newman was assigned to represent Petitioner Jose Padilla by Order of the Honorable Chief Judge Michael B. Mukasey.

5. Petitioner Donna R. Newman, seeks relief as "Next Friend" pursuant to the requirements of Whitmore v. Arkansas, 495 U.S. 149 (1990) which requires a "next friend" to provide an adequate explanation why the real party in action cannot appear on his own behalf, to be truly dedicated to the best interests of the person on whose behalf she seeks to litigate and for the "next friend" to demonstrate some significant relationship with the real party in interest.

6. In the instant matter, Petitioner Jose Padilla cannot appear because he is detained in the Consolidated Naval Brig in Charleston, South Carolina. Petitioner Jose Padilla cannot sign and verify the Amended Petition as counsel has been denied access to him by the Respondents. Petitioner Jose Padilla is not permitted to send or receive mail. Respondents have not permitted Petitioner Jose Padilla to communicate with anyone else including members of his family. Thus, Petitioner is without means or access to file a Petition on his own behalf.

7. Petitioner Donna R. Newman, as counsel to Jose Padilla has a significant relationship with the Petitioner Jose Padilla. After being assigned to represent, Jose Padilla on or about May 15, 2002, Petitioner Donna R. Newman filed and argued motions on his behalf and met with Mr. Padilla at the M.C.C. repeatedly and regularly as his attorney. Before Mr. Padilla was signed over to his current place of detention, Petitioner Donna R. Newman had established a attorney-client relationship with Jose Padilla. She has a professional obligation under the Code of Professional Ethics to zealously represent the best interests of her client. Attorneys have been permitted to act as "next friend." See Nash v. MacArthur, 184 F.2d 606 (D.C. Cir. 1950).

8. Respondent Bush is the President of the United States and Commander-in-Chief of the Armed Forces of the United States.

9. Respondent Rumsfeld is the United States Secretary of Defense and Respondent Marr's superior. He determines the conditions under which Petitioner Jose Padilla is held.

10. Respondent M.A. Marr is a Commander in the United States Navy and is in command of the Consolidated Naval Brig in Charleston, South Carolina. Respondent M.A. Marr receives orders with regard to Petitioner's custody from her superiors, including Respondents Bush and Rumsfeld. That Commander Marr could not obey an Order of this Court to release Petitioner Padilla without violating the order of a superior officer and thereby violating the Uniform Code of Military Justice. See 10 U.S.C §892.

11. Respondent Ashcroft is the Attorney General of the United States and is the superior to the Agents of the Federal Bureau of Investigation who initially seized Mr. Padilla and who on information and belief continue to interrogate Mr. Padilla in violation of his constitutional rights. Respondent Ashcroft is also the superior to the United States Attorney's Office for the Southern District of New York who, who on information and belief, assisted the Department of Defense in the seizure of Jose Padilla.

JURISDICTION

12. Petitioners bring this action under 28 U.S.C. §§2241 and 2242, and invoke this Court's jurisdiction under 28 U.S.C. §§1331, 1651, 2201 and 2202; as well as the under the Fourth, Fifth and Sixth Amendments to the United States Constitution.

13. This Court is empowered under 28 U.S.C. §§2241 to grant a Writ of Habeas Corpus and to entertain the Petition filed by Donna R. Newman, as Next Friend under 28 U.S.C. §§2242.

Venue

14. Venue is proper in the United States District Court for the Southern District of New York ("United States Attorney's Office") because this Court has unique familiarity with the facts and circumstances of this case and the resolution of the case does not require Padilla's presence. See, Braden v. 30th Judicial Circuit Court of Kentucky, 410 U.S. 484, 493–94, 35 L.Ed 2d 433, 93 S. Ct. 1123 (1973)(Traditional venue considerations apply to habeas cases; those include (1) where the material events occurred; (2) where records and witnesses pertinent to the claim are likely to be found; (3) the convenience of the forum for respondent and petitioner; and (4) the familiarity of the court with the applicable laws.).

STATEMENT OF FACTS

15. On May 8, 2002, Jose Padilla, an American citizen, was arrested by agents of the Federal Bureau of Investigation ["FBI"] at O'Hare Airport in Chicago, Illinois, upon a material witness warrant signed by the Honorable Michael B. Mukasey, Chief Judge of the United States District Court for the Southern District of New York.

16. The Court Order on which Mr. Padilla was arrested had been applied for by the United States Attorney's Office for the Southern District of New York.

17. On information and belief, Petitioner Jose Padilla was transported by agents of the FBI from Chicago to New York.

18. On or about May 15, 2002, Petitioner Jose Padilla appeared before the Honorable Michael B. Mukaey, who assigned Petitioner Donna R. Newman to represent Mr. Padilla pursuant to the Criminal Justice Act. 18 U.S.C. §3006A.

19. Petitioner Donna R. Newman met repeatedly and regularly with Mr. Padilla when he was being housed in the Metropolitan Correctional Center in New York, a prison operated by Department of Justice, Bureau of Prisons.

20. As an additional part of her representation of Mr. Padilla, Petitioner Donna R. Newman also appeared in court, filed and argued motions, and on his behalf consulted with both members of Mr. Padilla's family and representatives of the Government. She continues to consult with the Government and Mr. Padilla's family in her role as his attorney.

21. The motions filed sought Mr. Padilla's release, asserting his detention was illegal and contrary to his constitutional rights. The United States Attorney's Office for the Southern District of New York filed extensive papers in opposition to Padilla's motions. Judge Mukasey received all submissions and scheduled a hearing on Padilla's motion for June 11, 2002

22. On information and belief, on or about June 9, 2002, after consulting with the Respondent Ashcroft and a representative of Respondent Rumsfeld, George W. Bush, the President of the United States, acting as Commander-in-Chief, signed an order declaring Jose Padilla to be a "enemy combatant" and directing Respondent Rumsfeld to arrest Mr. Padilla and to detain him indefinitely for interrogation. See . . . transcript of Respondent Ashcroft's June 10, 2002 statement.

23. Despite requests to several government officials, the Government has refused to provide counsel for Respondent Padilla with a copy of the Order the President is reported to have signed. See Exhibit A, letters from Donna R. Newman requesting a copy of the Order on which Mr. Padilla was detained by military authorities.

24. On information and belief the term "enemy combatant" is not defined in either the United States Code or in the Uniformed Code of Military Justice.

25. On or about June 9, 2002, Petitioner Jose Padilla was transferred from the custody of the civilian authorities of the Department of Justice to the military authorities at the Consolidated Naval Brig at Charleston, South Carolina.

26. On information and belief, the Consolidated Naval Brig at Charleston, South Carolina is located on a United States Naval base where access is restricted to members of the military and other specifically designated individuals.

27. In the year 2002, the United States District Court for the Southern District of New York has been "opened for business" without interruption.

28. Petitioner Donna R. Newman was informed by representatives of the Department of Defense that she could not visit or speak with Jose Padilla.

29. On information and belief, from May 2002 through the time this Petition was filed a grand jury has been sitting in the Southern District of New York. No member of the United States Attorney's Office for the Southern District of New York has advised Petitioner Donna R. Newman that an indictment has been returned that charges Jose Padilla with any criminal conduct. Nor, on information and belief, has any complaint been filed in the United States District Court for the Southern District of New York that charges Jose Padilla with any criminal conduct.

30. As of the date of this Petition, Mr. Padilla has not been charged with any offense. Nor, according to press reports, are any criminal charges contemplated.

31. Respondent Rumsfeld has stated publicly that it is the Government's intention to detain Mr. Padilla indefinitely to interrogate him.

CLAIMS AS TO THE UNLAWFULNESS OF PETITIONER'S DETENTION

FIRST CLAIM FOR RELIEF
(DUE PROCESS —FOURTH, FIFTH AND SIXTH AMENDMENTS
TO THE UNITED STATES CONSTITUTION)

32. Petitioner incorporate paragraphs 1–28 by reference.

33. It is a violation of the Due Process Clause of the Fifth Amendment to the United States Constitution to hold an American citizen without giving notice of the basis for his detention.

34. By the action described above, Respondents, acting under color of law, have violated and continue to violate the Fourth, Fifth and Sixth Amendments to the United States Constitution. <u>See</u>, <u>e.g.</u>, <u>Zadvydas v. Davis</u>, 533 U.S. 678, 690 (2001)("Freedom from imprisonment – from government custody, detention, or other forms of physical restraint – lies at the heart of the liberty that the [Due Process] Clause protects. . . . And this Court has said that government detention violates that Clause unless the detention is ordered in a criminal proceeding with adequate constitutional protections . . .") Also see <u>Ex Parte Milligan</u>, 71 U.S. 2, 123 (1866)("[C]itizens of states where the courts are open, if charged with a crime, are guaranteed the inestimable privilege of trial by jury. This privilege is a vital principle, underlying the whole administration of criminal justice; it is not held by sufferance, and cannot be frittered away on pleas of state or political necessity.")

35. There is no authority to detain an American citizen without a finding of probable cause. <u>See</u>, <u>e.g.</u> <u>United States Ex Rel. Toth v. Quarles</u>, 350 U.S. 11, 14 (1955) an "assertion of miltary authority over civilians cannot rest on the President's power as commander-in-chief, or on any theory of martial law."

SECOND CLAIM FOR RELIEF

(SUSPENSION OF THE WRIT)

36. Petitioner incorporate paragraphs 1–28 by reference.

37. To the extent the Presidential Order on which Mr. Padilla is held as an "enemy combatant" disallows any challenge to the legality of Mr. Padilla's detention by way of habeas corpus, the Order and its enforcement constitutes an unlawful Suspension of the Writ, in violation of Article I of the United States Constitution.

THIRD CLAIM FOR RELIEF

(VIOLATION OF POSSE COMITATUS)

38. Petitioner incorporate paragraphs 1–28 by reference.

39. The Posse Comitatus Act, 18 U.S.C. §1385 prohibits Army and Air Force personnel from participating in civilian law enforcement activities. Members of the Army, Navy, Air Force and Marine Corps are prohibited from participation in civilian law enforcement activities by 10 U.S.C. §375 and as a matter of Department of Defense policy, see Department of Defense Directive 5525.5(C).

40. As the Courts of the United States are opened and no state of martial law exists, it is unlawful for an Jose Padilla, an American citizen to be held by the military at the Consolidated Naval Brig in Charleston, South Carolina.

PRAYER FOR RELIEF

WHEREFORE, Petitioners pray for the relief as follows:

1. Grant Petitioner Donna R. Newman, Next Friend status, as Next Friend of Jose Padilla;

2. Order Respondents to permit counsel to meet and confer with Jose Padilla;

3. Order Respondents to permit Jose Padilla to receive a copy of this Petition;

4. Order Respondents to cease all interrogations of Mr. Padilla, direct of indirect, while this litigation is pending;

5. Order and declare that Mr. Padilla is being held in violation of the Fourth, Fifth and Sixth Amendments to the United States Constitution.

6. To the extent Respondents contest any material factual allegation in this Petition, schedule an evidentiary hearing, at which Petitioners may adduce proof in support of their allegations;

7. Order that Petitioner Jose Padilla be released from Respondents' unlawful custody;

8. In the event that it is determined that venue does not properly lie in the Southern District of New York, that this matter be transferred to the appropriate United States District Court.

9. Such other relief as the Court may deem necessary and appropriate.

Dated: June 19, 2002

Respectfully submitted,

Jose Padilla, and Donna R. Newman, as Next Friend

By:
    Donna R. Newman, Esq.
       . . .

    Andrew G. Patel, Esq.
       . . .

. . .

IN THE UNITED STATES DISTRICT COURT
FOR THE SOUTHERN DISTRICT OF NEW YORK

JOSE PADILLA,   :
DONNA R. NEWMAN,   :
    as Next Friend of Jose Padilla   :
                                                 :
    Petitioners,   :
                                                 :
    v.   :   Civil Action
                                                 :   No. 4445
GEORGE W. BUSH,   :
DONALD RUMSFELD,   :
JOHN ASHCROFT,   :
COMMANDER M.A. MARR   :
                                                 :
    Respondents.   :

MOTION TO DISMISS
AMENDED PETITION FOR WRIT OF HABEAS CORPUS

JAMES B. COMEY
United States Attorney

PAUL D. CLEMENT
Deputy Solicitor General

DAVID B. SALMONS
Assistant to the Solicitor General

DEMETRA LAMBROS
Attorney

ERIC B. BRUCE
Assistant United States Attorney

. . .

Respondents hereby move to dismiss the amended petition for a writ of habeas corpus for lack of jurisdiction. The petition in this case seeks to interject this Court into the President's conduct of ongoing hostilities. Specifically, the petition makes the extraordinary request that this Court order respondents to return Jose Padilla (a/k/a Abdullah Al Muhajir) from Charleston, South Carolina – where he is being held by the United States military as an enemy combatant – to New York to then be released into the public. The petition, however, contains two independent – and equally fatal – jurisdictional defects that require this Court to dismiss the petition, or at a minimum, transfer this habeas action to South Carolina.

First, the Court lacks jurisdiction because the petition has not been properly brought on Padilla's behalf. The habeas statute requires that a detainee himself sign the petition or, if he is unable to do so (as here), that someone with "next friend" standing bring it on his behalf. Attorney Donna R. Newman asserts "next friend" status to bring this habeas action on behalf of Padilla. She does not, however, satisfy the "significant relationship" requirement for next-friend standing set forth by the Supreme Court in Whitmore v. Arkansas, 495 U.S. 149 (1990).

Second, and in any event, the Court lacks habeas jurisdiction because no proper respondent with "custody" over Padilla is present within this Court's territorial jurisdiction. The amended habeas petition names President Bush, Secretary of Defense Rumsfeld, Attorney General Ashcroft and Commander M.A. Marr as respondents. Only one – Commander Marr, the commanding officer of the Naval brig in South Carolina – is a proper respondent. And none of the named respondents – including Commander Marr – is within this Court's territorial jurisdiction. This Court therefore lacks habeas jurisdiction over the petition.[1]

BACKGROUND

On September 11, 2001, the al Qaida terrorist network launched a large-scale attack on the United States, killing approximately 3,000 persons, and specifically targeting the Nation's financial center and the headquarters of its Department of Defense. The September 11 attacks inflicted the loss of more American lives than the attack at Pearl Harbor, and were followed by a major military response. Shortly after the attacks, Congress authorized the President to use "force against the nations, organizations, or persons he determines planned, authorized, committed, or aided the terrorist attacks that occurred on September 11, 2001, or harbored such organizations or persons, in order to prevent any future acts of international terrorism against the United States by such nations, organizations, or persons." Authorization for Use of Military Force, Pub. L. No. 107-40, 115 Stat. 224 (2001). In authorizing such force, Congress emphasized the "unusual and extraordinary threat to the national security and foreign policy of the United States" posed by the forces responsible for the September 11 attacks, and that "the President has authority under the Constitution to take action to deter and prevent acts of international terrorism against the United States." Ibid.

The President, acting pursuant to his authority as Commander in Chief and with express congressional support, has dispatched the armed forces of the United States to Afghanistan to seek out and subdue the al Qaida terrorist network and the Taliban regime that had supported and protected that network. The ongoing military operations

---

[1] This motion to dismiss is addressed to the Court's lack of jurisdiction to entertain the petition and accompanying requests for relief. If the Court denies the motion to dismiss, it should transfer the action to South Carolina, where the Government would then address the merits of any of the claims raised in the petition. See 28 U.S.C. 1406 (a), 1631.

in Afghanistan and elsewhere – which are being conducted not only by thousands of men and women of the United States armed forces but also by coalition forces sent by our international allies – have, inter alia, resulted in the destruction of al Qaida training camps, removal of the Taliban regime that supported al Qaida, and gathering of vital intelligence concerning the plans, operations, and workings of al Qaida and its supporters. Numerous members of the military forces have lost their lives, and many others have suffered casualties as part of the campaign, which remains active and ongoing. See generally www.army.mil/enduringfreedom. While the military campaign is ongoing, the al Qaida network and those who support it remain a serious threat, as does the risk of future terrorist attacks on United States' citizens and interests carried out, as were the attacks of September 11, through covert infiltration of the United States by enemy belligerents. As explained below, Padilla is currently being held, consistent with the laws and customs of war, in the custody and control of the military as an enemy combatant in this ongoing armed conflict.

Padilla was arrested in Chicago on May 8, 2002, pursuant to a material witness warrant related to grand jury proceedings in the Southern District of New York. Pursuant to an order of this Court, Padilla was detained at the Metropolitan Correctional Center in New York City. See Amend. Pet. ¶¶15, 19.

On June 9, 2002, the President determined that Padilla was an enemy combatant and should be transferred to the control of the United States military. Thereafter, the Department of Justice requested that this Court vacate the material witness warrant. This Court vacated the warrant on June 9, and Padilla was transferred to the exclusive control of the United States military and transported to the Consolidated Naval Brig in Charleston, South Carolina for detention as an enemy combatant. The initial petition for habeas relief was filed on June 11, after this Court had vacated the material witness warrant and after the military had transferred Padilla to South Carolina for detention and questioning as an enemy combatant.

The authority of the United States to seize and detain enemy combatants is well settled – and vital to our core military objectives, including preventing enemies from rejoining the conflict and gathering intelligence to prevent attacks on Americans and U.S. interests. See Ex parte Quirin, 317 U.S. 1, 31, 35 (1942) ("[u]nlawful combatants" – or "those who during time of war pass surreptitiously from enemy territory into our own *** for the commission of hostile acts involving destruction of life or property" – are "subject to capture and detention"); see also In re Territo, 156 F.2d 142, 145 (9th Cir. 1946); Ex parte Toscano, 208 F. 938, 940 (S.D. Cal. 1913). The authority to capture and detain is not diminished by the fact that the enemy combatant is an American citizen. See Quirin, 317 U.S. at 37–38 ("[c]itizens who associate themselves with the *** enemy *** and with its aid, guidance and direction enter this country bent on hostile acts are enemy belligerents"); accord Colepaugh v. Looney, 235 F.2d 429, 432 (10th Cir. 1956); In re Territo, 156 F.2d at 145.

ARGUMENT

I.   ATTORNEY DONNA NEWMAN LACKS STANDING TO FILE THE PETITION AS PADILLA'S NEXT FRIEND.

This Court lacks jurisdiction over this petition because attorney Donna Newman lacks "next friend" standing to bring this habeas action on Padilla's behalf.[2]

---

[2] Attorney Newman signed the first petition purportedly as Padilla's lawyer. In her amended petition, she appears to acknowledge that a "next friend," not counsel, must bring the case on Padilla's behalf. That is correct.

. . .

Attorney Newman has not met her burden of establishing next-friend standing. Although she alleges that while briefly serving as his attorney for the material witness proceedings she met regularly with Padilla in New York, filed and argued motions on his behalf, and consulted with his family and the government, see Amend. Pet. ¶¶7, 19, 20, that is not sufficient to establish next-friend standing. Newman's entire prior relationship with Padilla lasted from May 15 to June 9, see 5/16/2002 Order (appointing Newman under Criminal Justice Act), Amend. Pet. ¶22 – or about three weeks. The fact that Newman has done her job as appointed counsel on a now dismissed material-witness matter for three weeks does not, without more, mean that she has established a "significant relationship" with the detainee.

. . .

Attorney Newman, thus, does not qualify as Padilla's "next friend." Her three-week representation of Padilla is not akin to the relationship between a prisoner and his parent, spouse, or sibling – or even like that between a long-standing lawyer and client. Moreover, the petition indicates that Attorney Newman has consulted with members of Padilla's family. Amend. Pet. ¶20. That there may be some genuine "next friends" available underscores the inappropriateness of conferring such status on Attorney Newman. See Hamdi, No. 02-6827, slip op. at 17 (lawyer's absence of significant relationship stood "in stark contrast to the close familial connection [of detainee's father] that was right around the corner").

II. THIS COURT LACKS HABEAS JURISDICTION BECAUSE IT LACKS TERRITORIAL JURISDICTION OVER PADILLA'S PROPER CUSTODIAN.

A. President Bush, Secretary Rumsfeld And Attorney General Ashcroft Are Not Proper Respondents.

In any event, even if Newman could satisfy the requirements of next-friend standing, this Court would still lack habeas jurisdiction over the petition. There is only one proper respondent for a habeas petition filed to challenge the detention of Padilla, and that is the commanding officer of the Naval Brig in South Carolina, Commander Melanie A. Marr, United States Navy. As discussed below, the proper habeas respondent is a prisoner's immediate, not ultimate, custodian. President Bush, Secretary of Defense Rumsfeld and Attorney General Ashcroft are therefore not proper respondents in this case.

By its terms, the federal habeas corpus statute provides that the writ "shall be directed to the person having custody of the person detained." 28 U.S.C. 2243. Thus, the proper respondent in a habeas case is the person who holds the petitioner in custody. Braden v. 30th Judicial Circuit Court, 410 U.S. 484, 494–95 (1973) ("([t]he writ of habeas corpus does not act upon the prisoner who seeks relief, but upon the person who holds him in what is alleged to be unlawful custody."); see also 28 U.S.C. 2242 (habeas petitioner must "allege *** the name of the person who has custody over him").

The habeas statute requires that an application "shall be in writing and verified by the person for whose relief it is intended or by someone acting in his behalf." 28 U.S.C. 2242 (emphasis added). As the Supreme Court has explained, the underscored words were intended to confer "next friend" standing on a third party where a detained prisoner is unable ("usually because of mental incompetence or inaccessibility") to seek relief himself. Whitmore v. Arkansas, 495 U.S. 149, 162–63 (1990). Thus, where a prisoner is inaccessible, only a proper "next friend" may file on his behalf. But for the reasons set forth herein, Newman cannot satisfy the vigorous restrictions on next-friend standing set forth by the Supreme Court in Whitmore.

In this case, Commander Marr is the immediate custodian and therefore the only proper respondent. See, e.g., Vasquez v. Reno, 233 F.3d 688, 693 (1st Cir. 2000) ("case law establishes that the warden of the penitentiary not the Attorney General is the person who holds a prisoner in custody for habeas purposes"), cert. denied, 122 S. Ct. 43 (2001); In re Hasred, 123 F.3d 922, 925 n.2 (6th Cir. 1997) (prison warden, not executive with ultimate authority over prisoner, is proper habeas respondent); Yi v. Maugans, 24 F.3d 500, 507 (3d Cir. 1994) (same; dismissing notion that Attorney General could be proper habeas custodian); Guerra v. Meese, 786 F.2d 414, 416 (D.C. Cir. 1986) (wardens at individual detention facilities, not Parole Commission, were proper custodians even though Commission had power to grant releases; otherwise, custodian could be "any person or entity possessing some sort of power to release" prisoner); Sanders v. Bennett, 148 F.2d 19, 20 (D.C. Cir. 1945) ("proper person to be served [in habeas action] is the warden of the penitentiary *** rather than an official in Washington, D.C. who supervises the warden").

As the Second Circuit has explained in an analogous context:

> [I]t would stretch the meaning of the term ["custodian"] beyond the limits *** to characterize the Parole Board as the 'custodian' of a prisoner who is under the control of a warden and confined in a prison *** At that point the prisoner's relationship with the Parole Board is based solely on the fact that it is the decision-making body which may, in its discretion, authorize a prisoner's release on parole.

Billiteri v. U.S. Board of Parole, 541 F.2d 938, 948 (2d Cir. 1976); see Henderson v. INS, 157 F.3d 106, 126 (2d Cir. 1998) ("Billiteri appears to bar the designation of a higher authority *** as a custodian when a habeas petitioner is under the day-to-day control of another custodian"). Indeed, the Second Circuit has pointedly noted that, although the Attorney General ultimately has control over all prisoners in the federal prison system, "no one seriously suggests that [he] is a proper respondent in prisoner habeas cases." Id. at 126.

Monk v. Secretary of the Navy, 793 F.2d 364 (D.C. Cir. 1986), is also instructive. There, a corporal in the Marine Corps brought a habeas action challenging his court-martial conviction, and named the Secretary of the Navy as the respondent. Id. at 368. He argued that because the Secretary was his "ultimate custodian," he was a proper habeas respondent. Id. at 369. The court of appeals flatly rejected the claim, and held that the "immediate" custodian (the local commandant of the facility in which Monk was incarcerated) was the proper respondent, not the Secretary. Ibid.

Further, as the First Circuit has explained, the very text of Section 2243, which provides that "[t]he writ *** shall be directed to the person having custody of the person detained" (emphasis added), indicates that there is only one proper respondent to a habeas petition – i.e., the immediate custodian:

> Section 2243 does not indicate that a petitioner may choose from among an array of colorable custodians, and there is nothing about the nature of habeas practice that would justify a court in stretching the statute's singular language to encompass so mischievous an interpretation.

Vasquez, 233 F.3d at 693.[3]

Accordingly, President Bush is not Padilla's custodian for habeas purposes. In any event, it is well settled that a court of the United States "has no jurisdiction *** to enjoin the President in the performance of his official duties" or otherwise to compel the

---

[3] ...

President to perform any official act. Franklin v. Massachusetts, 505 U.S. 788, 802–03 (1992) (plurality opinion) (citations omitted); id. at 825 (Scalia, concurring in part and concurring in the judgment).[4]

Nor is the Attorney General Padilla's habeas custodian. Indeed, the Attorney General is in no sense Padilla's custodian at all: as noted, when the President designated Padilla as an enemy combatant, he was transferred out of the control of the Justice Department and into the control of the military.[5]

Secretary Rumsfeld also does not qualify as Padilla's habeas custodian. Again, as the courts (including the Second Circuit and this Court) have repeatedly held, the proper custodian for habeas purposes is the "immediate custodian" – generally the local warden or superintendent – of the facility where a petitioner is detained.[6] That is because the warden has day-to-day control over the petitioner and is the one who can free the prisoner should the writ be granted. See Wang v. Reno, 862 F. Supp, 801, 811–12 (E.D.N.Y. 1994) ("[s]ince the result of an issuance of the writ is a direction to the respondent to "free the body" of the petitioner *** the court issuing the writ must have jurisdiction over the person holding the petitioner"); accord Henderson, 157 F.3d at 122. Although Secretary Rumsfeld may be among those who exercise some degree of control over Padilla, he is not Padilla's immediate custodian, and, hence, is not a proper respondent here.

. . .

B. The Only Proper Respondent Is Outside This Court's Territorial Jurisdiction.

The Court lacks habeas jurisdiction because Commander Marr, the only proper respondent in this case, is not within this Court's territorial jurisdiction. And as the Supreme Court has made clear, "the absence of [the] custodian is fatal to *** jurisdiction." Schlanger v. Seamans, 401 U.S. 487, 489 (1971).[7]

The federal habeas corpus statute contains an express territorial limitation that restricts the jurisdiction of district courts to granting the writ only "within their respective jurisdictions." 28 U.S.C. 2241(a) (emphasis added). Congress wrote the limitation into the habeas statute for several reasons:

> it was thought inconvenient, potentially embarrassing, certainly expensive and on the whole quite unnecessary to provide every judge anywhere with authority to issue the Great Writ on behalf of applicants far distantly removed from the courts whereon they sat.

---

[4] Although the Supreme Court has left open the question whether the President may be ordered to perform a purely "ministerial" duty, 505 U.S. at 802, the relief petitioner seeks – primarily, his release from custody – is far from "ministerial." See Mississippi v. Johnson, 71 U.S. 465, 499 (1866) ("duties [that] must necessarily be performed under the supervision of the President as commander-in-chief" are "in no just sense ministerial" but are "purely executive and political.").

[5] . . .

[6] . . .

[7] Nor are Secretary Rumsfeld and Attorney General Ashcroft within this Court's territorial jurisdiction, either. For purposes of habeas jurisdiction, those officials are "present" only at their official posts in Virginia (at the Pentagon) and Washington, D.C., respectively. See Monk, 793 F.2d at 369 & n.1 (rejecting claim that Secretary of Navy is proper habeas respondent but noting that Pentagon officials, in any event, are located in the Eastern District of Virginia); Demjanjuk v. Meese, 784 F.2d 1114, 1116 (D.C. Cir. 1986) (Bork, J., in chambers) (jurisdiction over Attorney General lies in D.C. Circuit in the "very limited and special circumstances" where location of prisoner was kept confidential). Thus, even if the Court were to find, contrary to settled precedent, that the Attorney General and Secretary are Padilla's habeas custodians, the Court would still lack jurisdiction over them and the petition.

Carbo v. United States, 364 U.S. 611, 617 (1961). Thus, when the Supreme Court considered whether a custodian "must be in the territorial jurisdiction of the District Court," Schlanger, 401 U.S. at 489, it unequivocally answered, "yes." Id. at 491.....

. . .

The Second Circuit's decision in Henderson does not counsel against this understanding of a district court's habeas jurisdiction. There, the Court assumed, without deciding, that a district court would have jurisdiction over a habeas respondent if the state long-arm statute could reach him. See Henderson, 157 F.3d at 123. This assumption was based on a statement in Braden, 410 U.S. at 495, that a custodian could "be reached by service of process." See Henderson, 157 F.3d at 122 (quoting Braden). Braden's reference to service, however, cannot be read to have altered the rule of Schlanger (requiring territorial jurisdiction over the custodian) – and to tacitly allow state long-arm statutes to trump the territorial limitations the federal habeas statute. To the contrary, Braden overruled a portion of Ahrens v. Clark, 325 U.S. 188 (1948), which had held that both the detainee and his custodian had to be within the district court's territorial jurisdiction. Id. at 189–93. While the Court in Braden held that a detainee need not be present in a court's territorial jurisdiction, it did not alter the settled requirement that the custodian be physically present in the district. Indeed, citing Schlanger, it found that the lower court had jurisdiction because the respondent was "properly served in that district." Braden, 410 U.S. at 500 (emphasis added).[8] Thus, Braden did not question, much less eliminate, the well-established principle (reaffirmed only two years earlier in Schlanger) that a habeas court must have territorial jurisdiction over a petitioner's custodian.

Furthermore, the Supreme Court has also explicitly rejected the suggestion that 28 U.S.C. 1391(e) – which permits nationwide service of process on government officers in civil cases – applies in habeas cases. See Schlanger, 401 U.S. at 490 n.4 (Section 1391(e) cannot serve to "exten[d] habeas corpus jurisdiction"); see also Dunne v. Henman, 875 F.2d 244, 248 (9th Cir. 1989) (section 1391(e) "does not extend habeas corpus jurisdiction to persons outside the territorial limits of the district court"). If a federal statute permitting nationwide service on federal officers does not trump the territorial limit on habeas jurisdiction, then a state long-arm statute cannot either.[9]

The proper custodian in this case, Commander Marr, is located at her duty station in Charleston, South Carolina. Thus, the only place where a habeas petition could be filed on Padilla's behalf is South Carolina, not New York.[10]

---

[8] The Court in Braden also embraced the dissenting opinion of Justice Rutledge in Ahrens. See 410 U.S. at 495. There, Justice Rutledge reviewed the history of the habeas statute, and, particularly, the words "within their respective jurisdictions." He concluded that, with this limitation, Congress meant to foreclose district judges from "issu[ing] process against jailers in remote districts" and also to ensure that "process does not run beyond the territorial jurisdiction of the issuing court." 335 U.S. at 204–05; see also id. at 205 (limitation intended to prevent district courts from "issu[ing] process to run through the country *** and thus to bring before them jailers without regard to distance.")

[9] Indeed, a state long-arm statute is invoked by a federal court via Fed. R. Civ. P. 4(e). And the federal rules make clear that they "shall not be construed to extend or limit the jurisdiction of the United States district courts." Fed. R. Civ. P. 82; see also Fed. R. Civ. P. 81(a) (2) (rules of civil procedure inapplicable in habeas cases to extent they would conflict with habeas statute).

[10] Jurisdiction, of course, is not to be confused with venue. And although, as the petition notes (Amend. Pet. ¶14), venue considerations also apply in habeas cases, such considerations do not point to this Court as the proper forum here. In the first place, and contrary to the petition's claim, this Court does not have "unique familiarity with the facts and circumstances of this case." Amend. Pet. ¶14. The matter that brought Padilla initially into this Court's jurisdiction was his arrest on a material witness warrant. That matter – and all the facts and issues that it raised – is now over. Padilla is no longer being detained as a material witness, pursuant to 18 U.S.C. 3144, but as an enemy combatant, pursuant to the laws of war. The petition for habeas corpus, filed after Padilla's transfer from this jurisdiction, challenges Padilla's detention in South Carolina as

CONCLUSION

This Court lacks jurisdiction over this habeas petition because attorney Newman does not have "next friend" standing to bring the case on Padilla's behalf. Moreover, the Court lacks habeas jurisdiction over this petition because the only proper respondent, Commander Marr, is outside this Court's territorial jurisdiction. President Bush, Attorney General Ashcroft, and Secretary Rumsfeld are not proper respondents and, in any event, they, too, are not within the Court's jurisdiction. Accordingly, the Court should dismiss the petition, or, at a minimum, transfer this habeas action to South Carolina.

Attorney Newman's lack of standing would, of course, deprive <u>any</u> court of jurisdiction over the petition. Accordingly, if this Court agrees that Newman lacks standing, it should dismiss the petition. If, however, the Court believes that Newman may maintain the action as Padilla's next friend (or that the next-friend issue may be resolved after transfer by a court with habeas jurisdiction), it should transfer the case to the district court in South Carolina, the only district court with jurisdiction over the proper respondent. See 28 U.S.C. 1406(a), 1631.

. . .

---

an enemy combatant. This is an entirely different case – involving different legal issues and implicating very different policy concerns. And although we agree that the resolution of the case does not require Padilla's presence (see Amend. Pet. ¶14), we also note that the petition elsewhere requests an evidentiary hearing. See id. at 9. However this case may play out in the future with regard to such a hearing, neither the issues implicated by the merits of the petition nor concerns about judicial economy make this district a better forum than the district of South Carolina.

UNITED STATES DISTRICT COURT
SOUTHERN DISTRICT OF NEW YORK
---x

JOSE PADILLA,   :
                                           :
DONNA R. NEWMAN, As Next   :   Petitioners'
Friend of Jose Padilla   :   Reply to Motion To Dismiss
                                           :   Petition For Writ of Habeas Corpus
            Petitioners,   :
                                           :   02 Civ. 4445 (MBM)
      -against-   :
                                           :
GEORGE W. BUSH   :
Ex officio Commander-in-Chief of US   :
Armed Forces   :
                    :   :
                    :   :
DONALD RUMSFELD   :
Secretary of the Defense   :
                                           :
                                           :
                                           :
JOHN ASHCROFT[1]   :
Attorney General   :
U.S. Department of Justice   :
                                           :
                                           :
                                           :
COMMANDER M.A. MARR   :
Consolidated Naval Brig   :
                                           :
                                           :
                                           :
            Respondents.   :
---x

Preliminary Statement

While denying Jose Padilla access to both this court and his counsel, the Government has the temerity to object to Donna R. Newman, Esq., acting as Mr. Padilla's "next friend" to institute this Petition for Writ of Habeas Corpus. It is respectfully submitted, that in light of Mr. Padilla's unavailability, Ms. Newman, who is Mr. Padilla's attorney, who has met with Mr. Padilla numerous times, appeared in court on his behalf, filed motions on his behalf, satisfies all the requirements to act as "next friend."

. . .

Respondent President Bush as Commander in Chief and Secretary of the Defense Rumsfeld, ordered[5] and directed, Padilla's arrest, the transfer of his custody from the

---

[1] Petitioners agree to remove Attorney General Ashcroft as a Respondent from this Petition.

[5] Attorney General Ashcroft in his announcement to the Press on June 10, 2002 referenced an Order issued by President Bush declaring Padilla an "enemy combatant" and which authorized Mr. Padilla's arrest and detention. Counsel has requested a copy of the Order from the Department of Defense, White House Counsel's Office, and the United States Attorney's Office for the Southern District of New York. She was advised that she would not be provided with a copy and would not be permitted to view this Order. At a minimum, this Court should order the government to provide the Court with a copy to be viewed "in camera" and ex parte to enable this Court to ascertain its relevance to the pending motion.

Department of Justice to the Department of Defense, the situs of his detention and the conditions of his detention. Based on the facts and circumstances of this case, Respondents Bush and Rumsfeld are Padilla's custodians. They can deliver the "body" while in fact Commander Marr lacks the authority to do so. Further, all Respondents have and had sufficient contacts to the Southern District of New York, through their activities, the activities of those within their chain of command and through the activities agents acting on their behalf, to make each amendable to process within the Southern District of New York. The Southern District of New York is the proper venue for this Petition, in light of the background of this case and for the convenience of the parties. This Court has jurisdiction over these Respondents and this petition. There is no jurisdictional bar to this Court deciding the merits of the habeas corpus petition.

Furthermore, Padilla's absence from this district and his inability to execute his habeas petition are due entirely to the action of these Respondents. This Court having had jurisdiction originally, in this instance should retain jurisdiction. Accordingly, it is respectfully submitted that the Government's motion to dismiss Padilla's writ of habeas corpus should be denied.

Facts[6]

Jose Padilla is an American citizen by virtue of having been born in Brooklyn, New York. Mr. Padilla was arrested outside of Chicago, Illinois at O'Hare International Airport on May 8, 2002, by agents of the Federal Bureau of Investigation. Mr. Padilla was not arrested on criminal charges, but rather was arrested on a material witness warrant for a grand jury which had been convened in the Southern District of New York. The order which authorized Mr. Padilla's arrest had been signed by the Honorable Michael B. Mukasey, Chief Judge of the United States District Court for the Southern District of New York.

On May 15, 2002, Mr. Padilla was produced in court before Judge Mukasey who assigned Donna R. Newman, Esq., to represent Mr. Padilla. Ms. Newman conferred with her client both when at Court and at the Metropolitan Correctional Center. She met with him on at least nine occasions for a total of approximately eighteen hours. She also met and conferred with the government, represented by United States Attorney's Office for the Southern District of New York about matters relating to her client's detention. She appeared before this Court at least two times with her client. Further, acting as Mr. Padilla's attorney, Ms. Newman filed motions with the Court contesting the legality of Mr. Padilla's detention as a potential grand jury witness. The government filed papers in opposition to the relief Ms. Newman sought for her client. Those motions were scheduled to be heard by this Court on the morning of Tuesday, June 11, 2002.

On Sunday June 9, 2002, before the court could rule on the pending motions, President Bush, in his role as Commander-in-Chief and acting on the advice of Attorney General Ashcroft and Secretary of Defense Rumsfeld, issued an Order finding Mr. Padilla to be an "unlawful combatant". Mr. Padilla, without notice to counsel, was transferred in the Southern District of New York from the custody of the Department of Justice to the custody of the Department of Defense. Mr. Padilla was placed under arrest by the Department of Defense for the purpose of his being interrogated. He was taken to South Carolina and placed in the brig at the Consolidated Naval Base.

The transfer of Mr. Padilla's custody and his arrest in this district was made possible through the efforts, assistance and cooperation of the United States Attorney's Office

---

6 ...

in this district. Among other things, to enable Mr. Padilla to be seized by agents from the Department of Defense, on June 9, 2002, the United States Attorney's Office had their grand jury material witness warrant withdrawn. Ms. Newman, while the afore-mentioned motions were still pending before this Court[7], filed a writ of habeas corpus on June 11, 2002 which was amended on June 20, 2002. The government has refused to respond to the merits of the writ and has brought a motion to dismiss the writ on jurisdictional grounds.

Mr. Padilla remains at the Naval Brig in Charleston, South Carolina. Ms. Newman has been informed that she will not be permitted to meet or communicate by any means with Mr. Padilla by representatives of the Department of Defense and the United States Attorney's Office for the Southern District of New York. Accordingly, Ms. Newman has been blocked from obtaining Mr. Padilla's signature on the petition. Mr. Padilla has not been charged with any offense under either civil or military law.

Other than the Government's unilateral decision to hold Mr. Padilla in Charleston, there is no nexus between South Carolina and this litigation. In other post-September 11th matters, the government has elected to criminally prosecute both John Phillip Walker Lindh (an American citizen taken into custody in Afghanistan) and Zacarias Moussaoui (a French national arrested in Minnesota) within the geographic area of the United States Court of Appeals for the Fourth Circuit. The Government has elected to hold Yaser Esam Hamdi (an American citizen taken into custody in Afghanistan) on a military base that is within the geographic area of the Fourth Circuit Court of Appeals. Now the Government has transferred Mr. Padilla from this district to Charleston, South Carolina which is also in the geographic area of the Fourth Circuit Court of Appeals.

. . .

Respectfully submitted,

_____

Donna R. Newman
Attorney for Jose Padilla

_____

Andrew G. Patel
Attorney for Jose Padilla

---

[7] The Court on June 13, 2002 determined that in light of the withdrawal of the material witness warrant, these motions were moot.

Declaration of Michael H. Mobbs
Special Advisor to the Under Secretary of Defense for Policy

Pursuant to 28 U.S.C. § 1746, I, Michael H. Mobbs, Special Advisor to the

Under Secretary of Defense for Policy, hereby declare that, to the best of my

knowledge, information and belief, and under the penalty of perjury, the following

is true and correct:

1. am a government employee (GS-15) of the U.S. Department of Defense and

    serve as a Special Advisor to the Under Secretary of Defense for Policy. The

    Under Secretary of Defense for Policy is appointed by the President and

    confirmed by the Senate. He is the principal staff assistant and advisor to the

    Secretary and Deputy Secretary of Defense for all matters concerning the

    formulation of national security and defense policy and the integration and

    oversight of DoD policy and plans to achieve national security objectives.

    The Under Secretary of Defense for Policy has directed me to head his

    Detainee Policy Group. Since mid-February 2002, I have been substantially

    involved with matters related to the detention of enemy combatants in the

    current war against the Al Qaeda terrorists and those who support and harbor

    them (including the Taliban).

2. As part of my official duties, I have reviewed government records and reports

    about Jose Padilla (also known as "Abdullah al Muhajir" and "Ibrahim Padilla")

    relevant to the President's June 9, 2002 determination that Padilla is an

    military forces as an enemy combatant.

3. The following information about Padilla's activities with the Al Qaeda terrorist

    network was provided to the President in connection with his June 9, 2002

    determination. This information is derived from multiple intelligence sources,

    including reports of interviews with several confidential sources, two of whom

were detained at locations outside of the United States.[1] The confidential
sources have direct connections with the Al Qaeda terrorist network and claim
to have knowledge of the events described. Certain aspects of these reports
were also corroborated by other intelligence information when available.

4. Padilla was born in New York. He was convicted of murder in Chicago in
approximately 1983 and incarcerated until his eighteenth birthday. In Florida
in 1991, he was convicted of a handgun charge and sent to prison. After his
release from prison, Padilla began referring to himself as Ibrahim Padilla.[2] In
1998, he moved to Egypt and was subsequently known as *I*

Muhajir. In 1999 or 2000 Padilla traveled to Pakistan. He also traveled to
Saudi Arabia and Afghanistan.

5. During his time in the Middle East and Southwest Asia, Padilla has been
closely associated with known members and leaders of the Al Qaeda terrorist
network.

6. While in Afghanistan in 2001, Padilla met with senior Usama Bin Laden
lieutenant Abu Zubaydah. Padilla and an associate approached Zubaydah
with their proposal to conduct terrorist operations within the United States.
Zubaydah directed Padilla and his associate to travel to Pakistan for training
from Al Qaeda operatives in wiring explosives.

---

[1] Based on the information developed by U.S. Intelligence and law enforcement agencies, it is
believed that the two detained confidential sources have been involved with the Al Qaeda terrorist
network. One of the sources has been involved with Al Qaeda for several years and is believed
to have been involved in the terrorist activities of Al Qaeda. The other source is also believed to
have been involved in planning and preparing for terrorist activities of Al Qaeda. It is believed
that these confidential sources have not been completely candid about their association with Al
Qaeda and their terrorist activities. Much of the information from these sources has, however,
been corroborated and proven accurate and reliable. Some information provided by the sources
remains uncorroborated and may be part of an effort to mislead or confuse U.S. officials. One of
the sources, for example, in a subsequent interview with a U.S. law enforcement official recanted
some of the information that he had provided, but most of this information has been
independently corroborated by other sources. In addition, at the time of being interviewed by
U.S. officials, one of the sources was being treated with various types of drugs to treat medical
conditions.

[2] Padilla's use of the name "Ibrahim Padilla" was not included in the information provided to the
President on June 9, 2002.

7. Padilla and his associate conducted research in the construction of a "uranium-enhanced" explosive device. In particular, they engaged in research on this topic at one of the Al Qaeda safehouses in Lahore, Pakistan.

8. Padilla's discussions with Zubaydah specifically included the plan of Padilla and his associate to build and detonate a "radiological dispersal device" (also known as a "dirty bomb") within the United States, possibly in Washington, DC. The plan included stealing radioactive material for the bomb within the United States. The "dirty bomb" plan of Padilla and his associate allegedly was still in the initial planning stages, and there was no specific time set for the operation to occur.

9. In 2002, at Zubaydah's direction,

with senior Al Qaeda operatives to discuss Padilla's involvement and participation in terrorist operations targeting the United States. These discussions included the noted "dirty bomb" plan and other operations including the detonation of explosives in hotel rooms and gas stations.[3] The Al Qaeda officials held several meetings with Padilla. It is believed that Al Qaeda members directed Padilla to return to the United States to conduct reconnaissance and/or other attacks on behalf of Al Qaeda.

10. Although one confidential source stated that he did not believe that Padilla was a "member" of Al Qaeda, Padilla has had significant and extended contacts with senior Al Qaeda members and operatives. As noted, he acted under the direction of Zubaydah and other senior Al Qaeda operatives, received training from Al Qaeda operatives in furtherance of terrorist activities, and was sent to the United States to conduct reconnaissance and/or other attacks on their behalf.

11. Padilla traveled from Pakistan to Chicago via Switzerland and was apprehended by federal officials on May 8, 2002, upon arrival in the United

---

[3] These attacks were to involve multiple, simultaneous attacks on such targets, and also included train stations. The additional facts in this footnote were not included in the information provided to the President on June 9, 2002.

States. Pursuant to court order, Padilla was held by the U.S. Marshals Service as a material witness in a grand jury investigation.

12. On June 9, 2002, George W. Bush, as President of the United States and Commander in Chief of the U.S. armed forces, determined that Jose Padilla is, and was at the time he entered the United States in May 2002, an enemy combatant in the ongoing war against international terrorism, including the Al Qaeda international terrorist organization. A redacted version of the President's determination is attached at Tab 1.

13. The President specifically determined that Padilla engaged in conduct that constituted hostile and war-like acts, including conduct in preparation for acts of international terrorism that had the aim to cause injury to or adverse effects on the United States.

14. The President further determined that Padilla posed a continuing, present and grave danger to the national security of the United States, and that detention of Padilla as an enemy combatant was necessary to prevent him from aiding Al Qaeda in its efforts to attack the United States or its armed forces, other governmental personnel, or citizens.

15. On June 9, 2002, the President directed the Secretary of Defense to detain Padilla as an enemy combatant.

16. On June 9, 2002, acting on the President's direction, the Secretary of Defense ordered the U.S. armed forces to take control of Padilla as an enemy combatant and to hold him at the Naval Consolidated Brig, Charleston, South Carolina.

Michael H. Mobbs

MICHAEL H. MOBBS
Special Advisor to the
Under Secretary of Defense for Policy

Dated: __27__ August 2002

```
UNITED STATES DISTRICT COURT
SOUTHERN DISTRICT OF NEW YORK
- - - - - - - - - - - - - - - - - - - - - - - - - - - - - - - -X
JOSE PADILLA, by                          :
Donna R. Newman, as next friend,          :
                                          :
                    Petitioner,           :  02 Civ.  4445  (MBM)
                                          :
        -against-                         :  OPINION AND ORDER
                                          :
                                          :
GEORGE W. BUSH, DONALD RUMSFELD,          :
and COMMANDER M.A. MARR,                  :
                                          :
                    Respondents.          :
- - - - - - - - - - - - - - - - - - - - - - - - - - - - - - -X
```

. . .

MICHAEL B. MUKASEY, U.S.D.J.

. . .

...[T]he government argues that the lawfulness of Padilla's custody is established by documents already before this court. Padilla argues that the President lacks the authority to detain him under the circumstances present here, including that he is a United States citizen arrested in the United States, and that in any event he must be permitted to consult with counsel.[2] The government has submitted a classified document in camera to be used, if necessary, in aid of deciding whether there exists evidence to justify the order directing that Padilla be detained.

For the reasons set forth below, the parties' applications and motions are resolved as follows: (i) Newman may pursue this petition as next friend to Padilla, and the government's motion to dismiss for lack of standing therefore is denied; (ii) Secretary Rumsfeld is the proper respondent in this case, and this court has jurisdiction over him, as well as jurisdiction to hear this case, and the government's motion to dismiss for lack of jurisdiction, or to transfer to South Carolina, is denied; (iii) the President is authorized under the Constitution and by law to direct the military to detain enemy combatants in the circumstances present here, such that Padilla's detention is not per se unlawful; (iv) Padilla may consult with counsel in aid of pursuing this petition, under conditions that will minimize the likelihood that he can use his lawyers as unwilling intermediaries for the transmission of information to others and may, if he chooses, submit facts and argument to the court in aid of his petition; (v) to resolve the issue of whether Padilla was lawfully detained on the facts present here, the court will examine only whether the President had some evidence to support his finding that Padilla was an enemy combatant, and whether that evidence has been mooted by events subsequent to his detention; the court will not at this time use the document submitted in camera to determine whether the government has met that standard.

---

[2] In addition, two sets of amici curiae have filed briefs. In one brief, the New York State and the National Association of Criminal Defense Lawyers have argued principally that this court has jurisdiction to review Padilla's detention, and that that detention on its current terms is unlawful. In another brief, the American and New York Civil Liberties Union Foundations, and the Center for National Security Studies (collectively "ACLU"), also argue principally that Padilla's detention on its current terms is unlawful.

I. FACTUAL BACKGROUND

The immediate factual and legal predicate for this case lies in the September 11, 2001 attacks on this country, and the government's response. On that date, as is well known, 19 terrorists associated with an organization called al Qaeda hijacked four airplanes, and succeeded in crashing three of them into public buildings they had targeted – one into each of the two towers of the World Trade Center in New York, and one into the Pentagon near Washington, D.C. The World Trade Center towers were destroyed and the Pentagon was seriously damaged. Passengers on the fourth airplane sought to overpower the hijackers, and in so doing prevented that airplane from being similarly used, although it too crashed, in a field in Pennsylvania, and all aboard were killed. In all, more than 3,000 people were killed in that day's coordinated attacks.

On September 14, 2001, by reason of those attacks, the President declared a state of national emergency. On September 18, 2001, Congress passed Public Law 107-40, in the form of a joint resolution that took note of "acts of treacherous violence committed against the United States and its citizens," of the danger such acts posed to the nation's security and foreign policy, and of the President's authority to deter and prevent "acts of international terrorism against the United States." The resolution, entitled "Authorization for Use of Military Force," (the "Joint Resolution") then provided as follows:

> That the President is authorized to use all necessary and appropriate force against those nations, organizations, or persons he determines planned, authorized, committed, or aided the terrorist attacks that occurred on September 11, 2001, or harbored such organizations or persons, in order to prevent any future acts of international terrorism against the United States by such nations, organizations, or persons.

Authorization for Use of Military Force, Pub. Law No. 107-40, §2(a), 115 Stat. 224, 224 (2001).[3] As the term "Public Law" connotes, the President signed the Joint Resolution.

On November 13, 2001, the President signed an order directing that persons whom he determines to be members of al Qaeda, or other persons who have helped or agreed to commit acts of terrorism aimed at this country, or harbored such persons, and who are not United States citizens, will be subject to trial before military tribunals, and will not have recourse to any other tribunal, including the federal and state courts of this country. He specifically cited the Joint Resolution in the preamble to that order. Mil. Order of Nov. 13, 2001, 66 Fed. Reg. 57,833, 57,833 (Nov. 16, 2001).

As previously noted, on May 8, 2002, this court, acting on an application by the Justice Department pursuant to 18 U.S.C. §3144,[4] based on facts set forth in the affidavit of Joseph Ennis, a special agent of the FBI, found that Padilla appeared to have knowledge

---

[3] The Joint Resolution provides also, in section 2(b)(1), that it "is intended to constitute specific statutory authorization within the meaning of section 5(b) of the War Powers Resolution." Authorization for Use of Military Force, Pub. Law No. 107-40, §2(b)(1), 115 Stat. 224, 224 (2001). That resolution was enacted in 1973 over Presidential veto, and purported to limit the President's authority and discretion to commit American troops to actual or potential hostilities without specific Congressional authorization. War Powers Resolution, Pub. Law No. 93-148, 87 Stat. 555 (1973) (codified at 50 U.S.C. §§1541 et seq.). Although President Bush signed the Joint Resolution the day it was passed, he did so while maintaining "the longstanding position of the executive branch regarding the President's constitutional authority to use force, including the Armed Forces of the United States and regarding the constitutionality of the War Powers Resolution." Press Release, Office of the Press Secretary, President Signs Authorization for Use of Military Force Bill (Sept. 18, 2001) (statement by the President), http://www.white house.gov/news/releases/2001/09/20010918-10.html. The constitutionality of the War Powers Resolution is a matter of debate, has never been tested in court – if indeed it could be – and need not be treated in this opinion.

[4] That section provides, in relevant part: "If it appears from an affidavit filed by a party that the testimony of a person is material in a criminal proceeding, and if it is shown that it may become impracticable to secure

of facts relevant to a grand jury investigation into the September 11 attacks. That investigation included an ongoing inquiry into the activities of al Qaeda, an organization believed to be responsible for the September 11 attacks, among others, and to be committed to and involved in planning further attacks. On May 15, 2002, following Padilla's removal from Chicago to New York, where he was detained in the custody of the Justice Department at the Metropolitan Correctional Center ("MCC"), he appeared before this court, and Donna R. Newman, Esq. was appointed to represent him. After Newman had conferred with Padilla at the MCC, and following another court appearance on May 22, 2002, Padilla, represented by Newman, moved to vacate the warrant. The motion to vacate the warrant included an affirmation from Padilla obviously drafted by Newman, albeit one that did not discuss any issue relating to the likelihood that he had information material to a grand jury investigation. (Padilla Affirmation) The motion was fully submitted for decision by June 7.

However, on June 9, 2002, the government notified the court ex parte that it was withdrawing the subpoena. Pursuant to the government's request, the court signed an order vacating the warrant. At that time, the government disclosed that the President had designated Padilla an enemy combatant, on grounds discussed more fully below, and directed the Secretary of Defense, respondent Donald Rumsfeld, to detain Padilla. The government disclosed to the court as well that the Department of Defense would take custody of Padilla forthwith, and transfer him to South Carolina, as in fact happened.

On June 11, 2002, Newman and the government appeared before this court at the time a conference had been scheduled in connection with Padilla's then-pending motion to vacate the material witness warrant. At that time, Newman filed a habeas corpus petition pursuant to 28 U.S.C. §2241[5], later to be amended. In response to an inquiry from the court, the government conceded that after the June 9 Order was signed, Department of Defense personnel took custody of Padilla in this district. (Tr. of 6/11/02 at 7; see also Tr. of 7/31/02 at 17) Newman's petition alleges the facts surrounding Padilla's initial capture and transfer to New York, Newman's activities in connection with representing him, proceedings relating to his motion to vacate the material witness warrant, and his subsequent transfer to South Carolina. (Am. Pet. ¶¶15–22, 25) Newman has averred that she was told she would not be permitted to visit Padilla at the South Carolina facility, or to speak with him; she was told she could write to Padilla, but that he might not receive the correspondence. (Newman Aff. of 9/24/02 ¶8)

In addition to having submitted the above-mentioned affirmation from Padilla in connection with the motion to vacate the material witness warrant, according to the amended petition, it appears that Newman consulted not only with Padilla but also with his family. (Am. Pet. ¶20) No criminal charges have been filed against Padilla.

The President's order, dated June 9, 2002 (the "June 9 Order"), is attached, in redacted form, to the government's dismissal motion, and sets forth in summary fashion

---

the presence of the person by subpoena, a judicial officer may order the arrest of the person and treat the person in accordance with the provisions of section 3142 of this title." 18 U.S.C. §3144 (2000).

[5] That section provides, in pertinent part:

> (a) Writs of habeas corpus may be granted by . . . the district courts . . . within their respective jurisdictions.
>
> . . . .
>
> (c) The writ of habeas corpus shall not extend to a prisoner unless–
>
> > (1) He is in custody under or by color of the authority of the United States . . . ; or
> >
> > . . . .
> >
> > (3) He is in custody in violation of the Constitution or laws or treaties of the United States[.]

28 U.S.C. §2241 (2000).

the President's findings with respect to Padilla. Attached as well is a declaration of Michael H. Mobbs ("Mobbs Declaration"), who is employed by the Department of Defense. The Mobbs Declaration sets forth a redacted version of facts provided to the President as the basis for the conclusions set forth in the June 9 Order. In addition to the redacted summary contained in the Mobbs Declaration, the government has submitted, under seal, an unredacted version of information provided to the President ("Sealed Mobbs Declaration"). As set forth more fully below, the government has argued that the Mobbs Declaration is sufficient to establish the correctness of the President's findings contained in the June 9 Order, although it has made the Sealed Mobbs Declaration available to the court to remedy any perceived insufficiency in the Mobbs Declaration. However, the government has maintained that the Sealed Mobbs Declaration must remain confidential. The government has taken the position that it would withdraw the Sealed Mobbs Declaration sooner than disclose its contents to defense counsel. (Respondents' Resp. to Petitioners' Supplemental Mem. at 11).

The June 9 Order is addressed to the Secretary of Defense, and includes seven numbered paragraphs setting forth the President's conclusion that Padilla is an enemy combatant, and, in summary form, the basis for that conclusion, including that Padilla: is "closely associated with al Qaeda," engaged in "hostile and war-like acts" including "preparation for acts of international terrorism" directed at this country, possesses information that would be helpful in preventing al Qaeda attacks, and represents "a continuing, present and grave danger to the national security of the United States." (June 9 Order ¶¶2–5) In addition, the June 9 Order directs Secretary Rumsfeld to detain Padilla. (Id. ¶6)

The Mobbs Declaration states that Padilla was born in New York and convicted in Chicago, before he turned 18, of murder. Released from prison after he turned 18, Padilla was convicted in Florida in 1991 of a weapons charge. After his release from prison on that charge, Padilla moved to Egypt, took the name Abdullah al Muhajir, and is alleged to have traveled also to Saudi Arabia and Afghanistan. (Mobbs Decl. ¶4) In 2001, while in Afghanistan, Padilla is alleged to have approached "senior Usama Bin Laden lieutenant Abu Zubaydeh" (id. ¶6) and proposed, among other things, stealing radioactive material within the United States so as to build, and detonate a "'radiological dispersal device' (also known as a 'dirty bomb') within the United States" (id. ¶8). Padilla is alleged to have done research on such a project at an al Qaeda safehouse in Lahore, Pakistan, and to have discussed that and other proposals for terrorist acts within the United States with al Qaeda officials he met in Karachi, Pakistan, on a trip he made at the behest of Abu Zubaydah. (See id. ¶¶7–9) One of the unnamed confidential sources referred to in the Mobbs Declaration said he did not believe Padilla was actually a member of al Qaeda, but Mobbs emphasizes that Padilla had "extended contacts with senior Al Qaeda members and operatives" and that he "acted under the direction of [Abu] Zubaydah and other senior Al Qaeda operatives, received training from Al Qaeda operatives in furtherance of terrorist activities, and was sent to the United States to conduct reconnaissance and/or conduct other attacks on their behalf." (Id. ¶10)

As mentioned above, Padilla was taken into custody on the material witness warrant on May 8, in Chicago, where he landed after traveling, with one or more stops, from Pakistan. (Id. ¶11)

Dealing with the contents of the Sealed Mobbs Declaration is problematic. Padilla argues that I should not consider it at all, at least unless his lawyers have access to it and, he argues, he has an opportunity to respond to its contents. The government argues that I must not disclose it, but that I need not consider it because the redacted version of what the President was told, as set forth in the Mobbs Declaration, is enough to justify the June 9 Order, unless for some reason I think otherwise, in which case I am invited to examine it in camera. Although neither the government nor Padilla mentions the point, the contents of the Sealed Mobbs Declaration could relate to another issue – whether, as the government claims, there is a reasonably cognizable risk to national security that could result from permitting Padilla to consult with counsel.

Although Padilla had been under arrest pursuant to the material witness warrant since May 8, his arrest was announced on June 10, after he was taken into Defense Department custody, by the President and by Attorney General John Ashcroft, who made his announcement during a trip to Moscow. See James Risen & Philip Shenon, Traces of Terror: The Investigation; U.S. Says it Halted Qaeda Plot to Use Radioactive Bomb, N.Y. Times, June 11, 2002, at A1.

Secretary Rumsfeld was questioned at a press briefing on Wednesday, June 12, during a trip to Doha, Qatar, about how close he thought Padilla and others were to being able to build a "dirty bomb," and whether he thought Padilla would be "court martialled."[6] News Briefing, Department of Defense (June 12, 2002), 2002 WL 22026773. In response, Secretary Rumsfeld described Padilla as "an individual who unquestionably was involved in terrorist activities against the United States." Id. He said that Padilla "will be held by the United States government through the Department of Defense and be questioned." Id. He then added that in order to protect the United States and its allies, "one has to gather as much [ ] intelligence information as is humanly possible." Id. Secretary Rumsfeld then summarized as follows how Padilla would be dealt with:

> Here is an individual who has intelligence information, and it is, in answer to the last part of your question – will be submitted to a military court, or something like that – our interest really in his case is not law enforcement, it is not punishment because he was a terrorist or working with the terrorists. Our interest at the moment is to try and find out everything he knows so that hopefully we can stop other terrorist acts.

Id.

Secretary Rumsfeld distinguished as follows the government's handling of Padilla from its handling of the usual case of one charged with breaking the law:

> It seems to me that the problem in the United States is that we have – we are in a certain mode. Our normal procedure is that if somebody does something unlawful, illegal against our system of government, that the first thing we want to do is apprehend them, then try them in a court and then punish them. In this case that is not our first interest.
>
> Our interest is to – we are not interested in trying him at the moment; we are not interested in punishing him at the moment. We are interested in finding out what he knows. Here is a person who unambiguously was interested in radiation weapons and terrorist activity, and was in league with al Qaeda. Now our job, as responsible government officials, is to do everything possible to find out what that person knows, and see if we can't help our country or other countries.

Id.

Secretary Rumsfeld offered anecdotal evidence to justify applying to Padilla procedures different from those applied to prisoners arrested in conventional cases:

> If you think about it, we found some material in Kandahar that within a week was used – information, intelligence information – that was used to prevent a[t] least three

---

[6] This was apparently an inartful reference to trial before a military tribunal, a procedure the President has already declared he will not apply to American citizens. See supra p. 6.

terrorist attacks in Singapore – against a U.S. ship, against a U.S. facility and against a Singaporean facility.

Now if someone had said when we found that information or person, well now let's us arrest the person and let's start the process of punishing that person for having done what he had did, we never would have gotten that information. People would have died.

So I think what our country and other countries have to think of is, what is your priority today? And given the power of weapons and given the number of terrorists that exist in the world, our approach has to [be] to try to protect the American people, and provide information to friendly countries and allies, and protect deployed forces from those kind of attacks.

I think the American people understand that, and that notwithstanding the fact that some people are so locked into the other mode that they seem not able to understand it, I suspect that . . . the American people will.

Id. Secretary Rumsfeld's quoted statements appear to show both his familiarity with the circumstances of Padilla's detention, and his personal involvement in the handling of Padilla's case.

It is not disputed that Padilla is held incommunicado, and specifically that he has not been permitted to consult with Newman or any other counsel.

Although the immediate predicate for this case lies in the events of September 11 and their consequences, that date did not mark the first violent act by al Qaeda directed against the United States. An indictment styled United States v. Bin Laden, No. 98 Cr. 1023, charged defendants allegedly affiliated with that organization in connection with the August 1998 bombing of United States embassies in Nairobi, Kenya and Dar-Es-Salaam, Tanzania. According to that indictment, which was tried to a guilty verdict in the summer of 2001, al Qaeda emerged in 1989, under the leadership of Usama Bin Laden. See United States v. Bin Laden, 92 F.Supp. 2d 225, 228–29 (S.D.N.Y. 2000). As summarized by Judge Sand, who presided at that trial, the indictment portrayed al Qaeda as a "vast, international terrorist network" that functioned on its own and in cooperation with like-minded groups to oppose the United States through the use of "violent, terrorist tactics." Id. "From time to time, according to the Indictment, Bin Laden would issue rulings on Islamic law, called 'fatwahs,' which purported to justify al Qaeda's violent activities." Id. at 229. Bin Laden has declared a "jihad" or holy war against the United States. Id. at 230.

In addition to the September 11 attack and the 1998 bombings in Kenya and Tanzania, al Qaeda is believed, at a minimum, to be responsible for the October 2000 bombing of the U.S.S. Cole that killed 17 U.S. sailors, and to have participated in the October 1993 attack on U.S. military personnel serving in Somalia that killed 18 soldiers. (Id.)

On October 8, 1999, al Qaeda was designated by the Secretary of State as a foreign terrorist organization, pursuant to section 219 of the Immigration and Nationality Act. See Designation of Foreign Terrorist Organizations, 64 Fed. Reg. 55,112 (1999). It has also been similarly designated by the Secretary of State under the International Emergency Economic Powers Act. See Additional Designations of Terrorism-Related Blocked Persons, 66 Fed. Reg. 54,404 (2001).

II. NEWMAN'S STANDING AS NEXT FRIEND

The first of the several issues presented by this petition concerns Newman's standing to assert a claim as next friend. The statute, 28 U.S.C. §2242 (2000), provides that an application for relief thereunder "shall be in writing signed and verified by the person for whose relief it is intended or by someone acting in his behalf." The Supreme Court has explained that this provision was intended to permit a third party to sue as next friend when a prisoner is unable to seek relief himself. See Whitmore v. Arkansas, 495 U.S. 149, 162 (1990) ("Most frequently, 'next friends' appear in court on behalf of detained prisoners who are unable, usually because of mental incompetence or inaccessibility, to seek relief themselves."). . . .

. . .

. . . Here, Newman had a preexisting relationship with Padilla that involved directly his apprehension and confinement. She had conferred with him over a period of weeks in aid of an effort to end that confinement. She submitted at least one affidavit that he signed, and was engaged in attacking the legal basis of his confinement when he was taken into custody by the Defense Department. She is at once the person most aware of his wishes in this case and the person best suited to try to achieve them. It is of no significance whatever that when she and Padilla formed their relationship he was in the custody of the Justice Department and now he is in the custody of a different executive department. The legal issues may have changed, but the nature of the relationship between Newman and her client has not.

Not only does Newman have a significant and relevant relationship with Padilla, but she appears also to have conferred with Padilla's relatives. (See Am. Pet. ¶20 ("As an additional part of her representation of Mr. Padilla, Petitioner Donna R. Newman . . . consulted with both members of Mr. Padilla's family and representatives of the Government. She continues to consult with the Government and Mr. Padilla's family in her role as his attorney.")) She is certainly neither an "intruder" nor an "uninvited meddler." Whitmore, 495 U.S. at 164.

Despite the government's casual suggestion that some other member of Padilla's family might serve as a next friend in this case (Mot. to Dismiss Am. Pet. at 10; Respondents' Reply in Supp. of Mot. to Dismiss Am. Pet. at 7–8), there is no indication here that any other member of Padilla's family, unlike the detainee's father in Hamdi, wishes to assume that role in place of Newman. . . .

. . .

Newman may act as next friend to Padilla here.

III. THIS COURT'S JURISDICTION

The government argues as well that this action must be dismissed, or transferred to the District of South Carolina because the only proper respondent in a case such as this is Padilla's custodian; Padilla's only custodian is Marr, the commander of the brig in South Carolina where Padilla is housed; and she is not within this court's jurisdiction. The government has moved to dismiss the petition against respondents other than Marr. For the reasons set forth below, that motion is granted with respect to the President and, mea sponte, as to Commander Marr, but is denied as to Secretary Rumsfeld.

The government's jurisdictional argument raises subsidiary issues: who is the proper respondent in a case such as this, whether this court has jurisdiction over that respondent, and whether this case should be transferred to South Carolina.

A.   Who Is A Proper Respondent?

As the government would have it, there is only one proper respondent to a habeas corpus petition, and that is the detainee's "immediate, not ultimate, custodian." (Mot. to Dismiss Am. Pet. at 11) The government points to language in 28 U.S.C. §2242 directing that a petitioner "shall allege...the name of the person who has custody over him," as well as language in 28 U.S.C. §2243, requiring that a writ or order to show cause "shall be directed to the person having custody of the person detained," and providing that, "the person to whom the writ is directed shall be required to produce at the hearing the body of the person detained," and argues, citing Vasquez v. Reno, 233 F.3d 688 (1st Cir. 2000), that this language "indicates that there is only one proper respondent to a habeas petition," id. at 693.

It is certainly true that in the usual habeas corpus case brought by a federal prisoner, courts have held consistently that the proper respondent is the warden of the prison where the prisoner is held, not the Attorney General. See, e.g., Sanders v. Bennett, 148 F.2d 19, 20 (D.C. Cir. 1945) ("But the Attorney General is not the person directly responsible for the operation of our federal penitentiaries. He is a supervising official rather than a jailer. For that reason, the proper person to be served in the ordinary case is the warden of the penitentiary in which the prisoner is confined rather than an official in Washington, D.C., who supervises the warden."). The government cites numerous cases to the same effect. (See Mot. to Dismiss Am. Pet. at 15 n.6) Similarly, as a general rule, the proper respondent to a petition brought by a military prisoner who challenges a court martial conviction is the warden of the facility where he is held. The government cites, for example, Monk v. Secretary of the Navy, 793 F.2d 364 (D.C. Cir. 1986), where the Court held "that for purposes of the federal habeas corpus statute, jurisdiction is proper only in the district in which the immediate, not the ultimate, custodian is located," id. at 369.

However, what makes the usual case usual is that the petitioner is serving a sentence, and the list of those other than the warden who are responsible for his confinement includes only people who have played particular and discrete roles in confining him, notably the prosecuting attorney and the sentencing judge, and who no longer have a substantial and ongoing role in his continued confinement. The warden becomes the respondent of choice almost by default. As discussed below, this is not the usual case.

. . .

Of the particular facts present here, the one that seems to me to bear most directly on the issue of who is a proper respondent is the personal involvement of the Cabinet-level official named as a respondent in the matter at hand. It was Secretary Rumsfeld who was charged by the President in the June 9 Order with detaining Padilla; it was plainly Secretary Rumsfeld who, in following that order, sent Defense Department personnel into this District to take custody of Padilla; it could only have been Secretary Rumsfeld, or his designee, who determined that Padilla would be sent to the brig in South Carolina, as opposed to a brig or stockade elsewhere; and, based on his own statements quoted above, see supra pp. 13–15, it would appear to be Secretary Rumsfeld who decides when and whether all that can be learned from Padilla has been learned, and, at least in part, when and whether the danger he allegedly poses has passed. This level of personal involvement by a Cabinet-level officer in the matter at hand is, so far as I can tell, unprecedented. Certainly, neither side, and no amicus, has cited a case even remotely similar in this respect. How "limited," Demjanjuk [v. Meese, 784 F.2d 1114,] 1116 [(D.C. Cir. 1986)], these circumstances may be – that is, in how many other cases, if any, the Secretary of Defense may have such personal involvement – I know not. However, when viewed in comparison to past cases, the circumstances present here seem at least "very special." Id. On these facts, the Secretary of Defense is the proper respondent.

As noted, Padilla has also sued the President. However, there are at least two reasons why the President should be dismissed as a party: first, Padilla does not seem to be seeking relief from the President; further, based on the authority cited below, the question of whether the President can be sued in this case raises issues this court should avoid if at all possible, and it is certainly possible to avoid them here.

. . .

. . . [T]he government has cited persuasive authority to the effect that this court has no power to direct the President to perform an official act. (Mot. to Dismiss Am. Pet. at 14) The relevant considerations are set forth in Franklin v. Massachusetts, 505 U.S. 788 (1992), quoted below, where the plurality reversed a district court injunction directing the President to recalculate the number of representatives of the State of Massachusetts, and reasoned as follows:

> While injunctive relief against executive officials like the Secretary of Commerce is within the courts' power, see Youngstown Sheet & Tube Co. v. Sawyer, supra, the District Court's grant of injunctive relief against the President himself is extraordinary, and should have raised judicial eyebrows. We have left open the question whether the President might be subject to a judicial injunction requiring the performance of a purely "ministerial" duty, Mississippi v. Johnson, 4 Wall. 475, 498–499 (1867), and we have held that the President may be subject to a subpoena to provide information relevant to an ongoing criminal prosecution, United States v. Nixon, 418 U.S. 683, 694 (1974), but in general "this court has no jurisdiction of a bill to enjoin the President in the performance of his official duties." Mississippi v. Johnson, supra, 4 Wall., at 501. At the threshold, the District Court should have evaluated whether injunctive relief against the President was available, and, if not, whether appellees' injuries were nonetheless redressable.
>
> For purposes of establishing standing, however, we need not decide whether injunctive relief against the President was appropriate because we conclude that the injury alleged is likely to be redressed by declaratory relief against the Secretary alone.

Id. at 802–03. . . . .

Although petitioner has named Commander Marr as a respondent, he and amici New York and National Criminal Defense Lawyers argue that she is not a necessary respondent in this case because she takes her orders from Secretary Rumsfeld and, indirectly, from President Bush, and cannot produce Padilla in violation of those orders without subjecting herself to a court martial. (Petitioners' Reply to Mot. to Dismiss Am. Pet. at 22–23) The government responds by pointing out that, "[n]o warden of any penal facility possesses independent power to release a prisoner, yet wardens are universally designated as the proper custodians in prisoner habeas cases." (Respondents' Reply in Supp. of Mot. to Dismiss Am. Pet. at 18) This debate now seems beside the point. I have already determined that Secretary Rumsfeld is a proper respondent, and there is nothing to indicate that he cannot or would not direct Commander Marr to obey any lawful order of this court, if necessary. Accordingly, the petition will be dismissed also as to Commander Marr.

B.   Territorial Jurisdiction

The habeas corpus statute, 28 U.S.C. §2241(a) (2000), permits the writ to be granted by district courts "within their respective jurisdictions." The government argues that this phrase operates to limit the jurisdiction of the court to grant the writ, beyond any limits otherwise imposed by the Federal Rules of Civil Procedure, and requires, at a minimum, that the respondent be physically present within this District in order for the court to grant relief. (Mot. to Dismiss at 17; Respondents' Reply in Supp. of Mot. to Dismiss Am. Pet. at 22) However, for the reasons set forth below, the government's reading of the statute is inconsistent with governing authority, and this court may grant relief under the statute if relief is otherwise warranted.

The subject phrase – "within their respective jurisdictions" – was read initially by the Supreme Court in Ahrens v. Clark, 335 U.S. 188 (1948), to require that a petitioner be physically present within the geographic boundaries of the district before a petition could be heard. However, the Court did away with that requirement in Braden v. 30th Judicial Circuit Court, 410 U.S. 484 (1973), where it held that a prisoner confined in an Alabama state prison following a felony conviction could seek habeas corpus relief in Kentucky to attack an indictment pending there, reasoning that in enforcing a Kentucky detainer, the Alabama warden was acting simply as the agent of the state of Kentucky, which was the real custodian. The Court said:

> Read literally, the language of §2241(a) requires nothing more than that the court issuing the writ have jurisdiction over the custodian. So long as the custodian can be reached by service of process, the court can issue a writ "within its jurisdiction" requiring that the prisoner be brought before the court for a hearing on his claim, or requiring that he be released outright from custody, even if the prisoner himself is confined outside the court's territorial jurisdiction.

Id. at 495. In Henderson v. INS, 157 F.3d 106 (2d Cir. 1998), the Second Circuit relied on Braden for the proposition that a New York district court would have jurisdiction to hear the §2241 petitions of detained aliens so long as it had jurisdiction over the petitioners' custodian through New York's long-arm statute, N.Y. C.P.L.R. §302(a) (1) (McKinney 1990): "A court has personal jurisdiction in a habeas case 'so long as the custodian can be reached by service of process.'" Id. at 122 (quoting Braden, 410 U.S. at 495)....

. . .

...[S]everal district courts in this Circuit have held that if a respondent can be reached through the forum state's long-arm statute, the court has jurisdiction to hear the petition, see, e.g., Barton v. Ashcroft, 152 F. Supp. 2d 235, 239 (D. Conn. 2001); Perez v. Reno, No. 97 Civ. 6712, 2000 WL 686369, at *3 (S.D.N.Y. May 25, 2000); as has a district court in the Sixth Circuit, see Roman v. Ashcroft, 162 F. Supp. 2d 755, 758 (N.D. Ohio 2001).

. . .

C.   Personal Jurisdiction

The question of whether New York's long-arm statute, N.Y. C.P.L.R. §302(a) (1) (McKinney 1990), reaches Secretary Rumsfeld is not complex. That section permits a court in New York to exercise personal jurisdiction, "[a]s to a cause of action arising from any of the acts enumerated" therein, "over any non-domiciliary . . . who in person or through an agent . . . transacts any business within the state." Id. The statute's "reference to 'business' is read broadly as 'purposeful activities,' without any limitation to commercial transactions." Perez, 2000 WL 686369, at *3 (citing Madden v. International Ass'n of Heat and Frost Insulators and Asbestos Workers, 889 F. Supp. 707, 710 (S.D.N.Y. 1995)). Section 302(a) (1) is a "single act statute": only one transaction is needed to confer jurisdiction, so long as the defendant's activities were purposeful and there is a substantial relationship between those activities and the claim in suit. See Kreutter v. McFadden Oil Corp., 71 N.Y.2d 460, 467, 527 N.Y.S.2d 195, 198–99 (1988). Here, Secretary Rumsfeld was directed by the President on June 9 to take custody of Padilla, and, as noted, the government has acknowledged that agents of the Department of Defense came into this district that day and did so. (Tr. of 6/11/02 at 7; see also Tr. of 7/31/02 at 17) That conduct, through agents, is sufficient to confer jurisdiction over Secretary Rumsfeld. There is no denial of due process in finding personal jurisdiction under these circumstances.

D.   Transfer to South Carolina

The government has moved in the alternative to transfer this case to the District of South Carolina. The principal arguments for transfer relate to issues already covered – principally, who is the proper respondent and whether this court has jurisdiction over that respondent and otherwise can hear this case. Those issues have been resolved in a way that favors keeping the case here.

Further, Padilla's lawyers are here, and Newman was here working to secure his release before he was taken to South Carolina. As a result of his having sent his agents into this district to take custody of Padilla, the Secretary can be reached through process issued by this court. Thus, he too is, in a legal if not quite a physical sense, here. Commander Marr is not here, but for reasons already explained there is no need that she be present in the jurisdiction where the action is pending. For current purposes, the Secretary will suffice. It may be, as set forth below, that it will be necessary for counsel to confer briefly with Padilla, which would entail a trip to South Carolina. However, as between taking a brief trip to South Carolina to confer with their client, and litigating the case in South Carolina, the convenience of counsel is served by keeping the case here. Insofar as the above cases suggest that considerations of convenience and practicality are relevant, see Henderson, 157 F.3d at 122, those considerations are served by keeping the case here. The government's motion to transfer the case to South Carolina therefore is denied.

IV. THE LAWFULNESS OF PADILLA'S DETENTION

The basic question dividing the parties is whether Padilla is lawfully detained. Like the question of whether this court has jurisdiction, that basic question unfolds into subsidiary questions: Does the President have the authority to designate as an enemy combatant an American citizen captured on American soil, and, through the Secretary of Defense, to detain him for the duration of armed conflict with al Qaeda? If so, can the President exercise that authority without violating 18 U.S.C. §4001(a),[9] which bars the detention of American citizens "except pursuant to an Act of Congress"? 18 U.S.C. §4001(a) (2000). If so, by whatever standard this court must apply – itself a separate issue – is the evidence adduced by the government sufficient to justify the detention of Padilla? As was true of the questions underlying the issue of jurisdiction, each of those questions subsumes its own set of questions.

---

[9] Padilla argues also that his detention by the military violates the Posse Comitatus Act, codified at 18 U.S.C. §1385. That statute makes it unlawful to use the military "as a posse comitatus or otherwise to execute the laws." First, it is questionable whether that statute is enforceable in a habeas corpus proceeding to secure release from custody. Cf. Robinson v. Overseas Military Sales Corp., 21 F.3d 502, 511 (2d Cir. 1994) (no private right of action to enforce Posse Comitatus Act). Moreover, the statute bars use of the military in civilian law enforcement. See United States v. Mullin, 178 F.3d 334, 342 (5th Cir. 1999) ("The [Posse Comitatus] Act is designed to restrict military involvement in civilian law enforcement."). Padilla is not being detained by the military in order to execute a civilian law or for violating a civilian law, notwithstanding that his alleged conduct may in fact violate one or more such laws. He is being detained in order to interrogate him about the unlawful organization with which he is said to be affiliated and with which the military is in active combat, and to prevent him from becoming reaffiliated with that organization. Therefore, his detention by the military does not violate the Posse Comitatus Act.

For the reasons set forth below, the answer to the first two of those questions is yes; a definitive answer to the third of those questions must await a further submission from Padilla, should he choose to make one, although the court will examine only whether there was some evidence to support the President's finding, and whether that evidence has been mooted by events subsequent to Padilla's detention.

A.   The President's Authority To Order That Padilla Be Detained As An Enemy Combatant

Neither Padilla nor any of the amici denies directly the authority of the President to order the seizure and detention of enemy combatants in a time of war. Rather, they seek to distinguish this case from cases in which the President may make such an order on the grounds that this is not a time of war, and therefore the President may not use his powers as Commander in Chief or apply the laws of war to Padilla, and that Padilla in any event must be treated differently because he is an American citizen captured on American soil where the courts are functioning.

The claim by petitioner and the amici that this is not a time of war has two prongs: First, because Congress did not declare war on Afghanistan, the only nation state against which United States forces have taken direct action, the measures sanctioned during declared wars, principally in Ex Parte Quirin, 317 U.S. 1 (1942), discussed below, are not available here. Second, because the current conflict is with al Qaeda, which is essentially an international criminal organization that lacks clear corporeal definition, the conflict can have no clear end, and thus the detention of enemy combatants is potentially indefinite and therefore unconstitutional. For the reasons discussed below, neither prong of the argument withstands scrutiny.

The first prong of the argument – that we are not in a war and that only Congress can declare war – does not engage the real issue in this case, which concerns what powers the President may exercise in the present circumstances. Even assuming that a court can pronounce when a "war" exists, in the sense in which that word is used in the Constitution, cf. Bas v. Tingy, 4 U.S. (4 Dall.) 37, 42 (1800) (determining whether France, with which the United States had engaged in an undeclared naval war, was an "enemy" within the meaning of a prize statute, but noting that whether there was a war in a constitutional sense was irrelevant: "Besides, it may be asked, why should the rate of salvage be different in such a war as the present, from the salvage in a war more solemn [i.e., declared] or general?"), a formal declaration of war is not necessary in order for the executive to exercise its constitutional authority to prosecute an armed conflict – particularly when, as on September 11, the United States is attacked. In The Prize Cases, 67 U.S. (2 Black) 635 (1862), the Supreme Court rejected a challenge to the President's authority to impose a blockade on the secessionist states – an act of war – when there had been no declaration of war. The Court acknowledged that the President "has no power to initiate or declare a war." Id. at 668. However, the Court recognized also that "war may exist without a declaration on either side," id., and that when the acts of another country impose a war on the United States, the President "does not initiate that war, but is bound to accept the challenge without waiting for any special legislative authority," id. The Court made it plain that what military measures were necessary was a political and not a judicial decision: "Whether the President in fulfilling his duties, as Commander-in-chief, in suppressing an insurrection, has met with such armed hostile resistance, and a civil war of such alarming proportions as will compel him to accord to them the character of belligerents, is a question to be decided by him, and this Court must be governed by the decisions and acts of the political department of the Government to which this power was entrusted." Id. at 670. It was the President, and not the Court, who:

> must determine what degree of force the crisis demands. The proclamation of blockade is itself official and conclusive evidence to the Court that a state of war existed which demanded and authorized a recourse to such a measure, under the circumstances peculiar to the case.

Id. Here, I agree completely with Judge Silberman who, after examining and quoting from The Prize Cases, wrote as follows:

> I read the Prize Cases to stand for the proposition that the President has independent authority to repel aggressive acts by third parties even without specific congressional authorization, and courts may not review the level of force selected.

Campbell v. Clinton, 203 F.3d 19, 27 (D.C.Cir. 2000) (Silberman, J., concurring); see also Johnson v. Eisentrager, 339 U.S. 763, 789 (1950) ("Certainly it is not the function of the Judiciary to entertain private litigation . . . which challenges the legality, wisdom, or the propriety of the Commander-in-Chief in sending our armed forces abroad or to any particular region."); Freeborn v. The Protector, 79 U.S. (12 Wall.) 700, 702 (1871) (treating executive proclamations as conclusive evidence of when the Civil War began and ended); Martin v. Mott, 25 U.S. (12 Wheat.) 19, 30 (1827) (Story, J.) ("We are all of opinion, that the authority to decide whether the exigency has arisen, belongs exclusively to the President, and that his decision is conclusive upon all other persons.").

The conclusion that the President may exercise his powers as Commander in Chief without a declaration of war is borne out not only by legal precedent, but also by even the briefest contemplation of our history. When one considers the sheer number of military campaigns undertaken during this country's history, declarations of war are the exception rather than the rule, beginning with the undeclared but Congressionally authorized naval war against France in the 1790's referred to in Bas v. Tingy, cited above. Taking into account only the modern era, the last declared war was World War II. Since then, this country has fought the Korean War, the Viet Nam War, the Persian Gulf War, and the Kosovo bombing campaign, as well as other military engagements in Lebanon, Haiti, Grenada and Somalia, to cite a random and by no means exhaustive list, with no appellate authority holding that a declaration of war was necessary. When confronted with challenges to the Viet Nam War, several appellate courts held specifically that no declaration of war was necessary. See, e.g., Mitchell v. Laird, 488 F.2d 611, 613–14 (D.C. Cir. 1973); Massachusetts v. Laird, 451 F.2d 26, 31–32 (1st Cir. 1971); Orlando v. Laird, 443 F.2d 1039, 1043 (2d Cir. 1971).

Further, even if Congressional authorization were deemed necessary, the Joint Resolution, passed by both houses of Congress, authorizes the President to use necessary and appropriate force in order, among other things, "to prevent any future acts of international terrorism against the United States," and thereby engages the President's full powers as Commander in Chief. Authorization for Use of Military Force §2(a).

The laws of war themselves, which the President has invoked as to Padilla, apply regardless of whether or not a war has been declared. What is sometimes referred to as the Third Geneva Convention – Geneva Convention Relative to the Treatment of Prisoners of War ("GPW"), Aug. 12, 1949, 6 U.S.T. 3316, 75 U.N.T.S. 135, to which the United States is a party and which therefore under the Supremacy Clause has the force of domestic law,[10] states that it applies, "to all cases of declared war or any other state of armed conflict." GPW, art. 2.

The question of when the conflict with al Qaeda may end is one that need not be addressed. So long as American troops remain on the ground in Afghanistan and Pakistan in combat with and pursuit of al Qaeda fighters, there is no basis for contradicting the President's repeated assertions that the conflict has not ended. See Ludecke v. Watkins, 335 U.S. 160, 167–69 (1948) (deferring to the President's position that a state of war continued to exist despite Germany's surrender to the Allies). At some point in the future, when operations against al Qaeda fighters end, or the operational capacity of al Qaeda is effectively destroyed, there may be occasion to debate the legality of continuing to hold prisoners based on their connection to al Qaeda, assuming such prisoners continue to be held at that time. See id. at 169 ("Whether and when it would be open to this Court to find that a war though merely formally kept alive had in fact ended, is a question too fraught with gravity even to be adequately formulated when not compelled.").

To the extent petitioner and the amici are suggesting that because the period of Padilla's detention is, at this moment, indefinite, it is therefore perpetual, and therefore illegal, the argument is illogical. Moreover, insofar as the argument assumes that indefinite confinement of one not convicted of a crime is per se unconstitutional, that assumption is simply wrong. In Kansas v. Hendricks, 521 U.S. 346 (1997), the Court upheld Kansas's Sexually Violent Predator Act, providing for civil commitment of those who, due to "mental abnormality" or "personality disorder" are likely to commit sexually predatory acts. Rejecting the argument that the statute imposed criminal sanctions in the guise of a civil remedy, the Court noted that "commitment under the Act does not implicate either of the two primary objectives of criminal punishment: retribution or deterrence." Id. at 361–62. The Court found that the statute was not retributive "because it does not affix culpability for prior criminal conduct," id. at 362, and that it was not intended as a deterrent because the targets of the statute were "unlikely to be deterred by the threat of confinement," id. at 362–63. See also United States v. Salerno, 481 U.S. 739, 748 (1987) ("We have repeatedly held that the Government's regulatory interest in community safety can, in appropriate circumstances, outweigh an individual's liberty interest. For example, in times of war and insurrection, when society's interest is at its peak, the Government may detain individuals whom the Government believes to be dangerous."); Moyer v. Peabody, 212 U.S. 78, 84 (1909) (upholding the detention of a union president without charge during an insurrection, reasoning: "Such arrests are not necessarily for punishment but are by way of precaution, to prevent the exercise of hostile power"). To be sure, the standard of proof in some of those cases may well have been higher than the standard ultimately will be found to be in this case, but the point is that there is no per se ban.

The Court recently raised constitutional doubts as to the permissible length of preventive detention when it considered a case involving aliens awaiting deportation, and therefore read the governing statute to limit such detention to the time reasonably necessary to secure the alien's removal, with six months presumed as a reasonable limit. Zadvydas v. Davis, 533 U.S. 678, 691–97, 701 (2001). However, even while doing so, the Court was careful to point out that the case before it did not involve "terrorism or other special circumstances where special arguments might be made for forms of preventive

---

[10] See U.S. Const. Art. VI, §2 ("This Constitution, and the laws of the United States which shall be made in pursuance thereof; and all Treaties made, or which shall be made, under the authority of the United States, shall be the supreme Law of the Land. . . .").

detention and for heightened deference to the judgments of the political branches with respect to matters of national security." Id. at 696.

Further, the notion that a court must be able now to define conditions under which the current conflict will be declared to be over, and presumably open its doors to parties who may wish to litigate before the fact what those conditions might be, defies the basic concept of Article III jurisdiction. Federal courts, it will be recalled, are not permitted to deal with any but actual "cases" and "controversies," U.S. Const., art. III, §2, as opposed to those disputes that live only on the agendas of interested parties. When and if the time comes that Padilla can credibly claim that he has been detained too long, whether due to the sheer duration of his confinement or the diminution or outright cessation of hostilities, the issue of how and whether such a claim can be adjudicated will have to be faced. I do not understand Padilla to be making that claim now, and therefore see no need to face that issue now.

Padilla and the amici challenge the President's authority to declare him an enemy combatant, and to apply to him the laws of war, citing his American citizenship and his capture on American soil at a time when the courts were functioning. Before examining directly the issue of the President's authority, it is necessary to examine what the designation "enemy combatant" means in this case. The laws of war draw a fundamental distinction between lawful and unlawful combatants. Lawful combatants may be held as prisoners of war, but are immune from criminal prosecution by their captors for belligerent acts that do not constitute war crimes. See United States v. Lindh, 212 F. Supp. 2d 541, 553 (E.D. Va. 2002) (citing numerous authorities); GPW, art. 87.

. . .

The Third Geneva Convention, referred to above, reaffirmed the distinction between lawful and unlawful combatants. Article 4 of that treaty uses the same standards as the Hague Regulations for distinguishing who must be treated as a prisoner of war from who enjoys no such protection. See GPW, art. 4(2). Although in the past unlawful combatants were often summarily executed, such Draconian measures have not prevailed in modern times in what some still refer to without embarrassment as the civilized world. See Manual of Military Law 242 (British War Office 1914) ("No law authorizes [officers] to have [any disarmed enemy] shot without trial; and international law forbids summary execution absolutely.").[11] Rather, as recognized in Quirin, unlawful combatants generally have been tried by military commissions. Quirin, 317 U.S. at 35. They are not entitled to prisoner of war status, either as a matter of logic or as a matter of law under the Third Geneva Convention. It is not that the Third Geneva Convention authorizes particular treatment for or confinement of unlawful combatants; it is simply that that convention does not protect them.

Although unlawful combatants, unlike prisoners of war, may be tried and punished by military tribunals, there is no basis to impose a requirement that they be punished.

---

[11] However, when they did prevail, in the practices of German troops during World War II, who often shot partisans summarily, certain of those tried after that war were found to have a valid defense based on the unlawful status of their victims. In one trial of Axis officials accused of murdering captured partisans in the Balkans, the Court wrote: "The [partisan] bands . . . with which we are dealing in this case were not shown by satisfactory evidence to have met the requirements [for lawful combatant status]. This means, of course, that captured members of these unlawful groups were not entitled to be treated as prisoners of war. No crime can be properly charged against the defendants for the killing of such captured members of the resistance forces, they being franc-tireurs [another term for unlawful combatants, dating from the Franco-Prussian War, when irregular French fighters captured by Prussian soldiers were summarily executed]." The Hostages Trial: Trial of Wilhelm List and Others (Case No. 47), 8 L. Rpts. of Trials of War Criminals 34, 57 (U.N. War Crimes Comm'n 1948).

Rather, their detention for the duration of hostilities is supportable – again, logically and legally – on the same ground that the detention of prisoners of war is supportable: to prevent them from rejoining the enemy. Under the Third Geneva Convention, the recognized purpose of confinement during an ongoing conflict is "to prevent military personnel from taking up arms once again against the captor state." ICRC, Commentary on the Geneva Conventions of 12 August 1949, Geneva Convention III Relative to the Treatment of Prisoners of War 547 (1960). Thus, Article 118 of the Third Geneva Convention provides, as to release of prisoners, only that "[p]risoners of war shall be released and repatriated without delay after the cessation of active hostilities." GPW, art. 118.

As noted, in the June 9 Order, the President designated Padilla an "enemy combatant" based on his alleged association with al Qaeda and on an alleged plan undertaken as part of that association. See supra p. 9. The point of the protracted discussion immediately above is simply to support what should be an obvious conclusion: when the President designated Padilla an "enemy combatant," he necessarily meant that Padilla was an unlawful combatant, acting as an associate of a terrorist organization whose operations do not meet the four criteria necessary to confer lawful combatant status on its members and adherents. See Ruth Wedgwood, Al Qaeda, Terrorism, and Military Commissions, 96 Am. J. Int'l L. 328, 335 (2002) ("Al Qaeda has failed to fulfill four prerequisites of lawful belligerency."); see also Quirin, 317 U.S. at 31 (describing an unlawful combatant as, inter alia, one "who without uniform comes secretly through the lines for the purpose of waging war by destruction of life or property"). Indeed, even the Taliban militia, who appear at least to have acted in behalf of a government in Afghanistan, were found by Judge Ellis in Lindh not to qualify for lawful combatant status. Lindh, 212 F. Supp. 2d at 557–58.

That brings us to the central issue presented in this case: whether the President has the authority to designate as an unlawful combatant an American citizen, captured on American soil, and to detain him without trial. Padilla and the amici argue that, regardless of what treatment is permitted under the Third Geneva Convention and otherwise for unlawful combatants, the Constitution forbids indefinite detention of a citizen captured on American soil so long as "the courts are open and their process unobstructed," Ex parte Milligan, 71 U.S. (4 Wall.) 2, 121 (1866). Padilla relies heavily on Milligan, a Civil War-era case in which Milligan was one of a group arrested in Indiana and tried before a military commission on a charge of conspiring against the United States by planning to seize weapons, free Confederate prisoners, and kidnap the governor of Indiana. Convicted and sentenced to death, he filed a habeas corpus petition challenging the jurisdiction of the military commission to try him. The Court set aside the conviction, declaring that the "[laws of war] can never be applied to citizens in states which have upheld the authority of the government, and where the courts are open and their process unobstructed." Id. The Court found that the military commission had unlawfully usurped the judicial function, id., reasoning that although the President had the power to suspend the writ of habeas corpus during the Civil War, all other rights remained intact, even in wartime. The Framers, the Court found, "limited the [power of] suspension to one great right [i.e., the right to petition for habeas corpus], and left the rest to remain forever inviolable." Id. at 126.

Milligan, however, received a narrow reading in Quirin, a case on which the government, not surprisingly, places heavy reliance. Petitioners in Quirin were German saboteurs put ashore in June 1942, during World War II, in two groups, from submarines off Amagansett, a village on Long Island, New York, and off Ponte Vedra Beach, Florida. They landed wearing German uniforms, which they quickly buried, and changed into civilian dress.[12] They intended to sabotage war industries and facilities in the United States, but were arrested before their plans ripened into action. See Quirin, 317 U.S. at 21. One of the saboteurs, Haupt, claimed United States citizenship, which the government disputed; the Court found the issue immaterial. Rather, the Court found that Haupt's belligerent status distinguished him from Milligan, noting that "the [Milligan] Court was at pains to point out that Milligan, a citizen twenty years resident in Indiana, who had never been a resident of any of the states of rebellion, was not an enemy belligerent either entitled to the status of a prisoner of war or subject to the penalties imposed upon unlawful belligerents." Id. at 45. The Court continued:

> We construe the Court's statement as to the inapplicability of the law of war to Milligan's case as having particular reference to the facts before it. From them the Court concluded that Milligan, not being a part of or associated with the armed forces of the enemy, was a non-belligerent, not subject to the law of war save as – in circumstances found not there to be present and not involved here – martial law might be constitutionally established.

Id. Because the Quirin Court found that the German saboteurs were not only attempting to harm the United States during an armed conflict but doing so as persons associated with an enemy's armed forces, the Court concluded that the saboteurs, unlike Milligan, could be treated as unlawful combatants. Padilla, like the saboteurs, is alleged to be in active association with an enemy with whom the United States is at war.

Although the particular issue before the Court in Quirin – whether those petitioners could be tried by a military tribunal – is not precisely the same as the one now before this court – whether Padilla may be held without trial, the logic of Quirin bears strongly on this case. First, Quirin recognized the distinction between lawful and unlawful combatants, and the different treatment to which each is potentially subject:

> By universal agreement and practice the law of war draws a distinction between . . . lawful and unlawful combatants. Lawful combatants are subject to capture and detention as prisoners of war by opposing military forces. Unlawful combatants are likewise subject to capture and detention, but in addition they are subject to trial and punishment by military tribunals for acts which render their belligerency unlawful.

Id. at 30–31. Second, if we revisit the last sentence quoted above, it appears that the Court touched directly on the subject at issue in this case when it said that "[u]nlawful combatants are likewise subject to capture and detention," id. at 31 (emphasis added). Although the issue of detention alone was not before the Court in Quirin, I read the quoted sentence to mean that as between detention alone, and trial by a military tribunal with exposure to the penalty actually meted out to petitioners in Quirin – death – or, at the least, exposure to a sentence of imprisonment intended to punish and deter, the Court regarded detention alone, with the sole aim of preventing the detainee from rejoining hostile forces – a consequence visited upon captured lawful combatants – as certainly the lesser of the consequences an unlawful combatant could face. If, as seems

---

[12] At first glance, it seems nearly perverse that the saboteurs, whose mission not only did not require uniforms but could be betrayed by them, would nonetheless land in uniforms and thereby impose on one of the most dangerous parts of the mission – the landing – when they were most vulnerable to detection, the time-consuming and complicated steps of having to change into civilian clothes and bury the uniforms. In fact, it was not perverse at all. Rather, it seems clear that those who organized the mission well understood the rules of war, and understood also that if the saboteurs were captured during the landing, when they were particularly vulnerable to detection, and were not wearing uniforms, they would have no hope of being classified as lawful combatants. The uniforms provided at least a measure of protection for the saboteurs against unlawful combatant status if they were captured during the landing. See supra pp. 57–60 and authority cited therein.

obvious, the Court in fact regarded detention alone as a lesser consequence than the one it was considering – trial by military tribunal – and it approved even that greater consequence, then our case is a fortiori from Quirin as regards the lawfulness of detention under the law of war. See also Colepaugh v. Looney, 235 F.2d 429, 432 (10th Cir. 1956) (American citizen who entered the United States to commit hostile acts in aid of Germany during World War II could be tried by military commission: "[B]oth the executive and judicial branches of the government have recognized a clear distinction between a lawful combatant subject to capture and detention as a prisoner of war, and an unlawful combatant, also subject to capture and detention, but in addition 'subject to trial and punishment by military tribunals for acts which render their belligerency unlawful.'" (citing Quirin, 317 U.S. at 31) (emphasis added)); In re Territo, 156 F.2d 142, 145 (9th Cir. 1946) (American citizen captured in Sicily while serving in enemy army could be held as prisoner of war in California for duration of hostilities).

Quirin spoke to the issue of Presidential authority as well, albeit obliquely, and not as Padilla and the amici would have me read that case. They argue that when the Court wrote that the Constitution "invests the President . . . with the power to wage war which Congress has declared," id. at 26, that was meant to confine the holding in that case to formally declared wars, such as World War II, and means that Quirin is irrelevant to this case. However, the logic of that argument requires a finding that Quirin sub silentio overruled the The Prize Cases, discussed at pages 50–51 above. That breathtaking conclusion is unwarranted, however, both because it is unreasonable to believe that the Court would deal so casually with its own significant precedents, and because, as noted above, The Prize Cases have been found authoritative since Quirin, and appear to be very much alive.

The Quirin Court found it "unnecessary for present purposes to determine to what extent the President as Commander in Chief has constitutional power to create military commissions without the support of Congressional legislation. For here Congress has authorized trial of offenses against the law of war before such commissions." Quirin, 317 U.S. at 29. However, the Court did suggest that the President's decision to try the saboteurs before a military tribunal rested at least in part on an exercise of Presidential authority under Article II of the Constitution:

> By his order creating the present Commission [the President] has undertaken to exercise the authority conferred upon him by Congress, and also such authority as the Constitution itself gives the Commander in Chief, to direct the performance of those functions which may constitutionally be performed by the military arm of the nation in time of war.

Id. at 28.

Here, the basis for the President's authority to order the detention of an unlawful combatant arises both from the terms of the Joint Resolution, and from his constitutional authority as Commander in Chief as set forth in The Prize Cases and other authority discussed above. Also as discussed above, no principle in the Third Geneva Convention impedes the exercise of that authority.

B. Is Padilla's Detention Barred by Statute?

Whatever may be the President's authority to act in the absence of a specific limiting legislative enactment, Padilla and the amici argue that 18 U.S.C. §4001(a) bars his confinement in the circumstances present here, and the ACLU argues that Padilla's confinement is barred as well by the USA Patriot Act, Pub. L. No. 107-56, 115 Stat. 272

(2001) (the "Patriot Act"). However, as set forth below, §4001(a), which by its terms applies to Padilla, bars confinement only in the absence of congressional authorization, and there has been congressional authorization here; the Patriot Act simply does not bear on this case.

Taking the second argument first, the Patriot Act permits the detention of aliens suspected of activity endangering the security of the United States, for a period limited to seven days. See 8 U.S.C. §1226A(a) (5) (2000). According to the ACLU, had Congress thought that American citizens or even aliens could be detained as enemy combatants, it would never have passed this provision of the Patriot Act. (See ACLU Br. at 8–9) The Patriot Act, however, cannot be read as a comprehensive guide to presidential powers under the Joint Resolution. Because the Patriot Act requires only that the Attorney General have a reasonable ground to believe that an alien is engaging in threatening activity, id. §1126A(a) (3), that Act can be applied to persons who could not be classified as enemy combatants under the law of war. See Quirin, 317 U.S. at 45 (acknowledging that a citizen may not be tried by military tribunal if he is not serving a recognized enemy); discussion at pages 58–59, above. The cited portion of the Patriot Act applies to persons as to whom there is alleged to be far less reason for suspicion than there is as to Padilla. Moreover, to accept the ACLU's reading of the cited portion of the Patriot Act is to read that statute as having been intended to undercut substantially the logic of Quirin. I refuse to read the statute to accomplish such a stark result.

Padilla's principal statutory argument is based on 18 U.S.C. §4001(a), which is broad and categorical:

> No citizen shall be imprisoned or otherwise detained by the United States except pursuant to an Act of Congress.

18 U.S.C. §4001(a) (2000); see Howe v. Smith, 452 U.S. 473, 480 n.3 (1981) ("[T]he plain language of §4001(a) proscrib[es] detention of any kind by the United States, absent a congressional grant of authority to detain.") (emphasis in original).

To avoid the reach of that statute, the government appears to lean heavily on statutory construction arguments that fail to confront the plain language of the statute, and to rest rather lightly on what seems to me the more persuasive position: that Padilla in fact is detained "pursuant to an Act of Congress." Thus, the government argues that reading §4001(a) to cover Padilla's detention would bring that section in conflict with Article II, section 2, clause 1 of the Constitution, which makes the President "Commander in Chief of the Army and Navy of the United States," U.S. Const., art. 2, §2, cl. 1, and has been interpreted to grant the President independent authority to respond to an armed attack against the United States. See The Prize Cases, 67 U.S. at 668 ("If a war be made by invasion of a foreign nation, the President is not only authorized but bound to resist force by force... without waiting for any special legislative authority."); see also Hamdi v. Rumsfeld, 296 F.3d at 281–82 ("The authority to capture those who take up arms against America belongs to the Commander in Chief under Article II, Section II."); Campbell 203 F.3d at 27 (Silberman, J., concurring) (collecting authorities for the proposition that "the President has independent authority to repel aggressive acts by third parties even without specific congressional authorization").

The government suggests that because reading the statute to impinge on the President's Article II powers, including detention of enemy combatants, creates a danger that the statute might be found unconstitutional as applied to the present case, a court should read the statute so as not to cover detention of enemy combatants, applying the canon that a statute should be read so as to avoid constitutional difficulty. See, e.g., Jones v. United States, 529 U.S. 848, 857 (2000) (citing "the guiding principle that 'where

a statute is susceptible of two constructions, by one of which grave and doubtful constitutional questions arise and by the other of which such questions are avoided, our duty
is to adopt the latter.'") (quoting United States ex rel. Attorney General v. Delaware &
Hudson Co., 213 U.S. 366, 408 (1909)).

However, this doctrine of constitutional avoidance "'has no application in the absence of statutory ambiguity.'" HUD v. Rucker, 535 U.S. 125, 122 S.Ct. 1230, 1235 (2002)
(quoting United States v. Oakland Cannabis Buyers' Cooperative, 532 U.S. 483, 494
(2001)). Any other approach, as pointed out in Rucker, "'while purporting to be an exercise in judicial restraint, would trench upon the legislative powers vested in Congress
by Art. I, §1, of the Constitution.'" Id. at 1235–36 (quoting United States v. Albertini, 472
U.S. 675, 680 (1985)). That is, if a court read an ambiguity into an unambiguous statute
simply for the purpose of avoiding an adverse decision as to the constitutionality of that
statute, the court would be exercising legislative powers and thereby usurping those
powers. There is no ambiguity here. The plain language of the statute encompasses
all detentions of United States citizens. Therefore, the constitutional avoidance canon
cannot affect how the statute is read.

The government argues also that because §4001(a) is in Title 18 of the United States
Code, and that title governs "Crimes and Criminal Procedure," Congress could not have
intended to impede the President's authority to use the military rather than the civilian
law enforcement arm of the government to detain unlawful combatants in wartime.
The government proffers, as additional textual evidence, that 18 U.S.C. §4001(b) gives
the Attorney General control over "Federal penal and correctional institutions, except
military or naval institutions," 18 U.S.C. §4001(b) (2000), and reasons that this shows
that Congress meant to exclude military detention from the reach of the section. However, §4001(b) simply limits the Attorney General's responsibility for prisons to those
that are not run by the military. The placement of this section within Title 18 is entirely
natural because most detentions result from arrest by law enforcement agencies. This
textual argument, too, cannot overcome the plain language of the statute, as read by the
Supreme Court in Howe v. Smith, cited above.

Although the government struggles unsuccessfully to avoid application of the
statute, the government is on firmer ground when it argues that even if §4001(a) applies, its terms have been complied with. The statute permits detention of an American
citizen "pursuant to an Act of Congress." 18 U.S.C. §4001(a) (2000). If the Military Force
Authorization passed and signed on September 18, 2001, is an "Act of Congress," and if
it authorizes Padilla's detention, then perforce the statute has not been violated here.

The Joint Resolution is not called an "Act," but that is the only respect in which
it is not an "Act." Joint resolutions generally, as their name would suggest, require the
approval of both Houses of Congress, and if signed by the President, have the force of
law. See Bowsher v. Synar, 478 U.S. 714, 756 (1986) ("The joint resolution, which is used
for 'special purposes and . . . incidental matters,' makes binding policy and 'requires an
affirmative vote by both Houses and submission to the President for approval' – the full
Article I requirements." (emphasis added) (citation omitted)). That is to say, there is
no relevant constitutional difference between a bill and a joint resolution; both require
bicameralism – passage by both Houses, and presentment – submission to the President
for signature.

Congress itself has intimated that a joint resolution qualifies as an "Act of Congress."
See Joint Resolution of Dec. 15, 1981, Pub.L. No. 97-92, §140, 95 Stat. 1183, 1200
("Notwithstanding any other provision of law . . . none of the funds appropriated by this
joint resolution or by any other Act shall be obligated or expended to increase, after
the date of enactment of this joint resolution, any salary of any Federal judge or Justice

of the Supreme Court, except as may be specifically authorized by Act of Congress hereafter enacted." (emphasis added)). A light smattering of cases suggests the same thing. See Acme of Precision Surgical Co. v. Weinberger, 580 F. Supp. 490, 501–02 (E.D. Pa. 1984) (calling joint resolutions "acts of Congress"); Louisville & Nashville R.R. v. Bass, 328 F.Supp. 732, 739 (W.D.Ky.1971) (equating a joint resolution with an "Act of Congress"); Berk v. Laird, 317 F.Supp. 715, 723 (E.D.N.Y. 1970) (calling the Gulf of Tonkin Resolution an "act of Congress").

Principally because the Joint Resolution complies with all constitutional require-ments for an Act of Congress, it should be regarded for purposes of §4001(a) as an "Act of Congress." Cf. Hamdi, 296 F.3d at 281 (concluding that the President acted with statu-tory authorization in designating Hamdi, an American citizen captured in Afghanistan, as an enemy combatant).

The authority conferred by the Joint Resolution itself is broad. It authorizes the President to "use all necessary and appropriate force against those . . . organizations, or persons he determines planned, authorized, committed or aided the terrorist at-tacks that occurred on September 11, 2001 . . . in order to prevent any future acts of international terrorism against the United States by such . . . organizations or persons." Authorization for Use of Military Force, Pub. Law No. 107-40, §2(a), 115 Stat. 224, 224 (2001). This language authorizes action against not only those connected to the sub-ject organizations who are directly responsible for the September 11 attacks, but also against those who would engage in "future acts of international terrorism" as part of "such . . . organizations." Id. As reflected, inter alia, in the President's November 13, 2001 order establishing military tribunals, al Qaeda is an organization the President has de-termined committed the subject acts. Mil. Order of Nov. 13, 2001, 66 Fed.Reg. 57,833 (Nov. 16, 2001). Indeed, in the June 9 Order directing Padilla's detention, the President refers to al Qaeda as "an international terrorist organization with which the United States is at war." June 9 Order at ¶2. As discussed above, Padilla is alleged in the June 9 Order to have been an unlawful combatant in behalf of al Qaeda. Also as discussed extensively above, the Third Geneva Convention does not forbid detention of unlawful combatants. Accordingly, the detention of Padilla is not barred by 18 U.S.C. §4001(a); nor, as discussed above, is it otherwise barred as a matter of law.

V. CONSULTATION WITH COUNSEL

The government has not disputed Padilla's right to challenge his detention by means of a habeas corpus petition. Although Padilla has the ability, through his lawyer, to challenge the government's naked legal right to hold him as an unlawful combatant on any set of facts whatsoever, he has no ability to make fact-based arguments because, as is not disputed, he has been held incommunicado during his confinement at the Consolidated Naval Brig in Charleston, and has not been permitted to consult with counsel. Therefore, unless I find that the only fact issue Padilla has a right to be heard on is whether the government's proffered facts, taken alone and without right of response, are sufficient to warrant his detention by whatever evidentiary standard may apply – an argument that can be presented by counsel without access to Padilla – I must address the question of whether he may present facts, and how he may do so. As explained below: (i) Padilla does have the right to present facts; (ii) the most convenient way for him to go about that, and the way most useful to the court, is to present them through counsel; and (iii) the government's arguments are insufficient to warrant denying him access to counsel. Therefore, to the extent set forth below, Padilla will be permitted to consult with counsel in aid of prosecuting this petition.

Padilla's right to present facts is rooted firmly in the statutes that provide the basis for his petition. Padilla has petitioned pursuant to 28 U.S.C. §2241, which, among other things, grants to district courts the power to issue writs of habeas corpus; a related section, 28 U.S.C. §2243, provides the skeletal outline of procedures to be followed in a §2241 case. It includes the following:

> Unless the application for the writ and the return present only issues of law the person to whom the writ is directed shall be required to produce at the hearing the body of the person detained.
>
> The applicant or the person detained may, under oath, deny any of the facts set forth in the return or allege any other material facts.

28 U.S.C. §2243 (2000). A related section, 28 U.S.C. §2246, allows the taking of evidence in habeas corpus cases by deposition, affidavit, or interrogatories.

Further, both the Federal Rules of Civil Procedure and the Rules Governing §2254 Cases may be applied in §2241 habeas corpus cases, in the discretion of the court. See Fed. R. Civ. P. 81(a)(2) (rules apply "to proceedings for... habeas corpus... to the extent that the practice in such proceedings is not set forth in statutes of the United States and... has heretofore conformed to the practice in civil actions"); Rules Governing §2254 Cases 1(b) (§2254 rules may apply in other habeas corpus cases "at the discretion of the United States district court"). This blend of procedures that may be applied makes a habeas corpus case different from the usual civil lawsuit. See, e.g., Harris v. Nelson, 394 U.S. 286, 293–94 (1969) ("It is, of course, true that habeas corpus proceedings are characterized as 'civil.' But that label is gross and inexact. Essentially, the proceeding is unique."). The Supreme Court has praised the flexibility of habeas corpus. See, e.g., Jones v. Cunningham, 371 U.S. 236, 243 (1963) ("It is not now and never has been a static, narrow, formalistic remedy.").

Quite plainly, Congress intended that a §2241 petitioner would be able to place facts, and issues of fact, before the reviewing court, and it would frustrate the purpose of the remedy to prevent him from doing so.

The habeas corpus statutes do not explicitly provide a right to counsel for a petitioner in Padilla's circumstances, but 18 U.S.C. §3006A(2) (B) permits a court to which a §2241 petition is addressed to appoint counsel for the petitioner if the court determines that "the interests of justice so require." 18 U.S.C. §3006A(2) (B) (2000). I have already so determined, and have continued the appointment of Newman and appointed also Andrew Patel, Esq., as co-counsel.

Of course, Padilla has no Sixth Amendment[13] right to counsel in this proceeding. The Sixth Amendment grants that right to the "accused" in a "criminal proceeding"; Padilla is in the custody of the Department of Defense; there is no "criminal proceeding" in which Padilla is detained; therefore, the Sixth Amendment does not speak to Padilla's situation. Beyond the plain language of the Amendment, "even in the civilian community a proceeding which may result in deprivation of liberty is nonetheless not a 'criminal proceeding' within the meaning of the Sixth Amendment if there are elements about it which sufficiently distinguish it from a traditional civilian criminal trial." Middendorf v. Henry, 425 U.S. 25, 38 (1976). Such "elements" are present here – notably, that Padilla's detention "does not implicate either of the two primary objectives of criminal punishment: retribution or deterrence." Hendricks, 521 U.S. at 361–62. Although Escobedo v. Illinois, 378 U.S. 478 (1964), recognized a Sixth Amendment right

---

[13] The Sixth Amendment to the Constitution states that "[i]n all criminal prosecutions, the accused shall enjoy the right... to have the Assistance of Counsel for his defence." U.S. Const., amend. VI.

against custodial interrogation without access to counsel, the remedy for violation of this right is exclusion of the fruits of the interrogation at a criminal trial, id. at 491. There being no criminal proceeding here, Padilla could not enforce this right now even if he had it.

Nor does the self-incrimination clause of the Fifth Amendment[14] provide any more help to Padilla than the Sixth Amendment in his effort to confer with counsel. Although the Supreme Court in Miranda v. Arizona, 384 U.S. 436 (1966), found in that clause a right to counsel, calling the presence of counsel "the adequate protective device necessary to make the process of police interrogation conform to the dictates of the privilege," id. at 466, and "[a]lthough conduct by law enforcement officials prior to trial may significantly impair that right [to avoid self-incrimination], a constitutional violation occurs only at trial." United States v. Verdugo-Urquidez, 494 U.S. 259, 264 (1990). That is of no help to Padilla, who does not face the prospect of a trial. But see Miranda v. City of Oxnard, 270 F.3d 852 (9th Cir. 2001) (holding that a plaintiff may bring a §1983 action alleging a violation of Fifth and Fourteenth Amendment rights to be free from police coercion in pursuit of a confession even though statements were not used against him at trial), cert. granted sub nom. Chavez v. Martinez, 122 S. Ct. 2326 (2002).

The Due Process Clause of the Fifth Amendment states that "[n]o person . . . shall be deprived of life, liberty, or property, without due process of law." U.S. Const., amend. V. Professor Laurence Tribe has commented that, "[w]hat emerges from [the] disparate cases and lines of thought [interpreting the Due Process Clause] is, quite clearly, less than a solidly grounded or coherently elaborated right of judicial access." Laurence H. Tribe, American Constitutional Law §§10–18, at 759 (2d ed. 1988). Finding guidance in the due process clause would require, at a minimum, locating the delicate balance between private and public interests that is the test for finding a due process right, as set forth in Mathews v. Eldridge, 424 U.S. 319 (1976):

> [I]dentification of the specific dictates of due process generally requires consideration of three distinct factors: First, the private interest that will be affected by the official action; second, the risk of an erroneous deprivation of such interest through the procedures used, and the probable value, if any, of additional or substitute procedural safeguards; and finally, the Government's interest, including the function involved and fiscal and administrative burdens that the additional or substitute procedural requirement would entail.

Id. at 335. That is not to say that there are no guides whatever to striking that balance. There are. See, e.g., Nat'l Council of Resistance of Iran v. Dep't of State, 251 F.3d 192, 209 (D.C. Cir. 2001) (holding that organizations designated by the Secretary of State as terrorist organizations must have "the opportunity to be heard at a meaningful time and in a meaningful manner," and must have "the opportunity to present, at least in written form, such evidence as those entities may be able to produce to rebut the administrative record or otherwise negate the proposition that they are foreign terrorist organizations"). However, as explained below, the provisions and characteristics of the habeas corpus statute and remedy discussed at pages 76–77 above, and the court's power under the All Writs Act, 28 U.S.C. §1651(a) (2000), to issue writs in aid of its jurisdiction, provide a statutory basis for decision. Considerations of prudence require that a court avoid a constitutional basis for decision when there exists a non-constitutional alternative. See Harris v. McRae, 448 U.S. 297, 306–07 (1980) (cautioning that when a

---

[14] That clause states that "[n]o person . . . shall be compelled in any criminal case to be a witness against himself." U.S. Const., amend. V.

case can be decided based on either a statute or the Constitution, the statute should provide the basis for decision).

Part of that non-constitutional alternative lies in the provisions of the habeas corpus statute, and the characteristics of the remedy, discussed at pages 76–77 above, which make it clear that Congress intended habeas corpus petitioners to have an opportunity to present and contest facts, and courts to have the flexibility to permit them to do so under proper safeguards. Padilla's need to consult with a lawyer to help him do what the statute permits him to do is obvious. He is held incommunicado at a military facility. His lawyer has been told that there is no guarantee even that her correspondence to him would get through. (Newman Aff. of 9/24/02 ¶8) Although it is not uncommon for habeas corpus cases to be pursued by petitioners pro se, such cases, usually involving challenges to either state convictions under 28 U.S.C. §2254 or federal convictions under 28 U.S.C. §2255, almost always are filed after the petitioners already have had the benefit of completed criminal proceedings, and appeals, in which they were represented by counsel. Padilla has had no such benefit here. It would frustrate the purpose of the procedure Congress established in habeas corpus cases, and of the remedy itself, to leave Padilla with no practical means whatever for following that procedure.

. . .

The government has argued that affording access to counsel would "jeopardize the two core purposes of detaining enemy combatants – gathering intelligence about the enemy, and preventing the detainee from aiding in any further attacks against America." (Respondents' Resp. to This Ct's 10/21/02 Order at 6) This would happen, the government argues, because access to counsel would interfere with questioning, and because al Qaeda operatives are trained to use third parties as intermediaries to pass messages to fellow terrorists, even if "[t]he intermediaries may be unaware that they are being so used." (Id. at 7)

However, access to counsel need be granted only for purposes of presenting facts to the court in connection with this petition if Padilla wishes to do so; no general right to counsel in connection with questioning has been hypothesized here, and thus the interference with interrogation would be minimal or nonexistent. As to the possibility that Padilla might use his lawyers to pass messages to others, there are several responses to that conjecture. First, accepting that conjecture at face value and across the board proves far too much: by the government's logic, no indicted member of al Qaeda facing trial in an Article III court should be allowed to consult with counsel – a result barred by the Sixth Amendment. Second, I have read both the Mobbs Declaration and the Sealed Mobbs Declaration, the latter only for the purpose of assessing the government's access-to-counsel argument; the government's conjecture is, on the facts presented to me in those documents, gossamer speculation. Although the government presents facts showing that Padilla had contact with and was acting on behalf of al Qaeda, there is nothing to indicate that Padilla in particular was trained to transmit information in the way the government suggests, or that he had information to transmit. Third, Padilla has already had meetings with counsel in New York, and thus whatever speculative damage the government seeks to prevent may already have been done. Fourth, there is no reason that military personnel cannot monitor Padilla's contacts with counsel, so long as those who participate in the monitoring are insulated from any activity in connection with this petition, or in connection with a future criminal prosecution of Padilla, if there should ever be one. The U.S. Bureau of Prisons has adopted such procedures with respect to incarcerated defendants who present a similar danger. See Prevention of Acts of Violence and Terrorism, 28 C.F.R. §501.3(a) (2002) (special procedures to be used if "there is a substantial risk that a prisoner's communications or contacts with persons could result in death or serious bodily harm to persons, or substantial damage to property that would entail the risk of death or serious bodily injury to persons"). One would think that such procedures would go a long way toward preventing Padilla from transmitting information through his lawyers to others. Finally, Padilla's lawyers themselves are members of this court's Criminal Justice Act panel who have appeared before this court in numerous cases. In addition to being able advocates, they have conducted themselves at all times in a fashion consistent with their status as – to use the antique phrase – officers of the court. There is nothing in their past conduct to suggest that they would be inclined to act as conduits for their client, even if he wanted them to do so.

Even giving substantial weight, as I do, to the President's statement in the June 9 Order that Padilla is "a continuing, present and grave danger to the national security of the United States" and that his detention "is necessary to prevent him from siding with al Qaeda in its efforts to attack the United States," there has been no fact presented to me that shows that the source of that danger is the possibility that Padilla will transmit information to others through his lawyers. By contrast, Padilla's statutorily granted right to present facts to the court in connection with this petition will be destroyed utterly if he is not allowed to consult with counsel. On the facts presented in this case, the balance weighs heavily in Padilla's favor.

I do not believe that the decision in Hamdi v. Rumsfeld, 296 F.3d 278 (4th Cir. 2002), alters the balance in the government's favor. In that case, the Court of Appeals for the Fourth Circuit reversed the order of a district court directing the government to permit unmonitored access by counsel to a detainee captured in Afghanistan and held at a Navy brig in Norfolk, Virginia. The order was rendered without benefit of briefing or argument, and with "little indication in the order (or elsewhere in the record for that matter) that the court gave proper weight to national security concerns." Id. at 282. According to the Fourth Circuit, "[t]he peremptory nature of the [District Court's] proceedings st[ood] in contrast to the significance of the issues before the court." Id. No such access is to be granted here, and the court has had the full benefit of the government's submissions, both sealed and unsealed. Further, Padilla's situation appears to differ from Hamdi's in that he had access to counsel after his capture but before his designation as an enemy combatant, and thus no potential prophylactic effect of an order barring access by counsel could have been lost.

Because this court has jurisdiction over Padilla's petition, and because the procedure outlined by the applicable statutes cannot be followed unless Padilla is permitted to consult with counsel, respondent Secretary Rumsfeld will be directed to permit Padilla to consult with counsel solely for the purpose of submitting to the court facts bearing upon his petition, under such conditions as the parties may agree to, or, absent agreement, such conditions as the court may direct so as to foreclose, so far as possible, the danger that Padilla will use his attorneys for the purpose of conveying information to others.

VI. THE STANDARD APPLICABLE TO THIS COURT'S REVIEW AND THE FACTS THE COURT MAY CONSIDER

Before Padilla consults with counsel for the purpose of submitting facts to the court in aid of his petition, it would seem essential for him to know what standard the court will apply in determining whether whatever facts the government has presented are sufficient to warrant the finding in the President's June 9 Order that Padilla is an unlawful combatant. In addition, it would be helpful for Padilla to know, at least in a general sense, what the court will consider in that calculus other than what appears in the Mobbs Declaration – in particular, whether the court will consider the Sealed Mobbs Declaration. Unless he has some idea as to both of these subjects, he cannot decide what sort of factual presentation he must make, or indeed whether he wishes to stand mute rather than try to present any facts at all. The standard the court will apply in deciding the sufficiency of the government's showing is described below. In addition, I do not believe it necessary to decide now whether to consider the Sealed Mobbs Declaration. For the reasons explained below, Padilla can determine whether to submit facts, and frame those facts, solely based on the Mobbs Declaration and without knowing precisely the content of the sealed submission.

A.   Deference Due the President's Determination

Padilla does not seem to dispute that courts owe considerable deference, as a general matter, to the acts and orders of the political branches – the President and Congress – in matters relating to foreign policy, national security, or military affairs. Nor could he. The Court of Appeals for the Fourth Circuit wrote as follows on that subject when it considered, and reversed, the order discussed immediately above, peremptorily granting to a detained combatant, captured during military operations in Afghanistan, unmonitored access to counsel:

> The order [under review] arises in the context of foreign relations and national security, where a court's deference to the political branches of our national government is considerable. It is the President who wields "delicate, plenary and exclusive power . . . as the sole organ of the federal government in the field of international relations – a power which does not require as a basis for its exercise an act of Congress." And where as here the President does act with statutory authorization from Congress, there is all the more reason for deference. Indeed, Articles I and II prominently assign to Congress and the President the shared responsibility for military affairs. See U.S. Const. art. I, §8; art. II, §2. In accordance with this constitutional text, the Supreme Court has shown great deference to the political branches when called upon to decide cases implicating sensitive matters of foreign policy, national security, or military affairs. This deference extends to military designations of individuals as enemy combatants in times of active hostilities, as well as to their detention after capture on the field of battle. The authority to capture those who take up arms against America belongs to the Commander in Chief under Article II, Section 2. As far back as the Civil War, the Supreme Court deferred to the President's determination that those in rebellion had the status of belligerents. And in World War II, the Court stated in no uncertain terms that the President's wartime detention decisions are to be accorded great deference from the courts.

Hamdi, 296 F.3d at 282 (citations omitted). Instead of disputing general principles, Padilla seeks to take his case outside their reach. Thus, he argues variously (i) that the President lacks statutory authority to act because Congress refrained in the Joint Resolution from declaring war, the Joint Resolution is limited only to those directly involved in the September 11 attacks, and the Patriot Act rather than the Joint Declaration should be read to control his case (Petitioners' Br. in Supp. of Am. Pet. and in Resp. to Respondents' Mot. to Dismiss at 9–12, 17–18); and (ii) the President lacks constitutional authority because his constitutional powers as Commander in Chief and as sole authority in the conduct of foreign affairs do not reach the capture of a United States citizen on American soil, and his detention as an enemy combatant (id. at 13–15, 16–17).

Padilla insists that this court conduct a "searching inquiry" into the factual basis for the President's determination that Padilla is an enemy combatant, lest the court "rubber stamp" the June 9 Order and thereby enforce a "Presidential whim." (Id. at 22, 32) In essence, Padilla argues that he is entitled to a trial on the issue of whether he is an unlawful combatant or not.[15]

However, as set forth above, Padilla has lost the legal arguments he relies on to remove this case from the reach of the principles described by the Fourth Circuit in Hamdi, cited above. The President, for the reasons set forth above, has both constitutional and statutory authority to exercise the powers of Commander in Chief, including the power to detain unlawful combatants, and it matters not that Padilla is a United States citizen captured on United States soil. See supra pp. 47–75. In his frequently-cited concurrence in Youngstown Sheet & Tube Co. v. Sawyer, 343 U.S. 579 (1952), Justice Jackson described three degrees of Presidential authority. First, when the President acts pursuant to express or implied authorization by Congress, "his authority is at its maximum, for it includes all that he possesses in his own right plus all that Congress can delegate." Id. at 635. Second, when he acts absent either approval or disapproval from Congress, "he can only rely upon his own independent powers, but there is a zone of twilight in which he and Congress may have concurrent authority, or in which its distribution is uncertain." Id. at 637. Third, when a President acts in a way incompatible with Congress's express or implied will, "his power is at its lowest ebb, for then he can rely only upon his own constitutional powers minus any constitutional powers of Congress over the matter." Id. In the decision to detain Padilla as an unlawful combatant, for the reasons set forth above, the President is operating at maximum authority, under both the Constitution and the Joint Resolution.

Notwithstanding Hamdi, and the cases it cites – which are, for the most part, the cases cited in support of the above findings as to the President's authority – it would be a mistake to create the impression that there is a lush and vibrant jurisprudence governing these matters. There isn't. Quirin offers no guidance regarding the standard to be applied in making the threshold determination that a habeas corpus petitioner is an unlawful combatant. Because the facts in Quirin were stipulated, see Quirin, 317 U.S. at 19, the Quirin Court moved directly to the legal principles applicable to unlawful combatants, and then to the application of those principles to the undisputed facts. Other controlling cases date to World War II, the Civil War, and even further back. As Justice Jackson observed in Sawyer, "[a] judge...may be surprised at the poverty of really useful and unambiguous authority applicable to concrete problems of executive power as they actually present themselves." Sawyer, 343 U.S. at 634. In this case, that poverty reflects, in part, a blessing – the blessedly placid history this country has enjoyed. The last time this country experienced widespread mayhem was during the Civil War; the last time a foreign army marched here was during the War of 1812.

However, if the case law seems sparse and some of the cases abstruse, that is not because courts have not recognized and do not continue to recognize the President's authority to act when it comes to defending this country. Recall that in Zadvydas v. Davis, cited above, even as the Supreme Court placed limits on the government's authority to detain immigrants awaiting deportation, Zadvydas, 533 U.S. at 691–97, 701, the Court

---

[15] In an affidavit submitted "on information and belief" (Newman Aff. of 9/24/02 ¶1), Newman states what appears to be her belief, although not the information that led to it, that Padilla had "traveled to Chicago to visit with his son," and then "planned to travel to Florida to visit other members of his family." (Id. ¶¶2, 3) That affidavit does not deny the allegations in the Mobbs Declaration relating to Padilla's activities in Afghanistan and Pakistan.

was careful to point out that the case before it did not involve "terrorism or other special circumstances where special arguments might be made for forms of preventive detention and for heightened deference to the judgments of the political branches with respect to matters of national security," id. at 696. The "political branches," when they make judgments on the exercise of war powers under Articles I and II, as both branches have here, need not submit those judgments to review by Article III courts. Rather, they are subject to the perhaps less didactic but nonetheless searching audit of the democratic process.

Zadvydas was decided at the end of June 2001, less than three months before the September 11 attacks, and the language now seems to convey ominous prescience. To the extent that the Court took pains to limit the rule it was creating so as to exclude cases involving "terrorism or other special circumstances" warranting "heightened deference to the judgments of the political branches," the quoted language cannot be dismissed as dictum. If it is dictum, it is the sort of considered dictum to which lower courts such as this one must pay particular heed. See Judge Newman's opinion in United States v. Oshatz, 912 F.2d 534, 540 (2d Cir. 1990) (distinguishing considered dictum from peripheral observations).

The deference to which the Supreme Court and the Fourth Circuit refer is due not because judges are not personally able to decide whether facts have been established by competent evidence, or whether those facts are sufficient to warrant a particular conclusion by a preponderance of evidence, or by clear and convincing evidence, or beyond a reasonable doubt. Indeed, if there is any task suited to what should be the job skills of judges, deciding such issues is it. Rather, deference is due because of a principle captured in another "statement of Justice Jackson – that we decide difficult cases presented to us by virtue of our commissions, not our competence." Dames & Moore v. Regan, 453 U.S. 654, 661 (1981). That principle applies equally to the case a judge feels unqualified for but must decide, as to the case a judge feels well qualified for but may not decide. The commission of a judge, as The Prize Cases, the other authority cited at pages 48–67 above, and the quoted language from Zadvydas suggest, does not run to deciding de novo whether Padilla is associated with al Qaeda and whether he should therefore be detained as an unlawful combatant. It runs only to deciding two things: (i) whether the controlling political authority – in this case, the President – was in fact exercising a power vouchsafed to him by the Constitution and the laws; that determination in turn, is to be made only by examining whether there is some evidence to support his conclusion that Padilla was, like the German saboteurs in Quirin, engaged in a mission against the United States on behalf of an enemy with whom the United States is at war, and (ii) whether that evidence has not been entirely mooted by subsequent events. The first determination – that there is some evidence of Padilla's hostile status – would support the President's assertion in the June 9 Order that he was exercising the power referred to above. That is the "some evidence" test suggested in the government's papers (Respondents' Resp. to and Mot. to Dismiss Am. Pet. at 17), and it will be applied once Padilla presents any facts he may wish to present to the court.

B.   The Sealed Mobbs Declaration

There remains the question of whether the court will consider the Sealed Mobbs Declaration not only to help decide whether Padilla presents a particular danger if he is allowed to consult with counsel, as has already been done, but also to help decide whether there was some evidence to support the President's decision to designate him an enemy combatant, and whether such evidence has not become moot. Padilla objects to my doing so, arguing that he has a fundamental right to avoid suffering serious injury based on facts that are not disclosed. Thus, he cites Greene v. McElroy, 360 U.S. 474 (1959), where the Supreme Court reversed denial of a security clearance to the employee of a defense contractor based on confidential reports, with Chief Justice Warren writing for the Court as follows:

> Certain principles have remained relatively immutable in our jurisprudence. One of these is that where governmental action seriously injures an individual, and the reasonableness of the action depends on fact findings, the evidence used to prove the Government's case must be disclosed to the individual so that he has an opportunity to show that it is untrue.

Id. at 496. Although the government has not discussed Greene in its reply papers, the case is distinguishable from this one on several bases, including that the confidential evidence was used before an executive agency and without explicit delegation from Congress or the President. Id. at 507.

Closer to the case at hand is United States v. Hayman, discussed at page 82 above, where a district court faced with a claim of ineffective assistance of counsel in a habeas corpus case held a hearing without having the petitioner present, and then found that counsel had engaged in the conflicted representation with the knowledge and consent of the petitioner. The Supreme Court disapproved and reversed, holding that the district court "did not proceed in conformity with Section 2255 when it made findings on controverted issues of fact relating to respondent's own knowledge without notice to respondent and without his being present." Hayman, 342 U.S. at 220; see also, Walker v. Johnson, 312 U.S. 275, 285 (1941) (holding that disputed issues of fact cannot be resolved based on affidavits and must be decided based on evidentiary hearings, "the only admissible procedure" for resolving such issues). Although, as the government argues, in military habeas corpus cases "the inquiry, the scope of matters open for review, has always been more narrow than in civil cases," Burns v. Wilson, 346 U.S. 137, 139 (1953) (plurality opinion), the Court in Burns went to some lengths to discuss the care with which military appellate courts had reviewed the petitioners' claims, id. at 144–45.

Judge Sand's opinion in United States v. Bin Laden, 126 F. Supp.2d 264 (S.D.N.Y. 2000), suggests that, rather than dealing with the problem at the level of abstract principle, it may be more useful to examine precisely what the nature is of the confidential submission so as to determine what rights, if any, are compromised if the court considers it. In Bin Laden, Judge Sand resolved a motion to suppress electronic surveillance without holding a hearing, based in part on "in camera, ex parte review of . . . sensitive material in the case." Id. at 287. He found, as required, that such review was necessary due to the damage that could be caused by disclosure of the subject information, id., and also that the issues before him were not factually complex and were predominantly legal, so that the "benefit [to the court] of holding an adversary hearing was substantially lessened," id. He noted that the question before him was whether the searches in question were conducted for foreign intelligence purposes or law enforcement purposes, and that resolving that question "required that the Court review a limited (and manageable) number of documents." Id. Judge Sand upheld withholding disclosure of the classified material before him even to defense attorneys who had clearance to review certain classified documents, noting that clearance to see certain classified documents does not necessarily mean clearance to see all such documents. Id. at 287 n. 27.

Of course, I recognize that Padilla is not pressing his objection simply to give the court the benefit of the adversary process, and that he raises an issue of fairness. However, the Sealed Mobbs Declaration does not engage issues of fairness to the extent that might at first be supposed because it does not broaden the nature of the accusations against Padilla beyond the bounds of the Mobbs Declaration itself, nor does it refer to conduct by Padilla that is not described in the Mobbs Declaration. Instead, other than identifying one or more of the sources referred to only in cryptic terms in the Mobbs Declaration, the sealed document simply sets forth objective circumstantial evidence that corroborates the factual allegations in the Mobbs Declaration. Padilla's access to the unclassified Mobbs Declaration gives him all the notice necessary to meet the allegations of whom he had contact with and what he did, or to explain why those allegations are now moot. Padilla is not in a position to dispute the government's claim that disclosure of the Sealed Mobbs Declaration "could compromise intelligence gathering crucial to the ongoing war effort by revealing sources and by divulging methods of collecting intelligence." (Respondents' Resp. to This Ct's 10/21/02 Order at 15)

Whatever outcome might result from the discussion above, I need not reach the issue of whether to consider the Sealed Mobbs Declaration now. If, after Padilla has had an opportunity to contest the unsealed Mobbs Declaration, I find that the government has failed to meet the some evidence standard, I will decide whether to consider the sealed document. At that point, I will have two options: (1) I could find that it is impermissible to use the sealed document without giving Padilla access to it, in which case the government will have the option of withdrawing the submission; or (2) I could consider the sealed document in camera. Before Padilla has disputed any facts, it would be premature to choose between these options.

*   *   *

To recapitulate: (i) Newman may pursue this petition as next friend to Padilla, and the government's motion to dismiss for lack of standing therefore is denied; (ii) Secretary Rumsfeld is the proper respondent in this case, and this court has jurisdiction over him, as well as jurisdiction to hear this case, and the government's motion to dismiss for lack of jurisdiction, or to transfer to South Carolina, is denied; (iii) the President is authorized under the Constitution and by law to direct the military to detain enemy combatants in the circumstances present here, such that Padilla's detention is not per se unlawful; (iv) Padilla may consult with counsel in aid of pursuing this petition, under conditions that will minimize the likelihood that he can use his lawyers as unwilling intermediaries for the transmission of information to others and may, if he chooses, submit facts and argument to the court in aid of his petition; (v) to resolve the issue of whether Padilla was lawfully detained on the facts present here, the court will examine only whether the President had some evidence to support his finding that Padilla was an enemy combatant, and whether that evidence has been mooted by events subsequent to his detention; the court will not at this time use the document submitted in camera to determine whether the government has met that standard.

. . .

SO ORDERED:

_____

Dated: New York, New York   Michael B. Mukasey
December 4, 2002   U.S. District Judge

Declaration of Vice Admiral Lowell E. Jacoby (USN)
Director of the Defense Intelligence Agency

Pursuant to 28 U.S.C. § 1746, I, Vice Admiral Lowell E. Jacoby, hereby declare that, to the best of my knowledge, information, and belief, and under penalty of perjury, the following is true and correct:

<u>Summary</u>

I submit this Declaration for the Court's consideration in the matter of <u>Jose Padilla v. George W. Bush et al.</u>, Case No. 02 Civ. 4445, pending in the United States District Court for the Southern District of New York. This Declaration addresses the following topics:

- my qualifications as an intelligence officer and Director of the Defense Intelligence Agency;
- the roles and mission of the Defense Intelligence Agency;
- the intelligence process;
- interrogations as an intelligence tool;
- interrogation techniques;
- use of interrogations in the War on Terrorism;
- intelligence value of Jose Padilla; and
- potential impact of granting Padilla access to counsel.

Based upon information provided to me in the course of my official duties, I am familiar with each of the topics addressed in this Declaration. I am also familiar with the interrogations of Jose Padilla ("Padilla") conducted by agents of the Federal Bureau of Investigation ("FBI") after his detention in Chicago on 8 May 2002 and by agents of the Department of Defense ("DoD") after DoD took control of Padilla on 9 June 2002. I have not included information obtained from any interrogations in this Declaration, however.

I assess Padilla's potential intelligence value as very high. I also firmly believe that providing Padilla access to counsel risks loss of a critical intelligence resource, resulting in a grave and direct threat to national security.

<u>Experience</u>

I am a Vice Admiral in the United States Navy, with more than 30 years of active federal commissioned service. I currently am the Director of the Defense Intelligence Agency. I report to the Secretary of Defense. In addition to other assignments, I have previously served as the Director of Intelligence (J2) for the Chairman of the Joint Chiefs of Staff; the Director of Intelligence for the Commander of the U.S. Pacific Command; the Commander of the Joint Intelligence Center Pacific; and the Commander of the Office of Naval Intelligence.

I have received the National Intelligence Medal of Achievement from the Director of Central Intelligence. My military decorations include two Defense Distinguished Service Medals, the Navy Distinguished Service Medal, the Defense Superior Service Medal, and two Legions of Merit. I hold a Masters degree in National Security Affairs from the Naval Postgraduate School.

The Defense Intelligence Agency

The Defense Intelligence Agency ("DIA") is a DoD combat support agency with over 7,000 military and civilian employees worldwide. DIA is a component of DoD and an important member of the United States Intelligence Community—a federation of 14 executive branch agencies and organizations that work separately and cooperatively to conduct intelligence activities necessary to protect the national security of the United States.

DIA activities include collection of information needed by the President and Vice President, the National Security Council, the Secretaries of State and Defense, and other Executive Branch officials for the performance of their duties and responsibilities. One of DIA's highest priorities is to collect intelligence on terrorists, including al Qaida members, by interrogation and other means.

The Defense HUMINT Service ("DHS"), under DIA's Directorate for Operations, handles all human-source intelligence collection within DoD.

The Intelligence Process

The security of this Nation and its citizens is dependent upon the United States Government's ability to gather, analyze, and disseminate timely and effective intelligence. DIA has expended considerable efforts to develop effective intelligence techniques.

Generally speaking, the intelligence cycle can be broken down into five basic steps:

1. **Planning and direction.** Senior United States policy makers establish the intelligence requirements for DIA. DIA formulates more specific plans and directions to meet those requirements. Finished intelligence products also generate new requirements.

2. **Collection.** Raw intelligence data can be gathered by various means. Human-Source Intelligence ("HUMINT") is the oldest and historically the primary method of collecting intelligence. HUMINT includes clandestine acquisition of materials as well as overt collection of information through methods such as interrogation.

3. **Processing and exploitation.** Intelligence data, including human-source reports, must be converted to a form and context to make them more comprehensible to the intelligence analysts and other users.

4. **Analysis and production.** Intelligence analysts absorb the incoming information, evaluate it, and prepare a variety of intelligence products.

5. **Dissemination.** After reviewing intelligence information and correlating it with other information available, analysts typically disseminate finished intelligence to various users.

One critical feature of the intelligence process is that it must be continuous. Any interruption to the intelligence gathering process, especially from an external source, risks mission failure. The timely, effective use of intelligence provides this Nation with the best chance of achieving success in combating terrorism at home and abroad, thus helping to prevent future catastrophic terrorist attacks.

Protecting the specific sources and methods used during the intelligence process is of paramount importance to the integrity of the process. DIA employs all available safeguards to ensure that its sources and methods are not intentionally or inadvertently made public or disclosed outside the Intelligence Community, because of the resulting damage to intelligence collection efforts.

Interrogation as an Intelligence Tool

Interrogation is a fundamental tool used in the gathering of intelligence. Interrogation is the art of questioning and examining a source to obtain the maximum amount of usable, reliable information in the least amount of time to meet intelligence requirements. Sources may include insurgents, enemy combatants, defectors, refugees, displaced persons, agents, suspected agents, or others.

Interrogations are vital in all combat operations, regardless of the intensity of conflict. Interrogation permits the collection of information from sources with direct knowledge of, among other things, plans, locations, and persons seeking to do harm to the United States and its citizens. When done effectively, interrogation provides information that likely could not be gained from any other source. Interrogations can provide information on almost any topic of intelligence interest.

The Department of the Army's Field Manual governing Intelligence Interrogation, FM 34-52, dated 28 September 1992, provides several examples of the importance of interrogations in gathering intelligence. The Manual cites, for example, the United States General Board on Intelligence survey of nearly 80 intelligence units after World War II. Based upon those surveys, the Board estimated that 43 percent of all intelligence produced in the European theater of operations was from HUMINT, and 84 percent of the HUMINT was from interrogation. The majority of those surveyed agreed that interrogation was the most valuable of all collection operations.

The Army Field Manual also notes that during OPERATION DESERT STORM, DoD interrogators collected information that, among other things, helped to:
- develop a plan to breach Iraqi defensive belts;
- confirm Iraqi supply-line interdiction by coalition air strikes;

- identify diminishing Iraqi troop morale; and
- identify a United States Prisoner of War captured during the battle of Kafji.

Interrogation Techniques

DIA's approach to interrogation is largely dependent upon creating an atmosphere of dependency and trust between the subject and interrogator. Developing the kind of relationship of trust and dependency necessary for effective interrogations is a process that can take a significant amount of time. There are numerous examples of situations where interrogators have been unable to obtain valuable intelligence from a subject until months, or even years, after the interrogation process began.

Anything that threatens the perceived dependency and trust between the subject and interrogator directly threatens the value of interrogation as an intelligence-gathering tool. Even seemingly minor interruptions can have profound psychological impacts on the delicate subject-interrogator relationship. Any insertion of counsel into the subject-interrogator relationship, for example—even if only for a limited duration or for a specific purpose—can undo months of work and may permanently shut down the interrogation process. Therefore, it is critical to minimize external influences on the interrogation process. Indeed, foreign governments have used these techniques against captured DoD personnel.

Even the Geneva Convention Relative to the Protection of Civilian Persons in Time of War of August 12, 1949—which the President has determined does not apply to enemy combatants such as Padilla—recognizes that a detainee's ability to communicate with members of his or her family or government may be suspended when such a person is suspected of engaging in activities hostile to the security of the detaining State.

Use of Interrogations in the War on Terrorism

Terrorism poses an asymmetric threat to the United States. "Asymmetric warfare" generally consists of unanticipated or non-traditional approaches to circumvent or undermine an adversary's strengths while exploiting its vulnerabilities through unexpected technologies or innovative means. "Asymmetric warfare" may also consist of leveraging inferior tactical or operational strength against American vulnerabilities to achieve disproportionate effect with the aim of undermining American will in order to achieve the asymmetric actor's strategic objectives.

Unlike any previous conflict, we face a foe that knows no borders and perceives all Americans, wherever they may be, as targets of opportunity. Our terrorist enemies have also clearly demonstrated their willingness—and in fact have expressed their intent—to use any type of potential weapon, including weapons of mass destruction.

This asymmetric threat creates difficult and unique challenges for DIA because of the many variables in identifying and addressing the threat. The complexities of the problem—and the dire consequences at stake—require innovative and aggressive solutions.

As explained above, the intelligence cycle is continuous. This dynamic is especially important in the War on Terrorism. There is a constant need to ask detainees new lines of questions as additional detainees are taken into custody and new information is obtained from them and from other intelligence-gathering methods. Thus, it is vitally important to maintain an ongoing intelligence process, including interrogations.

The United States is now engaged in a robust program of interrogating individuals who have been identified as enemy combatants in the War on Terrorism. These enemy combatants hold critical information about our enemy and its planned attacks against the United States that is vital to our national security.

These interrogations have been conducted at many locations worldwide by personnel from DIA and other organizations in the Intelligence Community. The results of these interrogations have provided vital information to the President, military commanders, and others involved in the War on Terrorism. It is estimated that more than 100 additional attacks on the United States and its interests have been thwarted since 11 September 2001 by the effective intelligence gathering efforts of the Intelligence Community and others.

In fact, Padilla's capture and detention were the direct result of such effective intelligence gathering efforts. The information leading to Padilla's capture came from a variety of sources over time, including the interrogation of other detainees. Knowledge of and disruption of al Qaida's plot to detonate a "dirty bomb" or arrange for other attacks within the United States may not have occurred absent the interrogation techniques described above.

Interrogating members of al Qaida, or those individuals trained by al Qaida, poses additional challenges and risks. Al Qaida is a highly dangerous and sophisticated terrorist organization that has studied and learned many counterintelligence techniques. An al Qaida training manual, "Military Studies in the Jihad Against the Tyrants," provides instructions regarding, among other things: the collection of intelligence; counter-interrogation techniques; and means of covert communication during periods of capture. As detainees collectively increase their knowledge about United States detention facilities and methods of interrogation, the potential risk to national security increases should those methods be released. Moreover, counsel or others given access to detainees could unwittingly provide information to the detainee, or be used by the detainee as a communication tool.

In summary, the War on Terrorism cannot be won without timely, reliable, and abundant intelligence. That intelligence cannot be obtained without robust interrogation efforts. Impairment of the interrogation tool—especially with respect to enemy combatants associated with al Qaida—would undermine our Nation's intelligence gathering efforts, thus jeopardizing the national security of the United States.

Intelligence Value of Jose Padilla

Padilla is currently being detained in the Naval Consolidated Brig, Charleston at Naval Weapons Station, Charleston, South Carolina. The President has determined that Padilla is closely associated with al Qaida, an international terrorist organization with which the United States is at war. The President has further determined that Padilla possesses intelligence, including intelligence about personnel and activities of al Qaida, that, if communicated to the United States, would aid our efforts to prevent further attacks by al Qaida on the United States, its armed forces, other government personnel, or its citizens.

Padilla has been implicated in several plots to carry out attacks against the United States, including the possible use of a "dirty" radiological bomb in Washington DC or elsewhere, and the possible detonation of explosives in hotel rooms, gas stations, and train stations.

As noted in the unclassified Declaration of Michael H. Mobbs, Special Advisor to the Under Secretary of Defense for Policy, dated 27 August 2002, Padilla has, among other things:
- met with senior Usama Bin Laden lieutenant Abu Zabaydah in Afghanistan about conducting terrorist operations in the United States;
- conducted research in the construction of a "uranium-enhanced" explosive device at an al Qaida safehouse in Pakistan;
- discussed plans to build and detonate a "radiological dispersal device" (also known as a "dirty bomb") within the United States;
- received training from al Qaida operatives in furtherance of terrorist activities;
- met with other senior al Qaida operatives to discuss Padilla's involvement and participation in terrorist activities targeting the United States; and
- spent time in Afghanistan, Pakistan, Saudi Arabia, Egypt, and Southwest Asia.

Thus, Padilla could potentially provide information about, among other things:
- details on any potential plot to attack the United States in which he has been implicated, including the identities and whereabouts of al Qaida members possibly still at large in the United States and elsewhere;
- additional al Qaida plans to attack the United States, its property, or its citizens;
- al Qaida recruitment;
- al Qaida training;
- al Qaida planning;
- al Qaida operations;
- al Qaida methods;
- al Qaida infrastructure;
- al Qaida capabilities, including potential nuclear capabilities;

- other al Qaida members and sympathizers; and
- al Qaida activities in Afghanistan, Pakistan, Saudi Arabia, Egypt, Southwest Asia, the United States, or elsewhere.

The information that Padilla may be able to provide is time-sensitive and perishable. As noted above, any information obtained from Padilla must be assessed in connection with other intelligence sources; similarly, Padilla is a potential source to help assess information obtained from other sources. Any delay in obtaining information from Padilla could have the severest consequences for national security and public safety.

Potential Impact of Granting Padilla Access to Counsel

Permitting Padilla any access to counsel may substantially harm our national security interests. As with most detainees, Padilla is unlikely to cooperate if he believes that an attorney will intercede in his detention: DIA's assessment is that Padilla is even more inclined to resist interrogation than most detainees. DIA is aware that Padilla has had extensive experience in the United States criminal justice system and had access to counsel when he was being held as a material witness. These experiences have likely heightened his expectations that counsel will assist him in the interrogation process. Only after such time as Padilla has perceived that help is not on the way can the United States reasonably expect to obtain all possible intelligence information from Padilla.

Because Padilla is likely more attuned to the possibility of counsel intervention than most detainees, I believe that any potential sign of counsel involvement would disrupt our ability to gather intelligence from Padilla. Padilla has been detained without access to counsel for seven months—since the DoD took control of him on 9 June 2002. Providing him access to counsel now would create expectations by Padilla that his ultimate release may be obtained through an adversarial civil litigation process. This would break—probably irreparably—the sense of dependency and trust that the interrogators are attempting to create.

At a minimum, Padilla might delay providing information until he believes that his judicial avenues of relief have been exhausted. Given the nature of his case, his prior experience in the criminal justice system, and the length of time that has already elapsed since his detention, Padilla might reasonably expect that his judicial avenues of relief may not be exhausted for many months or years.

Moreover, Padilla might harbor the belief that his counsel would be available to assist him at any point and that seven months is not an unprecedented time for him to be without access to counsel.

Any such delay in Padilla's case risks that plans for future attacks will go undetected during that period, and that whatever information Padilla may eventually provide will be outdated and more difficult to corroborate.

Additionally, permitting Padilla's counsel to learn what information Padilla may have provided to interrogators, and what information the interrogators may have provided Padilla, unnecessarily risks disclosure of the intelligence sources and methods being employed in the War on Terrorism.

In summary, the United States has an urgent and critical national security need to determine what Padilla knows. Padilla may hold extremely valuable information for the short-term and long-term security of the United States. Providing Padilla access to counsel risks the loss of a critical intelligence resource, and could affect our ability to detain other high value terrorist targets and to disrupt and prevent additional terrorist attacks.

LOWELL E. JACOBY, VADM, USN
Director of the Defense Intelligence Agency

Executed on 9 January 2003

UNITED STATES COURT OF APPEALS

FOR THE SECOND CIRCUIT

August Term, 2003

(Argued: November 17, 2003   Decided: December 18, 2003)

Docket Nos. 03-2235 (L); 03-2438 (Con.)

JOSE PADILLA, Donna R. Newman, as Next Friend of Jose Padilla,

Petitioner-Appellee-Cross-Appellant,

-v-

DONALD RUMSFELD,

Respondent-Appellant-Cross-Appellee.

• • •

POOLER and B.D. PARKER, *Circuit Judges*:

INTRODUCTION

This habeas corpus appeal requires us to consider a series of questions raised by Secretary of Defense Donald Rumsfeld and by Donna R. Newman, Esq., on behalf of Jose Padilla, an American citizen held by military authorities as an enemy combatant. Padilla is suspected of being associated with al Qaeda and planning terrorist attacks in this country. The questions were certified by the United States District Court for the Southern District of New York (Michael B. Mukasey, *C.J.*) and involve, among others: whether the Secretary of Defense is Padilla's "custodian" for habeas purposes, whether the Southern District of New York had jurisdiction over the petition, and whether the President has the authority to detain Padilla as an enemy combatant. We conclude that the Secretary of Defense is a proper respondent and that the District Court had jurisdiction. We also conclude that Padilla's detention was not authorized by Congress, and absent such authorization, the President does not have the power under Article II of the Constitution to detain as an enemy combatant an American citizen seized on American soil outside a zone of combat.

As this Court sits only a short distance from where the World Trade Center once stood, we are as keenly aware as anyone of the threat al Qaeda poses to our country and of the responsibilities the President and law enforcement officials bear for protecting the nation. But presidential authority does not exist in a vacuum, and this case involves not whether those responsibilities should be aggressively pursued, but whether the President is obligated, in the circumstances presented here, to share them with Congress.

Where, as here, the President's power as Commander-in-Chief of the armed forces and the domestic rule of law intersect, we conclude that clear congressional

734

authorization is required for detentions of American citizens on American soil because 18 U.S.C. §4001(a) (2000) (the "Non-Detention Act") prohibits such detentions absent specific congressional authorization. Congress's Authorization for Use of Military Force Joint Resolution, Pub. L. No. 107-40, 115 Stat. 224 (2001) ("Joint Resolution"), passed shortly after the attacks of September 11, 2001, is not such an authorization, and no exception to section 4001(a) otherwise exists. In light of this express prohibition, the government must undertake to show that Padilla's detention can nonetheless be grounded in the President's inherent constitutional powers. *See Youngstown Sheet & Tube Co. v. Sawyer*, 343 U.S. 579, 637–38 (Jackson, J., concurring). We conclude that it has not made this showing. In reaching this conclusion, we do not address the detention of an American citizen seized within a zone of combat in Afghanistan, such as the court confronted in *Hamdi v. Rumsfeld*, 316 F.3d 450 (4th Cir. 2003) (*"Hamdi III"*). Nor do we express any opinion as to the hypothetical situation of a congressionally authorized detention of an American citizen.

Accordingly, we remand to the District Court with instructions to issue a writ of habeas corpus directing Secretary Rumsfeld to release Padilla from military custody within 30 days, at which point the government can act within its legislatively conferred authority. For example, Padilla can be transferred to the appropriate civilian authorities who can bring criminal charges against him. If appropriate, he can also be held as a material witness in connection with grand jury proceedings. *See United States v. Awadallah*, 349 F.3d 42 (2d Cir. 2003). Under any scenario, Padilla will be entitled to the constitutional protections extended to other citizens.[1]

BACKGROUND

. . .

III. District Court Proceedings on the Habeas Petition

. . .

The District Court's order directed the parties to set conditions under which Padilla could meet with his counsel, but Secretary Rumsfeld declined to do so. Instead, more than a month after the *Padilla I* decision, the government moved for reconsideration of the portion of *Padilla I* that allowed him access to counsel, on the ground that no conditions could be set that would protect the national security. *Padilla ex rel. Newman v. Rumsfeld*, 243 F. Supp. 2d 42, 43–46 (S.D.N.Y. 2003) ("*Padilla II*"). Although Chief Judge Mukasey expressed doubts as to the procedural regularity of the motion, he nonetheless entertained it on the merits and denied it. *Id.* at 48–49, 57.

The government then moved for certification of the District Court's orders to obtain interlocutory review of the ruling on the issues on which it had lost. Chief Judge Mukasey certified his orders, identifying the following questions as "involv[ing] . . . controlling question[s] of law as to which there is substantial ground for difference of opinion" and the resolution of which "may materially advance the ultimate termination of the litigation." 28 U.S.C. §1292(b) (2000); *Padilla ex rel. Newman v. Rumsfeld*, 256 F. Supp. 2d 218, 222–23 (S.D.N.Y. 2003) ("*Padilla III*"):

    (1) Is the Secretary of Defense, Donald Rumsfeld, a proper respondent in this case?

    (2) Does this court have personal jurisdiction over Secretary Rumsfeld?

---

[1] Therefore, our holding effectively moots arguments raised by both parties concerning access to counsel, standard of review, and burden of proof.

(3) Does the President have the authority to designate as an enemy combatant an American citizen captured within the United States, and, through the Secretary of Defense, to detain him for the duration of armed conflict with al Qaeda?

(4) What burden must the government meet to detain petitioner as an enemy combatant?

(5) Does petitioner have the right to present facts in support of his habeas corpus petition?

(6) Was it a proper exercise of this court's discretion and its authority under the All Writs Act to direct that petitioner be afforded access to counsel for the purpose of presenting facts in support of his petition?

Id. at 223.

On June 10, 2003, this Court granted the parties' application for an interlocutory appeal.[5]

DISCUSSION

. . .

II. Power to Detain

A. Introduction

The District Court concluded, and the government maintains here, that the indefinite detention of Padilla was a proper exercise of the President's power as Commander-in-Chief. The power to detain Padilla is said to derive from the President's authority, settled by *Ex parte Quirin*, 317 U.S. 1 (1942), to detain enemy combatants in wartime – authority that is argued to encompass the detention of United States citizens seized on United States soil. This power, the court below reasoned, may be exercised without a formal declaration of war by Congress and "even if Congressional authorization were deemed necessary, the Joint Resolution, passed by both houses of Congress, . . . engages the President's full powers as Commander in Chief." *Padilla I*, 233 F. Supp. 2d at 590. Specifically, the District Court found that the Joint Resolution acted as express congressional authorization under 18 U.S.C. §4001(a), which prohibits the detention of American citizens absent such authorization. *Id.* at 598–99. In addition, the government claims that 10 U.S.C. §956(5), a statute that allows the military to use authorized funds for certain detentions, grants authority to detain American citizens.

These alternative arguments require us to examine the scope of the President's inherent power and, if this is found insufficient to support Padilla's detention, whether Congress has authorized such detentions of American citizens. We reemphasize, however, that our review is limited to the case of an American citizen arrested in the United States, not on a foreign battlefield or while actively engaged in armed conflict against the United States. As the Fourth Circuit recently – and accurately – noted in *Hamdi v. Rumsfeld*, "[t]o compare this battlefield capture [of Hamdi] to the domestic arrest in *Padilla v. Rumsfeld* is to compare apples and oranges." 337 F.3d 335, 344 (4th Cir. 2003) ("*Hamdi IV*") (Wilkinson, *J.*, concurring).

---

[5] Twelve amici submitted briefs in support of Petitioner and one in support of Respondent. Almost all of these briefs have been helpful to us. We particularly appreciate the amici's care in emphasizing different issues and thus eliminating much of the redundancy that would otherwise exist. At oral argument on November 17, 2003, we requested post-argument submissions concerning the legislative history of the congressional acts urged to be dispositive of this case. These submissions were received by the Clerk's office on November 28, 2003, and by chambers on December 2, 2003.

B. The <u>Youngstown</u> Analysis

. . .

Here, we find that the President lacks inherent constitutional authority as Commander-in-Chief to detain American citizens on American soil outside a zone of combat. We also conclude that the Non-Detention Act serves as an explicit congressional "denial of authority" within the meaning of *Youngstown*, thus placing us in *Youngstown*'s third category. Finally, we conclude that because the Joint Resolution does not authorize the President to detain American citizens seized on American soil, we remain within *Youngstown*'s third category.

i.   Inherent Power

The government contends that the President has the inherent authority to detain those who take up arms against this country pursuant to Article II, Section 2, of the Constitution, which makes him the Commander-in-Chief, and that the exercise of these powers domestically does not require congressional authorization. Moreover, the argument goes, it was settled by *Quirin* that the military's authority to detain enemy combatants in wartime applies to American citizens as well as to foreign combatants. There the Supreme Court explained that "universal agreement and practice" under "the law of war" holds that "[l]awful combatants are subject to capture and detention as prisoners of war by opposing military forces" and "[u]nlawful combatants are likewise subject to capture and detention, but in addition they are subject to trial and punishment by military tribunals for acts which render their belligerency unlawful." 317 U.S. at 30–31. Finally, since the designation of an enemy combatant bears the closest imaginable connection to the President's constitutional responsibilities, principles of judicial deference are said by the government to assume heightened significance.

We agree that great deference is afforded the President's exercise of his authority as Commander-in-Chief. *See Dep't of the Navy v. Egan*, 484 U.S. 518, 530 (1988). We also agree that whether a state of armed conflict exists against an enemy to which the laws of war apply is a political question for the President, not the courts. *See Johnson v. Eisentrager*, 339 U.S. 763, 789 (1950) ("Certainly it is not the function of the Judiciary to entertain private litigation – even by a citizen – which challenges the legality, the wisdom, or the propriety of the Commander-in-Chief in sending our armed forces abroad or to any particular region."); *The Prize Cases*, 67 U.S. (2 Black) 635, 670 (1862). Because we have no authority to do so, we do not address the government's underlying assumption that an undeclared war exists between al Qaeda and the United States. We have no quarrel with the former chief of the Justice Department's Criminal Division, who said:

> For [al Qaeda] chose not to violate the law but to attack the law and its institutions directly. Their proclaimed goal, however unrealistic, was to destroy the United States. They used powerful weapons of destructive force and openly declared their willingness to employ even more powerful weapons of mass destruction if they could lay hold of them. They were as serious a threat to the national security of the United States as one could envision.

Michael Chertoff, *Law, Loyalty, and Terror: Our Legal Response to the Post-9-11 World*, Wkly. Standard, Dec. 1, 2003, at 15.

However, it is a different proposition entirely to argue that the President even in times of grave national security threats or war, whether declared or undeclared, can lay claim to any of the powers, express or implied, allocated to Congress. The deference due to the Executive in its exercise of its war powers therefore only starts the inquiry;

it does not end it. Where the exercise of Commander-in-Chief powers, no matter how well intentioned, is challenged on the ground that it collides with the powers assigned by the Constitution to Congress, a fundamental role exists for the courts. *See Marbury v. Madison*, 5 U.S. (1 Cranch) 137 (1803). To be sure, when Congress and the President act together in the conduct of war, "it is not for any court to sit in review of the wisdom of their action or substitute its judgment for theirs." *Hirabayashi v. United States*, 320 U.S. 81, 93 (1943). But when the Executive acts, even in the conduct of war, in the face of apparent congressional disapproval, challenges to his authority must be examined and resolved by the Article III courts. *See Youngstown*, 343 U.S. at 638 (Jackson, J., concurring).

These separation of powers concerns are heightened when the Commander-in-Chief's powers are exercised in the domestic sphere. The Supreme Court has long counseled that while the Executive should be "indulge[d] the widest latitude of interpretation to sustain his exclusive function to command the instruments of national force, at least when turned against the outside world for the security of our society," he enjoys "no such indulgence" when "it is turned inward." *Youngstown*, 343 U.S. at 645 (Jackson, J., concurring). This is because "the federal power over external affairs [is] in origin and essential character different from that over internal affairs," and "congressional legislation which is to be made effective through negotiation and inquiry within the international field must often accord to the President a degree of discretion and freedom from statutory restriction which would not be admissible were domestic affairs alone involved." *Curtiss-Wright*, 299 U.S. at 319, 320. But, "Congress, not the Executive, should control utilization of the war power as an instrument of domestic policy." *Youngstown*, 343 U.S. at 644 (Jackson, J., concurring). Thus, we do not concern ourselves with the Executive's inherent wartime power, generally, to detain enemy combatants on the battlefield. Rather, we are called on to decide whether the Constitution gives the President the power to detain an American citizen seized in this country until the war with al Qaeda ends.

The government contends that the Constitution authorizes the President to detain Padilla as an enemy combatant as an exercise of inherent executive authority. Padilla contends that, in the absence of express congressional authorization, the President, by his June 9 Order denominating Padilla an enemy combatant, has engaged in the "lawmaking" function entrusted by the Constitution to Congress in violation of the separation of powers. In response, no argument is made that the Constitution expressly grants the President the power to name United States citizens as enemy combatants and order their detention. Rather, the government contends that the Commander-in-Chief Clause implicitly grants the President the power to detain enemy combatants domestically during times of national security crises such as the current conflict with al Qaeda. U.S. Const. art. II, §2.

As an initial matter, we note that in its explicit vesting of powers in Articles I and II, the Constitution circumscribes and defines the respective functions of the political branches. *INS v. Chadha*, 462 U.S. 919, 946 (1983) ("The very structure of the Articles delegating and separating powers under Arts. I, II, and III exemplifies the concept of separation of powers...."). The Constitution gives Congress the full legislative powers of government and at the same time, gives the President full executive authority and responsibility to "take care" that the laws enacted are faithfully executed. U.S. Const. art I, §1, art. II, §§1, 3; *Loving v. United States*, 517 U.S. 748, 758 (1996) ("[T]he lawmaking function belongs to Congress... and may not be conveyed to another branch or entity"); *Field v. Clark*, 143 U.S. 649, 692 (1892). Thus, while the President has the obligation to enforce laws passed by Congress, he does not have the power to legislate.

The propriety of a given branch's conduct does not turn on the labeling of activity as "legislative" or "executive." *See Mistretta v. United States*, 488 U.S. 361, 393 (1989). Legislative action depends "not on form but upon whether [it] contain[s] matter which is properly to be regarded as legislative in its character and effect." *Chadha*, 462 U.S. at 952 (internal quotation marks omitted). Thus, we must look to whether the exercise of power in question has been "subject to the carefully crafted restraints spelled out in the Constitution," *id.* at 959, to ensure that authority is exercised only by the branch to which it has been allocated. *See Youngstown*, 343 U.S. at 587–588.

The Constitution entrusts the ability to define and punish offenses against the law of nations to the Congress, not the Executive. U.S. Const. art. I, §8, cl. 10; *United States v. Arjona*, 120 U.S. 479, 483 (1887). Padilla contends that the June 9 Order mandating his detention as an "enemy combatant" was not the result of congressional action defining the category of "enemy combatant." He also argues that there has been no other legislative articulation of what constitutes an "enemy combatant," what circumstances trigger the designation, or when it ends. As in *Youngstown*, Padilla maintains that "[t]he President's order does not direct that a congressional policy be executed in a manner prescribed by Congress – it directs that a presidential policy be executed in a manner prescribed by the President." *Youngstown*, 343 U.S. at 588.

The Constitution envisions grave national emergencies and contemplates significant domestic abridgements of individual liberties during such times. *See Kennedy v. Mendoza-Martinez*, 372 U.S. 144, 159–60 (1963). Here, the Executive lays claim to the inherent emergency powers necessary to effect such abridgements, but we agree with Padilla that the Constitution lodges these powers with Congress, not the President. *See Youngstown*, 343 U.S. at 649–50 (Jackson, *J.*, concurring).

First, the Constitution explicitly provides for the suspension of the writ of habeas corpus "when in Cases of Rebellion or Invasion the public Safety may require it." U.S. Const. art. I, §9, cl. 2. This power, however, lies only with Congress. *Ex parte Bollman*, 8 U.S. (4 Cranch) 75, 101 (1807). Further, determinations about the scope of the writ are for Congress. *Lonchar v. Thomas*, 517 U.S. 314, 323 (1996).

Moreover, the Third Amendment's prohibition on the quartering of troops during times of peace reflected the Framers' deep-seated beliefs about the sanctity of the home and the need to prevent military intrusion into civilian life.[23] *See, e.g., Laird v. Tatum*, 408 U.S. 1, 15 (1972); *Katz v. United States*, 389 U.S. 347, 350 n.5 (1967). At the same time they understood that in times of war – of serious national crisis – military concerns prevailed and such intrusions could occur. But significantly, decisions as to the nature and scope of these intrusions were to be made "in a manner to be prescribed by law." U.S. Const. amend. III. The only valid process for making "law" under the Constitution is, of course, via bicameral passage and presentment to the President, whose possible veto is subject to congressional override, provided in Article I, Section 7. *See Chadha*, 462 U.S. at 946–51.

The Constitution's explicit grant of the powers authorized in the Offenses Clause, the Suspension Clause, and the Third Amendment, to Congress is a powerful indication that, absent express congressional authorization, the President's Commander-in-Chief

---

[23] The full text of the Third Amendment states: "No Soldier shall, in time of peace be quartered in any house, without the consent of the Owner, nor in time of war, but in a manner to be prescribed by law." U.S. Const. amend. III.

powers do not support Padilla's confinement. *See id.* at 946. The level of specificity with which the Framers allocated these domestic powers to Congress and the lack of any even near-equivalent grant of authority in Article II's catalogue of executive powers compels us to decline to read any such power into the Commander-in-Chief Clause. In sum, while Congress – otherwise acting consistently with the Constitution – may have the power to authorize the detention of United States citizens under the circumstances of Padilla's case, the President, acting alone, does not.[24] *See Youngstown*, 343 U.S. at 631–32 (Douglas, *J.*, concurring).

The government argues that *Quirin* established the President's inherent authority to detain Padilla. In *Quirin*, the Supreme Court reviewed the habeas petitions of German soldiers captured on United States soil during World War II. All of the petitioners had lived in the United States at some point in their lives and had been trained in the German Army in the use of explosives. *See* 317 U.S. at 20–21. These soldiers, one of whom would later claim American citizenship, landed in the United States and shed their uniforms intending to engage in acts of military sabotage. They were arrested in New York and Chicago, tried by a military commission as "unlawful combatants," and sentenced to death. The Court denied the soldiers' petitions for habeas corpus, holding that the alleged American citizenship of one of the saboteurs was immaterial to its judgment: "Citizenship in the United States of an enemy belligerent does not relieve him from the consequences of a belligerency which is unlawful because in violation of the law of war." *Id.* at 37. The government contends that *Quirin* conclusively establishes the President's authority to exercise military jurisdiction over American citizens.

We do not agree that *Quirin* controls. First, and most importantly, the *Quirin* Court's decision to uphold military jurisdiction rested on express congressional authorization of the use of military tribunals to try combatants who violated the laws of war. *Id.* at 26–28. Specifically, the Court found it "unnecessary for present purposes to determine to what extent the President as Commander in Chief has constitutional power to create military commissions without the support of Congressional legislation." *Id.* at 29.[25] Accordingly, *Quirin* does not speak to whether, or to what degree, the President may impose military authority upon United States citizens domestically without clear congressional authorization. We are reluctant to read into *Quirin* a principle that the *Quirin* Court itself specifically declined to promulgate.[26]

---

[24] The dissent misreads us to suggest that the President has no power to deal with imminent acts of belligerency on U.S. soil outside a zone of combat and absent express authorization from Congress. *See infra at* **[57–58]**. We make no such claim. As we have discussed, criminal mechanisms exist for dealing with such situations. We only hold that the President's Commander-in-Chief powers do not encompass the detention of a United States citizen as an enemy combatant taken into custody on United States soil outside a zone of combat.

[25] The dissent argues that *Quirin* located the President's authority to try the saboteurs before a military tribunal, in part, on his powers as Commander-in-Chief. 317 U.S. at 28. However, the Court clearly viewed the statutory basis as the primary ground for the imposition of military jurisdiction, and regarded any inherent executive authority, if indeed it existed, as secondary: "By his Order creating the present Commission [the President] has undertaken to exercise the authority conferred upon him by Congress, and also *such* authority as the Constitution itself gives the Commander in Chief . . . ." *Id.* The Court certainly did not find the President's Commander-in-Chief powers independently sufficient to authorize such military commissions. In fact, as noted above, the Court explicitly declined to reach this question.

[26] The government relies heavily on the factual parallels between the *Quirin* saboteurs and Padilla. Similar to the *Quirin* saboteurs, Padilla allegedly traveled overseas to Afghanistan and Pakistan, where he engaged in extended discussions with senior al Qaeda operatives about conducting hostile operations within the United States. Padilla is also alleged to have received explosives training and to have returned to the United States to advance prospective al Qaeda attacks against this country. We are not persuaded by these factual parallels that the President can act to place citizens in military detention absent congressional authorization because the *Quirin* Court relied on such authorization to justify the detention and military trial of the *Quirin* saboteurs, an authorization that we believe is lacking here.

Moreover, there are other important distinctions between *Quirin* and this case. First, when *Quirin* was decided in 1942, section 4001(a) had not yet been enacted. The *Quirin* Court consequently had no occasion to consider the effects of legislation prohibiting the detention of American citizens absent statutory authorization. As a result, *Quirin* was premised on the conclusion – indisputable at the time – that the Executive's domestic projection of military authority had been authorized by Congress. Because the *Quirin* Court did not have to contend with section 4001(a), its usefulness is now sharply attenuated.

Second, the petitioners in *Quirin* admitted that they were soldiers in the armed forces of a nation against whom the United States had formally declared war. The *Quirin* Court deemed it unnecessary to consider the dispositive issue here – the boundaries of the Executive's military jurisdiction – because the *Quirin* petitioners "upon the conceded facts, were plainly within those boundaries." *Id.* at 46. Padilla makes no such concession. To the contrary, he, from all indications, intends to dispute his designation as an enemy combatant, and points to the fact that the civilian accomplices of the *Quirin* saboteurs – citizens who advanced the sabotage plots but who were not members of the German armed forces – were charged and tried as civilians in civilian courts, not as enemy combatants subject to military authority. *Haupt v. United States*, 330 U.S. 631 (1947); *Cramer v. United States*, 325 U.S. 1 (1945).

In *Ex parte Milligan*, 71 U.S. (4 Wall.) 2 (1866), the government unsuccessfully attempted to prosecute before a military tribunal a citizen who, never having belonged to or received training from the Confederate Army, "conspired with bad men" to engage in acts of war and sabotage against the United States. 71 U.S. at 131. Although *Quirin* distinguished *Milligan* on the ground that "Milligan, not being a part of or associated with the armed forces of the enemy, was a non-belligerent, [and] not subject to the law of war," 317 U.S. at 45, a more germane distinction rests on the different statutes involved in *Milligan* and *Quirin*. During the Civil War, Congress authorized the President to suspend the writ of habeas corpus. *Milligan*, 71 U.S. at 4. However, it also limited his power to detain indefinitely "citizens of States in which the administration of the laws had continued unimpaired in the Federal courts, who were then held, or might thereafter be held, as prisoners of the United States, under the authority of the President, otherwise than as prisoners of war." *Id.* at 5.

This limitation was embodied in a requirement that the Executive furnish a list of such prisoners to the district and circuit courts and, upon request by a prisoner, release him if the grand jury failed to return an indictment. *Id.* The grand jury sitting when Milligan was detained failed to indict him. *Id.* at 7. The Court concluded that because "Congress could grant no . . . power" to authorize the military trial of a civilian in a state where the courts remained open and functioning, and because congress had not attempted to do so Milligan could not be tried by a military tribunal. *Id.* at 121–22. Thus, both *Quirin* and *Milligan* are consistent with the principle that primary authority for imposing military jurisdiction upon American citizens lies with Congress. Even though *Quirin* limits to a certain extent the broader holding in *Milligan* that citizens cannot be subjected to military jurisdiction while the courts continue to function, *Quirin* and *Milligan* both teach that – at a minimum – an Act of Congress is required to expand military jurisdiction.

The government's argument for the legality of Padilla's detention also relies heavily on the Fourth Circuit's decisions in *Hamdi II* and *Hamdi III*. These decisions are inapposite. The Fourth Circuit directly predicated its holdings on the undisputed fact that Hamdi was captured in a zone of active combat in Afghanistan. *Hamdi III*, 316 F.3d at 459 ("Because it is undisputed that Hamdi was captured in a zone of active combat in a foreign theater of conflict, we hold that . . . [n]o further factual inquiry is necessary or proper."). The court said:

> We have no occasion . . . to address the designation as an enemy combatant of an American citizen captured on American soil or the role that counsel might play in such a proceeding. We shall, in fact, go no further in this case than the specific context before us – that of the undisputed detention of a citizen during a combat operation undertaken in a foreign country."

Hamdi III, at 465 (internal citation omitted).

The dissent also relies on *The Prize Cases*, which, like *Milligan*, arose out of the Civil War, to conclude that the President has the inherent constitutional authority to protect the nation when met with belligerency and to determine what degree of responsive force is necessary. Neither the facts nor the holding of *The Prize Cases* supports such a broad construction.

First, *The Prize Cases* dealt with the capture of enemy property – not the detention of persons. The Court had no occasion to address the strong constitutional arguments against deprivations of personal liberty, or the question of whether the President could infringe upon individual liberty rights through the exercise of his wartime powers outside a zone of combat.

Second, the dissent would have us read *The Prize Cases* as resolving any question as to whether the President may detain Padilla as an enemy combatant without congressional authorization. The Court did not, however, rest its decision upholding the exercise of the President's military authority solely on his constitutional powers without regard to congressional authorization. Rather, it noted that the President's authority to "call[ ] out the militia and use the military and naval forces of the United States in case of invasion by foreign nations, and to suppress insurrection against the government" stemmed from "the Acts of Congress of February 28th, 1795, and 3d of March, 1807." *Id.* at 668. In any event, Congress's subsequent ratification of the President's wartime orders mooted any questions of presidential authority. *Id.* at 670. Finally, the Court in *The Prize Cases* was not faced with the Non-Detention Act specifically limiting the President's authority to detain American citizens absent express congressional authorization.

Based on the text of the Constitution and the cases interpreting it, we reject the government's contention that the President has inherent constitutional power to detain Padilla under the circumstances presented here.[27] Therefore, under *Youngstown*, we must now consider whether Congress has authorized such detentions.

ii. Congressional Acts

a.   The Non-Detention Act

As we have seen, the Non-Detention Act provides: "No citizen shall be imprisoned or otherwise detained by the United States except pursuant to an Act of Congress." 18 U.S.C. §4001(a). The District Court held that this language "encompasses all detentions of United States citizens." *Padilla I*, 233 F. Supp. 2d at 597.

We review this interpretation de novo. *United States v. Lucien*, 347 F.3d 45, 50 (2d Cir. 2003). In conducting our review, we must first examine the language of the statute

---

[27] The dissent expresses deep concern that our holding means that the President lacks inherent authority to detain a terrorist in the face of imminent attack. The President's authority to detain such a person is not an issue raised by this case. The dissent's concerns overlook the fact that Padilla was detained by the military while a maximum security inmate at the MCC. Thus, issues concerning imminent danger simply do not arise in this case.

and assume that its "ordinary meaning . . . accurately expresses the legislative purpose." *Id.* at 51 (internal quotation marks omitted). If the plain language is unambiguous, "judicial inquiry ends, except in 'rare and exceptional circumstances,' and legislative history is instructive only upon 'the most extraordinary showing of contrary intentions.'" *Id.* (quoting *Garcia v. United States*, 469 U.S. 70, 75 (1984)).

We read the plain language of section 4001(a) to prohibit all detentions of citizens – a conclusion first reached by the Supreme Court. *Howe v. Smith*, 452 U.S. 473, 479 n.3 (1981) (characterizing the Non-Detention Act as "proscribing detention *of any kind* by the United States" (emphasis in original)). Not only has the government not made an extraordinary showing of contrary intentions, but the legislative history of the Non-Detention Act is fully consistent with our reading of it. Both the sponsor of the Act and its primary opponent repeatedly confirmed that the Act applies to detentions by the President during war and other times of national crisis. The legislative history is replete with references to the detentions of American citizens of Japanese descent during World War II, detentions that were authorized both by congressional acts and by orders issued pursuant to the President's war power. This context convinces us that military detentions were intended to be covered. Finally, the legislative history indicates that Congress understood that exceptions to the Non-Detention Act must specifically authorize *detentions*.

Section 4001(a) was enacted in 1971 and originated as an amendment to legislation repealing the Emergency Detention Act of 1950, former 50 U.S.C. §§811–26 (1970), which authorized the detention by the Attorney General during an invasion, a declared war, or "an insurrection within the United States in aid of a foreign enemy" of "each person as to whom there is reasonable ground to believe that such person probably will engage in, or probably will conspire with others to engage in, acts of espionage or of sabotage." 50 U.S.C. §§812(a), 813(a) (1970). Congress referred to section 4001(a) as the Railsback amendment for its drafter, Representative Railsback. The Railsback amendment emerged from the House Judiciary Committee and was opposed by the House Internal Security Committee, which offered other alternatives.

Congressman Ichord, the chair of the House Internal Security Committee and the primary opponent of the Railsback amendment, argued that it would tie the President's hands in times of national emergency or war. He characterized the amendment as "this most dangerous committee amendment" and as "depriv[ing] the President of his emergency powers and his most effective means of coping with sabotage and espionage agents in war-related crises." 117 Cong. Rec. H31542 (daily ed. Sept. 13, 1971). Representative Ichord's alarm stemmed from his belief that *Youngstown* "teaches that where the Congress has acted on a subject within its jurisdiction, sets forth its policy, and asserts its authority, the President might not thereafter act in a contrary manner." *Id.* at H31544; *see id.* at H31549 ("I do feel that the language of the amendment drafted by [Representative Railsback] under the Youngstown Steel case would prohibit even the picking up, at the time of a declared war, at a time of an invasion of the United States, a man whom we would have reasonable cause to believe would commit espionage or sabotage.").

No proponent of the Railsback amendment challenged Representative Ichord's interpretation. In fact, in a striking exchange between Representatives Ichord and Railsback, he ratified Representative Ichord's interpretation. Representative Ichord asked: "Does [Representative Railsback] believe that in this country today there are people who are skilled in espionage and sabotage that might pose a possible threat to this Nation in the event of a war with nations of which those people are nationals or citizens?" *Id.* at H31551. Representative Railsback responded, "Yes." *Id.* Representative Ichord then asked: "Does the gentleman believe then that if we were to become engaged in a war with the country of those nationals, that we would permit those people to run at large without apprehending them, and wait until after the sabotage is committed?" *Id.* Railsback answered:

> I think what would happen is what J. Edgar Hoover thought could have happened when he opposed the actions that were taken in 1942. He suggested the FBI would have under surveillance those people in question and those persons they had probable cause to think would commit such actions. Does the gentleman know that J. Edgar Hoover was opposed to detention camps, because be thought he had sufficient personnel to keep all these potential saboteurs under surveillance, and that they could prosecute the guilty in accordance with due process?

Id. at H31551–52. Railsback also suggested to Congress that the President could seize citizens only pursuant to an Act of Congress or during a time of martial law when the courts are not open. *Id.* at 31755.[28]

Congress's passage of the Railsback amendment by a vote of 257 to 49 after ample warning that both the sponsor of the amendment and its primary opponent believed it would limit detentions in times of war and peace alike is strong evidence that the amendment means what it says, that is that no American citizen can be detained without a congressional act authorizing the detention.

In addition, almost every representative who spoke in favor of repeal of the Emergency Detention Act or adoption of the Railsback amendment or in opposition to other amendments, described the detention of Japanese-American citizens during World War II as the primary motivation for their positions. *See, e.g., id.* at H31537 (Rep. Railsback); *id.* at H31541 (Rep. Poff); *id.* at H31549 (Rep. Giaimo); *id.* at H31555 (Rep. Eckhardt); *id.* at H31556 (Rep. Mikva); *id.* at H31560 (Rep. Lloyd); *id.* at H31565 (Rep. Edwards); *id.* at H31568 (Rep. Wyatt); *id.* at H31571–72 (Rep. Matsunaga); *id.* at H31573 (Rep. Johnson); *id.* at H31757 (Rep. Wright); *id.* at H31760 (Rep. Holifield); *id.* at H31770–71(Rep. Hansen); *id.* at H31772–73 (Rep. Anderson); *id.* at H31779 (Reps. Drinan and Pepper). Because the World War II detentions were authorized pursuant to the President's war making powers as well as by a congressional declaration of war and by additional congressional acts, *see Endo*, 323 U.S. at 285–90, the manifest congressional concern about these detentions also suggests that section 4001(a) limits military as well as civilian detentions.

Finally, a statement by Representative Eckhardt demonstrates that Congress intended to require its express authorization before the President could detain citizens. He said: "You have got to have an act of Congress to detain, and the act of Congress *must authorize detention*." *Id.* at H31555 (emphasis added). Based primarily on the plain language of the Non-Detention Act but also on its legislative history and the Supreme Court's interpretation, we conclude that the Act applies to all detentions and that precise and specific language authorizing the detention of American citizens is required to override its prohibition.

---

[28] Railsback and Ichord's shared view of the scope of the Non-Detention Act was echoed by another opponent of the bill. *See, e.g., id.* at 31554 (Representative Williams stating that "I do not want to see the President's hands tied by the language of the [Railsback] proposal which would require an Act of Congress before any likely subversive or would-be saboteur could be detained"). However, another opponent of the bill and member of the Internal Security Committee argued that even with the Railsback amendment, the President could declare a national emergency and act to detain citizens using his inherent powers. *See id.* at 31547 (remarks of Representative Ashbrook). We address the President's inherent powers *supra* at Section II.B.ii.

Despite its plain language, the government argues that section 4001(a) is intended to preclude only detentions by the Attorney General, not by the military. Its first argument is a constitutional one: to construe section 4001(a) to include military detentions would, in the government's view, risk construing it as an unconstitutional abridgement of the President's war powers. Its second argument is a statutory "placement" argument, which the government claims is supported in two ways. First, it contends that because section 4001(a) appears in a section governing the management of prisons, it does not constrain the President's war power. Second, it maintains that because section 4001(a) immediately precedes section 4001(b)(1), which vests authority to manage prisons in the Attorney General but specifically excludes military prisons from his purview, section 4001(a) must be read to exclude military detentions.

The District Court correctly declined to construe section 4001(a) to apply only to civilian detentions in order to avoid a construction of the statute that would unconstitutionally limit the President's war power. It held that the "doctrine of constitutional avoidance 'has no application in the absence of statutory ambiguity.'" *Padilla I*, 233 F. Supp. 2d at 597 (quoting *HUD v. Rucker*, 535 U.S. 125, 134 (2002)). We agree. For the reasons discussed above, we have found that the statute is unambiguous. Moreover, this interpretation poses no risk of unconstitutionally abridging the President's war powers because, as we have also discussed above, the President, acting alone, possesses no inherent constitutional authority to detain American citizens seized within the United States, away from a zone of combat, as enemy combatants.[29]

Nor are we persuaded by the government's statutory placement argument. No accepted canon of statutory interpretation permits "placement" to trump text, especially where, as here, the text is clear and our reading of it is fully supported by the legislative history. While we, of course, as the government argues, read statutes as a whole to determine the most likely meaning of particular provisions or terms, this principle has no application here. *Greater New York Metro. Food Council, Inc. v. Giuliani*, 195 F.3d 100, 105 (2d Cir. 1999). Section 4001(b)(1) was enacted many decades prior to the Emergency Detention Act as part of entirely different legislation. The government points to nothing suggesting the two subsections share a common origin or meaning rather than simply a common code designation. In any event, reliance on subsection (b)(1) suggests a conclusion opposite to the one the government proposes. Subsection (b)(1) provides:

> The control and management of Federal penal and correctional institutions, except military or naval institutions, shall be vested in the Attorney General, who shall promulgate rules for the government thereof, and appoint all necessary officers and employees in accordance with the civil-service laws, the Classification Act, as amended and the applicable regulations.

---

[29] If the President's Commander-in-Chief powers were plenary in the context of a domestic seizure of an American citizen, the government's argument that the legislature could not constitutionally prohibit the President from detaining citizens would have some force. *Cf. Hamdi III*, 316 F.3d at 468 (stating that " §4001(a) functioned principally to repeal the Emergency Detention Act [which] had provided for the preventive 'apprehension and detention' of individuals *inside* the United States 'deemed likely to engage in espionage or sabotage' during 'internal security emergencies'" and that "[t]here is no indication that §4001(a) was intended to overrule the longstanding rule that an armed and hostile American citizen *captured on the battlefield* during wartime may be treated like the enemy combatant that he is" (quoting H.R. Rep. No. 92-116, at 2 (1971)) (emphases added)). In view of the plain language of the Act, it might have been preferable to hold that Congress could not intrude on the President's Commander-in-Chief power on the battlefield rather than to interpret the Act as the Fourth Circuit did. We do not have to reach that issue, however. As we have previously noted, Judge Wilkinson, one of the authors of *Hamdi III*, remarked in his later concurrence to the decision not to rehear *Hamdi III* en banc that "[t]o compare this battlefield capture to the domestic arrest in *Padilla v. Rumsfeld* is to compare apples and oranges." *Hamdi IV*, 337 F.3d at 344.

18 U.S.C. §4001(b)(1). In subsection (b)(1), Congress explicitly distinguished between military and civilian jurisdiction by authorizing the Attorney General to control all prisons except military institutions. The lack of any such distinction in subsection (a) suggests that none exists and that the Non-Detention Act applies to both civilian and military detentions.

b. *Specific Statutory Authorization*

Since we conclude that the Non-Detention Act applies to military detentions such as Padilla's, we would need to find specific statutory authorization in order to uphold the detention. The government claims that both the Joint Resolution, which authorized the use of force against the perpetrators of the September 11 terrorist attacks, and 10 U.S.C. §956(5), passed in 1984, which provides funding for military detentions, authorize the detention of enemy combatants. It is with respect to the Joint Resolution that we disagree with the District Court, which held that the Joint Resolution must be read to confer authority for Padilla's detention. It found that the "language [of the Joint Resolution] authorizes action against not only those connected to the subject organizations who are directly responsible for the September 11 attacks, but also against those who would engage in 'future acts of international Terrorism' as part of 'such . . . organizations.'" *Padilla I*, 233 F. Supp. 2d at 598–99.

We disagree with the assumption that the authority to use military force against these organizations includes the authority to detain American citizens seized on American soil and not actively engaged in combat. First, we note that the Joint Resolution contains no language authorizing detention. It provides:[30]

> That the President is authorized to use all necessary and appropriate force against those nations, organizations, or persons he determines planned, authorized, committed, or aided the terrorist attacks that occurred on September 11, 2001, or harbored such organizations or persons, in order to prevent any future acts of international terrorism against the United States by such nations, organizations or persons.

Joint Resolution §2(a).

Because the government seeks to read into the Joint Resolution authority to detain American citizens on American soil, we interpret its language in light of the principles enunciated in *Ex parte Endo*, 323 U.S. at 298–300. The *Endo* Court first recognized that "the Constitution when it committed to the Executive and to Congress the exercise of the war power necessarily gave them wide scope for the exercise of judgment and discretion so that war might be waged effectively and successfully." *Id.* at 298–99. It then said: "At the same time, however, the Constitution is as specific in its enumeration of many of the civil rights of the individual as it is in its enumeration of the powers of his government. Thus it has prescribed procedural safeguards surrounding the arrest, detention and conviction of individuals." *Id.* at 299. Therefore, the Court held: "[i]n interpreting a war-time measure we must assume that [the purpose of Congress and the Executive] was to allow for the greatest possible accommodation between those liberties and the exigencies of war." *Id.* at 300. The Court added: "We must assume, when asked to find implied powers in a grant of legislative or executive authority, that the law makers intended to place no greater restraint on the citizen than was *clearly* and *unmistakably* indicated by the language they used." *Id.* (emphasis added).

The plain language of the Joint Resolution contains nothing authorizing the detention of American citizens captured on United States soil, much less the express

---

30 . . .

authorization required by section 4001(a) and the "clear," "unmistakable" language required by *Endo*. While it may be possible to infer a power of detention from the Joint Resolution in the battlefield context where detentions are necessary to carry out the war, there is no reason to suspect from the language of the Joint Resolution that Congress believed it would be authorizing the detention of an American citizen already held in a federal correctional institution and not "arrayed against our troops" in the field of battle. *Hamdi III*, 316 F.3d at 467.[31]

Further, the Joint Resolution expressly provides that it is "intended to constitute specific statutory authorization within the meaning of . . . the War Powers Resolution." Joint Resolution §2(b); 50 U.S.C. §1541 *et seq.* The War Powers Resolution requires the President to cease military operations within 60 days unless Congress has declared war or specifically authorized the use of the armed forces. 50 U.S.C. §1544(b). It is unlikely – indeed, inconceivable – that Congress would expressly provide in the Joint Resolution an authorization required by the War Powers Resolution but, at the same time, leave unstated and to inference something so significant and unprecedented as authorization to detain American citizens under the Non-Detention Act.

Next, the Secretary argues that Padilla's detention is authorized by 10 U.S.C. §956(5), which allows the use of appropriated funds for "expenses incident to the maintenance, pay, and allowances of prisoners of war, other persons in the custody of the Army, Navy or Air Force whose status is determined by the Secretary concerned to be similar to prisoners of war, and persons detained in the custody of [the Armed Services] pursuant to Presidential proclamation." 10 U.S.C. §956(5). The Fourth Circuit found that section 956(5) along with the Joint Resolution sufficed to authorize Hamdi's detention. *Hamdi III*, 316 F.3d at 467–68. With respect to Section 956(5), the court said: "It is difficult if not impossible to understand how Congress could make appropriations for the detention of persons 'similar to prisoners of war' without also authorizing their detention in the first instance." *Id.*

At least with respect to American citizens seized off the battlefield, we disagree. Section 965(5) authorizes nothing beyond the expenditure of money. *Endo* unquestionably teaches that an authorization of funds devoid of language "clearly" and "unmistakably" authorizing the detention of American citizens seized here is insufficient. *See* 323 U.S. at 303 n.24 (acknowledging that Congress may ratify past actions of the Executive through appropriations acts but refusing to find in the appropriations acts at issue an intent to allow the Executive to detain a citizen indefinitely because the appropriation did not allocate funds "earmarked" for that type of detention). In light of *Endo*, the Non-Detention Act's requirement that Congress specifically authorize detentions of American citizens, and the guarantees of the Fourth and Fifth Amendments to the Constitution, we decline to impose on section 956(5) loads it cannot bear.

---

[31] The debates on the Joint Resolution are at best equivocal as to the President's powers and never mention the issue of detention. Therefore, even assuming they could overcome the lack of a specific grant to the President, they do not suggest that Congress authorized the detention of United States citizens captured on United States soil. Some legislators believed the President's authority was strictly limited. *See, e.g.,* 147 Cong. Rec. H5639 (Rep. Lantos: "to bring to bear the full force of American power abroad"). Supporters of the President's power argued that it was too limited. *See, e.g., id.* at H5653 (Rep. Barr arguing that in addition to the joint resolution, Congress should declare war to "[g]ive the President the tools, the absolute flexibility he needs under international law and The Hague Convention to ferret these people out wherever they are, however he finds them, and get it done as quickly as possible"); *id.* at H5654 (Rep. Smith: "This resolution should have authorized the President to attack, apprehend, and punish terrorists whenever it is in the best interests of America to do so. Instead, the resolution limits the President to using force only against those responsible for the terrorist attacks last Tuesday. This is a significant restraint on the President's ability to root out terrorism wherever it may be found.")

CONCLUSION

In sum, we hold that (1) Donna Newman, Esq., may pursue habeas relief on behalf of Jose Padilla; (2) Secretary of Defense Rumsfeld is a proper respondent to the habeas petition and the District Court had personal jurisdiction over him; (3) in the domestic context, the President's inherent constitutional powers do not extend to the detention as an enemy combatant of an American citizen seized within the country away from a zone of combat; (4) the Non-Detention Act prohibits the detention of American citizens without express congressional authorization; and (5) neither the Joint Resolution nor 10 U.S.C. §956(5) constitutes such authorization under section 4001(a). These conclusions are compelled by the constitutional and statutory provisions we have discussed above. The offenses Padilla is alleged to have committed are heinous crimes severely punishable under the criminal laws. Further, under those laws the Executive has the power to protect national security and the classified information upon which it depends. *See, e.g.,* 18 U.S.C. app. §3. And if the President believes this authority to be insufficient, he can ask Congress – which has shown its responsiveness – to authorize additional powers. To reiterate, we remand to the District Court with instructions to issue a writ of habeas corpus directing the Secretary of Defense to release Padilla from military custody within 30 days. The government can transfer Padilla to appropriate civilian authorities who can bring criminal charges against him. Also, if appropriate, Padilla can be held as a material witness in connection with grand jury proceedings. In any case, Padilla will be entitled to the constitutional protections extended to other citizens.

. . .

WESLEY, Circuit Judge, concurring in part, dissenting in part.

I respectfully dissent from that aspect of the majority's opinion that concludes the President is without authority from Congress or the Constitution to order the detention and interrogation of Mr. Padilla.[1] In my view, the President as Commander in Chief has the inherent authority to thwart acts of belligerency at home or abroad that would do harm to United States citizens. But even if Mr. Padilla's status as a United States citizen on United States soil somehow changes the constitutional calculus, I cannot see how the Non-Detention Act precludes an affirmance.

. . . I would affirm the thoughtful and thorough decision of Chief Judge Mukasey. . . . .

. . .

My disagreement with the majority is two-fold. In my view, the President, as Commander in Chief, has inherent authority to thwart acts of belligerency on U.S. soil that would cause harm to U.S. citizens, and, in this case, Congress through the Joint Resolution specifically and directly authorized the President to take the actions herein contested. The majority concludes the President is without inherent authority to detain Padilla. They agree that "great deference is afforded the President's exercise of his authority as Commander-in-Chief," **Maj. at 27** (citing *Dep't of the Navy v. Egan*, 484 U.S. 518, 530 (1988)), and concede the judiciary has no authority to determine the political question of whether the nation is at war. *Id.* They recognize that the President and Congress often work cooperatively during times of armed conflict. However, the majority contends that separation of powers concerns are heightened when the President's powers are exercised in the "domestic sphere" and that Congress, not the Executive, controls utilization of war powers when invoked as an instrument of domestic policy. **Maj. at 28.**

. . .

---

[1] . . .

No. 03-1027

In the Supreme Court of the United States

DONALD H. RUMSFELD, SECRETARY OF DEFENSE,
PETITIONER

v.

JOSE PADILLA AND DONNA R. NEWMAN,
AS NEXT FRIEND OF JOSE PADILLA

---

*ON PETITION FOR A WRIT OF CERTIORARI
TO THE UNITED STATES COURT OF APPEALS
FOR THE SECOND CIRCUIT*

REPLY BRIEF FOR THE PETITIONER

THEODORE B. OLSON
*Solicitor General
Counsel of Record
Department of Justice*

---

* Redaction on this page has been added for privacy purposes. – *Eds.*

. . .[6]

---

[6] As counsel for petitioners explained during oral argument before the court of appeals in November 2003, the Department of Defense (DOD), as a matter of discretion and military policy, has adopted a policy of permitting access to counsel by an enemy combatant who is a United States citizen and who is detained by the military in the United States, when DOD has determined that such access will not compromise the national security of the United States, and when DOD has determined either that it has completed intelligence collection from the enemy combatant or that granting access to counsel would not interfere with such intelligence gathering. See 11/17/03 Tr. 82–84, 113, 123–124. In accordance with DOD's policy and the military's ongoing evaluation of Padilla's detention, DOD has determined that Padilla may be permitted access to counsel subject to appropriate security restrictions. See http:// www.defenselink.mil/releases/2004/nr20040211-0341.html. That decision, along with the Second Circuit's own recognition that its broad ruling rendered arguments concerning access to counsel "effectively moot," counsel in favor of confining review to the questions presented in the petition.

No. 03-1027

In The

Supreme Court of the United States

DONALD RUMSFELD,

Petitioner,

v.

JOSE PADILLA AND DONNA R. NEWMAN,
AS NEXT FRIEND OF JOSE PADILLA,

Respondent.

On Petition for a Writ of Certiorari to the
United States Court of Appeals
for the Second Circuit

SUPPLEMENTAL BRIEF OF RESPONDENT

DAVID W. DeBRUIN
JENNER & BLOCK LLP

JENNY S. MARTINEZ

DONNA R. NEWMAN
Counsel of Record

ANDREW G. PATEL

WILSON-EPES PRINTING CO., INC.

---

* Redactions on this page have been added for privacy purposes. – *Eds.*

SUPPLEMENTAL BRIEF OF RESPONDENT

Pursuant to Supreme Court Rule 15.8, respondent submits this supplemental brief to call attention to intervening matter not available at the time of respondent's last filing.

The Government's assertion in this case of a novel and unprecedented Presidential power to imprison Jose Padilla indefinitely without any charges or trial necessarily raises fundamental questions concerning the scope of that authority, including: to whom this power may be applied; what type of conduct would subject an individual to this authority; what proof of that conduct is required and how is it reviewed; and whether there are limits on the duration of the detention. It is meaningless to ask whether the President has "authority" in this case without attempting to define what that authority is. And these questions necessarily must be considered in the context of this actual case, where the Government asks this Court to find authority for the President's continued detention of Mr. Padilla and to reverse the judgment of the Court of Appeals that – after 20 months of imprisonment in a military jail – Padilla either must be charged with a crime, detained as a material witness, or released.

The obvious need for the Court to consider these questions is not affected by the Government's surprise announcement earlier this week, as referenced in its reply brief filed that same day, *see* Reply Br. at 7 n.6, that Padilla suddenly would be allowed highly limited access to counsel. Two points are important.

First, the Government continues to deny that Padilla has any right to consult with the lawyers appointed by the District Court. As the Department of Defense (DoD) press release cited by the Government states: "DoD is allowing Padilla access to counsel as a matter of discretion and military authority. Such access is not required by domestic or international law and should not be treated as a precedent."[1] Thus, the Government may change its allegedly discretionary decision at any time.

Second, the conditions that the Government seeks to impose on any meeting between counsel and Padilla are so restrictive that such a meeting cannot be viewed in any meaningful sense as an attorney-client meeting. A DoD official will be present during any conversation, and the conversation will be videotaped and monitored by intelligence officials.[2]

For these reasons, the new facts created by the Government and disclosed in its reply brief should have no bearing on this Court's consideration and disposition of the Petition.

. . .

---

[1] News Release, *Padilla Allowed Access to Lawyers* (Feb. 11, 2004), at http://www.defenselink.mil/releases/2004/nr20040211-0341.html.

[2] *See* Shannon McCaffrey, *Alleged Dirty Bomb Plotter Given Access to Lawyer*, Knight-Ridder Newspapers, Feb. 11, 2004, *at* http://www.realcities.com/mld/krwashington/7931181.htm.

No. 03-1027

In the Supreme Court of the United States

Donald H. Rumsfeld, Secretary of Defense, Petitioner

v.

Jose Padilla and Donna R. Newman, as Next Friend of Jose Padilla

*ON WRIT OF CERTIORARI
TO THE UNITED STATES COURT OF APPEALS
FOR THE SECOND CIRCUIT*

BRIEF FOR THE PETITIONER

Theodore B. Olson
Solicitor General
Counsel of Record

Paul D. Clement
Deputy Solicitor General

Sri Srinivasan
David B. Salmons
Assistants to the Solicitor General

Jonathan L. Marcus
Attorney
Department of Justice

_____

* Redaction on this page has been added for privacy purposes. – *Eds.*

QUESTIONS PRESENTED[*]

1. Whether the district court has jurisdiction over the proper respondent to the amended habeas petition.

2. Whether the President has authority as Commander in Chief and in light of Congress's Authorization for Use of Military Force, Pub. L. No. 107-40, 115 Stat. 224, to seize and detain a United States citizen in the United States based on a determination by the President that he is an enemy combatant who is closely associated with al Qaeda and has engaged in hostile and war-like acts, or whether 18 U.S.C. 4001(a) precludes that exercise of Presidential authority.

. . .

ARGUMENT

I. THE DISTRICT COURT LACKS JURISDICTION OVER THE PROPER RESPONDENT TO THE AMENDED HABEAS PETITION

This case presents questions of exceptional national significance concerning the authority of the Commander in Chief to wage the ongoing conflict against al Qaeda. The court of appeals' approach to those issues was seriously flawed and warrants reversal. But the court also erred as an antecedent matter in holding that the district court properly asserted jurisdiction over the amended habeas petition. In a case raising sensitive questions of the magnitude and character presented here, it is especially important that a court be assured of its jurisdiction lest it pronounce on the merits of such questions without any authority to do so. See *Hamdi* v. *Rumsfeld*, 294 F.3d 598, 606–607 (4th Cir. 2002). That is what happened below.

The habeas statutes dictate, in the context of core habeas challenges to present, physical confinement, that the proceedings take place in the federal district of confinement. The habeas laws effectuate that territorial constraint through two complementary requirements. First, the detainee must bring his challenge to his present, physical detention against his immediate, on-site custodian rather than a supervisory official located in another, potentially far-removed district. Second, in such cases, a district court can issue the writ only within its territorial jurisdiction rather than reaching out to issue the writ against custodians located in other judicial districts. Those settled rules direct that the amended petition in this case should have been filed against Padilla's immediate custodian and heard in the District of South Carolina, not the Southern District of New York. The court of appeals misconceived both aspects of the jurisdictional inquiry.

A. The Proper Respondent To The Amended Habeas Petition Is Padilla's Immediate Physical Custodian, Commander Marr

1. The proper respondent in a habeas challenge to present, physical confinement is the person with day-to-day physical control over the detainee – *i.e.*, the immediate, on-site custodian, typically the warden or Commanding Officer of the facility. That settled rule is dictated by the terms of the habeas statutes. Those laws have long specified that the writ "shall be directed to *the person* having custody of the person detained." 28 U.S.C. 2243 (emphasis added); see Act of Feb. 5, 1867, ch. 28, §1, 14 Stat. 386. The focus on "the person" with control over the detainee is reinforced by the requirements that the

---

[*] The questions presented are listed here in the reverse order from the petition for certiorari. – *Eds.*

petitioner "allege *** the name of the person who has custody over him," 28 U.S.C. 2242, and that, in appropriate situations, "the person to whom the writ is directed shall *** produce at the hearing the body of the person detained," 28 U.S.C. 2243.

. . .

2. The court of appeals' contrary conclusion was based on a mistaken belief that the requirement to name the immediate custodian is inapplicable when the petitioner is "detained for reasons other than federal criminal violations." ..... However, there is a single federal habeas statute for criminal and non-criminal detentions, and the terms of the statute require the writ to be directed to the person with day-to-day physical control over the detainee. Nothing in the relevant statutory language suggests any pertinent distinction between criminal and non-criminal detentions. See *Vasquez* [v. *Reno*], 233 F.3d [688,] 693 [(1ˢᵗ Cir. 2000), cert. denied, 534 U.S. 816 (2001)]. In either case, the proper respondent is the "person having custody of the person detained," who is best situated to "produce *** the body of the person detained" if necessary. 28 U.S.C. 2243.

The court of appeals also emphasized . . . that Secretary Rumsfeld owns "the legal reality of control" because he is in a position to advise the President concerning when Padilla's detention as an enemy combatant may no longer be necessary. But that argument does not distinguish this case from any other habeas proceeding: *no* prison warden or facility commander has independent authority to determine the duration of a detainee's confinement. As the Seventh Circuit explained in *Al-Marri*, "there is a difference between authorizing and exercising custody." 2004 WL 415279, at *1. A host of officials from the sentencing judge to the prosecutor may play a role in determining the length of a detainee's confinement, but "for an inmate of a brig, jail, or prison, the 'custodian' is the person in charge of that institution." *Id.* at *1.

. . .

B. A Habeas Court Cannot Reach Respondents Located Beyond The Court's Territorial Jurisdiction

The habeas laws confine a district court to issuing the writ within the territorial boundaries of the judicial district. 28 U.S.C. 2241(a). Because Padilla's immediate custodian, Commander Marr, is located in the District of South Carolina, the district court lacked jurisdiction over the amended petition. Indeed, because Secretary Rumsfeld is located in the Eastern District of Virginia, see *Monk*[v. *Secretary of the Navy*], 793 F.2d [364,] 369 n.1 [D.C. Cir. 1986)], the district court would have lacked jurisdiction even if Secretary Rumsfeld were a proper respondent.

1. The terms of the habeas laws establish a strict territorial limitation on the reach of a district court's habeas jurisdiction, specifying that "[w]rits of habeas corpus may be granted by" the "district courts *** *within their respective jurisdictions*." 28 U.S.C. 2241(a) (emphasis added). That express territorial constraint originated in Congress's 1867 revision of the habeas laws. §1, 14 Stat. 235.

Congress added the language confining district courts' habeas authority to "their respective jurisdictions" to address concerns that, without the amendment, "a judge of a United States court in one part of the Union would be authorized to issue a writ of *habeas corpus* to bring before him a person confined in another and a remote part of the Union." Cong. Globe, 39th Cong., 2d Sess. 790 (1867) (remarks of Sen. Trumbull); see *Carbo* v. *United States*, 364 U.S. 611, 616–617 (1961). As this Court has explained, Congress thought it "inconvenient, potentially embarrassing, certainly expensive and on the whole quite unnecessary to provide every judge anywhere with authority to issue the Great Writ on behalf of applicants far distantly removed from the courts whereon they sat." *Id.* at 617. The result is that the "Great Writ" is "issuable only in the district of [the challenged] confinement." Id. at 618; see *Al-Marri*, 2004 WL 415279, at *5; *Monk*, 793 F.2d at 369.

2. The court of appeals gave short shrift to the argument that Section 2241(a) requires a habeas petition to be brought in the district where the immediate custodian is located, *i.e.*, the district of the challenged confinement. . . . . According to the court of appeals, a district court's habeas jurisdiction extends to *any* custodian within reach of the court's process in an ordinary civil action, which is generally defined by the long-arm statute of the state in which the court sits. . . . . That capacious understanding of habeas jurisdiction is flatly incompatible with the terms and purposes of the habeas statute.

a. If a habeas court's jurisdiction were defined by the reach of the state long-arm statute, district courts in every district with the requisite contacts with the custodian would have jurisdiction over a particular habeas action. Such overlapping and duplicative habeas jurisdiction is squarely foreclosed by the statutory restriction that district courts may issue the writ only "within their respective jurisdictions." 28 U.S.C. 2241(a). Indeed, Congress's entire purpose in adding that language was precisely to foreclose a district court from issuing process beyond the district's territorial borders. Congress thus required in Section 2241(a) that a habeas action be brought in the district of the challenged confinement. See *Carbo*, 364 U.S. at 616–618.[9]

The habeas laws elsewhere reinforce the conclusion that there is only one district court with territorial jurisdiction in any given habeas case. The statutes prescribe that the "Supreme Court, any justice thereof, and any circuit judge may decline to entertain an application for a writ of habeas corpus and may transfer the application *** to *the* district court having jurisdiction to entertain it." 28 U.S.C. 2241(b) (emphasis added). To the same effect, a habeas application "addressed to the Supreme Court, a justice thereof or a circuit judge" must "state the reason for not making application to *the* district court of the district in which the applicant is held." 28 U.S.C. 2242 (emphasis added). The Federal Rules likewise provide that an "application for a writ of habeas corpus must be made to *the* appropriate district court." Fed. R. App. P. 22(a) (emphasis added).

Conversely, when Congress intends to vest habeas jurisdiction in more than one district court, it does so explicitly. For instance, the habeas statutes provide that when the petitioner is "in custody under the judgment and sentence of a State court of a State which contains two or more Federal judicial districts, the application may be filed" not only "in the district court for the district wherein such person is in custody," but also "in the district court for the district within which the State court was held which convicted and sentenced him," and "each of such district courts shall have *concurrent jurisdiction* to entertain the application." 28 U.S.C. 2241(d) (emphasis added). That provision would have been unnecessary if the court of appeals' understanding of the scope of habeas jurisdiction were correct. See *Al-Marri*, 2004 WL 415279, at *3.[10]

b. The court of appeals assumed that a habeas court remains "within [its] respective jurisdiction[]" under the habeas statutes (28 U.S.C. 2241(a)) as long as the Federal Rules of Civil Procedure would permit the court to reach the respondent in a general civil action. See Pet. App. 23a. That approach confuses the basic question of statutory

---

[9] See also Cong. Globe, 39th Cong., 2d Sess. 790 (1867) (remarks of Sen. Johnson) (observing that addition of phrase "within their respective jurisdictions" addresses "practical evil" that would result if a habeas court could "issue process [that] extends all over the Union").

[10] The same conclusion follows with respect to 28 U.S.C. 2255, which was added to enable federal prisoners to bring post-conviction challenges in the sentencing court rather than in the district of confinement. See *United States* v. *Hayman*, 342 U.S. 205, 212–219 (1952).

jurisdiction with the separate issue of the procedures for service of process. See *Al-Marri*, 2004 WL 415279, at *3. The Federal Rules themselves make clear that they do not "extend or limit the jurisdiction of the United States district courts." Fed. R. Civ. P. 82; accord *Kontrick* v. *Ryan*, 124 S. Ct. 906, 914 (2004). And with respect to habeas jurisdiction in particular, the Rules provide that they apply in habeas proceedings only "to the extent that the practice in such proceedings is not set forth in statutes of the United States." Fed. R. Civ. P. 81(a)(2). As a result, the Federal Rules cannot alter the territorial constraint established by Congress in Section 2241(a).

This Court made the point clear in *Schlanger* v. *Seamans*, 401 U.S. 487 (1971). After reaffirming that "jurisdiction over [a habeas] respondent [is] territorial," *id*. at 490, the Court held that the territorial constraint on district courts was unaffected by the enactment of 28 U.S.C. 1391(e), the statute providing for nationwide service of process against federal officials. The Court explained that the statute "was enacted to broaden the venue of civil actions which could previously have been brought only in the District of Columbia," but there was no "indication that Congress extended habeas corpus jurisdiction." 401 U.S. at 490 n.4. If a federal *statute* providing for nationwide service of process fails to relax the territorial limits on habeas courts, a federal *rule* providing for service of process under long-arm statutes necessarily leaves those territorial constraints unaffected.[11]

c. Contrary to the court of appeals' view..., nothing in this Court's decisions in *Braden* or *Strait* [v. *Laird*, 406 U.S. 341 (1972)] suggests that the district court could venture beyond its territorial jurisdiction to reach respondents located elsewhere. In *Braden*, because the challenge was to the petitioner's legal custody under the Kentucky detainer, the relevant custodian was located in Kentucky, and the petition was filed in Kentucky. Although the Court observed that habeas jurisdiction lies "[s]o long as the custodian can be reached by service of process," 410 U.S. at 495, the Court went on to explain that "the respondent was properly served *in that district*," *i.e.*, within the district's territorial boundaries, *id*. at 500 (emphasis added). *Braden* thus had no occasion to consider service against custodians located outside the judicial district in which suit was brought. See *Al-Marri*, 2004 WL 415279, at *5 ("Braden sued his Kentucky custodian in Kentucky, just as §2241(a) provides."); see *also Guerra* v. *Meese*, 786 F.2d 414, 417 (D.C. Cir. 1986) ("The *Braden* decision in no way stands for the proposition *** that federal courts may entertain a habeas corpus petition when the custodian is outside their territorial jurisdiction.").

Strait, as explained, involved an unattached reservist not subject to physical confinement. The Court permitted the petitioner to file in California, where he resided and "where he had had his only meaningful contact with the Army." 406 U.S. at 343. The Court found that it would "exalt fiction over reality" to require him to seek relief in Indiana, the location of the "nominal custodian" who held his records, and where the petitioner had never been. *Id*. at 344. Because Strait permits filing where the effects of custody in fact were felt by the petitioner, the decision provides no authority for extending jurisdiction beyond the district of custody, particularly in a case involving physical confinement rather than a mere "nominal" custodian. See *Al-Marri*, 2004 WL 415279, at *5; *Vasquez*, 233 F.3d at 695 n.6.[12]

---

[11] The court of appeals' evisceration of the territorial constraints on habeas jurisdiction not only is foreclosed by the statute, but it creates the potential for "one idiosyncratic district or appellate court anywhere in the nation [to] insist that the entire federal government dance to its tune." *Al-Marri*, 2004 WL 415279, at *3.

[12] This Court's decision in *Endo*, like *Braden* and *Strait*, refers to service of process, see 323 U.S. at 307, but as explained (note 8, *supra*), *Endo* involved a petition initially filed within the territorial jurisdiction of the

Consequently, neither *Strait* nor *Braden* affect the statutory restriction that district courts may issue the writ only "within their respective jurisdictions." 28 U.S.C. 2241(a). That provision forecloses the district court's assertion of habeas jurisdiction in this case.

II.   THE PRESIDENT HAS AUTHORITY AS COMMANDER IN CHIEF AND PURSUANT TO CONGRESS'S AUTHORIZATION FOR USE OF MILITARY FORCE TO ORDER PADILLA'S DETENTION AS AN ENEMY COMBATANT

The President, explicitly invoking both his constitutional authority as Commander in Chief and the authority recognized by Congress in its Authorization of Force, determined that Padilla is "closely associated with al Qaeda," has engaged in "hostile and war-like acts," and "represents a continuing, present and grave danger to the national security," and that it therefore "is in the interest of the United States" that Padilla be detained by the military as an enemy combatant. App., *infra*, 5a–6a. That determination was the product of a careful, thorough, and multi-layered process of review incorporating independent recommendations based on all available intelligence information and legal and policy analyses of, among others, the Central Intelligence Agency, the Department of Defense, the Department of Justice, the White House Counsel and, ultimately, the President of the United States. See 150 Cong. Rec. S2701, S2703–S2704 (daily ed. Mar. 11, 2004) (reprinting Feb. 24, 2004 remarks of Alberto Gonzales, White House Counsel, before the American Bar Association's Standing Committee on Law and National Security). The President's determination lies at the heart of his constitutional powers as Commander in Chief, and it is fully supported by Congress's broad grant of authority to the President. The court of appeals' decision setting aside a core wartime determination of the Commander in Chief was both unprecedented and fundamentally in error.

A.   The Authority Of The Military To Seize And Detain Enemy Combatants In Wartime Is Well Settled

1. "This Court has characterized as 'well-established' the 'power of the military to exercise jurisdiction over *** enemy belligerents [and] prisoners of war." *Johnson* v. *Eisentrager*, 339 U.S. 763, 786 (1950) (quoting *Duncan* v. *Kahanamoku*, 327 U.S. 304, 313 (1946)). The capture and detention of enemy combatants is an essential aspect of warfare, and represents a core exercise of the President's constitutional powers as Commander in Chief. Accordingly, the United States military has seized and detained enemy combatants in virtually every significant armed conflict in the Nation's history, including in the current conflict against al Qaeda. That settled historical practice is deeply rooted in the laws and customs of war.

As this Court recognized in *Ex parte Quirin*, 317 U.S. 1 (1942), the "universal agreement and practice" under the "law of war" holds that enemy combatants are "subject to capture and detention *** by opposing military forces." *Id.* at 30–31. While all enemy combatants are subject to capture and detention for the duration of an armed conflict, the "law of war" draws a "distinction between *** those who are lawful and unlawful combatants." *Ibid.* "Lawful" combatants, so named because they adhere to the conditions of lawful belligerency such as wearing fixed insignia and openly displaying arms, are immune from prosecution for their hostile acts and entitled to treatment as

---

district of detention. When the detainee was subsequently moved, the court where the petition was initially and properly filed did not lose jurisdiction.

prisoners of war when detained. *Id*. at 31.... "Unlawful combatants are likewise subject to capture and detention, but in addition they are subject to trial and punishment by military tribunals for acts which render their belligerency unlawful." 317 U.S. at 31; *see Hamdi* v. *Rumsfeld*, 316 F.3d 450, 463 (4th Cir. 2003), cert. granted, 124 S. Ct. 981 (2004); *Colepaugh* v. *Looney*, 235 F.2d 429, 432 (10th Cir. 1956), cert. denied, 352 U.S. 1014 (1957*); In re Territo*, 156 F.2d 142, 145 (9th Cir. 1946); *Ex parte Toscano*, 208 F. 938, 940 (S.D. Cal. 1913).

2. The detention of enemy combatants serves two vital purposes directly connected to prosecuting the war. First, detention prevents captured combatants from rejoining the enemy and continuing the fight. See *Hamdi*, 316 F.3d at 465; *Territo*, 156 F.2d at 145. Second, detention enables the military to gather critical intelligence from captured combatants concerning the capabilities and intentions of the enemy. See J.A. 75–88 (Jacoby Decl.); see also Int'l Comm. of the Red Cross, Commentary III, Geneva Convention Relative to the Treatment of Prisoners of War 163–164 (Jean S. Pictet & Jean de Preux eds. 1960) ("[A] state which has captured prisoners of war will always try to obtain information from them."); United States Dep't of the Army, *The Law of Land Warfare*, Field Manual 27-10, ¶48 (1956) ("[T]he employment of measures necessary for obtaining information about the enemy and the country are considered permissible."). Those war-related purposes categorically distinguish the military's detention of enemy combatants in wartime from detention at the hands of civilian authorities. The detention of enemy combatants is "neither a punishment nor an act of vengeance," but is a "simple war measure." William Winthrop, *Military Law and Precedents* 788 (2d ed. 1920); see *Hamdi*, 316 F.3d at 465.

The intelligence-gathering function is especially critical in prosecuting the current conflict. As the September 11 attacks starkly illustrate, the enemy is composed of combatants who operate in secret and aim to launch surprise, sporadic, and large-scale attacks against the civilian population. The military estimates that intelligence collected from combatants seized in the current conflict has helped to thwart numerous potential attacks against the United States and its interests. See J.A. 82 (Jacoby Decl.). And in this case, the President determined not only that Padilla's detention as an enemy combatant is "necessary to prevent him from aiding al Qaeda in its efforts to attack the United States," but also that Padilla "possesses intelligence, including intelligence about personnel and activities of al Qaeda that, if communicated to the U.S., would aid U.S. efforts to prevent attacks by al Qaeda on the United States or its armed forces, other governmental personnel, or citizens."....

B. The Military's Authority To Detain Enemy Combatants Is Fully Applicable In The Circumstances Of This Case

1. The settled authority of the military to capture and detain enemy combatants fully applies to a combatant who is an American citizen and is seized within the borders of the United States. In *Quirin, supra*, this Court upheld the President's exercise of military jurisdiction over a group of German combatants who were seized in the United States before carrying out plans to sabotage domestic war facilities during World War II. Each of the eight saboteurs had lived in the United States at some point, and one was assumed to be an American citizen. 317 U.S. at 20. All of them affiliated with the enemy's forces and underwent training in Germany on the use of explosives. See *id*. at 21. They came ashore in the United States in two groups, the first arriving on June 13, 1942, and the second four days later. *Ibid*. They then proceeded in civilian clothing to various points, but were seized within days in Chicago and New York by FBI agents.

Ibid. On July 2, 1942, the President, in his capacity as Commander in Chief, appointed a military commission to try the combatants for violating the laws of war, whereupon the FBI transferred custody over them to the military. *Id.* at 22–23.

The saboteurs sought habeas relief in this Court, contending that the President lacked authority under the Constitution and federal law to subject them to military detention and trial by commission, and that they were entitled to be detained as civilians and tried in the civilian courts. 317 U.S. at 24. The Court denied the saboteurs' claims. Of particular significance, the Court rejected their reliance on *Ex parte Milligan*, 71 U.S. (4 Wall.) 2 (1866), which had held that the military lacked authority to subject to trial by military commission a citizen who was alleged to have "conspired with bad men" (*id.* at 131) against the United States during the Civil War. The *Quirin* Court found *Milligan* "inapplicable" to the circumstances before it, explaining that Milligan, "not being a part of or associated with the armed forces of the enemy, was a non-belligerent, not subject to the law of war." 317 U.S. at 45. By contrast, because the *Quirin* saboteurs not only conspired to harm the United States but did so as persons associated with the enemy's forces, they were enemy combatants subject to military jurisdiction under the laws and customs of war. *Id.* at 45–46; see *id.* at 30–31, 35–38.

2. The Court's opinion in *Quirin* confirms the military's authority to detain Padilla as an enemy combatant. First, the Court held that the authority to detain an enemy combatant is undiminished by the individual's American citizenship. As the Court explained, "[c]itizenship in the United States of an enemy belligerent does not relieve him from the consequences of [his] belligerency." 317 U.S. at 37. Rather, "[c]itizens who associate themselves with the military arm of the enemy government, and with its aid, guidance and direction enter this country bent on hostile acts, are enemy belligerents within the meaning of *** the law of war." *Id.* at 37–38; accord *Colepaugh*, 235 F.2d at 432; *Territo*, 156 F.2d at 142–143. Padilla fits squarely within the Court's language: the President determined that Padilla is "closely associated with al Qaeda," that he has "engaged in *** hostile and war-like acts, including conduct in preparation for acts of international terrorism that had the aim to cause injury to or adverse effects on the United States," and that his detention "is necessary to prevent him from aiding al Qaeda in its efforts to attack the United States." . . . .

In addition, the *Quirin* Court specifically rejected the suggestion that the saboteurs were "any the less belligerents if, as they argue, they have not actually *** entered the theatre or zone of active military operations." 317 U.S. at 38. There thus is no merit to respondent's submission (Br. in Opp. 16) that "there is a profound difference between" the circumstances of this case and the "historical practice of detention of prisoners of war on the field of battle." Respondent likewise errs in attaching significance to the fact that Padilla was "not engaged in imminent hostilities" at the moment of his initial seizure. *Id.* at 18. The *Quirin* Court found it immaterial that the combatants in that case had not "committed or attempted to commit any act of depredation" when they were captured. 317 U.S. at 38. Nor is it significant (see Br. in Opp. 18) that Padilla was initially seized and detained by civilian authorities before his transfer to military control. The combatants in *Quirin* similarly were seized by the FBI and detained by civilian authorities before the President ordered their transfer to military custody. 317 U.S. at 21–23.

Indeed, the factual parallels between *Quirin* and this case are striking. The *Quirin* combatants affiliated with German forces during World War II, received explosives training in Germany, entered the United States with plans to destroy certain of the United States' war facilities, and were seized by FBI agents in Chicago and New York. Padilla was in Afghanistan and Pakistan after the attacks of September 11, he engaged there in extended discussions with senior al Qaeda operatives about conducting terrorist operations in the United States, he researched explosive devices at an al Qaeda safehouse and received training on wiring explosives, he returned to the United States to advance the conduct of further al Qaeda attacks, and he was seized by law enforcement agents in Chicago. . . . . The Court's conclusion in *Quirin* that the saboteurs were enemy combatants subject to military detention and jurisdiction thus is equally applicable in this case.

3. The court of appeals reasoned that *Quirin* "rested on express congressional authorization" that is absent here. Pet. App. 37a. The President's actions in this case, however, are fully supported by Congress. See Section II.C., *infra*. Moreover, the provisions of the Articles of War discussed in *Quirin* and relied on by the court of appeals as a basis to distinguish *Quirin* in fact remain in effect today. *Quirin* focused on Article 15 of the Articles of War that were then in effect, which recognized the scope of the President's authority as Commander in Chief and provided for trial by military commission of offenses against the laws of war. See 317 U.S. at 28. The same provision is currently codified as Article 21 of the Uniform Code of Military Justice, 10 U.S.C. 821.

While the *Quirin* saboteurs were tried by commission pursuant to that provision, whereas no such charges have been brought against Padilla, the issue in *Quirin* was not merely whether the military had jurisdiction to try the saboteurs for violating the laws of war, but whether the military had authority to detain them in the first place. Accordingly, the Court framed the question in the case as whether "the *detention* and trial of petitioners – ordered by the President in the declared exercise of his powers as Commander in Chief of the Army in time of war and of grave public danger – *** are in conflict with the Constitution or laws of Congress." 317 U.S. at 25 (emphasis added); see *id*. at 18–19 ("question for decision is whether the detention of petitioners *** for trial by Military Commission *** is in conformity to the laws and Constitution of the United States").

The Court's opinion in *Quirin* likewise makes clear that the military's authority to try an enemy combatant for violating the laws of war necessarily includes the lesser authority to detain him in the course of the conflict. The Court explained that all enemy combatants "are subject to capture and detention *** by opposing military forces," but that unlawful combatants are "*in addition* subject to trial and punishment by military tribunals for acts which render their belligerency unlawful." 317 U.S. at 31 (emphasis added); see *Colepaugh*, 235 F.2d at 432. The Commander in Chief thus retains "the option to detain until the cessation of hostilities *** in either case," *Hamdi*, 316 F.3d at 469, and the overwhelming share of combatants detained in the course of a conflict are never charged with violations of the laws of war, see *id*. at 465. The President's authority to detain Padilla as an enemy combatant therefore follows "*a fortiori* from *Quirin*." Pet. App. 133a.[13]

C. The President's Exercise Of Commander-In-Chief Authority In This Case Comes With The Broad Support of Congress

Quirin settles that the Constitution raises no absolute prohibition against the detention of an American citizen as an enemy combatant in the circumstances of this case. The court of appeals did not suggest otherwise. The court instead concluded that Congress alone possesses power to authorize the detention as an enemy combatant of a citizen

---

[13] Respondent, like the court of appeals, would distinguish *Quirin* on the ground that the combatants in that case did not dispute their affiliation with the German forces. See Br. in Opp. 17. . . . But the court of appeals in this case concluded that the President lacked authority to detain Padilla even *assuming* that, as the President's determination and the Mobbs Declaration elaborate, Padilla is closely associated with al Qaeda and trained with al Qaeda forces and then came to the United States intending to advance the conduct of further hostile actions by al Qaeda. The context in which this case comes to the Court thus precisely parallels the undisputed facts in *Quirin*.

seized on United States soil, and that Congress has not done so here, and indeed, has precluded it.

The court reasoned, in particular, that: (i) the President lacks independent authority as Commander in Chief to detain a United States citizen seized within the borders of the United States; (ii) Congress's Authorization of Force does not supply the requisite statutory predicate for the President's order in this case; and (iii) the provisions of 18 U.S.C. 4001(a) reflect Congress's determination that the detention of an American citizen as an enemy combatant is unlawful absent specific statutory authorization. The court's analysis is deeply flawed at every turn.

1. *The President's Commander-in-Chief power squarely applies in the circumstances of this case*

Because the President's actions in this case are fully supported by Congress, the court of appeals' extended discussion of the President's independent powers as Commander in Chief . . . is largely beside the point. But the Court seriously misconstrued the nature of the President's constitutional authority.

The Commander-in-Chief Clause grants the President authority to defend the Nation when it is attacked and to determine the appropriate military response. The President's exercise of that core Article II power is not conditioned on any action by Congress. Rather, "[i]f a war be made by invasion of a foreign nation, the President is not only authorized but bound to resist force by force. He *** is bound to accept the challenge without waiting for any special legislative authority." *The Prize Cases*, 67 U.S. (2 Black) 635, 668 (1862). An essential aspect of the President's authority in that regard is determining the character of the military measures to be applied: "He must determine what degree of force the crisis demands." *Id.* at 670 (internal quotation marks omitted); see *id.* at 669–670.In short, "the President has independent authority to repel aggressive acts by third parties even without specific congressional authorization, and courts may not review the level of force selected." *Campbell* v. *Clinton*, 203 F.3d 19, 27 (D.C. Cir.) (Silberman, J., concurring), cert. denied, 531 U.S. 815 (2000); see *Eisentrager*, 339 U.S. at 789; *Martin* v. *Mott*, 25 U.S. (12 Wheat.) 19, 30 (1827).

The court of appeals nonetheless held that the President lacks any inherent power to decide whether Padilla should be seized and detained as an enemy combatant, reasoning that the Commander-in-Chief authority is strictly confined in the "domestic sphere." . . . . The court rested its conclusion in large part . . . on *Youngstown Sheet & Tube Co.* v. *Sawyer*, 343 U.S. 579 (1952). There, President Truman ordered the Secretary of Commerce to seize and assume control over the Nation's steel mills based on concerns that a work stoppage could jeopardize the production of war materials for the Korean War. See *id.* at 582–583. The government acknowledged that the President had acted without support from Congress, *id.* at 586, and argued that the President's authority "should be implied from the aggregate of his powers under the Constitution," *id.* at 587, including in part the Commander-in-Chief power because of the potential implications for the availability of war materials. This Court disagreed. With respect to the government's reliance on the Commander-in-Chief authority, the Court found that the President lacked independent "power as such to take possession of private property in order to keep labor disputes from stopping production." *Ibid.* The Court deemed that a job for "lawmakers, not *** military authorities." *Ibid.*

This case involves a decidedly different question. President Truman's order to seize the steel mills was not addressed to the military. The order instead called for action in the *civilian* sector in the form of a directive to the Secretary of *Commerce* to assume control over private industry. In sharp contrast, an order directed to the military to detain an individual as an enemy combatant is a quintessentially *military* measure concerning the military's actions towards the enemy's forces. And the military's actions vis-a-vis the enemy's forces lie at the core of the Commander-in-Chief authority. See *Quirin*, 317 U.S. at 28–29 ("An important incident to the conduct of war is the adoption of measures by the military command not only to repel and defeat the enemy, but to seize and subject to disciplinary measures those enemies who in their attempt to thwart or impede our military effort have violated the law of war."); *Hirota* v. *MacArthur*, 338 U.S. 197, 215 (1949) (Douglas, J., concurring) ("[T]he capture and control of those who were responsible for the Pearl Harbor incident was a political question on which the President as Commander-in-Chief *** had the final say."). Because the authority to detain enemy combatants is part and parcel of the conduct of war, the logic of the decision below would hamstring the President's authority to respond to attacks on United States soil or to take action to deter such attacks.

The court of appeals' attempt to cabin the Commander-in-Chief authority to the conduct of combat operations on a traditional battlefield . . . is particularly ill-considered in the context of the current conflict. The President's power as Commander in Chief "is vastly greater than that of troop commander. He *** has full power to repel and defeat the enemy; *** and to punish those enemies who violated the law of war." *Hirota*, 338 U.S. at 208 (Douglas, J., concurring). The "full power to repel and defeat the enemy," contrary to the court of appeals' suggestion . . . , is not confined to a "foreign battlefield." See *United States* v. *McDonald*, 265 F. 754, 764 (E.D.N.Y. 1920), appeal dismissed, 256 U.S. 705 (1921) ("With the progress made in obtaining ways and means for devastation and destruction, the territory of the United States was certainly within the field of active operations."). The September 11 attacks not only struck targets on United States soil; they also were launched from inside the Nation's borders. The "full power to repel and defeat the enemy" thus necessarily embraces determining what measures to take against enemy combatants found within the United States.

As the September 11 attacks make manifestly clear, moreover, al Qaeda eschews conventional battlefield combat, yet inflicts damage that, if anything, is more devastating. Al Qaeda combatants assimilate into the civilian population and plot to launch large-scale attacks against civilian targets far from any traditional battlefield. Confining the President's authority to traditional combat zones thus would substantially impair the ability of the Commander in Chief to engage and defeat the enemy's forces. The President's authority under Article II should not "be made almost unworkable, as well as immutable, by refusal to indulge some latitude of interpretation for changing times," but should be given the "scope and elasticity afforded by what seem to be reasonable, practical implications instead of the rigidity dictated by a doctrinaire textualism." *Youngstown Sheet*, 343 U.S. at 640 (Jackson, J., concurring). The Commander in Chief therefore has authority to seize and detain enemy combatants wherever found, including within the borders of the United States.

2. *The President's actions in this case are fully supported by Congress's Authorization for Use of Military Force*

Although the President's decision to detain Padilla as an enemy combatant falls squarely within his Commander-in-Chief power, that question is not directly at issue here in light of Congress's specific authorization of military force against the forces responsible for the September 11 attacks. Congress's Authorization of Force supplies an ample statutory basis for the President's decision to seize and detain Padilla as an enemy combatant.

Because "the President act[ed] pursuant to an express or implied authorization from Congress," his power is at its maximum, and its exercise is "supported by the strongest of presumptions." *Dames & Moore* v. *Regan*, 453 U.S. 654, 668 (1981) (quoting *Youngstown Sheet*, 343 U.S. at 635 (Jackson, J., concurring)); accord *Hamdi*, 316 F.3d at 467.

a. Congress recognized virtually unanimously in its Authorization of Force that "the President has authority under the Constitution to take action to deter and prevent acts of international terrorism against the United States." Preamble, 115 Stat. 224.[14] With that explicit recognition of the President's broad constitutional powers as a guidepost, Congress authorized the President "to use *all* necessary and appropriate force against those nations, organizations, or persons he determines planned, authorized, committed, or aided the terrorist attacks that occurred on September 11, 2001, *** in order to prevent *any* future acts of international terrorism against the United States by such nations, organizations or persons." §2(a), 115 Stat. 224 (emphasis added).

Because seizing and detaining enemy combatants has long been recognized as an essential part of warfare, the authority to use "all necessary and appropriate force *** to prevent any future acts of international terrorism against the United States" (§2(a), 115 Stat. 224) necessarily embraces the capture and detention of enemy combatants. See *Hamdi*, 316 F.3d at 467; cf. *Moyer* v. *Peabody*, 212 U.S. 78, 84–85 (1909) (construing statute granting authority to "repel or suppress" an invasion as necessarily encompassing "the milder measure of seizing the bodies of those *** consider[ed] to stand in the way of restoring peace").

That conclusion is fortified by the terms of 10 U.S.C. 956(5), which authorize the military to use appropriated funds for "the maintenance, pay, and allowances for prisoners of war" and "other persons in the custody of the [military] whose status is determined by the Secretary to be similar to prisoners of war," as well as "persons detained in the custody of the [military] pursuant to Presidential proclamation." "It is difficult if not impossible to understand how Congress could" authorize the use of funds "for the detention of persons 'similar to prisoners of war' without also authorizing their detention in the first instance." *Hamdi*, 316 F.3d at 467–468.[15]

b. The court of appeals determined . . . that the Authorization of Force "contains nothing authorizing the detention of American citizens captured on United States soil," even going so far as to conclude . . . that the Authorization "contains no language authorizing detention." That reading is insupportable.

The court's conclusion that the Authorization of Force fails to authorize detentions under any circumstances strains credulity. The detention of enemy combatants is an inherent part of warfare and thus is necessarily encompassed by the authorization to use "all necessary and appropriate force." §2(a), 115 Stat. 224; see Pet. App. 70a–71a

---

[14] The vote in favor of the Authorization of Force was unanimous in the Senate, while only one Congressman cast a vote against the Authorization in the House. See 147 Cong. Rec. H5683, S9421 (daily ed. Sept. 14, 2001).

[15] The court of appeals erred in discounting the relevance of 10 U.S.C. 956(5) based on *Endo*. . . . . *Endo* found that a "lump appropriation" in World War II for the "overall program" of the War Relocation Authority did not amount to ratification of the particular aspect of the Authority's programs involving detention of concededly loyal citizens. See U.S. at 303 n.24. The Court explained that "Congress may support the effort to take care of these evacuees without ratifying every phase of the program," and that "no sums were earmarked for the single phase of the total program whch is here involved." *Ibid.* This case, by contrast, does not involve a lump sum appropriation, or even an appropriation at all. Instead, 10 U.S.C. 956(5) grants specific authorization for the military to extend appropriate funds on the detention of persons "similar to prisoners of war" and persons detained "pursuant to Presidential proclamation." 10 U.S.C. 956(5). That statute demonstrates Congress' specific and explicit understanding that the use of military force inherently entails the detention of enemy forces.

(Wesley, J., dissenting) ("It would be curious if the [Authorization of Force] authorized the interdiction and shooting of an al Qaeda operative but not the detention of that person.").

There also is no basis for reading the broad language of Congress's Authorization to contain an unstated exception for enemy combatants captured within the United States. Congress recognized the President's authority to "take action to deter and prevent acts of international terrorism against the United States," and Congress specifically noted that it was "necessary and appropriate that the United States exercise its rights *** to protect United States citizens both *at home* and abroad." Preamble, 115 Stat. 224 (emphasis added). Indeed, Congress was acting in direct response to attacks that took place on United States soil and were initiated by combatants located within the borders of the United States. Congress cannot be assumed to have intended to withhold support for the use of force against forces identically situated to those that perpetrated the September 11 attacks. To the contrary, Congress recognized that the September 11 attacks "continue to pose an unusual and extraordinary threat to the national security," *ibid.*, and the enemy remains committed to launching further attacks within the Nation's borders, see note 1, *supra*.[16]

In addition, nothing in the Authorization of Force suggests that Congress sought to withhold support for the President's use of force against enemy combatants who are American citizens. Congress supported the President's use of force against "organizations" and "persons" that "*he determines*" were responsible for the September 11 attacks "in order to prevent any future acts of international terrorism" by those "organizations or persons." Preamble, 115 Stat. 224 (emphasis added). There is no suggestion of an intention to condition the President's use of force against persons "he determines" are associated with the enemy on a secondary determination of a person's citizenship. Indeed, whereas Congress broadly authorized the use of force against "persons" and "organizations," Congress specifically used the narrower term "citizen" elsewhere in the Authorization, recognizing that "acts of treacherous violence were committed against the United States and its citizens" on September 11 and that it is necessary to "protect United States citizens both at home and abroad." *Ibid.* Moreover, the "well-settled presumption [is] that Congress understands the state of existing law when it legislates," *Bowen* v. *Massachusetts*, 487 U.S. 879, 896 (1988), and *Quirin* established long ago that the military's authority to seize and detain enemy combatants fully applies to a United States citizen, including a citizen seized within the Nation's borders.

The court of appeals evidently would require Congress to have legislated to a level of detail so as specifically to have addressed the use of force against those enemy combatants who happen to be American citizens and are found within the United States. But Congress understandably saw the need to move expeditiously to express its support of the President within days of September 11; and even in less pressing circumstances, "Congress cannot anticipate and legislate with regard to every possible action the President may find it necessary to take or every possible situation in which he might act." *Dames & Moore*, 453 U.S. at 678. That is particularly true in the present context: "Such failure of Congress *** does not, 'especially . . . in the areas of foreign policy and national

---

[16] The debates in Congress reflect the understanding that the President may be required to take action against the enemy within the Nation's borders. See 147 Cong. Rec. H5660 (daily ed. Sept. 14, 2001) ("This will be a battle unlike any other, fought with new tools and methods; fought with intelligence and brute force, rooting out the enemies among us and those outside our borders.") (remarks of Rep. Menendez); *id.* at H5669 ("We are facing a different kind of war requiring a different kind of response. We will need more vigilance at home and more cooperation abroad.") (remarks of Rep. Velasquez).

security,' imply 'congressional disapproval' of action taken by the Executive." *Ibid*. (quoting *Haig* v. *Agee*, 453 U.S. 280, 291 (1981)).[17]

c. Even if there were any doubt on the scope of Congress's Authorization of Force, the President specifically found that his actions in this case were "consistent with" the Authorization. . . . There is no warrant for second-guessing the President's judgment in that regard. The court of appeals approached the issue of whether the President's actions are supported by Congress's Authorization as if it were confronting an abstract question of statutory interpretation in the first instance. But Congress wrote the Authorization of Force as an affirmative grant of authority to the President, expressly recognized the President's "authority under the Constitution to take action to deter and prevent acts of international terrorism against the United States," Preamble, 115 Stat. 224, and entrusted the President with broad discretion to "use all necessary and appropriate force against" the forces that "he determines" were responsible for the September 11 attacks "in order to prevent any future acts of international terrorism against the United States by" those forces, §2(a), 115 Stat. 224.

When Congress grants the President broad discretionary authority in that fashion, particularly in an area in which the President possesses independent constitutional powers, the courts can set aside the President's exercise of his authority as beyond the discretion conferred by Congress only in exceptionally narrow situations, if at all. See *Dames & Moore*, 453 U.S. at 68 ("[T]he enactment of legislation closely related to the question of the President's authority in a particular case which evinces legislative intent to accord the President broad discretion may be considered to 'invite' 'measures on independent presidential responsibility.'") (quoting *Youngstown Sheet*, 343 U.S. at 637 (Jackson, J., concurring)). Cf. *Dalton* v. *Specter*, 511 U.S. 462, 477 (1994) ("Where a statute *** commits decisionmaking to the discretion of the President, judicial review of the President's decision is not available."). Those considerations are magnified in this case by the traditional reluctance of courts "to intrude upon the authority of the Executive in military and national security affairs." *Department of the Navy* v. *Egan*, 484 U.S. 518, 530 (1988). Judged by those principles, there is no question that the President's decision to detain Padilla as an enemy combatant falls comfortably within the broad sweep of Congress's Authorization of Force.[18]

---

[17] The court of appeals relied . . . on this Court's statement in *Endo* that, "[w]e must assume, when asked to find implied powers in a grant of legislative or executive authority, that the law makers intended to place no greater restraint on the citizen than was clearly and unmistakably indicated by the language they used." 323 U.S. at 300. That observation has no application here. A conclusion that the Authorization of Force embraces the detention of enemy combatants does not require "implying" a power to impose a "greater restraint" than is authorized by the statute's "clear" and "unmistakable" terms. The Authorization broadly supports the use of "all necessary and appropriate force," §2a, 115 Stat. 224, and the authority to detain enemy combatants therefore is necessarily encompassed by its *explicit* terms. Moreover, as Judge Wesley observed, the power to detain enemy combatants, while part and parcel of the use of force and thus expressly authorized by Congress, is a far lesser "restraint" than the authority to shoot them, which the Authorization also grants. . . . . *Endo* in no way suggests that an authority to detain is lacking in those circumstances. In fact, the Court specifically observed that the "fact that the Act and the orders are silent on detention does not of course mean that any power to detain is lacking." 323 U.S. at 301. The Court found that a statute with the "single aim" of "protect[ing] the war effort against espionage and sabotage" did not support detention of a "concededly loyal" citizen, explaining that a person "who is loyal by definition [is] not a spy or a saboteur" and that "detention which has no relationship to" the statute's "objective is unauthorized." *Id*. at 300, 302.

[18] Respondent argues . . . that Padilla lies beyond the reach of the Authorization because Padilla *himself* did not "plan [], authorize[], commit[], or aid[] the terrorist attacks that occurred on September 11, 2001," §2(a), 115 Stat. 224. That argument is specious. Congress supported the President's use of "all necessary and appropriate force" against, *inter alia*, "organizations" that "he determines planned, authorized, committed, or aided" the September 11 attacks. *Ibid*. Al Qaeda indisputably is such an "organization," and the President determined that Padilla is "closely associated" with al Qaeda and has engaged in "hostile and war-like acts," . . . bringing Padilla squarely within the sweep of the Authorization. See Pet. App. 68a–70a (Wesley, J., dissenting).

3.   *Section 4001(a) does not constrain the military's detention of enemy combatants*

The court of appeals erred in concluding that Congress prohibited Padilla's detention in the provisions of 18 U.S.C. 4001(a). Section 4001(a) states that "[n]o citizen shall be imprisoned or otherwise detained by the United States except pursuant to an Act of Congress." 18 U.S.C. 4001(a). Padilla's detention could not raise any potential issue under that statute, because the Authorization of Force is an "Act of Congress" that authorized the detention. See Section II.C.2, *supra*. In any event, as is made clear by Congress's purpose in enacting Section 4001(a), by the nature of the statute it repealed, and by the terms of its neighboring provisions, Section 4001(a) pertains solely to the detention of American citizens by *civilian* authorities. It has no bearing on the settled authority of the *military* to detain enemy combatants in a time of war.

a.   Congress enacted Section 4001(a) in 1971. Act of Sept. 25, 1971, Pub. L. No. 92-128, 85 Stat. 347. The explicit purpose was to repeal the Emergency Detention Act of 1950, former 50 U.S.C. 811–826 (1970). See 85 Stat. 348. Under the Emergency Detention Act, if the President declared an "Internal Security Emergency" due to an invasion, insurrection, or declaration of war, the Attorney General was authorized to detain persons for whom there were reasonable grounds to believe that they would engage in acts of espionage or sabotage. 50 U.S.C. 812(a), 813(a) (1970). Although the authority under the Emergency Detention Act had never been invoked, Congress sought to eliminate concerns that the Act could become "an instrumentality for apprehending and detaining citizens who hold unpopular beliefs and views." H.R. Rep. No. 116, 92d Cong., 1st Sess. 2 (1971). In addition, Congress was particularly concerned with avoiding a recurrence of the World War II program of detention camps for Japanese-American citizens. See *ibid.*; . . . .

In the court of appeals' view, because the Emergency Detention Act authorized the detention of suspected spies and saboteurs in times of invasion or war, and because the World War II detentions of Japanese-American citizens likewise constituted war-related measures aimed to curb espionage and sabotage, Section 4001(a) was intended to "limit[] military as well as civilian detentions." . . . . That is incorrect. Section 4001(a) "must be understood against the backdrop of what Congress was attempting to accomplish in enacting" it. *Reves v. Ernst & Young*, 494 U.S. 56, 63 (1990). And both the Emergency Detention Act and the World War II detentions of Japanese-Americans involved detention by *civilian* authorities, not detention by the military under the laws of war. There is no indication that Section 4001(a) was intended to apply outside the context of civilian detentions.

The Emergency Detention Act assigned the detention authority to a civilian official, the Attorney General. See 50 U.S.C. 813 (1970). Moreover, the procedures for detentions under the Act – such as the requirement to obtain a warrant based upon probable cause and the provisions for administrative and judicial review – are characteristic of civilian detentions and did not involve the laws of war. See 50 U.S.C. 814, 819, 821 (1970).

The detention of Japanese-American citizens in World War II likewise was administered by civilian authority. As this Court explained in *Ex Parte Endo*, those detentions were conducted "by a civilian agency, the War Relocation Authority, *not by the military*." 323 U.S. 283, 298 (1944) (emphasis added).[19] In fact, the Court explicitly distinguished the circumstances in *Quirin*, observing that it was not confronting "a question such as

---

[19] The War Relocation Authority was established within the Office for Emergency Management of the Executive Office of the President and was later transferred to the Department of the Interior. See *Endo*, 323 U.S. at 287, 290 n.4.

was presented in *** *Quirin*" concerning "the jurisdiction of military tribunals to try persons according to the law of war." *Id*. at 297. Because the case before it involved civilian rather than military detentions, the Court explained, "no questions of military law are involved." *Id*. at 298. Consistent with *Endo*, Congress recognized when enacting Section 4001(a) that the detention of Japanese-American citizens in World War II involved the exercise of civilian authority rather than military authority. See H.R. Rep. No. 1599, 91st Cong., 2d Sess. 7 (1970) ("It appears that the controlling impetus for taking such action was not in fact military, but civilian.").

b. Congress's focus at the time of enacting Section 4001(a) was limited exclusively to civilian detentions. By that time, *Quirin* had long settled that "[c]itizenship in the United States of an enemy belligerent does not relieve him from the consequences of [his] belligerency." 317 U.S. at 37; see *Colepaugh*, 235 F.2d at 432; *Territo*, 156 F.2d at 142. While the legislative materials are replete with confirmation of Congress's intent to address civilian detention camps, like the ones instituted for Japanese-Americans in World War II, they do not address *Quirin* (or *Territo* or *Colepaugh*) or the military's established authority to seize and detain enemy combatants who are American citizens. If Congress had intended for Section 4001(a) to "override this well-established precedent and provide American belligerents some immunity from capture and detention, it surely would have made its intentions explicit." *Hamdi*, 316 F.3d at 468.[20]

Congress reconfirmed its intention to speak solely to civilian detentions when it chose to place Section 4001(a) within Title 18, which concerns "Crimes and Criminal Procedure," and elected to add Section 4001(a) to a provision addressed to the control of the Attorney General over federal prisons. See 85 Stat. 347. Before the addition of Section 4001(a), 18 U.S.C. 4001 (1970) consisted of two paragraphs that are now renumbered as Sections 4001(b)(1) and (b)(2). *Ibid*. The terms of those provisions, which remain unchanged, stated then (as now) that the "control and management of Federal penal and correctional institutions, *except military or naval institutions*, shall be vested in the Attorney General." 18 U.S.C. 4001(b)(1) (emphasis added).

Section 4001 "should not be read as a series of unrelated and isolated provisions." *Gustafson* v. *Alloyd Co.*, 513 U.S. 561, 570 (1995). The most natural conclusion from Congress's decision to add Section 4001(a) to a provision addressing the Attorney General's control over federal prisons – and specifically excluding military institutions – is that Section 4001(a) likewise is directed solely to civilian detentions and has no bearing on the military detention of enemy combatants under the laws of war. A contrary conclusion "simply is not tenable in light of the *** surrounding provisions." *Gade* v. *National Solid Waste Mgmt. Ass'n*, 505 U.S. 88, 99 (1992).

c. The court of appeals deemed dispositive that the words of Section 4001(a), standing alone and without regard to the language of the neighboring provisions, contain no exception for detentions by the military under the laws of war. Pet. App. 43a–44a. But as this Court has reminded, "[l]ooking beyond the naked text for guidance is perfectly proper when the result it apparently decrees is difficult to fathom or where it seems inconsistent with Congress' intention." *Public Citizen* v. *Department of Justice*, 491 U.S. 440, 455 (1989). The court of appeals' reading of Section 4001(a) not only fails to square with Congress's intentions, but it also is "difficult to fathom." *Ibid*. Under the court of

---

[20] It was so clear that military detentions lay beyond Congress's consideration that, when the Department of Defense was asked to submit its views on various initial proposals for repealing the Emergency Detention Act, the Department elected not to comment, explaining: "Inasmuch as the Act is administered by the Attorney General, this Department defers to the Department of Justice as to the merits of the bills." H.R. Rep. No. 1599, *supra*, at 26.

appeals' interpretation, Section 4001(a) would preclude the military's detention even of an American citizen seized while fighting for the enemy in the heat of traditional battlefield combat. Congress cannot be assumed to have intended that remarkable result. See *Hamdi*, 316 F.3d at 468.[21]

The court of appeals' construction would raise serious constitutional questions concerning whether Congress can constrain the basic power of the Commander in Chief to seize and detain enemy combatants in wartime. The canon of constitutional avoidance applies with added force when the "constitutional issues *** concern the relative powers of coordinate branches of government." *Public Citizen*, 491 U.S. at 467; see *American Foreign Serv. Ass'n v. Garfinkel*, 490 U.S. 153, 161 (1989) (per curiam). With particular respect to the Commander-in-Chief power, moreover, *Quirin* instructs that a "detention *** ordered by the President in the declared exercise of his powers as Commander in Chief" is "not to be set aside by the courts without the *clear conviction* that [it is] in conflict with the *** laws of Congress." 317 U.S. at 25 (emphasis added).

The substantial constitutional doubts raised by a construction of Section 4001(a) that would limit the President's authority as Commander in Chief to detain enemy combatants can be avoided in either of two ways. First, Congress's Authorization of Force can be construed consistent with its plain terms and the well-established principle that the authority to detain enemy combatants is part and parcel of the use of military force, thus supplying whatever statutory authority Section 4001(a) may require. Second, Section 4001(a) can be construed, consistent with its evident purpose, structure, and location in the Code, to limit detentions by civilian authorities but not to limit the authority of the military. The court below eschewed both of those saving constructions, adopting instead an unduly narrow construction of the Authorization and an unduly broad construction of Section 4001(a). That was error.

* * * * *

Because Section 4001(a) does not pertain to Padilla's detention as an enemy combatant, because Congress in any event broadly supported the President's actions through its Authorization of Force, and because the President has authority as Commander in Chief to protect the Nation against enemy combatants who infiltrate the borders of the United States, Padilla's detention is lawful.

CONCLUSION

The judgment of the court of appeals should be vacated and the case should be remanded with instructions that the amended petition be dismissed for lack of jurisdiction. In the alternative, the judgment should be vacated and the case should be remanded for further proceedings consistent with the Court's opinion.

. . .

---

[21] This Court observed in a footnote in *Howe v. Smith*, 452 U.S. 473, 479 n.3 (1981), that Section 4001(a) "proscrib[es] detention *of any kind* by the United States" absent statutory authorization. But *Howe* involved civilian detentions, and the Court had no occasion to consider whether Section 4001(a) should be construed to apply to the very distinct context of the military's detention of enemy combatants.

No. 03-1027

IN THE

Supreme Court of the United States

DONALD RUMSFELD,

Petitioner,

v.

JOSE PADILLA AND DONNA R. NEWMAN,
AS NEXT FRIEND OF JOSE PADILLA,

Respondent.

**On Writ of Certiorari to the
United States Court of Appeals
for the Second Circuit**

BRIEF OF RESPONDENT

DAVID W. DEBRUIN
WILLIAM M. HOHENGARTEN
MATTHEW HERSH
DUANE C. POZZA
SCOTT B. WILKENS
JENNER & BLOCK LLP

JENNY S. MARTINEZ

DONNA R. NEWMAN
Counsel of Record

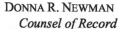
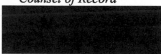

ANDREW G. PATEL

JONATHAN M. FREIMAN
WIGGIN AND DANA

WILSON-EPES PRINTING CO., INC. —

· · ·

---

* Redactions on this page have been added for privacy purposes. – *Eds.*

SUMMARY OF ARGUMENT

The Executive today seeks to validate an unprecedented new system of extrajudicial military imprisonment of citizens. It seeks to do so absent any authorization by Congress defining the permissible scope and duration of such imprisonments, absent any meaningful review by the courts, and absent any charge or trial or procedural protections of any kind. The Government argues that the President and his advisers have considered the situation carefully and the courts should defer, completely, to their determination that Padilla's detention is necessary for national security. But in our constitutional system, it is not enough to trust that our leaders act in good faith, for ours is "a government of laws, and not of men." *Marbury v. Madison*, 5 U.S. (1 Cranch) 137, 163 (1803). As this Court wrote in rejecting claims that the rule of law should give way to military necessity during the crisis of the Civil War:

> The Constitution of the United States is a law for rulers and people, equally in war and in peace, and covers with the shield of its protection all classes of men, at all times, and under all circumstances. No doctrine, involving more pernicious consequences, was ever invented by the wit of man than that any of its provisions can be suspended during any of the great exigencies of government.

Ex parte Milligan, 71 U.S. (4 Wall.) 2, 120–21 (1866). Terrorism presents a grave threat. But even – indeed especially – in times of peril, efforts to eviscerate our most basic constitutional safeguards must be rejected.

The Framers of our Constitution carefully divided power among the three branches of government to better preserve liberty. They placed stringent limits on the Executive's powers of detention and took care that the Nation's military power should be limited in scope and subordinated to the will of Congress. This Court has carefully policed the boundaries of military jurisdiction throughout our history, and has made clear that even citizens suspected of plotting to engage in hostile acts in wartime generally cannot constitutionally be subject to military jurisdiction where "the courts are open and their process unobstructed." *Milligan*, 71 U.S. at 121.

A system of domestic military detention for citizens suspected of plotting violent acts would violate the constitutional boundary recognized in Milligan. But in any event, it would represent such a dramatic departure from our Nation's constitutional traditions that, at a minimum, it must be authorized by a clear and unequivocal statement by Congress, explicitly delineating the scope of such detentions, and the procedures to accompany them. The courts then could review that system to determine if its scope and procedures were consistent with the Constitution. In the absence of a clear statement from Congress authorizing such detentions, it is premature for this Court to pass on their constitutionality.

Indeed, throughout the Nation's history, this Court has required clear congressional authorization for detention of citizens. *See, e.g., Ex parte Endo*, 323 U.S. 283, 300 (1944); *Duncan v. Kahanamoku*, 327 U.S. 304, 315 (1946). This fact alone renders inapposite this Court's decision in *Ex parte Quirin*, 317 U.S. 1 (1942), which rested on clear and explicit congressional authorization of trials of enemy soldiers by military commissions – authorization that was separate and distinct from the general authorization to use military force contained in the Declaration of War against Germany. Moreover, Congress has underscored its intent to exercise the full scope of its power over detention by enacting a statute specifying that "[n]o citizen shall be imprisoned or otherwise detained by the United States except pursuant to an Act of Congress." 18 U.S.C. §4001(a). Neither of the statutes relied on by the Government here – the Authorization for Use of Military

Force ("AUMF") and 10 U.S.C. §956(5) – provides the necessary clear authorization for detention.

Because the AUMF does not authorize Padilla's military detention, and §4001(a) expressly prohibits it, the President's "power is at its lowest ebb, for then he can rely only upon his own constitutional powers minus any constitutional powers of Congress over the matter." *Youngstown Sheet & Tube Co. v. Sawyer*, 343 U.S. 579, 637 (1952) (Jackson, J., concurring). Neither *Quirin* nor the law and customs of war on which that decision rests give the President the inherent power under the Commander-in-Chief Clause to detain citizens like Padilla as "enemy combatants."

In *Quirin*, the prisoners were given a trial and the opportunity to defend themselves with the assistance of counsel. Contrary to the Government's argument, the power to detain without trial is not *lesser* than the power to put on trial, for detention without trial carries a greater risk of error and abuse. These risks, moreover, are exacerbated in the "war on terror," where the persons the Government alleges to be combatants are indistinguishable from the civilian population.

Moreover, the petitioners in *Quirin* were, upon the conceded facts, soldiers in the German Army. Membership in the "armed forces" of an "enemy government" is a significant limiting principle for military jurisdiction, and it was critical to *Quirin's* distinction of *Milligan* – in which military jurisdiction had been held unconstitutional notwithstanding the fact that the petitioner was likewise alleged to have plotted to engage in violent acts in wartime, but in conjunction with a secret paramilitary organization rather than as a soldier in a government army. In light of this Court's reiteration even after *Quirin* that *Milligan* remains "one of the great landmarks in this Court's history," *Reid v. Covert*, 354 U.S. 1, 30 (1957) (plurality), and in light of the Court's caution in *Quirin* that it had "no occasion now to define with meticulous care the ultimate boundaries" of military jurisdiction in the absence of congressional legislation or for individuals differently situated, 317 U.S. at 45–46, the Court should decline the Government's invitation to extend *Quirin* far beyond its facts.

If the Government's position were accepted, it would mean that for the foreseeable future, any citizen, anywhere, at any time, would be subject to indefinite military detention on the unilateral order of the President. That would upset our constitutional system in a way that the legislatively authorized trial by military commission of admitted German soldiers simply did not. Equally important, the expansion of the law of war far beyond its historical boundaries and internal limits would be a fundamentally legislative act, yet is one that our legislature has not undertaken. *See Youngstown*, 343 U.S. at 587 (Jackson, J., concurring) ("In the framework of our Constitution, the President's power to see that the laws are faithfully executed refutes the idea that he is to be a lawmaker").

In addition, the power to detain asserted by the Government is so vast that it cannot, consistent with the Due Process Clause, be based solely on "a determination by the President," Questions Presented, US Br. (I), that the individual is an "enemy combatant." In light of the liberty interest at stake, the risk of error, and traditional principles of habeas corpus jurisdiction, the courts must have authority to determine *de novo* the "jurisdictional facts" that subject an individual to military rather than civilian jurisdiction. Ordinarily, a deprivation of liberty of the sort at issue here could never be accomplished without at least clear and convincing evidence presented at an adversarial heating before a neutral fact-finder where the accused is assisted by counsel. Again, however, this Court need not define in the first instance the process by which a citizen may be determined to be an enemy combatant and subject to military detention; that is a legislative act for Congress.

Nor should the Court compound the unchecked executive power asserted in this case by adopting new and technical personal jurisdiction rules for habeas corpus that would allow the Government to funnel cases to the judicial district it desires. The traditional standards applied by the Court of Appeals are flexible enough to take account of practical concerns related to the administration of justice under the unique facts of this case.

ARGUMENT

I. THE PRESIDENT LACKS AUTHORITY TO SUBJECT PADILLA TO MILITARY DETENTION.

A. The President's Claim of Power Must Be Evaluated in Light of Established Limitations on Executive Detention and Military Authority.

Throughout history, rulers have asserted the unilateral authority to imprison without trial those among their citizens deemed to be enemies of the state posing threats to national security. The Framers of our Constitution rejected such power as incompatible with a free and democratic society. Through numerous constitutional provisions, the Framers created structural and procedural protections that constrain the Government's power to deprive citizens of liberty. Similarly wary of the danger that military power could substitute for the rule of law, the Framers subordinated the military to civilian government, ensuring that the Constitution's checks and balances could not be evaded through the backdoor of military necessity. Throughout the Nation's history, this Court has remained faithful to these constitutional bedrocks by carefully scrutinizing extra-judicial detentions and policing the limits of military jurisdiction. The President's claim of an extraordinary power to subject citizens to military detention must be evaluated in light of these long-standing constitutional boundaries.

1. Executive detention is a core concern of the Constitution, as demonstrated by basic constitutional history and the number of constitutional provisions aimed specifically at this problem. The Constitution's frontline protections against executive detention include the Due Process Clause, the criminal procedure protections of the Bill of Rights, and the structural separation of powers. Ordinarily, these provisions ensure that a citizen can only be deprived of liberty pursuant to a law duly enacted by the *legislature* that defines the precise conduct prohibited; upon a prosecution initiated by the *executive*; following a *judicial* trial by jury at which the defendant is entitled to be represented by counsel and to present evidence in his defense. The President's assertion of the right to define, implement, and review Padilla's detention is fundamentally at odds with the Framers' "central judgment" that "within our political scheme, the separation of governmental powers into three coordinate Branches is essential to the preservation of liberty." *Mistretta v. United States*, 488 U.S. 361, 380 (1989). It also violates due process and the procedural safeguards of the Fourth, Fifth, and Sixth Amendments.

The Government claims that this case is extraordinary and outside the normal constitutional framework because the Nation is at war. But the Constitution is no less concerned with executive detention in times of war, and if anything demonstrates the Framers' concern that assertions of national security not be used as justification for unchecked executive power.

The Constitution establishes the primacy of legislative and judicial control over the power of detention even in wartime through the Habeas Suspension Clause. As Justice

Jackson explained: "Aside from the suspension of the privilege of habeas corpus in time of rebellion or invasion," the Framers "made no express provision for exercise of extraordinary power because of a crisis," and "I do not think we rightfully may amend their work." *Youngstown*, 343 U.S. at 649–50 (Jackson, J., concurring); *accord Milligan*, 71 U.S. at 125–26. The Suspension Clause expressly contemplates a "Rebellion or Invasion" in which the "Public Safety may require" detention without trial, and it gives *Congress*, not the President, the power temporarily to suspend the writ, which is tantamount to authorizing extrajudicial executive detention. U.S. Const. art. I, §9, cl. 2; *Ex parte Bollman*, 8 U.S. (4 Cranch) 75 (1807); *cf. INS v. St. Cyr*, 533 U.S. 289, 298–303 (2001).[4] This allocation of power ensures that even in times of crisis, no one branch has the power to deprive citizens of liberty. *See Youngstown*, 343 U.S. at 652 (Jackson, J., concurring) ("emergency powers are consistent with free government only when their control is lodged elsewhere than in the Executive who exercises them").

Historically, the Great Writ evolved as a tool to limit executive detention – a power that frequently had been abused by the Crown based on claims that such detention was necessary to protect the security of the realm in time of emergency. *See Darnel's Case*, III How. St. Tr. 2, 44–45 (1627); William F. Duker, *A Constitutional History of Habeas Corpus* 141 (1980) (describing how Parliament "refused to accept [the King's] claim to emergency power of arrest and detention," enacting first the Petition of Right and then the acts guaranteeing habeas corpus). The great struggles between the King and Parliament in the 17th Century eventually established that only Parliament could suspend habeas corpus. *See* 1 William Blackstone, Commentaries on the Laws of England 136 (photo reprint, Univ. of Chi. Press 1979) (1765). These struggles were well known to the Framers and continued into the colonial era. But limits on the King's power were sufficiently established by then that even King George did not claim an executive or military power to detain subjects suspected of treason during the American Revolution. Though the colonists had armed themselves and plotted to expel the Crown with violent acts, the King recognized he could not detain these combatants without charge absent an Act of Parliament suspending habeas corpus, which he sought and received. 17 Geo. 3 c. 9 (1777).

This history negates the notion that the President has broad inherent powers of detention absent legislative authorization. Even in wartime, detention must take place within a framework of positive law enacted by Congress. The Executive's unilateral detention of Padilla is directly contrary to this tradition.

2. The President's assertion of military power over Padilla also runs afoul of our Nation's established limits on military jurisdiction. The Framers had a "fear and mistrust of military power." *Reid*, 354 U.S. at 29 (plurality). This was born of the fact that "the King had endeavored to render the military superior to the civil power." *Duncan*, 327 U.S. at 320; Decl. of Ind. para. 14 (1776).[5] As a result, the Framers made the military "subordinate to civil authority." *Reid*, 354 U.S. at 30. By dividing war powers between Congress and the President, they also sought to ensure that military power would not become a tool of oppression.[6] As set forth by Justice Jackson in his seminal concurrence

---

[4] Similarly, the Treason Clause, which contemplates citizens "levying War against" the United States and "adhering to their Enemies," U.S. Const. art. III, §3, cl. 1, establishes *heightened* requirements for conviction of such crimes before an Article III court.

[5] *See also Loving v. United States*, 517 U.S. 748, 762 (1996) ("The political disorders of the 17th century ushered in periods of harsh military justice, with soldiers and at times civilian rebels punished, even put to death, under the summary decrees of courts-martial") (quotation marks omitted).

[6] The Framers allocated to Congress power to "define and punish . . . Offences against the Law of Nations" (U.S. Const. art. I, §8, cl. 10); powers over war and the militia, including the power to "declare War . . . and make Rules concerning Captures on Land and Water" (*id.*, art. I, §8, cl. 11); power to "make Rules for the

in *Youngstown*, particularly in the domestic sphere, the extent of the President's authority depends on whether he is acting pursuant to, absent, or contrary to congressional authorization. 343 U.S. at 635–38; *Dames & Moore v. Regan*, 453 U.S. 654, 668–69 (1981).

Throughout the Nation's history, this Court has carefully policed the boundaries of military jurisdiction and has struck down incursions of martial law into civilian life. The most important of these cases grew out of the Civil War, when the very existence of our Republic was threatened and large swaths of the country became battlefields. In the context of that grave crisis, the Court nevertheless held that military jurisdiction could not extend to civilians in areas "where the courts are open and their process unobstructed." *Milligan*, 71 U.S. at 121; *see also id*. at 141–42 (Chase, C.J., concurring) (military jurisdiction could not extend to civilians except where martial law had been lawfully imposed); *Duncan*, 327 U.S. at 322. Padilla's case fits squarely within the framework of *Milligan*.

. . .

Throughout its brief, the Government paints the limited military jurisdiction over trials of German soldiers upheld in *Ex parte Quirin* . . . as the general rule, to which *Milligan* forms a narrow exception. But that framework is exactly backwards. *Quirin* was a narrow decision, explicitly confined to the precise facts before the Court. 317 U.S. at 19–20. Since *Quirin*, this Court has continued to refer to *Milligan* as "one of the great landmarks in this Court's history." *Reid*, 354 U.S. at 30 (plurality). It has reaffirmed the principles of *Milligan* numerous times when the government has claimed that a threat to national security justifies the arrest, detention, or trial of an American citizen by the military. *See Duncan*, 327 U.S. at 324 (rejecting military jurisdiction to try civilians even under statute authorizing martial law); *Reid*, 354 U.S. at 33–34 & n.60 (plurality) (notwithstanding statute, rejecting on constitutional grounds military jurisdiction outside "active hostilities" or "occupied enemy territory," and rejecting argument that "concept 'in the field' should be broadened . . . under the conditions of world tension which exist at the present time"); *United States ex rel. Toth v. Quarles*, 350 U.S. 11, 23 (1955) (rejecting military authority to arrest and try discharged former soldier); *Endo*, 323 U.S. at 299 (rejecting power to detain loyal American citizen of Japanese descent during World War II). As *Reid* noted:

> Throughout history many transgressions by the military have been called "slight" and have been justified as "reasonable" in light of the "uniqueness" of the times. We cannot close our eyes to the fact that today the peoples of many nations are ruled by the military.

354 U.S. at 40 (plurality). But "[w]e should not break faith with this nation's tradition of keeping military power subservient to civilian authority, a tradition which we believe is firmly embodied in the Constitution." *Id*. In contrast, the two-year, ongoing military detention of Jose Padilla is fundamentally at odds with that tradition.

B.   Congress Has Not Authorized Padilla's Military Detention.

A statute that authorized the military detention of an American citizen based on untested allegations of his "association" with a terrorist group and "loose talk" of future acts of violence would present grave constitutional questions. The Court need not resolve those questions today, however, for there is no such statute. In reviewing deprivations of individual liberty, this Court consistently has required, at a minimum, the clearest

---

Government and Regulation of the land and naval Forces" (*id*., art. I, §8, cl. 14); power "to provide for calling forth the Militia to . . . suppress Insurrections, and repel Invasions" (*id*., art. I, §8, cl. 15); and the obligation to prescribe by law the quartering of soldiers in any private home, even in time of war (*id*., amend. III).

authority from Congress. The Court of Appeals correctly found that such authority is lacking in this case.

1. "In traditionally sensitive areas...the requirement of clear statement assures that the legislature has in fact faced, and intended to bring into issue, the critical matters involved in the judicial decision." *Gregory v. Ashcroft*, 501 U.S. 452, 461 (1991) (quotation marks omitted); *Greene v. McElroy*, 360 U.S. 474, 507 (1959) ("explicit action [by lawmakers], especially in areas of doubtful constitutionality, requires careful and purposeful consideration by those responsible for enacting and implementing our laws"). This "clear statement" requirement applies most forcefully in the context of restraints on personal liberty – particularly physical incarceration like that here. "Where the liberties of the citizen are involved...we will construe narrowly all delegated powers that curtail or dilute them." *Gutknecht v. United States*, 396 U.S. 295, 306–07 (1970) (citation and quotation marks omitted).

The clear statement rule does not disappear in times of war or emergency; to the contrary, in such times the Court has been especially vigilant. In our early years, the Court held that a congressional declaration of war does not grant the President authority to confiscate enemy persons or property found domestically, without an additional clear authorization of those seizures by Congress. *Brown v. United States*, 12 U.S. (8 Cranch) 110 (1814). Chief Justice Marshall explained that even a "declaration of war does not, of itself, authorize proceedings against the persons or property of the enemy found, at the time, within the [domestic] territory." *Id.* at 126; *see also Little v. Barreme*, 6 U.S. (2 Cranch) 170, 177–78 (1804) (Marshall, C.J.) (striking down wartime seizure of ship traveling *from* a French port because congressional statute authorized seizure of ships traveling *to* a French port). The Court reiterated this principle after the Civil War, finding that "[t]he clearest language would be necessary to satisfy us that Congress intended" to grant the military power to determine judicial questions, because "[i]t is an unbending rule of law, that the exercise of military power, where the rights of the citizen are concerned, shall never be pushed beyond what the exigency requires." *Raymond v. Thomas*, 91 U.S. 712, 715–16 (1875) (ruling that statutes that gave "very large governmental power to the military commanders" during Reconstruction were not sufficient to authorize military to void local court decree).

The Court has adhered to this clear statement requirement in modern wartime cases. In *Endo*, the Court construed a Congressional enactment and prior Executive Order concerning the Japanese-American internment camps of World War II. After reviewing the requirements of the Fifth and Sixth Amendments and the Habeas Suspension Clause and citing *Milligan*, the Court emphasized: "We must assume, when asked to find implied powers in a grant of legislative or executive authority, that the law makers intended to place no greater restraint on the citizen than was clearly and unmistakably indicated by the language they used." 323 U.S. at 300. Because the statute did not use "the language of detention," no authority to detain existed. *Id.*

. . .

2. . . . .

. . .

Detention without charge poses far greater risks of error and abuse than trials do. And those risks become even sharper in the "war on terror," where suspected saboteurs cannot readily be distinguished from the general civilian population. . . . . Indefinite detention – especially in solitary confinement, incommunicado, and subject to coercive interrogation – plainly raises unique constitutional problems not presented by the adversarial trial of defendants represented by counsel. . . . . The unchecked power to detain claimed and exercised by the Executive here is simply without precedent in our Nation's history, and it has never been sanctioned by this or any other Court. It certainly is not authorized by the Court's passing reference in *Quirin* to the capture and detention of combatants as the necessary prerequisites to the saboteurs' trials that promptly ensued. *See* 317 U.S. at 31.[11]

3. The clear statement rule is buttressed here by the Non-Detention Act, enacted by Congress is 1972. The Act provides: "*No citizen* shall be imprisoned or otherwise detained by the United States *except pursuant to an Act of Congress.*" 18 U.S.C. §4001(a) (emphasis added). Both courts below correctly held that §4001(a) plainly applies to Padilla's military imprisonment, and that the statute therefore clearly prohibits Padilla's detention absent specific authorization from Congress for that detention. . . . .

In response, the Government contends that §4001(a) applies only to *civilian*, not *military*, detentions of citizens. US Br. 45–48. But as this Court has recognized, "the plain language of §4001(a) proscrib[es] detention *of any kind* by the United States, absent a congressional grant of authority to detain." *Howe v. Smith*, 452 U.S. 473, 479 n.3 (1981) (emphasis in original). The statute cannot be twisted to say that only detentions of citizens by civilian authorities are impermissible (absent authority from Congress), but this prohibition may be avoided if citizens are imprisoned by the military instead. The Government's attempt to rewrite the statute must be directed to Congress, not this Court.

In light of the statute's plain language, no recourse to extra-textual materials is needed or proper. Nonetheless, the history and purpose of the Act confirm its plain meaning. . . . . Section 4001(a) was enacted to repudiate the experience of the notorious Japanese-American internment camps of World War II and to repeal the Emergency Detention Act of 1950 ("EDA"). *See* H.R. Rep. No. 92-116 at 1 (1971), *reprinted in* 1971 U.S.C.C.A.N. 1435, 1435–36 ("H. Rep."). Contrary to the Government's astounding claims, those internment camps were not wholly civilian. Although they were *administered* by a civilian agency, they were directly and heavily controlled by military commanders.[12]

Section 4001(a) also repealed the EDA, which likewise was directed toward the detention of persons believed to be a threat to the security of the country, including in times of war. The EDA authorized the President, in time of invasion, declared state of war, or insurrection in aid of a foreign enemy, to proclaim an "Internal Security Emergency" and to apprehend and detain persons as to whom there was reasonable ground to believe that they "probably will engage in, or probably will conspire with others to engage in, acts of espionage or of sabotage." Pub. L. No. 81-831, codified at 50

---

[11] Indeed, the only decision we are aware of upholding military detention of an American citizen without trial, *In re Territo*, 156 F.2d 142 (9th Cir. 1946), is distinguishable in multiple ways, including the critical fact that Territo was held to be an *enemy alien* notwithstanding his American citizenship, *id.* at 145, and he was captured on the battlefield in Italy wearing part of an Italian army uniform, *id.* at 143. In addition, Territo was afforded a full habeas corpus hearing in which witnesses were heard and he was assisted by counsel.

[12] Ms. Endo "was evacuated from Sacramento, California, in 1942, pursuant to certain *military orders* which we will presently discuss. . . ." 323 U.S. at 284–85 (emphasis added). Those military orders are discussed at length at pages 285 through 290 of the opinion. Among other things, it was a Proclamation of the *Secretary of War* that "provided that all persons of Japanese ancestry in [designated military] areas were required to remain there unless written authorization to leave was obtained from the Secretary of War or the Director of the War Relocation Authority. It recited that the United States was subject to 'espionage and acts of sabotage, *thereby requiring the adoption of military measures* necessary to establish safeguards against such enemy operations emanating from within as well as from without the national boundaries.'" *Id.* at 289 n.3 (emphasis added, citation omitted). Every citizen of Japanese ancestry who was permitted to leave a camp "was said to remain in the 'constructive custody' of the *military* commander in whose jurisdiction the Relocation Center was located." *Id.* at 291 n.9 (emphasis added). The internment detentions can hardly be described as "civilian" merely because the military ordered citizens into camps that were administered by civilian agents.

U.S.C. §§812, 813, 64 Stat. 1021 (1950).[13] Section 4001(a) *repealed* the Executive's right to detain such persons. Although those detentions were to have been administered by the Attorney General, there is no indication that Congress would have been satisfied had the same wartime spies and saboteurs covered by the EDA simply been detained instead by military authorities.

Indeed, Congress recognized that "the constitutional validity" of the EDA was "subject to grave challenge." H. Rep. at 5, *reprinted in* 1971 U.S.C.C.A.N. 1435, 1438. As explained in the House Report, the criteria for detention in the statute "would seem to violate the Fifth Amendment by providing imprisonment not as a penalty for the commission of an offense, but on mere suspicion that an offense may occur in the future. The Act permits detention without bail even though no offense has been committed or is charged." *Id.* Moreover, Congress specifically rejected the initial proposal for a simple *repeal* of the EDA, without adding the explicit prohibition of §4001(a): "Repeal alone might leave citizens subject to arbitrary executive action, *with no clear demarcation of the limits of executive authority*." *Id.* (emphasis added). Ironically, what the Government seeks to uphold with respect to Padilla – imprisonment without charge during an alleged war based upon suspicion that an offense may occur in the future – is precisely what Congress feared could occur under the EDA and enacted §4001(a) to prevent. Yet the Government claims §4001(a) and the repeal of the EDA are wholly irrelevant.

4. The Government contends that authority for Padilla's detention is conferred by the Authorization for Use of Military Force, Pub. L. No. 107-40, 115 Stat. 224 (2001) ("AUMF")..., enacted by Congress following the attacks of September 11, and by an appropriations statute for the Department of Defense, 10 U.S.C. §956(5). Neither law authorizes the military detention of citizens like Padilla.

a. The AUMF says *nothing* about military detentions of citizens, and it simply cannot be viewed as authority – let alone a "clear statement" of authority – for such an unbounded and extensive curtailment of individual liberties. The AUMF does not mention detention, much less define who is subject to being detained, how the detention decisions shall be made or reviewed, how long such persons may be imprisoned, or what rights they shall have while confined. Basic constitutional rights of trial by jury, civilian over military rule, and judicial review of executive detention cannot simply be eliminated by implication. The President's scheme for detaining citizens indefinitely in military prisons is unprecedented, yet there is no discussion whatsoever in the legislative history of the AUMF of the lawfulness or wisdom of such a system. The obvious explanation for this lack of debate is that Congress did not contemplate or intend to authorize such a scheme.

The Government principally relies on the Preamble of the AUMF, *see* US Br. 2, 15, 38, 40, 41, 43, which states that "the President has authority under the Constitution to take action to deter and prevent acts of international terrorism against the United States."....But while the Preamble recognizes that the President *has* authority to deter and prevent acts of terrorism, it does not begin to identify what that authority *is*, much less state that it includes detentions like that here. Under the Government's view, the general language of the Preamble recognized or created executive authority to do *anything* that could be said to "deter and prevent acts of international terrorism against the United States." The Preamble cannot reasonably be interpreted as conveying such unlimited power to the President, which would present grave constitutional questions.

---

[13] The EDA originally was enacted in response to a legislative finding that a "world Communist movement" was engaged in covert operations within the United States, through operatives in the United States whose mission was to engage in "treachery...espionage, sabotage, [and] terrorism." Id. §§2(1), 2(7), 101(1), 101(6), 64 Stat. 987–88, 1019–20.

　　The Government also relies on §2(a) of the AUMF, which provides that the President is authorized to use "all necessary and appropriate force" against those nations, organizations, or persons he determines were responsible for the September 11 attacks, "in order to prevent any future acts of international terrorism against the United States by such nations, organizations or persons." *Id*. at 60a. This authorization to use "necessary" and "appropriate" force does authorize the President to use military power; indeed, the AUMF itself provides that "this section is intended to constitute specific statutory authorization within the meaning of section 5(b) of the War Powers Resolution." Pet. App. 60a; *see* 50 U.S.C. §1541 *et seq*.[14] But there is nothing in the AUMF to suggest that Congress intended to displace the criminal laws (and protections associated with those laws) with a wholly new, unbounded scheme of preventive military detention by executive fiat. The AUMF simply is not a "clear statement" of congressional intent to curtail the fundamental rights of citizens against military detentions without trial. *See Endo*, 323 U.S. at 300 (finding no authority where statute did not use "the language of detention").[15]

. . .

Congress's subsequent enactments also confirm that the AUMF did not authorize Padilla's detention. Just one month after passing the AUMF, the same Congress passed the Patriot Act, Pub. L. No. 107-56, 115 Stat. 272 (Oct. 26, 2001). Unlike the AUMF, the Patriot Act expressly gave the Executive authority to detain without criminal charge *aliens* suspected of terrorist activity, for short periods of time before the initiation of criminal or removal proceedings.[16] Although there were extensive debates on this topic, there was no discussion of the parallel detention of *American citizens* suspected of terrorist activity.[17] If, as the Government claims, the AUMF had already delegated to the Executive unfettered discretion to detain any suspected terrorist without trial, whether or not a citizen, the Patriot Act's provisions would have been redundant. For it not to be so, one would have to conclude that Congress deliberately enacted §1226a of the Patriot Act to provide aliens with *more* protections than citizens. This is simply implausible.[18]

. . .

C. The President Lacks Authority to Detain Padilla for the Additional Reason that He Is a Civilian Citizen Not Subject to Military Jurisdiction.

Even if the President possessed some authority to order the military to arrest and detain suspected "combatants," that authority would not permit the exercise of military jurisdiction over Padilla, because he does not fit into any traditional or recognized category of "combatant" subject to military instead of civilian authority. In arguing to the contrary, the Government again relies exclusively on *Quirin*. But *Quirin* involved clear congressional authorization of the precise executive action taken – the opposite of the

---

[14] . . .

[15] . . .

[16] The Patriot Act authorizes executive detention of terrorist aliens, but requires the Executive either to put an alien in removal proceedings, charge him with a criminal offense, or release him "not later than 7 days after the commencement of such detention." 8 U.S.C. §1226a(5). The Attorney General may seek to renew the detention on an immigration violation charge, but that renewal request is subject to judicial oversight, and the detainee has a continuing ability to challenge the detention. *Id*. §§1226a(6) & §1226a(b).

[17] *See* Christopher Bryant and Carl Tobias, *Youngstown Revisited*, 29 Hastings Const. L.Q. 373, 386–91 (2002). The Patriot Act also greatly expanded federal criminal prohibitions on terrorism, as requested by the President. *See* Pub. L. No. 107-56, §§802, 803, 805, 808, amending 18 U.S.C. §§2331, 2339, 2339A, 2339B. These provisions appear specifically to encompass the unlawful acts attributed to Padilla. The Government contends that, instead of utilizing these provisions, the President simply may detain without trial anyone he suspects may have planned or committed a terrorist act within the United States.

[18] . . .

clear *prohibition* here. In addition to that dispositive distinction, the ambit of the military jurisdiction permitted in *Quirin* – whether to try and punish through a military commission, or even if to detain without trial – does not extend to this case.[20]

. . .

3. . . . .

. . .

Other democratic nations such as the United Kingdom and Israel have addressed the threat of organized terrorist networks through detailed legislation, carefully defining the circumstances under which suspected terrorists may be preventively detained and establishing procedural safeguards, including time limits and robust judicial review.[28] The model of a unilateral and unlimited executive power to detain, as claimed by the Government here, not only is contrary to our own constitutional principles but would set a disturbing worldwide precedent. Certainly, Congress's decision in the days following September 11 to authorize the President to use military force simply does not reveal any intent by Congress to create a comprehensive scheme for preventive detention of suspected terrorists. And it does not reflect the kind of deliberation and democratic consensus that ought to be present before this Court passes on the constitutionality of such a dramatic departure from our traditions.

. . .

II. ANY MILITARY POWER TO DETAIN PADILLA CANNOT BE BASED SOLELY ON A DETERMINATION BY THE PRESIDENT.

. . .[33]

III. ON THE UNIQUE FACTS HERE, SECRETARY RUMSFELD IS A PROPER RESPONDENT SUBJECT TO PERSONAL JURISDICTION IN NEW YORK.

In an attack on personal jurisdiction rejected by every judge below, the Government claims absolute control over the location where challenges to its actions may be heard.

---

[20] Significantly, the Government itself does not define consistently what it means by "enemy combatant." In this case, it defines the "legal standard" for "enemy combatant status" as follows: "'Citizens who associate themselves with the military arm of the enemy government, and with its aid, guidance and direction enter this country bent on hostile acts, are enemy belligerents within the meaning of . . . the law of war.'" US Br. 6 (quoting *Quirin*, 317 U.S. at 37–38 (ellipses inserted by Government)). In its Brief in *Hamdi v. Rumsfeld*, No. 03-6696 (U.S. filed Mar. 30, 2004), however, the Government defines "enemy combatant" quite differently: "When an individual is captured, commanders in the field, using all available information, make a determination as to whether the individual is an enemy combatant, *i.e.*, whether the individual 'was part of or supporting forces hostile to the United States or coalition partners, and engaged in an armed conflict against the United States.' Individuals who are not enemy combatants are released." *Id.* at 3 (citation to DoD fact sheet omitted).

[28] *See* Stephen J. Schulhofer, *Checks and Balances in Wartime*, 102 Mich. L. Rev. (forthcoming) *available in abridged form at* http://www.law.nyu.edu/faculty/workshop/spring2004/schulhofer.pdf.

[33] There are many examples of erroneous accusations of terrorist activity, which underscores the need for strong procedural safeguards. *See, e.g., In re United States for Material Witness Warrant*, 214 F. Supp. 2d 356 (S.D.N.Y. 2002) (ordering government investigation into erroneous September 11-related charges brought against individual based on deliberately false statements by security guard); *Kiareldeen v. Reno*, 71 F. Supp. 2d 402 (D.N.J. 1999) (granting writ of habeas corpus in case where detention was based on secret and false accusations of terrorism connections by ex-wife and detainee was able to effectively rebut accusations). There are, unfortunately, also cases where the Government has misled the courts. *See Korematsu v. United States*, 584 F. Supp. 1406, 1417 (N.D. Cal. 1984) (writ of *coram nobis* granted and conviction vacated based upon, *inter alia*, finding that "the government knowingly withheld information from the courts when they were considering the critical question of military necessity in this case").

It contends that Padilla's habeas corpus petition was filed improperly in New York, even though the Government itself chose to bring Padilla there and then sent agents of the military to seize him there – after Padilla had been placed in custody by a federal judge on a grand jury warrant, and after the judge had scheduled a hearing on motions challenging that warrant. The Government contends that a habeas corpus action can only be brought where the soldiers chose to take Padilla. The issue here, however, is the legality of the seizure that occurred on Chief Judge Mukasey's doorstep.

. . .

1. The Government first contends that suit is improper in New York because a "settled rule" requires that a "detainee must bring his challenge to his present, physical detention against his immediate, on-site custodian." US Br. 16. In fact, there is no such absolute requirement. The habeas corpus statute, 28 U.S.C. §2243, requires that the writ "shall be directed to the person having custody of the person detained," but it does not define *who* may be considered a proper custodian. *See, e.g., Eisel v. Secretary of the Army*, 477 F.2d 1251, 1258 (D.C. Cir. 1973) ("[n]owhere does the statute speak of an *immediate* custodian") (emphasis added).

. . .

To justify its immediate custodian rule, the Government reaches back to *Wales v. Whitney*, 114 U.S. 564 (1885), a case this Court subsequently overruled as a "stifling formalism." *Hensley v. Municipal Court*, 411 U.S. 345, 350 & n.8 (1973). *Wales* held that habeas corpus relief was not available to a petitioner released on bail because the habeas provisions "contemplate a proceeding against some person who has the immediate custody of the party detained, with the power to produce the body." 114 U.S. at 574. *Wales*'s reference to immediate custody was thus a corollary of a now-outmoded physical custody requirement. *Jones v. Cunningham*, 371 U.S. 236, 240 (1963); *Developments in the Law – Federal Habeas Corpus*, 83 Harv. L. Rev. 1072, 1073–75 (1970).

In finding that the Secretary was an appropriate respondent here, the courts below emphasized the narrow and unique circumstances of this case. . . . . This case involves an unprecedented *military* seizure in New York, pursuant to a presidential order directed to the Secretary of Defense, and involving a detention over which he, not Commander Marr, is directly responsible. As recognized below, it is the Secretary who (1) removed Padilla from the Southern District of New York, (2) determined that Padilla should be taken to the military brig in South Carolina, and (3) has the power to "decide [] when and whether all that can be learned from Padilla has been learned, and, at least in part, when and whether the danger he allegedly poses has passed." *Id.* at 105a. Secretary Rumsfeld, not Commander Marr, has the ultimate ability to "produce the body."

. . .

2. Personal jurisdiction over the Secretary can be exercised in New York on the specific facts here. The courts below correctly held, consistent with this Court's modern teaching, that jurisdiction over a respondent is determined by the limits of service of process and not antiquated notions of territoriality.

Section 2241 provides that "[w]rits of habeas corpus may be granted by . . . the district courts . . . within their respective jurisdictions." 28 U.S.C. §2241. Consistent with modern, contacts-based notions of personal jurisdiction, this Court has repeatedly interpreted "respective jurisdictions" to mean reachable by service of process, and has rejected the requirement that respondents be physically located within the territory of the court. While a divided Court had embraced the territorial view in *Ahrens v. Clark*, 335 U.S. 188 (1948), *but see id.* at 193 (Rutledge, J., dissenting), it broke from that approach over 30 years ago in *Braden v. 30th Judicial Circuit Court*, 410 U.S. 484 (1973). Citing statutory and judicial developments that cut against an "inflexible territorial rule, dictating the choice of an inconvenient forum," *id.* at 500, *Braden* concluded in plain language that §2241(a) "requires nothing more than that the court issuing the writ have jurisdiction over the custodian. *So long as the custodian can be reached by service of process*, the court can issue a writ 'within its jurisdiction.'" *Id.* at 495 (emphasis added).

. . .

Upholding the jurisdictional determination below will not allow courts around the country to reach out and decide disputes with which they have no connection, as the Government contends. US Br. 25 n.11. It is not *Padilla* who has reached out for "one idiosyncratic district or appellate court anywhere in the nation" to force "the entire federal government [to] dance to its tune," *id.* (quotation marks omitted), and it is disingenuous for the Government even to suggest that here. Padilla, through his New York counsel as next friend, filed this action in New York because the Government had brought him there, because counsel was appointed to represent him there, and because the military unlawfully seized him there. It is the Government that has sought to force all litigation into "one idiosyncratic district or appellate court."

. . .

CONCLUSION

The judgment of the Court of Appeals should be affirmed.

. . .

**Remarks of Deputy Attorney General
James Comey Regarding Jose Padilla
Tuesday, June 1, 2004**

Good afternoon. On April 22nd, Senator Orrin Hatch, the chairman of the Senate Judiciary Committee, sent a letter to the Attorney General asking the Department of Justice and the Department of Defense to supply whatever information we could about American citizens being held as enemy combatants here in the United States.

As you know, there are two such people: Yaser Esam Hamdi and Jose Padilla. Much is known about Hamdi, who was captured on the battlefield in Afghanistan; much less is known about Jose Padilla, in part because rules about classification have long restricted what we could say about him publicly.

For months, even before getting Senator Hatch's letter, we have been working to compile and declassify what we know about Padilla from his own statements, from the statements of other al Qaeda detainees around the world, and from intelligence sources around the world. Senator Hatch's request energized that process, which involved the Department of Justice, the Department of Defense, along with the FBI and other members of the intelligence community.

Because so many important questions have been raised about the detention of Jose Padilla, held after being captured on American soil, all those agencies have worked as hard as they possibly can to declassify as much as they possibly can. And while some information remains classified about Padilla, those efforts of those agencies have resulted in an answer to Senator Hatch's question that is remarkable for its scope, its clarity and its candor.

That answer, which was provided to Senator Hatch earlier today, and also provided to Padilla's lawyers and to our own Department of Justice lawyers handling his case in court, enables us for the first time to tell the full story of Jose Padilla. It will allow the American people to understand the threat he posed and also understand that the president's decision was and continues to be essential to the protection of the American people.

It will also serve to underscore the danger that we still face from al Qaeda, and why that terrorist organization so badly wants operatives who can move freely into and out of the United States.

Let me tell you the sobering story of Jose Padilla.

In 1998, Padilla flew from Miami to Cairo, where he spent the next year and a half. He has admitted that in March of 2000 he attended the religious pilgrimage, the hajj, in Saudi Arabia, and there he met a man from Yemen who was a recruiter for al Qaeda and they discussed the training opportunities al Qaeda offered in Afghanistan. Two months later, at this recruiter's request, Padilla traveled in May of 2000 to Yemen, where the recruiter introduced him to a sponsor, somebody who could arrange for his training in Afghanistan by al Qaeda.

In June of 2000 Padilla made that journey. He went to Pakistan and then traveled over land to Kandahar, Afghanistan. He has admitted that there he completed an application to receive training at an al Qaeda camp, sponsored by the man he met in Yemen who helped him fill out the paperwork. The FBI found Padilla's application to the al Qaeda training camp. They found it in a binder that contained 100 other such applications, typewritten, each with the title at the top, "Mujahideen Identification Form/New Applicant Form." Padilla's application was dated July 24th of 2000, and bears one of his aliases, "Abu Abdullah Al-Muhajir." It bears his date of birth, October 18th, 1970. It shows that he is an American citizen; that he speaks Spanish and English and is proficient at Arabic; that he has traveled through Afghanistan, Yemen, Saudi Arabia and Egypt.

Padilla has admitted that after filling out his application he attended the al-Farouq training camp in September and October of 2000, using the name Abdullah Al-Espani. Padilla says he went to the camp with the understanding that he would be sent to Chechnya to fight for jihad, although he recognized that the recruits of al Qaeda were offered no guarantees. According to Padilla, his training included weapons instruction on AK-47, on G-3, M-16, Uzi and other machine guns.

Training on topography; communications; camouflage; clandestine surveillance; explosives, including C-4 plastic explosives, dynamite and mines; as well as physical fitness and religious training. Padilla completed this basic terrorist training successfully and then spent three months in the fall of 2000 with other new al Qaeda recruits, guarding a Taliban outpost north of Kabul, Afghanistan.

Padilla admits that he first met al Qaeda's military commander, Abu Hafs al-Masri, better known as Mohammed Atef. He met him in Afghanistan when Atef approached this American in the al-Farouk camp and checked him out to gauge his suitability and his commitment to the cause. Atef no doubt spotted the tremendous value this American terrorist offered because he met with him again several times, even giving Padilla money to go back to Egypt to visit his wife.

In early 2001, Padilla walked into the American consulate in Karachi, Pakistan and said his passport had been lost in a market in Karachi and got a new one, a classic act of al Qaeda tradecraft designed to eliminate suspicious travel stamps and cover the nature of the traveler's work.

In April 2001, having completed his basic terrorist training and having found a mentor in the military leader of al Qaeda, Mohammed Atef, Padilla departed Karachi, Pakistan and returned to Egypt, ending his first trip to Afghanistan.

Two months later, in June of 2001, Padilla returned to Afghanistan and sought out Mohammed Atef. He met with Atef at a safe house that was reserved for the instructors and the leaders of al Qaeda. According to Padilla, about a month later his mentor, Atef, asked him a question. He asked him if he was willing to undertake a mission to blow up apartment buildings in the United States using natural gas. Padilla told him he would do it.

Atef then sent Padilla to a training site near the Kandahar airport, where Padilla would train under the watchful eye of an al Qaeda explosives expert and be trained with a man who was to be his partner in this mission to destroy apartment buildings, another al Qaeda operative. When Padilla saw this other operative, he recognized him immediately because he had known him from Florida. Padilla and the other operative trained under the guidance of this explosives expert and learned about switches and circuits and timers. They learned how to seal an apartment to trap the natural gas and to prepare an explosion using that gas that would have maximum yield and destroy an apartment building.

I told you that Padilla recognized this other al Qaeda expert who -- excuse me, this al Qaeda operative who was to be his partner, recognized him immediately. And you will too, because that other operative was Adnan Shukrijuma, also known as Jafar or Jafar the Pilot, a man that the Attorney General and the FBI director told this country about last week, one of the seven we want so badly to find.

Padilla and Jafar, though, could not get along. That personality conflict led them to abandon this operation, although only temporarily, after Padilla reported to Atef that he didn't think he could work with Jafar and he couldn't work this operation alone.

As I continue with Padilla's story, let me note, as the attorney general and Director Mueller did last week, that Jafar took another path and remains out there somewhere and is extraordinarily dangerous; an explosives expert who is also an experienced commercial pilot.

Padilla admits that after this specialized explosives training, he spent much of September of 2001, including after the attacks of September 11th, staying with Mohammed Atef at Atef's safe house near Kandahar. That was the same safe house were Atef was killed by American forces after it was bombed in November of 2001 in a military raid. Padilla's life was spared only because he happened that night to be staying at the safe house run by his explosives teacher. But he returned and dug his mentor Atef's body out of the rubble.

And then, according to Padilla, a decision was made that all Arab fighters had to be moved out of Afghanistan because the Americans were coming. Padilla, armed with his assault rifle, joined many other armed al Qaeda fighters in moving to the Pakistan border to escape the American forces. At that border, Padilla met Abu Zubaydah. Abu Zubaydah, one of the most important and powerful members of al Qaeda, was in charge at that border of sorting the fighters into two groups: those who should continue on and be relocated to Pakistan, and those who should be sent back into Afghanistan.

Padilla admits that after crossing into Pakistan he met Zubaydah again at a safe house in Lahore, Pakistan, and then met with him yet again at another house in Faisalabad, Pakistan. Padilla says it was at the place in Fasialabad that he and a new accomplice, a new partner, approached Abu Zubaydah with an operation in which they proposed to travel to the United States to detonate a nuclear improvised bomb that they had learned to make from research on the Internet. Padilla says that Zubaydah was skeptical about the idea of them building and deploying a nuclear bomb, but nonetheless, told them he would send them on to see Khalid Sheik Mohammed, also known as KSM, the operational leader of al Qaeda and the mastermind behind September the 11th.

We know separately that Zubaydah did think the nuclear bomb idea was not feasible, but he did think, as well, that another kind of radiological device was very feasible -- uranium wrapped with explosives to create a dirty bomb.

Zubaydah believed this was feasible, and encouraged Padilla and his accomplice to pursue it. He warned them, though, that it would not be as easy as they might think, but they seemed convinced that they could do it without getting caught.

Zubaydah's plan was to use Padilla and his accomplice for Zubaydah's own operations in the future. But they were so eager, so intent on carrying out an operation in the United States that in March of 2002 he sent them to see Khalid Sheikh Mohammed, even going so far as to write a reference letter to Khalid Shcikh Mohammed about Padilla, giving Padilla and his accomplice money, and urging them to seek out KSM about the dirty bomb plot. Zubaydah separately called Khalid Sheikh Mohammed, told him about the dirty bomb project, and also told him he didn't think it was practical, but he wanted Khalid Sheikh Mohammed to check it out himself and to evaluate it. He told Khalid Sheikh Mohammed that he was free to use Padilla in his operations in the United States if he wished.

Mohammed did meet with Padilla and his accomplice, and he was, as Zubaydah was, skeptical about the dirty bomb plot. Instead, he suggested to Padilla and his accomplice that they undertake the apartment building operation that had originally been conceived by the now-dead Mohammed Atef, the former military leader of al Qaeda. KSM suggested that they enter the United States by way of Mexico or by way of Puerto Rico, and that once in the country they locate high-rise apartment buildings that had natural gas supplied to all floors, that they rent two apartments in each building, seal those apartments, turn on the gas, and set timers to detonate and destroy the buildings simultaneously at a later time. This was precisely the mission that Padilla and Jafar had trained for, and now Padilla had a new accomplice.

Khalid Sheikh Mohammed gave Padilla full authority to conduct an operation if he and his partner succeeded in entering the United States. I should note that Khalid Sheikh Mohammed was not himself sure which operation Padilla intended to carry out. By that I mean in Khalid Sheikh Mohammed's mind, it was still possible that Padilla was going to pursue the dirty bomb plot. What KSM knew for sure, however, was that he had authorized this explosives-trained al Qaeda operative to mount an attack in the United States.

Padilla, for his part, admits that he presented the dirty bomb plot to Khalid Sheikh Mohammed, just as he admits he presented it to Abu Zubaydah.

Padilla says that Mohammed wanted him to hit apartment buildings in New York, although they also talked about Florida and Washington, D.C. Padilla was given the discretion about choosing the apartment targets.

According to Padilla's new accomplice, who is also in custody, the one who replaced Jafar, Khalid Sheik Mohammed wanted them to blow up 20 apartment buildings simultaneously. In response, Padilla pointed out that he could not possibly rent that many apartments without drawing attention to himself, and that he might have to limit this operation to the destruction of two or three entire apartment buildings. Padilla, by his own admission, accepted this terrorist assignment, although as our answer to Senator Hatch notes, he continues to maintain that he was not in the United States for that reason, and he was never really planning to go through with it. He does admit, however, that after accepting Khalid Sheik Mohammed's assignment, Ramzi Bin al-Shibh, who was the coordinator and organizer of the 19 hijackers on September 11th, trained Padilla in using telephones securely, and in al Qaeda's e-mail protocol. And Khalid Sheik Mohammed himself, according to Padilla, gave $5,000 cash to Padilla. And then Ammar al-Baluchi, who is Khalid Sheik Mohammed's right-hand man, give Padilla another $10,000 in cash, travel documents, a cell phone, an e-mail address to be used to notify al-Baluchi when the operative, Padilla, reached the United States.

Padilla also said something else remarkable. He says that the night before his departure, he and his accomplice attended a dinner with Khalid Sheik Mohammed, with Ramzi Bin al-Shibh, and with Ammar al-Baluchi. That is, the night before Jose Padilla left on his mission to the United States, he was hosted at a farewell dinner by the mastermind of September the 11th and the coordinator of those attacks.

After that dinner, Padilla departed Pakistan on April the 5th, 2002, bound for the United States by way of Zurich. After spending a month in Egypt, Padilla traveled on and arrived at Chicago's O'Hare International Airport on May the 8th of 2002. He was carrying over $10,000 in U.S. currency given to him by his al Qaeda handlers. He was carrying the cell phone provided to him by Ammar al-Baluchi, Khalid Sheikh Mohammed's right-hand man. He was carrying the names and telephone numbers of his recruiter and his sponsor, and the e-mail address for Ammar al-Baluchi, who he was to contact upon safely reaching the United States.

Padilla was arrested by the FBI in Chicago on a material witness warrant authorized by a federal judge in New York.

And he was transferred to Manhattan, where I was then the United States attorney. He was appointed a lawyer at public expense, and we set about trying to see if he would tell the grand jury what he knew about al Qaeda. With time running out in that process, on June the 9th of 2002, just about two years ago, the president of the United States ordered that Padilla be turned over to the custody of the Department of Defense as an enemy combatant, where he remains.

We have decided to release this information to help people understand why we are doing what we are doing in the war on terror, and to help people understand the nature of the threat we face, and in particular to help people understand why it is so important that we find Jafar, Adnan Shukrijuma, the pilot trained with Padilla in explosive destruction.

Much of this information has been uncovered because Jose Padilla has been detained as an enemy combatant and questioned. We have learned many things from Padilla that I'm not going to discuss today and that we did not include in our answer to Senator Hatch.

Had we tried to make a case against Jose Padilla through our criminal justice system, something that I as the United States attorney in New York could not do at that time without jeopardizing intelligence sources, he would very likely have followed his lawyer's advice and said nothing, which would have been his constitutional right. He would likely have ended up a free man, with our only hope being to try to follow him 24 hours a day, seven days a week and hope -- pray, really -- that we didn't lose him.

But Jose Padilla was more than a criminal defendant with the broad menu of rights that we offer in our great criminal justice system. On May the 8th of 2002, a soldier of our enemy, a trained, funded and equipped terrorist, stepped off that plane at Chicago's O'Hare; a highly trained al Qaeda soldier who had accepted an assignment to kill hundreds of innocent men, women and children by destroying apartment buildings; an al Qaeda soldier who still hoped and planned to do even more by detonating a radiological device, a dirty bomb, in this country; an al Qaeda soldier who was trusted enough to spend hour after hour with the leaders of al Qaeda: Mohammed Atef, Abu Zubaydah, Khalid Sheikh Mohammed; an al Qaeda soldier who had vital information about our enemy and its plans; and lastly an al Qaeda soldier who, as an American citizen, was free to move in, within and out of this country.

Two years ago, the president of the United States faced a very difficult choice. After a careful process, he decided to declare Jose Padilla for what he was: an enemy combatant, a member of a terrorist army bent on waging war against innocent civilians. And the president's decision was to hold him to protect the American people and to find out what he knows.

We now know much of what Jose Padilla knows, and what we have learned confirms that the president of the United States made the right call, and that that call saved lives.

Thank you for your time.

NOTICE: This opinion is subject to formal revision before publication in the preliminary print of the United States Reports. Readers are requested to notify the Reporter of Decisions, Supreme Court of the United States, Washington, D. C. 20543, of any typographical or other formal errors, in order that corrections may be made before the preliminary print goes to press.

SUPREME COURT OF THE UNITED STATES

No. 03–1027

DONALD H. RUMSFELD, SECRETARY OF DEFENSE, PETITIONER v. JOSE PADILLA AND DONNA R. NEWMAN, AS NEXT FRIEND OF JOSE PADILLA

ON WRIT OF CERTIORARI TO THE UNITED STATES COURT OF APPEALS FOR THE SECOND CIRCUIT

[June 28, 2004]

CHIEF JUSTICE REHNQUIST delivered the opinion of the Court.

Respondent Jose Padilla is a United States citizen detained by the Department of Defense pursuant to the President's determination that he is an "enemy combatant" who conspired with al Qaeda to carry out terrorist attacks in the United States. We confront two questions: First, did Padilla properly file his habeas petition in the Southern District of New York; and second, did the President possess authority to detain Padilla militarily. We answer the threshold question in the negative and thus do not reach the second question presented.

Because we do not decide the merits, we only briefly recount the relevant facts. On May 8, 2002, Padilla flew from Pakistan to Chicago's O'Hare International Airport. As he stepped off the plane, Padilla was apprehended by federal agents executing a material witness warrant issued by the United States District Court for the Southern District of New York (Southern District) in connection with its grand jury investigation into the September 11th terrorist attacks. Padilla was then transported to New York, where he was held in federal criminal custody. On May 22, acting through appointed counsel, Padilla moved to vacate the material witness warrant.

Padilla's motion was still pending when, on June 9, the President issued an order to Secretary of Defense Donald H. Rumsfeld designating Padilla an "enemy combatant" and directing the Secretary to detain him in military custody. App. D to Brief for Petitioner 5a (June 9 Order). In support of this action, the President invoked his authority as "Commander in Chief of the U.S. armed forces" and the Authorization for Use of Military Force Joint Resolution, Pub.L. 107-40, 115 Stat. 224 (AUMF),[1] enacted by Congress on September 18, 2001. June 9 Order 5a. The President also made several factual findings explaining his decision to designate Padilla an enemy combatant.[2] Based

---

[1] The AUMF provides in relevant part: "[T]he President is authorized to use all necessary and appropriate force against those nations, organizations, or persons he determines planned, authorized, committed, or aided the terrorist attacks that occurred on September 11, 2001, or harbored such organizations or persons, in order to prevent any future acts of international terrorism against the United States by such nations, organizations or persons." 115 Stat. 224.

[2] In short, the President "[d]etermine[d]" that Padilla (1) "is closely associated with al Qaeda, an international terrorist organization with which the United States is at war;" (2) that he "engaged in . . . hostile and warlike acts, including . . . preparation for acts of international terrorism" against the United States; (3) that he

on these findings, the President concluded that it is "consistent with U.S. law and the laws of war for the Secretary of Defense to detain Mr. Padilla as an enemy combatant." *Id.*, at 6a.

That same day, Padilla was taken into custody by Department of Defense officials and transported to the Consolidated Naval Brig in Charleston, South Carolina.[3] He has been held there ever since.

On June 11, Padilla's counsel, claiming to act as his next friend, filed in the Southern District a habeas corpus petition under 28 U.S.C. §2241. The petition, as amended, alleged that Padilla's military detention violates the Fourth, Fifth, and Sixth Amendments and the Suspension Clause, Art. I, §9, cl. 2, of the United States Constitution. The amended petition named as respondents President Bush, Secretary Rumsfeld, and Melanie A. Marr, Commander of the Consolidated Naval Brig.

The Government moved to dismiss, arguing that Commander Marr, as Padilla's immediate custodian, is the only proper respondent to his habeas petition, and that the District Court lacks jurisdiction over Commander Marr because she is located outside the Southern District. On the merits, the Government contended that the President has authority to detain Padilla militarily pursuant to the Commander in Chief Clause of the Constitution, Art. II, §2, cl. 1, the congressional AUMF, and this Court's decision in *Ex parte Quirin*, 317 U.S. 1 (1942).

The District Court issued its decision in December 2002. *Padilla ex rel. Newman v. Bush*, 233 F. Supp. 2d 564. The court held that the Secretary's "personal involvement" in Padilla's military custody renders him a proper respondent to Padilla's habeas petition, and that it can assert jurisdiction over the Secretary under New York's long-arm statute, notwithstanding his absence from the Southern District.[4] *Id.*, at 581–587. On the merits, however, the court accepted the Government's contention that the President has authority to detain as enemy combatants citizens captured on American soil during a time of war. *Id.*, at 587–599.[5]

The Court of Appeals for the Second Circuit reversed. 352 F.3d 695 (2003). The court agreed with the District Court that Secretary Rumsfeld is a proper respondent, reasoning that in cases where the habeas petitioner is detained for "other than federal criminal violations, the Supreme Court has recognized exceptions to the general practice of naming the immediate physical custodian as respondent." *Id.*, at 704–708. The Court of Appeals concluded that on these "unique" facts Secretary Rumsfeld is Padilla's custodian because he exercises "the legal reality of control" over Padilla and because

---

"possesses intelligence" about al Qaeda that "would aid U.S. efforts to prevent attacks by al Qaeda on the United States"; and finally, (4) that he "represents a continuing, present and grave danger to the national security of the United States," such that his military detention "is necessary to prevent him from aiding al Qaeda in its efforts to attack the United States." June 9 Order 5a–6a.

[3] Also on June 9, the Government notified the District Court *ex parte* of the President's order; informed the court that it was transferring Padilla into military custody in South Carolina and that it was consequently withdrawing its grand jury subpoena of Padilla; and asked the court to vacate the material witness warrant. *Padilla ex rel. Newman v. Bush*, 233 F. Supp.2d 564, 571 (SDNY 2002). The court vacated the warrant. *Ibid.*

[4] The court dismissed Commander Marr, Padilla's immediate custodian, reasoning that she would be obliged to obey any order the court directed to the Secretary. 233 F. Supp. 2d. at 583 The court also dismissed President Bush as a respondent, a ruling Padilla does not challenge. *Id.*, at 582–583.

[5] Although the District Court upheld the President's authority to detain domestically captured enemy combatants, it rejected the Government's contentions that Padilla has no right to challenge the factual basis for his detention and that he should be denied access to counsel. Instead, the court held that the habeas statute affords Padilla the right to controvert alleged facts, and granted him monitored access to counsel to effectuate that right. *Id.*, at 599–605. Finally, the court announced that after it received Padilla's factual proffer, it would apply a deferential "some evidence" standard to determine whether the record supports the President's designation of Padilla as an enemy combatant. *Id.*, at 605–608.

he was personally involved in Padilla's military detention. *Id.*, at 707–708. The Court of Appeals also affirmed the District Court's holding that it has jurisdiction over the Secretary under New York's long-arm statute. *Id.*, at 708–710.

Reaching the merits, the Court of Appeals held that the President lacks authority to detain Padilla militarily. *Id.*, at 710–724. The court concluded that neither the President's Commander in Chief power nor the AUMF authorizes military detentions of American citizens captured on American soil. *Id.*, at 712–718, 722–723. To the contrary, the Court of Appeals found in both our case law and in the Non-Detention Act, 18 U.S.C. §4001(a),[6] a strong presumption against domestic military detention of citizens absent explicit congressional authorization. 352 F.3d, at 710–722. Accordingly, the court granted the writ of habeas corpus and directed the Secretary to release Padilla from military custody within 30 days. *Id.*, at 724.

We granted the Government's petition for certiorari to review the Court of Appeals' rulings with respect to the jurisdictional and the merits issues, both of which raise important questions of federal law. 540 U.S. __ (2004).[7]

The question whether the Southern District has jurisdiction over Padilla's habeas petition breaks down into two related subquestions. First, who is the proper respondent to that petition? And second, does the Southern District have jurisdiction over him or her? We address these questions in turn.

I

The federal habeas statute straightforwardly provides that the proper respondent to a habeas petition is "the person who has custody over [the petitioner]." 28 U.S.C. §2242; see also §2243 ("The writ, or order to show cause shall be directed to the person having custody of the person detained"). The consistent use of the definite article in reference to the custodian indicates that there is generally only one proper respondent to a given prisoner's habeas petition. This custodian, moreover, is "the person" with the ability to produce the prisoner's body before the habeas court. *Ibid.* We summed up the plain language of the habeas statute over 100 years ago in this way: "[T]hese provisions contemplate a proceeding against some person who has the *immediate custody* of the party detained, with the power to produce the body of such party before the court or judge, that he may be liberated if no sufficient reason is shown to the contrary." *Wales* v. *Whitney*, 114 U.S. 564, 574 (1885) (emphasis added); see also *Braden* v. *30th Judicial Circuit Court of Ky.*, 410 U.S. 484, 494–495 (1973) ("The writ of habeas corpus" acts upon "the person who holds [the detainee] in what is alleged to be unlawful custody," citing *Wales, supra,* at 574); *Braden, supra,* at 495 (" '[T]his writ . . . is directed to . . . [the] jailer,'" quoting *In the Matter of Jackson*, 15 Mich. 417, 439–440 (1867)).

In accord with the statutory language and *Wales'* immediate custodian rule, long-standing practice confirms that in habeas challenges to present physical confinement – "core challenges" – the default rule is that the proper respondent is the warden of the facility where the prisoner is being held, not the Attorney General or some other remote supervisory official. See, *e.g., Hogan* v. *Hanks*, 97 F.3d 189, 190 (CA7 1996), *Brittingham* v. *United States*, 982 F.2d 378, 379 (CA9 1992); *Blango* v. *Thornburgh*, 942 F.2d 1487,

---

[6] Section 4001(a) provides that "[n]o citizen shall be imprisoned or otherwise detained by the United States except pursuant to an Act of Congress."

[7] The word "jurisdiction," of course, is capable of different interpretations. We use it in the sense that it is used in the habeas statute, 28 U.S.C. §2241(a), and not in the sense of subject-matter jurisdiction of the District Court.

1491–1492 (CA10 1991) (*per curiam*); *Brennan* v. *Cunningham*, 813 F.2d 1, 12 (CA1 1987); *Guerra* v. *Meese*, 786 F.2d 414, 416 (CADC 1986) (*per curiam*); *Billiteri* v. *United States Bd. of Parole*, 541 F.2d 938, 948 (CA2 1976); *Sanders* v. *Bennett*, 148 F.2d 19, 20 (CADC 1945); *Jones* v. *Biddle*, 131 F.2d 853, 854 (CA8 1942).[8] No exceptions to this rule, either recognized[9] or proposed, see *post*, at 4–5 (KENNEDY, J., concurring), apply here.

If the *Wales* immediate custodian rule applies in this case, Commander Marr – the equivalent of the warden at the military brig – is the proper respondent, not Secretary Rumsfeld. See *Al-Marri* v. *Rumsfeld*, 360 F.3d 707, 708–709 (CA7 2004) (holding in the case of an alleged enemy combatant detained at the Consolidated Naval Brig, the proper respondent is Commander Marr, not Secretary Rumsfeld); *Monk* v. *Secretary of the Navy*, 793 F.2d 364, 369 (CADC 1986) (holding that the proper respondent in a habeas action brought by a military prisoner is the commandant of the military detention facility, not the Secretary of the Navy); cf. 10 U.S.C. §951(c) (providing that the commanding officer of a military correctional facility "shall have custody and control" of the prisoners confined therein). Neither Padilla, nor the courts below, nor JUSTICE STEVENS' dissent deny the general applicability of the immediate custodian rule to habeas petitions challenging physical custody. *Post*, at 4. They argue instead that the rule is flexible and should not apply on the "unique facts" of this case. Brief for Respondents 44. We disagree.

First, Padilla notes that the substantive holding of *Wales* – that a person released on his own recognizance is not "in custody" for habeas purposes – was disapproved in *Hensley* v. *Municipal Court, San Jose-Milpitas Judicial Dist., Santa Clara Cty.*, 411 U.S. 345, 350, n. 8 (1973), as part of this Court's expanding definition of "custody" under the habeas statute.[10] Padilla seems to contend, and the dissent agrees, *post*, at 7, that because we no longer require physical detention as a prerequisite to habeas relief, the immediate custodian rule, too, must no longer bind us, even in challenges to physical custody. That argument, as the Seventh Circuit aptly concluded, is a "non sequitur." *Al-Marri*, *supra*, at 711. That our understanding of custody has broadened to include restraints short of physical confinement does nothing to undermine the rationale or statutory foundation of *Wales'* immediate custodian rule where physical custody *is* at issue. Indeed, as the cases cited above attest, it has consistently been applied in this core habeas context within the United States.[11]

---

[8] In *Ahrens* v. *Clark*, 335 U.S. 188 (1948), we left open the question whether the Attorney General is a proper respondent to a habeas petition filed by an alien detained pending deportation. *Id.*, at 189, 193. The lower courts have divided on this question, with the majority applying the immediate custodian rule and holding that the Attorney General is not a proper respondent. Compare *Robledo-Gonzales* v. *Ashcroft*, 342 F. 3d 667 (CA7 2003) (Attorney General is not proper respondent); *Roman* v. *Ashcroft*, 340 F. 3d 314 (CA6 2003) (same); *Vasquez* v. *Reno*, 233 F. 3d 688 (CA1 2000) (same); *Yi* v. *Maugans*, 24 F. 3d 500 (CA3 1994) (same), with *Armentero* v. *INS*, 340 F. 3d 1058 (CA9 2003) (Attorney General is proper respondent). The Second Circuit discussed the question at some length, but ultimately reserved judgment in *Henderson* v. *INS*, 157 F. 3d 106 (1998). Because the issue is not before us today, we again decline to resolve it.

[9] We have long implicitly recognized an exception to the immediate custodian rule in the military context where an American citizen is detained outside the territorial jurisdiction of any district court. *Braden* v. *30th Judicial Circuit Court of Ky.*, 410 U.S. 484, 498 (1973) (discussing the exception); *United States ex rel. Toth* v. *Quarles*, 350 U.S. 11 (1955) (courts-martial convict detained in Korea named Secretary of the Air Force as respondent); *Burns* v. *Wilson*, 346 U.S. 137 (1953) (court-martial convicts detained in Guam named Secretary of Defense as respondent).

[10] For other landmark cases addressing the meaning of "in custody" under the habeas statute, see *Garlotte* v. *Fordice*, 515 U.S. 39 (1995); *Carafas* v. *LaVallee*, 391 U.S. 234 (1968); *Peyton* v. *Rowe*, 391 U.S. 54 (1968); *Jones* v. *Cunningham*, 371 U.S. 236 (1963).

[11] Furthermore, Congress has not substantively amended in more than 130 years the relevant portions of the habeas statute on which *Wales* based its immediate custodian rule, despite uniform case law embracing the *Wales* rule in challenges to physical custody.

The Court of Appeals' view that we have relaxed the immediate custodian rule in cases involving prisoners detained for "other than federal criminal violations," and that in such cases the proper respondent is the person exercising the "legal reality of control" over the petitioner, suffers from the same logical flaw. 352 F. 3d, at 705, 707. Certainly the statute itself makes no such distinction based on the source of the physical detention. Nor does our case law support a deviation from the immediate custodian rule here. Rather, the cases cited by Padilla stand for the simple proposition that the immediate physical custodian rule, by its terms, does not apply when a habeas petitioner challenges something other than his present physical confinement.

In *Braden*, for example, an Alabama prisoner filed a habeas petition in the Western District of Kentucky. He did not contest the validity of the Alabama conviction for which he was confined, but instead challenged a detainer lodged against him in Kentucky state court. Noting that petitioner sought to challenge a "confinement that would be imposed in the future," we held that petitioner was "in custody" in Kentucky by virtue of the detainer. 410 U.S. at 488–489. In these circumstances, the Court held that the proper respondent was not the prisoner's immediate physical custodian (the Alabama warden), but was instead the Kentucky court in which the detainer was lodged. This made sense because the Alabama warden was not "the person who [held] him in what [was] alleged to be unlawful custody." *Id.*, at 494–495 (citing *Wales*, 114 U.S., at 574); *Hensley*, *supra*, at 351, n. 9 (observing that the petitioner in *Braden* "was in the custody of Kentucky officials for purposes of his habeas corpus action"). Under *Braden*, then, a habeas petitioner who challenges a form of "custody" other than present physical confinement may name as respondent the entity or person who exercises legal control with respect to the challenged "custody." But nothing in *Braden* supports departing from the immediate custodian rule in the traditional context of challenges to present physical confinement. See *Al-Marri*, *supra*, at 711–712; *Monk*, *supra*, at 369. To the contrary, *Braden* cited *Wales* favorably and reiterated the traditional rule that a prisoner seeking release from confinement must sue his "jailer." 410 U.S., at 495 (internal quotation marks omitted).

For the same reason, *Strait* v. *Laird*, 406 U.S. 341 (1972), does not aid Padilla. *Strait* involved an inactive reservist domiciled in California who filed a §2241 petition seeking relief from his military obligations. We noted that the reservist's "nominal" custodian was a commanding officer in Indiana who had charge of petitioner's Army records. *Id.*, at 344. As in *Braden*, the immediate custodian rule had no application because petitioner was not challenging any present physical confinement.

In *Braden* and *Strait*, the immediate custodian rule did not apply because *there was no* immediate physical custodian with respect to the "custody" being challenged. That is not the case here: Commander Marr exercises day-to-day control over Padilla's physical custody. We have never intimated that a habeas petitioner could name someone other than his immediate physical custodian as respondent simply because the challenged physical custody does not arise out of a criminal conviction. Nor can we do so here just because Padilla's physical confinement stems from a military order by the President.

It follows that neither *Braden* nor *Strait* supports the Court of Appeals' conclusion that Secretary Rumsfeld is the proper respondent because he exercises the "legal reality of control" over Padilla.[12] As we have explained, identification of the party exercising legal control only comes into play when there is no immediate physical custodian with

---

[12] The Court of Appeals reasoned that "only [the Secretary] – not Commander Marr – could inform the President that further restraint of Padilla as an enemy combatant is no longer necessary." 352 F. 3d 695, 707 (CA2 2003). JUSTICE STEVENS' dissent echoes this argument. *Post*, at 7–8.

respect to the challenged "custody." In challenges to present physical confinement, we reaffirm that the immediate custodian, not a supervisory official who exercises legal control, is the proper respondent. If the "legal control" test applied to physical-custody challenges, a convicted prisoner would be able to name the State or the Attorney General as a respondent to a §2241 petition. As the statutory language, established practice, and our precedent demonstrate, that is not the case.[13]

At first blush *Ex parte Endo*, 323 U.S. 283 (1944), might seem to lend support to Padilla's "legal control" argument. There, a Japanese-American citizen interned in California by the War Relocation Authority (WRA) sought relief by filing a §2241 petition in the Northern District of California, naming as a respondent her immediate custodian. After she filed the petition, however, the Government moved her to Utah. Thus, the prisoner's immediate physical custodian was no longer within the jurisdiction of the District Court. We held, nonetheless, that the Northern District "acquired jurisdiction in this case and that [Endo's] removal ... did not cause it to lose jurisdiction where a person in whose custody she is remains within the district." 323 U.S., at 306. We held that, under these circumstances, the assistant director of the WRA, who resided in the Northern District, would be an "appropriate respondent" to whom the District Court could direct the writ. *Id.*, at 304–305.

While *Endo* did involve a petitioner challenging her present physical confinement, it did not, as Padilla and JUSTICE STEVENS contend, hold that such a petitioner may properly name as respondent someone other than the immediate physical custodian. *Post*, at 7–8 (citing *Endo* as supporting a "more functional approach" that allows habeas petitioners to name as respondent an individual with "control" over the petitioner). Rather, the Court's holding that the writ could be directed to a supervisory official came not in our holding that the District Court initially acquired jurisdiction – it did so because Endo properly named her immediate custodian and filed in the district of confinement – but in our holding that the District Court could effectively grant habeas relief despite the Government-procured absence of petitioner from the Northern District.[14] Thus, *Endo* stands for the important but limited proposition that when the Government moves a habeas petitioner after she properly files a petition naming her immediate custodian, the District Court retains jurisdiction and may direct the writ to any respondent within its jurisdiction who has legal authority to effectuate the prisoner's release.

Endo's holding does not help respondents here. Padilla was moved from New York to South Carolina before his lawyer filed a habeas petition on his behalf. Unlike the District Court in *Endo*, therefore, the Southern District never acquired jurisdiction over Padilla's petition.

Padilla's argument reduces to a request for a new exception to the immediate custodian rule based upon the "unique facts" of this case. While Padilla's detention is undeniably unique in many respects, it is at bottom a simple challenge to physical custody

---

[13] Even less persuasive is the Court of Appeals' and the dissent's belief that Secretary Rumsfeld's "unique" and "pervasive" personal involvement in authorizing Padilla's detention justifies naming him as the respondent. 352 F. 3d, at 707–708 (noting that the Secretary "was charged by the President in the June 9 Order with detaining Padilla" and that the Secretary "determined that Padilla would be sent to the brig in South Carolina"); *post*, at 8. If personal involvement were the standard, "then the prosecutor, the trial judge, or the governor would be named as respondents" in criminal habeas cases. *Al-Marri v. Rumsfeld*, 360 F. 3d 707, 711 (CA7 2004). As the Seventh Circuit correctly held, the proper respondent is the person responsible for maintaining – not authorizing – the custody of the prisoner. *Ibid.*

[14] As we explained: "Th[e] objective [of habeas relief] may be in no way impaired or defeated by the removal of the prisoner from the territorial jurisdiction of the District Court. That end may be served and the decree of the court made effective if a respondent who has custody of the [petitioner] is within reach of the court's process." 323 U.S., at 307.

imposed by the Executive – the traditional core of the Great Writ. There is no indication that there was any attempt to manipulate behind Padilla's transfer – he was taken to the same facility where other al Qaeda members were already being held, and the Government did not attempt to hide from Padilla's lawyer where it had taken him. *Infra*, at 20–21, and n. 17; *post*, at 5 (KENNEDY, J., concurring). His detention is thus not unique in any way that would provide arguable basis for a departure from the immediate custodian rule. Accordingly, we hold that Commander Marr, not Secretary Rumsfeld, is Padilla's custodian and the proper respondent to his habeas petition.

II

We turn now to the second subquestion. District courts are limited to granting habeas relief "within their respective jurisdictions." 28 U.S.C. §2241(a). We have interpreted this language to require "nothing more than that the court issuing the writ have jurisdiction over the custodian." *Braden*, 410 U.S., at 495. Thus, jurisdiction over Padilla's habeas petition lies in the Southern District only if it has jurisdiction over Commander Marr. We conclude it does not.

Congress added the limiting clause – "within their respective jurisdictions" – to the habeas statute in 1867 to avert the "inconvenient [and] potentially embarrassing" possibility that "every judge anywhere [could] issue the Great Writ on behalf of applicants far distantly removed from the courts whereon they sat." *Carbo* v. *United States*, 364 U.S. 611, 617 (1961). Accordingly, with respect to habeas petitions "designed to relieve an individual from oppressive confinement," the traditional rule has always been that the Great Writ is "issuable only in the district of confinement." *Id.*, at 618.

Other portions of the habeas statute support this commonsense reading of §2241(a). For example, if a petitioner seeks habeas relief in the court of appeals, or from this Court or a Justice thereof, the petition must "state the reasons for not making application to *the* district court of the district *in which the applicant is held.*" 28 U.S.C. §2242 (emphases added). Moreover, the court of appeals, this Court, or a Justice thereof "may decline to entertain an application for a writ of habeas corpus and may transfer the application . . . to *the* district court having jurisdiction to entertain it." §2241(b) (emphasis added). The Federal Rules similarly provide that an "application for a writ of habeas corpus must be made to *the* appropriate district court." Fed. Rule App. Proc. 22(a) (emphasis added).

Congress has also legislated against the background of the "district of confinement" rule by fashioning explicit exceptions to the rule in certain circumstances. For instance, §2241(d) provides that when a petitioner is serving a state criminal sentence in a State that contains more than one federal district, he may file a habeas petition not only "in the district court for the district wherein [he] is in custody," but also "in the district court for the district within which the State court was held which convicted and sentenced him"; and "each of such district courts shall have concurrent jurisdiction to entertain the application." Similarly, until Congress directed federal criminal prisoners to file certain postconviction petitions in the sentencing courts by adding §2255 to the habeas statute, federal prisoners could litigate such collateral attacks only in the district of confinement. See *United States* v. *Hayman*, 342 U.S. 205, 212–219 (1952). Both of these provisions would have been unnecessary if, as the Court of Appeals believed, §2241's general habeas provisions permit a prisoner to file outside the district of confinement.

The plain language of the habeas statute thus confirms the general rule that for core habeas petitions challenging present physical confinement, jurisdiction lies in only one district: the district of confinement. Despite this ample statutory and historical pedigree,

Padilla contends, and the Court of Appeals held, that the district of confinement rule no longer applies to core habeas challenges. Rather, Padilla, as well as today's dissenters, *post*, at 8–10, urge that our decisions in *Braden* and *Strait* stand for the proposition that jurisdiction will lie in any district in which the respondent is amenable to service of process. We disagree.

Prior to *Braden*, we had held that habeas jurisdiction depended on the presence of both the petitioner and his custodian within the territorial confines of the district court. See *Ahrens v. Clark*, 335 U.S. 188, 190–192 (1948). By allowing an Alabama prisoner to challenge a Kentucky detainer in the Western District of Kentucky, *Braden* changed course and held that habeas jurisdiction requires only "that the court issuing the writ have jurisdiction over the custodian." 410 U.S., at 495.

But we fail to see how *Braden*'s requirement of jurisdiction over the respondent alters the district of confinement rule for challenges to present physical custody. *Braden* itself did not involve such a challenge; rather, Braden challenged his future confinement in Kentucky by suing his Kentucky custodian. We reasoned that "[u]nder these circumstances it would serve no useful purpose to apply the *Ahrens* rule and require that the action be brought in Alabama." *Id.*, at 499. In habeas challenges to *present* physical confinement, by contrast, the district of confinement is *synonymous* with the district court that has territorial jurisdiction over the proper respondent. This is because, as we have held, the immediate custodian rule applies to core habeas challenges to present physical custody. By definition, the immediate custodian and the prisoner reside in the same district.

Rather than focusing on the holding and historical context of *Braden*, JUSTICE STEVENS, *post*, at 8, like the Court of Appeals, seizes on dicta in which we referred to "service of process" to contend that the Southern District could assert jurisdiction over Secretary Rumsfeld under New York's long-arm statute. See *Braden*, 410 U.S., at 495 ("So long as the custodian can be reached by service of process, the court can issue a writ 'within its jurisdiction'... even if the prisoner himself is confined outside the court's territorial jurisdiction"). But that dicta did not indicate that a custodian may be served with process *outside* of the district court's territorial jurisdiction. To the contrary, the facts and holding of *Braden* dictate the opposite inference. Braden served his Kentucky custodian in Kentucky. Accordingly, we concluded that the Western District of Kentucky had jurisdiction over the petition "since the respondent was properly served *in that district*." *Id.*, at 500 (emphasis added); see also *Endo, supra*, at 304–305 (noting that the court could issue the writ to a WRA official "whose office is at San Francisco, which is in the jurisdiction of the [Northern District of California]"). Thus, *Braden* in no way authorizes district courts to employ long-arm statutes to gain jurisdiction over custodians who are outside of their territorial jurisdiction. See *Al-Marri*, 360 F.3d, at 711; *Guerra*, 786 F.2d, at 417. Indeed, in stating its holding, *Braden* favorably cites *Schlanger v. Seamans*, 401 U.S. 487 (1971), a case squarely holding that the custodian's absence from the territorial jurisdiction of the district court is fatal to habeas jurisdiction. 410 U.S., at 500. Thus, *Braden* does not derogate from the traditional district of confinement rule for core habeas petitions challenging present physical custody.

The Court of Appeals also thought *Strait* supported its long-arm approach to habeas jurisdiction. But *Strait* offers even less help than *Braden*. In *Strait*, we held that the Northern District of California had jurisdiction over Strait's "nominal" custodian – the commanding officer of the Army records center – even though he was physically located in Indiana. We reasoned that the custodian was "present" in California "through the officers in the hierarchy of the command who processed [Strait's] application for discharge." 406 U.S., at 345. The *Strait* Court contrasted its broad view of "presence" in the case of a nominal custodian with a "'commanding officer who is responsible for the day to day control of his subordinates,'" who would be subject to habeas jurisdiction only in the district where he physically resides. *Ibid.* (quoting *Arlen* v. *Laird*, 451 F.2d 684, 687 (CA2 1971)).

The Court of Appeals, much like JUSTICE STEVENS' dissent, reasoned that Secretary Rumsfeld, in the same way as Strait's commanding officer, was "present" in the Southern District through his subordinates who took Padilla into military custody. 352 F. 3d, at 709–710; *post*, at 8. We think not.

Strait simply has no application to the present case. *Strait* predated *Braden*, so the then-applicable *Ahrens* rule required that both the petitioner and his custodian be present in California. Thus, the only question was whether Strait's commanding officer was present in California notwithstanding his physical absence from the district. Distinguishing *Schlanger, supra*, we held that it would "exalt fiction over reality" to require Strait to sue his "nominal custodian" in Indiana when Strait had always resided in California and had his only meaningful contacts with the Army there. 406 U.S., at 344–346. Only under these limited circumstances did we invoke concepts of personal jurisdiction to hold that the custodian was "present" in California through the actions of his agents. *Id.*, at 345.

Here, by contrast, Padilla seeks to challenge his present physical custody in South Carolina. Because the immediate-custodian rule applies to such habeas challenges, the proper respondent is Commander Marr, who is also present in South Carolina. There is thus no occasion to designate a "nominal" custodian and determine whether he or she is "present" in the same district as petitioner.[15] Under *Braden* and the district of confinement rule, as we have explained, Padilla must file his habeas action in South Carolina. Were we to extend *Strait*'s limited exception to the territorial nature of habeas jurisdiction to the context of physical-custody challenges, we would undermine, if not negate, the purpose of Congress in amending the habeas statute in 1867.

The proviso that district courts may issue the writ only "within their respective jurisdictions" forms an important corollary to the immediate custodian rule in challenges to present physical custody under §2241. Together they compose a simple rule that has been consistently applied in the lower courts, including in the context of military detentions: Whenever a §2241 habeas petitioner seeks to challenge his present physical custody within the United States, he should name his warden as respondent and file the petition in the district of confinement. See *Al-Marri, supra*, at 710, 712 (alleged enemy combatant detained at Consolidated Naval Brig must file petition in the District of South Carolina; collecting cases dismissing §2241 petitions filed outside the district of confinement); *Monk*, 793 F. 2d, at 369 (court-martial convict must file in district of confinement).[16]

This rule, derived from the terms of the habeas statute, serves the important purpose of preventing forum shopping by habeas petitioners. Without it, a prisoner could name

---

[15] In other words, Commander Marr is the equivalent of the "commanding officer [with] day to day control" that we distinguished in *Strait*, 406 U.S., at 345 (internal quotation marks omitted).

[16] As a corollary to the previously referenced exception to the immediate custodian rule, n. 8, *supra*, we have similarly relaxed the district of confinement rule when "American citizens confined overseas (and thus outside the territory of any district court) have sought relief in habeas corpus." *Braden*, 410 U.S., at 498 (citing cases). In such cases, we have allowed the petitioner to name as respondent a supervisory official and file the petition in the district where the respondent resides. *Burns* v. *Wilson*, 346 U.S. 137 (1953) (courts-martial convicts held in Guam sued Secretary of Defense in the District of Columbia); *United States ex rel. Toth* v. *Quarles*, 350 U.S. 11 (1955) (court-martial convict held in Korea sued Secretary of the Air Force in the District of Columbia).

a high-level supervisory official as respondent and then sue that person wherever he is amenable to long-arm jurisdiction. The result would be rampant forum shopping, district courts with overlapping jurisdiction, and the very inconvenience, expense, and embarrassment Congress sought to avoid when it added the jurisdictional limitation 137 years ago.

III

JUSTICE STEVENS' dissent, not unlike the Court of Appeals' decision, rests on the mistaken belief that we have made various exceptions to the immediate custodian and district of confinement rules whenever "exceptional," "special," or "unusual" cases have arisen. *Post*, at 1, 4, 8, n. 5. We have addressed most of his contentions in the foregoing discussion, but we briefly touch on a few additional points.

Apparently drawing a loose analogy to *Endo*, JUSTICE STEVENS asks us to pretend that Padilla and his immediate custodian were present in the Southern District at the time counsel filed the instant habeas petition, thus rendering jurisdiction proper. *Post*, at 4–5. The dissent asserts that the Government "depart[ed] from the time-honored practice of giving one's adversary fair notice of an intent to present an important motion to the court," when on June 9 it moved *ex parte* to vacate the material witness warrant and allegedly failed to immediately inform counsel of its intent to transfer Padilla to military custody in South Carolina. *Ibid.*; cf. n. 3, *supra*. Constructing a hypothetical "scenario," the dissent contends that if counsel had been immediately informed, she "would have filed the habeas petition then and there," while Padilla remained in the Southern District, "rather than waiting two days." *Post*, at 4–5. Therefore, JUSTICE STEVENS concludes, the Government's alleged misconduct "justifies treating the habeas application as the functional equivalent of one filed two days earlier." *Post*, at 5 ("[W]e should not permit the Government to obtain a tactical advantage as a consequence of an *ex parte* proceeding").

The dissent cites no authority whatsoever for its extraordinary proposition that a district court can exercise statutory jurisdiction based on a series of events that did not occur, or that jurisdiction might be premised on "punishing" alleged Government misconduct. The lower courts – unlike the dissent – did not perceive any hint of Government misconduct or bad faith that would warrant extending *Endo* to a case where both the petitioner and his immediate custodian were outside of the district at the time of filing. Not surprisingly, then, neither Padilla nor the lower courts relied on the dissent's counterfactual theory to argue that habeas jurisdiction was proper. Finding it contrary to our well-established precedent, we are not persuaded either.[17]

---

[17] On a related note, the dissent argues that the facts as they actually existed at the time of filing should not matter, because "what matters for present purposes are the facts available to [counsel] at the time of filing." *Post*, at 4–5, n. 3. According to the dissent, because the Government "shrouded... in secrecy" the location of Padilla's military custody, counsel was entitled to file in the district where Padilla's presence was "last officially confirmed." *Ibid.* As with the argument addressed above, neither Padilla nor the District Court – which was much closer to the facts of the case than we are – or the Court of Appeals ever suggested that the Government concealed Padilla's whereabouts from counsel, much less contended that such concealment was the basis for habeas jurisdiction in the Southern District. And even if this were a valid legal argument, the record simply does not support the dissent's inference of Government secrecy. The dissent relies solely on a letter written by Padilla's counsel. In that same letter, however, counsel states that she "was informed [on June 10]" that her client had been taken into custody by the Department of Defense and "detain[ed] at a naval military prison." App. 66. When counsel filed Padilla's habeas petition on June 11, she averred that "Padilla is being held in segregation at the high-security Consolidated Naval Brig in Charleston, South Carolina." Pet. for Writ of Habeas Corpus, June 11, 2002, p. 2. The only reasonable inference, particularly in light of Padilla's

The dissent contends that even if we do not indulge its hypothetical scenario, the Court has made "numerous exceptions" to the immediate custodian and district of confinement rules, rendering our bright-line rule "far from bright." *Post*, at 6. Yet the dissent cannot cite *a single case* in which we have deviated from the longstanding rule we reaffirm today – that is, a case in which we allowed a habeas petitioner challenging his present physical custody within the United States to name as respondent someone other than the immediate custodian and to file somewhere other than the district of confinement.[18] If JUSTICE STEVENS' view were accepted, district courts would be consigned to making ad hoc determinations as to whether the circumstances of a given case are "exceptional," "special," or "unusual" enough to require departure from the jurisdictional rules this Court has consistently applied. We do not think Congress intended such a result.

Finally, the dissent urges us to bend the jurisdictional rules because the merits of this case are indisputably of "profound importance," *post*, at 1,7. But it is surely just as necessary in important cases as in unimportant ones that courts take care not to exceed their "respective jurisdictions" established by Congress.

The District of South Carolina, not the Southern District of New York, was the district court in which Padilla should have brought his habeas petition. We therefore reverse the judgment of the Court of Appeals and remand the case for entry of an order of dismissal without prejudice.

It is so ordered.

. . .

JUSTICE KENNEDY, with whom JUSTICE O'CONNOR joins, concurring.

Though I join the opinion of the Court, this separate opinion is added to state my understanding of how the statute should be interpreted in light of the Court's holding. The Court's analysis relies on two rules. First, the habeas action must be brought against the immediate custodian. Second, when an action is brought in the district court, it must be filed in the district court whose territorial jurisdiction includes the place where the custodian is located.

---

failure to argue to the contrary, is that counsel was well aware of Padilla's presence in South Carolina when she filed the habeas petition, not that the Government "shrouded" Padilla's whereabouts in secrecy.

[18] Instead, JUSTICE STEVENS, like the Court of Appeals, relies heavily on *Braden*, *Strait*, and other cases involving challenges to something other than present physical custody. *Post*, at 7–10; *post*, at 7–8, n. 4 (citing *Garlotte* v. *Fordice*, 515 U.S. 39 (1995) (habeas petitioner challenging expired sentence named Governor as respondent; immediate custodian issue not addressed); *Middendorf* v. *Henry*, 425 U.S. 25 (1976) (putative habeas class action challenging court-martial procedures throughout the military; immediate custodian issue not addressed)); *post*, at 9–10 (citing *Eisel* v. *Secretary of the Army*, 477 F.2d 1251 (CADC 1973) (allowing an inactive reservist challenging his military status to name the Secretary of the Army as respondent)). *Demjanjuk* v. *Meese*, 784 F.2d 1114 (CADC 1986), on which the dissent relies, *post*, at 4, is similarly unhelpful: When, as in that case, a prisoner is held in an undisclosed location by an unknown custodian, it is impossible to apply the immediate custodian and district of confinement rules. That is not the case here, where the identity of the immediate custodian and the location of the appropriate district court are clear.

The dissent also cites two cases in which a state prisoner proceeding under 28 U.S.C. §2254 named as respondent the State's officer in charge of penal institutions. *Post*, at 7, n. 4 (citing *California Dept. of Corrections* v. *Morales*, 514 U.S. 499 (1995); *Wainwright* v. *Greenfield*, 474 U.S. 284 (1986)). But such cases do not support Padilla's cause. First of all, the respondents did not challenge their designation as inconsistent with the immediate custodian rule. More to the point, Congress has authorized §2254 petitioners challenging present physical custody to name either the warden *or* the chief state penal officer as a respondent. Rule 2(a) of the Rules Governing Section 2254 Cases in the United States District Courts; Advisory Committee's Note on Rule 2(a), 28 U.S.C., pp. 469–470 (adopted in 1976). Congress has made no such provision for §2241 petitioners like Padilla.

These rules, however, are not jurisdictional in the sense of a limitation on subject-matter jurisdiction. *Ante*, at 5, n. 7. That much is clear from the many cases in which petitions have been heard on the merits despite their noncompliance with either one or both of the rules. See, *e.g.*, *Braden* v. *30th Judicial Circuit Court of Ky.*, 410 U.S. 484, 495 (1973); *Strait* v. *Laird*, 406 U.S. 341, 345 (1972); *United States ex rel. Toth* v. *Quarles*, 350 U.S. 11 (1955); *Burns* v. *Wilson*, 346 U.S. 137 (1953); *Ex parte Endo*, 323 U.S. 283 (1944).

In my view, the question of the proper location for a habeas petition is best understood as a question of personal jurisdiction or venue. This view is more in keeping with the opinion in *Braden*, and its discussion explaining the rules for the proper forum for habeas petitions. 410 U.S., at 493, 500 (indicating that the analysis is guided by "traditional venue considerations" and "traditional principles of venue"); see also *Moore* v. *Olson*, 368 F.3d 757, 759–760 (CA7 2004) (suggesting that the territorial-jurisdiction rule is a venue rule, and the immediate-custodian rule is a personal jurisdiction rule). This approach is consistent with the reference in the statute to the "respective jurisdictions" of the district court. 28 U.S.C. §2241. As we have noted twice this Term, the word "jurisdiction" is susceptible of different meanings, not all of which refer to the power of a federal court to hear a certain class of cases. *Kontrick* v. *Ryan*, 540 U.S. __ (2004); *Scarborough* v. *Principi*, 541 U.S. __ (2004). The phrase "respective jurisdictions" does establish a territorial restriction on the proper forum for habeas petitions, but does not of necessity establish that the limitation goes to the power of the court to hear the case.

Because the immediate-custodian and territorial-jurisdiction rules are like personal jurisdiction or venue rules, objections to the filing of petitions based on those grounds can be waived by the Government. *Moore, supra,* at 759; cf. *Endo, supra,* at 305 ("The fact that no respondent was ever served with process or appeared in the proceedings is not important. The United States resists the issuance of a writ. A cause exists in that state of the proceedings and an appeal lies from denial of a writ without the appearance of a respondent"). For the same reason, the immediate-custodian and territorial rules are subject to exceptions, as acknowledged in the Court's opinion. *Ante*, at 7, n. 9, 9–13, 16–18. This does not mean that habeas petitions are governed by venue rules and venue considerations that apply to other sorts of civil lawsuits. Although habeas actions are civil cases, they are not automatically subject to all of the Federal Rules of Civil Procedure. See Fed. Rule Civ. Proc. 81(a)(2) ("These rules are applicable to proceedings for…habeas corpus…to the extent that the practice in such proceedings is not set forth in statutes of the United States, the Rules Governing Section 2254 Cases, or the Rules Governing Section 2255 Proceedings"). Instead, these forum-location rules for habeas petitions are based on the habeas statutes and the cases interpreting them. Furthermore, the fact that these habeas rules are subject to exceptions does not mean that, in the exceptional case, a petition may be properly filed in any one of the federal district courts. When an exception applies, see, *e.g.*, *Rasul* v. *Bush, post,* p. __, courts must still take into account the considerations that in the ordinary case are served by the immediate-custodian rule, and, in a similar fashion, limit the available forum to the one with the most immediate connection to the named custodian.

I would not decide today whether these habeas rules function more like rules of personal jurisdiction or rules of venue. It is difficult to describe the precise nature of these restrictions on the filing of habeas petitions, as an examination of the Court's own opinions in this area makes clear. Compare, *e.g.*, *Ahrens* v. *Clark*, 335 U.S. 188 (1948), with *Schlanger* v. *Seamans*, 401 U.S. 487, 491 (1971), and *Braden, supra,* at 495. The precise question of how best to characterize the statutory direction respecting where the action must be filed need not be resolved with finality in this case. Here there has been no waiver by the Government; there is no established exception to the immediate-custodian rule or to the rule that the action must be brought in the district court with authority over the territory in question; and there is no need to consider some further exception to protect the integrity of the writ or the rights of the person detained.

For the purposes of this case, it is enough to note that, even under the most permissive interpretation of the habeas statute as a venue provision, the Southern District of New York was not the proper place for this petition. As the Court concludes, in the ordinary case of a single physical custody within the borders of the United States, where the objection has not been waived by the Government, the immediate-custodian and territorial-jurisdiction rules must apply. *Ante*, at 23. I also agree with the arguments from statutory text and case law that the Court marshals in support of these two rules. *Ante*, at 5–6, 13–14. Only in an exceptional case may a court deviate from those basic rules to hear a habeas petition filed against some person other than the immediate custodian of the prisoner, or in some court other than the one in whose territory the custodian may be found.

The Court has made exceptions in the cases of nonphysical custody, see, *e.g.*, *Strait*, 406 U.S., at 345, of dual custody, see, *e.g.*, *Braden*, 410 U.S., at 500, and of removal of the prisoner from the territory of a district after a petition has been filed, see, *e.g.*, *Endo*, 323 U.S., at 306; see also *ante*, at 11–12, 15–16. In addition, I would acknowledge an exception if there is an indication that the Government's purpose in removing a prisoner were to make it difficult for his lawyer to know where the habeas petition should be filed, or where the Government was not forthcoming with respect to the identity of the custodian and the place of detention. In cases of that sort, habeas jurisdiction would be in the district court from whose territory the petitioner had been removed. In this case, if the Government had removed Padilla from the Southern District of New York but refused to tell his lawyer where he had been taken, the District Court would have had jurisdiction over the petition. Or, if the Government did inform the lawyer where a prisoner was being taken but kept moving him so a filing could not catch up to the prisoner, again, in my view, habeas jurisdiction would lie in the district or districts from which he had been removed.

None of the exceptions apply here. There is no indication that the Government refused to tell Padilla's lawyer where he had been taken. The original petition demonstrates that the lawyer knew where Padilla was being held at that time. *Ante*, at 21, n. 17. In these circumstances, the basic rules apply, and the District of South Carolina was the proper forum. The present case demonstrates the wisdom of those rules.

Both Padilla's change in location and his change of custodian reflected a change in the Government's rationale for detaining him. He ceased to be held under the authority of the criminal justice system, see 18 U.S.C. §3144, and began to be held under that of the military detention system. Rather than being designed to play games with forums, the Government's removal of Padilla reflected the change in the theory on which it was holding him. Whether that theory is a permissible one, of course, is a question the Court does not reach today.

The change in custody, and the underlying change in rationale, should be challenged in the place the Government has brought them to bear and against the person who is the immediate representative of the military authority that is detaining him. That place is the District of South Carolina, and that person is Commander Marr. The Second Circuit erred in holding that the Southern District of New York was a proper forum for Padilla's petition. With these further observations, I join the opinion and judgment of the Court.

. . .

Justice Stevens, with whom Justice Souter, Justice Ginsburg, and Justice Breyer join, dissenting.

The petition for a writ of habeas corpus filed in this case raises questions of profound importance to the Nation. The arguments set forth by the Court do not justify avoidance of our duty to answer those questions. It is quite wrong to characterize the proceeding as a "simple challenge to physical custody," *ante*, at 13, that should be resolved by slavish application of a "bright-line rule," *ante*, at 21, designed to prevent "rampant forum shopping" by litigious prison inmates, *ante*, at 19. As the Court's opinion itself demonstrates, that rule is riddled with exceptions fashioned to protect the high office of the Great Writ. This is an exceptional case that we clearly have jurisdiction to decide.

I

In May 2002, a grand jury convened in the Southern District of New York was conducting an investigation into the September 11, 2001, terrorist attacks. In response to an application by the Department of Justice, the Chief Judge of the District issued a material witness warrant authorizing Padilla's arrest when his plane landed in Chicago on May 8.[1] Pursuant to that warrant, agents of the Department of Justice took Padilla (hereinafter respondent) into custody and transported him to New York City, where he was detained at the Metropolitan Correctional Center. On May 15, the court appointed Donna R. Newman, a member of the New York bar, to represent him. She conferred with respondent in person and filed motions on his behalf, seeking his release on the ground that his incarceration was unauthorized and unconstitutional. The District Court scheduled a hearing on those motions for Tuesday, June 11, 2002.

On Sunday, June 9, 2002, before that hearing could occur, the President issued a written command to the Secretary of Defense concerning respondent. "Based on the information available to [him] from all sources," the President determined that respondent is an "enemy combatant," that he is "closely associated with al Qaeda, an international terrorist organization with which the United States is at war," and that he possesses intelligence that, "if communicated to the U.S., would aid U.S. efforts to prevent attacks by al Qaeda" on U.S. targets. App. A to Pet. for Cert. 57a. The command stated that "it is in the interest of the United States" and "consistent with U.S. law and the laws of war for the Secretary of Defense to detain Mr. Padilla as an enemy combatant." *Id.*, at 58a. The President's order concluded: "Accordingly, you are directed to receive Mr. Padilla from the Department of Justice and to detain him as an enemy combatant." *Ibid.*

On the same Sunday that the President issued his order, the Government notified the District Court in an *ex parte* proceeding that it was withdrawing its grand jury subpoena, and it asked the court to enter an order vacating the material witness warrant. *Padilla ex rel. Newman* v. *Bush*, 233 F.Supp.2d 564, 571 (SDNY 2002). In that proceeding, in which respondent was not represented, the Government informed the court that the President had designated respondent an enemy combatant and had directed

---

[1] As its authority for detaining respondent as a material witness, the Government relied on a federal statute that provides: "If it appears from an affidavit filed by a party that the testimony of a person is material in a criminal proceeding, and if it is shown that it may become impracticable to secure the presence of the person by subpoena, a judicial officer may order the arrest of the person and treat the person in accordance with the provisions of section 3142....Release of a material witness may be delayed for a reasonable period of time until the deposition of the witness can be taken pursuant to the Federal Rules of Criminal Procedure." 18 U.S.C. §3144.

the Secretary of Defense, petitioner Donald Rumsfeld, to detain respondent. *Ibid.* The Government also disclosed that the Department of Defense would take custody of respondent and immediately transfer him to South Carolina. The District Court complied with the Government's request and vacated the warrant.[2]

On Monday, June 10, 2002, the Attorney General publicly announced respondent's detention and transfer "to the custody of the Defense Department," which he called "a significant step forward in the War on Terrorism." Amended Pet. for Writ of Habeas Corpus, Exh. A, p. 1, Record, Doc. 4. On June 11, 2002, presumably in response to that announcement, Newman commenced this proceeding by filing a petition for a writ of habeas corpus in the Southern District of New York. 233 F. Supp. 2d, at 571. At a conference on that date, which had been originally scheduled to address Newman's motion to vacate the material witness warrant, the Government conceded that Defense Department personnel had taken custody of respondent in the Southern District of New York. *Id.*, at 571–572.

II

All Members of this Court agree that the immediate custodian rule should control in the ordinary case and that habeas petitioners should not be permitted to engage in forum shopping. But we also all agree with Judge Bork that "special circumstances" can justify exceptions from the general rule. *Demjanjuk* v. *Meese*, 784 F.2d 1114, 1116 (CADC 1986). See *ante*, at 22, n. 18. Cf. *ante*, at 2 (KENNEDY, J., concurring). More narrowly, we agree that if jurisdiction was proper when the petition was filed, it cannot be defeated by a later transfer of the prisoner to another district. *Ex parte Endo*, 323 U.S. 283, 306 (1944). See *ante*, at 12–13.

It is reasonable to assume that if the Government had given Newman, who was then representing respondent in an adversary proceeding, notice of its intent to ask the District Court to vacate the outstanding material witness warrant and transfer custody to the Department of Defense, Newman would have filed the habeas petition then and there, rather than waiting two days.[3] Under that scenario, respondent's immediate

---

[2] The order vacating the material witness warrant that the District Court entered in the *ex parte* proceeding on June 9 terminated the Government's lawful custody of respondent. After that order was entered, Secretary Rumsfeld's agents took custody of respondent. The authority for that action was based entirely on the President's command to the Secretary – a document that, needless to say, would not even arguably qualify as a valid warrant. Thus, whereas respondent's custody during the period between May 8 and June 9, 2002, was pursuant to a judicially authorized seizure, he has been held ever since – for two years – pursuant to a warrantless arrest.

[3] The record indicates that the Government had not *officially* informed Newman of her client's whereabouts at the time she filed the habeas petition on June 11. Pet. for Writ of Habeas Corpus 2, ¶4 ("On information and belief, Padilla is being held in segregation at the high-security Consolidated Naval Brig in Charleston, South Carolina"); Letter from Donna R. Newman to General Counsel of the Department of Defense, June 17, 2002 ("I understand *from the media* that my client is being held in Charleston, South Carolina in the military brig" (emphasis added)), Amended Pet. for Writ of Habeas Corpus, Exh. A, p. 4, Record, Doc. 4. Thus, while it is true, as the Court observes, that "Padilla was moved from New York to South Carolina before his lawyer filed a habeas petition on his behalf," *ante*, at 13, what matters for present purposes are the facts available to Newman at the time of filing. When the Government shrouded those facts in secrecy, Newman had no option but to file immediately in the district where respondent's presence was last officially confirmed.

Moreover, Newman was appointed to represent respondent by the District Court for the Southern District of New York. Once the Government removed her client, it did not permit her to counsel him until February 11, 2004. Consultation thereafter has been allowed as a matter of the Government's grace, not as a matter of right stemming from the Southern District of New York appointment. Cf. *ante*, at 4–5 (KENNEDY, J., concurring). Further, it is not apparent why the District of South Carolina, rather than the Southern District of New York, should be regarded as the proper forum to determine the validity of the "change in the Government's

custodian would then have been physically present in the Southern District of New York carrying out orders of the Secretary of Defense. Surely at that time Secretary Rumsfeld, rather than the lesser official who placed the handcuffs on petitioner, would have been the proper person to name as a respondent to that petition.

The difference between that scenario and the secret transfer that actually occurred should not affect our decision, for we should not permit the Government to obtain a tactical advantage as a consequence of an *ex parte* proceeding. The departure from the time-honored practice of giving one's adversary fair notice of an intent to present an important motion to the court justifies treating the habeas application as the functional equivalent of one filed two days earlier. See *Baldwin* v. *Hale*, 1 Wall. 223, 233 (1864) ("Common justice requires that no man shall be condemned in his person or property without notice and an opportunity to make his defence"). "The very nature of the writ demands that it be administered with the initiative and flexibility essential to insure that miscarriages of justice within its reach are surfaced and corrected." *Harris* v. *Nelson*, 394 U.S. 286, 291 (1969). But even if we treat respondent's habeas petition as having been filed in the Southern District after the Government removed him to South Carolina, there is ample precedent for affording special treatment to this exceptional case, both by recognizing Secretary Rumsfeld as the proper respondent and by treating the Southern District as the most appropriate venue.

Although the Court purports to be enforcing a "bright-line rule" governing district courts' jurisdiction, *ante*, at 21, an examination of its opinion reveals that the line is far from bright. Faced with a series of precedents emphasizing the writ's "scope and flexibility," *Harris*, 394 U.S., at 291, the Court is forced to acknowledge the numerous exceptions we have made to the immediate custodian rule. The rule does not apply, the Court admits, when physical custody is not at issue, *ante*, at 8, or when American citizens are confined overseas, *ante*, at 19, n. 16, or when the petitioner has been transferred after filing, *ante*, at 12–13, or when the custodian is "'present'" in the district through his agents' conduct, *ante*, at 17. In recognizing exception upon exception and corollaries to corollaries, the Court itself persuasively demonstrates that the rule is not ironclad. It is, instead, a workable general rule that frequently gives way outside the context of "'core challenges'" to executive confinement. *Ante*, at 6.

In the Court's view, respondent's detention falls within the category of "'core challenges'" because it is "not unique in any way that would provide arguable basis for a departure from the immediate custodian rule." *Ante*, at 13. It is, however, disingenuous at best to classify respondent's petition with run-of-the-mill collateral attacks on federal criminal convictions. On the contrary, this case is singular not only because it calls into question decisions made by the Secretary himself, but also because those decisions have created a unique and unprecedented threat to the freedom of every American citizen.

"[W]e have consistently rejected interpretations of the habeas corpus statute that would suffocate the writ in stifling formalisms or hobble its effectiveness with the manacles of arcane and scholastic procedural requirements." *Hensley* v. *Municipal Court, San Jose-Milpitas Judicial Dist., Santa Clara Cty.*, 411 U.S. 345, 350 (1973). With respect to the custody requirement, we have declined to adopt a strict reading of *Wales* v. *Whitney*, 114 U.S. 564 (1885), see *Hensley*, 411 U.S., at 350, n. 8, and instead have favored a more functional approach that focuses on the person with the power to produce the body,

---

rationale for detaining" respondent. *Ante*, at 5. If the Government's theory is not "a permissible one," *ibid.*, then the New York federal court would remain the proper forum in this case. Why should the New York court not have the authority to determine the legitimacy of the Government's removal of respondent beyond that court's borders?

see *Endo*, 323 U.S., at 306–307.[4] In this case, the President entrusted the Secretary of Defense with control over respondent. To that end, the Secretary deployed Defense Department personnel to the Southern District with instructions to transfer respondent to South Carolina. Under the President's order, only the Secretary – not a judge, not a prosecutor, not a warden – has had a say in determining respondent's location. As the District Court observed, Secretary Rumsfeld has publicly shown "both his familiarity with the circumstances of Padilla's detention, and his personal involvement in the handling of Padilla's case." 233 F. Supp. 2d, at 574. Having "emphasized and jealously guarded" the Great Writ's "ability to cut through barriers of form and procedural mazes," *Harris*, 394 U.S., at 291, surely we should acknowledge that the writ reaches the Secretary as the relevant custodian in this case.

. . .

When this case is analyzed under those traditional venue principles, it is evident that the Southern District of New York, not South Carolina, is the more appropriate place to litigate respondent's petition. The Government sought a material witness warrant for respondent's detention in the Southern District, indicating that it would be convenient for its attorneys to litigate in that forum. As a result of the Government's initial forum selection, the District Judge and counsel in the Southern District were familiar with the legal and factual issues surrounding respondent's detention both before and after he was transferred to the Defense Department's custody. Accordingly, fairness and efficiency counsel in favor of preserving venue in the Southern District. In sum, respondent properly filed his petition against Secretary Rumsfeld in the Southern District of New York.

III

Whether respondent is entitled to immediate release is a question that reasonable jurists may answer in different ways.[8] There is, however, only one possible answer to the question whether he is entitled to a hearing on the justification for his detention.[9]

---

[4] For other cases in which the immediate custodian rule has not been strictly applied, see *Garlotte* v. *Fordice*, 515 U.S. 39 (1995) (prisoner named Governor of Mississippi, not warden, as respondent); *California Dept. of Corrections* v. *Morales*, 514 U.S. 499 (1995) (prisoner named Department of Corrections, not warden, as respondent); *Wainwright* v. *Greenfield*, 474 U.S. 284 (1986) (prisoner named Secretary of Florida Department of Corrections, not warden, as respondent); *Middendorf* v. *Henry*, 425 U.S. 25 (1976) (persons convicted or ordered to stand trial at summary courts-martial named Secretary of the Navy as respondent); *Strait* v. *Laird*, 406 U.S. 341, 345–346 (1972) ("The concepts of 'custody' and 'custodian' are sufficiently broad to allow us to say that the commanding officer in Indiana, operating through officers in California in processing petitioner's claim, is in California for the limited purposes of habeas corpus jurisdiction"); *Burns* v. *Wilson*, 346 U.S. 137 (1953) (service members convicted and held in military custody in Guam named Secretary of Defense as respondent); *United States ex rel. Toth* v. *Quarles*, 350 U.S. 11 (1955) (next friend of ex-service member in military custody in Korea named Secretary of the Air Force as respondent); *Ex parte Endo*, 323 U.S. 283, 304 (1944) (California District Court retained jurisdiction over Japanese-American's habeas challenge to her internment, despite her transfer to Utah, noting absence of any "suggestion that there is no one within the jurisdiction of the District Court who is responsible for the detention of appellant and who would be an appropriate respondent").

[8] Consistent with the judgment of the Court of Appeals, I believe that the Non-Detention Act, 18 U.S.C. §4001(a), prohibits – and the Authorization for Use of Military Force Joint Resolution, 115 Stat. 224, adopted on September 18, 2001, does not authorize – the protracted, incommunicado detention of American citizens arrested in the United States.

[9] Respondent's custodian has been remarkably candid about the Government's motive in detaining respondent: "'[O]ur interest really in his case is not law enforcement, it is not punishment because he was a terrorist or working with the terrorists. Our interest at the moment is to try and find out everything he knows so that

At stake in this case is nothing less than the essence of a free society. Even more important than the method of selecting the people's rulers and their successors is the character of the constraints imposed on the Executive by the rule of law. Unconstrained executive detention for the purpose of investigating and preventing subversive activity is the hallmark of the Star Chamber.[10] Access to counsel for the purpose of protecting the citizen from official mistakes and mistreatment is the hallmark of due process.

Executive detention of subversive citizens, like detention of enemy soldiers to keep them off the battlefield, may sometimes be justified to prevent persons from launching or becoming missiles of destruction. It may not, however, be justified by the naked interest in using unlawful procedures to extract information. Incommunicado detention for months on end is such a procedure. Whether the information so procured is more or less reliable than that acquired by more extreme forms of torture is of no consequence. For if this Nation is to remain true to the ideals symbolized by its flag, it must not wield the tools of tyrants even to resist an assault by the forces of tyranny.

I respectfully dissent.

---

hopefully we can stop other terrorist acts.'" 233 F. Supp. 2d 564, 573–574 (SDNY 2002) (quoting News Briefing, Dept. of Defense (June 12, 2002), 2002 WL 22026773).

[10] See *Watts v. Indiana*, 338 U.S. 49, 54 (1949) (opinion of Frankfurter, J.). "There is torture of mind as well as body; the will is as much affected by fear as by force. And there comes a point where this Court should not be ignorant as judges of what we know as men." *Id.*, at 52.

UNITED STATES DISTRICT COURT
DISTRICT OF SOUTH CAROLINA

\-x

JOSE PADILLA   :

                                            :   04 Civ._____

            Petitioner,

                                            :

        -against-

                                            :

COMMANDER C.T. HANFT, USN
Commander, Consolidated Naval Brig   :

███████████████████████████████

                                            :

            Respondent.   :

\-x

PETITION FOR WRIT OF HABEAS CORPUS

1. Jose Padilla, a citizen of the United States of America, has been unlawfully imprisoned without trial for over two years as an "enemy combatant" in violation of his rights under the laws and Constitution of the United States of America. He respectfully requests that this Court issue a writ of habeas corpus.

2. A Petition for Writ of Habeas Corpus on Padilla's behalf was previously filed with Southern District of New York. That Petition was ordered dismissed without prejudice by the U.S. Supreme Court on the grounds that it should have been brought in the District of South Carolina rather than New York. Rumsfeld v. Padilla, __ U.S. __, bench op. at 23 (June 28, 2004). In light of the two years of unlawful confinement Petitioner has already suffered, this Court should act expeditiously to grant the writ and order his release.

PARTIES

3. Petitioner Jose Padilla is an American citizen presently incarcerated and unlawfully held by Respondent at the Consolidated Naval Brig in Charleston, South Carolina.

4. Respondent C.T. Hanft is a Commander in the United States Navy and is in command of the Consolidated Naval Brig in Charleston, South Carolina. Commander Hanft is Padilla's immediate custodian and the proper respondent in this proceeding. See Rumsfeld v. Padilla, __ U.S. __ , bench op. at 13.

. . .

VENUE

7. Venue is proper in the United States District Court for the District of South Carolina, the district in which Padilla is currently detained as well as the location of

---

* Redaction on this page has been added for privacy purposes. – *Eds.*

Commander Hanft, the person with day to day control over Padilla. See Rumsfeld v. Padilla, __ U.S. __, bench op. at 23.

STATEMENT OF FACTS

. . .

18. As of the date of this Petition, Padilla has been imprisoned for more than two years without being charged with any criminal offense. On information and belief, since his designation as an "enemy combatant," no grand jury sitting in any district in the United States has returned an indictment charging him with any criminal conduct, including treason. No complaint has been filed in any United States District Court that charges him with any criminal conduct, including treason.

19. Padilla's court-appointed attorney, acting as next friend, filed a habeas petition on his behalf in the Southern District of New York while Padilla was being held in incommunicado military detention. That petition was ordered dismissed without prejudice by the U.S. Supreme Court on June 28, 2004, on the grounds that it should have been brought in the District of South Carolina. Rumsfeld v. Padilla, __ U.S. __, bench op. at 23.

CLAIMS AS TO THE UNLAWFULNESS OF PETITIONER'S DETENTION

FIRST CLAIM FOR RELIEF
PETITIONER'S DETENTION WITHOUT CRIMINAL CHARGES VIOLATES THE UNITED STATES CONSTITUTION, INCLUDING THE FOURTH, FIFTH AND SIXTH AMENDMENTS, THE HABEAS SUSPENSION CLAUSE OF ARTICLE I, AND THE TREASON CLAUSE OF ARTICLE III

20. Petitioner incorporates paragraphs 1–19 by reference.

21. Petitioner's ongoing detention without criminal charges violates the Fourth, Fifth and Sixth Amendments to the United States Constitution, as well as the Treason Clause of Article III, and the Habeas Suspension Clause of Article I. See Ex Parte Milligan, 71 U.S. 2, 122–23 (1866).

22. Although the U.S. Supreme Court ordered Padilla's habeas petition dismissed without prejudice on the grounds it had been brought in the wrong district, the Court's opinions in Rumsfeld v. Padilla and Hamdi v. Rumsfeld, __U.S.__ (2004), clearly indicate absent a valid suspension of habeas corpus by Congress, American citizens arrested in the U.S. can only be deprived of liberty through criminal process. See Milligan, 71 U.S. at 123; Hamdi, __ U.S. __, bench op. at 12. Neither the Constitution nor the laws of the United States authorize Padilla's detention as an "enemy combatant." Congress has not suspended the writ of habeas corpus pursuant to Article I, §9, cl.2 of the Constitution. Accordingly, Padilla must be charged with a crime or released immediately.

SECOND CLAIM FOR RELIEF
PETITIONER'S DETENTION VIOLATES THE NON-DETENTION ACT,
U.S.C. §4001(a)

23. Petitioner incorporates paragraphs 1–22 by reference.

24. The Non-Detention Act, 18 U.S. 4001(a), prohibits the detention of any American citizen "except pursuant to an Act of Congress."

25. Congress has enacted no legislation authorizing the detention of American citizens arrested on American soil as "enemy combatants."

THIRD CLAIM FOR RELIEF
DUE PROCESS AND RIGHT TO COUNSEL

26. Petitioner incorporates by reference the allegations of paragraphs 1–25.

27. In violation of his rights under the Due Process Clause of the Fifth Amendment of the U.S. Constitution, Petitioner has been imprisoned for more than two years without receiving "notice of the factual basis for his classification, and a fair opportunity to rebut the Government's factual assertions before a neutral decisionmaker." Hamdi, __ U.S. __, bench op. at 26 (O'Connor, J.) (plurality op.)

28. Petitioner disputes the factual allegations underlying the Government's designation of him as an "enemy combatant" and is entitled to a hearing on those allegations and is entitled to be released if the Government fails to establish that he is an "enemy combatant" by a standard of proof that comports with the Constitution.

29. Petitioner also "unquestionably has the right to access to counsel." Hamdi, __ U.S. __, bench op. at 32 (O'Connor, J.) (plurality op.) Petitioner is constitutionally entitled to communicate freely with his lawyers about any topic without restriction imposed by the executive, and those conversations are entitled to protection under the attorney-client privilege.

FOURTH CLAIM FOR RELIEF
INTERROGATION

30. Petitioner incorporates by reference the allegations of paragraphs 1–29.

31. A majority of the U.S. Supreme Court has indicated that prolonged detention for interrogation purposes is unlawful. Hamdi, __ U.S. __, bench op. at 13 (O'Connor, J., plurality op.)

32. The interrogation of a prisoner throughout two years of incommunicado detention shocks the conscience and violates fundamental principles of justice that are implicit in ordered liberty. The ongoing interrogation of Padilla violates his rights under the Fifth, Sixth and Eighth Amendments to the U.S. Constitution, including the right against self-incrimination, the right to counsel, the right not to be subject to cruel or unusual punishment, and substantive and procedural due process.

PRAYER FOR RELIEF

WHEREFORE, Petitioners pray for the relief as follows:

1. Pursuant to Counts 1 and/or 2 of this petition, grant the writ of habeas corpus, declare that. Petitioner is being held in violation of the Fourth, Fifth and Sixth Amendments, the Treason Clause, and the Habeas Suspension Clause of the U.S. Constitution, as well as the Non-Detention Act, 18 U.S.C. §4001(a), and order that he immediately be released or charged with a crime.

2. In the alternative, pursuant to Count 3 of this petition, grant Petitioner the opportunity to contest the Government's factual allegations at an evidentiary hearing in this Court;

3. Pursuant to Count 3 of the petition, order Respondent to permit counsel to meet and confer with Petitioner freely and under the shield of the attorney-client privilege, and to freely transmit to Petitioner all documents related to this litigation.

4. Pursuant to Count 4 of this petition, order Respondent to cease all interrogation of Petitioner while this litigation is pending.

5. Such other relief as the Court may deem necessary and appropriate.

Dated: Charleston, South Carolina
June 30, 2004

Respectfully submitted,

_____

Jose Padilla

. . .

IN THE UNITED STATES DISTRICT COURT
FOR THE DISTRICT OF SOUTH CAROLINA

Jose Padilla,	)	
	)	
Petitioner	)	
	)	
v.	)	C/A No. 02:04-2221-26AJ
	)	
Commander C.T. Hanft,	)	Respondent's Answer to the
U.S.N. Commander,	)	Petition for Writ of Habeas Corpus
Consolidated Naval Brig,	)	
	)	
Respondent	)	
	)	

Respondent Commander C.T. Hanft, Commanding Officer of the Consolidated Naval Brig in Charleston, South Carolina, by and through undersigned counsel, respectfully submits this Answer to the petition for writ of habeas corpus. The petition challenges the legality of petitioner's detention as an enemy combatant, alleging, *inter alia*, that petitioner's detention violates the Fourth, Fifth, and Sixth Amendments to the United States Constitution, the Suspension Clause of Article I, the Treason Clause of Article III, and 18 U.S.C. 4001(a). Those legal challenges fail. As is made clear by the Supreme Court's decisions in *Hamdi* v. *Rumsfeld*, 124 S. Ct. 2633 (2004) and *Ex parte Quirin*, 317 U.S. 1 (1942), the President has authority as Commander in Chief and pursuant to Congress's Authorization for Use of Military Force (AUMF), Pub. L. No. 107-40, 115 Stat. 224 (2001), to detain petitioner as an enemy combatant in the course of the ongoing conflict against al Qaeda.

. . .

ARGUMENT

I. The President Has Authority As Commander In Chief And Pursuant To Congress's AUMF To Detain Petitioner As An Enemy Combatant.

Petitioner's first claim is that his detention as an enemy combatant "without criminal charges" infringes the Constitution, and that "American citizens arrested in the U.S. can only be deprived of liberty through criminal process." Pet. 4–5, ¶¶20–22. That claim lacks merit. The Supreme Court's decisions in *Hamdi*, 124 S.Ct. at 2633, and *Quirin*, 317 U.S. at 1, confirm the military's long-settled authority – independent of and distinct from criminal process – to detain enemy combatants for the duration of an aimed conflict. Those decisions also establish that the authority is fully applicable in the factual circumstances of this case.

A. The military has authority to detain enemy combatants in the course of the conflict against al Qaeda.

1. *Hamdi* makes clear that the military has authority to seize and detain enemy combatants for the duration of the present conflict. The decision upholds the President's authority to detain as an enemy combatant a presumed American citizen who "was 'part of or supporting forces hostile to the United States or coalition partners' in Afghanistan and

who 'engaged in an armed conflict against the United States' there." 124 S.Ct. at 2639 (plurality). The Court did not reach the question whether the President has "plenary authority to detain pursuant to Article II of the Constitution," resting its decision instead on the conclusion that "Congress has in fact authorized Hamdi's detention, through the AUMF." *Ibid.*; see *id.* at 2679 (Thomas, J., dissenting) (agreeing with plurality that AUMF authorizes Hamdi's detention). The plurality opinion of Justice O'Connor is the controlling opinion with respect to the President's authority to detain enemy combatants because Justice Thomas concurred on grounds that were even more deferential to the President. See *id.* at 2674–2685 (Thomas, J., dissenting).

As the Court's controlling opinion explains, the "capture and detention of lawful combatants and the capture, detention, and trial of unlawful combatants, by 'universal agreement and practice' are 'important incident[s] of war.'" 124 S.Ct. at 2640 (plurality) (quoting *Quirin*, 317 U.S. at 28); accord *id.* at 2679 (Thomas, J., dissenting); see *Johnson* v. *Eisentrager*, 339 U.S. 763, 786 (1950) ("This Court has characterized as 'well-established' the 'power of the military to exercise jurisdiction over *** enemy belligerents [and] prisoners of war.'") (quoting *Duncan* v. *Kahanamoku*, 327 U.S. 304, 313 (1946)). The Executive's long-settled authority to detain combatants is not for the purpose of imposing criminal or other punishment, but instead serves to "prevent captured individuals from returning to the field of battle and taking up aims once again." *Hamdi*, 124 S.Ct. at 2640 (plurality).

"Because detention to prevent a combatant's return to the battlefield is a fundamental incident of waging war," the *Hamdi* Court held, "it is of no moment that the AUMF does not use specific language of detention." *Id.* at 2641 (plurality); see *id.* at 2679 (Thomas, J., dissenting). Rather, "Congress' grant of authority for the use of 'necessary and appropriate force' *** include[s] the authority to detain for the duration of the relevant conflict," an "understanding *** based on longstanding law-of-war principles." *Id.* at 2641 (plurality); see *id.* at 2679 (Thomas, J., dissenting). It therefore is clear after *Hamdi* that the President has authority pursuant to the AUMF to detain enemy combatants for the duration of the current conflict.[1]

2. Because the *Hamdi* Court concluded that the detention was authorized by the AUMF, the Court found no occasion to address the President's independent authority as Commander in Chief to detain a citizen as an enemy combatant. See 124 S.Ct. at 2639 (plurality). The issue likewise need not be reached in this case because the AUMF supplies an ample statutory predicate for petitioner's detention as an enemy combatant. See pp. 18–21, *infra*.

Nonetheless, Congress specifically recognized in the AUMF that "the President has authority under the Constitution to take action to deter and prevent acts of international terrorism against the United States," Preamble, 115 Stat. 224, and that authority supplies an independent basis for petitioner's detention as an enemy combatant. The

---

[1] The Court's holding that the AUMF encompasses the detention of Hamdi, a Taliban combatant, applies *a fortiori* to al Qaeda combatants. As the controlling opinion explains, "[t]here can be no doubt that individuals who fought against the United States in Afghanistan as part of the Taliban, an organization known to have supported *the al Qaeda terrorist network responsible for those attacks*, are individuals Congress sought to target in passing the AUMF." 124 S.Ct. at 2640 (emphasis added). There could be even less doubt that Congress in the AUMF sought to target combatants for al Qaeda, the organization directly responsible for the September 11 attacks. See §2(a), 115 Stat. 224 (supporting use of "all necessary and appropriate force against," *inter alia*, those "organizations" that the President "determines planned, authorized, committed, or aided the terrorist attacks that occurred on September 11, 2001"); see also President's Order, ¶2 (stating that "al Qaeda" is "an international terrorist organization with which the United States is at war").

Commander-in-Chief Clause grants the President authority to defend the Nation when it is attacked, and the President "is bound to accept the challenge without waiting for any special legislative authority." *The Prize Cases*, 67 U.S. (2 Black) 635, 668 (1862). An essential aspect of the President's authority in that regard is to "determine what degree of force the crisis demands." *Id.* at 670; see *Campbell* v. *Clinton*, 203 F.3d 19, 27 (D.C. Cir.) (Silberman, J., concurring) ("[T]he President has independent authority to repel aggressive acts by third parties even without specific congressional authorization, and courts may not review the level of force selected."), cert. denied, 531 U.S. 815 (2000). The President's decision to detain petitioner as an enemy combatant represents a basic exercise of his authority as Commander in Chief to determine the level of force needed to prosecute the conflict against al Qaeda.

B. The President's authority to detain enemy combatants in the current conflict is fully applicable in the circumstances of this case.

After *Hamdi*, the petition could not, and does not, challenge the President' s authority to detain enemy combatants in the course of the ongoing conflict against al Qaeda. The petition instead argues that, for various reasons, the President's authority does not extend to the particular circumstances of this case. Those arguments cannot be squared with the Supreme Court's decisions in *Hamdi* and *Quirin*.

1. The petition contends that, "absent a valid suspension of habeas corpus by Congress, American citizens arrested in the U.S. can only be deprived of liberty through criminal process." See Pet. 5, ¶22. That is incorrect. Neither a combatant's American citizenship nor his capture within the United States diminishes the military's authority to detain him for the duration of the conflict. With respect to citizenship, *Hamdi* involved a presumed American citizen, and the Court reiterated the long-settled rule that "[t]here is no bar to this Nation's holding one of its own citizens as an enemy combatant." 124 S.Ct. at 2640 (plurality); accord *id.* at 2679 (Thomas, J., dissenting); see *Quirin*, 317 U.S. at 37 ("Citizenship in the United States of an enemy belligerent does not relieve him from the consequences of [his] belligerency."); *Colepaugh* v. *Looney*, 235 F.2d 429, 432 (10th Cir. 1956), cert. denied, 352 U.S. 1014 (1957); *In re Territo*, 156 F.2d 142, 142–143 (9th Cir. 1946).

With respect to the location of a combatant's capture, because *Hamdi* involved a citizen who "engaged in an armed conflict against the United States" in Afghanistan, the Court described its holding in those particular terms. See 124 S.Ct. at 2639 (plurality). But nothing in *Hamdi* suggests that the authority to detain enemy combatants in the current conflict would be inapplicable in the context of a citizen captured within the United States's borders. To the contrary, the Court strongly reaffirmed its prior decision in *Quirin*, see *id.* at 2642–2643 (plurality); *id.* at 2682 (Thomas, J., dissenting), which had recognized the military's authority to seize and detain enemy combatants in factual circumstances indistinguishable from this case; and the Court relied on the AUMF, a congressional response to attacks launched from within the United States.

. . .

b. In light of the Supreme Court's decision in *Quirin*, petitioner errs in relying (Pet. 5, ¶22) on the Court's prior decision in *Ex parte Milligan*, 71 U.S. (4 Wall.) 2 (1866). *Milligan* held that the military lacked authority to subject to trial by military commission a citizen who was alleged to have conspired against the United States in the Civil War. Unlike petitioner and the *Quirin* combatants, Milligan had not affiliated or trained with enemy forces (and in fact had never resided in any State in the Confederacy). See *id.* at 121–122.

In *Quirin*, the Court unanimously confined *Milligan* to its specific facts, "constru[ing] the Court's statement as to the inapplicability of the law of war to Milligan's case as having particular reference to the facts before it." 317 U.S. at 45. The Court found *Milligan* "inapplicable" to the circumstances in *Quirin*, explaining that Milligan, "not being a part of or associated with the armed forces of the enemy, was a non-belligerent, not subject to the law of war." *Ibid*. Petitioner, by contrast, was closely associated with al Qaeda, and his actions directly parallel those of the *Quirin* combatants. Accordingly, petitioner, as much as the *Quirin* saboteurs, is an "enemy belligerent[] within the meaning of *** the law of war." *Id*. at 38.

Hamdi fortifies that conclusion. The controlling opinion in *Hamdi* explains that "*Quirin* was a unanimous opinion" and "both postdates and clarifies *Milligan*, providing us with the most apposite precedent that we have on the question of whether citizens may be detained in such circumstances." 124 S.Ct. at 2643 (plurality); see *id*. at 2682 (Thomas, J., dissenting). *Hamdi* cautions that "[b]rushing aside such precedent – particularly when doing so gives rise to a host of new questions never dealt with by this Court – is unjustified and unwise." *Id*. at 2643 (plurality). *Hamdi* also confirms that, while *Quirin* involved the detention of enemy combatants for trial by military commission, the authority recognized in *Quirin* necessarily includes the basic authority to detain for the duration of a conflict without bringing any such charges. See *id*. at 2640 (plurality) ("While Haupt was tried for violations of the law of war, nothing in *Quirin* suggests that his citizenship would have precluded his mere detention for the duration of the relevant hostilities.").

c. In light of *Hamdi* and *Quirin*, there is no merit to petitioner's contention that he "must be charged with a crime or released immediately." Pet. 5, ¶22. To be sure, a dissenting opinion in *Hamdi* expressed the view of two Justices that, in the absence of a suspension of the writ, an American citizen detained in the United States must be afforded criminal process. See 124 S.Ct. at 2660–2674 (Scalia, J., joined by Stevens, J., dissenting). No other Justice adopted that approach, however, and a majority of the Court specifically rejected it. See *id*. at 2643 (plurality) (rejecting approach "in which the only options are congressional suspension of the writ of habeas corpus or prosecution for treason or some other crime"); *id*. at 2682 (Thomas, J., dissenting) (rejecting "conclusion that the Government must choose between using standard criminal processes and suspending the writ"). This Court need go no further to reject petitioner's claim.

2. . . .

. . .

b. The circumstances surrounding petitioner's initial seizure upon arriving in Chicago likewise are indistinguishable from those in *Quirin*. Although the petition submits that the seizure occurred in a "civilian setting" rather than "on a foreign battlefield" (Pet. 3, ¶16), the *Quirin* saboteurs similarly were seized by civilian authorities in Chicago and New York before the President later ordered their transfer to military control. 317 U.S. at 21–23. Moreover, the *Quirin* Court rejected any suggestion that the saboteurs were "any the less belligerents if, as they argue, they have not actually committed or attempted to commit any act of depredation or entered the theatre or zone of active military operations." *Id*. at 38. And while petitioner was not carrying explosives when he was seized, the *Quirin* saboteurs likewise were not armed with explosives when arrested because they had buried their explosives upon coming ashore in the

United States. *Id*. at 21.[3] Consequently, the Court's conclusion in *Quirin* that the sabo-teurs were enemy combatants subject to military detention is equally applicable in this case.

II. Section 4001(a) Does Not Constrain The President's Authority To Detain Petitioner As An Enemy Combatant.

Petitioner's second claim (Pet. 5, ¶¶23–25) is that his detention as an enemy combatant violates 18 U.S.C. 4001(a), which states that "[n]o citizen shall be imprisoned or other-wise detained by the United States except pursuant to an Act of Congress." That claim lacks merit. Petitioner's detention could raise no issue under Section 4001(a) because the AUMF is an "Act of Congress" that authorizes the detention. Petitioner's claim also fails for the independent reason that Section 4001(a) does not apply to the military's wartime detention of enemy combatants.

A. The President's determination that petitioner should be detained as an enemy combatant falls squarely within the authority conferred by the AUMF.

The Supreme Court held in *Hamdi* that the AUMF authorizes Hamdi's detention, and that the detention therefore is "pursuant to an Act of Congress" within the meaning of Section 4001(a). 124 S.Ct. at 2639–2640 (plurality); *id*. at 2679 (Thomas, J., dissent-ing). While *Hamdi* thus establishes that the AUMF authorizes the detention of enemy combatants who are American citizens, the petition seeks to distinguish *Hamdi* on the ground that Congress did not authorize "the detention of American citizens arrested on American soil." Pet. 5, ¶25. Petitioner's reading of the AUMF is untenable.

. . .

III. There Is No Warrant For Granting Relief On Petitioner's Remaining Claims.

In addition to seeking petitioner's release under the first two claims for relief, the petition also seeks: (a) an evidentiary hearing and unimpeded counsel-client interactions, in connection with the third claim for relief; and (b) a cessation by the military of any interrogations of petitioner, in connection with the fourth claim for relief. There is no warrant for granting relief on those claims at this time.

A. Petitioner argues in his third claim for relief that he is entitled to notice of the factual basis for his detention as an enemy combatant and an opportunity to contest those facts, and that he has a right to access to counsel, including an entitlement to unrestricted communications with his lawyers and unrestricted transfer of documents related to the litigation. Pet. 5–6, ¶¶27–29. The government does not dispute that petitioner is entitled to "receive notice of the factual basis for his classification, and a fair oppor-tunity to rebut the Government's factual assertions before a neutral decisionmaker." *Hamdi*, 124 S.Ct. at 2648 (plurality). This answer, and the declaration attached hereto,

---

[3] At the time of their arrest, the *Quirin* combatants were in possession of "substantial sums in United States currency" that had been given to them by the German government. 317 U.S. at 21–22. Petitioner likewise had been given $15,000 by al Qaeda operatives and was carrying over over $10,000 when arrested. See Rapp Dec. ¶¶12–13.

provide the requisite notice of the factual basis for petitioner's detention. While the petition seeks an evidentiary hearing to challenge the government's factual assertions, there is no need to determine the nature of any evidentiary proceedings that may be necessary to resolve the petition until petitioner has reviewed the government's factual submission and has specified the extent of any factual challenges. See *id.* at 2652 ("We anticipate that a District Court would proceed with the caution that we have indicated is necessary in this setting, engaging in a factfinding process that is both prudent and incremental.").

Nor is there any ripe issue with respect to access to counsel. Although petitioner's counsel executed (under protest) agreements allowing the government to monitor counsel-client interactions and review documents, the government has not attempted to monitor counsel's meetings with petitioner and has no plans at present to do so. In addition, the government will no longer review documents relating to the litigation sent between counsel and petitioner. Accordingly, there is no need grant to the relief sought by petitioner or to address any issues concerning restrictions on counsel's interactions with petitioner, unless such issues in fact were to arise in a concrete factual context permitting the Court's informed consideration. Cf. *Hamdi*, 124 S.Ct. at 2652 (plurality) (noting that Hamdi "is now being granted unmonitored meetings" with counsel "and '[n]o further consideration of this issue is necessary at this stage of the case'").

B. Petitioner argues in the petition's fourth claim for relief that his "ongoing interrogation" violates various constitutional provisions, and seeks as relief an order requiring cessation of interrogation. Pet. 6, ¶¶30–32; Pet. 7, ¶4. The military has ceased its interrogation of petitioner, however, and has no present intention to resume interrogation of him. There thus is no warrant for addressing petitioner's claims concerning the legality of such interrogations in the abstract, or for granting the relief sought by petitioner until the issue is squarely raised.

In any event, there is no merit to petitioner's contention that the interrogation of enemy combatants could infringe the Fifth, Sixth, or Eighth Amendments. For instance, the Sixth Amendment applies only to "criminal prosecutions," U.S. Const. amend. VI, and its protections do not attach until the initiation of formal criminal proceedings. See, *e.g., Texas* v. *Cobb*, 532 U.S. 162, 167–168 (2001); cf. *Middendorf* v. *Henry*, 425 U.S. 25, 38 (1976) ("[A] proceeding which may result in deprivation of liberty is nonetheless not a 'criminal proceeding' within the meaning of the Sixth Amendment if there are elements about it which sufficiently distinguish it from a traditional civilian criminal trial."). Similarly, the right to counsel associated with the Self-Incrimination Clause of the Fifth Amendment (see *Miranda* v. *Arizona*, 384 U.S. 436 (1966)) is a "trial right of criminal defendants." *United States* v. *Verdugo-Urquidez*, 494 U.S. 259, 264 (1990). And while that right might limit the government's ability to use the fruits of interrogations in a criminal trial, it would afford no basis for enjoining ongoing interrogations. See *ibid.* (A "constitutional violation occurs only at trial.").

With respect to the Eighth Amendment, neither the detention of enemy combatants nor their interrogation while detained constitutes "punishment," see *Hamdi*, 124 S.Ct. at 2640 (plurality), let alone punishment that is "cruel and unusual." See Int'l Comm. of the Red Cross, Commentary III, Geneva Convention Relative to the Treatment of Prisoners of War, 163–164 (Jean S. Pictet & Jean de Preux eds. 1960) ("[A] state which has captured prisoners of war will always try to obtain information from them."). Finally, in view of the long-settled historical practice of attempting to elicit information from detained enemy combatants, such interrogations could not be found to infringe general principles of due process. See *Herrerra* v. *Collins*, 506 U.S. 390, 407–408 (1993); *Medina* v. *California*, 505 U.S. 437, 445–446 (1992).[5]

CONCLUSION

The petition should be denied.

Respectfully submitted,

J. STROM THURMOND, JR.
  United States Attorney
  District of South Carolina

SRI SRINIVASAN
  Assistant to the Solicitor General

STEPHAN E. OESTREICHER, JR.
  Attorney, Department of Justice

_____

MILLER SHEALY
  Assistant United States Attorney
  District of South Carolina

. . .

_____

[5] Although the plurality in *Hamdi* observed that "indefinite detention for the purpose of interrogation is not authorized," 124 S. Ct. at 2641, that observation has no application here. The plurality made no suggestion that combatants detained for the purpose of preventing their re-engagement with enemy forces are entitled to be immune from interrogation during their detention. In addition, by "indefinite detention," the Court was referring to detentions that continue beyond the "duration of the relevant conflict," *ibid.*, and petitioner does not suggest that the conflict against al Qaeda has ended. At any rate, nothing in *Hamdi* suggests that petitioner's "two years of *** detention" (Pet. 6, ¶32) is impermissibly "indefinite."

EXHIBIT B

Declaration of Mr. Jeffrey N. Rapp
Director, Joint Intelligence Task Force for Combating Terrorism

1. Pursuant to 28 U.S.C. § 1746, I, Jeffrey N. Rapp, hereby declare, to the best of my knowledge, information, and belief, and under penalty of perjury, that the following is true and correct:

Preamble

2. I submit this Declaration for the Court's consideration in the matter of Jose Padilla v. Commander C.T. Hanft, USN, Commander, Consolidated Naval Brig, Case Number 04-CV-2221-26AJ, pending in the United States District Court for the District of South Carolina.

3. Based on information that I have acquired in the course of my official duties, I am familiar with all the matters discussed in this Declaration. I am also familiar with the circumstances surrounding Jose Padilla's ("Padilla") arrest at Chicago's O'Hare International Airport and interrogations by agents of the Department of Defense ("DoD") after DoD took control of Padilla on 9 June 2002. The information in this declaration concerning Padilla and his activities with the al-Qaeda terrorist organization is derived from the circumstances surrounding his arrest and Padilla's statements during post-capture interrogation.

Professional Experience as an Intelligence Officer

4. I am a career Defense Intelligence Agency Defense Intelligence Senior Executive Service member appointed by the Director of the Defense Intelligence Agency. I report to the Director of the Defense Intelligence Agency. My current assignment is as the Director of the Joint Intelligence Task Force for Combating Terrorism (JITF-CT). JITF-CT directs collection, exploitation, analysis, fusion, and dissemination of the all-source foreign terrorism intelligence effort within DoD. In addition to my current assignment, I have previously served as the first Director of the National Media Exploitation Center and as the civilian Deputy Director for the Iraq Survey Group in Qatar.

5. My active duty military intelligence career in the United States Army included service as the senior intelligence officer for 1st Infantry Division, when deployed to Bosnia-Herzegovina, Commander of the 101st Military Intelligence Battalion, 1st Infantry Division, Fort Riley Kansas, and the forward-deployed 205th Military Intelligence

Brigade in Europe, and Deputy Director for the Battle Command Battle Lab, U.S. Army

Intelligence Center at Fort Huachuca, Arizona. I also directed a South Asia regional

analytic division in the Defense Intelligence Agency Directorate for Analysis and

Production that was awarded the National Intelligence Meritorious Unit Citation for its

accomplishments.

6. My military decorations include the Legion of Merit, Defense Superior Service Medal,

Defense Meritorious Service Medal, and Army Meritorious Service Medal. I am a

graduate of the U.S. Army War College. I hold a Masters degree in strategic intelligence

from the Joint Military Intelligence College.

Padilla's Background

7. Padilla, also known as Abdullah al Muhajir, is a U.S. citizen of Hispanic ethnicity

who spent time in a juvenile detention facility as a teenager. He joined a local street gang

when he was 13 years old, and was arrested for murder in 1985. During his early life in

Chicago and Florida he was arrested for a number of offenses including cannabis

possession, weapons charges, and assault. In 1995, he converted to Islam while serving a

state prison sentence in Florida. After his release from prison, he joined a mosque in

Florida that sponsored his first trip to Egypt in September 1998. While in Egypt, Padilla

agreed to an arranged marriage to an Egyptian woman and fathered two sons. He has

another son as a result of a previous relationship in Chicago. Padilla studied Arabic in

Cairo while earning a subsistence income as a handyman working odd jobs. In February

2000, he traveled to Mecca, Saudi Arabia to complete the Muslim Hajj pilgrimage. At

that time, he met with an al Qaeda recruiter, and discussed training opportunities in

Afghanistan. In June 2000, Padilla traveled to Yemen to continue his Islamic studies.

Overview of Padilla's al Qaeda Activities

8. In the summer of 2000, Padilla first entered Pakistan, and traveled to a Taliban

safehouse in Quetta. From there, he traveled across the border to Kandahar, Afghanistan

in the company of Taliban operatives and five other recruits to train for jihad. In July

2000, Padilla completed a training camp application using his alias, Abdullah al Muhajir.

Padilla then traveled to the al Qaeda-affiliated training camp, al-Farouq, north of

Kandahar. In September and October of 2000, at al-Farouq, he received training in the

use of firearms and other weapons, explosives, land navigation, camouflage techniques,

communications, and physical conditioning. While at the camp, Padilla met several
times with Mohammed Atef ("Atef"), who was a senior al Qaeda operative and military
commander. After completing this initial training, Padilla and other recruits were
returned to Kandahar and later transported to Kabul. For approximately three months in
the fall of 2000, Padilla and other recruits guarded what he understood to be a Taliban
outpost north of Kabul. Padilla was armed with a Kalashnikov assault rifle and
ammunition for that purpose. He subsequently returned to Pakistan and, from there,
traveled back to Egypt to reunite with his wife in the spring of 2001.

9. In June 2001, Padilla again left his family in Egypt and traveled to Quetta where he
stayed in an al Qaeda safehouse before traveling back to Kandahar. During the summer,
Padilla received additional training relating to future plots to attack U.S.-based apartment
buildings described below. In the fall of 2001, Padilla was staying at an al Qaeda
safehouse in or near Kandahar when he and his fellow al Qaeda operatives learned of the
September 11 terrorist attacks on the United States. Padilla spent much of September
2001, including after the September 11 attacks, with Atef at an al Qaeda safehouse in or
near Kandahar. Once the United States commenced combat operations against the
Taliban and al Qaeda in Afghanistan, Padilla and his fellow al Qaeda operatives began
moving from safehouse to safehouse in an effort to avoid being bombed or captured by
U.S. or coalition forces.

10. In mid-November 2001, an air strike destroyed a safehouse in Afghanistan and killed
Atef. Padilla was staying at a different al Qaeda safehouse that day, but he and other al
Qaeda operatives participated in an attempt to rescue survivors and retrieve Atef's body
from the rubble. After this attack, Padilla, armed with an assault rifle, along with
numerous other al Qaeda operatives, began moving toward the mountainous border with
Pakistan near Khowst, Afghanistan, in a further effort to avoid U.S. air strikes and
capture by U.S. forces. Padilla was thus armed and present in a combat zone during
armed conflict between al Qaeda/Taliban forces and the armed forces of the United States
and its coalition partners. After taking cover in a network of caves and bunkers near
Khowst, the al Qaeda operatives, including Padilla, were escorted by Taliban personnel
across the border into Pakistan in groups of 15 to 20. Padilla crossed into Pakistan in
January 2002. After crossing into Pakistan, Padilla met with senior Osama bin Laden

lieutenant Abu Zubaydah ("Zubaydah") at a safehouse in Lahore, Pakistan, and met

Zubaydah again at a safehouse in Faisalabad, Pakistan. Padilla discussed with Zubaydah

the idea of conducting terrorist operations involving the detonation of explosive devices

in the United States. While in Pakistan, he conducted what he called "research" on the

construction of an atomic bomb at an al Qaeda safehouse in Pakistan.

Padilla's Plan to Kill Apartment Building Residents

11. Padilla admits that he was first tasked with an operation to blow up apartment

buildings in the United States with natural gas by Atef at a meeting in Kandahar in the

summer of 2001. Padilla accepted this tasking. Atef advised Padilla that he was

sending Padilla to a location outside the Kandahar Airport where Padilla would train

with, a still at large, senior al Qaeda explosives expert ("Explosives Expert) and another,

still at large al Qaeda operative, El Shukri Jumah ("Jumah") aka Jaffar al-Tayyar.

Padilla and Jumah trained with Explosives Expert at the Kandahar Airport on switches,

circuits, and timers. Padilla recognized Jumah as someone he had met in the United

States before departing for Egypt. Padilla and Jumah also spent time learning how to

prepare and seal an apartment in order to obtain the highest explosive yield, and thereby

obtain the highest number of casualties among apartment residents.

However, the mission was apparently abandoned after the training because Padilla and

Jumah could not get along and Padilla told Atef he could not do the operation on his own.

12. Padilla admits that the apartment building plan was resurrected when he first met

senior al Qaeda operational planner and 11 September 2001 mastermind Khalid Sheikh

Mohammad ("KSM") in Karachi, Pakistan after Zubaydah sent Padilla and another

accomplice, ("Accomplice"), an al-Qaeda operative, there in March 2002 to present the

atomic bomb operation. Zubaydah gave Padilla money and wrote a reference letter to

KSM about Padilla. Padilla was taken to a safehouse by al Qaeda facilitator and planner

Ammar al-Baluchi ("al-Baluchi"). Al-Baluchi is also a nephew of KSM. Padilla

presented the atomic bomb idea to KSM, who advised that the idea was a little too

complicated. KSM wanted Padilla to revive the plan to kill apartment building residents

originally discussed with Atef. KSM wanted Padilla to hit targets in New York City,

although Florida and Washington, D.C. were discussed as well. Padilla had discretion in the selection of apartment buildings. KSM gave Padilla full authority to conduct the operation if Padilla and Accomplice were successful in entering the United States. Padilla admits that he accepted the mission. Al Qaeda operative and unindicted 9/11 co-conspirator Ramzi Bin al-Shibh ("al-Shibh") trained Padilla on telephone call security and e-mail protocol. KSM gave Padilla $5,000 for the operation and al-Baluchi gave him $10,000, travel documentation, a cell-phone, and an e-mail address to notify him when Padilla arrived in the United States. Al-Baluchi instructed Padilla to leave on the mission through Bangladesh. Al-Baluchi told Padilla to call him before entering the Karachi airport. The night before his departure, Padilla and Accomplice attended a dinner with KSM, al-Baluchi, and al-Shibh.

Operational Deployment to the United States

13. Padilla departed Pakistan on 5 April 2002, bound for the United States. After spending a month in Egypt, Padilla entered the United States at Chicago's O'Hare International Airport on 8 May 2002. Padilla was carrying $10,526 in U.S. currency he had received from al Qaeda, but declared only approximately $8,000. Padilla had in his possession the cell-phone provided to him by al-Baluchi, the names and telephone numbers of his recruiter and his sponsor, and e-mail addresses for al-Baluchi and Accomplice. At the time of his capture by the FBI at O'Hare International Airport, Padilla was an operative of the al Qaeda terrorist organization with which the United States is at war.

14. When interviewed by FBI agents upon his arrival in Chicago, Padilla falsely denied he had ever been to Afghanistan. Padilla also lied about the source of the money he was carrying and the purpose of his return to the United States. Padilla was arrested by the FBI on a material witness warrant. On 9 June 2002, Padilla was transferred to DoD custody after the President of the United States determined that Padilla is an enemy combatant.

Conclusion

15. As an al Qaeda operative, Padilla participated in numerous al Qaeda activities over a nearly two-year period, including military training and armed battlefield activities in Afghanistan, and plans to attack the United States for the purpose of killing large

numbers of American civilians. He admits to meeting with numerous key al-Qaeda leadership figures and senior operational planners, and to planning plots against the United States with them. Padilla proposed using an atomic bomb in the United States and explosives and natural gas to blow up apartment buildings in the United States.

Jeffrey N. Rapp
Director, Joint Intelligence Task Force for
Combating Terrorism

Executed on 27 August 2004 at the Pentagon,
Washington, D. C.

IN THE UNITED STATES DISTRICT COURT
FOR THE DISTRICT OF SOUTH CAROLINA
CHARLESTON DIVISION

JOSE PADILLA, Petitioner,	§ § §	
vs.	§ §	CIVIL ACTION NO. 2:04-2221-26AJ
COMMANDER C.T. HANFT, USN Commander, Consolidated Naval Brig, Respondent.	§ § § §	

MEMORANDUM OPINION AND ORDER

I.   INTRODUCTION

This is a 28 U.S.C. §2241 *habeas corpus* action. The Court has jurisdiction over the matter pursuant to 28 U.S.C. §1331. Pending before the Court is Petitioner's Motion for Summary Judgment as to Counts One and Two.[1] The sole question before the Court today is whether the President of the United States (President) is authorized to detain an United States citizen as an enemy combatant under the unique circumstances presented here.

. . .

V.   DISCUSSION

A.   *Three Supreme Court cases*

Respondent maintains that the decisions of the Supreme Court in *Hamdi* v. *Rumsfeld*, 124 S.Ct. 2633 (2004) and *Quirin*, 317 U.S. 1 "reaffirm the military's long-settled authority – independent of and distinct from the criminal process – to detain enemy combatants for the duration of a given armed conflict, including the current conflict against al Qaeda." Respondent's Opposition at 8. According to Respondent, "[t]hose decisions squarely apply to this case." *Id.* Petitioner, on the other hand, maintains that *Ex parte Milligan*, 71 U.S. (4 Wall) 2 (1866) is controlling. The Court will consider each case in turn.

1.   *Hamdi*

The petitioner in *Hamdi* was an American citizen captured while on the battlefield in Afghanistan. In that case, the Supreme Court had before it the threshold question

---

[1] . . .

of "whether the Executive has the authority to detain citizens who qualify as 'enemy combatants.'" *Hamdi*, 124 S.Ct. at 2639.

. . .

...[I]t is true that, under some circumstances, such as those present in *Hamdi*, the President can indeed hold an United States citizen as an enemy combatant. Just because something is sometimes true, however, does not mean that it is always true. The facts in this action bear out that truth.

In the instant case, Respondent would have this Court find more similarities between Petitioner here and the petitioner in *Hamdi* than actually exist. As two other courts have already found, however, the differences between the two are striking.

The first to distinguish the difference was Judge Wilkinson when he noted that "[t]o compare this battlefield capture [in *Hamdi*] to the domestic arrest in *Padilla v. Rumsfeld* is to compare apples and oranges." *Hamdi v. Rumsfeld*, 337 F.3d 335, 344 (4th Cir. 2003) (Wilkinson, J., concurring). Not long thereafter, the Supreme Court, in responding to Justice Scalia's dissent, specifically noted "Justice Scalia largely ignores the context of [*Hamdi*]: a United States citizen captured in a *foreign* combat zone." *Hamdi*, 124 S.Ct at 2643 (emphasis in original).[8]

Nevertheless, Respondent would have the Court find that the place of capture is of no consequence in determining whether the President can properly hold Petitioner as an enemy combatant. According to that view, it would be illogical to find that Petitioner could evade his detention as an enemy combatant status just because he returned to the United States before he could be captured. The cogency of this argument eludes the Court.

In *Hamdi*, the petitioner was an American citizen who was captured on the battlefield. Petitioner is also an American citizen, but he was captured in an United States airport. He is, in some respects, being held for a crime that he is alleged to have planned to commit in this country.[9] No one could rightfully argue that "[t]he exigencies of military action on the battlefield present an entirely different set of circumstances than the arrest of a citizen arriving at O'Hare International Airport." Brief of *Amici Curiae* Janet Reno et al. at 5, *Padilla*, 124 S.Ct. 2711, (No. 03-1027).

It cannot be disputed that the circumstances in *Hamdi* comport with the requirement of the AUMF, which provides that "the President is authorized to use all *necessary*

---

[8] In fact, in the plurality opinion, Justice O'Connor noted at least nine additional times that the Court's holding that Mr. Hamdi's detention as an enemy combatant was constitutionally permissible was limited to the facts of that case. *Id.* at 2635 ("Congress authorized the detention of combatants in the *narrow circumstances* alleged here.") (emphasis added); *Id.* at 2639 ("We therefore answer only the *narrow question* before us.") (emphasis added); *Id.* at 2639–40 ("[W]e conclude that the AUMF is explicit congressional authorization for the detention of individuals in the *narrow category* we describe.") (emphasis added); *Id.* at 2640 ("We conclude that the detention of individuals falling within the *limited category* we are considering...is an exercise of the 'necessary and appropriate force' Congress has authorized the President to use.") (emphasis added); *Id.* at 2641 ("Congress has clearly and unmistakably authorized detention in the *narrow circumstances* considered here.") (emphasis added); *Id.* at 2642 ("*Ex parte Milligan* ... does not undermine our holding about the Government's authority to seize enemy combatants, *as we define that term today.*") (emphasis added); *Id.* at 2642 n.1 ("Here the basis asserted for detention by the military is that Hamdi was *carrying a weapon against American troops on a foreign battlefield;* that is, that he was an enemy combatant.") (emphasis added); *Id.* at 2643 (noting with disapproval that "Justice Scalia finds the *fact of battlefield capture* irrelevant....") (emphasis added); *Id.* ("Justine Scalia can point to no case or other authority for the proposition that those *captured on a foreign battlefield* ... cannot be detained outside the criminal process.") (emphasis added).

[9] The Court finds Respondent's argument concerning whether Petitioner had actually entered the country unavailing. Respondent has not provided, and this Court has not found, any case law that supports Respondent's position that an United States citizen, is not "in" the United States when he or she is "in" a United States airport. Such a failure is fatal to the claim.

and appropriate force against those ... persons, in order to prevent attacks by al Qaeda on the United States." That is, the President's use of force to capture Mr. Hamdi was necessary and appropriate. Here, that same use of force was not.

Again, Petitioner in this action was captured in the United States. His alleged terrorist plans were thwarted at the time of his arrest. There were no impediments whatsoever to the Government bringing charges against him for any one or all of the array of heinous crimes that he has been effectively accused of committing. Also at the Government's disposal was the material witness warrant. In fact, the issuance of a material witness warrant was the tool that the law enforcement officers used to thwart Petitioner's alleged terrorist plans. Therefore, since Petitioner's alleged terrorist plans were thwarted when he was arrested on the material witness warrant, the Court finds that the President's subsequent decision to detain Petitioner as an enemy combatant was neither necessary nor appropriate. As accurately observed by counsel for Petitioner,

> [i]t's not necessary because the criminal justice system provides for the detention power. Nothing makes that clearer than the facts of this case. There was a warrant issued from a grand jury for Mr. Padilla's arrest. Mr. Padilla was arrested by law enforcement officials, civilian law enforcement officials. He was brought before a civilian judge. He was imprisoned in a civilian facility in New York. Everything occurred according to the civilian process in the way it is supposed to. And it's not only not necessary, but not appropriate. It's not appropriate because it directly conflicts with the limits on detention that [C]ongress has set by statute and the limits that the framers set on presidential power.

Transcript of January 5, 2005 hearing, at 5:6-5:17.

2. *Quirin*

. . .

Although seemingly similar to the instant case, *Quirin* is, in fact, like *Hamdi*, starkly different. As the Second Circuit has already noted, "the *Quirin* Court's decision to uphold military jurisdiction rested on the express congressional authorization of the use of military tribunals to try combatants who violated the law." *Hamdi*, 352 F.3d 695, 715–16.

> From the very beginning of its history this Court has recognized and applied the law of war as including that part of the law of nations which prescribes, for the conduct of war, the status, rights and duties of enemy nations as well as of enemy individuals. By the Articles of War, and especially Article 15, Congress has explicitly provided, so far as it may constitutionally do so, that military tribunals shall have jurisdiction to try offenders or offenses against the law of war in appropriate cases. Congress, in addition to making rules for the government of our Armed Forces, has thus exercised its authority to define and punish offenses against the law of nations by sanctioning, within constitutional limitations, the jurisdiction of military commissions to try persons for offenses which, according to the rules and precepts of the law of nations, and more particularly the law of war, are cognizable by such tribunals. And the President, as Commander in Chief, by his Proclamation in time of war has invoked that law. By his Order creating the present Commission he has undertaken to exercise the authority conferred upon him by Congress, and also such authority as the Constitution itself gives the Commander in Chief, to direct the performance of those functions which may constitutionally be performed by the military arm of the nation in time of war.

Quirin, 317 U.S. at 27–28 (footnote omitted).

Respondent goes to great lengths to argue that the Court is *Quirin* did not rest its decision on a "clear statement from Congress." Respondent's Opposition at 22. The Court is unconvinced.

Contrary to Respondent's argument, it is clear from *Quirin* that the Court found that Congress had "explicitly provided, so far as it may constitutionally do so, that military tribunals shall have jurisdiction to try offenders or offenses against the law of war in appropriate cases." *Id.* at 28. Therefore, since no such Congressional authorization is present here, Respondent's argument as to the application of *Quirin* must fail.[10]

3.   *Ex parte Milligan*

The Constitution of the United States is a law for rulers and people, equally in war and in peace, and covers with the shield of its protection all classes of men, at all times, and under all circumstances. No doctrine, involving more pernicious consequences, was ever invented by the wit of man than that any of its provisions can be suspended during any of the great exigencies of government. Such a doctrine leads directly to anarchy or despotism, but the theory of necessity on which it is based is false; for the government, within the Constitution, has all the powers granted to it, which are necessary to preserve its existence.

Id. at 12–21.

. . .

While not directly on point, and limited by *Quirin*, *Milligan*'s greatest import to the case at bar is the same as that found in *Quirin*: the detention of a United States citizen by the military is disallowed without explicit Congressional authorization.

B.   *The Non-Detention Act, 18 U.S.C. §4001(a)*

The Non-Detention Act, also referred to as the "Railsback Amendment," named after its author Representative Railsback, provides that "No citizen shall be imprisoned or otherwise detained by the United States except pursuant to an Act of Congress." 18 U.S.C. §4001(a).

Respondent asserts that the Non-Detention Act does not constrain the President's authority to detain Petitioner as an enemy combatant. He contends that 1) the Joint Resolution for Authorization for Use of Military Force (AUMF), passed by Congress on September 18, 2001, is an "Act of Congress" authorizing Petitioner's detention and 2) the Non-Detention Act does not apply to the military's wartime detention of enemy combatants. The Court finds these contentions to be without merit.

. . .

---

[10] Other differences include, but are not limited to, the fact that:

> 1) In *Quirin*, the petitioner was charged with a crime and tried by a military tribunal. In the instant case, Petitioner has not been charged and has not been tried.
>
> 2) *Quirin* involves a prisoner whose detention was punitive whereas Petitioner's detention is purportedly preventative.
>
> 3) *Quirin* is concerned more with whether the petitioner was going to be tried by a military tribunal or a civilian court. The case at bar is concerned with whether Petitioner is going to be charged and tried at all.
>
> 4) The decision in *Quirin* preceded the Non-Detention Act.
>
> 5) *Quirin* involved a war that had a definite ending date. The present war on terrorism does not.

1. *Authorization*

. . .

In sum, "[i]n interpreting a war-time measure we must assume that [the purpose of Congress and the Executive] was to allow for the greatest possible accommodation between those liberties and the exigencies of war." *Ex parte Endo*, 323 U.S. 283, 300 (1944). "We must assume, when asked to find implied powers in a grant of legislative or executive authority, that the law makers intended to place no greater restraint on the citizen than was clearly and unmistakably indicated by the language they used." *Id.* In the case *sub judice*, there is no language in the AUMF that "clearly and unmistakably" grants the President the authority to hold Petitioner as an enemy combatant. Therefore, Respondent's argument must fail.[12]

Respondent next argues that,

> Even if there were any doubt about whether the AUMF encompasses combatants seized within the United States, such doubt would be resolved in favor of the President's determination that Congress did in fact authorize petitioner's detention. President's Order, Preamble (declaring that petitioner's detention is "consistent with the laws of the United States, including the Authorization for Use of Military Force").

Respondent's Opposition at 26.

Certainly Respondent does not intend to argue here that, just because the President states that Petitioner's detention is "consistent with the laws of the United States, including the Authorization for Use of Military Force" that makes it so. Not only is such a statement in direct contravention to the well settled separation of powers doctrine, it is simply not the law. Moreover, such a statement is deeply troubling. If such a position were ever adopted by the courts, it would totally eviscerate the limits placed on Presidential authority to protect the citizenry's individual liberties.

2. *Application to wartime detention*

In arguing that the Non-Detention Act has no application to Petitioner, Respondent first maintains that the placement the Act – in Title 18 ("Crimes and Criminal Procedure"), with directions regarding the Attorney General's control over federal prisons, and not in Title 10 ("Armed Forces") or Title 50 ("War and National Defense") – indicates that it speaks only to civilian detentions. Second, Respondent argues that the legislative history of the Non-Detention Act renders the same result. The Court is unpersuaded by either argument. Simply stated, the statute is clear, simple, direct and unambiguous. It forbids *any* kind of detention of an United States citizen, except that it be specifically allowed by Congress. Therefore, since Petitioner's detention has not been authorized by Congress, Respondent's argument must again fail.

C. *Inherent authority*

Having found that the Non-Detention Act expressly forbids the President from holding Petitioner as an enemy combatant, and that the AUMF does not authorize such detention, neither explicitly nor by implication, the Court turns to the question of whether the President has the inherent authority to hold Petitioner.

. . .

---

[12] To the extent that Respondent maintains that the Non-Detention Act was impliedly repealed by the AUMF, the Court rejects the argument. It is black letter law that repeal of a statute by implication is strongly disfavored in the law.

Simply stated, Respondent has not provided, and this Court has not found, any law that supports the contention that the President enjoys the inherent authority pursuant to which he claims to hold Petitioner. The *Prize* cases are chiefly concerned with enemy property, not enemy combatants, and *Campbell* concerns air strikes in another country. Obviously, neither of those issues are present here. Thus, the Court finds the two cases of little guidance.

. . .

Accordingly, and limited to the facts of this case, the Court is of the firm opinion that it must reject the position posited by Respondent. To do otherwise would not only offend the rule of law and violate this country's constitutional tradition, but it would also be a betrayal of this Nation's commitment to the separation of powers that safeguards our democratic values and individual liberties.

For the Court to find for Respondent would also be to engage in judicial activism. This Court sits to interpret the law as it is and not as the Court might wish it to be. Pursuant to its interpretation, the Court finds that the President has no power, neither express nor implied, neither constitutional nor statutory, to hold Petitioner as an enemy combatant.

D. Other matters and concerns

1. A law enforcement matter

. . .

Simply stated, this is a law enforcement matter, not a military matter. The civilian authorities captured Petitioner just as they should have. At the time that Petitioner was arrested pursuant to the material arrest warrant, any alleged terrorist plans that he harbored were thwarted. From then on, he was available to be questioned – and was indeed questioned – just like any other citizen accused of criminal conduct. This is as it should be.

. . .

> [I]n declaring Padilla an enemy combatant, the President relied upon facts that would have supported charging Padilla with a variety of offenses. The government thus had the authority to arrest, detain, interrogate, and prosecute Padilla apart from the extraordinary authority it claims here. The difference between invocation of the criminal process and the power claimed by the President here, however, is one of accountability. The criminal justice system requires that defendants and witnesses be afforded access to counsel, imposes judicial supervision over government action, and places congressionally imposed limits on incarceration.

Amici Curiae at 3.

2. Suspension of the writ of habeas corpus

"The Privilege of the Writ of *Habeas Corpus* shall not be suspended, unless when in Cases of Rebellion or Invasion the public Safety may require it." Const. Art. 1, §9, cl. 2. This power belongs solely to Congress. Since Congress has not acted to suspend the writ, and neither the President nor this Court have the ability to do so, in light of the findings above, Petitioner must be released.

3. *Other measures*

If the law in its current state is found by the President to be insufficient to protect this country from terrorist plots, such as the one alleged here, then the President should prevail upon Congress to remedy the problem. For instance, if the Government's purpose in detaining Petitioner as an enemy combatant is to prevent him from "returning to the field of battle and taking up arms once again[,]" *Hamdi*, 124 S.Ct at 2640, but the President thinks that the laws do not provide the necessary and appropriate measures to provide for that goal, then the President should approach Congress and request that it make proper modifications to the law. As Congress has already demonstrated, it stands ready to carefully consider, and often accommodate, such significant requests.

VI. CONCLUSION

In light of the foregoing discussion and analysis, it is the judgment of this Court that Petitioner's Motion for Summary Judgment on Counts One and Two of the Petition, as well as his Petition for a writ of *habeas corpus* must be **GRANTED**. Accordingly, Respondent is hereby directed to release Petitioner from his custody within forty-five (45) days of the entry of this Order.[14]

IT IS SO ORDERED.

Signed this 28th day of February, 2005, in Spartanburg, South Carolina.

s/ Henry F. Floyd
_____

HENRY F. FLOYD
UNITED STATES DISTRICT JUDGE

---

[14] Of course, if appropriate, the Government can bring criminal charges against Petitioner or it can hold him as a material witness.

PUBLISHED

UNITED STATES COURT OF APPEALS
FOR THE FOURTH CIRCUIT

JOSE PADILLA, *Petitioner-Appellee,* v. C. T. HANFT, U.S.N. Commander, Consolidated Naval Brig., *Respondent-Appellant.* --- WASHINGTON LEGAL FOUNDATION; THE ALLIED EDUCATIONAL FOUNDATION, *Amici Supporting Appellant,* NATIONAL ASSOCIATION OF CRIMINAL DEFENSE LAWYERS; COMPARATIVE LAW SCHOLARS AND EXPERTS ON THE LAWS OF THE UNITED KINGDOM AND ISRAEL; PEOPLE FOR THE AMERICAN WAY FOUNDATION AND THE RUTHERFORD INSTITUTE; THE BRENNAN CENTER FOR JUSTICE AT THE NEW YORK UNIVERSITY SCHOOL OF LAW; AMERICAN CIVIL LIBERTIES UNION; NEW YORK CIVIL LIBERTIES UNION; AMERICAN CIVIL LIBERTIES UNION OF SOUTH CAROLINA; AMERICAN CIVIL LIBERTIES UNION OF VIRGINIA; ORIGINAL CONGRESSIONAL SPONSORS OF 18 U.S.C. SECTION 4001(A); JANET RENO; PHILIP B. HEYMANN; ERIC H. HOLDER, JR.; JEFFREY H. SMITH; CENTER FOR NATIONAL SECURITY STUDIES; CONSTITUTION PROJECT, *Amici Supporting Appellee.*	No. 05-6396

PADILLA v. HANFT

Appeal from the United States District Court
for the District of South Carolina, at Charleston.
Henry F. Floyd, District Judge.
(CA-04-2221-26AJ)

Argued: July 19, 2005

Decided: September 9, 2005

Before LUTTIG, MICHAEL, and TRAXLER, Circuit Judges.

Reversed by published opinion. Judge Luttig wrote the opinion for the
Court, in which Judge Michael and Judge Traxler joined.

. . .

LUTTIG, Circuit Judge:

. . .

The exceedingly important question before us is whether the President of the United States possesses the authority to detain militarily a citizen of this country who is closely associated with al Qaeda, an entity with which the United States is at war; who took up arms on behalf of that enemy and against our country in a foreign combat zone of that war; <u>and</u> who thereafter traveled to the United States for the avowed purpose of further prosecuting that war on American soil, against American citizens and targets.

We conclude that the President does possess such authority pursuant to the Authorization for Use of Military Force Joint Resolution enacted by Congress in the wake of the attacks on the United States of September 11, 2001. Accordingly, the judgment of the district court is reversed.

. . .

II.

A.

. . .

As the AUMF authorized Hamdi's detention by the President, so also does it authorize Padilla's detention. Under the facts as presented here, Padilla unquestionably qualifies as an "enemy combatant" as that term was defined for purposes of the controlling opinion in *Hamdi*. Indeed, under the definition of "enemy combatant" employed in *Hamdi*, we can discern no difference in principle between Hamdi and Padilla. Like Hamdi, Padilla associated with forces hostile to the United States in Afghanistan. *Compare* J.A. 19–23 (detailing Padilla's association with al Qaeda in Afghanistan and Pakistan), *with Hamdi*, 124 S.Ct. at 2637 (describing Hamdi's affiliation with the Taliban in Afghanistan). And, like Hamdi, Padilla took up arms against United States forces in that country in the same way and to the same extent as did Hamdi. *Compare* J.A. 21 (averring that Padilla was "armed and present in a combat zone during armed conflict between al Qaeda/Taliban forces and the armed forces of the United States"), *and id*. at 20–21 (alleging that Padilla was "armed with an assault rifle" as he escaped to Pakistan), *with Hamdi*, 124 S.Ct. at 2642 n.1 (noting that the asserted basis for detaining Hamdi was that he "carr[ied] a weapon against American troops on a foreign battlefield"), *and id*. at 2637 (quoting Mobbs Affidavit that Hamdi had "'surrender[ed] his Kalishnikov assault rifle'" to Northern Alliance forces (alteration in original)). Because, like Hamdi, Padilla is an enemy combatant, and because his detention is no less necessary than was Hamdi's in order to prevent his return to the battlefield, the President is authorized by the AUMF to detain Padilla as a fundamental incident to the conduct of war.

Our conclusion that the AUMF as interpreted by the Supreme Court in *Hamdi* authorizes the President's detention of Padilla as an enemy combatant is reinforced by the Supreme Court's decision in *Ex parte Quirin*, 317 U.S. 1 (1942), on which the plurality in *Hamdi* itself heavily relied. In *Quirin*, the Court held that Congress had authorized the military trial of Haupt, a United States citizen who entered the country with orders from the Nazis to blow up domestic war facilities but was captured before he could execute those orders. *Id*. at 20–21, 28, 46. The Court reasoned that Haupt's citizenship was no bar to his military trial as an unlawful enemy belligerent, concluding that "[c]itizens who associate themselves with the military arm of the enemy government, and with its aid, guidance and direction enter this country bent on hostile acts, are enemy belligerents within the meaning of . . . the law of war." *Id.* at 37–38.

Like Haupt, Padilla associated with the military arm of the enemy, and with its aid, guidance, and direction entered this country bent on committing hostile acts on American soil. J.A. 22–23. Padilla thus falls within *Quirin's* definition of enemy belligerent, as well as within the definition of the equivalent term accepted by the plurality in *Hamdi*. *Compare Quirin*, 317 U.S. at 37–38, (holding that "[c]itizens who associate themselves with the military arm of the enemy government, and with its aid, guidance and direction enter this country bent on hostile acts, are enemy belligerents within the meaning of . . . the law of war"), *with Hamdi*, 124 S. Ct. at 2639 (accepting for purposes of the case the government's definition of "enemy combatants" as those who were "'part of or supporting forces hostile to the United States or coalition partners'" in Afghanistan and who "'engaged in an armed conflict against the United States'" there").

We understand the plurality's *reasoning* in *Hamdi* to be that the AUMF authorizes the President to detain all those who qualify as "enemy combatants" within the meaning of the laws of war, such power being universally accepted under the laws of war as necessary in order to prevent the return of combatants to the battlefield during conflict. *Id.* at 2640–41. Given that Padilla qualifies as an enemy combatant under both the definition adopted by the Court in *Quirin* and the definition accepted by the controlling opinion in *Hamdi*, his military detention as an enemy combatant by the President is unquestionably authorized by the AUMF as a fundamental incident to the President's prosecution of the war against al Qaeda in Afghanistan.[3]

B.

Padilla marshals essentially four arguments for the conclusion that his detention is unlawful. None of them ultimately is persuasive.

1.

Recognizing the hurdle to his position represented by the Supreme Court's decision in *Hamdi*, Padilla principally argues that his case does not fall within the "narrow circumstances" considered by the Court in that case because, although he too stood alongside Taliban forces in Afghanistan, he was seized on American soil, whereas Hamdi was captured on a foreign battlefield. In other words, Padilla maintains that capture on a foreign battlefield was one of the "narrow circumstances" to which the plurality in *Hamdi* confined its opinion. We disagree. When the plurality articulated the "narrow question" before it, it referred simply to the permissibility of detaining "an individual who . . . was "'part of or supporting forces hostile to the United States or coalition partners'" in Afghanistan and who "'engaged in an armed conflict against the United States'" there." *Id.* at 2639. Nowhere in its framing of the "narrow question" presented did the plurality even mention the locus of capture.

The actual reasoning that the plurality thereafter employed is consistent with the question having been framed so as to render locus of capture irrelevant. That reasoning was that Hamdi's detention was an exercise of "necessary and appropriate force" within

---

[3] Under *Hamdi*, the power to detain that is authorized under the AUMF is not a power to detain indefinitely. Detention is limited to the duration of the hostilities as to which the detention is authorized. 124 S. Ct. at 2641–42. Because the United States remains engaged in the conflict with al Qaeda in Afghanistan, Padilla's detention has not exceeded in duration that authorized by the AUMF.

the meaning of the AUMF because "detention to prevent a combatant's return to the battlefield is a fundamental incident of waging war." *Id*. at 2641. This reasoning simply does not admit of a distinction between an enemy combatant captured abroad and detained in the United States, such as Hamdi, and an enemy combatant who escaped capture abroad but was ultimately captured domestically and detained in the United States, such as Padilla. As we previously explained, Padilla poses the same threat of returning to the battlefield as Hamdi posed at the time of the Supreme Court's adjudication of Hamdi's petition. Padilla's detention is thus "necessary and appropriate" to the same extent as was Hamdi's.

Padilla directs us to a passage from the plurality's opinion in *Hamdi* in which, when responding to the dissent, the plurality charged that the dissent "ignore[d] the context of th[e] case: a United States citizen captured in a *foreign* combat zone." *Id*. at 2643. Padilla argues that this passage proves that *capture on a foreign battlefield* was one of the factual circumstances by which the Court's opinion was limited. If this language stood alone, Padilla's argument as to the limitation of *Hamdi* at least would have more force, though to acknowledge that foreign battlefield capture was part of the *context* of the case still is not to say (at least not necessarily) that the locus of capture was essential to the Court's *reasoning*. However, this language simply cannot bear the weight that Padilla would have it bear when it is considered against the backdrop of both the quite different limitations that were expressly imposed by the Court through its framing of the question presented, and the actual reasoning that was employed by the Court in reaching its conclusion, which reasoning was consistent with the question having been framed so as to render an enemy combatant's point of capture irrelevant to the President's power to detain. In short, the plurality carefully limited its opinion, but not in a way that leaves room for argument that the President's power to detain one who has associated with the enemy and taken up arms against the United States in a foreign combat zone varies depending upon the geographic location where that enemy combatant happens to be captured.

Our conclusion that the reasoning in *Hamdi* does not support a distinction based on the locus of capture is buttressed by the plurality's analysis of *Quirin*. Although at issue in *Quirin* was the authority of the President to subject a United States citizen who was also an enemy combatant to military trial, the plurality in *Hamdi* went to lengths to observe that Haupt, *who had been captured domestically*, could instead have been permissibly *detained* for the duration of hostilities. *See id*. at 2640. That analysis strongly suggests, if it does not confirm, that the plurality did not regard the locus of capture (within or without the United States) as relevant to the President's authority to detain an enemy combatant who is also a citizen, and that it believed that the detention of such a combatant is not more or less a necessary incident of the President's power to wage war depending upon the locus of eventual capture.

Given the lack of any reference to locus of capture in the plurality's articulation of the "narrow question" before it, the absence of any basis in *Hamdi's* reasoning for a distinction between foreign and domestic capture of one who has both associated with the enemy and taken up arms against the United States on behalf of that enemy in a foreign combat zone, and the plurality's understanding of and reliance upon *Quirin* as a precedent that would permit the detention of an enemy combatant who had been captured domestically, we simply cannot ascribe to the rejoinder to Justice Scalia the significance, much less the dispositive significance, that Padilla urges.[4]

---

[4] Padilla also argues that the locus of capture should be legally relevant to the scope of the AUMF's authorization because there is a higher probability of an erroneous determination that one is an enemy combatant when the seizure occurs on American soil. It is far from clear that this is actually the case. In any event, Padilla's

2.

Padilla also argues, and the district court held, that Padilla's military detention is "neither necessary nor appropriate" because he is amenable to criminal prosecution. . . . . Related to this argument, Padilla attempts to distinguish *Quirin* from his case on the grounds that he has simply been detained, unlike Haupt who was charged and tried in *Quirin*. Neither the argument nor the attempted distinction is convincing.

As to the fact that Padilla can be prosecuted, the availability of criminal process does not distinguish him from Hamdi. If the mere availability of criminal prosecution rendered detention unnecessary within the meaning of the AUMF, then Hamdi's detention would have been unnecessary and therefore unauthorized, since he too was detained in the United States and amenable to criminal prosecution. We are convinced, in any event, that the availability of criminal process cannot be determinative of the power to detain, if for no other reason than that criminal prosecution may well not achieve the very purpose for which detention is authorized in the first place – the prevention of return to the field of battle. Equally important, in many instances criminal prosecution would impede the Executive in its efforts to gather intelligence from the detainee and to restrict the detainee's communication with confederates so as to ensure that the detainee does not pose a continuing threat to national security even as he is confined – impediments that would render military detention not only an appropriate, but also the necessary, course of action to be taken in the interest of national security.

The district court acknowledged the need to defer to the President's determination that Padilla's detention is necessary and appropriate in the interest of national security. *See id.* at 179. However, we believe that the district court ultimately accorded insufficient deference to that determination, effectively imposing upon the President the equivalent of a least-restrictive-means test. To subject to such exacting scrutiny the President's determination that criminal prosecution would not adequately protect the Nation's security at a very minimum fails to accord the President the deference that is his when he acts pursuant to a broad delegation of authority from Congress, such as the AUMF.

As for Padilla's attempted distinction of *Quirin* on the grounds that, unlike Haupt, he has never been charged and tried by the military, the plurality in *Hamdi* rejected as immaterial the distinction between detention and trial (apparently regarding the former as a lesser imposition than the latter), noting that "nothing in *Quirin* suggests that [Haupt's United States] citizenship would have precluded his *mere detention* for the duration of the relevant hostilities." *Hamdi*, 124 S. Ct. at 2640 (emphasis added).

3.

Padilla, citing *Ex parte Endo*, 323 U.S. 283 (1944), and relying upon *Quirin*, next argues that only a clear statement from Congress can authorize his detention, and that the AUMF is not itself, and does not contain, such a clear statement.

In *Endo*, the Court did state that, when asked to find implied powers in a wartime statute, it must assume that "the law makers intended to place no greater restraint on the citizen than was clearly and unmistakably indicated by the language [the law makers] used." *Id.* at 300. The Court almost immediately thereafter observed, however, that the "fact that the Act" at issue was "silent on detention [did] not of course mean that any

---

argument confuses the scope of the President's *power* to detain enemy combatants under the AUMF with the *process* for establishing that a detainee is in fact an enemy combatant. *Hamdi* itself provides process to guard against the erroneous detention of non-enemy combatants. 124 S. Ct. at 2648–52.

power to detain [was] lacking," *id.* at 301, an observation that proves that the Court did not adopt or even apply in that case a "clear statement" rule of the kind for which Padilla argues.[5]

Padilla contends that *Quirin* also supports the existence of a clear statement rule. However, in no place in *Quirin* did the Court even purport to establish a clear statement rule. In its opinion, the Court did note that Congress had "explicitly" authorized Haupt's military trial. *See* 317 U.S. at 28. But to conclude from this passing note that the Court required a clear statement as a matter of law would be unwarranted. In fact, to the extent that *Quirin* can be understood to have addressed the need for a clear statement of authority from Congress at all, the rule would appear the opposite:

> [T]he detention and trial of petitioners – ordered by the President in the declared exercise of his powers as Commander in Chief of the Army in time of war and of grave public danger – are not to be set aside by the courts without the clear conviction that they are in conflict with the Constitution or laws of Congress constitutionally enacted.

Id. at 25.

Of course, even were a clear statement by Congress required, the AUMF constitutes such a clear statement according to the Supreme Court. In *Hamdi*, stating that "it [was] of no moment that the AUMF does not use specific language of detention," 124 S. Ct. at 2641, the plurality held that the AUMF "clearly and unmistakably authorized" Hamdi's detention, *id.* Nothing in the AUMF permits us to conclude that the Joint Resolution clearly and unmistakably authorized Hamdi's detention but not Padilla's. To the contrary, read in light of its purpose clause ("in order to prevent any future acts of international terrorism against the United States") and its preamble (stating that the acts of 9/11 "render it both necessary and appropriate . . . to protect United States citizens both at home and abroad"), the AUMF applies even more clearly and unmistakably to Padilla than to Hamdi. Padilla, after all, in addition to supporting hostile forces in Afghanistan and taking up arms against our troops on a battlefield in that country like Hamdi, *also* came to the United States in order to commit future acts of terrorism against American citizens and targets.

These facts unquestionably establish that Padilla poses the requisite threat of return to battle in the ongoing armed conflict between the United States and al Qaeda in Afghanistan, and that his detention is authorized as a "fundamental incident of waging war," *id.*, in order "to prevent a combatant's return to the battlefield," *id.* Congress "clearly and unmistakably," *id.*, authorized such detention when, in the AUMF, it "permitt[ed] the use of 'necessary and appropriate force,'" *id.*, to prevent other attacks like those of September 11, 2001.

4.

Finally, Padilla argues that, even if his detention is authorized by the AUMF, it is unlawful under *Ex parte Milligan*, 71 U.S. (4 Wall.) 2 (1866). In *Milligan*, the Supreme Court held that a United States citizen associated with an anti-Union secret society but unaffiliated

---

[5] At issue in *Endo* was the detention of a "concededly loyal" citizen, not an enemy combatant. 323 U.S. at 302. In the face of the statute's silence on detention, the Court looked to the statute's purpose – the prevention of espionage and sabotage – to determine whether Endo's detention was authorized. *See id.* at 300–02. The Court concluded that it was not, because detention of a concededly loyal citizen bore no relation to the prevention of espionage and sabotage. *Id.* at 302. Padilla's detention, by contrast, emphatically does further the purpose of the AUMF – "to prevent any future acts of international terrorism against the United States," Pub. L. No. 107-40, §2(a), 115 Stat. 224 (2001).

with the Confederate army could not be tried by a military tribunal while access to civilian courts was open and unobstructed. *Id*. at 6–7, 121. *Milligan* purported to restrict the power of Congress as well as the power of the President. *Id*. at 121–22 ("[N]o usage of war could sanction a military trial . . . for any offence whatever of a citizen in civil life, in nowise connected with the military service. Congress could grant no such power . . ."). *Quirin*, however, confirmed that *Milligan* does not extend to enemy combatants. As the Court in *Quirin* explained, the *Milligan* Court's reasoning had "particular reference to the facts before it," namely, that Milligan was not "a part of or associated with the armed forces of the enemy." *See* 317 U.S. at 45. The *Hamdi* plurality in turn reaffirmed this limitation on the reach of *Milligan*, emphasizing that *Quirin*, a unanimous opinion, "both postdates and clarifies *Milligan*." 124 S. Ct. at 2643. Thus confined, *Milligan* is inapposite here because Padilla, unlike Milligan, associated with, and has taken up arms against the forces of the United States on behalf of, an enemy of the United States.

III.

The Congress of the United States, in the Authorization for Use of Military Force Joint Resolution, provided the President all powers necessary and appropriate to protect American citizens from terrorist acts by those who attacked the United States on September 11, 2001. As would be expected, and as the Supreme Court has held, those powers include the power to detain identified and committed enemies such as Padilla, who associated with al Qaeda and the Taliban regime, who took up arms against this Nation in its war against these enemies, *and* who entered the United States for the avowed purpose of further prosecuting that war by attacking American citizens and targets on our own soil – a power without which, Congress understood, the President could well be unable to protect American citizens from the very kind of savage attack that occurred four years ago almost to the day.

The detention of petitioner being fully authorized by Act of Congress, the judgment of the district court that the detention of petitioner by the President of the United States is without support in law is hereby reversed.

REVERSED.

11/20/2005: MEMO TRANSFERRING PADILLA FROM DEPARTMENT OF DEFENSE TO DEPARTMENT OF JUSTICE

THE WHITE HOUSE

WASHINGTON

November 20, 2005

MEMORANDUM FOR THE SECRETARY OF DEFENSE

SUBJECT: Transfer of Detainee to Control of the Attorney General

Based on the information available to me,   [REDACTED]

I hereby determine that it is in the interest of the United States that Jose Padilla be released from detention by the Secretary of Defense and transferred to the control of the Attorney General for the purpose of criminal proceedings against him.

Accordingly, by the authority vested in me as President by the Constitution and the laws of the United States, I hereby direct you to transfer Mr. Padilla to the control of the Attorney General upon the Attorney General's request. This memorandum supersedes my directive to you of June 9, 2002, and, upon such transfer, your authority to detain Mr. Padilla provided in that order shall cease.

PUBLISHED

Filed December 21, 2005

UNITED STATES COURT OF APPEALS
FOR THE FOURTH CIRCUIT

JOSE PADILLA,
        Petitioner-Appellee,

v.

C. T. HANFT, U.S.N. Commander,
Consolidated Naval Brig.,
        Respondent-Appellant.

No. 05-6396
(CA-04-2221-26AJ)

ORDER

The motion filed by the government for authorization to transfer petitioner from military custody in the state of South Carolina to civilian law enforcement custody in the state of Florida is denied. The suggestion that the court's opinion of September 9, 2005, be withdrawn is denied.

Judge Luttig wrote an opinion in which Judge Michael concurred. Judge Traxler wrote a separate opinion concurring in part.

For the Court

/s/ Patricia S. Connor
Clerk

LUTTIG, Circuit Judge:

Before the court is the government's motion pursuant to Supreme Court Rule 36 for authorization to transfer Jose Padilla immediately out of military custody in the State of South Carolina and into the custody of federal civilian law enforcement authorities in the State of Florida, together with its suggestion that we withdraw our opinion of September 9, 2005, in which we held that the President possesses the authority under the Authorization for the Use of Military Force to detain enemy combatants who have taken up arms against the United States abroad and entered into this country for the purpose of attacking America and its citizens from within.

Because we believe that the transfer of Padilla and the withdrawal of our opinion at the government's request while the Supreme Court is reviewing this court's decision of September 9 would compound what is, in the absence of explanation, at least an appearance that the government may be attempting to avoid consideration of our decision by the Supreme Court, and also because we believe that this case presents an issue of such especial national importance as to warrant final consideration by that court, even if only by denial of further review, we deny both the motion and suggestion. If the natural progression of this significant litigation to conclusion is to be pretermitted at this late date under these circumstances, we believe that decision should be made not by this court but, rather, by the Supreme Court of the United States.

I.

The relevant events preceding the government's motion are as follows.

The government has held Padilla militarily for three and a half years, steadfastly maintaining that it was imperative in the interest of national security that he be so held. However, a short time after our decision issued on the government's representation that Padilla's military custody was indeed necessary in the interest of national security, the government determined that it was no longer necessary that Padilla be held militarily. Instead, it announced, Padilla would be transferred to the custody of federal civilian law enforcement authorities and criminally prosecuted in Florida for alleged offenses considerably different from, and less serious than, those acts for which the government had militarily detained Padilla. The indictment of Padilla in Florida, unsealed the same day as announcement of that indictment, made no mention of the acts upon which the government purported to base its military detention of Padilla and upon which we had concluded only several weeks before that the President possessed the authority to detain Padilla, namely, that Padilla had taken up arms against United States forces in Afghanistan and had thereafter entered into this country for the purpose of blowing up buildings in American cities, in continued prosecution of al Qaeda's war of terrorism against the United States.

The announcement of indictment came only two business days before the government's brief in response to Padilla's petition for certiorari was due to be filed in the Supreme Court of the United States, and only days before the District Court in South Carolina, pursuant to our remand, was to accept briefing on the question whether Padilla had been properly designated an enemy combatant by the President.

The same day as Padilla's indictment was unsealed in Florida, the government filed with us a motion pursuant to Supreme Court Rule 36 for authorization to transfer Padilla to Florida, a motion that included no reference to, or explanation of, the difference in the facts asserted to justify Padilla's military detention and those for which Padilla was indicted. In a plea that was notable given that the government had held Padilla militarily for three and a half years and that the Supreme Court was expected within only days either to deny certiorari or to assume jurisdiction over the case for eventual disposition on the merits, the government urged that we act as expeditiously as possible to authorize the transfer. The government styled its motion as an "emergency application," but it provided no explanation as to what comprised the asserted exigency.

When we did not immediately authorize Padilla's transfer as requested, the government, rather than file its response to Padilla's petition for certiorari as scheduled, sought and received from the Supreme Court an extension of time until December 16 within which to file that response.

Instead of simply granting the motion for immediate authorization to transfer Padilla, we directed the parties to brief the question whether, in light of the difference in the facts asserted to justify Padilla's military detention on which our decision was premised and the facts underlying the charges in Padilla's indictment in Florida, our opinion should be vacated in the event of Padilla's transfer. In response to our request for briefing, the government has now taken the position that our decision of September 9 should be withdrawn entirely.

II.

Under Supreme Court Rule 36, the custodian of a habeas petitioner whose case is pending before the Supreme Court "may not transfer custody to another person unless the transfer is authorized under this Rule." Rule 36 further provides that "[u]pon application by a custodian, the court, Justice, or judge who entered the decision under review may authorize transfer and the substitution of a successor custodian as a party." There is no articulated purpose for this rule, the rule does not specify a standard upon which a requested transfer should be authorized or denied, and it is unclear to us what the applicable standard ought to be or whether the rule even applies in a circumstance such as this. This said, to the extent our authorization is needed, we believe there are two reasons for us to deny the government's motion, as well as its suggestion for vacatur of our opinion.

A.

First, the government's actions since this court's decision issued on September 9, culminating in and including its urging that our opinion be withdrawn, together with the timing of these actions in relation both to the period for which Padilla has already been held and to the government's scheduled response to Padilla's certiorari petition in the Supreme Court, have given rise to at least an appearance that the purpose of these actions may be to avoid consideration of our decision by the Supreme Court.

We are not in a position to ascertain whether behind this appearance there is the actual fact, because the government has not explained its decisions either publicly or to the court. The media has variously reported that the government's abrupt change in course was prompted by its concern over Supreme Court review of our decision and/or its concern for disclosure of the circumstances surrounding its receipt of the information regarding Padilla's plans to blow up buildings in American cities or of the identities and locations of the persons who provided that information. In one instance, immediately after we had initially declined to act on the government's transfer motion, these concerns were detailed in the press and attributed to former and current Administration officials speaking on the condition of anonymity. It was even reported that the government had considered transfer and criminal prosecution of Padilla before its argument in this court that military detention of Padilla was necessary in the interest of national security. No such explanations have been provided to the court, however.

It should go without saying that we cannot rest our decisions on media reports of statements from anonymous government sources regarding facts relevant to matters pending before the court, nor should we be required to do so or to speculate as to facts based upon such reports. The information that the government would provide to the media with respect to facts relevant to a pending litigation, it should be prepared to provide to the court. Nevertheless, even if these were the government's concerns, neither concern would justify the intentional mooting of the appeal of our decision to the Supreme Court after three and a half years of prosecuting this litigation and on the eve of final consideration of the issue by that court.

As for the first of these reported concerns, we would regard the intentional mooting by the government of a case of this import out of concern for Supreme Court consideration not as legitimate justification but as admission of attempted avoidance of review. The government cannot be seen as conducting litigation with the enormous implications of this litigation – litigation imbued with significant public interest – in such a way as to select by which forum as between the Supreme Court of the United States and an inferior appellate court it wishes to be bound.

As for the second reported concern, the means by which the government may have come by its information concerning Padilla, as well as the current locations of any persons who might have provided that information, are legally irrelevant to the appeal of our decision now pending before the Supreme Court. These concerns would be relevant, if at all, only at the hearing required by *Hamdi* v. *Rumsfeld* to determine the legitimacy of the President's designation of Padilla as an enemy combatant. And if the government did fear "sensitive evidentiary issues" that might arise in this hearing, it could have sought a stay from the district court, continued to pursue its argument before the Supreme Court that the President possesses the authority from Congress to detain persons such as Padilla, and transferred Padilla to civilian law enforcement custody and initiated prosecution only after final Supreme Court resolution of the pending appeal, whether favorable or unfavorable. Thus, in the end, concerns over evidentiary issues could no more justify the government's actions than could an interest in avoiding Supreme Court review.

That neither of these speculated reasons would have justified the government's actions is not to say that there are not legitimate reasons for those actions. There may well be. For example, the government could have come to believe that the information on which Padilla has been detained is in fact not true or, even if true, is not sufficiently reliable to justify his continued military detention (although to serve as legitimate basis for its actions the government would have had to come to such belief based upon information or intelligence acquired since the issuance of our decision). Of course, if the government had come to so believe, it is expected that it would have informed this court or the Supreme Court and *then* proceeded as it has. But any legitimate reasons are not evident, and the government has not offered explanation. Absent explanation, our authorization of Padilla's transfer under the circumstances described and while the case is awaiting imminent consideration by the Supreme Court would serve only to compound the appearance to which the government's actions, even if wholly legitimate, have inescapably given rise.

B.

Second, apart from the need to protect the appearance of regularity in the judicial process, we believe that the issue presented by the government's appeal to this court and Padilla's appeal to the Supreme Court is of sufficient national importance as to warrant consideration by the Supreme Court, even if that consideration concludes only in a denial of certiorari.

For four years, since the attack on America of September 11, 2001, a centerpiece of the government's war on terror has been the President's authority to detain militarily persons who, having engaged in acts of war against the United States abroad, have crossed our borders with the avowed purpose of attacking this country and its citizens from within – the kind of persons who committed the atrocities of September 11. The President himself acted upon the belief that he possessed such authority and that such authority was essential to protect the Nation from another attack like that of September 11 when he designated Padilla an enemy combatant, declared that Padilla "represent[ed] a continuing, present and grave danger to the national security of the United States," and directed the Secretary of Defense to assume and maintain custody over Padilla. The government's belief in the indispensability to our national security of the President's authority to detain enemy combatants such as Padilla was reaffirmed by the Attorney General when he stated at the time that our opinion issued that "the authority to detain enemy combatants like Jose Padilla plays an important role in protecting American citizens from the very kind of savage attack that took place almost four years ago to the day." And though we limited our holding to the circumstance where the President detains persons who have associated with enemy forces abroad, taken up arms on behalf of such forces, and thereafter entered into this country with the avowed purpose of prosecuting war against America on her own soil, we ourselves recognized the "exceeding importance" of the issue presented, even as so limited.

On an issue of such surpassing importance, we believe that the rule of law is best served by maintaining on appeal the status quo in all respects and allowing Supreme Court consideration of the case in the ordinary course, rather than by an eleventh-hour transfer and vacatur on grounds and under circumstances that would further a perception that dismissal may have been sought for the purpose of avoiding consideration by the Supreme Court.

Accordingly, for the reasons stated, we deny both the government's motion for authorization to transfer and its suggestion of vacatur of our opinion of September 9, and thereby maintain for the Supreme Court the status quo while it considers the pending petition for certiorari.

III.

Because of their evident gravity, we must believe that the consequences of the actions that the government has taken in this important case over the past several weeks, not only for the public perception of the war on terror but also for the government's credibility before the courts in litigation ancillary to that war, have been carefully considered. But at the same time that we must believe this, we cannot help but believe that those consequences have been underestimated.

For, as the government surely must understand, although the various facts it has asserted are not necessarily inconsistent or without basis, its actions have left not only the impression that Padilla may have been held for these years, even if justifiably, by mistake – an impression we would have thought the government could ill afford to leave extant. They have left the impression that the government may even have come to the belief that the principle in reliance upon which it has detained Padilla for this time, that the President possesses the authority to detain enemy combatants who enter into this country for the purpose of attacking America and its citizens from within, can, in the end, yield to expediency with little or no cost to its conduct of the war against terror – an impression we would have thought the government likewise could ill afford to leave extant. And these impressions have been left, we fear, at what may ultimately prove to be substantial cost to the government's credibility before the courts, to whom it will one day need to argue again in support of a principle of assertedly like importance and necessity to the one that it seems to abandon today. While there could be an objective that could command such a price as all of this, it is difficult to imagine what that objective would be.

For the reasons stated, the government's motion to transfer and the suggestion that our opinion of September 9, 2005, be vacated are denied.

. . .

1/04/2006: SUPREME COURT ORDER GRANTING TRANSFER

(ORDER LIST: 546 U.S.)

WEDNESDAY, JANUARY 4, 2006

ORDER IN PENDING CASE

05A578   HANFT, C.T. V. PADILLA, JOSE

Jose Padilla has filed a petition for certiorari, seeking review
of the Fourth Circuit's judgment upholding his detention by military
authorities. See *Padilla* v. *Hanft*, No. 05-533 (filed Oct. 25, 2005). On
November 22, 2005, the Government filed a motion before the Fourth Circuit,
seeking approval to transfer Padilla from military custody to the custody of
the warden of a federal detention center in Florida, to face criminal charges
contained in an indictment filed November 17, 2005. See Supreme Court Rule
36.1 ("Pending review in this Court of a decision in a habeas corpus
proceeding. . . the person having custody of the prisoner may not transfer
custody to another person unless the transfer is authorized under this
Rule."). Padilla agreed that the transfer should be approved. The Fourth
Circuit denied the request, citing a concern that transfer might affect this
Court's consideration of the pending petition for certiorari and concluding
that the "decision should be made not by this court but, rather, by the
Supreme Court of the United States." Order at 3, *Padilla* v. *Hanft*,
No. 05-6396 (CA4 Dec. 21, 2005).

The Solicitor General has now filed with this Court an Application
Respecting the Custody and Transfer of Jose Padilla, seeking the same
authorization previously sought from the Court of Appeals. Padilla has filed
a response, arguing instead that the Court should delay his release from
military custody and consider his release along with his petition for
certiorari. The Government's application presented to the Chief Justice and
by him referred to the Court is granted. The Court will consider the pending
petition for certiorari in due course.

SUPREME COURT OF THE UNITED STATES

JOSE PADILLA v. C. T. HANFT, UNITED STATES NAVY COMMANDER, CONSOLIDATED NAVAL BRIG

ON PETITION FOR WRIT OF CERTIORARI TO THE UNITED STATES COURT OF APPEALS FOR THE FOURTH CIRCUIT

No. 05–533.　Decided April 3, 2006

The petition for a writ of certiorari is denied. JUSTICE SOUTER, JUSTICE GINSBURG, and JUSTICE BREYER would grant the petition for a writ of certiorari.

JUSTICE KENNEDY, with whom THE CHIEF JUSTICE and JUSTICE STEVENS join, concurring in the denial of certiorari.

The Court's decision to deny the petition for writ of certiorari is, in my view, a proper exercise of its discretion in light of the circumstances of the case. The history of petitioner Jose Padilla's detention, however, does require this brief explanatory statement.

Padilla is a United States citizen. Acting pursuant to a material witness warrant issued by the United States District Court for the Southern District of New York, federal agents apprehended Padilla at Chicago's O'Hare International Airport on May 8, 2002. He was transported to New York, and on May 22 he moved to vacate the warrant. On June 9, while that motion was pending, the President issued an order to the Secretary of Defense designating Padilla an enemy combatant and ordering his military detention. The District Court, notified of this action by the Government's *ex parte* motion, vacated the material witness warrant.

Padilla was taken to the Consolidated Naval Brig in Charleston, South Carolina. On June 11, Padilla's counsel filed a habeas corpus petition in the Southern District of New York challenging the military detention. The District Court denied the petition, but the Court of Appeals for the Second Circuit reversed and ordered the issuance of a writ directing Padilla's release. This Court granted certiorari and ordered dismissal of the habeas corpus petition without prejudice, holding that the District Court for the Southern District of New York was not the appropriate court to consider it. See *Rumsfeld* v. *Padilla*, 542 U.S. 426 (2004).

The present case arises from Padilla's subsequent habeas corpus petition, filed in the United States District Court for the District of South Carolina on July 2, 2004. Padilla requested that he be released immediately or else charged with a crime. The District Court granted the petition on February 28, 2005, but the Court of Appeals for the Fourth Circuit reversed that judgment on September 9, 2005. Padilla then filed the instant petition for writ of certiorari.

After Padilla sought certiorari in this Court, the Government obtained an indictment charging him with various federal crimes. The President ordered that Padilla be released from military custody and transferred to the control of the Attorney General to face criminal charges. The Government filed a motion for approval of Padilla's transfer in the Court of Appeals for the Fourth Circuit. The Court of Appeals denied the motion, but this Court granted the Government's subsequent application respecting the transfer. *Hanft* v. *Padilla*, 546 U.S.__ (2006). The Government also filed a brief in opposition to certiorari, arguing, among other things, that Padilla's petition should be denied as moot.

The Government's mootness argument is based on the premise that Padilla, now having been charged with crimes and released from military custody, has received the principal relief he sought. Padilla responds that his case was not mooted by the Government's voluntary actions because there remains a possibility that he will be redesignated and redetained as an enemy combatant.

Whatever the ultimate merits of the parties' mootness arguments, there are strong prudential considerations disfavoring the exercise of the Court's certiorari power. Even if the Court were to rule in Padilla's favor, his present custody status would be unaffected. Padilla is scheduled to be tried on criminal charges. Any consideration of what rights he might be able to assert if he were returned to military custody would be hypothetical, and to no effect, at this stage of the proceedings.

In light of the previous changes in his custody status and the fact that nearly four years have passed since he first was detained, Padilla, it must be acknowledged, has a continuing concern that his status might be altered again. That concern, however, can be addressed if the necessity arises. Padilla is now being held pursuant to the control and supervision of the United States District Court for the Southern District of Florida, pending trial of the criminal case. In the course of its supervision over Padilla's custody and trial the District Court will be obliged to afford him the protection, including the right to a speedy trial, guaranteed to all federal criminal defendants. See, *e.g.*, U.S. Const., Amdt. 6; 18 U.S.C. §3161. Were the Government to seek to change the status or conditions of Padilla's custody, that court would be in a position to rule quickly on any responsive filings submitted by Padilla. In such an event, the District Court, as well as other courts of competent jurisdiction, should act promptly to ensure that the office and purposes of the writ of habeas corpus are not compromised. Padilla, moreover, retains the option of seeking a writ of habeas corpus in this Court. See this Court's Rule 20; 28 U.S.C. §§1651(a), 2241.

That Padilla's claims raise fundamental issues respecting the separation of powers, including consideration of the role and function of the courts, also counsels against addressing those claims when the course of legal proceedings has made them, at least for now, hypothetical. This is especially true given that Padilla's current custody is part of the relief he sought, and that its lawfulness is uncontested.

These are the reasons for my vote to deny certiorari.

Cite as: 547 U. S. ____ (2006)

SUPREME COURT OF THE UNITED STATES

JOSE PADILLA *v.* C. T. HANFT, UNITED STATES NAVY COMMANDER, CONSOLIDATED NAVAL BRIG

ON PETITION FOR WRIT OF CERTIORARI TO THE UNITED STATES COURT OF APPEALS FOR THE FOURTH CIRCUIT

No. 05–533.   Decided April 3, 2006

JUSTICE GINSBURG, dissenting from the denial of certiorari.

This case, here for the second time, raises a question "of profound importance to the Nation," *Rumsfeld* v. *Padilla*, 542 U.S. 426, 455 (2004) (STEVENS, J., dissenting): Does the President have authority to imprison indefinitely a United States citizen arrested on United States soil distant from a zone of combat, based on an Executive declaration that the citizen was, at the time of his arrest, an "enemy combatant"? It is a question the Court heard, and should have decided, two years ago. *Ibid.* Nothing the Government has yet done purports to retract the assertion of Executive power Padilla protests.

Although the Government has recently lodged charges against Padilla in a civilian court, nothing prevents the Executive from returning to the road it earlier constructed and defended. A party's voluntary cessation does not make a case less capable of repetition or less evasive of review. See *Spencer* v. *Kemna*, 523 U.S. 1, 17 (1998) (the capable-of-repetition exception to mootness applies where "(1) the challenged action [is] in its duration too short to be fully litigated prior to *cessation* or expiration, and (2) there [is] a reasonable expectation that the same complaining party [will] be subject to the same action again" (emphasis added)) (citations and internal quotation marks omitted); cf. *United States* v. *Concentrated Phosphate Export Assn., Inc.*, 393 U.S. 199, 203 (1968) (party whose actions threaten to moot a case must make "absolutely clear that the allegedly wrongful behavior could not reasonably be expected to recur"); *United States* v. *W. T. Grant Co.*, 345 U.S. 629, 632–633 (1953) (voluntary cessation of illegal activity will not render case moot unless there is "no reasonable expectation that the wrong will be repeated" (internal quotation marks omitted)). See also *Lane* v. *Williams*, 455 U.S. 624, 633–634 (1982) (applying "capable of repetition, yet evading review" in a habeas case (internal quotation marks omitted)). Satisfied that this case is not moot, I would grant the petition for certiorari.

Case Update: April 2008

On August 16, 2007, in the Federal District Court in Miami, Jose Padilla was convicted of conspiracy to injure property of a foreign government, conspiracy to defraud the United States, and providing material support to terrorists. He was sentenced on January 22, 2008, to 17 years and four months in prison. Although the prosecutors had asked for a life sentence, Judge Marcia Cooke noted that there was no evidence linking Padilla or his co-defendants to any specific acts of terrorism or that anyone had died as a result of their actions. Moreover, Judge Cooke subtracted the three and a half years Padilla had already spent in detention, stating that the time served warranted consideration because of the harsh conditions under which he had been held. Prosecutors have filed to appeal the sentence.

al-Marri v. Hanft

On June, 23, 2003, Ali Saleh Kahlah al-Marri became the second person in the United States to be declared an "enemy combatant" and the first criminal defendant in American history to be denied a trial because the president ordered his transfer to military custody. He is a citizen of Qatar who came to the United States in September 2001 with his wife and five children to obtain a master's degree at Bradley University in Peoria, Illinois. The following December, he was arrested at home on a material witness warrant and, two months later, was indicted on credit card fraud and other charges. He pled not guilty and vigorously contested the charges, with the assistance of New Jersey defense attorneys Mark A. Berman and Lawrence S. Lustberg. Days before a hearing in federal court on Mr. al-Marri's motion to suppress illegally seized evidence, and less than a month before his trial was scheduled to commence, the president circumvented the criminal justice system by militarizing Mr. al-Marri's domestic arrest and prosecution through the mere stroke of a pen.

The president's redacted one-page order declaring Mr. al-Marri an "enemy combatant" marks a crossing of the constitutional Rubicon. In essence, the president claims the power to subject individuals arrested in the United States to secret and indefinite military detention based on the proposition that the entire country is a battlefield in a perpetual and ubiquitous "war on terrorism." If accepted, this sweeping view of executive power would eliminate any meaningful distinction between civilians living in Peoria, Illinois, and combatants seized in foreign war zones. Based upon the president's order, the district judge dismissed the pending criminal case and the Defense Department took custody of Mr. al-Marri and imprisoned him in the Naval Consolidated Brig in Charleston, South Carolina.

He disappeared for the next 16 months. No one had any contact with him or any way of knowing whether he was still alive. Even the International Committee for the Red Cross was prohibited from visiting him at the brig, where he was held completely incommunicado. The administration's goal in declaring Mr. al-Marri an enemy combatant was unmistakable: to create a prison beyond the law in the United States, where a person could be detained without due process and interrogated under highly coercive conditions without any oversight or restrictions. Only later, after finally winning the right to visit him in October 2004, would we begin to learn about the abuses Mr. al-Marri was enduring: solitary confinement in a six-foot by nine-foot cell for 24 hours a day, seven days a week; denial of all contact with his family and the outside world; the use of stress positions and extreme sensory deprivation; denial of basic necessities like a toothbrush, toilet paper, soap, and a mattress; denial of basic religious materials (including at times the Koran); and threats of violence and death against him and his family. Every aspect of his environment was manipulated to create a sense of hopelessness.

At times, the isolation and deprivation became so severe that Mr. al-Marri felt he was losing his mind. He still remains in isolation today, having gained improvements in his conditions through the pressure of legal action and the good will of brig staff members who, unlike the high-level administration officials who set the policies, recognize that detainees are human beings.

After Mr. al-Marri was declared an "enemy combatant," we challenged his detention by filing a habeas corpus petition in federal court, though he did not know any legal action had been taken on his behalf until we gained the right to see him in October 2004. His habeas petition raises some of the most important issues of the post-9/11 era, testing the limits of the president's exercise of military power on American soil. Does the president have the legal authority to indefinitely imprison without charge an individual arrested in the United States in a "war on terrorism" unlimited in scope, duration, and all other criteria that traditionally separate a state of war from a state of peace? Can the president indefinitely detain such a person based solely upon the multiple hearsay statement of a faceless government official without a hearing, without actual or admissible evidence, without a right to confront any witnesses and without any opportunity to show his detention was based on evidence gained through torture? If the government were ultimately to prevail in this case, it would eviscerate the most basic right in the Constitution – the right to be charged and tried in a judicial proceeding – guaranteed to all individuals in this country. Military law would swallow civilian law, and the president would have created a system of unchecked detention in the United States.

As the case progressed through the courts, the administration's assertions grew more extreme. (I joined Mr. al-Marri's legal team in January 2005, and serve as lead counsel in his challenge to his detention as an "enemy combatant"). While Mr. al-Marri's appeal was pending in the U.S. Court of Appeals for the Fourth Circuit, the government sought to dismiss his case entirely. It argued that under a recently enacted statute, the Military Commissions Act of 2006 ("MCA"), federal courts no longer had jurisdiction to hear his habeas corpus action. The MCA, the government claimed, deprived the federal courts of jurisdiction to consider the habeas corpus petition of any foreign national whom the executive labeled an "enemy combatant." While the government has also asserted that the MCA eliminates habeas corpus jurisdiction over the petitions of the hundreds of detainees at Guantanamo Bay, the implications in Mr. al-Marri's case are particularly chilling. Under the government's view, any of the millions of immigrants living in the United States, including longtime permanent residents, could be snatched off the streets and imprisoned for years by the military without charge or access to a court. Such sweeping detention power contradicts the most basic principles of our Constitution and system of government. While we maintain that Congress did not intend to deprive the federal courts of jurisdiction over Mr. al-Marri's case, if it did the MCA must be invalidated as an unconstitutional suspension of the writ of habeas corpus.

I argued Mr. al-Marri's appeal before the Fourth Circuit on February 1, 2007, and, on June 11, 2007, the court issued its decision. In an opinion by Judge Diana Gribbon Motz, the court ruled that the MCA did not repeal jurisdiction over the habeas petitions of lawful resident aliens like Mr. al-Marri and that the president lacked legal authority to detain Mr. al-Marri as an "enemy combatant." Judge Motz said that the United States had to charge Mr. al-Marri in the civilian justice system or release him, and that his prolonged military detention must cease. The full court of appeals, however, subsequently granted the government's petition to rehear the case en banc. I argued the appeal before the full court on October 31, 2007, and the case is still pending.

It is important to remember that behind this important legal battle is a human story. At the time of this writing, Mr. al-Marri has been imprisoned in a navy jail for more than four years in legal limbo: without charge, trial, or a definitive ruling on his status. Throughout this time, he has remained in complete isolation, denied any socialization and prohibited from seeing or speaking with his family. Moreover, letters between him and his family in Qatar often take more ten months to arrive due to delays in the government's screening process. Other than occasional visits from the Red Cross, which the military now permits, Mr. al-Marri's attorneys have been his only contact with individuals outside the brig. Here, it is important to recognize the selfless dedication and zealous advocacy of my co-counsel, South Carolina attorney Andrew J. Savage, III, and his wife and colleague Cheryl Savage. Their regular letters and visits to our client have played a vital role, preventing Mr. al-Marri from falling into a state of utter hopelessness and despair.

Too often, we restrict our understanding of torture to graphic physical abuse, the proverbial rack and screw employed in the Tower of London by absolute monarchs centuries ago. Certainly, abuses like those documented at Abu Ghraib or secret CIA "black sites" capture the public's attention. And, in doing so, they dramatically illustrate the consequences of the United States' decision to abandon its commitment to human rights and the rule of law after September 11. Yet, for Mr. al-Marri (as for many detainees at Guantanamo and elsewhere), the legal limbo of indefinite detention without charge or due process may be been the most pernicious consequence of the administration's detention policies. Those reading this book now might pause to consider whether they could spend two days locked alone in a cell without any human contact or anything else to distract them from their total isolation. Then, consider being detained for more than 1,600 days under these conditions, with no prospect of when, if ever, this ordeal will end. Remarkably, the government denies that this mind-numbing isolation and physical and emotional deprivation is punishment, arguing instead that it represents a "simple war measure" to prevent Mr. al-Marri's "return to the battlefield" even though Mr. al-Marri is not accused of ever having taken up arms or ever having been anywhere near, let alone on, a battlefield. Yet, through all this, Mr. al-Marri has somehow managed to maintain his faith and ability to go on, trusting that one day justice will be done.

To be sure, the government's allegations against Mr. al-Marri are serious. The government alleges that he is an al Qaeda "sleeper agent" who entered the United States to engage in unspecified terrorist activity. Yet, the government has never presented any evidence to support its accusations other than untested third-hand allegations of a single official, many of which appear to have been gained through torture and other abuse. Mr. al-Marri has asked for no special favors or treatment. Rather, he seeks only the right to be tried in a court of law before being deprived – potentially for life – of his liberty. In the face of the president's untrammeled and unprecedented assertions of executive power, it is legal challenges such as these that test America's commitment to its most cherished freedoms.

Jonathan Hafetz
Litigation Director, Liberty and National Security Project
Brennan Center for Justice at NYU School of Law
New York, New York December 15, 2007

On September 10, 2001, Ali Saleh Kahlah al-Marri brought his wife and children to Peoria, Illinois, from Qatar, ostensibly to pursue a master's degree at Bradley University. He had received his bachelor's degree from Bradley in 1991. On December 12, 2001, Mr. al-Marri was arrested in his home in Peoria by FBI agents as a material witness in the investigation of the attacks of September 11th. He was held at the Peoria County Jail and later transferred to the Metropolitan Correctional Center in New York City, a detention facility which generally houses inmates awaiting trial or awaiting transfer to another facility.

In February 2002, Mr. al-Marri was charged with possession of unauthorized or counterfeit credit card numbers with intent to defraud, to which he pled not guilty. In late January 2003, he was additionally charged with two counts of making false statements to the FBI, three counts of making a false statement in a bank application and one count of using a means of identification of another person for the purpose of influencing the action of a federally insured financial institution. He pled not guilty to these charges as well. In May 2003, all of the charges were dismissed for lack of venue by the federal District Court for the Southern District of New York, and Mr. al-Marri was returned to the Peoria County Jail.

In Illinois, he was indicted on all of the charges which had been dismissed in New York. He again pled not guilty, and his trial was set for July 21, 2003. On or about May 29, 2003, the government began to deny his lawyers access. On June 20, 2003, the court scheduled a hearing to argue pre-trial motions, including a motion to suppress evidence which Mr. al-Marri claimed had been obtained by torture. That hearing was scheduled for July 2. On June 23, 2003, President Bush signed an order finding him to be an enemy combatant, and the government moved ex parte to dismiss the indictment and transfer him to military detention. The motion was granted and he was transferred to the Naval Consolidated Brig in South Carolina.

On July 8, 2003, Mr. al-Marri's attorneys filed a petition for habeas corpus in the federal District Court for the Central District of Illinois. That court dismissed the petition for improper venue on August 1, 2003. The Seventh Circuit affirmed the dismissal on March 8, 2004, holding that the district court in Illinois had no jurisdiction because Mr. al-Marri's custodian was located elsewhere. Mr. al-Marri's attorneys re-filed his habeas petition in South Carolina on July 8, 2004.

THE WHITE HOUSE

WASHINGTON

TO THE SECRETARY OF DEFENSE AND THE ATTORNEY GENERAL:

Based on the information available to me from all sources,

FILED

JUN 2 3 2003

JOHN M. WATERS, Clerk
U.S. DISTRICT COURT
CENTRAL DISTRICT OF ILLINOIS

REDACTED

In accordance with the Constitution and consistent with the laws of the United States, including the Authorization for Use of Military Force Joint Resolution (Public Law 107-40);

I, GEORGE W. BUSH, as President of the United States and Commander in Chief of the U.S. armed forces, hereby DETERMINE for the United States of America that:

(1) Ali Saleh Kahlah al-Marri, who is under the control of the Department of Justice, is, and at the time he entered the United States in September 2001 was, an enemy combatant;

(2) Mr. al-Marri is closely associated with al Qaeda, an international terrorist organization with which the United States is at war;

(3) Mr. al-Marri engaged in conduct that constituted hostile and war-like acts, including conduct in preparation for acts of international terrorism that had the aim to cause injury to or adverse effects on the United States;

(4) Mr. al-Marri possesses intelligence, including intelligence about personnel and activities of al Qaeda that, if communicated to the U.S., would aid U.S. efforts to prevent attacks by al Qaeda on the United States or its armed forces, other governmental personnel, or citizens;

(5) Mr. al-Marri represents a continuing, present, and grave danger to the national security of the United States, and detention of Mr. al-Marri is necessary to prevent him from aiding al Qaeda in its efforts to attack the United States or its armed forces, other governmental personnel, or citizens;

(6) it is in the interest of the United States that the Secretary of Defense detain Mr. al-Marri as an enemy combatant; and

(7) it is,   REDACTED   consistent with U.S. law and the laws of war for the Secretary of Defense to detain Mr. al-Marri as an enemy combatant.

Accordingly, the Attorney General is directed to surrender Mr. al-Marri to the Secretary of Defense, and the Secretary of Defense is directed to receive Mr. al-Marri from the Department of Justice and to detain him as an enemy combatant.

DATE:
White House Office-controlled Document

6/23/03

FILED *LR*

JUL - 8 2004

LARRY W. PROPES, CLERK
CHARLESTON, SC

UNITED STATES DISTRICT COURT
DISTRICT OF SOUTH CAROLINA

ALI SALEH KAHLAH AL-MARRI,
and MARK A. BERMAN, ESQ.,
as Next Friend,

Petitioner,

- vs -

C.T. HANFT, Commander, Naval
Consolidated Brig, ▆▆▆▆▆▆▆

Respondents.

Docket No.

2 04 2257 26AJ

PETITION FOR WRIT OF HABEAS CORPUS

Petitioner Ali Saleh Kahlah al-Marri, a civilian designated an "enemy combatant" by the President on June 23, 2003, is being held in military custody in Charleston, South Carolina without basis, without charge, without access to counsel, and without being afforded any process by which he might challenge his designation and detention, by color of the authority of the President, and in violation of the Constitution, laws, and treaties of the United States. Accordingly, this Court should issue a Writ of Habeas Corpus.

PARTIES

1.   Petitioner Ali Saleh Kahlah al-Marri, a citizen of the State of Qatar who was lawfully resident in the State of Illinois at the time of his initial detention by the government, is presently detained incommunicado at the Naval Consolidated Brig, Charleston, South Carolina, and has been so detained since June 23, 2003.

2.   Respondent C.T. Hanft, a commander in the United States Navy, is in command of the Naval Consolidated Brig, Charleston,

---

* Redactions on this page and in the signature block have been added for privacy purposes. – *Eds.*

South Carolina, and exercises immediate custody over Petitioner pursuant to orders issued by the President and the Secretary of Defense.

NEXT FRIEND

3.   Lawrence S. Lustberg and Mark A. Berman (collectively, "Counsel") are partners in the law firm of Gibbons, Del Deo, Dolan, Griffinger & Vecchione, P.C., One Riverfront Plaza, Newark, New Jersey. Counsel have represented Petitioner since on or about February 4, 2003.

4.   On that date, Counsel met with Petitioner in the Special Housing Unit ("SHU") at the Metropolitan Correctional Center, in New York City ("MCC-NY"). At that time, Petitioner was the only defendant named in two criminal indictments pending in the Southern District of New York.

5.   Counsel vigorously defended Petitioner in the Southern District of New York by successfully moving to consolidate, and then to dismiss, the Southern District of New York indictments, and by making other applications to the court regarding the conditions of Petitioner's confinement.

6.   During Petitioner's confinement in New York, Counsel met with him on numerous occasions at MCC-NY. Counsel also met with Petitioner numerous times in the courtroom, including once when court was not in session (as permitted by the court), or in the lockup attached to the courtroom, as well as several times in the Office of the United States Attorney for the Southern District of New York. Counsel spoke with Petitioner by telephone on a weekly basis after the court (upon Counsel's application) directed the guards at MCC-NY not to interfere with such telephone calls.

7.   During the course of many conversations, Petitioner and Counsel discussed a wide variety of topics and, thereby, developed

a substantial relationship. For example, Petitioner shared with Counsel his concerns regarding, among other matters, the welfare of his wife, children, and family members, as well as the discriminatory treatment to which he was subjected in prison.

8. Counsel also discussed with Petitioner the possibility that he might be designated an enemy combatant by President Bush. Specifically, on February 13, 2003, Counsel met with Petitioner's prior counsel, who voiced his concern that, if Petitioner did not agree to cooperate with the government, he might be designated an enemy combatant by the President, as had been the case with others.

9. Thereafter, Counsel and Petitioner discussed prior counsel's concern that the President might designate him an enemy combatant. Petitioner made clear that he intended to establish his innocence at trial.

10. On March 14, 2003, after meeting with Petitioner at MCC-NY, Counsel met with Assistant U.S. Attorney Michael G. McGovern, the lead prosecutor in the Southern District of New York. At that time, Counsel raised with AUSA McGovern the possibility that Petitioner might be designated an enemy combatant. AUSA McGovern stated that he had never threatened such a designation, which was beyond the scope of his authority, but that the case was being closely monitored by other officials in the Bush Administration.

11. On March 27, 2003, Counsel met with Petitioner and shared with him the substance of this conversation with AUSA McGovern, and specifically discussed the possibility that the President might one day designate Petitioner an enemy combatant. Counsel told Petitioner that, should such contingency come to pass, Counsel would challenge Petitioner's detention by filing a petition for a writ of habeas corpus in his behalf. Petitioner responded that he wished and, indeed, expected Counsel to do so.

12. On May 8, 2003, Petitioner and Counsel met at the U.S. Attorney's Office with then-Deputy U.S. Attorney David E. Kelley, who had requested an opportunity to speak with Petitioner personally before the government was required to respond to Petitioner's then-pending motion to dismiss the New York federal indictments on constitutional venue grounds. At that meeting, Mr. Kelley told Petitioner that one possible ramification of his insisting upon the dismissal of the New York federal indictments was that the already severe conditions of his confinement would be made even worse.

13. Counsel next met with Petitioner at MCC-NY on May 14, 2003, by which time the New York federal indictments had been dismissed, and Petitioner had been charged in a new criminal complaint in the Central District of Illinois. At that time, Counsel recounted to Petitioner Mr. Kelley's statement that the conditions of his confinement would become more severe, and reminded Petitioner that this could mean that the President might designate him an enemy combatant. Petitioner and Counsel again agreed that, in such event, Counsel would continue to act in Petitioner's behalf by pursuing all legal measures necessary to represent Petitioner's interests and to obtain his release.

14. Counsel continued to represent Petitioner after he was returned to, and re-indicted in, the Central District of Illinois, and has continued to represent him even after June 23, 2003, by filing a habeas petition in his behalf in the United States District Court for the Central District of Illinois, and litigating that petition to the United States Supreme Court.

15. Counsel last met with Petitioner on May 29, 2003, in the United States Marshal's lockup in the Federal Courthouse in Peoria.

Since that time, however, the government has denied Petitioner access to counsel.

16. Even if Petitioner had not shared his express wishes with Counsel, which he did, Counsel's relationship with Petitioner was sufficiently close that Counsel is certain that Petitioner would have expected Counsel to file the instant petition in his behalf both as counsel and as his next friend.

JURISDICTION

17. Petitioner brings this action under 28 U.S.C. § 2241 and invokes this Court's jurisdiction under 28 U.S.C. §§ 1331, 1651, 2201 and 2202, as well as Articles I and III of, and the Fifth and Sixth Amendments to, the Constitution of the United States.

VENUE

18. Venue is proper in the United States District Court for the District of South Carolina because Petitioner is confined at the Naval Consolidated Brig, in Charleston, South Carolina, which is under the command of Respondent. See Rumsfeld v. Padilla (No. 03-1027); al-Marri v. Rumsfeld, 360 F.3d 707, 708-09 (7th Cir. 2004).

STATEMENT OF FACTS

19. On September 10, 2001, Petitioner lawfully entered the United States, with his wife and five children, for the purpose of obtaining a master's degree from Bradley University in Illinois, the same institution from which he had earned a bachelor's degree in 1991.

20. On December 12, 2002, Petitioner was arrested by the Federal Bureau of Investigation ("FBI") in Peoria, Illinois, at the direction of the United States Attorney's Office for the Southern District of New York, as an alleged material witness in the

government's investigation of the terrorist attacks of September 11, 2001.

21. Thereafter, the government transported Petitioner from the Peoria County Jail to MCC-NY.

22. On February 6, 2002, the government charged Petitioner in a one-count indictment with possession of 15 or more unauthorized or counterfeit credit card numbers, with intent to defraud, in violation of 18 U.S.C. § 1029(a)(3). On February 8, 2002, Petitioner entered a plea of "not guilty" to this indictment and thereby asserted his innocence.

23. On January 22, 2003, Petitioner was charged in a second, six-count indictment with two counts of making a false statement to the FBI, in violation of 18 U.S.C. § 1001, three counts of making a false statement in a bank application, in violation of 18 U.S.C. § 1014, and one count of using a means of identification of another person for the purpose of influencing the action of a federally insured financial institution, in violation of 18 U.S.C. § 1028(a)(7). On January 24, 2003, Petitioner entered a plea of "not guilty" to this second indictment and thereby asserted his innocence.

24. On May 12, 2003, the United States District Court for the Southern District of New York granted a motion filed by Counsel in Petitioner's behalf to dismiss the indictments then pending in that district on venue grounds.

25. On or about May 20, 2003, Petitioner was removed from MCC-NY to the Peoria County Jail.

26. On May 22, 2003, a federal grand jury sitting in the Central District of Illinois returned a new indictment against Petitioner alleging the same seven counts as had been charged in

the dismissed Southern District of New York indictments. On May 29, 2003, Petitioner entered a plea of "not guilty" to this indictment and thereby asserted his innocence to the charges. The court set a July 21, 2003 trial date.

27. On Friday, June 20, 2003, the court directed the parties to be prepared to proceed with a suppression hearing on July 2, 2003, in connection with pretrial motions that Counsel had filed in Petitioner's behalf.

28. On Monday morning, June 23, 2003, the government moved <u>ex parte</u> to dismiss the indictment based upon a redacted declaration, signed by Respondent Bush which: i) designated Petitioner an enemy combatant; ii) directed the Attorney General to surrender Petitioner to the custody of the Secretary of Defense; iii) directed the Secretary of Defense to detain Petitioner as an enemy combatant. The court granted the government's motion, ultimately, entering an order dismissing the indictment with prejudice.

29. Petitioner was then removed from the custody of the United States Marshal's Service at the Peoria County Jail, into the custody of the Department of Defense at the Naval Consolidated Brig in Charleston, South Carolina.

30. Petitioner has been denied access to counsel since on or about May 29, 2003, despite repeated requests by Counsel to meet with him, all of which were ignored by the government. The last such request was made by Counsel in Petitioner's behalf on June 29, 2004, a day after the Supreme Court issued its decision in <u>Hamdi v. Rumsfeld</u>, 542 U.S. __, Slip Op. at 32 (2004) (holding that enemy combatant must be afforded access to counsel). The government has ignored that request, as well.

31. Petitioner is in fact a civilian, not a combatant. Indeed, he was treated as such by the government for over one year and a half prior to his designation as an enemy combatant by the President on June 23, 2003.

32. Since that date, Petitioner has been detained by the military without basis, without charge, without access to counsel, and without being afforded any process by which he can challenge his detention or his designation as an enemy combatant.

CLAIMS AS TO THE UNLAWFULNESS OF PETITIONER'S DETENTION

FIRST CLAIM

(Unlawful Detention)

33. Petitioner incorporates by reference all preceding paragraphs as if set forth fully herein.

34. Petitioner is a civilian, not a combatant, and disputes the factual allegations underlying the President's June 23, 2003 Order which designated him an "enemy combatant."

35. A civilian seized in the United States may not be detained by the military unless Congress has suspended the writ of habeas corpus, which it has not. See Ex Parte Milligan, 71 U.S. 2 (1866).

36. Therefore, the detention of Petitioner by the military is in violation of the Constitution and laws of the United States.

SECOND CLAIM

(Right To Counsel)

37. Petitioner incorporates by reference all preceding paragraphs as if set forth fully herein.

38. The Supreme Court has held that even an individual alleged by the government to have been captured on a foreign battlefield while bearing arms, and, thereafter, detained as an

enemy combatant, has the right to counsel and to challenge his designation. See Hamdi v. Rumsfeld, 542 U.S. __, Slip Op. at 32 (2004).

39. Neither the Constitution nor the laws of the United States allow the President or the military to detain an individual seized within the United States, and not on an active field of battle, without access to counsel, simply by designating such individual an enemy combatant.

40. Petitioner has the constitutional right to communicate freely with counsel, without government-imposed restrictions, and such communications are entitled to protection under the attorney-client privilege.

41. Therefore, the detention of Petitioner without unimpeded access to counsel is in violation of the Constitution and laws of the United States.

THIRD CLAIM

(Right To Be Charged)

42. Petitioner incorporates by reference all preceding paragraphs as if set forth fully herein.

43. Since June 23, 2003, Petitioner -- a civilian lawfully present in the United States at the time he was seized by the government -- has been detained by the military, upon Order of the President, without charge.

44. Absent suspension of the Writ of Habeas Corpus by Congress, the military may not detain an individual seized within the United States without charge.

45. Therefore, the detention of Petitioner without charge is in violation of the Constitution and laws of the United States.

FOURTH CLAIM

(Right To Process)

46.   Petitioner incorporates by reference all preceding paragraphs as if set forth fully herein.

47.   Since June 23, 2003, Petitioner has been detained by the military as an enemy combatant, upon Order of the President, at the Naval Consolidated Brig in Charleston, South Carolina.

48.   Petitioner denies that he is an enemy combatant.

49.   Petitioner has the right to receive "notice of the factual basis for his classification, and a fair opportunity to rebut the Government's assertions before a neutral decisionmaker." Hamdi, 542 U.S. at __, Slip Op. at 26.

50.   Petitioner has not been afforded any process by which he might challenge his designation by the President as an enemy combatant designation, or his continued detention by the military on that basis.

51.   Therefore, the detention of Petitioner without process is in violation of the Constitution and laws of the United States.

FIFTH CLAIM

(Interrogation)

52.   Petitioner incorporates by reference all preceding paragraphs as if set forth fully herein.

53.   Upon information and belief, Petitioner was designated an enemy combatant so that the government could interrogate him and Petitioner has in fact been interrogated by the government for over one year while incarcerated incommunicado at the Naval Consolidated Brig in Charleston, South Carolina.

54.   The United States Supreme Court has indicated that indefinite detention for the purpose of interrogation is unlawful. See Hamdi, 542 U.S. at __, Slip Op. at 13.

55.   Therefore, the indefinite detention and interrogation of Petitioner is in violation of the Constitution and laws of the United States.

PRAYER FOR RELIEF

WHEREFORE, Petitioner prays that the Court enter an Order:

1)   declaring that Petitioner is being held in violation of the Constitution, laws, and treaties of the United States;

2)   directing Respondent to allow Petitioner to meet and confer freely with Counsel, and to allow Counsel to transmit to Petitioner all documents related to their representation of him;

3)   directing Respondent to cease all interrogation of Petitioner while this litigation is pending;

4)   directing Respondent to charge Petitioner with a criminal offense or to release him;

5)   directing Respondent to: i) release Petitioner from custody; or ii) schedule a hearing at which Respondent is compelled to present evidence establishing that Petitioner is, in fact, an enemy combatant, and at which Petitioner is afforded an opportunity to challenge such designation with the assistance of counsel; and

6)   such other relief as the Court may deem just.

Respectfully submitted in behalf of
Petitioner Ali Saleh Kahlah al-Marri,

Lawrence S. Lustberg, Esq.
Mark A. Berman, Esq.
**GIBBONS, DEL DEO, DOLAN,
GRIFFINGER & VECCHIONE**
A Professional Corporation

Dated: July 7, 2004

. . .

IN THE UNITED STATES DISTRICT COURT
FOR THE DISTRICT OF SOUTH CAROLINA

Ali Saleh Kahlah Al-Marri, and)
Mark A. Berman as next friend)
)
    Petitioners)
)
v.)   C/A No. 02:04-2257-26AJ
)
Commander C.T. Hanft,)   Respondent's Answer to the
    U.S.N. Commander,)   Petition for Writ of Habeas Corpus
    Consolidated Naval Brig,)
)
    Respondent)
)

Respondent Commander C.T. Hanft, Commanding Officer of the Consolidated Naval Brig in Charleston, South Carolina, by and through undersigned counsel, respectfully submits this Answer to the petition for writ of habeas corpus pursuant to 28 U.S.C. 2241.

STATEMENT
. . .

3. On June 23, 2003, President Bush, invoking his constitutional authority as Commander in Chief as well as the authority granted to him by Congress through the Authorization for Use of Force, made a formal determination that petitioner "is, and at the time he entered the United States in September 2001 was, an enemy combatant." President's Order, ¶1.... That determination was the culmination of a thorough deliberative process in the Executive Branch involving several layers of review and evaluation by various agencies, including the Central Intelligence Agency (CIA), the Department of Defense (DoD), and the Department of Justice.... Through that careful evaluation process, the President specifically determined that petitioner "is closely associated with al Qaeda," id., ¶2, has "engaged in *** hostile and war-like acts" against the United States, id., ¶3, "possesses intelligence" about al Qaeda that "would aid U.S. efforts to prevent attacks by al Qaeda on the United States,"id., ¶4, and "represents a continuing, present, and grave danger to the national security" such that his detention is necessary to prevent him from aiding al Qaeda in its efforts to attack the United States," id., ¶5. The President thus directed the Secretary of Defense to "receive [petitioner] from the Department of Justice and detain him as an enemy combatant." Id. at 1.

Also on June 23, 2003, the district court dismissed the pending charges against petitioner with prejudice on motion of the government. 274 F. Supp.2d at 1004–1005. Petitioner was moved to the Naval Consolidated Brig in Charleston, South Carolina. Ibid.

4. On July 8, 2003, petitioner's counsel filed on petitioner's behalf a petition for a writ of habeas corpus in the Central District of Illinois. 273 F.Supp.2d at 1005. On July 16, 2003, the government filed a motion to dismiss that petition. On August 1, 2003,

the district court granted the government's motion on the ground that the petition had been filed in an improper venue. The district court found that the habeas petition should have been filed in this District – the district of al-Marri's present, physical confinement – rather than in the Central District of Illinois. On August 25, 2003, the district court denied a motion for reconsideration filed by petitioner.

5. The court of appeals unanimously affirmed. Al-Marri v. Bush, 360 F.3d 707 (7th Cir. 2004). On April 9, 2004, petitioner petitioned the Supreme Court of a writ of certiorari; that petition remains pending before the Court.[1]

6. On July 8, 2004, petitioner filed a petition for a writ of habeas corpus in this Court.....

ARGUMENT

Petitioner is properly detained as an enemy combatant. The President, after an elaborate and careful evaluation process involving multiple layers of review from various Executive Branch agencies . . . made an individualized determination that al-Marri is an enemy combatant who is "closely associated with al-Qaeda" and has "engaged in *** hostile and war-like acts" against the United States on behalf of al-Qaeda.[2] See President's Order, ¶1. Contrary to petitioner's principal claim that the government has no authority to hold him without filing criminal charges, Pet. 11, ¶¶42–45, the Executive Branch powers implicated by this case are not the President's law-enforcement powers, but his congressionally authorized and constitutionally-based war powers.

The authority to capture and hold enemy combatants for the duration of the conflict, without charges, for the purposes of incapacitation and protecting the nation's security is part and parcel of the war power.[3] That proposition was recognized by the Supreme Court in Ex Parte Quirin and was reaffirmed by the Supreme Court just this year in Hamdi v. Rumsfeld, 124 S.Ct. 2633 (2004) (plurality). Id. at 2639–2643 (plurality) (reaffirming Quirin); id. at 2682–2683 (Thomas, J., dissenting) (same).[4] . . . .

. . .

---

[1] . . .

[2] The Supreme Court has recently noted that "[t]he permissible bounds of the [enemy-combatant] category will be defined by the lower courts as subsequent cases are presented to them." Hamdi v. Rumsfeld, 124 S. Ct. 2633, 2642 n.1 (2004) (plurality). For the purposes of this case, an enemy combatant can be considered a person who "has become a member or associated himself with hostile enemy forces" and has entered the Country bent on hostile acts. Detention of Enemy Combatants in the War of Terrorism, 150 Cong. Rec. S2701, S2704 (March 11, 2004) (remarks by Alberto R. Gonzales, Counsel to the President, to the American Bar Association, Standing Committee on Law and National Security); see also Ex parte Quirin 317 U.S. 1, 37–38 (1942) ("Citizens who associate themselves with the military arm of the enemy government, and with its aid, guidance and direction enter this country bent on hostile acts are enemy belligerents within the meaning of *** the law of war.")

[3] The proposition that enemy combatants may be held for the duration of armed hostilities is as old as recorded history. For example, the ancient Greek historian Thucydides notes that in 425 b.c. after the battle of Pylos during the Peloponnesian War, "the Athenians determined to keep [the captured Spartan combatants] in prison until the peace." Robert B. Strassler, The Landmark Thucydides: A Comprehensive Guide To The Peloponnesian War, 244, ch. 4.41 (Richard Crawley trans., 1998).

[4] Justice O'Connor's plurality opinion in Hamdi is controlling in that Justice Thomas differed with the plurality on grounds that were more deferential to the President than the plurality's. 124 S.Ct. at 2674–2685 (Thomas, J., dissenting).

I.   **Petitioner Is Lawfully Detained As An Enemy Combatant.**

. . .

  A.   **The Military's Detention of Enemy Combatants During Wartime Serves Critical National-Security Objectives.**

. . .

When an enemy combatant is lawfully detained by the military, detention may serve another objective, namely, allowing our armed forces to gather military intelligence. It is widely recognized that lawfully detained enemy combatants maybe interrogated by the military to obtain vital information to further the war effort. See L. Oppenheim, International Law 368–369 (H. Lauterpachted., 7th ed. 1952); see also Hamdi, 296 F.3d at 282 (overturning district court order allowing counsel unmonitored access to citizen enemy combatant, noting that the district court failed to consider "what effect petitioner's unmonitored access to counsel might have upon the government's ongoing gathering of intelligence"); see generally W. Winthrop, [Military Law and Precedents] 788 [(rev. 2d ed. 1920)].

  B.   **The President's Actions are Authorized by the Constitution, Congress, and Supreme Court Precedent.**

. . .

Petitioner suggests that because he was initially detained within the United States, the military does not have authority to continue to detain him. Pet. 11, ¶44. That argument is meritless. The fact that petitioner was taken into custody in the United States in now way takes him outside the scope of Congress's authorization to use force. In the Authorization for Use of Force itself, moreover, Congress observed that al-Qaeda and its supporters "continue to pose an unusual and extraordinary threat to the national security," and Congress specifically expressed that it was "necessary and appropriate that the United States exercise its rights *** to protect United States citizens both at home and abroad." Preamble, 115 Stat. 224 (emphasis added). Nor, in light of the nature of the September 11 attacks, can it be seriously argued that Congress in authorizing the use of force was less concerned about protecting the United States from attack than about rooting out terrorism abroad. The September 11 hijackers themselves were alien enemy combatants secreted within the United States when they murdered over 3,000 people. Thus, there can be no serious claim that Congress intended the Authorization for Use of Force, which was enacted as a direct response to the September 11 attacks, to authorize the detention of citizen enemy combatants captured abroad but not individuals identically situated to the perpetrators of the September 11 attacks – i.e., alien enemy combatants found in the United States. See Reyes v. Ernst & Young, 494 U.S. 56, 63 (1990) (a statute "must be understood against the backdrop of what Congress was attempting to accomplish in enacting" it).

. . .

  C.   **Deference To The President's Determination That Petitioner Is An Enemy Combatant Is Constitutionally Required.**

. . .

The Supreme Court's cautionary admonitions are especially apt in a case such as this where the President has made a wartime determination that a non-citizen should be detained by the military as an enemy combatant. In fact, the President's authority as Commander in Chief to detain an enemy combatant is particularly clear, the detainee's entitlement to intrusive judicial review of the President's determination is more questionable, and the judiciary's need to defer to the President's authority is correspondingly great, where the detainee, as here, is an alien enemy. Indeed, deference is particularly appropriate to the President's handling of alien enemy combatants, because in dealing with alien enemies the President acts "not only as Commander-in-Chief but also the guiding organ in the conduct of our foreign affairs. He who was entrusted with such vast powers in relation to the outside world was also entrusted by Congress, almost throughout the whole life of the nation, with the disposition of alien enemies during a state of war." Ludecke, 335 U.S. at 173. As the Supreme Court explained in Eisentrager, "Executive power over enemy aliens *** has been deemed throughout our history, essential to war-time security." 339 U.S. at 774. Although the Alien Enemy Act, 50 U.S.C. 21, which was at issue in Ludecke and discussed in Eisentrager, does not have direct application to this case, the Eisentrager Court stressed that during wartime aliens, whether or not resident in the United States, are "constitutionally" subject to different treatment than citizens. 339 U.S. at 775. The Eisentrager Court additionally noted that "[a]t common law alien enemies have no rights, no privileges, unless by the king's special favour, during the time of war." 339 U.S. at 774 n.6 (citation and internal quotation marks omitted); cf. Hamdi, 124 S. Ct. at 2663 ("[A] plurality of this Court, asserts that captured enemy combatants (other than those suspected of war crimes) have traditionally been detained until the cessation of hostilities and then released. That is probably an accurate description of wartime practice with respect to enemy aliens.") (Scalia, J., dissenting) (citation omitted). The extent to which alien enemy combatants have less legal protections than citizens enemy combatants is strongly illustrated by the fact that none of the concurring or dissenting opinions in Hamdi would preclude the detention of alien enemy combatants.[12]

. . .

D. The Evidence Underlying the President's Designation of Petitioner as an Enemy Combatant Amply Supports that Determination.

The President correctly designated petitioner an enemy combatant. As the accompanying declaration demonstrates, that designation is fully supported by the evidence and is predicated on an elaborate and careful set of evaluation procedures that were applied to petitioner's case.

The Executive Branch evaluation process that petitioner underwent was essentially the same as that for United States citizens suspected of being enemy combatants. See generally 150 Cong. Rec. S2701, S2703–S2704 (daily ed. March 11, 2004) (reprinting Feb. 24, 2004, remarks of Alberto R. Gonzales, Counsel to the President, before the American Bar Association's Standing Committee on Law and National Security); Rapp Decl. ¶6. Under the process, following an initial assessment that a detainee is an enemy combatant, the Director of Central Intelligence forwards to DoD a recommendation concerning whether DoD should take the detainee into custody. The Director's recommendation includes a written assessment of the intelligence available concerning the detainee. The Secretary of Defense then produces a second written assessment based

---

[12] In this connection, petitioner repeatedly relies on the plurality's description of the procedural rights of citizen detainees in Hamdi to challenge his detention as an enemy combatant, see Pet. ¶¶38, 49, 54, but that reliance is misplaced. The Hamdi plurality takes pains to clarify that its holding concerns only citizen detainees. See, e.g., 124 S.Ct. at 2635, 2648, 2651; accord id. at 2672 ("Several limitations give my views in this matter a relatively narrow compass. They apply only to citizens, accused of being enemy combatants, who are detained within the territorial jurisdiction of a federal court.") (Scalia, J., dissenting).

on the CIA's information and intelligence developed by DoD, and forwards that assessment (accompanied by the CIA and DoD reports) to the Attorney General. The Attorney General, in turn, provides DoD with a recommendation concerning whether the detainee should be taken into custody as an enemy combatant, as well as a legal opinion concerning the propriety of such an action. In addition to the CIA and DoD reports, the Attorney General's recommendation is informed by a memorandum from the Department of Justice's Criminal Division setting forth factual information concerning the detainee supplied by the FBI and a formal legal opinion from the Department's Office of Legal Counsel (OLC) analyzing whether petitioner is appropriately designated an enemy combatant. The Secretary forwards to the President a package containing all of the forgoing material. Upon receipt of the Secretary's package by the White House, it is further reviewed by White House counsel, who provides the entire set of materials (including his own assessment) to the President.

Having reviewed the materials and information generated by this process, on June 23, 2003, the President determined that petitioner was an enemy combatant. Among the findings made by the President concerning petitioner are that petitioner is "closely associated with al Qaeda"; engaged in conduct that constituted hostile and war-like acts, including conduct in preparation for acts of international terrorism that had the aim to cause injury to or adverse effects on the United States; "possesses intelligence, including intelligence about personnel and activities of al Qaeda that, if communicated to the U. S., would aid U.S. efforts to prevent attacks by al Qaeda ***"; and "represents a continuing, present, and grave danger to the national security of the United States" whose "detention is necessary to prevent him from aiding al Qaeda in its efforts to attack the United States." President's Order, ¶5.

The evidence underlying the President's findings is more than ample. The factual basis for petitioners continued detention as an enemy combatant is elaborated in the attached declaration, which make clear that petitioner is "part of or associated with the armed forces of" al Qaeda. Quirin, 317 U.S. at 45.

The declaration shows, for example, that petitioner met with al-Qaeda members, including Osama Bin Laden, and offered to be a martyr in al-Qaeda's war against the United States and its allies; that he received training in al-Qaeda terrorist camps, including poisons training; that he was tasked by al-Qaeda with entering the United States prior to the September 11 attacks to serve as a sleeper agent to facilitate terrorist operations and future attacks against the United States that would follow on the September 11 attacks; and that he accepted those tasks and took numerous actions, including obtaining false identities and credit card information to assist other al-Qaeda sleeper agents within the United States and researching poisonous chemicals and information about the location and capacity of water reservoirs within the United States. As the declaration demonstrates, moreover, this information about petitioner and his relationship with and activities on behalf of al-Qaeda has been obtained from and corroborated by multiple intelligence sources.

In sum, as the declaration makes clear, petitioner's conduct, and the President's findings based on that conduct, establish that petitioner is an enemy combatant subject to detention by the military to ensure that petitioner does not continue engaging in hostile and war-like acts against the United States and its allies while hostilities against al-Qaeda remain ongoing. For the reasons set forth herein, that detention is consistent with the Constitution, Congress's Authorization for Use of Force, the laws of war, and the Supreme Court's decisions in Hamdi and Quirin.

II.   Petitioner's Remaining Claims Do Not Merit Relief.

In addition to challenging the legality of his detention, see Pet. 9–10,¶¶33–36; id. at 11, ¶¶42–45, petitioner also challenges certain conditions of his confinement. Regarding his second claim for relief, Pet. 10–11, ¶¶37–41, petitioner prays for an order "allow[ing] Petitioner to meet and confer freely with counsel *** ," id. at 13, ¶2. Petitioner's fourth claim for relief states that he "has the right to receive 'notice of the factual basis of for his classification, and a fair opportunity to rebut the Government's assertions before a neutral decisionmaker.'" Id. at 12, ¶49 (quoting Hamdi, 124 S.Ct. at 2648). Petitioner thus prays for an order "directing Respondent to: i) release Petition from custody; or ii) schedule [an evidentiary] hearing." Pet. 13, ¶5. Finally, with regard to his fifth claim for relief, petitioner prays for an order "directing Respondent to cease all interrogation of Petitioner while this litigation is pending." Id. at 13,¶3; see id. at 12, ¶¶52–55.

These claims do not warrant relief. First, petitioner's access-to-counsel claims are moot in view of the fact that the military has in fact granted him access to counsel. This Court found as much in its August 4, 2004 Oral Order concerning petitioner's July 19, 2004 motion for immediate access to counsel. While there remains the potential for disputes about the conditions of access to counsel, any possible further issues concerning counsel access, such as government monitoring of counsel-client interactions, are not ripe for review at this time. . . . .

. . .

Finally, petitioner's prayer for an order "directing Respondent to cease all interrogation of Petitioner while this litigation is pending," id. at 13,¶3, is not ripe as the military is not currently interrogating him. More importantly, as explained above, interrogation of detained enemy combatants is recognized as permissible under the laws of war. See supra at 8. . . . Nothing in Hamdi suggests that a validly detained enemy alien during wartime cannot be questioned, and petitioner cites no authority whatever suggesting that it is unlawful to interrogate such persons to obtain vital military intelligence.[16]

CONCLUSION

The petition should be denied.

Respectfully submitted,

> J. STROM THURMOND, JR.
> United States Attorney
> District of South Carolina
>
> DAVID B. SALMONS
> Assistant to the Solicitor General

---

[16] Petitioner characterizes his detention as "indefinite." Pet. 12, ¶¶54–55. But the detention of enemy combatants during World War II was just as "indefinite" while that war was being waged. Given the unconventional nature of the current conflict, it is unlikely to end with a formal cease-fire agreement, but that does not mean that petitioner will not be released. The military has no intention of holding captured enemy combatants any longer than is necessary in the interests of national security, and it has already released scores of enemy combatants. In any event, the plurality in Hamdi found just a few months ago that the issue of the indefiniteness of the detention is premature while combat operations are ongoing. 124 S.Ct. at 2641–2642, see ibid. (upholding military detention of enemy combatants without charges "for the duration of the relevant conflict"). Petitioner does not and cannot dispute that the United States is currently engaged in active military operations against al Qaeda. See, e.g.,http://www.cnn.com/2004/WORLD/asiapcf/03/19/Pakistan.alqaeda/ ("Battle Rages With Al Qaeda Fighters") (May 6, 2004) (reporting that U.S. assisting Pakistan in meeting armed resistence of al Qaeda fighters along Afghan border).

JOHN A. DRENNAN
    Attorney, Criminal Division,
    Department of Justice

MILLER SHEALY
    Assistant United States Attorney
    District of South Carolina
    . . .

. . .

ATTACHMENT B

Unclassified Declaration of Mr. Jeffrey N. Rapp
Director, Joint Intelligence Task Force for Combating Terrorism

Pursuant to 28 U.S.C. § 1746, I, Jeffrey N. Rapp, hereby declare that, to the best of my knowledge, information and belief, and under the penalty of perjury, the following is true and correct:

Preamble

1. I submit this Declaration for the Court's consideration in the matter of Al-Marri v. Hanft, Case Number 2:04-2257-26AJ, pending in the United States District Court for the District of South Carolina.

2. Based on the information that I have acquired in the course of my official duties, I am familiar with all the matters discussed in this Declaration. I am also familiar with the interviews of Ali Saleh Mohamed Kahlah Al-Marri (Al-Marri) conducted by agents of the Federal Bureau of Investigation and by personnel of the Department of Defense (DoD) once DoD took custody of Al-Marri on 23 June 2003 after he was declared an enemy combatant by the President of the United States.

Professional Experience as an Intelligence Officer

3. I am a career Defense Intelligence Agency Defense Intelligence Senior Executive Service member appointed by the Director of the Defense Intelligence Agency. I report to the Director of the Defense Intelligence Agency. My current assignment is as the Director of the Joint Intelligence Task Force for Combating Terrorism (JITF-CT). JITF-CT directs collection, exploitation, analysis, fusion, and dissemination of the all-source foreign terrorism intelligence effort within DoD. In addition to my current assignment, I have previously served as the first Director of the National Media Exploitation Center and as the civilian Deputy Director for the Iraq Survey Group in Qatar.

4. My active duty military intelligence career in the United States Army included service as the senior intelligence officer for the 1st Infantry Division, when deployed to Bosnia-Herzegovina; Commander of the 101st Military Intelligence Battalion, 1st Infantry Division, Fort Riley Kansas; Commander of the forward-deployed 205th Military Intelligence Brigade in Europe; and Deputy Director for the Battle Command Battle Lab, U.S. Army Intelligence Center at Fort Huachuca, Arizona. I also directed a South Asia regional analytic division in the Defense Intelligence Agency Directorate for Analysis and Production that was awarded the National Intelligence Meritorious Unit Citation for its accomplishments.

5. My military decorations include the Legion of Merit, Defense Superior Service Medal, Defense Meritorious Service Medal, and Army Meritorious Service Medal. I am a graduate of the U.S. Army War College. I hold a Masters degree in strategic intelligence from the Joint Military Intelligence College.

Declaration of Al-Marri as an Enemy Combatant

6. On June 23, 2003, President George W. Bush determined that Al-Marri is an enemy combatant. The President's determination was based on information derived from several Executive Branch agencies in a multi-layered Executive Branch evaluation. The evaluation process applied to Al-Marri is essentially the same as that for United States citizens suspected of being enemy combatants. See generally 150 Cong. Rec. S2701, S2703-S2704 (daily ed. March 11, 2004) (reprinting Feb. 24, 2004, remarks of Alberto R. Gonzales, Counsel to the President, before the American Bar Association's Standing Committee on Law and National Security). As a general matter, the process involves assessments by the following agencies: Central Intelligence Agency, Department of Defense, Department of Justice, and the White House. First, following an initial assessment that a detainee might be an enemy combatant, the Director of Central

Intelligence makes a written recommendation to DoD concerning whether DoD should take the detainee into custody. The Secretary of Defense then makes a second written assessment based on the CIA's report and intelligence developed by DoD, and provides that assessment (accompanied by the CIA and DoD reports) to the Attorney General. The Attorney General, in turn, provides DoD with a recommendation concerning whether the detainee should be taken into custody as an enemy combatant, as well as an opinion concerning the lawfulness of such an action. The Attorney General's recommendation is informed by the CIA and DoD reports as well as a memorandum from the Department of Justice's Criminal Division setting forth factual information concerning the detainee supplied by the FBI, and a formal legal opinion from the Department's Office of Legal Counsel (OLC) analyzing whether petitioner is appropriately designated an enemy combatant. The Attorney General's recommendation package to the Secretary includes the Criminal Division's fact memorandum and OLC's legal opinion. The Secretary forwards to the President a package containing all of the foregoing material. White House counsel reviews the package, makes his own assessment, and provides the materials (including his own assessment) to the President. The President then determines on the basis of the foregoing whether the detainee is an enemy combatant.

Overview

7. Al-Marri, also known as Abdulkareem A. Almuslam, is currently being detained in the Naval Consolidated Brig in Charleston, South Carolina. The President of the United States has determined that he is an enemy combatant that is closely associated with al Qaeda, an international terrorist organization with which the United States is at war, and that he has engaged in hostile and war-like acts against the United States. Multiple intelligence sources confirm that Al-Marri is an al Qaeda "sleeper" agent sent to the United States for the purpose of engaging in and facilitating terrorist activities subsequent

to September 11, 2001, and exploring ways to hack into the computer systems of U.S.
banks and otherwise disrupt the U.S. financial system. Prior to arriving in the United
States on September 10, 2001, Al-Marri was trained at an al Qaeda terror camp. He met
personally with Usama Bin Laden (Bin Laden) and other known al Qaeda members and
volunteered for a martyr mission or to do anything else that al Qaeda requested. Al-Marri
was assisted in his al Qaeda assignment to the United States by known al Qaeda members
and traveled to the United States with money provided for him by al Qaeda. Al-Marri
currently possesses information of high intelligence value, including information about
personnel and activities of Al Qaeda.

Al-Marri's Background and Training

8. Al-Marri is a dual national of Saudi Arabia and Qatar. Al-Marri attended college in
the United States; in 1991, he obtained a bachelor's degree in business administration
from Bradley University in Peoria, Illinois.

9. Multiple sources have confirmed that Al-Marri attended an al Qaeda terror training
camp.

10. Al-Marri entered the United States with his family on September 10, 2001,
purportedly to pursue a graduate degree in computer science at Bradley University.
School officials at Bradley reported that Al-Marri contacted them in July 2001 about
beginning his studies during the Fall 2001 semester. By mid-December 2001 he had
rarely attended classes and was in failing status.

Al-Marri's al Qaeda Activities

Analysis of Laptop Computer

11. The FBI interviewed Al-Marri on October 2, 2001, and again on December 11, 2001.
Subsequent to the second of these interviews, the FBI conducted a forensic examination

of Al-Marri's laptop computer. The results of that examination are discussed by category

below.

Chemical Research

12. Al-Marri was trained by al Qaeda in the use of poisons. In the hard drive of Al-

Marri's laptop, FBI agents discovered a folder entitled "chem," which contained

bookmarked Internet sites of industrial chemical distributors. Analysis revealed that Al-

Marri had visited a number of sites related to the manufacture, use and procurement of

hydrogen cyanide.

Communication Tactics

13. On September 22, 2001, five email accounts, which Al-Marri later stated belonged to

him, were created from the same computer during one log-on session. The computer on

which these email accounts were created was part of the network operated by Western

Illinois University in Macomb, Illinois.

14. Among the messages located in three of these email accounts were identical draft

messages written in English on September 22, 2001, which read as follows, with all

errors as in the originals:

> "hi
>
>> I hope every thing is ok with you and your family. I have started school
>> ok. It is hard but I had to take 9 hours to meet the school standard. Me
>> and my family are ok. I want to here from you soon can you contact me
>> by email or on 701-879-6040.
>> P.S.
>> I have tried to contact you at your uncle ottowa but I could not get in."

15. In the United States, the area code 701 is assigned to North Dakota. However,

subscriber checks for telephone number 701-879-6040 were negative. Upon further

analysis, it was determined that telephone number 701-879-6040 is a coded message.

Additional Computer Files

16. Analysis of Al-Marri's laptop revealed computer files containing Arabic lectures by Bin Laden and his associates on the importance of jihad and martyrdom, and the merits of the Taliban regime in Afghanistan. These lectures instructed that Muslim scholars should organize opposition to Jewish and Christian control of Palestine, Lebanon, and Saudi Arabia; that ordinary Muslims should train in Bin Laden camps in Afghanistan by entering through Pakistan; and that clerics who claim that Islam is a religion of peace should be disregarded. There were also computer files containing lists of websites titled "Jihad arena," "Taliban," "Arab's new club - Jihad club," "Tunes by bullets," and "martyrs." Other computer folders contained additional favorite bookmarked websites, including sites related to weaponry and satellite equipment.

17. Photographs of the September 11, 2001 terrorist attacks on the World Trade Center were also discovered on the computer along with various photographs of Arab prisoners of war held by authorities in Kabul, Afghanistan; an animated cartoon of an airplane flying at the World Trade Center; and a map of Afghanistan.

18. In addition, Al-Marri's laptop computer contained numerous computer programs typically utilized by computer hackers; "proxy" computer software which can be utilized to hide a user's origin or identity when connected to the internet; and bookmarked lists of favorite websites apparently devoted to computer hacking.

Telephone Communications

19. After the terrorist attacks of September 11, 2001, calling cards attributed to Al-Marri were utilized in attempts to contact the United Arab Emirates (UAE) telephone number of an al Qaeda financier, Mustafa Ahmed Al-Hawsawi (the "Al-Hawsawi number"). Analysis of Al-Marri's cellular telephone records indicated that Al-Marri utilized cell sites during some of the same times and in the same geographical areas, as the attempted calls to the Al-Hawsawi number.

20. On September 23, 2001, a telephone call was attempted from a pay telephone in a store in Peoria, Illinois to the Al-Hawsawi number. The calling card used for that call was used again four days later, on September 27, 2001, from a cellular telephone subscribed to by Al-Marri. Thereafter, on October 14, 2001 the same calling card was used again from a pay telephone in a gas station in Springfield, Illinois (approximately sixty-five miles from Peoria) to the Al-Hawsawi number. During the same time period and on the same day, Al-Marri's cellular telephone utilized cell sites in Springfield, and Lincoln (approximately 20 miles north of Springfield), Illinois.

21. Approximately three weeks later, on November 4, 2001, a different calling card was used from a pay telephone in Chicago, Illinois to attempt a call to the Al-Hawsawi number. On the same day, Al-Marri's telephone records indicate that Al-Marri's cellular telephone utilized sites in Chicago to access its voicemail system and to call Al-Marri's home telephone number. The calling card used on November 4, 2001, was then used again three days later to place a call from Al-Marri's home telephone number.

Credit Card Theft

22. Upon the seizure of his laptop computer, Al-Marri provided the computer carrying case to the FBI. Inside the case, agents found a folded two-page handwritten document that listed approximately thirty-six credit card numbers, the names of the account holders, an indication as to whether each credit card number was Visa or Mastercard, and the expiration dates. The expiration dates on the list reflected past expiration dates for each of the cards. Al-Marri was not listed as the account holder for any of the approximately thirty-six cards. Approximately seventeen of the thirty-six credit card numbers were issued by domestic banks. Based on the records of the issuing domestic banks, the credit card numbers were either currently valid or were once valid and were issued to persons other than Al-Marri.

23. During the previously mentioned forensic examination of Al-Marri's laptop computer, computer files containing over 1,000 apparent credit card numbers were found stored in various computer files. The examination of Al-Marri's laptop computer also revealed computer folders called "hack," "id," "crack," "final," and "online store," among others. These computer folders contained a list of numerous favorite bookmarked internet websites relating to computer hacking; fake driver's licenses and other fake identification cards; buying and selling credit card numbers; and processing credit card transactions. When agents visited an internet website that was bookmarked in the "hack" folder of Al-Marri's laptop computer, the internet website appeared to be an electronic bulletin board that allows internet users to post and advertise messages. Topics advertised on this website included: "sale CC," "I buy cc (with exp. data not less than 2003)"; "I will buy credit Card"; "I sell new creditcard (Visa, maser, expres. . .)"; "Credit card for sae. 0.3 $/1cc w/o CVV"; and "I sell #cc without cvv2." As a result of the information discovered within Al-Marri's laptop computer and carrying case, the material witness warrant was vacated and Al-Marri was immediately taken into custody pursuant to a charge of unauthorized possession of credit card numbers with intent to defraud, in violation of 18 USC §1029(a)(3). In February 2002, Al-Marri was indicted on this charge in the SDNY.

Analysis of Credit Card Numbers

24. Fraudulent purchases at "AAA Carpet" were identified on several of the credit card numbers that were in Al-Marri's possession. "AAA Carpet" has been determined to be a fraudulent business for which an individual named Abdulkareem A. Almuslam opened bank accounts in Macomb, Illinois, in July and August 2000. Signature cards and account applications from the three banks in Macomb, Illinois, at which Almuslam

opened accounts have significant similarities to the signatures of Al-Marri on his passport and other documents. In addition, an eye doctor in the area identified Al-Marri in a photographic array as a patient the doctor treated under the name Almuslam. Latent print analysis of original documents from the banks and the eye doctor's office has resulted in three positive fingerprint identifications of Al-Marri. During this time period, Al-Marri, aka Almuslam, also opened an account to process credit card transactions for AAA Carpet; records for this account indicate that twelve credit cards were processed for AAA Carpet during the time the account was active. All twelve transactions were later voided after the true cardholders notified their credit card providers of the fraudulent charges. Investigation to date has confirmed six of the twelve credit cards that received charges to AAA Carpet were found within Al-Marri's laptop computer. Al-Marri, aka Almuslam, also created an account on June 13, 2000 with PayPal.com, an internet service that allows the electronic transfer of funds to anyone who possesses an email account.

25. As a result of the above investigation, a second indictment was filed in SDNY on January 22, 2003 against Al-Marri alleging two counts of making false statements to federal agents for denying his calls to the UAE telephone number of Al-Hawsawi and for not advising of his travel to the United States in 2000, in violation of 18 USC §1001(a)(1) and (2); three counts of making false statements to a financial institution for opening bank accounts under a false name, in violation of 18 USC §1014; and one count of using a means of identification of another person for unauthorized use of a social security account number to open a bank account, in violation of 18 USC §1028(a)(7). The two indictments against Al-Marri were subsequently consolidated. In April 2003, Al-Marri withdrew his waiver of venue, which allowed him to be tried in the SDNY; he was then indicted on May 22, 2003 in the Central District of Illinois on the same seven charges.

Conclusion

26. In conclusion, investigation has determined that Al-Marri was an active al Qaeda operative at the time of his entry into the United States on September 10, 2001. Al-Marri was sent to the United States at the behest of al Qaeda. Upon his arrival in the United States, Al-Marri engaged in conduct in preparation for acts of international terrorism intended to cause injury or adverse effects on the United States. Al-Marri's status has been subject to a rigorous review process and it has been determined that Al-Marri represents a continuing grave danger to the national security of the United States. Al-Marri must be detained to prevent him from aiding al Qaeda in its efforts to attack the United States, its armed forces, other governmental personnel, or citizens.

Jeffrey N. Rapp
Director, Joint Intelligence Task
Force for Combating Terrorism

Executed on _9_ September 2004 in
Washington, D.C.

IN THE UNITED STATES DISTRICT COURT
FOR THE DISTRICT OF SOUTH CAROLINA

Ali Saleh Kahlah Al-Marri, and	)	
Mark A. Berman as next friend,	)	
	)	
Petitioners,	)	
	)	C/A No. 02:04-2257-26AJ
v.	)	
	)	Petitioners' Reply (Traverse) to
Commander C.T. Hanft,	)	Respondent's Answer to the Petition
U.S.N. Commander,	)	for Writ of Habeas Corpus
Consolidated Naval Brig,	)	
	)	
Respondent.	)	
	)	

Petitioner Ali Saleh Kahlah Al-Marri, by and through undersigned counsel, respectfully submits this Reply (Traverse) to Respondent Commander C.T. Hanft's Answer to the petition for writ of habeas corpus. Petitioner denies the factual assertions underlying his classification as an "enemy combatant" and maintains that he is an innocent civilian unlawfully detained in violation of the Constitution and laws of the United States.

PRELIMINARY STATEMENT AND TRAVERSE

Petitioner Ali Saleh Kahlah al-Marri was lawfully residing with his family in Peoria, Illinois, when, on December 12, 2001, the FBI arrested him as an alleged material witness in its investigation of the terrorist attacks of September 11, 2001. He was subsequently indicted on criminal charges, including possession of unauthorized or counterfeit credit card numbers, with intent to defraud, and making false statements to the FBI and in a bank application. For sixteen months, his case proceeded through the criminal justice system. Then, on June 23, 2003, shortly before his trial date, and with the district court poised to conduct a suppression hearing in connection with pre-trial motions counsel had filed on Mr. al-Marri's behalf, the government moved to dismiss the indictments based upon a redacted "declaration" by President Bush, designating Mr. al-Marri an "enemy combatant" and directing the Secretary of Defense to detain him. Pursuant to the President's order, Mr. al-Marri was transferred from the custody of the United States Marshal's Service to the custody of the Department of Defense at the Naval Consolidated Brig outside of Charleston, South Carolina, where he was interrogated without access to counsel, and where he remains to this day in solitary confinement.

This Court, at the current time, is considering the case of *Padilla v. Hanft*, C/A No. 02:04-2221-26AJ, which involves the only other individual presently detained in the United States by the military as an "enemy combatant." It is, of course, aware of the Supreme Court's consideration last Term of *Hamdi v. Rumsfeld*, 124 S. Ct. 2633 (2004), which also involved an "enemy combatant" captured overseas but detained by the military in the United States. Although Mr. al-Marri is not a U.S. citizen, his case presents as serious a threat to individual liberty, the separation of powers, and the rule of law as do those other "enemy combatant" cases. Unlike Padilla, Mr. al-Marri was not arrested while trying to enter the United States; unlike Hamdi, he was not captured on a foreign battlefield or while engaged in armed combat. Instead, he was lawfully present in the United States, living in Peoria, Illinois, and was designated an "enemy combatant" by the President while in the midst of a criminal proceeding in which he had pled his innocence. His potentially lifelong military confinement is now premised solely upon the hearsay declaration of a Department of Defense functionary, which is itself based upon purported statements from a single witness, whose identity and whereabouts have been classified by the government, who has never been subject to cross-examination in a court of law, and who is widely believed to have been tortured while in custody. Mr. al-Marri, detained in the United States and protected by the U.S. Constitution, has been afforded even *less* process than individuals seized on a foreign battlefield and detained at Guantanamo Bay, Cuba. His continued military detention without charges represents an unprecedented erosion of the most basic guarantees afforded to those inside the United States, citizen and non-citizen alike.

Even assuming *arguendo* that the allegations against Mr. al-Marri are true, the President lacks the authority to detain him as an "enemy combatant," as the military clearly intends to do until a court directs otherwise; therefore, the government must charge him, or release him forthwith. Alternatively, Mr. al-Marri is entitled to a fair opportunity to rebut the factual assertions on which his classification as an "enemy combatant" is based and to an evidentiary hearing conducted consistent with the fundamental requirements of due process, including, most importantly, the right to confront and cross-examine the witnesses against him. Anything less would make his right to due process illusory.

I.   PETITIONER IS UNLAWFULLY DETAINED AS AN "ENEMY COMBATANT"

The government argues that the President has properly detained Petitioner al-Marri as an "enemy combatant" pursuant to the Authorization for Use of Military Force ("AUMF"), Pub. L. No. 107-40, 115 Stat. 224 (Sept. 18, 2001), and his inherent authority as commander-in-chief under Article II of the United States Constitution. For purposes of *this case*, the government defines an "enemy combatant" as "a person who 'has become a member or associated himself with hostile enemy forces' and has entered the Country bent on hostile acts." Answer at 5 n.2. This definition is taken from neither statute nor caselaw but, rather, remarks made to the American Bar Association by then-White House Counsel and now-Attorney General Alberto R. Gonzales. *See* Detention of Enemy Combatants in the War on Terror, 150 Cong. Rec. S2701, S2704 (Mar. 11, 2004) (remarks by Alberto R. Gonzales, Counsel to the President, to the American Bar Association, Standing Committee on Law and National Security).[1] And, to justify the President's actions, the government relies on a handful of wartime precedents which it rips from their original context and twists beyond all recognition. Indeed, the government can

---

[1] The government's definition of "enemy combatant" has repeatedly changed to accommodate its immediate purposes, and to justify executive detention on an ad hoc basis, *Hamdi v. Rumsfeld*, _U.S. _, 124 S. Ct. 2633, 2639 (2004) (plurality opinion) ("[T]he Government has never provided any court with the full criteria that it uses in classifying individuals as ['enemy combatants].""). *Compare* Answer at 5 n.2, with *Hamdi v. Rumsfeld*, _ U.S. _, 124 S. Ct. 2633, 2657 (2004) (Souter, J., concurring in part, dissenting in part, and concurring in the judgment) ("[T]he Government here repeatedly argues that [the petitioner's] detention [as an "enemy combatant"] amounts to nothing more than customary detention of a captive taken on the field of battle."); Memorandum for the Secretary of the Navy, Order Establishing Combatant Status Review Tribunal ¶a (July 7, 2004) ("the term 'enemy combatant' shall mean an individual who was part of or supporting Taliban or al Qaeda forces, or associated forces that are engaged in hostilities against the United States or its coalition partners"); News Briefing on Military Commission by William J. Haynes II, General Counsel of the Department of Defense (Mar. 21, 2002) (describing "enemy combatants" as individuals "captured *on the battlefield* seeking to harm U.S. soldiers or allies") (emphasis added).

point to no case in which an individual, arrested inside the United States, and claiming to be an innocent civilian, was transferred to military custody in the middle of a criminal proceeding and then confined indefinitely without charges being filed against him. Yet, under the government's interpretation of executive authority, the President could seize any civilian present in the United States, and detain him in solitary confinement in a Navy brig for the rest of his life, by the simple expedient of declaring him an "enemy combatant." The Court should reject this shocking attempt to expand executive power at the expense of individual liberty and fundamental constitutional safeguards, and order that Mr. al-Marri be charged by the government or released forthwith.

A.   The AUMF Does Not Authorize Petitioner's Detention

. . .

1.   Petitioner Cannot Be Detained Absent A Clear Statement From Congress.

. . .

. . . In *Ex parte Endo,* 323 U.S. 283 (1944), the Court reviewed a congressional statute and Executive Order relating to the relocation and internment of persons of Japanese ancestry in the United States during World War II. *Id.* at 285–89. Although the Court recognized that the statute was "a war measure" to protect the nation against espionage and sabotage, during a conflict in which actual enemy combatants infiltrated the United States, it nevertheless concluded that the power to detain had not been authorized because the statute failed to use "the language of detention." *Id.* at 300. This holding was premised upon the core constitutional guarantee prohibiting detention without trial, a guarantee which applies to all individuals in the United States. *Id.* at 299 ("[T]he Constitution is as specific in its enumeration of many of the civil rights of the individual as it is in its enumeration of the powers of his government."); *see also id.* (describing "the approach which we think should be made to an Act of Congress or an order of the Chief Executive that touches the sensitive area of rights specifically guaranteed by the Constitution"), including the guarantees surrounding "the arrest, detention and conviction of individuals" provided by the Sixth Amendment, the Due Process Clause of the Fifth Amendment, and the Suspension Clause of Article I, *id*, which extend to non-citizens in the United States. *See, e.g., Wong Wing v. United States,* 163 U.S. 228, 238 (1896) (non-citizens protected by the Fifth and Sixth Amendments to the Constitution); *INS v. St. Cyr,* 533 U.S. 289, 301–02 & n.16 (2001) (non-citizens able to invoke the protections of habeas corpus since before the nation's founding).

The *Endo* Court did not construe the statute to prohibit the detention of Japanese aliens in the United States because Congress had already expressly provided for their detention under the Alien Enemies Act. *See* Act of July 6, 1798, ch. 66, §1, 1 Stat. 577; *see also Ludecke,* 335 U.S. at 162 ("The Alien Enemy Act has remained the law of the land, virtually unchanged since 1798."). Yet, as the government concedes, Mr. Al-Marri is not an "enemy alien." Answer at 17. *See* 1 Stat. 577 (defining "alien enemy" as non-citizens who are "natives, citizens, denizens, or subjects of the hostile *nation or government* against which the United States has declared war or which has invaded or threatened to invade the United States) (emphasis added); *see also Johnson v. Eisentrager,* 339 U.S. 763, 772 (1950) ("[I]n war, every individual of the one nation must acknowledge every individual of the other nation as his own enemy – because the enemy of his country.") (citation omitted). Therefore, he may not be detained by the military under that statute.

The clear statement rule was reaffirmed two years after *Endo* in *Duncan v. Kahanamoku,* 327 U.S. 304 (1946), when the Court considered a congressional enactment permitting the Governor of Hawaii to "'suspend the privilege of the writ of habeas corpus, or place the Territory...under martial law.'" *Id.* at 307 n.1 (quoting Hawaiian Organic Act, §67, 31 Stat. 141 (1900) (repealed 1959)). The Court in *Duncan* construed the enactment narrowly to prevent "the supplanting of [civilian] courts by military tribunals." *Id.* at 324. The Court's decision did not turn on the citizenship of the petitioners but, rather, on their status as civilians and the danger the unwarranted assertion of military power posed to the constitutional right to trial by jury guaranteed to all persons in the United States. *Id.* at 322–24; *id.* at 324 n.21 (constitutional guarantee of jury trial "protects not only the citizens of States which are within the Union, but it shields *every human being* who comes or is brought under our jurisdiction") (citation omitted and emphasis added). Moreover, even the government acknowledged in *Duncan* that, since the privilege of the writ of habeas corpus had subsequently been restored to Hawaii, and martial law terminated, there was no basis for the military to continue to detain the individuals. *Id.* at 313 n.5.

During the height of the Cold War, the government sought the authority to detain potentially dangerous individuals seized in the United States without criminal charges during a time of domestic peril. In accordance with the clear statement rule, Congress enacted the Emergency Detention Act, which expressly authorized the Attorney General, during "an [i]nvasion of the territory of the United States or its possessions," a "[d]eclaration of war by Congress," or an "[i]nsurrection within the United States in aid of a foreign enemy," to "apprehend and...detain...each person as to whom there is reasonable ground to believe that such person probably will engage in, or probably will conspire with others to engage in, acts of espionage or of sabotage." Pub. L. No. 81-831, tit. II, §§102–103, 64 Stat. 1021 (Sept. 23, 1950). Congress's purpose was to give the executive otherwise unauthorized means to defend the nation against "a different kind of threat from that of a strictly military act," [Jennifer K.] Elsea, ["Presidential Authority to Detain 'Enemy Combatants,'" 33 *Presidential Studies Q.* 568,] 586 [(2003)], including terrorism, 64 Stat. at 1019, by allowing the preventive detention of those it suspected were enemy agents, but who fell outside the definition of "alien enemies" under the 1798 act. Elsea, *supra*, at 588–89. Thus, Congress's enactment of the Emergency Detention Act, including the language used, demonstrates that it speaks clearly when it intends to authorize the detention of any individual present in the United States.

Congress repealed the Emergency Detention Act in 1971. *See* Pub. L. 92–128, 85 Stat. 348 (Sept. 25, 1971). At that time, it made clear that "[n]o citizen shall be imprisoned or otherwise detained by the United States except pursuant to an Act of Congress." *Id.* (codified at 18 U.S.C. §4001(a)). This provision was added to ensure that the shameful internment of Japanese-American citizens during World War II would not be repeated, while at the same time preserving the long-standing statutory authority to detain noncitizens under the Alien Enemies Act. *See Padilla v. Rumsfeld*, 352 F.3d 695, 720 (2d Cir. 2003) ("[A]lmost every representative who spoke in favor of repeal of the Emergency Detention Act...described the detention of Japanese-American citizens during World War II as the primary motivation for their positions.") (citing legislative history of 18 U.S.C. §4001(a)), *rev'd on other grounds*, 124 S. Ct. 2711 (2004). Thus, after the repeal of the Emergency Detention Act, aliens in the United States may only be detained under the Alien Enemies Act, or pursuant to some other congressional statute clearly authorizing their detention.

More recently, in *Zadvydas v. Davis*, 533 U.S. 678 (2001), the Court construed a statute expressly providing for the detention beyond a prescribed 90-day period of certain criminal aliens who had been ordered removed from the country, where the Attorney General determined they posed "'a risk to the community.'" *Id.* at 682 (quoting 8 U.S.C. §1231(a)(6)). Even though Congress had used the specific language of detention, the

Court nonetheless found that the statute did not authorize the indefinite, potentially permanent detention sought by the Executive because of the "serious constitutional threat" such detention would pose. *Id*. at 699. Instead, it held that the statute did not permit an alien's detention beyond the period in which his removal from the country was "reasonably foreseeable," and presumptively limited that period to six months. *Id*. at 701. And, just last month, the Supreme Court found that the same provision did not authorize the indefinite detention of even non-admitted criminal aliens in the United States. *Clark v. Suarez Martinez*, ＿U.S.＿, 125 S. Ct. 716, 723, 727 (2005) (adopting *Zadydas'* six-month presumptive limit on detention).

Although the Court said in *Zadvydas* it was not considering "terrorism or other special circumstances where special arguments might be made for forms of preventive detention," 533 U.S. at 696, it also did not hold that an alien could be detained indefinitely in such circumstances absent express authorization by Congress, nor did it consider the constitutional limitations on any such asserted detention power. Notably, in response to *Zadvydas*, and six weeks after the attacks of September 11, 2001, Congress issued a clear statement in the PATRIOT Act, authorizing the detention of aliens who cannot be removed from the country, but who are suspected of terrorist activities or affiliations, beyond this six-month period. 8 U.S.C. §1226a(a)(6) (and also establishing specified review procedures, *id*. §1226a(b)). *See also infra* Section I.A.2 (discussing PATRIOT Act). Thus, here too, executive authority to detain suspected alien terrorists was established only when Congress used the clear language of detention.

By contrast, the AUMF does not contain the type of clear statement required to authorize the executive detention of non-citizens arrested in the United States. The government relies on the AUMF's Preamble, Answer at 9–10, which states that "the President has authority under the Constitution to take action to deter and prevent acts of international terrorism against the United States," to bolster its view that the seizure and military detention of *any* non-citizen in the United States is permissible based upon mere executive say-so. Yet, the Preamble does not specifically authorize the military to seize and detain persons inside the United States. Indeed, Congress never even mentioned, let alone debated, the issue of detention. *Padilla*, 352 F.3d 723 n.31. But, the fundamental protection against detention without charges which extends to *all* individuals present in this country may not be abolished by mere implication.[3] Had Congress intended such a radical shift in constitutional authority when it enacted the AUMF, it would have spoken clearly, as it was required to do.

The government also relies on the "necessary and appropriate force" language of section 2(a) of the AUMF. Answer at 9–10. The AUMF states, however, that "this section is intended to constitute specific statutory authorization within the meaning of section 5(b) of the War Powers Resolution," *id*., which requires the President to consult with Congress and to cease military operations within 60 days unless Congress has declared war or specifically authorized the use of the armed forces. 50 U.S.C. §§1542, 1544(b). Quite clearly, the AUMF authorized the President to go to war in Afghanistan and, in the process, to seize enemy combatants on foreign battlefields. But, there is no indication, however, that Congress intended the phrase "necessary and appropriate force" to authorize the seizure by the military of individuals inside the United States, and outside an immediate theater of war, let alone of an individual who was actually being

---

[3] While non-citizens may also be detained pending their removal on immigration charges, that detention is expressly authorized by statute. 8 U.S.C. §1226(a) ("On a warrant issued by the Attorney General, an alien may be *arrested and detained* pending a decision on whether the alien is to be removed from the United States.") (emphasis added).

prosecuted in a civilian court on criminal charges. In short, the AUMF does not provide the clear statement from Congress required to authorize the executive detention of non-citizens arrested in the United States, and, therefore, cannot provide a lawful basis for Mr. al-Marri's continued military confinement.

2. Congress's Enactment Of The PATRIOT Act Demonstrates That It Did Not Authorize Petitioner's Detention By The Military

Congress's enactment of the PATRIOT Act also demonstrates that the AUMF does not authorize Mr. al-Marri's detention. *See* Uniting and Strengthening America by Providing Appropriate Tools Required to Intercept and Obstruct Terrorism Act of 2001, Pub. L. No. 10756, 115 Stat. 272 (Oct. 26, 2001) ("PATRIOT Act"). Signed into law five weeks after the AUMF, the PATRIOT Act expressly authorizes the Executive Branch to detain aliens in the United States who pose a threat to national security. *Id.* §412(a), 115 Stat. at 350 (codified at 8 U.S.C. §1226a(a) (2000 ed. Supp. II)). It states that the Attorney General "shall take into custody" any alien he certifies he has "reasonable grounds to believe" is engaged in terrorist activities, 8 U.S.C. §1226a(a)(1),(3)(A), or "in any other activity that endangers the national security of the United States." *Id.* §1226a(a)(1),(3)(B). Congress also included explicit definitions circumscribing the category of persons who fall within the scope of this new executive detention authority, *id.* §1226a(a)(3), and limited how long any such person may be detained without charges by requiring the Attorney General to place him in removal proceedings, to charge him with a criminal offense, or to release him "not later than 7 days after the commencement of such detention." *Id.* §1226a(a)(5). Congress expressly authorized detention for additional six-month periods where the alien is ordered removed but his removal is not reasonably foreseeable and his release "will threaten the national security of the United States or the safety of the community or any person." *Id.* §1226a(a)(6).

The PATRIOT Act clearly authorizes the Executive Branch to detain for a statutorily limited period of time persons like Mr. al-Marri: non-citizens inside the United States believed by the government to be associated with al Qaeda. Answer at 20 & Exhibit A. Of course, the President chose not to detain Mr. al-Marri under this law. The significant point, however, is that if Congress had authorized the limitless detention of such persons by the military in the AUMF, it would not have expressly provided for their detention – including their possible indefinite detention – five weeks later in the PATRIOT Act. *See, e.g.*, *Meghrig v. KFC Western, Inc.*, 516 U.S. 479, 484–85 (1996) (when later legislation shows Congress knows how to provide for a desired result, but did not provide for that result in previous legislation, it suggests Congress did not intend to provide for that result in that earlier legislation).

In addition, other provisions of the PATRIOT Act demonstrate that Congress intended to for terrorism inside the United States to be combated through the civil justice system. As evidenced by its name, Congress enacted the PATRIOT Act to provide additional tools to civil law enforcement officers "to wage war on the terrorists in our midst," and viewed those tools as *"the domestic complement* to the weapons our military is currently bringing to bear on the terrorists associates overseas." 147 *Cong. Rec.* S10990, S11015 (2001) (statement of Sen. Hatch) (emphasis added). Those tools include dramatically enhanced power to engage in electronic surveillance (including for acts relating to terrorism), to conduct searches, and to obtain records and other documents in terrorism-related investigations. While Congress obviously recognized that "[t]errorism has come to America," *id.* at S11048 (statement of Sen. Biden), it responded through comprehensive legislation that specifically addressed the detention of suspected terrorists and other national security threats through the civilian justice system, and that enhanced the power of civilian law enforcement to combat terrorism through the civilian courts. The PATRIOT Act thus makes clear that Congress *never* authorized the Executive Branch to detain suspected terrorists arrested in the United States as "enemy combatants." Rather, that authority has been arrogated unto itself by the Executive Branch in this, and other, cases.

3. Well-Established Precedents Prohibit The Military Detention Of Individuals Arrested in Civilian Settings In the United States.

. . .

...[A]lthough the government characterizes Mr. al-Marri's detention as non-punitive and, hence not warranting the constitutional guarantee of criminal process,[4] the confinement of alleged terrorists has – as a historical matter – not been regarded as a "classic example of nonpunitive detention." *Kansas v. Hendricks*, 521 U.S. 346, 363 (1997); *see also Hamdi*, 124 S. Ct. at 2662 (Scalia, J., dissenting) ("civil commitment of the mentally ill" and "temporary detention in quarantine of the infectious" are two "limited" and "well-recognized exceptions" that did not mandate the protections guaranteed by ordinary criminal process). Congress has created a "well-stocked statutory arsenal of defined criminal offenses covering the gamut of actions" for which an individual might be prosecuted for engaging in, conspiring to engage in, or supporting terrorist activities against the United States. *Hamdi*, 124 S. Ct. at 2657 (Souter, J., concurring in part, dissenting in part, and concurring in the judgment) (citing statutes). And, acts of terrorism on American soil – as Congress was well aware when it enacted the AUMF – have regularly been prosecuted in this Nation's criminal courts. *See, e.g.*, *United States v. Moussaoui*, 365 F.3d 292, 295–96 (4th Cir 2004) (pending prosecution for defendant's alleged involvement in attacks of September 11, 2001); *United States v. Yousef*, 327 F.3d 56 (2d. Cir. 2003) (affirming convictions of defendants involved in 1993 World Trade Center bombing and conspiracy to bomb airliners); *United States v. Rahman*, 189 F.3d 88, 123 (2d Cir. 1999) (affirming conviction of Sheikh Omar Abdel Rahman and his followers for, *inter alia*, plotting a "day of terror" against New York City landmarks); *Kasi v. Virginia*, 508 S.E. 2d 57 (Va. 1998) (affirming conviction of foreign national who murdered CIA employees). It was against this backdrop that Congress enacted the AUMF, and there is no indication that Congress intended to deviate from the well-established limits on the exercise of military authority inside the United States.

The government principally relies on *Hamdi* and *Ex parte Quirin*, 317 U.S. 1 (1942), for its expansive interpretation of the AUMF, but neither supports its position. *Hamdi* addressed only the "narrow question" of whether the government could detain as an "enemy combatant" an "individual who, it alleges, was part of or supporting forces hostile to the United States or coalition partners *in Afghanistan* and *who engaged in an armed conflict against the United States there*." 124 S. Ct. at 2639 (plurality opinion) (citation omitted and emphases added). The plurality concluded that the AUMF authorized

---

[4] The government's characterization of his confinement as "non-punitive" is specious. Mr. al-Marri was designated an "enemy combatant" after he asserted his innocence in a criminal proceeding and refused to cooperate with the government. Because Mr. al-Marri continues to assert his innocence, he has been held in solitary confinement for over nineteen months, for most of that time, without access to counsel or family. He has been interrogated by military and civilian interrogators, denied religious and other reading materials, subjected to coercive tactics and verbal harassment, and provided with inadequate medical care. Although not necessary to the decision on this motion, he is quite clearly being punished for not behaving in the manner desired by the government.

the detention of individuals, including United States citizens, in that "narrow category." *Id*. at 2639–40; *see also id*. at 2640 (AUMF reaches "individuals who fought against the United States in Afghanistan as part of the Taliban, an organization known to have supported the al Qaeda terrorist network responsible for those attacks").[5] Specifically, even though the AUMF does not specifically authorize the detention of individuals, the plurality construed it to permit the detention of this "limited category" of persons because the capture and detention of combatants on a foreign battlefield is "by 'universal agreement and practice . . . [an] important incident[] of war.'" *Id*. at 2640 (quoting *Quirin*, 317 U.S. at 28); *see also id*. at 2641 ("In light of these principles, it is of no moment that the AUMF does not use specific language of detention.").

This interpretation of the AUMF was thus rooted in the particular factual context of *Hamdi* – an enemy soldier who was participating in armed conflict and captured on foreign battlefield. *Id*. at 2642 n.1 ("[T]he basis asserted for detention by the military is that Hamdi was carrying a weapon against American troops on a foreign battlefield; that is, that he was an enemy combatant."). In such situations, detention is "a simple war measure" intended "to prevent captured individuals from returning *to the field of battle and taking up arms* once again." *Id*. at 2640 (citations omitted and emphasis added). This same reasoning, however, does not apply, nor has it ever been applied, to the military detention of unarmed individuals, arrested in civilian settings in the United States, who deny that they are combatants.

. . .

Although the government seeks to characterize Mr. al-Marri's detention as "a simple war measure," Answer at 8 (citation omitted), seizing a person lawfully present in the United States, and confining him for life to a Navy brig, is not "simple" in the way that capturing an armed soldier on a battlefield is a simple "incident of war." Mr. al-Marri is not an admitted soldier of a sovereign nation against which Congress has declared war, *cf. Quirin*, 317 U.S. at 21, 36, was not captured bearing arms in a foreign combat zone, *cf. Hamdi*, 124 S. Ct. at 2636–37, 2640–41 (plurality opinion), and was not seized at the border while attempting to enter the United States. *Cf. Padilla*, 352 F.3d at 699. To the contrary, Mr. al-Marri was arrested in a civilian setting, indicted on criminal charges, and prosecuted for over sixteen months before the President designated him an "enemy combatant" and banished him to a military brig.

This is no "simple war measure," and the AUMF did not authorize this unprecedented displacement of basic constitutional rights by executive fiat. The AUMF neither uses the language of detention nor can it be construed to authorize detention in these circumstances. Although Congress must have envisioned that the use of military force

---

[5] Moreover, an equal number of justices rejected the proposition that the government had the authority to detain Hamdi as an "enemy combatant." 124 S. Ct. at 2653, 2660 (Souter, J., concurring in part, dissenting in part, and concurring in the judgment) (AUMF does not authorize Hamdi's detention); *id*. at 2660–61 (Scalia, J., dissenting) (Constitution prohibits Hamdi's detention as an "enemy combatant"). While Justice Thomas agreed with the plurality that the AUMF would authorize Hamdi's detention based upon the alleged facts, 124 S. Ct. at 2679–80 (Thomas, J., dissenting), he was the only justice to disagree with the "eight members of the Court rejecting the Government's position." *Id*. at 2660 (Souter, J., concurring in part, dissenting in part, and concurring in the judgment). Justice Thomas's virtually limitless view of the President's wartime detention power does not provide the necessary vote for a majority. *Marks v. United States*, 430 U.S. 188, 193 (1977) (internal quotation omitted) (where no opinion commanded a majority, "the holding of the Court may be viewed as that position taken by those Members who concurred in the judgment[] on the narrowest grounds"), *reiterated with approval by Grutter v. Bollinger*, 539 U.S. 306, 325 (2003). The limitation of the concurrence to "someone in Hamdi's position," 124 S. Ct. at 2660, underscores the limits of the plurality's own analysis. Were there any doubt about the plurality's own limits, those doubts should resolved in favor of the "narrowest grounds," *Marks*, 430 U.S. at 193, and restricted to "someone in Hamdi's position." 124 S. Ct. at 2660.

would include the detention of enemy soldiers seized on a foreign battlefield where American troops are engaged in combat operations, as the Supreme Court recognized in *Hamdi*, it did not silently eradicate the most fundamental protections of individual liberty in the Constitution.

B. The President Lacks Inherent Constitutional Authority To Detain Petitioner.

. . .

1. The Authority Asserted By The President Usurps Congress's War Powers.

. . .

The Alien Enemies Act of 1798, discussed above, which provides for the wartime detention of enemy aliens, was enacted by Congress pursuant to its war powers. *See* Act of July 6. 1798, ch. 66, §1, 1 Stat. 577 (authorizing the detention of enemy aliens during "a declared war between the United States and any foreign nation or government"). Such congressional authorization was necessary because, even in a declared war against a foreign nation or government, the President lacks the inherent authority to detain enemy aliens inside the United States. *See Brown* [*v. United States*], 12 U.S. [110,] 126 [(1814)] ("The act concerning alien enemies, which confers on the president very great discretionary powers . . . affords a strong implication that he did not possess those powers by virtue of the declaration of war.") (Marshall, C.J.); *see also Ludecke*, 335 U.S. at 165 (President's power to detain and remove "enemy aliens" was "vested" in him by Congress through the passage of Alien Enemies Act); Madison's Report on the Virginia Resolutions, *in* 4 *Debates on the Federal Constitution* 554 (J. Elliot ed. 1836) (hereinafter "*Elliot's Debates*") ("[T]he Constitution ha[s] expressly delegated to Congress the power to declare war against any nation, and . . . to treat it and all its members as enemies."). Indeed, Chief Justice Marshall made clear in *Brown* that the President lacked authority to detain alien enemies during a declared war, *id.*, 12 U.S. at 126, even though their detention – as opposed to the detention of aliens from friendly or neutral nations – had been permitted at common law. *Eisentrager*, 339 U.S. at 769 n.2, 774–75 n.6; 1 William Blackstone, *Commentaries* *372 ("alien-enemies" are subjects of an enemy nation in time of war; all other aliens are "alien-friends"). *See also Ex parte Gilroy*, 257 F. 110 (S.D.N.Y. 1919) (challenge by German alien arrested under the Alien Enemies Act, in which the government emphasized the Act's importance to protecting national security by allowing the President to detain German agents bent on sabotage in the United States, but never suggested that the President had inherent authority as commander-in-chief to detain such individuals without trial as "enemy combatants") (discussed in Elsea, *supra*, at 575).

Similarly, the infamous Alien Act of 1798, which Congress enacted at the same time as the Alien Enemies Act, specifically authorized the President to remove from the country any aliens he deemed "dangerous to the peace and safety of the United States" or had "reasonable grounds to suspect [we]re concerned in any treasonable or secret machinations against the government thereof." Act of June 25, 1798, ch. 58, §1, 1 Stat. 570–71. Its enactment shows the long-established understanding that the President has no power to remove, let alone detain, allegedly dangerous aliens from the country during wartime absent express congressional authorization. Indeed, even though authorized by Congress, the Alien Act was "vigorously and contemporaneously attacked as unconstitutional" by Thomas Jefferson and James Madison. *See Ludecke*, 335 U.S. at 171–72 n.18; Madison's Report on the Virginia Resolutions, *in* 4 *Elliot's Debates*, *supra*, at 554. The Alien Act was allowed to expire in 1800, and no President has asserted such sweeping authority since.

In sum, there is no support for the government's contention that the President possesses inherent constitutional authority to detain individuals in the United States during wartime. The government's claim is not only unprecedented but contrary to the limits on the President's power imposed by Article I of the Constitution.

2.   Petitioner's Detention By The Military Contravenes The Suspension Clause.

The protection of individual liberty afforded by the Suspension Clause further demonstrates the supremacy of legislative and judicial control over the Executive's power to detain alleged enemies of the state inside the Nation's borders. *See* U.S. Const., art. §9, cl. 2. For centuries, the writ of habeas corpus has served as the preeminent safeguard against executive detention without trial. *E.g., Brown v. Allen*, 344 U.S. 443, 533 (1953) (Jackson, J., concurring in the result) ("The historic purpose of the writ has been to relieve detention by executive authorities without judicial trial."); *see also Hamdi*, 124 S. Ct. at 2661 (Scalia, J., dissenting) (writ historically secured fundamental right to judicial trial guaranteed by the Due Process Clause); *Swain v, Pressley*, 430 U.S. 372, 386 (1977) (Burger, C.J., concurring) ("[T]he traditional Great Writ was largely a remedy against executive detention."). As Alexander Hamilton explained, the writ's protection against the supreme example of arbitrary government – imprisonment without accusation and trial – made the Habeas Corpus Act of 1679 "the bulwark of the British Constitution." *The Federalist* No. 84, at 512 (Alexander Hamilton) (C. Rossiter ed. 1961) (quoting 4 William Blackstone, *Commentaries* *438). *See also* Rollin C. Hurd, *A Treatise on the Right of Personal Liberty, and on the Writ of Habeas Corpus* 266 (2d ed.1876) ("It was the hateful oppressiveness of long and close confinement, and not the dread of a trial by his peers, which made the suffering prisoner of state exclaim: 'The writ of habeas corpus is the water of life to revive from the death of imprisonment.'") (emphases omitted).

This fundamental right is effectively guaranteed in America by the Suspension Clause, which represents the only "express [constitutional] provision for exercise of extraordinary authority because of a crisis." *Youngstown*, 343 U.S. at 650 (Jackson, J., concurring). In the event of "Rebellion or Invasion," U.S. Const. art. I., §9, cl. 2, Congress alone possesses the authority to suspend the writ. *Ex parte Bollman*, 8 U.S. (4 Cranch) 75, 101 (1807) (Marshall, C.J.) ("If at any time the public safety should require the suspension of the powers vested by this act in the courts of the United States, it is for the legislature to say so."); *Ex parte Merryman*, 17 F. Cas. 144, 148–49 (C.C.D. Md. 1861) (No. 9,487); *see also* [Joseph] Story, [*Commentaries on the Constitution of the United States*] §1342, at 214–15 [R. Rotunda & J. Nowack eds. 1987)]. Thus, even in situations of rebellion in or invasions of the United States, the President lacks the "inherent" power to detain indefinitely.[6] Thus, the Suspension Clause reinforces the requirement of congressional authorization to detain an individual without charges amid domestic peril. *Milligan*, 71 U.S. at 135 (Chase, C.J.).

By prohibiting executive detention without congressional authorization, the Suspension Clause thus preserves fundamental rights – including due process – guaranteed

---

[6] This case does not involve the separate question of the President's authority to temporarily detain individuals where martial law has been declared, a situation which, historically, acted as a suspension of habeas corpus. [William] Winthrop, [*Military Law and Precedents*]...828 [(2d ed. 1920)] ("[T]he suspending of the writ by military authority is essentially an exercise of the power of martial law. Thus, the two powers are closely connected, the one substantially including or involving the other...."); *see also Hamdi*, 124 S. Ct. at 2659 (Souter, J.) (stating that, "in a moment of genuine emergency, when the Government must act with no time for deliberation, the Executive may detain a citizen if there is reason to fear he is an imminent threat to the safety of the Nation and its people").

to all persons in the United States. Further, non-citizens present in the United States possess the same right against imprisonment without trial as citizens, *Wong Wing*, 163 U.S. at 237–38, and their indefinite detention by the Executive is no less "oppressive and lawless." *Shaughnessy v. United States ex rel. Mezei*, 345 U.S. 206, 218 (Jackson, J., dissenting). Indeed, this guarantee is regarded as "one of the bulwarks of the Constitution." Henry M. Hart, Jr., "The Power of Congress to Limit the Jurisdiction of Federal Courts: An Exercise in Dialectic," 66 *Harv. L. Rev.* 1362, 1387 (1953). It extends to all persons in the United States who claim they are noncombatants and who are seized outside a theater of war, as long as "the courts are open, and in the proper and unobstructed exercise of their jurisdiction," *Milligan*, 71 U.S. at 127, including non-citizens. *See, e.g., Carlisle v. United States*, 83 U.S. 147, 154–55 (1872) (even temporarily domiciled aliens owe obligation of fidelity and obedience, and are subject to criminal prosecution for treason and other offenses as are citizens); 8 *Annals of Cong.* 2012 (1798) ("It is an acknowledged principle of the common law, the authority of which is established here, that alien friends . . . residing among us, are entitled to the protection of our laws, and that during their residence they owe a temporary allegiance to our Government. If they are accused of violating this allegiance, the same laws which interpose in the case of a citizen must determine the truth of the accusation, and if found guilty they are liable to the same punishment.") (statement of Edward Livingston in the House debate on the Alien Act of 1798) (emphasis added); Madison's Report on the Virginia Resolutions, *in* 4 *Debates on the Federal Constitution, supra*, at 557 ("alien friends" cannot be treated like "alien enemies," but instead must be subjected to punishment under the laws of the United States).

The government's claim that the President can, without authorization from Congress, direct the military to seize a person off the streets of the United States and confine him indefinitely, without charges, in a military prison contravenes the Suspension Clause's protection against the arbitrary exercise of executive power. The President cannot circumvent this constitutional guarantee simply by labeling Mr. al-Marri an "enemy combatant."

3.   Petitioner's Detention Threatens The Supremacy Of Civilian Authority.

The President's assertion of inherent detention power also contravenes the fundamental principle of the supremacy of civilian authority over the military. This principle can be traced to the Nation's founding, when colonial leaders listed the supremacy of the military as one of the abuses rendered by the King of England against the American colonists. *The Declaration of Independence* para. 14 (U.S. 1776) ("[The King] has affected to render the Military independent of and superior to the Civil power."). The supremacy of civilian over military authority inside the United States is at the core of *Milligan*, where the Court rejected the exercise of military jurisdiction based upon charges that Milligan had joined and aided a secret paramilitary group for purposes of overthrowing the government, communicated with the enemy, and conspired to seize munitions, liberate prisoners of war, and commit other violent acts in an area under constant threat of invasion (but not actually invaded) by the enemy. 71 U.S. at 6–7 (statement of case); *id.* at 140 (Chase, C.J., concurring). The Court there determined that the constitutional protections of the Fourth, Fifth, and Sixth Amendments apply "equally in war and in peace" and are not "suspended during any of the great exigencies of government," 71 U.S. at 120–21, except where Congress has suspended habeas corpus. *Id.* at 125. Although Milligan was an American citizen, the Court's decision turned on the fact that he was a non-combatant outside an active theater of war. 71 U.S. at 127 ("If, in foreign invasion or civil war, the courts are actually closed, and it is impossible to administer criminal justice according to law, *then*, in the theatre of active military operations, where war really prevails, there is a necessity to furnish a substitute for the civil authority, thus overthrown, . . . [and] to govern by martial rule until the laws can have their free course.") (emphasis in original); *see also Hamdi*, 124 S. Ct. at 2642 (plurality opinion) (suggesting military jurisdiction was rejected in *Milligan* because petitioner "was not a prisoner of war, but a resident of Indiana arrested while at home there" and was not seized carrying arms "on a Confederate battlefield").

Since *Milligan* was decided, the Court has consistently affirmed the supremacy of civilian rule by limiting the reach of military jurisdiction. *See, e.g., Duncan*, 327 U.S. at 324 (rejecting military jurisdiction to try civilians even under statute providing for martial law); *Reid*, 354 U.S. at 33–34 (plurality opinion) (rejecting military jurisdiction over civilians and contrasting military's "broad power over persons on the battlefront" with its lack of power over persons where "active hostilities" were not underway). Congress, as well, enacted the Posse Comitatus Act in 1878, criminalizing the military's involvement in domestic law enforcement activities in order to curb abuses by the military in the sphere of civilian rule. 18 U.S.C. §1385 (2000). The President's assertion of inherent constitutional authority in this case to remove an individual from a pending judicial process that is a hallmark of civilian rule, and to confine him without charges in a Navy brig, possibly for the duration of his natural life, flouts the supremacy of civilian over military rule. The entire United States does not become a battlefield, and all those lawfully within it "enemy combatants," simply because the Commander-in-Chief says so.

The government cites only a handful of cases in support of its argument that the President possesses inherent detention authority under the instant circumstances, none of which – including *Quirin* – bears any resemblance to Mr. al-Marri's situation. As noted above, *Quirin* did not involve the indefinite executive detention of persons who claimed to be civilians but, rather, a military trial of admitted enemy soldiers, based upon express statutory authorization by Congress. 317 U.S. at 21, 28; *see also Rasul v. Bush*, __U.S.__, 124 S. Ct. 2686, 2700 (2004) (Kennedy, J., concurring) (contrasting indefinite detention of "enemy combatants" with trial of combatants for violations of the law of war by military commission). In fact, in *Quirin* the government acknowledged and relied on the distinction between civilians and combatants to justify its assertion of military jurisdiction. *See* Brief for Respondent in *Ex parte Quirin* at 10 ("Milligan never wore the uniform of the armed forces at war with the United States. The [*Quirin*] petitioners did."); *id.* at 45 ("Milligan was a civilian; the present defendants are imprisoned combatants of an enemy nation."). Thus, whereas the United States military could have lawfully shot the enemy German soldiers in *Quirin* on sight after they landed in the United States, the government makes no such claim with respect to Mr. al-Marri; if he really were an "enemy combatant," however, it would have been justified in shooting him upon discovery as well. *See* Dep't of the Army, *The Law of Land Warfare*, Field Manual 27-10, para 31 (1956) (authorizing attacks on "individual soldiers or officers of the enemy whether in the zone of hostilities, occupied territory, or elsewhere"). In sum, *Quirin* does not provide a basis for the President's sweeping assertion of inherent executive detention authority in this case.

The government's reliance on *The Prize Cases*, 67 U.S. 635 (1862), *see* Answer at 9, is likewise misplaced. *The Prize Cases* involved the capture of enemy property, not the detention of persons, and the Supreme Court did not suggest in those cases that the President could deprive an individual of liberty through the exercise of his wartime powers outside a zone of combat. *Padilla*, 352 F.3d at 717–18. Also, the Court in *The Prize Cases* carefully distinguished between belligerents and insurgents based upon its understanding of war as a conflict between sovereignty-claiming entities acting "*as States*" within a defined boundary. 67 U.S. at 673 (emphasis in original). Moreover, the Court did not base its decision upholding the President's exercise of military authority solely on his independent constitutional powers but, rather, stated that the President's authority "to call[] out the militia and use the military and naval forces of the United States in case of invasion by foreign nations, and to suppress insurrection against the government" derived from two acts of Congress. *Id*. at 668 (citing Acts of February 28, 1795, and March 3, 1 807). In any event, Congress's subsequent ratification of the President's wartime orders mooted any issues of independent presidential authority. *Id*. at 670.

In support of its argument, the government also cites the Fourth Circuit's decision in *Hamdi* that deference to the Executive's designation of individuals as "enemy combatants" was required, and that "enemy combatants" have no right of access to counsel. *See* Answer at 9 (citing *Hamdi v. Rumsfeld*, 296 F.341 278, 281 (4th Cir. 2002)). The Fourth Circuit, however, limited its holding to the detention of individuals "capture[d] on the field of battle." 296 F.3d at 281. And, in any event, the Supreme Court rejected the Fourth Circuit's conclusions on these issues. 124 S. Ct. at 2652 (plurality opinion). The only other case cited by the government in support of its inherent presidential authority argument, *Durand v. Hollins*, 8 F. Cas. 111 (C.C.S.D.N.Y. 1860) (No. 4,186), was a damages action by a U.S. citizen for destruction of his property abroad due to the bombardment by a naval commander acting pursuant to a presidential order. *Id*. It provides no basis for the President's indefinite military detention of individuals seized in civilian settings in the United States.

. . .

II.   PETITIONER HAS THE RIGHT TO AN EVIDENTIARY HEARING BEFORE THIS COURT THAT IS CONSISTENT WITH THE FUNDAMENTAL REQUIREMENTS OF DUE PROCESS.

In the event the Court determines that Mr. al-Marri may be detained by the military as an "enemy combatant," he is entitled – as the Supreme Court held in *Hamdi*, 124 S. Ct. at 2650–51 (plurality opinion) – to a constitutionally sufficient process through which he can challenge his detention. The government argues that, even if Mr. al-Marri were entitled to the some due process, the President's determination that he is an "enemy combatant," and this Court's deferential review of that unilateral determination, constitute "all the process he is due." . . . Thus, in the government's view, a person can be seized in the United States by the military, thrown in a Navy brig, and detained indefinitely without charges and without access to counsel, based solely upon a multiple hearsay certification signed by a Department of Defense functionary. The government thus seeks to eliminate any meaningful role for the Judiciary in reviewing the potentially life-long detention at issue here even though this argument was squarely rejected by the Supreme Court in *Hamdi*.

If he is to be detained as an "enemy combatant," Mr. al-Marri is entitled under the Constitution to challenge the allegations underlying that determination in an evidentiary hearing that adheres to the fundamental requirements of due process. At a minimum, Mr. al-Marri has the right to see all of the government's inculpatory evidence (including classified information contained in the aforementioned certification that counsel has been prohibited from sharing with Petitioner), to obtain from the government and present exculpatory evidence, to confront and cross-examine the government's witnesses against him, and to compel the government to prove its case by clear and convincing evidence, an appropriately stringent burden of proof in light of the significant deprivation of liberty which is at stake. Anything less would make a mockery of this country's commitment to due process and the rule of law.

A.   Petitioner Is Entitled To Due Process.

"[T]he Due Process Clause applies to all 'persons' within the United States, including aliens, whether their presence here is lawful, unlawful, temporary, or permanent." *Zadvydas*, 533 U.S. at 693; *see also Plyer v. Doe*, 457 U.S. 202, 210 (1982) ("Aliens, even aliens whose presence in this country is unlawful, have long been recognized as 'persons' guaranteed due process of law by the Fifth and Fourteenth Amendments."); *Kwong Hai Chew v. Colding*, 344 U.S. 590, 596 (1953) (resident alien is a "person" within the meaning of the Fifth Amendment); *Wong Wing*, 163 U.S. at 238 ("all persons within the territory of the United States are entitled to the protection [of the Due Process Clause]"); *see also Yick Wo v. Hopkins*, 118 U.S. 356, 369 (1886) (protections of Fourteenth Amendment "are universal in their application, to all persons within the territorial jurisdiction" of the United States). Aliens present in the United States have a right to due process even during wartime. *Joint Anti-Fascist Refugee Committee v. McGrath*, 341 U.S. 123, 162 (1951) (Frankfurter, J., concurring) ("The requirement of 'due process' is not a fair-weather or timid assurance. It must be respected in periods of calm and in times of trouble; it protects aliens as well as citizens."); *see also Rasul*, 124 S. Ct. at 2699 (Kennedy, J., concurring) ("Physical presence in the United States 'implie[s] protection.'") (quoting *Eisentrager*, 339 U.S. at 777–78); *Khalid v. Bush*, _F. Supp. 2d_ , Nos. 04-1142 & 04-1166, 2005 WL 100924, at *7 (D.D.C. Jan. 19, 2005) (recognizing that constitutional protections extend to "alien[s] . . . within [the United States'] territorial jurisdiction"). And, the right asserted here of "[f]reedom from imprisonment – from government custody, detention, or other forms of physical restraint – lies at the heart of the liberty that [the Due Process] Clause protects." *Zadvydas*, 533 U.S. at 690 (citation omitted); *see also In re Guantanamo Detainee Cases*, _F. Supp. 2d_, 2005 WL 195356, at *19 (D.D.C. Jan, 31, 2005) ("There is no practical difference between incarceration at the hands of one's own government and incarceration at the hands of a foreign government; significant liberty is deprived in both situations regardless of the jailer's nationality.").[7]

The Court in *Hamdi* held that the petitioner, an American citizen, was entitled to due process even though he was an enemy soldier captured bearing arms on a foreign battlefield. 124 S. Ct. at 2648 (plurality opinion); *id*. at 2660 (Souter, J., concurring in part, dissenting in part, and concurring in the judgment). Even if non-citizens seized and detained *outside* the United States might be beyond the protections of the Due Process Clause – a question this Court need not decide, *but see Rasul*, 124 S. Ct. at 2698 n.15; *In re Guantánamo Detainee Cases*, 2005 WL 195356, at *18 (finding that "there can be no question" that the Due Process Clause extends to individuals detained as "enemy combatants" at Guantanamo Bay, Cuba) – non-citizens seized and detained inside the United States fall squarely within the Due Process Clause's protections. *Zadvydas*, 533 U.S. at 690; *see also Eisentrager*, 339 U.S. at 771. Thus, any individual arrested in the United States and detained as an "enemy combatant" is entitled, at a minimum,

---

[7] The government cites *United States v. Verdugo-Urquidez*, 494 U.S. 259 (1990), to suggest that the Due Process Clause does not guarantee Mr. al-Marri the right to a meaningful judicial inquiry into the legality of his continued detention. Answer at 18 n.13. *Verdugo-Urquidez*, however, involved the *extraterritorial* application of the Fourth Amendment to the search of a foreign national's residence in Mexico by federal agents. 494 U.S. at 261; *see also id.* at 278 (Kennedy, J., concurring) ("All would agree, for instance, that the dictates of the Due Process Clause of the Fifth Amendment protect the defendant."). That, of course, is not at issue here.

to the "essential constitutional promises" of "notice of the factual basis for [that] classification, and a fair opportunity to rebut the Government's factual assertions before a neutral decisionmaker." *Hamdi*, 124 S. Ct. at 2648–49 (plurality opinion); *see also id.* at 2660 (Souter, J., concurring in part, dissenting in part, and concurring in the judgment). Thus, Mr. al-Marri not only has the right to, but unquestionably must be afforded, a non-illusory process by which he can challenge his continued detention by the military.

B. Petitioner Has Been Denied Due Process.

On June 23, 2003, the President determined that petitioner was an "enemy combatant" and ordered his detention by the military. This determination was based solely on vague and conclusory allegations relying on unidentified sources. Now, over a year later, the government has provided the declaration of a Department of Defense functionary which contains the only "evidence" to support the President's unilateral determination. *See* Declaration of Jeffrey N. Rapp. This declaration and, hence, the fact of Mr. al-Marri's detention, turns upon the hearsay statements of a single witness who has been detained incommunicado, who is reported to have been subjected to extreme methods of coercion, who has never given sworn testimony in a court of law, and whom Mr. al-Marri has not had the opportunity to confront or cross-examine.

Since June 2003, when he was taken, without notice to counsel, from a pending criminal proceeding in federal district court to isolated confinement in the military brig where he remains today, Mr. al-Marri has not been afforded any non-Executive Branch process. Indeed, he has been afforded *less* process than even those minimal procedures imposed upon the alleged "enemy combatants" captured outside the United States and detained at Guantánamo Bay, Cuba. *In re Guantanamo Detainee Cases*, 2005 WL 195356, at *5 (describing Combatant Status Review Tribunal). Rather, the only "process" provided to Mr. al-Marri has been the same internal Executive Branch determination that the Court found constitutionally deficient in *Hamdi*, 124 S. Ct. at 2648 (plurality opinion) (rejecting government's argument that no further fact-finding was required); *see also id.* at 2660 (Souter, J., concurring in part, dissenting in part, and concurring in the judgment).

The Due Process Clause guarantees every individual the right "to be heard 'at a meaningful time and in a meaningful manner.'" *Mathews v. Eldridge*, 424 U.S. 319, 333 (1976) (quoting *Armstrong v. Manzo*, 380 U.S. 545, 552 (1965)); *see also In re Oliver*, 333 U.S. 257, 273 (1948) ("A person's right to reasonable notice of a charge against him, and an opportunity to be heard in his defense – a right to his day in court – are basic in our system of jurisprudence...."). Unlike the capture of enemy soldiers on a battlefield, Mr. al-Marri's detention by the military at a time he was being prosecuted by a civilian authority inside the United States is not a "fundamental and accepted" incident of war but, rather, a threat to core constitutional values. *See supra* Sections I.B.2 & 1.B.3. Moreover, Mr. al-Marri's indefinite confinement lacks the protections against prolonged detention inherent in battlefield captures, which can be assessed by the traditional yardstick of ongoing military operations in the foreign combat zone. *See Hamdi*, 124 S. Ct. at 2642 (plurality opinion). Mr. al-Marri's detention, according to the government's own view, may well last a lifetime. *In re Guantanamo Detainee Cases*, 2005 WL 195356, at *19 (describing government's view of the duration of the "war on terrorism"). Other than a death sentence, lifetime incarceration "is the ultimate deprivation of liberty," and its mere specter "may be even worse than if [a] detainee[] had been tried, convicted, and definitively sentenced to a fixed term." *Id.* Under such circumstances, the Due Process Clause mandates even greater procedural protections than in *Hamdi*.

There is simply no case in the history of this country in which an individual was arrested in the United States, charged and prosecuted criminally, and then seized and detained indefinitely by the military, without charges, based solely upon the hearsay declaration of a single government bureaucrat. For Mr. al-Marri, a meaningful opportunity to rebut the factual assertions underlying the President's determination that he is an "enemy combatant" requires a process both familiar and established, that is, one which includes: (i) an evidentiary hearing in this Court, (ii) at which Mr. al-Marri is assisted by counsel, (iii) the government bears an appropriately stringent burden of proof, and (iv) perhaps most fundamentally, Mr. al-Marri has the opportunity to confront and examine the witnesses against him. Anything less would not satisfy the dictates of the Due Process Clause.

First, as *Hamdi* makes clear, this Court must conduct an evidentiary hearing in which Mr. al-Marri has the opportunity to rebut the government's factual assertions on which his "enemy combatant" classification is based. *Hamdi*, 124 S. Ct. at 2649 (holding that a district court that receives a habeas corpus petition "must itself ensure that the minimum requirements of due process are achieved"); *see also Rasul*, 124 S. Ct. at 2699 (district court must "consider in the first instance the merits of petitioners' claims"). Although the government contends that due process would be satisfied "by this Court's proper exercise of its habeas jurisdiction to review [his] claims," Answer at 23, the Court in *Hamdi* rejected precisely this argument. 124 S. Ct. at 2651 (plurality opinion). Indeed, the *Hamdi* plurality rejected the deferential "some evidence" test advanced by the government which, it pointed out, "primarily has been employed by courts in examining an administrative record developed *after an adversarial proceeding*" consistent with due process, and not where "a habeas petitioner has received no prior proceedings before any tribunal and had no prior opportunity to rebut the Executive's factual assertions before a neutral decisionmaker." *Id.* (emphasis added). In order to address just such a situation, the federal habeas statute expressly provides for evidentiary hearings. *See, e.g., Walker v. Johnston*, 312 U.S. 275, 285 (1941) (obligation of habeas court to "hold a hearing at which evidence is received" to resolve factual disputes); *see also Harris v. Nelson*, 394 U.S. 286, 299 (1969) (recognizing power of district courts to "fashion appropriate modes of procedure" to allow a habeas petitioner to "secure[e] facts where necessary to accomplish the objective of the proceedings").

The government further suggests that an evidentiary hearing at this stage is unwarranted because of Mr. al-Marri's "vague and conclusory factual assertions." Answer at 23 n.15. An assertion of innocence, however, is neither vague nor conclusory; it is the plea that has always protected the individual against executive tyranny by putting the government to its burden of proving by a sufficiently high evidentiary standard those facts claimed by the state to warrant imprisonment. *In re Winship*, 397 U.S. 358, 361–64 (1970) (by imposing upon the government the burden of proving its case, a plea of "not guilty" safeguards individual liberty and prevents unlawful imprisonment). The two cases cited by the government, *David v. United States*, 134 F.3d 470 (1st Cir. 1998), and *Machibroda v. United States*, 368 U.S. 487 (1962), illustrate precisely this point. Both involved motions under 28 U.S.C. §2255 to collaterally attack the sentences of prisoners who *already had already been convicted* in a criminal proceeding consistent with the guarantees of due process, including the requirement that the government meet its burden of proof. They do not describe the obligations of a habeas court to determine the factual disputes in the case of a petitioner, like Mr. al-Marri, who maintains his innocence but has received no judicial process whatsoever. *Hamdi*, 124 S. Ct. at 2651 (plurality opinion). As Mr. al-Marri has been detained for over nineteen months without any judicial process, he is now entitled to an evidentiary hearing in this Court.[8]

Second, due process demands that Mr. al-Marri be afforded counsel to assist him. *Hamdi*, 124 S. Ct. at 2652 (plurality opinion) (petitioner "unquestionably has the right to access to counsel"). The government claims that Mr. al-Marri's access to counsel claims "are moot" since – following the *Hamdi* decision – it was compelled to grant Petitioner access to counsel. Answer at 22. Although counsel reached an agreement with the government to have unmonitored visits with Mr. al-Marri, his attorneys have been allowed to meet with Mr. al-Marri only in a room equipped with microphones and a functioning surveillance camera, and still have not permitted to share with Petitioner the substance of the government's classified response against him. In any event, even if Mr. al-Marri has access to counsel *now*, it does not remedy the fact that the government asks to uphold Mr. al-Marri's detention based upon a deferential review of an "Executive Branch evaluation process" in which the participation of counsel was totally prohibited.....

Due process includes the right to counsel in the first instance. *Goldberg v. Kelly*, 397 U.S. 254, 270 (1970) ("The right to be heard would be, in many cases, of little avail if it did not comprehend the right to be heard by counsel.") (quoting *Powell v. Alabama*, 287 U.S. 45, 68–69 (1932)); *see also, e.g.*, *Mosley v. St. Louis Southwestern Railway*, 634 F.2d 942, 945 (5th Cir. 1981) ("The right to the advice and assistance of retained counsel in civil litigation is implicit in the concept of due process, ... and extends to administrative, as well as courtroom, proceedings.") (citation omitted). Even persons seized in armed combat on a foreign battlefield and detained outside the United States have a due process right to have counsel participate in the process established to determine whether they are, in fact, "enemy combatants." *In re Guantanamo Detainee Cases*, 2005 WL 195356, at *26. Thus, due process demands that Mr. al-Marri be given the opportunity for counsel to participate in a *de novo* factual hearing before this Court in which he may, with the assistance of counsel, see the government's evidence and confront and cross-examine the witnesses against him.

Third, the Due Process Clause requires the government to prove by clear and convincing evidence that Mr. al-Marri is, in fact, an "enemy combatant." "In cases involving individual rights, whether criminal or civil, [t]he standard of proof [at a minimum] reflects the value society places on individual liberty.'" *Addington v. Texas*, 441 U.S. 418, 425 (1979) (quoting *Tippett v. Maryland*, 436 F.2d 1153, 1166 (4th Cir. 1971) (Soboloff, J., concurring in part and dissenting in part)). The Supreme Court has held that the "clear and convincing" standard is mandated "when the individual interests at stake ... are both particularly important and more substantial than mere loss of money." *Cruzan v. Director, Missouri Dep't of Health*, 497 U.S. 261, 282 (1990) (citation omitted). Thus, the Court has compelled the government to meet this higher burden in those circumstances in which it seeks to preventively detain individuals inside the United States based upon their alleged dangerousness. *E.g.*, *United States v. Salerno*, 481 U.S. 739, 750–52 (1987); *Foucha v. Louisiana*, 504 U.S. 71, 81, 85 (1992); *Addington*, 441 U.S. at 433; *see also Hendricks*, 521 U.S. at 356 (statute providing for preventive detention requires proof of dangerousness by clear and convincing evidence). Even if this standard does not apply to an enemy soldier seized on a foreign battlefield, *see Hamdi*, 124 S. Ct. at 2649

---

[8] The government also argues that due process would be fully satisfied were Mr. al-Marri tried before a military tribunal. Answer at 22–23 (citing *Hamdi*, 124 S. Ct. at 2651 (plurality opinion)). This issue is not before this Court because Mr. al-Marri has not been charged by, let alone tried before, a military tribunal. He has not been charged with any crime whatsoever.

(plurality opinion), it has consistently been applied to the preventive detention of individuals seized in civilian settings in the United States, citizen and non-citizen alike. *E.g.*, *Zadvydas*, 533 U.S. at 690–91 (Supreme Court has "upheld preventive detention based on dangerousness only when limited to specially dangerous individuals and subject to strong procedural protections," including requirement of proof of dangerousness by clear and convincing evidence). It should be applied here, as well.

Fourth, and perhaps most fundamentally, Mr. al-Marri is constitutionally entitled to confront and cross-examine the witnesses against him. Our system of justice is premised upon the firmly held conviction that cross-examination is "the greatest legal engine ever invented for the discovery of truth." *California v. Green*, 399 U.S. 149, 158 (1970) (internal citation omitted). The Supreme Court has "frequently emphasized that the right to confront and cross-examine witnesses is a fundamental aspect of procedural due process." *Jenkins v. McKeithen*, 395 U.S. 411, 428 (1969). The notion that an individual arrested on the streets of the United States could be held in solitary confinement in a Navy brig for the rest of his life without *any* opportunity to confront and cross-examine the single witness on whose statements his military confinement hinges is offensive to deep-seated principles of American justice.

As the Supreme Court recently held, "[i]t is a rule of the common law, founded on natural justice, that no man shall be prejudiced by evidence which he had not the liberty to cross examine." *Crawford v. Washington*, 541 U.S. 36, 124 S. Ct. 1354, 1363 (2004) (Scalia, J.) (citation omitted). This fundamental right has never been limited to criminal cases.

> Certain principles have remained relatively immutable in our jurisprudence. One of these is that where governmental action seriously injures an individual, and the reasonableness of the action depends on fact findings, the evidence used to prove the Government's case must be disclosed to the individual so that he has an opportunity to show that it is untrue. While this is important in the case of documentary evidence, it is even more important where the evidence consists of the testimony of individuals whose memory might be faulty or who, in fact, might be perjurers or persons motivated by malice, vindictiveness, intolerance, prejudice, or jealousy. We have formalized these protections in the requirements of confrontation and cross-examination. They have ancient roots. . . . This Court has been zealous to protect these rights from erosion. It has spoken out not only in criminal cases, . . . but also in all types of cases where administrative and regulatory actions were under scrutiny.

Greene v. McElroy, 360 U.S. 474, 496–97 (1959) (citations and footnote omitted); *see also In re Oliver*, 333 U.S. at 273 (right to notice of the charge and opportunity to be heard in one's defense "are basic in our system of jurisprudence" and include one's "right to examine the witnesses against him"). In this regard, the right to confront and cross-examine witnesses has been guaranteed in each of the preventive detention schemes the Supreme Court has upheld. *E.g.*, *Hendricks*, 521 U.S. at 353 (preventive detention of extremely violent sexual predators); *Salerno*, 481 U.S. at 742, 751 (preventive pre-trial detention of particularly dangerous felons). Indeed, this right is so basic to our understanding of due process that it cannot be dispensed with even when the private interest is far less significant than the indefinite loss of liberty. *Goldberg*, 397 U.S. at 270 (right to confront and cross-examine witnesses in hearing for termination of welfare benefits). If the President were permitted to do away with this due process right by the simple expedient of labeling someone an "enemy combatant," it would render meaningless the Constitution's guarantee of individual liberty, and would make the Judiciary the mere handmaiden of the Executive.

The question of the government's use of coercive interrogation tactics, and the credibility of evidence obtained through the use of such tactics, bears directly on Mr. al-Marri's right to confront and cross-examine adverse witnesses. The government states that Mr. al-Marri is not *presently* being interrogated by the military, . . . but does not deny that it has previously interrogated him, or that his detention is based upon information obtained from at least one other person who has been interrogated and detained under severe conditions. Detention for the purpose of interrogation is unlawful. *Hamdi*, 124 S. Ct. at 2641 (plurality opinion); see also *In re Guantanamo Detainee Cases*, 2005 WL 195356, at *28 (same). And, if any evidence was obtained by the government as the result of abusive interrogation tactics, that evidence cannot, as a matter of due process, be used to support Mr. al-Marri's indefinite detention as an "enemy combatant" regardless of its purported "reliability." *E.g., Chavez v. Martinez*, 538 U.S. 760, 788 (2003) (Stevens, J., concurring part and dissenting in part) (coercive interrogation tactics are "a classical example of a violation of a constitutional right implicit in the concept of ordered liberty") (internal quotation marks omitted); *Miller v. Fenton*, 474 U.S. 104, 109 (1985) ("This Court has long held that certain interrogation tactics . . . are so offensive to a civilized system of justice that they must be condemned under the Due Process Clause. . . ."); *Brown v. Mississippi*, 297 U.S. 278, 286 (1936) (coercive interrogation techniques are "revolting to the sense of justice"); *see also In re Guantanamo Detainee Cases*, 2005 WL 195356, at *26 ("[D]ue process requires a thorough [judicial] inquiry into the accuracy and reliability of statements alleged to have been obtained through torture."). At a minimum, due process requires that the Court learn how this information was obtained by the government by affording Mr. al-Marri the opportunity to confront and cross-examine the single witness on whose statements his detention rests. Otherwise, the Court cannot fulfill its obligation of assessing and weighing the evidence to determine, as it must, whether Mr. al-Marri is being unlawfully detained.

In sum, due process demands that Mr. al-Marri be afforded a meaningful opportunity to challenge the factual basis for his detention in this Court, including the right to confront and cross-examine the witnesses against him. Anything less would fall short of the constitutional guarantees that protect those within the United States from unlawful detention.

CONCLUSION

The government's position in this and other "enemy combatant" cases has been and remains that the courts must defer to the President. . . . . The Supreme Court in *Hamdi*, however, expressly rejected the government's position. 124 S. Ct. at 2650 (plurality opinion) ("[The Constitution] most assuredly envisions a role for *all three branches* when individual liberties are at stake."). A "state of war is not a blank check for the President" when he directs the military to act abroad, *id.*, and, all the more so, when he directs the military to act within the United States itself. *See Youngstown*, 343 U.S. at 645 (Jackson, J., concurring) (Executive should be "indulge[d] the widest latitude of interpretation to sustain his exclusive function to command the instruments of national force, at least when turned against the outside world for the security of our society [b]ut, when it is turned inward, . . . it should have no such indulgence"). Accordingly, the Court should embrace this opportunity to underscore the critical role played by Congress and the Judiciary as checks against the abuse of executive power, and as guarantors of individual liberty. *See The Federalist* No. 47, at 301 (James Madison) (C. Rossiter ed. 1961) ("The accumulation of all powers, legislative, executive, and judiciary, in the same hands . . . may justly be pronounced the very definition of tyranny.").

For these reasons, this Court should order Respondent to release Mr. al-Marri from detention or, alternatively, conduct an evidentiary hearing consistent with the fundamental requirements of due process in which he may challenge his classification as an "enemy combatant."

Respectfully submitted,

Andrew J. Savage, III, Esq.
SAVAGE & SAVAGE, P.A.

. . .

Lawrence S. Lustberg, Esq.
Mark A. Berman, Esq.
Jonathan L. Hafetz, Esq.
GIBBONS, DEL DEO, DOLAN,
GRIFFINGER & VECCHIONE
A Professional Corporation

. . .

Attorneys for Petitioner Ali al-Marri

By: _____
Andrew J. Savage, III

. . .

Charleston, South Carolina
February 11, 2005

IN THE UNITED STATES DISTRICT COURT
FOR THE DISTRICT OF SOUTH CAROLINA
CHARLESTON DIVISION

ALI SALEH KAHLAH AL-MARRI, and	§	
MARK A. BERMAN, as Next Friend,	§	
Petitioners,	§	
	§	
vs.	§	CIVIL ACTION NO. 2:04-2257-HFF-RSC
	§	
COMMANDER C.T. HANFT,	§	
USN Commander, Consolidated Naval Brig,	§	
Respondent.	§	

MEMORANDUM OPINION AND ORDER

I.   INTRODUCTION

This is a 28 U.S.C. §2241 *habeas corpus* action. The Court has jurisdiction over the matter pursuant to 28 U.S.C. §1331. Pending before the Court is Petitioner Ali Saleh Kahlah al-Marri's (Petitioner)[1] motion for summary judgment as to counts one and three of his petition.[2] The sole question before the Court today is whether the President of the United States (President) is authorized to detain a non-citizen as an enemy combatant under the unique circumstances presented here.

II.   FACTUAL AND PROCEDURAL HISTORY

. . .

On July 8, 2004, Petitioner filed the present petition for writ of *habeas corpus*, raising five claims: 1) unlawful detention; 2) right to counsel; 3) right to be charged; 4) denial of due process; and 5) unlawful interrogation. Subsequently, on March 3, 2005, Petitioner filed the present motion for summary judgment as to counts one and three.

. . .

---

* On February 28, 2005, the District Court for the District of South Carolina held in *Padilla v. Hanft* that the government lacked the ability to hold Jose Padilla as an enemy combatant (which was later reversed). Al-Marri's attorneys filed a motion for summary judgment regarding detention based on *Padilla*. This opinion is in response to that motion. – *Eds*.

[1] Technically, there are two Petitioners in this case, one of whom is Ali Saleh Kahlah al-Marri's Next Friend. Mr. Berman is not being held as an enemy combatant. Thus, all references herein to "Petitioner" will be to Mr. al-Marri.

[2] In counts one and three of the petition, Petitioner claims that his detention without being criminally charged violates the United States Constitution, including the Fourth, Fifth and Sixth Amendments, as well as the *habeas* suspension clause found in Article Two.

IV. CONTENTIONS OF THE PARTIES

Petitioner posits that the President possesses neither statutory nor constitutional authority to subject civilians, albeit non-citizens, to indefinite military detention as enemy combatants.

Respondent counters that both the Authorization for Use of Military Force (AUMf), Pub.L. No. 107-40, 115 Stat. 24, and the President's inherent constitutional authority allow for Petitioner's detention.

V. DISCUSSION

A. *Padilla v. Hanft*

Petitioner relies heavily on this Court's recent opinion in *Padilla v. Hanft*, No. 2:04-2221-26AJ, 2005 WL 465691 (D.S.C. Feb.28, 2005), for his contention that "the critical issue is not citizenship but, rather, the specific circumstances surrounding Petitioner's seizure by the military." . . . . Respondent, on the other hand, asserts that this Court "repeatedly recognized the significance of Padilla's citizenship in its decision granting him summary judgment." . . . . This Court agrees with Respondent.

First, throughout the *Padilla* order, the Court is careful to note that its holding is limited to the facts of the case. *E.g.*, *Padilla*, 2005 WL 465691, at * 1 ("The sole question before the Court today is whether the President of the United States [ ] is authorized to detain an United States citizen as an enemy combatant under the unique circumstances presented here."); *Padilla*, 2005 WL 465691, at *17 (relying on the "narrow circumstances presented here"); and *Padilla*, 2005 WL 465691, at *20 (stating the holding is "limited to the facts of this case").

Next, and most importantly, unlike Petitioner, Mr. Padilla is an United States citizen. Although Petitioner would have this Court hold that the issue of whether an enemy combatant can be detained turns, not on citizenship, but on the location of his capture, the holding in *Padilla* does not support such an assumption. Of course, in distinguishing Mr. Padilla from Mr. Hamdi,[4] this Court did recognize the fact that Mr. Padilla was captured on American soil. *Padilla*, 2005 WL 465691, at *6 (noting that the "cogency" of Respondent's argument that place of capture is of no consequence "eludes the Court"). Nevertheless, the holding was not limited to that fact alone, and the Court repeatedly acknowledged the importance of Mr. Padilla's citizenship to its holding. For instance, when relying on *Ex parte Milligan*, 71 U.S (4 Wall.) 2 (1866), this Court stressed that "*Milligan*'s greatest import to the case at bar is the same as that found in *Quirin*: the detention of an United States citizen by the military is disallowed without explicit Congressional authorization." *Padilla*, 2005 WL 465691, at *9.

The Court's reliance on the Non-Detention Act, 18 U.S.C. §4001(a), in *Padilla* further indicates the significance of Mr. Padilla's citizenship. The Non-Detention Act provides that "[n]o citizen shall be imprisoned or otherwise detained by the United States except pursuant to an Act of Congress." *Id*. In response to the Government's argument that the AUMF satisfied the Non-Detention Act's requirement for an act of Congress, this Court noted that "'[it] must assume, when asked to find implied powers in a grant of legislative

---

[4] Mr. Hamdi is an United States citizen who was captured during military operations in Afghanistan and detained as an enemy combatant. The Supreme Court, in a plurality opinion, held that Mr. Hamdi was properly detained pursuant to the Authorization for Use of Military Force, Pub.L. No. 107-40, 115 Stat. 24. *Hamdi v. Rumsfeld*, 124 S.Ct. 2633, 2635 (2004).

or executive authority, that the law makers intended to place no greater restraint on the *citizen* than was clearly and unmistakably indicated by the language they used.'" *Padilla*, 2005 WL 465691, at *10 (quoting *Ex parte Endo*, 323 U.S. 283, 300 (1944)) (emphasis added). In light of such precedent, this Court held that the AUMF did not authorize the detention of Mr. Padilla. *Padilla*, 2005 WL 465691, at *9.

To continue to rely on *Padilla* in light of the distinct and crucial differences between that case and the present, Petitioner must, and does, assert that his status as a resident alien is irrelevant to the legality of his detainment. To yield to such an argument, the Court must accept the premise that aliens to this country, at all times, have access to the same constitutional protections as its citizens. This it cannot do. Both Supreme Court precedent and statutory law require the failure of such a premise.

B. *Citizen Status v. Alien Status*

1. *Johnson v. Eisentrager*

In *Johnson v. Eisentrager*, 339 U.S. 763 (1950), the Supreme Court[,]...holding that *habeas corpus* protection was not afforded to these parties,[5] ... began by measuring the differences between the status of citizens and that of aliens. The Court explained that

> [t]he alien, to whom the United States has been traditionally hospitable, has been accorded a generous and ascending scale of rights as he increases his identity with our society. Mere lawful presence in the country creates an implied assurance of safe conduct and gives him certain rights; they become more extensive and secure when he makes preliminary declaration of intention to become a citizen, and they expand to those of full citizenship upon naturalization.

Id. at 770. The Court also noted that

> [m]odern law has come a long way since the time when outbreak of war made every enemy national an outlaw, subject to both public and private slaughter, cruelty and plunder. But even by the most magnanimous view, our law does not abolish the inherent distinctions recognized throughout the civilized world between citizens and aliens, nor between aliens of friendly and of enemy allegiance....

Id. at 769 (footnote omitted).

The central focus of *Eisentrager* is on the differences between the rights of resident aliens and non-resident aliens. However, in establishing that the extension of constitutional protections beyond citizenry requires the alien's presence within the jurisdiction, the Court limited the reach of such protections to resident aliens...

2. *Alien Enemy Act of 1798*

Further indicia of the decreased rights of enemy aliens arises from the Alien Enemy Act of 1798, 1 Stat. 577, as amended, 50 U.S.C. §21, *et seq.*, which has remained virtually unchanged since it was enacted. This act provides, in relevant part, that

> [w]henever there is a declared war between the United States and any foreign nation or government, or any invasion or predatory incursion is perpetrated, attempted, or threatened against the territory of the United States by any foreign nation or government, and the President makes public proclamation of the event, all natives, citizens, denizens, or subjects of the hostile nation or government, being of the age of fourteen years and

---

5 ...

upward, who shall be within the United States and not actually naturalized, shall be liable to be apprehended, restrained, secured, and removed as alien enemies.

Id.

The constitutionality of this act was upheld in *Ludecke v. Watkins*, 335 U.S. 160, 173 (1948), in which the Court stated,

[h]e who was entrusted with such vast powers in relation to the outside world was also entrusted by Congress, almost throughout the whole life of this nation, with the disposition of alien enemies during a state of war. Such a page in history is worth more than a volume of rhetoric."

Id.

That the Alien Enemy Act does not have direct application to this case is simply a result of the nature of the war on terrorism, which is not a "declared war" against a "foreign nation or government." Nevertheless, the AEA has the significance of establishing that the authority to detain enemy aliens in times of war is not a novel concept to the executive branch of our government.[6]

. . .

C.   *Authorization for Use of Military Force*

. . .

As Respondent recognizes, "aliens who come to the United States to support al Qaeda terror operations . . . are in the same position as the September 11th hijackers when the hijackers arrived in the United States. . . . [T]he AUMF emphasizes that the individuals and groups responsible for the 'acts of treacherous violence' that were committed on September 11, 2001, 'continue to pose an unusual and extraordinary threat to the national security and foreign policy of the United States.'" . . . . Assuming for purposes of this motion only that all the facts asserted by Respondent are true, Petitioner attended an al Qaeda terror training camp and later, on September 10, 2001, entered this country to continue the battle that the September 11th hijackers began on American soil.[7] . . . Accordingly, this Court holds that Petitioner's detention is proper pursuant to the AUMF and, thus, declines to reach the issue of whether the President possesses inherent authority to detain Petitioner.

D.   *Other Concerns*

1.   *Petitioner's Criminal Charges*

Petitioner makes much of the fact that he was designated as an enemy combatant sixteen months after he was indicted on criminal charges. According to Petitioner, his detention as an enemy combatant was not necessary to thwart any war-like acts he may commit since he was already being held on criminal charges. However, Respondent maintains that the facts that led the President to designate Petitioner as an enemy combatant were developed while he was in custody on the pending criminal charges. Once that determination was made, Petitioner fell within military jurisdiction.

---

[6] The proposition that citizens and non-citizens possess different degrees of constitutional rights has been established in other areas of the law as well. For example, in *Matthews v. Diaz*, 426 U.S. 67, 79–80 (1976), the Court explained that "[i]n the exercise of its broad power over naturalization and immigration, Congress regularly makes rules that would be unacceptable if applied to citizens."

[7] It is important to note that Petitioner has been labeled by the President an enemy combatant, not because he is a Qatari citizen, but because of his alleged association with al-Qaeda terrorist activities.

Such a situation can be likened to charges pending in state court: if, during the pendency of and investigation into the state charges, it is revealed that the defendant's actions implicate federal charges, the state charges can be dismissed and the matter can be transferred to federal jurisdiction. It is unreasonable to think that federal charges cannot be brought against an individual simply because he is being held on pending state charges. The argument that Petitioner's criminal charges necessarily preclude military jurisdiction is equally unsatisfactory.

Petitioner's argument also fails because the purpose of detaining enemy combatants is not only to thwart any ongoing activities of terrorism, but, as stated above, to preclude the detainee from returning to those activities. *Hamdi*, 124 S.Ct. at 2640. It is certainly possible that Petitioner could have been acquitted of the criminal charges against him, thus allowing him to, as Respondent maintains, return to the service of the enemy.[8] Accordingly, this Court declines to find that Petitioner's criminal charges prevent his present detainment as an enemy combatant.

This Court stated in *Padilla* that [t]here can be no debate that this country's laws amply provide for the investigation, detention and prosecution of citizen and non-citizen terrorists alike." *Padilla*, 2005 WL 465691, at * 12. Within that statement, however, is no implication that other options are unavailable to the Government when detaining non-citizens. In fact, the cited portion of Justice Scalia's dissent in *Hamdi* is prefaced with the assertion that "citizens have been charged and tried in Article III courts for acts of war against the United States even when their noncitizen co-conspirators were not." *Hamdi*, 124 S.Ct. at 2664 (Scalia, J., dissenting) (citing *United States v. Fricke*, 259 F. 673 (S.D.N.Y. 1919); *United States v. Robinson*, 259 F. 685 (S.D.N.Y. 1919); *United States ex rel. Wessels v. McDonald*, 265 F. 754 (E.D.N.Y. 1920); *Ex parte Quirin*, 317 U.S. 1 (1942)). Thus, this Court's statement in *Padilla* does not foreclose Petitioner's detention.

2. *Fact-finding Process*

Of course, today's ruling does not close the door of this Court to Petitioner. As stated above, this ruling is based upon the assumption that all the facts asserted by Respondent are true. It does not foreclose Petitioner's opportunity to challenge those facts. "For more than a century the central meaning of procedural due process has been clear: '[p]arties whose rights are to be affected are entitled to be heard.'" *Fuentes v. Shevin*, 407 U.S. 67, 80 (1972) (quoting *Baldwin v. Hale*, 1 Wall. 223, 233 (1864).

. . .

VI. CONCLUSION

In light of the foregoing discussion and analysis, it is the judgment of this Court that Petitioner's motion for summary judgment on counts one and three of his petition must be **DENIED.**

IT IS SO ORDERED.

Signed this 8th day of July, 2005, in Spartanburg, South Carolina.

s/ Henry F. Floyd

HENRY F. FLOYD
UNITED STATES DISTRICT JUDGE

---

[8] This Court recognizes the natural response to this reasoning that, when a defendant is acquitted of criminal charges, society should not assume that he ever did nor that he will, in the future, engage in the activities for which he was charged. In this case, however, Petitioner was not charged with crimes of terrorism, and thus, an acquittal of various fraud charges does not lead to the conclusion that he will not, in the future, engage in acts of terrorism as alleged by the government.

IN THE UNITED STATES DISTRICT COURT
FOR THE DISTRICT OF SOUTH CAROLINA
CHARLESTON DIVISION

ALI SALEH KAHLAH AL-MARRI, and MARK A. BERMAN, as next friend, 　　　　Petitioners, vs. COMMANDER C.T. HANFT, USN Commander, Consolidated Naval Brig, 　　　　Respondent.	§ § § § §　C. A. NO. 2:04-2257-HFF-RSC § § § § §

REPORT AND RECOMMENDATION

I.　INTRODUCTION

Pending before the Court is the petition of Ali Saleh Kahlah al-Marri's (al-Marri or Petitioner)[1] in accord with 28 U.S.C. §2241 for *habeas corpus* relief. . . . .

. . .

II.　STANDARD OF REVIEW

. . .

. . . [T]he standard of review at this level is limited to determining which is more persuasive on the issue of whether the petitioner falls outside the enemy combatant criteria, the government's credible evidence or the responsive rebuttal evidence which the petitioner wishes to present. The purpose being to address the "risk of erroneous deprivation." Hamdi v. Rumsfeld, 542 U.S. 507, 124 S.Ct. 2633 at 2649 (2004), (quoting Mathews v. Eldridge, 424 U.S. 319 at 335 (1976)). . . . .

. . .

VI.　DISCUSSION

It plainly appears from the pleadings, the attached exhibits, and the various declarations that the moving party is not entitled to relief, and the petition must be dismissed.

As noted the issue here is which is more persuasive on the issue of whether the petitioner falls outside the enemy combatant criteria, the government's credible evidence or the responsive rebuttal evidence which the petitioner wishes to present, with special attention to the "risk of erroneous deprivation." Here the petitioner presents nothing but a general denial to the Executive's assertion of facts. Although he apparently has evidence he believes relevant, he refuses to present it before this court stating, "Petitioner respectfully declines *at this time* the Court's invitation to assume the burden of proving his own innocence, a burden that is unconstitutional, unlawful and un-American." Petitioner's Response filed May 4, 2006 (Docket Number 68) (emphasis added).

---

[1] . . .

The petitioner mistakes an order of this court for an invitation. He also forgets his status as the petitioner in a civil proceeding under 28 U.S.C. §2241 which he is obligated to prosecute. This failure to prosecute alone would justify dismissal of his petition. Davis v. Williams, 588 F.2d 69, 70 (4th Cir. 1978).

Al-Marri brought this action and has now refused to participate in a meaningful way. As a result, there is nothing specific before the court to dispute even the simplest of assertions which al-Marri could easily dispute, were they not accurate.....

· · ·

In deciding which is more persuasive, the undersigned has not considered such things as the number of declarations for one party or the other, or for that matter given weight based upon the source of the declarations or pleadings. Nor has greater weight been given to one pleading or the other based upon credibility since none of the declarations were sworn to, hearsay predominated and none carried any other independent indicia of truthfulness. The court did consider the extent to which the parties provided details within their capacity to provide them, how specific the assertions or denials were, how direct the responses were to the issues in this matter, and the extent to which a factual assertion tends to establish falsity in a pleading or points to the possibility of an erroneous deprivation.

· · ·

The petitioner here has been given notice and opportunity, but has responded with merely a general denial and an election not to further participate in these proceedings.

Neither due process nor the rule of law in general grant a party the right to participate only in the court procedures he deems best or to present his proof whenever it suits him. The petitioner's refusal to follow "at this time" the orders of the court establishing fact-finding procedures that are intended to be both prudent and incremental is either a sophomoric approach to a serious issue, or worse, an attempt to subvert the judicial process and flout due process. The petitioner has squandered his opportunity to be heard by purposely not participating in a meaningful way.

VII. CONCLUSION

Accordingly, while recognizing the importance of respecting the acts of the Executive Branch in times of national emergency, and after providing the petitioner a threshold opportunity reasonable under the circumstances to contest the Executive Branch's actions and factual assertions in an incremental and deliberate manner, it appears to the court that the Executive Declaration is more persuasive than Petitioner's general denial on the issue of whether the petitioner meets the enemy combatant criteria, and there is no basis for concluding that an erroneous deprivation has occurred.

Therefore it is recommended that the petition for *habeas corpus* relief herein be dismissed without further action.

Respectfully Submitted,

Robert S. Carr
United States Magistrate Judge

Charleston, South Carolina
May 8, 2006

IN THE UNITED STATES DISTRICT COURT
FOR THE DISTRICT OF SOUTH CAROLINA

Ali Saleh Kahlah Al-Marri, and	)	
Mark A. Berman as next friend,	)	
	)	
Petitioners,	)	
	)	**C/A No. 02:04-2257-26AJ-HFF-RSC**
v.	)	
	)	
Commander S.L. Wright,	)	
U.S.N. Commander,	)	
Consolidated Naval Brig,	)	
	)	
Respondent.	)	
	)	

PETITIONER ALI SALEH KAHLAH AL MARRI'S SUPPLEMENTAL MEMORANDUM ADDRESSING THE IMPACT OF *HAMDAN V. RUMSFELD*

INTRODUCTION

On June 29, 2006, the United States Supreme Court issued its decision in *Hamdan v. Rumsfeld*, 548 U. S. __, 2006 WL 1764793 (June 29, 2006). This Court subsequently directed the parties to submit memoranda addressing the impact, if any, of *Hamdan* on the issues before the Court.

. . . Though *Hamdan* addressed a different question – the trial of an "enemy combatant" captured by the military in a foreign war zone and detained at Guantánamo Bay, and not the indefinite detention without charge or due process of a civilian arrested and detained inside the United States – the decision nevertheless underscores why Petitioner's detention is unlawful.

THE *HAMDAN* DECISION

. . .

Thus, as discussed at greater length below, the significance of *Hamdan* to the instant case is threefold. Specifically, the Supreme Court reiterated that: 1) the authority of the President to infringe upon the liberty of individuals detained by the military is not unlimited but, rather, is subject to significant restraints; 2) the Executive Branch's detention of individuals is constrained by and must adhere to the procedural and evidentiary protections established under law; and 3) the federal courts continue to play an essential role in ensuring that the President does not overreach, as he has in this case, and that persons detained by the military are afforded the full protection of applicable constitutional, statutory, and treaty rights.

ARGUMENT

I. Petitioner's Detention Is Unlawful.

In *Hamdan*, the Supreme Court invalidated the military commissions for their "striking" and "glaring" procedural shortcomings. 2006 WL 1764793, at *30. For example, the

907

commissions deny a defendant's right to be present at his hearing and to see and hear all the evidence against him. *Id.* at *30, *35; *see also id.* at *39 at n.67 (plurality op. of Stevens, J.) ("[T]he Government suggests no circumstances in which it would be 'fair' to convict the accused based on evidence he has not seen or heard."). The commissions also fully admit "testimonial hearsay and evidence obtained through coercion." 2006 WL 1764793, at *30; *see also id.* at *49 (Kennedy, J., concurring) (commission rules "permit admission of multiple hearsay and other forms of evidence generally prohibited on grounds of unreliability"). Indeed, the commission regulations specifically contemplate admission of "unsworn written statements" and "make no provision for exclusion of coerced declarations save those established to have been made as a result of torture." *Id.* at *49 (Kennedy, J., concurring). Under commission rules, moreover, a defendant and his civilian counsel may be denied access to evidence in the form of "protected information," a broad category which includes not only classified information but also "information concerning other national security interests." 2006 WL 1764793, at *30. The commission rules thus permit the reception of testimony from a confidential informant without the defendant's ever being "permitted to hear the testimony, see the witness's face, or learn his name." *Id.* at *30 n.43.

For more than three years, ever since he was unilaterally removed by the President from the civil justice system and detained in the Consolidated Naval Brig, Petitioner has been denied these same protections even though he is indisputably protected by the Due Process Clause of the Fifth Amendment and even though the Federal Rules of Evidence apply to his domestic habeas proceeding. . . . .

Petitioner has also been denied procedural safeguards that were afforded to Hamdan, even though Hamdan was captured in a foreign war zone and is detained at Guantánamo Bay, Cuba. For example, Hamdan was entitled to a presumption of innocence by the military commission; the government was obligated to bear the burden of proving its case against him beyond a reasonable doubt; and Hamdan was guaranteed an evidentiary hearing. Here, by contrast, the Magistrate Judge established a presumption in favor of the government's multiple-hearsay Rapp Declaration and sanctioned Petitioner's indefinite detention by the military without insisting upon the presentation of any actual evidence and without convening an evidentiary hearing at which the government's assertions might have been tested. Objections at 17–27.

. . .

II. The Federal Rules of Evidence Apply to This Case.

In *Hamdan*, the Court decided that a general authorization to create military commissions does not give the President unfettered power to set the rules for those commissions. 2006 WL 1764793, at *21; *see also id.* at *21 n.23 ("Whether or not the President has independent power, absent congressional authorization, to convene military commissions, he may not disregard limitations that Congress has, in proper exercise of its own war powers, placed on his powers.") (citing *Youngstown Sheet & Tube Co. v. Sawyer*, 343 U.S. 579, 637 (1952) (Jackson, J., concurring)). . . . . By holding that the commissions were invalid because they violated both the UCMJ, *Hamdan*, 2006 WL 1764793, at *34–*35; *id.* at *50 (Kennedy, J. concurring) ("Hamdan's military commission exceeds the bounds Congress has placed on the President's authority. . . ."), and the Geneva Conventions, *id.* at *36, the Court subjected the Administration's sweeping assertions of executive power to the rule of law. . . . .

. . .

Further, as in *Hamdan*, here "there is no suggestion . . . of any logistical difficulty in securing properly sworn and authenticated evidence or in applying the usual principles of relevance and admissibility." *Hamdan*, 2006 WL 1764793, at *35; *see also id.* at *46

(Kennedy, J., concurring) (no "exigency requiring special speed or precluding careful consideration of evidence"). Indeed, the Court in *Hamdan* expressly rejected the suggestion that the "danger posed by international terrorism" justified departing from the established rules governing the admissibility of evidence. *Id.* at *35. That reasoning applies even more forcefully here, where the Petitioner was arrested in the United States – and not on a foreign battlefield – and where civilian law enforcement agencies developed evidence for the very purpose of criminally prosecuting Petitioner in federal court. If the government's evidence is insufficient, or if the government is unwilling to prove its case, then Petitioner should be released.

III.   The AUMF Does Not Authorize Petitioner's Detention.

The Supreme Court determined in *Hamdan* that the AUMF provided at most general authorization to use military commissions in appropriate circumstances but lacked the necessary specificity to authorize Hamdan's trial by military commission. In addition, the Court found that the President's exercise of authority under the AUMF is subject to the constraints imposed by other domestic statutes.....

. . .

Even assuming the AUMF "activated the President's war powers," *Hamdan*, 2006 WL 1764793, at *21; *Hamdi v. Rumsfeld*, 542 U.S. 507 (2004), it did not authorize the indefinite military detention of suspected terrorists arrested in the United States by civilian law enforcement authorities. Indeed, as the *Hamdan* Court noted, in *Ex parte Quirin*, 317 U.S. 1 (1942), the Court "looked beyond Congress' declaration of war and accompanying authorization for use of force during World War II," relying instead on a statute independently and explicitly authorizing the military commission there at issue. *Hamdan*, 2006 WL 1764793, at *21 n.24. Here, not only does no other such statute authorize Petitioner's unilateral detention by the President but, in enacting the PATRIOT Act, Congress explicitly rejected the proposition that an individual arrested inside this country could be held indefinitely without charge. Certainly in the aftermath of *Hamdan*, the government's argument that Petitioner's detention is authorized by the AUMF must fail. Objections at 42–43.

   In addition, *Hamdan* reaffirms that the AUMF is limited by the law of war itself. 2006 WL 1764793, at *21; *see also id.* at *44 (Kennedy, J., concurring) (where government "invokes the law of war" to charge individual, it is bound by the limits the law of war imposes); *accord Hamdi*, 542 U.S. at 520 (plurality op.) ("Congress' grant of authority for the use of 'necessary and appropriate force' to include the authority to detain for the duration of the relevant conflict . . . is based on longstanding law-of-war principles."). As previously explained, Petitioner's detention is not authorized under the AUMF because the law of war does not apply to him. Objections at 37–42.[1] . . . .

. . .

CONCLUSION

For the foregoing reasons, the Supreme Court's decision in *Hamdan v. Rumsfeld* further supports Petitioner's claims that his detention is unlawful, and that he is otherwise entitled to a process more robust than that afforded to him by the Magistrate Judge.

---

[1] Assuming *arguendo*, however, that the law of war applies to him, Petitioner's incredibly harsh and punitive conditions of confinement, including his near complete isolation at the Brig for more than three years and other mistreatment, violate Common Article 3 of the Geneva Conventions, which prohibits "[o]utrages on personal dignity, in particular humiliating and degrading treatment." *See* Complaint filed in *al Marri v. Rumsfeld et al.*, C/A No. 2:05-2259-HFF-RSC.

Respectfully submitted,

Lawrence S. Lustberg   Andrew J. Savage, III
Mark A. Berman   **SAVAGE & SAVAGE, P.A.**
GIBBONS, DEL DEO, DOLAN,   . . .
GRIFFINGER & VECCHIONE,
A Professional Corporation
        . . .

Jonathan Hafetz   By: /s/ Andrew J. Savage, III
BRENNAN CENTER FOR JUSTICE   Andrew J. Savage, III
AT NYU SCHOOL OF LAW   . . .
        . . .

Attorneys for Petitioner Ali Saleh Kahlah al-Marri

Dated: Charleston, South Carolina
       July 12, 2006

**IN THE UNITED STATES DISTRICT COURT
FOR THE DISTRICT OF SOUTH CAROLINA**

ALI SALEH KAHLAH AL-MARRI, and
MARK A. BERMAN, as next friend,
 	
               Petitioners,
 	
v.
 	
COMMANDER S.L. WRIGHT,
U.S.N. Commander, Consolidated Naval Brig,
 	
               Respondent.
	Civil Action No.
	2:04-2257-HFF

**RESPONDENT'S RESPONSE TO PETITIONER AL-MARRI'S MEMORANDUM
ADDRESSING THE IMPACT, IF ANY, OF *HAMDAN* V. *RUMSFELD* ON HIS
PETITION**

Respondent, by and through undersigned counsel, respectfully submits this response to petitioner Al-Marri's supplemental memorandum addressing the impact, if any, of Hamdan v. Rumsfeld, 548 U. S. __, 126 S. Ct. 2749 (2006), on his petition for a writ of habeas corpus. For the reasons explained below and in respondent's initial response to this Court's June 29, 2006 Order, the Hamdan decision does not materially affect al-Marri's challenge to his detention as an enemy combatant.

Al-Marri's reliance on Hamdan to support his objections to the Magistrate Judge's report is misplaced for the fundamental reason that Hamdan pointedly did not address the President's authority to detain enemy combatants during the ongoing conflict with al Qaeda. See 126 S. Ct. at 2798. Moreover, nothing in Hamdan calls into question any aspect of the controlling opinion in Hamdi v. Rumsfeld, 542 U.S. 507 (2004), which set out a framework for judicial review of habeas petitions filed by citizen enemy combatants seeking to challenge their detention during the ongoing armed conflicts with al Qaeda and the Taliban, and on which the Magistrate Judge relied in recommending that al-Marri's petition be dismissed.

. . .

Nothing in Hamdan undermines the President's authority to detain captured enemy combatants during the ongoing war, as opposed to subject them to trial and punishment by military commission as presently constituted. Indeed, the Court specifically "emphasized" that it was not addressing "the Government's power to detain [Hamdan] for the duration of active hostilities in order to prevent [great] harm." 126 S. Ct. at 2798. And the Court in no way called into question its recent decision in Hamdi dealing with the different question of the President's authority to detain captured combatants, such as al-Marri, during the ongoing conflict.[1]

---

[1] The Hamdan Court found it unnecessary to address the question of whether the President could rely on his inherent war powers to convene military commissions in the absence of congressional action, because Congress had chosen to regulate them. See 126 S. Ct. at 2774 & n.23.

Al-Marri's attempt to find support in Hamdan to challenge his wartime detention lacks merit. First, al-Marri complains . . . that certain court-martial rules that the President decided not to apply in military commissions, such as prohibitions on the admission of certain forms of hearsay, similarly do not apply in his habeas proceeding. That complaint has no merit because petitioner is not on trial or subject to criminal punishment that could extend his detention beyond the cessation of hostilities, but rather is being detained as an enemy combatant. See Hamdi, 542 U.S. at 518 ("The purpose of detention is to prevent captured individuals from returning to the field of battle and taking up arms once again."). In the detention context presented here, the Supreme Court in Hamdi has already set out the procedural framework that governs challenges filed by citizen enemy combatants to their detention. See Hamdi, 542 U.S. at 524–539.

. . . As we have explained in our previous pleadings, at a minimum, an alien enemy combatant such as al-Marri is entitled to no greater process than the Hamdi plurality ruled must be accorded to citizen-combatants.

Al-Marri's further contention . . . that Hamdan supports his claim that the AUMF does not authorize his detention is equally meritless. The Hamdan Court did not question the Hamdi plurality's ruling that "the AUMF activated the President's war powers," 126 S. Ct. at 2775, including the powers to detain and prosecute enemy combatants. The Hamdan Court's conclusion that the AUMF did not authorize military commissions does not undermine Hamdi's conclusion that it authorized the detention of captured combatants. Al-Marri suggests . . . that Hamdan requires additional congressional action to authorize his detention. That is a misreading of the Hamdan decision and ignores Hamdi, which Hamdan did not purport to limit, let alone overrule. . . . .

. . .

CONCLUSION

For the reasons stated above and in respondent's initial response to this Court's June 29, 2006 Order, the Hamdan decision provides no support for al-Marri's habeas petition challenging his detention as an enemy combatant. Accordingly, this Court should adopt Magistrate Judge Carr's Report and Recommendation that the petition be dismissed.

Respectfully submitted.

REGINALD I. LLOYD
UNITED STATES ATTORNEY

s/ Kevin F. McDonald
Kevin F. McDonald . . .
Assistant United States Attorney
. . .

David. B. Salmons
Assistant to the Solicitor General
United States Dept. of Justice
. . .

July 19, 2006

IN THE UNITED STATES DISTRICT COURT
FOR THE DISTRICT OF SOUTH CAROLINA
CHARLESTON DIVISION

ALI SALEH KAHLAH AL-MARRI, and	§	
MARK A. BERMAN, as next friend,	§	
Petitioners,	§	
	§	
vs.	§	CIVIL ACTION NO. 2:04-2257-HFF
	§	
COMMANDER S.L. WRIGHT,	§	
USN Commander, Consolidated Naval Brig,	§	
Respondent.	§	

MEMORANDUM OPINION AND ORDER

. . .

IV. DISCUSSION

A. *Burdens of Production and Persuasion*

As the Magistrate Judge notes, there is no binding standard for reviewing the factual basis supporting the detention of an alleged enemy combatant. . . . . What little guidance is available comes from the Supreme Court's plurality opinion in *Hamdi v. Rumsfeld*, 542 U.S. 507 (2004). In *Hamdi*, a plurality of the Court held that the President has the authority to detain a United States citizen captured while taking up arms against the United States in support of the Taliban or Al-Qaeda. The plurality also held, however, that "a citizen-detainee seeking to challenge his classification as an enemy combatant must receive notice of the factual basis for his classification, and a fair opportunity to rebut the Government's factual assertions before a neutral decisionmaker." *Id.* at 533. . . . . Describing this process as "both prudent and incremental," the plurality noted that the "full protections that accompany challenges to detentions in other settings may prove unworkable and inappropriate in the enemy-combatant setting." *Id.* at 535.

Petitioner now seeks to escape the framework outlined by the *Hamdi* Court and asserts that Respondent should be required to bear both the burdens of production and persuasion under a standard more closely approximating that used in a criminal trial. . . . . Petitioner contends that the Constitution does not permit any presumption in favor of the Government . . . that any evidence produced by the Government must be admissible under the Federal Rules of Evidence . . . and that he is entitled to discovery. . . . In short, Petitioner advocates a "full-blown adversary process." . . . .

Petitioner's principal contention is that *Hamdi* does not apply here because the "constitutional balance" it struck is limited to cases where the alleged enemy combatant is captured on a foreign battlefield. The Court finds this argument unconvincing.

. . .

Petitioner's attempt to limit *Hamdi*'s scope likewise finds little support in the few subsequent cases which have analyzed challenges to detention. The United States District Court for the District of Columbia, for example, observed that *Hamdi* "considered the process that is owed under the Constitution for United States citizens detained as enemy combatants." *Khalid v. Bush*, 355 F.Supp.2d 311, 323 n.16 (D.D.C.2005). Importantly, the court made this statement while reviewing the claims of alleged enemy combatants defined as:

> individual[s] who [were] part of or supporting Taliban or al Qaeda forces, or associated forces that are engaged in hostilities against the United States or its coalition partners. This includes any person who has committed a belligerent act or has directly supported hostilities in aid of enemy armed forces.

Id. at 315 n.2. This definition makes no reference to the location of any hostile act or the place of capture. In noting that any due process rights possessed by the *Khalid* detainees afford "much of the same process" available to Hamdi, the court implicitly recognized the broad applicability of the due process standards set out in *Hamdi*.

Similarly, in *Padilla v. Hanft*, the Fourth Circuit viewed *Hamdi* as addressing the authority of the Executive "to detain citizens who qualify as 'enemy combatants.'" 423 F.3d 286, 391 (4th Cir. 2005) (quoting *Hamdi*, 542 U.S. at 516). While it is true that *Hamdi* and *Padilla* defined "enemy combatants" as "individual[s] who . . . [were] part of or supporting forces hostile to the United States or coalition partners in Afghanistan and who engaged in an armed conflict against the United States there," *Padilla*, 423 F.3d at 391 (citing *Hamdi*, 542 U.S. at 516) (internal punctuation omitted) (alteration in original), this definition was expressly used only for "purposes of this case," *Hamdi*, 542 U.S. at 516; *see also Padilla*, 423 F.3d at 391. *Hamdi* itself recognized that "there is some debate as to the proper scope" of the term "enemy combatant." *Hamdi*, 542 U.S. at 516. The Court further observed that "[t]he legal category of enemy combatant has not been elaborated in great detail. The permissible bounds of the category will be defined by the lower courts as subsequent cases are presented to them." *Id.* at 522. It is clear, then, that the term "enemy combatant" is not limited to the definition used in *Hamdi*. This Court, in fact, recognized as much when it denied Petitioner's motion for summary judgment. *Al-Marri*, 378 F.Supp.2d at 676–77 (holding that Petitioner's status as an alien, rather than his place of capture, justifies his detention by the President). As *Hamdi* has been interpreted as supporting the authority of the President to designate Padilla, 423 F.2d at 391, and al-Marri, 378 F.Supp.2d at 676–77, as enemy combatants and to order their detention, it makes little sense to cast aside the framework it announced for analyzing the factual evidence supporting that detention. The Court concludes, then, that the due process requirements outlined in *Hamdi* apply here.

Having determined that *Hamdi* applies, the question becomes what burdens it places on the Government and on an alleged enemy combatant during the initial phase of an enemy combatant proceeding. While the plurality opinion does not indicate precisely how the burdens of production and persuasion are to be allocated, it does offer much guidance. First, as already noted, it indicates that the Constitution permits "a presumption in favor of the Government's evidence." *Hamdi*, 542 U.S. at 534. Second, once the Government puts forth "credible evidence" that the petitioner is an enemy combatant, the burden shifts to petitioner to rebut that showing with "more persuasive evidence." *Id.*

B.   Factual Evidence

1.   *Government's Burden*

Using the framework announced in *Hamdi*, the Court begins its inquiry by examining the evidence put forth by the Government in support of Petitioner's detention. Here, Respondent bases Petitioner's designation as an enemy combatant and his continued detention solely on the "Declaration of Mr. Jeffrey N. Rapp, Director, Joint Intelligence Task Force for Combating Terrorism" ("Rapp Declaration" or "the Declaration"), which consists of a summary of the intelligence gathered on Petitioner's activities in the United States. Before considering the import of the Rapp Declaration, the Court turns to Petitioner's objection to the Magistrate Judge's conclusion that the Declaration can be considered by the Court in support of Respondent's argument that Petitioner is an enemy combatant.

a.   *Petitioner's Objections*

Petitioner's principal objection to the Court's consideration of the Rapp Declaration centers on the hearsay status of the Declaration. . . . .

In making this argument, Petitioner and amici misread *Hamdi* and misunderstand the nature of the current proceedings. As already observed, *Hamdi* indicated that enemy combatant proceedings should be "both prudent and incremental." 542 U.S. at 539. The Court further indicated that the first increment consists of a simple examination of the available evidence and an opportunity for rebuttal by the detainee. *Id.* at 538. At this stage, a court can quickly separate out "the errant tourist, embedded journalist, or local aid worker," *id.* at 534, after a quick comparison of the evidence presented by the Government and the rebuttal offered by the detainee. A process of this sort, then, prevents an "erroneous deprivation of a detainee's liberty interest" while eliminating procedures which unduly burden the Government. *Id.* Incumbent in this process is the detainee's burden of presenting rebuttal evidence sufficient to overcome the Government's factual basis for detaining the alleged combatant. Therefore, the question at this stage is whether the factual notice provided by the Government can consist of hearsay or whether it must meet a more stringent evidentiary standard.

On this point, *Hamdi* is unequivocal: hearsay may be used to satisfy the Government's burden of providing an alleged enemy combatant with notice of the factual allegations against him. In *Hamdi*, the Supreme Court repeatedly indicated that hearsay may be considered at the initial phase of enemy combatant proceedings. The Court, for example, expressly rejected the district court's view which "disapproved of the hearsay nature of the Mobbs Declaration." 542 U.S. at 528, 532. The Court further held that "[h]earsay . . . may need to be accepted as the most reliable available evidence from the Government in such a proceeding." *Id.* at 533–34. This hearsay could exist of, among other things, a summary of official records created by "a knowledgeable affiant." *Id.* at 534. Finally, the Court gave specific approval to the admission of these affidavits, holding that "a habeas court in a case such as this may accept affidavit evidence like that contained in the Mobbs Declaration, so long as it also permits the alleged combatant to present his own factual case to rebut the Government's return." *Id.* at 538.

As with his earlier contention that *Hamdi's* allocation of the burdens of production and persuasion does not apply here, Petitioner's primary argument for distinguishing *Hamdi's* teaching on the consideration of hearsay statements is that *Hamdi* applies only when an alleged enemy combatant has been detained on a foreign battlefield. Having rejected this distinction earlier, the Court refuses to revive it now. As *Hamdi* applies to support Petitioner's detention as an enemy combatant, its instructions as to the process to which Petitioner is entitled also apply.[6]

. . .

b.   *Rapp Declaration*

Once it is determined that the Rapp Declaration may be considered by the Court at this stage, it is apparent that the Declaration satisfies Respondent's burden of providing Petitioner with the factual basis supporting his detention as an enemy combatant. . . . . Affording this evidence a favorable presumption, as *Hamdi* directs, the Court finds that the Government has met its burden of providing a factual basis in support of Petitioner's classification and detention as an enemy combatant.

2.   *Petitioner's Burden*

. . .

In the instant case, the parties dispute the exact burden which each party bears. Respondent, for example, objects to the Magistrate Judge's conclusion that the Government at all times bears the burden of justifying Petitioner's detention by clear and convincing evidence. . . . . Petitioner, in objecting to *Hamdi's* application here, objects to any presumption in favor of the Government's evidence and to any burden being placed on Petitioner. . . . . Although Petitioner's position must be – and has already been – rejected, the Court finds it unnecessary to detail with exactness the burdens faced by the parties. This is so because the Government, by presenting the Rapp Declaration, has satisfied its initial burden of providing the factual basis for Petitioner's detention while Petitioner has offered nothing more than a general denial in support of his burden of presenting "more persuasive evidence." . . . .

Despite being given numerous opportunities to come forward with evidence supporting this general denial, Petitioner has refused to do so. . . . .

Given Petitioner's refusal to participate in the initial evidentiary process and his failure to offer *any* evidence on his behalf, it is beyond question that he has failed to present "more persuasive evidence" to rebut Respondent's classification and detention of him as an enemy combatant. Further, given the imbalance between the evidence presented by the parties, the Government clearly meets any burden of persuasion which could reasonably be imposed on it at this initial stage. Proceeding incrementally, as *Hamdi* directs, the Court need go no further today. Accordingly, under *Hamdi's* outline of the procedures applicable in enemy combatant proceedings, the Court finds that Petitioner has received notice of the factual basis supporting his detention and has been afforded a meaningful opportunity to rebut that evidence. As a review of that evidence does not indicate that an "erroneous deprivation" has occurred, *Hamdi*, 542 U.S. at 534, this petition should be dismissed.

V.   CONCLUSION

Therefore, pursuant to the standard set forth above, the Court overrules Petitioner's objections to the Report, adopts the Report, and incorporates it herein to the extent that it does not contradict the terms of this Order. It is the judgment of this Court that this petition be, and the same is hereby, **DISMISSED.**

---

[6] . . .

IT IS SO ORDERED.

Signed this 8th day of August, 2006, in Spartanburg, South Carolina.

> s/ Henry F. Floyd
> HENRY F. FLOYD
> UNITED STATES DISTRICT JUDGE

DEPUTY SECRETARY OF DEFENSE

███████████

NOV 1 3 2006

MEMORANDUM FOR DIRECTOR, OFFICE FOR THE ADMINISTRATIVE
REVIEW OF THE DETENTION OF ENEMY COMBATANTS

SUBJECT: Combatant Status Review Tribunal

    You are directed to provide Ali Saleh Kahlah Al-Marri with a Combatant Status
Review Tribunal upon dismissal of his pending habeas litigation based on Section 7 of
Military Commissions Act of 2006. This Combatant Status Review Tribunal shall follow
the procedures contained in the "Implementation of Combatant Status Review Tribunals
for Enemy Combatants Detained at U.S. Naval Base Guantanamo Bay, Cuba," dated July
14, 2006. In accordance with those procedures, the Combatant Status Review Tribunal
shall determine, based on the complete record before it, whether a preponderance of the
evidence supports the conclusion that, notwithstanding any prior designation, al-Marri
meets the criteria set forth in those procedures to be designated an enemy combatant.

Gordon England (signature)

IN THE UNITED STATES COURT OF APPEALS
FOR THE FOURTH CIRCUIT

ALI SALEH KAHLAH AL-MARRI,	)
	)
Petitioner-Appellant,	)
	)
and	)
	)
MARK A. BERMAN, as next friend,	)
	)
Petitioner,	) No. 06-7427
	)
v.	)
	)
COMMANDER S.L. WRIGHT,	)
USN Commander, Consolidated Naval Brig.,	)
	)
Respondent-Appellee.	)

RESPONDENT-APPELLEE'S MOTION TO DISMISS FOR LACK
OF JURISDICTION AND PROPOSED BRIEFING SCHEDULE

. . .

As explained below, the Military Commissions Act of 2006 (MCA), Pub. L. No. 109-366 . . . , which took effect on October 17, 2006, removes federal court jurisdiction over pending and future habeas corpus actions and any other actions filed by or on behalf of detained aliens determined by the United States to be enemy combatants, such as petitioner-appellant al-Marri, except as provided in Section 1005(e)(2) and (e)(3) of the Detainee Treatment Act (DTA). In plain terms, the MCA removes this Court's jurisdiction (as well as the district court's) over al-Marri's habeas action. Accordingly, the Court should dismiss this appeal for lack of jurisdiction and remand the case to the district court with instructions to dismiss the petition for lack of jurisdiction.

Background

Exercising, inter alia, its "plenary authority to regulate federal court jurisdiction," In re B-727 Aircraft Serial No. 21010, 272 F.3d 264, 269 (5th Cir. 2001), Congress enacted the DTA – the predecessor to the MCA – on December 30, 2005, to remove federal court jurisdiction over applications for a writ of habeas corpus and any other actions filed by alien enemy combatants held in military custody at Guantanamo Bay. . . . .

In Hamdan v. Rumsfeld, 126 S. Ct. 2749 (2006), the Supreme Court held that the DTA did not divest the federal courts of jurisdiction over habeas actions, such as Hamdan's, which were pending when the DTA was enacted and which challenged the legitimacy of the military commissions established by the President. The Court went on to hold that the military commission that was convened to try Hamdan for a violation of the law of war was not authorized by Congress.

In response to <u>Hamdan</u>, Congress enacted the MCA both to provide the statutory authorization for military commissions the Court found lacking in <u>Hamdan</u> and to amend the DTA to make clear that the provision eliminating habeas jurisdiction applies to all <u>pending</u> habeas actions and, as most relevant here, to extend the DTA's elimination of habeas jurisdiction to any action (other than the exclusive review provided in the D.C. Circuit) filed on behalf of any alien enemy combatant held by the United States, regardless of the location of the detention.

· · ·

Argument

The MCA divests this Court and the district court of jurisdiction over al-Marri's habeas petition. In pertinent part, the jurisdiction-removing provisions apply to "<u>all cases, without exception</u>" that were "<u>pending</u> on or after" October 17, 2006, and "which relate to <u>any aspect of the</u> detention, *** of an alien detained by the United States since September 11, 2001." MCA §7(b) (emphasis added). Al-Marri's petition for a writ of habeas corpus meets these three conditions. First, the petition was filed on July 8, 2004, see <u>Al-Marri</u> v. <u>Wright</u>, 443 F. Supp. 2d 774, 777 (D.S.C. 2006), and was still pending on October 17, 2006. Second, the petition challenges the legality of al-Marri's detention as an enemy combatant. <u>Ibid.</u>

Third, al-Marri is an "alien detained by the United States" within the meaning of the MCA, because he has "been determined by the United States to have been properly detained as an enemy combatant or is awaiting such determination." MCA §7(a). . . . . Moreover, even if, contrary to fact, al-Marri had not been determined by the United States to have been properly detained as an enemy combatant, the MCA would still apply to al-Marri's petition because al-Marri is also "awaiting" such a determination within the meaning of the MCA. The Department of Defense has ordered, upon dismissal of this habeas action for lack of jurisdiction, that al-Marri be provided with a Combatant Status Review Tribunal (CSRT), in accordance with the existing procedures governing such tribunals. . . . .[1] If the CSRT's finding is adverse to al-Marri, he may avail himself of the DTA's exclusive review scheme by filing a claim in the District of Columbia Circuit.[2]

· · ·

Conclusion

For the reasons stated above, this court should dismiss this appeal and remand the case to the district court with instructions to dismiss al-Marri's habeas petition for lack of jurisdiction.

---

[1] Although the order makes clear that al-Marri is alternatively covered by the jurisdictional provision <u>both</u> as an alien determined to be properly held as an enemy combatant and as an alien awaiting such a determination, the order is not the event that eliminated this Court's jurisdiction and is not necessary to the government's argument that jurisdiction is lacking. This Court lost jurisdiction over this action on the effective date of the MCA; the order indicates only how the government plans to handle al-Marri in the event the courts agree that the MCA divested the courts of jurisdiction.

[2] Under the DTA, al-Marri may challenge whether the CSRT's determination was "consistent with the standards and procedures specified by the Secretary of Defense for [CSRTs]," including "the requirement that the conclusion of the Tribunal be supported by a preponderance of the evidence." DTA §1005(e)(2)(C)(i). Also, "to the extent the Constitution and laws of the United States are applicable," al-Marri may challenge "whether the use of such standards and procedures to make the [combatant] determination is consistent with the Constitution and laws of the United States." DTA §1005(e)(2)(C)(ii).

Respectfully submitted,

PAUL D. CLEMENT
Solicitor General

REGINALD I. LLOYD
United States Attorney
District of South Carolina

GREGORY G. GARRE
Deputy Solicitor General

DAVID B. SALMONS
JONATHAN L. MARCUS
Assistants to the Solicitor General

_____

KEVIN F. MCDONALD . . .
Assistant United States Attorney

. . .

November 13, 2006

RECORD NO. 06-7427

In The

United States Court of Appeals
For The Fourth Circuit

ALI SALEH KAHLAH AL-MARRI;
MARK A. BERMAN, as next friend,

Petitioners - Appellants,

v.

COMMANDER S.L. WRIGHT, USN Commander,
Consolidated Naval Brig.,

Respondent - Appellee.

ON APPEAL FROM THE UNITED STATES DISTRICT COURT
FOR THE DISTRICT OF SOUTH CAROLINA
AT CHARLESTON

APPELLANTS' RESPONSE TO
APPELLEE'S MOTION TO DISMISS FOR
LACK OF JURISDICTION

Jonathan Hafetz	Andrew J. Savage, III	Lawrence S. Lustberg
BRENNAN CENTER FOR JUSTICE	SAVAGE & SAVAGE, P.A.	Mark A. Berman
AT NYU SCHOOL OF LAW		GIBBONS, DEL DEO, DOLAN,
		GRIFFINGER & VECCHIONE,
		A Professional Corporation
Counsel for Appellants	*Counsel for Appellants*	*Counsel for Appellants*

THE LEX GROUP ◆

. . .

---

* Redactions on this page have been added for privacy purposes. – *Eds*.

INTRODUCTION AND SUMMARY OF ARGUMENT

On November 13, 2006, the government moved to dismiss the appeal of Petitioner Ali Saleh Kahlah al-Marri ("al-Marri"), arguing that section 7 of the Military Commissions Act of 2006, Pub. L. No. 109-366 ("MCA") deprives the federal courts of subject matter jurisdiction over his habeas corpus petition and this appeal. Disregarding the grave constitutional issues at stake, the government contends that Congress eliminated the right of lawful resident aliens to challenge their executive detention by way of habeas corpus. As a result, the government argues, neither this Court, nor the Supreme Court, has jurisdiction to hear the fundamental questions raised on this habeas appeal:

1) whether the President has the authority to detain as an "enemy combatant," and without charge, a civilian arrested in his home in Peoria, Illinois; and,

2) if so, whether the President may imprison such person indefinitely in a Navy Brig based solely upon a multiple-hearsay declaration from a government bureaucrat, without a hearing and without any witnesses.

Instead, under the government's view, the President is now free "to handle" al-Marri as he sees fit. He can prolong indefinitely al-Marri's 3½-year military imprisonment without charge, and now exercises complete and unfettered control over al-Marri's ability to challenge the lawfulness of that imprisonment in an Article III court.

The government's arguments should be rejected. Like American citizens, aliens in the United States have a constitutional right to habeas corpus. Thus, absent a valid suspension of the writ, Congress could not repeal habeas jurisdiction over the petition of a lawful resident alien like al-Marri without providing an adequate and effective substitute. Yet, the MCA, in the government's view, not only eliminates jurisdiction over al-Marri's habeas petition and appeal, but fails to provide *any* substitute that guarantees al-Marri review by an Article III court of the lawfulness of his prolonged executive detention. Further, contrary to the government's suggestion, the future possibility of review by another circuit of a summary military hearing that may never occur and that fails to satisfy the most basic requirements of due process cannot provide an adequate or effective substitute for habeas corpus.

As set forth below, section 7 of the MCA plainly does not repeal jurisdiction over habeas petitions filed by or on behalf of resident aliens, like al-Marri, whose constitutional entitlement to the Great Writ and Due Process has long been recognized. If, however, this Court construes section 7 as purporting to eliminate jurisdiction over al-Marri's habeas petition, it must invalidate this provision under the Suspension, Due Process, and Equal Protection Clauses of the Constitution.

ARGUMENT

A. Al-Marri Has A Constitutional Right To Habeas Corpus.

Habeas corpus is "the highest safeguard of liberty" within our legal tradition, *Smith v. Bennett*, 365 U.S. 708, 712 (1961), and has provided a judicial remedy that "has been for centuries esteemed the best and only sufficient defense of personal freedom." *Lonchar v. Thomas*, 517 U.S. 314, 324 (1996) (citation omitted). Long known as the Great Writ, habeas corpus is "a writ antecedent to statue, ... throwing its root deep into the genius of our common law. ..." *Rasul v. Bush*, 542 U.S. 466, 473 (2004) (citation omitted).

Although thought of today as a post-conviction remedy, habeas was historically "a remedy against executive detention." *Swain v. Pressley*, 430 U.S. 372, 386 (1977) (Burger, C.J., concurring); *see also, e.g., Brown v. Allen*, 344 U.S. 443, 533 (1953) (Jackson, J., concurring) ("The historic purpose of the writ has been to relieve detention by executive authorities without judicial trial."). Indeed, it is precisely in reviewing the lawfulness of executive detention that the writ's "protections have been strongest." *INS v. St. Cyr*, 533 U.S. 289, 301 (2001).

Our nation's Founders took great care to ensure that access to habeas corpus would never depend upon executive or legislative grace by ensuring the Writ's protections in the Constitution's Suspension Clause. *See St. Cyr*, 533 U.S. at 304 n.24 (Suspension Clause protects against loss of right to pursue habeas claim "by either the inaction or the action of Congress") (citing *Ex parte Bollman*, 8 U.S. (4 Cranch) 75 (1807)); *The Federalist*, No. 84, at 511 (Alexander Hamilton) (Clinton Rossiter ed. 1961) (affirming importance of Constitution's "establishment of the writ of *habeas corpus*"). Under the Suspension Clause, "[t]he Privilege of the Writ of Habeas Corpus shall not be suspended, unless when in Cases of Rebellion or Invasion, the public Safety may require it." U.S. Const. art. I, §9, cl. 2.

The Suspension Clause protects not only citizens, but all persons arrested and detained in the United States. *See, e.g., Hamdi v. Rumsfeld*, 542 U.S. 507, 525 (2004) (plurality opinion) ("[A]bsent suspension, the writ of habeas corpus remains available to *every* individual detained inside the United States.") (emphasis added); *St. Cyr*, 533 U.S. at 305 (elimination of habeas review over deportation of aliens would raise "a serious Suspension Clause issue"). Thus, regardless of whether the Constitution's guarantee of habeas corpus extends to aliens captured and detained outside the United States – a question not before this Court – it certainly encompasses an individual like al-Marri, who was seized and has at all times been detained inside this country. *See Johnson v. Eisentrager*, 339 U.S. 763, 771 (1950) ("[The Supreme] Court has been at pains to point out that it was the alien's presence within its territorial jurisdiction that gave the Judiciary power to act."); *id.* at 777–78; *Rasul*, 542 U.S. at 475–79.[1]

Indeed, as the government has previously acknowledged, the right to habeas corpus for aliens arrested and detained inside the United States has been virtually unquestioned. *See, e.g.*, Argument Transcript, *Rasul v. Bush*, 542 U.S. 466 (2004), 2004 WL 943637, at *40–*41 (Solicitor General Olson agreeing that petitioner's right to invoke federal court's habeas jurisdiction and rights under Due Process Clause "[w]ould . . . be entirely different" if he were detained within sovereign territory of the United States).

. . .

B. Congress Has Not Suspended, And Could Not Validly Suspend, Habeas Corpus In Order To Eliminate Jurisdiction Over Al-Marri's Habeas Petition.

The Suspension Clause limits Congress's ability to interfere with the federal courts' essential role in protecting individual liberty, "serving as an important judicial check on the Executive's discretion in the realm of detentions." *Hamdi*, 542 U.S. at 536 (plurality opinion). The Constitution expressly prohibits suspension except in cases of actual "Rebellion or Invasion," and, even then, only when "the public Safety" so requires. U.S. Const. art. I, §9, cl. 2.

Cognizant of the Constitution's clear limits on its power to curtail the Great Writ, Congress has suspended habeas "[o]nly in the rarest of circumstances." *Hamdi*, 542 U.S.

---

[1] . . .

at 525 (plurality opinion); *see also* William F. Duker, *A Constitutional History of Habeas Corpus* 149, 178 n.190 (1980) (suspension authorized only four times in American history). Each time, Congress expressly stated that it was authorizing suspension, and each suspension was effected amid an ongoing insurrection or invasion. *See id.*[3] "At all other times, [the Writ] has remained a critical check on the Executive, ensuring that it does not detain individuals except in accordance with law." *Hamdi*, 542 U.S. at 525 (plurality opinion) (citing *St. Cyr*, 533 U.S. at 301).

In enacting the MCA, Congress did not clearly state that it intended to suspend the constitutional right to habeas corpus, and it did not invoke the necessary grounds for suspension. *See, e.g.*, 152 Cong. Rec. S10368 (daily ed. Sept. 28, 2006) (statement of Sen. Specter) ("Fact No. 3, uncontested. We do not have a rebellion or invasion."). Furthermore, the MCA's elimination of habeas jurisdiction contains no temporal limitation; it purports to be permanent. This Court, therefore, cannot and should not conclude that Congress sought to suspend all aliens' constitutional right to habeas corpus. *See generally St. Cyr*, 533 U.S. at 299 ("[W]hen a particular interpretation of a statute invokes the outer limits of Congress' power, we expect a clear indication that Congress intended that result."); *Gregory v. Ashcroft*, 501 U.S. 452, 461 (1991) ("In traditionally sensitive areas, . . . the requirement of [a] clear statement assures that the legislature has in fact faced, and intended to bring into issue, the critical matters involved in the judicial decision.").

C.   The MCA Does Not Divest This Court Of Jurisdiction Over Al-Marri's Appeal.

Section 7 of the MCA amends 28 U.S.C. 2241 by eliminating jurisdiction over habeas corpus petitions "filed by or on behalf of an alien detained by the United States" who either:

(i)   "has been determined by the United States to have been properly detained as an enemy combatant"; or

(ii)   "is awaiting such determination."

MCA §7(a). As set forth below, section 7(a) does not apply to al-Marri because he does not fall within either category, and because section 7(a) does not retroactively strip the federal courts of jurisdiction over his pending habeas case. If, however, this Court construes the MCA to apply to al-Marri, it must invalidate the statute under the Suspension, Due Process, and Equal Protection Clauses.

---

[3] *See also* Act of Mar. 3, 1863, ch. 81, §1, 12 Stat. 755 (authorizing President Lincoln during Civil War "to suspend the privilege of the writ of habeas corpus in any case throughout the United States, or any part thereof" for duration of "the present rebellion" and where "the public safety may require it"); Act. of Apr. 20, 1871, ch. 22, §4, 17 Stat. 14 (authorizing President Grant amid armed rebellion in Reconstruction South "to suspend the privileges of the writ of habeas corpus" for "the continuance of such rebellion" and where "the public safety shall require it"); Act of July 1, 1902, ch. 1369, §5, 32 Stat. 692 (authorizing President or Governor amid armed rebellion in Philippines to "suspend" the "privilege of the writ of habeas corpus" for duration of "rebellion, insurrection, or invasion" and where "during such period the necessity for such suspension shall exist"); *Duncan v. Kahanamoku*, 327 U.S. 304, 307–08 (1946) (recognizing that Hawaiian Organic Act, ch. 339, §67, 31 Stat. 153 (1900), expressly authorized suspension of habeas corpus immediately after attack on Pearl Harbor).

1. *Al-Marri Has Not "Been Determined by the United States To Have Been Properly Detained As An Enemy Combatant."*

While al-Marri may be "an alien detained by the United States," he has not "been determined by the United States to have been properly detained as an enemy combatant." This prong of section 7(a) describes the two-step process to which Guantanamo detainees have been subjected: (i) initial detention as an "enemy combatant"; and (ii) subsequent determination by a Combatant Status Review Tribunal ("CSRT") that such detention is proper. *See In re Guantanamo Detainee Cases*, 355 F. Supp. 2d 443, 450 (D.D.C. 2005) (describing CSRT).[4] Section 7(a), however, does not apply to al-Marri because he has never been "determined by the United States to have been properly detained as an enemy combatant" within the meaning of the MCA. Rather, whether al-Marri was properly detained as an "enemy combatant" based upon the President's June 23, 2003 order is precisely the question at issue in this appeal. The government's position, therefore, would resolve by circular reasoning the very issue presented for this Court's determination.

The government, nevertheless, makes two arguments as to why this prong of section 7(a) applies to al-Marri. Both arguments, however, fail to provide the "specific and unambiguous statutory directive[]" necessary to repeal habeas jurisdiction over al-Marri's habeas petition. *St. Cyr*, 533 U.S. at 299; *accord Demore v. Kim*, 538 U.S. 510, 517 (2003). Both arguments, moreover, would raise serious constitutional questions that this Court should avoid where, as here, "an alternative interpretation of the statute is 'fairly possible.'" *St. Cyr*, 533 U.S. at 299–300 (quoting *Crowell v. Benson*, 285 U.S. 22, 62 (1932)).

The government first contends . . . that al-Marri was "determined by the United States to have been properly detained as an enemy combatant" when the President unilaterally issued his redacted June 23, 2003 order declaring him an "enemy combatant" and directing that he be transferred from civilian to military custody. . . . . But the President's order determined only that al-Marri *should be* detained as an "enemy combatant," not that he had "been properly detained as an enemy combatant" by the United States. As the President stated:

> I, GEORGE W. BUSH, as President of the United States and Commander in Chief of the U.S. armed forces, hereby DETERMINE for the United States of America that . . . Ali Saleh Kahlah al-Marri, who is under the control of the Department of Justice [as a criminal defendant], is, and at the time he entered the United States in September 2001 was, an enemy combatant. . . .
>
> . . . .
>
> Accordingly, the Attorney General is directed to surrender Mr. al-Marri to the Secretary of Defense, and the Secretary of Defense is directed to receive Mr. al-Marri from the Department of Justice and *to detain him as an enemy combatant.*

JA 54 (emphasis added).

The President's order, therefore, did not, and could not, determine that al-Marri had been "properly detained as an enemy combatant" because al-Marri *had never before*

---

[4] Section 7(a) also describes the two-step process used to determine whether other aliens captured and held elsewhere outside the United States, such as at Bagram Air Base in Afghanistan, have been properly detained as enemy combatants. *See* Respondents' Response to Order to Show Cause and Motion to Dismiss for Lack of Jurisdiction, Decl. of Col. Rose M. Miller ¶ 11, *Ruzatullah v. Rumsfeld*, No. 06-CV-1707 (GK) (D.D.C.) ("By direction of the Secretary of Defense, within 90 days of a detainee being brought under DoD control, the detaining commander, or his designee, shall review the initial enemy combatant determination made in the field [to determine whether the detention is proper].").

been detained as an "enemy combatant." Rather, al-Marri had been arrested by the FBI, and was being detained as a criminal defendant by the Department of Justice in a Peoria County Jail, pending trial on credit card fraud and other charges. Whether al-Marri was "properly detained" as an "enemy combatant" is the precise question at issue here, just as it was in *Padilla*, the only other case involving the detention of an "enemy combatant" by order of the President. *See Padilla v. Hanft*, 432 F.3d 582, 586–87 (4th Cir. 2005) ("the President's authority to detain militarily persons" like Padilla and al-Marri has been "a centerpiece of the government's war on terror" and is "an issue of . . . surpassing importance"); *Padilla v. Hanft*, 423 F.3d 386, 389 (4th Cir. 2005) (stating that "[t]he exceedingly important question before [the Court]" is whether Padilla can be lawfully detained by the military based upon the president's order declaring him an "enemy combatant"). Plainly, section 7 instead addresses detainees at Guantanamo and other prisons outside the United States who were "determined . . . to have been properly detained" as enemy combatants after they had already been detained by the military.

The President's June 23, 2003 order also cannot affect this Court's jurisdiction for another, more fundamental reason. The whole purpose of habeas corpus is for an individual detained "by the United States" (by the Executive) to obtain an independent adjudication (by the Judiciary) of the lawfulness of his detention. *See Rumsfeld v. Padilla*, 542 U.S. at 441 (challenge to detention as enemy combatant lies at "the traditional core of the Great Writ"); *Hamdi*, 542 U.S. at 536 (plurality opinion); Paul M. Bator, *Finality in Criminal Law and Federal Habeas Corpus for State Prisoners*, 76 Harv. L. Rev. 441, 475 (1963) ("[T]he classical function of habeas corpus was to assure the liberty of subjects against detention by the executive or the military without any court process at all. . . ."). Thus, under the government's view, Congress eliminated the right of a lawful resident alien, arrested in his home in the United States, to seek review by an Article III court of the lawfulness of the President's order subjecting him to indefinite military detention without charge. There could be no plainer violation of the Suspension and Due Process Clauses.

The government's second argument is equally flawed. Specifically, it contends . . . that al-Marri was "determined by the United States to have been properly detained as an enemy combatant" when the district court issued its decision denying his habeas corpus petition. . . . . But a determination by a federal district judge is not a determination "by the United States." Section 7(a)'s reference to a determination "by the United States" does not apply to al-Marri, who never received a CSRT or any other determination "by the United States" that he had been "properly detained" as an "enemy combatant" following his transfer from civilian custody to the Navy Brig on June 23, 2003. Rather, section 7(a) refers unmistakably to aliens detained at Guantanamo Bay, who have been determined by a CSRT to have been "properly detained" as enemy combatants. *See* Govt's Supp. MCA Brief in *Boumediene v. Bush & Al Odah v. United States*, Nos. 05-5062, 05-5063 & 05-5064, 05-5095 through 05-5116, at 6 n.1 (D.C. Cir.) (Govt's D.C. Cir. MCA Br.) ("The United States, through the CSRTs, has determined that petitioners are 'properly detained' as enemy combatants [under the MCA]."). The government's reading of the MCA, therefore, not only contradicts the statute's plain language but also fails to provide the clear statement necessary to eliminate jurisdiction over al-Marri's habeas corpus petition.

The district court's determination cannot serve as the basis for eliminating this Court's jurisdiction for several additional reasons. *First*, if Congress intended the MCA to divest the federal courts of jurisdiction over habeas petitions like this one, as the government contends . . . , the district court's decision, too, is null and void. *See, e.g., Steel Co. v. Citizens for a Better Env't*, 523 U.S. 83, 94 (1998) ("Without jurisdiction, the court cannot proceed at all in any case. Jurisdiction is power to declare the law, and when it ceases to exist, the only function remaining to the court is that of announcing the fact and dismissing the cause.") (quoting *Ex parte McCardle*, 74 U.S. 506, 514 (1868)); *Elliott v. Peirsol's Lessee*, 26 U.S. 328, 340 (1828). Hence, there has been no valid determination in this case that al-Marri is "properly detained" as an enemy combatant, the pre-requisite for eliminating habeas relief.

Second, if, as the government argues, the district court's determination is sufficient under the MCA because the district court had jurisdiction to determine whether al-Marri was properly detained as an "enemy combatant" at the time it issued its decision, but no longer possesses jurisdiction by virtue of the MCA, this Court then necessarily retains jurisdiction under 28 U.S.C. 1291 to review that decision on appeal, as nothing in the MCA affected that distinct jurisdictional provision. *Cf. Bruner v. United States*, 343 U.S. 112, 115 (1952) (statute withdrawing jurisdiction of district court did not affect jurisdiction of court of claims). This Court would also retain authority under the All Writs Act to grant "all writs necessary or appropriate in aid" of that jurisdiction, including to order al-Marri's release if it concludes that his detention as an "enemy combatant" is unlawful. *See* 28 U.S.C. 1651; *Pennsylvania Bureau Corr. v. U.S. Marshals Serv.*, 474 U.S. 34, 43 (1985) (All Writs Act confers broad authority on federal courts "to fashion extraordinary remedies when the need arises").[5]

Third, al-Marri has a right to appeal the district court's decision denying his habeas petition to this Court and to the Supreme Court. *See Hamdi v. Rumsfeld*, 542 U.S. 507 (2004); *Rumsfeld v. Padilla*, 542 U.S. 426 (2004). The Supreme Court has long required Congress to speak with unmistakable clarity if it exercises its Article III power to make exceptions to that Court's appellate jurisdiction. *See, e.g., Ex parte Yerger*, 75 U.S. 85, 106 (1868) (declining to conclude that Supreme Court's appellate jurisdiction had been repealed "without the expression of such intent, and by mere implication"). The Supreme Court, moreover, has been especially hesitant to construe a statute as withdrawing its jurisdiction to review decisions in habeas cases. Thus, *Ex parte Yerger* found it:

> too plain for argument that the denial to this court of appellate jurisdiction in this class of cases must greatly weaken the efficacy of the writ . . . and seriously hinder the establishment of that uniformity in deciding upon questions of personal rights which can only be attained through appellate jurisdiction. . . . We are obliged to hold, therefore, that in all cases where a Circuit Court . . . caused a prisoner to be brought before it, and has, after inquiring into the cause of detention, remanded him to the custody from which he was taken, this court, in the exercise of its appellate jurisdiction, may, by the writ of *habeas corpus*, aided by the writ of *certiorari*, revise the decision of the Circuit Court, and if it be found unwarranted by law, relieve the prisoner from the unlawful restraint to which he has been remanded.

Id. at 102–03. Indeed, every time the Supreme Court has upheld a congressional limitation under the Exceptions Clause, U.S. Const. art. III, §2, it has emphasized that an alternative avenue of contemporaneous appellate review was available. *See Felker*, 518

---

[5] The 1789 Judiciary Act specified that "all the . . . courts of the United States, shall have power to issue writs of *scire facies, habeas corpus*, and all other writs not specifically provided for by statue." Judiciary Act of 1789, §14, 1 Stat. 81–82. In 1948, in what is now 28 U.S.C. 1651, Congress replaced "all other writs not specifically provided for by statute" with "all writs." This suggests that while a specific statute might have limited writs under the 1789 Act, the new act eliminates those limits – permitting a court to issue even a writ of habeas corpus in an appropriate case. Indeed, Congress expanded the Act in 1948 to permit courts to issue not only "necessary" writs but instead "necessary or appropriate" ones, a change that suggests that section 1651 was intended to broaden the Act.

U.S at 661–62; *id*. at 667 (Souter, J., concurring) ("[I]f it should later turn out that statutory avenues other than certiorari for reviewing [a lower court's denial of habeas] were closed, the question whether the statute exceeded Congress's Exceptions Clause power would be open."); *Yerger*, 75 U.S. at 105–06; *McCardle*, 74 U.S. at 515. No such avenue of appellate review is guaranteed to al-Marri under the MCA.

Thus, under the government's circular reasoning, the MCA eliminated all appellate jurisdiction to review the lawfulness of the very determination – the district court's denial of al-Marri's habeas petition – that the government insists forecloses that review. As in *Yerger*, it is "too plain for argument" that Congress did not except the Supreme Court's appellate jurisdiction to review al-Marri's pending habeas action based upon the very district court determination that forecloses that review. 75 U.S. at 102; *see also Hamdan v. Rumsfeld*, 126 S. Ct. 2749, 2764 (2006) (statute will not be held to revoke Supreme Court's habeas jurisdiction "absent an unmistakably clear statement to the contrary").

2. *Al-Marri Is Not "Awaiting Such Determination"*

In addition to not having been determined by the United States to have been properly detained as an enemy combatant, al-Marri was not and is not "awaiting such determination" within the meaning of the MCA. Rather, al-Marri, the only remaining "enemy combatant" detained in the United States, was – and is – awaiting a determination by the federal courts, and by this Court in particular, with respect to the merits of his habeas petition challenging his detention by the President.

The government, nonetheless, asserts . . . that al-Marri is "awaiting such determination" under the MCA because, on November 13, 2006 – the date the government filed its motion to dismiss – the Defense Department ordered that al-Marri be provided with a CSRT in the event this Court dismisses his habeas petition for lack of jurisdiction. . . . . Thus, when Congress enacted the MCA on October 17, 2006, the Defense Department had never convened a CSRT for al-Marri, had never ordered that a CSRT be convened for al-Marri, and had never announced any intention to convene a CSRT for al-Marri. *Cf. Defense Department Ordered to Take Custody of High-Value Detainees*, Sept. 6, 2006 (http://www.defenselink.mil/Releases/Release.aspx?ReleaseID=9909) (announcing, before MCA's passage, that the fourteen "high-value" terrorist suspects transferred from CIA custody to Guantanamo would "undergo" CSRTs). No statute or government regulation required then, or requires now, that the Defense Department ever convene and conclude a CSRT for al-Marri, and the CSRT procedures themselves expressly apply only to aliens "detained by the Department of Defense *at the U.S. Naval Base Guantanamo Bay, Cuba.*" *See* Memorandum from Deputy Secretary of Defense on Implementation of Combatant Status Review Tribunal Procedures for Enemy Combatants Detained at U.S. Naval Base Guantanamo Bay, Cuba, at 1, July 14, 2006 ("CSRT Memorandum") (http://www.defenselink.mil/news/Aug2006/d20060809CSRTProcedures. pdf) (emphasis added). Because the MCA and Detainee Treatment Act, Pub. L. No. 109-148, 119 Stat. 2680 (2005) ("DTA"), limit judicial review exclusively to aliens detained as "enemy combatants" who have received final CSRT decisions, *see* MCA §7(a); DTA §1005(e)(2), Congress, in the government's view, necessarily eliminated al-Marri's right to habeas corpus without guaranteeing him any other access to an Article III court to challenge the lawfulness of his executive detention. Indeed, the government's construction of the MCA leads to the absurd result whereby Congress guaranteed an alternative avenue of review by an Article III court for prisoners captured abroad and detained at Guantanamo, but eliminated habeas corpus without guaranteeing any such review for a resident alien, arrested and detained in the United States, whose constitutional rights have long been recognized.

In an eleventh-hour attempt to avoid the unconstitutional result of its own inter-pretation, the government (Mot. at 5 n.1) now tells the Court "how [it] plans to handle al-Marri in the event the courts agree that the MCA divested the courts of jurisdiction." But the government cannot remedy a suspension of the Writ after the fact. Further, if a CSRT were the adequate and effective substitute for habeas that the government will inevitably say it is, the government would have given al-Marri a CSRT already, instead of telling the Court what it "plans" to do, as an act of grace, gamesmanship, or mere convenience, if the Court accepts its invitation to dismiss al-Marri's appeal. The Exec-utive cannot defeat habeas with a promise of future review that could be revoked as easily as it was made, and that does not ensure an adequate and effective substitute for the Writ.

The government, in short, attributes to Congress an intent to eliminate a pending habeas action without providing any substitute, let alone the adequate and effective substitute for habeas that the Suspension Clause requires. *See Swain*, 430 U.S. at 381; *infra* Point D. Indeed, if Congress properly divested the federal courts of habeas juris-diction over al-Marri's petition, any alien could be snatched off the streets of the United States at any time and imprisoned forever in a Navy Brig without charge and without access to counsel based solely upon the speculative possibility of future federal court review that is not guaranteed by law and that the Executive has the unfettered dis-cretion to permit, delay, or deny. Congress certainly did not intend such a result, and the MCA lacks the clear statutory directive necessary to repeal habeas jurisdiction over this case. *See Demore*, 538 U.S. at 517 ("[W]here Congress intends to preclude judicial review of constitutional claims its intent to do so must be clear.") (quoting *Webster v. Doe*, 486 U.S. 592, 603 (1988)); *St. Cyr*, 533 U.S. at 300 (reading statute to "entirely preclude review of a pure question of law by any court would give rise to substantial constitutional questions"). If, however, the Court finds that Congress did seek to repeal jurisdiction over al-Marri's habeas petition, it must strike down section 7 of the MCA as an unconstitutional suspension of the Writ.

3.   *The MCA Does Not Apply Retroactively To Al-Marri's Habeas Action.*

The government's argument that Congress intended the MCA to reach al-Marri's habeas action also violates the longstanding rule that statutes affecting substantive rights must be presumed to apply prospectively. *See, e.g., Lindh v. Murphy*, 521 U.S. 320, 327–28 (1997); *Landgraf v. USI Film Prods.*, 511 U.S. 244, 280 (1994). Thus, a statute that would retroactively alter a party's rights in a pending case "does not govern absent clear con-gressional intent favoring such a result." *Hamdan*, 126 S. Ct. at 2765 (quoting *Landgraf*, 511 U.S. at 280). Construing the MCA to apply to al-Marri would retroactively eliminate his fundamental right to habeas corpus and due process. As set forth above, there is no unequivocal statement that Congress intended such a result.

. . .

. . . [T]he MCA, in the government's view, retroactively deprived al-Marri of any right to challenge his indefinite military detention. The MCA does not even arguably shift the forum that can hear al-Marri's habeas case to the District of Columbia Circuit, as the government says the MCA and DTA do for the Guantanamo Bay detainee cases. *See* Govt's D.C. Cir. MCA Br. at 32 (arguing that pending appeals of district court decisions in Guantanamo detainee habeas cases should be "converted into petitions for review under section 1005(e)(2) of the DTA," to the extent authorized by that statute, and decided on the merits). Rather, the government argues, the MCA stripped this Court of all jurisdiction to hear the legal and constitutional claims presented by al-Marri's habeas appeal without guaranteeing jurisdiction over those claims in any other court. There is no evidence of the clear congressional intent necessary to effect that repeal.

. . .

4. *The MCA's Extension Of The DTA's Guantanamo Bay-Specific Repeal Of Habeas Jurisdiction Does Not Reach The Petition Of A Resident Alien Like Al-Marri.*

The government . . . argues that the MCA extended the Guantanamo Bay-specific repeal of habeas jurisdiction in section 1005(e)(1) of the DTA to encompass "any alien enemy combatant held by the United States, regardless of the location of the detention." MCA §7(a). That argument contradicts not only the language and intent of section 7 but also longstanding rules of statutory construction that forbid repeals of habeas corpus absent an unmistakably clear directive from Congress and that require courts to avoid serious constitutional problems where an alternative interpretation of a statute is fairly possible, as it is here.

The MCA's extension of the DTA's habeas repeal beyond Guantanamo was never intended to sweep so broadly to encompass a lawful resident alien, like al-Marri, who has a constitutional right to the Writ. Congress instead enacted the MCA in response to the Supreme Court's decision in *Hamdan* and against the background of an unbroken line of cases establishing that resident aliens in the United States have constitutional rights, including the right to habeas corpus and due process. *See, e.g., Sanchez-Llamas v. Oregon*, 126 S. Ct. 2669, 2681–82 (2006) (Roberts, C.J.); *St. Cyr*, 533 U.S. at 299–300; *Zadvydas v. Davis*, 533 U.S. 678, 693 (2001); *United States v. Verdugo-Urquidez*, 494 U.S. 259, 270–71 (1990); *Eisentrager*, 339 U.S. at 771, 777–78; *Wong Wing v. United States*, 163 U.S. 228, 238 (1896). In *Hamdan*, the Court ruled that the DTA did not eliminate jurisdiction over pending habeas petitions filed by or on behalf of Guantanamo detainees, 126 S. Ct. at 2762–69, and that the military commissions set up by the President to try suspected terrorists lacked the requisite congressional authorization, *id.* at 2786. The MCA amended the habeas statute in response to that decision.

The MCA also extended the DTA's repeal of habeas corpus from that of "an alien detained by the Department of Defense at Guantanamo Bay, Cuba," DTA §1005(e)(1), to that of "an alien detained by the United States," MCA §7(a). But the MCA did not, and could not, entirely eliminate jurisdiction over the pending habeas action of a lawful resident alien like al-Marri, who was arrested and has at all times been detained inside the United States, and whose rights under the Constitution have long been recognized. Rather, the MCA amended the federal habeas statute to limit its reach to aliens who, Members of Congress who voted for the bill believed, did not have a constitutional right to the Writ. *See* 152 Cong. Rec. H7944 (daily ed. Sept. 29, 2006) (statement of Rep. Sensenbrenner) ("The Supreme Court has never held that the Constitution's protections, including habeas corpus, extend to noncitizens held outside the United States."); 152 Cong. Rec. S10268 (daily ed. Sept. 27, 2006) (statement of Sen. Kyl) ("*Eisentrager* and *Verdugo* are still the governing law in this area. These precedents hold that aliens who are either held abroad or held here but have no other substantial connection to this country are not entitled to invoke the U.S. Constitution."); 152 Cong. Rec. S10407 (daily ed. Sept. 28, 2006) (statement of Sen. Sessions) ("The [Supreme] Court concluded [in *Rasul*] only that the federal habeas statute confers jurisdiction on federal district courts to hear claims brought by aliens detained at Guantanamo Bay. The Court nowhere suggested that the Constitution grants such aliens a right of access to American courts.").

The MCA, accordingly, addresses habeas petitions filed by or on behalf of aliens captured and detained outside the United States, including prisoners at Guantanamo and in Afghanistan and Iraq, where military operations are ongoing. *See* 152 Cong. Rec. S10267 (daily ed. Sept. 27, 2006) (statement of Sen. Warner) ("Well, if [habeas] is actionable in Guantanamo . . . what about 18,000 in our custody in Iraq now?").[7] Indeed, during floor debates, Members of Congress repeatedly made clear that they sought to eliminate habeas only for non-resident aliens who could claim only a statutory, not a constitutional, right to habeas. *See, e.g.*, 152 Cong. Rec. S10367 (daily ed. Sept. 28, 2006) (statement of Sen. Graham) (MCA does not eliminate habeas for alleged enemy combatants whose right to habeas is guaranteed by Constitution). As Representative Sensenbrenner, Chairman of the Judiciary Committee and co-manager of the bill stated:

> There are two types of habeas corpus: one is the constitutional great writ. We are not talking about that here. . . . The other is statutory habeas corpus, which has been redefined time and time again by the Congress. That is what we are talking about here, and we have constitutional power to redefine it.

152 Cong Rec. H7548 (statement of Rep. Sensenbrenner) (daily ed. Sept. 27, 2006); *see generally* Brief for Center for National Security Studies *et al.* as *Amici Curiae*.

Accordingly, whatever effect the MCA might have on the habeas corpus petitions filed by or on behalf of aliens captured abroad and detained at Guantanamo or elsewhere outside the United States, it does not terminate the habeas action of a lawful resident alien, like al-Marri, whose rights under the Constitution have long been established. At most, Congress removed the DTA's references to Guantanamo Bay in order to restrict the habeas rights of aliens captured abroad regardless of where the United States decides to imprison them. *See, e.g.*, 152 Cong. Rec. S10355 (daily ed. Sept. 28, 2006) (statement of Sen. Kyl) (discussing treatment of "a suspected enemy combatant captured on the battlefield"). Whether such aliens would gain constitutional rights by virtue of their involuntary presence in the United States is irrelevant here because al-Marri, who lawfully entered and resided in this country, unquestionably has those rights. *See Verdugo-Urquidez*, 494 U.S. at 271 ("[O]*nce an alien lawfully enters and resides in this country* he becomes invested with the rights guaranteed by the Constitution to all people within our borders.") (quoting *Kwong Hai Chew v. Colding*, 344 U.S. 590, 596 n.5 (1953)) (emphasis in original).

The MCA, therefore, did not – and could not – strip the federal courts of jurisdiction over the habeas petition of a resident alien like al-Marri. If, however, this Court were to hold that section 7 of the MCA was intended by Congress to apply to al-Marri, it must invalidate this provision.

D. The MCA Violates The Suspension And Due Process Clauses If Applied To Al-Marri.

. . . The MCA . . . would repeal habeas jurisdiction over al-Marri's case without guaranteeing any substitute, let alone the adequate and effective substitute that the Constitution requires. This Court, therefore, cannot dismiss this appeal based upon the contingencies

---

[7] Notably, habeas corpus petitions were filed on behalf of 25 of the approximately 500 detainees at Bagram Air Base before the MCA's passage. *See* Warren Richey, *New lawsuits challenge Congress's detainee act*, Christian Science Monitor, Oct. 6, 2006, at 1.

and uncertainties of a process that has not happened and may never happen; that does not guarantee review by an Article III court of the lawfulness of al-Marri's detention, but instead places complete and unilateral control over any such review in the hands the detaining power (in this case, the President of the United States); and that is constitutionally deficient on its face.

1. *The MCA Deprives Al-Marri Of His Right To Judicial Review Of His Legal And Constitutional Claims.*

... The MCA would eliminate al-Marri's constitutional right to raise that challenge in any federal court.

Instead, the MCA subjects al-Marri's access to an Article III court to the unilateral control and sole discretion of the Executive. Under the MCA, al-Marri no longer has any right to judicial review since such review depends entirely upon the military's decision to conduct and conclude a CSRT. *See* MCA §7(a); DTA §1005(e)(2)(C)(i). Al-Marri has been detained by the military for more than 3½ years, and the military has never convened a CSRT to review his detention. Indeed, no statute or government regulation requires the military to conduct or conclude a CSRT, and the CSRT procedure expressly states that it "is not intended to, and does not, create any right or benefit, substantive or procedural, enforceable at law or in equity by any party against the United States, its departments, agencies, instrumentalities or entities, its officers, employees or agents, or any person." *See* CSRT Memorandum, Encl. (1), at 1.

Thus, if the MCA strips the Court of jurisdiction over this appeal, al-Marri's right to a determination by the Judiciary of the lawfulness of his detention by the President not only will be indefinitely delayed, but may never occur. The protections of the Great Writ of liberty, however, cannot hinge on Executive whim or the vagaries of an *ad hoc* military process that remains completely within the Executive's control. *Cf. Harris v. Nelson*, 394 U.S. 286, 290–91 (1969) (habeas corpus is "the fundamental instrument for safeguarding individual freedom against arbitrary and lawless state action"); 3 William Blackstone, *Commentaries* *131 (habeas corpus is "the great and efficacious writ in all manners of illegal confinement").

. . .

2. *If The MCA Repeals Jurisdiction Over This Habeas Appeal, There Is No Certainty A Court Will Ever Review The Lawfulness Of The President's June 23, 2003 Order Declaring Al-Marri An "Enemy Combatant."*

The MCA's repeal of jurisdiction over this case would be impermissible for another reason. Even if a CSRT were provided, there is no certainty a federal court would ever address the lawfulness of the President's June 23, 2003 order declaring al-Marri an "enemy combatant," which provided the basis for his indefinite military detention. The CSRT would determine only whether, "notwithstanding any prior designation," al-Marri meets the criteria set forth in CSRT procedures defining an "enemy combatant." .... The District of Columbia Circuit's review would then be limited to whether the CSRT's determination was "consistent with the [CSRT's] standards and procedures" and "supported by a preponderance of the evidence," DTA §1005(e)(2)(C)(i), and whether the "use of such standards and procedures ... is consistent with the Constitution and laws of the United States," *id.* §1005(e)(2)(C)(ii). The District of Columbia Circuit, therefore, would be confined to reviewing the CSRT's findings and CSRT's use of its standards and procedures. It would not necessarily and, indeed, potentially could never review the very challenge al-Marri asserts here to the President's June 23, 2003 order ousting him from the civilian criminal justice system and the constitutional protections it provides to all individuals living in this country. *See, e.g., Milligan*, 71 U.S. at 121–22, 126–27. Instead, if the MCA repeals jurisdiction over al-Marri's habeas petition, al-Marri would, at best, be subjected to a military status hearing designed for battlefield combatants without review by an Article III court of his legal claim that, as a civilian arrested by the FBI at home in the United States, he is not subject to military jurisdiction at all. Foreclosing such review would transgress the Suspension Clause. *Cf. St. Cyr*, 533 U.S. at 301.

3. *Even If Al-Marri Were Provided A CSRT, And Prevailed, He Would Remain Detained Based Upon The President's June 23, 2003 Order Without Review By An Article III Court.*

The MCA would also repeal habeas jurisdiction without providing an adequate and effective substitute by denying al-Marri the right to release from unlawful detention, an essential element of habeas. *See generally, e.g., Fay v. Noia*, 372 U.S. 391, 400 (1963), *overruled on other grounds by Wainwright v. Sykes*, 433 U.S. 72 (1977). Even if al-Marri were provided a CSRT, and prevailed, he would still remain detained based upon the President's June 23, 2003 order declaring him an "enemy combatant." . . . . Nowhere in its motion does the government acknowledge that al-Marri would have a right to release if a CSRT determined that he was not an "enemy combatant" or otherwise suggest that the President's June 23, 2003 order no longer binds the Executive branch. Instead, the President would remain free, as the government suggests (Mot. 5 n.1), "to handle al-Marri" however he sees fit.

4. *The CSRT, And Review Of The CSRT Under The DTA, Would Deprive Al-Marri Of His Right To The Meaningful Factual Inquiry Guaranteed By The Suspension And Due Process Clauses.*

This Court cannot dismiss this habeas appeal unless it first establishes that there is an adequate and effective substitute for the Writ. *See Swain*, 430 U.S. at 381. Al-Marri has not been given a CSRT and, even if he had, this Court would have no jurisdiction under the DTA to review the CSRT's decision. This Court, however, cannot consistent with the Suspension Clause, dismiss al-Marri's habeas petition based upon the future possibility of a fundamentally flawed proceeding in which al-Marri's access to review by an Article III court remains within the sole discretion and control of the Executive power that continues to detain him.

To uphold the MCA's repeal of habeas over this case, therefore, this Court must first determine that the CSRT and DTA review, which the government suggests . . . al-Marri, perhaps one day, "may avail himself of," guarantees an adequate and effective substitute for the Writ. As explained below, this scheme, on its face, violates both the Suspension Clause and the Due Process Clause, which the Suspension Clause protects. *See Hamdi*, 542 U.S. at 536–37 (plurality opinion); *see also id.* at 555–56 (Scalia, J., dissenting) (writ of habeas corpus, guaranteed by the Suspension Clause, is "the instrument by which due process" is secured). Specifically, it denies al-Marri the right to: (i) a meaningful inquiry into the factual basis for his detention; (ii) the assistance of counsel; (iii) see the government's evidence; (iv) confront and cross-examine witnesses; (v) be free from detention based on evidence gained by torture; (vi) discovery of the basis for the government's allegations; and (vii) a neutral decisonmaker. This Court, accordingly, should avoid these "serious constitutional problem[s]" by finding that the MCA does not apply to al-Marri. *See Zadvydas*, 533 U.S. at 690. If, however, the Court finds that section 7 of the MCA sought to repeal jurisdiction over al-Marri's petition, it must invalidate this provision.

. . .

The CSRT makes no attempt to mask its glaring inadequacies. It is a self-described "non-adversarial proceeding to determine whether each detainee . . . meets the criteria to be designated as an enemy combatant." CSRT Memorandum, Encl. (1), at 1. Review of that proceeding under the DTA, moreover, does not appear to provide any judicial inquiry into disputed facts. DTA §1005(e)(2)(C); *see also* 152 Cong. Rec. S10271 (daily ed. Sept. 27, 2006) (statement of Sen. Kyl) ("It is not for the courts to decide if someone is an enemy combatant, regardless of the standard of review. It is simply not the role of the courts to make that decision. . . . The only thing the DTA asks the courts to do is check that the record of the CSRT hearings reflect that the military has used its own rules."). Indeed, as the government maintains, the DTA limits the District of Columbia Circuit's review to the CSRT "record" and "does not authorize fact finding" by any court in "any . . . circumstances." *See* Response in Opposition to Motion to Compel at 14–15, *Bismullah v. Rumsfeld*, No. 06-1197 (D.C. Cir.). The District of Columbia Circuit, according to the government, decides only "whether the CSRT followed appropriate procedures and rendered a decision supported by sufficient evidence." *Id.* at 12. Thus, under the DTA, al-Marri would have no right to the meaningful hearing and opportunity to be heard that due process requires.

The *Hamdi* plurality, of course, contemplated that when the military captures a soldier amid combat on a foreign battlefield, the process due could be provided in the first instance by "an appropriately authorized and properly constituted military tribunal." 542 U.S. at 538 (plurality opinion). But *Hamdi* never suggested, and due process does not allow, the same process for a civilian, whether citizen or alien, arrested at home inside the United States. . . . . *Hamdi* further states that "[i]n the absence of such process, . . . a court that receives a petition for writ of habeas corpus from an alleged enemy combatant must itself ensure that the minimum requirements of due process are achieved." 542 U.S. at 538 (plurality opinion). Just like Hamdi and Padilla, al-Marri had not received any process when he filed his habeas petition. And, just like in *Hamdi* and *Padilla*, al-Marri has the right to a hearing consistent with due process, as a habeas proceeding can provide.

. . .

Second, the MCA denies al-Marri the assistance of counsel, a right essential to due process. *See, e.g., Powell v. Alabama*, 287 U.S. 45, 69 (1932) ("right to be heard" would be of "little avail if it did not comprehend the right to be heard by counsel"); *Johnson v. Zerbst*, 304 U.S. 458, 462 (1938) (assistance of counsel "necessary to ensure fundamental human rights of life and liberty"). As the Supreme Court has made clear, al-Marri "unquestionably has the right to access to counsel" in challenging his detention as an "enemy combatant." *See Hamdi*, 542 U.S. at 539 (plurality opinion); *see also id.* at 553 (opinion of Souter, J.). Yet, the government – which unilaterally and illegally deprived al-Marri of access to counsel for 16 months after his transfer from civilian to military detention – again seeks to deprive him of that fundamental constitutional right.

The CSRT does not permit representation by counsel. Rather, the CSRT provides only a "personal representative." CSRT Memorandum, Encl. (1) at 2 & Encl. (3) at 1–3. The personal representative is neither a detainee's attorney nor his advocate. "[N]o confidential relationship exists or may be formed between the detainee and the Personal Representative." *Id.* Encl. (3) at 1. Instead, the personal representative's function is to explain the CSRT process and to assist the detainee in collecting "reasonably available information." *Id.* Encl. (3) at 1. In the overwhelming majority of cases, personal representatives meet with detainees only once, sometimes in meetings as short as 10 minutes. *See* Mark Denbeaux et al., *No-Hearing Hearings; CSRT: The Modern Habeas Corpus?* 4 (summarizing records in 78 per cent of 393 CSRTs for which U.S. had produced records) (http://law.shu.edu/news/final_no_hearing_hearings_report.pdf) (*"No-Hearing Hearings"*). Personal representatives, moreover, freely comment on classified information outside a detainee's presence to "aid the [CSRT's] deliberations," CSRT Memorandum, Encl. (3) at 2, often advocating against detainees, *No-Hearing Hearings*, *supra*, at 6. A CSRT personal representative, in short, is no attorney and no substitute for one. *See In re Guantanamo Detainee Cases*, 355 F. Supp. 2d at 471–72 (CSRT's denial of assistance of counsel violates due process). The DTA, moreover, limits judicial review to a CSRT record developed without the assistance of counsel, compounding the due process violation and denying the meaningful opportunity to be heard that the Constitution requires.

Third, the MCA denies al-Marri meaningful notice of the factual basis for his detention by eliminating his right to review the government's allegations. The CSRT permits the use of classified and secret evidence that a detainee cannot see or rebut. CSRT Memorandum at 7–8. In the vast majority of cases, CSRT decisions have been based upon such evidence. *See No-Hearing Hearings*, *supra*, at 5. As the lower court already concluded here, the use of secret evidence to detain al-Marri would violate due process. JA 388, 396–98; *see also In re Guantanamo Detainee Cases*, 355 F. Supp. 2d at 472 (holding, in habeas cases, that CSRT's reliance on classified information that detainees cannot see violates due process); *cf. Rafeedie v. INS*, 880 F.2d 506, 516 (D.C. Cir. 1989) (individual must be able to see "undisclosed evidence" to rebut it).

Fourth, the MCA denies al-Marri the right to confront and cross-examine witnesses. As al-Marri has explained at length, this right is essential to due process..... Al-Marri would have no right to confront and cross-examine witnesses in a CSRT, which, moreover, could freely consider multiple hearsay. CSRT Memorandum, Encl. (1) at 6. Review by the District of Columbia Circuit, in turn, would be confined to the record of a proceeding which necessarily lacked this *sine qua non* of due process. Therefore, the MCA, if it repeals jurisdiction over al-Marri's habeas petition, would necessarily violate due process and cannot provide an adequate and effective substitute for the Writ.

Fifth, the MCA would allow the use of evidence obtained by torture and other mistreatment. Such evidence is not merely inherently unreliable but, by definition, derives from "interrogation techniques ... so offensive to a civilized system of justice that they must be condemned under the Due Process Clause." *Miller v. Fenton*, 474 U.S. 104, 109 (1985); *see* Brief of Appellants at 53–55. In designating al-Marri an "enemy combatant," the President appeared to rely on information gained from individuals who have been tortured and mistreated, including Khalid Sheikh Mohammed. *See* Brief of Appellants at 53. The CSRT, however, fails to provide any meaningful "inquiry into the accuracy and reliability" of such hearsay statements to determine whether, in fact, they were obtained by torture or other abuse. *In re Guantanamo Detainee Cases*, 355 F. Supp. 2d at 473; *see also* Brief of *Amici Curiae* Retired Federal Jurists in Support of Petitioners' Supplemental Brief Regarding the Military Commissions Act of 2006, at 6, *Boumediene v. Bush & Al Odah v. United States*, Nos. 05-5062, 05-5063 & 05-064, 05-095 through 05-5116 (D.C. Cir.) (finding, based upon review of hundreds of CSRT records, that "CSRT neither examined allegations of torture *before* [an] individual was adjudicated an enemy combatant, nor did it exclude such evidence from its consideration") (emphasis in original).

Assuming a CSRT were ever convened for al-Marri, it would merely "assess, to the extent practicable, whether any statement derived from or relating to [him] was obtained as a result of coercion and the probable value, if any, of any such statement." CSRT Memorandum, Encl. (10) (implementing DTA §1005(b)(1)). The CSRT, therefore, would be under no obligation to assess whether a statement was gained through torture. Further, the CSRT would not only be free to rely upon statements obtained through torture, but it would assess such statements' "reliability" without any examination by al-Marri of the witnesses against him. Such reliance on unexamined hearsay statements gained from custodial interrogations flouts due process. *See, e.g., Crawford v. Washington*, 541 U.S. 36, 50–53 (2004); Brief of Appellants at 51–52.

Further, the District of Columbia Circuit would have no power under the DTA to inquire into the factual basis for al-Marri's detention, but would instead be limited to the CSRT record. As a result, the government could freely launder coerced statements without any factual inquiry by an Article III court, in violation of the rights guaranteed to al-Marri by the Due Process Clause and secured by the Suspension Clause.

Sixth, the MCA would deprive al-Marri of his right to obtain discovery, including discovery related to the circumstances under which the evidence against him was obtained. Habeas courts have the power to grant discovery to enable the petitioner to "secur[e] facts where necessary to accomplish the objective of the proceedings." *Harris*, 394 U.S. at 299; Brief of Appellants at 60–64. The CSRT, however, denies any right to discovery, including discovery of exculpatory evidence, contrary to the requirements of habeas and due process. *See* Brief of Appellants at 63. And the DTA, unlike a habeas court, would necessarily be confined to a record in which the detainee had no right to discovery and, therefore, no opportunity to obtain the facts necessary to show his detention was unlawful, including because it was based on statements obtained through torture or other abuse.

Seventh, the MCA would deny al-Marri his due process right to a determination by a neutral decisionmaker. *See Hamdi*, 542 U.S. at 533 (plurality opinion); *id.* 553 (opinion of Souter, J.). A CSRT, assuming one is ever convened, can never be a neutral decisionmaker in this case. The government asserts . . . that al-Marri has already been properly determined to be an "enemy combatant" by the President of the United States. . . . . No tribunal of three subordinate military officials – who answer to the President in the military chain of command – can reject a determination by the Commander-in-Chief that al-Marri should be detained as an "enemy combatant." In addition, due process mandates a "neutral and detached judge in the first instance," not a tribunal convened after years of detention and an elaborate secret process to confirm a determination already made. *See Concrete Pipe & Prods. v. Constr. Laborers Pension Trust*, 508 U.S. 602, 617 (1993) (quoting *Ward v. Vill. of Monroeville*, 409 U.S. 57, 61–62 (1972)). Therefore, the only neutral decisionmaker that can satisfy al-Marri's right to due process in challenging his executive detention is a federal habeas court. *See Hamdi*, 542 U.S. at 533, 536 (plurality opinion). The MCA would impermissibly take away that right.

5. *The MCA Would Deprive Al-Marri Of His Right To Challenge The Jurisdiction Of A Military Commission.*

Under the MCA, a CSRT determination would do more than subject al-Marri to indefinite detention without due process; it would also expose him to trial by military commission without any opportunity to challenge the commission's jurisdiction over him. The MCA states that a CSRT finding "that a person is an unlawful enemy combatant is dispositive for the purposes of jurisdiction for trial by military commission under this chapter." MCA §3(a)(1) (adding 10 U.S.C. 948d(c)). The military commission itself is not permitted to consider whether it lacks jurisdiction over a detainee on the ground that the basis for his unlawful enemy combatant decision was erroneous. Thus, the MCA would foreclose the jurisdictional inquiry that has been central to the habeas process for centuries – the inquiry into whether the military commission properly has jurisdiction over the prisoner. *See, e.g., Milligan*, 71 U.S. at 118; *Yamashita*, 327 U.S. at 8 (investigating "the lawful power of the commission to try the petitioner for the offense charged"); *United States v. Grimley*, 137 U.S. 147, 150 (1890) (habeas corpus secures right to challenge military tribunal's jurisdiction). . . . .

> 6. *The MCA Would Suspend The Writ By Denying Al-Marri The Right To Invoke The Protections Of The Geneva Conventions In Any Habeas Proceeding.*

The MCA would also effect a suspension of the Writ by impermissibly denying al-Marri the right to assert the protections of the Geneva Conventions in any habeas action, including as a defense to a charge by military commission to which he would be subject if found to be an "enemy combatant" by a CSRT. The MCA provides that "[n]o person may invoke the Geneva Conventions or any protocols thereto in any habeas corpus or other civil action or proceeding to which the United States, or a current or former officer, employee, member of the Armed Forces, or other agent of the United States is a party as a source of rights in any court of the United States or its States or territories." MCA §5(a). The Geneva Conventions have the status of federal law as "treaties of the United States" under Article VI of the Constitution, and thus provide a source of rights enforceable in a habeas proceeding. *See* 28 U.S.C. 2241(c)(3); *Mali v. Keeper of the Common Jail*, 120 U.S. 1, 17–18 (1887); *Saint Fort v. Ashcroft*, 329 F.3d 191, 201 (1st Cir. 2003).

. . .

E. The MCA Violates Equal Protection.

The Constitution's guarantee of equal protection applies to all persons in the United States, regardless of citizenship. *See, e.g., Plyer v. Doe*, 457 U.S. 202, 210 (1982) ("[A]liens whose presence in this country is unlawful, have long been recognized as 'persons' guaranteed [equal protection]."); *Yick Wo v. Hopkins*, 118 U.S. 356, 369 (1886) ("The [Equal Protection Clause of the] Fourteenth Amendment to the Constitution is not confined to the protection of citizens. . . . [Its protections] are universal in their application, to all persons within the territorial jurisdiction. . . ."). The "equal protection obligations imposed by the Fifth and Fourteenth Amendment [are] indistinguishable." *See, e.g., Adarand Constructors, Inc. v. Pena*, 515 U.S. 200, 217 (1995).

As a resident alien, therefore, al-Marri is guaranteed equal protection of the law. The MCA, however, threatens to create a second-class justice system in the United States, in which any of the millions of aliens lawfully residing in this country may be swept off the streets and imprisoned in a Navy Brig indefinitely without the right to judicial review guaranteed to citizens. The Constitution forbids that result.

. . .

> 2. *The MCA Improperly Discriminates Based Upon Alienage.*

. . .

. . . [T]he right to challenge one's indefinite detention by habeas corpus is not a government benefit that can divided unequally between citizens and aliens. Rather, it is an indivisible and fundamental right of constitutional dimension that belongs to all individuals in this country. *Cf. Milligan*, 71 U.S. at 120–21; *Quirin*, 317 U.S. at 37.....

For Congress to deprive al-Marri of this right because he is an alien would engender precisely the unequal treatment the Constitution forbids, selectively targeting the weak and vulnerable. *Cf. Ry Express Agency, Inc. v. New York*, 336 U.S. 106, 112–13 (1949) (Jackson, J., concurring) ("[N]othing opens the door to arbitrary action so effectively as to allow ... officials to pick and choose only a few to whom they will apply legislation and thus to escape the political retribution that might be visited upon them if larger numbers were affected."); *A. v. Sec'y of the State of the Home Dep't* [2004] UKHL 56 A.C. 68 (appeal from Eng.) (U.K.) (invalidating United Kingdom's anti-terror legislation because, *inter alia*, it discriminated against suspected terrorists who were not British citizens). If, as this Court recognized in *Hamdi v. Rumsfeld*, 316 F.3d 450 (4th Cir 2003), *overruled on other grounds*, 542 U.S. 507 (2004), the President cannot remove a citizen from "the Great Writ's purview" by declaring him an "enemy combatant," *id.* at 465, the President also cannot remove a resident alien from the Writ's purview, as such aliens have the same fundamental rights and are protected by the same Constitution as citizens. Such blatant discrimination not only fails to satisfy strict scrutiny but is palpably arbitrary, and violates equal protection under any standard.

CONCLUSION

For the foregoing reasons, Congress did not eliminate jurisdiction over al-Marri's habeas petition. But, if this Court finds that Congress did, it should strike down section 7 of the MCA as unconstitutional. Accordingly, the government's motion to dismiss al-Marri's appeal for lack of jurisdiction should be denied.

. . .

BRENNAN CENTER FOR JUSTICE
AT NYU SCHOOL OF LAW

December 15, 2006

Ms. Patricia S. Connor
Clerk, United States Court of Appeals
for the Fourth Circuit

███████████████████████

Re: *Al-Marri v. Wright*, No. 06-7427

Dear Ms. Connor:

Appellant al-Marri submits this letter, pursuant to Federal Rule of Appellate Procedure 28(j), to advise the Court of supplemental authority. On December 13, 2006, the United States District Court for the District of Columbia ruled that section 7 of the Military Commissions Act of 2006 ("MCA") deprived it of subject matter jurisdiction over the habeas petition of a Guantanamo detainee. Slip. Op. in *Hamdan v. Bush*, No. 04-1519 (D.D.C. Dec. 13, 2006) (opinion attached).

The district court's decision directly supports al-Marri's argument (Response at 3-10, 28-33) that the MCA would violate the Suspension Clause if construed to eliminate habeas jurisdiction here. The court determined: "[T]he Great Writ [protected by the Suspension Clause] has survived the Military Commissions Act. If and to the extent that the MCA operates to make the writ unavailable to a person who is constitutionally entitled to it, it must be unconstitutional." Slip. Op. at 15; *see also id.* at 7-15.

The district court found that Guantanamo detainees are not constitutionally entitled to habeas relief because they are aliens captured and detained outside the sovereign territory of the United States. In its view, *Johnson v. Eisentrager*, 339 U.S. 763 (1950), "appears to provide the controlling authority on the availability of constitutional habeas to enemy aliens." Slip Op. at 19. The petitioners in *Eisentrager*, it stated, "had no constitutional entitlement to habeas relief in U.S. Courts because 'at no relevant time were [they] within any territory over which the United States is sovereign, and the scenes of their offense, their capture, their trial, and their punishment were all beyond the territorial jurisdiction of any court of the United States.'" *Id.* at 19 (quoting *Eisentrager*, 339 U.S. at 778); *see also id.* at 21 ("[Hamdan] ... does not enjoy the 'implied protection' that accompanies presence on American soil.") (quoting *Eisentrager*, 339 U.S. at 777-79). The district court, however, expressly agreed with al-Marri's position that, by contrast, an alien arrested and detained in this country, like al-Marri, is constitutionally entitled to habeas relief, and that the MCA would impermissibly suspend the Writ if construed to eliminate jurisdiction over his appeal.

Respectfully submitted,

Jon Hafetz

Jonathan Hafetz

cc: Gregory G. Garre, Esq.
     David B. Salmons, Esq.
     Kevin F. McDonald, Esq

---

* Redaction on this page has been added for privacy purposes. – *Eds*.

PUBLISHED

UNITED STATES COURT OF APPEALS
FOR THE FOURTH CIRCUIT

ALI SALEH KAHLAH AL-MARRI,
Petitioner-Appellant,

and

MARK A. BERMAN, as next friend,
Petitioner,

v.

COMMANDER S. L. WRIGHT, USN
Commander, Consolidated Naval
Brig,

Respondent-Appellee.

SPECIALISTS IN THE LAW OF WAR;
PROFESSORS OF EVIDENCE AND
PROCEDURE; UNITED STATES CRIMINAL
SCHOLARS AND HISTORIANS; FORMER
SENIOR JUSTICE DEPARTMENT
OFFICIALS; CENTER FOR NATIONAL
SECURITY STUDIES; AMERICAN-ARAB
ANTI-DISCRIMINATION COMMITTEE;
ASIAN-AMERICAN JUSTICE CENTER;
NATIONAL IMMIGRANT JUSTICE
CENTER; HUMAN RIGHTS FIRST;
HUMAN RIGHTS WATCH;
PROFESSORS OF CONSTITUTIONAL
LAW AND FEDERAL JURISDICTION;
HATE FREE ZONE; MUSLIM
ADVOCATES; WORLD
ORGANIZATION FOR HUMAN RIGHTS
USA,
Amici Supporting Appellant.

No. 06-7427

2 AL-MARRI v. WRIGHT

Appeal from the United States District Court
for the District of South Carolina, at Charleston.
Henry F. Floyd, District Judge.
(2:04-cv-002257-HFF)

Argued: February 1, 2007

Decided: June 11, 2007

Before MOTZ and GREGORY, Circuit Judges, and
Henry E. HUDSON, United States District Judge for the
Eastern District of Virginia, sitting by designation.

Reversed and remanded by published opinion. Judge Motz wrote the
opinion, in which Judge Gregory joined. Judge Hudson wrote a dissenting opinion.

COUNSEL

ARGUED: Jonathan L. Hafetz, BRENNAN CENTER FOR JUS-
TICE, New York University School of Law, New York, New York,
for Appellant. David B. Salmons, Assistant to the Solicitor General,
UNITED STATES DEPARTMENT OF JUSTICE, Office of the
Solicitor General, Washington, D.C., for Appellee. **ON BRIEF:**
Andrew J. Savage, III, SAVAGE & SAVAGE, P.A., Charleston,
South Carolina; Lawrence S. Lustberg, Mark A. Berman, GIBBONS,
DEL DEO, DOLAN, GRIFFINGER & VECCHIONE, P.C., Newark,
New Jersey, for Appellant. Paul D. Clement, Solicitor General, Regi-
nald I. Lloyd, United States Attorney, District of South Carolina,
Gregory G. Garre, Deputy Solicitor General, Kevin F. McDonald,
Assistant United States Attorney, Claire J. Evans, UNITED STATES
DEPARTMENT OF JUSTICE, Criminal Division, Appellate Section,
Washington, D.C., for Appellee. Jenny S. Martinez, Stanford, Califor-
nia; Allison Marston Danner, Nashville, Tennessee; Valerie M. Wag-
ner, Daniel B. Epstein, DECHERT, L.L.P., Palo Alto, California, for

4   AL-MARRI v. WRIGHT

Specialists in the Law of War, Amicus Supporting Appellant. Jona-

• • •

Law Student Contributors: Melissa Keyes (U. of CA at Hastings Law School), Charles Wait, Aaron Clark-Rizzio, Kennon Scott, Binish Hasan, Maria Tennyson, Olivia Maginley and Meredith Angelson (New York Univ. Law Sch.), Simon Moshenberg, Jesse Townsend, Stephanie Hays, Sameer Ahmed and Nicholas Pederson (Yale Law School), Matt Sadler (B.C. Law School), for World Organization for Human Rights USA, Amicus Supporting Appellant. David H. Remes, Enrique Armijo, John F. Coyle, COVINGTON & BURLING, L.L.P., Washington, D.C., for David M. Brahms, Brigadier General, Donald J. Guter, Rear Admiral, Merrill A. McPeak, Retired General, Amici Supporting Appellant.

OPINION

DIANA GRIBBON MOTZ, Circuit Judge:

For over two centuries of growth and struggle, peace and war, the Constitution has secured our freedom through the guarantee that, in the United States, no one will be deprived of liberty without due process of law. Yet more than four years ago military authorities seized an alien lawfully residing here. He has been held by the military ever since – without criminal charge or process. He has been so held despite the fact that he was initially taken from his home in Peoria, Illinois by civilian authorities, and indicted for purported domestic crimes. He has been so held although the Government has never alleged that he is a member of any nation's military, has fought alongside any nation's armed forces, or has borne arms against the United States anywhere in the world. And he has been so held, without acknowledgment of the protection afforded by the Constitution, solely because the Executive believes that his military detention is proper.

While criminal proceedings were underway against Ali Saleh Kahlah al-Marri, the President ordered the military to seize and detain him indefinitely as an enemy combatant. Since that order, issued in June of 2003, al-Marri has been imprisoned without charge in a military jail in South Carolina. Al-Marri petitions for a writ of habeas corpus to secure his release from military imprisonment. The Government defends this detention, asserting that al-Marri associated with al Qaeda and "prepar[ed] for acts of international terrorism." It maintains that the President has both statutory and inherent constitutional authority to subject al-Marri to indefinite military detention and, in any event, that a new statute – enacted years after al-Marri's seizure – strips federal courts of jurisdiction even to consider this habeas petition.

We hold that the new statute does not apply to al-Marri, and so we retain jurisdiction to consider his petition. Furthermore, we conclude that we must grant al-Marri habeas relief. Even assuming the truth of the Government's allegations, the President lacks power to order the military to seize and indefinitely detain al-Marri. If the Government accurately describes al-Marri's conduct, he has committed grave crimes. But we have found no authority for holding that the evidence offered by the Government affords a basis for treating al-Marri as an enemy combatant, or as anything other than a civilian.

This does not mean that al-Marri must be set free. Like others accused of terrorist activity in this country, from the Oklahoma City bombers to the surviving conspirator of the September 11th attacks, al-Marri can be returned to civilian prosecutors, tried on criminal charges, and, if convicted, punished severely. But the Government cannot subject al-Marri to indefinite military detention. For in the United States, the military cannot seize and imprison civilians – let alone imprison them indefinitely.

I.

Al-Marri, a citizen of Qatar, lawfully entered the United States with his wife and children on September 10, 2001, to pursue a master's degree at Bradley University in Peoria, Illinois, where he had obtained a bachelor's degree in 1991. The following day, terrorists hijacked four commercial airliners and used them to kill and inflict grievous injury on thousands of Americans. Three months later, on December 12, 2001, FBI agents arrested al-Marri at his home in Peoria as a material witness in the Government's investigation of the September 11th attacks. Al-Marri was imprisoned in civilian jails in Peoria and then New York City.

In February 2002, al-Marri was charged in the Southern District of New York with the possession of unauthorized or counterfeit credit-card numbers with the intent to defraud. A year later, in January 2003, he was charged in a second, six-count indictment, with two counts of making a false statement to the FBI, three counts of making a false statement on a bank application, and one count of using another person's identification for the purpose of influencing the action of a federally insured financial institution. Al-Marri pleaded not guilty to all of these charges. In May 2003, a federal district court in New York dismissed the charges against al-Marri for lack of venue.

The Government then returned al-Marri to Peoria and he was re-indicted in the Central District of Illinois on the same seven counts, to which he again pleaded not guilty. The district court set a July 21, 2003 trial date. On Friday, June 20, 2003, the court scheduled a hearing on pre-trial motions, including a motion to suppress evidence against al-Marri assertedly obtained by torture. On the following Monday, June 23, before that hearing could be held, the Government moved *ex parte* to dismiss the indictment based on an order signed that morning by the President.

In the order, President George W. Bush stated that he "DETERMINE[D] for the United States of America that" al-Marri: (1) is an enemy combatant; (2) is closely associated with al Qaeda; (3) "engaged in conduct that constituted hostile and war-like acts, including conduct in preparation for acts of international terrorism;" (4) "possesses intelligence . . . that . . . would aid U.S. efforts to prevent attacks by al Qaeda;" and (5) "represents a continuing, present, and grave danger to the national security of the United States." The President determined that al-Marri's detention by the military was "necessary to prevent him from aiding al Qaeda" and thus ordered the Attorney General to surrender al-Marri to the Secretary of Defense, and the Secretary of Defense to "detain him as an enemy combatant."

The federal district court in Illinois granted the Government's motion to dismiss the criminal indictment against al-Marri. In accordance with the President's order, al-Marri was then transferred to military custody and brought to the Naval Consolidated Brig in South Carolina.

Since that time (that is, for four years) the military has held al-Marri as an enemy combatant, without charge and without any indication when this confinement will
end. For the first sixteen months of his military confinement, the Government did not
permit al-Marri any communication with the outside world, including his attorneys,
his wife, or his children. He alleges that he was denied basic necessities, interrogated
through measures creating extreme sensory deprivation, and threatened with violence.
A pending civil action challenges the "inhuman, degrading" and "abusive" conditions of
his confinement. *See* Complaint at 1, *Al-Marri v. Rumsfeld*, No. 2:05-cv-02259-HFF-RSC
(D.S.C. Aug. 8, 2005).

On July 8, 2003, counsel for al-Marri petitioned on his behalf (because it was undisputed that he was unavailable to petition) for a writ of habeas corpus in the Central
District of Illinois. The district court dismissed the petition for lack of venue, *Al-Marri
v. Bush*, 274 F. Supp. 2d 1003 (C.D. Ill. 2003); the Seventh Circuit affirmed, *Al-Marri
v. Rumsfeld*, 360 F.3d 707 (7th Cir. 2004); and the Supreme Court denied certiorari,
al-Marri v. Rumsfeld, 543 U.S. 809 (2004). On July 8, 2004, al-Marri's counsel filed
the present habeas petition on al-Marri's behalf in the District of South Carolina. On
September 9, 2004, the Government answered al-Marri's petition, citing the Declaration of Jeffrey N. Rapp, Director of the Joint Intelligence Task Force for Combating
Terrorism, as support for the President's order to detain al-Marri as an enemy combatant.

The Rapp Declaration asserts that al-Marri: (1) is "closely associated with al Qaeda,
an international terrorist organization with which the United States is at war"; (2)
trained at an al Qaeda terrorist training camp in Afghanistan sometime between 1996
and 1998; (3) in the summer of 2001, was introduced to Osama Bin Laden by Khalid
Shaykh Muhammed; (4) at that time, volunteered for a "martyr mission" on behalf of al
Qaeda; (5) was ordered to enter the United States sometime before September 11, 2001,
to serve as a "sleeper agent" to facilitate terrorist activities and explore disrupting this
country's financial system through computer hacking; (6) in the summer of 2001, met
with terrorist financier Mustafa Ahmed Al-Hawsawi, who gave al-Marri money, including funds to buy a laptop; (7) gathered technical information about poisonous chemicals
on his laptop; (8) undertook efforts to obtain false identification, credit cards, and bank-
ing information, including stolen credit card numbers; (9) communicated with known
terrorists, including Khalid Shaykh Muhammed and Al-Hawsawi, by phone and e-mail;
and (10) saved information about jihad, the September 11th attacks, and Bin Laden on
his laptop computer.

The Rapp Declaration does *not* assert that al-Marri: (1) is a citizen, or affiliate of
the armed forces, of any nation at war with the United States; (2) was seized on or near
a battlefield on which the armed forces of the United States or its allies were engaged
in combat; (3) was ever in Afghanistan during the armed conflict between the United
States and the Taliban there; or (4) directly participated in any hostilities against United
States or allied armed forces.

On October 14, 2004, the Government permitted al-Marri access to his counsel for
the first time since his initial confinement as an enemy combatant sixteen months before. Al-Marri then submitted a reply to the Government's evidence, contending that he
is not an enemy combatant; he then moved for summary judgment. The district court
denied the summary judgment motion and referred the case to a magistrate judge for
consideration of the appropriate process to be afforded al-Marri in light of *Hamdi v.
Rumsfeld*, 542 U.S. 507 (2004). The magistrate judge ruled that the Rapp Declaration
provided al-Marri with sufficient notice of the basis of his detention as an enemy combatant and directed al-Marri to file rebuttal evidence.

In response to the magistrate's ruling, al-Marri again denied the Government's allegations, but filed no rebuttal evidence, contending that the Government had an initial burden to produce evidence that he was an enemy combatant and that the Rapp Declaration did not suffice. The magistrate judge recommended dismissal of al-Marri's habeas petition because al-Marri had failed to rebut the allegations in the Rapp Declaration. In August 2006, the district court adopted the magistrate judge's report and recommendation and dismissed al-Marri's habeas petition. A few days later, al-Marri noted this appeal.[1]

II.

On November 13, 2006, three months after al-Marri noted his appeal, the Government moved to dismiss this case for lack of jurisdiction, citing section 7 of the recently enacted Military Commissions Act of 2006 (MCA), Pub. L. No. 109-366, 120 Stat. 2600.

A.

Section 7 of the MCA amends 28 U.S.C. §2241(e) – a provision Congress added to the federal habeas corpus statute in the Detainee Treatment Act of 2005 (DTA), Pub. L. No. 109-148, §1005(e)(1), 119 Stat. 2680, 2741–42. Congress enacted the DTA in response to the Supreme Court's holding, in *Rasul v. Bush*, 542 U.S. 466 (2004), that the federal habeas corpus statute, 28 U.S.C. §2241(a), (c), granted the federal courts jurisdiction over habeas petitions filed by aliens held at Guantanamo Bay.

In the DTA, Congress amended 28 U.S.C. §2241 by adding a new subsection, 2241(e), which removed the statutory grant of federal jurisdiction over actions filed by alien enemy combatants held at Guantanamo Bay. DTA §1005(e)(1). Through the DTA, Congress sought to replace the procedures that Rasul had upheld with a substitute remedy. In place of the statutory right to petition for habeas directly to a federal district court in §2241(a), Guantanamo Bay detainees would receive a Combatant Status Review Tribunal (CSRT) conducted "pursuant to applicable procedures specified by the Secretary of Defense," followed by review by the United States Court of Appeals for the District of Columbia Circuit. See DTA §1005(e)(2)(A) ,(B); *id.* §1005(a).

The Supreme Court considered the reach of the DTA in *Hamdan v. Rumsfeld*, 126 S. Ct. 2749, 2762–69 (2006). It held that the DTA did not divest the federal courts of jurisdiction over §2241 habeas actions filed by Guantanamo Bay detainees that were *pending* when the DTA was enacted in December 2005.

On October 17, 2006, in response to *Hamdan*, Congress enacted the MCA, in part to clarify that it wished to remove §2241 jurisdiction over pending and future habeas cases from detainees whom it believed had only a "*statutory* right of habeas." *See, e.g.,* 152 Cong. Rec. S10267 (daily ed. Sept. 27, 2006) (statement of Sen. Graham) (emphasis added). Thus, section 7 of the MCA replaces the habeas provision added by the DTA and substitutes the following:

> (e)(1) No court, justice, or judge shall have jurisdiction to hear or consider an application for a writ of habeas corpus filed by or on behalf of an alien detained by the United States who has been determined by the United States to have been properly detained as an enemy combatant or is awaiting such determination.

---

[1] Numerous amici have submitted briefs to us, both on the jurisdictional and merits questions. Many of these briefs have been helpful and we are especially grateful for the care exhibited in focusing on different issues, thus avoiding redundancy.

(2) Except as provided in paragraphs (2) and (3) of section 1005(e) of the [DTA], no court, justice, or judge shall have jurisdiction to hear or consider any other action against the United States or its agents relating to any aspect of the detention, transfer, treatment, trial, or conditions of confinement of an alien who is or was detained by the United States and has been determined by the United States to have been properly detained as an enemy combatant or is awaiting such determination.

MCA §7(a) (codified at 28 U.S.C.A. §2241(e) (West 2006)). The new statute expressly provides that this amendment to §2241(e) "shall take effect on the date of the enactment of this Act [October 17, 2006], and shall apply to all cases, without exception, pending on or after the date of the enactment of this Act. . . ." MCA §7(b).

B.

The Government asserts that the MCA divests federal courts of all subject matter jurisdiction over al-Marri's petition. Al-Marri maintains that the MCA, by its plain terms, does not apply to him and that if we were to hold it does, the MCA would be unconstitutional.

Al-Marri's constitutional claim is a serious one. As an alien captured and detained within the United States, he has a right to habeas corpus protected by the Constitution's Suspension Clause. *See Hamdi v. Rumsfeld*, 542 U.S. 507, 525 (2004) ("All agree that, absent suspension, the writ of habeas corpus remains available to every individual detained within the United States."). The Supreme Court has explained that "at the absolute minimum, the Suspension Clause protects the writ as it existed in 1789," *INS v. St. Cyr*, 533 U.S. 289, 301 (2001) (internal quotation marks omitted), and "[a]t common law, courts exercised habeas jurisdiction over the claims of aliens detained within sovereign territory of the realm," *Rasul*, 542 U.S. at 481.

Al-Marri argues persuasively that the MCA, which simply amended a federal statute – 28 U.S.C. §2241 – is not, and could not be, a valid exercise of Congress's powers under the Suspension Clause. *See, e.g., Hamdan*, 126 S. Ct. at 2764; *St. Cyr*, 533 U.S. at 298–99. Moreover, although Congress may remove federal jurisdiction over habeas petitions without suspending the writ *if* it provides an "adequate and effective" substitute, *Swain v. Pressley*, 430 U.S. 372, 381 (1977), Al-Marri maintains that Congress has provided him no substitute at all. Thus, he argues, if the MCA is read to strip our jurisdiction over his petition, it violates the Suspension Clause.

The Government seems to concede that al-Marri has a right to habeas corpus protected by the Suspension Clause, and acknowledges that "the touchstone of habeas corpus," and thus any substitute remedy, is "[j]udicial review of constitutional claims and questions of law." The Government asserts, however, that Congress has provided al-Marri a constitutionally adequate habeas substitute through the DTA and MCA scheme – an administrative determination by a CSRT followed by limited review of the CSRT's decision in the D.C. Circuit. Since al-Marri has never been afforded a CSRT and neither the DTA, the MCA, nor any other statute, regulation, or policy guarantees that he be granted one, it is not immediately apparent how this statutory arrangement could provide al-Marri a substitute remedy. Al-Marri has also raised substantial questions as to whether this statutory arrangement – were it available to him – would be constitutionally adequate. *Cf. Boumediene v. Bush*, 476 F.3d 981, 1004–07 (D.C. Cir. 2007) (Rogers, J., dissenting) (stating that a CSRT followed by limited D.C. Circuit review is not an adequate habeas substitute), *cert. denied*, 127 S. Ct. 1478 (2007).

We need not, however, resolve these difficult constitutional questions because we conclude that the MCA does not apply to al-Marri. The Supreme Court has instructed that when it is "fairly possible" to read a statute to avoid serious constitutional problems a court must do so. *Crowell v. Benson*, 285 U.S. 22, 62 (1932) ("When the validity of an act of the Congress is drawn in question, and even if a serious doubt of constitutionality is raised, it is a cardinal principle that this Court will first ascertain whether a construction of the statute is fairly possible by which the question may be avoided."); *Ashwander v. Tenn. Valley Auth.*, 297 U.S. 288, 347 (1936) (Brandeis, J. concurring) ("It is not the habit of the Court to decide questions of a constitutional nature unless absolutely necessary to a decision of the case." (internal quotation marks omitted)); *see also St. Cyr*, 533 U.S. at 299–300 (applying this principle in the context of habeas jurisdiction). In this case, ordinary principles of statutory interpretation demonstrate that the MCA does not apply to al-Marri.

C.

As always in interpreting an act of Congress, we begin with the plain language of the statute. *See, e.g.*, *Watt v. Alaska*, 451 U.S. 259, 265 (1981). The MCA eliminates habeas jurisdiction under §2241 only for an alien who "has been determined by the United States to have been properly detained as an enemy combatant or is awaiting such determination." MCA §7(a). Thus, the MCA does not apply to al-Marri and the Government's jurisdictional argument fails *unless* al-Marri (1) "has been determined by the United States to have been properly detained as an enemy combatant," or (2) "is awaiting such determination."

The Government asserts that al-Marri "has been determined by the United States to have been properly detained" through the President's order of June 23, 2003, designating al-Marri an enemy combatant. Alternatively, the Government argues that because the Department of Defense claims that if this court dismisses his habeas action al-Marri will be provided with a CSRT, al-Marri is "awaiting" such a determination for the purposes of the MCA. We find neither argument persuasive.

1.

In his order of June 23, 2003, the President "DETERMINE[D] for the United States of America that" al-Marri was an enemy combatant and ordered al-Marri detained by the Department of Defense. This Presidential order may well constitute a "determination" by the President, for the United States, that al-Marri *is* an enemy combatant. But the plain language of the MCA requires more than this initial determination to divest federal courts of jurisdiction under §2241. The statute does not eliminate §2241 jurisdiction in cases filed by an alien whom "the United States has determined is an enemy combatant" *or* who "has been detained as an enemy combatant." Rather the MCA only eliminates §2241 jurisdiction over a habeas petition filed by an alien who "*has been determined* by the United States *to have been properly detained* as an enemy combatant" (emphasis added).

The statute's use of the phrase "has been determined . . . to have been properly detained" requires a two-step process to remove §2241 jurisdiction: (1) an initial decision to detain, followed by (2) a determination by the United States that the initial detention was proper. The President's June 23 order only constitutes an initial decision to detain. To read the statute as the Government proposes would eliminate the second step and render the statutory language "has been determined . . . to have been properly detained" superfluous – something courts are loathe to do. *See, e.g.*, *Mackey v. Lanier Collection Agency & Serv., Inc.*, 486 U.S. 825, 837 (1988) ("[W]e are hesitant to adopt an interpretation of a congressional enactment which renders superfluous another portion of that same law.").

Other provisions of the DTA and MCA similarly demonstrate that Congress intended to remove jurisdiction only in cases in which the Government followed this two-step process. For those detainees to whom the DTA-MCA scheme applies, a CSRT (or similar tribunal) determines whether a person's initial detention as an enemy combatant is proper. In fact, Congress recognized that the very purpose of a CSRT is to "determine" whether an individual has been "properly detained." Thus, Congress delineated some basic procedural requirements for the CSRTs, *see* DTA §1005, and required the Secretary of Defense to submit to it within 180 days "the procedures of the Combatant Status Review Tribunals... that are in operation at Guantanamo Bay, Cuba, for *determining the status of the detainees*." DTA §1005(a)(1)(A) (emphasis added). The Department of Defense's CSRT procedures, in turn, explain that the CSRT process was established "to *determine*, in a fact-based proceeding, whether the individuals *detained* by the Department of Defense at the U.S. Naval Base Guantanamo Bay, Cuba, are *properly* classified as enemy combatants." Memorandum from Deputy Secretary of Defense Gordon England to Secretaries of the Military Departments et al. 1 (July 14, 2006) [hereinafter CSRT Procedures Memorandum] (emphasis added).

Moreover, the DTA and MCA provisions establishing D.C. Circuit review of CSRT final decisions are entitled "Review of decisions of combatant status review tribunals of *propriety of detention*." *See* DTA §1005(e)(2); MCA §10 (emphasis added). These provisions allow for D.C. Circuit review only of a final decision of a "Combatant Status Review Tribunal that an alien is *properly detained* as an enemy combatant." DTA §1005(e)(2)(A) (emphasis added). These procedures reinforce the plain language of section 7 of the MCA. Congress intended to remove federal courts' §2241 jurisdiction only when an individual has been detained *and* a CSRT (or similar Executive Branch tribunal) has made a subsequent determination that the detention is proper.[2]

Thus, the plain language of the MCA does not permit the Government's interpretation – i.e., that the President's initial order to detain al-Marri as an enemy combatant constitutes *both* a decision to detain al-Marri *and* a determination under the MCA that al-Marri *has been* properly detained as an enemy combatant. The MCA requires both to eliminate our jurisdiction.

2.

The Government's remaining jurisdictional contention is that even if al-Marri has not yet "been determined by the United States to have been properly detained," the Government plans to provide him with a CSRT in the future, and so under the MCA he is "awaiting such determination." Al-Marri maintains that Congress intended the term "awaiting such determination" to apply only to new detainees brought to Guantanamo Bay, or to those captured and held elsewhere outside the United States, and that the Government reads the term far more broadly than Congress intended.

---

[2] For these reasons, the Government's brief suggestion that the district court's denial of habeas relief to al-Marri could constitute the determination "by the United States" that he had "been properly detained" is inconsistent with legislative intent. For under the system Congress enacted, a CSRT or similar *Executive Branch* tribunal makes that determination "by the United States." Indeed, the Government has informed the federal courts of precisely this point in other litigation involving the MCA. *See* Government's Supplemental Br. Addressing the Military Commissions Act at 6 n.1, *Boumediene*, 476 F.3d 981 (D.C. Cir. 2007) (Nos. 05-5062, 05-5063, 05-5064, and 05-5095 through 05-5116) (noting that "[t]he United States, through the CSRTs, has determined that petitioners are 'properly detained' as enemy combatants" under the MCA). And, of course, the Government has repeatedly and vehemently asserted that the Executive Branch, not the Judiciary, determines a person's enemy combatant status. *See, e.g., Hamdi*, 542 U.S. 507. Moreover, the very purpose of section 7 of the MCA is to eliminate the jurisdiction of federal judges over certain enemy combatant cases. Hence, adoption of the Government's argument would mean that Congress empowered federal judges to make a "determination [for] the United States" in the very cases in which those judges had no jurisdiction. Congress could not have intended such a result.

Neither the DTA-MCA nor any other law or policy requires that al-Marri receive a CSRT, or even indicates that Congress believed he would be eligible for a CSRT and so could be "awaiting" one. At the same time, Congress did not expressly prohibit al-Marri from receiving a CSRT. To the extent that the plain language of the MCA does not clearly state who is "awaiting" a determination, its context and legislative history make clear that this phrase does not apply to persons, like al-Marri, captured and held within the United States. *See, e.g., King v. St. Vincent's Hosp.*, 502 U.S. 215, 221 (1991) ("[A] cardinal rule [is] that a statute is to be read as a whole...since the meaning of statutory language, plain or not, depends on context." (citation omitted)); *Crandon v. United States*, 494 U.S. 152, 158 (1990) ("In determining the meaning of the statute, we look not only to the particular statutory language, but to the design of the statute as a whole and to its object and policy.").

In enacting the MCA, Congress distinguished between those individuals it believed to have a *constitutional* right to habeas corpus, and those individuals it understood had been extended the right of habeas corpus only by *statute*, i.e., 28 U.S.C. §2241. The supporters of the MCA consciously tracked the distinction the Supreme Court had drawn in *Johnson v. Eisentrager*, 339 U.S. 763, 777–78 (1950), and *United States v. Verdugo-Urquidez*, 494 U.S. 259, 271 (1990), between aliens within the United States who become "'invested with the rights guaranteed by the Constitution to all people within our borders,'" *Verdugo-Urquidez*, 494 U.S. at 271 (*quoting Kwong Hai Chew v. Colding*, 344 U.S. 590, 596 n.5 (1953)), and aliens who have no lawful contacts with this country and are captured and held outside its sovereign territory. *See, e.g.,* 152 Cong. Rec. S10268 (daily ed. Sept. 27, 2006) (statement of Sen. Kyl); 152 Cong. Rec. S10406–07 (daily ed. Sept. 28, 2006) (statement of Sen. Sessions).

Congress sought to eliminate the statutory grant of habeas jurisdiction for those aliens captured and held outside the United States who could not lay claim to constitutional protections, but to preserve the rights of aliens like al-Marri, lawfully residing within the country with substantial, voluntary connections to the United States, for whom Congress recognized that the Constitution protected the writ of habeas corpus. As the Chairman of the House Judiciary Committee and floor manager for the MCA in the House explained, "There are two types of habeas corpus: one is the constitutional great writ. We are not talking about that here.... The other is statutory habeas corpus, which has been redefined time and time again by the Congress. That is what we are talking about here...." 152 Cong. Rec. H7548 (daily ed. Sept. 27, 2006) (statement of Rep. Sensenbrenner); *see also* H.R.Rep. No. 109-664, pt. 2, at 5–6 (2006) (noting that "aliens receive constitutional protections when they have come within the territory of the United States and developed substantial connections with this country" and that the MCA "clarifies the intent of Congress that statutory habeas corpus relief is not available to alien unlawful enemy combatants held outside of the United States" (internal quotation marks omitted)).

In fact, notwithstanding its posture in this case,[3] the Government has otherwise demonstrated that it shares this understanding of the scope of the MCA. On January

---

[3] Consistent with its litigation strategy, the Government briefly suggests that al-Marri "is on the same footing as alien enemy combatants at Guantanamo" because the DTA does not provide Guantanamo detainees with "a statutory right to a CSRT." This contention misses the mark. First, Congress knew when it enacted the MCA that the Executive had already provided CSRTs to all Guantanamo Bay detainees, and that the CSRT procedures – which Congress required be provided it, DTA §1005(a)(1)(A) – were designed to apply only to Guantanamo detainees. In contrast, when Congress enacted the MCA on October 17, 2006, the Government had never indicated any intention to convene a CSRT for anyone like al-Marri, captured and held within the United States. Moreover, and just as importantly, although Congress believed that the Guantanamo detainees

18, 2007, while al-Marri's appeal was pending, the Attorney General himself testified before Congress that the MCA did *not* affect any habeas rights historically protected by the Constitution. Citing *Eisentrager* in written testimony to the Senate Judiciary Committee, he explained: "The MCA's restrictions on habeas corpus petitions did not represent any break from the past. Indeed, it has been well-established since World War II that enemy combatants *captured abroad* have no constitutional right to habeas petitions in the United States courts." *Oversight of the U.S. Dep't of Justice: Hearing Before the S. Comm. on the Judiciary*, 110th Cong. (Jan. 18, 2007) (statement of Alberto Gonzales, Att'y Gen. of the United States) (emphasis added).

Furthermore, the Government's treatment of al-Marri suggests that, despite its litigation posture, it does not actually believe that the CSRT process in the DTA and MCA applies to al-Marri. In the four years since the President ordered al-Marri detained as an enemy combatant, the Government has completed CSRTs for each of the more than five hundred detainees held at Guantanamo Bay. Yet it was not until November 13, 2006, the very day the Government filed its motion to dismiss the case at hand, that the Government even suggested that al-Marri might be given a CSRT. At that time the Government proffered a memorandum from Deputy Secretary of Defense Gordon England directing that al-Marri be provided a CSRT "upon dismissal" of this case. This memorandum is too little too late.

The CSRT procedures, which the England memorandum suggests would govern al-Marri's hypothetical tribunal, by their own terms only apply to aliens detained "at the Guantanamo Bay Naval Base, Cuba." CSRT Procedures Memorandum, Enclosure (1), at 1. Moreover, the DTA and MCA provide for limited D.C. Circuit review only to detainees for whom a CSRT "has been conducted, pursuant to *applicable procedures* specified by the Secretary of Defense." DTA §1005(e)(2)(B)(ii) (emphasis added); *see* MCA §10. Because the procedures that would govern al-Marri's hypothetical CSRT are "applicable" only to persons detained at Guantanamo Bay, even were al-Marri to receive a CSRT pursuant to them, he might not be eligible for judicial review.

Given these provisions, the Government's argument that the phrase "awaiting such determination" covers persons confined within the United States yields a strange result. It would mean that Congress assured that Guantanamo Bay detainees were provided with an administrative factfinding process (the CSRT) followed by judicial review in the D.C. Circuit when eliminating habeas jurisdiction over their cases – but that Congress provided neither any substitute administrative procedure nor any form of judicial review when eliminating the habeas rights of those captured and detained within the United States. The Government offers nothing to indicate that Congress embarked on this strange course, and the legislative history of the MCA renders that theory untenable.

Perhaps because the Government knows that Congress did not intend the CSRT process to apply to persons like al-Marri, the England memorandum neither convenes

---

had no constitutional right to habeas corpus, and so believed it had no constitutional need to provide them a statutory alternative, Congress recognized that aliens captured and held within the United States did have a constitutional right to habeas. If Congress had intended to provide an adequate substitute for the constitutional protections of aliens within the United States, surely it would have enacted legislation to do so.

For these same reasons, the Government's attempt to find significance in the MCA's removal of the DTA's limiting references to "Guantanamo Bay, Cuba" is also misplaced. In fact, that change merely allowed the MCA to apply to aliens captured and held in other places outside the United States, for example in Iraq and Afghanistan, *see, e.g.,* 152 Cong. Rec. S10267 (daily ed. Sept. 27, 2006) (statement of Sen. Graham), and made clear in the face of public discussion about closing Guantanamo Bay that the rights of detainees moved from Guantanamo would not change. Even the Government ultimately concedes that the "amendment may have been designed to underscore the absence of habeas for aliens detained abroad at locations other than Guantanamo, as opposed to aliens detained in the United States."

nor even schedules a CSRT for al-Marri. Indeed, in its motion to dismiss, the Government acknowledges that the England memorandum only indicates "how the government plans to handle al-Marri in the event the courts agree that the MCA divested the courts of jurisdiction." Thus, the England memorandum makes al-Marri's CSRT at best conditional – triggered only "in the event" that we dismiss this litigation. In other words, the memorandum says only that al-Marri might receive a CSRT if this court dismisses his petition because he is awaiting a CSRT, but al-Marri will be awaiting a CSRT only if we dismiss his petition.

If al-Marri is "awaiting" a CSRT it is only because he might, through the good graces of the Executive, some day receive one. But he might not. After all, the Government's primary jurisdictional argument in this case is that the President's initial order to detain al-Marri constitutes the sole "determination" that he is due. And so under the Government's view, al-Marri might well be "awaiting" a determination of the propriety of his detention for the rest of his life – a result Congress could not have countenanced for an individual it understood to have a constitutional right to habeas corpus.

In sum, the Government's interpretation of the MCA is not only contrary to legislative intent, but also requires reading the phrase "awaiting such determination" so broadly as to make it meaningless. We are not at liberty to interpret statutes so as to render them meaningless. *See Scott v. United States*, 328 F.3d 132, 139 (4th Cir. 2003) ("[W]e must . . . avoid any interpretation that may render statutory terms meaningless. . . .") (*citing Freytag v. Comm'r Internal Revenue*, 501 U.S. 868, 877 (1991)). The phrase "awaiting such determination" gains meaning only if it refers to alien detainees captured and held outside the United States – whom Congress both believed had no constitutional right to habeas and expected would receive a CSRT based on the larger DTA-MCA scheme. Al-Marri is not such a detainee; therefore he is not "awaiting such determination" within the terms of the MCA.

3.

For these reasons, we must conclude that the MCA does not apply to al-Marri. He was not captured outside the United States, he is not being held at Guantanamo Bay or elsewhere outside the United States, he has not been afforded a CSRT, he has not been "determined by the United States to have been properly detained as an enemy combatant," and he is not "awaiting such determination." The MCA was not intended to, and does not, apply to aliens like al-Marri, who have legally entered, and are seized while legally residing in, the United States. Accordingly, the Government's jurisdictional argument fails and we turn to the merits of al-Marri's petition.

III.

Al-Marri premises his habeas claim on the Fifth Amendment's guarantee that no person living in this country can be deprived of liberty without due process of law. He maintains that even if he has committed the acts the Government alleges, he is not a combatant but a civilian protected by our Constitution, and thus is not subject to military detention. Al-Marri acknowledges that the Government can deport him or charge him with a crime, and if he is convicted in a civilian court, imprison him. But he insists that neither the Constitution nor any law permits the Government, on the basis of the evidence it has proffered to date – even assuming all of that evidence is true – to treat him as an enemy combatant and subject him to indefinite military detention, without criminal charge or process.

The Government contends that the district court properly denied habeas relief to al-Marri because the Constitution allows detention of enemy combatants by the military without criminal process, and according to the Government it has proffered evidence that al-Marri is a combatant. The Government argues that the Authorization for Use of Military Force (AUMF), Pub. L. No. 107-40, 115 Stat. 224 (2001), as construed by precedent and considered in conjunction with the "legal background against which [it] was enacted," empowers the President on the basis of that proffered evidence to order al-Marri's indefinite military detention as an enemy combatant. Alternatively, the Government contends that even if the AUMF does not authorize the President to order al-Marri's military detention, the President has "inherent constitutional power" to do so.

A.

Each party grounds its case on well established legal doctrine. Moreover, important principles guiding our analysis seem undisputed. Before addressing the conflicting contentions of the parties, we note these fundamental principles, which we take to be common ground.

The Constitution guarantees that no "person" shall "be deprived of life, liberty, or property, without due process of law." U.S. Const., amend. V; *see also id.* amend. XIV, §1. The text of the Fifth Amendment affords this guarantee to "person[s]," not merely citizens, and so the constitutional right to freedom from deprivation of liberty without due process of law extends to all lawfully admitted aliens living within the United States. *See Wong Wing v. United States*, 163 U.S. 228, 238 (1896); *see also Verdugo-Urquidez*, 494 U.S. at 271.

To be sure, our Constitution has no "force in foreign territory unless in respect of our citizens." *United States v. Curtiss-Wright Export Corp.*, 299 U.S. 304, 318 (1936). But, as Chief Justice Rehnquist explained, a long line of Supreme Court cases establish that aliens receive certain protections – including those rights guaranteed by the Due Process Clause – "when they have come within the territory of the United States and developed substantial connections with this country." *Verdugo-Urquidez*, 494 U.S. at 271; *see also Kwong Hai Chew*, 344 U.S. at 596 n.5 (noting that "once an alien lawfully enters and resides in this country he becomes invested with . . . rights . . . protected by . . . the Fifth Amendment[ ] and by the due process clause of the Fourteenth Amendment") (internal quotation marks omitted); *Wong Wing*, 163 U.S. at 238 (holding that "all persons within the territory of the United States are entitled to the protection guaranteed by" the Due Process Clause of the Fifth Amendment); *Yick Wo v. Hopkins*, 118 U.S. 356, 369 (1886) (explaining that the Due Process Clause of the Fourteenth Amendment protects "all persons within the territorial jurisdiction" of the United States). Thus, the Due Process Clause protects not only citizens but also aliens, like al-Marri, lawfully admitted to this country who have established substantial connections here in al-Marri's case by residing in Illinois for several months, with his family, and attending university there.[4]

"Freedom from imprisonment – from government custody, detention, or other forms of physical restraint – lies at the heart of the liberty that [the Due Process] Clause protects." *Zadvydas v. Davis*, 533 U.S. 678, 690 (2001); *see also Foucha v. Louisiana*, 504 U.S. 71, 80 (1992). This concept dates back to Magna Carta, which guaranteed that "government would take neither life, liberty, nor property without a trial in accord with the law of the land." *Duncan v. Louisiana*, 391 U.S. 145, 169 (1968) (Black, J., concurring). The "law of the land" at its core provides that "no man's life, liberty or property be

---

[4] Hence, the case at hand involves – and we limit our analysis to – persons seized and detained within the United States who have constitutional rights under the Due Process Clause.

forfeited as a punishment until there has been a charge fairly made and fairly tried in a public tribunal." *In re Oliver*, 333 U.S. 257, 278 (1948). Thus, the Supreme Court has recognized that, because of the Due Process Clause, it "may freely be conceded" that as a "'general rule'... the government may not detain a person prior to a judgment of guilt in a criminal trial." *United States v. Salerno*, 481 U.S. 739, 749 (1987).

The Court, however, has permitted a limited number of specific exceptions to this general rule. Although some process is always required in order to detain an individual, in special situations detention based on process less than that attendant to a criminal conviction does not violate the Fifth Amendment. *See, e.g., Kansas v. Hendricks*, 521 U.S. 346, 358 (1997) (civil commitment of mentally ill sex offenders); *Salerno*, 481 U.S. 739 (pretrial detention of dangerous adults); *Schall v. Martin*, 467 U.S. 253 (1984) (pretrial detention of dangerous juveniles); *Addington v. Texas*, 441 U.S. 418, 427–28 (1979) (civil commitment of mentally ill); *Humphrey v. Smith*, 336 U.S. 695 (1949) (courts martial of American soldiers). Among these recognized exceptions is the one on which the Government grounds its principal argument in this case: Congress may constitutionally authorize the President to order military detention, without criminal process, of persons who "qualify as 'enemy combatants,'" that is, fit within that particular "legal category." *Hamdi v. Rumsfeld*, 542 U.S. 507, 516, 522 n.1 (2004) (plurality).[5]

The act of depriving a person of the liberty protected by our Constitution is a momentous one; thus, recognized exceptions to criminal process are narrow in scope, and generally permit only limited periods of detention. *See, e.g., Jackson v. Indiana*, 406 U.S. 715, 738 (1972). And, of course, the Government can never invoke an exception, and so detain a person without criminal process, if the individual does not fit within the narrow legal category of persons to whom the exception applies. For example, the Supreme Court has explained that the Constitution does not permit the Government to detain a predatory sex criminal through a civil commitment process simply by establishing that he is dangerous. The civil commitment process may only be substituted for criminal process for such a criminal if the Government's evidence establishes "proof of dangerousness" *and* "proof of some additional factor, such as a 'mental illness' or 'mental abnormality.'" *Hendricks*, 521 U.S. at 358.

In *Hamdi*, the plurality explained that precisely the same principles apply when the Government seeks to detain a person as an enemy combatant. Under the habeas procedure prescribed in *Hamdi*, if the Government asserts an exception to the usual criminal process by detaining as an enemy combatant an individual with constitutional rights, it must proffer evidence to demonstrate that the individual "qualif[ies]" for this exceptional treatment. 542 U.S. at 516, 534. Only *after* the Government has "put[ ] forth credible evidence that" an individual "meets the enemy-combatant criteria" does "the onus" shift to the individual to demonstrate "that he falls outside the [enemy combatant] criteria." *Id.* at 534. For in this country, the military cannot seize and indefinitely detain an individual – particularly when the sole process leading to his detention is a

---

[5] Case law also establishes that during times of war Congress may constitutionally authorize the President to detain "enemy aliens," also known as "alien enemies," defined as "subject[s] of a foreign state at war with the United States." *Eisentrager*, 339 U.S. at 769 n.2 (internal quotation marks omitted); *see Ludecke v. Watkins*, 335 U.S. 160 (1948). And, the Government can detain potentially dangerous resident aliens for a limited time pending deportation. *See, e.g., Carlson v. Landon*, 342 U.S. 524, 537–42 (1952); *cf. Zadvydas v. Davis*, 533 U.S. 678 (2001) (construing a statute's authorization of post-removal-period detention to not permit indefinite detention of aliens, to avoid serious doubt as to its constitutionality). But, as the Government recognizes, the Alien Enemy Act, the statute the Court considered in *Eisentrager* and *Ludecke*, does not apply to al-Marri's case – in fact, al-Marri is not an "enemy alien" but a citizen of Qatar, with which the United States has friendly diplomatic relations; and the Government does not seek to deport al-Marri. Therefore neither of these exceptions is offered by the Government as a basis for holding al-Marri without criminal charge, and neither is applicable here.

determination by the Executive that the detention is necessary[6] – unless the Government demonstrates that he "qualif[ies]" for this extraordinary treatment because he fits within the "legal category" of enemy combatants. *Id.* at 516, 522 n. 1.

Moreover, when the Government contends, as it does here, that an individual with constitutional rights is an enemy combatant, whose exclusive opportunity to escape indefinite military detention rests on overcoming presumptively accurate hearsay, courts must take particular care that the Government's allegations demonstrate that the detained individual is not a civilian, but instead, as the Supreme Court has explained, "meets the enemy-combatant criteria." *Id.* at 534. For only such care accords with the "deeply rooted and ancient opposition in this country to the extension of military control over civilians." *Reid v. Covert*, 354 U.S. 1, 33 (1957) (plurality).

These principles thus form the legal framework for consideration of the issues before us. Both parties recognize that it does not violate the Due Process Clause for the President to order the military to seize and detain individuals who "qualify" as enemy combatants for the duration of a war. They disagree, however, as to whether the evidence the Government has proffered, even assuming its accuracy, establishes that al-Marri fits within the "legal category" of enemy combatants. The Government principally contends that its evidence establishes this and therefore the AUMF grants the President *statutory* authority to detain al-Marri as an enemy combatant. Alternatively, the Government asserts that the President has inherent *constitutional* authority to order al-Marri's indefinite military detention. Al-Marri maintains that the proffered evidence does not establish that he fits within the "legal category" of enemy combatant and so the AUMF does not authorize the President to order the military to seize and detain him, and that the President has no inherent constitutional authority to order this detention. We now turn to these contentions.

B.

The Government's primary argument is that the AUMF, as construed by precedent and considered against "the legal background against which [it] was enacted," i.e. constitutional and law-of-war principles, empowers the President to order the military to seize and detain al-Marri as an enemy combatant. The AUMF provides:

> . . . the President is authorized to use all necessary and appropriate force against those nations, organizations, or persons he determines planned, authorized, committed, or aided the terrorist attacks that occurred on September 11, 2001, or harbored such organizations or persons, in order to prevent any future acts of international terrorism against the United States by such nations, organizations or persons.

115 Stat. 224.[7] In considering the Government's AUMF argument, we first note the limits the Government places on its interpretation of this statute, and then consider the Government's central contention.

---

[6] *Hamdi* recognizes that the sole process that the Government need provide in order to initially detain an enemy combatant is a presidential determination that the detention is necessary. 342 U.S. at 518. Of course, *Hamdi* also reaffirms that the writ of habeas corpus provides a remedy to challenge collaterally the legality of the ongoing detention. *Id.* at 525–26. Although the habeas remedy follows from the Suspension Clause, the *Hamdi* plurality borrowed the due process balancing approach from *Mathews v. Eldridge*, 424 U.S. 319 (1976), to design the specific requirements of this habeas remedy. *Hamdi*, 542 U.S. at 525–35.

[7] Although the Government asserts in a footnote that the MCA "buttresses" the President's "inherent authority" to detain al-Marri, it does not assert that the MCA provides statutory authority to detain enemy combatants. Plainly, the MCA provides no such authority, for it addresses only whether a detained individual is an *unlawful* enemy combatant subject to military trial, not whether an individual with constitutional rights seized in this country qualifies as an enemy combatant in the first instance.

1.

Tellingly, the Government does *not* argue that the broad language of the AUMF authorizes the President to subject to indefinite military detention anyone he believes to have aided any "nation[ ], organization[ ], or person[ ]" related to the September 11th attacks. Such an interpretation would lead to absurd results that Congress could not have intended. Under that reading of the AUMF, the President would be able to subject to indefinite military detention anyone, including an American citizen, whom the President believed was associated with any organization that the President believed in some way "planned, authorized, committed, or aided" the September 11th attacks, so long as the President believed this to be "necessary and appropriate" to prevent future acts of terrorism.

Under such an interpretation of the AUMF, if some money from a nonprofit charity that feeds Afghan orphans made its way to al Qaeda, the President could subject to indefinite military detention any donor to that charity. Similarly, this interpretation of the AUMF would allow the President to detain indefinitely any employee or shareholder of an American corporation that built equipment used by the September 11th terrorists; or allow the President to order the military seizure and detention of an American-citizen physician who treated a member of al Qaeda.

To read the AUMF to provide the President with such unlimited power would present serious constitutional questions, for the Supreme Court has long recognized that the Due Process Clause "cannot be . . . construed as to leave congress free to make any process 'due process of law,' by its mere will." *See Murray's Lessee v. Hoboken Land & Improvement Co.*, 59 U.S. (18 How.) 272, 276–77 (1855).

2.

We need not here deal with the absurd results, nor reach the constitutional concerns, raised by an interpretation of the AUMF that authorizes the President to detain indefinitely – without criminal charge or process – anyone he believes to have aided any "nation[ ], organization[ ], or person[ ]" related to the September 11th terrorists. For the Government wisely limits its argument. It relies only on the scope of the AUMF as construed by precedent and considered in light of "the legal background against which [it] was enacted." Specifically, the Government contends that "[t]he Supreme Court's and this Court's prior construction of the AUMF govern this case and compel the conclusion that the President is authorized to detain al-Marri as an enemy combatant."

i.

The precedent interpreting the AUMF on which the Government relies for this argument consists of two cases: the Supreme Court's opinion in *Hamdi*, 542 U.S. 507, and our opinion in *Padilla v. Hanft*, 423 F.3d 386 (4th Cir. 2005). The "legal background" for the AUMF, which it cites, consists of two cases from earlier conflicts, *Ex Parte Quirin*, 317 U.S. 1 (1942) (World War II), and *Ex Parte Milligan*, 71 U.S. (4 Wall.) 2 (1866) (U.S. Civil War), as well as constitutional and law-of-war principles.

With respect to the latter, we note that American courts have often been reluctant to follow international law in resolving domestic disputes. In the present context, however, they, like the Government here, have relied on the law of war – treaty obligations including the Hague and Geneva Conventions and customary principles developed alongside them. The law of war provides clear rules for determining an individual's status during an international armed conflict, distinguishing between "combatants" (members of a nation's military, militia, or other armed forces, and those who fight alongside them) and "civilians" (all other persons).[8] *See, e.g.*, Geneva Convention Relative to the Treatment of Prisoners of War (Third Geneva Convention) arts. 2, 4, 5, Aug. 12, 1949, 6 U.S.T. 3316, 75 U.N.T.S. 135; Geneva Convention Relative to the Protection of Civilian Persons in Time of War (Fourth Geneva Convention) art. 4, Aug. 12, 1949, 6 U.S.T. 3516, 75 U.N.T.S. 287. American courts have repeatedly looked to these careful distinctions made in the law of war in identifying which individuals fit within the "legal category" of "enemy combatants" under our Constitution. *See, e.g., Hamdi*, 542 U.S. at 518; *Quirin*, 317 U.S. at 30–31 & n.7; *Milligan*, 71 U.S. at 121–22; *Padilla*, 423 F.3d at 391.

In the case at hand, the Government asserts that the construction given the AUMF in *Hamdi* and *Padilla* – based on these law-of-war principles – "compel[s] the conclusion that the President is authorized [by the AUMF] to detain al-Marri as an enemy combatant." In other words, the Government contends that al-Marri fits within the "legal category" of persons that the Supreme Court in *Hamdi*, and this court in *Padilla*, held the AUMF authorized the President to detain as enemy combatants. Thus, we examine those cases to determine whether the interpretation of the AUMF they adopt does indeed empower the President to treat al-Marri as an enemy combatant.

In *Hamdi*, the Supreme Court looked to precedent and the law of war to determine whether the AUMF authorized the President to detain as an enemy combatant an American citizen captured while engaging in battle against American and allied armed forces in Afghanistan as part of the Taliban. *See Hamdi*, 542 U.S. at 518–22. In support of that detention, the Government offered evidence that Yaser Esam Hamdi "affiliated with a Taliban military unit and received weapons training," "took up arms with the Taliban," "engaged in armed conflict against the United States" in Afghanistan, and when captured on the battlefield "surrender[ed] his Kalishnikov assault rifle." *Hamdi*, 542 U.S. at 510, 513, 516 (internal quotation marks omitted). Hamdi's detention was upheld because in fighting against the United States on the battlefield in Afghanistan with the Taliban, the de facto government of Afghanistan at the time,[9] Hamdi bore arms with the army of an enemy nation and so, under the law of war, was an enemy combatant. *Hamdi*, 542 U.S. at 518–20.

The *Hamdi* Court expressly recognized that the AUMF did not explicitly provide for detention. *Id.* at 519; *see also id.* at 547 (Souter, J., concurring). It concluded, however, "in light of" the law-of-war principles applicable to Hamdi's battlefield capture, that this was "of no moment" in the case before it. *Id.* at 519 (plurality). As the plurality

---

[8] Thus, "civilian" is a term of art in the law of war, not signifying an innocent person but rather someone in a certain legal category, not subject to *military* seizure or detention. So too, a "combatant" is by no means always a wrongdoer, but rather a member of a different "legal category" who is subject to military seizure and detention. *Hamdi*, 542 U.S. at 522 n. 1. For example, our brave soldiers fighting in Germany during World War II were "combatants" under the law of war, and viewed from Germany's perspective they were "enemy combatants." While civilians are subject to trial and punishment in civilian courts for all crimes committed during wartime in the country in which they are captured and held, combatant status protects an individual from trial and punishment by the capturing nation, unless the combatant has violated the laws of war. *See Hamdi*, 542 U.S. at 518; *Quirin*, 317 U.S. at 28–31. Nations in international conflicts can summarily remove the adversary's "combatants," i.e. the "enemy combatants," from the battlefield and detain them for the duration of such conflicts, but no such provision is made for "civilians." *Id.*

[9] *See* White House Fact Sheet: Status of Detainees at Guantanamo (Feb. 7, 2002), http://www.pegc.us/archive/White_House/20020207_WH_POW_fact_sheet.txt; *see also* Protocol Additional to the Geneva Conventions of 12 August 1949, and Relating to the Protection of Victims of International Armed Conflicts (Protocol I), June 8, 1977, arts. 43–44, 1125 U.N.T.S. 3 (defining combatants in conflicts between nations as members, other than chaplains and medical personnel, of "all organized armed forces, groups and units which are under a command responsible to that [nation] for the conduct of its subordinates").

explained, "[b]ecause detention to prevent a combatant's *return to the battlefield* is a fundamental incident of waging war, in permitting the use of 'necessary and appropriate force,' Congress has clearly and unmistakably authorized detention in the *narrow circumstances considered here*." *Id.* (emphasis added). Thus, the *Hamdi* Court reached the following limited holding: "the AUMF is explicit congressional authorization for the detention of individuals in the *narrow category* we describe," that is, individuals who were "part of or supporting forces hostile to the United States or coalition partners in Afghanistan and who engaged in an armed conflict against the United States there." *Hamdi*, 542 U.S. at 516–17 (plurality) (internal quotation marks omitted) (emphasis added); *accord id.* at 587 (Thomas, J., dissenting). Indeed, the plurality expressly explained that its opinion "only finds legislative authority to detain under the AUMF once it is sufficiently clear that the individual is, in fact, an enemy combatant." *Id.* at 523 (plurality) (emphasis added).

In *Padilla*, we similarly held that the AUMF authorized the President to detain as an enemy combatant an American citizen who "was armed and present in a combat zone" in Afghanistan as part of Taliban forces during the conflict there with the United States. 423 F.3d at 390–91 (internal quotation marks omitted). The Government had not been able to capture Jose Padilla until he came to the border of the United States, but because the Government presented evidence that Padilla "took up arms against United States forces in [Afghanistan] in the same way and to the same extent as did Hamdi" we concluded that he "unquestionably qualifies as an 'enemy combatant' as that term was defined for the purposes of the controlling opinion in *Hamdi*." 423 F.3d at 391.[10] We too invoked the law of war, upholding Padilla's detention because we understood "the plurality's *reasoning* in *Hamdi* to be that the AUMF authorizes the president to detain all who qualify as 'enemy combatants' within the meaning of the laws of war." *Id.* at 392. We also noted that Padilla's detention, like Hamdi's, was permissible "'to prevent a *combatant's return to the battlefield* . . . a fundamental incident of waging war.'" *Id.* at 391 (*quoting Hamdi*, 542 U.S. at 519) (emphasis added).

Supreme Court precedent offered substantial support for the narrow rulings in *Hamdi* and *Padilla*. In *Quirin*, which the *Hamdi* plurality characterized as the "most apposite precedent," 542 U.S. at 523, the Supreme Court upheld the treatment, as

---

[10] Although our opinion discussed Padilla's association with al Qaeda, we *held* that Padilla was an enemy combatant because of his association with Taliban forces, i.e. Afghanistan government forces, on the battlefield in Afghanistan during the time of the conflict between the United States and Afghanistan. *Padilla*, 423 F.3d at 391. Al-Marri urges us to ignore *Padilla* in light of its subsequent history. *See Padilla v. Hanft*, 432 F.3d 582, 583 (4th Cir. 2005) (noting that the Government's transfer of Padilla to civilian custody for criminal trial after arguing before this court that he was an enemy combatant created "an appearance that the government may be attempting to avoid consideration of our decision by the Supreme Court"). That history is troubling but we see no need to avoid *Padilla*'s narrow holding.

We do wish to respond to points concerning *Padilla* raised by our friend in dissent. First, we do not, as the dissent suggests, *post* at 80–81, ignore *Padilla*'s holding that an individual qualifying as an "enemy combatant" may be captured and detained in the United States. *Padilla* provides no precedent for al-Marri's military capture and detention in this country because al-Marri, for the reasons explained in text, is *not* an enemy combatant. We emphasize the place of al-Marri's capture and detention only to establish that, as an alien lawfully residing in this country, he is protected by the Due Process Clause and so cannot be seized and indefinitely detained by the military unless he qualifies as an enemy combatant. Second, we do not hold, in conflict with *Padilla*, that al-Marri cannot be detained in military custody because the Government could criminally prosecute him. *Id.* at 80–81. If al-Marri, like Padilla, did qualify as an enemy combatant, then the Government could choose to either detain him or prosecute him (if it established that he was not entitled to immunity from criminal prosecution as a lawful combatant). That said, given the dissent's acknowledgment, *id.* at 82, that unlike Padilla, al-Marri has never been "in a combat zone," we do not see how his detention as an enemy combatant could achieve the asserted purpose of such detention, i.e. "the prevention of return to the field of battle." *Id.* at 81 (*quoting Padilla*, 423 F.3d at 394–95).

enemy combatants, of men directed, outfitted, and paid by the German military to bring explosives into the United States to destroy American war industries during World War II. The *Quirin* Court concluded that even a petitioner claiming American citizenship had been properly classified as an enemy combatant because "[c]itizens who associate themselves with the military arm of the enemy government, and with its aid, guidance and direction enter this county bent on hostile acts, are enemy belligerents [combatants] within the meaning of . . . the law of war." *Quirin*, 317 U.S. at 37–38. The Court cited the Hague Convention "which defines the persons to whom belligerent [i.e. combatant] rights and duties attach," *id.* at 30–31 n. 7, in support of its conclusion that the *Quirin* petitioners qualified as enemy combatants. Given the "declaration of war between the United States and the German Reich," *id.* at 21, and that all the *Quirin* petitioners, including one who claimed American citizenship, were directed and paid by the "military arm" of the German Reich, the Court held that the law of war classified them as enemy belligerents (or combatants) and so the Constitution permitted subjecting them to military jurisdiction. *Id.* at 48.

Hamdi and *Padilla* ground their holdings on this central teaching from *Quirin*, i.e., enemy combatant status rests on an individual's affiliation during wartime with the "military arm of the enemy government." *Quirin*, 317 U.S. at 37–38; *Hamdi*, 542 U.S. at 519; *see also Padilla*, 423 F.3d at 391. In *Quirin* that enemy government was the German Reich; in *Hamdi* and *Padilla*, it was the Taliban government of Afghanistan.

Hamdi and *Padilla* also rely on this principle from *Quirin* to distinguish (but not disavow) *Milligan*. In *Milligan*, the Court rejected the Government's impassioned contention that a presidential order and the "laws and usages of war," 71 U.S. at 121–22, justified exercising military jurisdiction over Lamdin Milligan, an Indiana resident, during the Civil War. The Government alleged that Milligan had communicated with the enemy, had conspired to "seize munitions of war," and had "join[ed] and aid[ed] . . . a secret" enemy organization "for the purpose of overthrowing the Government and duly constituted authorities of the United States." *Id.* at 6. The Court recognized that Milligan had committed "an enormous crime" during "a period of war" and at a place "within . . . the theatre of military operations, and which had been and was constantly threatened to be invaded by the enemy." *Id.* at 7, 130. But it found no support in the "laws and usages of war" for subjecting Milligan to military jurisdiction as a combatant, for although he was a "dangerous enem[y]" of the nation, he was a civilian, and had to be treated as such. *Id.* at 121–22, 130.

Quirin, *Hamdi*, and *Padilla* all emphasize that *Milligan*'s teaching – that our Constitution does not permit the Government to subject *civilians* within the United States to military jurisdiction – remains good law. The *Quirin* Court explained that while the petitioners before it were affiliated with the armed forces of an enemy nation and so were enemy belligerents, Milligan was a "non-belligerent" and so "not subject to the law of war." 317 U.S. at 45. The *Hamdi* plurality similarly took care to note that *Milligan* "turned in large part on the fact that Milligan was not a prisoner of war" (i.e. combatant) and suggested that "[h]ad Milligan been captured while he was assisting Confederate soldiers by carrying a rifle against Union troops on a Confederate battlefield, the holding of the Court might well have been different." 542 U.S. at 522. And in *Padilla*, we reaffirmed that "*Milligan* does not extend to enemy combatants" and so "is inapposite here because Padilla, unlike Milligan, associated with, and has taken up arms against the forces of the United States on behalf of, an enemy of the United States." 423 F.3d at 396–97. Thus, although *Hamdi*, *Quirin*, and *Padilla* distinguish *Milligan*, they recognize that its core holding remains the law of the land. That is, civilians within this country (even "dangerous enemies" like Milligan who perpetrate "enormous crime[s]" on behalf of "secret" enemy organizations bent on "overthrowing the Government" of this country) may not be subjected to military control and deprived of constitutional rights.[11]

In sum, the holdings of *Hamdi* and *Padilla* share two characteristics: (1) they look to law-of-war principles to determine who fits within the "legal category" of enemy combatant; and (2) following the law of war, they rest enemy combatant status on affiliation with the military arm of an enemy nation.

ii.

In view of the holdings in *Hamdi* and *Padilla*, we find it remarkable that the Government contends that they "compel the conclusion" that the President may detain al-Marri as an enemy combatant. For unlike Hamdi and Padilla, al-Marri is not alleged to have been part of a Taliban unit, not alleged to have stood alongside the Taliban or the armed forces of any other enemy nation, not alleged to have been on the battlefield during the war in Afghanistan, not alleged to have even been in Afghanistan during the armed conflict there, and not alleged to have engaged in combat with United States forces anywhere in the world. *See* Rapp Declaration (alleging none of these facts, but instead that "Al-Marri engaged in conduct in preparation for acts of international terrorism intended to cause injury or adverse effects on the United States").

In place of the "classic wartime detention" that the Government argued justified Hamdi's detention as an enemy combatant, *see* Br. of Respondents at 20–21, 27, *Hamdi*, 542 U.S. 507 (No. 03-6696), or the "classic battlefield" detention it maintained justified Padilla's, *see* Opening Br. for the Appellant at 16, 20, 29, 51, *Padilla*, 432 F.3d 386 (No. 05-6396), here the Government argues that al-Marri's seizure and indefinite military detention in this country are justified "because he engaged in, and continues to pose a very real threat of carrying out, . . . acts of international terrorism." And instead of seeking judicial deference to decisions of "military officers who are engaged in the serious work of waging battle," *Hamdi*, 542 U.S. at 531–32, the Government asks us to defer to the "multi-agency evaluation process" of government bureaucrats in Washington made eighteen months after al-Marri was taken into custody. Neither the holding in *Hamdi* nor that in *Padilla* supports the Government's contentions here.

In arguing to the contrary, the Government confuses certain secondary arguments it advanced in *Hamdi* and *Padilla* with the actual holdings in those cases. As discussed above, both *Hamdi* and *Padilla* upheld the President's authority pursuant to the AUMF to detain as enemy combatants individuals (1) who affiliated with and fought on behalf

---

[11] Because of this important principle, the Supreme Court has hailed *Milligan* as "one of the great landmarks in th[e] Court's history." *Reid*, 354 U.S. at 30. Although the Government largely avoids *Milligan*, it implicitly acknowledges this point and so attempts to distinguish *Milligan* from the case at hand on the ground that Milligan was a citizen, and al-Marri an alien. In some circumstances the Constitution does afford aliens less protection than citizens. *See, e.g., Hamdi*, 542 U.S. at 558–59 (Scalia, J., dissenting) (suggesting that during war the constitutional rights of an "enemy alien," whom the Supreme Court has defined as a "subject of a foreign state at war with the United States," *Eisentrager*, 339 U.S. at 769 n.2 (internal quotation marks omitted), differ from those of a treasonous citizen); *Verdugo-Urquidez*, 494 U.S. at 274–75 (holding that the Fourth Amendment does not apply to searches by United States agents of property owned by aliens *in* foreign countries). But the distinction between citizens and aliens provides no basis for depriving an alien like al-Marri, lawfully resident within the United States and not the subject of an enemy nation, of those rights guaranteed by the Due Process Clause. Rather, the Supreme Court has repeatedly held that aliens situated like al-Marri have an unquestioned right to the due process of law. *See Wong Wing*, 163 U.S. at 238; *see also Verdugo-Urquidez*, 494 U.S. at 271; *id.* at 278 (Kennedy, J., concurring) (observing that "[a]ll would agree . . . that the dictates of the Due Process Clause of the Fifth Amendment protect" an alien lawfully within the United States). The Government does not dispute or distinguish these cases; it simply ignores them.

of Taliban government forces, (2) against the armed forces of the United States and its allies, (3) on the battlefield in Afghanistan. In both cases, however, the Government also contended that the AUMF provided the President with even broader authority to subject to military detention, as enemy combatants, persons otherwise involved "in the global armed conflict against the al Qaeda terrorist network." Br. of Respondents at 20–21, *Hamdi*, 542 U.S. 507 (No. 03-6996); see Opening Br. for the Appellant at 17–18, *Padilla*, 423 F.3d 386 (No. 05-6396).

But neither the Supreme Court in *Hamdi*, nor this court in *Padilla*, accepted the Government's invitation to fashion such a broad construction of the AUMF. Instead, the Hamdi plurality emphasized the narrowness of its holding, *id.* at 509, 516, 517, and the "limited category" of individuals controlled by that holding, *id.* at 518. In *Padilla*, we similarly saw no need to embrace a broader construction of the AUMF than that adopted by the Supreme Court in *Hamdi*. Indeed, the Government itself *principally* argued that Padilla was an enemy combatant because he, like Hamdi, "engaged in armed conflict" alongside the Taliban "against our forces in Afghanistan." *See* Opening Br. for the Appellant at 22–23, 27, *Padilla*, 423 F.3d 386 (No. 05-6396).[12]

Thus, the Government is mistaken in its representation that *Hamdi* and *Padilla* "recognized" "[t]he President's authority to detain 'enemy combatants' during the current conflict with al Qaeda." No precedent recognizes any such authority. *Hamdi* and *Padilla* evidence no sympathy for the view that the AUMF permits indefinite military detention beyond the "limited category" of people covered by the "narrow circumstances" of those cases. Therefore the Government's primary argument – that *Hamdi* and *Padilla* "compel the conclusion" that the AUMF authorizes the President "to detain al-Marri as an enemy combatant" – fails.

3.

The Government offers no other legal precedent, rationale, or authority justifying its position that the AUMF empowers the President to detain al-Marri as an enemy combatant. The *Hamdi* plurality, however, noted that because it had not "elaborated" on "[t]he legal category of enemy combatant," "[t]he permissible bounds of the category will be defined by the lower courts as subsequent cases are presented to them." *Hamdi*, 542 U.S. at 522 n.1. As a "lower court" in this "subsequent case[ ]," we have searched extensively for authority that would support the Government's contention that al-Marri fits within the "permissible bounds" of "the legal category of enemy combatant." As explained below, we have found none. Certainly, the Supreme Court's most recent terrorism case, *Hamdan*, 126 S. Ct. 2749, and the law-of-war principles it identifies provide no support for that contention. Moreover, contrary to the Government's apparent belief, no precedent and nothing in the "legal background against which the AUMF was enacted" permits a person to be classified as an enemy combatant because of his criminal conduct on behalf of an enemy organization. And, the AUMF itself neither classifies

---

[12] In doing so, the Government acknowledged, *id.* at 29–30, our distinguished colleague Judge Wilkinson's statement that "[t]o compare [Hamdi's] battlefield capture to the domestic arrest in *Padilla v. Rumsfeld* is to compare apples and oranges," *Hamdi v. Rumsfeld*, 337 F.3d 335, 344 (4th Cir. 2003) (Wilkinson, J., concurring in the denial of rehearing en banc), but explained that Judge Wilkinson's observation came *before* the Government had proffered any evidence that Padilla had carried arms alongside the Taliban against United States armed forces during the conflict in Afghanistan. In other words, at the time Judge Wilkinson differentiated Hamdi from Padilla, the Government's allegations against Padilla mirrored its allegations against al-Marri here – that he had associated with al Qaeda and engaged in conduct in preparation for acts of terrorism. We agree with Judge Wilkinson's characterization: to compare Hamdi's battlefield capture to the domestic arrest of al-Marri is indeed "to compare apples and oranges." *Id.*

certain civilians as enemy combatants, nor otherwise authorizes the President to subject civilians to indefinite military detention.

i.

Rather than supporting the Government's position, the Supreme Court's most recent terrorism case provides an additional reason for rejecting the contention that al-Marri is an enemy combatant. In *Hamdan*, the Court held that because the conflict between the United States and al Qaeda in Afghanistan is not "between nations," it is a "'conflict not of an international character'" – and so is governed by Common Article 3 of the Geneva Conventions. *See* 126 S. Ct. at 2795; *see also id.* at 2802 (Kennedy, J., concurring). Common Article 3 and other Geneva Convention provisions applying to non-international conflicts (in contrast to those applying to international conflicts, such as that with Afghanistan's Taliban government) simply do *not* recognize the "legal category" of enemy combatant. *See* Third Geneva Convention, art. 3, 6 U.S.T. at 3318. As the International Committee of the Red Cross – the official codifier of the Geneva Conventions – explains, "an 'enemy combatant' is a person who, either lawfully or unlawfully, engages in hostilities for the opposing side in an *international* armed conflict;" in contrast, "[i]n non-international armed conflict combatant status *does not exist*." Int'l Comm. of the Red Cross, Official Statement: The Relevance of IHL in the Context of Terrorism, at 1, 3 (Feb. 21, 2005), http://www.icrc.org/Web/Eng/siteeng0.nsf/htmlall/terrorism-ihl-210705 (emphasis added).[13]

Perhaps for this reason, the Government ignores *Hamdan*'s holding that the conflict with al Qaeda in Afghanistan is a non-international conflict, and ignores the fact that in such conflicts the "legal category" of enemy combatant does not exist. Indeed, the Government's sole acknowledgment of *Hamdan* in its appellate brief is a short footnote, in which it asserts that "the Court took it as a given that Hamdan was subject to detention as an enemy combatant during ongoing hostilities." The weakness of this response is apparent. Not only does it avoid the holding in *Hamdan* that the conflict between the United States and al Qaeda is a non-international conflict, but also it suggests that the Supreme Court approved Hamdan's detention when the legality of that detention was not before the Court, and in fact, the legality of the detention of those like Hamdan, captured and detained in the conflict with al Qaeda *outside* the United States, is still being litigated. *See, e.g., Boumediene*, 476 F.3d 981.

Moreover, even were the Supreme Court ultimately to approve the detention of Hamdan and those like him, that would not bolster the Government's position at all in the case at hand.[14] This is so because, since the legal status of "enemy combatant"

---

[13] Notwithstanding this principle, we recognize that some commentators have suggested that "for such time as they take a *direct* part in hostilities," participants in non-international armed conflicts may, as a matter of customary international law, be placed in the formal legal category of "enemy combatant." *See, e.g.*, Curtis A. Bradley & Jack L. Goldsmith, *Congressional Authorization and the War on Terrorism*, 118 Harv. L. Rev. 2047, 2115 & n.304 (2005) (internal quotation marks omitted). No precedent from the Supreme Court or this court endorses this view, and the Government itself has *not* advanced such an argument. This may be because even were a court to follow this approach in *some* cases, it would not assist the Government here. For the Government has proffered no evidence that al-Marri has taken a "*direct* part in hostilities." Moreover, the United States has elsewhere adopted a formal treaty understanding of the meaning of the term "direct part in hostilities," which plainly excludes al-Marri. *See* Message from the President of the United States Transmitting Two Optional Protocols to the Convention on the Rights of the Child, S. Treaty Doc. No. 106-37, at VII (2000) (distinguishing between "immediate and actual action on the battlefield" and "indirect participation," including gathering and transmitting military information, weapons, and supplies).

[14] The Supreme Court has yet to hold that there is a non-international armed conflict between the United States and al Qaeda *within the United States*. Non-international conflicts "occur[ ] in the territory of *one of*

does not exist in non-international conflicts, the law of war leaves the detention of persons in such conflicts to the applicable law of the detaining country. In al-Marri's case, the applicable law is our Constitution. Thus, even if the Supreme Court should hold that the Government may detain indefinitely Hamdan and others like him, who were captured *outside* the United States and lacked substantial and voluntary connections to this country, that would provide no support for approving al-Marri's military detention. For not only was al-Marri seized and detained *within* the United States, he also has substantial connections to the United States, and so plainly is protected by the Due Process Clause.

ii.

The core assumption underlying the Government's position, notwithstanding *Hamdi*, *Padilla*, *Quirin*, *Milligan*, and *Hamdan*, seems to be that persons lawfully within this country, entitled to the protections of our Constitution, lose their civilian status and become "enemy combatants" if they have allegedly engaged in criminal conduct on behalf of an organization seeking to harm the United States. Of course, a person who commits a crime should be punished, but when a civilian protected by the Due Process Clause commits a crime he is subject to charge, trial, and punishment in a civilian court, *not* to seizure and confinement by military authorities.

We recognize the understandable instincts of those who wish to treat domestic terrorists as "combatants" in a "global war on terror." Allegations of criminal activity in association with a terrorist organization, however, do not permit the Government to transform a civilian into an enemy combatant subject to indefinite military detention, any more than allegations of murder in association with others while in military service permit the Government to transform a civilian into a soldier subject to trial by court martial. *See United States ex rel. Toth v. Quarles*, 350 U.S. 11, 23 (1955) (holding that ex-servicemen, "like other civilians, are entitled to have the benefit of safeguards afforded those tried in the regular courts authorized by Article III of the Constitution").

To be sure, enemy combatants may commit crimes just as civilians may. When an enemy combatant violates the law of war, that conduct will render the person an "unlawful" enemy combatant, subject not only to detention but also to military trial and punishment. *Quirin*, 317 U.S. at 31. But merely engaging in unlawful behavior does not make one an enemy combatant. *Quirin* well illustrates this point. The *Quirin* petitioners were first enemy combatants – associating themselves with the military arm of the German government with which the United States was at war. They became *unlawful* enemy combatants when they violated the laws of war by "without uniform com[ing] secretly through the lines for the purpose of waging war." *Id.* By doing so, in addition to being subject to military detention for the duration of the conflict as enemy combatants, they also became "subject to trial and punishment by military tribunals for acts which render their belligerency illegal." *Id.* Had the *Quirin* petitioners never "secretly and without uniform" passed our "military lines," *id.*, they still would have been enemy combatants, subject to military detention, but would not have been *unlawful* enemy combatants subject to military trial and punishment.

---

the High Contracting Parties," *Hamdan*, 126 S. Ct. at 2795 (*quoting* Third Geneva Convention, 6 U.S.T. at 3318) (emphasis added) – and *Hamdan* only found there to be a conflict between the United States and al Qaeda *in Afghanistan*. Of course, al-Marri is not a participant in any conflict involving the United States in Afghanistan. Although the Government alleges that al-Marri attended an al Qaeda training camp in Afghanistan years before September 11th, it has proffered no evidence that al-Marri was involved in the conflict between the United States and al Qaeda *in Afghanistan* – nor could it, for al-Marri has not been in Afghanistan at any point during that conflict.

Neither *Quirin* nor any other precedent even suggests, as the Government seems to believe, that individuals with constitutional rights, unaffiliated with the military arm of any enemy government, can be subjected to military jurisdiction and deprived of those rights solely on the basis of their conduct on behalf of an enemy organization.[15] In fact, *Milligan* rejected the Government's attempt to do just this. There, the Court acknowledged that Milligan's conduct – not "mere association" with, *cf. post* at n.3, but also "joining and aiding" a "secret political organization, armed to oppose the laws, and seek[ing] by stealthy means to introduce the enemies of the country into peaceful communities, there to...overthrow the power of the United States" – made him and his co-conspirators "dangerous enemies to their country." 71 U.S. at 6, 130. But the Government did not allege that Milligan took orders from any enemy government or took up arms against this country on the battlefield. And so the Court prohibited the Government from subjecting Milligan to military jurisdiction for his "enormous crime." *Id.*

Although Milligan was an "enem[y]" of the country and associated with an organization seeking to "overthrow[ ] the Government" of this country, he was still a civilian. *Id.* Milligan's conduct mirrors the Government's allegations against al-Marri. If the Government's allegations are true, like Milligan, al-Marri is deplorable, criminal, and potentially dangerous, but like Milligan he is a civilian nonetheless.[16]

---

[15] The distinction between organizations and nations is not without rationale. The law of war refuses to classify persons affiliated with terrorist organizations as enemy combatants for fear that doing so would immunize them from prosecution and punishment by civilian authorities in the capturing country. *See, e.g.*, Message from the President of the United States Transmitting the Protocol II Additional to the 1949 Geneva Conventions, and Relating to the Protection of Victims of Noninternational Armed Conflicts, S. Treaty Doc. No. 100-2, at IV (1987) (explaining President Reagan's recommendation against ratifying a treaty provision that "would grant combatant status to irregular forces" and so "give recognition and protection to terrorist groups"). Moreover, a rule permitting indefinite military detention as "enemy combatants" of members of an "armed" organization, even one "seek[ing]...to...overthrow" a government, in addition to being contrary to controlling precedent, *Milligan*, 71 U.S. at 130, could well endanger citizens of this country or our allies. For example, another nation, purportedly following this rationale, could proclaim a radical environmental organization to be a terrorist group, and subject American members of the organization traveling in that nation to indefinite military detention.

The dissent properly recognizes the distinction between an organization and a nation's armed forces, acknowledging that an allegation of "mere association" with an organization, including al Qaeda, does not necessarily establish enemy combatant status permitting detention under the AUMF. *Post* at n.3. The dissent suggests, however, that if the Government alleges that a person affiliates with an organization and commits criminal acts with the "*purpose* of...facilitating terrorist activities," *id.* (*quoting* Rapp Declaration (emphasis added)), that would qualify him for enemy combatant status, permitting military detention under the AUMF. But the *Hamdi* plurality outlined a procedure to verify an individual's *status*, not to determine whether he harbored a particular purpose or intent. In this country, the only appropriate way to determine whether a person can be imprisoned for harboring a particular purpose or intent is through the criminal process.

[16] The Government's treatment of al-Marri, i.e. subjecting him to military detention, which the Government insists "is not 'punishment,'" is at odds with the Government's repeated recognition that criminal terrorist conduct by aliens *in this country* merits punishment by a civilian court, not indefinite military detention as an enemy combatant. *See, e.g., United States v. Abdi*, 463 F.3d 547, 550 (6th Cir. 2006) (civilian prosecution of suspected al-Qaeda terrorist who allegedly "indicated a desire to 'shoot up' a Columbus shopping mall with an AK-47"); *United States v. Moussaoui*, 382 F.3d 453 (4th Cir. 2004) (civilian prosecution of surviving al Qaeda conspirator involved in the September 11th attacks); *United States v. Reid*, 369 F.3d 619, 619-20 (1st Cir. 2004) (civilian prosecution of terrorist allied with Bin Laden who attempted to destroy airplane with explosives); *United States v. Goba*, 240 F. Supp. 2d 242, 244 (W.D.N.Y. 2003) (civilian prosecution of associates of al Qaeda, including those who met with Bin Laden and trained in terrorist camps in Afghanistan). Moreover, the Government is now prosecuting Jose Padilla in civilian court for his crimes. This practice is hardly new. Even the civilian co-conspirators of the *Quirin* petitioners were tried for their crimes in civilian courts. *See Cramer v. United States*, 325 U.S. 1 (1945); *United States v. Haupt*, 136 F.2d 661 (7th Cir. 1943).

The Government's treatment of others renders its decision to halt al-Marri's criminal prosecution – on the eve of a pre-trial hearing on a suppression motion – puzzling at best. Al-Marri contends that the Government

iii.

Finally, we note that the AUMF itself contains nothing that transforms a civilian into a combatant subject to indefinite military detention. Indeed, the AUMF contains only a broad grant of war powers and lacks any specific language authorizing detention. For this reason, the *Hamdi* plurality explained that its opinion "only finds legislative authority to detain under the AUMF once it is sufficiently clear that the individual *is*, in fact, an enemy combatant." *Hamdi*, 542 U.S. at 523 (emphasis added). Although the military detention of enemy combatants like Hamdi is certainly "a fundamental incident of waging war," *id.* at 519, the military detention of civilians like al-Marri just as certainly is not. Notably, even the Government does not contend that the AUMF transforms civilians into combatants or authorizes the President to classify civilians as enemy combatants and so detain them in military custody.

Moreover, assuming the Constitution permitted Congress to grant the President such an awesome and unprecedented power, if Congress intended to grant this authority it could and would have said so explicitly. The AUMF lacks the particularly clear statement from Congress that would, at a minimum, be necessary to authorize the classification and indefinite military detention of *civilians* as "enemy combatants." *See, e.g.*, *Greene v. McElroy*, 360 U.S. 474, 508 (1959) (rejecting Government argument that Executive Orders and statutes permitted deprivation of liberty rights absent "explicit authorization" in them); *Duncan v. Kahanamoku*, 327 U.S. 304, 324 (1946) (rejecting Government argument that statute authorized trial of civilians by military tribunals because Congress could not have intended "to exceed the boundaries between military and civilian power, in which our people have always believed"); *Ex Parte Endo*, 323 U.S. 283, 300 (1944) (rejecting Government argument that a "wartime" executive order and statute permitted detention of citizen of Japanese heritage when neither "use[d] the language of detention"); *Brown v. United States*, 12 U.S. (8 Cranch) 110, 128–29 (1814) (rejecting Government argument that declaration of war authorized confiscation of enemy property because it did not clearly "declare[ ]" the legislature's "will"). We are exceedingly reluctant to infer a grant of authority that is so far afield from anything recognized by precedent or law-of-war principles, especially given the serious constitutional concerns it would raise.

Furthermore, shortly after Congress enacted the AUMF, it enacted another statute that did explicitly authorize the President to arrest and detain "terrorist aliens" living within the United States believed to have come here to perpetrate acts of terrorism. *See* Uniting and Strengthening America by Providing Appropriate Tools Required to Intercept and Obstruct Terrorism (USA PATRIOT ACT) Act of 2001 (hereinafter "Patriot Act"), Pub. L. No. 107-56, 115 Stat. 272. However, that statute only authorizes detention for a limited time pending deportation or trial, pursuant to *civilian* law enforcement processes, and accompanied by careful congressional oversight. *See infra* Section III.C.1. The explicit authorization for limited detention and criminal process in civilian courts

---

has subjected him to indefinite military detention, rather than see his criminal prosecution to the end, in order to interrogate him without the strictures of criminal process. We trust that this is not so, for such a stratagem would contravene *Hamdi*'s injunction that "indefinite detention for the purpose of interrogation is not authorized." 542 U.S. at 521. We note, however, that not only has the Government offered no other explanation for abandoning al-Marri's prosecution, it has even propounded an affidavit in support of al-Marri's continued military detention stating that he "possesses information of high intelligence value." *See* Rapp Declaration. Moreover, former Attorney General John Ashcroft has explained that the Government decided to declare al-Marri an "enemy combatant" only after he became a "hard case" by "reject[ing] numerous offers to improve his lot by . . . providing information." John Ashcroft, *Never Again: Securing America and Restoring Justice* 168–69 (2006).

in the Patriot Act provides still another reason why we cannot assume that Congress silently empowered the President in the AUMF to order the indefinite military detention without any criminal process of civilian "terrorist aliens" as "enemy combatants."

We note that this does *not* mean that we accept al-Marri's contention that the Patriot Act affirmatively prohibits the detention of all suspected terrorist aliens within this country as enemy combatants. Plainly, the Patriot Act does not eliminate the statutory authority provided the President in the AUMF to detain individuals who fit within the "legal category" of enemy combatant; thus, if an alien "qualif[ies]" as an enemy combatant, then the AUMF authorizes his detention. *Hamdi*, 542 U.S. at 516. But if there were any conflict between the Patriot Act and the AUMF as to the legality of the detention of terrorist alien *civilians* within the United States, we would have to give precedence to the Patriot Act – for while the Patriot Act's explicit and specific focus is on detention of terrorist aliens within the United States, the AUMF lacks any language permitting such detention. *See Hamdi*, 542 U.S. at 519. And the Supreme Court has instructed that "a more specific statute will be given precedence over a more general one, regardless of their temporal sequence." *Busic v. United States*, 446 U.S. 398, 406 (1980); *see also Edmond v. United States*, 520 U.S. 651, 657 (1997).

In sum, the Government has not offered, and although we have exhaustively searched, we have not found, any authority that permits us to hold that the AUMF empowers the president to detain al-Marri as an enemy combatant. If the Government's allegations are true, and we assume they are for present purposes, al-Marri, like Milligan, is a dangerous enemy of this nation who has committed serious crimes and associated with a secret enemy organization that has engaged in hostilities against us. But, like Milligan, al-Marri is still a civilian: he does not fit within the "permissible bounds of" "[t]he legal category of enemy combatant." *Hamdi*, 542 U.S. at 522 n.1. Therefore, the AUMF provides the President no statutory authority to order the military to seize and indefinitely detain al-Marri.

C.

Accordingly, we turn to the Government's final contention. The Government summarily argues that even if the AUMF does not authorize al-Marri's seizure and indefinite detention as an enemy combatant, the President has "inherent constitutional authority" to order the military to seize and detain al-Marri. The Government maintains that the President's "war-making powers" granted him by Article II "include the authority to capture and detain individuals involved in hostilities against the United States." In other words, according to the Government, the President has "inherent" authority to subject persons legally residing in this country and protected by our Constitution to military arrest and detention, without the benefit of any criminal process, if the President believes these individuals have "engaged in conduct in preparation for acts of international terrorism." *See* Rapp Declaration. This is a breathtaking claim, for the Government nowhere represents that this "inherent" power to order indefinite military detention extends only to aliens or only to those who "qualify" within the "legal category" of enemy combatants.

To assess claims of presidential power, the Supreme Court has long recognized, as Justice Kennedy stated most recently, that courts look to the "framework" set forth by Justice Jackson in *Youngstown Sheet & Tube Co. v. Sawyer*, 343 U.S. 579, 635–38 (1952) (Jackson, J., concurring). *See Hamdan*, 126 S. Ct. at 2800 (Kennedy, J., concurring). Justice Jackson explained that "Presidential powers are not fixed but fluctuate, depending upon their disjunction or conjunction with those of Congress." *Youngstown*, 343 U.S. at 635 (Jackson, J., concurring). "When the President acts pursuant to an express or implied authorization of Congress, his authority is at its maximum," *id.*, but "[w]hen the President takes measures incompatible with the expressed or implied will of Congress, his power is at its lowest ebb," *id.* at 637. Hence, to evaluate the President's constitutional claim we must first look to the "expressed or implied will of Congress" as to detention of aliens captured within the United States alleged to be engaged in terrorist activity.

1.

In fact, in the Patriot Act, Congress carefully stated how it wished the Government to handle aliens believed to be terrorists who were seized and held within the United States. In contrast to the AUMF, which is silent on the detention of asserted alien terrorists captured and held within the United States, the Patriot Act, enacted shortly after the AUMF, provides the Executive with broad powers to deal with "terrorist aliens." But the Patriot Act *explicitly prohibits* their indefinite detention.

Section 412 of the Patriot Act, entitled "Mandatory Detention of Suspected Terrorists," permits the short-term "[d]etention of [t]errorist [a]liens." Patriot Act §412(a). The statute authorizes the Attorney General to detain any alien whom he "has reasonable grounds to believe" is "described in" certain sections of the United States Code. *Id.* These code sections, in turn, "describe" aliens who: (1) "seek[ ] to enter the United States" to "violate any law of the United States relating to espionage or sabotage" or to use "force, violence, or other unlawful means" in opposition to the government of the United States; or (2) have "engaged in a terrorist activity;" or (3) the Attorney General reasonably believes are "likely to engage after entry in any terrorist activity," have "incited terrorist activity," are "representative[s]" or "member[s]" of a "terrorist organization" or are "representative[s]" of a "group that endorses or espouses terrorist activity," or have "received military-type training" from a terrorist organization. 8 U.S.C.A. §1182(a)(3)(A) and (B) (West 2007); *see also* 8 U.S.C. §§1227(a)(4)(A)(I), (iii); 1227(a)(4)(B) (West 2007). In addition, the Patriot Act authorizes the Attorney General to detain any other alien who "is engaged in any other activity that endangers the national security of the United States." Patriot Act §412(a). In particular, the Patriot Act permits the Attorney General to "take into custody" any "terrorist aliens" based only on the Attorney General's "belie[fs]" as to the aliens' threat, with *no* process or evidentiary hearing, and judicial review only through petition for habeas corpus. *Id.* §412(a).

Recognizing the breadth of this grant of power, however, Congress also imposed strict limits in the Patriot Act on the duration of the detention of such "terrorist aliens" within the United States. Thus, the Patriot Act expressly prohibits unlimited "indefinite detention;" instead it requires the Attorney General either to begin "removal proceedings" or to "charge the alien with a criminal offense" "not later than 7 days after the commencement of such detention." *Id.* §412(a). If a terrorist alien's removal "is unlikely for the reasonably foreseeable future," he "may be detained for additional periods of up to six months" if his release "will threaten the national security of the United States." *Id.* But no provision of the Patriot Act allows for unlimited indefinite detention. Moreover, the Attorney General must provide the legislature with reports on the use of this detention authority every six months, which must include the number of aliens detained, the grounds for their detention, and the length of the detention. *Id.* §412(c).

Therefore, the Patriot Act establishes a specific method for the Government to detain aliens affiliated with terrorist organizations, who the Government believes have come to the United States to endanger our national security, conduct espionage and sabotage, use force and violence to overthrow the government, engage in terrorist activity, or even who are believed likely to engage in any terrorist activity. Congress could not have better described the Government's allegations against al-Marri – *and* Congress decreed that individuals so described are *not* to be detained indefinitely but only for a limited time, and by civilian authorities, prior to deportation or criminal prosecution.

In sum, Congress has carefully prescribed the process by which it wishes to permit detention of "terrorist aliens" within the United States, and has expressly prohibited the indefinite detention the President seeks here. The Government's argument that the President may indefinitely detain al-Marri is thus contrary to Congress's expressed will. "When the President takes measures incompatible with the expressed or implied will of Congress, his power is at its lowest ebb, for then he can rely only upon his own constitutional powers minus any constitutional powers of Congress over the matter." *Youngstown*, 343 U.S. at 637 (Jackson, J., concurring). As the Supreme Court explained just last term, "[w]hether or not the President has independent power . . . he may not disregard limitations that Congress has, in proper exercise of its own war powers, placed on his powers." *Hamdan*, 126 S. Ct. at 2774 n.23 (*citing Youngstown*, 343 U.S. at 637 (Jackson, J., concurring)). In such cases, "Presidential claim[s]" to power "must be scrutinized with caution, for what is at stake is the equilibrium established by our constitutional system." *Youngstown*, 343 U.S. at 638 (Jackson, J., concurring).

2.

In light of the Patriot Act, therefore, we must "scrutinize[ ] with caution," *id.*, the Executive's contention that the Constitution grants the President the power to capture and subject to indefinite military detention certain civilians lawfully residing within the United States. The Government nowhere suggests that the President's inherent constitutional power to detain does not extend to American citizens. Yet it grounds its argument that the President has constitutional power to detain al-Marri on his alien status. The Government apparently maintains that alien status eliminates the due process protection applicable to al-Marri, and for this reason permits the President to exercise special "peak" authority over him. The Government can so contend only by both ignoring the undisputed and relying on the inapposite.

It is undisputed that al-Marri had been legally admitted to the United States, attending an American university from which he had earlier received an undergraduate degree, and legally residing here (with his family) for several months before the Government arrested him at his home in Peoria. The Government's refusal to acknowledge these undisputed facts dooms its contention that al-Marri's status as an alien somehow provides the President with special "peak" authority to deprive al-Marri of constitutional rights. For, as we have noted within, the Supreme Court has repeatedly and expressly held that aliens like al-Marri, i.e. those lawfully admitted into the United States who have "developed substantial connections with this country," are entitled to the Constitution's due process protections. *Verdugo-Urquidez*, 494 U.S. at 271; *see Kwong Hai Chew*, 344 U.S. at 596; *Wong Wing*, 163 U.S. at 238. No case suggests that the President, by fiat, can eliminate the due process rights of such an alien.

Without even a mention of these undisputed facts and controlling legal principles, the Government relies on two sorts of inapposite cases as assertedly establishing special presidential authority over aliens like al-Marri. The first of these, *Eisentrager*, 339 U.S. at 769 n.2, and *Ludecke*, 335 U.S. at 161–62, involves "enemy aliens." In those cases, the Supreme Court specifically defined "enemy aliens," but the Court did *not* define them as aliens who commit crimes against our country and so are enemies, as the Government seems to suggest. Rather, the Supreme Court defined "enemy aliens" as "subject[s] of a foreign state at war with the United States." *Eisentrager*, 339 U.S. at 769 n.2. Al-Marri plainly is *not* the "subject of a foreign state at war with the United States" and so is *not* an "enemy alien," but rather a citizen of Qatar, a country with which the United States has friendly relations. Thus *Eisentrager* and *Ludecke* provide no basis for asserting authority over al-Marri. In fact, elsewhere in its brief the Government concedes, as it must, that *Eisentrager* and *Ludecke* do not "have direct application" to al-Marri.

The other inapposite cases on which the Government relies involve *congressional* authority over aliens stemming from Congress's power over naturalization and immigration – not some special "inherent" constitutional authority enjoyed by the President over aliens. *See Mathews v. Diaz*, 426 U.S. 67, 79–80 (1976); *Harisiades v. Shaughnessy*, 342 U.S. 580, 588–91 (1952). These cases do not speak to the powers of the President acting alone – let alone contrary to an Act of Congress – and certainly do not suggest that the President has the power to subject to indefinite military detention an alien lawfully residing in this country, like al-Marri.

In sum, al-Marri is not a subject of a country with which the United States is at war, and he did not illegally enter the United States nor is he alleged to have committed any other immigration violation. Rather, after lawfully entering the United States, al-Marri "developed substantial connections with this country," *Verdugo-Urquidez*, 494 U.S. at 271, and so his status as an alien neither eliminates due process rights, nor provides the President with extraordinary powers to subject al-Marri to seizure and indefinite detention by the military. The President's constitutional powers do not allow him to order the military to seize and detain indefinitely al-Marri without criminal process any more than they permit the President to order the military to seize and detain, without criminal process, other terrorists within the United States, like the Unabomber or the perpetrators of the Oklahoma City bombing.

3.

In light of al-Marri's due process rights under our Constitution and Congress's express prohibition in the Patriot Act on the indefinite detention of those civilians arrested as "terrorist aliens" within this country, we can only conclude that in the case at hand, the President claims power that far exceeds that granted him by the Constitution.[17]

We do not question the President's war-time authority over enemy combatants; but absent suspension of the writ of habeas corpus or declaration of martial law, the Constitution simply does not provide the President the power to exercise military authority over civilians within the United States. *See Toth*, 350 U.S. at 14 ("[A]ssertion of military authority over civilians cannot rest on the President's power as commander-in-chief, or on any theory of martial law."). The President cannot eliminate constitutional protections with the stroke of a pen by proclaiming a civilian, even a criminal civilian, an enemy combatant subject to indefinite military detention. Put simply, the Constitution does not allow the President to order the military to seize civilians residing within the United States and detain them indefinitely without criminal process, and this is so even if he calls them "enemy combatants."

A "well-established purpose of the Founders" was "to keep the military strictly within its proper sphere, subordinate to civil authority." *Reid*, 354 U.S. at 30. In the Declaration of Independence our forefathers lodged the complaint that the King of Great Britain had "affected to render the Military independent of and superior to the Civil power" and objected that the King had "depriv[ed] us in many cases, of the benefits

---

[17] Because Congress has not empowered the President to subject civilian alien terrorists within the United States to indefinite military detention, *see supra* Part II, we need not, and do not, determine whether such a grant of authority would violate the Constitution. Rather, we simply hold that the Constitution does not provide the President acting alone with this authority.

of Trial by Jury." *The Declaration of Independence* paras. 14, 20 (U.S. 1776). A resolute conviction that civilian authority should govern the military animated the framing of the Constitution. As Alexander Hamilton, no foe of Executive power, observed, the President's Commander-in-Chief powers "amount to nothing more than the supreme command and direction of the military and naval forces." The Federalist No. 69, at 386 (Alexander Hamilton) (Clinton Rossiter ed., 1961). "That military powers of the Commander in Chief were not to supersede representative government of *internal affairs* seems obvious from the Constitution and from elementary American history." *Youngstown*, 343 U.S. at 644 (Jackson, J., concurring) (emphasis added). For this reason, the Supreme Court rejected the President's claim to "inherent power" to use the military even to seize property within the United States, despite the Government's argument that the refusal would "endanger the well-being and safety of the Nation." *Id.* at 584 (majority opinion).

Of course, this does not mean that the President lacks power to protect our national interests and defend our people, only that in doing so he must abide by the Constitution. We understand and do not in any way minimize the grave threat international terrorism poses to our country and our national security. But as *Milligan* teaches, "the government, within the Constitution, has all the powers granted to it, which are necessary to preserve its existence." *Milligan*, 71 U.S. at 121. Those words resound as clearly in the twenty-first century as they did in the nineteenth.

Thus, the President plainly has plenary authority to deploy our military against terrorist enemies overseas. *See Curtiss-Wright*, 299 U.S. at 319–20; *see also Eisentrager*, 339 U.S. at 789. Similarly, the Government remains free to defend our country against terrorist enemies within, using all the considerable powers "the well-stocked statutory arsenal" of domestic law affords. *Hamdi*, 542 U.S. at 547 (Souter, J., concurring in the judgment) (citing numerous federal statutes criminalizing terrorist acts). Civilian law enforcement officers may always use deadly force whenever reasonable. *See Scott v. Harris*, 127 S. Ct. 1769, 1776–78 (2007). Furthermore, in the wake of September 11th, Congress has specifically authorized the President to deploy the armed forces at home to protect the country in the event of actual "terrorist attack[s] or incident[s]" within the United States meeting certain conditions. *See* 10 U.S.C.A. §333(a) (A) (2007) (amending the Insurrection Act to provide the President with this authority, notwithstanding the Posse Comitatus Act, 18 U.S.C. §1385).

But in this nation, military control cannot subsume the constitutional rights of civilians. Rather, the Supreme Court has repeatedly catalogued our country's "deeply rooted and ancient opposition...to the extension of military control over civilians." *Reid*, 354 U.S. at 33; *see also Laird v. Tatum*, 408 U.S. 1, 15 (1972) (Burger, C.J.) (recognizing "a traditional and strong resistance of Americans to any military intrusion into civilian affairs" that "has deep roots in our history and found early expression...in the constitutional provisions for civilian control of the military"). The Court has specifically cautioned against "break[ing] faith with this Nation's tradition" – "firmly embodied in the Constitution" – "of keeping military power subservient to civilian authority." *Reid*, 354 U.S. at 40. When the Court wrote these words in 1957, it explained that "[t]he country ha [d] remained true to that faith for almost one hundred seventy years." *Id*. Another half century has passed but the necessity of "remain[ing] true to that faith" remains as important today as it was at our founding.

The President has cautioned us that "[t]he war on terror we fight today is a generational struggle that will continue long after you and I have turned our duties over to others." Pres. George W. Bush, State of the Union Address (Jan. 23, 2007). Unlike detention for the duration of a traditional armed conflict between nations, detention for the length of a "war on terror" has no bounds. Justice O'Connor observed in *Hamdi* that "[i]f the practical circumstances of a given conflict are entirely unlike those of the conflicts that informed the development of the law of war," the understanding that combatants can be detained "for the duration of the relevant conflict" "may unravel." 542 U.S. at 521. If the indefinite military detention of an actual combatant in this new type of conflict might cause the thread of our understandings to "unravel," the indefinite military detention of a civilian like al-Marri would shred those understandings apart.

In an address to Congress at the outset of the Civil War, President Lincoln defended his emergency suspension of the writ of habeas corpus to protect Union troops moving to defend the Capital. Lincoln famously asked: "[A]re all the laws, but one, to go unexecuted, and the government itself to go to pieces, lest that one be violated?" Abraham Lincoln, Message to Congress in Special Session (July 4, 1861), *in Abraham Lincoln: Speeches and Writings 1859–1865* at 246, 254 (Don E. Fehrenbacher ed., 1989). The authority the President seeks here turns Lincoln's formulation on its head. For the President does not acknowledge that the extraordinary power he seeks would result in the suspension of even one law and he does not contend that this power should be limited to dire emergencies that threaten the nation. Rather, he maintains that the authority to order the military to seize and detain certain civilians is an inherent power of the Presidency, which he and his successors may exercise as they please.

To sanction such presidential authority to order the military to seize and indefinitely detain civilians, even if the President calls them "enemy combatants," would have disastrous consequences for the Constitution – and the country. For a court to uphold a claim to such extraordinary power would do more than render lifeless the Suspension Clause, the Due Process Clause, and the rights to criminal process in the Fourth, Fifth, Sixth, and Eighth Amendments; it would effectively undermine all of the freedoms guaranteed by the Constitution. It is that power – were a court to recognize it – that could lead all our laws "to go unexecuted, and the government itself to go to pieces." We refuse to recognize a claim to power that would so alter the constitutional foundations of our Republic.

IV.

For the foregoing reasons, we reverse the judgment of the district court dismissing al-Marri's petition for a writ of habeas corpus. We remand the case to that court with instructions to issue a writ of habeas corpus directing the Secretary of Defense to release al-Marri from military custody within a reasonable period of time to be set by the district court. The Government can transfer al-Marri to civilian authorities to face criminal charges, initiate deportation proceedings against him, hold him as a material witness in connection with grand jury proceedings, or detain him for a limited time pursuant to the Patriot Act. But military detention of al-Marri must cease.

REVERSED AND REMANDED

HUDSON, District Judge, dissenting:

I regret that I am unable to concur in the majority opinion, except to the extent that I agree that this Court has jurisdiction over this appeal. Although I do not embrace all aspects of the majority's jurisdictional reasoning, I agree that Section 7 of the Military Commission Act of 2006 (MCA) does not divest this Court of its constitutional jurisdiction, under Article I, Section 9, to review habeas corpus decisions involving individual detainees within the United States. *See Hamdi v. Rumsfeld*, 542 U.S. 507, 525, 124 S. Ct. 2633, 2644 (2004). The MCA may, however, foreclose a right of statutory review. Beyond the jurisdictional question, the majority and I part company.

While I commend the majority on a thoroughly researched and impressively written opinion, I must conclude that their analysis flows from a faulty predicate. In my view, the appellant was properly designated as an enemy combatant by the President of the United States pursuant to the war powers vested in him by Articles I and II of the United States Constitution and by Congress under the Authorization to Use Military Force (AUMF). *See Hamdi v. Rumsfeld*, 296 F.3d 278, 281–82 (4th Cir. 2002).[1] I am also of the opinion that al-Marri has received all due process entitlements prescribed by existing United States Supreme Court precedent. I would therefore vote to affirm the district court's dismissal of al-Marri's Petition for Writ of Habeas Corpus.

The wellspring of the majority's reasoning is the notion that a non-military person arrested on U.S. soil, outside the zone of battle, for providing active aid to the enemy at time of war, cannot be declared an enemy combatant and detained for the duration of the hostilities, but must be prosecuted in the civilian courts of the United States. In fact, the majority would even go further and find that the language of the AUMF does not include organizations, such as al Qaeda, that are not affiliated with recognized nation states. The clear congressional intent underlying the AUMF was to afford the President of the United States all the powers necessary to suppress those individuals or organizations responsible for the terrorist attack on September 11, 2001. This broad language would certainly seem to embrace surreptitious al Qaeda agents operating within the continental United States. The AUMF provided as follows:

> [T]he President is authorized to use all necessary and appropriate force against those nations, *organizations, or persons* he determines planned, authorized, committed, or aided the terrorist attacks that occurred on September 11, 2001, or harbored such organizations or persons, in order to prevent any future acts of international terrorism against the United States by such nations, organizations or persons.

Pub. L. No. 107-40, §2(a), 115 Stat. 224, 224 (2001) (emphasis added). History has proven that al Qaeda, an international terrorist organization with which the United States is at war, falls squarely within that definition. *See Hamdi v. Rumsfeld*, 316 F.3d 450, 459 (4th Cir. 2003), vacated and remanded on other grounds, *Hamdi v. Rumsfeld*, 542 U.S. 507, 124 S. Ct. 2633 (2004).

Central to the majority's analysis is the locus of his arrest. Unlike the petitioners in *Hamdi v. Rumsfeld*, 542 U.S. 507, 124 S. Ct. 2633 (2004), and *Hamdan v. Rumsfeld*, 126 S. Ct. 2749 (2006), al-Marri is a lawful resident alien who was not taken into custody in a battle zone. He was arrested in Peoria, Illinois, where he was residing on a student visa. Despite powerful evidence of his connection to al Qaeda, the majority believe the President is without power to declare him an enemy combatant. They believe he

---

[1] In *Hamdi v. Rumsfeld*, the U.S. Supreme Court found that the AUMF provided congressional authority for the President to detain Hamdi as an enemy combatant under the narrow facts of that case. The critical elements of the court's definition of an "enemy combatant", for the purposes of that case, were the petitioner's being: 1) "part of a supporting force hostile to the United States or coalition partner", and (2) "engaged in an armed conflict against the United States." *Hamdi*, 542 U.S. at 526, 124 S. Ct. at 2645 (internal quotation marks omitted).

The boundaries of activity qualifying for "enemy combatant" status staked out in *Hamdi* were not meant to be immutable. The obvious impact of the limiting language was to confine the court's holding to the immediate facts before them.

While al-Marri was not captured while armed in a formal theater of war, the evidence would certainly support the conclusion that he was actively supporting forces hostile to the United States – and that the forces he was supporting were actively engaged in armed conflict against the United States.

Given the unconventional nature of the conflict that the United States is engaged in with al Qaeda, the exact definitions of "enemy combatants" and "enemy belligerents" are difficult to conceptualize and apply with precision.

must be indicted and tried for crimes against the United States. Although definitive precedent is admittedly sparse, in my opinion, this position is unsupported by the weight of persuasive authority.

In *Padilla v. Hanft*, 423 F.3d 386 (4th Cir. 2005), a panel of this Court unanimously rejected the argument that the locus of capture was relevant to the President's authority to detain an enemy combatant. *See id.* at 394. Padilla, a U.S. citizen, was arrested by FBI agents upon his arrival at O'Hare International Airport in Chicago, Illinois. *Id.* at 388. A close associate of al Qaeda, Padilla had been "armed and present in a combat zone during armed conflict between al Qaeda/Taliban forces and the armed forces of the United States." *Id.* at 390 (internal quotation marks omitted). Moreover, "Padilla met with Khalid Sheikh Mohammad, a senior al Qaeda operations planner, who directed Padilla to travel to the United States for the purpose of blowing up apartment buildings, in continued prosecution of al Qaeda's war of terror against the United States." *Id.*

This Court in *Padilla* reversed the holding of the district court that the President lacked authority under the AUMF to detain Padilla, and that Padilla must be either criminally prosecuted or released. *Id.* With respect to Padilla's argument that the circumstances of his detention mandated only the option of criminal prosecution, this Court noted:

> . . . We are convinced, in any event, that the availability of criminal process cannot be determinative of the power to detain, if for no other reason than that criminal prosecution may well not achieve the very purpose for which detention is authorized in the first place – the prevention of return to the field of battle. Equally important, in many instances criminal prosecution would impede the Executive in its efforts to gather intelligence from the detainee and to restrict the detainee's communication with confederates so as to ensure that the detainee does not pose a continuing threat to national security even as he is confined – impediments that would render military detention not only an appropriate, but also the necessary, course of action to be taken in the interest of national security.

Id. at 394–95.

Military detention during time of war and criminal prosecution serve discrete functions. The object of criminal prosecution is to punish for legal transgression. The purpose of military detention is to immobilize the enemy during hostilities. *Hamdi*, 542 U.S. at 518, 124 S. Ct. at 2640. Such detention is also intended "to prevent the captured individual from serving the enemy." *In re Territo*, 156 F.2d 142, 145 (9th Cir. 1946).

The only significant fact that distinguishes the justification for Padilla's detention from that of al-Marri is that Padilla at some previous point in time had been armed and present in a combat zone. There was no indication, however, that Padilla was ever a soldier in a formal sense, particularly while acting on U.S. soil.

Like Padilla, al-Marri, an identified al Qaeda associate, was dispatched to the United States by the September mastermind as a "sleeper agent" and to explore computer hacking methods to disrupt the United States' financial system. Moreover, al-Marri volunteered for a martyr mission on behalf of al Qaeda, received funding from a known terrorist financier, and communicated with known terrorists by phone and e-mail. Decl. of Jeffrey N. Rapp, Director, Joint Intelligence Task Force for Combating Terrorism, ¶7, Sept. 9, 2004. It is also interesting to note that al-Marri arrived in the United States on September 10, 2001. *Id.*

The district court in this case credited the Declaration of Rapp, which was unrebutted, and found by a preponderance of the evidence, that al-Marri had been properly classified and detained as an enemy combatant. *See Al-Marri v. Wright*, 443 F. Supp. 2d 774, 784 (D.S.C. 2006).[2]

The standard employed by the district court to determine al-Marri's qualifications for enemy combatant status was analogous to that invoked by the United States Supreme Court in *Ex Parte Quirin*, 317 U.S. 1, 63 S. Ct. 2 (1942). In *Quirin*, the Court explained,

> [E]ntry upon our territory in time of war by enemy belligerents, including those acting under the direction of the armed forces of the enemy for the purpose of destroying property used or useful in prosecuting the war, is a hostile and war-like act. . . .
>
> . . . .
>
> . . . Citizens who associate themselves with the military arm of the enemy government, and with its aid, guidance and direction enter this country bent on hostile acts are enemy belligerents within the meaning of . . . the law of war. . . .

Id. at 36–38. The *Quirin* Court further provided that "[i]t is without significance that petitioners were not alleged to have borne conventional weapons or that their proposed hostile acts did not necessarily contemplate collision with the Armed Forces of the United States." *Id.* at 37. "Nor are petitioners any the less belligerents if, as they argue, they have not actually committed or attempted to commit any act of depredation or entered the theatre or zone of active military operations." *Id.* at 38.

Ex Parte Milligan, 4 Wall. 2, 71 U.S. 2 (1866), does not undermine the district court's decision. Milligan did not associate himself with a rebellious State with which the United States was at war. *See Milligan*, 71 U.S. at 131; *Quirin*, 317 U.S. at 45, 63 S. Ct. at 19 (noting that the Court in *Milligan* "concluded that Milligan [was] not . . . a part of or associated with the armed forces of the enemy"). In this case, the unrebutted evidence shows that al-Marri associated himself with and became an agent of al Qaeda, the organization targeted by the AUMF and the enemy with which the United States is at war. *See Rapp Decl.* ¶7 ("Al-Marri is an al Qaeda 'sleeper agent' . . . was trained at an al Qaeda terror camp . . . met personally with Usama Bin Laden . . . and volunteered for a martyr mission.").[3] As noted above, it is without significance that al Marri did not himself carry a conventional weapon in a zone of active military operations. *See Quirin*, 317 U.S. at 37–38.

In *Hamdi*, the Supreme Court considered the due process requirements for a citizen being held in the United States as an enemy combatant. *See Hamdi*, 542 U.S. at 509, 124 S. Ct. at 2635. Hamdi was an American citizen captured in Afghanistan for allegedly taking up arms with the Taliban in a combat zone. *Id.* at 510, 124 S. Ct. at 2635. Like al-Marri, Hamdi was being detained at the Naval Brig in Charleston, South Carolina. *Id.* at 510, 124 S. Ct. 2636. After applying a balancing of interest calculus, the Court observed, "a citizen-detainee seeking to challenge his classification as an enemy combatant must receive notice of the factual basis for his classification, and a fair opportunity to rebut the Government's factual assertions before a neutral decisionmaker." *Hamdi*, 542 U.S.

---

[2] Al-Marri not only failed to offer any evidence on his behalf, he refused to even participate in the initial evidentiary process. *Al-Marri*, 443 F. Supp. 2d at 785.

[3] Just as mere presence is not sufficient to make one a part of a criminal conspiracy or an accomplice to a crime, I agree with the majority that mere association with al Qaeda or an organization that supports al Qaeda does not necessarily make one an enemy combatant. *See Milligan*, 71 U.S. at 131 (stating that "[i]f in Indiana [Milligan] conspired with bad men to assist the enemy, he is punishable for it in the courts of Indiana"). This is not a case, however, of mere association. Al-Marri trained with and became an agent of al Qaeda and, operating under its guidance and direction, entered the United States on September 10, 2001, "for the purpose of engaging in and facilitating terrorist activities subsequent to September 11," the very activities that the AUMF was intended to prevent. Rapp Decl. ¶7; *see AUMF* §2(a).

at 533, 124 S. Ct. at 2648. "It is equally fundamental that the right to notice and an opportunity to be heard must be granted at a meaningful time and in a meaningful manner." *Id.* at 533, 124 S. Ct. at 2649 (internal quotation marks omitted).

After upholding the power of the President to detain al-Marri under the AUMF, the district court, after providing him with all due process entitlements articulated in *Hamdi*, found that his continued detention as an enemy combatant was proper and dismissed his petition. *See Al-Marri*, 443 F. Supp. 2d at 785. In addition, al-Marri was represented by counsel at all stages of the proceedings below.

I believe the district court correctly concluded that the President had the authority to detain al-Marri as an enemy combatant or belligerent. Although al-Marri was not personally engaged in armed conflict with U.S. forces, he is the type of stealth warrior used by al Qaeda to perpetrate terrorist acts against the United States. Al-Marri's detention is authorized under the AUMF "to prevent any future acts of international terrorism against the United States." AUMF §2(a). Furthermore, setting aside the amorphous distinction between an "enemy combatant" and an "enemy belligerent," there is little doubt from the evidence that al-Marri was present in the United States to aid and further the hostile and subversive activities of the organization responsible for the terrorist attacks that occurred on September 11, 2001.

I therefore vote to affirm the district court.

Case Update: April 2008

On August 22, 2007, the Fourth Circuit granted a motion requesting a rehearing of the case before a full panel of judges. Oral arguments were held in Richmond, Virginia, on October 31, 2007. A decision is pending.

Cases of Note

Braden v. 30th Judicial Circuit Court of Kentucky, 410 U.S. 484 (1973) – Braden, a prisoner in Alabama, petitioned for habeas corpus in a Kentucky court, alleging that he had been denied his right to a speedy trial on a Kentucky state charge. The Supreme Court held that a habeas petitioner does not need to be present in a court's territorial jurisdiction when challenging future custody there, although the custodian does. Since it was the legality of the Kentucky, rather than Alabama, custody that Braden was challenging, the claim was properly brought in Kentucky. This case upheld the traditional rule that a prisoner challenging his custody must sue his immediate custodian (with regards to that custody).

Duncan v. Kahanamoku, 327 U.S. 304 (1946) – Two civilians were sentenced to prison by military tribunals in Hawaii and appealed their detention. The government argued that the Hawaii Organic Act, which permitted the governor of Hawaii to "suspend the privilege of the writ of habeas corpus, or place the Territory... under martial law," barred their challenge. The Court determined that, despite the congressional enactment authorizing marital law, Congress could not have intended "to exceed the boundaries between military and civilian power, in which our people have always believed," by supplanting civilian courts with military tribunals. Since civilian courts were operational and available to the defendants, their trial should take place there.

Ex parte Endo, 323 U.S. 283 (1944) – Endo sought to be discharged from a Japanese internment camp, alleging that she had been improperly detained. The Court, after examining a statute and executive order authorizing relocation and internment of people of Japanese descent, found that the authorizations did not give the War Relocation Agency the power to detain her. The authorizations, the Court found, failed to use the "language of detention" necessary to override the constitutional safeguard against detention without trial, and that such authorizations need to be clear and unmistakable.

INS v. St. Cyr, 533 U.S. 289 (2001) – St. Cyr, a lawful permanent United States resident, pled guilty to selling a controlled substance, a criminal charge for which he was deportable. The Anti-Terrorism and Effective Death Penalty Act of 1996 was passed between his arrest and his removal proceedings. The government argued that several provisions of the act, including one entitled "Elimination of Custody Review by Habeas Corpus," should be construed as stripping his (as well as other petitioners') right to habeas review of their removal proceedings. The Court rejected this position, noting that the writ had been available to non-enemy aliens since 1789. Construing the statutes to suspend habeas corpus, the Court said, would raise grave constitutional doubts under the Suspension Clause. While the government argued that the writ was not unlawfully suspended if Congress had given statutory authorization to do so, the Court held that the suspension would not be lawful unless Congress had made its intention to do so patently clear, and that these statutes did not meet that threshold.

Johnson v. Eisentrager, 339 U.S. 763 (1950) – In 1945, after Germany's unconditional surrender, 21 German nationals were arrested by U.S. forces in China. After hostilities ceased, they were tried in China by a U.S. military tribunal for violations of the laws of war, including continuing intelligence activities for Japanese forces after Germany's surrender. After conviction, the prisoners were sent to Germany to serve their sentences. They petitioned for a hearing in the D.C. District Court. The petition was denied on the basis that the court lacked jurisdiction over the prisoners. The Supreme Court held that the Federal Courts did not have jurisdiction over foreign enemy aliens whose crimes had not been committed in and who were not held in the territorial jurisdiction of the United States.

Korematsu v. United States, 323 U.S. 214 (1944) – Korematsu was convicted of violating a military order requiring people of Japanese descent living on the West Coast to leave their homes. The military order had been issued pursuant to an authorizing executive order. Korematsu challenged his conviction, arguing that the military order improperly impinged on his fundamental rights. The Court upheld the order, and the statute which made its violation a crime, holding that the congressional and the executive constitutional war powers allowed both branches to propagate such rules while the country was at war with Japan. The order was justified by a "definite and close relationship to the prevention of espionage and sabotage," the Court said.

Ludecke v. Watkins, 335 U.S. 160 (1948) – Ludecke, a German enemy alien, was captured on American soil in 1941. The Court ruled that the President has the power, under the Alien Enemy Act, to detain and deport such enemy aliens for the duration of hostilities. The Court deferred to the President in defining when those hostilities were officially over, saying that to determine whether war exists "when the guns are silent but the peace of Peace has not come … are matters of political judgment for which judges have neither technical competence nor official responsibility."

Mathews v. Eldridge, 424 U.S. 319 (1976) – This case set out a three-part test for determining whether or not due process had been given to a defendant under the Constitution. The court held that the relevant considerations were: "[f]irst, the private interest that will be affected by the official action; second, the risk of an erroneous deprivation of such interest through the procedures used, and the probable value, if any, of additional or substitute procedural safeguards; and finally, the Government's interest, including the function involved and fiscal and administrative burdens that the additional or substitute procedural requirement." The Court later applied the *Mathews* test in *Hamdi*.

Ex parte Milligan, 71 U.S. (4 Wall.) 2 (1866) – Milligan, a Confederate sympathizer, was seized in his home in Indiana and brought before a military tribunal. He was accused of conspiring in a variety of plots against the Union and its war efforts, along with four others. Upon being found guilty and sentenced to be hanged, Milligan appealed on the grounds that as a civilian he ought not to be tried by a military commission. The Supreme Court unanimously overturned Milligan's conviction. A five-justice majority found that while the suspension of habeas corpus by President Lincoln and the Congress was proper, martial rule cannot be imposed in places, such as Indiana, which are far from active combat and which have functioning civil courts. The remaining four justices agreed that Milligan should receive a civil trial, but they ruled much more narrowly. They argued that it would have been permissible to try Milligan before a military commission if Congress had explicitly given authorization for it, because Congress' power to make rules for military courts trumps "the fifth [and] any other amendment."

The Prize Cases (**Brig Amy Warwick**), **67 U.S.** (**2 Black**) **635** (**1863**) – The Court upheld the President's right to carry out an act of war against the secessionist states by imposing a blockade on their ports and then impounding their ships, even though war had not been declared by Congress. The Court observed that "war may exist without a declaration on either side," and that when the President responds to an act of war, he "does not initiate that war, but is bound to accept the challenge without waiting for any special legislative authority." The Court also said that the President had the authority to decide what military measures were necessary and that the Court would not review that authority.

Ex parte Quirin, **317 U.S. 1** (**1942**) – In 1942, a group of German soldiers snuck into the United States by submarine with explosives and detonators. Upon their apprehension by the FBI, President Roosevelt appointed a military commission to try the prisoners, declaring on the same day that military tribunals would try all such cases. The defendants challenged the constitutionality of the President's proclamation, arguing that domestic courts should have jurisdiction over the case and that the President lacked the authority to call the commission. The Supreme Court found that in times of war and grave public danger, decisions regarding the detention and trial of prisoners are "not to be set aside by the courts without the clear conviction that they are in conflict with the Constitution or laws of Congress constitutionally enacted." In this case, the Court stated that Congress, in the Articles of War, had specifically found that violations of the laws of war could be tried by military tribunal. The Court reserved the question as to whether the President could appoint a commission without direct statutory authority. Further, the Court found that although the military tribunals did not include all the 5th and 6th Amendment protections provided by civil courts, they were not unconstitutional. The Court stated that military tribunals existed without jury trial at the time of the signing of the Constitution, and that the Constitution meant to ensure a continuance of jury trials in civilian courts (where jury trials already existed at its enactment), but did not intend to expand jury trials to areas where they did not exist.

Reid v. Covert, **354 U.S. 1** (**1957**) – Covert, a civilian, was convicted by a military tribunal set up under the Uniform Code of Military Justice (UCMJ) of killing her husband, a member of the Air Force stationed in England. She challenged the jurisdiction of the tribunal through habeas corpus proceedings. The Court held that the UCMJ could not reach civilians outside of the United States for capital offenses during peacetime. The Court stressed that military trials, unlike those in Article III courts, permitted the President to exercise "legislative, executive and judicial powers.... Such blending of functions in one branch of the Government is the objectionable thing which the draftsmen of the Constitution endeavored to prevent by providing for the separation of governmental powers."

In re Territo, **156 F.2d 142** (**9th Cir. 1946**) – Territo was born in West Virginia and later served in the Italian Army. He was captured in Sicily during the Second World

War and detained as an enemy combatant. He challenged his detention through habeas corpus, arguing that he could not be held as an enemy combatant because he was an American citizen. The ninth circuit, citing *Quirin*, found that his association with an enemy of the United States and his seizure on the battlefield made him an enemy combatant, notwithstanding his citizenship. The court also affirmed the legitimacy and importance of the United States' power to detain such combatants in preventing them from continuing to serve the enemy.

In re Yamashita, 327 U.S. 1 (1946) – Yamashita was a Japanese general captured during the American liberation of the Philippines (a U.S. territory) at the end of World War II. He was tried by a military commission and sentenced to death. He then challenged the military commission's validity. The Court emphasized its own power to review "whether the detention complained of is within the authority of those detaining the petitioner," and said that the executive branch could not withdraw its ability to review the commission's authority absent a suspension of the writ of habeas corpus. The Court then upheld the commissions as being properly installed by Congress under the Articles of War, saying that "an important incident to the conduct of war is the adoption of measures by the military commander . . . [to] subject to disciplinary measures those enemies who, in their attempt to thwart or impede our military effort, have violated the law of war."

Youngstown Sheet & Tube Co. v. Sawyer, 343 U.S. 579 (1952) – In the midst of the Korean War, the Steelworkers' Union gave notice of a nationwide strike. Believing that a strike in the steel industry would harm national defense, President Truman issued an executive order directing the Secretary of Commerce to seize the steel mills. The steel companies responded by suing the Secretary of Commerce, arguing that the seizure was unlawful and beyond the powers of the President. Justice Black's opinion for the majority of the Court agreed, stating that even in wartime there are some limits to the President's power. However, the case is most often cited for Justice Jackson's concurring opinion, wherein Justice Jackson laid out a framework for judging whether or not the President has overstepped his authority. Under this framework, there are three zones of Presidential action. In the first zone, Congress has expressly authorized action and in that case the President's actions are allowable. In the third zone, Congress has expressly forbidden some action, in which case the President may not act unless Congress has tried to limit some power directly granted in the Constitution. However, in the second zone, the so-called "zone of twilight," Congress has not ruled one way or another. In this zone it is difficult to determine whether the President may act, so Jackson warns that courts should try to avoid this zone.

Zadvydas v. Davis, 533 U.S. 678 (2001) – Zadvydas, a resident alien who had been or-dered to be deported, brought a habeas petition seeking release after the INS held him beyond the 90-day removal period. The Court said that "an indefinite, perhaps perma-nent, deprivation of human liberty without any [judicial] protection" raised "serious constitutional problem[s]." Due process, the Court said, applied to everyone within the nation's borders, regardless of their immigration status. In particular, the Court said, "Freedom from imprisonment – from government custody, detention, or other forms of physical restraint – lies at the heart of the liberty that the Clause protects." The Court noted that the case did not involve "terrorism or other special circumstances where special arguments might be made for forms of preventive detention and for heightened deference to the judgments of the political branches with respect to matters of national security."

Frequently Cited Precedent

Ahrens v. Clark, 335 U.S. 188 (1948)

Baker v. Carr, 369 U.S. 186 (1962)

Balzac v. Porto Rico, 258 U.S. 298 (1922)

Braden v. 30th Judicial Circuit Court of Kentucky, 410 U.S. 484 (1973)

Chicago & Southern Air Lines, Inc. v. Waterman S.S. Corp., 333 U.S. 103 (1948)

Colepaugh v. Looney, 235 F.2d 429 (10th Cir. 1956)

Duncan v. Kahanamoku, 327 U.S. 304 (1946)

Ex parte Endo, 323 U.S. 283 (1944)

Head Money Cases (*Edye v. Robertson*), 112 U.S. 580 (1884)

Hirota v. MacArthur, 338 U.S. 197 (1948)

INS v. St. Cyr, 533 U.S. 289 (2001)

Johnson v. Eisentrager, 339 U.S. 763 (1950)

Korematsu v. United States, 323 U.S. 214 (1944)

Loving v. United States, 517 U.S. 748 (1996)

Ludecke v. Watkins, 335 U.S. 160 (1948)

Madsen v. Kinsella, 343 U.S. 341 (1952)

Mathews v. Eldridge, 424 U.S. 319 (1976)

Ex parte Milligan, 71 U.S. (4 Wall.) 2 (1866)

Murray v. Schooner Charming Betsy, 6 U.S. (2 Cranch) 64 (1804)

Preiser v. Rodriguez, 411 U.S. 475 (1973)

The Prize Cases (*Brig Amy Warwick*), 67 U.S. (2 Black) 635 (1863)

Ex parte Quirin, 317 U.S. 1 (1942)

Ralpho v. Bell, 569 F.2d 607 (D.C. Cir. 1977)

Reid v. Covert, 354 U.S. 1 (1957)

Schlesinger v. Councilman, 420 U.S. 738 (1975)

Swain v. Pressley, 430 U.S. 372 (1977)

Tel-Oren v. Libyan Arab Republic, 726 F.2d 774 (D.C. Cir. 1984)

In re Territo, 156 F.2d 142 (9th Cir. 1946)

United States v. Curtiss-Wright Export Corp., 299 U.S. 304 (1936)

United States v. Robel, 389 U.S. 258 (1967)

United States v. Spelar, 338 U.S. 217 (1949)

United States v. Verdugo-Urquidez, 494 U.S. 259 (1990)

Ex parte Vallandigham, 68 U.S. (1 Wall.) 243 (1864)

Vermilya-Brown Co. v. Connell, 335 U.S. 377 (1948)

In re Yamashita, 327 U.S. 1 (1946)

Ex parte Yerger, 75 U.S. (8 Wall.) 85 (1868)

Youngstown Sheet & Tube Co. v. Sawyer, 343 U.S. 579 (1952)

Zadvydas v. Davis, 533 U.S. 678 (2001)

Index

Index of Cases of Note

Afterword – *Boumediene v. Bush*

Whether so-called "enemy combatants" could petition the federal courts via habeas corpus has been a primary focus of the five cases covered in this volume. On June 12, 2008, the Supreme Court, by a 5-4 margin, decided *Boumediene v. Bush* and settled the issue in favor of the detainees. The decision invalidates a core premise of the two principal legislative efforts that endeavored to deny the detainees habeas corpus access to the U.S. courts: the Detainee Treatment of 2005 and the Military Commissions Act of 2006. This decision has provided some closure to the debate that has involved a three-way exchange between the Congress, the Court, and the Executive.

Now that the Supreme Court has spoken definitively, it will be the responsibility of Congress, the Executive, and, ultimately, the American people to decide the future of enemy combatants held by the United States. Questions concerning due process, the interaction between habeas and military proceedings, and whether the constitutional provisions extend to military commissions, to the Combatant Status Review Tribunals, and to those held outside of Guantanamo Bay remain.

Opinion of the Court

SUPREME COURT OF THE UNITED STATES

Nos. 06–1195 and 06–1196

LAKHDAR BOUMEDIENE, ET AL., PETITIONERS
06–1195   *v.*
GEORGE W. BUSH, PRESIDENT OF THE UNITED
STATES, ET AL.

KHALED A. F. AL ODAH, NEXT FRIEND OF FAWZI
KHALID ABDULLAH FAHAD AL ODAH, ET AL.,
PETITIONERS
06–1196   *v.*
UNITED STATES ET AL.

ON WRITS OF CERTIORARI TO THE UNITED STATES COURT OF
APPEALS FOR THE DISTRICT OF COLUMBIA CIRCUIT

[June 12, 2008]

JUSTICE KENNEDY delivered the opinion of the Court.

Petitioners are aliens designated as enemy combatants and detained at the United States Naval Station at Guantanamo Bay, Cuba. There are others detained there, also aliens, who are not parties to this suit.

Petitioners present a question not resolved by our earlier cases relating to the detention of aliens at Guantanamo: whether they have the constitutional privilege of habeas corpus, a privilege not to be withdrawn except in conformance with the Suspension Clause, Art. I, §9, cl. 2. We hold these petitioners do have the habeas corpus privilege. Congress has enacted a statute, the Detainee Treatment Act of 2005 . . . , that provides certain procedures for review of the detainees' status. We hold that those procedures are not an adequate and effective substitute for habeas corpus. Therefore §7 of the Military Commissions Act of 2006 (MCA) . . . operates as an unconstitutional suspension of the writ. We do not address whether the President has authority to detain these petitioners nor do we hold that the writ must issue. These and other questions regarding the legality of the detention are to be resolved in the first instance by the District Court.

. . .

III

In deciding the constitutional questions now presented we must determine whether petitioners are barred from seeking the writ or invoking the protections of the Suspension Clause either because of their status, *i.e.*, petitioners' designation by the Executive Branch as enemy combatants, or their physical location, *i.e.*, their presence at

Guantanamo Bay. The Government contends that noncitizens designated as enemy combatants and detained in territory located outside our Nation's borders have no constitutional rights and no privilege of habeas corpus. Petitioners contend they do have cognizable constitutional rights and that Congress, in seeking to eliminate recourse to habeas corpus as a means to assert those rights, acted in violation of the Suspension Clause.

. . .

IV

. . .

. . .[F]or purposes of our analysis, we accept the Government's position that Cuba, and not the United States, retains *de jure* sovereignty over Guantanamo Bay. As we did in *Rasul*, however, we take notice of the obvious and uncontested fact that the United States, by virtue of its complete jurisdiction and control over the base, maintains *de facto* sovereignty over this territory. See 542 U.S., at 480; *id.*, at 487 (KENNEDY, J., concurring in judgment).

Were we to hold that the present cases turn on the political question doctrine, we would be required first to accept the Government's premise that *de jure* sovereignty is the touchstone of habeas corpus jurisdiction. This premise, however, is unfounded. For the reasons indicated above, the history of common-law habeas corpus provides scant support for this proposition; and, for the reasons indicated below, that position would be inconsistent with our precedents and contrary to fundamental separation-of-powers principles.

. . .

B

The Government's formal sovereignty-based test raises troubling separation-of-powers concerns as well. The political history of Guantanamo illustrates the deficiencies of this approach. The United States has maintained complete and uninterrupted control of the bay for over 100 years. . . . . [A]lthough it recognized, by entering into the 1903 Lease Agreement, that Cuba retained "ultimate sovereignty" over Guantanamo, the United States continued to maintain the same plenary control it had enjoyed since 1898. Yet the Government's view is that the Constitution had no effect there, at least as to noncitizens, because the United States disclaimed sovereignty in the formal sense of the term. The necessary implication of the argument is that by surrendering formal sovereignty over any unincorporated territory to a third party, while at the same time entering into a lease that grants total control over the territory back to the United States, it would be possible for the political branches to govern without legal constraint.

Our basic charter cannot be contracted away like this. . . . .

. . .

C

. . .

Based on . . . language from *Eisentrager*, and the reasoning in our other extraterritoriality opinions, we conclude that at least three factors are relevant in determining the reach of the Suspension Clause: (1) the citizenship and status of the detainee and the adequacy of the process through which that status determination was made; (2) the nature of the sites where apprehension and then detention took place; and (3) the practical obstacles inherent in resolving the prisoner's entitlement to the writ.

· · ·

It is true that before today the Court has never held that noncitizens detained by our Government in territory over which another country maintains *de jure* sovereignty have any rights under our Constitution. But the cases before us lack any precise historical parallel. They involve individuals detained by executive order for the duration of a conflict that, if measured from September 11, 2001, to the present, is already among the longest wars in American history. . . . . The detainees, moreover, are held in a territory that, while technically not part of the United States, is under the complete and total control of our Government. Under these circumstances the lack of a precedent on point is no barrier to our holding.

We hold that Art. I, §9, cl. 2, of the Constitution has full effect at Guantanamo Bay. If the privilege of habeas corpus is to be denied to the detainees now before us, Congress must act in accordance with the requirements of the Suspension Clause. Cf. *Hamdi*, 542 U.S., at 564 (SCALIA, J., dissenting) ("[I]ndefinite imprisonment on reasonable suspicion is not an available option of treatment for those accused of aiding the enemy, absent a suspension of the writ"). This Court may not impose a *de facto* suspension by abstaining from these controversies. See *Hamdan*, 548 U.S., at 585, n. 16 ("[A]bstention is not appropriate in cases . . . in which the legal challenge 'turn[s] on the status of the persons as to whom the military asserted its power'" (quoting *Schlesinger* v. *Councilman*, 420 U.S. 738, 759 (1975))). The MCA does not purport to be a formal suspension of the writ; and the Government, in its submissions to us, has not argued that it is. Petitioners, therefore, are entitled to the privilege of habeas corpus to challenge the legality of their detention.

V

· · ·

B

We do not endeavor to offer a comprehensive summary of the requisites for an adequate substitute for habeas corpus. We do consider it uncontroversial, however, that the privilege of habeas corpus entitles the prisoner to a meaningful opportunity to demonstrate that he is being held pursuant to "the erroneous application or interpretation" of relevant law. *St. Cyr*, 533 U.S., at 302. And the habeas court must have the power to order the conditional release of an individual unlawfully detained–though release need not be the exclusive remedy and is not the appropriate one in every case in which the writ is granted. . . . These are the easily identified attributes of any constitutionally adequate habeas corpus proceeding. But, depending on the circumstances, more may be required.

· · ·

Where a person is detained by executive order, rather than, say, after being tried and convicted in a court, the need for collateral review is most pressing. A criminal conviction in the usual course occurs after a judicial hearing before a tribunal disinterested in the outcome and committed to procedures designed to ensure its own independence. These dynamics are not inherent in executive detention orders or executive review procedures. In this context the need for habeas corpus is more urgent. The intended duration of the detention and the reasons for it bear upon the precise scope of the inquiry. Habeas corpus proceedings need not resemble a criminal trial, even when the detention is by executive order. But the writ must be effective. The habeas court must have sufficient authority to conduct a meaningful review of both the cause for detention and the Executive's power to detain.

To determine the necessary scope of habeas corpus review, therefore, we must assess the CSRT process, the mechanism through which petitioners' designation as enemy combatants became final. . . . . What matters is the sum total of procedural protections afforded to the detainee at all stages, direct and collateral.

. . .

Although we make no judgment as to whether the CSRTs, as currently constituted, satisfy due process standards, we agree with petitioners that, even when all the parties involved in this process act with diligence and in good faith, there is considerable risk of error in the tribunal's findings of fact. This is a risk inherent in any process that, in the words of the former Chief Judge of the Court of Appeals, is "closed and accusatorial." See *Bismullah III*, 514 F.3d, at 1296 (Ginsburg, C. J., concurring in denial of rehearing en banc). And given that the consequence of error may be detention of persons for the duration of hostilities that may last a generation or more, this is a risk too significant to ignore.

For the writ of habeas corpus, or its substitute, to function as an effective and proper remedy in this context, the court that conducts the habeas proceeding must have the means to correct errors that occurred during the CSRT proceedings. This includes some authority to assess the sufficiency of the Government's evidence against the detainee. It also must have the authority to admit and consider relevant exculpatory evidence that was not introduced during the earlier proceeding. . . . .

Consistent with the historic function and province of the writ, habeas corpus review may be more circumscribed if the underlying detention proceedings are more thorough than they were here. . . . .

. . . We do hold that when the judicial power to issue habeas corpus properly is invoked the judicial officer must have adequate authority to make a determination in light of the relevant law and facts and to formulate and issue appropriate orders for relief, including, if necessary, an order directing the prisoner's release.

C

. . .

. . . To hold that the detainees at Guantanamo may, under the DTA, challenge the President's legal authority to detain them, contest the CSRT's findings of fact, supplement the record on review with exculpatory evidence, and request an order of release would come close to reinstating the §2241 habeas corpus process Congress sought to deny them. The language of the statute, read in light of Congress' reasons for enacting it, cannot bear this interpretation. Petitioners have met their burden of establishing that the DTA review process is, on its face, an inadequate substitute for habeas corpus.

Although we do not hold that an adequate substitute must duplicate §2241 in all respects, it suffices that the Government has not established that the detainees' access to the statutory review provisions at issue is an adequate substitute for the writ of habeas corpus. MCA §7 thus effects an unconstitutional suspension of the writ. In view of our holding we need not discuss the reach of the writ with respect to claims of unlawful conditions of treatment or confinement.

VI

. . .

A

. . .

The cases before us . . . do not involve detainees who have been held for a short period of time while awaiting their CSRT determinations. Were that the case, or were it probable that the Court of Appeals could complete a prompt review of their applications, the case for requiring temporary abstention or exhaustion of alternative remedies would be much stronger. These qualifications no longer pertain here. In some of these cases six years have elapsed without the judicial oversight that habeas corpus or an adequate substitute demands. And there has been no showing that the Executive faces such onerous burdens that it cannot respond to habeas corpus actions. To require these detainees to complete DTA review before proceeding with their habeas corpus actions would be to require additional months, if not years, of delay. The first DTA review applications were filed over a year ago, but no decisions on the merits have been issued. While some delay in fashioning new procedures is unavoidable, the costs of delay can no longer be borne by those who are held in custody. The detainees in these cases are entitled to a prompt habeas corpus hearing.

Our decision today holds only that the petitioners before us are entitled to seek the writ; that the DTA review procedures are an inadequate substitute for habeas corpus; and that the petitioners in these cases need not exhaust the review procedures in the Court of Appeals before proceeding with their habeas actions in the District Court. The only law we identify as unconstitutional is MCA §7 . . . . Accordingly, both the DTA and the CSRT process remain intact. Our holding with regard to exhaustion should not be read to imply that a habeas court should intervene the moment an enemy combatant steps foot in a territory where the writ runs. The Executive is entitled to a reasonable period of time to determine a detainee's status before a court entertains that detainee's habeas corpus petition. The CSRT process is the mechanism Congress and the President set up to deal with these issues. Except in cases of undue delay, federal courts should refrain from entertaining an enemy combatant's habeas corpus petition at least until after the Department, acting via the CSRT, has had a chance to review his status.

. . .

*   *   *

. . .

. . . Security depends upon a sophisticated intelligence apparatus and the ability of our Armed Forces to act and to interdict. There are further considerations, however. Security subsists, too, in fidelity to freedom's first principles. Chief among these are freedom from arbitrary and unlawful restraint and the personal liberty that is secured by adherence to the separation of powers. It is from these principles that the judicial authority to consider petitions for habeas corpus relief derives.

Our opinion does not undermine the Executive's powers as Commander in Chief. On the contrary, the exercise of those powers is vindicated, not eroded, when confirmed by the Judicial Branch. Within the Constitution's separation-of-powers structure, few exercises of judicial power are as legitimate or as necessary as the responsibility to hear challenges to the authority of the Executive to imprison a person. Some of these petitioners have been in custody for six years with no definitive judicial determination as to the legality of their detention. Their access to the writ is a necessity to determine the lawfulness of their status, even if, in the end, they do not obtain the relief they seek.

. . .

. . . The laws and Constitution are designed to survive, and remain in force, in extraordinary times. Liberty and security can be reconciled; and in our system they are reconciled within the framework of the law. The Framers decided that habeas corpus, a right of first importance, must be a part of that framework, a part of that law.

. . .

JUSTICE SOUTER, with whom JUSTICE GINSBURG and JUSTICE BREYER join, concurring.

. . .

. . . JUSTICE SCALIA is . . . correct that here, for the first time, this Court holds there is (he says "confers") constitutional habeas jurisdiction over aliens imprisoned by the military outside an area of *de jure* national sovereignty . . . . But no one who reads the Court's opinion in *Rasul* could seriously doubt that the jurisdictional question must be answered the same way in purely constitutional cases, given the Court's reliance on the historical background of habeas generally in answering the statutory question. . . . . Indeed, the Court in *Rasul* directly answered the very historical question that JUSTICE SCALIA says is dispositive . . . ; it wrote that "[a]pplication of the habeas statute to persons detained at [Guantanamo] is consistent with the historical reach of the writ of habeas corpus," 542 U.S., at 481. JUSTICE SCALIA dismisses the statement as dictum . . . but if dictum it was, it was dictum well considered, and it stated the view of five Members of this Court on the historical scope of the writ. Of course, it takes more than a quotation from *Rasul*, however much on point, to resolve the constitutional issue before us here, which the majority opinion has explored afresh in the detail it deserves. But whether one agrees or disagrees with today's decision, it is no bolt out of the blue.

. . .

. . . The several answers to the charge of triumphalism might start with a basic fact of Anglo-American constitutional history: that the power, first of the Crown and now of the Executive Branch of the United States, is necessarily limited by habeas corpus jurisdiction to enquire into the legality of executive detention. And one could explain that in this Court's exercise of responsibility to preserve habeas corpus something much more significant is involved than pulling and hauling between the judicial and political branches. Instead, though, it is enough to repeat that some of these petitioners have spent six years behind bars. After six years of sustained executive detentions in Guantanamo, subject to habeas jurisdiction but without any actual habeas scrutiny, today's decision is no judicial victory, but an act of perseverance in trying to make habeas review, and the obligation of the courts to provide it, mean something of value both to prisoners and to the Nation. . . . .

. . .

CHIEF JUSTICE ROBERTS, with whom JUSTICE SCALIA, JUSTICE THOMAS, and JUSTICE ALITO join, dissenting.

Today the Court strikes down as inadequate the most generous set of procedural protections ever afforded aliens detained by this country as enemy combatants. The political branches crafted these procedures amidst an ongoing military conflict, after much careful investigation and thorough debate. The Court rejects them today out of hand, without bothering to say what due process rights the detainees possess, without explaining how the statute fails to vindicate those rights, and before a single petitioner has even attempted to avail himself of the law's operation. And to what effect? The majority merely replaces a review system designed by the people's representatives with a set of shapeless procedures to be defined by federal courts at some future date. One cannot help but think, after surveying the modest practical results of the majority's ambitious opinion, that this decision is not really about the detainees at all, but about control of federal policy regarding enemy combatants.

. . .

I

. . .

If the CSRT procedures meet the minimal due process requirements outlined in *Hamdi*, and if an Article III court is available to ensure that these procedures are followed in future cases, see [542 U.S.], at 536; *INS* v. *St. Cyr*, 533 U.S. 289, 304 (2001); *Heikkila* v. *Barber*, 345 U.S. 229, 236 (1953), there is no need to reach the Suspension Clause question. Detainees will have received all the process the Constitution could possibly require, whether that process is called "habeas" or something else. The question of the writ's reach need not be addressed.

. . .

II

. . .

A

. . .

. . . First of all, the majority is quite wrong to dismiss the Executive's determination of detainee status as no more than a "battlefield" judgment, as if it were somehow provisional and made in great haste. In fact, detainees are designated "enemy combatants" only after "multiple levels of review by military officers and officials of the Department of Defense." Memorandum of the Secretary of the Navy, Implementation of Combatant Status Review Tribunal Procedures for Enemy Combatants Detained at Guantanamo Bay Naval Base (July 29, 2004) . . . .

The majority is equally wrong to characterize the CSRTs as part of that initial determination process. They are instead a means for detainees to *challenge* the Government's determination. . . . . . The CSRTs operate much as habeas courts would if hearing the detainee's collateral challenge for the first time: They gather evidence, call witnesses, take testimony, and render a decision on the legality of the Government's detention. . . . If the CSRT finds a particular detainee has been improperly held, it can order release. . . .

. . .

. . . CSRT review is just the first tier of collateral review in the DTA system. The statute provides additional review in an Article III court. Given the rationale of today's decision, it is well worth recalling exactly what the DTA provides in this respect. The statute directs the D.C. Circuit to consider whether a particular alien's status determination "was consistent with the standards and procedures specified by the Secretary of Defense" *and* "whether the use of such standards and procedures to make the determination is consistent with the Constitution and laws of the United States." DTA §1005(e)(2)(C), 119 Stat. 2742. That is, a *court* determines whether the CSRT procedures are constitutional, and a *court* determines whether those procedures were followed in a particular case.

. . .

D

. . .

. . . In the event a detainee alleges that he has obtained new and persuasive exculpatory evidence that would have been considered by the tribunal below had it only been available, the D.C. Circuit could readily remand the case to the tribunal to allow that body to consider the evidence in the first instance. The Court of Appeals could later review any new or reinstated decision in light of the supplemented record.

If that sort of procedure sounds familiar, it should. Federal appellate courts reviewing factual determinations follow just such a procedure in a variety of circumstances.

. . . .

A remand is not the only relief available for detainees caught in the Court's hypothetical conundrum. The DTA expressly directs the Secretary of Defense to "provide for periodic review of any new evidence that may become available relating to the enemy combatant status of a detainee." DTA §1005(a)(3). Regulations issued by the Department of Defense provide that when a detainee puts forward new, material evidence "not previously presented to the detainee's CSRT," the Deputy Secretary of Defense "'will direct that a CSRT convene to reconsider the basis of the detainee's . . . status in light of the new information.'" Office for the Administrative Review of the Detention of Enemy Combatants, Instruction 5421.1, Procedure for Review of "New Evidence" Relating to Enemy Combatant (EC) Status 4(a)(1), 5(b) (May 7, 2007); Brief for Federal Respondents 56, n. 30. Pursuant to DTA § 1005(e)(2)(A), the resulting CSRT determination is again reviewable in full by the D.C. Circuit.[2]

. . .

III

For all its eloquence about the detainees' right to the writ, the Court makes no effort to elaborate how exactly the remedy it prescribes will differ from the procedural protections detainees enjoy under the DTA. The Court objects to the detainees' limited access to witnesses and classified material, but proposes no alternatives of its own. Indeed, it simply ignores the many difficult questions its holding presents. What, for example, will become of the CSRT process? The majority says federal courts should *generally* refrain from entertaining detainee challenges until after the petitioner's CSRT proceeding has finished. . . . . But to what deference, if any, is that CSRT determination entitled?

. . .

*   *   *

So who has won? Not the detainees. The Court's analysis leaves them with only the prospect of further litigation to determine the content of their new habeas right, followed by further litigation to resolve their particular cases, followed by further litigation before the D.C. Circuit – where they could have started had they invoked the DTA

---

2 . . .

procedure. Not Congress, whose attempt to "determine – through democratic means – how best" to balance the security of the American people with the detainees' liberty interests, see *Hamdan* v. *Rumsfeld*, 548 U.S. 557, 636 (2006) (BREYER, J., concurring), has been unceremoniously brushed aside. Not the Great Writ, whose majesty is hardly enhanced by its extension to a jurisdictionally quirky outpost, with no tangible benefit to anyone. Not the rule of law, unless by that is meant the rule of lawyers, who will now arguably have a greater role than military and intelligence officials in shaping policy for alien enemy combatants. And certainly not the American people, who today lose a bit more control over the conduct of this Nation's foreign policy to unelected, politically unaccountable judges.

I respectfully dissent.

. . .

JUSTICE SCALIA, with whom THE CHIEF JUSTICE, JUSTICE THOMAS, and JUSTICE ALITO join, dissenting.

Today, for the first time in our Nation's history, the Court confers a constitutional right to habeas corpus on alien enemies detained abroad by our military forces in the course of an ongoing war. . . . . The writ of habeas corpus does not, and never has, run in favor of aliens abroad; the Suspension Clause thus has no application, and the Court's intervention in this military matter is entirely *ultra vires*.

. . .

I

. . .

The game of bait-and-switch that today's opinion plays upon the Nation's Commander in Chief will make the war harder on us. It will almost certainly cause more Americans to be killed. That consequence would be tolerable if necessary to preserve a time-honored legal principle vital to our constitutional Republic. But it is this Court's blatant *abandonment* of such a principle that produces the decision today. The President relied on our settled precedent in *Johnson* v. *Eisentrager*, 339 U.S. 763 (1950), when he established the prison at Guantanamo Bay for enemy aliens. Citing that case, the President's Office of Legal Counsel advised him "that the great weight of legal authority indicates that a federal district court could not properly exercise habeas jurisdiction over an alien detained at [Guantanamo Bay]." Memorandum from Patrick F. Philbin and John C. Yoo, Deputy Assistant Attorneys General, Office of Legal Counsel, to William J. Haynes II, General Counsel, Dept. of Defense (Dec. 28, 2001). Had the law been otherwise, the military surely would not have transported prisoners there, but would have kept them in Afghanistan, transferred them to another of our foreign military bases, or turned them over to allies for detention. Those other facilities might well have been worse for the detainees themselves.

In the long term, then, the Court's decision today accomplishes little, except perhaps to reduce the well-being of enemy combatants that the Court ostensibly seeks to protect. In the short term, however, the decision is devastating. At least 30 of those prisoners hitherto released from Guantanamo Bay have returned to the battlefield. See S. Rep. No. 110-90, pt. 7, p. 13 (2007) (Minority Views of Sens. Kyl, Sessions, Graham, Cornyn, and Coburn) (hereinafter Minority Report). Some have been captured or killed. See *ibid.*;

see also Mintz, Released Detainees Rejoining the Fight, Washington Post, Oct. 22, 2004, pp. A1, A12. But others have succeeded in carrying on their atrocities against innocent civilians. . . . .

These, mind you, were detainees whom *the military* had concluded were not enemy combatants. Their return to the kill illustrates the incredible difficulty of assessing who is and who is not an enemy combatant in a foreign theater of operations where the environment does not lend itself to rigorous evidence collection. Astoundingly, the Court today raises the bar, requiring military officials to appear before civilian courts and defend their decisions under procedural and evidentiary rules that go beyond what Congress has specified. . . . .

. . .

II

. . .

B

. . .

There is simply no support for the Court's assertion that constitutional rights extend to aliens held outside U.S. sovereign territory, see *Verdugo-Urquidez*, 494 U.S., at 271, and *Eisentrager* could not be clearer that the privilege of habeas corpus does not extend to aliens abroad. By blatantly distorting *Eisentrager*, the Court avoids the difficulty of explaining why it should be overruled. See *Planned Parenthood of Southeastern Pa.* v. *Casey*, 505 U.S. 833, 854–855 (1992) (identifying *stare decisis* factors). The rule that aliens abroad are not constitutionally entitled to habeas corpus has not proved unworkable in practice; if anything, it is the Court's "functional" test that does not (and never will) provide clear guidance for the future. *Eisentrager* forms a coherent whole with the accepted proposition that aliens abroad have no substantive rights under our Constitution. Since it was announced, no relevant factual premises have changed. It has engendered considerable reliance on the part of our military. And, as the Court acknowledges, text and history do not clearly compel a contrary ruling. It is a sad day for the rule of law when such an important constitutional precedent is discarded without an *apologia*, much less an apology.

C

What drives today's decision is neither the meaning of the Suspension Clause, nor the principles of our precedents, but rather an inflated notion of judicial supremacy. The Court says that if the extraterritorial applicability of the Suspension Clause turned on formal notions of sovereignty, "it would be possible for the political branches to govern without legal constraint" in areas beyond the sovereign territory of the United States. . . . . That cannot be, the Court says, because it is the duty of this Court to say what the law is. . . . . It would be difficult to imagine a more question-begging analysis. "The very foundation of the power of the federal courts to declare Acts of Congress unconstitutional lies in the power and duty of those courts to decide cases and controversies *properly before them*." *United States* v. *Raines*, 362 U.S. 17, 20–21 (1960) (citing *Marbury* v. *Madison*, 1 Cranch 137 (1803); emphasis added). Our power "to say what the law is" is circumscribed by the limits of our statutorily and constitutionally conferred jurisdiction. See *Lujan* v. *Defenders of Wildlife*, 504 U.S. 555, 573–578 (1992). And that is precisely the question in these cases: whether the Constitution confers habeas jurisdiction on federal courts to decide petitioners' claims. It is both irrational and arrogant to say that the answer must be yes, because otherwise we would not be supreme.

. . .

III

. . .

...[B]ecause I conclude that the text and history of the Suspension Clause provide no basis for our jurisdiction, I would affirm the Court of Appeals even if *Eisentrager* did not govern these cases.

*   *   *

Today the Court warps our Constitution in a way that goes beyond the narrow issue of the reach of the Suspension Clause, invoking judicially brainstormed separation-of-powers principles to establish a manipulable "functional" test for the extraterritorial reach of habeas corpus (and, no doubt, for the extraterritorial reach of other constitutional protections as well). It blatantly misdescribes important precedents, most conspicuously Justice Jackson's opinion for the Court in *Johnson* v. *Eisentrager*. It breaks a chain of precedent as old as the common law that prohibits judicial inquiry into detentions of aliens abroad absent statutory authorization. And, most tragically, it sets our military commanders the impossible task of proving to a civilian court, under whatever standards this Court devises in the future, that evidence supports the confinement of each and every enemy prisoner.

The Nation will live to regret what the Court has done today. I dissent.